Great Pages in History from the Wisconsin State Journal 1852-2002

What Is a Newspaper?

written in 1962 by the late Fred J. Curran, former night city editor at the Wisconsin State Journal

What, the little girl asked, is a newspaper?
It's a paper with words and pictures on it.
It is made up of a lot of people, including ourselves.
It's a big event and a little event, about folks far away and folks next door.
It's happiness and tragedy, a laugh, a cry, and a song that's heard again.

It's government, from the president to Congress, from the governor to the Legislature, from the mayor to the City Council, and all their branches – with a quizzical fellow looking over their shoulders.
It's a policeman, a fireman, and others in dangerous jobs.
It's business, it's industry; it's a front window for merchants to display their goods. It's an ad for a lost dog.
It's a record of what happened to people, of who did what, when, where, and why.

It's a description of a bride's dress; it's a newly married couple looking for an apartment.
It's a welcome to a new pastor, a church dedication, a farewell to someone retiring after long service.
It's a home run, a long pass, a team's box score, a well-rolled bowling game.
It's a hint of a recipe, a plan for home improvement, a bit of advice for someone who's troubled.

It's the first snow, awakening spring, the hottest day of the year, and an autumn day with edges as crisp as the fallen leaves.
It's about a youngster, scuffling to and from school, and about the things he learns and does with his teachers.
It's about playgrounds and vacations, and places to go and how to get there.
It's the summer fishin' hole and the beach; it's just lazin' around.

It's growth and it's progress, new products and old standbys.
It's professional help and service; it's a note on what hospitals and clinics do.
It's a bulletin for a church, a temple, a synagogue.
It's a note on a veteran's organization, a service club, an afternoon tea.
It's the greatest daily collection of words and pictures ever assembled.

It's a big story, a little story, a feature story. It's a pretty picture, a stark photo, a page of pictures of big events. It's an editor's view, a reader's disagreement, a columnist's reasoning. It's an explanation of many things. It's a crossword puzzle, a comic, a game.
It's writing that is not always literary, but it's the language people speak, because much of it is what people said.

It's a pressman in a funny paper hat, a printer deftly putting type together, an advertising salesman showing a merchant how to tell his story, a reporter busy at a typewriter, a deskman reading copy and writing headlines, a photographer trying for one more shot. It's a newsboy whistling up the street (quietly in the morning).

It's a mirror of life, a part of life, as essential as the clock and the calendar.
It's paper with words and pictures on it.
Like this.

GREAT PAGES IN HISTORY

FROM THE

Wisconsin State Journal

1852 – 2002

James W. Hopson, publisher

Frank M. Denton, editor

Edited by William C. Robbins

The University of Wisconsin Press

The University of Wisconsin Press
1930 Monroe Street
Madison, Wisconsin 53711

www.wisc.edu/wisconsinpress/

3 Henrietta Street
London WC2E 8LU, England

5 4 3 2 1

Printed in Canada

Library of Congress Cataloging-in-Publication Data available

For 150 years, generations of Wisconsinites have viewed the world through the pages of the Wisconsin State Journal.

Through most of those years, the newspaper was the only real source for news beyond the reader's personal daily experience. Even later, as radio, television and the Internet offered more sources for news, the State Journal has remained the authoritative source for the most comprehensive, and comprehensible, news in our part of the world.

This collection of our most noteworthy pages is a celebration of 150 years of the Wisconsin State Journal as a daily newspaper. Actually, the paper is 163 years old, founded as the weekly Madison Express on Dec. 2, 1839. David Atwood converted the successful publication into a daily on Sept. 30, 1852.

These pages, among the hundreds of thousands published over the years, were selected because they reflect the great events of three centuries. Beyond that, they are the contemporaneous portraits of the times, reflecting the lives not only of leaders and officials, the famous and infamous, but also of ordinary citizens. It has been said that most people get their names in the newspaper only twice: when they are born and when they die. In fact, the pages of the State Journal are packed with the names of people of all sorts who have built our state and our communities, whether as leaders or as laborers.

Through these years, the Wisconsin State Journal has been the community's daily chronicler, reporting important events, telling the people's stories, helping them navigate the days, offering advice, celebrating their accomplishments, duly noting the shortcomings, mixing in all sorts of news and information.

These pages are rich with fascinating detail and insights. Look beyond the big stories and experience the texture of life in that time. Or pick a major historical event and see how we reported it. Sometimes, you will find, the news did not seem as important at the time as it later became. For example, the birth of flight was reported Dec. 18, 1903, but only at the bottom of the front page, much less prominently than a report on state taxes.

Our beacon, as inspiration and guiding light, has been the First Amendment. Keep in mind as you scan these pages that they are not an official record of history; they are the best truth-seeking by journalists of the era, unfettered by official control. At times, you will see that the journalism itself was the catalyst for change.

In that spirit, this book is dedicated to the thousands of journalists who have crafted the Wisconsin State Journal, day in and day out, over 150 years. Like almost everything else, the tools of journalism have evolved, from the telegraph and lead type to computers, color and solution-oriented journalism. But our job has remained the same: Find the truth as best we can every day, and put it in the newspaper for everyone to read.

Please enjoy these reminiscences, and celebrate our sesquicentennial with us.

Frank M. Denton, editor

Table of Contents

1800s

1900

1920

1930

1940

1950

1960

Table of Contents

WISCONSIN DAILY JOURNAL.

BY DAVID ATWOOD. Published every Day except Sunday. $4 per Annum, in Advance.

VOLUME 1. MADISON, WISCONSIN, SEPTEMBER 30, 1852. NUMBER 1.

Official Directory.

UNITED STATES GOVERNMENT.

President—MILLARD FILLMORE.
Sec'y of State—DANIEL WEBSTER.
Sec'y Treasury—THOMAS CORWIN.
Sec'y Interior—ALEX. H. H. STUART.
Sec'y of War—CHARLES M. CONRAD.
Sec'y of Navy—JOHN P. KENEDY.
P. M. General—SAMUEL D. HUBBARD.
Att'y General—JOHN J. CRITTENDEN.
Vice Pres. pro tem—WILLIAM R. KING.
Speaker of the House—LYNN BOYD.

UNITED STATES SUPREME COURT.

Chief Justice—ROGER B. TANEY,
Assoc. Justice—JOHN McLEAN,
" " JAMES M. WAYNE,
" " JOHN CATRON,
" " PETER V. DANIEL,
" " SAMUEL NELSON,
" " ROBERT C. GRIER,
" " BENJAMIN R. CURTIS,
Reporter—BENJAMIN C. HOWARD.

WISCONSIN STATE OFFICERS.

Governor—LEONARD J. FARWELL.
Lieut. Governor—TIMOTHY BURNS.
Sec'y State—CHARLES D. ROBINSON.
Treasurer—EDWARD H. JANNSSEN.
Att'y Gen.—EXPERIENCE ESTABROOK.
Superin. Pub. Ins. AZEL P. LADD.

SUPREME AND CIRCUIT JUDGES.

I. EDWARD V. WHITON, of Janesville.
II. LEVI HUBBELL, of Milwaukee.
III. CHAS. H. LARRABEE, of P. Wash'n.
IV. TIMOTHY O. HOWE, of Green Bay.
V. MORTIMER M. JACKSON, of Min'l Pt.
VI. WYRAM KNOWTON, Prairie du Chien.

UNITED STATES SENATORS.

HENRY DODGE, of Dodgeville, Iowa Co.
ISAAC P. WALKER, of Milwaukee.

REPRESENTATIVES IN CONGRESS.

I. CHARLES DURKEE, Kenosha.
II. BEN C. EASTMAN, of Plattville.
III. JAMES DUANE DOTY of Me[illegible]

BOARD OF PUBLIC WORKS.

PETER H. PRAME,
WILLIAM RICHARDSON,
ANDREW PROUDFIT.

UNITED STATES LAND OFFICE.

MILWAUKEE.
JOHN P. SMITH, Register.
CHARLES H. WILLIAMS, Recei[ver].

MINERAL POINT.
GEO. H. SLAUGHTER, Register.
——— STEVENSON, Receiver.

WILLOW RIVER.
MOSES S. GIBSON, Register,
FRANCIS P. CATLIN, Receiver.

MENASHA.
ALEXANDER SPAULDING, Re[gister].
EDGAR CONKLIN, Receiver.

STATE LAND OFFICERS.

BENJAMIN O. HENNING, Register,
JAMES MURDOCK, Receiver.

STATE AGRICULTURAL SOCIETY.

Hon. HENRY M. BILLINGS, President.
N. B. CLAPP, O. DENSMORE, M. WEBSTER, } Vice Presidents.
ALBERT C. INGHAM, Rec. & Cor. Sec'y.
SIMEON MILLS, Treasurer.
WARREN CHASE, ELIAB B. DEAN, SAM. J. DAGGETT, J. D. MERRETT, H. B. HAWLEY, } Executive Com.

Officers of Dane County.

County Judge—NATHANIEL B. EDDY.
Clerk of Circuit Court—ELISHA BURDICK.
Clerk B'd Supervisors—SYLVESTER GILES.
Sheriff—ALFRED MAIN.
Treasurer—EZRA L. VARNEY.
Prosecuting Attorney—GEORGE [illegible] SMITH.
Surveyor—DAVID B. TRAVIS.
Coroner—CHARLES L. WILSON.

OFFICERS OF THE TOWN OF MADISON.

PHILO DUNNING, Ch'n. } JAMES R. LARKIN, X. JORDAN, } Supervisors.
JAMES DONELLAN, Town Clerk.
CASPER ZWICKEY, Town Treasurer.

CORPORATION OFFICERS.

CHAUNCEY ABBOTT, Pres't.
HORACE A. TENNEY,
P. H. VAN BERGEN,
EZRA L. VARNEY,
MEYER FRIEND,
F. G. TIBBITTS, } [Trus]tees.
JOHNSON J. STARKS, Treasurer.
ROBERT L. REAM, Clerk.

From Arthur's Home Gazette.

THE MAIDEN'S ROCK.

AN INDIAN LEGEND.

BY AN OLD PIONEER.

There is love and romance in real life as well as in fiction; and sentiment and despair are not wholly confined to civilized man. With all the apathy and stoicism attributed to the Indian race, there are few well attested instances of as enduring affection as can be found amongst the refined "pale faces." A residence of more than thirty years on the confines of the West, and no small intercourse with the tribes of red-men, who are fast fading away before the march of civilization, have made the writer familiar with many a thrilling story of Indian character and suffering. None, however possess a deeper interest than the one we are about to narrate.

Passing up the Mississippi beyond what until within four years past, was the boundary of civilization, and about equidistant between Prairie du Chien and St. Paul, is Lake Pepin. This body of water would be regarded merely as an expansion of the river if it were not several fathoms deep, and destitute of a current. This lake is about twenty-four miles long, and from two to five broad, and, unlike the Mississippi, wholly destitute of islands. No description we can give will impress the imagination of the reader with the beauty and sublimity of its scenery, in the quiet hour of a summer's morning. When the air is calm, the sky clear, and the soft light of the ascending sun first tinges the water, not a ripple disturbs the surface, and the traveler exclaims, involuntarily,—"How beautiful!"

Its course is from west-northwest to east-south-east, and its waters are enclosed with an amphitheatre of bluffs and cliffs, presenting every form, and elevated several hundred feet; and broken occasionally by a ravine, or the indentation of a plateau of an alluvial deposit. From the tops of these bluffs the view is grand and imposing.—The traveler on the steamboats while gazing upward to these cliffs, feels his curiosity excited to know what lies beyond. A stranger to the structure of this region would hardly imagine that from the summit of is region of bluffs, on either side, lies an extensive champaign country. Those who, having never seen a prairie country, and having imbibed the erroneous impression that it is low, wet land, may [readi]ly learn the facts by ascending some [pin]nacle along the shore of this lake.—[Look]ing in a westerly direction, he will per[ceive] a wide expanse of prairie, rolling in gentle undulations, interspersed with groves of timber, and extending far as the eye can reach. Beneath him several hundred feet, is the deep, blue lake; and across the opposite range of bluffs eastward, is a more rolling country, with the pine-clad hills of the Chippewa river in the far distant perspective.

About half way up the lake, its north-eastern shore rises to the height of four hundred feet; one hundred and fifty feet is a perpendicular cliff of magnesian limestone, and the remainder is a very abrupt and precipitous slope, which extends from the base of the cliff to the water's edge; and covered with erratic rocks, and a few scattered shrubs and trees. This point projects some distance into the lake, and on either hand are basins of low ground, through which small streams or brooks pass.

The scenery is peculiarly wild, and the voyager, who has gazed on the high bluffs he has already passed, is struck with peculiar interest in beholding the spot. In no instance along the banks of the Mississippi has he seen a high, precipitous crag, resting on almost a steep bluff, whose base is washed by a wide expanse of water, the calmness of which gives such a wonderful contrast to the savage wildness of the landscape. This has long been known to the Canadian *voyageurs* as the *Cap de Sioux*; and has been much celebrated in the annals of *Dah-co-tos* as the *Win-no-ke-yah In-yan*,—The Maiden's Rock.

The interesting and gloomy legend has been told in divers ways, with considerable variations, but we have no doubt it is substantially true, and that the tragedy occurred about the middle of the last century. While narrating the general characters already told by others, we shall give such additions as Indian traditions and the legendary lore of the *voyageurs* have handed down to the present time.

The legend runs thus:—

This spot, which for grandeur, sublimity, and wildness, is now so much admired, was the scene of a most tragical event.

In the village and tribe of *Wa-pa-sha*, or the Red Leaf, there was an Indian girl, known far and near amongst the *Dah-co-tas* [the allied people] as *Wee-no-nah*, or the "First-born." From her birth she had enjoyed the affections of her family and was the idol of the village. Stout hearted "braves" sought to win her confidence by acts of prowess and danger, and gallant hunters brought to her father's lodge the choicest spoils of the chase. A young hunter, graceful in his person and skillful in his calling, won her regard, and gave those "signs" which an Indian maiden so well understands, of ardent, enduring affection. The feeling was reciprocated, and after repeated meetings, pledges of that union in which all their hopes centered, were exchanged. But Indian marriages, especially among the Dah-co-tas, are less the result of the attachment and choice of the parties than the cold, calculating policy and authority of the parents. Feeble as may be the bonds of legal administration among Indians, the law of custom and established usage is so strong, and executed with such unrelenting power, that escape from parental domination is seldom attempted, and more rarely successful.

Te-os-cate, her lover, found a formidable rival in the person of *Muck-wah*, or the Bear, who was twice the age of Wee-no-nah, rough in his manners, blood-thirsty, cruel and vengeful in his disposition, and who had two wives already in his lodge.—This person was a successful and popular warrior in the Wapasha band, and could show more Chippewa scalps in his smoky lodge than any other savage in this marauding tribe. He had acquired his popularity and fame by the services he had rendered his village, when attacked by the Chippewas. He desired the possession of Wee-no-nah (as a third and of course an inferior wife) that he might strengthen his position in the tribe, by attaching to his interest her father, her younger brothers, and a large family connection. Her parents and relatives encouraged this ill assorted match, which, aside from her sincere attachment to Te-os-ca-te, the hunter, was most disgusting to her feelings, and destructive to all her hopes of happiness. In firm, but respectful language to her parents and relations, she remonstrated against this outrage on her sensitive nature, gave an emphatic denial to the solicitations of the warrior, and persisted in her determination to marry the hunter. To the entreaties of her friends and their recommendations of Muck-wah, she argued that having chosen a man that was a hunter for her companion for life, his time would be spent with his family, and his industry and skill devoted to secure her comfort and subsistence; while the warrior would be absent, intent on martial exploits, and neglect her and his too numerous family. She added expostulations, prayers and tears, but to no purpose.

"What folly," said her father, "that a silly girl should be induldged in such a fancy as to marry a hunter, in preference to a great warrior!"

By various persecutions, and denials of access to her presence, they drove her lover to the haunts of the buffalo and moose, on a long hunting excursion, with the vain hope that his absence might bring quiet to his betrothed, in whose enduring fidelity he had the utmost confidence. From childhood Wee-no-nah had enjoyed the affections of her father and family, and had received far more indulgence than is common to females among Indians. She had been a favorite with her brothers, and the other young braves of the family connection; all of whom were anxious to gain her consent to the projected union by persuasive means, rather than by harsh and compulsive measures. In order to remove some of her objections, they adopted measures to provide for her comfortable maintainance and pledged their skill in supplying her lodge with a hunter's share in all their excursions; and purchased of the traders the various articles of finery so much coveted by Indian damsels.

About that time, and during the absence of her lover, a party ascended the river from Wapasha village to Lake Pepin to provide a store of the blue clay found in bluffs, which is used by the Indians in painting their bodies on gala days. Wee-no-nah and her friends were of the party who encamped on the little plain below the cliff. There was an arrangement for Muck-wah, the warrior, to meet them at that spot, and to bestow, as is customary with distinguished braves, the wedding gifts which always complete the negotiations. Here he again addressed her; and as is customary, came into her lodge after she had retired, with the lighted torch; which, if the visitor is accepted, the female extinguishes. But firm in her purpose, and resolved rather to suffer death than violate her espousal with the hunter, and become the wretched companion of the hateful Bear, she covered her face with her buffalo robe, rnd gave signs of indignation and disgust. This was too humiliating to the proud and vengeful warrior, and he was now determined to have her treated as the meanest slave.

Vexed with her obstinancy, her father remonstrated in strong and resentful language, to which he added severe threats to compel her to obedience. In these measures her mother, brothers, and the whole family joined. She even yielded so far as to promise to relinquish Te-os-ca-te, return to him the pledge tokens of their union, and live and die a maiden. But this only strengthened their determination to consummate the union with Muck-wah. Her reply was solemn but fearfully indignant.

"Since this is your love to me, let it be so; but soon you will have no daughter to love or fear you—no sister or relative to torment you with false professions of affection."

[TO BE CONTINUED.]

Home Impressions.

Mrs. H. M. Tracy, now Mrs. Cutler, returned a few days ago from a visit of something over a year to Europe. She went out as a delegate from Ohio to the Peace Congress, and remained in England and France, principally in the former, actively engaged in good works and in examining and comparing the condition, characteristics, and prospects of the Old World with the New.—During her absence Mrs. T. wrote a series of interesting letters to the Ohio Statesman, and in an epistle from New York she thus gives sensation. and impressions in returning to her native land:

But after seventeen days, we found ourselves in sight of land, American land. I would not let my heart bound up as it would have delighted to, for I said, You have looked as coldly as possible on other countries, seeking out their faults; now do not take it for granted that all is right at home just because it is your native land, but weigh well its defects against its beauties, and then you can know more fully, whether you and your country people are the egregious boasters they are said to be by their trans-atlantic uncles and aunts. So, as we came up the Deleware, I looked out with the cold eye of a critic, comparing the shades of green, the forms of trees, the aspect of houses in the distance, in short, the whole landscape, to see if it were worthy the eulogiums that I had been wont to lavish upon it in the old world. Nearer, nearer, our gallant ship made for the land, and higher and higher swelled my bosom with pride and gratitude that this was my own country, my dear native land. Then as we neared the city, vessel after vessel glided by with its graceful awnings raised, and its hundreds of happy looking passengers looking out and waving us welcome. Multitudes of white sails were spread to a soft sighing land breese, and all seemed like a land of enchantment.

Then rose the beautiful city of Penn upon the geen banks, embowered in its shades of green, a city without smoke or dust, and as you passed its streets, there seemed no poverty, and none of those evidences of degradation that we meet in the cities of the Old World.

The delicate beauty and grace of the women and children first struck me as I passed through the streets. What a contrast to what I had daily seen in the Old World.—Then I had not vainly boasted, it was true, all true, and more than true, what I said and boasted of in the Old World. We were not faultless, but we possessed elements of general happiness and refinement in a higher degree than any other land.

I went out through the city, into the midst of its green shade, and looked upon the works of men's hands, where wealth had reared stately domes, and benevolence had consecrated them to the good of humanity. Did the finest specimens of architectural art in the cities of the Old World so entirely eclipse all that I here saw? No, there was the Asylum for Orphans reared by the munificence of Girard, which would almost vie with the temple of glory which Napoleon intended to have consecrated to his heroes. Such was one temple of glory here, the fruits of the toils of a once poor laborer, devoted to the good of homeless children. Then I went to see the Water Works at Fairmount, and as the last shades of day faded into the gloom of twilight, I looked down upon the waters with their beautiful surroundings, and my heart said, never have I met in the old world such a scene of surpassing loveliness.

Then I again embarked upon the river and floated towards New York, beautiful and enchanting as any of the Old World cities, for, though it cannot boast of its Champs de Elysee, it can of its Battery, unrivaled in a beauty all its own.

It is said by some tourist, that the most beautiful sight that a traveler ever witnesses, is the first sight of his native land on returning to it. So I am sure all travelers will pardon my extravagance, even if I did, as I passed by steam up the river and over the railway, give vent to my emotions in a faint effort at poetry, the only true language of emotion.

Gazed ye ever, gazed ye ever
On a scene so fair as this,
In the old world where you've wandered,
Questioning of human bliss?

Tell me not of palace grandeur,
Crowning hills along the Rhine,
Where relics of their splendor,
Sublimer seem thro' lapse of time.

Tell me not that France more lovely,
Spreads her valleys to the sky,
Where her towering trees of Freedom,
Lift their stately heads on high—

That her vine-clad hills are fairer,
With her peasent's lowly homes—
That her cities boast more splendor,
Freer light-winged Fancy roams.

England, with her soft green hedges,
Like a garden all doth seem,
Where, thro' meadows rich in vendure,
Courses many a blue waved stream—

Peasent homes whose lowly beauty,
Like the flowers that round them twine,
Tell of those who yield meek duty,
To their lords of ancient line.

Here rise halls of princely grandeur,
Castle,s towers that jeer at time,
Grand when reared, but with the ages,
Rendered even more sublime.

Ruins of the days of Cæsars—
Moss grown abbeys—ivy-twined—
Cities, with their pomp and splendor,
And their squalor, and their crime.

Ireland, rising like an emerald,
From the bosom of the sea,
I have marked thy hills of beauty,
And the greenness of thy lea.

But from all these alluring,
To each far-famed foreign strand,
Turns my soul, with love enduring,
To my thrice-dear native land!

Homeward, over Ocean's billows,
How the watcher's heart beats wild,
When the first land breeze that kisses,
Whispers—"Welcome home my child!"

Where the Delaware throws open
Her broad arms of living green—
Firts Cape May, and then Henlopen,
Stretched like welcoming hands they seem.

Now we mark the willows bending,
Till they kiss the laughing wave,
And the broad green fields extending
Till their very lips they lave.

And the fairy barks whose canvass
Spreads like white wings o'er the tide,
While, deep-mirrored in the waters,
Like a double life they glide.

Born amid the rugged mountains,
Thro' a rocky channel thrown,
Dreamed the first gush of its fountains,
Thro' such soft scenes o'er to roam?

Like a childhood full of sorrow,
Struggling, toiling, onward, lone,
Strength came with the boding morrow,
Till all woes were overcome.

Such thy childhood, O my nation,
Born amid the Old World's scorn,
But thy present, like this river,
Calm and mighty, glideth on.

Fairer seem to me thy children
Than the sons of other lands—
None so proud, and none so servile,
Stronger, purer, Virtue stands.

Yonder rise their homes of beauty,
Reared by Love and honest toil,
Flowers round them, trees embower them,
Blest, thrice blest—my native soil!

H. M. TRACY

Wisconsin   State Journal.

VOLUME IX. MADISON, WIS., WEDNESDAY MORNING, NOVEMBER 7, 1860. NUMBER 36.

The State Journal.

WEDNESDAY MORNING, NOVEMBER 7.

ABRAHAM LINCOLN, THE PRESIDENT ELECT.

Wisconsin good for 15,000 majority!

The Reception of the Returns.

SUPREME COURT DECISIONS.

BY TELEGRAPH.

REPORTED EXPRESSLY FOR THE WISCONSIN STATE JOURNAL.

The Republican Avalanche!

THE "SLOGAN" HEARD AT LAST!!

The Earthquake Tread of the People!

FREEDOM HAS TRIUMPHED!!

Thunder from the Prairies of the West!

50,000 Majority in New York!

Reverberations from the Alleghanies!!

Connecticut all Right!

Little Rhody's Voice is Heard!

Splendid gains in Indiana, Michigan, and Ohio!!

IOWA'S VOICE JOINS THE CHORUS!

Three Republican Congressmen Elected.

Effects of Douglas' Speeches in Milwaukee and the Third District.

Dane County Probably Redeemed!!

All Hail Illinois!

Hurrah for Delaware!

VERMONT FOREVER!

LET THE WELKIN RING!!!

New York.--3 o'clock A. M.--Sufficient returns are received to give the State to the Republicans by upwards of 50,000 majority.

NEW YORK MARKET.

New Advertisements.

TO THE PUBLIC.

WISCONSIN STATE JOURNAL.

VOLUME XII. MADISON, WIS., SATURDAY, NOVEMBER 21, 1863. NUMBER 56.

STATE JOURNAL.

THE OFFICIAL STATE PAPER.

SATURDAY, NOVEMBER 21, 1863.

READING MATTER ON EVERY PAGE.

5 O'CLOCK

SECOND EDITION.

Losses of the 23d Wisconsin.

We publish to-day a letter from Lt. CARL JUSSEN, giving a list of the losses of the 23d Wisconsin in the recent battle in Louisiana. It will be seen that the regiment lost heavily, though largely in prisoners.

Col. GUPPY is wounded and a prisoner.

The 23d was largely composed of Dane county men.

The Gettysburg Battle Cemetery Consecration—Remarks of the President.

It is estimated that from 30,000 to 50,000 people were present on Thursday at the consecration of the Cemetery of those who fell in battle for the Union at Gettysburg in last July. The oration of EDWARD EVERETT, occupied over two hours in its delivery.

The President made a few remarks at the conclusion, which are reported by telegraph as follows:

Four score and seven years ago, our fathers established upon this continent a Government conceived in liberty and dedicated to the fundamental principle that all mankind are created equal by a good God, [applause] and now we are engaged in a great contest.

We are contesting the question whether this nation, or any nation so conceived, so dedicated, can longer remain.

We are met on a great battle-field of the war. We are met here to dedicate a portion of that field as the final resting place of those who have given their lives to that nation that it might live. It is altogether fitting and proper that we should do this. But in a large sense we cannot dedicate, we cannot consecrate, we cannot hallow this ground. The brave men lying dead, who struggled here, have consecrated it far above our poor power to add or to detract. [Great applause.] The world will little heed, nor long remember, what we say here; but it will not forget what they did here. [Immense applause.] It is for us rather, the living, to be dedicated here to the unfinished work that they have thus far so nobly carried forward. It is rather for us here to be dedicated to the great task remaining before us; for us to renew our devotion to that cause for which they gave the full measure of their devotion. Here let us resolve that what they have done shall not have been done in vain. That the nation shall, under God, have a new birth. That the Government the people founded, by the people shall not perish.

THE present management of the New York Central Railroad, has excited serious opposition among a portion of the stockholders. A determined effort is to be made to put it under the control of a different set of men from those who now manage it. It is charged against the present officers that they have prostituted the interests of the road to advance political and personal objects. Mr. CORNING, the President, receives no direct salary, but in lieu of it, a firm, of which he is a member, is allowed to supply the road with all articles necessary for its operation. This monopoly, while it greatly enhances the cost of running the road, is believed to be worth not less than $200,000 a year, and perhaps more, which is a very handsome substitute for a salary.

THE action of our Government in forwarding food for the Union prisoners in Richmond, is probably without a parallel in history. Nothing more vividly illustrates the sheer and monstrous sham which the insurrectionists are attempting to palm off upon the world as a new nationality, than the fact that they are unable to feed their prisoners. With gaunt famine stalking through the streets of their Capital city, and without the means of subsisting the prisoners they have captured, they may well cease to look for recognition from foreign powers.

☞ "PUMP" virtually confesses the correctness of the account we gave of his efforts to get out of the draft last year, by declaring that we pretend to have it from some physician, and then administering a hint that physicians who are so unprofessional as to divulge the secrets of their patients will soon lose their practice. We said nothing about the source of our information, but the fact that PUMP immediately suspects that the touching narrative came from a physician, is tantamount to a confession of its substantial fidelity.

"PUMP" makes us a proposition in regard to going into the army, which looks very much as if he has a new attack of his old abdominal complaint. If he has the slightest intention of anything beyond talk and bluff, we can make our arrangements for entering the service of Uncle Sam best by going before a competent attorney and there arranging the preliminaries. If bonds are to be given they must be given on his side as well as ours.

LITERARY NEWS.—Dicken's new serial, to be completed in twenty parts, will be published by Messrs. Chapman and Hall, in London. The first number will be issued on the 1st of May next.

WILKIE COLLINS has been seriously ill for eighteen months past, and is now in Italy, incapable of work.

☞ Mysterious intimations are given out by secession sympathizers from Maryland that Gov. BRADFORD is going to refuse certificates of election to the Congressmen from that State. They declare that CRESWELL will be refused a certificate, on the ground of military interference with the election.

THREE CHILDREN BURNED TO DEATH.—Three children of Mr LAWRENCE DUFFY, of Poysippi, Waushara county, aged four, two and a half, and one and a half years, respectively, were burned to death, one evening last week, while their parents were absent, the bed in which they slept being accidentally set on fire by one of the older children.

☞ The Chicago *Times* has concluded that "a want of thought" is one of the peculiarities of the American people. As the highest evidence in favor of its position it might have quoted the fact that the American people support such a newspaper as the Chicago *Times.*

☞ HON. JONATHAN BOWMAN, Senator from Columbia county, and Hon. G. W. HAZELTON, his predecessor are both drafted.

The Battle of Buzzard's Prairie—Killed, Wounded and Prisoners of the 23d Wisconsin.

HEADQUARTERS 23d R. W. V. I.,
Vermillion Bayou, La., Nov. 6.

Editors State Journal:—Enclosed find list of killed, wounded and missing in the late action at Buzzard's Prairie. Of the 228 men and officers available for line of battle on that morning we lost 128. We have now for duty and available for line of battle 108 men and 17 officers. Total 115.

Respectfully, CARL JUSSEN,
Act Adjutant.

CASUALTIES OF THE 23D WISCONSIN.

The following is the report of the killed, wounded and missing of the 23d Wisconsin Volunteer Infantry in the battle of Buzzard Prairie, Nov. 3d, 1863:

FIELD AND STAFF.

Col. Joshua J. Guppy, wounded in leg slight and prisoner; Act. S. M. John L. Jolley, wounded slightly in abdomen and right arm.

COMPANY A.

Killed.—Alonzo G. Jack.—1.

Wounded.—Sergt. William Carey, in left hand, slight; Corp. Stephen Jex, in side, severe; Thomas Whamby, in side, serious.—3.

Prisoners.—Lieut. Alex. Atkinson, Corp. John G. Memhard, Corp. Halver E. Hanson, Christian H. Beyler, Joseph Byer, Edmund Quinn, Niels Thompson, James A. Wells, Oscar P. Whitney, Wallace Davis.—10.

COMPANY B.

Wounded—Sergt. Francis Scott, in left arm, severely; Philip Nugent, in right wrist, severely; Edward Kennedy, in left side, slightly.—3.

Prisoners.—Corp. A. F. McConnell, Edmund Stolt, Patrick Griffin, John Waters, William Griffin, Ernst F. Stauch, Michael Hogan, Pat. Hickey, John Hannahan, Philip McCoy, Chas. Tabor, Chas Puffer.—12.

COMPANY C.

Wounded.—Corp. Fred'k Ford, in shoulder slight; Porter Langdon, in neck; Silas J Packard. in arm.—3.

Prisoners.—Captain Oliver H. Sorenson, wounded in shoulder, slight; Wm. Edwards, Peter Anderson, Peter Boll, Israel J. Cannon, Greenleaf Ackerman, James Whitney, Henry Mattey, John Robins.—9.

COMPANY D.

Killed.—Ole Oleson.—1.

Wounded.—Sergt. Henry Morton, leg amputated above knee.—1.

Prisoners.—Corp. Clarence R. Taft, Corp. Fred E. Zimmerman, Corp. George W. Pomeroy, Stephen S. Bell, Jared M. Fuller, John G. Klyter, Herman Roll, David F. Scidmore, John Waldschocky (wounded severely), Wm. H. Outhouse, Drummer H. R. Bird.—11.

COMPANY E.

Wounded.—Corp. Harrison M. Thompson, in left leg severely—1.

Prisoners.—Capt. James M. Bull, Privates Franklin Lees, Loern D. Parker, Cornelius Ford, Austin Laughlin, Wm. Clinton, Wm. Roberts, Orrin L. Huie, Joseph Harman, Winfield S. Colby, Edward Blackmore and John Wells—11.

COMPANY F.

Wounded—Sergt. Joseph N. Savage, slightly in right shoulder; Corp. Henry C. Stanley, slightly in right arm; Elisha W. Ellis, severely in right thigh.—3.

Prisoners—1st Lieut. D. C. Stanley, Z. M. Palmer, George Dustin, M. E. Jopp —4,

Killed—Jabez Williams.

Wounded.—Serg. J. F. Kent, in right breast, slight; Corp'ls Peter J. Harger, in right thigh, severe; and Edward Gray, in back, slight; Privates Franklin Fisher, in face, severe; Daniel O'Rouke, in right thigh, severe; Seth Trask, in left hand, finger amputated; and Henry Russell, in right breast, severe —7.

Prisoners.—Corp. Daniel C. Cooper, Privates Hugh Hall, Byron Van Walker, Chas. J. Wilder, George Etscheit, Ole J. Oleson, and John Waggoner—7.

COMPANY H.

Wounded.—Serg. Byron Waffle, in leg, slight; Privates Hugh Lindsay, in left arm, slight; and Joseph F. Fisher—3.

Prisoners.—Corp'ls John W. Paul, Thomas Farber, Robert Giller, and E. O. Waterbury, Privates John Cavanaugh, James W. Dever, James Quin, Leanddr Wells, Ernest Degrur, George Phinney, Edwin C. Riddle, and Musician Joseph Eells, jr.—12.

COMPANY I.

Wounded.—Serg. L. D. Frost, in hip, severe; Corp. Elijah McGinley, leg, severe; Privates Moses Flesh, in arm, severe; Iver Johnson, in face and hip, severe; Anthony Questa, in arm, slightly; John B. Inskeep, in hand, slight—6.

Prisoners.—Serg'ts John G. Smith, and Jesse L. Myers, Corp. W. L. Matts, Privates Charles Bitney, Gunder Edwards, and Roderick J. Park.

COMPANY K.

Killed.—Serg. James H. Hilliard, Privates James McKeever, and William M. Ballard—3.

Wounded—1st Serg. Alexander McGinnis, in left leg, slighty; Serg'ts George W. Johnson, in thigh, and Wm. H. Harris, in left wrist; Corp. John C. Link, in left hand; Privates Henry D. Stickl, in left arm—5.

Prisoners—Privates Jefferson L. Daggett, and Randolph Brown.

RECAPITULATION.

COMMISSIONED OFFICERS.

Prisoners 5

ENLISTED MEN.

Killed 6
Wounded 34
Prisoners 81

Total 128

How the Soldiers Vote.

The following table shows the vote of the soldiers so far as received:

Regiment.	Lewis.	Palmer.
1st in Tenn., complete	82	4
2d in Virginia, "	181	7
3d in Alabama, "	280	2
4th in Louisiana, 8 Co's	317	2
5th in Virginia, complete	418	1
6th " "	107	6
7th " "	222	1
8th in Miss., "	334	14
9th in Arkansas, 8 Co's,	149	54
10th in Tenn., complete	34	0
12th in Miss., "	510	12
11th in Louisiana "	265	3
13th in Tenn., "	411	17
14th " "	230	0
15th " four Co's	41	0
16th in Miss., complete	202	1
17th " "	27	220
18th " 2 Co's	29	0
19th in Va., eight Co's,	142	47
21st in Tenn., complete	155	2
22d " "	433	10
23d in Louisiana, 3 Co's	55	0
24th in Tenn., complete	181	17
25th in Arkansas, "	275	0
27th " 8 Co's	182	10
28th " 6 Co's	229	10
30th in Wisconsin 9 Co's	505	20
31st in Tenn. complete	390	41
32d " six Co's,	295	4
33d in Miss., complete,	340	5
1st Cav. in Tenn. "	213	4
2d Cav. in Miss. "	115	0
3d Cav. on frontier 1 Co.	60	0
Benton Hussars,	83	0
Berdan's Sharpshoot's	27	0
1st Battery,	52	0
2d "	25	8
3d "	60	0
4th "	7	17
5th "	64	0
7th "	104	0
8th "	41	0
9th "	56	0
Battery A, Heavy Artill'y	83	24
" B, " "	29	17
" D, " "	49	0
	8,330	586

The 9th Reg. cast 67 votes for SALOMON.

☞ We have never claimed to be more loyal than other people.—*Patriot.*

And certainly nobody has ever suspected you of anything of the kind.

LOCAL MATTERS.

OFFICIAL PAPER OF DANE COUNTY.

NEW CIDER—*A Genuine Article.*—The best cider we have seen in market has just been received by Messrs MITCHELL & STILLWELL, at their new grocery on Pinkney street, next below KLAUBER'S corner. It was manufactured by Mr. STILLWELL'S brother in Michigan, and is the pure juice of the apple. Those who want a first-rate and reliable article better secure it of Messrs. M. & S. without delay.

THE VARIAN CONCERT.—Persons who are intending to attend the Concert of Madame VARIAN, on Monday evening, should secure seats without delay. This can be done by calling at MOSELEY'S Bookstore, where a diagram of the City Hall is kept, and the seats selected will be reserved.

Madame VARIAN'S reputation as a vocalist will doubtless call out a large audience.

FRANK LESLIE'S ILLUSTRATED.—The last number, received from MOSELEY'S, has a great variety of illustrations, including the battle of Rappahannock Station, Centerville and the Bull Run battle field, a recent skirmish in Louisiana, portraits of marshall Forey and Gen. Averill, with a caricature of New York Democracy.

FRANK LESLIES' ALMANAC.—Frank Leslie has been getting out an illustrated Almanac, something after the style of the London Almanacs. It contains a great variety of interesting information, portraits, &c., and can be procured of HOSKINS, at the Post Office, for a quarter.

VANITY FAIR.—Some of the numbers for 1860 and 1861, have been put together in yellow, and its old time hits are interesting curiosities. It can be had at the Post Office News Depot, with the newest song books, novels, &c., &c.

AMUSEMENTS FOR NEXT WEEK.—Madame VARIAN gives concerts on Monday and Tuesday evenings. On Wednesday and Thursday the levees of TOM THUMB and his petit bride, with Commodore NUTT and MINNIE WARREN, are held.

GOING TO THE WARS.—C. E. REDFIELD, Esq., editor and publisher of the Waupacca *Spirit*, is in town to-day. He has come here to enlist as a volunteer in the 8th Wisconsin, in which regiment he already has a brother.

☞ The Young People's Prayer Meeting will be held to-morrow afternoon at 3 o'clock precisely, in the lecture room of the Presbyterian church. The young of the city are cordially invited to attend.

MARRIED.

ATWOOD—WIGGINTON.—At the residence of the bride's mother, on the 12th of November, 1863, by Rev. Mr. Dunlap, Mr. J. BRUCE ATWOOD, of Chicago, to Miss CECILIA P. WIGGINTON, of La Grange, Missouri.

BY TELEGRAPH.

OUR NIGHT DISPATCHES.

Exclusively for the Wisconsin State Journal.

ITEMS FROM SOUTHERN PAPERS.

Warm Times at Charleston.

250 Shot Thrown into the City.

MONITORS EXPLORING CHANNEL.

One Reported Badly Battered.

Rebel Reports from Tennessee.

A $500,000 Rebel Ram Worthless.

REMOVAL OF UNION PRISONERS

Probable Exchange of Surgeons.

AFFAIRS IN MEMPHIS AND VICINITY.

Burnside's Position Impregnable.

Bragg Reported as Retiring to Rome.

NEWS FROM REBEL SOURCES.

NEW YORK, Nov. 20.

Richmond papers of the 16th contain the following:

An Atlanta, Georgia, dispatch, dated Nov. 13th, says a party of the Georgia State troops and Indians killed the notorious Bryson and thirty-four of his men, a short time since, on the line between Georgia and North Carolina.

A special to the *Register*, dated Sweetwater, Tenn., Nov. 12th, says the federals have removed all their supplies to Knoxville for safety, and are living on half rations.

A special to the Atlanta *Intelligencer* says that Yankee officers, who deserted and came into our lines, report that Grant expects soon to assault Lookout Mountain. His army is on half rations.

About 2,100 of the Yankee prisoners in Richmond have been sent to console the good people of Danville.

The escape of the notorious Dr. Rucker from jail, has removed the difficulty with regard to the exchange of surgeons. It is probable that the next flag of truce steamer from the North, which is expected at City Point, daily, will bring up a large number of our surgeons held as prisoners at the North. The Libby prison contains 84 Yankee surgeons, which is quite as great a number as the Yankees hold. These will be sent forward as soon as ours are received.

No news was received here yesterday from the Chowan. We have heard a rumor that the enemy were fortifying at Winton, but the rumor wants confirmation. We should not be surprised at any time, however, to hear of an advance on Weldon, in that direction.

The great ram *Missouri*, built at Shreveport, La., is a failure. She cost the Confederate Government half a million of dollars.

The Richmond *Examiner*, in a recent editorial, shows the worthlessness of the rebel currency, and says: Government is gradually feeling its way to a system of forced loans. The bakers of Richmond have raised the price of the pound loaf of bread, from 25 to 50 cents.

A rebel report says the Yankees recently came to Jonesville, Lee Co., Va., from the Rappahanuock, and burnt the Academy and Masonic Hall, and committed all sorts of depredations.

From rebel accounts it appears that a calcium light is used by Gen. Gilmore, at Fort Gregg, to obtain greater accuracy in firing at night.

The city council of Richmond has appropriated $60,000, to purchase a family residence for Gen. Lee.

FROM CHARLESTON.

FORT MONROE, Nov. 20.

A Richmond paper of the 16th says:

The bombardment of Fort Sumter last night continued as usual. Slow firing is going on this morning. The enemy fired 250 shots into the city, doing no material damage. It is reported that their gun bursted at the last fire. There has been slow firing on Sumter all day. Present indications are that the enemy intend more extensive operations. No Monitors were in action.

The Richmond *Examiner* of the 18th contains the following:

CHARLESTON, Nov. 17.—Two of the Monitors engaged are not seen this morning. A report from Moultrie states that the leading Monitor in the fight had her smoke stacks and turret perforated. A report from Sumter states that four Monitors took their position to-day near Cummings Point and afterwards passed up the channel. It is believed they carried heavy weights suspended at certain depths below the water, to ascertain if there was a passage for vessels of certain drafts.

FROM THE SOUTHWEST.

MEMPHIS, Nov. 17.

Gen. Hurlbut's order, reported yesterday, directing a conscription of the able-bodied men here, caused great excitement in this city, especially among the Jews, a large number of whom are liable. The conscription order is generally approved of among military men. The soldiers are especially jubilant at the general consternation of the citizens.—The lines are completely closed and all intercourse with the interior suspended for the present.

Chalmers' forces are again gathering upon the Tallahatchie for another raid. They are reported from 6,000 to 8,000 strong, with ten pieces of artillery, having been reinforced from Alabama. A warm reception awaits them.

The railroad from Jackson, Mississippi, to Grenada, has been repaired by the rebels, and trains commenced running to the latter point on the 8th.

Bragg is reported to be falling back on Rome. The foundry at Selma is said to be casting 120 pounder guns, and large quantities of shells.

BURNSIDE'S SITUATION.

NEW YORK, Nov. 20.

A special to the *Post* from Washington says advices have been received at the War Department this morning from Gen. Burnside. He says his position is impregnable and he has no fear of the rebels under Longstreet.

OUR MIDNIGHT DISPATCHES.

Exclusively for the Wisconsin State Journal.

Later from Europe.

Palmerston on the American Question.

A European Congress to be Held.

UNION PRISONERS AT RICHMOND.

Delivery of Supplies for Them.

Everything they Need Sent Forward.

LATER FROM NEW ORLEANS.

Banks' Complete Success in Texas.

Gen. Hartsuff at Lexington.

No Communication with Knoxville.

GEN. MEAGHER'S NEW COMMAND.

Russian Fleet to Leave New York.

Reasons for the Rise in Gold.

FROM EUROPE.

CAPE RACE, Nov. 20.

The steamer *City of Baltimore* from Liverpool Nov. 11th via Queenstown 12th, passed here this morning.

Lord Palmerston in a speech at the Lord Mayor's banquet deplored the American war. He said England would have interfered but for the belief that it would have been in vain. She therefore would yield neither to blandishment or menaces, but would remain strictly neutral. Regarding Poland he said England had done her duty by remonstrating, but although these remonstrences failed, he hoped Russia would cease to pursue an offensive course. Lord Palmerston's reception was significantly enthusiastic.

Mr. Vellians, a prominent supporter of the government, had been speaking in defense of the Federal Government.

A Paris telegram says that Matamoras is not blockaded, but contraband of war is not allowed to be landed.

The Emperor's proposal for a European Congress attracts universal attention. Fifteen powers are invited. It is supposed that a greater number will acquiesce.

The drain of gold from England still continued. A further advance in rates of discount was anticipated.

OUR PRISONERS AT RICHMOND.

FORT MONROE, Nov. 20.

The steamer has arrived from City Point. Col. Irving states that he has satisfactorily transferred our government rations, also the Baltimore American relief fund and provisions to Commissioner Ould.

Richmond papers say that 600 more Yankee prisoners were sent to Danville Tuesday, and that on Monday night 115 Yankee prisoners were received at Libby prison from Charleston, among them the sailors and marines captured on the last night of the assault on Sumter's battered walls.

WASHINGTON, Nov. 20.

The *Star* of this afternoon says, we learn through recent correspondence up to the 17th instynt from Richmond, between Robert Ould, the rebel commissioner, and our own, which has reached this city, that the rebel authorities are faithfully executing their promise to give our prisoners in their hands the food and everything our government has forwarded to Richmond. To that end our hospital department here, through Acting Surgeon Barnes, has come forward to add medicines to the stores thus furnished our suffering heroes in Richmond by the government. The rebel authorities will not permit our government agents to accompany the goods within their lines, substituting rebel commissiaries in their stead where the flag of truce boats meet.

THE TEXAS EXPEDITION.

NEW YORK, Nov. 20.

The steamer *Morning Star*, from New Orleans 14th, via Havana 17th arrived to-night.

The expedition sent by water, accompanied by Gen. Banks, has been a great success. Brasos Island, Brownville and Point Isabell were captured, and are now in our possession. The enemy threw away their guns and fled to San Antonio. The casualties on either side are not mentioned.

Reports of heavy fighting in western Louisiana are untrue. There had been slight skirmishing, but nothing decisive. Our forces are still in the vicinity of Vermilionville and everything is quiet.

FROM KENTUCKY.

LEXINGTON, Ky., Nov. 20.

Maj. Gen. Hartsuff, commanding the 20th Army Corps, has arrived here. The change of position of the bullet in his hip, received at the battle of Antietam, disables him from active field duty for the present. He has been ordered to Cincinnati, to preside over a court-martial of high rank. The command of the District or Department of Ohio will probably be tendered him, should the disability continue.

There is nothing new from Cumberland Gap, and the line east of that point is still interrupted, it is supposed from the recent rain.

MISCELLANEOUS ITEMS.

NEW YORK, Nov. 20.

Report says that Gen. Meagher has been made a Major General, and is to command the old Irish and Excelsior Brigades, recruited to their full standard.

The Russian Admiral and fleet leave New York on Monday for Fort Monroe, where they expect to pass the winter.

A letter from the blockading squadron off Mobile reports that a rebel ram recently attacked the fleet, but after receiving three shots from the *Colorado* and two from the *Genesee*, ran back under the guns of Fort Morgan.

THE RISE IN GOLD.

NEW YORK, Nov. 20.

The gold market was excited to-day, by unfavorable rumors as to Burnside, and reports that a French war vessel took out to-day, $2,700,000 for Vera Cruz, and that to-morrow's shipment to Europe would be heavy. Gold at one time reached $1.54¼, but closed at 1.53¼. A large firm operating in gold, failed to-day.

MORNING DISPATCHES.

All Sorts of Items.

The Reconstruction Question.

Freedom and Equality the Basis.

MORE ABOUT UNION PRISONERS.

Exchange of Correspondents.

AFFAIRS IN VIRGINIA.

MEADE'S ARMY AT MADISON C. H.

Lee's Forces Still Retreating.

French War Steamer at New York.

Union Ticket Successful in Idaho.

FROM WASHINGTON.

WASHINGTON, Nov. 20.

Special to Tribune—The attention of the President and more prominent members of the cabinet and other gentlemen, has been largely given of late to the consideration of the important questions connected with the recall to the Union of the truant Southern states, several of which may soon be knocking at the door.

The precise course to be adopted is not yet determined. Several theories claim the President's ear, but he is amply engaged in maturing a practical plan by which to secure reunion upon the only practicable basis—the basis of freedom and equality before the law for all. Recent utterances of the President and instructions to recently commissioned representatives of the Government in districts of the South, now in our possession, leave no doubt that the policy of the Administration, to permit none of the vagrant States to come back with a slave constitution, is fixed. The present discussion relates to the ways and means of effecting the result.

THE PRISONER QUESTION.

NEW YORK, Nov. 21.

The *World's* Washington dispatch says:

The Indiana State Agent reached here to-night from Fort Monroe, bringing with him a letter from Commissioner Ould, in reply to one of his own, stating that the rebel authorities will promptly receive and deliver to all Indiana soldiers in the Confederacy all clothing and supplies which may be forwarded to them, and for which he (Ould) will give due notice to the Indiana authorities from time to time as such may be delivered and accounted for.

A proposition has been made to the Richmond authorities to release, unconditionally without parol or exchange, all newspaper correspondents in prison, provided a similar release of the same number of civilians is made here.

FROM THE POTOMAC ARMY.

NEW YORK, Nov. 21.

The *Herald* has the following:

ARMY POTOMAC, Nov. 20.—The guerillas around Warrenton having fired upon our pickets quite frequently of late, the citizens have been notified that on the first recurrence of picket shooting Warrenton will be shelled.

BRANDY STATION, Nov. 20.—A squadron of the Sixth, Seventh, and Third Virginia cavalry, of Buford's command, under Captain Conger of the latter regiment, made a reconnoissance yesterday in the direction of Sperryville and captured a rebel herd of 232 cattle, 14 horses and 15 tenders.

WASHINGTON, Nov. 20.

It is reported here that Meade's army occupies Madison Court House and that the rebels are retreating.

Advices from the front to-night state that no collision has yet occurred. The rebels have made no new demonstration within a day or two, but seem to be still strengthening their earthworks.

FROM NEW ORLEANS.

NEW YORK, Nov. 21,

The New Orleans correspondent, of the 14th, to the *Herald* states that yesterday the U. S. Marshal and his deputies seized all the cotton now in New Orleans. The seizure was made on the order of Mr. Rufus Wofles, the U. S. District Attorney. Rumor says that the seizure was made on information derived from secret police that most of the cotton now in store and in transit was purchased from disloyal parties, and that before it can be released the present owners must prove that the parties from whom they purchased it are loyal to the U. S. Government.

GOLD FOR MEXICO.

NEW YORK, Nov. 21.

The *World* says that the French war steamer *Milan* has just arrived at this port from Vera Cruz and Havana. She will return directly to the former port, having been ordered to New York expressly to take out to Mexico $4,000,000 in gold, purchased in this city on account of the French Government by the house of Belmont & Co.

SALES OF 5-20s.

WASHINGTON, Nov. 20.

Sales of 5-20s during the last ten days amount to over $9,000,000. The Treasury Department is nearly $33,000,000 behind in the delivery of coupon bonds, some of the orders of Oct. 30th being yet unfilled. This delay, like that of last August is in consequence of the non-completion of the new series of bonds.

N. Y. CENTRAL R. R. DIVIDEND.

ALBANY, Nov. 20.

The directors of the Central Railroad, at a meeting held in this city to-day, determined to declare next month a semi-annual dividend for the current six months ending January 31, 1864, of 5 per cent. with a confident hope that this rate can be hereafter maintained.

IDAHO ELECTION.

SAN FRANCISCO, Nov. 18.

The Portland *News* says that partial returns from the late Idaho election are sufficient to warrant the assurance that Governor Wallace, the Union candidate for Delegate to Congress, has been elected by a handsome majority.

THE CASE OF THE ALEXANDRA.

WASHINGTON, Nov. 20.

Advices from Mr. Adams, our minister in England, confirm the news that a new trial is granted by the Court of Exchequer in the case of the *Alexandra.*

AFTERNOON DISPATCHES.

THE TEXAS EXPEDITION.

The Occupation of Brownsville.

Recent Skirmishing on the Rapidan.

FROM THE TEXAS EXPEDITION.

NEW YORK, Nov. 21.

The *Tribune's* letter from Brazos, Texas, Nov. 8th, says, on the arrival of Banks, the character of the expedition being known, rebel sympathizers threw the armament of the fort into the Rio Grande and burned the greater portion of the dwellings of Brownsville, leaving the Unionists in possession of the place. The rebels took the cotton on the Texas side across the river, after ferrying over all owned by the Confederate government. A general destruction of the cotton remaining took place. The 94th Illinois regiment raised their flag at Brownsville, on Thursday, at 10 A. M.

Gen. Banks arrived soon after. At the last accounts seven regiments had arrived there.

FROM THE ARMY OF THE POTOMAC.

NEW YORK, Nov. 21.

A *Times'* special from the Army of the Potomac dated the 20th, says the enemy's movement on Wednesday seems to have been a concerted plan along the whole front to ascertain our position. A force of infantry crossed a short distance below Raccoon Ford, and attempted to cut off the 1st Michigan cavalry, but Maj. Brewer discovered them before an attack could be made. The enemy crossed the river during the night and exposed themselves just at dawn. After skirmishing one or two hours and finding their plans discovered, they returned to the opposite bank.

COMMERCIAL.

Milwaukee Market.

MILWAUKEE, Nov. 21.

Flour, unchanged.

Wheat, dull. Sales of 27,300 bushels No. 1 spring, winter receipts, at 1,10; do, fall receipts, 1.09½; do, delivered, 1.11; choice do, 1.11½.

Oats, in store, 61@62c.

Corn, delivered, 95c.

Barley, good to choice, 1.15@1.25; do, interior, 90c@1.00.

Rye in store, 73c.

Gold touched 1,54¾ at one time yesterday in New York, and closed firm at 1,53¾. The opening price, as telegraphed this morning, was 1,53¾. The range here is from 1,51@1,51½.

Chicago Market.

CHICAGO, Nov. 20.

Wheat—No. 1 is 1.10; No. 2, 1.05½.

Corn, 53c.

Oats, 63½@65c, and better.

Freights, 9c on wheatto Buffalo.

Market steady.

New York Market.

EVENING REPORT.

NEW YORK, Nov. 20.

Flour—Is 5@10c better and not very active at 6.40@6.45 for Extra State; 7.50@7.60 for Round Hooped Ohio; 7.65@9.30 for Trade Brands, the market closing quiet.

Wheat—Opened at 1@2c better, but with only a limited demand, and closed dull—buyers generally refusing to pay any advance—at 1.41@1.46 for Chicago Spring; 1.42@1.46 for Milwaukee Club; 1.47 for Milwaukee Amber; 1.50@1.60 for Winter Red Western; 1.61@1.65 for Amber Michigan.

Corn—Is much excited and 3@4c higher, with a strong speculative demand at 1.14@1.16 for Shipping Mixed Western in store; 1.14@1.14½ for Western Yellow in store.

Oats—Are excited and 2@3c higher, at 89@90c for Western and State.

NEW YORK, Nov. 21

Flour—More active and 5c higher, at 6.45@6.50 for Extra State; 7.55@7.60 for Round Hooped Ohio.

Wheat—Receipts 95,244 bushels; market about 1c better, quoted at 1.42@1.46 for Chicago Spring and Milwaukee Club; 1,47@1,48 for amber Mil.; 1.52@1.56 for Winter Red.

Corn—Receipts 9,570 bushels; market excited and 4c better, at 1,16@1,20 in store.

Oats—Excited and 2@3c higher at 90@92½c.

Pork and lard quiet.

Whiskey—Irregular and excited, at 70@75c, the latter for small lots.

New York Stock Market.

SECOND BOARD.

NEW YORK, Nov. 20.

Money—Is less stringent at 7 per cent.

Sterling Exchange—Is firmer but quiet at 1.07 @1.68.

Gold—Is firmer but very irregular and unsettled, opening at 1.53½, declining to 1.51½, advancing to 1.54, and closing firm at 1.53½.

Government Stocks—Are quiet and steady.

NEW YORK, Nov. 21.

Stocks, better, but not active.

Money, quiet at 7 per cent.

Sterling exchange, quiet, 1.69 asked.

Gold, 1.53½.

U. S. 6s of '81, with coupons, 1.09½; 5s of '74, with coupons, 98c; endorsed 7-30s 1.06½; 1 year certificates, 1.02¼.

WISCONSIN STATE JOURNAL.

VOLUME XIII. MADISON, WIS., WEDNESDAY, NOVEMBER 9, 1864. NUMBER 45.

STATE JOURNAL.

WEDNESDAY, NOV. 9, 1864.

THE OFFICIAL STATE PAPER.

No General News.

The disagreeable rain which has prevailed for the last 36 hours, not only in this State but all over the North, has almost silenced the telegraph to-day, reducing the quantity of election returns and preventing the reception of any general news whatever.

The Election Yesterday—Result in the State.

The returns of the election in this State as far as heard from will be found in to-day's papers. The storm has impeded to some extent the transmission of news by telegraph, and prevented the bringing in of returns from many of the back towns that would have otherwise been heard from.

The complexion of the returns indicates with certainty the success of the general ticket, but perhaps by a reduced majority, as compared with the vote of last year. In some places we have gained handsomely, but in many others we lose considerably upon last year's majorities.

We are disappointed in this result; we had hoped to keep up our majority to the high mark of last year; but there were several causes conspiring to reduce it, without any actual change in public sentiment. The very fact of carrying the State last year by over 25,000 majority rendered the Union voters confident, and diminished the sense of the importance of a single vote. The storm yesterday was also unfavorable to getting out the full vote of the rural districts, where our majorities reside. We have also sent some 20,000 men into the army since last year, four fifths of whom have been Union men, and would have voted for LINCOLN if at home.—The soldiers vote will, therefore, probably be increased so as to make up in part for the falling off in the home vote.

At the very worst our majority on the home vote will not fail below 5,000 while it may reach 10,000, though we hardly expect to attain so high a figure. To this, unless the rebels kept our troops busy on election day, there will be 12,000 to 15,000 majority on the soldiers vote to be added.

Sufficient returns from the Congressional districts have not been received to form the basis for any absolute judgment respecting the result on Congress. In all probability however, we shall elect five out of the six members. The returns from the 4th district indicate the re-election of ELDREDGE (copper,) by a considerable majority. This, however, is not unexpected.

Both houses of the Legislature will be largely Union.

The General Result.

It may be set down as an undoubted fact that the people of the United States signified at the ballot-box on yesterday their deliberate preference for ABRAHAM LINCOLN as their President for four years more, rejecting the peace and surrender platform, and announcing their unalterable resolution to stand by the Union and the flag.

There is some cloud of doubt yet resting over the result in New York, where the gigantic election fraud, arrested before it was fully consummated, may have been partially successful. Every other free State has doubtless gone for the Union ticket, unless it be New Jersey, and even there the prospects are favorable to the Union ticket.

Result in the City—Well done for Madison.

The Union men of the Capital city did themselves honor by their exertions and achievements yesterday, reducing the opposition majority nineteen below what it was last year, giving MCDOUGALL, the *Union* candidate for Sheriff, a majority of 24, and coming within six votes of tying the Copperhead candidate for the Assembly. With the soldiers vote added we shall probably carry the city for the Union electoral ticket by a small majority. We could hardly hove hoped to do better than this.

Result in this County.

The returns from Dane county indicate the success of the entire Union County ticket, by majorities ranging from 200 to 600 on the home vote.

Some of the towns have done nobly, among them we may mention Rutland, Vienna, Windsor, and Medina, and especially Christinia and Pleasant Springs, towns chiefly settled by Norwegians, who show by their votes a fidelity to their adopted land worthy of all praise.

Dane county will be represented in the next Legislature by the following persons:—*Senate*, Thos. Hood and Willard H. Chandler, both Union. *Assembly*, Wm. M. Colladay, A. A. Boyce, John S. Frary and James Ross, Union, and David Ford, copperhead.

The Second Congressional District.

The Copperhead candidate for Congress in this district was vain enough to imagine that in consequence of his personal attractions and Ciceronian eloquence he would be elected. A majority of from 3,000 to 4,000 on the home vote against him is the response of the people to his great expectations.

THE PIRATE SEMMES AGAIN AT SEA.—A letter from THOS. H. DUDLEY, our Consul at Liverpool, states that the screw steamer *Laurel*, of 300 tons burthen, sailed from Liverpool on Sunday, the 9th ult., with Captain SEMMES, eight other Confederate officers, and about one hundred men. She had six 68-pounder guns, in cases in her hold, with gun carriages ready for mounting.

It is thought probable that there is somewhere another vessel of a more formidable character, to which the men and guns will be transferred.

☞ The *Patriot*, before the election, told the people that the Union candidate for the Assembly in this district was an exceedingly incompetent person—without property ability or anything else to recommend him. Nevertheless his opponent falls almost a hundred behind his ticket, showing that even the Democrats preferred Ross.

STRAIGHT UNION.—The Postmaster at Evansville sends us the vote of Union, Rock county, giving 314 Union and 20 Democratic straight through, except that J. R. BENNETT, Union, runs one ahead for District Attorney. Union is worthy of her name.

THE ELECTIONS!

A GLORIOUS VICTORY!

THE VOICE OF THE PEOPLE!

UNION TO BE PRESERVED

LIBERTY THROUGHOUT LAND.

Lincoln and Johnson Elected.

The Little Mackerels Skinned.

NEW ENGLAND IS A UNIT.

ALL RIGHT IN THE CENTER.

Gains on October and September.

The West Piling up Union Majorities.

Slave States Wheeling into Line.

CLEAN SWEEP EVERYWHERE.

Big States and Little States go Alike

COPPERHEADS NOT SURE OF A STATE.

Wisconsin Stands by Union.

DANE COUNTY IS ALL SOUND.

Ross Elected to the Assembly.

Money Don't "Make the Mare go."

Geo. B. and Vilas Started up Salt River

WISCONSIN.

The following are the returns from this State, as far as received. They indicate a Union majority of about 10,000:

Special Dispatch to the State Journal.

MILWAUKEE, Nov. 8.

Milwaukee city gives 2,880 for McClellan. The county is probably 3,500. DeWitt Davis for Assembly is elected in the 4th ward by 90 majority over Taylor. All the other Assemblymen are Democratic.

Carey is ahead in the district probably 500 on the home vote. The soldiers vote will most likely elect Paine.

Ross' friends in Milwaukee are jubilant.

The Union men carry the 4th and 7th wards. C.

DANE COUNTY.

CITY OF MADISON.

	1st W'd.	2d W'd.	3d W'd.	4th W'd.	Maj.
Lincoln	236	191	137	141	....
McClellan	276	136	241	154	102
J. McMynn	236	194	140	141	....
J. B. Parkinson	279	135	243	156	102
J. C. Sloan	236	189	138	140	....
Geo. B. Smith	279	141	242	156	115
Jas. Ross	241	201	162	155	....
Wm. F. Vilas	271	130	221	143	6
G. W. McDougal	259	200	142	170	24
A. M. Hanchett	256	180	238	123	....
L. W. Hoyt	237	198	145	142	....
J. E. Mann	275	131	237	154	75
A. Pickarts	251	185	150	132	....
J H. Clark	263	144	232	165	86
H. A. Lewis	234	183	132	139	....
C. Habich	281	145	250	157	145
S. Foote	251	191	148	141	....
A. S. Sanborn	264	140	239	135	47
J. A. Johnson	238	196	143	142	....
J. Keenan	277	134	239	155	86
H. M. Warner	236	194	137	139	....
P. McCabe	278	136	245	157	109
W. M. Colladay	237	194	139	141	....
A. Patten	278	136	243	157	103

DANE COUNTY.

	LINCOLN.	MCCLELLAN.
Albion		
Berry		135 maj.
Black Earth	94	25
Blooming Grove		52 maj.
Blue Mounds		
Bristol	46 maj.	
Burke		3 maj.
Christiana	140	75
Cottage Grove	87	126
Cross Plains		161
Dane	123	59
Deerfield	77	64
Dunkirk	7 maj.	
Dunn		1 maj.
Fitchburg	125	79
Madison, Town	55	76
Madison, City		
Mazomanie	88 maj.	
Medina	47	
Middleton	96	187
Montrose		
Oregon	97 maj.	
Perry		
Primrose	95 maj.	
Pleasant Spring	82 maj.	
Roxbury		
Rutland	171	
Springdale		50
Springfield		
Sun Prairie	67 maj.	
Vienna	117	34
Verona		16
Vermont	42	
Westport	101	
Windsor	121	26
York		

DEERFIELD.

Lincoln	77	McClellan	64
McMynn	76	Parkinson	65
Sloan	77	Smith	64
Chandler	77	Dow	64
Boyce	77	Noyes	64
McDougal	76	Hanchett	65
Hoyt	77	Mann	64
Pickarts	79	Clark	62
Lewis	77	Habich	65
Foote	78	Sanborn	63
Johnson	77	Keenan	64
Warner	77	McCabe	68
Colloday	77	Patten	64

BLACK EARTH.

Lincoln	94	McClellan	25
McMynn	94	Parkinson	25
Sloan	94	Smith	25
McDougal	88	Hanchett	28
Hoyt	94	Mann	25
Pickarts	93	Clark	24
Lewis	94	Habich	25
Foote	94	Sanborn	25
Johnson	94	Keenan	25
Warner	92	McCabe	25
Colladay	94	Patten	25

TOWN OF MADISON.

Lincoln	55	McClellan	77
McMynn	52	Parkinson	79
Sloan	55	Smith	77
Ross	57	Vilas	72
McDougall	59	Hanchett	72
Hoyt	55	Mann	74
Pickarts	57	Clark	74
Lewis	54	Habich	77
Foote	58	Sanborn	73
Johnson	55	Keenan	76
Warner	55	McCabe	76
Colliday	55	Patten	76

MIDDLETON.

Lincoln	96	McClellan	187
McMynn	96	Parkinson	187
Sloan	96	Smith	186
Davis	99	Ford	184
McDougal	101	Hanchett	182
Hoyt	100	Mann	183
Pickarts	102	Clark	181
Lewis	96	Habich	187
Foot	96	Sanborn	187
Johnson	96	Keenan	187
Warner	96	McCabe	187
Colladay	96	Patten	187

FITCHBURG.

Lincoln	79	McClellan	125
McMynn	78	Parkinson	126
Sloan	78	Smith	126
Frary	79	Flick	125
McDougal	79	Hanchett	125
Hoyt	78	Warner	121
Pickarts	74	Clark	130
Lewis	78	Habich	126
Foote	78	Sanborn	126
Johnson	74	Keenan	130
Warner	78	McCabe	126
Colladay	78	Patten	126

WINDSOR.

Lincoln	121	McClellan	26
McMynn	120	Parkinson	29
Sloan	122	Smith	27
Chandler	119	Dow	25
Boyce	123	Noyes	25
McDougal	114	Hanchett	34
Hoyt	124	Mann	26
Pickarts	122	Clark	27
Lewis	124	Habich	24
Foote	122	Sanborn	27
Johnson	121	Keenan	27
Warner	122	McCabe	27
Colladay	122	Patten	27

VIENNA.

Lincoln	117	McClellan	34
McMynn	117	Parkinson	34
Sloan	117	Smith	34
Chandler	117	Dow	34
Boyce	118	Noyes	33
McDougal	117	Hanchett	34
Hoyt	117	Mann	34
Pickarts	117	Clark	34
Lewis	116	Habich	34
Foote	117	Sanborn	34
Johnson	117	Keenan	34
Warner	117	McCabe	34
Colladay	117	Patten	34

CHRISTIANA.

Lincoln	140	McClellan	75
McMynn	140	Parkinson	75
Sloan	141	Smith	75
Chandler	141	Dow	73
Colladay	141	Morton	75
McDougal	140	Hanchett	76
Hoyt	141	Mann	75
Pickarts	141	Clark	75
Foote	141	Sanborn	75
Lewis	141	Habich	75
Johnson	143	Keenan	73
Colladay	111	Patten	75

COTTAGE GROVE.

Lincoln	87	McClellan	126
McMynn	87	Parkinson	126
Sloan	87	Smith	126
Chandler	87	Dow	126
Colladay	88	Morton	125
McDougal	93	Hanchett	120
Hoyt	88	Mann	125
Pickarts	90	Clark	123
Lewis	85	Habich	128
Foote	90	Sanborn	123
Johnson	88	Keenan	125
Warner	94	McCabe	119
Colladay	88	Patten	125

DANE.

Lincoln	123	McClellan	59
McMynn	123	Parkinson	59
Sloan	123	Smith	59
Davis	121	Ford	61
McDougal	123	Hanchett	59
Hoyt	122	Mann	59

Rest of ticket, 123 to 59.

VERMONT.

The whole number of votes cast is 148. The following are the Union majorities, which, considering how many voters have gone to the war, is doing very well:

Lincoln	42
McMynn	42
Davis	49
McDougal	38
Hoyt	42
Pickarts	42
Lewis	42
Foote	43
Johnson	48
Warner	52
Colladay	42

PLEASANT SPRINGS.

Union .... 115 Democratic 33

Union majority 81 on the whole ticket.

Oregon gives the following majorities: Lincoln 97, McMynn 97, I. C. Sloan 97, Frary 101, McDougal 104, Hoyt 97, Pickarts 91, Lewis 97, Foote 96, Johnson 98, Warner 97, Colladay 97.

BROWN COUNTY.

Green Bay city, 22 majority for Lincoln.

Howard, 6 majority for Lincoln.

COLUMBIA.

Randolph, 75 Union majority.

Newport, 64 majority for Lincoln and Sloan.

Courtland, 131 Union majority.

Portage, 73 Democratic majority.

Wyocena, 81 Union majority.

Lodi, Lincoln, 194, McClellan, 53; Sloan for Congress, 194, Smith, 54; Bowman for Senator, 193, Wood, 55; Barden for Assembly, 194, McGregor, 54.

Columbus, 163 Union majority.

Hampden, 22 Union majority.

CRAWFORD.

Prairie du Chien, 109 majority for McClellan; 105 for Rodolph for Congress.

Marietta, 8 Union majority.

DODGE.

Waupun, South ward, Lincoln 110 majority; A. S. Sloan, 105.

Hubbard, 214 Democratic majority.

Oak Grove, 86 majority for Lincoln; 84 for Sloan.

Burnett, 31 majority for Lincoln.

Westford, 9 majority for McClellan and Eldredge.

Fox Lake, 31 majority for Lincoln and 34 for Sloan.

Chester, 56 majority for Lincoln.

Trenton, 76 majority for Lincoln.

FOND DU LAC.

Sawyer, Union candidate for the Assembly in the 3d district, is elected.

Ripon, 258 majority for Lincoln.

Waupun, village, north ward, 7 majority for Lincoln; 5 for Sloan.

Oakfield, 123 majority for Lincoln and Sloan.

Friendship, 59 Democratic majority.

Waupun, town, 172 majority for Lincoln.

Alto, 80 majority for Lincoln.

GRANT.

Boscobel, 115 Union majority.

Marion, 40 Union majority.

Hickory Grove, 50 Union majority.

Watertown, 33 for Lincoln, all the votes cast.

Muscoda, 10 Union majority.

GREEN.

Brooklyn, 99 Union majority.

GREEN LAKE.

Berlin city, 408 votes polled. Lincoln, 356; McClellan, 52. Congressman same.

Berlin town, 129 majority for Lincoln.

IOWA.

Pulaski, 16 majority for McClellan; 14 for Rodolph (Dem.) for Congress; Madden (Dem.) for Senate, 12; Parkinson (Dem.) for State Superintendent, 16. County ticket the same.

Arena, 3 Union majority.

JEFFERSON.

Palmyra, 194 Union majority.

Watertown, 450 Democratic majority.

Cold Spring, 41 Union majority.

JUNEAU.

New Lisbon, 60 majority for Lincoln; 12 for Dunn (Dem.) for Assembly.

Mauston, 40 Union majority.

KENOSHA.

Kenosha, 61 majority for Lincoln and Paine.

Pleasant Prairie, 30 Union majority.

LA CROSSE.

La Crosse City 42 Union majority.

Neshonoc, 134 for Lincoln, 12 for McIndoe.

MILWAUKEE.

Milwaukee city complete, McClellan 2,880 Democratic majority, Democratic gain of 807. Cary, Dem., for Congress 2,390.

Wauwatosa, 260 majority for McClellan.

Granville, 245 Democratic majority.

Majority in County on President and Congress about 3,500.

MONROE.

Sparta, Lincoln 350; McClellan 147; McIndoe, Union, for Congress, 190 maj.; Tarr, Union, for Assembly, 209.

Angelo, 36 majority for Lincoln, 37 for McIndoe.

Leon, 51 majority for Lincoln and McIndoe; 83 for Chandler, Union, for Senate.

Tomah, 37 majority for Lincoln.

OUTAGAMIE.

Appleton city, 86 majority for Lincoln and Sawyer.

RACINE.

Racine, Lincoln and Paine, 290 majority.

RICHLAND.

Buena Vista, 35 Union majority.

Orion, 118 Union majority.

Eagle, 16 Union majority.

ROCK.

Janesville City, 304 Union majority.

Harmony, 133 Union majority.

La Prairie, 130 Union majority, only one "rebel" vote.

Janesville town, 65 Union majority.

Rock, 52 Union majority.

Turtle, 170 Union majority.

Union, 314 Union, 20 Democratic.

Beloit City, 313 Union majority.

Clinton, 168 Union majority.

Plymouth, 53 Union majority.

Center, 93 Union majority.

The county will probably give about 3,000 for Old Abe.

SAUK.

Spring Green, 80 Union majority.

New Buffalo, 124 majority for Lincoln and Sloan.

Prairie du Sac, 9 Union majority.

Baraboo, 223 Union majority.

Westfield, 10 Union majority.

Washington, 61 Union majority.

Excelsior, 43 Union majority.

WALWORTH.

Whitewater, Lincoln 320 majority, 337 for Paine for Congress.

Delavan, 330 majority for Lincoln, 327 for Paine.

La Grange, 130 Union majority.

Sugar Creek, 40 Union majority.

Richmond, 75 Union majority.

Sharon, 258 Union majority.

WASHINGTON.

Richfield, 229 majority for McClellan and Eldrege.

WAUKESHA.

Waukesha, 93 majority for Lincoln, 98 for Paine, 101 for McMynn for State Supt.

Eagle, 11 majority for Lincoln and Paine.

Oconomowoc, Lincoln 34 majority, Paine 37.

Brookfield, 146 Democratic majority.

Pewaukee 24 Union majority.

Delafield, 33 Union majority.

Lisbon, 6 Union majority.

Ottawa, 1 Democratic majority.

Genesee, 13 Democratic majority.

Vernon, 63 Union majority.

WINNEBAGO.

Oshkosh city, Lincoln 88 majority, Sawyer, Union for Congress, 91 majority.

Menasha, 22 majority for McClellan, 30 for Bouck, Union gain of 50.

Neenah, 97 majority for Lincoln and Sawyer.

NEW YORK.

BUFFALO, Nov. 8.

No official returns are received here yet from New York City, but it is reported to have gone about 30,000 for McClellan.

Albany is about 2,500 the same way.

The Eastern lines are working very hard.

This city gives about 500 democratic majority.

Rochester is 62 democratic, a Union gain of 127 over last year.

The rural districts vote about as in 1860. Union men claim the State for Lincoln.

NEW YORK, Nov. 8.

The total vote of this city, is Lincoln 36,442; McClellan 73,329; one ward, the 15th, gave Lincoln a majority of 274. The total majority for McClellan in this city is 36,618.

The vote of this city for Lieutenant-Governor is Alvord, 36,064; Jones, 73,790. It is reported that Fernando Wood is defeated for Congress, by Darling, Republican.

R. J. Conkling, Republican, is elected to Congress, over Kernan. Raymond in the 6th District, and Humphrey in the 3d District, (Brooklyn,) both Republicans, are certainly elected. Taylor (Dem.) in the 5th District and Chandler (Dem.) in the 7th District are elected to Congress.

For Governor, this city gives Seymour 73,727; Fenton, 36,122.

Returns from 105 towns and 2 counties give Lincoln 20,704 majority.

In 83 towns and cities, including Albany, Buffalo, Troy, Schenectady and Utica, and also three counties, McClellan has 16,094 majority.

NEW YORK, Nov. 9—1:30 a. m.

Troy city complete gives McClellan over Lincoln, 788; Seymour over Fenton, 802.

ILLINOIS.

SPRINGFIELD, ILL., Nov. 8.

The State has probably gone Republican, and will probably give a small Republican majority on the Legislature. It is thought the Democrats lose congressmen in the 8th, 13th, and 7th districts, and probably Harris in the 4th. The Republicans elect a State Senator in Madison and St. Clair counties.

Returns from the eastern part of the State show Republican gains.

CHICAGO, Nov. 8.

The Union ticket has a majority in this city of 1,745. The majority in the county will probably not be less than 4,000. Partial returns from the State show Union gains compared with the vote of 1860, and indicate a Republican majority for Lincoln of 20,000. The Republicans will have a majority in the Legislature, and probably gain two congressmen.

SPRINGFIELD, Nov. 5—3 A. M.

It is now believed that the Republicans have a majority in both branches of the Legislature and elect a Congressman at large.

INDIANA.

INDIANAPOLIS, Nov. 8.

Election returns heard from show large Union gains over the October election. Lincoln's majority will be from 30,000 to 35,000.

The vote of the Ohio soldiers here stood as follows: Lincoln, 202; McClellan, 13.

CHICAGO, Nov. 8.

Returns from Indiana show increased Union majorities, compared with October, and indicate a Union majority of 35,000.

INDIANAPOLIS, Nov. 8, Midnight.

Returns show that the Union majority in this State will not be less than 27,000 to 30,000.

MISSOURI.

ST. LOUIS, Nov. 8.

Returns are meagre. The Republicans estimate Lincoln's majority in this county at between 4,000 and 5,000 on the home vote. The Democrats give 1,500 to 2,000. Henry T. Blow, present representative in the 2d District, is re-elected by a large majority. Large numbers of refugees in this city voted for McClellan and the Democratic State ticket. Lincoln is undoubtedly elected in this State. A Radical triumph on the State ticket is regarded as certain.

KENTUCKY.

LOUISVILLE, Nov. 8, 10:30 P. M.

Partial returns from 28 counties in Kentucky, including Jefferson, give Lincoln two hundred and fifty majority.

Louisville official gives McClellan 4,873, Lincoln 1,649.

Lexington gives 12 Union Majority, Falmouth 695, Covington 601, Paris gives 63 Democratic majority, Cynthiana 126.

Returns are meager, but indicate a Democratic majority.

MAINE.

PORTLAND, ME., Nov. 8, 9 P. M.

There is a heavy rain, and the telegraph works badly, and there has been no returns received from the eastern towns. We have 28 towns, which give Lincoln 13,264, McClellan 7,994, a Union gain of 380 on the September election. The vote of Portland foots up Lincoln 2,858, McClellan 879, a Union loss of 63 votes since September.

PENNSYLVANIA.

PHILADELPHIA, Nov. 8.

All but 2 wards gave 10,200 republican majority. Partial returns from 13 counties show a republican gain of 1,209. The full vote is not given. Erie gives 294 Union majority, a Union gain of 72. The vote as far as received shows Union gains. Pennsylvania is conceded to have gone for Lincoln.

OHIO.

TOLEDO, Nov. 8.

This city gives 242 Union majority.

CLEVELAND, O., Nov. 8.

Scattering returns from Ohio show Union gains over the October election, and indicate that Lincoln has carried the State by a heavy majority.

CINCINNATI, Nov. 8.

The Union majority on the home vote will be about 35,000.

MINNESOTA.

ST. PAUL, Nov. 8.

Minneapolis, Hennepin county, gives Lincoln a majority of 618; Donnelly, republican, Congressman, a majority of 217.

Richard, Hennepin county, gives Lincoln a majority of 77; Donnelly, 78.

MICHIGAN.

DETROIT, Nov. 8—10 p. m.

Returns are scattering and meagre. The republicans claim the State by 15,000 maj. Detroit gives about 900 democratic majority and Wayne county about 1,650 democatic majority.

NEW HAMPSHIRE.

CONCORD, Nov. 8.

One hundred and ten towns and cities in New Hampshire give Lincoln 22,895; McClellan, 20,291; a Democratic gain of 2,050. The above embraces nearly two-thirds of the entire vote of the State.

DELAWARE.

NEW YORK, Nov. 8.

Private dispatches from Philadelphia say Delaware gives Lincoln her electoral vote.

WILMINGTON, Nov. 8.

This city gives 800 Union majority, a Union gain of 500.

NEW JERSEY.

NEW YORK, Nov. 8.

Essex county has gone Union by over 150, making a Union gain of over 1,000 over last year. The legislative delegation is six Union to three Democratic.

MASSACHUSETTS.

BOSTON, Nov. 8—11:30 P. M.

One hundred and seventy-six towns in Massachusetts foot up Lincoln, 90,000; McClellan, 36,631.

It is raining heavily here.

VERMONT.

MONTPELIER, Nov. 8.

Fifty towns give Lincoln 16,644; McClellan, 4,869; a Union gain over September of 8,741. Vermont is good for *thirty thousand* for Lincoln.

RHODE ISLAND.

PROVIDENCE, Nov. 9—3 P. M.

Returns from nearly the whole State show a majority for Lincoln of about 5,000.

CONNECTICUT.

NEW YORK, Nov. 8.

Two counties in Connecticut give Lincoln 5,276, McClellan 5,047.

MARYLAND.

NEW YORK, Nov. 8.

It is reported that Maryland has undoubtedly gone for Lincoln.

How the Soldiers Vote.

CAMP RANDALL, Nov. 8.

EDITORS STATE JOURNAL: The following is the result of the general election held at Camp Randall, Madison, Wis., by Co. B, 45th regiment Wis. inf'y, to day:

PRESIDENT.

Lincoln, 52; McClellan, 11.

CONGRESS.

Fifth District—Philetus Sawyer, 43; G. Bouck, 8.

Fourth District—Charles A. Eldredge, 3.

Third District—Amasa Cobb, 1.

Second District—A. Scott Sloan, 1.

STATE SUPERINTENDENT.

John G. McMynn, 50; Parkinson, 1.

SENATOR.

Nineteenth District—Oscar Koch, 49; George Reed, 2.

Respectfully,

JACOB LEISEN,

Cap't Com'g Com.

The following is the vote of Battery G, Wisconsin Heavy Artillery, at Camp Randall:

Lincoln, 33; McClellan 14.

I. C. Sloan, for Congress, 11 majority.

A. S. Sloan, do 5 do

Sawyer, do 19 do

McIndoe, do 6 do

Senator, 29th District—Horatio S. Thomas, 1; G. Dewitt Elwood, 17.

Senator, 1st District—John E. Thomas, 3; John A. Bently 19.

The Dane county Union ticket has 8 majority.

From Sauk County.

BARABOO, Nov. 8th, 1864.

Editors State Journal:—The vote of Baraboo is as follows:

Union 309; Copperhead 33.

Yours, &c., T. D. LANG.

PRAIRIE DU SAC, Nov. 9, 1864.

Editors of State Journal: GENTLEMEN:—The result of the election in this town is as follows: Union, 168; Democratic, 159—being 9 Union majority. Pretty good for this Democratic stronghold of Sauk county.

H. KLEINPELL.

THE NEW STATE OF NEVADA.—The State is called "Nevada," from the old Spanish nomenclature, that word signifying "snowy," from the word "nieve," which means snow in the Castilian language.

The Territory was organized on the 2d of March, 1861. The capital, now the chief city of the State, is Carson City. The whole estimated area of the country embraced in the new State is 83,500 square miles, and in 1863 its white population was put down at 40,000.

GEN. SWEET.—The Chicago papers abound in warm eulogies upon the energy and vigilance shown by Col. B. J. SWEET, of the Veteran Reserved Corps, who is the commandant of the post in that city, in detecting and nipping in the bud the conspiracy of the secession emissaries and copperheads for releasing the rebel prisoners at Camp Douglas, and introducing a carnival of blood in their peaceful streets.

LOCAL MATTERS.

OFFICIAL PAPER OF THE CITY & COUNTY.

RAILROAD TIME TABLES.

Mil. and Prairie du Chien.

	ARRIVE.		DEPART.
Chi. & Mil.	4:10 P. M.	Going East.	9:35 A. M.
" "	4:30 A. M.	" "	1:15 P. M.
North	5:50 P. M.	" "	10:25 P. M.
West	1:00 P. M.	" West.	4:40 A. M.
"	10:05 P. M.	" "	4:30 P. M.

☞ The 10:25 P. M. train for the East on Prairie du Chien road leaves daily except Saturdays.

☞ The 4:40 A. M. train for the West on the Prairie du Chien road leaves daily except Mondays.

Chicago & Northwestern.

	ARRIVE.		DEPART.
From Chicago.	7:30 P. M.	Going South.	5:30 A. M.
" "	10:20 P. M.	" "	7:30 A. M.

WHERE TO BUY YOUR OYSTERS.—The celebrated Baltimore oysters, fresh and delicious, can be obtained at P. H. SPENCER'S grocery, in the United States block. Mr. SPENCER has been appointed agent for their sale in this city, and receives them regularly by express. Price 90 cents per can.

Mr. SPENCER has forwarded to us some of the oysters in question, put up in neat tin packages—the original packages—and what we say of them is based upon an actual test of their excellent quality.

A HIGH COMPLIMENT.—"Barney," the favorite horse of the late lamented Brig. General RANSOM, and which has borne his heroic rider through much hard service and many hard fought battles, arrived here yesterday with his trappings and accoutrements, having been in the most delicate manner presented by the General's mother, to his late Aid de Camp, Lieut. J. D. TREDWAY, of this city.

ATTENTION SIR KNIGHTS.—There will be a regular meeting of Robert Macoy Commandery to-morrow, (Thursday) evening, at 7½ o'clock. A general attendance is particularly requested.

STATE LIBRARY.—We are requested to give notice to the Bar and others interested, that the State Library will be kept open evenings during the session of the Supreme Court.

☞ The sale of A. C. DAVIS' furniture at BRUCE'S, advertised for to-day, is postponed until Saturday next, at 1 o'clock.

A YOUTHFUL COUPLE.—The oldest man in Wisconsin was married a few weeks since.—His name is JAMES STEEL, of Newport, Sauk county. He is 100 years old. The bride, a Mrs. MADDON, is aged 88. In D. S. DURRIE'S genealogy of the STEEL family, we find this notice of Mr. STEEL:

"In the town of Newport, Columbia Co., Wisconsin, resides James STEEL. He was born at Snickers Gap, Snickersville, Loudon Co., Va., in the year 1764. He has been west of the lakes 65 years. Four years ago (this was written in 1858) he rode a young, spirited horse at a race, that no younger man could be induced to mount, and says he would have won the race if the horse had not 'bolted.'"

New Advertisements.

LIST OF LETTERS

Remaining unclaimed in the Post Office at Madison, State of Wisconsin, on the 9th day of November, 1864.

☞ To obtain any of these letters, the applicant must call for "advertised letters," give the date of this list, and pay one cent for advertising.

☞ If not called for within one month, they will be sent to the dead letter office.

1. Direct letters plainly to the street and number, as well as the post office and state.

2. Head letters with the writer's post office and state, street and number, sign them plainly, with full name, and request that answers be directed accordingly.

3. Letters to strangers or transient visitors in a town or city, whose special address may be unknown, should be marked, in the lower left hand corner, with the word, "Transient."

4. Place the postage stamp on the upper right hand corner, and leave space between the stamp and direction for post-marking without interfering with the writing.

N. B.—A request for the return of a letter to the writer, if unclaimed within 30 days or less, written or printed with the writer's name, post office and State, across the left-hand end of the envelope, on the face side, will be complied with at the usual prepaid rate of postage, payable when the letter is delivered to the writer.—*Sec. 28, Laws of 1863.*

LADIES' LIST.

A — Allen Miss Catharine. B — Bressford Mrs Anna V; Baird Miss C; Bellemann Mrs Elmyra; Bittinger Mrs Jane 2; Blackwell Miss Josephene; Burke Miss Myry; Bailey Mrs M L; Briggs Mrs Mary M; Burt Martha; Bird Mrs Susan; Brown Miss Sarah Catharine. C — Cox Mrs A; Cox Miss Anna; Cooper Miss Caty M; Camp Miss Delia; Cheney, Miss; Cooper Miss Fanny; Coody Mrs J; Cole Mrs Margaret R; Cody Miss Mary; Cutler Mrs P; Cleveland Mrs P A; Campbell Mrs Susan; Casselman Mrs S A; Carpenter Mrs S; Carenter Mrs Susan C. D — Daily Mrs Bridget; Dodge Mrs John D; Downey Ann; Daley Miss Jane H; Daley Miss Jane; Dowery Mrs Mary S; Davis Mrs Oliver. E — Ellsworth Mrs Josie; Earl Mrs Martha. F — Faringer Mrs Mary E; Flangan Miss Margaret. G — Graham Miss Maggie; Gardner Mrs Maria R. H — Hale Mrs Julia; Healms Miss Maria. J — Jones Miss Susan. K — Kellogg Miss Amanda; Kellogg Miss A J; Kelley Miss Jane; Knapp Miss J Maria; Kinney Mrs Mary. L — Lewis Miss Richel; Lyon Miss Emeline; Lake Mrs E. M — Meckey Mrs M; Morton Miss Georgia; Mandi Miss Harriet G 2; Mason Mrs Nancy; Myles Nellie; McKinney Miss Mary 2.

GENTLEMEN'S LIST.

A — Adams James; Adams C H; Ainsworth Dr E D; Anderson Andrew; Arnold Wm Curtis; Arnolt Wm. B — Brabson Wm R; Brown Wm S; Brodie Robert; Burdick Morice; Barrington Michael; Bowen M L; Blanch J H; Bean John J; Brainard James A; Blair James A; Blessinger Joseph; Blackstone J W; Bliss Irving V; Butler J C; Bennett Jacob; Bieler John; Brundage Hiram A; Badger Henry C; Brunelle H N; Bliss Henry; Bond George; Baird H S; Briggs Dighton T; Bonner Lewis; Barns John H; Beedle Jacob 3; Breuer Henry; Bruce David; Balthaser Benton; Beaman Alonzo; Baker Charles; Bartlett Hiram; Buisely Benj F; Bigelow Horace; Brockman Lewis; Bowman Wm W; Bush Daniel L. C — Carter Wm F; Crosby & Cooper; Canady Wm; Carey Wm; Clayton Samuel; Cornell Timothy; Cooper Spencer H; Cullinan Patrick; Calligan Mathew; Conroy Michael; Creed Lyman; Casey James; Clohasy Joseph; Caldwell E F; Code Elak Sarg't; Cole Daniel; Coleman D N; Conrath A; Castleman Dr A; Campbell Andrew; Cram Sidney 2; Campbell Porter H; Cole Bennie; Christensen Claus 2; Clark Chas T; Court Edward; Campbell Wm C; Connelly James; Campbell Joseph; Croft Charles; Cowles Elba L; Cook Clinton. D — De Lapp Thomas 2; Dixon Theron; Decker Samuel; Davis G W; Dunn Martin; Doyle Joseph; Dixon E B; Davenport George; De Haven G W; Douglas Fredrick 3; Dury George; Duffey Bernard; Dewey A; Dun Wm W; Doot Ambrose; Draves Andrew; Davey J J; Dickenson E W; Drews Fritz; Delves John R; Denure Jerome; Dickinson E C; Derenger Sigesmund; Doherty James. E — Ewing Mathew; Ellis Hiram E. F — Flagler Sylvester; Fay Patrick; French M; Forthan Louis; Fox John; Farnam Jacob; Freman Henry; Ford Hiram; Fresse Henry; Fuller E; Fox F; Freeman Dacre; Fleetwood Charles; Fello Peter; French James; Frazer Geo H; Fuller Jesse J; French Sames; Fairbanks Sylvester 2. G — Gibson John; Gibson David A; Gill Alex; Goodchild Wm; Gill Wm; Green Milton; Gay Jesse; Grady John; Graton Michael; Gibson Elie; Gaven John. H — Herron James; Halston J; Hunt John; Huntley J A; Heath John; Aubert F; Hamilton F B; Heeran John; Halgen F A; Haley Dennis; Hess George; Haskin Andrew 2; Hayward Richard L; Hodgson Dempster; Hubert Jacob; Hudson Adolphus; Hart Seth; Hanes S W; Harris Enoch. I — Irish Henry P; Irish Lyman D. J — Johnson; Jones Richard W; Jones Mike P; Johnson John O; Johnson John; Jackson James A; Johnson John; Jolce Hugh; Jenke Henry. K — Kelson Wm; Keenie John; Kneeland John; Kerr J J; Kellogg H E; Krugher Charles; Kingsland C F; Kelsey Dennis; Keescher E A; Kadon John; Kranz Daniel; Kirscher John C; Kleinlein John 2; Kloess George; Kulas John. L — Laughter James; Lane John B; Lomis Lange; Loude Lange; Lodach Samuel T; Lowe Dennis G; Lawrence Henry T; Lot Christian; Lon Bernard; Lewis Lester; Lewis Lawton; Lovette Adam; Liddall James 1. M — Merwin D G 2; Murphy James E; Mefailo W; Moor Wilhelm; Minor Horace Jun; McIntyre W E; Moore Joseph; Morville John T; Martin Edward Henry; McQuarty Wm; Martin Oscar; Mathews James; Moore James M; Merton James M; Marsh Joel O; McKey J; Mathews John; Mike E; McGrath Dennis; McLeod David; McManus Allen; McManus Albert. N — Nelson Dominikus; Noble E P. O — Norton Christopher; Neuskinkin Anton. P — Phillips Jason F; Parson Henry; Perry John P; Pickett A K M; Pfaff Michael; Pollet Luther. R — River John; Rogue Peter S; Riley Philip; Ridling Frederick; Rhodes Frederick; Rungles Leroy; Riley Edward; Riley Thomas; Rickerman Henry; Rawden Minor; Rodgers Jacob. S — Sexton Charles; Smith William; Scotten John H; Sullivan P; Sumner Alfred G; Stanton Daniel J; Shaddel Jacob; Sanders Nathan F; Smith Albert E H; Shelley James; Skellar James; Steele F R; Spittmaner Daniel; Shepard Wm M; Smith James W. T — Thompson Edward; Tyler F H; Thomas John W; Toket Frederick; Thompson N S; Thelen Wendel. W — Willson John; Watson Frederick; Wellsen W C; Willard Henry C.

E. W. KEYES, P. M.

WISCONSIN STATE JOURNAL.

VOLUME XIII. MADISON, WIS. THURSDAY, MARCH 23, 1865. NUMBER 164.

STATE JOURNAL.

THURSDAY, MARCH 23, 1865.

THE OFFICIAL STATE PAPER.

READING MATTER ON EVERY PAGE

For Judge of the Ninth Circuit—

ALVA STEWART.

The News.

Owing to the interruption of the telegraph lines east of Chicago, we have no night dispatches.

To-day's dispatches bring no news of victories won, but show that SHERMAN'S army has been swelled by reinforcements to overwhelming strength, which will enable him to crush all before him, and important news may soon be expected.

From every quarter we hear the muttering thunders of the storm which is about to break on the rebels, and the despairing cries of defeated traitors.

Gold, this noon, was $1.54 in New York.

Legislative Summary.

THURSDAY, March 23—*Senate.*—After some warm discussion between Senators BOWMAN and SESSIONS relative to the effect it would have on the lumbering interests, the bill authorizing the construction of a dam three feet high, with proper safe-guards, across the Wisconsin river at Kilbourn City, by a vote of 20 to 10 was returned to the Assembly. The Committee on the Judiciary reported against the amendment to the Constitution abolishing the Grand Jury system.

Most of the session was taken up in the consideration of the Agricultural College bill, which was ably advocated by Senators W. H. CHANDLER, HARRIS and VAN WYCK.—The Senate refused to indefinitely postpone the bill by one majority. The vote on ordering it to a third reading resulted as follows:

Ayes—Senators W. H. Chandler, Cole, Harris, Hood, Ketchum, Lawrence, Lincoln, Littlejohn Smith, Van Wyck, Wescott, Wilkinson, A. H. Young, M. K. Young—15.

Nays—Senators Barnum, Bentley, Blair, Budlong, J. A. Chandler, Clark, Ellis, Elwood, Morgan, Read, Reynolds, Sessions, Webb, Wheeler, Wilson—15.

Lieut. Gov. SPOONER gave his casting vote in favor of the bill, on the ground that it gave the industrial classes an opportunity to be heard in regard to their desire for such an institution as was proposed.

The bill as it now stands proposes—

1st. That the 240,000 acres of land granted by Congress, be offered for sale by the 1st of August next, by the School Land Commissioners, who are to have the entire control of the same, in the same manner as they have the care of other State lands. All lands not sold to be subject to private entry at not less than $1.25 per acre.

2d. The proceeds of the lands to be invested by the commissioners in Government or State stocks, preference being given to Wisconsin stocks, and the annual interest to be devoted to the support of the College, under the direction of a board of Trustees to be appointed by the Governor, approved by the Senate, in the first instance, and afterwards by the Governor, from nominations made by Agricultural and Industrial institutions.

3d. Appropriates $3,000 for the purpose of defraying the necessary expenses of soliciting subscriptions, selecting location &c., and if $30,000 is actually subscribed and paid, then $10,000 yearly for three years to aid in the support of the institution.

Senate bills passed appropriating to the State Reform School 18,500; to the Institute for the Education of the Deaf and Dumb 18,000; to the Institute for the Blind 26,000; to Charles H. Larkin 808.80, for expenses in defending himself against charges for malfeasance in office.

Assembly.—Petitions were presented for bi-ennial sessions and for the passage of the insurance bill.

A resolution to hold afternoon sessions of the Assembly for the remainder of the session was adopted.

Several local bills were passed, and the remainder of the forenoon session spent in discussing the insurance bill. Though not a political question, the Assembly appears to be nearly divided, according to its political sentiments, Union men supporting and Democrats opposing the bill. The only exception we have noted is that of Mr. SIMMONS (Union) of Kenosha, who opposes it.

Circuit Judge.

The Judicial Convention which met in this city yesterday was very meagerly attended. Only twelve delegates were present, two of whom were authorized to cast the full vote of their respective districts, making fourteen votes in all. Four, moreover, of these were instructed to oppose any nomination, and to withdraw from the Convention in case a majority insisted upon making a nomination. No delegates were present from Sauk county.

Under these circumstances, after some discussion, the Convention, by an unanimous vote adjourned without making a nomination. This leaves Judge STEWART the only candidate thus far presented for the suffrages of the people.

The result is very generally satisfactory in this portion of the circuit. Judge STEWART, during his brief occupancy of the bench, has given very general satisfaction. He is a good lawyer, an upright citizen, a man of sound judgment, and will, we doubt not, make an impartial, dignified, able and pains-taking Judge. We put up his name to-day and shall give him a sincere and cordial support, and we trust that he may receive the earnest and undivided support of the people of the circuit.

THANKS.—We are requested on behalf of Mrs. EWING to return thanks to Mrs. Ross and Mrs. HALL for collecting means, amounting to $10, and making clothing for her daughter MARY ROBINSON, on the occasion of the funeral of her grandmother, Mrs. ROBINSON.

☞ The Chicago people recently attempted to get permission to enlist a couple of thousand repentant rebels in Camp Douglas to the credit of that city. Secretary STANTON refused.

☞ HENRY J. RAYMOND of the New York *Times*, and JOHN MULLALY, Editor of the *Metropolitan Record*, were among the drafted recently in New York city.

☞ Parson BROWNLOW has had twenty thousand dollars awarded him for damages done by secessionists, and the secessionists have to pay it.

☞ There was a tremendous storm in Indiana on the 20th.

Judicial Convention.

The Union Convention, called for the purpose of nominating a candidate for Judge of the 9th Judicial District, met pursuant to notice, at the Court House, in Madison, on Wednesday, March 22d.

The convention was called to order by L. W. Barden, and on motion, H. W. Tenny was elected Chairman, and H. B. Gallup, Secretary.

The following gentlemen were appointed by the chair a Committee on Credentials, viz: L. W. Barden, H. M. Lewis, and D. C. Bush. The committee reported the following persons as entitled to seats as delegates in the convention:

Horace Rublee, D. C. Bush, 26th Senatorial District, Dane Co.

J. P. Bacon, J. N. Flannigan, North-east Assembly District, Dane Co.

W. H. Chandler, A. A. Boyce, 11th Senatorial District.

H. W. Tenny, H. M. Lewis, 5th Assembly District, Dane Co.

John D. Jones, Columbia Co. Senatorial District.

L. W. Barden, Western District, Columbia County.

H. B. Gallup, Daniel Hall, 1st Assembly District, Jefferson Co.

Alanson Pike, 2 votes, Fort Atkinson District.

A motion for the admission of Wm. Owen to act as delegate for the 2d Assembly District of Columbia Co., was lost.

On motion of Mr. Barden, it was resolved that a committee of five should be appointed, of which committee each county should have one, for the purpose of calling conventions to nominate candidate for Judge of the 9th District.

The chair announced as such committee, L. W. Barden, of Columbia; E. W. Keyes and W. H. Chandler, of Dane; C. C. Remington, of Sauk, and H. Barber, Jr., of Jefferson.

On motion, the convention adjourned.

H. W. TENNEY, Ch'n.

H. B. GALLUP, Sec'y.

GREAT DECLINE IN PRICES.—The decline in prices during the present week has been unexampled. The Chicago *Tribune* states that during the week ending on Tuesday evening, flour had declined $1 per barrel; wheat 17c; Corn, 7c; Oats, 6a8c; Rye, 18c; and Barley, 5a6c per bushel. In provisions, mess pork has fallen $5 per barrel; prime mess pork, 4.50 per barrel; bulk meats, 2a3c per lb, and lard 3a3½c per lb. Highwines have declined 7c per gallon; tea, 10c per lb; coffee, 5c per lb; sugar, 2a3c per lb; wool, 8a10c per lb; nails, 1.00 per keg; iron, ½c per lb; tallow, 1c per lb; clover seed, 50a65c per bushel, timothy seed, 25a30c per bushel; prints and sheetings, 3a5c a yard.

The following table shows the closing prices of railroad stocks in New York up to Tuesday, compared with the corresponding day of last week and last month:

	Mar. 21.	Mar. 14.	Feb 21.
New York Central.....	99¾	105¾	115¾
Chicago & N. Western.	23¾	32	24¾
Chicago & N. W. preferd	50¾	60¾	64
Erie (common)........	60	63¾	74
Erie (preferred)......	87	90¾	92
Cleveland & Pittsburg.	58¾	69¾	84
Mich. Southern (com).	57	84¾	65¾
Mich. Southern (guar).	133	135	....
Pittsb'gh, Ft. W. & Chi	82¾	85¾	95¾
Michigan Central......	98¾	108	111¾
Chicago & Alton (com).	....	87¾	91
Chicago & Alton (pref).	88	93	93¾
Rock Island..........	90¾	98¾	96¾
Burlington & Quincy...	....	117	117
Quicksilver..........	63	76	85
Cleveland & Toledo...	102¾	108	113¾
Hudson River.........	100¾	109¾	112
Illinois Central......	101¾	111¾	118¾
Reading Railroad......	97¾	106¾	....

THE FORTY-NINTH.—A business note from Capt. CHENEY, of the 49th Regiment, dated Rolla, Mo., March 19th, informs us that Co. B was at St. James' Iron Works, some ten miles distant; Co. E doing provost duty in Rolla, and Co. K was doing guard duty at Fort Wyman, near Rolla. The weather was fine and the regimet healthy.

DEATHS IN NEW ORLEANS HOSPITALS.—From Mr. GEO. W. STURGES, military agent at St. Louis, we have the following list of deaths of Wisconsin soldiers at New Orleans:

Wm. O. Howard, K, 20th.
Wm. Millain, B, 29th.
Thos. Meredith, D, 4th.
Michael Hinchman, A, 30th.

DEPARTURE OF THE FORTY-EIGHTH.—The *Wisconsin* says the 48th regiment left Camp Washburn Wednesday afternoon for the seat of war. The regiment was nearly full to the maximum. It is an unusually good regiment, and made a most soldier-like appearance as they marched through the city for the cars.

DAMAGE TO THE LA CROSSE RAILROAD.—The Milwaukee *Sentinel* says the flood carried away a bridge on the La Crosse railroad between Sparta and Hurseyville, another between Salem and La Crosse, and two or three culverts torn up. Trains were interrupted for a day or two.

CONSUL TO HAYTI.—Prof. H. E. PECK, of the Oberlin College, Ohio, has been appointed commissioner and consul-general to the republic of Hayti, vice B. F. WHIDDEN, resigned. The salary is seven thousand five hundred dollars.

THE RACINE ROAD.—We learn that the Racine railroad was so much damaged by the recent flood, that some members of the Legislature, from the Southeastern portion of the State, were delayed two or three days in getting here.

WISCONSIN LEGISLATURE.

SENATE.

THURSDAY, March 23.

Prayer by Rev. Mr. JOHNSON.

Numerous reports were made from Committees, on which no action was taken, among others, one from the Judiciary Committee, in favor of the indefinite postponement of the joint resolution to amend the Constitution so as to abolish the Grand Jury system.

REMONSTRANCES.

Senator POPE presented several remonstrances, numerously signed, against any amendment to the Assembly bill, No. 24, so as to compel the Tomah & Lake St. Croix R. R. Company to build its road on the old survey of the La Crosse & Milwaukee R. R. Co.

THE KILBOURN CITY DAM.

The bill to incorporate the Columbia Manufacturing Company having been returned from the Assembly, on request of the Senate, Senator BOWMAN moved that it be again returned to the Assembly. He repelled intimations that any unfair means had been resorted to to secure or hasten the passage of the bill and that there were no provisions in the bill which would authorize anything to be done which would prejudice any other interests. He reviewed the history of the attempts to build a dam at Kilbourn City, and claimed that this would not interfere with the navigation of the river, and denied that lumbermen had any exclusive right to the Wisconsin river which should interfere with the improvement of this magnificent water power, in which the citizens of Kilbourn City and the surrounding country were so deeply interested, which would not obstruct the running of lumber.

Senator SESSIONS defended his action in seeking to recall the bill from the Assembly, and earnestly argued that its passage would be most prejudicial to the lumbering interests, claiming that it was in violation of the ordinance of 1787, declaring the Wisconsin a navigable stream, and an attempt to build up Kilbourn City at the expense of the lumbering regions. He spoke at some length.

Senator BOWMAN replied, forcibly advocating the propriety of building such a dam as was proposed, three feet high, and claimed that it was the opinion of experienced lumbermen that it would not obstruct navigation.

The motion to return the bill to the Assembly prevailed by a vote of 20 to 10.

THE AGRICULTURAL COLLEGE BILL.

On motion of Senator M. K. YOUNG, the special order, being the bill to incorporate the State Agricultural College, was taken up.

Sundry amendments reported by the committee on claims were adopted.

The report of the minority of the Committee on Claims, against the passage of the bill was read.

Senator WHEELER moved to indefinitely postpone.

Senator W. H. CHANDLER advocated the passage of the bill, as demanded by the agricultural interests, stating the differences between it as originally introduced and as amended by the Committee on Claims, and opposed the plan of transferring the grant to any private institution. He thought the industrial and agricultural classes ought to have an opportunity of declaring their wishes on this subject and contributing to the establishment of such an institution.

Senator HARRIS had had some doubts as to the propriety of establishing a State Agricultural College, but thought the present proposition was fair and eminently worthy of support. He referred to the resolution which he had introduced relative to this matter, and disclaimed any hostility to this measure in so doing.

Senator VAN WYCK said he thought it proper that all friends of the education of the industrial classes should have an opportunity to express themselves on this measure, and declared his own convictions decidedly in favor of using the grant for the establishment of a separate institution, as what the act of Congress contemplated; as the only means by which the attendance of those expecting to be engaged in manual labor could be secured where its true dignity was recognized; that education in these pursuits might be under the charge of practical men. He answered the various objections to the institution, and adduced many arguments against giving the grant to any existing institution.—His remarks were very able and eloquent and no synopsis would do it justice.

The Senate then refused to indefinitely postpone the bill by a vote of 15 to 16.

The vote on ordering it to a third reading, resulted in a tie vote, 15 to 15, and the Lieutenant Governor giving his casting vote in the affirmative, the bill was ordered to a third reading.

ASSEMBLY BILL PASSED.

A bill to authorize the town of Watertown, in Jefferson county, to pay certain moneys to the families of drafted men and persons furnishing substitutes.

SENATE BILLS PASSED.

To appropriate to the State Reform School $13,500.

To appropriate to the Institute for the education of the deaf and dumb $18,000.

To appropriate to the Institute for the Blind $26,000.

To appropriate to Charles H. Larkin $806, 80, for expenses. (The vote was 19 to 11.)

To Clark & Co $47.45 for goods.

Adjourned.

ASSEMBLY.

THURSDAY, March 23, 1865.

Prayer by Rev. Mr. BLETSCH.

PETITIONS PRESENTED.

By Mr. SLADE, remonstrance of Geo. C. Cole and others against the bill amending the Sheboygan city charter.

By Mr. GILBERT, petition of B. Caspar and others for biennial sessions; also of A. Miner and others for the passage of the insurance bill.

By Mr. COBB, frm citizens of Winnebago county for biennial sessions.

AFTERNOON SESSIONS.

The resolution for afternoon sessions was amended, on motion of Mr. UTT, so as to provide for meeting at 9½ o'clock a. m. and 3 o'clock p. m. from and after to-day, and adopted.

NORMAL SCHOOL BILL.

The Normal School bill, on motion of Mr. TILTON, was referred to the Committee on Education.

BILLS PASSED.

To amend the charter of the Mechanic's Mutual Insurance Company of Milwaukee.

To vacate certain streets in Beaver Dam.

To authorize the St. John's Evangelical Lutheran Grace Church and German Evangelical Grace Church of Milwaukee to acquire real estate.

To amend the city charter of Racine.

For the preservation of fish in and near Lake Koshkonong.

To authorize Lyman Howe and John Rablin to maintain a boom on the Wisconsin River, in Wood county.

WIS. TELEGRAPH CO.

The bill amending the charter of the Wisconsin Telegraph Company was postponed until Tuesday next.

WAY FREIGHT.

Mr. CADBY offered a substitute for the bill to compel railroad companies to attach a car for way freight to one train over their roads daily, which was referred to a select committee of five.

THE INSURANCE BILL.

The insurance bill and substitute, reported by the Judiciary Committee, was taken up.

Mr. JONES moved to indefinitely postpone—lost.

Mr. JONES then stated that he wished to make remarks on the bill, but desired that its consideration might be postponed in order to give him opportunity to procure some statistics which he desired to produce here.

He moved to go into committee of the whole on the substitute—lost.

Mr. JONES addressed the House in opposition to the bill, as a burden unjustly placed on insurance companies for the purpose of maintaining the credit of the bonds of the State. It was conceded that the bonds of this State had no market value. Now it was proposed to thrust upon the people of the State, as security for insurance companies, bonds so utterly worthless that there was no one who would buy them. There was no object sought by this bill to secure policy holders; that was a mere pretence; the sole object of the bill was to create an artificial market for our State bonds. Who was to be benefitted by the passage of this bill? It was claimed that it was for the interest of the holders of Wisconsin bank bills. If this bill would accomplish what is claimed for it, and would induce the insurance companies to purchase our bonds at par, he admitted that its effect would be to protect bill holders. But the insurance companies would withdraw from the State rather than submit to such a burden. The proper method of meeting the present financial crisis was the levy of such a tax, payable in Wisconsin currency, as will enable us to take up the bonds.

The speaker continued at some length, arguing that the large interest the State would have to pay insurance companies on their bonds, and the immensely increased rates of insurance such companies would be obliged to demand, would prove exceedingly burdensome to the people.

Mr. FULTON advocated the bill as a measure in itself perfectly right, and which ought long ago to have been adopted by the state, but made especially requisite by the exigencies of the present time. Companies were undoubtedly doing business in this state to-day on fraudulent statements of their assets, and that if they were to incur a loss of $10,000 would not be able to pay it. He believed the bill would be an advantage to insurance companies themselves, by increasing the confidence felt in them by the people.

Mr. JONES moved to amend the bill by adding after "bonds of Wisconsin," the words, "or of the United States."

Mr. THOMAS did not expect anything he could say would influence those who had made up their minds to oppose this bill. Some gentlemen, he understood, went further than the gentleman from Dodge (Mr. Jones) and not only declared the bonds unconstitutional but expressed their wish that they should never be paid. He (the speaker) had yet to hear of any measure to prevent a financial crash in this State which did not encounter the opposition of the gentleman from Dodge and of his party.

Mr. HADLEY, (interrupting) called attention to the fact that such was not his position, and that promptly on the first symptom of financial difficulty, he introduced a bill here to maintain the credit of our bonds.

Mr. THOMAS said he was willing to except the gentleman. From many of his acts here this winter, he, Mr. T. was satisfied that the gentleman sympathized with the party to which he, Mr. T., had the honor to belong.—He hoped and he expected that gentleman would vote for this bill.

Mr. T. continued, denouncing the attempt to create an opinion that the State bonds were unconstitutional. It was a humbug.—Those bonds were good and would be faithfully redeemed. And the insurance companies laughed at the idea that this bill was an oppressive one. What this bill required was a mere trifle for them to do, in view of the heavy receipts which they receive for premiums in this State. He also pointed out other measures in progress for taking up the State bonds. At the farthest, the companies probably would not be required to hold them more than two years, and if they were so paltry mean as at this time to refuse to render this small service to the State, they were not worthy of the patronage of our people. Like the genleman from St. Croix, he believed that aside from all temporary considerations, the principle of this bill was right, and that it would be well to adopt it as a permanent policy.

Mr. JONES renewed his opposition to the bill. If this policy was adopted by states; if we require insurance companies to buy our inconvertible bonds; if Illinois and other States compel them to purchase their inconvertible bonds, the companies would soon be unable to pay losses.

Mr. ROSS advocated the passage of the bill and showed that it would not be burdensome on the Insurance Companies.

Mr. JUDD spoke at considerable length in favor of the bill as essential to the public interest, and defended our state bonds from the imputation cast upon them.

Mr. SIMMONS was opposed to the bill, regarding it in the nature of a forced loan, only justifiable on the ground of necessity. The State was not, in his opinion, reduced to a condition which warranted a resort to such expedients.

Mr. WINSOR supported the bill, explaining its details and replying to the proposition made by its opponents in favor of immediate taxation to take up the State bonds. Such a tax at this time he thought would be oppressive. They had already all the taxation they could well bear. He was in favor of relieving them from unnecessary burdens. Such additional taxation would be oppressive and injurious. The people had been heavily taxed of late in addition to State and National taxes by taxes levied to pay bounties to soldiers. He called attention to the fact that if the securities for the Wisconsin currency were permitted to depreciate it would not be the wealthy who would lose, but the heaviest losses would fall on the poorer classes.

Our state bonds were perfectly good. Even those who intimated they were unconstitutional dare not say, they will not and ought not to be paid. They bear 6 per cent. interest. It was no hardship to ask these wealthy insurance companies, doing business in the State to take the quantity of bonds required by the substitute, and hold them for a year or two. If there was such a company, he would willingly bid it good bye. The sooner it withdrew from the State the better.

Mr. STARKS recounted the circumstances under which, immediately after the fall of Fort Sumter, the State bonds were issued, and the manner in which they were sold. With the money thus raised, our first regiments were equipped and sent to the field. There were then a certain class opposed to issuing the bonds, and ever since they had shown a peculiar hostility to them. He could not believe that any man here would say that those bonds were comparatively worthless. The assets of most of the insurance companies were largely made up of State stocks, and was it not fair to require them to take some proportion of the bonds of this State. He thought it was, and hoped the bill would pass.

Adjourned.

LOCAL MATTERS.

Peat Meeting.

We are requested to give notice that there will be a meeting of citizens at the State Agricultural Society's rooms, in Porter's Block, on Friday (to-morrow) evening, at 7½ o'clock, to take into consideration measures for the manufacture of fuel from peat, valuable beds of which exist in this vicinity.

Prof. CARR, of the State University, will be present, and will explain the qualities and uses of peat.

All those who take an interest in this subject, which in view of the prices of wood and coal, is one of great importance to this locality, are requested to be present.

PERSONAL.—We were happy to receive a call this morning from our old friend, J. W. BLACKSTONE, Jr., the popular county judge of Lafayette county. He is a candidate for re-election, Mr. AUGUSTUS MURPHY being run by the Democrats against him.

Col. CLARK, Lieut. Col. BRYANT and Surgeon VIVIAN, of the 50th, arrived here from the west to-day, having been detained two or three days by the storm.

Adjutant JENKINS, of the 21st Regiment, a prisoner in rebel hands since Chickamauga, has arrived here.

Hon. I. C. SLOAN, our worthy member of Congress, is in the city.

Gen. DAVID ATWOOD, the senior editor of this paper, returned home last evening, having been detained two or three days by the floods in New York.

D. R. CAMERON, of Culver, Page & Hoyne, Chicago, is stopping at the Capital House.

ANOTHER SWORD PRESENTATION.—We learn that on Monday evening, March 2d, the members of Co. B, 50th Regiment, presented to their captain and first Lieut. each, an elegant and costly sword. A delegation was sent the officers at their quarters, requesting them to appear at the company barracks, which they did, notwithstanding the inclemency of the weather. It may be, they suspected the liberality of the company. At any rate they came, and were rewarded by the gift already mentioned. Private A. A. SUMNER, of De Soto, Wis., made an eloquent off-hand presentation speech, exactly suited to the occasion. This was appropriately responded to by Capt. ROGERS and Lieut. NEWELL, who are worthy of the noble company they command. The scene then closed, and the officers withdrew amid the good wishes of their company.

SENATOR VAN WYCK'S LECTURE THIS EVENING.—This morning the Assembly appointed a committee to wait upon Senator VAN WYCK and make arrangements for his lecture on "Italy" in the Assembly Chamber this evening. The committee, consisting of Messrs. ROSS, THOMPSON and WOOSTER have made arrangements for the lecture this evening and cordially invite citizens of Madison, and the general public, to come and enjoy with the legislature the intellectual treat. The lecture will commence at 7:30 P. M.

SUIT FOR DAMAGES.—We learn that on yesterday Judge HARVEY BRIGGS brought a civil action, before Court Commissioner LAMB against Major SMITH BROWN, for arbitrarily arresting him, and laid his damages at $5,000. On the usual affidavit, stating the facts, and that Major BROWN was a non-resident, an order was issued for his arrest. He was released, however on $2,500 bail. It should be understood that Major B.'s action in arresting the substitute brokers, was taken at the request of the State authorities, and under orders of the Secretary of War.

A SELF-ADJUSTING LANTERN.—We are indebted to R. L. GARLICK of the Madison Crockery Store, for one of Woodward's self-adjusting lanterns, a new and very convenient invention, admirably adapted for dark nights and muddy streets. It burns kerosene, gives a bright light, is very convenient to open and trim, durable, and withal cheap. We advise every one who wants a good lantern, to procure one of Woodward's self-adjusting.

BILLIARDS.—Mr. ALF. MERRILL, of Madison, has accepted S. A. TUSTIN's billiard challenge to play with any resident of Wisconsin who has resided in the State one year, to a match game of 1500 points up, the American four ball carron game, to be played on a four pocket table made by C. E. WILCOX of Milwaukee. The match will be for $250 a side, and will come off in this city Tuesday afternoon, April 25, at the City Hall.

DEMOCRATIC CITY CONVENTION.—In the absence of any Democratic newspaper in this city, we publish and invite the attention of our readers to the call of the Democratic City Committee for a convention to meet at Court House, on the 1st of April next, to nominate Democratic candidates for Mayor and City Treasurer.

HARPER'S WEEKLY.—The last number, received from the Post Office News Depot, illustrates the grand "Triumph" in New York recently, over our victories, Gen. SHERIDAN'S march, gives portraits of the new Secretaries and others, and several sketches.

ALL RIGHT.—We learn that the damages to the Mil. and Prairie du Chien Railway, and the Beloit Branch of the Northwestern, have been repaired, and the first trains went over the breaks this morning.

FRANK LESLIE.—The last number, received from MOSELEY'S, gives fine pictures of the present appearance of Fort Sumter, several street views in Charleston, a view of Richmond, &c.

☞ See notice of Capt. VAN SLYKE, United States Quartermaster, who wants a large number of horses, for which he offers a high price, in cash.

☞ It is cool and clear to-day, with a strong March wind, which is beginning to dry up the mud a little.

☞ Teams have ceased crossing the lakes on the ice, but foot passengers still venture.

☞ Prof. CARR's first lecture takes place Saturday evening, not this evening.

MARRIED.

POUND—MILES.—In this city on the evening of the 21st inst., by Rev. J. E. Johnson, Mr. SAMUEL POUND to Mrs. HANNAH MILES, both of Porter, Rock county.

BY TELEGRAPH.

MORNING DISPATCHES.

THE WAR IN NORTH CAROLINA.

Movement of Sherman's Left.

Going Toward Raleigh.

Thousands of Refugees Coming in.

Organization of North Carolina Unionists.

Immense Amounts of Stores Taken.

Richmond is Being Evacuated.

Probably be Ours Without a Battle.

Talk of Rebel Stand at Danville.

Jeff. Davis Denounced by Rebel Congress.

GEN. SHERMAN'S CAMPAIGN.

NEW YORK, March 23.

The *Herald's* Washington special says "an officer from Fayetteville, reports that the column which Raleigh papers mentioned as moving towards Hillsboro, is Sherman's left wing, moving toward the North Carolina R. R., to destroy the bridge over the Neuse between Raleigh and Goldsboro. Thousands of refugees are on the way to Wilmington, and the wharves of all the lands between Fayetteville and Wilmington are filled with rosin, turpentine, cotton, &c. The value of property captured amounts to millions.

The *Herald's* Kinston correspondent says the ram *Neuse*, destroyed by the rebels, had a crew, exclusive of officers, of 90 men, who surrendered. On the ram were 21 hermetically sealed cans of powder of 200 pounds each, and two 68-pounder rifled guns. The rebels, before leaving Kinston, placed torpedoes all about the place, some of which have done execution on our troops.

The *Herald's* Second Corps correspondent of the 20th, reports an army of rebel deserters in western North Carolina under lead of one Kirk. They are all armed and organized for protection against conscripting officers, and to inflict such injury on the rebel cause as will best contribute to the speedy termination of the war and enable them to return home.

THE SITUATION.

NEW YORK, March 23.

The *Tribune's* correspondent avers, upon what he deems to be the best authority, that Richmond is now being evacuated as fast as possible, and that in a few days it will be occupied by Union troops without a battle.

The *Tribune's* Washington special says it is believed by military men there that the rebels will evacuate Raleigh and make their stand at Danville, if they fight at all south of Richmond.

The *World's* Washington special says Grant some time since told H. S. Cox he believed Lee desired to evacuate Richmond but did not think it could be done. It is very doubtful whether Lee could so much as begin a movement without Grant's knowledge, and once known our armies would immediately move.

FROM REBELDOM.

NEW YORK, March 23.

Richmond papers of the 20th contain a long reply made by a select committee relative to Mr. Davis, in which the Senators charge that it was he who was guilty of tardiness, inefficiency and want of decision. They say that with very few exceptions, every law that he suggested was speedily enacted, and all that he asked was readily granted; that on matters which he charges them with neglecting, he failed to give them the information requested, and which was necessary to enable them to act intelligently.

Mr. Hunter publishes a card to let the people know he is still opposed to a reconstruction of the Union.

THE WAR IN VIRGINIA.

NEW YORK, March 23.

The *Herald's* 5th Corps correspondence of the 20th, says heavy rumbling, as of trains crossing pontoon bridges, is heard every night from within the enemy's lines, showing that they are actively engaged in some movement.

ERRATA.—In publishing the report of the Treasurer of Bounty Fund Committee, several errors occurred.

R. A. Vilas, 1st Ward, received bounty—$290—erroneously printed $310.

Joseph Dubre received bounty—$310—erroneously printed $810.

These errors *in no manner* affect the balance sheet, *or the general account with the several wards*, as the error was not carried forward.

Some few of the 1st Ward accountants fail to see through the balance sheet. It is very simple to understand, taking the report together. Twenty-four men were enlisted and paid from the *private* fund; five of these were for the 1st Ward. This ward, through its note, made full provision for 46 men—its quota. The city paid back to the private fund the $1,000—$200 per man, city bounty—and of course this amount belonged to that ward, to apply on its note. In other words, the 1st Ward raised $1,000 more than was required, in respect to the city bounty, the city having subsequently repaid to the treasurer its $1,000 on five men. Now the private fund must make up the excess of cost of volunteers over $200. This is deficient.—The same fact, as to nine men, or $1,800, is true of the 3d Ward, only that this ward raised a surplus of private subscription.

The 4th Ward note was not enough to pay $200 per man. Hence the deficiency. The private subscription was ample.

J. L. Lewis, enrolled in 1st ward, residing in 4th ward, paid $30; in classifying names, his was omitted. This sum affects the footings, and adds to 1st ward subscriptions, and asserts a "better claim" than my own to $30 of boasted "surplus assets."

The following named 3d Ward subscribers have come to light: D. Kessler, $10; Klauber & Ott, $10; Mr. Zwang, $10; Mr. Matthias, $5; John Offert, $15; and M. Foss, $10, making $60. This is part of the $155; names not given.

I must ask the sub-committee of the 3d Ward, and all others in the 3d and 1st Wards, to excuse me from any further trouble with names. I am uncertain as to my own.

W. WELCH, Treasurer.

MADISON, March 23, 1865.

☞ See notice of new saloon.

AFTERNOON DISPATCHES.

IMPORTANT from SHERMAN

HE IS STILL MARCHING ON.

His Army Largely Reinforced.

Its Numbers Overwhelming.

A Battle Thought to be Imminent.

Rebels Must Fight or Surrender.

Address of the Rebel Congress.

The Wail of Defeated Traitors.

THE NORTH CAROLINA CAMPAIGN.

NEW YORK, March 23.

The steamer *Varuna*, from Beaufort, N. C., the 20th, brings important intelligence.

The news of the capture of Goldsboro, was received in the city, soon after the victory, by dispatches from Gen. Sherman, who, it was reported, called for reinforcements for his army during their further march northward.

Immense numbers of troops were promptly sent in response from Beaufort, by rail and other roads, to Goldsboro, preparatory to meeting the main army of Sherman. It was believed that a battle was imminent, and hence Gen. Sherman's army was swelled to an overwhelming force, the extent of which may lead to a general retreat or surrender of the enemy. Reinforcements and supplies had also been sent from Newbern to join Sherman's army.

Refugees at Beaufort and Morehead City declare that the rebel troops were demoralized, and that their supplies are beginning to fail. It was also reported that part of Lee's army had gone to reinforce Gen. Johnston, and that his main force was about five miles north of Raleigh.

FROM REBELDOM.

NEW YORK, March 23.

The rebel Congress, before taking its recent hasty leave of Richmond, and after refusing to adopt any of the measures urged by Davis as requisite to save the rebel cause, issued an address to the Southern people.

It begins by saying that they cannot have peace except by the sacrifice of independence and property, that confiscation and extermination are the only terms they can get. It refers to what it regards the evils of Union and makes an appeal to Southern manhood.

It gives a rose-colored view of the resources of the South and calls upon the people to drive into ranks again absentees and skulkers. It congratulates the country upon the appointment of Lee as General-in-chief, and apologizes for the heavy burdens of taxation which they have obliged to impose.

They believe the people of the United States have become tired of the war, and can at any time have peace by abandoning the wicked attempt at subjugation. They recite again their grievances under the old government, and call upon the people to emulate the example of the Russians when Napoleon invaded their territory.

They wind up with a stirring appeal, saying success is within their reach, that the battle is not to the strong, and that the shades of their martyred heroes hover over and beckon them on.

COMMERCIAL.

Milwaukee Market.

MILWAUKEE, March 23.

Wheat less active and ½c lower, with No. 1 spring in store at 1.14@1.14½.

Oats dull and nominally lower.

Gold is buying at 1.50@1.52.

Chicago Market.

CHICAGO, WEDNESDAY EVENING, March 22.

The rally in gold and the improved tone of the New York dispatches strengthened the leading markets to some extent to-day, and prices were a shade better for one or two articles.

In flour there was nothing done, and the market was nominal at 9.00@10.00 for White Winter wheat brands, and 6.00@7.00 for medium to choice Spring Extras.

There was a fair speculative movement in wheat, and an advance of 1@2c. No. 1 Spring sold at from 1.17½@1.19, and No. 2 Spring at 1.06. At the close the market ruled steady and firm at 1 18½ for No. 1.

Corn was dull and easier, with rejected at 60@63. No. 1 corn nominal at 73@74c.

Oats moderately active. Strictly fresh receipts of No. 1 sold at 51@51½c, but the general range was from 49@50½c.

There were no buyers for rye, and the market is nominal at 74@78c.

For barley there was but a limited inquiry, and sales were meagre at 1.00 for new No. 2, and 95c for rejected in South Side houses.

Highwines improved 3c per gallon, but the demand was light, and only 200 bbls sold at 2.08.

Seeds declined 10@15c on Timothy and Flax, and 50c on Clover, with sales of Timothy at 3.25@3.70; Flax at 2.25@2.40, and Clover at 11.50@11.75.

Provisions dull and heavy, and declined 25@50c per bbl on pork, with sales of mess at 24.50, and prime mess at 23.50@24.25—closing at 24.00 for prime mess from slaughtered hogs. Lard was neglected and nominal at 17c for prime city steam.

New York Market.

NEW YORK, March 23.

Flour is dull and 10c lower, at 9.75@9.85 for extra State; 10.30@10.40 for round-hoop Ohio.

Wheat unsettled and irregular, at 2.10 for amber Michigan.

Corn dull, at 1.54 for new mixed western.

Oats quiet, at 97c for western.

Pork is lower.

New York Stock Market.

NEW YORK, March 23.

Stocks lower and dull.

Gold opened at 1.57 and closed at 1.54.

U. S. 6s of '81, with coupons, 1.07; 5-20s, with coupons, 1.07; do new issue 1.06½; 10 40s with coupons, 93; 1 year certificates, 97.

WISCONSIN STATE JOURNAL.

VOLUME XIII. MADISON, WIS. MONDAY, APRIL 10, 1865. NUMBER 179.

STATE JOURNAL.

MONDAY, APRIL 10, 1865.

THE OFFICIAL STATE PAPER.

Our Paper To-day.

The publication of a village charter, and work in getting up a tax list, obliges us to postpone till to-morrow various matter.

The line east of Janesville has been out of order to-day, so that we have been unable to obtain any later dispatches than those of last night for our paper to-day. Interesting, isn't it?

Saturday evening's report will be found on the second page, also a letter giving some account of the glorious part taken by the 38th Regiment in the recent battles near Petersburg, with a list of losses.

The Crowning Victory.

Once more the great heart of the land pulsates with the mighty joy of victory. Once more the cannons boom. Once more the bonfires blaze. Once more the steeples rock with peals of gladness. Once more from a thousand cities and hamlets, across the continent, there goes up the clamorous rejoicings of a people thrilled and electrified with the news of a final triumph over mortal foes.

LEE has surrendered the Army of Virginia on conditions prescribed by GRANT! In that brief sentence all is told. It means the end of war and the dawn of peace. It means that all formidable resistance to the Constitution and laws of the United States has terminated. It means the complete triumph of nationality over secession. It means no more calls for men, no more sanguinary battles, no more sacrifice of precious lives, no more wounding and maiming of our fathers and brothers and sons; but a speedy return of "the boys in blue," covered with the laurels of victory, to the blessings of peaceful homes, with "Liberty and Union now and forever."

It is true there yet remains under JOHNSTON a rebel army of considerable strength. But what can it accomplish? Note its situation. It is penned in beween the mountains and the sea, with GRANT's victorious legions at the North and the invincible hosts of SHERMAN pressing on it from the South. It may as well lay down its arms at once, and doubtless it will. Otherwise it will speedily learn how dangerous it is

> —"When the baser nature comes,
> Between the pass and fell incensed points
> Of mightiest opposites,"

When LEE surrendered, the last prop which supported the tottering "Confederacy" gave way. He was the last hope of the enemies of the Union. No other man retained the confidence of any considerable portion of the Southern people. When Richmond fell there still lingered a hope that LEE might find some means of restoring the shattered fortunes of the rebellion. He had been raised to the position of Dictator. The Southern people had trusted all to him. But he could not escape the inexorable pursuit of Gen. GRANT. With the army that has caused so much trouble, and cost us so much blood, he has surrendered. *It is an end of the war.*

Well may the loyal men and women of this land rejoice,—they who have stood faithful in all the crises of an unparalleled struggle—who have resisted every solicitation to a dishonorable peace—who have risked their lives and freely given of their substance for the support of the old flag—and who have never, in the darkest hour, wavered, or despaired of the Republic. Their gladness is of a kind that can find no adequate expression in words—a profound and solemn emotion—no vulgar exultation, such as might accompany an ordinary triumph, but a sentiment that swells the heart like grief, while filling it with a holy and religious joy:

> "Now praise and thanks for ever more,
> The long and dreary night has passed!
> The trials of the land are o'er;—
> The giant stands erect at last!
>
> "O weary hours! O night of years!
> What storms our darkling pathway kept,
> When beating back our thronging fears,
> By faith alone our march we kept.
>
> "Awake! awake! my Fatherland!
> It is thy Northern light that shines!
> This stirring march of Freedom's band,
> The storm-song of thy mountain pines!
>
> "O prisoners in your house of pain!
> Dumb, toiling millions bought and sold,
> Look! stretched o'er southern vale and plain,
> The Lord's delivering hand behold!"

☞ The pontoon train on which our army crossed the Appomattox on their entry into Petersburg, was laid under the direction of Maj. W. H. Paine, of the Topographical Engineers at Gen. Meade's headquarters. Maj. Paine is a resident of Sheboygan in this State.

REBEL ATTEMPTS TO ARM NEGROES.—The attempt to organize and arm negroes was the most laughable and ridiculous failure of the war, and was so decided by the rebels themselves. There were never more than 800 organized.

☞ The recent heavy rains in California, raising the rivers to an unprecedented height, brought down an immense quantity of gold dust from the mountains, which the miners are now sifting from the slime of the subsided waters.

THE GREAT SHOWMAN TURNED LEGISLATOR.—P. T. BARNUM was chosen a member of the Connecticut Legislature from Fairfield, on Monday week.

☞ The city of Grand Rapids, Michigan, hitherto democratic, was carried clean for the republican ticket on Monday week by majorities ranging from 14 to 118.

☞ At a meeting of rejoicing over the fall of Richmond held in Faneuil Hall, Boston, Robert C. Winthrop and Fred. Douglass were among the speakers.

MRS. JEFF DAVIS is reported to have left Richmond for Galveston, Tex., on Wednesday of last week.

Final Adjournment of the Legislature.

In pursuance of the joint resolution, the Legislature adjourned at 11 o'clock to-day. A large number of bills were acted upon Saturday, both houses remaining in session till midnight and passing and killing bills by wholesale, but generally with a clear understanding of what they were about. In the Assembly quite a number of bills failed to receive final consideration, but mostly of a private and local character.

About all important measures were disposed of. The appropriation bills all passed, except that of $30,000 for the enlargement of the Hospital for the Insane, and also the bills for a temporary loan and special tax of $850,000 for war purposes, and a general tax of $350,000 for general expenses. The bill increasing the rate of interest was defeated in the Assembly, also the bill allowing the Racine & Mississippi railroad to build branches to Milwaukee and Chicago.

The following is a summary of this mornings proceedings in the two Houses:

In the Senate, the following resolution, offered by Senator CLARK, was unanimously adopted:

Resolved, That the thanks of the Senate are due and are hereby tendered to the Hon. Wyman Spooner and to Hon. W. H. Chandler for the able, kind and impartial manner they have each conducted the deliberations of this body during its present session.

On motion of Senator ELLIS, the following resolution was also unanimously adopted:

Resolved, That the thanks of the Senate are hereby tendered to Frank M. Stewart, Esq., Chief Clerk, and his assistants, and Nelson Williams, Esq., Sergeant-at-Arms, for the able, courteous, and satisfactory manner in which they have discharged their respective duties.

In response to these resolutions Lt. Governor Spooner and president *pro tem* W. H. Chandler made some eloquent remarks which will be published to-morrow.

Senator Clark offered a resolution for a joint committee to wait on the Governor to inquire if he had any further communication to make to the Legislature, and Senators Clark and Littlejohn appointed. After the lapse of a short time Senator Clark returned and said the Governor had a communication in course of preparation which he desired to make to the Legislature, and would send it in before the hour of adjournment.

About 10.45 A. M. Gov. Lewis transmitted the following message:

STATE OF WISCONSIN,
EXECUTIVE DEPARTMENT,
MADISON, April 10, 1865.

To the Honorable the Legislature:

Four years ago, on the day fixed for adjournment, the sad news of the fall of Fort Sumter was transmitted to the Legislature.

To-day, thank God, and next to Him the brave officers and soldiers of our Army and Navy, I am permitted to transmit to you the official intelligence, just received, of the surrender of Gen. Lee and his army—the last prop of the rebellion.

Let us rejoice and thank the Ruler of the Union for Victory, and the prospects of an honorable Peace.

JAMES T. LEWIS.

The accompanying dispatches, which will be found in our telegraphic columns, were read by the clerk and received most enthusiastically. On their conclusion, on motion of Senator WESCOTT the Senate gave three cheers for Gen. GRANT and the glorious army under his command.

Senator W. H. CHANDLER then, at 11 a. m., in pursuance of the joint resolution, declared the Senate adjourned *sine die.*

In the Assembly the usual resolutions of thanks to the officers were adopted, various speeches of congratulation made, and a highly appropriate farewell address delivered by Speaker FIELD, the publication of which is unavoidably postponed till to-morrow.

Wisconsin Losses in Recent Battles.

We compile the following list of Wisconsin men wounded in recent battles in Virginia and North Carolina, from our exchanges.

We find the following names of Wisconsin men wounded in the battles before Petersburg up to Saturday:

6th Regiment.—Thomas Fardy, B, thorax; Edward Butler, H, hip; James M. Pegg, M, thigh; Wm. Gibberson, B, slight; Geo. Ferguson, H, slight; Francis Franis, B, amputated arm; H. Koch, B, leg; Chas. Heusler, F, head; F. McCabe, B, back; George Seldon, A, arm; W. V. Hammah, B, arm; G. H. Farcrook, E, hand; John Stelin, A, hand; H. R. Conard, B, hand; John Stiller, A, hand; Sergt. A. Rolfe, D, foot; Wm. Friss, F, thorax; Capt. H. Scheldt, F, face; Frederick Lockeman, arm; Henry Cook, leg; A. G. Beecker, foot; Peter Muller, D, slight; Walter Wieds, G, head; Fred. Lockman, B, face and arm; A. Burchell, I, face; Henry Revels, face and arm; John Gunderman, E, hand; D. Barnard, A, severe; H. H. Palmer, A, thigh; G. Mathews, hip; A. Davis, K, leg amputated. Thos. Sweet, H, hip; Sergt. C. A. Wenser, shoulder, severe; Ferdinand Lennesdary, D, face; H. Hoesle, G, arm; M. T. Wall, G, head.

7th Regiment.—Jno. Krase, B, leg amputated; Geo. Miners, G, leg; Corp. T. W. Reilly, foot; Henry Shelter, D, thigh; A. Kellogg, A, thorax; Sergt. Thos. Strageway, A, back; L. Noetch, F, leg; M. R. Leach, A, slight; W. D. Bennett, K, hand; Sergt. J. C. Morgan, K, leg; Lt. Oneisure, shoulder; Patrick Gleason, hand; Henry Decke, head; A. H. Powell, E, amputated thigh; Monroe Hyatt, arm; Frank Stewell, K, slight; John Stadler, shoulder; D. A. McLinn, leg; Thos. Boucher, B, foot; Nathan Muriger, slight; Corp. F. W. Isham, D, leg amputated; Jas. H. Rice, A, leg; Lewis Rowe, E, arm; J. T. Wilson, I, hand; Jno. R. Armes, H, do, shoulder; Isaiah Shaller, G, arm; John H. Hepper, E, leg; Sergt. J. C. Morgan, D, leg fractured; Jas. Baulis, I, shoulder; Sergt. W. H. Walker, hip and fore arm; M. Thomas, E, arm; Samuel Hukeny, B, leg; Irwin Flagg, E, arm fractured; Chauncy Elisthorpe, A, hand; F. M. McKee, K, arm; Corp. Geo. Horar, A, thigh; H. Dunk, do; Eugene Cole, arm; J. Loby, G; J. M. Roberts, F, bowels.

37th Regiment.—Henry Sholand, arm.

The following is a list of wounded in Wisconsin regiments at the recent battle of Averysboro, North Carolina:

3d Regiment.—Edwin C. Williams, right knee; Chas. S. Wilson; arm; Patrick Silione, back; Merritt Wilsey, left foot; William White left femur; Willard Allen, thigh; Wm. Townsend, head; Alfred Gillette, thigh; George Lovel, 31st, arm; Jas. Brentner, scalp; Geo. W. Norton, thigh; August Rasin, leg; Peter Bowers, shoulder; Eugene Cossette, thigh; Ole Hanson, Groin; W. H. Holmes, left thigh; Theo. Bomhardt, femur; Chas. A. Hart, thighs; Sergt. Geo. B. Bennett, left ankle; Corp. Jaspar Woodford, right hand; James Alling, left thigh; Leonard Heabener, right thigh; Ole Goodsitte, arm; John Seymour, left hand; Richard Geardoe, thigh; Ole Hanson, abdomen.

22d Regiment.—Ira Barrows, left leg; David Williams, left arm; Edwin Parkhurst, left thigh.

31st Regiment.—Levi Limburger, left thigh; Geo. Lovell, arm; Chas. E. Bivader, thorax; Jas. Grenville, thigh; Geo. T. Crumwell, thorax; Jas. McBride, hand; Geo. Beitz, arm; A. F. McDermott, foot; Edwin Thompson, hand; Henry Carter, hand; Gardner Stearns, femur; Sergt. John Richards, foot; Martin Bassart, back; C. B. Helen, head; Henry Goeldener, arm; Thos. Crabtree, hand; Jas. A. Porter, shoulder; Alfred Cothren, scalp; Chas. Weed, groin; Geo. H. Beaumont, leg; Sergt. A. C. Parkinson, arm; Theophilis Case, shoulder; Geo. W. Newton, thigh; Benj. Edwards, R. M. Thomas, abdomen.

THE PRESIDENT AT RICHMOND.—A Richmond letter of the 5th says: "President Lincoln walked up yesterday from the flag-ship *Malvern,* which landed at the city, amid a vast concourse of the inhabitants, and was welcomed by the mayor and citizens." He is not expected to return until the middle of next week.

THE FIRE AT RICHMOND.—The Richmond *Whig* says the damage by the fire which the rebels started as they were leaving will amount to many hundred millions of dollars. Nearly 1,000 buildings were destroyed. By the blowing up of a powder magazine in the suburbs, some 80 lives were lost.

Presentation to Speaker Field and Chief Clerk Dean.

On Saturday evening the members and officers of the Assembly made presentations of silver tea services to their worthy officers, Speaker FIELD and Chief Clerk DEAN. The services were placed on one of the reporters' tables, and their design and richness was admiringly commented on, especially by the many ladies present. The Speaker's contained eight pieces, the largest showing the following inscription: "Presented to Hon. W. W. FIELD as a slight testimonial of the regard of the Members and Officers of the Seventeenth Assembly." The Chief Clerk's contained six pieces, one of them showing a similar inscription to the inscribed piece of the Speaker's. Both sets were supplied by Mr. BELDEN, of this city, and they are worthy of his tastefully stocked establishment.

When the Assembly was called to order, Mr. Ross rose and spoke as follows:

MR. SPEAKER:—It is probably known to you, sir, that a number of your esteeming friends in this Assembly, unite in tendering you the testimonial of their regard which I have the pleasure to present for your acceptance. This silver tea-service is not given to increase your worldly gifts, but to add to your mental joys an association that may be grateful and inspiring to you. The hope of the donors is, that you will ever regard it as an humble expression of the feelings of admiration and friendship which your ability as a presiding officer, and qualities as a man, have raised in their hearts. As a Speaker you are completely appreciated within these walls, and the knowledge of your manly qualities and walk is not limited to the boundaries of this state.

"Act well your part, there all the honor lies." Is nobly exemplified by you; therefore the gift honors the giver as much as the recipient and each donor feels that it does.

Similar presentations to this have been made in this chamber and among them one to yourself while Speaker of the last Assembly, but on those occasions the war was raging without any decisive sign of the end. The spirit of this occasion is heightened by the victory that so completely perches on the national banner, bringing the peace that will warmly cherish and preserve the remembrance of this genial time.

During our official intercourse on this floor, nothing has occurred to disturb our mutual good will, and I believe that the recollections of the intercourse will be as agreeable to you as to us. When it shall have ceased and you are at home in the bosom of your family, the sight of our gift as you sit with it before you, after the useful labor of one of your well spent days, will probably sometimes bring us to mind with our various attributes and you will think and talk of us, investing our memories with your good wishes, and be assured that prayers for your welfare and happiness will always mingle with our "Auld Lang Syne" remembrances of you and this session.

MR. SPEAKER FIELD responded as follows:

GENTLEMAN FROM DANE, MR. ROSS—SIR—I sincerely thank you for this beautiful, ornamental and useful present which you have been pleased to bestow upon me, on behalf of the members and officers of the Assembly over which I have the pleasure of presiding. If I have discharged those delicate and responsible duties pertaining to my position, in a manner which meets your approval, it has in a great measure been due, to the aid afforded, and the kindness and courtesy extended to me by the members and officers you here represent. Having simply, with your aid, discharged my duty. I cannot appreciate that I merit this public notice, and token of regard at you hands; but, sir, as you have been pleased to confer this testimonial of esteem upon me, I accept it with pleasure, gratitude and pride. I accept it, sir, as a public demonstration of approbation and esteem for my humble services as your presiding officer during this session. I shall ever deem it a private treasure of inestimable value, prized for the kinn and friendly feelings ever manifested towards me by you, sir, and the members and officers of this Assembly, and which has prompted the bestowal of this elegant gift upon me. As I shall sit with my little family, and I trust often numerous friends, around the table upon which stands this gift of friendship, and sip the infusion of "Old Java" made into a delicious beverage by the accompaniments contained in other articles composing this beautiful silver tea sett, my thoughts will inevitably revert to this happy occasion, and it will ever be an incentive to good and praiseworthy deeds, and of renewed exertion on my part to merit a continuance of the confidence and esteem here expressed, and the approbation of those with whom I may be associated in private or public life. I again thank you for this testimonial of your regard, and through you those numerous friends, members and officers of the Assembly, who have made me the happy recipient on this occasion.

Mr. WINSOR, of Walworth, then rose and spoke as follows:

MR. CHIEF CLERK:—Only a few moments ago did I know that I had been selected by my fellow members of the Legislative Assembly to the honor of making the presentation to you of this beautiful silver tea service.

I have no studied language or set phrase of speech to make on this pleasant occasion. This beautiful gift is presented to you by my fellow members as a sligh. testimonial of the esteem which they entertain for you personally, and for the creditable manner in which you have discharged the laborious duties of Chief Clerk of this Assembly during the session now about to close.

Most of us met at the opening of this session for the first time. We were strangers to you and to each other—we were unskilled in the science of legislation—you, sir, had long experience in that department of this Hall belonging to your desk, and through your ever willing and courteous aid in our legislative inexperience we have been enabled to perform the duties assigned to us in a much more efficient and creditable manner than we otherwise could. Nor would I here omit to mention the high personal regards we entertain for you, for the many social and moral qualities you have displayed throughout your entire intercourse with us at this session. As we are about separate to our several homes and families, we did not feel that we could do so without doing you an injustice if we did not, in some humble manner, intimate to you our kind regards, by some appropriate testimonial, and we could think of none more fitting or acceptable to you than this beautiful service of silver. Though the gift is a small one, and of no intrinsic value, nevertheless we hope and believe you will not deem it so insignificant that our kindly feelings and respect for you, should be measured by the metalic value of the offered gift.

We hope, in after years, when you shall cast your eyes upon this simple present, it will bring back to your mind pleasant and agreeable reminiscences of the legislative Assembly of 1865. In that retrospect we fondly hope that each one of your faces may be gazed upon with the same genial countenance that now reflects back our own gaze on this pleasant occasion.

In conclusion, then, permit me in behalf of my fellow members of the Assembly, to present to you this beautiful tea service, with the kindest wishes for your future health, prosperity and happiness.

Mr. Chief Clerk then responded as follows:

HR. WINSOR AND GENTLEMEN OF THE ASSEMBLY: I thank you very heartily for this handsome present. It is as undeserved as unexpected on my part, for whatever satisfaction I may have given in the performance of my duties, you had a right to expect that I should serve you to the best of my ability.

It is gratifying to know that I have merited your approbation, as this presentation would indicate; and, in accepting this gift, I can but feel that it is an implied compliment not only to myself but to the clerical force of this Assembly. Although my own labors have been more prominent perhaps, (from the nature of my position,) yet, whatever success has attended me, has been due in a great degree to the invaluable services rendered by my assistants. In this connection, it is a pleasure to say, that I have been peculiarly fortunate at this session, in the selection of my associates.

I have occupied the position of assistant and chief clerk for eight successive years, but never has a session passed away more pleasantly, never has my own labor been so light, and my intercourse between each and every member has been of that friendly nature that I shall always look back with pleasing recollections to the winter of 1865.

As the day of adjournment draws near, and we shall soon part, some of us to meet no more, allow me to tender to each one of you my sincere and heartfelt thanks for the kindness and courtesy extended to me during the session, and for the additional pleasure which has called forth these remarks.

This terminated the interesting proceedings, and the Assembly began its regular business.

Presentation to the Sergeant-at-Arms of the Senate.

The subordinate officers of the Senate, in the Sergeant-at-Arms Department on Saturday evening, presented Sergeant-at-Arms WILLIAMS with a large and beautiful Family Bible on Saturday evening. The presentation was made by Postmaster LELAND, who accompanied the book with the following note:

WISCONSIN LEGISLATURE,
SENATE CHAMBER,
MADISON, April 8th, 1865.

NELSON WILLIAMS, Esq., *Sergeant-at-Arms of the Senate:*

DEAR SIR:—The officers and employees of your department of this body, being desirous of in some way expressing their appreciation of your character as a man and an officer, take pleasure in presenting to you this Bible as a memento of their regard. Being thus desirous of in some manner expressing to you our appreciation of your many courtesies and uniform kindness to your subordinates, all agreed that we could not better do so, and perpetuate a memory of the pleasant relations that have existed between us during the present session of the Legislature, more appropriately, than in presenting you with a family Bible, and here allow us to say, that in this selection they have shown themselves worthy employees of an honorable body, and have expressed a high appreciation of your character as a man. Trusting that you and yours may profit by the glorious and truthful teachings of this Book of books which has survived all time and all opposition, and its truths shine more bright and glorious to-day than ever before; that the law given to Moses upon Mount Sinai, written by the fingers of Jehovah, and which is the ground work of all other just laws, may be the law of your life; that you may read the sublime and poetic teachings of God's holy prophets with profit to yourself and those you hold dear; that you may be guided by the teachings of Him who "spake as man never spake," and took upon Himself the form of frail humanity and suffered, and "was tempted in all points as we are," and hence, in our hours of trial and bitter anguish, when no human heart can soothe, He is "touched with a feeling of our infirmity," in brief, that this blessed book may be a "lamp to your feet" and a "guide to your life," all through its journey, and that its teachings may guide you to that haven of eternal rest of which it affords so many glorious glimpses,

We are truly your friends,

J. L. WILDER,	FRANK LELAND,
J. P. MILLER,	D. B. SNODY,
CHARLES ERKTON,	NORMAN McBEATH,
AUGUST VANDRY,	ROSWELL STOWE,
W. P. BURROUGHS,	C. C. FREY,
A. ISING,	RUFUS ROYS,
S. STOUGHTON.	H. W. SPOONER.

Mr. Williams responded as follows:

MY FRIENDS: It is a pleasure to be remembered as we are about to part, and I feel very grateful for this expression of kindness and regard on your part, by this presentation. I accept it with a thankful heart, and shall ever keep it in remembrance of those with whom I have been so pleasantly connected the past winter.

You, and each of you, have discharged the duties pertaining to your respective positions to my entire satisfaction, and I trust to the satisfaction of the Senate. I again thank you, and wish you all a long life of good health and prosperity.

LOCAL MATTERS.

REJOICINGS LAST NIGHT.—The news of LEE's surrender reached this city between 9 and 10 o'clock last evening. The intelligence was immediately announced in the Assembly Chamber by Hon. Z. G. SIMMONS, of Kenosha, and spread as only such news will spread throughout the city.

A national salute was ordered to be fired in the park by the Governor, under the direction of the State Armourer, JOHN MCFARLAND, while the bells of the Churches and City Hall pealed joyfully out, arousing the whole people.

A large bonfire was speedily kindled at the head of Wisconsin avenue, near the Capital House, and a crowd collected there. Speeches were made, and the city was uproarious with the noise of rejoicing till late into the night.

The law office of Mr. KEYES, our mayor elect, on the same floor with the telegraph office, was crowded with people to whom our dispatches were read as they were received. The crowd amused themselves when not hearing dispatches by singing the "Star-Spangled Banner," "John Brown," "When Johnny Comes Marching Home," "Praise God from Whom All Blessings Flow," &c., &c. The proceedings were protracted till between one and two o'clock in the morning.

SERMON ON THE FALL OF RICHMOND.—An eloquent and impressive sermon was preached at the Congregational church last evening by the pastor, Rev. L. E. MATSON, on the fall of the rebel capital. His text was from the second chapter of St. Luke: "Glory to God in the highest, and on earth peace and good will to men." The church was packed with people, every seat and every inch of standing room being occupied, while the vestibule, the steps outside, and even the sidewalk in front of the church was crowded. We may be able to give some extracts from the sermon hereafter.

At the close of the sermon, after a brief and eloquent appeal, a collection of $184 was taken up for the Christian Commission.

A GOOD DEED.—Mr. EVAN KNUDSON, who has been employed as a fireman about the Assembly this winter, handed us $4 this morning which he desired us to place where it would be used for the relief of the soldiers wounded in the recent battles. As we knew no better disposition, we have added it to the collection for the Christian Commission which was taken up at the close of Mr. MATSON's sermon last night.

AT THE UNIVERSITY.—The students at the University testified their joy over the good news last night by a bonfire, serenading the Professors and other demonstrations. This morning when the students assembled they were patriotically addressed by different members of the Faculty and given a holiday. The buildings are to be illuminated to-night.

PATRIOTIC.—The engine on the eastern train was covered with flags to-day, showing how heartily the railroad men sympathized in the general joy. We have no more patriotic citizens.

DAMAGED.—The break in the dam of Lake Mendota near Farwell's mill, has resulted in washing out a bad break in the road along the Catfish below the mill. The water is running five or six feet deep where the road was, rendering it of course impassible.

☞ The mud has all dried up and the roads are getting in an excellent condition.

BY TELEGRAPH.

SUNDAY NIGHT'S DISPATCHES

VICTORY!

GLORIOUS NEWS.

LEE'S ARMY SURRENDERS

ON TERMS OFFERED BY GRANT

THE MEN TO BE PAROLED.

ARE TO RETURN TO HOMES.

ALL ARMS ARE TO BE GIVEN UP.

The End Approaches.

Glory to God in the Highest.

On Earth Peace and Good Will.

Correspondence Between Grant and Lee

Grant Makes First Proposition

Lee was Reluctant to Yield.

National Honor to our Army.

OPERATIONS AGAINST MOBILE

All Progressing Favorably.

Affairs in Virginia.

President and Mrs. Lincoln at Richmond.

LEADING REBELS ASKING FOR TERMS.

WAR DEPARTMENT,
WASHINGTON, April 9—9 P. M.

To Gov. James T. Lewis:

THIS DEPARTMENT HAS RECEIVED OFFICIAL REPORT OF THE SURRENDER THIS DAY OF GEN. LEE AND HIS ARMY TO LIEUT. GEN. GRANT ON THE TERMS PROPOSED BY GEN. GRANT.

EDWIN M. STANTON, Sec. of War.

HEADQUARTERS OF U. S. ARMY,
April 9—4:30 P. M.

To Hon. Edwin M. Stanton, Sec. of War:

Gen. Lee surrendered the army of Northern Virginia this afternoon, upon the terms proposed by myself. The accompanying correspondence will show the conditions fully.

U. S. GRANT, Lt. Gen.

APRIL 9, 1865.

To Lt. Gen. Grant, Commanding U. S. A:

GENERAL:—I received your note of this morning on the picket line, whither I had come to meet you and ascertain definitely what terms were embraced in your proposition of yesterday, with reference to the surrender of this army. I now request an interview, in accordance with the offer contained in your letter of yesterday for that purpose.

Very respectfully your ob't servant,
R. E. LEE, General.

APRIL 9TH, 1865.

To Gen. R. E. Lee, Commanding Confederate States' Armies:

Your note of this date is but this moment, 11:50 A. M., received, in consequence of my having passed from the Richmond & Lynchburg road to the Farmville & Lynchburg road. I am at this writing about four miles west of Walters Church and will push forward to the front for the purpose of meeting you. Notice sent to me on this road where you wish the interview to take place will meet me. Very respectfully,

Your ob't servant,
U. S. GRANT, Lt. Gen.

APPOMATTOX CHURCH, April 9, 1865.

Gen. R. E. Lee, Commanding C. S. A.:

In accordance with the substance of my letter to you of the 8th inst., I propose to receive the surrender of the army of Northern Virginia on the following terms, to wit:

Rolls of all the officers and men to be made in duplicate, one copy to be given to an officer designated by me, the other to be retained by such officer as you may designate, the officers to give their individual paroles not to take up arms against the government of the United States, until properly exchanged, and each company or regimental commander sign a like parole for the men of their commands; the arms, artillery and public property to be parked and stacked and turned over to the officers appointed by me to receive them. This will not embrace the side arms of the officers, nor their private horses or baggage.

This done, each officer and man will be allowed to return to their homes, not to be disturbed by the U. S. authorities so long as they observe their parole and the laws in force where they may be residing.

Very respectfully,
U. S. GRANT, Lt. Gen.

HEADQUARTERS ARMY OF NORTHERN VIRGINIA,
April 9, 1865.

Lt. Gen. U. S. Grant, Commanding U. S. A.:

GEN.—I have received your letter of this date, containing the terms of surrender of the Army of Northern Virginia as proposed by you. As they are substantially the same as those expressed in your letter of the 8th inst., they are accepted. I will proceed to designate the proper officers to carry the stipulations into effect.

Very respectfully,
Your obd't serv't,
R. E. LEE, Gen.

The following is the previous correspondence between Lieut. Gen. Grant and Gen. Lee, referred to in the foregoing telegram to the Secretary of War:

CLIFTON HOUSE, VA., April 7, 1865.

To Hon. Edwin M. Stanton, Secretary of War:

The following correspondence has taken place between Gen. Lee and myself. There has been no relaxation in the pursuit during its pendency.

(Signed) U. S. GRANT, Lieut. Gen.

CLIFTON HOUSE, VA., April 7.

To Gen. R. E. Lee, Commanding C. S. A.:

GENERAL: The result of the last week must convince you of the hopelessness of further resistance on the part of the army of Northern Virginia in this struggle. I feel that it is so, and regard it as my duty to shift from myself the responsibility of any further effusion of blood, by asking of you the surrender of that portion of the C. S. A. known as the army of Northern Virginia.

Very respectfully,
Your ob't servant,
U. S. GRANT, Lieut. Gen.,
Commanding the Armies of the U. S.

April 7th, 1865.

To Lt. Gen. U. S. Grant, Commanding Armies of the U. S.

GEN.—I have received your note of this date. Though not entirely of the opinion you express of the hopelessness of further resistance on the part of the Army of Northern Virginia, I reciprocate your desire to avoid useless effusion of blood, and therefore, before considering your proposition, ask the terms you will offer on condition of its surrender.

R. E. LEE, Gen.

April 8th, 1864.

Gen. R. E. Lee, Commanding C. S. A.

GEN.—Your note of last evening, in reply to mine of the same date, asking on what conditions I will accept the surrender of the army of Northern Virginia, is received. In reply I would say that peace being my first desire, there is but one condition that I insist upon, viz.: that the men surrendered shall be disqualified from taking up arms again against the Government of the United States until properly exchanged. I will meet you, or designate officers to meet any officers you may name for the same purpose, at any point agreeable to you for the purpose of arranging definitely the terms upon which the surrender of the army of Northern Virginia shall be received.

Very respectfully, your obd't serv't,
U. S. GRANT,
Lt. Gen., Com'g Armies of U. S.

APRIL 8, 1865.

To Lieut. Gen. Grant:

GEN.—I received at a late hour your note of today in answer to mine of yesterday. I did not intend to propose the surrender of the Army of Northern Virginia, but to ask the terms of your proposition. To be frank, I do not think the emergency has arisen to call forth the surrender, but as the restoration of peace should be the sole object of all, I desire to know whether your proposals would tend to that end. I cannot, therefore, meet you with a view to surrender the Army of Northern Virginia, but as far as your proposition may affect the C. S. A. forces under my command and tend to the restoration of peace, I should be pleased to meet you at 10 o'clock A. M. to-morrow on the old stage road to Richmond, between the picket lines of the two armies.

Very respectfully, &c.,
R. E. LEE.

APRIL 9.

To Gen. R. E. Lee, Commanding C. S. A:

GENERAL:—Your note of yesterday is received. As you have no authority to treat on the subject of peace the meeting proposed for 10 A. M. to-day could lead to no good. I will state however, General, that I am equally anxious for peace with yourself and the whole North entertain the same feeling. The terms upon which peace can be had are well understood: by the south laying down their arms they will hasten that most desirable event, save thousands of human lives and millions of dollars worth of property not yet destroyed. Sincerely hoping that all our difficulties may be settled without the loss of another life, I subscribe myself

Very respectfully &c.
U. S. GRANT, Lt. Gen.

WAR DEPARTMENT,
WASHINGTON, April 9th—8:30 P. M.

To Lieut. Gen. Grant:

All thanks be to Almighty God for the great victory with which he has this day crowned you, and the gallant army under your command. The thanks of this Department and of the Government and of the people of the United States have been deserved, and will be rendered to you and the brave soldiers and gallant officers of your army for all time.

EDWIN M. STANTON,
Secretary of War.

WAR DEPARTMENT,
WASHINGTON, April 9th—10 P. M.

ORDERED, That a salute of 200 guns be fired at the headquarters of every army and navy department, and at every post and arsenal in the United States, and at the Military Academy at West Point, on the day of the receipt of this order, in commemoration of the surrender of Gen. R. E. Lee and the Army of Northern Virginia to Lieut. Gen. Grant and the army under his command, report of the receipt and execution of this o.der to be made to the Adjutant General at Washington.

E. M. STANTON, Secretary of War.

MOBILE.

NEW YORK, April 9.

The *Herald* has Mobile Bay correspondence up to the 31st ult.

It appears that Granger's and Smith's corps marched from Danby's Mills on the 25th for Blakely, meeting slight opposition only on the first day.

On the 26th the 13th corps moved toward the Spanish Fort, a strong earth work commanding Minnette Bay, encountering and driving in the rebel cavalry, and in the evening Granger encamped on the left of that fort. The 16th corps continued on toward Blakely, encamping at Sibley's Mills, five miles from that town on the 26th.

On the morning of the 27th our forces advanced on the Spanish Fort, driving in the rebels, capturing rifle pits and establishing our batteries within 400 yards of the fort. On the 29th our forces were entrenched within 70 yards of the fort. Several lives had been lost by torpedoes, which are thickly strewn around. Our loss averages 15 per day. Some three hundred of the enemy had been cut off by a portion of our forces, but not yet captured, owing to their taking refuge in the swamps.

Early on the morning of the 30th the rebels made an attack, but were handsomely repulsed.

The rebel fleet of gun boats are on the extreme right within musket range of our troops, and the earth work is being completed to mount seige guns. Our losses to the 31st were about 800. Five of our monitors and the gun boat *Octarcora* have crossed Blakely bar and others were arriving. On the 31st, seige guns and mortars having been placed in position, heavy cannonading was opened on the Spanish Fort and continued all day, but the result is not known.

Steele's column left Pensacola on the 19th. He captured two trains of cars at Greenwood. At Pollard, Ala., two rebel cavalry regiments were routed and Brig. Gen. Clauson, 22 officers, 400 men and 450 horses captured. On the 29th Col. Spurling with a detachment of the 2d Maine and West Florida cavalry cut the Mobile & Montgomery Railroad, captured two wagon trains and 100 prisoners. Gen. Steele and force had arrived at Blakely, six miles from Spanish Fort and would soon unite with Canby.

A naval letter to the *Herald* states that the monitor *Milwaukee* was blown up by a torpedo on the 28th, and the *Osage* on the 29th, while operating with other monitors against Spanish Fort. Four sailors were killed on the *Osage,* and six seriously injured. Only one was injured on the *Milwaukee.* One of the turrets of the *Milwaukee* is still out of the water and in working order, and is used.—The *Osage* is submerged too deep to be used. They will probably be raised. The rebels are busy sending down torpedoes and fire-rafts.

The force in Spanish Fort is estimated at 6,000 or 8,000, it having been reinforced from Mobile by water on the night of the 29th. It is rumored also that Forrest and his whole command had reached Blakely. The rebel ram *Nashville* and the gunboats *Tuscaloosa, Morgan* and *Natchez* are in Blakely river, evidently intending giving battle to our monitors. On the west of the bay our gunboats have had several skirmishes with water batteries, driving the enemy from their guns. The rebel troops in Spanish Fort are commanded by Maury.

AFFAIRS IN VIRGINIA.

WASHINGTON, April 8.

A notice is posted at the War Department that no passes to Richmond are granted under any circumstances.

On Thursday President Lincoln paid another visit to Richmond, accompanied by his wife, Senators Sumner and Harlan, and others of the party.

NEW YORK, April 9.

The *Times'* Petersburg correspondent contradicts the statement that the railroad to Richmond was nearly repaired. Not a workman has been put upon it. The South Side Railroad is to have its gauge changed so as to take upon it our rolling stock. Petersburg was in command of Gen. Warren until the 5th when Gen. Hartsuff was assigned to the command as military Governor.

The *Herald's* Richmond correspondent says: "Mr. Lincoln was on the 4th informed by Gens. Weitzel and Shepley that prominent rebels desired an interview with him. He replied that he was willing to grant the interview, but in presence of a friend. After the reception of the officers of the army and navy it was announced to the President that Judge Campbell, the Assistant rebel Secretary of War and Mr. Myers, member of the late rebel Congress were awaiting an audience with the President in another room.—The President, accompanied by Gen. Weitzel immediately retired to the room and held a conference which lasted but a short time, and was adjourned to the flag ship *Malvern.* The result of these conferences cannot be made known, but auspicious results are known to be about to occur from them.

PRISONERS OF WAR.

NEW YORK, April 9.

The steamer *Matanzas* arrived from City Point this morning with 900 rebel prisoners, part of those captured at Bentonville, Goldsboro and Columbia. Among the prisoners is Col. Rhett, of Fort Sumter notoriety.

WASHINGTON, April 9.

Over 500 rebel officers of all grades are now in the old capitol prison.

Information is received that 5,000 Union prisoners, of those held by the rebel in Georgia, have arrived at or near Dalton to be delivered to us.

COMMERCIAL.

Milwaukee Market.

MILWAUKEE, April 8, 2 P. M.

Wheat in good demand, with No. 1 spring at 1.09@1.10, and No. 2 spring at 90c.

Flour steady at 5.00@5.75 for extra spring; 5.75 @6.00 for double extra; and 6.00@7.00 for winter wheat brands.

Oats nominal at 48@50c delivered.

Corn, shelled, nominal at 65c delivered.

Rye, nominal, at 70@75c delivered.

Barley, No. 2, in store, 80@85c.

Butter 15@23.

Cheese—21@24.

Beans—Dull at 1.00@1.30.

Eggs—Dull at 17@18 for fresh.

Lard—15@17c.

Tallow—9½@10c.

Sugars—12½@20c, according to quality.

Coffee—32@44.

Teas—75@2 00.

Salt—$2 30@6 50.

Seeds—Timothy, $3 25@3.75; Clover, 13.00@14.00; Flax, 2.00@2.40.

LiveStock—Beef Cattle, $4 00@8 00, according to quality; Sheep, $7 00@8 00; Hogs, $9 00@10 50.

Hides—Green 5@6c; Salted, 5½@6½c; Full cured and trimmed, 6@7c; dry salted, 11@13c; dry flint, 14@16c.

Chicago Market.

CHICAGO, FRIDAY EVENING, April 8.

The markets to-day, generally speaking, were dull, but in most cases firmer.

Wheat advanced 1@2c, and No. 1 spring closed steady at 1.07½.

Flour was inactive.

Corn dull, with light sales at 55@58c for rejected, and at 67c for No. 1.

Oats firm and 1c higher, closing quiet at 41c.

Rye and Barley inactive and nominal.

Highwines were nominal at 2.00.

Provisions flat and nominally 50c@1.00 per barrel lower on pork. Mess pork sold at 25.00, and there were sellers of prime mess at 24.00.

Beef Cattle advanced 25@50c per 100 lbs., with sales of prime to extra government and shipping steers at 8.50@9.75 per 100 lbs.; fair government cattle at 7.25@8.25, and butcher's and stock steers, common cows, etc., at 4.00@6.50 ℔ 100 lbs.

Live Hogs firmer, with an advance of 25c per 100 lbs at 9.80@11.00.

New York Market.

EVENING REPORT.

NEW YORK, April 8.

Flour heavy and 3@5c lower, at 8.10@8.15 for state; 8.60@8.70 for round-hoop Ohio; 8.80@9.75 for trade brands, the market closing heavy without decided change.

Wheat, amber Michigan 1.80; winter red western 1.75; No. 1 Milwaukee spring 1.63.

Corn dull and heavy, with new yellow and white 1.40.

Oats selling retail at 89c for western.

Pork dull and heavy, at 26.50@26.87½ for new mess, closing at 26.75 cash, 24 00@24.50 for 1863 and 1864 mess, closing at 24.25 cash; 24.50 for prime.

New York Stock Market.

SECOND BOARD.

NEW YORK, April 8.

Money easy at 6@7 per cent.

Sterling exchange quiet at 108¾@109¼ for specie or first-class bills.

Gold without decided change, opening at 150, advancing to 150¾, declining to 148¾, and closing at 148¾. The market is quiet, the demand being confined chiefly to the ordinary wants of importers. There is no apparent desire to engineer the market for either a rise or fall, the chances of fluctuating being now so slight as to discourage such operations.

U. S. 5.20s, with coupons, 1.07; 6s of '81, with coupons, 1.07.

BOOTS STOLEN.—We hear that the porter's room at the Capital House was entered last evening and a number of pairs of boots belonging to guests and boarders stolen. All attempts to recover the stolen property have thus far proved *bootless.*

☞ We understand that a large number of our leading citizens have united in inviting Rev. L. E. MATSON of this city to deliver an address in the Assembly Chamber, on the evening of the 14th inst., the anniversary of the surrender of Fort Sumter.

A WAKENER.—The salute in honor of the fall of Richmond Sunday night awakened people 20 miles distant.

☞ Most of the Members of the Legislature have lef

MARRIED.

FOGES—BEYER.—By the Rev. Mr. Steckemesser, April 9th, 1865, Mr. CHARLES FOGES to Miss SUSANNA BEYER, all of this city.

DIED.

BELDEN.—At one o'clock this morning, CLARA REMINGTON, eldest daughter of Chas. A. and Caroline E. Belden, aged 10 years and 9 months.

The sympathies of a large circle of friends attend the bereaved parents amid the deep darkness of their sad affliction.

Funeral services at the Congregational Church at two o'clock to-morrow afternoon.

LUSE.—In Camp Fry, Chicago, March 11th, 1865, of measles, HEATON LEANDER LUSE, private in Co. A. 153d Reg. Ill. Vols., aged 16 years and 8 months.

> Death is the parting of rainbow drops
> From the dark and dismal cloud,—
> White mists stealing up from the mountain tops,
> While shadows the valleys enshroud.

WISCONSIN STATE JOURNAL.

VOLUME XIII. MADISON, WIS. SATURDAY, APRIL 15, 1865. NUMBER 184.

STATE JOURNAL.

SATURDAY, APRIL 15, 1865.

THE OFFICIAL STATE PAPER.

The Great Tragedy.

The appalling news of the death of the President of the United States and of the Secretary of State, by assassination has filled the whole land with horror.

The details of this astounding tragedy will be found in our telegraphic columns. The story reads like some horrid fiction of the old dramatists. History hardly furnishes a parallel to this monstrous atrocity, the news of which will send a shudder through Christendom.

It sets the crowning seal of guilt upon the fiendish traitors who have assailed our country. Foiled in its infamous attempt upon the life of the Republic, Treason wounded unto death and dying, summons to its aid assassination, not to save its cause, but in a spirit of mere wanton, aimless, frenzied vengeance.

The assassins selected their victims with a care that shows they struck under the direction of some one above themselves. They aimed at LINCOLN, SEWARD and GRANT, the three lives most precious at this time to the country. Thank God the General-in-Chief escaped their fiendish designs. And thank God, too, that the fate of this great nation does not depend upon the lives of any one or two men. It will survive this blow, though it is the most terrible yet inflicted.

No other man had secured such a rooted hold upon the confidence and affections of the American people as ABRAHAM LINCOLN. Far-sighted, upright, merciful, the people loved him as a father. And next to him, we relied upon the sagacity, coolness, even-balanced judgment of SEWARD. Both are gone. They are added to the long list of the martyred dead who have fallen victims to the fell spirit of the slaveholders' rebellion.

God save the Republic.

Military Items.

Gen. THOMAS A. DAVIS, recently in service in Kansas, has arrived here to take command of a district composed of this State. He was formerly Colonel of the 16th New York and has rendered distinguished service at the first battle of Bull Run. He was in command of the 2d division of the Army of the Tennessee during 1863, and is the battles which took place there in October of that year. He is a distinguished and able officer. He is accompanied by two of his staff, Capt. D. J. CRAIGIE, A. A. G. and Lt. E. BUCKMASER, A. D. C.

There have been 218 men mustered into the U. S. service this week.

Orders have been received to discharge all men drafted under the call of Dec. 19th, who have not been forwarded to the general rendezvous, (the order not to apply to substitutes already mustered in) and also to muster no more men, and send forward no more troops till further orders.

The tenth company of the 50th has not yet been organized.

Five companies of the 51st have been organized, and four have now been sent forward, two within the week.

Four companies for each of the 52d and 53d have been organized, and two of each left for St. Louis Friday evening. The two regiments will probably be consolidated.

There are 115 men for the First Army Corps still remaining in the State, who were to have gone forward last week, but have been detained.

A NOTICE TO FOREIGN POWERS.—Now that the rebellion is subdued the United States government is able to assert its rights and dignity, and show that it no longer proposes to submit to insults which have been impatiently endured because they could not be cured. President LINCOLN has issued a proclamation setting forth that, for some time past vessels of war of the United States have been refused, in certain ports, privileges to which they were entitled by treaty, public law, or the comity of nations, at the same time that vessels of war of the country in which the same privileges and immunities have been withheld have enjoyed them fully and uninterruptedly in the ports of the United States, which condition of things has not been forcibly resisted by the United States, although, on the other hand they have not at times failed to protest against and declare their dissatisfaction with the same; and that now at least, whatever claim or pretence may have existed heretofore, the United States are entitled to claim an entire and friendly equality of rights and hospitalities with all maritime nations, and therefore a refusal of privileges to Union war vessels in foreign ports will be met by measures of a similar character on the part of the United States government toward the war vessels of the power offending.

THE RECIPROCITY TREATY.—The State Department has promulgated the following:—"Formal notices of the abrogation of the reciprocity treaty was given by Mr. Adams to the British on the 17th of March, and its receipt acknowledged on that day. Therefore, in accordance with stipulations contained in the treaty, it will expire in twelve months from that date, viz: the 17th of March, 1866."

A TRAGIC DEATH.—The New York Times correspondent says, that in a skirmish, Gen. THEODORE READ on our side and Gen. DEERING on the rebel side, met, and in full view of the forces held a tournament of death, fighting with pistols until, almost simultaneously, READ fell dead and DEERING mortally wounded.

☞ It is said that Jeff. Davis has for some had in contemplation a trans-Mississippi confederacy, comprising Arkansas, Texas, Western Louisiana, and some of the Mexican States.

Mosby has notified the Federal commander at Fairfax Station that, notwithstanding the surrender of LEE, he is determined to fight as long as he has a man left.

☞ It is currently reported that Secretary STANTON will resign as soon as peace is declared.

☞ The French consul at Richmond has gone to Washington to lay claim to the French tobacco.

REORGANIZATION OF SHERMAN'S ARMY.—Gen. SHERMAN has issued an order giving the following as the organization of his army:

Right wing: Army of the Tennessee, 15th and 17th corps, Maj. Gen. O. O. Howard, commanding.

Left wing: Army of Georgia, 14th and 20th corps, Maj. Gen. H. A. Slocum, commanding.

Centre: Army of Ohio, 10th and 23d corps, Maj. Gen. J. W. Schofield, commanding.

Cavalry: Brevet Maj. Gen. J. Kilpatrick, commanding.

Maj. Gen. Joseph A. Mower, subject to the approval of the President, is appointed to command the 20th corps, vice Slocum, promoted to a command of an army in the field.

☞ Gen. WEITZEL has been sent with his colored troops to Petersburg.

COMMERCIAL.

Madison Produce Market.

MADISON, Saturday, April 15.

The wheat market has somewhat improved since our last quotations. It seems to be the general opinion that the bottom has been touched, prices having been fully discounted in expectation of the great victories of the past two weeks.

Wheat—No. 1, 90c; No. 2, 80c; rejected, 65c.

Coarse Grains have steadily advanced, during the past week, in Chicago. Oats have advanced fully 7@10c.

Oats—40c.

Barley—1.00.

Rye—60c.

Corn—Shelled, 50@60c.

Salt—3.00.

Beans—1.00.

Hides—Green, 4c; grubby, ½ off; dry, 12@14c.

Wool—Washed 50c; unwashed ⅓ off.

Butter—20@25c.

Eggs—15@18c.

Hay—Timothy, $16.00; red top, $15.00; clover $5.00; marsh, $12.00 @ 14.00.

Straw—Oat, 4.00 per load; wheat, 3.00.

Wood—White or black oak, $8.00; burr oak 7.50; stove length, $8.50 @ 9.00 per cord.

New York Market.

NEW YORK, April 14.

Flour without decided change, with moderate business in extra state, at 7.25@7.35; 8.40@8.55 for round hoop Ohio; 8.55@9.00 for trade brands.

Whisky dull and decidedly lower.

Wheat firmer for spring, and steady for good winter. Other grains quiet.

Pork firmer, but nothing doing.

New York Stock Market.

NEW YORK, April 14.

There were no exchange, gold or stock boards to-day.

Money easy, at 5@6 per cent.

Stocks nominal.

Gold dull, without decided change; opening at 1.45½, declining to 1.45, advancing to 1.46¼, and closing at 1.46.

Government stocks firm.

Chicago Market.

CHICAGO, FRIDAY EVENING, April 14.

Wheat firm, at 1.12¼.

Corn dull, at 65c. for No. 1, and 60c. for rejected.

Oats firm at 40c.

Whisky neglected, and entirely nominal.

Freights dull, at 11c. on corn to Buffalo.

LOCAL MATTERS.

THE FEARFUL NEWS.—On the reception of the terrible news of President LINCOLN'S death, the general regard and respect of our lamented Chief Magistrate, was shown by the signs of profound grief in every face, and the words of sorrow and bitter indignation on every tongue.

Judge STEWART adjourned the Circuit Court till Tuesday, the 25th.

All offices at the Capitol are closed.

Business is almost entirely suspended, the public buildings are draped with mourning and flags are hung at half-mast. The bells were tolled at noon.

Some formal demonstration of sorrow and of respect for the memory of the honored dead will doubtless soon take place.

The terrible news leaves us little heart to prepare anything for our columns.

THE MEETING OF REJOICING.—The Assembly Chamber, floor and galleries, was crowded last night to express joy over recent victories and to listen to a discourse by the Rev. L. E. MATSON on our great triumph. The Assembly Chamber was decorated with the battle-rent flags of our veteran regiments, bearing the names of Antietam, Shiloh, South Mountain, Chickamauga, and other fields of carnage, flags torn with shot and shell, flags that have streamed over dying men on the perilous edge of battle, but which have never been dishonored. Under them were a number of rebel colors captured in different battles by Wisconsin regiments.

The Glee Club opened the proceedings by singing "Marching through Georgia."

Treasurer HASTINGS then made some very appropriate introductory remarks, referring to the progress of the war and the great changes it had wrought in public sentiment; referring particularly to the change in views of such men as BUTLER, and to the fact that WILLIAM LLOYD GARRISON, the despised abolitionist, now by invitation of a prominent officer of the Government was to be present in Charleston harbor at the raising of the old flag over Fort Sumter.

Mr. MATSON then delivered a very eloquent and appropriate address, of which we proposed publishing a full report, but have been prevented by the sad news of the day. He reviewed the origin of the conflict and eloquently recounted how "the first gun was fired" and how Sumter fell. The great issues decided by the contest were well set forth, and its lessons earnestly urged. The speaker avowed himself in favor of the severest punishment to the leaders of the rebellion, and paid a glowing tribute to the soldiers of the Union, living and dead.

After the close of the address the glee club sang some other pieces, including "The Ship of State."

Mr. J. W. JOHNSON was loudly called for and made some most eloquent and appropriate remarks, partly humorous and partly serious, which were received with much applause.

The exercises were closed by singing the Doxology to the tune of Old Hundred.

The Circuit Court.

In the Circuit Court to-day the intelligence of the assassination of President LINCOLN and Secretary SEWARD was announced in feeling terms by Hon. GEO. B. SMITH, who moved that court adjourn for one week.

Judge STEWART remarked that he had no words to express his grief at this terrible calamity, and that in accordance with the motion of Mr. SMITH he would adjourn the court until Tuesday, April 25th.

The following is a continuation of the proceedings in the Circuit Court up to date:

Carl W. Moemmer vs. Henry Cook. Action of trespass. Tried April 12. Verdict for defendant.

Henry W. Livingston vs. Wm. H. Angell. Action for damages against defendant for pay purchased as agent, an inferior quality of wool. Tried April 14. Verdict for defendant. Motion for new trial made.

Charles H. King, as administrator, and Mary A. Cook, as Administratrix of the estate of Wm. G. Cook, deceased, vs. George P. Delaplaine. Action of ejectment. Tried April 15. Verdict for defendant. Motion for a new trial made.

ARTEMUS WARD.—The "show" at the City Hall last evening, considering the circumstances, was very largely attended. The Hall was very well filled, and those who were there felt as if they were well paid for attending. The views of scenery in Utah are very fine, the paintings of Salt Lake and the proposed Mormon temple, rarely excelled. Mr. BROWN gave a great deal of useful information and kept his audience on a broad grin and in a roar of laughter most of the time.

☞ There will be a special meeting of the Common Council of the city of Madison this evening in the Council Chamber, at which the citizens are invited be present, by order of the Mayor.

Immediately on the reception of the dreadful news this morning, Mayor LEITCH caused all the saloons of the city to be closed.

☞ The benefit ball for the German Catholic church, which was to come off Monday evening, will be postponed on account of the sad news of the death of the President.

PRESBYTERIAN CHURCH.—Prof. J. D. BUTLER will preach in the Presbyterian Church to-morrow morning. Services commence at 10½ o'clock.

☞ The services at the Methodist church to-morrow evening will have special reference to the nation's sad bereavement.

POSTPONED.—The benefit at Turner's Hall for H. JUNGMAN is postponed until further notice.

THE 44TH REGIMENT.—The 44th Wisconsin, Col. SYKES, has gone to Paducah, Ky., where it is at present stationed.

MADISON HORTICULTURAL SOCIETY.—The regular meeting will be held in the State Agricultural Rooms on Monday evening, April 17th. JOSEPH HOBBINS, Rec. Sec.

BY TELEGRAPH.

OUR NIGHT DISPATCHES.

AFFAIRS IN VIRGINIA.

Gen. Lee is Back in Richmond.

A Rush to Take the Oath.

Gen. Weitzel Superseded by Ord.

Gen. Grant in Washington.

SHERMAN'S ARMY IS IN MOTION.

FROM WASHINGTON.

BALTIMORE, April 15.

The Richmond *Whig* of yesterday, contains little news of importance. It announces the arrival of General Lee the night previous.

The publishers of the *Whig* have taken the oath of allegiance, which it says citizens will be required to swear and subscribe to. The Provost Marshal's office is crowded with people anxious to take it, and the only question among citizens seems to be who shall be first to renew their citizenship.

NEW YORK, April 14.

A special to the *Commercial* from Washington says:

"It is believed here in certain quarters that the movement for the return of Virginia to the Union covers an effort of the States Rights politicians of that state to obtain possession of the State government.

"The order for reduction of the army has spread consternation among the political generals, who, it is understood, are to be first thrown overboard.

"Gen. Grant keeps himself secluded since his arrival in the city. He has had several interviews with the President and head of the War Department."

"Most comprehensive measures for the pacification of the South are known to be in contemplation.

"Gen. Ord having made Richmond the headquarters of the Army of the James, takes command, outranking Weitzel. Gen. Lee arrived in Richmond on Wednesday, and proceeded at once to his home.

The *Post's* Washington special says Gen. Weitzel has been superseded in command at Richmond. Rumors were afloat this morning that he had been removed because the Government disapproved his action in granting sub-contracts to the rebels.

SHERMAN'S ARMY.

NEW YORK, April 14.

Advices just received from Goldsboro, report that Sherman's army moved on the 10th inst.

TO-DAY'S DISPATCHES.

Horror! Horror!

MOST DREADFUL NEWS.

ASSASSINATION

Pres. Lincoln Shot.

HE DIED THIS MORNING.

SEWARD STABBED.

HE DIED THIS FORENOON.

HIS TWO SONS BADLY HURT.

PLOT TO KILL STANTON.

Harrowing Details of the Affair.

THE ASSASSINS ESCAPE.

EFFORTS TO SECURE THEM.

Vice President at Washington,

Has Been Sworn in as President.

WAR DEPARTMENT,
WASHINGTON, April 15—1:30 A. M.

To Maj. Gen. Dix:

This evening about 9:30 A. M., while at Ford's Theatre, the President while sitting in his private box with Mrs. Lincoln, Mrs. Rogers and Major Rathburn, was shot by an assassin who suddenly entered the box and approached behind the President. The assassin then leaped upon the stage, brandishing a large dagger or knife and made his escape in the rear of the theatre.

The pistol balls all entered the back of the President's head, and penetrated nearly through the head. The wound is mortal. The President has been insensible ever since it was inflicted, and is now about dying.

About the same hour an assassin, whether the same or not is not known, entered Mr. Seward's apartments, and under pretence of having a prescription, was shown to the Secretary's secret chamber. The assassin immediately rushed to the bed and inflicted two or three stabs on the throat, and two on the face.

It is hoped that the wounds may not be mortal. My apprehension is that they will prove fatal.

The nurse alarmed Mr. Fred. Seward who was in an adjoining room, and hastened to the door of his father's room, where he met the assassin, who inflicted upon him one or more dangerous wounds.

The recovery of Fred. Seward is doubtful. It is not probable that the President will live through the night.

Gen. Grant and wife were advertised to be at the theatre this evening, but he started to Burlington, New Jersey, at 6 o'clock this evening.

At a cabinet meeting, at which Gen. Grant was present, the subject of the state of the country and the prospect of a speedy peace was discussed. The President was very cheerful and hopeful, and spoke very kindly of Gen. Lee and others of the confederacy, and of the establishment of a government in Virginia.

All the members of the Cabinet, except Mr. Seward, are now in attendance upon the President.

I have seen Mr. Seward, but he and Frederick were both unconscious.

(Signed) E. M. STANTON,
Secretary of War.

WAR DEPARTMENT,
WASHINGTON, April 15—4:10 P. M.

To Maj. Gen. Dix:

The President continues insensible, and is sinking.

Secretary Seward remains without change. Frederick Seward's skull is fractured in two places, besides a severe cut on the head. The attendant is still alive, but hopeless. Maj. Seward's wound is not dangerous.

It is now ascertained with reasonable certainty that two assassins were engaged in the horrible crimes, Wilkes Booth being the one that shot the President, and the other an accomplice whose name is not known but whose description is so clear that he can hardly escape.

It appears from a letter found in Booth's trunk that the murder was planned before the 4th of March, but fell through then because the accomplice backed out until Richmond could be heard from. Booth and his accomplice were at the livery stable at six o'clock last evening, and left there with their horses about 10 o'clock, or shortly before that hour.

It seems that the assassins had for several days been watching their chance, but for some unknown reason it was not carried into effect until last night. One of them has evidently made his way to Baltimore; the other has not yet been traced.

(Signed) EDWIN M. STANTON.

WAR DEPARTMENT,
WASHINGTON, April 15, 1865.

To Maj. Gen. Dix:

ABRAHAM LINCOLN DIED THIS MORNING AT TWENTY-TWO MINUTES AFTER SEVEN O'CLOCK.

E. M. STANTON, Sec. of War.

CHICAGO, April 15.

Dispatches just received here say Secretary Seward died at 9:30 this morning.

THE ASSASSINATION.

WASHINGTON, April 15.

President Lincoln and wife, with other friends, this evening visited Ford's Theater, for the purpose of witnessing the performance of "Our American Cousin." It was announced in the papers that Gen. Grant would also be present, but that gentleman took the late train of cars for New Jersey. The theatre was crowded full, and everybody seemed pleased with the scene before them. During the third act, and while there was a temporary pause for one of the actors to enter, a sharp report of a pistol was heard, which attracted attention, but was supposed to be nothing serious, until a man rushed to the front of the President's box, waving a large dagger in his hand and exclaiming, "*Sic Semper Tyrannis*," immediately leaped from the box, which was in the rear, on to the stage beneath and ran across to the opposite side of the stage, making his escape amid the bewilderment of the audience from the rear of the theatre, and mounting a horse fled.

The screams of Mrs. Lincoln first disclosed the fact to the audience that the President had been shot, when all present rose to their feet and rushed towards the stage, many exclaiming, "Hang him." The excitement was of the wildest possible description, and of course there was an abrupt termination of the theatrical performance.

There was a rush towards the President's box, when cries were heard to "stand back, and give him air"—"has any one stimulants?"

On examination it was found that the President had been shot through the head, above and back of the temporal bone, and that some of the brains were oozing out. He was removed to a private house, opposite the Theatre, and the Surgeon General of the army and other surgeons sent for to attend to his condition.

On an examination of the private box, blood was discovered on the back of the cushioned rocking-chair in which the President had been sitting, also on the partition and on the floor.

A common single barrel horse-pistol was found on the carpet.

A military guard was placed in front of the private residence to which the President had been conveyed. It had been previously announced that the wound was mortal, but all hoped otherwise. The shock to the community was terrible.

Although the Cabinet, Messrs. Sumner, Farnsworth, Judge Bates, Gov. Oglesby, Senator Morgan, Col. Hay and a few personal friends, with Surgeon General Barnes and his immediate assistants were around his bedside, the President was in a state of syncope, totally insensible, and breathing slowly. The blood oozed from the wound at the back of his head. The surgeon exhausted every possible effort of medical skill, but all hope was gone.

The parting of his family with the dying President is too sad for description.

The President and Mrs. Lincoln did not start for the theatre until 15 minutes after 8 o'clock. Speaker Colfax was at the White House at the time. The President stated to him that he was going, although Mrs. Lincoln had not been well, because the papers had announced that Gen. Grant was to be present, and as General Grant had gone North, he did not wish the audience to be disappointed. He went with apparent reluctance, and urged Mr. Colfax to go with him, but that gentleman had made other engagements, and with Mr. Ashmun of Massachusetts, bid him good-bye.

When the excitement at the theatre was at its wildest height reports were circulated that Secretary Seward had also been assassinated. On reaching this gentleman's residence, a crowd and a military guard were around the door, and, on entering, it was ascertained that the reports were based on truth, and everybody there was so excited that scarcely an intelligent word could be gathered, but the facts are substantially as follows:

About 10 o'clock a man rang the bell and the call having been answered by a colored servant, he said he had come from Dr. Viele, Secretary Seward's family physician, with a prescription, at the same time having in his hand a small piece of folded paper, and saying, in answer to a refusal, that he must see the Secretary, as he was instructed with particular directions concerning the medicine. He insisted on going up, and although repeatedly informed that no one could enter the chamber, he pushed the servant one side and walked heavily toward the Secretary's room. He was then met by Fred. Seward, of whom he demanded to see the Secretary, making the same explanation which he did to the servant. What further passed in the way of colloquy is not known, but the man struck him on the head with a billy, severely injuring the skull and beating him almost insensible.

The assassin then rushed into the chamber and attacked Maj. Seward, Paymaster U. S. A., and Mr. Hansdill, a messenger in the State Department, and the nurse, and disabled them. He then rushed upon the Secretary who was lying in bed in the same room and inflicted three stabs in the neck. He bled profusely. The assassin then rushed down stairs, mounted his horse at the door and rode off before an alarm could be sounded, and in the same manner as the assassin of the President.

It is believed that the injuries of the Secretary are not fatal, nor those of the others, although both the Secretary and the assistant are very severely injured.

Secretaries Stanton and Welles, and other prominent officers of the government visited Secretary Seward's house to inquire into his condition, and there heard of the assassination of the President. They then proceeded to the house where he was lying. The excitement of course is intense, and deep anxiety and solicitude is felt. An immense crowd was gathered in front of the President's house and a strong guard was also stationed there. Many persons evidently supposed he would be brought home. The city to-night presented a scene of wild excitement, accompanied by earnest expressions of indignation and profoundest sorrow. Many shed tears.

The military authorities have despatched mounted patrols in every direction, in order, if possible, to arrest the assassins, and the whole metropolitan police are likewise vigilant for the same purpose.

The assassination, both at the theater and at Secretary Seward's house, took place at about the same hour, 10 o'clock, thus showing a preconcerted plan to assassinate those gentlemen then.

Some evidence of the guilty party who attacked the President are in possession of the board of police.

Vice President Johnson is in the city and his headquarters are guarded by troops.

WASHINGTON, April 15.

The assassin of President Lincoln left behind him his hat and a spur. The hat was picked up in the President's box, and has been identified by parties to whom it has been shown as the one belonging to the suspected man, and accurately described by other parties not allowed to see it before describing it. The spur was discovered on the stage, and that also has been identified as the one from a stable where the same man hired a horse in the evening.

Two gentlemen who went to the Secretary of War to apprise him of the attack on Mr. Lincoln, met at the residence of the former a man muffled in a cloak, who, when accosted by them, hastened away. It had been Mr. Stanton's intention to accompany Mr. Lincoln to the theatre and occupy the same box, but the press of business prevented. It therefore seems evident that the aim of the plotters was to paralyze the country by at once striking down the head, the heart and the arm of the country.

As soon as the dreadful events were announced in the street, the chief of police and his assistants were at work to discover the assassins. In a few moments the telegraph had aroused the whole police force of the city. Mayor Richards and several members of the city government were soon on the spot and every precaution was taken to preserve order and quiet in the city. Every street in Washington was patrolled. At the request of Mr. Richards Gen. Augur sent horses to mount the police, and every road leading out of Washington was strongly picketed and every possible avenue of escape was thoroughly guarded. Steamers about to depart down the Potomac were stopped.

The *Daily Chronicle* says it is suspected that the conspiracy originated in Maryland. The telegraph flashed the mournful news to Baltimore, and all the cavalry was immediately put on active duty. Every road was picketed and every precaution taken to prevent the escape of the assassins.

A preliminary examination was made by Mayor Richards and his assistants. Several persons were called to testify, and the evidence as elicited before an informal tribunal and not under oath, was conclusive to this point: the murderer of President Lincoln was John Wilkes Booth. His hat was found in the private box, and identified by several persons who had seen him within the last two days, and the spur which he dropped in excitement after he jumped to the stage, was identified as one of those which he had obtained from the stable where he hired his horse.

This man Booth has played more than once at Ford's Theatre and is of course acquainted with its exit and entrance and the ease with which he escaped behind the scenes is easily understood.

The person who attacked Secretary Seward left behind him a slouched hat and an old navy revolver, the chambers of which were broken loose from the barrel as if done by striking.

The following circular has been issued:

WAR DEPARTMENT,
PROVOST MARSHAL GENERAL'S BUREAU,
WASHINGTON, April 15—3:40 A. M.

It is believed that the assassins of the President and Secretary Seward are attempting to escape to Canada. You will make a careful and thorough examination of all persons attempting to cross from the United States into Canada, and will arrest all suspected persons. The most vigilant scrutiny on your part, and the force at your disposal, is demanded. A description of the parties supposed to be implicated in the murder will be telegraphed to you to-day; but, in the mean time, be active in procuring the arrest of any suspicious persons.

By order of the Secretary of War.

H. L. JEFFRIES, Brev. Brig. Gen'l,
Acting Pro. Mar. Gen'l.

NEW YORK, April 15—12:40 P. M.

A dispatch from Washington says Frederick Seward is not dead, but in a critical condition.

THE NEW PRESIDENT.

WASHINGTON, April 15—1:30 P. M.

Andrew Johnson was sworn into office as President of the United States by Chief Justice Chase to-day at 11 o'clock. Secretary McCulloch and Attorney General Speed and others were present.

GEN. GRANT.

BURLINGTON, N. J., April 15.

Lieut Gen. Grant left here for Washington at six o'clock this morning.

MRS. U. S. GRANT.

WISCONSIN STATE JOURNAL.

VOLUME XIII. | MADISON, WIS. THURSDAY, APRIL 27, 1865. | NUMBER 194.

STATE JOURNAL.

THURSDAY, APRIL 27, 1865.

THE OFFICIAL STATE PAPER.

The News.

The item of paramount interest in to-day's news is the discovery and shooting of BOOTH, the assassin, and the arrest of HAROLD, his accomplice. They were lurking in a swamp in one of the secesh districts of Maryland. BOOTH was shot through the head and died soon after.

The progress of the remains of the murdered President, attracting thousands at every point where the train conveying the body stops, continues to form a prominent feature of our dispatches.

The restrictions on visiting Richmond have been removed, and Gov. PIERPONT, of the loyal state organization, will probably convene a legislature of Union men in that city about the 1st of June.

Gens. THOMAS, MEADE, and other Union commanders, have been ordered to wholly disregard the unwarranted negotiations of Gen. SHERMAN, and to push upon the enemy, wherever found, with all vigor. Efforts are also being made to intercept JEFF. DAVIS, and the money he has robbed and stolen from Richmond. It is one of the saddest events of the war that Gen. SHERMAN should have so far forgotten what was due to his country and his own name as to have rendered such orders necessary.

Our Gallant Badger Boys.

On the next page we publish a letter from Chaplain HAMMOND detailing the part borne by the gallant 5th Wisconsin in the recent grand events in the vicinity of Richmond, and also a letter from Col. RICHARDSON of the veteran 7th, to the Adjutant General, giving an account of the operations of that brave and tried regiment.

A letter from Col. ALLEN to Adjutant General GAYLORD furnishes some additional particulars respecting the 5th. In the attack on the rebel lines before Petersburg on the 1st, the colors of the 5th Wisconsin were first planted on the enemy's works, and Lt. Col. BULL, in command of the skirmish line, was the first to enter Petersburg from that side.

Col. ALLEN recommends for promotion and medals, for distinguished gallantry on the occasion, the following:

Lt. Col. J. M. Bull, Capt. Henry Curran, Sergt. Angus Cameron, Co. C, Color Sergeant Robert F. Langdon, Co. F, Sergt. R. Elwell, Co. K, Sergt. H. M. Lowe, K, Corp. Aug. Frantz, A, Corp. Francis Lee, A, Private Wm. Shumacker, Sergt. A. Q. Smith, B, Sergt. Fred. J. Smith, B, Corp. Alex. Carboneaux, B, Corp. Aug. Brocker, C, Alex Johnson, C, Sergt. James Young, D, Corp Olin Bean, D, Sergt. Wm. B. Harshaw, E, Corp. J. B. Freeman, E, Corp. S. Brunhall, F, Corp. A. E. Brown, F, Corp. L. A. Day, G Private James Conlin, G, Corp. John Graham, H, Private Louis Ossawa, H, Corp. F. H. Cornwall, I, Sergt. H. T. Lacey, I. The Colonel says the men and officers of the new companies vied with the old veterans in gallantry.

In the fight at Little Sailor's Creek, near Burkeville, Capt. HENRY CURRAN and Lieut. EVAN R. JONES, commanding the skirmish lines, won special mention from Col. ALLEN.

Col. C. E. WARNER, of the heroic 36th, sends a brief and modest account to the Adjutant General of the part taken by his regiment, than which no other has seen more or harder service since it was organized. It was engaged on the 30th and 31st of March, and on the 1st of April. On the 2d, with the 19th Massachusetts, it charged and carried a rebel fort mounting three guns, and took 150 prisoners. It was in the pursuit of LEE, and engaged in several skirmishes. On the 9th it had the satisfaction of being present at the surrender and disbandment of LEE's army.—Two days after it moved back to Burke's Station. It was singularly fortunate during this campaign, the only casualties being as follows: Corp. DANNA HAMILTON severely wounded, and Corp. L. DOUGLAS and privates I. GOKEE and WM. RECOB slightly wounded.

IMPORTANT DECISION BY ATTORNEY GENERAL SPEED.—The Attorney General of the United States has decided that, under the terms of capitulation, LEE's officers have no right to come to loyal States; that former residents of Washington, who have been in the civil service of the rebellion; and that rebel officers have no right to wear their uniforms in loyal States.

The great clock that stands on the walk in front of the Fifth Avenue House, New York and which had not stopped since the building was erected, is now motionless, and the hands indicate 22 minutes past 7—the point of time when Mr. LINCOLN breathed his last.

☞ What is known as the Mather place at Springfield, with adjoining lots, has been purchased for the burial grounds of Mr. LINCOLN. The price paid was $53,000.

☞ Navigation on Lake Erie, near Buffalo, was obstructed by ice as late as the 25th. The straits of Mackinaw have been open for some days.

☞ The family of JOHN C. RIVES, of Virginia, has subscribed $1,000 for a fund for the family of Mr. LINCOLN.

☞ An elegant porcelain set, captured at Jeff. Davis residence at Richmond, has been presented to President Johnson.

☞ The cessation of the government demand for coal is expected to lower its price materially within a short time.

☞ A man has just been sentenced in New York for stealing crape from buildings.

☞ The Suez canal, connecting the Mediterranean and Red seas, is completed.

DIED

TULLIS.—At 10 o'clock this morning, SIBBIE, daughter of D. H. and H. W. TULLIS, aged five years and ten months.

Funeral services from their residence corner of Carroll and Clymer streets, Friday morning at 10½ o'clock.

BILLINGS.—In Burke, April 20th, MARIA O., wife of Lorenzo Billings, aged 48 years and 1 month.

HAWKES.—In the town of Bristol, April 5, 1865, MAGGIE, youngest daughter of James R., and Mary Hawkes, aged 9 years and 5 mos.

Wisconsin Soldiers in Washington Hospitals.

WASHINGTON, April 18.

His Excellency James T. Lewis, Governor of Wisconsin:

SIR:—Within the past few days I have visited nearly all of the persons whose names appear in the subjoined list; and with a few exceptions, have found them doing well, and as comfortable as their circumstances would permit. The list shows a large number of amputations, and many cases of very severe wounds. Respectfully, yours,

D. OSTRANDER,
State Agent.

STANTON HOSPITAL.

E. A. Allen, F, 5th.
H. S. Tully, I, 5th.
D. W. Head.
G. Olson, B, 6th.
P. Brown, C, 6th.
John Boyne, E, 6th.
E. H. Parker, I, 6th.
Benjamin Ballard, E, 36th.
Wm. Coughlin, B, 7th.
G. Anderson, B, 7th.
X. Eutz, E, 7th.
E. Becker, G, 7th.
Geo. Newell, H, 7th.
J. O. Moon, I, 7th.
John Cavanaugh, amputation, discharged.

JUDICIARY SQUARE HOSPITAL.

Chas. A. Walker, M, 2d U. S. Cavalry.
D. H. Miller, 47th Co. V. R. C.
Levi R. Croisant, C, 5th.
Isaac Vansky, I, 5th.
Corp. G. W. Baker, I, 5th.
Wilson D. Moffatt, D, 6th.
Abraham Wolf, I, 38th, left leg amputated.

DOUGLAS HOSPITAL.

A. A. Stillwell D, 7
Merrit Stanley, B, 36th.
Corp. W. Rowe, do
W. De Long, E, 37th.
S. M. Du Bois, B, 36th.
A. Heisen, F, 37th.
Isaac L. Miller, F, 37th.
Valentine Scaerod, F, 6th.
Terence McColve, B, 6th.

CAMPBELL HOSPITAL.

Corp. H. Powell, K, 2d.
Sergt. J. R. Peterson, C, 36th.
Corp. Fred. Isham, D, 7th, left leg amputated.
Fred. Lanesdorf, D, 6th.
John W. Elder, H, 7th.
August Hagerman, C, 6th.
Lewis E. Miller, C, 5th.
C. Woltreon, E, 6th.
A. Kellogg, A, 7th.
Wm. Johnson, E, 7th.
Edwin Angelo, H, 7th.
N. Leach, C, 7th.
Corp. W. Brown, I, 38th.
R. S. Bingham, H, 6th.
F. Sewell, K, 7th.
Jos. Pratt, I, 36th.
A. H. Hoyt, D, 7th.
E. Rumys, G, 5th.
A. Van Allen, C, 7th.
A. Gould, I, 7th.
Joseph Du Point, G, 37th.
Francis Troucey, B, 5th, left arm amputated.
D. A. McLin, H, 7th.
M. Werlin, K, 7th.
Geo. F. West, I, 5th, left leg amputated.
H. Housel, G, 6th, left arm amputated.
C. Langner, H, 7th.
Robert Blair, B, 38th.
Corp. J. M. Sargent, B, 38th.
Corp. C. Carman, E, 7th.
Wm. Fuss, F, 6th.
H. Jones, F, 7th.
Corp. Jno. E. Wess, E, 38th.
E. S. Spaulding, D, 36th.
James Pigg, K, 6th.

CARVER HOSPITAL.

Geo. Hafner, F, 37th.
Herman Ecke, E, 37th.
Joseph Cook, G, 38th.
Corp. L. W. Sherman, G, 38th.
Wm. T. Barr, C, 38th, right arm amputated.
W. T. Dunn, H, 38th.
Corp. Robert A. Lawrence, F, 38th.
Eben Ewen, B, 38th.
S. H. Lomorad, K, 38th.
Nelson Vannie, K, 38th.
Corp. L. W. Hardwick, G, 38th.
Martin A. Grow, G, 38th.
Wm. Haynes, G, 38th, right hand amputated.
Wm. Greenwood, G, 38th.
Corp. A. J. Fish, K, 38th.
Jas. S. Bates, C, 5th.
Sergt. J. Scanlan, A, 5th.
John Whorton, E, 7th.
E. Barth, A, 7th, left arm amputated.
E. B. Parish, A, 36th.
J. H. Hart, D, 38th.
Pat Manning, K, 38th.
Corp. Pat McCarty, D, 38th.
F. Underwood, I, 5th.
Thomas Roach, G, 5th.
Joseph Dunn, I, 5th.

COLUMBIA HOSPITAL.

M. Reily, C, 6th.
M. H. Baker, H, 5th.
A. Berker, A, 6th.
Thomas Sweet, H, 6th.
C. A. Winsor, A. 6th.
A. P. Conrad, B, 6th.
H. Matson, B, 6th.
H. Ellis, A. 7th.
L. Lipman, I, 7th.
B. Peck, G, 7th.
John Krase, B, 7th, amputation of right thigh.
J. Gunderson, F, 6th.
E. Vanhorn, H, 6th.
O. Iverson, B, 6th.
C. Amos, D, 37th.
L. W. Weatherbee, K, 38th.
S. F. Fraser, K, 38th.
John Stile, A, 6th.

MT. PLEASANT HOSPITAL.

E. M. Helk, A, —, died April 7, 1865.
E. C. Cavanaugh, I, 7th.
J. Hefferman, B, 7th.
J. D. Fowler, C, 38th.
T. L. Caughley, D, 38th.
Marion Flick, F, 37th.

ARMORY SQUARE HOSPITAL.

L. H. Moses, A, 37th.
John Rising, K, 6th.
W. Blackburn, D, 6th.
A. Donaldson, B, 7th.
A. Wolford, I, 6th.
J. Haynes, F, 6th.
H. Shelter, B, 7th.
A. B. Bronson, K, 38th, left leg amputated.
L. B. Thomas, H, 7th.
E. Marlett, F, 3d.
Lieut. C. S. Wood, G, 38th, wounded in right hand.
Capt. A. A. Kelley, F, 38th, wounded in back.

ACTION OF THE DANE PRESBYTERY ON THE RESIGNATION OF MR. GREEN.—The Dane Presbytery at its late meeting in this city, after accepting the resignation of the Rev. W. L. GREEN as pastor of the Presbyterian Church, adopted the following minute:

That while we reluctantly sever the connection so long and so happily existing between the Rev. W. L. Green and the Presbyterian Church in Madison, we desire to have it distinctly understood that we agree to the disolution of the pastoral relation on the ground of the enfeebled health of our beloved brother. The Church and the Presbytery yield to the necessity of the present case because our brother is physically unable to fulfill the duties of the office, and in this connection we would express our joy in the great and good work which has been accomplished in Madison by the instrumentality of brother Green. We part here with heartfelt sorrow, and with earnest wishes for his future usefulness.

M. A. FOX, Moderator.

Circuit Court.

APRIL 26th, 1865.

G. W. Lusk vs. H. J. Smith, action for recovery of money, jury disagreed.

State of Wisconsin vs. Clarence McCarty, indicted for robbery and larceny.

Change of venue to Rock County, ordered the prisoner having sworn that he believed the court was prejudiced against him. Most of the day was occupied in the trial of the case of John Flick vs. Jonathan Weatherbee, which was not completed when court adjourned.

THURSDAY, April 27, 1865.

Peter F. Walser vs A. Courvoisier. Judgment of non-suit.

State of Wisconsin vs. Byron P. Chamberlain. Indicted for forgery. Continued till November term. Bail fixed at $400.

John Flick vs Jonathan Weatherbee. Trial completed. Verdict for plaintiff. Damages $90.

LOCAL MATTERS.

Special Train for Chicago.

With a view to giving our people a comfortable trip to Chicago, to witness the reception of the remains of the late President LINCOLN, in that city, the Northwestern Railway Company will run a special train from this city, on Sunday evening, at 8 o'clock, as will be seen by the following notice of their gentlemanly Superintendent of the Madison Division:

CHICAGO AND NORTHWESTERN RAILWAY.—A special train will leave Madison on Sunday evening, at 8 o'clock, for the purpose of enabling passengers to attend the reception of the remains of our late President, which will arrive at Chicago on Monday morning.

W. ABEEL,
Sup't Madison Division.

Mr. ABEEL is doing all he can to accommodate the people of this city; and this arrangement is a step in the right direction. It has been put on through his agency entirely, and adds to the many obligations due from our people to Mr. ABEEL, for kind favors.

This train will stop at Harvard for supper, where a most excellent meal will be provided, by one of the most zealous Union men in the country. The train will arrive in Chicago early Monday morning. It will afford a very pleasant trip.

THE PEAT MEETING.—At the Peat meeting, last evening, Mr. GEO. P. DELAPLAINE, from the committee appointed to correspond with parties at the East, and report whether any suitable machinery exists for the economical manufacture of compressed peat for fuel, &c., submitted an interesting paper, giving the result of his inquiries.

After treating of the character of peat as a fuel, and showing that the condensed article if it can only be produced cheaply enough is ton for ton more valuable for many purposes than the best coal, the report stated that the only machine suitable for the purpose that the committee had heard of was that used by the American Peat Company of Boston. That company had a machine patented which they claimed would manufacture from 20 to 100 tons of compressed peat per day, according to the size of the machine used, at a cost of from $4 to $5 per ton. Such a machine was about to be put in operation at Lexington, Mass.

After some discussion, Hon. S. D. HASTINGS, who is abou visiting the East, was requested to make a personal inspection of the machinery at Lexington, and report to a future meeting.

RELETTING OF THE STATE PRINTING.—The bids for doing the State Printing from the 1st of June next till January 1st, 1867, were opened at noon to-day. But three bids were in, as follows:

C. L. SHOLES, 16 per cent. less than the maximum.

ATWOOD & RUBLEE, 45 per cent. less than the maximum.

W. J. PARK. 52 per cent. less than the maximum.

Mr. PARK, being the lowest bidder, will take the work.

SWIMMING SCHOOL AND BATHING ESTABLISHMENT.—Mr. A. KULEMAN is about opening a swimming school and bathing establishment on Lake Monona, provided he finds sufficient encouragement. His terms will be $3 for season bathing tickets, and $8 for teaching proficiency in the art of swimming. Mr. K. will call on our citizens for subscriptions tomorrow, and in case any are omitted who would like season tickets, they can subscribe by calling at the store of HUCHTING Brothers, Pinckney street. It is desirable that as many tickets as possible should be immediately subscribed for in order that Mr. K. may know what he can do.

HEINOUS.—A young man in this city of respectable connections and hitherto bearing a good character, was recently guilty of the following violent and outrageous perversion of his mother tongue. He inquired of a companion why the eldest son of the Emperor of Mexico is like a man kissing a young lady who is to inherit a million of property. The companion, as a matter of course, gave it up. "Because," said the unfeeling young man, "he smacks a million's heir!"

THE ILLUSTRATED PAPERS.—This week the supply was not equal to the demand. *Harper's Weekly* and *Frank Leslie's* from MOSELEY'S, both give different illustrations in connection with the murder of President LINCOLN, and have a variety of Richmond scenes. *Harper* has two fine allegorical pictures, one Columbia weeping over the dead LINCOLN, the other "The Eve of War" and "Dawn of Peace."

☞ Chaplain WALTER, of the 20th regiment Wisconsin Infantry, will speak to-morrow night in the Assembly Chamber, at 7½ o'clock, in behalf of our soldiers at Mobile, Ala. He will give his experience in the army as chaplain.

BENEFIT BALL.—A Ball is to be given on Monday Evening next, at the Turner Hall, for the benefit of the German Lutheran St. Paul's Church and School. The city band is engaged for the occasion, and good refreshments will be furnished.

NEW GOODS AT FRIEND'S.—See the advertisement of M. FRIEND, Esq., in to-day's paper. He is just receiving a fine assortment of furnishing goods of the latest and most fashionable styles.

☞ Wild pigeons are selling at 50 cents per dozen in the streets. Eggs are cheaper than they have been—selling at retail for 15 cents per dozen.

☞ A pair of horses attached to a wagon took fright and ran away last evening near the City Hall. They managed to break thing up pretty generally before they were stopped.

☞ The team of goats belonging to the show now exhibiting at the City Hall, attracted a large crowd, as they were driven through the streets last evening.

☞ We hear that the Pound Master is about making a grand raid upon all hogs found running at large. This is a good move.

☞ A warm steady rain set in at about ten o'clock this morning and has continued during the day.

LAST NIGHT.—This evening is the second and last of the exhibition of the "Little Folks." Go and see them at the City Hall.

BY TELEGRAPH.

OUR NIGHT DISPATCHES.

President's Remains at Albany.

Thousands Throng to See Them.

Rumor Concerning Mexico

BLOCKADE ON MARYLAND SHORE.

A Riot at Danville.

People Plunder Rebel Stores.

Terrible Explosion and Loss of Life.

VAPORING OF "EXTRA-BILLY" SMITH.

SORROWING IN CHARLESTON OVER PRESIDENT'S DEATH

Ex-Gov. Aiken Addresses the People

Arrests in California.

Collision between Soldiers & Rebel Sympathizers

CENTRAL AMERICAN AFFAIRS.

Texas Blockade Running.

Cortinas Declares against Maximillian

No Restrictions on Visiting Richmond

Gov. Pierpont and Loyal Legislature

Gen. Johnston Cannot Escape

FROM WASHINGTON.

WASHINGTON, April 26.

The Richmond *Whig* and *Times* of yesterdty have been received. The *Whig* has the following from gentlemen of intelligence who have reached that city on foot from Danville:

"We have some interesting particulars of events that occurred there after the surrender of Lee's army. When this event became known in town and the surrounding country, a crowd of citizens of all classes and ages, and a large number of soldiers collected around the buildings in which were stored immense quantitites of commissary stores, and after a short deliberation made a general rush upon the establishments. The parties in charge of the stores at first attempted to resist the mob, but were quickly forced to desist, and seek their own safety in flight. The mob scattered throughout every part of the buildings, each person plundering according to his or her fancy.

In one of the buildings it appears there was a large quantity of ammunition, gunpowder in kegs and percussion caps. The soldiers and country people swarmed around the powder kegs to secure it for fowling purposes. While they were thus engaged by some means fire communicated to the powder, and in an instant the building and its contents, including over fifty persons, was blown to atoms.

The horrible tragedy for a time put a check upon the plundering, which, however, soon commenced again but with somewhat more circumspection.

Ex-Gov. Extra Billy Smith was in Danville when our informant left. He had been vaporing a good deal about his determination never to surrender, saying that sooner than succumb he would turn bushwhacker, guerrilla, or something of that sort. Notwithstanding this, our informant learned, just before leaving, that Extra Billy had sent a flag of truce to Gen. Meade, the object of which had not transpired. We will mention in connection a report which has obtained circulation here, that the citizens of Lynchburg either requested or compelled the Ex-Governor to leave the town.

FROM ALBANY.

ALBANY, April 26.

From the time last night the remains of of President Lincoln were deposited in the capitol till now, persons have been pressing thither to see the honored dead. This morning the line of people extends at least a mile, one half of those composing it being ladies. The coffin has been again strewn by ladies with flowers. The cars and steamboats this morning have brought additional thousands to the city. The funeral party are entertained by the corporate authorities, at the Delavan House. All the buildings are draped with mourning. Among the most touching mottoes on house fronts are the following:

"The heart of the Nation throbs heavily at the portals of the tomb."

"Let us resolve that the martyred dead shall not have died in vain."

The latter is believed to be an extract from Lincoln's Maryland Fair remarks.

A low estimate fixes the number of strangers here to-day at 30,000. All the morning extra trains and excursion boats brought large numbers of people from the surrounding country, many coming a distance of 100 or 200 miles. Never before were such multitudes gathered at the Capital. Everybody seemed to participate in the solemnities of the occasion.

At one o'clock the military, the fire department and civic societies began to form and at 2 o'clock the coffin was closed. From 1 A. M. all that night, and until 2 P. M. the stream of people pouring through the capitol to take a last look at the distinguished dead was constant, and yet thousands were standing in line awaiting their turn when the hour for replacing the cover arrived. Nearly 50,000 men, women and children visited the remains.

Soon after 2, the procession having been formed commenced to move over the prescribed route. It was composed of the 18th and 25th regiments of this city, the 24th and the light horse battery of Troy. The state and city authorities, the fire department and a large number of civic societies. The military was about 2,000 strong. The hearse elegantly and elaborately furnished, trimmed with white silk and adorned richly with silver mountings, surmounted by the eagle drawn by white horses.

FROM NEW YORK.

NEW YORK, April 26.

The *Commercial's* Washington special says, Marshal Roberts has offered 10,000 dollars toward a national fund for the family of the late President.

It is believed on what appears trustworthy authority that our relations with Mexico will soon assume a new and important aspect.

WASHINGTON, April 26.

A special to the New York *Post* says the precautions taken in North Carolina by government will arrest any serious consequences that might arise from Sherman's action.

No vessels are allowed to land on the western shore of Maryland in order to prevent the escape of Booth in that section. It is reported that two men attempting to cross the river in a small boat were captured off Maryland point yesterday.

FROM NEW YORK.

NEW YORK, April 26.

The *Post's* special says restriction on visiting Richmond have been removed, and any one can go there.

Advices from Richmond say Governor Pierpont will probably convene the loyal legislature by the 1st of June.

It is believed that if Johnston refuses unconditional surrender that he can't escape.

Several rebel officers, rather than go South, have taken the oath.

FROM HAVANA.

NEW YORK, April 26.

The steamer *Columbian* brings Havana dates to the 24th.

The blockade runners arrived on the 23d from Galveston with cotton.

Jno. G. Williams, who was carrying $54,000 dollars, state money, from Goliad to Clinton, Texas, was robbed by a band of thieves.

The blockade runner, Eliza Catherine, loaded with cotton, sunk on a bar at Brazos river, drowning the captain, mate, and three others.

By way of Matamoras it was reported that Cortinas had declared against the empire, and was preparing to attack Gen. Mejea, who is in Matamoras with 4000 or 5000 men.—Mejea is cut off from communication with the interior. He will either surrender or retreat, and if he does the latter he is lost.—Cortinas has from 6000 to 7000 troops.

FROM CALIFORNIA.

SAN FRANCISCO, April 25.

The military have arrested 12 or 15 men in Solona and Colusa counties for rejoicing at the assassination of President Lincoln.

Upon the receipt of the news of the President's death at Green Valley, Solona county, a number of secessionists met to rejoice over the event. A body of troops attempted to break up the meeting, but as they approached the ringleaders of the secessionists fortified themselves in a house and fired at the soldiers, wounding two of them. The fire was returned by the soldiers, and several of the secessionists were wounded. The whole party then surrendered.

The ship *Bacchante*, for Hong Kong, takes a quarter of a million of dollars.

FROM CENTRAL AMERICA.

NEW YORK, April 26.

The steamer *Ariel* from Panama the 6th has arrived. Beyond the circulation of idle rumors of fresh revolutionary uprisings, keeping the timid in suspense, nothing has occurred worthy of note from Central America.

We learn the death of Gen. Carrera, President of Gautamayla was expected, and a crisis was expected to follow the event. Carrera was President for life with power to name his successor. He has named Gen. Cerau, late governor of Chiquimula.

It was thought Carrera's death would be the signal for Gen. Barios to renew his claims to the Presidential chair. The President of Honduras had issued a decree of non-intercourse with Costa Rica, for affording Barios asylum.

FROM CHARLESTON.

NEW YORK, April 26.

By the steamer *Fulton* we have Charleston papers of the 22d.

On the 21st a meeting was held in Charleston, on the subject of the assassination of President Lincoln. It was addressed by Ex-Gov. Aiken, and appropriate resolutions were adopted. A meeting was also held at Port Royal, which was addressed by Gen. Littlefield, and resolutions were adopted.

FINANCIAL.

NEW YORK, April 26.

Transactions in gold are light, but feeling favors an upward tendency of price asked; was $1.55, but immediately declined to $1.52 @1.51½.

The principal dealings are in cash; gold to cover contracts.

COMMERCIAL.

Milwaukee Market.

MILWAUKEE, April 27.

Flour dull and 25c lower; extra spring at 5.75.
Wheat declined 3@4c, at 1.77@1.77¼.
Gold buying at 1.44@1.45.

Chicago Market.

CHICAGO, WEDNESDAY EVENING, April 26.

The demand for flour was more active. Good brands of spring extras sold at from 6.25@6.50; choice winter wheat flour at 9.25@9.50, and spring superfine flour at from 4.00@5.00.

The was a good speculative and some shipping inquiry for wheat, and at the opening sales of No. 1 spring were made at 1.23, but the market subsequently was less firm and receded 1.22@1.22¼, closing a shade better, with sellers at 1.22¼ and buyers at 1.21¾. No. 2 spring was in better demand at 1.11@1.12. Sales of rejected spring were meagre at 98c. Winter wheat is scarce, and but little more than nominal. Small sales were reported at 1.70 for No. 1 white and 1.50 for No. 1 red.

Corn at 71½c for No. 1 and 64½c for rejected in store.

Oats declined 1½c per bushel. Sales ranged from 43¾@45¼c, and at the close prices were weak at 41c.

Rye was quiet but firm, with sales of No. 2 at 78c in store—an advance of 2c per bushel.

There was more firmness in the barley market at the opening, but at the close there was an easier feeling. No. 2 in store sold at from 90@95c.

The market for Highwines was firm and closed steady at 2.10.

Seeds were firm, and the market ruled steady at previous quotations.

Provisions were in active request, and we note a further advance of 50@1.00 per barrel on pork; ½c per lb. on sweet pickled hams, and ½c per lb. on dry salted shoulders. Sales were made at 27.50@28.00 for mess pork; 24.75@25.00 for prime mess; 17½@18c for sweet pickled hams; 16c for clear sides boxed, and at 15c for dry salted shoulders. At the close first class city brands of mess pork were firmly held at 28 00, and dry salted shoulders at 15½c.

Dry goods are active and firm, and prices are higher for nearly all descriptions.

Lake freights at 8c for oats to Cleveland, and 10c for corn to Buffalo, and at 8c for oats to Collingwood.

The receipts of Beef Cattle were light, and business generally quiet. 335 head at 7.25@8.00 per 100 lbs. for fair government grades; and at 4.00@6.75 for common to medium cows, steers, rough oxen, etc.

Hogs in fair supply. Market firmer at an advance of 12½@25c per 100 lbs. on yesterday's quotations. Entered sales, 1,796 head at 8.12½@9.50, chiefly at 8.50@9.00 per 100 lbs.

New York Market.

NEW YORK, April 26.

EVENING REPORT.

Flour heavy and 5c lower on common grades, and a shade firmer for better kinds, and more active, at 7.40@7.65 for extra state; 8.25 for round hooped Ohio, and 8.30@9.60 for trade brands, market closing quiet.

Whiskey steady; Western 2.13@2.14.

Wheat steady and firmer; winter red western at 1.61@1.75; choice amber Michigan 1.85.

Rye a shade firmer with western at 1.02@1.05.

Barley and barley malt quiet.

Corn shade firmer, at 1.38 for new white Western; 1.40 for old mixed Western.

Oats nominal at 85@86c for western.

NEW YORK, April 27.

Flour dull and 5@10c lower on common grades.

Wheat quiet and without decided change, at 1.65 for No. 1 Mil.; 1.83@1.85 for amber Michigan; 1.72 @1.75 winter red western.

Corn 1@2c better.

Oats dull and 1@2c lower, at 82@83 for western.

Pork firmer.

New York Stock Market.

NEW YORK, April 26.

SECOND BOARD.

Money easy, at 4@5 per cent.

Sterling quiet, at 1.09¾@1.09¾.

Gold firmer, opening at 1.52, declining to 1.50¾, and closing at 1.50¾.

Government stocks more active and firmer.

NEW YORK, April 27.

Money 4@5 per cent.

Gold closed at 1.48¾.

U. S. 6's of '81 registered, 1.09¾; do. with coupons, 1.10¾; 5-20's registered, 1.04; do. with coupons, 1.09¾; do. new issue, 1.09¾; 6's of '80 with coupons, 1.07½; 10-40's, 97¾; one year certificates, 99¾.

MORNING DISPATCHES.

Sherman and Johnston's Negotiations.

Further Details of the Affair.

Vance sends Commissioners to Sherman.

Precautions of Pres't Johnson.

Funeral Train at Rochester,

SHERMAN.

NEW YORK, April 27.

The *Herald's* Raleigh correspondent of the 17th says Johnston first proposed to surrender his army on the terms granted to Lee, and requested Sherman to send the proposition to Washington. Sherman replied that he was empowered to act, and it was unnecessary to send to Washington, thus causing delay. An interview was had next day, when Johnston made inquiry as to what terms would be yielded to members of the Confederate Government. Sherman refused to recognize the authorities of any such Government, but was prepared to treat with Johnston as an officer of the insurgent forces.

A second meeting was had at which Breckinridge, recognized as a Maj. Gen. and not as a rebel Secretary of War, was president. It was at this conference that Sherman permitted the introduction of the objectionable propositions which it is said was dictated by Jeff Davis. Sherman heard of the President's assassination before negotiating, and communicated the intelligence to the rebels who appeared to have the profoundest regret at the event.

Gen. Stoneman, who was reported at Greensboro, was permitted to come through Johnston's line to Raleigh.

Johnston's army, probably 30,000 strong, is better supplied wild field guns and horses than any army the Confederacy ever had. Many of the rank and file, however,—not willing to await the formal surrender, are leaving for their homes.

The *Herald's* Raleigh correspondent says a commission consisting of Ex-Gov. Swain, Surgeon General Warren and Col. Burr, were sent by Gov. Vance to see what arrangement could be made with Sherman on the part of the State for a cessation of hostilities, and to ascertain what was the state of the State government and its officers under the new regime. The commission had the assent of Gen. Hardee to visit Sherman, Johnston not being at hand, but Wade Hampton intercepted them and sent them back. Kilpatrick being in the rear, captured them, and Hampton having retreated, sent them on their mission. They had an interview with Sherman, who gave them a protection paper for the Governor and State officers so long as no hostilities were shown by them.

Sherman told them he had no information as to how the status of State Governments was affected. That question did not come under his province; that he did not consider North Carolina out of the Union, as the question of secession had not been submitted to the people; that he would respect every man that was not an original secessionist, and show them every consideration. Still he must march through the state in pursuit of Johnston, and people must necessarily suffer by that march. Johnston's army was inferior to his, and every man slain in future was an unnecessary sacrifice. Johnston and not himself would he responsible for sacrifices and sufferings entailed on the people of N. C. The civilised world would pronounce Johnston's course inhuman and illegitimate.

The statement that President Johnson declines all precautions for his personal safety is erroneous. He has not given any special directions for guards to be placed about his person, but he opposed the precautions taken by the authorities which embrace the continuance upon duty of law. The President's body-guard is commanded by Lt. J. B. Jameson, of Ohio. This company consists of one man selected from each county in Ohio, and numbers nearly one hundred, a sufficient force of these guards is upon duty at all times, and a visitor who calls upon the President at his temporary mansion is confronted at once upon approaching the door by three or four soldiers, who do not permit him to advance further until his name has been sent in and the order given by the President to admit him. In the hall adjuining the reception room are also found soldiers of gentle deportment who quietly remain about the entrance within a few feet of Mr. Johnson.—Sentinels also constantly surround the house and upon the street and in the lot upon which the buildings stands. In fact every reasonable precaution is taken to prevent any violence being attempted upon President Johnson.

FUNERAL SOLEMNITIES.

ROCHESTER, April 27.

The funeral train arrived at 3:20 A. M. Minute guns were fired and the bands performed funeral dirges. The 54th N. Y. regiment, 1st Co. V. R. C., hospital soldiers lately attached to the 26th brigade Union Blues Independent, were in line in the depot on the north side of the track, the Mayor and 26 of the Common Council, with other civic organizations. The bells of the city churches are being tolled, and as the train leaves the city, the multitude show marked signs of sorrow and respect. Thus far there has been no accident. Ten thousand people are present.

BATAVIA, N. Y., April 27.

The remains of Abraham Lincoln arrived at Batavia at 5:18. Two thousand of the inhabitants were assembled at this place. During the time we remained here a choir of male and female voices sung a requiem.—Bells were tolled and minute guns fired.

BUFFALO, April 27.

Funeral party arrived at 7 A. M., escorted by the 74th regiment, a company of light artillery, the committee of arrangements, the city government, and others, to St. James Hall. Services opened by dirges sung by the St. Creilias society; afterwards the public were admitted. Full accounts will be sent this evening.

Capital City Base Ball Club.

An adjourned meeting of the Capital City Base Ball club will be held at their room in the basement of the capitol at seven and a half o'clock P. M., Friday, the 28th inst. All members are requested to be present. By Order. ap27d2t

AFTERNOON DISPATCHES.

THE ASSASSIN BOOTH.

He is Hunted Down and Shot!

His Accomplice Harold is Secured.

Important Orders from War Department

Union Generals Directed to Disregard Sherman's Arrangement.

Ordered to Push the Enemy.

Important Dispatch from Halleck.

Generals Ordered not to Obey Sherman.

Measures to Cut off Jeff. Davis' Specie.

Particulars of the Killing of Booth

OFFICIAL DISPATCHES.

WAR DEPARTMENT,
Washington, April 27—9:20 A. M.

Maj. Gen. Dix:

J. Wilkes Booth and Harold were chased from a swamp in St. Mary's county, Md., to Garrett's farm, near Port Royal, on the Rappahannock, by Col. Baker's force.

The barn in which they took refuge was fired.

Booth was shot and killed and Harold captured.

Booth's body and Harold are now here.

E. M. STANTON,
Secretary of War.

WAR DEPARTMENT,
WASHINGTON, April 27—9 30 A. M.

Maj. Gen. Dix:

The Department has received the following dispatch from Maj. Gen. Halleck, commanding the military division of the James. Generals Canby and Thomas were instructed, some days ago, that Sherman's arrangement with Johnston was disapproved by the President, and they were ordered to disregard it, and to push the enemy in every direction.

EDWIN M. STANTON, Sec'y of War.

RICHMOND, VA., 9 P. M., April 26th.

Hon. E. M. Stanton:

Gens. Meade, Sheridan and Wright are acting under orders to pay no regard to any truce or orders of Gen. Sherman respecting hostilities, on the ground that Sherman's agreement could bind his own command only and no others. They are directed to push forward regardless of orders from any one except Gen. Grant, and cut off Johnston's retreat.

Beauregard has telegraphed to Danville that a new arrangement has been made with Sherman, and the advance of the 6th corps was to be suspended until further orders.

I have telegraphed back to obey no orders of Sherman, but to push forward rapidly as possible.

The bankers here have information to-day that Davis' specie is moving south from Goldsboro in wagons as fast as possible. I suggest that orders be telegraphed through Gen. Thomas, that Wilson obey no orders from Sherman, and notifying him and Canby and all commanders on the Mississippi to take measures to intercept the rebel chiefs and their plunder. The specie taken with them is estimated at from $6,000,000 to $13,000,000.

H. W. HALLECK,
Maj. Gen. Com.

FROM WASHINGTON.

WASHINGTON, April 24.

Yesterday morning a squadron of the 6th N. Y. Cavalry traced Booth and Harald to a barn between Bowling Green and Front Royal, near Fredericksburg, Va.

The barn was surrounded and a demand made for their surrender, which Harold was in favor of doing, but upon Booth calling him a coward he refused to do so.

The barn was then set on fire, and, on its getting too hot, Harold again presented himself, and put his hands through the door to be handcuffed. While this was going on, Booth fired upon the soldiers, upon which a sergeant fired at him. The ball of the sergeant took effect in the head of Booth, killing him.

Harold was taken alive. He and Booth's body were brought to the Washington Navy Yard last night.

Booth was discovered in the barn by the cavalry. He declared his intention never to surrender, and said he would fight the whole squad, consisting of 28 men, if they would permit him to place himself twenty yards distant.

The scouting party was under the command of Lieut. Edward Dougherty. Booth was on a crutch, and was lame. He lived two hours after he was shot, whispering blasphemies against the Government and sending a farewell message to his mother.

At the time he was shot it is said he was leaning on his crutch and preparing to fire again upon his captors.

The *Star* has the following particulars of the capture of Booth:

To Col. L. C. Baker, special detective of the War Department, and his admirably trained detective force, and to the 16th N. Y. cavalry, active participants in the seizure of the assassins, the country owe a debt of gratitude for this timely service.

It seems that a detachment of the 16th N. Y. cavalry numbering about 25 men, was despatched from this city on Monday, under the direction of Col. Baker, in command of Lieut. Dougherty, accompanied by some of Col. Baker's officers, who captured and killed Booth and captured Harold, one of his accomplices, alive.

The cavalry, after leaving here, landed at Belle Plain in the night, and at once started out in pursuit of Booth and Harold, having previously ascertained from a colored man that they had crossed the river into Virginia at Swan Point in a small canoe hired by Booth for $300.

Proceeding on toward Bowling Green, some three miles from Port Royal, Lt. Dougherty, who was in command of the cavalry, discovered that Booth and Harold were secreted in a large barn owned by a man named Garrett, and were well armed.

The cavalry then surrounded the barn and summoned Booth and Harold to surrender.

The City Hall—Unsafe Condition of the Cornice.

Editors State Journal:—I wish to call the attention of our City Fathers to the *unsafe* condition of the cornice work in the City Hall. I went to see the "Little Folks" last evening, and while enjoying a speech of the Commodore's a piece of plastering weighing some three pounds came down within three feet of me. Only a few weeks ago I was at the same Hall, though in another part of it, and a piece fell, which had it struck on any one's head, death would have been the consequence. I have a presentiment that some fatal results will happen if it is neglected much longer. It would be sad in the midst of the amusements oftimes enjoyed in the City Hall to witness such a tragedy, and I sincerely hope that attention which can avert such scenes will be the consequence of this correspondence.

CITIZEN.

WISCONSIN STATE JOURNAL.

VOLUME XVII. MADISON, WIS., WEDNESDAY AFTERNOON, MAY 12, 1869. NUMBER 206.

STATE JOURNAL.

THE OFFICIAL STATE PAPER.

Hon. Philetus Sawyer—Letter from Sen. T. O. Howe.

A correspondent of the Fond du Lac *Journal*, an ultra Democratic sheet, has been villifying Hon. PHILETUS SAWYER, the able, influential and honest representative in Congress from the 5th District in this State, charging him with "ambition, stupidity and vanity," and accusing him of a want of education, &c. This paper has been brought to the notice of Hon. T. O. HOWE, United States Senator, who volunteers a letter in defence of Mr. SAWYER, which is alike honorable to the distinguished Senator, as it is truthful in its reference to the faithful Representative. In this State, Mr. SAWYER needs no defence. He is an old and highly respectable citizen, whose nobleness of character has made him conspicuous with the people of the entire State, and his acts in various public positions have given him a deservedly high reputation, as a sagacious, energetic, efficient, practical, honest and faithful representative of his people, in whatever capacity he assumes. As the Senator intimates, every day Mr. SAWYER remains in public life, he does it at a pecuniary sacrifice, which most of his constituents know and appreciate; but they can illy afford to lose the services of so valuable a man in Congress—one who so well understands the wants of the district, and is so successful in procuring all proper legislation in reference to it—as Mr. SAWYER has proved himself to be, since he became a member. But our object at this time was not to speak especially of Mr. SAWYER'S merits as a man and public officer, but to publish what Senator HOWE volunteers to say of him. Here is his letter, copied from the Green Bay *Gazette:*

MESSRS. EDITORS:—I have recently received from two different sources, both unknown to me, copies of the Fond du Lac *Journal* of the 29th ultimo.

My attention is thus persistently called to some editorial remarks, introductory to a communication purporting to come from Neenah. The communication and the remarks have reference to Mr. Sawyer, the Representative from this Congressional District. The editor is pleased not only to charge him with "ambition, stupidity and vanity," but to stigmatize him as an "illiterate boor." Now I desire to submit a few observations to the good people of this District in reference to Mr. Sawyer.

Mr. Sawyer never would have been a candidate for Congress, but for the earnest solicitations of friends who believed he would serve the District well. Of these friends I was one. He would have retired from the position long since, but for the same kind of solicitations. Whatever my testimony may be worth I give it to this effect, that no District in the United States has sent to Washington an honester man, or a more faithful or efficient Representative. I don't know of an interest in the District that he has abused or neglected. At the same time I do not know a man more tolerant of or generous to his political opponents than he is.

Now, I submit that such a man is entitled to fair treatment. Mr. Sawyer's early education was limited; but he was born a gentleman and he has lived like a gentleman in all the relations of life. And in spite of lack of culture, he is to-day as widely and familiarly known to the picked men who represent the States of this Great Republic, in Congress, and is as universally respected too, as any man in either House. In spite of his alleged "stupidity" he has at three successive elections made the Democratic party of this District bite the dust, and he can do it again.

But every day he has been in the public service has been a day of pecuniary loss to him. He knows that and all who know anything of his private business know it. He has given public notice of his intention to retire from the public service at the close of the present Congress. I know such is his purpose. I do not know but that purpose is unalterable. But unless he can be treated with something of the respect always due to honest and unoffending worth, even when "illiterate," I for one shall try to alter that purpose. If he is to be followed in private life by this vituperation from the press of a party to which he has given no cause of offense, except by not joining it; if the misfortune of his youth be visited upon him as if it were a crime of his manhood, I shall earnestly hope that his retirement will be deferred to some more distant and dispassionate time.

Very respectfully, T. O. HOWE.

Personal News.

— RISTORI is going to Brazil.

— NAPOLEON is healthy, hopeful, and 61.

— SPRAGUE has gone South, leaving Rhody desolate.

— Miss ADELAIDE PHILLIPS is going to Paris for two years.

— Five girls have been admitted to the Iowa Agricultural College.

— Among the income tax returns published in the Washington papers occurs the following: "U. S. GRANT, $565."

— It is announced on the authority of Mr. DICKENS' doctors that he will not be able to read for several months.

— BEECHER says he receives about $25,000 a year, and gives one-third of it in charity and to applications for aid.

— The Empress CARLOTTA'S health has, within the last month, changed notably for the worse, and it is supposed that she cannot survive the summer.

— Mr. SUMNER'S speech is in greater demand than any speech ever before delivered by him. He is in the daily receipt of letters from all parts of the country soliciting copies.

— It is probable that OLIVER WENDELL HOLMES will write an ode for the opening of the Musical Festival, which will be sung by ten thousand voices to the accompaniment of the great organ and an orchestra of a thousand pieces.

— Count WALEWSKI'S widow is getting up a Book of Common Prayer for her fellow-widows. Its completion depends upon the conduct of the marriageable old Counts of Europe. That is, they must refrain from proposing marriage to the Countess.

— Minister E. B. WASHBURNE, before starting for France, obtained leave of absence to visit the German watering places. He will pass several weeks at Hamburg (celebrated for its healing waters and its gambling saloons), where he has engaged apartments.

— The Hon. HORACE GREELEY says: "I did once sue two Democratic editors who had libeled me without stint; but I was heartily ashamed of it when cool reflection came, and, accepting very poor apologies for retractions, ordered that my suits be withdrawn."

— There is some talk of the Prince Imperial not accompanying the rest of the BONAPARTE family to Corsica, but remaining in Paris as the honorary President of a Council of Regency, the idea being that this will accustom the Prince to the people and the people to the Prince.

— The poet WHITTIER has received several rare birds from the Emperor of Brazil. They are of the *alma perdida*, whose cry, WHITTIER says, in a poem, is not the cry of a bird, but of

"The pained soul of some infidel
Or cursed heretic that cries from hell."

This poem so interested the Emperor of Brazil, that he translated it very faithfully and poetically into Portugese, and sent an autograph copy to WHITTIER. It was also translated by PEDRO LINZ, a Brazilian poet, and published widely in South America.

— The Empress EUGENIE conversed, a few weeks since with some working men whom she met near St. Cloud. She asked them if they were making money. The men, who evidently did not know her, replied in the negative. "But," said the Empress, "you are not idle. Do you not get good wages?" "Yes, we do," was the answer, "but under the Empire, everything has become so dear that we are much worse off than we were twenty years ago with lower wages." The Empress, instead of preserving her *incognito* was imprudent enough to say who she was. The workingmen bowed to her, but said that what they had told her was nothing but the truth.

Wisconsin Items.

—The Milwaukee *Wisconsin* says Frank Roetsch, a well known German in that city, committed suicide on Tuesday morning.—Shortly after 6 o'clock he was heard to go into the stable, and an hour after when the drivers went in to look after their teams, they found Roetsch hanging by the neck to a ring in the ceiling and dead. The cause of the suicide is only surmised, the deceased being in good circumstances. He was married only a few months since. He was 37 years of age....On 'Change yesterday it was figured up that Miles, the defaulter who run away the other day, had forged bills of lading to the amount of 10,000 barrels of flour, which at $5 per barrel would amount to $50,000....The city authorities are "going for" the velocipedes in Milwaukee.... One of the men employed at the rolling mill when in the act of cleaning one of the pulleys, was caught by the belt and had his arm torn off below the elbow.

—The Oshkosh *Northwestern* says the Fox river has not been as high this year as last by 18 inches. The small lumber streams have not been high enough to overflow their banks. The river at Oshkosh has not varied three inches in its minimum and maximum spring and fall height for 14 years.

—The Augusta *Herald* reports that a little daughter of T. W. Richards fell one day last week and dislocated her shoulder....A little boy about four years old, son of Mr. Jas. Lynn, of that place, eat a quantity of wild parsnip, last Tuesday, which came very near ending his life.

—The Dunn County *News* says the spring continues very backward and the weather unfavorable for seeding. Farmers are behind with their spring's work, and there is still a large amount of grain to be sown.

—The great attraction in the Chippewa Valley at present is a jam of logs above the Falls. The river is completely blockaded, bridged and dammed with pine logs, hemmed, jammed and wedged together, averaging from twenty to fifty tiers in depth, and forming a complete gorge thirty-five rods in width, entirely obliterating and rendering invisible the water for a distance of over two miles. The amount of logs contained in the jam is variously estimated, and will probably exceed 100,000,000 feet. The oldest lumbermen of that section say it is the largest collection of logs they ever witnessed in one body and under similar circumstances. If the jam is not broken before the water of the present spring freshet goes down, it will certainly greatly embarrass the business prospects of the entire Chippewa Valley.

YOUNG MEN'S ASSOCIATION OF MILWAUKEE.—The annual election of the Young Men's Association was held on Monday afternoon and evening. There were three tickets in the field, and considerable excitement was manifested. The contest was conducted in most friendly spirit throughout. Nearly a thousand votes were cast. The vote on the opening of the rooms on Sunday showed a majority of 216 in its favor. Mr. JENKINS, the candidate for President, had no opposition, and received 130 votes. The following officers were elected:

President—Jas. G. Jenkins.
Vice President—John E. Eldred.
Secretary—J. M. Whaling.
Treasurer—Frank G. Bigelow.
Trustees—Alfred L. Cary, Chas. L. Pierce, Henry C. Payne, Alex. C. Botkin, James M. Chivas, Sam. Chandler, and R. C. Hopkins.

The interest felt in the election indicates that a new life will characterize the society for the year to come.

VELOCIPEDE RIDING.—The last sensation in velocipede riding was produced at the Boston Velocipede Rink, last week, when Master JOHN REARDON rode a velocipede with grooved wheels along a rope stretched from one end of the rink to the other, about 20 feet from the floor. In addition to this, a trapeze was hung to the velocipede, and Mr. HENRY M. STEVENS performed a variety of feats upon it while the velocipede was moving along the rope. Two little girls, aged 3 and 5 years, rode velocipedes around the rink with the ease of experts.

PLAYING OUT.—"Brick" POMEROY has got tired of experimenting with a morning paper in New York, and has changed his *Democrat* back into an evening paper. Strange as it may seem, the Democracy of New York are not quite bad enough to support so foul a sheet as this; and for the honor of journalism, we rejoice that it is so.

☞ The mining regions of the "far west," including California, during the year 1868, produced an aggregate of $66,580,000 of the precious metals. This rich mineral country, by the completion of the Pacific Railroad, is now brought into our very doors.

The Pacific Railroad—Scenes at Promontory Point.

A special correspondent of the Chicago *Tribune* gives a very interesting description of the scenes connected with the completion of the Pacific Railroad on Monday last. The special dispatch is dated at "Promontory Summit," Utah, May 10th. From it we glean some interesting particulars. The preparation for formally uniting the two grand divisions of the great trans-continental railway were all completed early on the morning of the 10th, and Governor STANFORD with friends from the Pacific coast were on the ground impatiently awaiting the arrival of the Directors of the Union Pacific from the East to commence the ceremony.

The day was clear and beautiful, and the little gathering of less than 1,000 people, representing all classes of our people, from the humblest citizen to the highest civil and military authorities, every State from the Atlantic to the Pacific, Canada and Mexico, met to enact the last scene in the mighty drama of peace on a little grassy plain surrounded by green-clad hills, with the snow-clad summit of the Wasatch Mountains looking down on the placid blue water of the inland sea of America, in the distance formed a scene that will not be forgotten by the beholder. The Occident and Orient, North and South, Saxon, Celt, Mongolian, each clad in his peculiar costume, met and mingled on common ground. All personal and sectional animosities, all distinctions of class, all prejudices, race and nationality were forgotten for the moment in the all absorbing interest of the grand event of history and civilization about to take place.

THE JUNCTION.

Both parties being in readiness, the ties were thrown down on the open space of about one hundred feet, and the employes, two companies, approached with the rails to fill the gap. J. H. Stenbridge, sub-contractor, who has had charge of the building of the Central Pacific from the laying of the first rail on the bank of the Sacramento, commanding a party of Chinese track-layers, advanced from the west with Assistant General Superintendent Corning, who had the general supervision and final arrangement. The Chinamen, conscious that the strangers from the East were watching their movements with curious eyes, wielded the pick, shovel and sledge with consummate dexterity; but their faces wore an appearance of unconcern and indifference wonderful if real, and not the less so if affected. White laborers from the East did their best work, but with more indication of a desire to produce an effect, and at 11 a. m. the European and Asiatic private soldiers of civilization stood face to face in the heart of America, each proudly conscious that the work was well done, each exultant over the victory nobly won.

The locomotives from the different divisions of the road were each richly decorated with flags and evergreens, and, when they approached within one hundred feet of each other, gave a salute with exultant screams.

The following dispatches were sent to President Grant and Vice President Colfax:

PROMONTORY POINT, Utah, May 10.
His Excellency U. S. Grant, President of the United States:
We have the honor to report the last rail laid, the last spike driven. The Pacific Railroad is finished.
LELAND STANFORD,
President Central Pacific Railroad.
THOS. C. DURANT,
Vice President Union Pacific Railroad.

PROMONTORY SUMMIT, Utah, May 10.
To Vice President Colfax:
The rails were connected to-day. The prophecy of Benton is to-day a fact. This is the way to India.
G. M. DODGE,
JOHN DUFF,
SIDNEY DILLON,
T. C. DURANT.

IMPORTANCE OF THE TELEGRAPH DEMONSTRATED.

Superintendent Vandenburgh now attached the telegraph wires to the last rail so that each blow of the sledge should cause a corresponding blow struck on the bell in the City Hall at San Francisco, and the last one fire a cannon in the batteries at Fort Point, a signal to dwellers in the city by the Golden Gate that the great work of years was done, and bid all the guns which guard the western ports of our land pour from their black throats the roar of exultation.

ARIZONA'S OFFERING.

General A. K. P. Safford, in behalf of the Territory of Arizona, presented a spike composed of iron, gold and silver, as an offering by Arizona, with the remarks:

"Ribbed with iron, clad in silver, and crowned with gold, Arizona presents her offering to the enterprise that has banded every continent and dictated a new pathway to commerce."

PRESIDENT STANFORD'S REMARKS.

Hon. Leland Stanford responded as follows:

GENTLEMEN: The Pacific Railroad Companies accept with pride and satisfaction these golden and silver tokens of your appreciation of the importance of our enterprise to the material interests of the sections which you represent on this occasion, and to the material interests of our whole country, East and West, North and South, these gifts shall receive a fitting place in the superstructure of our road. And before laying the ties and driving the spikes in completion of the Pacific Railroad, allow me to express the hope that the great importance which you are pleased to attach to our undertaking may be in all respects fully realized. This line of rails connecting the Atlantic and Pacific, and affording to commerce a new transit, will prove, we trust, the speedy forerunner of increased facilities. The Pacific Railroad will, as soon as commerce shall begin fully to realize its advantages, demonstrate the necessity of such improvements in railroading as to render practicable the transportation of freights at much less rates than are possible under any system which has thus far been anywhere adopted. The day is not far distant when three tracks will be found necessary to accommodate the commerce which will seek a transit across this continent. Freights will then move only one way on each track, and rates of speed that will answer the demands of cheapness and time. Cars and engines will be light or heavy, according to the speed required and weight to be transported. In conclusion, I will add, we hope to do what is now impossible. On long lines transport ore and products for all distances at living rates to trade. Now, gentlemen, with your assistance, we will proceed to lay the last rail, the last tie, and drive the last spike.

AN IMPRESSIVE SCENE.

The crowd fell back at the request of Gen. Casement, and the artist for the Union Railroad photographed the scene, with locomotives confronting each other, and Chinese and Caucasian laborers confronting the work. It was now announced that the last blow was to be struck. Every head was uncovered in reverential silence.

Rev. Dr. Todd, of Pittsfield, Mass., then offered up the following brief and deeply impressive invocation:

Almighty God, our Heavenly Father and God of the creation, and the waters of the earth, in whom we move, and live and have our being, we acknowledge Thee to be the God of creation, of the human mind, with its power and successes on this beautiful day. In presence of these lovely hills and golden summit we render thanks that Thou hast, by this means brought together the East and the West, and bound them together by this stronger band of union. We implore Thee that Thou will bless this work of our hands, which we have now completed; this movement of our labor, and [illegible] together. And we thank Thee for the blessings Thou hast conferred on us and other nations; bless our future and those whom Thou hast appointed to conduct us. To Thee, to Thy Son Jesus Christ, be all honor and glory ascribed, world without end, Amen.

THE LAST RAIL.

The magnificent rail of laurel, on which was a commemorative plate of silver, was brought forward, put in place, and Dr. Harkness, in behalf of the State of California, presented Governor Stanford the gold spike, with the following address:

REMARKS OF DR. H. W. HARKNESS, OF SACRAMENTO.

The last rail needed to complete the greatest enterprise of the world is about to be laid. The last spike needed to unite the Atlantic and Pacific by a new line of commerce and travel is about to be driven to its place. To perform these acts the East and West have come together. Never since history commenced her record of human events, has she been called upon to note the completion of a work so magnificent in conception, so marvellous in execution. When Venice was mistress of the seas, and her argosies let go their anchors in every part, it was the custom of her days to propitiate the Genii of the Seas by wedding the Adriatic with a costly jewel. More proudly than Venice can America boast of her power and progress, of her wealth and commerce. Not the sea only, but the continent is thus made a pathway. Unlike the Doges of Venice we have no Genii of the Seas to propitiate, but in emulation of their example we may fitly ornament and decorate with gold and silver these iron rails on which to a large degree the trade and traffic of a continent is about to roll, and it is in this mode that California, within whose borders and by whose citizens the Pacific Railroad was inaugurated, desires to express her appreciation of the vast importance to her and her sister States of the great enterprise which, by your joint action, is about to be consummated. From her mines of gold she has forged a spike; from her laurel woods she has hewn a tie, and by the hands of her citizens she offers them to become a part of the great highway which is about to unite her in close fellowship with her sisters of the Atlantic. From her bosom was taken the first rail. Let hers be the last tie and the last spike. With them accept the hopes and wishes of her people, that the success of your enterprise may not stop short of its brightest promises.

THE SILVER SPIKE.

Hon. F. A. Tritle, from the State of Nevada, presented a silver spike on behalf of the citizens of Nevada, with the following remarks:

"To the iron of the East and the gold of the West, Nevada adds her link of silver to span the continent and wed the irons."

REMARKS OF GENERAL DODGE.

General DODGE in behalf of the Union Pacific then responded as follows:

Gentlemen:—"The great Benton prophesied that some day a granite statue of Columbus would be erected on the highest peak of the Rocky Mountains pointing westward, denoting this as the great route across the continent. You have made that prophesy this day. Accept this as the way to India."

Thereupon Superintendent Coe, in behalf of the Pacific Union Express, presented the sledge with which to drive the last spike. Governor Stanford and Vice President Durant now advanced, took in hand the sledge, and drove the last spike, while the multitude stood silent. Edgar Miles, of Sacramento, who was elected Chairman of the meeting, announced the great work done. The silence of the multitude was broken and a great cheer went forth which, while it yet quivered on the gladened air, was caught up by the willing lightning, and borne to the uttermost parts of the earth. Cheer followed cheer for the union of the Atlantic and Pacific, the two Pacific Railroad Companies and their officers, and the President of the United States. All was over. Glory be to God in the highest; on earth peace and good will toward men.

COMMERCIAL.

Milwaukee Market.

MILWAUKEE, May 12.

Freights unchanged—Buffalo 6c and Oswego 11c.

Flour quiet, firm and unchanged. Receipts 3,000 brls.; Shipments 3,000 brls.

Wheat steady at 1.18¼ for No. 1, and 1.13¾ for No. 2. Receipts 53,000 bus.; Shipments 54,000 bus.

Corn nominally unchanged. Receipts none; Shipments 200 bus.

Oats nominal. Receipts 3,600 bus.; Shipments 200 bus.

New York Market.

NEW YORK, May 12.

Flour, shipping grades improved, at 5.20@6.70 for superfine; 6.20@6.70 for state; 6.25@7.00 for western, and 6.40@7.50 for round hoop Ohio.

Wheat firmer, but quiet.

Rye quiet.

Corn—Old firmer; new dull and heavy. Sales at 80@82½c for new mixed western; 85c for old; 85@86½c in store.

Barley dull.

Oats at 80½c for western in store.

Pork dull and heavy at 30.75@31.00 for new mess.

New York Stock Market.

NEW YORK, May 12.

Gold 1.38⅜.

United States bonds are quoted as follows:

United States 6s 1881	@120
United States 5-20s, '62	@119⅜
United States 5-20s, '64	@115¼
United States 5-20s, '65	@116⅝
United States 5-20s, new	@117¾
United States 5-20s, '67	@117⅛
United States 5-20's '68	@117⅜
United States 10-40s	@108⅜

Chicago Market.

CHICAGO—TUESDAY EVENING, May 11.

Flour has been in moderate request, and prices rule steady at about the same figures as yesterday.

Wheat has been moderately active, and the market closes 2½c higher than yesterday. There is but little cash wheat offering, and with a moderate inquiry, prices were firm, and as the advices from Liverpool, New York and Milwaukee indicated higher figures at those points the market here advanced from 1.12¾, the opening figure, to 1.13⅝, closing at one o'clock at 1.13¼@1.13⅛ for cash. There has been an active business done in options, which ranged about ½c below cash for seller the month, closing at 1.13, seller May. Seller June has sold at 1.11@1.11¼. No. 1 has been in fair demand at 1.16@1.18 according to location. No. 3 has sold at 1.04@1.06. Rejected is nominal at 95c. No grade is reported at 88c.

Corn was in moderate request and prices rule higher notwithstanding the decline reported in New York and Liverpool. Sales of No. 1 were made early at 58c, advancing to 59¼c, and closed at one o'clock at 59½c.

Oats have been in fair demand and steady, at 61@61½c, closing at 61c for regular. Rejected have sold at 58½@59c. Options are reported at 60½c seller May, and 59c seller June.

Rye has been quiet and easier, with sales at 1.15@1.16¼ for No. 1, closing at 1.15@1.15¼. No. 2 has sold at 1.12¼@1.13¼.

Barley continues dull, and we only note the sale of one car load of No. 2, at the Illinois Central, at 1.68.

Seeds continue very dull as the season is nearly gone and the sales are very meagre.

Highwines are weaker, with sales at 89@90c for wood bound and 90½c for iron bound.

Cheese is in fair demand, and the new coming in is held at 22@23c for New York factory.

Nails continue firm, and so far as we can learn, all dealers are selling at 4.25 rates.

We have no particular change to note in the provision trade. The demand was mainly for mess pork for the jobbing trade, and 31.00 was the market. For choice brands of lard 17½c was bid, also 17¼ for regular brands, though small lots of butchers' rendering could have been had at 17¼c. There was a better inquiry for shoulders, and lots that suited, readily brought 11¾c. There were no rough sides or short rib offering; held at 14¾@15¼c. Sweet pickled hams can be had, at 15@15½c, according to quality. Yet there are brands held as high as 16c.

CHICAGO, May 12.

The market is generally dull, wheat, 119¾ for No. 2.

Corn, 59c for No. 1; 55c for No. 2.

Oats unchanged.

Fruits unchanged.

[illegible]

BY TELEGRAPH.

EXCLUSIVELY TO THE STATE JOURNAL

NEWS FROM WASHINGTON

Through Mails by Pacific R. R.

Instructions to Revenue Officers.

A Splendid Gift to Washington.

CUBAN MATTERS.

Official Announcement that the Rebellion is Suppressed.

Other Side of the Story.

Anniversary Meetings

Opening of New York Canals.

European News.

The Mayor of Cork Resigned.

Miscellaneous Items.

FROM WASHINGTON.

WASHINGTON, May 11.

A general order has been issued from headquarters of the army assigning a large number of officers to duty as Indian superintendents and agents. They are officers who were left out of their regimental organizations by the consolidation of the infantry regiments.

The Postoffice Department has received a telegram from Promontory Point stating the mails have been delivered at that place to the Central Pacific road, and that the through line has been regularly established. The Butterfield Company were last week informed that their contract would close when the junction was formed. The cost by the Butterfield route for transporting the mails was $1,100 per mile, by the railroad $200 a mile per annum.

The President has appointed Mr. Pixley, United States Attorney for California; Bartlett Bert postmaster at Middletown, Conn.; W. Preityman postmaster at Marietta; Geo. M. Cleft postmastmaster at Savannah, Ga.

About thirty clerks were removed to-day from the office of the 6th Auditor of the Treasury, and several other dismissals in other branches are to take place immediately. The appointment clerk has issued stringent instructions to subordinates in his office, forbidding to give any information concerning the removals under his supervision, either previous to or after they have been made. The object of this is to prevent any parties designated for removal to trouble that officer with importunities to be reinstated.

A letter of instruction has been issued by the Secretary of the Treasurer to the Internal Revenue officers relative to the tax on foreign capital, and prescribing the following addition regulations relative to taxes paid the Government from the dividend interest or profits due to non-residents prior to March 10th, 1866, requiring the annexed evidence in addition to that heretofore required.

First. The affidavit of the non-resident setting forth his present place of residence, also his alienage and place of residence at the time when the taxes in question were withheld, and that he is the identical person entitled to receive the amount so withheld, also, specifying the amount which he or the bond company, or corporation is entitled to have refunded.

Second. Or an affidavit of a creditable person, that he is well acquainted with "such non-resident alien, and knows him to be the person described, and to have been a non-resident alien as claimed."

Third. The officers before whom these affidavits are verified, must certify that he knows the persons so verifying before him, to be a creditable person.

Fourth. A certificate of the consul of consular agent or other official representatives of the United States, in the country in which the affidavits that the attestation to such affidavits are genuine, and made in accordance with the form of the law, by duly authorized officers.

Fifth. When applications are made by the bank company or corporation, satisfactory proof will be required of the fact, that the bank and corporation has paid to a non-resident alien or his legal representatives, withheld from him under section 120 or section 122 of the act of June 30, 1864.

Sixth. When an application is made directly to the Commissioner of Internal Revenue, by a non-resident alien, he will be required to prove that by the insolvency of the bank, company or corporation by which the amount of tax was withheld, or other sufficient cause, he is unable to obtain payment from such bank, company or corporation.

Seventh. In all such cases, evidence of the receipt of the money by the United States required by existing regulations on the subject of refunding, must be furnished, in case of the death of a non-resident alien, the facts relating to him herein above required to be verified by his own affidavit of the legal representative of the estate of the deceased or other creditable person cognizant of the facts of the case with the same corroborative evidence as is above required.

Information coming to the knowledge of Gen. Smith, Second Assistant Postmaster General, that certain Western contractors were in the habit of throwing off the mails in order to make room for passengers, he has fined two of them $1,000 each, and will apply this rule in all cases. The department will also withhold payment in every case where the trip is not performed, no matter what may be the cause.

Commissioner Delano decides that when parties are engaged in the manufacture of goods of any description by furnishing the material, paying for the work, etc., though not personally engaged in the process of manufacture, but conducting it through agents and superintendents, they are liable to the tax imposed by the act of March 31, 1868, on manufacturers.

The rush to the Executive mansion of male and female visitors, who have no actual business with the President, but who are influenced by mere curiosity, will probably lead to a curtailment of the time now set apart for public receptions.

Col. Corcoran has executed a deed transferring to a board of nine trustees the building erected by him some years ago, near the War Department, for an art depository, together with the ground on which it is situated, and all the back rents due on account of its use and occupancy by the Government as the Quartermaster's Department, to be held by them in perpetuity as a free picture gallery for the city of Washington. He has also added his large collection of paintings and other works of art. The value of the property is estimated at $1,000,000. It is stated that August Belmont, of New York, has written to Corcoran, authorizing the trustees, when they shall have entered upon the trust, to choose from his collection twelve pictures, which he will thereupon convey to them, to be added as the Belmont contribution.

Owing to the high charges by the authorities of St. Thomas for the use of a coal depot at that station, this Government has, as a matter of economy, taken measures to transfer the coaling station to Samanca Bay.

The Cabinet to-day had a long consultation in regard to Virginia matters. It was finally determined that an order should be issued submitting the test oath and disfranchisement clauses of the constitution to a separate vote. No exceptions will be made regarding the county and township organization clauses. It is understood, however, that these clauses may possibly be included in the exceptions before the order is issued.

ANTI-SLAVERY SOCIETY.

NEW YORK, May 11.

The anniversary meeting of the American Anti-Slavery Society commenced to-day at Steinway Hall. The attendance was slim, Wendell Phillips called the meeting to order, congratulating the society on the favorable auspices under which they met, and declaring that Heaven's bright and every sign of the times were on the side of anti-slavery. The financial report was favorable, showing a balance cash on hand of $2,500. Resolutions were adopted urging the adoption of the 15th amendment to the Constitution approving Gen. Grant's inauguration, appointing colored men to office, deprecating the social and political prescription of the colored race, upbraiding on the church and press for neglecting to put an end to it, praising Cuban patriots for abolishing slavery, calling on the Government to recognize them, asserting that reconstruction must be based on education, and blaming the Government for not more promptly and vigorously protecting the union people in the South, and denouncing the proposed restrictions upon the elective franchise in the District of Columbia. Speeches were made throughout the day and evening by Wendell Phillips, Lucy Stone Blackwell, G. M. Sims, an expelled colored member of the Georgia Legislature, Stevens, Foster and Fred Douglas. Mr. Phillips predicted that the time would come when the colored man would be in the Cabinet, the Legislature, and Foreign legation. He urged the adoption of the 15th amendment as it would confer incalculable benefit upon the nation. Mrs. Brown introduced the question of woman's rights and discussed it at length.

The American Christian Union held their annual meeting at the Bible House, Rev. Dr. Thomas in the chair. The annual report is very encouraging in regard to the success of mission work abroad in German Catholic countries, especially in South America and Southern Europe. The treasurer's report shows the receipts at $111,700; expenditures $112,150. Rev. D. Dewitt was re-elected president and Rev. J. R. Cadder, secretary.

CUBAN.

NEW YORK, May 11.

A Washington special says the Spanish Minister received last night a sub-marine cable dispatch from Gen. Dulce announcing the final suppression of the rebellion in Cuba. It is asserted by Dulce that only 200 insurgents are under arms in detached bodies without any leaders or concert of action. The news was submitted to the State Department. It does not receive great credit here and is supposed to be promulgated to discourage American sympathy with Cuba and prevent filibustering schemes. Cubans here affirm the ability of their countrymen to held out against the Spaniards for an indefinite time. They claim the armed bodies alleged to be wandering around constitute neuclus of concentrating officers, and there are over 10,000 men working on the farms and plantations that can be concentrated at any time to strike a decisive blow.

HAVANA, May 11.

The *Diaro* to-day publishes a meagre report of the engagement which took place between the Spanish troops and the insurgents at Atla Grecia. Report says the rebels offered more determined resistance than in any previous battle and acknowledged that the Spaniards lost a colonel, captain and 6 privates, killed, and 30 wounded. It claims that the rebel losses are heavy but does not give the number. The insurgents have burned the village of San Miguel, near Nuevitas. Puerto Principe is reported to be plentifully supplied with provisions. It is expected that the *Premsa* of this city will soon suspend publication and probably withdraw entirely from the field.

The steamer *Columbia* arrived at noon to-day from New York with Mr. Plum, the new Consul General of United States for Havana, as passenger.

FROM NEW YORK.

NEW YORK, May 11.

The Cleveland, Ohio, and Lumberman's Insurance Company, of Chicago, lose $10,000 each by the fire in Broadway last night.

The Troy *Times* of last evening says that water let into the canal Saturday night, and navigation would have promptly opened this morning, but it was found that a boat laden with iron, lying in the Three Mile Level between here and Schenectady, could not float, and consequently the water had to be drawn off. The boat was removed at 1'clock to-day. The canal was two-thirds full, and the prospect was that the first boat would pass up early this evening. Everything, as far as heard from, is all right between here and Buffalo.

The North German emigrant ship *Cristel* arrived to-day, 36 days from Bremen, with 422 pessengers. She had 13 cases of small pox on board, and had four deaths from that disease during her passage. She is in quarantine.

At the meeting of the Anti-Slavery Society to-night, Frederick Douglass was the first speaker. He said what the negro race claimed was fairplay and no favor, the right to vote and be voted for. He incidentally alluded to the amalgamation of the white and negro races, which, he said, was certain to follow the negroes to social and political equality, notwithstanding its disavowal by some of the friends of the negro, he believed it would produce beneficial results. Senators Wilson and Stuart, of Nevada, were present and spoke briefly in favor of the 15th constitutional amendment. Wendell Phillips advocated the public policy of justice for all nationalities and races, whether negroes, Indians, Chinese, German or Irish. The United States could afford to absorb all and deal justly with all. The meeting adjourned at 11 o'clock.

PRICES OF CABLE DISPATCHES.

NEW YORK, May 11.

The announcement heretofore made of the proposed reduction in the price of dispatches on the Atlantic cable from and after June have been incorrect in some respects. The rates to the general public on and after the first of June are to be one dollar per word for each and every word, including the address, date and signature, but no message will be charged a less sum than $10. A reduction of 50 per cent. from these rates on political and general news for the press is also proposed, but one of the companies interested has not yet given its assent to this proposition.

FIRE.

PITTSFIELD, May 11.

Burbank's Block, occupied by Messrs. Storrs & Hall, was destroyed by fire this morning. Loss $35,000; insurance $14,000. The county offices were in the same building, and a portion of the law library and all the plans of the new Court House were consumed.

RACES.

LONDON, May 11.

At the York races, the Zealand stakes was won by the filly Adventurer. The Great Northern Handicap was won by Ploughboy.

FROM NEW ORLEANS.

NEW ORLEANS, May 12.

The trouble between Governor Warmouth and Auditor Wyckliff is practically at an end. Warmouth is reported to have stated that he will take no further steps against the Auditor, and the latter will be restored to his office as soon as the necessary legal steps can be taken.

The Chamber of Commerce met to-night to receive the delegation of the St. Louis Grain Dealers Association. They were introduced by Gen. Herron, and were received by Pres't Oglesbee with a brief and patriotic welcome address. Mr. L. R. Shyock followed, and stated that St. Louis had succeeded in interesting President Grant in the movement, and that the appointment of a St. Louis merchant, Henry T. Blow, to the Brazilian mission was in furtherance of the effort to reclaim the South American trade with the Mississippi Valley. He read some interesting statistics relative to the trade previous to the war. Gov. Stanard followed with a pungent and interesting speech. He closed by saying that he wished to see an organization similar to the St. Louis Grain Association. There were other speakers who followed in the same strain.

FROM CANADA.

OTTAWA, May 11.

In the House of Commons last night, Mr. Harrison moved an address and petition regarding the seizure of the schooner *Marzata* at Detroit in 1864, the owner of which had never been compensated by the American Government. The motion was carried.

Mr. Savoy moved for copies of the proclamation, &c., requiring the assimilation of the currency, and urged that the Government pass a bill making United States or British currency the standard in the Dominion.

Mr. Rose said that France, England and the United States would probably make a uniform currency on the basis of the English sovereign, and he thought it best not to make any change until other countries could understand the matter.

The motion was withdrawn.

FOREIGN NEWS.

LONDON, May 11.

Mr. O'Sullivan, Mayor of Cork, has resigned his office. Mr. Maguire, member for Cork, announced the fact in the House of Commons to-day, and stated that O'Sullivan had taken this action to prevent a re-election. The bill introduced by the Attorney General disqualifying a mayor from acting as a magistrate was in consequence postponed one month.

ST. PETERSBURG, May 11.

The Government is considering a plan for the reorganization of the Roman Catholic Church throughout the empire.

FROM BOSTON.

BOSTON, May 11.

The Central Church of this city has extended a unanimous call to the Rev. A. S. Storrs, of Brooklyn, New York, to become their pastor.

A grand rehearsal of all Boston societies and independent classes intending to participate in the great oratorio chorus of the National Peace Jubilee, will take place at Music Hall on the 19th inst. Boston alone will furnish 5,000 singers, who have been rehearsing in sections for the past two months.

PRIZE FIGHT.

NEW YORK, May 11.

Jim Gallagher, of New Haven, and Andy Hanley, of New York, had a fight on the shores of Long Island Sound, about six hours sail from New Haven, yesterday. Gallagher got the battle after 43 rounds were fought.

It is stated that Gen. Banks had an interview with Secretary Fish yesterday, urging the prompt recognition of the Cuban patriots, and claiming that further procrastination is ruinous folly.

FROM GEORGIA.

AUGUSTA, May 11.

James Atkins, Radical Senator from Warren county, was shot in the abdomen, yesterday afternoon, near Thompson. Reports assign the cause to a private difficulty, growing out of a *crim. con.* case. It is believed that Atkins' wound would be mortal.

There is considerable discussion as to the propriety of extending the Georgia Railroad to Blue Ridge, to form a connection with Cincinnati, by the Southern Railroad.

FITTING FOR WAR.

WASHINGTON, May 11.

It is known here that the *Grapeshot*, which recently sailed from Florida, is at a Southern port engaged in fitting out with arms and munitions of war for Cuba, and that several Cuban sympathizers have engaged passage on her. The Government authorities have issued instructions to the officials in New York to keep close watch on her movements.

CUBAN PROCLAMATION.

NEW YORK, May 12.

The Cuban General Miramon has issued a proclamation responsive to the Spaniard General Valmazeda, in which he declares war to death against the Spanards.

CUBAN PRIVATEER.

PHILADELPHIA, May 12.

The iron clad *Atlanta*, formerly a rebel craft has been sold. It is understood that, after getting to sea, to raise the Cuban flag.

STEAMER BURNED.

CINCINNATI, May 12.

Six steamboats were burned at the landing this morning. Loss heavy. Particulars at noon.

WISCONSIN STATE JOURNAL.

VOLUME XX. MADISON, WIS., TUESDAY AFTERNOON, OCTOBER 10, 1871. NUMBER 32.

STATE JOURNAL.

THE OFFICIAL STATE PAPER.

REPUBLICAN NOMINATIONS.

FOR GOVERNOR—
GEN. C. C. WASHBURN,
OF LA CROSSE.

FOR LIEUTENANT GOVERNOR—
MILTON H. PETTIT,
OF KENOSHA.

FOR SECRETARY OF STATE—
LLYWELYN BREESE, of Columbia

FOR STATE TREASURER—
Maj. HENRY BÆTZ, of Manitowoc

FOR ATTORNEY GENERAL—
S. S. BARLOW, of Sauk.

FOR STATE PRISON COMMISSIONER—
G. F. WHEELER, of Fond du Lac.

FOR STATE SUPT. OF PUBLIC INSTRUCTION—
SAMUEL FALLOWS, of Milwaukee

FOR COMMISSIONER OF IMMIGRATION—
OLE C. JOHNSON, of Rock,

FOR MEMBERS OF THE ASSEMBLY.
3d Dist.—JOHN BROSEMER, of Roxbury.
4th " —PHINEAS BALDWIN, of Oregon.

Appointments for Hon C. G. Williams.

The appointments of Hon. CHAS. G. WILLIAMS have been changed to the following places, in the evening:

Black River Falls, Oct. 14.
Eau Claire, Oct. 16.
Chippewa Falls, Oct. 17.
Menomonee, Oct. 18.
Hudson, Oct. 19.
Osceola, Oct. 31.

E. W. KEYES, Chairman.

Appointments for Senator T. O. Howe.

Beloit, Friday, Oct. 13.
Darlington, Tuesday, Oct. 17.
Platteville, Wednesday, Oct. 18.
Dodgeville, Thursday, Oct. 19.
Prairie du Chien, Friday, Oct. 20.
La Crosse, Monday, Oct. 23.
Eau Claire, Wednesday, Oct. 25.
Madison, Friday, Oct. 27.
Berlin, Tuesday, Oct. 31.
Fond du Lac, Wednesday, Nov. 1.
Evening meetings.

E. W. KEYES, Chairman.

Appointments for Hon. J. A. Barber and Hon. Geo C. Hazleton.

Hon. J. A. BARBER, M. C., and the Hon. GEO. C. HAZLETON will speak to the citizens of the following places at the time stated:

Richland Center, October 25.
Sauk City, October 26.
Baraboo, October 27.
Prairie du Chien, October 30.
Evening meetings.

E. W. KEYES, Chairman.

Republican Meetings

Will be held at
Spring Green, October 16.
Lone Rock, October 17.
To be addressed by W. W. Likens, Esq., of Iowa, and Nelson Wheeler, Esq., of Sauk.
Arena, October 18.
Avoca, October 19.
Boscobel, October 20.
Muscoda, October 21.
To be addressed by NELSON WHEELER, Esq., and Col. ED. E. BRYANT.
Viroqua, Oct. 19th.
To be addressed by W. W. Likens, Esq., and Gen. J. S. Kellogg. All evening meetings.

The Great Fire in Chicago.

We have a few brief dispatches in regard to the Chicago fire, stating its origin and limits, and aggregating the amount of loss at the enormous sum of five hundred million dollars.

Messrs. J. L. HILL, of the Bank of Madison, J. H. GARNHART, B. J. STEVENS, EUGENE A. JONES, Dr. E. B. RICE, GILBERT DUTCHER, now of Saint Paul, and others, have come up from Chicago since the fire, some of them having been there while it was raging. They say no words can possibly convey an adequate idea of the horrors of the fearful conflagration, and the enormous devastation it has caused, nor of the scenes of wild frenzy, making a pandemonium of the city while it raged. They say the half has not been told.

The heat far distant from the fire was so intense as to set buildings on fire, and the flames traveled with the speed of the whirlwind. Within an hour after church services closed at the Methodist block, opposite the Court House, it was in flames. The Sherman House was hardly known to be on fire till it was a sheet of flames, and the inmates, with great difficulty, escaped. It is reported that Hon. DAVID A. GAGE lost his life there. Many people betook themselves with such goods as they could carry to Lincoln Park, in the northern part of the city, thinking it a place of safety, but the flames swept through it as over a prairie, and it is reported many children perished there.

The river was a sheet of flame with oil melted from great heaps of coal, shooting up many feet.

Among the elegant residences destroyed were those of Messrs. DUNLAP, PERRY H. SMITH, and ELLIS, well known here, and hardly any of their valuable contents were saved.

Rush street bridge was the last between North and South side to go, and Mr. HILL thinks that by the efforts of a crowd he rallied, its destruction was averted till it had proved an avenue of escape for 20,000 people, who would otherwise have been cut off.

It is thought there must have been thousands of lives lost, especially of the young and helpless.

Men seemed frenzied and apathetic in view of their losses, and all manner of violence, robbery and extortion is reported.

It is thought the money and valuables of many of the banks were saved. We are glad to learn that everything from the Second National Bank of Messrs. TINKHAM & ELLIS was saved, and the cashier has arrived safely in Milwaukee and deposited it with MARSHALL & ILLSLEY.

The greatest destitution and suffering prevails among those who are left, and thousands are without shelter, food or drink, the water works having been destroyed.

A letter from a friend of one of the editors, living on the West Side, far beyond the reach of the fire, whose house is filled with refugee friends from the North Side, written yesterday, says:

CHICAGO, Oct. 9.

I cannot attempt to describe the ruin that has been and is being wrought. Nearly all the South Side, (scarcely if any exception), north of Harrison street, has been burned. How much was saved in the way of goods, books, &c., there is no means of knowing. Fire-proof buildings fell with the rest. The one remark is that "all North Side is burned up." The expression is not a great exaggeration.

Great Fires.

A friend has kindly furnished us with some statistics of great fires, to which we have added others.

In speaking of the burning of Chicago, reference is made to the great London fire, over two centuries ago. That city then contained less than two-thirds the population of Chicago, for the plague which visited London in June, 1665, and raged until December of that year, swept off 68,596 people, nearly one third of the population. The next year, September 2, 1666, the great fire broke out and lasted four days and nights. It took 13,2000 buildings, swept 400 streets, and was only extinguished by blowing up the surroundings. Five-sixths of the whole city within the walls were reduced to ashes. The *Encyclopedia Britannica* says the ruin covered a space more than a mile long and half a mile wide, and the value of the buildings and goods consumed was estimated at ten or twelve million pounds sterling. But though severe at the time, this visitation contributed materially to the improvement of the city. It was rebuilt on a more commodious plan, by Sir CHRISTOPHER WREN, in about four years.

It will be seen that the Chicago fire covers a much greater extent of territory than that of London, and the loss instead of being fifty or sixty millions, we have heard estimated by careful business men at hundreds of millions.

The memorable fire in New York city in 1835, consumed six hundred warehouses, and the loss was estimated at twenty million dollars. That city in 1830 contained less than 203,000 people; in 1840 less than 313,000, and Chicago by the last census was reported to contain about 299,000 inhabitants.

In 1845, one thousand buildings were burned in Pittsburg; loss about ten million dollars. The same year, April 10th, fifteen hundred dwellings were burned in Quebec, and the next month, May 28th, thirteen hundred more buildings were destroyed in the same city. A fire in New York that year destroyed three hundred and nine buildings.

In 1849, the great fire in Albany burned six hundred buildings, covering twenty-four acres. The estimated loss was three million dollars.

The Philadelphia fire of 1854 burned three hundred buildings. Troy, New York, has suffered from two serious conflagrations, but we have not the statistics by us showing the extent of the damages. Our impression is that the last one burned the bridge across the Hudson and over twenty blocks of buildings. The great fire in Portland occurred July 4th, 1866. A space about one mile and a half long and a quarter of a mile wide was burned over. A great number of buildings were blown up to check the flames. The fire continued nearly two days. Portland contained about fifty thousand inhabitants. The United States authorities sent two thousand tents to the sufferers.

It will be seen from the above that Chicago has a larger population than either New York or London had at the time of their great fires. The extent of territory burned over at Chicago, which was estimated yesterday at nine square miles, is much greater than at all the above fires, and the magnitude of the loss is probably many times that suffered by all the above cities, including London.

The buildings were, many of them, costly and magnificent structures, better than any that have been recently destroyed in any city, except those burned by the communists in Paris this year.

The Chicago fire will rank as the greatest, or one of the greatest in history.

—The latest reports say that two thousand acres are burned over, and the loss is estimated at five hundred million dollars!

Wisconsin Legislative Nominations.

— N. D. LOOMIS has been nominated for the Assembly by the Democrats of La Crosse.

— The Republicans of the Second Assembly district of Fond du Lac have nominated ELIHU COLMAN candidate for the Assembly. The *Daily* says he is "a native of Wisconsin, thirty years of age, a lawyer by profession, an energetic, well informed man, and a staunch Republican. He will do credit to the district. He was a good soldier in our late war, graduated at Lawrence University, and is a good man for the position he seeks."

— The Republicans of the Third Assembly district of Winnebago county, have nominated Hon. R. J. JUDD candidate for the Assembly—the humorous, eloquent and versatile member who so distinguished himself in the Assembly last winter.

JUDGE ORTON AT THE NORTHERN FAIR.—The Oshkosh *Journal* thus highly speaks of Judge ORTON's address at the Northern Wisconsin Fair:

At 2 P. M., Hon. H. S. Orton delivered the annual address. It was a masterly effort, and the best we ever listened to upon the fair ground. It was short but pithy, and to the point. We do not remember of ever hearing an address where there were so much expressed in so few words as were contained in Mr. O's address. He did credit to himself and to the society.

—The *Northwestern*, giving a brief synopsis, says:

The address was full of humor, and was delivered in the orator's favorable style, and was throughout replete with practical sense which was highly appreciated by the listeners.

☞ The Secretary of the Treasury has directed the Treasurer and Assistant Treasurers to pay the November coupons upon rebate interest to October 25, and on and after that day to pay the interest due to November 1st without rebate.

☞ Foreign letters report the completion of the alliance between Germany, Austria and Italy, with an army of 2,250,000 men for the insurance of European peace.

☞ Incredible as such fiendishness appears, it is said men were caught yesterday setting new fires, in Chicago, for purposes of plunder, and shot in the act.

THIS is election day in Pennsylvania, Ohio and Iowa. The returns will be delayed on account of the Chicago fire.

WASHBURN—DOOLITTLE.

Second Discussion, at Fond du Lac.

Another Republican Victory.

The second discussion between the rival candidates for Governor took place at Fond du Lac on Saturday, the 7th, and according to all accounts, resulted in a victory for WASHBURN, and the making of votes for the Republican party. The correspondent of the *Wisconsin* says: "The discussion brought out 3,000 people—farmers from the country, workmen from shop and mill, and what is significant, three-fourths, if not five-sixths, were Republicans. There is no mistake about this. DOOLITTLE don't draw. His oratory falls dead. The *Sentinel* correspondent says a band of music escorted the speakers to the stand, which were lined with eager people, a large audience gathering near the debate. The *News* says the Democrats formed a large majority of the meeting.

GEN. WASHBURN'S SPEECH.

Gen. WASHBURN was introduced to the audience by Hon. E. H. GALLOWAY, the Republican President, and he proceeded to deliver the opening address of an hour, of which we make up the following report from different papers:

He said he was glad to meet the people of Fond du Lac county, and while here he hoped to learn something of their wants, that he might know best how to promote their interests after the 1st of January. Last Tuesday he, with his friend Judge D., was up at Oshkosh, and he had demonstrated that the people of Wisconsin had no occasion to change their administration. He hesitated not to declare that Wisconsin was the model State of the Union. Nothing has been said, and nothing can be said by my friend against it. It was not alleged that every department had not been honestly, economically, faithfully and ably managed. The same might be said in regard to the national administration, and Judge D. had not ventured to assail it, except in what he denominated its tendency to centralization. He had shown that the Democracy had entirely abandoned the ground they occupied three years ago, and for the sake of obtaining power, that they were willing to recognize the 14th and 15th amendments. To day he should have no time to follow in the line he had marked out at Oskosh, as he had there promised to define his position here to-day, on the tariff question, on which he said:

Judge Doolittle, at Oshkosh, represented that I was a high tariff man, and proud of it. By what authority he made the statement I do not know. Certainly not from any utterance of mine or record of mine in the *Congressional Globe*. I suppose he must have derived his information from the Milwaukee *News*, the same paper which he declared in 1863 was more dangerous than the Alabama pirates and menace of foreign intervention combined, but which has since become his political Bible. The tariff question has properly no business in this discussion. First, because the Governor of Wisconsin had nothing to do with providing revenue for the Government; and, next, because the Democratic party had no defined policy that is accepted throughout the country on this question. The last National Democratic Convention proclaimed itself in favor of incidental protection; in this State they are for revenue only; in Illinois for free trade and direct taxation; in New York for free trade in iron, wool, woolens, and some other articles; in Pennsylvania for the highest rates of protection. Judge Doolittle attacked the present tariff without provocation. I propose to notice his attack and show that whatever its merits or demerits, any attack upon it now ill becomes him. The present tariff was passed while Doolittle was in the Senate, and received his support. I have looked in vain for the record of any attempt made by him to amend it or make it less burdensome. It was passed in war times, when we needed all the revenue we could obtain by a tariff granted, but the war closed in 1866, and a revision of the war tariff was for months pending in the Thirty-ninth Congress, but I have looked over the debates in vain for evidence that he sought to correct its abuses. If some of its features are abuses now, they were then, and so continued to be until he left the Senate, March 4, 1869. While I absolutely disclaim being in favor of a high tariff, or any tariff at all not absolutely demanded by the wants of the Government, I believe in allowing those articles of prime necessity consumed by all classes of the people to come in at a low rate of duty. In accordance with that belief, I voted to reduce the tariff on tea, coffee, coal and salt, and many other articles, placed upon them by Judge Doolittle, and which remained there without remonstrance while he was in Congress, and until he appeared in the present campaign." He charged that Doolittle was absent when a tariff was passed to increase a wool tariff, and added: "The tariff on luxuries I would have placed at a high rate. The true doctrine in other respects is this: that the tariff should be placed high enough on articles that can be produced here as well as elsewhere, but for the difference in the cost of labor, to enable the laborer here to be well paid, well clothed, well housed, and well fed, and be able to compete with the ill-paid and ill-fed laborer of the old world, but at the same time should not be so high as to be prohibitory, and prevent fair competition."

The industries of Wisconsin should be diversified. Look at the city of Milwaukee, that most beautiful of all the western cities, and one in which every citizen of Wisconsin has a just and honorable pride, and tell me what has caused her wonderful growth in population, wealth and power. It is her manufacturing industry, which, according to the report of the State Agricultural Society, reached the enormous sum of $18,000,000 last year. The value to a city of one such establishment as Bay View can hardly be estimated, and if the enterprising gentlemen who have placed their capital there shall find it a source of profit, I shall rejoice with them, and shall look to see that city occupy the same relative position to Chicago, that Philadelphia does to New York.

It is a popular idea that the tariff is now maintained for the benefit of New England. There was never a greater mistake. New England has arrived at that stage of development that it is fast becoming in favor of free trade, as old England is, and for the same reason. What she now wants is the market, and she sees with regret the present system of manufactures growing up in the South and West. She knows that if this state of things continues, her supremacy in factories is gone. Those who have noticed the discussion on the Schenck tariff bill have noticed that not a New England man opened his head in favor of protection. Gen. Butler, in his recent canvass, opposed protection, and Edward Atkinson, a manufacturer and a leader of that ring in the Republican party, in writing and speaking against it, attacked the common fallacy that a duty on a given article is so much added to its price, and cited many instances to show that many articles had been largely reduced in price by the introduction of their manufacture in this country.

The General anew repudiated the allegation that his nomination was the result of Executive or Federal dictation, and said: "My friend, DOOLITTLE, is running on a platform now with but a single plank, and that is Federal Dictation and Centralization, and it is necessary to hold his plank together by every means in his power. He sees an office-holder haunting him everywhere, and I think that he gently hinted that the offices ought to be filled without office-holders. He didn't think so once, when he was a United States Senator, and had the entire control of all the offices in Wisconsin.

The remainder of his opening speech was devoted to San Domingo. He said that he had a right to speak on it, having uniformly opposed the acquisition of outlying territory. He opposed the acquisition of Alaska, which his opponent favored, and of St. Thomas, since destroyed by an earthquake, which his opponent went to Copenhagen to purchase, and he claimed to have aided in the defeat of that project, which was to have cost $7,500,000 in gold. The President had a right to make the treaty for the acquisition of San Domingo, and the Senate had a right to reject it. The President did not act without knowledge, as Mr. Seward did in the purchase of Alaska. The report of the San Domingo Commission vindicated the President from the charges of improper conduct in the negotiation, and no evidence implicating any officer of the Government in making the treaty was ever found.

The *Sentinel* correspondent says: "The General spoke extemporaneously, referring to his notes but little, and was perfectly at home in his speaking, his hearers listening with undivided interest until he closed. * His effort was exceedingly able, and well delivered; and his fairness, candor and open-hearted manner could but be satisfactory to all who heard him. He closed with the applause of the entire crowd."

JUDGE DOOLITTLE'S REPLY.

As to the reply, the *Sentinel* correspondent says:

Gen. Washburn having occupied his allotted hour, Judge Doolittle was introduced to the audience by Judge R. Flint, the Democratic president of the meeting. The Judge had voluminous documents, and was evidently well prepared for the encounter. The Judge opened with his usual readiness, but it was not "an earnest man talking to earnest men" this time. He occupied his hour and a half in replying to the address of his opponent, and the conclusive manner in which the first speaker had elaborated his good points, put the ex-Senator to his best paces in endeavoring to do away with them."

The *Wisconsin's* correspondent says:

Mr. Doolittle went off into a general tirade on taxes, but could find no fault nor pick any flaws in Mr. Washburn's record or policy. If he had any practical views, any line of his own, he failed to give them. On the question of amnesty he agreed that Mr. Washburn took liberal and advanced grounds. He hadn't a word of censure or reproof for the Ku Klux. He rained torrents on the carpet baggers. He emptied volcanoes on the government despots at Washington."

From the *News* report we judge the speech is much the same as that made by Judge DOOLITTLE at Oshkosh, reiterating his claims of superiority for the Democratic Republican party; figuring up increased expenses of the State under Republican rule; repeating the story of Gen. WASHBURN's nomination at the dictation of the Federal office holders under the able lead of the Postmaster at Madison; attempting to defend his own action and assail that of Gen. WASHBURN on the tariff, and dwelling at length on what he claimed to be the hardships of the tariff; lamenting the disfranchisement of southern whites and the ascendancy of negroes and carpet-baggers; again by implication justifying the Kuklux outrages; denouncing the San Domingo purchase; quoting Gustavus Adolphus again on breaking chains; defending the New York Democracy, and again bewailing the centralizing tendency of the party in power.

WASHBURN'S REJOINDER.

As to Gen. WASHBURN's reply, the *Wisconsin* correspondent says:

Mr. Washburn, in his last half hour, dropped his notes, and opened right and left. He reviewed Doolittle's course in Congress, and his indirect apology for those Ku-Klux rascals at the South, who, the report of the Congressional Committee will show, have murdered thousands in cold blood for simply being friends of the Union. Congress believed the Ku-Klux bill constitutional and demanded by the necessities of the hour. At this point General Washburn put the following question:

"All who believe this Government has not the right, and that it is not its duty to protect its citizens everywhere on the face of the earth, where local authorities are unable or unwilling to do so, or who think the Ku-Klux assassins should be apologized for and excused as they have been to-day, will please to answer aye."

A few feeble responses were heard in the affirmative.

"All of the contrary opinion, say no."

One sweeping response of "NO" went up from the whole audience that seemed to open the vault of heaven. That settled the Ku-Klux question.

A man in the crowd, who proved to be a Democratic bummer, called out to General Washburn just before he closed, "Why did you not vote to give land to soldiers?" General Washburn thanked him for the question, as it gave him an opportunity to relieve the anxiety and distress of the copperhead press, which was in the habit of denouncing Lincoln hirelings until the war ended, and also of certain claim agents, who had been engaged in robbing the soldiers since the war ended. The Court of Military Affairs, of which Gen. Logan, the head of the Grand Army of the Republic, was Chairman, reported a homestead bill for the soldiers. It gave them the right to take 160 acres of land within the limits of any railway grant, when no other citizen could take but 80 acres, and in addition it allowed the time they served in the army to be deducted from the time all other persons were required to reside on the land. In fact, it was the same bill that the Grand Army of the Republic in this State had asked to have passed. It passed, and by the help of his vote. While it was pending, a Democratic representative from Indiana, and a steady opponent of the war, offered an amendment proposing to issue to each soldier a 160 acre land warrant, or 2,000,000 in all, covering 320,000,000 acres of the public land. Gen. Logan, Gen. Stoughton, a soldier from Michigan, who was shot all to pieces during the war, and other soldiers on the committee, opposed the amendment, and assured the House that the bill reported by the committee was satisfactory to the soldiers, and that it was better for them, in their judgment, than the amendment proposed. It is well known what the effect has heretofore been when even a small amount of warrants have been issued. When less than 10,000,000 acres of college scrip was issued, the price went down to about fifty or sixty cents, and there can be no shadow of doubt that had we issued $320,000,000 as the bill contemplated, that the price would have gone down to 10 cents on the dollar. The holder would have got his warrant, but he would have nothing left after paying the claim agent to procure it. It is two or three claim agents who have been robbed of a rich harvest that are trying to make a little capital for Democracy. I have seen no Democratic paper yet of any standing that has said that my vote was not a proper vote, or that I ought to have voted otherwise. Had $320,000,000 of such warrants been issued they would have fallen into the hands of few persons who would have bought them up for a trifling sum, and eventually they would have absorbed all the most desirable public lands, so that neither lands for homesteads nor pre emptions would have been left for soldiers or other people to settle upon. Among those who voted with me were Gens. Logan, Butler, Banks, Barry, Asper, Brock, Buckley, Clark, Cobb, Garfield, Hawley, Ketchum, Moore, Morey, Negley, Newsham, Packard, Packer, Paine, Pierce, Platt, Prosser, Stevens, Stokes, Stoughton, Tanner and Van Slyck. Among those who voted for the bill were such staunch Union men and friends of the soldier, as Fernando Wood, Dan Vorhees, Samuel Marshall, Charles A. Eldridge, G. W. Woodward, and many more of the same sort. Of course the soldiers will understand that their true friends are among those last named.

At the close of the half hour, three wild, rousing cheers were given for Mr. Washburn. One poor scared fellow started a cheer for Doolittle, but never a soul responded.

West Wisconsin Methodist Episcopal Conference.

We have the following additional report of the session at Mineral Point:

The Missionary services of Friday afternoon and evening—second day—were unusually interesting, and attended by a crowded house. Rev. WM. STURGES preached in the afternoon, and Revs. J. D. SEARLES, of Hudson, L. A. W. JEWETT, of Galena, Dr. J. M. WALDEN, of Chicago, and Dr. G. M. STEELE, of Lawrence University, addressed the audience in the evening. The lay delegates also held a preliminary meeting for social purposes.

THIRD DAY.

The conference opened with the usual religious services. Applications for local ordination were received and disposed of. Resolutions instructing the delegates to General Conference to resist changes in the Discipline as to Bishops and Presiding Elders were passed. After several ballots, the four delegates to General Conference were elected as follows: J. B. BACHMMAN, J. B. REYNOLDS, A. BRUNSON and T. M. FULLERTON. R. DUDGEON and P. S. MATHER were made reserves.

A Sunday School Anniversary was held in the afternoon, and Revs. M. B. BALCH, S. S. BENEDICT and H. S. RICHARDSON, addressed the large gathering of children.

A crowded house greeted that prince of song, PHILIP PHILIPS, in the evening.

The Laymen's Electorial Conference organized with Maj. J. H. ROUNTREE in the chair, and JAS. T. PYOR, Jr., Secretary. A committee on resolutions was appointed, and Maj. J. H. ROUNTREE and Hon. J. E. STILLMAN were elected delegates to the General Conference; Judge J. STEEL and Dr. A. BELL were held as reserves.

S. S. B.

GEN. WASHBURN AT SHEBOYGAN.—In a notice of an address of Gen. WASHBURN to a large meeting of city and county people at Sheboygan on the 7th the *Herald* says:

Hon. B. Williams was called upon to preside over the meeting, and in introducing Gen. Washburn said he was glad to introduce a man who had always been true to his principles; who had proved himself the firm friend of the people and the opponent of monopolies; a man in favor of a railroad tariff. Gen. Washburn made a long and elaborate speech, discussing the political questions of the day in an able and masterly manner. He has thousands of true friends in Sheboygan county who may be depended upon in November.

MISTAKEN IDENTITY.—The Omro *Union* tells the following true story of one of the Democracy of Oshkosh:

It is reported that a certain attorney at Oshkosh, who was to receive Judge Doolittle at the cars on the 3d inst., mistook the Hon. C. C. Washburn for the Judge, shook hands with the Hon. C. C., calling him Judge Doolittle; then he, said attorney, calling to one of his friends who was standing near, whom he introduced to the Hon. C. C. saying, "Allow me to introduce you to Judge Doolittle, our next Governor," to which the Hon. C. C. responded: "A part of what you say may be true, but I am not Judge Doolittle." Comment is unnecessary.

THE NORTHERN FIRES.—A dispatch to the Milwaukee *Wisconsin*, dated Green Bay the 9th, says:

The fires are still raging in the north and surrounding country. The people of this city are going into the country to help the farmers, and we can hear nothing from the north. The steamer *Dunlap*, that was due here on Sunday at 3 P. M., is not yet in. Mr. Bliss and Mr. Smith are in the north. Heavy weather we suppose is the cause of the delay to the *Dunlap*. There is no truth in the report of Saturday, about thirty men being burned, and the burning of the mill, etc., at Pensaukee. Lamb and Watson's mill, with store, boarding houses and logs at New Franklin, were destroyed last night by fire.

WHY DIDN'T THEY COME?—The Madison *Democrat* and Milwaukee *News* are informed that three-fourths of the people in attendance on the discussion in this city between Washburn and Doolittle were Republicans. The charge that the Republicans attempted to keep people away is utterly without foundation. We published and advertised, and wrote specials, every day for weeks, and urged our friends to attend. Bills were also got out jointly by the Republicans and Democrats. The crowd was larger than we had a right to expect, considering the fact that many were making entries at the Fair ground, that our business men could not leave their business in the middle of the day. If we kept Republicans away, let the *News* tell us who kept the Democrats away. There were not more than 150 or 200 of that denomination present, and many of them acknowledged that Washburn placed his opponent *hors du combat* in fine style. The reason the Democrats did not turn out better was that they felt sold out by their leaders and had no hopes for the future. Those who were present went away terribly disappointed.—*Oshkosh Northwestern.*

BY TELEGRAPH.

NIGHT DISPATCHES.

THE CHICAGO FIRE

MORE RUIN WROUGHT.

Whole Business Center Gone.

Wide Desolation.

Terrible Loss and Suffering.

No Water but from River and Lake

Not One Newspaper Left.

Only One Depot Remaining.

Principal Hotels Destroyed.

Thousands Without Shelter or Food

Milwaukee Freely Sending Aid.

The West Side Still Spared.

THE CHICAGO FIRE.

MILWAUKEE, Oct. 9—4 P. M.

Believe everything and you can realize nothing compared with the situation at Chicago.

The entire North Side has gone or is in flames. The West Side depot grounds are yet safe, but the heat from the other side of the river is intense, and the shipping is beginning to burn. The Galena division of the Northwestern railroad has lost three elevators, with over one million bushels of wheat, depots, offices, &c. Both the Union and Michigan Southern depots are burned. The South Side is destroyed as far south as Van Buren street, and this includes every principal hotel in the city.

For miles outside the city the ground is covered with vehicles of every description, conveying goods and people to places of safety. There is no water in the city except what can be drawn from the river or lake. The whole central, eastern and north side business portions are consumed, and the fire is still under full headway. All the newspaper offices are destroyed. The city is being abandoned by the citizens as fast as possible. The Milwaukee firemen have arrived and are at work.

W. J. Swan, of the Milwaukee and St. Paul railroad sends the following to S. S. Merrill, General Manager:

CHICAGO, Oct. 9—5:15 P. M.

"The fire on the South Side has worked back to Twelfth street, taking all before it. The West Side is comparatively safe yet, unless the fire crosses from the North Side about three quarters of a mile north of the depot. Our Milwaukee engines are doing noble duty, in keeping the fire from catching on the West Side of the river. Not a newspaper building was standing at 6 o'clock this morning. Such a fire would not have left a stone standing. If the fire extends to the West Side by a change of wind, before rain falls, all will be lost and utterly desolate. I cannot find my own people. Though the suffering is so great and general, only the poor people complain.

There is nothing we can do at present, unless to open our homes to the sufferers. Ruins mark their late residences, and it is not possible that anything but life could be saved from the awful grasp of the fire fiend."

AT MILWAUKEE.

The public and private buildings are thrown open to the Chicago sufferers, and food and supplies sent by extra trains. The utmost sympathy is expressed here for them. There was full ten car loads of provisions forwarded from here this morning.

Hon. C. H. Larkin, who went in charge of the provisions, telegraphs to the Mayor of Milwaukee that they arrived safely with the supplies, and will distribute them at once. Thousands of people are on the prairies without shelter or food.

We suggest to our citizens that to-morrow they send provisions on the first train. You cannot send too much.

There was a slight rain here this afternoon, but none has fallen in Chicago up to this hour, 9 o'clock.

The fires are raging within three miles of this city.

TO-DAY'S DISPATCHES.

THE GREAT FIRE.

UNEQUALED IN HISTORY.

2,000 ACRES BURNED OVER.

Best Part of Chicago.

The Loss $500,000,000.

HOW THE FIRE BEGAN.

A Lamp Kicked Over by a Cow.

Limits of the Conflagration.

Its March Now Arrested.

A Timely Rain Last Night.

THE CHICAGO FIRE.

CHICAGO, Oct. 10—8 A. M.

The conflagration which has swept over this city for the last forty eight hours has been nearly checked. A heavy rain last night, helped greatly. The West Side has mainly escaped.

CHICAGO, Oct. 10.

The great fire commenced on the corner of Twelfth and DeKoven streets, at half past 9 o'clock, occasioned, it is said, by a cow kicking over a lamp. The fire spread rapidly in an easterly and northeasterly direction, to Jefferson street and Clinton, and from Clinton and Canal it swept onward, crossing Canal street to the river, everything going down in its terrible path, until it reached Van Buren street, where it ceased between these streets, and burned to the river. Everything on the river front, from Taylor street to Van Buren street, was burned. At 3 o'clock, A. M., the great National Elevator caught fire and was consumed, throwing a lurid sheet of flame high up into the heavens.

The raging element crossed the river about twelve o'clock near Taylor street and with its fiery tongue licked up, as if it were a feast, as it advanced, whatever was within its reach. Still onward it marched, right through this portion of the doomed city northward and eastward to Harrison street, thence north to the river and lake, consuming all the principal business portion of the city upon Van Buren, Jackson, Adams, Monroe, Madison, Washington, Randolph, Lake and South Water streets, and upon Market, Franklin, Wells, La Salle, Clark, Dearborn, State, Wabash and Michigan avenues.

All this portion of the city, wherein was its vast wealth and most beautiful and costly structures, full of merchandise and valuable property of every description, which made it the pride of our western world, went down in the general havoc and ruin. Crossing at Wells street bridge, the fire fiend sped onward, taking a northeasterly direction to Lincoln Park, full two and a half miles from this last point, involving all that portion of the city east to the lake, in total destruction, and the latest dispatches left the consuming scourge creeping westerly towards the North Branch, upon which are large rolling mills, furnaces, tanneries, distilleries and coal yards. The whole of this great conflagration, covers over 2,000 acres of ground of the most valuable portions of Chicago, and involves a loss of $500,000,000.

Washburn and Doolittle—Joint Discussion.

The following times and places of meeting have been fixed upon for the joint discussion between Gen. Washburn and ex-Senator Doolittle:

Portage City—Tuesday, Oct. 10.
Eau Claire—Saturday, Oct. 14.
La Crosse—Thursday, Oct. 19.
Janesville—Saturday, Oct. 21.
Mineral Point—Wednesday, Oct. 25.
Lancaster—Friday, Oct. 27.
Milwaukee—Tuesday, Oct. 31.

These discussions are to take place in the afternoon, commencing about one o'clock. The speakers alternate at the different places, the opening to occupy one hour, the one following to occupy one hour and a half, the one who opened to occupy one hour in reply, and the other to conclude in half an hour. These meetings to be presided over by two Presidents, one to be named by the friends of each, and during the afternoon of the discussion no other political meetings are to be held in the same town.

Appointments for Governor Fairchild and Hon. G. W. Hazleton.

Gov. FAIRCHILD and Hon. G. W. HAZLETON, M. C., will speak at the following places and at the times stated. Evening meetings.

Mauston, Oct. 11.
Clinton Junction, October 16.
Genova, October 17.
Brodhead, October 18.
Monroe, October 19.
Albany, October 20.
Lodi, October 23.
Baraboo, October 24.
Palmyra, October 25.
Omro, October 27th, Friday.
Berlin, October 28th, Saturday.
Wautoma, October 30th, Monday.
Waupaca, October 31st, Tuesday.
Stevens Point, November 1st, Wednesday.
Grand Rapids, November 2d, Thursday.
New Lisbon, November 3d, Friday.

Appointments for General Washburn.

Gen. C. C. WASHBURN will speak at the following places during the ensuing canvass, viz:

Watertown, October 9.
Baraboo, October 11.
Jefferson, October 12.
Tomah, October 16.
Monroe, October 23.
Darlington, October 24.
Platteville, October 26.
Menomonee, November 2.
Hudson, November 3.
River Falls, November 4.

Such meetings to be held in each case in the evening.

Appointments for Hon. Geo. C. Hazleton Hon. Wm. Pitt Dewey and Nelson Wheeler.

Hon. GEO. C. HAZLETON Hon. WM. PITT DEWEY and NELSON WHEELER will speak at—

Bloomington, October 12.
Glen Haven, October 13.
Beetown, October 14.

Appointments of Attorney General Barlow.

Attorney General BARLOW will speak at the following places:

Lake Mills, October 17.
Fort Atkinson, October 18.
Evansville October 20.
Prairie du Sac, October 23.
Viroqua, October 26.

Second Assembly District Convention.

A Republican Convention for the Second Assembly District of Dane County, comprising the towns of Blooming Grove, Burke, Dunn, Windsor and the city of Madison, will be held at the Court House, in the city of Madison, on Saturday, October 21st, at 2 o'clock P. M., for the purpose of nominating a candidate for Member of Assembly, and to transact such other business as may be deemed proper.

Each town and ward will be entitled to five delegates in said Convention.

ANDREW SEXTON, Chairman District Committee.

MADISON, Oct. 6, 1871.

Republican Caucus—Blooming Grove.

A Republican Caucus for the town of Blooming Grove, will be held at the office of Judge Bryant, at the Court House, in the city of Madison, on Saturday Oct. 14, at 2 o'clock P. M., for the purpose of electing delegates to attend the Assembly District Convention.

By order of the Committee.

WISCONSIN STATE JOURNAL.

VOLUME XXIII. MADISON, WIS., TUESDAY AFTERNOON, JUNE 1, 1875. NO. 228.

STATE JOURNAL.

THE OFFICIAL STATE PAPER.

Republican State Convention.

MADISON, Wis., May 20, 1875.

A State Convention representing the Republican Party of Wisconsin, is hereby called to meet at the Capitol, in Madison, at 12 o'clock M., on

Wednesday, July 7, 1875,

for the purpose of placing in nomination candidates for election for State officers to be supported by the party at the next general election, and to transact such other business as may be deemed appropriate.

Each Senate and Assembly District will be entitled to two delegates in the convention.

E. W. KEYES, Chairman.

FRANK LELAND, ELIHU COLEMAN,
J. T. MOAK, ROBERT MCCURDY,
J. H. VIVIAN, H. B. COLES,
I. M. BEAN, J. T. KINGSTON,

Republican State Central Committee.

The Third Term Bugaboo.

The action of the Pennsylvania Republicans in pronouncing emphatically against a third term, has brought out a letter from the President. We give it in full. He is not a candidate for renomination, and would not accept unless under extraordinary circumstances, which he frankly says are "not likely to arise."

The Democrats, who are disappointed by this letter, intended to silence their third term thunder, pretend to doubt its sincerity. They doubtless judge him by his first Democratic opponent, ex-Gov. SEYMOUR, who said he could not be the candidate of the Democrats, and then put his whole strength into the struggle to secure the executive office. But President GRANT means what he says, in declaring that he is not a candidate, and people will take him at his word. Ninety-nine in every hundred Republicans, the vast majority of the people who speak plainly, saying what they mean, will believe the President means precisely what he says.

THE MECKLENBURG DECLARATION.—Prof BUTLER was Chairman of the meeting in the Historical Rooms when Secretary DRAPER read an exhaustive and very valuable paper on the Mecklenburg resolutions, yesterday. Mr. DRAPER has devoted much time to this subject. He visited the place and has examined all accessible records, whether in print or manuscript. The alleged declaration of the 20th was never taken to Congress, or published in a paper until 1819. No one ever professed to have the original. That of the 31st was taken to Congress, and was published in four contemporary papers, and it was a retraction to a great extent of the supposed declaration of independence of the 20th, that is, it looked to a reconciliation with Britain. The phraseology of the first declaration was so far identical with the one drawn by JEFFERSON that one or the other must have been a plagiarism. When it was published in 1819, both JEFFERSON and ADAMS doubted its genuineness. BANCROFT repudiates it.

These points, presented with elaborate minuteness, convinced those present that the so-called declaration of the 20th was bogus. The paper is to be published, and will be an important contribution to historical literature of special interest at this time.

THE Democrats of North Carolina are not satisfied with reconstruction. One of the leading organs of the party, the Charlotte *Democrat*, says: "No North Carolinian would say that he is willing to surrender his claim for damages in the unlawful emancipation and deprivation of personal property, although we are all now opposed to re-establishing slavery in any shape." This was written in denunciation of a legislative act providing for calling a constitutional convention wherein it is declared that no plan, "or amendment or scheme of compensation to the owners of emancipated slaves shall be adopted." The Democrats insist on their right to claim pay for slaves. They cling to this as one of their inalienable privileges, after the late amendments to the constitution are declared null and void.

REVENUE ARRESTS.—The *Wisconsin* reports Court Commissioner BLOODGOOD busy on Monday. The cases of PHILIP WEIMER, AUGUST BERGENTHAL, AARON SCHOENFELDT, VICTOR SCHILTZ and W HOVEY were continued. WM. H. RODDIS, United States Gauger, was arrested on the charge of making false gauges. He marked a barrel, it is said as containing 5 gallons, which contained 45 gallons, when it reached Rock Island. He was held in bonds of $2,500, the Commissioner being busy with the RINDSKOPF Brothers, brought before him for examination. The counsel for defendants claimed that the complaint was not properly drawn in this last case, as it gave a copy of the law, instead of making specific charges.

CAPTURED AT LAST.—The La Crosse *Democrat* states that Gen. VAN STEENWYK, ex-mayor, ex-bank comptroller, and for many years president of the Batavian Bank of that city, was married a week or two since in Geneva, Switzerland, to a young lady formerly of Madison, but now of Chicago, who is traveling in Europe with relations.

☞ The report of M. L. HALE, Special Agent of the Treasury Department, on the custom service, shows that a large number of the interior ports of entry and delivery do not pay expenses, and it is not improbable that several of them will be abolished.

☞ The Secretary of State has received a letter from Minister WASHBURNE, at Paris, stating that SEVALLION BROWN, the Chief Clerk of the State Dypartment, who left for Europe for his health, is lying very low of consumption.

☞ The Secretary of the Treasury has instructed the Assistant Treasurer of the United States at New York to sell $500,000 in gold each Thursday during June. Total amount to be sold, $2,000,000.

☞ Peaches promise finely in the Michigan fruit belt, owing to late rains.

PRESIDENT GRANT'S LETTER

Settling Third Term Question.

Why He Speaks Now and Not Before.

President GRANT has written a letter to Gen. HARVEY WHITE, President of the recent Pennsylvania Republican State Convention, in regard to which a Washington dispatch to the Chicago *Tribune* says:

Gen. Grant is not and never has been a candidate for the Presidency for a third term. The President to-night, over his own name, has forever closed the third-term discussion. The simple words which he spoke to the Indians on Thursday, when he said he wanted to have such provision made for them as would be respected by his successor, and other administrations in future, were a reflex of his thought upon the third term. He had then in mind the letter which now appears. A draft of a portion of it was written before the Pennsylvania Convention. After the adoption of the third-term resolution by the Pennsylvania Convention, the President decided to complete the letter, which he had so long contemplated. To this fact the President refers in his letter when he says that he had determined to take no notice of the agitation of this question so long as it was confined to Opposition newspapers, but when the State which is second in rank in the Union, through the Republican party Convention, considered it worthy of notice, he thought it was time to speak. The letter, which was begun several days ago, was completed to-day. This afternoon some of the Cabinet officers were called to hear it read, and were furnished with copies. This evening it was taken to the office of the Associated Press, and given to the country. It is as follows:

EXECUTIVE MANSION,
WASHINGTON, D. C., May 29, 1875.

DEAR SIR: A short time previous to the Presidential election of 1872 the press, a portion of it hostile to the Republican party, and particularly so to the Administration, started the cry of "Cæsarism" and the "Third Term," calling lustily for me to define my position on the latter subject. I believed it to be beneath the dignity of the office which I have been twice called upon to fill, to answer such a question before the subject should be presented by competent authority to make a nomination, or by a body of such dignity and authority as not to make a reply a fair subject of ridicule. In fact I have been surprised that so many sensible persons in the Republican party should permit their enemy to force upon them and their party an issue which cannot add strength to the party, no matter how met. But a body of the dignity and party authority of a convention to make nominations for State officers of the second State in the Union having considered this question, I deem it not improper that I should now speak.

In the first place, I never sought the office for a second, nor even for a first, nomination. To the first I was called from a life position, one created by Congress expressly for me for supposed services rendered to the Republic. The position vacated I liked. It would have been most agreeable to me to have retained it until such time as Congress might have consented to my retirement with the rank and a portion of the emoluments, which I so much needed, to a home where the balance of my days might be spent in peace and the enjoyment of domestic quiet, relieved from cares which have oppressed me so constantly now for fourteen years. But I was made to believe that the public good called me to make the sacrifices. Without seeking the office for the "second term," the nomination was tendered to me by a unanimous vote of the delegates of all the States and Territories selected by the Republicans of each to represent their whole number for the purpose of making their nomination. I cannot say that I was not pleased at this and at the overwhelming indorsement which their action received at the election following. But it must be remembered that all the sacrifices, except that of comfort, had been made in accepting the "first term." Then, too, such a fire of personal abuse and slander had been kept up for four years, notwithstanding the conscientious performance of my duties to the best of my understanding, though I admit, in the light of subsequent events, many times subject to fair criticism. Then, an indorsement from the people, who alone govern republics, was a gratification that it is only human to have appreciated and enjoyed.

Now, for the "third term." I do not want it any more than I did the first. I would not write or utter a word to change the will of the people in expressing and having their choice. The question of the number of terms allowed to any one Executive can only come up fairly in the shape of a proposition to amend the Constitution,—a shape in which all political parties can participate,—fixing the length of time or the number of terms which any one person shall be eligible for the office of President. Until such an amendment is adopted the people cannot be restricted in their choice by resolution further than they are now restricted as to age, nationality, etc. It may happen in the future history of the country that to change an Executive because he has been eight years in office will prove unfortunate, if not disastrous. The idea that any man could elect himself President, or even nominate himself, is preposterous. It is a reflection upon the intelligence and patriotism of the people to suppose such a thing possible. Any man can destroy his chances for the office, but no one can force an election or even nomination. To recapitulate: I am not nor have I ever been a candidate for renomination. I would not accept a nomination if it were tendered, unless it should come under such circumstances as to make it an imperative duty—circumstances not likely to arise. I congratulate the Convention over which you presided for the harmony which prevailed, and for the excellent ticket put in the field, and which I hope may be triumphantly elected. With great respect, your obedient servant, U. S. GRANT.

To GEN. HARRY WHITE, President Pennsylvania Republican State Convention.

The Madison Mutual.

The best evidence of the soundness of an insurance company, is found in its prompt payment of losses. In this respect, the Madison Mutual Insurance Company has always stood in the front rank. We copy below an article from the Oshkosh *Times* of the 29th ult., and would commend it to the attention of the people of the state. The *Times* says:

SOUND COMPANY.—The Madison Mutual Insurance Company has demonstrated that it has backbone, and ranks among the best companies in the state. Some of the "adjusters" for other companies, when they would run across a person who had lost his property, and his only hope was a policy he held in the Madison, they would shake their heads and hint that they would not give much for said policy, and finally when George A. Mason, one of the most substantial citizens of Madison, appeared in the city as adjuster for the Madison company, and settled the losses without the usual wrangling, the looks of astonishment that came over said opposition agents' faces was good to behold. The Madison company lost some $28,499, and in the July fire, 1874, they paid $23,807.12. It should be a matter of pride for the citizens to sustain the Madison Mutual, as they pay their losses without grumbling. The Madison Mutual stands well in Oshkosh.

THE NAVAL ACADEMY.—The annual examination of cadet midshipmen will commence at the naval academy on the 10th of June, and will close about the 20th, after which the graduating class will go on the usual cruise, on the *Constellation*. The graduating class this year numbers 32. There are about 75 candidates for admission to the academy. Their examination will begin about the 21st of June, and will close about the end of the month.

BARNUM'S FAT WOMAN DEAD.—Mrs. Rohm, the fat woman of Barnum's show, died at her residence in East Baltimore, May 28th, aged 29. Her weight was 583 pounds, height 6 feet 4 inches, and span around waist 72 inches. She was born in Licking county, Ohio. Her maiden name was Hannah Jane Duck.

WHISKEY SEIZURE.—About 1,000 barrels of whiskey have been seized at New York, 20 barrels belonging to Rindskopf Brothers, of the First District of Wisconsin, 10 barrels to L. Tuescher, of the First District of Missouri, and 210 to R. W. Ulrich, of St. Louis.

GRASS HOPPERS DROWNED OUT.—A telegram from Kansas City, dated Thursday, says rain had fallen over an area of one hundred miles for twenty four hours. The torrent flooded and washed out the lowlands in some localities, damaged fences and railroad embankments, and also injured the growing crops slightly. But the damage is trifling compared with the benefit, caused by the wholesale destruction of grasshoppers by the rain. They were drowned out by millions. The gutters and sewers at Kansas City, and all the streams within the area of the rain fall, were full of the little pests. The Missouri river opposite Kansas City has been black with them, and the engineer of the railroad bridge reports that hardly any estimate of the number that has floated past is possible. Hundreds of people have witnessed this gratifying sight. There is no question but the bulk of the insects have been destroyed by the flood, and there is every prospect there will be few left to trouble the farmers in the open fields. The ground in places is thick with dead grasshoppers that have been killed by the beating rain.

DEATH IN A STREET CAR.—The following pathetic story is told by the San Francisco *Bulletin* of May 12th: A sad incident occurred to-day in a Fourth street car. On Kearny street, some distance beyond the City Hall, a lady stepped aboard the car, having in her arms a babe some five or six weeks old. The child was evidently in pain, and moaned and writhed in the mother's arms. She seemed to suffer accutely from anxiety for the little one, whose face was turning rapidly to a livid deathly color. The passengers were interested in the painful anxiety of the woman, and when she burst into tears and pressed the infant to her arms and kissed the cold lips, there was not a dry eye in the car. It had died apparently without any strong spasm of agony. For a few moments before it breathed its last it was perfectly quiet. The car stopped at Mission and Fourth streets, and the weeping mother left with the infant's body in her arms.

THE WISCONSIN CENTRAL. — At the annual election of Directors of the Wisconsin Central Railroad in Milwaukee, on the 27th, Gardner Colby was re-elected President, Charles L. Colby, Vice-President; and E. N. Abbott, Secretary and Treasurer. Three Directors retired, namely, George Reed, Samual Gould, and M. Wadleigh, and the two latter were re-elected, H. L. Palmer being elected in the place of Reed. Immediately after the meeting, Reed, who was formerly Vice-President and lately counsel for the road, went over to Hon. Matt H. Carpenter and instructed Carpenter & Murphy to commence suit against President Colby for $300,000. This is understood to be a claim for certain portions of the property, stock in trust, etc., now held by Colby, but really belonging to Reed and the interests represented by him.

NEWSPAPER FAILURES.—Rowell's forthcoming "Newspaper Directory" shows the failure of over 1,000 newspapers in this country during the past year, the loss to publishers, subscribers and advertisers amounting to over $8,000,000, the *Republic*, of New York, alone losing half a million. Among those who went into the newspaper business and lost heavily thereby were 275 merchants and adventurers, 315 school teachers, 57 lawyers, 4 blacksmiths, 33 plasterers, 10 farmers, 200 fanatics of various classes afflicted with literary lesion, 100 ambitious but visionary young men who drew upon their fathers, and thus suddenly exhausted large margins of paternal capital, and six lottery men.

RESPECTFULLY DECLINES.—An overture by the General Assembly of the Presbyterian Church, inviting the various branches of the Reformed Church to unite in holding an Ecumenical Council, is declined by the General Synod of the Reformed Church now in session at Fort Wayne. The latter body, while cordially sympathizing with the proposed movement, respectfully refuses to take part in it, for the reason that the Reformed Church represented by the Synod recognizes the Heidelberg Catechism as the only confession of binding authority, while the proposed Council contemplates participation only by such Churches as hold to the Westminster Confession.

FRIDAY'S FIRES.—The business portion of Great Bend, in Susquehanna county, Pa., was destroyed by an incendiary fire Friday night; loss $100,000. Two banks and ten stores are included in the destruction. Portland, a suburb of St. John, N. B., was almost entirely consumed Friday; 68 houses and shops and much other property were destroyed; loss $250,000. An extensive furniture factory at Worcester, Mass., was destroyed Friday night; loss, $262,000; also a woolen factory at Cleveland, O.; loss, $60,000; a nail factory at Wheeling, W. Va.; loss, $75,000. Great fires are raging in the Michigan pine forests in the vicinity of Bay City and Grand Haven.

THE ISTHMUS CANAL.—The surveying party sent out by the Government to locate the line of the proposed ship canal across the Isthmus of Panama, having completed the work, have returned. The expedition was subjected to numerous hardships and dangers to health, but there was no loss of life among the officers or men. The early estimate of $56,000,000 for the completion of the work is not now regarded as sufficient. The Napipi Atrato route is the shortest, but requires five and one half miles of tunnelling.

AN IOWA TRAGEDY.—At Moulton, Iowa, on the 27th ult., A. McAaron was shot by Major Moore, of that place. Mr. McAaron received three wounds, one of which, being in the region of the heart, caused his death in a few hours. Major Moore is now under arrest. An old feud between the men was the cause of the quarrel. Both were respectable citizens of the place, McAaron being a druggist, and Moore a dry goods merchant. Great excitement prevails over the affair.

A BANK HERO.—A hero has been found in the person of a bank cashier. His name is Deland, of the National Mahawie Bank, of Great Barrington, Mass. A band of masked burglars captured him and the bank's keys, at his residence, and forced him to accompany them to the bank and to open its doors, but he persistently refused to unlock the vaults for them. They then left him in the bank, and returning to his house, robbed it and escaped. That cashier deserves to be immortalized.

PRESIDENTIAL FAMILY PERSONALS.—The President's son-in-law, Mr. Sartoris, has decided to enter the banking firm of Grant & Sherman, and will reside permanently in Washington. He will occupy the Drexel cottage at Long Branch this summer. Rumor says the President will shortly be a grandfather.

— Potter Palmer and family, with Mrs. Colonel Grant, have been guests at the White House all the week.

☞ A gang of counterfeiters, five Italians and one woman, were captured at New Orleans on Saturday evening. They had $500 in counterfeit nickles, dies, plates, etc.

PIONEER PUBLIC LIBRARY.

MADISON LEADS THE STATE.

AN AUSPICIOUS OPENING.

Large Audience at City Hall.

Many Additions of New Books

Interesting Addresses by Prest. Ford, Mayor Pinney, Prest. Bascom, State Supt. Searing, and Prof. J. D. Butler.

Monday evening, May 31st, was a most auspicious occasion for Madison, the inauguration of her Free City Library, the first in the state. Though there had been rain late in the afternoon and more was threatened, the air was pleasant, and the people seemed easily disposed to leave their homes and to demonstrate by their presence, the lively interest they feel in the establishment of an institution that cannot but prove to our city a beneficent means of social and intellectual growth and progress. Some time before the hour appointed for the meeting, the rooms of the old Madison Institute Library were thrown open, and were thronged with citizens, who had come to contribute books, at the invitation of the directors of the new library, to join in the ceremonies and listen to the able and interesting addresses prepared for the occasion. After examining the excellent and quite extensive library, the custody and use of which, by the munificence of the Madison Institute, has now been transferred to the city, and adding some two hundred volumes to it, by voluntary contribution, the crowd passed on to the spacious hall, and soon filled every available seat with which it is provided. The stage was occupied by Mayor PINNEY, several members of the City Council, Judge BRALEY, G. P. DELAPLAINE, J. C. FORD, Esq., President of the Board of Directors of the Library, and the speakers of the occasion. The Lake City Cornet Band, which had taken their position in the gallery opposite them, struck up a lively air, after the excellent execution of which Mr. FORD read the following:

PRESIDENT'S ADDRESS.

FELLOW CITIZENS:—We have met this evening to celebrate the opening of our Free Library. In December, 1874, our City Council, acting under the authority granted by chapter 80 of the laws of 1872, passed an ordinance establishing a Public Library and Reading Room, and levied a tax for its support and maintenance, and the Mayor, with the consent of the Council, has appointed a board of directors, who have organized, elected their officers, and adopted rules and regulations for the government of the Library. Printed copies of these rules and regulations can be had by applying to the Librarian, at the Library rooms in the City Hall. The Library will open to-morrow, and will be open hereafter every day—Sundays and legal holidays excepted—from 10 to 12 o'clock in the forenoon, and from half-past 2 to half-past 5 in the afternoon. By the provisions of the act of the Legislature, before referred to, any Library and Reading Room established under said act, *shall be free to all the inhabitants of the city or village where such library is located*, subject only to such regulations as are deemed necessary by the Board of Directors, to render such Library and Reading Room of the greatest benefit to the greatest number. The only limitation the Directors have seen fit to make, that it is necessary to mention here, is that of age. Applicants for books must be of the age of 15 years and upwards. The reason of such a rule will be apparent to everyone. The Directors have not as yet opened the Reading Room contemplated by the law, but expect to do so as soon as rooms are provided for that purpose by the city. This we have good reason to believe will soon be done.

The sum raised by taxation is not large, and yet it is sufficient, with economy in the current expenses, to make handsome additions to the library each year. But we do not start upon this appropriation as our sole capital. To-night we take formal possession of the library of the Madison Institute, a library of nearly 3,500 volumes, and, which, for the excellence of its selections, I venture the assertion is not equaled by any library of its size in the State. With this surrender of its library, the Madison Institute steps down and out, and with this act closes a long and useful career. Organized in 1854, by some of our public spirited citizens (one of whom—Gen. DELAPLAINE—is with us to-night), it has continued for 21 years to be one of our cherished institutions. It was the lyceum and library combined. It has maintained a course of lectures for a long succession of years. It has maintained a debating department, and it has built up a library. Many of you remember the course of lectures instituted by it; how the tediousness of our long winter evenings was relieved by the lectures of EMERSON, and CHAPIN, and GILES, and TAYLOR, and EVERETT, and STARR KING, and GREELEY, and others, who then had something to say which we were glad to listen to. You remember, too, with pleasure, the festivals given by the ladies for the benefit of the library, where with fruits and flowers and their own presence, they made this hall for the time an enchanted place. You remember also the tableaux and charades and dramatic entertainments given by the friends of the Institute for the benefit of the library. And many of us remember the debating department, where our young lawyers and business men waged hot debate on questions which stirred and thrilled the country, but which are no longer questions, but accomplished facts.

As we turn from the minutes of the debates, how the faces of those eager young men stand out before us. There are HASKELL and RUBLEE, and JOHNSON and MAYHEW, and MCFARLAND and ROLLINS, and SPRAGUE and BALTZELL, and WAKELY and FIRMIN, and LEWIS. The bland MAYHEW is in the chair, and the contestants range themselves on either side; the debate waxes warm. But we cannot tarry; the debates are ended; the lectures have ceased: the flowers of the festivals have withered; the boys are growing old, but their works do follow them, and to-day the city reaps the fruit of their labors in the library which fills the shelves in the room below.

To-day the city takes possession of this valuable donation, and at the same time assumes the burden of its support. By the generosity of the members of the Institute and the wise action of our City Council we have a Public Library which is and shall remain *free to all our citizens*. I take great pleasure in announcing to this audience, and through it, to the public that the library is now *open*. And in behalf of the Directors I invite all our citizens, both young and old; both rich and poor, to avail themselves of its advantages. It is the earnest wish that the library may be used by all our citizens who love and need books. The Directors feel that they will be abundantly compensated for any labor of theirs in behalf of the library, when its books shall be in general use.

One more request we have to make. The Free Library is now a public institution, owned and controlled by the citizens of Madison—through its Mayor and Council for its existence and prosperity, then it *depends on the public favor*. Henceforth *public opinion* makes or unmakes it. I therefore invoke your influence in its behalf. The library is now a part of our educational system, and its public support is to be vindicated on the same grounds as our common school system. To the Mayor and Common Council of the city of Madison we owe our thanks for establishing and providing for the maintenance of this Free Library. I believe this Council will be remembered with gratitude by our citizens for this act of theirs. We hope and believe that in its administration, and the appointment of its directors, all political considerations will be ignored, and that its managers will be appointed solely in the interest of the library and its objects. *One word more.* The Directors wish it distinctly understood that this is a *Free Library* in a double sense: That it is *free to receive* as well as *free to give*. Its doors hang on double hinges and swing both ways. They will let you in as well as out. If any of you have a book which you have done with, here is the place for it. If any of you are about to travel, and know not where to place your library for safe keeping, leave it here. If any of you, when about to close your earthly career, are anxious to know how to dispose of your property so that it may be of permanent use to your fellow men, give your library to this association, and insert a clause in your will giving a few thousand dollars to be used in erecting a building for the accommodation of the library. So will you do good and your name be remembered.

MAYOR PINNEY'S ADDRESS.

On concluding his own remarks, the President introduced Hon. S. U. PINNEY, Mayor of the city, who read the following:

MR. PRESIDENT, LADIES AND GENTLEMEN—The founding and opening of a free library, which is to diffuse its advantages and confer its blessings on all alike, whether rich or poor, of whatever condition, is an enterprise and an event of marked public interest and importance.

The successful establishment of such an institution cannot but be regarded as an era in the history of this city, securing as it does all those signal advantages and beneficent influences which such and all similar institutions, when judiciously conducted, necessarily confer.

Many of us know, and others have been made acquainted, with the enterprising and praiseworthy efforts on the part of the founders, officers and prominent members of the Madison Institute, in securing to its membership the privilege of a library of over 3,500 volumes of useful and well selected books. This institution has served as a nucleus for the successful organization of the Free Library, which, under the most favorable auspices, is inaugurated to-night, and opens its doors to its wealth of knowledge and literary treasures to all our citizens. The custody and use of the Institute Library have been generously transferred to the Free Library, which now takes its place as an established institution of our city. In addition, a large number of new and judiciously selected books have been purchased with the funds of the new institution, derived from the last years' tax for its benefit; and this addition will, no doubt, be increased by about 1,000 volumes voluntarily donated by public-spirited citizens of our city who never fail to promptly respond to all such meritorious calls on their generosity.

The proceedings on this interesting occasion, without suitable mention of the disinterested and well directed action of the founders, prominent members and officers of the Madison Institute, would be singularly deficient, and to our citizens upon whom the duty of sustaining the *free* library is now devolved, they look, and justly too, for a full realization of all they had designed and so far and so well executed, to promote the important interests to be subscribed by such an institution.

For what they have done in founding the library of the Institute and in transferring to it, and in establishing the *free* one, which promises so much of usefulness in the future, they deserve the thanks and grateful remembrance of our people.

The *free* library which we inaugurate to-night and dedicate to the use of our people, is the first organized under the act of 1872, and to this city belongs the honor of founding and opening *the first free library in the State*—a distinction of which we will hereafter have reason to be justly proud, in that degree, in which we support and sustain it. The law provides for an annual tax of one-tenth of a mill on each dollar of valuation to increase the library and add to its efficiency and usefulness; a tax which was promptly levied by the Council of last year, to whom belongs the credit of passing the ordinance establishing our free library. This tax is a mere pittance in comparison with the benefits it will confer, and the duty to annually levy and collect it is no less obligatory and sacred than to provide for the support of our common schools. No good citizen will for a moment object to the exercise of the power of taxation for so beneficent a purpose, and any city officer, who, having the power, fails to see that this institution receives a generous and ample support—one commensurate with the intelligence, liberality and public spirit, in which it is founded, and which in the past have characterized the history of our city, will fall short, very far short, indeed, of an intelligent and wise discharge of public duty. I think that it may be safely asserted, that since the organization of our city, no act or ordinance has been passed by its Common Council which will in the future bring to the public more of real, substantial benefit and advantage than the ordinance establishing this our *free* library—the pioneer free library of Wisconsin.

I most heartily commend this institution thus organized, and managed as it is by a competent and eminently judicious directorship, to the generous confidence and liberal support of our people: and I particularly invite all our citizens to avail themselves of the excellent advantages it will afford. I believe it will be their pleasure and their pride to carry on successfully the work which has been so well begun, until soon we will have one of the most useful libraries in the northwest, embracing the wealth of informatinn and of literature of the English language, and of languages of all nationalities spoken in our midst, with a library room and lecture hall and all the appropriate adornments of art.

The influences of such an institution cannot but be beneficial and in the right direction; sending forth to all classes its wealth of knowledge and literary cheer, to quicken and enlighten the intellects, to correct the tastes, to improve the morals and mature the judgments of our people.

The necessity and demand of the country is not so much earnest and active labor, as it is labor intelligent, well and wisely directed; and in its capacity to supply this necessity, the importance and usefulness of this institution cannot be overestimated.

As a most important adjunct and auxiliary to this great system of popular education, reaching as it will those who, from mature years or other causes, have passed beyond the benefit of ordinary public educational advantages, it cannot but commend itself most favorably.

The earliest library of which any account remains, it is said, was founded in ancient Memphis, in the early days of antiquity, by an Egyptian King of the 12th dynasty, who placed it in a division of his palace, inscribing over the entrance the words, "The healing of the soul." Books are said to be the monuments of lives; and so of libraries—Free Libraries, such as this; they are the monuments of the progress and history of communities, of cities and of States; the most enduring in the lessons they teach and the influences they send forth, which any age or civilization can read.

Again, then, I most heartily commend this new enterprise, this Free Library, born of a liberal public spirit, to the patronage, support and confidence of a generous and intelligent city, trusting that our hopes and our labors will not be in vain; that it will speedily become one of the most useful, thoroughly supported, and highly prized of all our institutions; most completely filling its appropriate sphere of usefulness, and teaching only those lessons, and asserting those influences, which make men and communities intelligent, prosperous, wise and good.

PRESIDENT BASCOM,

of the State University, was next introduced, and made a short and spirited speech without notes, and of which we can only give a brief report.

Among our public institutions there are few that do us more honor than our public libraries; few that better express our private munificence and public wisdom; few that exert a more beneficent influence on the people in the diffusion of knowledge. He was in favor of restricting the power of the government so that individual wisdom and enterprise should have the largest scope, and believed the world had been governed and the people enervated by too much help. Government, however, should not withhold any means of public education, and much more might wisely be done in that direction than had been. It was not enough to give the elements of an education, but like plants started in hot beds, care should be taken in transplanting and fitting for life in the outer world. To supplement the school: the pulpit, the press, and the public libraries were most important in diffusing knowledge and stimulating intelligence, and the latter were of special value and their establishment most beneficial. In the Eastern States during the past few years much attention had been paid to this matter and many free libraries founded, so that there was scarcely a city of any size that had not its public library. The circulation of their volumes had rapidly increased and a growing interest was manifested. Many of these libraries were the result of private munificence. In Massachusetts there was a provision of law that dogs should be taxed and the proceeds devoted to popular education or public libraries, and as schools were generally well provided for otherwise, the avails were largely devoted to libraries, with excellent result. If he could feel that every dog he encountered on passing through the streets of Madison, every dog whose yelp he heard on the night air, was contributing to such a library as this, he should be glad.

In the future this library and its condition would be a certain index to the intelligence and common sympathy of the citizens of Madison, and it would do good work in every household. He gave his hand heartily to it. He was proud that Madison was the first city of the State to avail itself of the law providing for such libraries, and that the Capital occupies the van in the free library movement, so auspicious of good to the State.

After music by the band

STATE SUPT. SEARING

was introduced as the next speaker, and very impressively delivered the following address, which was very well received:

MR. PRESIDENT:—I hold that the founding of a Public Library is one of the most admirable enterprises that can engage the attention of a community. Before costly public buildings, before parks, before plans for laying out and adorning streets, before all other efforts at mere physical convenience or grace in city or village should be surely and wisely provided means for the culture of the people who dwell in it or are to dwell in it. The school and the library should be the first creation and care. The school usually is the first. For this the founders of an American State or city usually make immediate provision. Certain sections of land in the State or certain lots in the city are sacredly dedicated in the very beginning to the purpose of public instruction. Few public buildings in either antedate those of the school.

I have coupled the school and the library. Indeed these were so coupled—were recognized as twin necessities—by the founders of our own State, who, in the organic constitution, made joint provision for "common schools" *and libraries*, for "academies and normal schools" *and libraries*,—as if the library were an indispensable adjunct to the school of whatever grade. I think those founders were right. Libraries are indispensable adjuncts or supplements to schools, if the latter are to be, in anything like the highest sense, fruitful in good results. Merely to kindle a love for knowledge, and to show how knowledge can be obtained, without providing a source *whence* it may be obtained, is like lighting a lamp that is nearly destitute of oil; or it is to emulate the unwisdom of those who too frequently plant trees, and think that in the planting alone they have fulfilled the whole law; whereas, neglecting all but its first requirement, securing no permanent conditions of growth, the fierce suns and moisture-robbing winds of later summer parch the earth, and the buds and leaves of the earlier season droop and perish untimely. Oh! foolish planters of trees, losing the reward of one labor because neglecting another consequent but easier one. Oh! foolish founders of schools, seeking to make good and wise and happy men by a little formal instruction in a few arts or sciences in childhood, and then dooming the instructed to perpetual isolation from the great fountain of knowledge, and light, and wisdom, and joy flowing from books. The best that the common school can do, beyond imparting the mystery of two or three practically useful arts, is to qualify its pupils for an intelligent and joyful use of good books. A nobler, happier result I cannot conceive. It is well to be thoroughly conversant with the various branches of school lore, but it is decidedly better to be thoroughly in love with reading. Could the schools merely arouse this love in every youthful breast, their mission would be beneficent far beyond the present fact.

Not in the least extravagant were the words of Sir JOHN HERSCHELL. "If I were to pray for a taste," said he, "which should stand me in stead, under every variety of circumstances, and be a source of happiness and cheerfulness to me through life, and a shield against its ills, however things might go amiss, and the world frown upon me, it would be a taste for reading. Give a man this taste and you place him in contact with the best society in every period of history—with the wisest and the wittiest, with the tenderest, the bravest, and the finest characters which have adorned humanity. You make him a denizen of all nations, a contemporary of all ages. The world has been created for him. It is hardly possible but that his character should take a higher and better tone from the constant habit of associating with a class of thinkers, to say the least of it, above the average of human nature." Nor in the least extravagant was the speech of FENELON, when he said that "If all the riches of both the Indians; if the kingdoms of Europe were laid at his feet, in exchange for his love of reading, he would spurn them all." RUFUS CHOATE said: "Happy is he who has laid up in youth, and held fast in all fortune, a genuine and passionate love of reading. True balm of hurt minds; of surer and more healthful charm than 'poppy or mandragora, or all the drowsy syrups of the world';—by that single taste, by that single capacity, he may bound in a moment into the still region of delightful studies and be at rest."

With such sentiments book lovers everywhere are in hearty sympathy. A humbler, but no less devoted and enthusiastic lover of reading myself, I can add personal testimony that to this taste I owe the most substantial and enduring happiness I have known. And I will go further and say that looking back from my present standpoint over the past years of my life, I owe to the quiet reading and study of books out of school life, much more than to the formal work of my technical education. The latter was probably as good as the average, but the best part of it was the acquirement of the ability to make good use of books after school and college life was left. No man here is a more faithful, a more grateful devotee of reading. No one can rejoice more heartily in the enterprise that is here formally inaugurated to-night. No one believes more profoundly in its great and increasing value to the people of this city. Madison is not behind other cities in useful and honorable enterprise, but Madison, in thus founding a large public library—free to all her citizens alike, rich and poor—performs the noblest act in her history. A new source of just pride is opened to her people—may I say it is a source of more personal pride. Nature made her charming lakes and almost unrivaled landscapes. The state built her graceful Capitol and adorned her delightful park. But to the city itself is due all the honor of establishing this Free Library, which like Minerva from the brain of Jove, appears to spring into being with full stature and panoply.

For the city I rejoice at it. With the city I shall be proud of it. But with just pride and rejoicing come some other considerations of anxiety and regret. If I love books, I love rural life as much. The city has some peculiar charms for me, but the country has more. I love its quiet, its freedom, its healthful scenes and associations, its people. It appears to me that the country is a far better place in which to rear children than the city. Feeling and believing thus, I am jealous of the attractions of cities, and I look with sorrow and apprehension upon the change from rural to urban life, which is in all sections of the Union depleting the country of its best citizens. From farms to cities and villages are constantly going the most intelligent families, the most enterprising and useful. They go for the superior means of education, for better society, for a score of advantages which cities possess and the country does not, but might and ought to possess. It is my conviction that when in this country, as of old in the Roman Empire, all the intelligence and wealth shall be in cities, and the country shall be given over to mere laborers—unintelligent, unprogressive, serf-like—then the perils that beset Republicanism will be much greater and more numerous than they are to-day. And the drift appears to be in this direction. New England shows melancholy evidences of it. Even here in the newer West we see the manifest beginnings of the change.

To seek to give more advantages and attractions to rural life appears to me one of the first and plainest duties of patriotism in this Republic. Under this view the educational facilities of the country ought to be trebled. Facilities for better and higher instruction ought to be devised. To this end it occurred to me that a system of Town High Schools and a system of Town Libraries might be inaugurated which should be a means of giving greater value, dignity and permanence to country life. The High School plan received the approval of the last legislature and promises to become a success. The Library scheme is the chief educational effort of the present year and will be the leading feature of the next annual report of the department of instruction.

In this matter, however, I find I was so fully anticipated by a distinguished predecessor, and now honored resident of this city, that I hope to find comparatively easy the revival of a law that once, through his efforts, had place upon the statute book, that would have wrought for Wisconsin the great blessing this Free Library will bring to its Capital, but for the accident of a civil war, and that I trust will yet be in substance restored.

I hope the report of the proceedings here to-night will fly on the wings of the wind, to every section of the State, will stir up emulation in many another city more destitute of books and book-lovers than this, and will aid somewhat in the speedy establishment of a State Library system that shall at no distant day, bless every village and township within its fair borders.

PROF. BUTLER'S ADDRESS.

President FORD said he was glad to be able to announce, on the authority of Judge BALTZELL, that the Library had already received additions by contributions of over 200 new books, many of them quite valuable. The next speaker would be Prof. J. D. BUTLER. If we could have him with us always to consult, there would be less need of libraries, but as we could not, it was desirable to obtain from him all we could, and the audience would now have an opportunity for half or three quarters of an hour, to get from him a little of his learning. Prof. BUTLER then proceeded to deliver the principal address of the evening, which was listened to with close attention, and called forth frequent applause and laughter:

LIBRARIES AS LEAVEN.

My subject is, LIBRARIES AS LEAVEN, or the relation of Libraries to the increase and diffusion of knowledge.

What is a Library? It is the knowledge of all brought within the reach of each one. It is an expanded encyclopædia, or the books which are, or ought to be, consulted in compiling a perfect encyclopedia.

Human knowledge,—and hence the books in which it is treasured up,—is divided by some authors into forty departments. I have their names here all written down,—but I dare not read them. [See Note.] You would give no more quarter to such a catalogue—than the lover gave to the mercantile inventory of his sweetheart's charms, when itemized as "two lips indifferent red," "two gray eyes with lids to them," and so on.

But all these forty classes of knowledge ought to be represented in a Library, and the more largely the better. They should also mingle there in due proportion, "parts into parts reciprocally shot, and all so forming a harmonious whole." "If the whole body were an eye, where were the hearing?"

I once lived in a town of a thousand families, where, through a legacy, one copy of some single author was annually presented to each family. But, with the same money, a thousand different works might have been every year purchased, and all kept accessible by all the families. The result would have been a feast as appetizing to all palates as the miraculous manna which the rabbins tell us tasted to each Jew like that particular dainty which he loved best.

It is no objection to a Library that no man will ever read it through. No man will read through his dictionary. The day is not long enough for a man to read all words in the daily *Tribune*. Nor will any customer exhaust a store. Yet he demands an assortment from which to select the little that he needs. In every Library most authors, bound up in congenial calf, sleep soundly in their own sheets. Yet the dust of dead men's bones at the touch of genius comes forth in a new life. How much that is best in MACAULAY and BUCKLE is extracted from bibliothecal rubbish,—or reading which had never been read. Hence even SAMSON could not say to the jaw-bone of an ass: "I have no need of you." The wise thank God for fools. They get their living out of them, and mostly out of the greatest fools. In truth no Library is large enough. GUIZOT and MICHELET complain of inability to consult certain books, even in that Parisian Library, where books are as plenty as water in the deluge, and the shelves would reach from here to Milwaukee.

A library should be a cosmos; but it is a chaos, till arrangement, catalogues and librarians bring us at once the volume we desire, and which, without them, would be as hard to fish up as the Atlantic cable lost in mid-ocean.

"Thus war-like arms in magazines we place,
All ranged in order and disposed with grace;
Not thus alone the curious eye to please,
But to be *found*, when need requires, with ease."

In some libraries, however, books are arranged on a system which seems borrowed from Spanish hospitals, where patients are arranged according to religious creeds, rather than bodily complaints. Every library has more volumes than I can master; but no library, though it be the conflux of all civilizations, has so many volumes as I may need to consult.

Chief Justice STORY used to assert that no

WISCONSIN STATE JOURNAL.

VOLUME XXIV. MADISON, WIS., SATURDAY AFTERNOON, JULY 8, 1876. NO. 268.

STATE JOURNAL.

THE OFFICIAL STATE PAPER.

REPUBLICAN TICKET.

FOR PRESIDENT—

R. B. Hayes,

OF OHIO.

FOR VICE-PRESIDENT—

William A. Wheeler,

OF NEW YORK.

PRESIDENTIAL ELECTORS—

At Large—W. H. HINER, Fond du Lac.
FRANCIS CAMPBELL, Lafayette.
First District—T. D. WEEKS, Walworth.
Second do T. D. LANG, Sauk.
Third do J. H. MINER, Richland.
Fourth do C. M. SANGER, Milwaukee.
Fifth do CHAS. LULING, Manitowoc.
Sixth do J. H. FOSTER, Winnebago.
Seventh do C. B SOLBERG, La Crosse.
Eighth do JOHN H. KNAPP, Dunn.

CAMPAIGN STATE JOURNAL.

Newspapers are the Best Campaign Documents.

A Word to Patriotic Politicians.

The pending Presidential Campaign will be an exciting one. The result deeply concerns every good citizen, and a weighty responsibility rests upon all voters—upon all who can influence electors. Men who want to increase the vote in their town, county or district, will find that a Newspaper does the best of work. It lasts beyond the present.

The most effective of all agencies in a campaign is a political paper, and now is the time to present the facts, and make correct impressions on the minds of readers.

The STATE JOURNAL will contain important speeches, documents, letters and political intelligence, besides the general and local news of the day. It is offered at the following reduced rates for the campaign:

Daily four months, - - - -	$3-35
Tri-Weekly four months, - - -	1.65
Weekly four months, - - - -	50

It will be mailed, post paid, at the above rates, to single subscribers and clubs.

A paper sent to a non-reading or non-voting neighbor, afflicted with apathy or involved in doubt, may prove his political salvation. The salvation of a soul, politically, is worth more than fifty-cents to his neighborhood and to the public generally. Try it. Address

ATWOOD & CULVER,
Madison, Wis.

Tilden as a Protestant.

With the possible exception of JAMES BUCHANAN, the Democratic party never had a man so slippery as SAMUEL J. TILDEN. Whenever he is cornered on a bad record, his response, through the medium of a proxy, is that he protested at the time, or didn't know, or wasn't responsible. For instance, TILDEN moved, in the Chicago Convention, for a Committee to prepare a platform, and he was made a member of the Committee that drew the infamous peace plank as follows:

"*Resolved*, That this Convention does explicitly declare, as the sense of the American people, that, after four years of failure to restore the Union by the experiment of war,—during which, under the pretense of a military necessity of war power higher than the Constitution, the Constitution itself has been disregarded in every part, and public liberty and private right alike trodden down, and the material prosperity of the country essentially impaired,—justice, humanity, liberty and the public welfare demand that immediate efforts be made for a cessation of hostilities, with a view to an ultimate Convention of the States, or other peaceable means, to the end that at the earliest practicable moment peace may be restored on the basis of the Federal States."

No word of public protest was heard from TILDEN against this, but when the Chicago *Times* referred to it fourteen years afterwards, and declared or intimated that it would utterly ruin TILDEN's chances in the Presidential race, Slippery SAM obtained a statement from a zealous friend, that he had protested against the plank. Was he afraid to protest at the time, or so weak and worthless that his protest amounted to nothing? If he was not able fourteen years ago to control Northern Democrats, who called for peace when we were in a mighty struggle to save the Union, will he be able now to control Northern Democrats, with all the Southern fire-eaters of the BEN HILL and BOB TOOMBS school added?

Again, he was hand and glove with TWEED when that great thief was gorging himself with plunder and stuffing ballot boxes, to perpetuate the reign of Democracy. TILDEN was the guide, advisor, friend and Chairman of the Central Committee. Was he so stupid as not to know or suspect that TWEED was stealing millions and millions of dollars right under his nose? If so, he is utterly unfit to be President. The thieves would steal the treasury empty with a President as blind, inefficient or willing as TILDEN was in TWEED's days of high handed robbery.

We recently published a circular signed by TILDEN as Chairman, calling on Democrats to telegraph immediately at the close of the polls in 1868, to WM. M. TWEED an estimate of results. The plain object and intent of this circular was to get information as to what the honest vote was, so that TWEED & Co. might return a sufficient number of fraudulent votes in New York to carry the election. And now we have a declaration that "Slippery Sam's" circular was "issued without his knowledge." When he heard of it, "he protested at once against such a use of his name, or the issue of the document itself." So this poor tool of TWEED lifted up his hands and protested in vain, did he? This hero of Democracy, who is to "*reform*," "REFORM," "REFORM," was a mere nose of wax in the fingers of the big thief. It is very likely that the chairman of the Central Committee would assent to the forgery of his name and allow the State to be shingled with the circular "without his knowledge." He is a nice man to run for President. We want some one who has sufficient force and shrewdness to prevent pirates from stealing the Treasury dry and forging his name to all sorts of papers.

But let us turn to the testimony of one who is greater than "Wingate" or any one else yet heard from, to-wit: the Democratic candidate for President in the year of grace 1872—HORACE GREELEY. He fixes the responsibility, and he does this from a full knowledge of what he is talking about, one year after the frauds were perpetrated. From an open letter to TILDEN, written by HORACE GREELEY in 1869, we take the following:

Mr. Tilden, you cannot escape responsibility by saying, with the guilty Macbeth,

"Thou can'st not say I did it; never shake
Those gory locks at me!"

For you were, at least, a passive accomplice in the great frauds of last November. Your name was used, without public protest on your part, in circulars sowed broadcast over the State, whereof the manifest intent was to "make assurance doubly sure" that the frauds here perpetrated should not be overborne by the honest vote of the rural districts. And you, not merely by silence, but by positive assumption, have covered those frauds with the mantle of your respectability. On the principle that "the receiver is as bad as the thief." YOU ARE AS DEEPLY IMPLICATED IN THEM TO-DAY AS THOUGH YOUR NAME WERE TWEED, O'BRIEN, OR OAKEY HALL.

* * * *

And though our city has largely increased its population, the lower wards were quite as populous then (1840) as they are to day, several of them more so. * * *

Now, look at the vote of four of these wards in 1840 and 1868, respectively:

	President, 1840.		Governor, 1868.	
Four Wards......	4,793	5,521	2,840	20,283

Van Buren's majority, 726; Hoffman's majority, 17,443.

Mr Tilden, you know what this contrast attests. Right well do you comprehend the means whereby the vote of 1868 was thus swelled out of all proportions. There are not 12,000 legal voters living in those Wards to-day, though they gave Hoffman 17,443 majority.

This is one of the most pointed condemnations ever penned. No words can add to the force of this terrible arraignment of TILDEN as an accomplice in the gigantic election frauds, which says to him: "You are as deeply implicated in them to-day as though your name were TWEED."

SOUTHERN CLAIMS.—A plank referring to soldiers and sailors is found in each platform. The Republican plank is as follows:

The pledges which the nation has given our soldiers and sailors must be fulfilled. The grateful people will always hold those who periled their lives *for the country's preservation* in the kindest remembrance.

The Democratic plank studiously abstains from this pointed reference to "the country's preservation." There is no distinction made between rebels and Unionists in referring to those who have fallen in battle, as will be observed:

Resolved, That the soldiers and sailors of *the republic*, and the widows and orphans of those *who have fallen in battle*, have a just claim upon the care, protection and gratitude of their fellow citizens.

These words were deliberately written and carefully considered. Southern papers and speakers have insisted that widows and orphans of Southern soldiers, and the maimed rebels who survive have a just claim to consideration. And if the Constitution was amended after the Republicans came in power, why may it not be amended when the Democrats gain control, if anything stands in the way of their avowed principles? No one can tell how many hundreds of millions of dollars would be demanded to pay Southern claims under Democratic rule.

RICHLAND NARROW GUAGE.—The Narrow Gauge Railway, laid with maple rails, from Lone Rock to Richland Center, is open for traffic. An excursion train left the latter place June 30th, heavily loaded with people. On reaching Lone Rock the following dispatch was received by the General Manager of the Narrow Guage road, Hon. N. L. JAMES, of Richland Center:

MILWAUKEE, June 30.

To JAMES, KROUSKOP AND DOWNS:

Please accept these three bottles of Extra Dry; hoping they will cheer and not inebriate. Let us continue the exercises on this happy occasion by singing

Broad is the way that leads to Milwaukee.
But Richland builds a Narrow Gauge with local aid and maple rails.
Three cheers for Richland.

JOHN C. GAULT.

Senator KROUSKOP, President of the Road, invited responses, and speeches were made by Senator D. L. DOWN, ex-Senator H. L. EATON, J. WALWORTH and others.

The Company have a locomotive and nine cars, and we believe the road and equipments cost less than $3,800 a mile.

We heartily congratulate the enterprising people of that section on their success.

THE DEAD LOCK.—The Senate and House are no nearer an agreement on the Legislative, Executive and Judicial Appropriation bill than three weeks ago, the point of difference being that the House insists upon a reduction of various salaries fixed by law, while the Senate disputes the right of the House to put legislation of this kind into an appropriation bill. The committee held a meeting on the 6th, but there was an utter lack of conciliating spirit manifested, so that there was as much antagonism displayed as upon any previous session of the conference committee. The meeting broke up in despair of any agreement. The feeling engendered in committee followed the conference report into the House. In the discussion there was a marked increase of partisan warmth and bitterness displayed in discussing the economies proposed by the Democrats, that indicates a tightening of the dead-lock beyond anything that has happened within the last week or ten days. There are at present over 100 members absent on leave.

THE CUSTER DISASTER.—We have little additional information to-day in regard to the butchery of CUSTER and his men by the Indians. An official account seems to have been sent to the authorities, which failed to reach them.

A dispatch this afternoon says that the Bismarck *Tribune* extra gives a list of the killed and wounded. The following is a summary of the killed:

Commissioned officers..................	14
Acting Assistant Surgeon..............	1
Enlisted men...........................	237
Civilians...............................	5
Indian Scouts..........................	3

The Centennial.

A Magnificent Spectacle.—Incidents of the Day.—Terribly hot Weather.—Illness of Governor Ludington.—The Wisconsin Home.

PHILADELPHIA, July 5, 1876.

The great Centennial 4th has passed and the hundreds of thousands of the good people of the country, representing the whole nation, rejoice thereat! They rejoice that it is over, and many of them rejoice that they were present. It has been a most glorious Fourth! The demonstration here was all that could have been expected, or even desired. The city was full of people all anxious to witness the great spectacle. The weather being very warm there was much sweltering and suffering, but the people were wonderfully good natured, while the crowd was so immense that it was next to impossible to see or hear any of the public exercises. This condition of things was accepted as a part of the grand whole, and enjoyed to the fullest extent. There was wonderful equality exhibited in all places. In the streets were men, women and children, of all nations, of all colors, of all ages, and of all stations in life, enjoying all the privileges of the occasion, in the full spirit of freedom, of the great Declaration that was promulgated in this city, one hundred years ago.

It is not my purpose to give any description of what has taken place here. I could not do it if I had time and strength, neither of which can I claim to possess; and it is unnecessary, as the telegraph will give the readers the main features of the grand occasion, at an earlier day than this letter could reach them. It is enough to say that the celebration was all that the patriotic people of this nation could desire it should be. The demonstration during the night of the 3d was immense! A procession was formed at eight o'clock in the evening, and proceeded through Broad street some four miles and back, then down Chestnut, and at midnight the head of the procession reached Independence Hall, when a grand new bell, just hung there, proclaimed the commencement of the Second Century since the immortal Declaration of Independence was promulgated. On the entire line of the procession the streets were crowded with people, the houses were filled and every available space on balconies, house tops, etc., was used by the people, anxious to witness the passing of the procession. The Emperor of Brazil, foreign Commissioners, Governors of States, and all classes of officials, as well as the masses of the people, were represented in this grand procession. Houses and business blocks were illuminated and decorated in splendid style. Indeed nothing was omitted to cause the spectacle to be a grand one in all respects.

The ceremonies on the 4th were carried on in a most satisfactory manner. The reception of the original copy of the Declaration of Independence was grand. The Mayor of the city brought it forth, and holding it up before the people, it received the huzzas of at least one hundred thousand people, over and over again! And it was pleasant to notice that our foreign friends joined heartily in the applause — the English representatives vieing with their American brethren in their demonstrations of joy! All were happy, and the past seems to have been entirely forgotten. The poem, by BAYARD TAYLOR, and the address of WM. M. EVARTS, have been printed and can be read by all. Those who were present will need to read them as well as those who were absent, in order to know what they contain. To hear, was impossible, although as good order was maintained as was possible with such an immense concourse of people as was congregated in and around old Independence Square.

The military display was very superior, and gave much satisfaction to the people. The fire-works in the evening were grand! We have thus glanced at the main points of the Centennial celebration on the glorious 4th. The labors of the occasion have used up our strength, too much to admit of writing more on this theme. No pen could do the subject anything like justice!

Wisconsin people will deeply regret that its excellent Governor, Hon. HARRISON LUDINGTON, though in the city, was not able to take part in the great celebration. He was quite ill, and confined to his room. He is improving nicely, and in a day or two will be on the move again.

One of the pleasant features of the day was the reception given by Governor HAYES at the Ohio headquarters. Many friends called on the Governor, and were most cordially received by that gentleman. All were pleased with the man. He has the appearance of a true gentleman in every movement. He made a most favorable impression upon all who called on him. He is evidently a man of fine ability, with an evenly balanced mind, that will make him a grand and noble head of this great Nation for four years from the 4th of March next; a position he is sure to occupy and adorn!

The weather is very warm, and amidst the pleasure here, there is much suffering on account of the great heat. The State buildings afford much relief to such sufferers; and none is more popular in this respect than the Wisconsin Home. Here people flock by hundreds every day, and find comfort. Col. E. STARR, of Milwaukee, is always on had, and makes all who come to our quarters comfortable and happy.

But I cannot write. The readers must take the will for the deed. I would like to say much. I may feel more like doing it hereafter.

A.

BOARD OF HEALTH.—We publish the address of Dr. E. L. GRIFFIN, of Fond du Lac, President of the State Board of Health and Vital Statistics. It is a brief statement of the objects of this important Board which will well repay perusal. Dr. GRIFFIN is evidently the right man in the right place. The Board meets again in Madison, July 11.

THE WAR WITH THE SIOUX.

Sitting Bull and His Outrages.

The Washington correspondent of the Chicago *Tribune* gives some valuable information in regard to the causes of the expedition against the Sioux, which has had so terrible a check, and some information of value in regard to Sitting Bull, the hostile Chief, who has been guilty of so many outrages and now of this butchery of Custer and his men. He says:

For many years a number of hostile Sioux have been roaming through the northern portion of Dakota under the leadership of Sitting Bull, Crazy Horse, and a few other Chiefs. Two years ago, their number was estimated at 7,000, but subsequently about 4,000 of these Indians went into the Agencies of Standing Rock, Spotted Tail, and Cheyenne River, reducing the number who might properly be called hostile to about 3,000. The War Department estimates Sitting Bull's band at about 3,500. The number of warriors in these bands could not originally have exceeded between 400 and 500. All attempts to induce these Indians to go upon reservations have thus far failed, and last fall Gen. Crook visited Washington for the purpose of consulting the Administration in regard to its future treatment of them. With the Secretary of War and Gen. Cowen, Acting Secretary of the Interior, Gen. Crook visited the President and proposed that an expedition be sent against these Indians during the winter, when they would be less prepared than at any other time to resist it.

His recommendation was favorably considered, and a message was sent to Sitting Bull and the Chiefs who were operating with him, ordering them to report at the reservation before the 1st of January, 1876, the alternative being that if they did not, the United States would make war against them. This step was considered necessary not only on account of the numerous murders of white people committed by these Indians, but because they were making constant attacks on the Bannock and other friendly Indians whose reservations were in their vicinity, and were inciting other Sioux to hostility. The uneasiness of the Red Cloud and the Spotted Tail Indians on account of the invasion of the Black Hills, and the scarcity of supplies furnished them, also made it very dangerous to allow these hostile bands to remain any longer beyond the control of the United States authorities. They might at any time be led to join in a general war which it would require the entire available military power of the United States to quell, and in which there might be a great sacrifice of life and property. The hostile Sioux paid no attention whatever to the orders directing them to report at the reservation, and preparations were made in the meantime to send an expedition against them.

There was a fight of no importance in January, and about the 20th of June another with CROOK's command, which gave the hostile Indians much encouragement, and enabled them to add to their numbers many discontented savages. The country where the conflict took place is cut up into ravines and is very favorable to ambuscades by the Indians and very difficult for successful cavalry operations.

The *Tribune* correspondent gives some interesting statements by Delegate MCGINNIS, of Montana, from which we take the following:

The cause of this war, or rather of these expeditions, for this war with these Indians has been going on for fifteen or more years, may be summed up in the words, "Sitting Bull and the outlaw Sioux." We have never had peace or even treaty relations with these bands. After the Spirit Lake massacre in Iowa and the great Sioux massacre in Minnesota, all the more turbulent spirits banded together. After Gen. Sibley's expedition in 1863, they crossed the Missouri, and endeavored to concentrate for another invasion of Minnesota, but the next year Sully followed them across the Missouri, and after several running fights they retreated across the Bad Lands into the Big Horn country, and he followed to the Yellowstone and established Fort Buford. Upon this post, and on the steamboats, and immigrants to Montana, they kept up unceasing war, often keeping the garrison at Buford in a state of siege for weeks at a time, and murdering every straggler who went outside the post. An attempt was made to treat with them in 1866, but, after accepting the presents and securing ammunition, Sitting Bull broke up the council, and the Commissioners escaped to the fort across the river. When Red Cloud and Spotted Tail made peace at Laramie, Sitting Bull refused to come in. All that year he made war on the steamboats and commerce of the Missouri, massacreing several small boat-loads of returning miners, and capturing large quantities of gold dust which he traded for arms to the Northern half-breeds. In 1867 he threatened the Gallatin Valley, in Montana, when the Montana Volunteers were raised to meet him. In 1868 he attacked the settlement of Muscle-Shell and suffered defeat, losing thirty-six warriors. The settlers having notice of his coming, ambuscaded him in a ravine outside the town. Although the attack was made by the Sioux on the village, this battle was denounced as a massacre by a portion of the Eastern press. After this he lost prestige. During 1869 and 1870 he devoted himself princpally to the slaughter of the Crows, the Mandans, the Rees, the Shoshone, and all other tribes friendly to the whites, varying it by an occasional attack on the Missouri river forts. In 1870, Gen. Hancock, then commanding that department, thought of organizing an expedition to bring him to terms, but as there was a prospect of the extension of the Northern Pacific Railway, which would simplify operations, he recommended another attempt to buy peace with him until that road should be pushed into the Big Horn country. On this recommendation, backed by the assurances of the Peace Commissioners and the Interior Department, Congress voted half a million dollars to make peace and subsist him. This was the famous Teton-Sioux appropriation, Sitting Bull himself claiming to be a Teton, though his followers are outlaws and hard customers from all the bands of the Sioux Nation. Considerable criticism has been made on the expenditure of this appropriation. It resulted in bringing to the Fort Peck Agency a part of his followers, but he refused to treat himself. Next year Gen. Custer went out with the Northern Pacific surveying party, and twice defeated Sitting Bull, and at least repulsed his attacks. One of his bands invaded the Gallatin Valley in 1872, and carried off 500 head of horses, after murdering a number of farmers. In 1873, he made a night attack on Col. Baker, but was repulsed and pursued. In 1874, he drove the Crows from their reservation agency, and made war on all peaceable Indians.

The Peace Commission, finding him intractable, now began to demand that the army should take the offensive and subdue him, and this request has frequently been repeated by the Peace Commission and the Indian Department, until the War Department has acted on it. Last year some of his followers went down to meet the Commission in Conference with the Red Cloud Sioux, and came near precipitating a massacre of the Commission. Sitting Bull himself refused to go in, and spent the summer in attacks on the Crow Agency, and on the frontier settlers. He captured a Government wagon-train on the Carroll Road, murdered a number of recruits going to the Montana posts, and captured the stock of the Carroll Stage Company.

Such have been his exploits up to the bloody history of the present year. He defies the government and hopes that he can get the Sioux nation to join him. If they will only do this he promises to drive the whites back into the sea, out of which they came, and utterly disbelieves the reports of Red Cloud and others who have visited the coast as to the number of whites they saw. He says their eyes were dazzled by bad medicine, "magic." How many followers has he ordinarily? Not more than 200 or 300 lodges, but there is no doubt that his numbers are now swelled by recruits from all the Agencies. The northern Cheyennes are with him, and a large portion of the Ogallallahs, and probably he has had 2,000 or more well armed and well mounted warriors in these late fights. There were times last winter when he could not have gathered 800 men, but young bucks have slily slipped away from the Agency where they wintered, and where the old people and women and children are being fed by the government, and they will remain with him during the summer.

This war, then, has no connection with the Black Hills trouble; none whatever. It has been waged defensively on our part for many years before the Black Hills were entered by anybody. The Black Hills troubles may be used for a pretext to induce the treaty Sioux to join him. Of course, he is anxious to confederate all the Sioux tribes and bands in a general war. He has been trying to do this for years, and has made repeated advances to the Crows and Black Feet. This is one reason why the Peace Commissioners urged that he must be subdued, lest he should demoralize all the treaty Indians, and bring on a general war. Of course the government has no alternative except to bring him to terms. Any other course would be a cowardly and wicked surrender of our frontier. Settlers and our friendly Indian allies would be subject to a barbarous and determined enemy.

DECLINES TO ANSWER.—Ex-Secretary BRISTOW was before the sub committee of the House special committee on the whiskey trials on Thursday. The sub-committee consists of only two members—COCHRANE, of Pennsylvania, a Democrat, and PLAISTED, of Maine, a Republican. The result was that when, after a few questions of a general nature, BRISTOW refused to answer inquiries by COCHRANE as to what happened in Cabinet meetings touching the trials at St. Louis, there was a dead lock on a small scale, COCHRANE insisting on an answer and PLAISTED sustaining BRISTOW in his refusal to divulge Cabinet proceedings. The question was brought before the full committee, of which PROCTOR KNOTT is Chairman, there being no quorum present no action was taken. It is stated that whatever may be the decision of the Committee, BRISTOW will maintain his position.

TILDEN WILL CARRY KENTUCKY.—Statesmen of the blue grass region boast that TILDEN will carry Kentucky by a large majority. Their souls are on fire for the war a failure and "peace platform" candidate. They still think the "war a failure" down that way, we judge, from the following paragraph in the *Inter-Ocean:*

They celebrated in Kentucky on the Fourth. A mob of patriotic souls surrounded the house of the widow of a Union soldier, and compelled her, under threat of destroying her home, to haul down the American flag which she had displayed from the housetop. Of course these are the sort of men to take charge of the Government. *They* are for reform! They are unanimous for Tilden and Hendricks, and will declare to you on their sacred honors that there is not a single case of outrage in the entire South!

THE BELKNAP IMPEACHMENT.—The BELKNAP impeachment trial was resumed by the Senate Thursday and several witnesses were examined, among whom were H. F. CROSBY, Chief Clerk of the War Department, and Gen. MCDOWELL, and the examination will continue from day to day. The House managers expect to have all of their evidence in by Monday evening. But it will require about ten days to hear the evidence for the defense. The trial is expected to last a month at least Yesterday it was interrupted for action on an appropriation bill.

MR. BLAINE'S HEALTH.—Mr. BLAINE has now been home ten days. So far there has been no special change in his case. The nervous prostration is still a marked characteristic. He is not able to leave his room, and is almost entirely confined to his bed. His physician thinks it will be many weeks before he will resume active work. A European trip is strongly recommended as soon as his strength is sufficient.

SANTA ANNA DEAD.—SANTA ANNA, the old Mexican President, Dictator and General, who for nearly fifty years was a conspicuous figure in Mexican politics, is dead. He died in the City of Mexico on the 24th of June, at the age of 84. He was the leader of the Mexicans in their war with the United States, and had a life of vicissitudes. Of late years he had almost subsided from public view.

UNSAFE.—Cincinnati's old Exposition Hall has been ordered pulled down at once, being unsafe for occupancy. In it have been held, among other meetings the Liberal Convention of 1872 and the Republican Convention of 1876. There would have been some trepidation if its condition had been known while the latter was in session.

☞ From many towns and cities in the Northwest come complaints of annoyances from "tramps." At Rock Island and Davenport several hundred of them are reported, and unusual precautions are deemed necessary to keep them under restrait. A suggestion to send them into the Indian country meets with favor.

☞ Volunteers are offering their services to the War Department from every quarter to fight old Sitting Bull and the Sioux savages.

BY TELEGRAPH.

CUSTER'S DEATH.

EXCITEMENT INCREASING.

Indignation Meetings Held

The Government Offered Aid

To Thoroughly Punish Indians.

Washington News.

Morrill Explains Follies of House.

THE TURKO-SERVIAN WAR.

Both Sides Claim Advantage.

MISCELLANEOUS ITEMS.

The Indian War.

WASHINGTON, July 7.

There was a consultation at the White House to-night on the subject of the Indian war, and Gen. Sherman, who reached here from Philadelphia this afternoon, and the President, discussed the matter at considerable length. An impression is felt in the highest quarters that the troops now in the West near the scene of present operations against the Indians, are numerically, as well as in every other respect, able to enforce the demands of the Government upon the hostile tribes, and to inflict proper chastisement upon them.

To-morrow morning, Gen. Sheridan will leave Philadelphia for his headquarters at Chicago, to which place he has been ordered by Gen. Sherman, owing to the recent Indian disaster.

YANKTON, July 7.

An immense mass meeting was held at the Court House to-night, presided over by Mayor Sieback, to take action concerning the massacre of Custer and his brave comrade. Stirring addresses were delivered by Gen. Tripp, Dr. Burleigh, Gen. Beadle, Acting Governor Yond, and others. Dr. Burleigh spoke of a recent trip down the Missouri river from Bismarck, during which he satisfied himself that the Sioux warriors had left all the agencies and gone to join Sitting Bull, while full rations were still issued for them, and that these warriors had left their reservation well armed and provisioned. The following resolutions were unanimously adopted:

Resolved, That we have heard with the deepest sorrow of the disaster which has befallen our national armies in the slaughter of the gallant Gen. Geo. Custer and his entire brave command, while discharging the duty imposed on them by the government, by outlaw bands of savages, which have so long infested our borders and robbed and brutally murdered our defenseless people.

Resolved, That we extend our most profound sympathy to the wives and families of the officers and men of the 7th cavalry, who bravely fought, and as bravely died in the defense of our frontier.

Resolved, That the Governor of this Territory be requested to tender to the Secretary of War a regiment of mounted troops to aid in the vigorous prosecution of the present war, and for such other services as shall be required by the General Government.

DENVER, Col., July 7.

Gov. Routt has telegraphed to the President as follows:

"Can raise one regiment of frontiermen in ten days for service against the Indians, if the Government will arm and equip them. If you accept, telegraph orders."

ST. LOUIS, July 7.

The *Republican's* Kansas City special says Joe O. Shelby, a noted Confederate general of that State, sent the following telegram to President Grant to-day:

"Gen. Custer has been killed We once fought him, now we purpose to avenge him. Should you determine to call volunteers, allow Missouri to raise one thousand."

From Washington.

WASHINGTON, July 7.

The examination of Secretary Robeson has been concluded by the committee. In reference to the deficiency supposed to exist in the funds of certain bureaus, he made a statement of the reason why certain appropriations had been exhausted. These found their origin last fall in the threatened trouble with Spain, at which time it became necessary, in view of our foreign relations, to put the navy in position to carry out any policy our Government might adopt. Owing to this unexpected state of affairs, the appropriations which would otherwise have been ample were rapidly exhausted, leaving some contracts which had been previously made, unprovided for.

Senator Morrill, of Maine, made a forcible speech this morning against the assumption of the exclusive power of the House to not only fix the amount of the appropriations, but to enact general laws, by forcing the consent of the Senate, under the threat of stopping the wheels of government. He showed conclusively that the Senate had concurred with the House in every reduction in expenses that could be made without crippling the Government. The Senate has conceded to the House every reduction claimed, excepting eight million, which cannot be assented to without injury to the country and government.

The House Judiciary Committee has adopted a report of the sub-committee declaring that the House has jurisdiction in the cases of King and Schumacher, in connection with the Pacific Mail subsidy. It was voted to report to the House and refer the matter to the Committee on Civil Service Reform for investigation.

Tilden Ratification.

CHICAGO, July 6.

A Tilden and Hendricks ratification meeting was held in this city to-night. Speeches were made by Sen. Doolittle, of Wisconsin, and W. F. Coolbaugh, of this city.

Hayes' Acceptance.

COLUMBUS, O., July 7.

It is understood here that Gov. Hayes' letter of acceptance will be ready for the papers Monday morning. It will probably be brief.

Don Carlos.

RICHMOND, July 7.

A party of strangers arrived here this morning via the Peidmont Air Line Railroad, en route for the Centennial, said to be Don Carlos and suite traveling *incog.*

From Europe.

PARIS, July 7.

The *Journal des Debats* has the following latest news from the seat of war: The Servians have occupied Rochkar, General Techernoff compelling the Turks to withdraw beyond Palanka. The balance of the advices so far are slightly favorable to the Servians. An official telegraphic dispatch received at Belgrade announces that after ten hours' desperate fighting at Rochkar, the Turks have fled to Novibalor. The Servians occupied the territory between Rochkar and Novibalor. The Servian loss was inconsiderable. The army under Gen. Zack crossed the frontier near Yavar on Thursday. They found the Turks entrenched in very favorable positions, and were unable to dislodge them, after five hours' severe fighting.

CONSTANTINOPLE, July 7.

The Porte has sent to its representatives abroad the following: "Moukhtar Pasha telegraphs details of the last engagements at Bellina. The enemy's loss exceeds the first estimate. There were 200 of their killed left in the village of Bellina and 700 in the neighborhood. Among the dead are their commander and several officers. A large Turkish force is now concentrated at Bellina."

The journals here assert that the Softas at their own request are about to be armed and will be sent to the frontier.

LONDON, July 7.

The *Standard's* dispatch from Belgrade, dated July 6, says that 130 wounded Servians of the army of the Drino have arrived there. They report that during the fighting at Bellina the garrison of the Turkish guard house and the inhabitants defended themselves to the utmost against the Servians in the streets of the town. A terrible massacre ensued, in which almost all the inhabitants perished. The prisoners of Belgrade have been ordered to give information to the authorities relative to a quantity of provisions in other houses. A bombardment by Turkish boats is feared. An American general and three Prussian officers have entered the Servian army. There have 5,000 militia men left Belgrade for Alexanterz.

Another despatch dated Belgrade the 7th, evening, says detailed reports of the encounter near Bellina contradict the first telegrams announcing a victory. The Turks have assumed the offensive and surprised the Servian camp at Rochkar. The Turks hold Bellina, and are concentrating a strong corps there. No news had been published in Belgrade for four days from the Servian army at Alexanterz.

VIENNA, July 7.

The *Political Correspondence* is informed that the Prince of Montenegro arrived on Thursday before Gatschka, where a considerable number of Turks are entrenched. The Bosnian Catholics intend to appeal to Austria to protect their interests against Servia.

BELGRADE, July 7.

The insurrection in Bulgaria is reported to have become general. The Servian troops have captured Saguera, on the Drina. Other Turkish reverses are reported.

BERNE, July 7.

A passenger train from this city, for Lausanne, came in collision to-day, at Palezieux, with another coming from Lausanne. Both engines were destroyed, several cars demolished and ten persons killed.

COLORADO, the great silver and grazing State, her domain including a broad section of the back bone of the continent, and containing some of the richest mines yet discovered, enjoys the proud distinction of being the Centennial State. On the first of July she took her place as the thirty-eighth State in the Union. Her population of 80,000 will increase as her mineral resources become developed.

All hail to our new sister, wearing the shining silver star in her coronet. Come in; come in and stay forever.

STATE TEACHERS' ASSOCIATION.—This body adjourned its session in Milwaukee Thursday evening, the closing exercises being a lecture by Rev G. E. GORDON, "A Plea for Education from a Public Standpoint," at which Prof. EARTHMAN was chosen to preside, President HOWLAND having been taken ill in the afternoon.

As the Western Democrats find out more about TILDEN's black record they begin to understand why the leading New York Democrats who knew him best said it would be "suicidal to nominate him." They were correct.

RESIGNED.—Judge HENRY D. BARRON resigned his seat as member of the State Senate some days ago, and a Senator will have to be elected from the new district, in which he was left by the new appointment.

ARMY OF THE CUMBERLAND.—The society of this army has been holding its annual reunion in Philadelphia this week, and Gens. SHERMAN and SHERIDAN have been attending it as well as the Centennial 4th celebration.

THE CENTENNIAL EXPOSITION TO BE KEPT CLOSED SUNDAY.—Friday the Centennial Commission, after a long and warm debate, decided by a vote of 30 to 0, to keep the Centennial Exposition closed on Sunday.

☞ The subcription to the printers' monument of HORACE GREELEY has reached the sum of $3,233 76.

☞ The convicted members of the Milwaukee whisky ring were to be sentenced this afternoon.

BRITISH COTTON TRADE.—The Manchester (Eng.) *Guardian* says the cotton trade in Blackburn District is so depressed that a general resort to short time is stated to be probable. A meeting of employers in North and Northwestern Lincolnshire will shortly be held to consider proposals affecting both wages and hours of labor.

☞ A regular whiskey crusade has commenced at Iowa City, Iowa. The leading saloon-keepers of the place were up Wednesday for selling whiskey contrary to law. The Sheriff has nearly 100 of the prominent young men of the city subpœnaed to appear on the stand against the saloon-keepers.

JUDGE DAVIS' DENIAL.—Our Bloomington correspondent is authorized to state that Judge Davis has not, before or since the June convention, written a letter on the subject of politics. The report that the Judge has determined to bolt the St. Louis nominations is therefore presumably false.—*Inter-Ocean.*

☞ Damages, public and private, by the late storm in Dubuque will foot up not less than $100,000. A child of Mr. Utrich, living on the Flats, was drowned in its cradle before the parents knew the water was in their house.

WISCONSIN STATE JOURNAL.

VOLUME XXXIV. MADISON, WIS., WEDNESDAY AFTERNOON, MAY 5, 1886. NO. 219.

STATE JOURNAL.

THE OFFICIAL STATE PAPER.

From the Seat of War.

In Milwaukee, to-day, the Polack mob again moved on the Bay View mills, and on refusing to obey the orders of the militia to halt, the latter fired one volley, in which two rioters appear to have been killed and eight or nine wounded. The mob then returned to the city and sacked the residence of Captain Borchardt, of the Kosciusko guard, the local military company composed of the better class of Poles. The rioters then armed themselves and threatened to go back to Bay View and be revenged on the troops, but the troops still live, as The State Journal goes to press. Another scrimmage occurred at Best's brewery, but without bloodshed.

In Chicago, last night, dynamite bombs were thrown at 300 police sent to break up an anarchists' meeting on Desplaines street. About twenty officers were wounded, of whom one is dead and probably a dozen more will die. As many rioters were likewise injured. To-day, the leaders of the Chicago anarchists were jailed, and their organ, The Arbeiter Zeitung, raided by the police, publication being suspended, and all its force of printers arrested. Mobs in different parts of the city sacked a few stores, but otherwise quiet prevails. The mayor has not yet called on the militia to aid him.

The organizers of the Knights of Labor talk speciously, heralding their order as the organization of peace, good will and mutual improvement among workingmen. By this means they beguile honest laborers into their ranks, bind them by iron-clad oaths to obey the junto of the professional agitators who control the order, and then use them to carry out their nefarious socialistic schemes. The Knights of Labor started and conducted the disastrous strike on the Gould southwest system,—disastrous not only to themselves and their employers, but paralyzing the entire southwest, with its myriads of industries and financial interests. Directly out of the Gould strike grew the uprising at East St. Louis, with its terrible tragedy. The strike mania then became epidemic, and spread to nearly every large city in the country, in greater or less degree. It became the fashion to strike. Men threw up their jobs by the scores of thousands without definite cause. Novel complaints were made and demands formulated that were unthought of before the Knights of Labor crusaders began their rounds. Capital everywhere was assaulted as if it were a deadly enemy. Labor contracts were ruthlessly broken, the ties that had so long bound workingmen to their employers were broken. The splendid business prospects of two months ago have been shattered and the outlook for hard times stares us in the face. Trade has been demoralized, industry crippled. The Knights of Labor are alone responsible. They are responsible for such orders as have forced Kirk's workmen to gnaw the crust of idleness; for the shutting down of Allis' works; for the closing of McCormick's factory,—for the turning out of 10,000 men in Milwaukee and 25,000 in Chicago, who would willingly work, but are obliged to go out because the oath they have taken to obey Shilling and Powderly and the rest of the knightly gang, obliges them to stop the wheels of industry when told to do so for some secret reason unknown of honest men. The Knights of Labor are responsible for bringing about the condition of affairs that makes it possible for the socialists to unfurl their red flags and fire dynamite bombs into the ranks of the guardians of the peace in Chicago; for the Polack wharf-rats to raid the Bay View mills, to sack Captain Borchardt's residence, to organize a reign of terror in Milwaukee. No workingman who respects himself and understands the situation can afford to join the Knights of Labor. It is the enemy of industry, it is socialism in a most specious form, it is a device of blatherskites to upturn American institutions. No greater danger threatens American workingmen to-day than the rapid spread of this engine of demagoguery.

Monday evening, E. P. Allis applied to Mayor Wallber of Milwaukee for protection for his iron works, from threatened mob-rule. The mayor, instead of standing up to the rack and doing his duty to the full extent of his power, pleaded his inability to do anything, and advised Mr. Allis to close down. Of course, in the face of such weakness, the works had to be closed, and 1,200 hundred men who wanted to continue at their work and were amply satisfied with their treatment, were forced into idleness. It is no wonder that the press and the public of Milwaukee join Mr. Allis in his burst of indignation at the mayor's weak-kneed policy. This concession to mob-law greatly encouraged the rioters, and Tuesday's demonstrations were the direct result of it. The mayor, without sufficiently trying the power of his police force, finally managed to get up courage enough to call on the state for assistance and the governor responded with commendable promptness.

There is no foolishness in Governor Rusk's make-up. He will work his militiamen for all they are worth. Some 800 of the troops from the interior of the state are now on the field in Milwaukee, in addition to the four local companies. Yesterday there was a momentary show of weakness, in the spectacle of one of the Milwaukee companies firing over the heads of the mob instead of at their breasts, but in justice to the governor it should be borne in mind that the volley was the result of a temporary scare on the part of the company and was not ordered from headquarters. The troops are doing better work to-day, under definite instructions to aim to kill, when they do fire. We look for an effective handling of the state troops, under Governor Rusk and Adjutant General Chapman, and are confident that the Badger militiamen will acquit themselves with credit.

This Morning's Dispatches Condensed.

DISASTERS.

Joseph Whitwam, one of the best-known engineers on the lakes, was cut to pieces by a locomotive Tuesday at Toledo, Ohio. He was 60 years of age.

An Alton freight train of twenty-two cars broke in two at Delavan, Ill., early yesterday morning. Nine lumber-cars were thrown down an embankment, by which four men were instantly killed.

CRIMINAL.

Robert Harding, assistant postmaster at Cleveland, killed himself with a revolver.

Captain Huebler, a veteran member of the St. Louis police force, has been appointed to the chieftaincy.

Wm. Hammond, recently pastor of the Baptist church at Franklin, N. H., who robbed his wife, restored the money and then eloped to Canada, is suspected of having murdered his first wife, and of having burned his house at Wolf Lake, Ind., to get the insurance. It is known that he was warned to quit Ligonier, Ind., and that he bore an unsavory reputation as a traveling quack.

PERSONAL.

Hon. E. B. Washburne has returned to Chicago from California much improved in health.

Miss Jennie Barber, daughter of a wealthy citizen, dropped dead Tuesday afternoon at Shirland, Ill.

Judge W. T. Hopkins, a leading citizen of Grundy county, Ill., died yesterday at his home in Morris.

The Catholic clergy of Chicago have presented Vicar General Conway with a purse of $4,000. He is to leave this afternoon for Europe.

An application made in the supreme court at Buffalo for the release from the insane asylum of Amos Atwood, formerly a hardware merchant at Andover, alleges that he has been kept in confinement by his wife in order to control his property.

TRANSPORTATION NOTES.

The Lachine and Rideau canals are open for navigation.

A north wind dispersed the ice in Duluth harbor and opened navigation yesterday morning. A number of vessels arrived and cleared during the day.

The railroads centering at Keokuk, Iowa, have been ordered to discontinue switching on the levee in that city, for the reason that it is hurtful to the business of the retail dealers in the vicinity.

The Atchison railway system admits a decrease of $297,617 in its gross earnings since the year opened. The St. Paul road reports a decrease of $163,263 in its gross income for April.

Good beeves in the Chicago market sell at about the prices current a year ago. Common to choice qualities were yesterday 10 to 15 cents per hundred higher, because of the withholding of supplies by country shippers.

MISCELLANEOUS.

Marshalltown has been selected as the site for the soldiers' home in Iowa.

The Indians in the Northwestern territory are threatening trouble. They have asked Sitting Bull to join them.

The American Medical association began its seventh annual convention Tuesday at St. Louis with a very large attendance of delegates.

At the American Institute rink in New York, yesterday, was held an auction sale of Senator Stanford's California colts. Forty-seven head brought $46,835.

Some unknown vigilantes at Flushing, L. I., ducked in the village fountain a married man named Neil Howard, for remaining away from home late at nights.

League ball games Tuesday resulted: St. Louis 6, Chicago 5 (eleven innings); Boston 8, Washington 5; Philadelphia 11, New York 4. Rain prevented the Detroit-Kansas City game.

Rev. F. R. Scully, an ex-priest, now pastor of the Baptist church in Braddock, Pa., and Rev. Mr. O'Connor, an ex-priest of New York, are maturing a plan for a convention of all the Protestantized Catholics in the United States, to be held at Pittsburg, Pa., during the coming summer, to establish what they term "Reformed Catholic churches," in all the principal cities of the country where none exist.

The right to work is inalienable. It is one of the greatest of human rights. Any man who attempts to prevent another, either by threats or violence, from honestly earning his livelihood, is as great an enemy of society as the man who threatens or takes the life of another. The crime is only aggravated, when a mob commits it. It then becomes a revolution. When a man or a body of men is threatened with violence because of continuing at labor when other men choose to be idle, the utmost protection in the power of the government should be brought to bear. The first overt act should be instantly and vigorously repulsed. If necessary, every member of the mob should be shot down without mercy. There should be no nonsense. Every feeling of compassion must be smothered for the moment, for the central principle is this: A reputable man who desires to pursue his regular calling in the usual place and under the usual circumstances, must be protected at every hazard. It is better that a thousand ruffians be killed than that the rights of one honest citizen be trampled upon. It is the underlying principle in all these labor riots; to disguise it is folly; to allow other issues to be coupled with it to cloud the judgment, is unwise; to temporize with a mob is suicidal. That is where Mayor Wallber, of Milwaukee, made a grand mistake, in the case of the Allis works. He does not seem to have studied the bill of rights.

BY TELEGRAPH

BLOODSHED IN MILWAUKEE.

Two Rioters Killed by Militia at Bay View.

Capt. Bourchardt's Residence Completely Wrecked by the Mob.

Anarchist Leaders Jailed to-day in Chicago.

Headquarters of the Red Flag People Raided.

Several Shops Sacked, but No More Shooting.

Miscellaneous Domestic and Foreign Telegrams.

The Situation in Milwaukee.

YESTERDAY'S SUMMARY.

MILWAUKEE, May 5. — Armed with clubs, a mob of Polish strikers marched through the Kinnickinnic valley yester-morning, compelled all workmen whom they encountered to cease work, and brought up at the North Chicago Rolling Mill company's works in Bay View. After several conferences they prevailed upon the common laborers to strike, causing the works to shut down and throwing 1,200 men out of work. It being feared that the company's property would be damaged by the mob, the local companies of militia were called. A collision resulted, but though several volleys were given, there were no fatalities, for the militia fired over the heads of the mob. Several militiamen were injured, but not seriously, by missiles thrown by the crowd.

Mobs appeared at the Brand stove works and later at the Best Brewing company's plant on the west side during the evening, but accomplished nothing of consequence.

All day large crowds surrounded the Allis works, among them many of the strikers who attempted to storm the place on Monday. Two militia companies were stationed there, and no demonstration was made.

The labor disturbances have caused Gov. Rusk to summon the First regiment of the Wisconsin national guard to the city. The companies have arrived and are stationed at different manufacturing establishments.

It is estimated that the mob of Polish strikers who have marched through the streets the past few days have forced 4,500 workingmen to quit work against their will.

The Sentinel thus editorially summarizes some of the details:

This city presented a good deal of the appearance of a holiday, yesterday. Early in the morning the streets were full of rumors of the movements of the strikers, who had met with such success the day before. They were no doubt much encouraged by the force-out at the railroad shops and by the shutting down of the Allis works—for which Mr. Allis is in no way to blame, but the local authorities if anybody—and it was expected they would move upon the rolling mills at Bay View in increased force. The sounding of the signal bell at the central station brought the militiamen to the armory on Broadway, which was soon surrounded by crowds of curious citizens and some strikers and sympathizers. When a militia company left the armory to move to Bay View, the streets were lined with people, many of whom were anything but choice in their remarks to the young soldiers. The streets of the south side were very Sunday-like. On every corner was a group of idle workingmen, and about the Allis works a number of the workingmen lingered. At most of the houses idle workingmen sat on the steps, looking anything but cheerful. An occasional squad of workingmen, dinner-pails in hand, showed that the strike was still being recruited. Beyond the bridge near the mills, at Bay View, was an immense crowd of strikers, mostly foreigners, many of whom had sticks in their hands and all of whom were intensely interested in the outcome of the negotiations with the mill workers. The militia kept the crowd back from the fence surrounding the works, sometimes with considerable effort. The crowd was vociferous at times, and the truculence of some of the strikers was with difficulty held in check. They were bitter over the presence of the militia, which alone prevented a wholesale invasion of the works. The mill workers, who were seen in the distance, paid no attention to the shouts of the mob on the outside.

It was observable that the more intelligent working men among the strikers throughout the city took no part in the attempt to force out the mill-workers. They were either at their homes or in groups away from the mass of agitators. It must be said of the great majority of strikers that they studiously avoided the mob and were very far from giving encouragement to the Polish shovelers who made up the most aggressive part of the crowd near the bridge.

It was apparent that the moral effect of the militia was tremendous. After their success of Monday, there is no telling what would have been the end of yesterday's march of the shovelers but for the timely presence of the state troops. It was a strained situation. When it was determined to shut down the works and the militia moved toward the yards, a few of the more desperate of the mob begun to throw stones, and then the firing begun. It was the first suggestion to the mob that the militia could be induced to fire. The lesson was hardly thorough enough, but sent a good many of the rioters out of the crowd. But for the militia the works would have been destroyed.

THE OUTSIDE MILITIA.

MILWAUKEE, May 5.—Eleven military companies, numbering 432 men in all, arrived yesterday afternoon from different parts of the state. All excepting one—Company I, of the 2d regiment—belong to the 1st Wisconsin regiment. Following are the companies and the locations where they were stationed last night:

Company A, the Janesville guard, numbering thirty-nine men, under Capt. Newman, and Company B, the Bower City rifles of Janesville, numbering forty one, under Capt. F. H. Koeblin, were ordered to Bay View to reinforce the Fourth battalion, and reported to Maj. Traeumer.

Company C, the Custer rifles, of Whitewater, forty-three men, under Lieut. J. D. Hogan, and Company D, the Delavan guard, forty-five men, under Capt. R. J. Wilson, were sent to the West Milwaukee shops and were placed under the command of Maj. A. F. Caldwell, of the 1st regiment.

Company E, the Beloit City guard, fifty-three men, under Capt. Cham. Ingersoll; Company K, the Darlington rifles, forty men, under Capt. Geo. S. Anthony, and Company I, of the 2d regiment, the Watertown rifles, forty-four men, under Capt. A. Solliday, were stationed at Allis' works, under command of Lieut. Col. La Grange, of the 1st regiment.

The reserve force retained at the armory under command of Col. Sam Lewis comprised the following companies: Company F, the Racine Light guard, thirty-nine men under Capt. John T. Vaughan; Company G, the Garfield guard, of Racine, thirty-seven men under Capt. W. H. Brigham; Company H, the Monroe City guard, fifty-one men under Capt. S. B. Schadel; and Company I, the Governor's guard of Madison, fifty men under Capt. Wm. Helm.

The companies all responded promptly to the governor's call and arrived in the city on special trains over the St. Paul road.

The governor's and adjutant general's headquarters are at the armory. The governor was cool and collected, but determined, all day yesterday, and General Chapman is kept busy at his desk writing or dictating orders, and providing for the details of the military occupation.

A MOB FIRED ON.

MILWAUKEE, May 5—9 A. M.—Reports from Bay View say that the militia fired one round this morning on a mob marching towards Allis' works, which had started up under military protection this morning. The Light Horse squadron is on its way to the Allis works.

A large gathering of socialists is reported at Milwaukee garden. The police are on their way to the spot.

9:30 A. M.—The mob of socialists assembled at the Milwaukee garden have started for Best's brewery. Three companies of infantry, a platoon of cavalry and a platoon of police are on their way to intercept them.

9:50 A. M.—An eye witness of the shooting at Bay View this morning says that two men were killed outright, two mortally wounded and a number of others slightly hurt. The collision occurred at Deer creek bridge, close to the village of Bay View.

THE MOB FIRED ON, AT BAY VIEW.

MILWAUKEE, May 5.—The latest reports from Bay View show a much more serious condition of affairs than at first reported. Crowds of strikers commenced to form at 8:30 and moved towards the mills. Six military companies marched out of the grounds and were stationed in front of the works, and as the crowd approached, paying no attention to the orders to halt, a volley of bullets was poured into the crowd. The rioters beat a hasty retreat, when it was learned that five lives had been lost and several persons wounded. A school boy was among those killed.

Later.—The list of killed and wounded is as follows:

KILLED.

Franz Keinkiel.
Michael Ruhalski.

WOUNDED.

Martin Jonkazen.
A boy named Nowachek.
Casimer Dudek.
Albert Witmann.
And two or three others were dangerously wounded.

The firing of the militia and the fatal results resulted in dispersing the mob.

CAPT. BORCHARDT'S RESIDENCE SACKED.

The Polish rioters returned to the city and proceeded to sack the residence of Captain Borchardt, of the Kosciusko guards. The residence is a complete wreck. The Poles then assembled near the Polish church. It is rumored that they decided to arm themselves and make a raid on the militia at the Bay View mills this afternoon.

AT BEST'S BREWERY.

MILWAUKEE, May 5—11:30 A. M.—A large crowd of socialists assembled at Milwaukee garden, preparing to carry out the programme of riot and destruction. A platoon of sixty policemen and three infantry companies were dispatched there and cleared the premises. The mob then reassembled and proceeded to the Best brewery, and word has just been received at military headquarters that a disturbance took place there, in which it became necessary to resort to firing, and two persons were killed.

MILWAUKEE, May 5—12 M.—The rumor that two men were killed at the Best brewery is found to be untrue.

QUIET UP TO 2 P. M.

MILWAUKEE, May 5—2 P. M.—Up to this hour no fresh outbreak has been reported from Bay View. The militia are in readiness for a reappearance of the rioters.

Bloodshed in Chicago.

TWENTY POLICEMEN INJURED AND FIVE KILLED.

CHICAGO, May 5—6 A. M.—A dynamite bomb was last evening thrown into the ranks of 300 Chicago policemen who had formed at the Desplaines street station to suppress a socialistic gathering in the old Market square. The officers retaliated upon the mob with 100 or more shots. It is believed that fifteen officers were seriously injured, five being killed outright, and an equal number of strikers had their wounds dressed at neighboring drug stores.

Spies, Schwab, Parsons and Fielden, the chief socialistic leaders of the city, had been addressing a rough mob of some 1,500 anarchists. Fielden was talking when a huge gray wind-cloud, covering the entire north heavens, floated rapidly to the south, bringing a cold wave with it. Spies interrupted the speaker, and was about to have the meeting adjourned to Zeph's hall, but many had already left, and Fielden said he would not speak much longer. It was about ten minutes after 10 o'clock, and just at that moment a large squad of police moved up from the Desplaines street station, for the purpose of arresting the chief socialists, Spies, Schwab, Parsons and Fielden. There were loud cries of defiance from the socialists as the police formed about them, and in the next moment a dynamite bomb was exploded in their midst. There followed a wild scene of terror and confusion. All in the neighborhood were running for their lives, while pistol-shots were fired thick and fast in every direction. People fell in their haste and others fell over them, until they were four or five deep, and made desperate struggles to escape from the bullets and bombs which were feared at every point. There were fierce cries of desperation and pitiful moans of both police and civilians, who had been more or less mangled by the bomb or wounded by the bullets. In less than two minutes the street was clear, with the exception of those who lay wounded. The patrol-wagons, which were immediately summoned, were busy for a time removing the wounded policemen to the police station, and physicians were hurriedly sent for to dress their wounds

Capt. Ward at once telephoned to every police station in the city for reinforcements of all the men, and ordered the rifles brought up from the cellar. There was never a more exciting time in any police station of the city, as all the officers who were able were preparing for whatever emergency might arise, while so many of their brother officers were lying in blood and agony, some of them fatally wounded. There was a feeling of anxiety that the friends of the socialists would destroy the police station and make the night more hideous with their reckless murder, but this was not done.

A later account says that the list of casualties so far as can be learned foot up as follows: One socialist dead; two officers dead, four other officers who may not survive till morning, and thirty more police who have wounds, many of a most serious character. In addition to this, probably fifty people, nearly all members of the socialist crowd or citizens of the vicinity, were shot or otherwise wounded. The compilation of a detailed list is made almost impossible, the confusion and excitement is so great and the attention of officers and populace is so taken up with the care of the injured. A great number of these were quickly taken to different hospitals and to private houses, so that it may be days before the full extent of the casualties can be brought to light.

A number of wounded socialists are under arrest.

Mayor Harrison arrived at the station as soon as possible after the bombs had been thrown. He walked around among the wounded officers and spoke encouraging words to them. "I was," said he, at the meeting for a while during the time Parsons was speaking. I went from there to the Desplaines street station, and learning that there was no indication of trouble, I went home to bed. I had hardly done so when I heard of the bomb-throwing, and came directly to the station."

"What action will be taken to subdue the socialistic element?" was asked.

"I can't say now. I haven't had time to think of any plan since this affair. You can say, however, that the entire police force of the city will be used to maintain order, and unlawful gatherings at which speeches are made threatening life and property, will not be permitted."

FREIGHT HANDLERS.

CHICAGO, May 5.—The situation so far as the local railway freight-handlers are concerned was little changed yesterday. The officials held another meeting and duplicated the action of Monday, resolving to stand by each other and firmly refuse to grant any concessions. The managers seemed nervous, but say they apprehend no serious trouble. The Milwaukee & St. Paul and the Illinois Central moved considerable freight with the assistance of their clerical forces. The strikers say that as soon as they perfect their organization they will call upon the switchmen, brakemen, engineers and firemen to lend assistance in forcing their claims for a higher rate of wages.

MISCELLANEOUS TROUBLES.

CHICAGO, May 5. — Managers of the metal-working establishments of the city at a meeting yesterday, agreed that the eight-hour system was impracticable unless adopted universally throughout the country, and decided to close down Saturday, not to reopen until the employes agree to work ten hours. This is regarded by the trades assembly as the most serious blow the movement has yet received. The furniture-workers agreed to go to work on a basis of a 10 per cent. advance in wages, but the manufacturers are disposed to be stand-offish, and at a meeting yesterday decided to recognize no union, but only individuals, in receiving applications for employment. The lumbermen's committee flatly refused the demands of the men, and a member of the delegation calling on the committee was subsequently locked up for incendiary language. The men at a subsequent meeting decided to stay out till their demands were granted. A blockade exists along the river, attempts to unload the cargoes of upwards of 100 vessels now in port being repulsed by strikers.

GREAT POPULAR INDIGNATION.

CHICAGO, May 5—11 A. M.—The excitement of the general populace is very intense, growing out of the massacre planned and carried out by a small band of anarchists and their blind followers last night. The city is outwardly very quiet. In the street cars and at every point of gathering in the city the events of last night are being seriously discussed. A large and conservative element in the population, it is proper to say, has never seriously contemplated that an outbreak of such serious proportions and atrocious character could be meditated by any class in the community. Words heard on every side this morning are of an utter and abhorrent condemnation of the assault made on the police.

The occurrences of Monday and last night are ascribed in the public mind to the teachings and recent utterances, principally, of

THREE MEN:

August Spies, A. R. Parsons and Samuel Fielding, the speakers of last night. They have been pointed out by nearly every paper in the city during the past four days, and the tragic culmination on Desplaines street only appeared to emphasize these warnings. Their arrest has been repeatedly demanded. When the firing began last night, Parsons was the only man seen to be recognized. He was in a liquor store on the corner of Desplaines and Lake streets, the socialists' headquarters, within 150 feet of the point where the deadly bomb was thrown among the ranks of the police. The firing at the police came from the same direction, and it is surmised that the criminals obtained their guns and made Socialist hall their rendezvous, and from there they proceeded to make their assault. They were concealed

BEHIND BARRICADES

of boxes and barrels on the sidewalks, leveling their guns and firing during the confusion following the explosion of the bomb.

Parsons was seen in the place, accompanied by his negro wife, for only a moment, and then disappeared with the other anarchists.

The police searched for the three men all night, but did not succeed in finding them. A little after 8 o'clock this morning all three were found in a close room in the office of The Arbeiter Zeitung newspaper, at 107 Fifth avenue. They were in consultation. When

THE OFFICERS CAME UPON THEM

they exhibited alarm, but made no resistance. They were taken quickly to the central police station, a block away, and up to 9 o'clock the public had not been made aware of the arrest. They are kept closely guarded, and no one is permitted to see them.

It is not known what if any charges have been made against them, and what is the exact policy the city authorities intend to pursue. They have in evidence against Spies his guarded but inflammatory utterances in his newspaper, The Arbeiter Zeitung, in which he has within the past few days urged a dynamite warfare against the police and all regularly-constituted authorities. His direct connection and that of his companions, in the events of the past few days, appears very clear.

MAYOR HARRISON

reasserts his ability to preserve absolute peace in Chicago, without outside aid. He argues that the occurrence of last night could not have been foreseen, and was an unparalleled event in American history.

The entire police force is on duty to-day, and its numbers are apparently in first-class condition, while their duties have been arduous. The fact that the department is equipped with numerous patrol wagons, and that they have been able to reach scenes of disorder without the fatigue consequent upon a strictly marching body, has been in their favor. The police are accorded by the entire press the most unstinted praise for their discretion, bravery and excellent discipline in the face of unusual assaults by the criminal element.

The only published criticism upon the mayor was, in his not forbidding the assemblage last night and similar ones during the preceding three or four years. Thus far to-day no proclamation has been issued forbidding all future gatherings, but it is assumed by the press that this will end for some time any assembling by the red-flag advocates.

Another great strike was inaugurated this morning.

PROBABLY INTIMIDATED.

Seventeen hundred men employed in the Deering harvester works stopped without notice or warning of any character and without making any demands. Whether the men had been influenced by the recent riotous events directed against workingmen remaining at their posts is not known. The managers of the works have asked for police protection. The works are located in a district largely populated by foreign-speaking people.

THE RAILROAD SITUATION

was further complicated this morning by the strike of all the freight-handlers on the Lake Shore road. The switchmen on the same road also decided not to handle any freight-cars loaded by any persons other than strikers.

A DRUGGIST ATTACKED.

CHICAGO, May 5.—About 9 o'clock this morning a crowd of 30 persons made an assault on the drug store belonging to Samuel Rosenfeld. "Tear down the place," they yelled,—"kill Rosenfeld, he's a police spy," and other like expressions. The mob had the idea that the druggist was giving the police tips through his telephone. A wagon load of police was soon on the scene and conveyed Rosenfeld and family to the station, leaving a guard in the vicinity.

HE OUGHT TO HAVE BEEN LYNCHED.

CHICAGO, May 5.—Sam. Fielding, a rabid anarchist and the companion of August Spies, is under arrest. He it was who spoke the last words to the mob last night, which led to the slaughter. He was found this morning and safely caged at the central station. Fielding was suffering from a gun-shot wound in the leg.

NO SYMPATHY WITH SOCIALISTS.

CHICAGO, May 5.—Three thousand men employed in the great car shops at Pullman went out this morning, joining the strikers who quit yesterday. A mass meeting was held at 9 o'clock and resolutions adopted condemning the action of the socialists, declaring that they had no sympathy with that element or its methods, and counselling quiet and good order.

THE POLICE FORCE AMPLE.

Chief of Police Ebersold said this morning that the police force was amply able to deal with the trouble without outside assistance. The sheriff has not yet been called on.

Both the 1st and 2d regiments and the 1st cavalry and battery D are ready to turn out at short notice.

Between 300 and 400 Springfield rifles have been given out to a special squad of the police force. Every man on the force is armed with two 44-caliber revolvers.

The mayor has been in consultation all morning with the officers of the city law department and prominent citizens. The various city officers are preparing to take action regarding the murderous occurrences of last night.

EVIDENCE AGAINST THE ANARCHISTS.

CHICAGO, May 5.—The police are rapidly collecting evidence against the chief conspirators among the anarchists. They searched Spies' office this morning, and found absolute proof that the inflammatory circular mentioned in these dispatches, headed, "Revenge! Workingmen to Arms!" and another headed "Attention, Workingmen!" were printed at his office. They found the forms in type. These were taken possession of and locked up at the central station as evidence that Spies and Schwab directly incited the riot and bloodshed.

The anarchist Parsons has not yet been captured, as at first reported. He is still in hiding. Schwab was mistaken for him when the first arrests were made.

Inspector Bonfield raided Zepp's hall, corner of Lake and Desplaines streets, this morning. Here were found a lot of muskets, red flags and German books expounding socialistic doctrines.

Shortly after noon, the police made another raid on the office of The Arbeiter Zeitung. They arrested a man in the office who, upon being searched, produced a large revolver and a dirk. He were placed under arrest. In the office was discovered several boxes of dynamite and a number of red flags and incendiary banners. They were all seized.

SHOPS RAIDED.

A mob of from 6,000 to 8,000 persons reassembled near the corner of Eighteenth street and Center avenue, at noon, and raided Rosenfeld's drug store, carrying off everything portable. They then raided a liquor store in the near vicinity, kept by a man named Weeskopf, carrying away or drinking the liquor. Women and children joined in this raid.

The police returned to the scene and succeeded in dispersing the mob.

DEERING'S MEN.

The strikers at the Deering reaper works held an open-air meeting on the prairie near the factory at 10 o'clock this morning. They demand eight hours' work, ten hours' pay, double pay for over-time and 20 per cent. advance for piece-work.

It is learned that Schwab, one of the men now under arrest, addressed these strikers last night, urging this course.

NO PARADE OF FREIGHT-HANDLERS.

The striking freight-handlers intended making a parade to-day, but issued orders countermanding it. They also adopted resolutions condemning the anarchists and tendering their service, if needed, to preserve the public peace.

THE MAYOR'S PROCLAMATION.

It has finally been decided by the mayor to issue a proclamation. The document will call on all persons to keep off the streets after dark, and will warn the people not to gather in crowds on the streets, or in vacant lots.

TWO ROOSTS RAIDED.

Inspector Bonfield raided 54 West Lake street about 1 o'clock this afternoon. It is a notorious resort for socialists. One of the rooms was occupied by freight handlers. The police cleared the place.

The police raided the establishment kept by C. H. Bissell, at 15 South Clark street, this afternoon, carrying away ninety guns and revolvers. It is declared that Bissell has been supplying the socialists with guns.

THE ARBEITER ZEITUNG RAIDED.

CHICAGO, May 5.—Twenty-five printers were arrested in The Arbeiter Zeitung building and arraigned before Justice Meech, charged with murder. The cases were postponed till May 14. Bail was refused. Dynamite was found in The Arbeiter Zeitung office this morning. At noon to-day it was taken to the lake front and exploded. A piece the size of a hen's egg was placed in a coupling link and exploded. The heavy iron was shattered into fine bits.

The mayor, with several detectives, visited The Arbeiter Zeitung office and held a consultation with Oscar Neibe, employed to get out the paper. The mayor told him that the paper could not be issued until inspected by Mr. Hand, whom he would send for that purpose. Niebe promised that nothing of an inflammatory nature should appear in the paper. Before the paper was issued, a raid was made and twenty-five printers arrested.

THE INQUEST

upon the body of Police Officer John Diegan, killed last night, began at the city clerk's office this afternoon. It is thought the evidence will result in the indictment of Spies and other anarchists for murder.

THE LATEST.

2:30 P. M.—The city remains quiet up to this hour. The railway companies have sustained no molestation of any kind. With the exception of the Lake Shore, all are moving about all the freight offered. The Northwestern road has arranged to resume business operations to-morrow with a full force of men.

Forty-five wounded officers and men are at the county hospital. Officer Deagan is the only one dead, among the injured officers. The announcement of the death of Officers Burrell and Hanson is hourly expected.

At 2 o'clock Officer Barrett was reported dying and there appears to be little hope of the lives of Officers Miller, Jabob Hansen, Nelson Haben and Redden. Of the remaining twenty-four officers in the county hospital wards, all have a show of recovery, but some are extremely low.

Two rioters named Emil Lutz and John Lepland are in a very critical condition and it is expected they will die.

On the door leading up to The Arbeiter Zeitung, the following in German is posted:

The Arbeiter Zeitung will not be published for the next few days. All advertisements, etc., can be left in the saloon in the basement.

Nearly 10,000 has already been subscribed on 'change for the families of the wounded and dead police officers.

CHICAGO, Ill., May 5. — Colonel Knox, of the 1st regiment of Chicago has four hundred men in readiness at their armory, and a new gatling gun has been presented to the command. Major Tobey has a company of artillerymen guarding the gatling at battery D armory.

Labor Troubles Elsewhere.

KANSAS CITY TRACKMEN.

KANSAS CITY, Mo., May 5.—The trackmen in the various railway yards here with the exception of the Missouri Pacific, have gone on a general strike for an advance of 25 cents per day.

IT ASTONISHED HIM.

NEW YORK, May 5.—One of the anarchist strikers here was arrested for placing an obstruction in the way of the Third avenue cars. He had a fair trail before an intelligent jury, and was found guilty and sentenced to the penitentiary for six months by the judge. It is said that the striker was very much astonished at his sentence, but it is also said there have been no further obstructions to the business of the road.

MUSKEGON AFFECTED.

DETROIT, Mich., May 5. — The labor troubles in Chicago have resulted in a virtual suspension of business at Muskegon, from which port there was but one clearance Tuesday.

A SCHOOL STRIKE QUELLED.

CHICAGO, Ill., May 5. — Thirteen boys in an Arcola (Ill.) school went on a strike one day last week and refused to resume their studies. The principal summoned thirteen of the biggest girls in the school and ordered them to proceed to the playground and each bring in a boy. The order was promply obeyed and the strike ended.

BOYCOTTERS LOCKED UP.

NEW YORK, May 5.—Seventeen members of the Boseman bakers' union, engaged in boycotting Mrs. Landgrof, were arrested early this morning and locked up.

WORK RESUMED.

INDIANAPOLIS, May 5.—The Woodburn-Sarven Wheel company resumed work this morning, 500 of the old employes reporting for duty.

AT DETROIT.

DETROIT, May 5.—At an early hour this morning, over 500 strikers formed in line near the Michigan car shops and marched to the Peninsular car shops. The numbers increased until 1,500 men were in line. On the arrival of the strikers, the Peninsular shops shut down. The strikers then visited a number of other establishments, and succeeded in drawing out a thousand more men.

Washington News.

THE MORMON QUESTION.

WASHINGTON, May 5.—The hearing on the Mormon question was resumed by the sub-committee of the house committee on judiciary yesterday. Miss Kate Field and a number of women were present. Mr. West, a member of the Utah legislature, and Delegate Caine made addresses opposing the Edmunds bill.

A QUARANTINE PATROL.

In order to assist the local authorities in the maintenance against the introduction of infectious diseases the president has determined to establish by means of vessels of the revenue marine a national patrol of the coast of the United States so far as may be practicable under existing law and consistent with the other duties confided to that service.

THE HAWAIIAN TREATY.

The ship owners, ship builders and lumber dealers of the Pacific coast have memorialized congress asking that reciprocity with the Hawaiian islands be not abrogated.

GOV. SWINEFORD TO BE MARRIED.

WASHINGTON, May 5.—Gov. A. P. Swineford, of Alaska, is in the city. The primary object of his visit is to consummate an engagement of marriage between himself and a Washington lady. His confirmation as governor, he says, is not giving him the slightest concern. He proposes to return to Alaska and make it his future home whether he shall be confirmed or not. He regards Alaska as a country of wonderful possibilities. One serious drawback, he says, is the absence of land laws which will enable settlers to pre-empt a homestead. Under the existing circumstances mining claims only can be taken up. Gov Swineford thinks when these defects shall have been remedied a steady stream of immigration will start Alaskaward.

Miscellaneous Cable News.

LONDON, May 5.—Moriarty, an absconding official of the Hibernian bank of Dublin, was captured at Rotterdam, where he made three attempts to strangle himself.

The Spanish floating debt is 65,000,000 pesetas, a reduction since April 1 of 11,000,000. The Spanish government has decided to proceed with the consolidation of the Cuban debt as authorized by the cortes last year; also to renew negotiations for a treaty of commerce with the United States with a view of improving the trade and revenue of Cuba, in order to ease the burden of the guarantee.

The Greek Question.

ATHENS, May 5.—The powers have instructed their ministers at Athens to remain at their posts. It is believed that the powers will accept a guarantee from France that she will secure the disarmament of Greece and that they will not fix an actual period for its accomplishment.

THE WISCONSIN STATE JOURNAL: MADISON, JULY 10, 1890.

DR. BABCOCK'S TEST.

Simple Method of Determining the Quality of Milk.

FORTY TESTS IN TWO HOURS

Wisconsin Agricultural Experiment Station Demonstrates Its Practical Value.

Dr. S. M. Babcock, professor of agricultural chemistry at the state university, has just perfected a new test for milk which is practical, simple and accurate. For three months he has been working every day on this test and has succeeded so well that the result of his labors are about to be made public. A State Journal reporter visited Dr. Babcock's laboratory, yesterday afternoon, and obtained a description of the process and appliances used in determining the quality of the milk.

Seventeen and five-tenths centimeters of milk are taken up in a suction flask and dropped in a test bottle. An equal quantity of sulphuric acid is placed in the bottle. The decomposition of the milk by the acid heats the mixture quite hot. The test bottle is then placed in a compartment fastened to the inner rim of a centrifugal wheel. This wheel hangs over a pan containing water heated to boiling by a lamp beneath. After the bottle of decomposing milk is placed in its compartment the centrifugal wheel is driven for five minutes at the rate of 600 to 700 revolutions per minute. The butter fat, by which the quality of the milk is determined, will be found then to be separated from the milk and floating on the surface. The bottle is then taken out and a sufficient quantity of hot water is poured into it to bring the butter fat up in the neck of the bottle, on which is a graduated scale acurately measuring the percentage of butter fat to the given quantity of milk. This ends the test.

THE OLD SYSTEM.

Under the old gravo-metric process a good part of two days is occupied in making the test which by Dr. Babcock's process can be completed in a little over five minutes. By the old process fifty or sixty weighings by delicately balanced scales had to be made, and ether, one of the most expensive of chemicles, was largely employed in the work of separation. Dr. Babcock uses no balances, but has solved the problem of percentage by his method and proved it correct by comparison with the gravo-metric process. There is not the variation of one-tenth of one per cent. from the results obtained by the latter. The sulphuric acid used in the Babcock process does not cost over one-fifth of a cent to each test, hence the expensive chemicles are saved. The first apparatus made for Dr. Babcock cost him less than $50 and it can be made now for less than half that amount, as patterns had to be made and their cost is included in this sum. One balance alone in the old gravo-metric process is so delicate that it costs $100, and it is this expensiveness that has kept the old process from being available to creameries, etc.

THE TEST BOTTLES.

The test bottles are graduated perfectly when made, the scale on the neck measuring accurately the percentage of butter fat in 17.5 centimeters of milk. The centrifugal wheel is a common band wheel on the inner parimeter of which is fixed a series of compartments for the reception of the bottles of decomposing milk. Dr. Babcock's wheel has thirty compartments, so that he may make thirty tests at the same time. There is, however, no limit to the number of places for bottles except the size of the wheel. The bottle is taken while hot from the process of decomposition and put in the wheel; the lamp under the water-pan is lighted, and by the time the required number of revolutions have been made the water is boiling hot, so that the bottles have been kept at about an even temperature all through. Hot water is dipped from the water pan into the bottles to bring the floating butter fat up to the scale for measurement; thus it is seen there is no complicated machinery, no long chemical processes, no delicate weighings or tedious figuring, but when the three operations are finished the result stands out clear and accurate.

PROUD OF HIS SUCCESS.

Dr. Babcock is proud of his success in finding a cheap, simple and rapid method of determining the quality of milk, one that can be used by any person or with an apparatus which is within reach of dairymen. To demonstrate the rapidity of the process it is only necessary to state that in less than two hours, yesterday, forty tests were made at the labratory by Dr. Babcock, without any asststance,and with a centrifugal machine with a capacity for sixty bottles he could have doubled the number in less than fifteen minutes more time.

This scores another success for the Wisconsin university agricultural experiment station and will make the name Babcock noted among the dairymen of the world.

LETTERS FROM THE PEOPLE.

To THE EDITOR—*Sir:* Parties interested would be glad to know: 1st, Why the city library is closed for book-inspection at a time when so many people are at liberty to read? and 2d, Why the authorities do not take measures to relieve the Third Lake property owners of the annoyance caused by the stagnant water within the triangle?

Many Madisonians regret the non-appearance in print of Miss Giles' poem, delivered on Fourth of July. It was pronounced a most beautiful effort by the fortunate ones who heard it.

Madison, July 10. M. L. B.

Recovering from the Accident.

May Bennett, the little daughter of James Bennett, elevator engineer at the capitol, is recovering slowly from the effects of the burns she received, July 4. She set fire to a pin-wheel and fastened it to a tree. It jumped from the tree and caught on the front of the girl's waist, still sending out its fire. A neighbor lady saw the accident and hastening to the child picked her up, but she did not notice the burning wheel for a moment, so that by the time the wheel was pulled off the little one was badly burned about the chest, neck and the lower part of her face.

MINOR LOCAL TOPICS.

Items Worthy of Passing Notice by the Reporters.

Angell & Hastreiter's new city directory will not be ready for delivery before Aug. 1.

Haase & Son, of Oshkosh, have purchased the George F. Taylor stock of boots and shoes.

The case of the state against George Miller for burglary was put over until to-morrow morning.

Fred. Bartels is moving his grocery stock into the store on Pinckney street vacated by Gardner Snell.

W. H. Gallagher, of the Northern Pacific Express company, is paying Madison, his old home, a brief visit.

The work of pushing the chimney at the waterworks upward is suspended for the present. The scaffolding will have to be rebuilt.

The German Lutheran Sunday-school is picnicking at Winnequah to-day. A private picnic is being held at Schuetzen park, and another school picnic at Lakeside.

FOR SEVENTY YEARS.

DAVID H. WRIGHT'S LIFE ON EARTH

His Friends Surprise Him On the Anniversary of His Birth.

Last evening, the seventieth anniversary of the birth of David H. Wright was celebrated at his home on North Carroll street by a number of the genial gentleman's many friends. He is a prominent member of the Masonic fraternity, and his years of faithful work for the order were recognized by his brothers of the square, who brought with them to his residence a handsome easy chair. Other presents were left as a mark of the esteem in which Mr. Wright is held by his many friends.

The gathering of neighbors and friends was a complete surprise to the gentleman, but he entertained those who spent the evening under his roof-tree in a royal manner.

In his younger days David H. Wright was one of the first teachers in the Madison schools. Mr. Reuben G. Thwaites, in his history of Madison's public schools, says: "David H. Wright, a new-comer to Madison, was engaged. He commenced the spring term early in May [1844], and continued through the spring of the following year, 1845. Mr. Wright had in charge about fifty scholars, which sadly crowded the old school house, but he managed to stow them away after a fashion. Mr. Wright remembers that among his pupils were: William H. Joslin, George W. Stoner, William H. and Albert U. Wyman, William Pyncheon, Jr., Sinclair W. Botkin, Sabrina Pyncheon and the late Frank W. Bird. Col. George W. Bird was in the primary class, and among the most mischievous boys was Joseph N. P. Bird, who afterwards suffered the terrors of imprisonment at Andersonville."

In another connection Mr. Thwaites says: "The school-house was a one-story frame structure, sided with oak shakes, standing some 18x20 feet on the ground and costing about $70. It was located on the north corner of Pinckney and Dayton streets. * * * Around the room was constructed a continuous table of planed planks, two feet wide, akin to a mechanic's work bench. This was the general writing desk and alongside were the settees. When writing or studying the scholars turned outward to the table; when recitsng they faced the center, where the teacher sat with keen glance and solemn visage, open book in one hand and stout ruler in the other to bestow chastisement or impart instruction as occasion demanded. * * * Later the school was so crowded that a broad shelf was built upon brackets along one side of the room near the door. Here the children stowed their wraps and lunch baskets. In Wright's time this gallery became a sort of school section for the A. B. C. pupils. The stalwart Wright, in order to hasten matters at the opening of each session, was wont to toss the little ones up, two at a time, while at recess and when school closed they would clamber down upon his broad shoulders and thence to the ground — Lilliputians descending the Man Mountain."

Mr. Wright is and has been for years state carpenter. He is still a towering specimen of splendid physique, sturdy and lively of step. His seventy years sit lightly upon him, and beyond a slight silvering of the hair there is but little to mark the flight of time.

PERSONAL.

Thomas K. Beecher, of Elmira, N. Y., brother of the late famous Brooklyn divine, preached in the First Presbyterian church last Sunday. No announcement of his presence in the city was made, for the reason that the pastor, Mr. McAtee, did not know that Mr. Beecher would occupy the pulpit, and consequently only the usual congregation was present. On Monday Mr. Beecher left the city on his way to the Pacific coast. Although the gentleman has a national reputation as an orator and literateur, he has not occupied so prominent a place in the religious world as his deceased brother. Personally he has the distinguishing traits of the Beecher family and would be readily recognized as a man above the common run of humanity. In build he is not unlike Henry Ward, though he wears a full beard, while the former was always smooth-shaven. Mr. McAtee says he is endowed with a more philosophical and executive mind than his brother Henry, but has never courted notoriety. His church in Elmira, N. Y., is one of the largest and most flourishing in the country, and his Sunday-school, conducted somewhat on the plan of a public school, has a membership of 600. Mr. McAtee was married by Mr. Beecher and the two have always been on the most friendly terms. Mr. Beecher has not visited Madison before in fifteen years, when he delivered a lecture.

***

Sketches of Miss Ella A. Giles, and numerous selections from her pen, will soon appear in a volume now in press in Chicago, to be entitled "Local and National Poets of America," and in The Magazine of Poetry, a fine quarterly published in Buffalo. Although Miss Giles prefers writing prose, her poems of the past few years in eastern and southern papers have been of sufficient demand to prove remunerative.

***

Mr. and Mrs. J. H. Waggoner, of Eau Claire, are in the city for a few days, guests of Mr. and Mrs. T. Olson, at their residence on West Gilman street.

***

Father Knox officiated at the laying of the corner stone on the new St. Barnabas church at Mazomanie, this afternoon.

***

Gov. Hoard left last evening to attend the soldiers' encampment at Camp Douglass. He will return to-night.

***

Charles Cramer is home from his trip to Vermont and is again at his post at the Northwestern depot.

***

Joe Hobbins and wife left for a three weeks' outing to the northern fishing grounds, this morning.

***

A daughter has been born to Mr. and Mrs. Purder.

FAITH IN ITS FUTURE

Justice Bartholomew Gives a Pen Picture of Dakota.

FINE CROPS ITS SALVATION

Last Year's Drought Contributes to Decrease Emigration and to Discourage People—Prohibition.

J. M. Bartholomew, Bismarck, N. D., was written in a bold hand on the Park hotel register last evening.

"Who is this gentleman," said a State Journal representative to the clerk, as he placed his index finger on the name.

"I'm that fellow," responded a well-dressed, intelligent looking man, with a rotund well-proportioned form, who would tip the scales at not less than 175 pounds, and who was standing less than a foot away from the hotel desk, when the query was made.

The coincident paved the way for a talk about the crop prospects, politics, future growth and present status of affairs in the new state.

Mr. Bartholomew is an associate justice of the supreme court of North Dakota, and a brother-in-law of L. K. Luce, of Stoughton, assistant attorney-general, at whose home he expects to visit on his way east, and for which point he left late last night.

Mr. Bartholomew does not take a Utopian view of the future of the Dakotas, although he has faith that it will grow and prosper as its agricultural interests are developed. "The crop outlook, this year," said he, "were never better. Farmers are jubilant and predict the greatest yield of cereals ever known. The rains have been abundant and the growth of wheat and other products has so far advanced that hot wheather, should it continue from now on, is not going to reduce the percentage materially. The failure of crops last year and the subsequent distress in several counties was a serious drawback to emigration, this year. There was not so much suffering, except in a few isolated districts, as newspaper reports represented, but nevertheless the effect was to start emigration to other states especially to the Pacific coast, where the influx has been enormous.

"With this year's aboundent crop Mr. Bartholomew thinks that the faith in Dakota will be revived next year. The prohibitional feature of the constitution, he thinks, has also worked to the disadvantage of the prosperity of the state, especially in the large towns. The "original package" decision, however, has, in his opinion, counteracted some of this influence, and liquor is being sold at a good many points. As to whether prohibition was a good thing for Dakota on general principles Mr. Bartholomew was not prepared to say.

Speaking of the census enumeration, he said that Bismarck would not show a phenomenal growth; in fact it has lost in population since the boom caused by the location of the capitol has collapsed. The population of Pierre, which had also been inflated by the capitol boom, was also suffering from the reaction. In the Sioux reservation nothing like the scenes witnessed at the opening of the lands to settlers are now taking place. Affairs there have settled down to a legitimate basis. Mr. Bartholomew said he had doubts about the Sioux lands being more valuable or richer than other parts of the Dakotas. In fact, he had heard a good deal of it was poorer.

Concerning the political outlook of both North and South Dakota, Mr. Bartholomew thought that everything was favorable for republican success and for the ascendency of and control of affairs by the party in the future. The action of the Louisiana legislature on the lottery bill had he believed, settled an aggravating question for Dakota. But little railroad building, he says, is being done in Dakota the present year.

Early Closing.

We, the undersigned butchers of Madison, do hereby agree to close our markets at 7 o'clock each evening, excepting Saturday, on and after Monday, July 14, until August 18:

J. L. MILLER & Co.,	SPRECHER BROS.,
SOELCH & MENG,	SIGGLEKOW & KLEIN,
M. J. HOVEN,	WM. H. LANSING,
ROESCH BROS.,	GALLAGHER BROS.,
SOMMERS BROS.,	H. NOLTY & CO.,
MCARTHUR & CO.,	HENRY SCHELER.

857jy8d3t

Wanted.

A middle-aged man, perfectly responsible, to take the agency for the well-known Shaw Boiler Cleansing Compound, for keeping steam boilers free from scales, etc. Large inducements for the right man. Address The Shaw Manufacturing Co., 171 Broadway, New York City. 768je13dtf

For Rent.

The Store in State Journal block, for several years past occupied by McConnell & Son, grocers. Right on the market. Exceptionally fine location. If two good parties desire each to rent one-half the store, it can be divided by partition or not as they may determine. Enquire at State Journal office. dtf

The Savings, Loan and Trust Co.

is prepared to offer special inducements to investors and guaranties capital and prompt payment of semi-annual interest. Please call at the company's office for further particulars.

HALLE STEENSLAND, President.
809mar20dtf

CATARRH CURED, health and sweet breath secured, by Shiloh's Catarrh Remedy. Price 50 cents. Nasal Injector free. Sold by Dunning & Sumner.
1233nov5d&weow1y-B

For Rent.

Rooms and Dwellings. Inquire of F. J. Lamb, opposite Park Hotel.
853jy8d2w

Woman Wanted.

At Madison Hospital, a good strong woman to do cooking and general housework. Enquire at Madison Hospital immediately. 820je26dtf

Wanted.

A boy about 15 years of age wanted immediately at WALTZINGER'S.
860jy10dtf

Who are the best walkers in town? Those who wear Coward's Boots and Shoes, because their feet are fitted on the bottom. 861jy10d2t-thur-sat

Col. W. F. Vilas was 50 years old yesterday. He has gone to Ashland on legal business.

Mr. Sarles, of Minneapolis, father of Mrs. O. D. Brandenburg, is visiting in the city.

W. S. Dwinnell was down from Minneapolis a few days this week.

Gen. Burchard and Maj. Curran are at Camp Douglass.

ARTICLES OF ASSOCIATION.

Black Hawk Silver Mining Company, of Milwaukee.

The Milwaukee Ice company, of Milwaukee, filed an amendment fixing their capital at $10,000.

The Beloit Land and Investment company, of Beloit; capital, $50,000. The incorporators are Porter B. Rates, Torris Gesley, J. B. Dow, Chas. W. Merriman and A. N. Bort.

The Caledonia Building and Loan association, of Kenosha; capital, $1,000,000. The incorporators are Hugh Innis, W. W. Strong, Urben J. Lewis, James Pennefeather, John O'Donnell and James Cavanagh.

In the secretary of state's office the following articles of association were filed to-day: The Black Hawk Solid Silver Mining company, of Milwaukee; capital, $70,000. The incorporatore are Frank A. Woodford, Joshua Stark and Edwin F. Van Vechten.

IS HE INSANE?

PHYSICIANS THINK THAT HE IS.

A Man Blessed With Four Children in Two Years.

Hans Olson may or may not be insane, but his actions at Mazomanie were so peculiar that it was thought advisable to have his mental condition inquired into, and he was brought here this morning by Sheriff Vernon for that purpose. Drs. Keenan and Twitchell were called to the county court for the purpose of sounding the length and breadth of his mental caliber.

Hans lived down in the town of Perry. He says he has been married two years and has four children, a record which one wicked wag says would warrant a verdict of "justifiable insanity," if such a verdict could be rendered by the doctors. Hans says he has been abused by his wife since the second pair of twins entered on the race of life; that he has been compelled to take up his bed in the cellar, while she slept in the garret. These things, he suspects, may have made him cynical and worked upon him until he talked too much about it. He loves the dear children, but he thinks too many of them at one time would discourage any man that had to contribute to their support.

It is said that Mr. Francis Ritchie, register in probate, firmly believed the fellow to be sane until he made the announcement of four children in two years; then he backed down, declaring that the man would have to be unusually strong if he kept his mental balance under such a strain as that.

Denied the Application.

TOPEKA, Kas., July 10.—The State Board of Railway Commissioners has denied the application of the Farmer's alliance for a reduction of the local grain rate in Kansas to Missouri river points.

"TICKETS AT HALF RATES"

Via the Chicago, Milwaukee and St. Paul Railway.

For the Biennial Conclave of Knights of Pythias at Milwaukee, sale July 5th to 11th inclusive; return good on trains leaving Milwaukee July 9th to 19th inclusive. Fare, round trip, two dollars and forty-four cents ($2.44).

For the National Educational Association at St. Paul, sale July 1st to 7th, good to return from 11th to 14th, and can be extended on application. Fare one way for round trip, with two dollars ($2) added for membership fee.

L. D. STONE, T. & P. Agt., Madison.
A. V. H. CARPENTER, G. T. & P. Agt. 801je20dtd

An Enterprising Firm.

For many years the S. L. Sheldon Co., of this city, have been the leaders in the trade on Wheeled Vehicles, and their present stock of Fine Carriages, Phaetons and Surries, with either Extension or Canopy Tops exceeds any variety heretofore offered by them.

Not only do they excel in the above line, but their stock of Road Wagons, Skeleton and Phaeton Carts and Spring Wagons and everything in the vehicle line consists of the largest assortment and greatest variety in any one establishment in the state.

Their long experience in the trade enables them to select the latest and nobbiest styles of the best makers that the markets afford and they guarantee bottom prices and the fullest warrantee on the jobs sold by them. Go and see them and look over their stock.

They offer a Good Road Cart and Set of Single Harnees for Twenty Dollars Cash. A. S. Brown is in charge of the Vehicle Department. See him and get bargains. 805je21dtf

FRENCH & CLIFFORD are offering a few bargains in residence property located in different part of the city. They have a number of very desirable properties convenient to the University which can be had at reasonable prices. All property shown without charge to purchaser. They have a few houses to rent, desirably located. Give them a call, 14 East Mifflin street. 859jy9d12t

Milwaukee Market.

MILWAUKEE, July 10.—Wheat firm; No. 2 spring, cash, 87c; No. 1 northern, 90c.

Corn firm; No. 2 white, 35½c.

Oats firm; No. 2 white, 31½c.

Rye firm; No. 1, 50c.

Barley firm; No. 2, 53c.

Chicago Market.

CHICAGO, July 10—(Close).—Wheat easy; cash, 88¼c; seller September, 90c.

Corn steady; cash, 37½c; seller September, 38⅝c.

Oats firm; cash, 28⅝c; seller September, 28c.

Rye steady; 48½c.

Barley firm.

Prime timothy 1.35.

Flax 1.33.

Whisky; 1.09.

Pork dull; cash, 11.87½; seller September, 11.25.

Lard steady; cash, 5.75@5.77½; seller September, 5.97½@6.00.

CHICAGO, July 10.—Hogs: Receipts, 33,000; market generally active and lower; light, 3.75@3.95; heavy packing and shipping, 3.75@3.90.

Cattle: Receipts, 14,500; market slow and weak; inferior to fancy, 3.50@4.85; stockers and feeders 2.00@3.35; Texans 2.00@3.00.

Sheep: Receipts, 6,000; market strong; natives, 3.50@5.12½; stockers 3.00@4.00.

New York Stock and Money Markets.

NEW YORK, July 10—Noon—Money at 4@5 per cent.

Government securities: 4's coupon, 1.21½; Pacific 6's of '95, 1.13.

B., C. R. & N.	126	Northern Pacific	36
Chicago & Alton	131	do preferred	81¾
C. B. & Q.	136¼	Northwestern	110¾
do preferred		do preferred	143
Delaware & Lac	146¼	New York Central	108
Erie	25¼	Rock Island	90¼
do preferred	63	St. Paul	73⅝
Fort Wayne	155	do preferred	118
Illinois Central	116¼	St. P., M. & M.	110¾
Kansas & Texas	18¾	St. P. & O.	32¾
Lake Shore	109¼	do preferred	92
Louisville & N.	88½	Union Pacific	63
Michigan Central	97½	Fargo	140
New Jersey Central	20	Western Union	83¼

IN CIRCUIT COURT.

Ryan's Insurance Money Given to His Sisters.

THE BUTLER CASE DECIDED

The Business of the July Term Practically Done—Judge Clementson Has Finished.

Judgment was given to-day in the circuit court for the plaintiffs in the case of Alice Ryan and Mrs. Mary Lally against Mrs. Isabella Ryan, widow of Thomas Ryan, late of the Fourth ward, this city. Ryan was engaged to Emma Fitch, of Monroe, and made her the beneficiary of a policy for $2,000 in the Ancient Order of United Workmen. While he was still engaged to Miss Fitch he married a Sheboygan woman. Just before his death, it is alleged, he assigned the money to his two sisters, the plaintiffs in this action. The manner of this assignment was the ground of Mrs. Ryan's defense, but when the case was called to-day the defendant's counsel did not appear and judgment was taken in favor of the plaintiffs in default of appearance. The United Workmen paid the $2,000 into the hands of the clerk of the court, pending the decision of the case and this money will now be paid over to the sisters of the deceased.

OTHER CASES.

In the same court a stipulation has been filed settling the case of Charles Durst against John Schlimgen, in which the plaintiff sought to set aside the conveyance of property to which he would have been heir. Durst's father conveyed his property to Schlimgen and the plaintiff alleged that the old man was out of his head when the conveyance was made. Schlimgen pays $500 and costs to the boy in settlement of the case.

THE BUTLER CASE.

John Butler, by his guardian, A. M. Daggett, brought suit against his wife, Elizabeth Butler, asking the setting aside as null and void of a deed conveying to the defendant the title to the defendant the title to the homestead, situated in the Fifth ward. The case was heard by Judge Clementson, at the April term of the circuit court. The case many interesting phases. John Butler was divorced from his wife, Elizabeth Butler, and after a few years separation they remarried. After the second conjugal contract had been made Butler signed a deed giving Mrs. Butler the title to the homestead. Later he became demented and is at present in the state hospital for the insane.

Mrs. Susan M. Austin, who lives on South Bassett street, is a sister of Butler, and would be heir to his property if the second marriage and deed were void. She alleged that Butler was not in his right mind when he married his divorced wife and that he was also non compus mentis when he conferred the title to the homestead on his wife. She therefore brought suit in the name of the guardian of her brother, asking the court to declare the marriage and conveyance void. Judge Clementson, after carefully weighing the matter, decided that Butler was sane at the time he was married the second time to the woman, and holds the deed good and sufficient. This confirms Mrs. Butler in the right to the homestead, worth about $8,000.

Judge Clementson, this afternoon, finished the hearing of such cases as Judge Siebecker was interested in as attorney and he will return home, this evening. A few cases of fact for court remain to command Jude Siebecker's attention, but the work of the term is about finished.

☞ Palpitation of the heart, nervousness, tremblings, nervous headache, cold hands and feet, pain in the back, and other forms of weakness are relieved by Carter's Iron Pills, made specially for the blood, nerves and complexion.
196mar24dawly-d

Dr. Joseph Schneider, the Milwaukee oculist, will be abroad during July, August and September. His return will be duly announced. 806je23d1m

FOR SALE.

Choice Lake Lots. Prices low and terms easy. Madison Manufacturing Co.'s re-plat — one block from University. Inquire of J. W. Hudson or F. J. Lamb.
673may19dtf

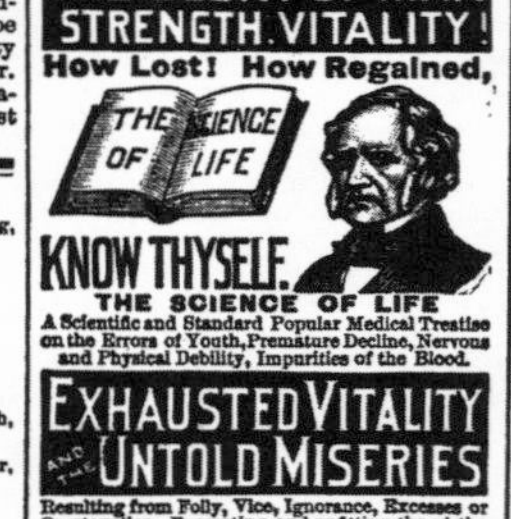

THE SCIENCE OF LIFE

A Scientific and Standard Popular Medical Treatise on the Errors of Youth, Premature Decline, Nervous and Physical Debility, Impurities of the Blood.

EXHAUSTED VITALITY AND THE UNTOLD MISERIES

Resulting from Folly, Vice, Ignorance, Excesses or Overtaxation, Enervating and unfitting the victim for Work, Business, the Married or Social Relation. Avoid unskillful pretenders. Possess this great work. It contains 300 pages, royal 8vo. Beautiful binding, embossed, full gilt. Price only $1.00 by mail, postpaid, concealed in plain wrapper. Illustrative Prospectus Free, if you apply now. The distinguished author, Wm. H. Parker, M. D., received the GOLD AND JEWELLED MEDAL from the National Medical Association for this PRIZE ESSAY on NERVOUS and PHYSICAL DEBILITY. Dr. Parker and a corps of Assistant Physicians may be consulted, confidentially, by mail or in person, at the office of THE PEABODY MEDICAL INSTITUTE, No. 4 Bulfinch St., Boston, Mass., to whom all orders for books or letters for advice should be directed as above.

WANTED—AN ACTIVE MAN for each section. Salary $75 to $100 to locally represent a successful New York Company, incorporated to supply Dry Goods, Clothing Shoes, Jewelry, etc., to consumers at cost. Also a Lady of tact, Salary $40, to enroll members (80,000 now enrolled, $100,000 paid in). References exchanged. Empire Co-Operative Association (credit well rated) Lock Box 610, New York.
88feb10deowly-mon

FARM FOR SALE.

Two hundred and forty acres, known as the Joseph Deming Farm, situated near the center of the town of Vienna, Dane county, Wisconsin, within five miles of four railroad stations: Waunakee, Dane, De Forest and Windsor.

An excellent place for a Stock Farm, having Good Pasture, Good Well with Windmill, Two Barns, Plenty of Timber and a Very Good House, For information in regard to terms, apply to

R. G. DEMING, Business College, Madison, Wis.
732je30d&woswfw-fri-45

ESTABLISHED A. D. 1853 — **THE STATE BANK** — MADISON, WIS.

LOANS MADE ON APPROVED REAL ESTATE SECURITY.

SAVINGS BANK DEPARTMENT paying Compound Interest on Time Deposits.

Money sent to *England, Ireland, Germany, Norway,* and to all accessible points in the United States.

DIRECTORS.

SAMUEL MARSHALL, L. S. HANKS, President, J. H. PALMER, Vice Pres.

S. H. MARSHALL, Cashier.

jan-dawly

SEVENTY-FIFTH SEMI-ANNUAL REPORT OF

THE STATE BANK,

MADISON, WIS.,

MONDAY MORNING, JULY 7, 1890.

RESOURCES:

Loans and discounts	$656,696 10
Due from directors or stockholders, nothing	....
Overdrafts	495 63
United States and other bonds and securities	25,213 26
Real estate, bank premises	10,000 00
Specie, Treasury notes and bank notes on hand	74,042 31
Due from banks	165,885 71
Total	$932,333 01

LIABILITIES:

Capital paid in	$100,000 00
Due depositors	818,250 75
Due to others	14,082 26
Total	$932,333 01

L. S. HANKS, President.
S. H. MARSHALL, Cashier.

Subscribed and sworn to before me, this 7th day of July, 1890.
850jy7d1w&w4w-48 E. O. KNEY, Notary Public, Dane Co., Wis.

BUSINESS DIRECTORY.

OLSON & VEERHUSEN.
CLOTHIERS. THE LARGEST display of Perfect Fitting Ready-Made Clothing. In Merchant Tailoring we are the leaders.

JULIUS ZEHNTER & CO.
WONDERFUL LOW PRICES in Dress Goods. Carpet Department displays Good Ingrains at 40, 50 and 60 cents per yard.

W. J. PARK & CO.
THE BEHR BROS.' PIANO IS still in the lead. The Burdett Organ, Western Cottage, Clough & Warren, Storey & Clark, and the Celebrated Æolian Organs.

WINDEN, GRINDE & SCHMEDEMAN
20 EAST MAIN ST. MEN'S Boys' and Youths' Ready-Made Clothing. Suits to order from the largest selection of Imported and Domestic Cloths.

NELSON & HENDERSON.
CLOTHIERS AND HATTERS. Corner of Pinckney St. and Washington Ave. Before buying your Spring Hats and Furnishing Goods, call and look over our goods and prices.

HOLLISTER'S PHARMACY.
PAINTS. ALL THE CHOICE New Tints for decorating the home, outside and in. Any lady can use them. Artists' Materials of all kinds.

MADISON MARKET DAY.
FIRST WEDNESDAY IN EACH Month. Two thousand letters have been sent to Livery Men, 'Bus Men and Street Car Companies in Chicago and Milwaukee.

JOSEPH S. KEYES.
FIRE INSURANCE. 555may3d1y

R. W. HURD.
DENTIST. NO. 23 SOUTH Pinckney St., Madison. 615may7d1y

ST. JULIAN RESTAURANT AND EUROPEAN HOTEL.
GAME, FISH, OYSTERS, Spring Chickens, Spring Lamb. Open after performances at Fuller Opera House. Thomas Morgan, Proprietor. Corner Main and Pinckney streets. 662may16d1y

THE FRANCIS WHITTAKER ST. LOUIS
HAMS AND BACON, THE Finest Cured Meats in the United States. For sale only at Harnden's, No. 111 West Main St. 667may17d1y

THE DEERING HARVESTERS.
JUNIOR STEEL BINDERS, New Deering Mowers. H. H. Beebe, General Agent, Madison, Wis., foot of Blair Street.

C. B. WELTON & CO.
CASH CLOTHING HOUSE. Hats and Gents Furnishing Goods.

M. L. NELSON,
GROCER, MAIN ST. FRUITS, Berries, Vegetables by Express daily. California Clarets and fine table Wines sold by the gallon or in quart or pint bottles. Hennesy Brandy and Rhine Wines. 675may20d1y

ALEX. FINDLAY.
TEAS, COFFEES, SYRUPS, Gilt Edge Flour. Manager Peoples' Bread Company. Send for Price List.

FESS HOUSE.
GEORGE E. FESS, MANAGER. Rates $1.00 per day. Nos. 113 and 119 East Doty Street.

ADVANCE THRESHERS.
E. H. HEATH, MANAGER Wisconsin Branch, Madison, Wis., foot of Blair Street.

FRED BARTELS.
TEAS, COFFEES, SYRUPS. Fancy Grades of Flour. Fresh Fruit and Vegetables Daily.

FOR SALE OR TRADE.
A GOOD BUSINESS IN PROSperous town, General Merchandise. Will sell on easy terms or trade for farm. Address State Journal Printing Co., Madison, Wis. 688may22d2w

J. H. D. BAKER & CO.
ENGLISH DECORATED DINner Sets, English Tea Sets, Gold Band Cups and Saucers, China Plates, Chamber Setts, China Fruit Plates, Jap Teapots, Piano Lamps. 683may22d1y.

DAYTON LOCKE
HAS A COMPLETE STOCK OF Ladies' Oxford Ties, Latest Styles; also Ladies' and Gents' Patent Leather and Tennis Goods, endless variety. Correct Styles, Lowest Prices. 704may27d1y

FANS, 300 STYLES.
GAUZE, PLAIN PAINTED, all the leading shades Ostrich Fans, at Dunning & Sumner's. The largest assortment of Novelty Handled Canes. 684may29d1y

SUMNER & MORRIS.
HARDWARE, GUNS, RIFLES, Fishing Tackle, Lawn Mowers, Spruce and Ash Oars. No. 11 Pinckney St. and 106 King St.

BOLEY, HINRICHS & THOMPSON.
DRY GOODS. OUR STOCK for the spring and summer season is complete in all departments. 27 East Main St.

ANDREW A. MAYERS.
PURE DRUGS, BEST MEDICinal Wines and Fresh Groceries. Nos. 108 King and 115 East Main streets. 709may29d1y

NEW YORK STORE.
DRY GOODS AND CARPETS, Full assortment of New and Seasonable Goods always on hand.

CITY MARKET.
COLD STORAGE REFRIGERators. Choice Meats, Fancy Roasts, French Chops, Spring Chickens, Tender Loin Steaks. Soelch & Menz, Main St. 688may16d1y

ADAM BLIND.
BOOTS AND SHOES. TWENty years in the Shoe trade in Madison. Ladies' Grover shoes, soft soles for tender feet. Men's $2 and $3 Calf Shoes. 104 King St., next to German Bank.

KLAUBER-ROWLEY CLOTHING CO.
MENS' AND BOYS' CLOTHing at Low Cash Prices.

DR. VANCE.
SPECIALIST. OFFICE THREE Doors South of Court House. Dr. Vance will be at home every day except Wednesdays.

ROYAL HOT AIR FURNACES,
STOVES, RANGES, CUTLERY, Tinware. at SCHIEBEL & KREHL'S, 842jy3d1y Washington Ave.

LADIES' FURNISHING PARLOR.
I HAVE OPENED PARLORS and have a Stock of Ladies' Furnishing Goods which I shall be pleased to have the ladies of Madison call and examine. Outing Suits, Divided Skirts, etc. Health Waists a Specialty. Repairing neatly done. Rooms open daily, and Tuesday, Thursday and Saturday evenings. Solicitors wanted in adjoining towns. Street Cars pass the door. MRS. JULIA D. THOMAS, 609may5d1y 929 University Ave.

Fuller Opera House.

One Night Only.

FRIDAY EVENING, JULY 11th.

SPECIAL ENGAGEMENT OF

FITZPATRICK'S SPECTACULAR

Rip Van Winkle Co.

Introducing the Eminent German Comedian,

JOHN P. HILL,

Supported by the Beautiful and Genteel Spanish Artist, Miss

ETHEL HODGSON,

THE TWO CHILD WONDERS,

Little Tillie and Edna Adams,

And 22 Artists of Recognized Merit.

ELABORATE SCENERY.
STARTLING MECHANICAL EFFECTS.
NEW AND ORIGINAL MUSIC.

A Grand Street Parade at 11:30.

PRICES:

Parquet, reserved	75c
Dress Circle, reserved	75c
Three Rows in Balcony, reserved	75c
Remaining Seats in Balcony	50c
Gallery	25c

☞ Box Office open Thursday at 9 a. m.
853jy8dtd

FIRST NATIONAL BANK.

UNITED STATES

DESIGNATED DEPOSITORY.

MADISON, - - WISCONSIN.

DIRECTORS:

N. B. VAN SLYKE, President. M. E. FULLER, Vice President.
WM. F. VILAS, B. J. STEVENS,
J. E. MOSELEY, F. F. PROUDFIT.
WAYNE RAMSAY, Cashier.

WM. H. ROGERS. F. HALL. ANTHONY DONOVAN.

ROGERS, HALL & DONOVAN,

Attorneys and Counsellors at Law,

Tenney Block, cor. Main and Pinckney Sts., MADISON, WIS.
849jy7d&w3m

We Have It, the Finest Soda Fountain,

COLD SODA.

HOLLISTER'S PHARMACY

TO RENT!

From September 1st, the 10-Room House, No. 719 State St., near the University. Large Lot. All the Modern Improvements.
Enquire on the premises. 840jy8tf

Northwestern EYE and EAR Infirmary

Surgical and Medical disease of Eye, Ear, Nose and Throat treated. Spectacles adjusted and Artificial Eyes inserted.

Dr. W. C. ABALY, Physician & Surgeon, Madison, Wis

CIRCUIT COURT—MILWAUkee County.

In the matter of Kate F. Sullivan, insolvent debtor.

To the creditors of Kate F. Sullivan, of the city of Milwaukee:

You are hereby notified that on June 2, 1890, on reading and filing the petition of the above named Kate F. Sullivan, praying that she may be adjudged an insolvent debtor, within the purview of chapter 179, of the revised statutes of Wisconsin, and that she be discharged in pursuance of the provisions of said chapter 179 from all her debts provable under the same, and the schedules and affidavit hereunto annexed, the judge of the above named court duly made an order on said day requiring all creditors of the said Kate F. Sullivan, to show cause, if any they have, before the circuit court of Milwaukee county, at the court house, in the city of Milwaukee, county of Milwaukee, and state of Wisconsin, on the first day of September, 1890, at 10 o'clock in the forenoon of that day, or as soon thereafter as the matter can be heard, why the said Kate F. Sullivan should not be adjudged to be an insolvent debtor within the purview of said chapter 179, of the revised statutes of Wisconsin, and why an assignment of the estate of such insolvent debtor, said Kate F. Sullivan, should not be made, and why such insolvent debtor, said Kate F. Sullivan, should not be discharged from her debts, and why such further and other order should not be made as shall be just and equitable in the premises.

Dated Milwaukee, June 2, 1890.

KATE F. SULLIVAN, Insolvent Debtor.

AUSTIN, BUNKEL & AUSTIN, Attorneys for Insolvent Debtor. [illegible]

THE STATE JOURNAL Is the Official State Paper of Wisconsin. It circulates all over the State. All laws and official publications appear first in its columns. Both Daily and Weekly editions offer superior inducements to advertisers.

WISCONSIN STATE JOURNAL.

VOL. 90. NO. 142. MADISON, WIS., WEDNESDAY AFTERNOON, FEBRUARY 16, 1898. PRICE FIVE CENTS.

HORROR AT HAVANA.

U. S. Battleship Maine Blown Up in the Harbor at 9:40 Last Night.

253 ARE DEAD OR MISSING.

All Officers are Saved but Two. Explosion Occurred in Magazine Under Men's Quarters.

CAUSE IS STILL A MYSTERY

All Accounts Indicate an Accident, Though There is No Explanation as to How It Could Occur—Sentry Was On Deck—Spanish Express Deep Sorrow and Give Every Assistance—De Lome Says Spaniards Love America. Capt. Sligsbee's Report—He Declines to Commit Himself as to Cause of Explosion.

Havana, Feb. 16.—Two officers and more than 200 of the crew of the battleship Maine, wrecked in this harbor by an explosion last night, are missing. Some of the crew who were able to swim kept afloat till picked up by boats. Six of the wounded crew and one officer have been taken to the military hospital by Gen. Blanco's orders.

CONSUL LEE'S REPORT.

Washington: Assistant Secretary of State Day received the following from Gen. Lee: "The Maine blew up at 9:40 last night. The explosion occurred well forward under the men's quarters, and consequently many are lost. It is believed all the officers are saved but Jenkins and Merritt, not accounted for. The cause of the explosion is yet to be investigated. The captain general and army and navy officers have rendered every assistance. Capt. Sigsbee and most of his officers are on board the steamer City of Washington. Others are on a Spanish gun boat and in the city. I am with Sigsbee, who has telegraphed the navy department."

THE COOK'S STORY.

New York: The Evening Telegram's correspondent says: "James Howe, the ship's cook, is the least injured of any of the Maine's crew brought in while I was there. I asked him how it happened. 'I don't know,' he replied, 'I turned into my hammock at 8 and heard three bells strike. I don't remember anything more until I felt myself turning over, and falling heavily upon the deck. I jumped overboard to keep from being drawn down by the suction. I was picked up by a boat from a Spanish man-of-war.'

"As far as I can learn now the explosion took place in the magazine used for storage of gun cotton for torpedoes. The vessel lies with her bows wholly submerged and only part of the stern showing. The explosion, which shook the city from end to end, created the wildest excitement. All the electric lights were put out by the shock. Fire engines rushed madly about. No one knew for certain from which direction the explosion came.

AT THE NAVY DEPARTMENT.

Washington: The navy department was the scene of intense excitement this morning. The first news came from Commandant Forsyth, at Key West, who wired he had been notified by Captain Sigsbee, of the Maine, to inform Admiral Sicard, in command of the North Atlantic squadron, that the Maine had been blown up and destroyed. He requested a light house tender be sent to Havana, and added that many are killed and wounded. Commandant Forsyth further said the light house tender Mangrove left Key West at 3 this morning for Havana, and the tug Fern would promptly follow her. A second dispatch said he had sent the torpedo boat Ericksson to Admiral Sicard at Dry Tortogus with a message concerning the disaster to the Maine.

Captain Dickins, chief of the navigation bureau, expressed the opinion that the explosion took place in the magazine of the Maine. This is evident for the reason that the ship was afloat an hour after the explosion. Had a torpedo been fired under the battleship she would have sunk immediately.

DISPATCH FROM GEN. BLANCO.

The news of the Maine disaster was learned at the Spanish legation with horror and was the occasion for many expressions of the most profound regret and condolence. Early Du Bosc, the charge d' affairs, received a message from Captain General Blanco, dated Havana, at 2 o'clock this morning, as follows: "With profound regret I have to inform you that the American ship Maine, in this harbor, blew up, by undoubtedly a chance accident. It is believed it resulted from the explosion of the boiler of a dynamo. Immediately following the accident all possible elements at the capitol hastened to the spot and rendered every aid possible. These included the force of the marine fire brigade and all the generals in Havana, among them my chief of staff. There have been deaths and wounded. I have sent an aide-decamp to offer every assistance to the American consul that he may wish for. I will forward further details as they become available.

"(Signed) BLANCO."

Du Bosco said to the Associated Press: "Of course I look at it with horror as due in every respect solely and simply to accident. That is the clear and unequivocal statement of the authorities at Havana, and all the evidence goes to sustain it." Du Bosc hastened to the state department for the purpose of expressing his deep condolence to the authorities.

CONGRESSMEN ARE RETICENT.

Greatest interest prevailed among the senators and representatives as to the extent of the Maine disaster. With only first reports before them, and recognizing the gravity of any utterances, there is a hesitancy to express opinions. The immense gravity of the situation in case later advices should show the disaster was not accidental, is admitted by all. Chairman Hitt, of the foreign affairs committee, Chairman Dingley, of the ways and means committee, and members of the naval committee of the house, all said they preferred to await fuller information before expressing themselves. Hitt said it would be well for the public to follow the cue given by Capt. Sigsbee and suspend judgment till the cause of the disaster is ascertained. Ex-Senator Butler, of South Carolina, member of the committee on foreign relations during his service, was of the opinion that some bold man had gone aboard among many doubtless allowed to visit the ship and placed a grenade with a slow match where it would explode the magazine. Members of both houses, as a rule, expressed the opinion for publication that the catastrophe was the result of accident; but there were some opinions, generally expressed under the breath with the admonition not to publish, to the effect that the affair looked very mysterious and doubtful.

DE LOME LOVES AMERICA.

New York: Ex-Spanish Minister De Lome heard the news of the disaster to the Maine at his hotel this morning. At first he refused to credit the news, but when the truth dawned upon him he said: "It is terrible. I pray God the news has been exaggerated. You may be sure of one thing, however, no Spaniard did this. The Spanish ministry and Spanish people have been greatly misunderstood in this country. They all desire peace; they all want peace with America and Americans, not only from motives of policy, but because they love America. I'm forced to say now by this terrible affair what I should have been precluded from saying before. There is no country in the world I love as I do America. I love the country and the people in it, and with the keenest regret I take my leave as the result of this unfortunate letter incident. Nearly all prominent Spaniards and men of influence in my country share my views in regard to America. Spain cannot afford to go to war with the United States. If only from motives of policy they are determined not to have war. Such a thing is out of the question. If the Maine was blown up in Havana harbor it was the result of accident. That is certain. There will be no war."

THE MADRID VERSION.

Madrid: The first news received here direct from Havana said the explosion on the Maine was caused by fire, and that the warship, enveloped in flames, afterwards sank.

CAPT. SIGSBEE'S REPORT.

Washington: While with the president, Secretary Long received the following from Captain Sigsbee: "I advise sending a wrecking vessel at once. The Maine is submerged except the debris. It is mostly work for divers now. Jenkins and Merritt are still missing and there is little hope of their safety. Those known to be saved are: Officers, 24; uninjured crew, 18. The wounded are now on board a Ward line steamer, in the city hospital and at a hotel, and number 59 as far as known. All the others went down on board or near the Maine. The total lost or missing is 253. With several exceptions, no officer or man has more than part of a suit of clothing, and that is wet with harbor water. The Ward steamer leaves for Mexico at 2 this afternoon. The officers saved are uninjured. The damage was in the compartments of the crew. I am preparing to telegraph a list of the wounded and saved. The Olivette leaves for Key West at 1 p. m. I will send by her to Key West the officers saved, except myself and Wainwright, Holman, Henneberger, Ray and Holden. I will turn over the three uninjured boats to the captain of the port, with the request for their safekeeping. I will send all wounded to the hospital at Havana. (Signed) SIGSBEE."

LOOKS LIKE ACCIDENT.

Two members of the cabinet who spent some time with the president, state that everything received indicates the loss of the Maine was due to accident. Captain Sigsbee declines to express an opinion

About noon Secretary Long received the following unsigned telegram from Havana: "The explosion was forward and by all indications in the magazine, but we cannot tell till investigation. The sentry on the poop deck reports that there were no boats in the vicinity when the explosion occurred."

A telegram from G. B. Rae, said to be a newspaper correspondent, said: "There is no excitement. All is quiet. The only feelings are sympathy and sorrow for the accident."

Secretary Long sent the following: "The president directs me to express for himself and the people of the United States profound sympathy with the officers and crew of the Maine, and desires that no expense be spared in providing for the survivors and care of the dead."

DROWNED IN THEIR QUARTERS.

New York: The Evening World's Havana special says officers of the Maine state the explosion was in the central magazine; the vessel was raised out of the water, and went partially to pieces. The dispatch continues: All but the surgeon were in the ward room at the moment of the explosion. Then came a stupendous shock. All the officers below rushed on deck, but could get no further forward than the middle superstructure. Only a very pitiable few of the 350 Jackies ever got from below. The water rushed over them and many were stunned and drowned, but not mangled. It is not likely more than 40 sailors were saved. The officers on deck narrowly escaped. In the junior officers' mess all had to clamber out through the water and wreckage waist deep. All agree that a double explosion occurred as the natural result of an under-water explosion of the magazines. Out of the dense smoke came anguished cries for help to those on land and water. Simultaneously with the cessation of the falling of fragments of iron and wood from the wreck, search-lights were thrown on it. Spanish boats from shore joined those of the steamer Washington in the rescue of those still alive.

ANOTHER ACCOUNT.

New York: A telegram from Havana say Captain Sigsbee was on deck when the explosion came. It was in the bow. A sentry stationed there was unhurt. He had seen nothing suspicious. One of the officers said: "When I got on deck fire had started forward. There was a good strong breeze. The call for all hands on deck was promptly obeyed, and men and officers were perfectly cool. All possible efforts were made to check the flames without avail. The flames spread rapidly and several explosions occurred. The magazines were burst open and explosives thrown overboard. In half an hour it was apparent that nothing could save the ship."

LEE SILENT AS TO CAUSE.

Washington: Lee has telegraphed from Havana: "I am not prepared yet to report on the cause of the explosion."

The coast survey steamer Bache, now at Key West, has been ordered to Havana with wrecking paraphernalia.

BLANCO SAYS ACCIDENT.

Madrid: Captain General Blanco has cabled the authorities here and at Washington, that the disaster to the Maine was due indisputably to an accident.

THE EFFECT ON STOCKS.

New York: The shadow of the Maine disaster was felt on the stock market, which opened a point off for many prominent shares. Part of the losses recovered on supporting orders, but the pressure was renewed later, the market becoming firmer.

London: American securities opened firm, owing to the belief that the Cuban difficulty was ended; later they broke rapidly on news of the Maine disaster.

NOT DISCUSSED IN CONGRESS.

Washington: The senate ignored the Maine disaster and considered the resolution to prevent the confirmation of the Kansas Pacific railroad agreement. The house took up the bankruptcy bill. Henderson, of Iowa, opened with a long explanatory speech.

WON'T SEND ANOTHER SHIP.

Washington: Among the matters discussed by the president and cabinet today was the question of the expediency of immediately sending one or more warships to Havana to take the place of the Maine. The conclusion was reached that at present such a course is not desirable.

It is authoritively stated at the White house that information so far received indicates the loss of the Maine is the result of accident, and in the absence of evidence to the contrary, this should be assumed to be a fact.

THE MAINE'S OFFICERS.

Washington: The following is a list of officers of the Maine: Captain, Charles D. Sigsbee, Washington; Lieutenant Commander, Richard Wainwright, Washington; lieutenant, G. F. Holman, California; lieutenant, John Hood, Florence, Ala.; Lieutenant Carl W. Jungen, New York; Lieutenants (junior grade) G. P. Blow, La Salle, Ill.; John Blandin, Greenwood, Md.; F. W. Jenkins, Allegheny City, Pa. Naval cadets: W. T. Cluverius, Jr., Louisiana; Amon Bronson, Nebraska; D. F. Boyd, Joy, Ala. Surgeon L. G. Heneberger, Harrisonburg, Va.; Paymaster C. M. Ray, Washington; Chief Engineer C. H. Powell, Goshen; Past Assistant Engineer, F. C. Bowers, Brooklyn; Assistant Engineers G. R. Morris, Oregon, Mo.; Darwin R. Merritt, Red Oak, Iowa; Engineer Cadets Pope, Washington, North Carolina; Arthur Crenshaw, Alabama; Chaplain J. P. Chadwick, New York city; First Lieutenant of Marines Albert W. Catlin, Minnesota.

SAW NEVADA BLOW UP.

Running for Shelter When Explosion Occurred — 25 Lost.

Victoria, B. C., Feb. 16.—Advices from Juneau, Alaska, say: George Beck, a resident of Seaward City, on Berner's Bay, says he was standing on the beach and saw the steamer Clara Nevada running for shelter. Suddenly there was a flash, and the vessel burst into flames and foundered in a few seconds It is supposed the boilers burst. All on board were lost, in number 25.

WILL CENSURE DE LOME.

But Spain is Surprised at Request for Official Explanation of Private Letter.

New York, Feb. 16.—The World's Madrid special says: The Spanish note will express surprise that the United States should expect an explanation concerning De Lome's private letter. It will strongly censure De Lome's remarks about the president.

WHEAT GOES UP.

Chicago, Feb. 16.—The wheat market is unusually active. The volume of trade is not large, but owing to light offerings the price moved up easily, May gaining 3¼ cents for the day, and July the same amount. Shortly after the close curb wheat sold at $1 05¼, while calls went to $1 10¼. It is expected prices will go still higher before the shorts cover all their orders.

KANSAS PACIFIC SALE SETTLED.

Topeka, Kas., Feb. 16.—The government lien on the Kansas Pacific road was wiped out this morning. It was bought in by the reorganization committee of the Union Pacific for $6,303,000, the amount agreed on with the government

DE LOME HAS LEFT US.

New York, Feb 16.—De Lome, the ormer Spanish minister, sailed for Liverpool today.

ORATORS ELECTED.

The Madison high school graduating class has elected Miss Nora McCue valedictorian and Harry Sauthoff salutatorian, Fred. De Lay has been chosen as orator for Arbor day, and Miss Gussie Billings girl representative of the fourth grade. Miss McCue is recognized as one of the gifted and popular young ladies of the high school, winning the honor on the merit of her scholastic attainments.

FOR RENT.

Suite of rooms over Alford Bros.' laundry, suitable for dressmaking parlors

Wanted—First-class cook; first-class wages; good references. 153 W. Gorham.

ALL FOR KLONDIKE.

Two Coaches Filled at Lancaster Pass Through Madison.

HALE AND HEARTY MEN.

Young Bride and Groom Join the Party Here—Eighty One Dogs Fill a Baggage Car.

A party of fifty-two men, two women, including a bride and groom, and about eighty dogs, all from Lancaster and vicinity, reached Madison at 12:10 today, on their way to Klondike. Their coming drew to the Chicago & Northwestern railway depot not less than 150 people eager to get a view of the adventurers. There was a great rush for the two coaches occupied by the Klondikers No married couple came to view. Mr. Edward Cathen of British Hollow, near Lancaster, and Miss Amelia Damm of the latter place, were married at the bride's home Monday and came direct to this city, and here they joined the party. They took section 8 in sleeper 499. The husband, a strong man of nearly 40 years, took great care of his rather attractive wife, 10 years his junior. Both appeared happy. The party was made up of husky fellows, varying in age from 25 to 45 years. They take their meals in the coaches they occupy, and sleep in them. There appears to be every comfort. Two porters look after them. Seventy seven dogs came on from Lancaster, four were taken on here and two will come on at St. Paul. A large baggage car furnishes quarters for the canine family. They will receive good care. All sorts of breeds are embraced in this kennel.

At 12:55 the train of four regular coaches, two of the Klondike party, and two baggage cars pulled out for St Paul. It was a double header, L Moran pulled the throttle of engine 191 and F. Farwell manipulated that of 294. Conductor A. A. Astruh had charge of the train, which will make a change at Elroy. The dog car bore a banner, "Alaska Expedition, Lancaster, Wis.," and the Klondike coaches displayed red, white and blue colors. The party expect to reach Seattle at 2 o'clock next Saturday afternoon.

CITY NEWS NOTES.

In the yacht race on Mendota today the Defender was winner in the first class, and U. H. D. in the second.

The days are lengthening apace; the sun rises a few minutes before 7 o'clock, and sets about 5:20.

The little sparrows sat by the side of their partially builded nests this morning, when the mercury was only 5 degrees above zero, and wondered if Valentine's day was the proper time for mating in this latitude.

Reports are that a great supply of ice will be needed from this point for southern cities; and that the Knickerbocker Ice company, on Lake Wingra, is preparing to ship thousands of tons to southern Illinois. There is hope that the ice harvest will be in full blast here in a short time.

It should be understood by the public that the Governor's Guards will treat their friends and patrons to real old time dancing, with the best of music. It will not be so much a masquerade as a dance of maskers. Prizes will be given for the best characters and costumes. See display in Klauber & Co.'s window.

Word comes from New York that Rev. Ralph O. Irish, son of Dr. and Mrs. J. E. Irish, lost all his household goods in the Atlantic, off the Azores, Nov. 30. The English ship Cromanty, on which the goods were shipped, went down, carrying her cargo with her. Mr. Irish had been four years on missionary work abroad, and among his loss was a library of 600 volumes and a large collection of curios. Mr. Irish is well known in Madison.

MR. AND MRS. ROTH HURT.

Last Sunday at noon when Mr. Agnalin Roth and his wife, who live about three miles north of the city, were driving home from church, near the malt house, a team behind belonging to Christ Capaul ran away and smashed into their rig, the horses of Capaul jumping over them and severely injuring Mr. and Mrs. Roth.

MEETINGS.

Regular meeting of Madison Home Forum No. 335 this evening at its hall in Brown's block.

DID YOU MAKE YOUR GRAIN-O THIS WAY?

Here are the latest directions: Use one tablespoonful of Grain-O to two cups of cold water. Mix the Grain-O with half an egg and add the water. (Be sure to measure.) After the water gets to the boiling point let boil for fifteen to twenty minutes. Use cream and sugar to suit the taste. If you have not cream use hot milk.

A lady said: "The first time I drank Grain-O I did not like it, but after using it for ten days and forming the habit, nothing would influence me to go back to coffee." This is the experience of all. If you will follow directions, measure it every time and make it the same, and try it for ten days, you will not go back to coffee.

WANTED.

Fifty girls at once, to sort tobacco at Farmers' warehouse, just east of the Yahara river, near railroad track.

SUTTER BROS., Madison.

FINE ORGAN PLAYING.

Mr. Eaton, of Milwaukee, Christens the Congregational Instrument. Mrs. Dreier Sings.

The Congregational church was cold last evening, as usual, and the programme was too long (2½ hours); but the seats were nearly all taken and it was an enjoyable evening. Bach, of Milwaukee, has been rebuilding the organ (which dates from 1874) since early December, and the $1,600 expended results in a superb instrument. It has 46 stops and 1,844 pipes. Guilmant, the French organist, whose selections were in favor last night by both Mr. Eaton and Prof. Sleeper, said of American organs, that he marvelled at their mechanical devices and variety, but noted a lack of sonority in the loud stops. If there is any criticism of the new organ it might be this generic charge against all home work.

Mr. Eaton (who is organist at the fashionable St. James' and also at Pabst theater, where the oratorios are given) had five numbers, some of them groups of three. He has a command of the instrument, his mechanism is fine; it was most enjoyable. The organ programme was classic, though the familiar strains of "William Tell" roused up people who had come as escorts, and Mendelssohn's "War March" set memory at work, for it is with this air that organists often regale the crowded church while the bride is on the way. Then, too, "pedelling" interests people, Mr. Eaton sometimes carrying along the thread of his story with his feet alone —great heavy rich tones responding to keys as skilfully and rapidly pressed as by the hand.

Perhaps there was a lack of tone shading in Mr. Eaton's work, due, no doubt, to lack of opportunity in his selections which were quite uniform in style. Prof. Sleeper, however, came to the rescue of those who love sustained harmonies and gentle, quiet things; and in "The Prayer and Cradle Song" scored a triumph. One could just see people stretch back their necks and close their eyes and let their thought go glimmering among the things that were. Prof. Sleeper excels in what the critics call tone color. Mrs. Dreier's song, "The Last Chord," he accompanied admirably, and delicate flute trills reinforcing the voice were sweet beyond words.

Miss Bliss led the church choir of 42 voices, young men and women, through Mendelssohn's difficult "Hear My Prayer." The rendition revealed faithful practice and the young soprano sang sweetly and with evidences of growing power and skill. Mrs. Dreier sang a number of times to much acceptance. She was in most brilliant evening dress of pink and green and being of dazzling beauty, the somber pulpit hangings formed a strange, wierd background. "Ich Grolle Nicht" (I'll ne'er complain), she has studied with George Henschel and perhaps showed her finest work. Her enunciation is marked and made much of by the critics. Those who have heard contraltos big of voice and majestic in execution prefer a more forceful and organ-like rendition of "The Last Chord;" but full of charming simplicity and warmth of expression were groups of songs which she sang. The velvety smoothness of her voice and its youthful freshness were especially displayed in the charming "Silver Ring," by Chaminade; and of course her singing of Prof. Sleeper's setting for "Thou Art Like Unto a Flower," was tumultuously received. The programme was a rare treat, musically, and we trust Prof. Sleeper may soon announce another one with Clarence Eddy, Schucke or other organist in the class with Mr. Eaton.

AUCTION.

Commencing Wednesday, Feb. 16th, we will sell at public auction our entire stock of clothing, hats, caps and furnishing goods.

As it is well known that we have handled nothing but the most reliable goods no one can fail to appreciate this rare opportunity for obtaining genuine bargains. Notwithstanding the large amount of goods sold by us during the last 60 days, our stock is still one of the largest in the city. As every article in the store must go, the sale will be *positive* and *without reserve*. Sale will commence at 1 o'clock p. m. on above date and continue every afternoon and Wednesday and Saturday evenings until the stock is closed. Four show cases, as good as new, and other store fixtures for sale.

C. B. WELTON & Co.

ONLY THREE DAYS TO CALIFORNIA.

Via "Sunset Limited" from Chicago and St. Louis Composite car with barber shop, bath room and library; ladies' parlor observation room car; compartment and drawing room sleeping cars and dining cars. An ideal winter route, not so far south but just south enough to escape high altitudes and snow blockades. Complete particulars and illustrated pamphlet mailed free to any address by your local agent or James Charlton, G P. A., C & A. R. R., Chicago, Ill., or H. C. Townsend, G. P. A., St. L., I. M. & S. Ry., St Louis, Mo.

THE MARKETS.

Chicago Board of Trade quotations, reported by Robt. Lindblom & Co., Board of Trade, Chicago, to Grant Thomas, Room 30, Pioneer block, Madison, Wis., Feb. 16, 1898:

Articles	Opening.	Highest.	Lowest.	Closing. Feb. 16.	Closing. Feb. 15.
Wheat.					
May..	99¾@1.00	1.03⅜	99¾	1.03¼	99⅝-¾
July..	85¾	89¼	86	89½	85¾
Corn.					
May..	31-¼	31⅝	30¾	31¼-⅜	30⅝-¾
July..	32¼	[illegible]	32-⅛	32⅛	31⅞-32
Oats.					
May..	27¼	27⅝	27	27⅜	27⅛-¼
Mess Pk.					
May..	11.05	11.22	11.00	11.10	11 15
Lard.					
May..	5.15	5.20	5.12	5.17	5.20
S.R.Sides					
May..	5.27	5.35	5.25	5.27	5.22

Chicago car lots Wheat, 49; corn, 253; oats 136.

Minneapolis and Duluth car lots: Wheat, 230.

Chicago hogs a shade lower; receipts today, 28,000; estimated tomorrow, 27,000.

Liverpool first cables, ½d higher; closing ½d higher.

Chicago curb, 1:45 p. m.: May wheat, 1.03¾ calls, 1.11; puts, 99¾c.

New York stocks are lower and weak.

BRYAN ON MEXICO.

Wants Americans to Behold the Wonders of Free Silver!

HIS N. Y. WORLD'S LETTER.

Everything Lovely as Seen Through His Eyes; and All the Credit Given to the Money System—He Seems to Forget That Unfolding Resources and Fresh Energies Would Quicken Any Country's Industry.

[Copyright, 1898, by the Press Publishing Co., New York World. All rights reserved.]

The reading which I did preparatory to my visit to Mexico revealed to me how little I had known of the history of that country, past and current. In this connection I acknowledge my indebtedness to Senor Romero, the Mexican minister at Washington, for advanced proofs of his book, just issuing from the press, descriptive of Mexico at the present time. Senor Romero, besides being a student of great industry and research, is thoroughly familiar with our language, and his book will be of great value to both republics in that it gives to the people of the United States full and authentic information with regard to our neighbor on the south. The readers of The World may be interested in a brief reference to some of the facts which came under my observation during a three weeks' stay in the land of the Aztecs

I found:

First.—That Mexico is a delightful place to visit. Travel on the main lines is as safe, as comfortable and as cheap as in the United States. The City of Mexico is within four days' ride of Kansas City and can be reached by three routes. The Mexican National leaves the Rio Grande at Laredo, the International at Eagle Pass and the Mexican Central at El Paso.

The weather is dry and pleasant during the winter months, and the temperature high enough to be inviting to those who find the cold of the north too rigorous. The descent from the City of Mexico to Vera Cruz can be made between sunrise and sunset, and in the course of the day the traveler has an opportunity to compare the flora of two zones. As both the Mexican and the Interoceanic railroads connect the capital with this seaport the tourist is enabled to vary the scenery without loss of time. The new railroad which is building from the City of Mexico to Acapulco rises 2,500 feet almost within sight of the City of Mexico, and then drops 5,000 feet to Cuernavaca, the present terminus. The three snow crowned peaks Popocatepetl, Iztaccihuatl and Orizaba are magnificent mountains. Popocatepetl and Iztaccihuatl are near the City of Mexico. The first named, the largest of the three, presents the best view from Cuernavaca. All three can be seen from a point on the Interoceanic road near Pueblo. Cathedrals built before the landing of the pilgrims, huge public buildings, differing entirely in architecture from our own; unique Chapultepec, a national art gallery, filled with rare and valuable paintings, and a museum containing innumerable relics of a civilization which antedates the discovery of the continent by Europeans—all these combine to interest and instruct.

Second.—That while our nation has more inhabitants, covers more territory and possesses greater wealth, we cannot surpass the Mexicans in hospitality or in the courtesy which they extend to strangers.

Mexico Friendly to the United States.

Third.—That the Mexican authorities entertain a very friendly feeling toward the citizens of the United States, and heartily desire a continuation of the amicable relations now existing between the two nations.

Fourth.—That Mexico is as firm as the United States in the support of the Monroe doctrine, having realized only 30 years ago the dangers attendant upon an attempt to extend monarchical institutions upon the western hemisphere.

Fifth.—That President Diaz is entirely deserving of the encomiums bestowed upon him by his own people, by resident Americans and by visitors. He has a genius for public affairs, understands the condition and needs of his people and has their confidence to a degree seldom enjoyed by an executive, either hereditary or elective. While the advantages of a stable government are now so generally recognized that his death or resignation would not disturb the existing order of things, yet his qualifications have been so amply proved and his administration so completely successful that his people are unanimous in the hope that he may yet enjoy many years of official life.

Hidalgo, the warrior priest, who led the movement which resulted in independence, is called the Mexican Washington. Juarez, who successfully defended his country against Maximilian, was the second great Mexican leader of the nineteenth century. President Diaz, himself a brave general, by restoring order, establishing the supremacy of the civil law and perfecting the system of public education has earned for himself and will enjoy in history a place by the side of Hidalgo and Juarez.

Sixth.—That the public men of Mexico are not inferior to our own in intelligence, education and general information. Senor Mariscal, secretary of foreign affairs, adds to great ability long experience as a diplomat and is worthy of comparison with the premiers of the leading nations of the world. Senor Limantaur, secretary of finance, is a most accomplished gentleman and has exhibited superior skill in the management of the fiscal affairs of the republic. The other cabinet officers, governors, members of the national and state congresses, mayors, etc., whom I met were, without exception, men of refinement and scholarly attainments.

Seventh.—That the English language is being taught more and more extensively each year and is now understood and spoken by most of the public men or by members of their families. I was

Continued on third page.

Royal has a larger sale than all other cream of tartar baking powders combined.

M.S.KLAUBER&Co

Clearance Sale.

IN ORDER TO MAKE ROOM FOR SPRING GOODS WE ARE GOING TO OFFER OUR ENTIRE LINE OF

Winter Suits AND Overcoats

At Greatly Reduced Prices.

20 Per Cent. Discount FOR CASH.

☞This is worth your consideration if in need of a Winter Garment

M. S. KLAUBER & CO.

You Know THAT DWIGHT'S FLOUR (At Findlay's)

enjoys an established reputation in this community. You naturally draw the (correct) inference that it's a

GOOD FLOUR

But, while others have tried it and are daily enjoying its use, You have continued to use Flashbury's "Comparative" or "Imperative," or Somebuoy's "Seven X" (Xs are cheap) simply from habit or because it is so easy to get the same kind as always.

You run no risk in trying Dwight's Flour. It costs you nothing if not suitable in every way. You do not even pay for what you have used in making experiments. But you run the chance of being better pleased and also perhaps of buy ng it at a lower figure than you pay now.

FINDLAY, King Street, 'Phones 40.

DISCOUNT SALE.

WE WILL CONTINUE OUR 20 Per Cent DISCOUNT SALE OFF LAMPS During February.

☞Our line of KITCHEN UTENSILS was never more complete.

H.B. McGOWAN

Mendota Block, 14 W. Mifflin St.

THE LARSON JEWELRY STORE

FEBRUARY SALE.—The Best Silver Plated Ware. Warranted Full Weight Plate on 21 per cent. Nickel Silver Base.

Rogers' Triple Plated Knives and Forks, per dozen $2 50
Rogers' Triple Plated Table Spoons, per set 2 00
Rogers' Triple Plated Dessert Spoons, per set 2 50
Rogers' Triple Plated Tea Spoons per set 1 50
Butter Knife and Sugar Spoon, gold bowl 1 00
Berry Spoon, gold bowl 1 25
Soup Ladle, $2.25 Gravy Ladle, gold bowl, $[illegible] Cream Ladle, gold bowl 75
Child's Knife, Fork and Spoon 1 70
Pie Knife, gold blade 1 50

It is only through buying in the largest quantities that we are enabled to offer the above goods at these extremely low prices, which are less than charged by Chicago Jobbers for the same goods.

As a special extra inducement so that you may become acquainted with their merit we will give a free premium with every sale of these goods during the month.

WISCONSIN STATE JOURNAL.

VOL. 95. NO. 36. MADISON, WIS., WEDNESDAY AFTERNOON, NOVEMBER 7, 1900. PRICE FIVE CENTS.

M'KINLEY 285; BRYAN 142.

Republican Landslide Greater Than in 1896.

THEN IT WAS M'KINLEY 271; BRYAN 176

Utah, Kansas, Wyoming, All for McKinley; Kentucky and Nebraska in Doubt; Lind Loses in Minnesota; Pettigrew Knocked Out.

	1896 McKinley	1896 Bryan	1900 McKinley	1900 Bryan
Alabama	...	11	...	11
Arkansas	...	8	...	8
California	8	1	9	...
Colorado	...	4	...	4
Connecticut	6	...	6	...
Delaware	3	...	3	...
Florida	...	4	...	4
Georgia	...	13	...	13
Idaho	...	3	...	...
Illinois	24	...	24	...
Indiana	15	...	15	...
Iowa	13	...	13	...
Kansas	...	10	10	...
Kentucky	12	1	...	...
Louisiana	...	8	...	8
Maine	6	...	6	...
Maryland	8	...	8	...
Massachusetts	15	...	15	...
Michigan	14	...	14	...
Minnesota	9	...	9	...
Mississippi	...	9	...	9
Missouri	...	17	...	17
Montana	...	3	...	3
Nebraska	...	8	...	...
Nevada	...	3	...	3
New Hampshire	4	...	4	...
New Jersey	10	...	10	...
New York	36	...	36	...
North Carolina	...	11	...	11
North Dakota	3	...	3	...
Ohio	23	...	23	...
Oregon	4	...	4	...
Pennsylvania	32	...	32	...
Rhode Island	4	...	4	...
South Carolina	...	9	...	9
South Dakota	...	4	4	...
Tennessee	...	12	...	12
Texas	...	15	...	15
Utah	...	3	4	...
Vermont	4	...	4	...
Virginia	...	12	...	12
Washington	...	4	4	...
West Virginia	6	...	6	...
Wisconsin	12	...	12	...
Wyoming	...	3	3	...
Totals	271	176	285	142

Boston.—Massachusetts gives McKinley 82,985 majority.

San Francisco.—McKinley's plurality will be 20,000..

Helena, Mont.—Bryan carries the state and Clark will be elected to the senate.

Portland, Ore.—The state is for McKinley by 14,105.

Nashville, Tenn.—The plurality for Bryan is 30,000.

Reno, Nevada, Nov. 7.—Bryan's majority will not fall far short of 1,500.

Charleston, W. Va., Nov. 7.—Republicans carried the state by 15,000 plurality.

NEBRASKA IN DOUBT.

Omaha, Nov. 7.—Nebraska is in doubt. Democrats claim it by 3,000; republicans by 5,000. The legislature is democratic.

POPULISTS CONCEDE KANSAS.

Topeka, Nov. 7.—Populists concede that the republicans have carried Kansas.

BRYAN HOLD MISSOURI.

St. Louis, Nov. 7.—Bryan carried the state by a reduced plurality. No complete figures can be given for some time.

PETTIGREW KNOCKED OUT.

Sioux Falls, S. D., Nov. 7.—McKinley has over 10,000 plurality. The republican majority is nearly 20 in the legislature, which assures the election of a republican to succeed Pettigrew.

Fargo, N. D., Nov. 7.—Returns seem to indicate that the republican plurality is over 10,000.

MORMONS FOR REPUBLICAN.

Salt Lake, Nov. 7.—McKinley carried the state by not less than 4,500. The legislature will be republican, also the congressman.

WASHINGTON REPUBLICAN.

Seattle, Wash., Nov. 7.—McKinley has carried the state. It is believed Cushman and Jones, republicans, for congress, are elected.

LIND MAY BE ELECTED.

St. Paul, Nov. 7.—The only uncertainty in Minnesota is the governorship. Both parties claim it. McKinley's majority increases as fuller returns come in.

INDIANA BY 30,000.

Indianapolis, Nov. 7.—Latest returns indicate that republicans carried the state by 28,000 to 30,000, and probably elected 11 out of 13 congressmen. The legislature is safe for the republicans.

OHIO 82,000.

Detroit, Nov. 7.—Latest figures give McKinley a plurality of 82,000. The state senate will be solid republican with but 11 democrats in the house. Constitutional amendment authorizing taxation of corporations on a cash value of property was overwhelming adopted.

NEW YORK 146,000.

New York, Nov. 7.—Returns this morning indicate that the republicans carried the state by 146,000. The democrats carried Greater New York by 27,500. Republicans gain in both houses of the legislature.

WISCONSIN 102,000.

Full Reports Not In—All Congressmen Republican.

Milwaukee, Nov. 7.—Figures from the state will not be known for some time, but a fair approximation shows republicans have a plurality of 102,000. All republican congressmen are elected. The legislature will be overwhelmingly republican.

McKinley and La Follette have carried Wisconsin by a plurality of about 110,000. It was evident by 10 o'clock Tuesday night that the majority was large. Ten republican congressmen are again elected. The democrats have made some important gains in some localities where they formerly had their large majorities in German-American communities indicating a disaffection on account of the new questions which have been raised, but these apparently have been more than overcome by republican gains in republican counties and through the farming districts.

The vote is lighter than it was four years ago. Chairman A. F. Warden, of the democratic state central committee at 10 o'clock Tuesday night said that Wisconsin had gone republican by about 75,000. National Committeeman T. E. Ryan also conceded the state. He fixed the plurality at 60,000.

Among those who were at republican state headquarters in Milwaukee watching the returns were Lieut. Gov. Stone of Watertown, Charles F. Pfister, Henry Fink, Edwin Coe and others.

The first sixty precincts received from different sections of the state before 9 o'clock showed a gain of 400 over the vote of 1896. The same ratio would give the state to the republicans by 110,000 plurality.

At 11 o'clock Gen. Bryant said: "Mr. La Follette is running even with the national ticket. When we get into Dane county he will go ahead of the national ticket.

The indications are that not a single democratic state senator has been elected and the only democrats in that body will be the two who hold over—H. I. Weed, Winnebago, and Michael A. Jacobs, Dodge. In the assembly the democrats will have not to exceed twenty members. Last year they had nineteen.

DAHLE RE-ELECTED

His Plurality in the District About 2,700, That of Dane County.

CARRIED MADISON BY 17.

Columbia and Dane Each Give Him About 2,500 — Dodge Gives Aylward 1,500.

Congressman Dahle is re-elected by about 2,700 plurality, according to the estimate of Chairman Zimmerman of the congressional committee, this being about the plurality by which he carried Dane county. The pluralities by counties as estimated are:

	Dahle.	Aylward.
Dane	2,500	....
Dodge	....	1,500
Columbia	2,530	....
Jefferson		800

Dahle's vote in this city was one of the surprises of the election. While he ran behind the ticket, as was expected, it being Aylward's home, he secured a plurality here of 17. Mr. Aylward and his friends had confidently expected a plurality of 500 in Madison.

Columbia county's plurality of over 2,500 for Dahle was about 1,000 more than was looked for. The figures given above for that county are accurate, being from the chairman of the county committee on full returns. Columbia gave La Follette a plurality of 2,733, McKinley 2,647.

H. B DAHLE.

Maryland 14,146 Republican.

Baltimore, Nov. 7.—With scattered precincts to hear from, Maryland's plurality for McKinley is 14,146. The official count may probably make it more than 15,000. A solid republican congressional delegation elected by handsome majorities.

CONNECTICUT COUNT COMPLETE.

For McKinley by 28,415—State Ticket the Same.

New Haven, Nov. 7.—With every district heard from Connecticut gives McKinley a plurality of 28 415. The republican state ticket is all elected. The legislature is republican overwhelmingly.

20 MAJORITY IN CONGRESS

Republicans Will Have Control in Lower House.

Chicago, Nov. 7.—Dispatches from 334 of 357 congressional districts show republicans elected 191; democrats 140; silverites 2; populists 1. Republican majority will be about 20.

MILWAUKEE NEARLY 9,000.

City for McKinley—La Follette Runs Even.

Milwaukee, Nov. 7.—Complete returns from Milwaukee county give McKinley a plurality of 8,973; La Follette's plurality is about the same.

Insane Sauk County Mother's Act.

Baraboo, Wis., Nov. 7.—Mrs. George Lee, of Merrimac, nearly killed her infant son by striking him against a table. A year ago she shot at her husband. She was just released from a sanitarium.

Fond du Lac Episcopal Consecration.

Fond du Lac, Nov. 7.—With becoming pomp arrangements for the consecration of Bishop Coadjutor Reginald Meber Weller, Jr., Thursday, will be carried out. Many dignitaries of the Episcopal church will be present.

REPUBLICANS SWEEP CITY.

McKinley Carries Madison by 413; La Follette by 896.

THUS BREAKING ALL PREVIOUS RECORDS.

Every Republican Candidate Has a Plurality in the City.

THE VOTE BY WARDS IN DETAIL.

Burmeister for Sheriff Carries the City by 526—Third Ward Republican for Most Candidates—Vote Shows Much "Splitting."

Madison went republican Tuesday by the biggest majority in history, giving McKinley a plurality of 413, and La Follette a splendid home endorsement in the shape of a plurality of 896, or 483 ahead of the ticket. Aylward for congress came nearer than any democrat to carrying the city, but he was beaten by a plurality of 17 for Dahle. On the county ticket Burmeister, for sheriff, ran ahead of McKinley in the city, receiving a plurality of 526.

One of the many surprises was the Third ward, supposedly a democratic stronghold, which gave McKinley a plurality of 16, and La Follette a plurality of 82. Aylward succeeded in carrying the ward by 3. Levis for assembly, who lives in the Third, got the largest democratic vote there, 242, a plurality of 22 only.

Miller for state senator carried the city by 243, and the first assembly district by 648. Stoughton have him a plurality of 473. His plurality in the county will probably be about 2,500.

The vote in the city was more than 1,000 more than two years ago, for governor, the total being 4,664, compared with 3,649 in 1898. The vote in each ward for president, governor, congressman and sheriff was:

WARD	McKinley.	Bryan.	La Follette.	Bohmrich.	Dahle.	Aylward.	Burmeister.	Engelke.
First	297	148	308	134	257	194	299	150
Second	384	200	423	163	336	252	379	199
Third	238	222	274	192	231	234	254	210
Fourth—1st prec't	205	141	240	104	177	164	213	124
2d prec't	161	195	186	168	153	203	174	182
Fifth—1st prec't	307	189	336	168	291	216	306	191
2d prec't	179	137	192	126	166	172	179	135
Sixth—1st prec't	219	225	219	120	207	228	215	225
2d prec't	145	93	148	90	142	85	144	94
Seventh	241	221	264	200	233	230	251	214
Eighth	160	353	190	319	158	356	167	331
Total	2,536	2,123	2,780	1,884	2,351	2,334	2,581	2,055
Plurality	413		896		17		526	

FIRST WARD.

(Pres. vote 1896: Dem. 123; Rep. 252.)

Bryan	148	McKinley	297
Bohmrich	134	La Follette	308
Woodnorth	142	Froehlich	305
Aylward	194	Dahle	257
Evans	161	Miller	282
Levis	152	Stevens	303
Rorge	142	Terwilliger	306
Wallace	159	Wilke	220
Engelke	150	Burmeister	299
Starck	148	Lynch	299
Dodge	147	Torgeson	302
Moran	146	Dudgeon	302
Hutter	147	Reindahl	300
Nader	152	Marcy	302

Smith, prohibition, for governor 13

SECOND WARD.

(Pres. vote 1896: Dem. 183; Rep. 361.)

Bryan	200	McKinley	384
Bohmrich	163	La Follette	423
Woodnorth	186	Froehlich	394
Aylward	254	Dahle	336
Evans	222	Miller	353
Levis	234	Stevens	348
Rorge	192	Terwilliger	388
Wallace	226	Wilke	353
Engelke	199	Burmeister	379
Starck	203	Lynch	374
Dodge	187	Torgeson	388
Moran	220	Dudgeon	360
Hutter	212	Reindahl	365
Nader	216	Marcy	371

THIRD WARD.

(Pres. vote 1896; Dem. 258; Rep. 223.)

Bryan	222	McKinley	238
Bohmrich	192	La Follette	274
Woodnorth	218	Froehlich	247
Aylward	234	Dahle	231
Evans	233	Miller	232
Levis	242	Stevens	220
Rorge	229	Terwilliger	235
Wallace	233	Wilke	231
Engelke	210	Burmeister	254
Starck	211	Lynch	249
Dodge	208	Torgeson	253
Moran	235	Dudgeon	229
Hutter	224	Reindahl	241
Nader	234	Marcy	233

Smith, prohibition, for governor ....

FOURTH WARD—1st PRECINCT.

(Pres. vote 1896: Dem. 137; Rep. 199.)

Bryan	141	McKinley	205
Bohmrich	104	La Follette	240
Woodnorth	123	Froehlich	...
Aylward	164	Dahle	177
Evans	133	Miller	200
Levis	142	Stevens	198
Rorge	134	Terwilliger	200
Wallace	153	Wilke	183
Engelke	124	Burmeister	213
Starck	123	Lynch	212
Dodge	122	Torgeson	213
Moran	146	Dudgeon	187
Hutter	150	Reindahl	195
Nader	159	Marcy	194

Smith, prohibition, for governor 4

FOURTH WARD—2D PRECINCT.

(Pres. vote 1896: Dem. 178; Rep. 136.)

Bryan	195	McKinley	161
Bohmrich	168	La Follette	186
Woodnorth	...	Froehlich	...
Aylward	203	Dahle	153
Evans	201	Miller	156
Levis	199	Stevens	158
Rorge	191	Terwilliger	163
Wallace	210	Wilke	148
Engelke	182	Burmeister	174
Starck	201	Lynch	154
Dodge	185	Torgeson	169
Moran	196	Dudgeon	159
Hutter	200	Reindahl	155
Nader	195	Marcy	159

Smith, prohibition, for governor ....

FIFTH WARD—1ST PRECINCT.

(Pres. vote 1896: Dem. 176; Rep. 177.)

Bryan	189	McKinley	307
Bohmrich	168	La Follette	336
Woodnorth	184	Froehlich	322
Aylward	216	Dahle	291
Evans	191	Miller	312
Levis	180	Stevens	322
Rorge	185	Terwilliger	318
Wallace	201	Wilke	302
Engelke	191	Burmeister	306
Starck	191	Lynch	312
Dodge	181	Torgeson	320
Moran	192	Dudgeon	310
Hutter	194	Reindahl	309
Nader	188	Marcy	314

Smith, prohibition, for governor 16

FIFTH WARD—2D PRECINCT.

(Pres. vote 1896: Dem. 139; Rep. 148.)

Bryan	137	McKinley	179
Bohmrich	126	La Follette	192
Woodnorth	185	Froehlich	177
Aylward	152	Dahle	166
Evans	144	Miller	169
Levis	136	Stevens	180
Rorge	136	Terwilliger	176
Wallace	149	Wilke	164
Engelke	185	Burmeister	179
Starck	185	Lynch	174
Dodge	135	Torgeson	172
Moran	134	Dudgeon	175
Hutter	144	Reindahl	167
Nader	133	Marcy	181

Smith, prohibition, for governor 9

Continued on fifth page.

WISCONSIN STATE JOURNAL.

VOL. 97. NO. 140. MADISON, WIS., FRIDAY AFTERNOON, SEPTEMBER 6, 1901. PRICE TWO CENTS.

McKINLEY SHOT!

ONCE IN SIDE AND ONCE IN THE CHEST AT BUFFALO EXPOSITION.

HIS CONDITION VERY SERIOUS.

Now In the Hospital--A Stranger the Assassin.

MC KINLEY WILL DIE.

Assassin Is Beaten to Jelly By the Crowd.

Buffalo, Sept. 6.—(Received 3:30 p. m.)—President McKinley was shot twice in the stomach here this afternoon at the Temple of Music. His condition is serious. Two shots took effect in his stomach. He is now in the hospital on the Pan-American grounds. He was shot by a stranger.

member of congress from 1876 to 1891, and became famous as chairman of the comittee on ways and means committee which reported the famous protective taric measure known as "the McKinley Bill."

McKINLEY IN MADISON.

McKinley was well known in Madison and had many friends here, personal and political. Before he was president he delivered an address at the Monona Lake assembly and attracted the largest crowd in the history of the assembly. During the last presidential campaign he made a short stop in Madison, speaking from the east steps of the capitol. He made a profound impression. Especially when speaking of the Philippine war, about which many of our people had their doubts, did his face wear an enxious evxpression, as he spoke of the "misguided men" (natives), etc. Judge Keyes knew McKinley well as did others. The news will come as a great shock to Senator Spooner. The latter enjoyed McKinley's confidence as did few.

Photo by Pach Bros., New York.

PRESIDENT M'KINLEY.

Buffalo—(Later)— McKinley was struck once in the chest and once in the groin. The mob rushed about the assassin and he was crushed to a jelly under the beating.

Buffalo—President was fatally injured.

Sketch of McKinley's Life.

President McKinley was born in Niles, Ohio, Jan. 29, 1843 ,and was educated at public schools, Poland academy and Allegheney college. He enlisted as a private in 23d Ohio volunteer infantry in 1861; commissary sergeant 1862; secind lieutenant 1863; first lientenant 1863; captain 1864; seevrd on staffs of Gens. R. B. Hayes, George Crok and Winfield S. Hancock: was breveted major of the U. S. volunteers by President Lincoln for galantry. McKinley studied law in Ohio and after a course at the Albany, N. Y. law school was admitted to practice in 1867

City Fathers Not Enough Protection.

Madison Democrat: The old assessment was some $8,000,000; the new, $18,000,000. The will of the common council alone stands between them and the virtual confiscation which the possible levy implies.

SECOND EDITION

ASSASSIN IS A POLISH ANARCHIST

He Gives His Name as Fred Nieman of Detroit.

BADLY INJURED BY THE CROWD

They Beat Him Badly--One Bullet Is EXtracted.

FOUR DOCTORS AT HIS BED SIDE

Taken to Hospital on Exposition Grounds.

SHOOK McKINLEY'S HANDS.

But Shot Him At Same Time—Well Dressed Miscreant.

Buffalo, Sept. 6.—McKinley was shot by a well dressed man who wore a high hat, and who, while shaking hands with the President, fired shots with the left hand. One shot took effect in the left breast, the other in the abdomen. The man is under arrest but unidentified.

DETROIT MAN DID IT.

Buffalo, Sept. 6.—The name of the President's assassin is said to be Fred Nieman; he is said to have come from Detroit. Nieman admits he is an anarchist and a resident of Detroit. He says he is of Polish nationality.

Photo copyright, 1900, by Clinedinst.

MRS. M'KINLEY.

BULLET EXTRACTED.

The One Lodged Against the Breast Bone—Resting Easier.

Buffalo, Sept. 6—(4:45 p. m.—The bullet which lodged against the breast bone is extracted. The president is resting easier.

LATEST VERSION—5 P. M.

Buffalo, Sept. 6.—President McKinley was shot twice here this afternoon. His condition is serious. One shot took effect in the breast and the other in the stomach. He was taken at once to the hospital in the Pan-American grounds. He was shot by a well-dressed man while shaking hands with him. The revolver was in the man's left hand covered with a handkerchief. The bulet which lodged against the breast bone was extracted and after the operation the president rested easier. The assassin was an anarchist and said he was of Polish nationality.

Four physicians are now with the president.

Famous Devotion to Wife.

McKinley's devotion to his wife is a romance of world-wide fame. He was as tender to her as to a child. She was an invalid and not strong-minded, in fact, dependent as a child. The McKinley's lost two children many years ago. His personal character was without stain.

Critics have sometimes charged him with lacking resisting powers and all the way along from his Ohio days the criticism has been made by his enemies that he was all things to all men; but his hold on the people shows that they did not believe this. He was the people's ideal up to the election of 1900 as shown by the fact that the leaders preferred some other man as the nominee. He was a gracious man who never lost his temper, and an orator of the slow, massive type—with little or no humor. His dignity never forsook him. His administration has been so rife with big events that careful students say it will rank with Lincoln's, and when one comes to think of the Cuban and Filipino wars, with new territories annexed, this may be so. McKinley being so attractive a man per-
and so judicious in his actions, he may go down to posterity with Lincoln and Washington. Time will do much to ecace temporary prejudices.

Political History of McKinley.

Elected governor of Ohio, 1891; reelected in 1893. Was delegate at large to National Republican convention dan member of committee on resolutions, 1884, and supported James G. Blaine; to that of 1888 supporting John Sherman; and was chairman comittee on resolutions; nominated for president at National Republican convention at St. Louis, June 18, 1896, receiving 661 out of total of 905 votes; elected Nov. 1896, by popular plurality of 600,000 votes, and received 271 electoral votes as against 176 for William J. Bryan.

IF McKINLEY DIES.

Roosevelt Will Become President—Is It Steady Enough?

Theodore Roosevelt, vice president, will succeed McKinley ,if the latter dies. Roosevelt is 43 years old, of a Dutch family in New York state. He has been governor of New York, and began his career in the New York assembly as a reformer. He attracted national attention as a police commissioner in New York, where he tackled all sorts of things and succeeded in conforming obedience to the Sunday saloon law something no one supposed was possible in New York city. He is popular with strenuous people, honest, literary, etc., but older men hesitate when they think of the impulsive young man at the head of the government.

What the doctors say:

Dr. W. W. Gill: "The danger to the president's life would result from injury to structural tissues caused by the bullet in the groin and from hemernhage resulting from in the chest. His age would scarcely be against him. He cannot recover if the vital tissues are injured."

Dr. Clarke Gapen: "In a man of his age, all the chances would be against him."

Dr. Updike's Expressions.

The attempt to take the life of McKinley causes the whole civilized world to shudder. He was a wise, good man. He has made a great president. No man since Lincoln has had such difficult problems to solve. He has done it most wisely. His death will be a nationa calamity.

SORROW IN MADISON.

Great Shoch to Citizens—Great Calamity at This Critical Time.

H. C. Adams: Too horrible to talk about.

Alderman Hanks: I can express no opinion. I am too badly shocked.

L. S. Hanks: I am so shocked that I cannot speak. It was the work of another crank, without a doubt.

Chas. Tenney: The greatest calamity that could befall the country at the present time.

James E. Moseley: I have always held President McKinley in the highest esteem. When he spoke at the Monona Assembly he impressed us all as a profound Christian gentleman.

J. A. Alyward: I think it is one of the worst things that could befall the country that the president should be shot at a public gathering.

Labor Commissioner Erickson: It is a very sad happening; a national calamity.

Ex-Senator George B. Burrows was today and was one of his guests at a private reception.

P. L. Spooner: Of all men it sems the most cruel that he should be chosen.

Col. Jerre Murphy: It is something too terrible to comprehend. No sane man would have committed an assault upon the pjresident.

Dick Petherick: It is a national calamity.

J. A. Alyward: It is too bad for the country that a president can be shot down in a crowd. It hurts Republican governments.

C. F. Spenseley: The greatest calamity that could befall a country is to lose its head by the hand of an assassin.

James Conklin: A terrible crime. They should kil the assassin. Hanging is too good for him.

Frank Currier: It is too terrible to talk about. It is a crime that the severest punishment is not enough for the assassin.

Judge Donovan: Too terrible to talk of.

Observations By Bystanders.

"Too bad they can't lock up those fellows on sight—all the crazy-looking ones."

"The assassin was a crank; there are many of them looking for what they call glory."

"He probably wanted to avenge some fancied wrong; perhaps he was out of work."

"McKinley was a man of such worth ,so near to all the people; it makes my heart ache."

SCHOOL BEGINS NEXT MONDAY

Many Improvements Have Been Made-- $4,000 Ventilating System in High School.

MORE PUPILS THIS YEAR.

Marked Increase Over Former Enrollments—Blackboards Retouched, New Finishing and Some Additions to Buildings.

Monday next begins the school year for the public schools of the city. At the High school building carpenters and furnace men are working overtime to have the building ready for use on Monday. At the Second ward building roofers are putting on the finishing shingles to a new roof, and in Greenbush Contractor Sayles has an extra force of men at work so that part of the school house will be ready for occupation when the bell rings and vacation is over.

The improvements at the High school are the most extensive. The American Foundry and Furnace company of Milwaukee has been putting in a new heating and ventilating system at a cost of $4,000. Four new furnaces are receiving the finishing touches from expert workmen and the ventilating pipes and fans are all being put in place. Their contract reads that the building is to be ready for occupation Monday next but it is doubtful if the work will be completed by that time.

The blackboards in some of the class rooms have been retouched, the woodwork repaired and new seats put in where they were needed. T' afternoon there was a force of some twenty men at work and everything was upside down ,although the foreman said that all would be in order tomorow night.

In Greenbush two new rooms have ben added to the school building. They will cost $5,400, but when the interior finishing is done the cost will reach $5,500. These new rooms will not be ready until October 15, but the old part of the building will be used after next Wednesday. In the Second ward the school house has had a new roof put on and interior repairs as they were needed.

There are seventy-five teachers in the employ of the city in the High school, seven ward schools, Greenbush and Northeast District. There have been many changes in the teaching force since the schools closed last spring, but Superintendent Dudgeon has assigned them to various schools and all will be in working order when the roll is called Monday. The High school wil have the greatest increase in numbers. Just what the number of pupils will be neither City Clerk Norsman nor Superintendent Dudgeon was prepared to state, except that it would be far in excess

We are fast getting the Semi-Centennial Edition into shape. Over fifty of the best brains in Madison are busy compiling special articles. See that the interests you represent are not overlooked or omitted.

WISCONSIN STATE JOURNAL.

TELEPHONES:
Business Office . . . 540.
Editorial Room . . . 76.
Job Room . . . . . . 476.

VOL. 100. NO. 31. MADISON, WIS., TUESDAY AFTERNOON, NOVEMBER 4, 1902. PRICE TWO CENTS.

WOMEN OUT

OVER TWO THOUSAND SEEN AT MILWAUKEE POLLS.

FAIR VOTE IN STATE

New York and Pennsylvania Show Heavy Balloting — President Out Early -- Day Passing Quietly.

[By Associated Press.]

Milwaukee, Wis., Nov. 4.—Specials from all parts of the state indicate the election is passing off quietly. The weather generally is threatening but little rain is falling. In the cities and towns quite a number of women are taking advantage of the first opportunity in the history of the state to exercise their right of suffrage, which is on school questions. In Milwaukee it is expected the fair sex will cast 2,000 votes. The usual off year vote is being polled.

HEAVY VOTE IN WINNEBAGO.

Oshkosh, Nov. 4.—Winnebago county votes for a state senator and three assemblymen, besides the state and congressional tickets. Early indications point to a heavy vote. Three hundred and fifty women will cast their ballots. The weather is threatening.

WOMEN VOTING IN LA CROSSE.

La Crosse, Wis., Nov. 4.—For the first time in the history of Wisconsin women are casting ballots today for school offices. Much interest has been manifested by Club Women but it has gone a little further than these circles.

HEAVY VOTING IN MILWAUKEE.

Milwaukee, Nov. 4—Cloudy and light showers marked the early part of the day. Great interest centers in the outcome of the election in this city, and a big vote was cast before seven. There is much scratching.

Racine, Nov. 4—Cloudy, with light showers. The women's vote on the constitutional amendment will be the largest ever cast. Indications are for a heavy vote.

Peoria, Ill., Nov. 4—Cloudy. The early vote is heavy. There is much interest in the result.

NEW YORK POLLING BIG VOTE.

New York, Nov. 4.—The weather is perfect and voters were out early in large numbers. In a number of assembly districts twenty-five per cent. of the registered votes had been cast at 8.30. In some districts the leaders predict that the entire vote will be cast by noon. About forty arrests for illegal voting were reported this morning. In one district the rival leaders came to blows. Policemen conducting several persons to the station house were attacked by a mob. In the struggle one prisoner escaped.

GREAT INTEREST IN PHILADELPHIA.

Philadelphia, Pa., Nov. 4.—A heavy vote was cast early. More interest is being taken in the election in this city than was expected.

Pittsburg, Nov. 4.—An unusually large early vote was polled. The weather throughout Western Pennsylvania is delightful.

Cleveland, Nov. 4.—It is ideal election weather. The voting was early and extremely heavy. There is much scratching. Reports from Northwestern Ohio show an average vote is being polled.

REPUBLICAN CANDIDATE IS OUT.

Boston, Nov. 4.—Reports from the state at noon indicate that Bates, republican, for governor, was being cut and Gaston, democrat, was running ahead of his ticket.

Atlanta, Ga., Nov. 4.—The Georgia legislature in joint session today re-elected United States Senator Clay.

Indianapolis, Nov. 4.—Reports from state show a heavy vote. In this city there was much scratching.

IT DEPENDS UPON COOK COUNTY.

Chicago, Nov. 4.—Reports from various points in the state indicate only a fair vote in the county districts. There will be a heavy vote for an off year in the towns and cities. At democratic headquarters it was state the result in the state for the state ticket as well as the legislature depends upon the vote of Cook county.

PENNSYLVANIA DEMOCRATS OUT.

Philadelphia, Nov. 4.—Reports from the state indicate an unusually heavy vote being polled in country districts. This is particularly the case with the Democratic vote, more apathy being shown by the Republicans than by their oppenents. Nearly fifty per cent. of the total vote had been polled at noon.

St. Louis, Nov. 4.—Balloting is proceeding throughout the state under leaden skies. The light vote in the rural districts will cause the Democrats some losses, but in all probability not enough to prevent them from coming to St. Louis with a majority of 15,000 to 20,000 over the Republicans.

INDIAN SUMMER DAY IN OHIO.

Columbus, Nov. 4.—Favorable conditions, including clear Indian Summer weather prevailed in Ohio today for election, but the reports up to noon indicated slow voting, except in the large cities and close congressional districts. Nothing today has occurred to indicate any change in the predictions that the Republicans will carry the state by a large plurality.

Reno, Nevada, Nov. 4.—The election in Nevada is passing quietly with a large vote being polled.

Boise, Idaho, Nov. 4.—Reports from all parts of the state show fair weather and a large vote.

Topeka, Nov. 4.—Reports from the state show early a heavy vote polled and much scratching.

(Continued on page six.)

The Polls Close Tonight at Seven (7) O'clock — not 8 O'clock, but 7.

MILWAUKEE VOTE VERY HEAVY.

Within Seven Thousand of That Cast At Presidential Election.

[Special to State Journal.]

Milwaukee, Nov. 4.—The vote cast at the polls here today at noon was 23,000 against 17,000 of four years ago and 30,000 two years ago, at the time of the presidential election. This shows a heavy vote for this year.

Antigo, Wis., Nov. 4.—Yesterday afternoon at the village of Polar, nine miles from this city, Henry Wade shot George Gould. Wade went after Gould with a double-barrel shot gun and discharged a barrel of buck-shot into Gould's left breast and face. Gould is in a very critical condition and Wade is still at large.

Middleton, Wis., Nov. 4—J. Atkinson, a notorious character of Middleton, this morning about three o'clock returned home and threatened to kill his wife and children with a large knife. His wife ran screaming out of the house. People went to her assistance, and after a fierce struggle the drunken man was secured

FIGHTING IN PORT AU PRINCE.

Fouchardists Enter City and Clash With Civil Authorities.

[By Associated Press.]

Port Au Prince, Nov. 4.—A troop of 1,200 Fouchardists which entered capital yesterday had a conflict with the civil authorities. There was heavy firing during the night. Seven persons were killed and many wounded. The situation is grave, threatening a new civil war.

The disorders continued during the day, another conflict occurring before the National bank at 11 o'clock. There were several victims. The entire population is very much alarmed and the foreigners are claiming protection. It is believed that the arrival of General Nord with 10,000 men, which is expected within the next few days, will put an end to the disturbance.

GOV. YATES IS MUCH WORSE.

His Condition Considered Very Alarmin At Springfield, Ill.

[By Associated Press.]

Springfield, Ill., Nov. 4.—The condition of Governor Yates is considered very alarming. He has been in a delirious condition all today. His temperature is 104 degrees. He is a very sick man.

TWO KILLED AND SIX INJURED.

Heavy Trolley Car in Kansas City Jumps the Track.

[By Associated Press.]

Kansas City, Mo., Nov. 4.—A heavy trolley car on the Broadway line jumped the track today at Fifth and Broadway and crashed into a saloon. Two passengers, a woman and a negro, were killed and six others were injured.

GAME WARDEN RECEIVES MONEY

NonResidents Eagerly are Picking Up Hunting Licenses.

C. D. Nelson, chief deputy game warden, reported that money is coming in fast for non-resident licences.

The number of licences taken out up to Nov. 4. this year shows a large increase over last year. On Nov. 4, 1900, seventy-six deer and small game licenses were taken out; eighty-five were issued in 1901, and 120 in 1902.

Small game licenses issued to Nov. 1, 1900, numbered 135; in 1901, the total was 196; and this year 243 have been taken out.

Are Opening Hospital Bids.

The meeting of the directors of the Greenbush hospital was held at 3:30 o'clock this afternoon in the offices of Tenney, Hall and Swenson. The bids were opened and considered by the members present, among whom were Prof. W. A. Henry, Mrs. J. W. Hobbins, John Corscot, Mrs. J. Jastrow, D. K. Tenney and Secretary S. W. Gilman.

The contract will not be let this afternoon.

TOOK $8,000

ROBBERS LOOT BANK VAULT AT GREENWOOD VILLAGE.

CITIZENS IN FIGHT

Shots Exchanged With Bandits, but They Escape Without Injury to Anyone-- Money in Gold.

[By Associated Press.]

Marshfield, Wis., Nov. 4.—The State bank of Greenwood, several miles from here, was entered by burglars early today and $8,000 in gold was stolen. Five men were implicated in the work. They blew open the two vaults with dynamite. The noise of the explosions attracted several citizens and a gun fight ensued. Several shots were exchanged.

No one was injured and the robbers escaped.

[Special to State Journal.]

WAS THE WORK OF PROFESSIONAL.

Marshfield, Nov. 4.—The robbery was seemingly the work of professionals. The door was blown off the safe, which was wrecked. Nitroglycerin was used in the work.

The robbers escaped, and dogs have been put on the trail.

NOT TO CONVENE ON THURSDAY.

Circuit Court Will Adjourn For One Week—Johnson Case.

The session of the circuit court which was to have convened Thursday of this week will be adjourned for one week. Judge Siebecker is now holding court in Baraboo and it will not be possible for him to get here for another week. The case of the Johnson estate will come before the court next week.

LAST OF FOX SISTERS IS DEAD.

Mrs. Maria Fox Smith Expires at Newark, N. Y., at Eighty-Five.

[By Associated Press.]

Newark, N. Y., Nov. 4.—Mrs. Maria Fox Smith, the last member of the family of Fox Sisters, originators of modern spiritualism, died today, aged 85.

ASK $10,000 BONUS

MASON-KIPP COMPANY WANTS PUBLIC TO TAKE STOCK.

Unless Assisted to Expand Business Will Leave City--Mayor Groves and Dr. Gapen Not Notified.

Can Madison invest $10,000 in a paying enterprise? "She will have to do it in order to retain our factory," says A. A. Stelting, secretary and manager of the Mason-Kipp Manufacturing company. "We have been offered the use of a building and site in Hopkins, a suburb of Minneapolis, free of charge if we will move our concern there, but if Madison people will buy enough capital stock in the company we will permanently locate here. It will take $10,000 worth of stock to insure the enterprise for Madison. I feel warranted in saying to prospective stockholders that we can declare a handsome dividend at the end of the season, for when the affairs of the Mason Lubricator company were consolidated with the O. G. Kipp Manufacturing company of Rockville, Ill., the company was able to declare a ten per cent dividend from March 1, 1902

HOPE TO BUILD MODERN PLANT.

"We have located temporarily in the Swenson planing mill, but as soon as we are put in a position to build a modern factory we will move into it. We have not decided where in the city we will build, although two sites have been offered us free of charge.

"If Madison people do not buy a sufficient amount of stock we will move our factory either to Minneapolis or to Peoria, Illinois.

A branch factory is to be established at Winnipeg, Manitoba, in order to take charge of the firm's enormous trade in the northwest."

The officers of the company are J. B. Bartholomew, of Peoria, Ill., president; Fred Jung, of Theresa, Wis., vice-president; A. A. Stelting, of Madison, secretary and manager; O. G. Kipp, of Rochelle, Ill., shop superintendent.

In a few days W. H. Putnam will start west to travel for the company in Nebraska, Kansas, Texas and Oklahoma.

MADE CONTRACTS IN CANADA.

Mr. Stelting has just returned from Canada, where he made contracts with a great many firms who handle traction engines, as the lubricator manufactured by the new company is a great favorite with makers of thresh-

(Continued on page six.)

VOTE HEAVY

DEMOCRATS WORKING FOR DUDGEON'S ELECTION.

WOMEN OUT STRONG

Weathor Propitious for Big Rural Vote--Spooner Will Save the Governor, Say the Stalwarts.

A heavy vote is being polled in every precinct in Dane county today. The day is ideal, the interest is wide-spread and every voter is splitting up his ticket so unfeelingly that prognostications are figuratively up in the air.

In the city male and female voters are out in great number. In some wards the voters linger over their ballots and do wholesale splitting while in others the men watching the process say that many are casting straight.

M. S. Dudgeon, candidate for assembly in this district, is going to be saved by the democrats.

Secretary Ernest N. Warner was given definite assurance this afternoon that the democrats in the Eighth and Third wards especially are cutting Ladd and openly working for Dudgeon. The stalwarts claim to be standing by him to the man, while the administration men are adhering to their promises and working like demons for Dudgeon to pull the stalwart vote for the county officers.

The female voters are piling over one another to vote for Mathie. The genial Wausau professor has made a hit with the women and they are openly asserting their intention to stand by the democratic nominee

MRS. LA FOLLETTE LEADS

Mrs. Robert M. La Follette was probably the first woman in Madison to vote at the polls. She reached the Fourth ward voting precinct at 8 oclock this morning accompanied by the governor and entered the booth without asking any questions. It was the work of an instant and she turned to hand her ballot to the inspector. "Mrs. Belle La Follette," he called, and the balot went into the box.

The First ward women lead in point of numbers as 50 female votes have there been cast. The other wards average 20 votes by women.

VOTING IN THE WARDS.

Up to the hour of 2 this afternoon the votes in the various wards had not equalled in number the balloting of 1900 but a heavy vote has been cast. The data for the wards follows:

First ward: 302 votes, 50 of which were cast by women. The women in this ward have openly declared themselves for Mathie.

Second ward: 312 votes, 38 women vote lighter than in 1900.

Third ward: 215 votes, 7 women, among whom were Mrs. Milo Sharp, Mrs. Jessie Troan, Miss Sena Troan, Mrs. Mary Hoyt, Mrs. Florence Thompson, Mrs. Ethel Calwell and Mrs. Elma Smith.

Fourth ward: 198 votes, 19 less than in 1900, 11 women, among whom were Mesdames R. M. La Follette, R. G. Siebecker, S. U. Pinney, Kate Chittenden, R. Monteith and Miss Monteith.

Fifth ward, 1st precinct: 300 votes, 23 women, among whom were Mesdames J. M. Olin, J. B. Parkinson and Lillian Kahlenberg.

Second precinct, Fifth ward: 177 votes, 17 women, among whom were: Mrs. Josephine Whitson, Miss Alice Cary, Mrs. Frank Ball, Mrs. Ida Oakey, Mrs. Troy, Mrs. A. W. Gratz, Mrs. William Millward, Mrs. Mary Stoner, Mrs. Owen Twitchell, Mrs. L. S. Smith and Mrs. Clara Henry.

Sixth ward: 255 votes, including 15 women among whom were: Miss L. Redel, Mrs. Frank Reed, Mrs. C. F. Lamb, Mrs. A. M. Frish, Miss Maude Parkinson, Miss Ida Oliver, Mrs. Elizabeth Graham and Mrs. Harriet Kroncke.

Seventh ward: 182 votes, including 14 women, vote equals that of last year. Eighth ward: 276 votes, including 15 women, among whom were: Mary A. King, Annie E. Lemon, Lizzie M. Deutch, Miss Martha Dodge, Mrs. Lovejoy, Mrs. S. B. W. Brown, Mrs. Hanchett, Mrs. Marietta and Miss Winona Merrick.

STALWART CUT VERY LIGHT.

If Robert M. La Follette is defeated by David S. Rose today it will be because the stalwarts of Wisconsin have more delicate palates than has their idol John C. Spooner. If Robert M. La Follette is elected, the stalwart banner will go up and dissenting republicanism will get up on its hind legs and yell "John Spooner saved the governor's scalp." And that is the honest conviction of the Wisconsin stalwarts today. They have thought the matter over and they have said: "If John C. Spooner can take the gall and wormwood on his palate and swallow La Follette principles and criticisms without flinching, then Wisconsin stalwarts can swallow the same dose without a scowl."

However the stalwarts do not concede the governor's election. Considering the railroad voter's cut, and the democratic revival, they figure that if the governor wins, he will win barely.

EXPECT BIG RURAL VOTE.

The rural vote polled in Dane county today will be larger than any year within the last six, according to the estimates made by the leading democratic and republican candidates. The overhanging clouds of today in contrast to the favorable weather of last week is looked upon, not as a democratic or republican omen, but as an indication of a big farmer vote. The roads are good and the work has been done up in order that the day may be spent at the voting polls of the precinct.

Secretary Edward J. Reynolds said this morning "I look for a much larger rural vote today than has been polled in years. The weather is unfavorable for work but not for driving, therefore the farmers will get out to the polls. We will not make any predictions. We are just sawing wood."

REPUBLICAN VICTORY SURE.

Candidate for district attorney on the republican ticket, Attorney Frank Gilbert, has made eighteen consecutive speeches in eighteen nights in various parts of the county. He knows more about the situation in the county than any other man. Attorney Gilbert said this morning:

"The dissatisfied republican voters who turn down Governor La Follette in Dane county today will be exceeded in number by the disgruntled democratic voter who will vote for the governor in preference to Rose. The democratic vote will help the governor and furthermore I think that the stalwart cut is going to be light. Out in the eastern part of the county, some of the Norwegians are cutting "Bob" McWatty but in this section and in the western district McWatty has strength enough to repulse the attack. I think Dudgeon will be elected in this assembly district."

CHAIRMAN GIVES ESTIMATE.

Chairman Geo. E. Bryant and A. F. Warden of the republican and democratic state central committees, gave out statements this morning, sizing up the situation as follows:

George E. Bryant, chairman republican state central committee—"I have had no reason to change my views regarding the pluralities that will be rolled up by the republican tickets and think that Governor La Follette and the state ticket will be elected by at least 40,000. The re-

(Continued on page six.)

KILL MANIA

ALAN G. MASON HELD FOR MURDEROUS ASSAULTS.

WOMEN HIS VICTIMS

Fifteen Struck Down in Suburbs of Boston Since June — Two Dead — Prisoner Is a Wealthy Man.

Boston, Nov. 4—In connection with the fifteen murderous assault cases which have occurred in Cambridge, Brookline and Somerville in the last few months, two of which resulted fatally, the police today arrested Alan G. Mason, of Boston, a well-known and wealthy business man, a member of the piano manufacturing firm of Mason & Hamlin, a prominent club member and a Harvard graduate. The police suspect, from evidence in their hands, that Mason has been involved in nearly all the cases referred to, as the circumstances have been very similar. Mr. Mason is a middle-aged man but he has been a victim of mental trouble, for which he was treated at the McLean asylum at Waverly. About a year ago he was permitted to leave the institution.

FREQUENTLY SEEN IN LOCALITIES.

The fact that he had been frequent-seen about the localities in which the assaults occurred, led to suspicion against him.

The peculiar cases, which have terrorized Cambridge and vicinity as well as other suburban sections, began last June. During the summer there were half a dozen victims of an unknown assailant, each of whom was struck down and beaten with a blunt instrument. Early in October Agnes McPhee was assaulted in Somerville and died from her injuries. An iron wrench was found and fixed upon as the weapon used.

EIGHT CASES IN ONE MONTH.

During the same month eight other cases followed, the last of which occurred last Saturday night, when Clara A. Morton, a laundress with the McLean asylum, was accosted on the grounds of that institution and beaten with a blunt instrument. Miss Morton died Sunday. Mr. Mason was taken into custody ot his mother's home. He made no objections on the way to the police headquarters.

It is said Mr. Mason admitted to the officers that he was in Somerville on the night on which Miss McPhee was fatally injured.

IS A COUSIN OF JOHN MASON.

Mr. Mason has a mother and three brothers, and is a cousin of John Mason, the well-known actor. While in college Mr. Mason displayed a pronounced musical taste and was president of the Glee club. He was also an athlete of some note.

HE PASSED COUNTERFEIT MONEY

William Farmer Will Appear on The Charge Tomorrow.

A man giving his name as William Farner was arrested this morning by Captain Thomas Shaughnessy for attempting to pass counterfeit money. Farner staid at the West Madison hotel last night and when he came to pay his bill, he gave the landlady the only dollar he possessed, which turned out to be lead.

Farner claims to be a printer by trade and says that he hired out to the Madisonian yesterday, but on account of a lame wrist was not able to go to work. He says that he did not know the dollar was counterfeit, that someone gave it to him in change.

SAILORS DEAD IN COLLISION.

Steamer Sampson Runs Down a Schooner off Cape Cod.

[By Associated Press.]

Boston, Nov. 4.—Steamer Admiral Sampson ran down and sank a schooner off Cape Cod today. Four of the schooner's crew were drowned.

MAN AND WOMAN ARE KILLED.

Bodies Found Strapped Together in The Oswego Canal.

[By Associated Press.]

Syracuse, N. Y., Nov. 4.—The bodies of a man and a woman, strapped together, were found in the Oswego canal near here today. Their identity is unknown. The man is about 65 and the woman considerably younger.

THE WEATHER.

The weather predictions for Wisconsin are: Rain this afternoon and in the east tonight cooler tonight and Wednesday; fair and cooler in the east.

ELECTION RETURNS.

Complete election returns will be received tonight by the STATE JOURNAL by special telegraph service, and the messages flashed upon a screen over the market place, opposite the JOURNAL building. Returns from state and county, and especially from the First assembly district, will be displayed in detail.

Well, anyway, the automobile scares more people than it really hurts.

HOW GREAT AUTHORITY RATES [illegible] — The Wisconsin State Journal has a higher circulation rating than is accorded to any other daily in Madison. — From Printer's Ink, Aug. 18, 1903 (page 48).

WISCONSIN STATE JOURNAL.

LAST EDITION

VOL. 102. NO. 69. MADISON, WIS., FRIDAY AFTERNOON, DECEMBER 18, 1903. PRICE TWO CENTS.

EXPRESS COMPANY ASSESSMENT IS OUT

State Tax Commission Submits Important Report to State Treasurer.

The state tax commission to-day submitted to the state treasurer its report of assessment and amount of taxes of sleeping car, express, freight line companies. The rate of tax levy is .01158. The total amount of assessment of express companies is $765,-555.21; sleeping car companies, $309,-291.64; equipment companies, $143,-654.98; freight line companies, $33,-582.33.

The first set of figures is the amount of assessment, the second the amount of tax:

SLEEPING CAR COMPANIES.

The Pullman Co., Chicago, $309,291-.64, $3,581.60.

EXPRESS COMPANIES.

American Express Co., N. Y., $481,-545.81, $5,576.80.

Adams Express Co., N. Y., $53,312.92, $640.52.

Northern Pacific Express Co., St. Paul, $5,886, $68.16.

United States Express Co., N. Y., $212,174.58, $2,456.98.

Western Express Co., St. Paul, $10,-635.90, $123.16.

American Fast Freight Line, Chicago, $3,422.22, $39.63.

American Refrigerator Transit Co., St. Louis, Mo., $455.47, $5.27.

Cudahy Packing Co., Omaha, Neb., $68.26, 79 cents.

Merchants' Despatch Transportation Co., New York, $11,613.61, $134.49.

National Car Co., St. Albans, $15,-440.16, $178.80.

Union Refrigerator Transit Co., St. Louis, $2,415.30, $27.97.

Western Refrigerator Line, St. Louis, $82.31, 95 cents.

Western Refrigerator Transit Co., St. Louis, $84.97, 98 cents.

EQUIPMENT COMPANIES.

Armour Car Lines, Chicago, $2,192, $25.38.

Arms Palace Horse Car Co., Chicago, $4,886.84, $56.59.

Chicago, New York & Boston Refrigerator Co., Chicago, $1,[illegible]89.72, $16.09.

Cold Blast Transportation Co., Chicago, $663, $7.68.

Cudahy Milwaukee Refrigerator Line, Cudahy, $14,305.64, $165.66.

Dairy Shippers' Despatch, Chicago, $285.61, $3.31.

Live Poultry Transportation Co., Chicago, $222, $2.57.

Lipton Car Lines, Chicago, $603.98, $6.99.

Morrell Refrigerator Co., Ottawa, Ia., $14.68, 17 cents.

National Car Line Co., Chicago, $68.70, 80 cents.

Produce Shippers' Despatch, Louisville, Ky., $38.53, 45 cents.

Provision Dealers' Despatch, Chicoga, $31.34, 37 cents.

St. Louis Refrigerator Car Co., St. Louis, Mo., $252.63, $2.93.

Streets' Western Stable Car Line, Chicago, $13,675.87, $158.37.

Swift Refrigerator Transportation Co., Chicago, $7,633.88, $88.40.

Union Tank Line, Brooklyn, $97,-390.01, $1,127.78.

GIRLS LEAP TO ESCAPE FIRE

Dayton, Ohio, Dec. 18.—To escape death from probable suffocation 12 girls leaped from the fifth story windows of the Canby building today, landing on the roof of a one story building below. At least half were caught in the arms of Dr. Lambert, who by breaking the force of their fall, probably saved their lives. The fire was an insignificant affair, but the smoke caused the panic among the girls.

GOTTEN FROM HORSES.

Secret of New Typhoid Serum Made Public.

New York, Dec. 18.—It has been learned that the new typhoid serum in use at Beth-Israel Hospital in this city, where thirty cases have already been successfully treated is prepared by immunizing horses, just as that for diphtheria is manufactured. It was discovered by Dr. Jez of Berne, Switzerland, and sent by him to the staff physician at the hospital.

CARDS LEAD TO THEFT.

Student of Brown University Makes Incriminating Confession.

Providence, R. I., Dec. 18.—Poker playing among students of Brown University has led to the arrest of Ralph F. Bancroft of Stoneham, Mass., on the charge of larceny. He was put on probation after the case was heard, but has been dismissed from the university. Members of the faculty declare the card playing which involved Bancroft did not take place in the college buildings. Bancroft confesed he has been stealing money and other valuables from the clothing of his fellow students who patronized the swimming pool. The proceeds ranged from small change up to $25 and Bancroft declares his losses at cards had drawn him into the trouble.

Dreyfus Not Restored.

Paris, Dec. 18.—Reports that War Minister Andre had announced the restoration of Dreyfus to the army are manifestly untrue. The case is now before a special commission of judges which has not concluded its sessions and has not rendered any decision.

IOWA AND LOUISIANA HAVING THEIR CENTENNIAL EXHIBITION

New Orleans, Dec. 18.—Under the auspices of the state of Louisiana, the city of New Orleans and the Louisiana Historical society, a series of official celebrations in commemoration of the centennial transfer of Louisiana territory from France to he United States was begun to-day, the day's feature being a review by Governor Heard and his party of distinguished guests of the French and American warships which have come here to assist in the ceremonies.

Des Moines, Dec. 18.—One hundred years ago today occurred the formal transfer of Iowa as a part of the Louisiana territory to the United States. In commemoration of the event 13,000 schools of the Hawkeye state are holding special services today, the plan suggested by Governor Cummins and Superintendent Barrett in a large pamphlet issued in October from the educational department being carried out.

FLYING MACHINE WORKS IN FACE OF STRONG WIND

Norfolk, Va., Dec. 18.—A successful trial of a flying machine was made yesterday near Kitty Hawk, N. C., by Wilbur and Orville Wright, of Dayton, Ohio. The machine flew for three miles in the face of a wind blowing at a registered velocity of 21 miles an hour, then gracefully descended to earth at a spot selected by a man in the navigator's car as a suitable landing place. The machine has no balloon attachment but gets its force from propellers worked by a small engine.

Preparatory to its flight the machine was placed upon a platform near Kitty Hawk, on a high sand hill. When all was in readiness, the fastenings to the machine were released and it started down the incline. Navigator Wilbur Wright then started a small gasoline engine which worked the propellors. When the end of the incline was reached the machine gradually rose until it obtained an altitude of 60 feet. In the face of the strong wind blowing it maintained an even speed of eight miles an hour.

The idea of a box kite has been adhered to in the basic formation of the flying machine. The huge frame work of the light timbers is 33 feet wide, 5 feet deep and 5 feet across the top forms of the machine proper. In the center is the navigator's car, and suspended just below the bottom plan is a small gasoline engine which furnishes motive power for propelling and elevating the wheels. There are two six blade propellors, one arranged just below the frame so as to exert an upward force when in motion, while the other extends horizontally to the rear from the center of the car, furnishing the forward impetus. Protruding from the center of the car is a huge fan-shaped rudder of canvas, stretched upon a frame of wood. This rudder is controlled by the navigator and may be moved to each side and raised or lowered.

HONDURAS IS NEXT IN LINE

Revolution Scheduled For Opening of New Year.

TO OUST PRESIDENT BONILLA.

People Dissatisfied With Conduct of Railroad Which Pays No Interest to Bondholders.

Mobile, Ala., Dec. 18.—Advices received here by steamer indicate that another revolution is imminent in Honduras soon after the first of the year. It is expected to be fostered by Ex-President Sierra, through special envoy, with the purpose of ousting President Bonilla. On his retirement from the executive chair Sierra named Senor Arias for president and he was given the position. Then Bonilla organized a revolution and overthrew Arias, who is now in exile and in prison at Teguclgaipa. It is said the people are dissatisfied with the conduct of the government, especially in the matter of the Honduras railroad built by English capitalists. Since its construction not a cent of interest or principal has been paid the bondholders and it is asserted the English government will take cognizance of the matter and enforce payment.

MUST ENFORCE MONROE DOCTRINE

Congressman Esch Makes a Significant Speech.

All EUROPE TRYING TO PLEASE.

But We Must Object to Attempts to Get Coaling Stations—Should Improve Consular Service.

New York, Dec. 18.—In an address at the annual banquet of Group 8 of the New York State Bankers association, Congressman John J. Esch, of Wisconsin, who discussed "Steps to Promote Trade," said:

"The battles of the future will not be on tented fields, but on the highways of commerce and in the marts of trade. In these battles that nation will best succeed which best solves the question of production, transportation and legislation.

"What ought we do to obtain our just share of South American commerce? We ought to enforce the Monroe doctrine and apply it to any European power that attempts to get a coaling station on or near the American continent.

"If we would improve our commerce we must improve our consular service. Our consuls are and ought to be 'scouts of our foreign trade.' To do this they should be keen, active, diplomatic men of business, men in maritime and commercial law and versed in the language of the people with whom they do business."

He also recommended strong efforts toward upbuilding our merchant marine, and declared, in closing, that the great powers of Europe are now vieing with one another as to who shall be our best friends.

DRIVERS GO ON BIG STRIKE

Chicago, Dec. 18.—Sixteen hundred livery drivers, backed by every teamsters' union in Chicago, struck to-day. Nearly 400 livery stables are completely tied up. The drivers demand an increase of $2 per week.

The first trouble occurred when an attempt was made to conduct a funeral at West Eighteenth and Alport streets. The undertaker secured enough conveyances to take the body and mourners to the church, but while the services were in progress pickets compelled the drivers of the hearse and carriages to desert under threats of violence.

TRANSPORT SHIP IS HARD AGROUND

Manila, Dec. 18.—The United States transport Kingsley is ashore at Murcielagos, North Mindanao, with a rock through her bottom.

Washington, Dec. 18.—A small British steamer Kingsley, sailed from Manila October 20, for the Philippine provincea. She may be a transport chartered by the authorities at Manila Otherwise there is no record of a United States transport named Kingsley.

RUSSIAN TROOPS MOVING.

Said to Be Going Night and Day Toward Port Arthur.

St. Petersburg, Dec. 18.—A traveler who just returned from Manchuria says Russian troops are still moving night and day towards Port Arthur.

BIDS FOR THE DUEL.

Mayville Wants to Entertain Milwaukee Belligerents.

Mayville, Wis., Dec. 18.—Herr Gustav Hoffman and Editor von Schleinitz are invited to fight in Mayville. They will be presented the free use of Ziegler's park, a guarantee of police protection, their choice of any style of weapons, and the assurance, backed by a bond, that if either falls in battle, his widow and orphans will be given $1,000 in cash. Should both fall, the sum will be made $2,000.

This proposition is made by the Alterthumforscher Verein, a German-American social organization, which formally adopted resolutions condemning the attitude of the Milwaukee grand jury toward the proposed battle.

The Verein specifies that should its offer be accepted, no admission fee shall be charged, and that the German army code of honor shall prevail. The invitation to the belligerents is signed by Anton Burger, M. M.; Emil Ziegler, first M. Z., and William Butter, first M.

GET 18 MONTHS FOR DEFRAUDING

Chicago, Dec. 18.—Judge Humphrey, in the federal court today, sentenced Julius M. Nisson and Arthur J. Herbst to the penitentiary for 18 months and imposed fines of $500 each. By representing themselves as Western Supply company representatives, the two men used the mails to defraud reputable business houses in all parts of the United States.

ALEXANDER EVADES IMPLICATING FIRM

New York, Dec. 18.—In the hearing of the United States Shipbuilding receivership case today Charles B. Alexander, of the firm of Alexander & Green, was the first witness. He told at length of the connection of his firm and himself with the early attempts to form a shipbuilding concern but parried successfully the most of Untermeyer's attempts to obtain any important sensational testimony about the final attempt.

SENATE ASKS FOR BETTER TYPE

Washington, Dec. 18.—The senate today passed a resolution offered by Sen. Hoar, instructing the committee on printing to ascertain whether it be not possible to have the congressional record printed in better type than at present. The reading of the resolution brought out the fact that the senators find it difficult to read the record.

SUSTAINS OPINION OF LOWER COURT

Philadelphia, Dec. 18.—Judge Gray in the federal court of appeals today handed down an opinion sustaining Judge Kirkpatrick of the United States district court of New Jersey in the case of Harry C. Spinks and other stockholders who appealed against the payment of the assessment called by receiver Tanall, of the Asphalt company of Africa. Kirkpatrick decided the assessment was legal.

CAMPAIGN PLAN IS OUTLINED

Paris, Dec. 18.—The "United Colombian committee" here gave out a statement today saying that Colombia would first seek through a commission to induce the United States to recognize Colombia's rights under the treaty of 1846; second, if the commission fails Colombia will ask for a submission of the question to The Hague arbitration court; third, if its submission to The Hague court is refused, Colombia will go to war and rely on Latin republics to come to her aid.

GREEN HELD ON FIVE INDICTMENTS

Binghamton, N. Y., Dec. 18.—United States Commissioner Hall today handed down a decision in the case of State Senator George E. Green, of this city, charged with bribery and conspiracy to defraud the government in connection with the sale of time recorders and cancellation machines. The defendant was held on all five indictments for trial in the city of Washington.

JOHN LEE MAHIN ON ADVERTISING

Famous Chicago Ad Man Addresses Students.

GOOD AD MUST TELL NEWS.

Says Something That Merely Catches the Eye Is Not Necessarily a Good Ad — Answers Many Questions.

Members of the Commercial Club (a students' organization) enjoyed a banquet and listened to a talk on advertising by Chicago's great advertising authority, John Lee Mahin, last night. The gathering was in Guild hall.

UNIQUE DECORATIONS.

"'Ad' Dinner" was the appropriate name given the event on the menu card. The bill of fare was made up of contributions of good things to eat from famous advertisers. Shredded wheat biscuit, Van Camp's Boston baked beans, Heinz pure food products were served. Madison palatable table items were Findlay's "dry-roast" coffee and his "Sealship" oysters. The Madison Candy Co., Oppel's Grocery and J. H. Snell's products were also served, and Grove's "Knox" cigars. The decorations were unique, consisting of a brilliant assortment of the advertising placards used by great advertisers.

Everyone wore a plaster of Paris Heinz pickle stick pin on his coat lapel.

MAHIN BETTER THAN DINNER.

The dinner was excellent, while the talk of Mr. Mahin, the speaker of the evening, was brilliant. He is a man of large, healthful appearance, quiet and engaging countenance—light hair and lots of it. His appearance is youthful for one who has pushed his way so far to the front in his profession.

LIVED IN WISCONSIN.

Mr. Mahin brought himself close to his audience in his first sentence, when he said that eighteen years ago he was a student in Wisconsin, at Beaver Dam.

The address proper was a little disappointing. He spoke with effort and a constant search after words. It looked as though he was one of those men who could do a thing better than tell how it is done.

FORTE IS ANSWERING QUESTIONS.

But when this set part of his speech was over and he gave the invitation to his hearers to ask questions, he was a different man. For over an hour he fascinated those present with his quick, accurate and brilliant analysis of problems opened up.

AD MUST TELL NEWS.

The majority of questions asked could be included in the one, "What is a good ad?" Mr. Mahin's answer to this was that a good ad was one that most clearly conveyed to the reader the strong points of the article being advertised.

An advertisement should contain news; it should tell the public some facts about the article offered for sale; it should tell it in a straightforward, sincere, interesting way that will invite notice to future ads.

CLEVERNESS NOT NEEDED.

The clever ad is not a good ad. If the ad tells news, facts and has ideas of interest, if it is cleverly phrased, the ad may be all the better for it; but the moment the other qualities are sacrificed to cleverness the ad is weakened.

He said advertising appropriations are often overestimated. A campaign can be carried over the entire country for $200,000. To illustrate how vast some of the advertising transactions are however, he stated that the right to use the new New York underground railway stations for street car advertising has been let to a man for $500,000 a year.

FAST PRESSES HAVE EFFECT.

As an illustration of factors that advertisers must consider Mr. Mahin stated that the character of advertisement plates used in magazines and in newspapers are today distinct. The continual stress of newspapers to increase speed of their presses as their circulation grows has made it impossible for advertisers to use the same kind of plates in big newspapers, as they do in smaller ones or in the magazines. In the papers printed on fast presses it is no longer possible to use fine half tone plates. Such plates can be used in slow running presses used by small papers and by magazines.

The talk ended at midnight. Among up-town men interested in advertising who were present were [illegible] Findlay and Otto Kney, Prof. [illegible]erman, Prof. W. A. Scott, Prof. S. [illegible] Sparling and W. D. Taylor of the university faculty were also present.

Great Wheat Increase.

Sydney, Dec. 14.—The official estimate of the wheat yield of New South Wales is 28,570,000 bushels, an increase of twelve and a half million bushels compared with the record of 1901. About eighteen and a half million bushels are available for export.

IS CALLED TO ANSWER

Washington, Dec. 18.—Secretary Root today requested Brigadier General H. C. Merriam, retired, to inform the department if he was quoted correctly in an alleged interview in Denver yesterday in which he is made to say the president's appointment of Leonard Wood to be major general was generally unpopular with army men and that such appointments tended to unsettle the army and impair its morality. The general was asked to make such explanation as he may deem proper.

UNION MUSICIANS REFUSE TO PLAY

DECLINE TO APPEAR ON PROGRAM WITH NON-UNION TALENT AT UNIVERSITY.

Unionism has invaded the university. Madison musicians who belong to the union turned down a request to play at a concert to be given by the students at Library hall next Monday evening, becuse they would not appear on the program with non-union players.

To complete the program of the concert, which is in charge of the young ladies' glee club of the university, it was requested of Prof. F. A. Parker that he ask some of the local musicians to participate. The instruments needed were three violins and a bass viol. Prof. Parker asked several members of the Madison union if they would assist in the entertainment, but learning that the players with whom they were to appear are not members of the musicians' union they immediately balked and declined their services.

After considerable trouble Prof. Parker secured student musicians who will fill the vacant places on the program.

SENTENCED FOR DEFRAUDING WOMEN

Chicago, Dec. 18.—Housewives from different parts of the United States were in attendance in the federal district court to-day and heard Judge Humphrey announce sentence in the case of Wilbur Leach, of six months in jail and a fine of $500. Under the guise of an organization known as the "Modern Supply club," Leach advertised he would furnish a sewing outfit and material and would pay ten cents for each apron made by the members of the club. Deposits of a dollar were required from each victim. The defendant was charged with keeping the money and omitting the payment for the women's work.

BIG FIRE IN A COAL MINE

Bloomington, Dec. 18.—The South Shaft coal mine at Lincoln was destroyed by fire today. The loss is $100,000, and one hundred and fifty miners are thrown out of employment.

Princess Has Not Cancer.

Berlin, Dec. 18.—The report from Paris that Princess Charlotte of Saxe Meiningen, sister of Emperor William is suffering from cancer is officially defined as "nonsense." The princess is not ill.

MADISON HOTEL MEN WARNED

Informed of Man Who is Passing Bogus Checks.

IT IS A SIGN OF HARD TIMES.

Same Party Did Capital City Hotel Proprietor Out of $15 — Is Also Wanted at Ripon.

Madison hotel proprietors, who are members of the Wisconsin State Hotel association, have received a letter of warning, advising them to be on the lookout for a man whose name is said to be E. E. Campbell, who is wanted at Ripon for passing a worthless check. The same party a short time ago did a Madison hotel man out of $15 in the same manner.

The man is described in the circular as being about 40 years old. He registered at the Hotel Foeste, Sheboygan, as E. E. Summers and there tried to pass a check but failed. Manager Warner, of the Foeste, requested the man to leave it for collection. A worthless check, it is stated in the circular, was passed at the Hotel Englebreght at Ripon. A description of the man, given by Herman O. Kleitsch, secretary of the hotel association, speaks of him as being tall, with dark moustache, slight stoop, sloping shoulders and wearing dark clothes.

SIGN OF HARD TIMES.

"It's a sign of hard times," said John A. Simon, one of the proprietors of Simon's hotel, the popular hostelry on South Butler street. "We have received three of these warnings in the last two months. When they begin to come it's a sign of failing prosperity."

The Madison members of the association are Frederick N. Simon and John A. Simon of Simon's hotel; Geo. A. Lougee, proprietor, and Ernest F. Bunn, manager of the Park hotel; W. H. Huppeler, proprietor of the Capital house; C. R. Willey, Avenue hotel.

LA FOLLETTE AT SUPERIOR

Governor La Follette will lecture at Superior January 12. His subject is announced as Hamlet. It will be given under the auspices of the Pilgrim Congregational church of that city and the proceeds will go to the liquidation of the church debt.

The governor is also slated to talk at Duluth on the preceding evening, the subject being his favorite discourse, Representative Government. The lecture at Duluth will be given in the Lyceum theater.

WOMAN DIES OF STARVATION

Mrs. Flaherty of Duluth, Whose Husband Is in Jail, Succumbs to Exposure.

St. Paul, Dec. 18.—Mrs. Geneva Flaherty, of Duluth, while on her way to Marston, Wisconsin, her brother's home, died on a Northern Pacific train today. The coroner's verdict was that death was due to starvation and exposure. Mrs. Flaherty was accompanied by her four children whose ages ranged from 15 months to ten years. Her husband is in the Duluth jail on a charge of non-support, and it was while struggling against ill-health and poverty to provide food for her babies that she starved herself to such an extent that death followed.

MANY CANDIDATES PROVING BAD OMEN FOR LA FOLLETTE

Governor La Follette will be forced to run for a third term, is the opinion of a prominent Stalwart leader in the city. If he could have his own way, continued the man who has a clear vision of the field, he would sit right down and dictate who should be the Halfbreed candidate for the office. But he does not feel that his forces are strong enough to do such a thing. If a candidate should develop sufficient strength in the gubernatorial campaign La Follette might withdraw and reserve his energies for the senatorial struggle against Senator Quarles. But there is no candidate to which the present governor can hitch and feel sure that the campaign would turn out successfully.

The only alternative for La Follette is that he shall enter himself actively in the race, which is considered much against his desire. This plan alone, it is believed, will give him any chance for success. There can be no doubt in the minds of politicians, both Halfbreeds and Stalwarts, that this is the crux of the political situation. The numerous gubernatorial candidates who are prominently mentioned as possibilities have seriously alarmed Governor La Follette. Of only there can be no question [illegible] forces did all in their power to keep Baensch and Cook from entering the field. But the fact that they could not be kept out of the race leads many to believe that the [illegible] political strength [illegible] one [illegible] for La Follette is [illegible] warning. The announcement of the possibility of Connors, the Marshfield millionaire, for the governor's chair also strikes a hard blow to the administration. It is reported that an effort will be made by those at present in the harness to sidetrack Connors by running him for congress in the ninth district against Congressman Brown.

Then, Ira Bradford, the Augusta statesman, has gubernatorial ambitions and this fact, too, is causing the administration leaders much worriment. How are political aspirations to be satisfied? Every day the gubernatorial situation assumes a more serious phase.

WISCONSIN STATE JOURNAL. LAST EDITION

VOL. 102. NO. 128. MADISON, WIS., SATURDAY AFTERNOON, FEBRUARY 27, 1904. PRICE TWO CENTS.

STATE CAPITOL BURNED THIS A. M.

Fire Starts at 2:45 A. M. From Gas Jet, Cloak Room, Second Floor.

PART OF NORTH WING ONLY FREE FROM FLAMES

No Insurance--Chief Bernard Seriously Hurt--Capitol Water Service Absolutely Useless--Hose from Remote City Hydrants Carried Light Pressure--Attorney General's Office, Land Office, Board of Control, Insurance Commissioner's and Supreme Court Rooms alone Escape Flames--Milwaukee Sends two Engines--Loss a Million Dollars--Extra Session of Legislature at Once.

Fire started at 2:45 on second story in center of building.

Building gutted except at North end (toward postoffice).

SAVED.

Attorney general's office.
Board of Control.
Land office.
Insurance commissioner's office.
Supreme Court office (on second floor.
All else gutted by fire.

THESE BURNED OUT.

On First Floor:
Secretary of State's.
State Treasurer's.
Supt. of Public Instruction.
Normal Regents.
State Tax Commission.
Erickson's Bureau of Statistics.
Dairy and Food.
J. M. True's Agriculture Bureau.
Boardman's National Guard Rooms.
Railroad Commissioner's Office.
Governor's Office.

SECOND STORY.

G. A. R. rooms.
State Library Commission.
Game Warden's.
Senate and Assembly Chambers, and Committee Rooms.
Everything upstairs except Supreme Court rooms burned.

Law Library saved by students.

Records in vaults saved, but much material not locked up.

THE FIRST CAPITOL IN 1837.

Loss $900,000 on tangible property (W. E. Main's estimate).

No Insurance.

Chief Bernard injured; also Coroner Lynch.

Governor has taken Board of Control's office at once.

University water service which supplies capitol fails.

Gov. La Follette calls a conference of state officers for Monday when matter of extra session will be taken up.

A fire which broke out between 2:30 and 3 o'clock this morning almost completely destroyed the state capitol building. The fire is believed to have been caused from a gas jet in the closet on the second floor, next to the assembly postoffice. It spread rapidly and in spite of the heroic work of the firemen, the entire building was shortly doomed. The flames spread rapidly and by 10 o'clock little was left of the splendid building but the great dome and the ruined walls, whose architectural beauty seemed enhanced when stripped of roof and woodwork. The north end alone was saved. The loss will be about a million dollars with no insurance, not considering many things, treasured in sentiment, which are above money value.

CRAMTON'S STATEMENT.

The fire originated from a gas jet in the cloak room on the second floor adjoining the assembly post office. The dynamo furnishing the electric light for the building is turned off at 11 o'clock. The only light then left for the watchman on the second floor is a gas jet in this cloak room. Nat Cramton, of Madison, is the watchman on this floor. Mr. Cramton said:

"I was downstairs temporarily when I smelled fire. I immediately rushed upstairs to my quarters and found that the ceiling had become ablaze from the gas jet. This jet was too near the ceiling which had been blackened from it before and I had called attention to the danger previously. I immediately grabbed a pail of water and dashed it up to the ceiling, but was not able to put it out. I immediately sent in an alarm to the city department which arrived promptly but the flames were then gaining fast."

SNELL SAVES NORTH WING.

The saving of the north wing of the Capitol was due to the heroic work of Jay H. Snell and his brave fellows. He stood at the head of the north hall on the second floor and kept two streams plying on the fire. He begged to have two men stay with him and they volunteered, though the smoke was stifling and blazing timbers were falling all around them. When this floor fell in he climbed upon the roof and kept two streams plying on the flames there and one from below and in this way fought the fire back, and saved the north end. The highest praise is given the Madison firemen.

MILWAUKEE TAKES ACTION.

News from Milwaukee is that the chamber of commerce has appointed a committee to look up legal opinions as to legality of removing the capitol.

Regent William F. Vilas immediately took action to place such university buildings as were available at the use of the state departments.

UNIVERSITY WATER FAILED.

The big capitol fire would undoubtedly have been averted had the water supply not failed. When the fire broke out the capitol employees prepared to use the hydrants and hose which are stationed about the building. When the nozzles were turned on the water failed to come. During this time the fire had been confined to a space of a few feet, and, had the water come,

(Continued on page six.)

GOV. LA FOLLETTE PROVES A HERO

Was Early On Hand Directing Work of Rescue.

VALUABLE RECORDS ARE SAVED.

Executive Though Soaked from Head to Foot Directs Work of Saving Records.

Gov. La Follette proved himself a hero and it was largely through his activities in directing the firemen and the labor force and citizens who quickly lent their help, that many valuable records were saved. He ran everywhere through the burning building.

At 4:30 he first learned of the fire through Fireman John Brahany, who, at Chief Bernard's order, telephoned him that the capitol building was afire and that assistance was wanted from Milwaukee. The governor immediately telephoned Milwaukee and a detachment of the department was immediately dispatched. It was the first that the governor heard of the fire and he was much surprised. He dressed immediately and came down, where he superintended the work of carrying out records from the treasurer's office and the office of the land commissioners.

He ran everywhere through the burning building, directing the work of rescue of valuable records and documents. Practically everything of value in the executive department was saved. The

(Continued on page five.)

MANY SIGHTSEERS.

View Fire Ruins and Attend Ski Tournament.

News of the big fire has attracted many people to the city from small neighboring towns. After viewing the ruins of the state capitol most of them attended the big ski tournament being pulled off on university hill this afternoon.

MAYOR GROVES ASSISTS GOVERNOR

Says City Water Service Doing Fine Work.

STATE OFFICERS BEING LOCATED

Governor Will Occupy Board of Control Room—Food for Tired Firemen—City Will Pay the Bill.

Mayor Groves was seen at 11 o'clock this morning and said that the city was doing all in its power to assist Governor La Follette in caring for the state official's property and the tired firemen: Despite the fact that the

(Continued on fifth page.)

CHIEF BERNARD WAS INJURED

Slewing Of Hose Cart Throws Him From Seat.

SUFFOCATED BY SMOKE.

Dr. D. B. Collins Called—Inquires of Wife Whether c[illegible] Fire is Under Control.

Chief Charles Bernard of the fire department lies at his home, 624 East Gorham street, in a precarious condition, as a result of injuries sustained in this morning's big fire. The slewing of a hosecart threw him from the seat shortly after the first alarm was sounded. The chief was thrown with terrific force against a huge tree. His right knee was badly injured, but the accident dazed the chief only a few moments. Despite the entreaties of the firemen the chief was peristent and well in front of his men he led them into the blazing capitol. Not for a moment did he falter and it was not until he fell unconscious, suffocated from smoke on the inside of the capitol did the seriousnes of his condition become known.

Dr. D. B. Collins was summoned without delay. The chief was tenderly laid in one of the hosecarts and driven to his home. At 10 o'clock this morning the chief was again himself and inquired anxiously of his wife whether or not the fire was under control. Many called at his home, but none were allowed to see him.

Mr. Bernard was made chief of Madison's fire department succeeding Wm. Hughes in March, 1890.

Dr. D. B. Collins, who is attending Chief Bernard of the fire department, said at 1 o'clock this afternoon that he did not consider his patient in a serious condition. He says, "when I first saw Mr. Bernard his lungs were full of smoke and his right knee was sprained. He was pale and weak and had all the appearances of a man badly injured."

DECLINES OFFER OF FOREIGN LOAN

Count Tolstoi Contributes Books for War Fund.

JAPAN LODGES A PROTEST.

No Truth In Report That French Minister Had Been Asked to Leave Korea.—War News.

St. Petersburg, Feb. 27.—The minister of finance, it is stated, has again declined firmly the offers of several groups of leading foreign banks to float the Russian loan on the ground that there is no need for adopting such a course.

Count Leo Tolstoi has contributed a thousand sets of his works, the profit from sale of which will be expended for the benefit of the troops taking part in the campaign in the far east.

WILL LODGE PROTEST.

The Hague, Feb. 27.—The Japanese minister here has been instructed by his government to lodge a protest with the president of the council of the permanent court of arbitration against the language used by M. Muravieff, president of the arbitration tribunal and the Russian minister of justice, in a speech he made after announcing the tribunal's decision in favor of blockading the powers as against Venezuela.

Chefoo, Feb. 27.—Several Japanese officers and sailors who landed here from an open boat early to-day refused to give any information as to where they came from. At the Japanese consulate it was given out they belong to a gunboat which was damaged during the fight off Port Arthur and which sank trying to reach this port.

Paris, Feb. 27.—There is no truth in the report that the Japanese minister at Seoul, Korea, had requested the Korean government to hand the French minister his passports.

St. Petersburg, Feb. 27.—The czar has received the following from Viceroy Alexieff, dated Port Arthur, Feb. 26:

"Early in the morning of the 25th the Retvizan repelled several attacks by the enemy's torpedo boats, two of which are believed to have been sunk in the open sea. Our topedo boats, unsupported, encountered and pursued the enemy's torpedo boat flotilla.

MACHEN TO PRISON

Bulletin. Washington, Feb. 27.—Justice Pritchard this afternoon sentenced August W. Machen, Diller B. Groff and George Lorenze each to two years' imprisonment in the penitentiary and to pay a fine of $10,000. The case of Samuel A. Groff has not been decided.

LATEST

Fond du Lac, Feb. 27.—The body of Mrs. Fredericks, an emigrant and a domestic, employed by John Edwards, of Rosendale, missing since Monday, was found Friday caught in a wire fence and frozen half mile from home. She lost her way in the storm. Her husband is in Germany. She had a son seven years old.

Oshkosh, Feb. 27.—John Loose, Jr., of Chilton, pleaded guilty today to the charge of assault with intent to kill on Joseph Koenig. He is a degenerate.

Bagley Going South.

Mr. W. R. Bagley expects to leave for Floria either Monday or Tuesday. He goes in hope of benefiting his health.

STATE GETS NOT A CENT INSURANCE

Present Administration Repealed Policy of Insuring State Property.

SCOFIELD'S $600,000 PROTECTION LAPSED

Policies of $500,000 Covering University Buildings Lapse Next Tuesday and Cannot be Renewed--Loss is Fully $1,000,000 But Experts Cut it Down to $800,000.

Not one cent of insurance will come to the state as a result of destruction by fire of the state capitol here today. The state staggers under a complete loss of a sum between $1,000,000 and $800,000.

Loss and ruin of many state documents, and destruction of such relics and mementos as those contained in Memorial Hall is irremediable, nor can they be valued in dollars. Estimates of men of judgment, who take into account everything in the way of tangible property, put the loss at fully $1,000,000.

W. E. MAIN SAYS $800,000.

W. E. Main, of the insurance firm of A. H. Main & Son, and who is an expert fire loss adjuster, estimates the loss at $800,000. "This is on the assumption that the walls cannot be saved in the new building—that a new capitol will have to be built complete," said Mr. Main.

$600,000 INS. JUST LAPSED.

A distressing circumstance of the loss is that the last insurance policy lapsed only three months ago. For several years the state had been carrying a total of $600,000 on the capitol and contents.

June 1, 1903, $510,000 of this lapsed. Dec. 1, 1903, the remaining $90,000 lapsed.

(Continued on page six.)

GREAT LOSS OF THE GRAND ARMY

All Records of Order in State Destroyed.

OLD ABE'S BODY IN ASHES.

Valuable Pictures and Mementoes Treasured Above All Cost Are No More.

I have been asked to tell about the loss to the Grand Army room in the capitol. It may be said, in the first place, that financially the state is little the worse off because of what was burned there. I suppose that a hundred dollars would easily pay for the furniture of the room.

But there are things beyond the price of money, things money cannot buy. There were all the Grand Army rec-

(Continued on fifth page.)

NOTES OF THE FIRE

At 9 o'clock several students went into the building with big cans of coffee for the firemen.

About 5:30 this morning two or three students ran up and down Langdon, State and Lake streets and Mendota court, shouting, "The capitol building is on fire. Turn out and save the law library." In less than half an hour over two hundred students were at work carying out the volumes.

It was noticed while the students were carrying out books from the law library several ladies were helping in the work.

Mr. Lathrop Smith and Edward Sumner of the Congregational church offered to Judge Siebecker the basement of the Congregational church to house the law library.

The priceless stereotyped plates of the state reports are in boxes in the basement of the capitol and believed to be safe. It is from them the State Journal prints the reports.

University professors and instructors were up town witnessing the fire as soon as the mob of students. Those members of the faculty who had classes cut them or dismissed the few students who came. Among them were Professors Frampton, Blyer, A. L. S. Brown and others.

As early as half past three and four this morning, people, excited at the two fire alarms, sent in, rushed to the scene of the fire. Among the first to arrive were the stenographers employed in the capitol, who made for the offices to fetch out their typewriters and other belongings. Practically all the things in this line were saved.

(Continued on page six.)

FIRE SCENE ONE OF GREATEST CHAOS

Insidious Flames Baffled All First Attempts.

ACCIDENTS NARROWLY AVERTED

Firemen and Police Prove Themselves Heroes—Many Narrow Escapes.

The fire which ruined the capitol of Wisconsin broke out on the western side of the south wing, close to the assembly chamber, at 3 o'clock this morning. The alarm was turned in and the fire department responded quickly. However, before they could accomplish much the fire had gained much headway. With the half dozen or more of streams playing on the burning south wing, the fire gained more headway, until the entire wing, including the assembly chamber, was enveloped in a mass of flames.

AID FROM MILWAUKEE.

Requests for aid were sent to Janesville and Milwaukee, and a second alarm was turned in. This brought out the entire local department and volunteers, including citizens of Madison of all classes who lent a helping hand. By this time a large number of Madison people had assembled and

(Continued on page five.)

THE CAPITOL BEFORE DESTROYED BY FIRE.

REGULAR AND LAST EDITION.

Subscribers not receiving their papers regularly will confer a favor by notifying this office PROMPTLY.

WISCONSIN STATE JOURNAL.

WEATHER PREDICTIONS
The weather predictions for Wisconsin are: Partly cloudy tonight and Thursday; warmer tonight; cooler west and north Thursday.

VOL. 107. NO. 15. MADISON, WIS., WEDNESDAY AFTERNOON, APRIL 18, 1906. PRICE TWO CENTS.

DEATH OF THOUSANDS AND LOSS OF $50,000,000 TOLL OF SAN FRANCISCO HORROR

Danger of Tidal Wave Adds to Fear that Entire Lower Section of the City May be Devastated---Mechanic's Pavilion is Chocked with Dead and Undertakers can Care for no More Victims---Shocks Felt in Many Sections of the Country.

MARTIAL LAW PREVAILS AND THE TROOPS GUARD CORPSES; WIND FANS THE FLAMES

LOS ANGELES, APRIL 18.—COMMUNICATION WITH SAN FRANCISCO WAS SEVERED AT 11:00 WHEN THE POSTAL TELEGRAPH COMPANY WAS FORCED TO DESERT ITS BUILDING. AT THAT HOUR THE PALACE AND GRAND HOTELS, AND THE CALL BUILDING HAD BEEN DESTROYED. THE EXAMINER, RIALTO, AND SOUTHERN PACIFIC BUILDINGS ARE ABLAZE.

[By the Associated Press.]

San Francisco, Cal., April 18.—Death, fire and rain swept the city today, in consequence of an earthquake which shook the entire district around here for miles at 5:10 o'clock this morning. The city is practically wrecked.

Up to noon 500 dead had been brought to Mechanics' pavilion, and more are coming in all the time.

The shocks are continuing at intervals. At 9:20 and 10 o'clock there were heavy shocks that did further damage and increased the panic.

The possibility of a devastating tidal wave is increasing.

The damage is roughly estimated at $50,000,000.

Another shock at 8:15 o'clock added to the terror, but caused no more material damage. To intensify the horror, the water system is completely tied up, and fires are raging in all directions. If the wind comes up later in the day the city will absolutely destroyed by the greatest conflagration of modern times.

Mayor Schmitz established headquarters at hall of justice has appointed a relief committee of fifty prominent citizens. The military is patroling the streets, guarding banks and other establishments. They have received orders to shoot any one on sight detected in theft.

The chief of police has closed all saloons.

The whole north end of the city is wrecked and the flames are spreading in all directions.

The fire has taken hold of the 16-story Call building on Third street. The building also is threatened on the Market street side.

The back of the 11-story Monadnock building, now nearing completion, has fallen out.

Fire is raging on all sides of the Palace hotel.

From present indications the entire business district, both wholesale and retail, will likely fall prey to the flames, which are increasing in intensity, fanned by a stiff breeze.

TWENTY-ONE BODIES HAVE BEEN TAKEN TO THE MORGUE, WHICH CANNOT ACCOMMODATE ANY MORE.

On Lower Market street the main thoroughfare of the city, block after block of substantial buildings has been destroyed. Practically the entire water front is on fire.

FEAR FOR TIDAL WAVE.

Rochester, N. Y., April 18.—"Another and even greater disaster than the earthquake threatens San Francisco. A tidal wave would not be unlooked for as an accompaniment to the present seismic disturbances," said Prof. H. L. Fairchild of the university of Rochester today. "Much of San Francisco is only twelve feet wide and this fact renders it particularly liable to destruction in such event."

The wildest rumors as to loss of life are coming into the newspapers, but it impossible to confirm them. No reports have been received outside San Francisco, but the damage about the bay must be enormous. Oakland is said to have suffered severely.

The chief building affected was the St. Nicholas Hotel, which was severely shaken. The walls collapsed in certain parts of the structure, patrons were thrown out of their beds and the furniture destroyed.

The gas works, south of Market street, has been blown up and that has started another big fire in that section.

A portion of the mission several miles from the business section is in flames.

The fire began at Twenty-Second street and is rapidly moving eastward. Gore Block, Market and Pine streets, will be a total loss.

At 10 o'clock the fire had reached Market and Third. The building next to the Claude Spreckles building was in flames and the fire extended along the south side of Market to Fourth street.

The following buildings on New Montgomery street have been entirely destroyed: Pacific States Telephone company, Rialto, Mission and Market; Natoma building on Second and Market. The twelve story Mutual Life building on California and Sansome has been destroyed.

The Valencia Hotel, a five-story frame bu... ng toppied into the street, burying 75 people in the debris. A house on Fourteenth street near Valencia was wrecked, killing two people. Many firehouses were damaged so badly it was impossible to get the fire apparatus out. A lodging house on ... street known as Kingsley was entirely collapsed. From 75 to 80 people are believed to be buried in the ruins.

At Eighteenth and Valencia there is crevice in the street six feet wide. Street car tracks are badly twisted. Throughout the southern section traffic is at a standstill.

Dynamite is used to stop the flames.

At the Southern Pacific hospital water is being carried in the building from outside sources for the use of patients. Many people suffering from injuries are seen on the streets making their way to the different hospitals.

The Episcopal church on Eleventh street and the Studebaker carriage factory on Tenth and Market streets, were badly wrecked.

It is reported three miles of the Southern Pacific track, near Benecia, 30 miles from San Francisco, has sunk down for a depth of about four feet.

Fire in the vicinity of Fourth and Stevenson streets got beyond the control of the firemen. The Winchester rooming house is on fire. Unless the flames are checked here the Palace hotel, a block distant, will be endangered. The water supply is entirely inadequate.

The rooms in the Palace hotel were vacated early in the morning. The guests are now returning to gather up their effects. The loss of life seems to have been confined to the poorer districts and manufacturing territory. For the benefit of eastern people who have friends in San Francisco, it is safe to say they have not been injured.

The Postal Telegraph company was the first to get a wire and its offices were besieged with people filing messages.

The Santa Fe roundhouse and machine shops at Point Richmond, across the bay, have collapsed.

The earthquake was not seriously felt at other points along the coast, so far as can be ascertained. At 10:15 a. m. the fire extends from Ferry to Front street on one side, and pretty much all south of Market street and out to about Seventh street, with sporadic fires in the park section and the western division. There is no way of estimating the number of dead. It may be hundreds or even thousands.

The Postal telegraph operators who are at their posts are taking their lives in their hands, as the building is collapsing, the fire being within half a block.

The Mechanics' Pavilion has been converted into a temporary hospital. Already several hundred victims of the disaster are being treated there by a corps of volunteer surgeons.

The entire water front is ablaze. The postoffice has entirely collapsed.

The fish market, corner Clay and Merchant streets, collapsed, killing six people. Fire Chief Sullivan and his wife were badly injured.

The Grand Opera house is burning fiercely. Several big buildings between the theatre and St. Patrick's church apparently are doomed. The people are fleeing from the Palace Hotel, taking their personal effects.

In Oakland five persons were killed by the collapse of the Empire building.

Power of every kind is gone and there are no lights, either of gas or electricity. Neither the Palace Hotel nor the St. Francis are destroyed, but inside the plastering is greatly damaged.

Between the postoffice and water front there has been great damage by a fire which is burning fiercely. Damage by the earthquake apparently extends all over the city. The residence districts are safe so far as heard from.

HUNDREDS KILLED

San Francisco, April 18.—The business section from Market street to Mission street from the bay back is almost completely wrecked.

The Call and Examiner buildings and many structures along Market and Mission streets, including department stores, were destroyed. Hundreds of people in the cheap tenement district are reported killed. Fires are raging owing to the scarcity of water and are practically beyond control.

The Associated Press building was wrecked. The residence portion was but slightly damaged although nearly every house was more or less injured.

FELT IN NEVADA.

New York, April 18.—At 11:05 a. m. the Western Union received a report that a serious fire is burning at Berkeley, where the state university is located. At the offices of the Frisco railroad in this city messages were received from the company's agent in Nevada saying the earthquake was felt throughout Nevada and all wires have been thrown down west of San Francisco.

FACTS ABOUT DEAD.

Up to noon 500 bodies had been brought to Mechanic's Pavilion and more are coming in every minute:

There is no way of estimating the number of dead. It may be hundreds or even thousands.

Twenty-one bodies have been taken to the morgue, which cannot accommodate any more.

In Oakland five persons were killed by the collapse of the Empir building.

The Valencia Hotel, a five-story frame building toppled into the street, burying seventy-five in the debris. A house on Fourteenth street near Valencia was wrecked, killing two people.

The fish market, corner Clay and Merchant streets, collapsed killing six people.

A lodging house on Seventh street known as Kingsley was entirely collapsed. From seventy-five to eighty people are believed to be buried in the ruins.

Hundreds of people in the cheap tenement district are reported killed.

The loss of life seems to have been confined to the poorer districts and manufacturing territory.

GOVERNMENT TO HELP

Washington, April 18.—Assistant Secretary of War Oliver telegraphed Major General Greeley, at San Francisco to co-operate with the local authorities and use all resources at his command to assist in alleviating the situation there.

FELT IN WASHINGTON

Washington, April 18.—The San Francisco earthquake has reached across the entire continent. The seismograph at the weather bureau here showed such violent agitation about 8:30 this morning that the pen passed off the recording sheet. The instrument at 10 o'clock was still under vibration, showing the earthquake had not ceased.

RAILROAD IS CRIPPLED

New York, April 18.—The Western Union has received a report from Sacramento that the Southern Pacific railroad will attempt to get a line into San Francisco from Sacramento and taking a roundabout route to Vallejo, on the bay at San Pablo. At that place the passengers will be taken by boat to San Francisco. This roundabout course was made necessary by the sinking of three mile section of the railroad company's tracks between Suisuan and Benecia which are in the direction of the line between Sacramento and San Francisco.

WORST EVER KNOWN.

New York, April 18.—The Western Union Telegraph office says it is the most severe shock ever known.

New York, April 18.—At 9:45 the Postal had communication with their San Francisco office, but lost the connection almost immediately. In the brief period the wire was working the Sa nFrancisco office reported a number of buildings had collapesed and

(Continued on page six.)

FACTS ABOUT DEVASTATION OF THE GOLDEN GATE CITY

Damage roughly estimated at $50,000,000.

A tidal wave is now the greatest menace to the city. The possibility of a repetition of the Galveston horror is very great.

Hundreds of people are killed and thousands injured. No figures obtainable.

Mechanics' Pavilion converted into a temporary hospital and already several hundred victims of the disaster are being treated by volunteer nurses and surgeons.

Martial law prevails. Troops in control of the city, with orders to shoot ghouls and thieves in sight.

The entire water front is ablaze. The postoffice has collapsed entirely. Six killed in the fish market.

Gas works blown up, starting another big fire.

Twelve-story Mutual Life building destroyed.

Three mile section of Southern Pacific sinks four feet just east of San Francisco.

Disastrous fire at Berkeley, near 'Frisco, where the state university is located.

Shock of the quake nearly ruined seismograph in the weather office at Washington, D. C.—over 3,000 miles. Nevada also suffered from the shock.

Greatest damage reported to be in Battery, Sansol, Montgomery, Kearney, Spear, Main, Beale and Fremont streets in San Francisco.

Secretary of war orders all available aids under his direction to the scene of the disaster.

MADISON PEOPLE ARE APPREHENSIVE

Many Have Relatives in San Francisco and Nearby Cities.

ANXIOUS INQUIRIES ARE MADE.

But Few Details of Great Disaster Received—Some Madisonians Now on the Coast.

Many Madison people have relatives in San Francisco and other cities and are much worried over there safety. When news of the earthquake spread over the city many called up the State Journa office to get what particulars they could. C. E. Zeidler has a brother, George, living in the city and a sister, Mrs. Jesse Calvert, a bride, had just arrived there. Another brother was also on the way there.

Mrs. A. C. Titus, wife of the assistant attorney general, is at Los Angeles, where a son, Robert H. Titus, is engaged in newspaper work.

Paul Findlay, the Madison merchant, is at Los Angeles with his family.

In far southern California Dr. Frank

(Continued on page six.)

FACTS ABOUT THE STRICKEN "QUEEN CITY" OF THE WEST

Richard Henry Dana describes San Francisco of 1835 as follows:

"It is about thirty miles from the mouth of the bay ,and on the southeast side is a high point upon which the presidio is built. Behind this is the harbor in which trading vessels anchor, and near it, the mission of San Francisco, and a newly begun settlement, mostly of Yankee Californians, called Yerba Buena, which promises well. Here, at anchor, and the only vessel, is the Russian America, which had come down to winter, and to take in a supply of tallow and grain, great quantities of which latter article are raised in the missions at the head of the bay."

* * * * * *

That was San Francisco of 1835. As late as 1846 the place had grown so little that not more than twenty or thirty houses of all descriptions lined the beach. Mud flats, laid bare at low tide, extended for some distance out from the shore, and the only landing place for boats was at Clark's Point, where the rocks jutted out into the water. This was near the present site of Broadway Wharf. A bay reached into the valley now traversed by market square, cutting across the present line of First street and penetrating as far as the border of Montgomery. But there was a sudden transition of this quiet little settlement into a lawless frontier town of America, and from that into a great metropolis where the commerce of the Pacific centers.

THE FAMOUS BAY.

"A free sweep of water navigable for the largest ocean vessels over a stretch of well nigh sixty miles; a land locked harbor with but a single passage, a mile in width leading to its sequestered waters; a haven cut off by hills and mountains from the ocean yet so accessible that the largest steamers can enter an all tides—such is San Francisco Bay with its 450 square miles of water!"

Such is the harbor which Portala first looked upon from the heights in 1769, and into which the little Spanish ship, San Carlos, said in 1775.

A BUSY PLACE.

San Francisco has been one of the United States' leading cities for years. There the busy scenes on State street, Chicago, and the great crowds on Broadway street, New York, are reproduced. It has long been a beautiful place, and the favorite spot of many who can afford to spend their winter where it is most always summer. The Bolinas Ridge, with the waters of the Golden Gates at its base; Grizzly Peak of the Berkely range; Goat Island, a green spot in the center of the bay; Fort Point and Point Bointa—these are all features of interest at San Francisco.

CITY AWAKENS.

For a time preceding the dawn of the new century, a lethargy seemed to settle upon the city of the Golden Gate. Northward, Seattle and Spokane were progressing with giant strides. To the southward, Los Angeles, had grown into a metropolis. Public spirit in San Francisco was at a low ebb. The population was at a standstill, houses were for rent, and the merchants displayed indifference. The city was staggered by the crash of '93. From this time on San Francisco took a brace. Everyone knows the result.

San Francisco occupies the strategic post of the world commerce of the twentieth century.

Like in '93, San Francisco has again been staggered, but rebuilding will doubtless begin soon.

The last earthquake that occurred in San Francisco was about the middle of January, 1900. Several distinct shocks were felt early in the morning, causing a vibration of buildings all over the city.

DO YOUR TRADING IN MADISON
WISCONSIN'S MARKET CENTER
CITY EDITION
THE WISCONSIN STATE JOURNAL

VOL. 119. NO. 14. MADISON, WIS., TUESDAY AFTERNOON, APRIL 16, 1912 PRICE TWO CENTS.

1,492 ARE LOST; 866 ARE RESCUED; TITANIC'S GRAVE IS 2 MILES DEEP

THE MESSAGE THAT BROUGHT THE NEWS

Six hundred and fifty, mostly women and children on board the liner Carpathia, are the only ones saved from the Titanic. Others went down with the ship and wreckage. Other rescue ships failed to find any more of Titanic's passengers.--Wireless received at Charlestown Navy Yard.

NOTABLES ABOARD TITANIC; COL. ASTOR, MAJ. BUTT AND WILLIAM STEAD IN NUMBER

SAD CROWDS IN NEW YORK SEEK NEWS

Crowds Storm Offices of White Star Line for Word From Relatives Aboard Titanic

ASTOR JR., ANXIOUS

Company is Accused of Suppressing the News, say Class was Counted in the Rescue

New York, April 16.—Utterly stunned by the weight of the terrible disaster that followed the loss of the giant liner Titanic on her maiden voyage, New York halted today.

It was hard to realize that the latest creation of marine architecture, the great steamship which only yesterday, when news that she had been in collision was received, was proudly branded by her owners as "unsinkable" now lay below the waters of the Atlantic off the banks of Newfoundland and had carried with her much of the flower of American and British manhood.

Not since the ill-fated French liner Bourgoyne was rammed and sent to the bottom with all of her company by the great iron freighter Cromartyshire on July 2, 1898, have such scenes been witnessed as were enacted at the offices of the White Star line on lower Broadway throughout the night and day. The men, women and children, many hysterical and weeping, stormed the offices and vainly begged for some word of comfort regarding the fate of their loved ones.

FEW GET WORD

Few got any satisfaction. For the great majority all that the company would say was that there had been loss of life, but they were hoping for the best. To relatives of noted passengers a private audience was granted and it was quiety whispered that the outlook was most serious. But even they did not get all the facts which the company had in its possession. For some inexplicable reason the White Star line has steadily refrained from making public facts in its possession and apparently it was able to muzzle the wireless, as messages sent direct to ships on the scene were held up.

Charges were freely made by relatives of the missing that the company not alone withheld news of the disaster, but that it was responsible for messages of comfort received yesterday saying all of the passengers had been rescued and the disabled liner was being towed to port. But the officials refused explanation.

When first announcement was made last night that the Titanic had sunk and that there "was probable loss of [illegible]" the officers of the line were immediately besieged by anxious men and women, all waiting for a word of [illegible] or assurance.

The word reached many while they were in the theaters and the restaurants and soon great automobiles and [illegible] of all descriptions were rolling [illegible] the offices and discharging their [illegible] of anxious humanity. Soon the [illegible] were called and the line extended [illegible] into the street. Among the [illegible] reach the offices of the line was [illegible] Astor, only son of Colonel John [illegible] Astor. He was worried but hopeful when he arrived and was admitted [illegible] private offices of Vice President Franklin. He was accompanied by J. [illegible] and the representative of the Astor estate. Half an hour later the young man emerged weeping and was assisted into his auto and hurried to his home.

Relatives of the missing continued to arrive and all were told that the list of survivors would be made public as soon as possible. This came to the

(Continued on fifth page)

Head of Famous Family and Young Wife Among the Passengers on Doomed Ocean Liner

SORROW AT CAPITOL

Taft's Aid Was Returning From Vacation Spent In Europe Where He Went For His Health

STEAD NOTED AUTHOR

Frank D. Millet, Artist, Had Contract to Paint Panels In Supreme Court at State Capitol

Wealth Represented Aboard Titanic

Name	Wealth
Col. John Jacob Astor	$150,000,000
J. Bruce Ismay	40,000,000
Col. W. Roebling	25,000,000
Isidor Straus	50,000,000
G. D. Widener	50,000,000
Benjamin Guggenheim	95,000,000
J. B. Thayer	10,000,000
Total	$420,000,000

New York, April 16.—Seldom in the history of navigation has a steamer carried so many noted persons as thronged the Titanic on her maiden trip.

Colonel John Jacob Astor, male head of the famous Astor family ranks as the largest individual land owner, so far as values are concerned in America.

Henry B. Harris is a power in the theatrical world, a native of St. Louis and an official in many managerial associations.

Isador Straus is a brother of Nathan and Oscar Straus and New York's most prominent Hebrew merchant.

William Stead, noted London author and for years editor of the Review of Reviews was enroute on a brief tour of the United States.

Charles Melville Hays, president of the Grand Trunk railroad, considered one of the most brilliant of railroad officials was returning from a business trip in England. Benjamin Guggenheim, fifth of the seven sons of Meyer Guggenheim, has for years been in charge of the Guggenheim mining interests.

Frank D. Millet, a noted artist and traveler, was returning from a trip to Italy where he was at the head of the American Academy at Rome.

Clarence Moore, one of Washington's most prominent society and sportsmen, was returning from England where, as master of the Chevy Chase hunt of Washington, he had purchased a new pack of hounds.

Major Archibald W. Butt, military aide to President Taft, had been abroad on a vacation for his health.

Jacques Futrelle, the writer of fiction had been on a pleasure trip with his wife.

J. Bruce Ismay, president of the International Mercantile Marine Co., which controls the White Star line, was also on board.

MEDICAL SOCIETY WILL MEET TONIGHT

The monthly meeting of the Dane County Medical Society will be held tonight at 8 o'clock in the chemical engineering building. One of the features of the meeting will be a demonstration of the work being done in the university school of medcine.

ANNOUNCE WINNER OF CONTEST TOMORROW

The winner of The State Journal slogan contest will be announced in tomorrow's issue.

Titanic Cross Section; Boat Compared With Dome

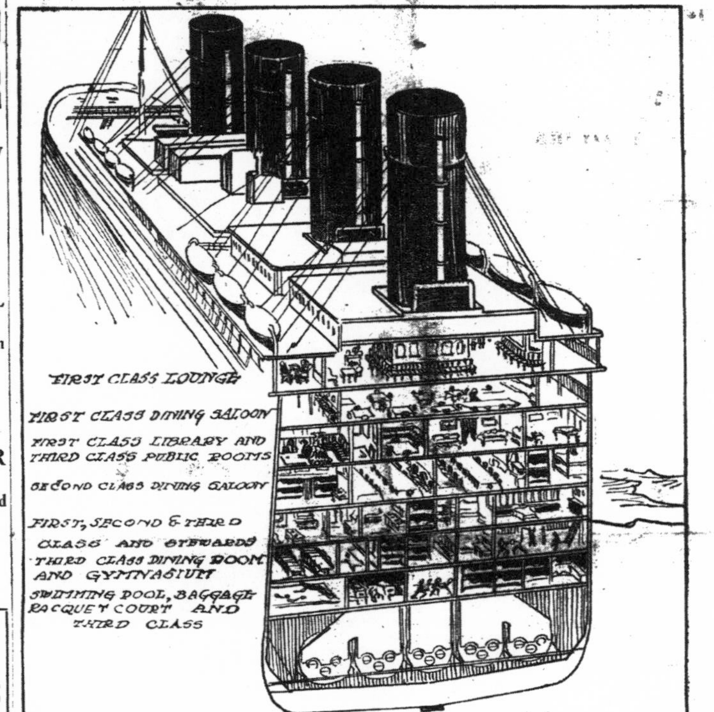

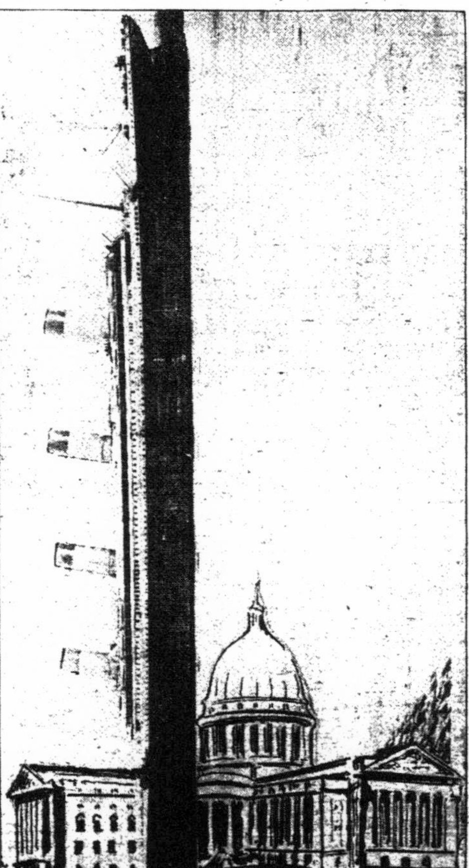

Capitol Dome Compared to Titanic's Length.

LOCAL BANK MERGER IS COMPLETED

Capital City, Bank of Wisconsin and Merchants Savings Bank Consolidate

CAPITAL $600,000

Location of New Bank and New Officers not Definitely Settled Upon

After pending for several weeks, the consolidation of the Capital City Bank, Bank of Wisconsin, and Merchants and Savings Bank, has finally been cosummated and it is now expected that it will be put into effect early in July.

The stockholders of the Bank of Wisconsin and the Merchants and Savings Bank decided in favor of consolidation several weeks ago but the proposition was held up by the stockholders of the Capital City bank who were unwilling to agree to a merger until some of the questions had been more definitely settled.

The probable location of the new bank as well as the officers has not been definietly settled as yet but it is understood that the directors have agreed on the name of the new bank as the "Wisconsin and Capital City Bank."

Before the merger can be brought about, however, it will be necessary for the Capital City and the Merchants and Savings Banks to give up their charters.

EXPECT VIRGINIAN WITH SURVIVORS

Boston, April 16.—The local office of the White Star line says that a wireless from St. Johns, N. B., says that the Allan liner Virginian is headed for that port. If that is true it is believed she must have on board survivors of the Titanic as she is a mail steamer and was eastward bound. Every effort is being made to speak to her and ascertain the facts.

ALL HOPE IS GONE WHEN WORD IS RECEIVED FROM TWO OF LINERS NEARBY

Survivors are Now Being Brought to New York on Board The Carpathia Which Went to Aid

ONLY 20 LIFE BOATS

Small Vessels Crowded to Limit With Women and Children; Sea's Code of Honor Is Observed

BOAT IS DUE FRIDAY

Stories of Experiences to Eclipse All In Fiction; Ice Floes Encircle Survivors Boats

Sea's Code of Honor

"Save the women and the children."

In every disaster the strict code of honor of the men who sail ships at sea has placed the safety of the weaker and the more helpless first.

And faithful to this code a thousand men gave up their lives in the sinking of the Titanic.

The list of survivors is made up largely of the names of women. And a great part of them were in the steerage. Under the leveling touch of danger, even the men of the first cabins seem to have stepped aside to place in the hazardous safety of the life boats the women of the emmigrant parties.

For the code is a greater thing than life itself.

New York, April 16.—Unable to withstand the wound she received yesterday when she crashed into a tramp iceberg the giant Titanic today lies in a watery grave two miles down in mid-ocean.

When she gave up the fight and sank into her last resting place, the mammoth liner carried 1,492 souls with her. Speeding toward New York on board the Carpathia are 866 persons—survivors of the most terrible tragedy recorded in oceanic history. Of these 886 are scores of wives and daughters of men—REAL MEN—men who followed to their death the unwritten code of honor of the seas: "Save the women and children first." When the big trans-Atlantic greyhound went down into the deep, helpless women and children strewn about in tiny lifeboats saw fathers and husbands swept from their sight forever.

Hope was practically abandoned this afternoon. Latest reports placed only 866 persons, and they chiefly women and children, on the Carpathia, while even the officials of the White Star line admitted there was practically no hope for the remaining 1,492 of the ship's company of 2,358 souls.

LIFEBOATS ARE SCARCE

That all would have had a chance of safety had there been life boats and rafts enough, was the general belief of navigators. But the liner, newest and greatest of trans-Atlantic ships, carried only 20 large, modern life boats, and they were loaded to the gunwales with the women and children, who in accordance with the unwritten law of the sea, had been put over the side of the ship.

Most of the men are missing. Colonel John Jacob Astor, Major Archie Butt, President Taft's aide; Benjamin Guggenheim, Jacques Futrelle, William T. Stead, F. D. Millet, Henry B. Harris—all of them all known personages whom had taken passage on the gala day of the Altanic's departure from her home port, were not included in the list of those reported saved. The inference was that they had remained on the ship and gone to the bottom with her, a sacrifice to the custom which fails to compel enough life boats and rafts on ocean steamers to take off everyone on board.

(Continued on fifth page)

JOHN HEIM TAKES SEAT AS MAYOR

New Administration Goes Into Office at Meeting at Noon Today

MANY APPOINTMENTS

Norsman Re-electedCity Clerk; but William Ryan Beats Out Vroman Mason for Attorney

Promptly at 12 o'clock noon John B. Heim became Mayor of Madison. He took the chair which had been occupied for six years by Joseph C. Schubert, and called the council to order.

In front of Mayor Heim reposed a huge bunch of American Beauty roses, presented to the new mayor by friends.

The council chamber was well filled shortly before the outgoing body took its seat for the last time.

Just before Mayor Schubert called the old council to order, a fine oak, roller top desk was carried into the chamber.

Alderman Prien took the floor and presented the desk to Mayor Schubert. The gift was from the members of the old council, in recognition of the services he had rendered the city and the council.

"Whenever I sit down at that desk I will remember the pleasant deliberations that we have had together" said Mr. Schubert in thanking the aldermen.

"I thought it would be an easy matter to lay down the burdens of public life, but I do not know whether it is easier to lay them down than it is to carry them."

Alderman Prien moved at 11:59 that the council adjourned sine die.

As Mayor Heim took his seat, former Mayor Schubert presented him with the official gavel.

In a short speech Mayor Heim said that he wanuted the co-operation of the new council in making Madison a better city.

NORSEMAN IS RE-ELECTED.

O. S. Norsman, who has been city clerk for about 23 years was unanimously re-elected. All the aldermen were present except Alderman Hobbins who is confined to his home by illness.

W. J. Ryan was elected city attorney over Vroman Mason, who was the choice of a joint caucus.

Immediately afte rthe election of Mr. Norsman, he announoed the appointment of George Nelson as his assistant.

The election of president of the council followed the selection of the city clerk. On the first ballot it was found that 20 ballots had been cast, while but

(Continued on fifth page)

The New Committees

Judiciary—Prien, Baker, Constantine, Dowling, Sommers.

Finance—Constantine, Kittleson, Bourke, McGregor, Prien, Steffen, Hobbins.

Claims — Stadelmann, Alford Bourke, Barry, Sullivan, Kittleson, McGregor.

City property — Barry, Marks, O'Neil, Simon, Utter.

Fire and Water—Simon, Behrend, Sommers, Quinn, Utter.

Police—Behrend, Dowling, Marks Prien, Simon.

Streets and sewers—Senior aldermen.

Street lighting—Junior aldermen.

Ordinances — Hobbins, Baker, Steffen, Sullivan, O'Neil.

License—Dowling, Behrend, Utter, Stadlemann, Barry.

Printing—Sommers, Barry, Hobbins, Baker Alford.

Public market—Quinn, Alford, Steffen, Stadlemann, Kittleson, O'Neil.

General hospital—Marks, Constantine.

The Wisconsin State Journal

CITY EDITION

VOL. 122. NO. 81. MADISON, WIS., TUESDAY AFTERNOON, JANUARY 6, 1914 PRICE TWO CENTS

BARNYARD BIRDS PREDOMINATE AT POULTRY EXHIBIT

But Silver Campines And Houdans With Latest Style of Headdress Are There

FORTY POUND GOBBLER

Single Combed Rhode Island Red Hen Brings Family With Her to The Show

A great variety of utility chickens —plain farmers' breeds—are shown by the Wisconsin Poultry association at its tenth annual exhibition in the stock pavilion of the college of agriculture. The exposition opened Tuesday forenoon and will be continued until Friday. The pavilion will be open to the public from 8 o'clock a. m. until 10 p. m.

Turkey Weighs 40 Pounds

Four bronze turkeys which were too good to die during the recent holiday season were expected to arrive on Tuesday and they have been heralded as enormous birds. The large male bird weighs forty pounds. A few Buff Orpington ducks and a few Pekin and Indian Runner ducks are on exhibition, but the rest of the collection is made up of chickens.

Standard breeds are in the majority, including Plymouth Rocks, Rhode Island Reds, Wyandottes, Leghorns, Langshan and Orpingtons. These entries include: Barred Plymouth Rocks, 67; White Plymouth Rocks, 58; Buc Plymouth Rocks, 70; Partridge Plymouth Rocks, 44; Buff Wyandottes, 72; Silver Wyandotte, 71; White Wyandottes, 90; Partridge Wyandotte, 69; Single Comb Rhode Island Reds, 108; Rose Comb Rhode Island Reds, 81; Black Langshan, 65; Single Comb White Leghorn, 115; Single Comb Brown Leghorn, 49; Buff Orpington, 57; White Orpington, 82; Black Orpington, 35.

New Breed Appears

Twenty-one Silver Campines, Belgian chickens, are new birds in the exhibition and have never been shown here before. Lakenvelders, Holland chickens, and Rhode Island Whites, are among the other new breeds.

Other breeds in smaller exhibits include Buff Brahmas, Columbian Rocks, Black and Golden Wyandottes, Light Brahmas, Anconas, Silver Duck Wings, Houdans, Single Rose Comb Black Minorcas, Silver Speckled Hamburgs and among the Leghorns, Rose Comb White, Single Comb Brown, Rose Comb Brown, Single and Rose Comb Buff, and Single Comb Black.

Latest Fashions Represented

Among the various organizations which have offered prizes for exhibitors among their members and in which classes the entries are large, are, the White Plymouth Rock, the American Buff Plymouth Rock, the Rhode Island Red, National Partridge Wyandotte, National White Wyandotte, American Buff Wyandotte, Silver Wyandotte Club of America, National Single Comb Buff Orpington and American Orpington Clubs.

The Silver Campines are black and white chickens, with the color in the feathers giving the effect of a pin stripe. The cocks have long white hackel feathers and the combs are bright looking birds with black and neat looking birds with black and white feathers. The hens' feathers are largely white with little black tufts all over them. The cocks have black tail and black hackel feathers.

The birds which have the most peculiar appearance are the Houdans, which are black birds, big and fluffy which look just as if they have been out in a big snow storm and a few flakes have stuck to their feathers,—for every now and then there is a white tipped feather. These birds have large hoods and beards so that their heads are entirely covered.

Brings Family Along

In the Black Orpington and Black Langshan class there are a number of very large birds. Until Tuesday only one hen with chicks had been entered. It was a Single Comb Rhode Island Red.

Judging for prizes will begin on Wednesday morning. A large number of birds will arrive late and the contest will not be closed until all of the birds have arrived.

The latest style incubators wire coops and all sorts of poultry feed are being shown by local exhibitors.

OPEN WATER ON LAKE WINNEBAGO

OSHKOSH, Wis., Jan. 6.—For the first time within the memory of the oldest inhabitants here, there was open water in Lake Winnebago in January today. The mercury hovered around twenty degrees and weather bureau records shows there has been no zero weather this winter.

RACINE GIRL THROWN ONTO STREET, RUINED

RACINE, Wis., Jan. 6.—Frank Tomacek, 25 years old, is in jail, charged with having inveigled a young immigrant girl into a trail marriage, at the instiation of his own mother, and then throwing her on the street after effecting her ruin.

"CINDRELLA" FINDS TINY SLIPPER LOST YESTERDAY; WISCONSIN STATE JOURNAL WANT AD, MODERN "PRINCE"

A MODERN CINDRELLA

And her 12 1-2—A Child's size slipper, recovered through a modern fairy prince—a want ad.

LOST

LOST Between Keeley, Neckerman Kessenich Co. and the Park hotel one lady's satin slipper 12 1-2 child's size. Reward if returned to the Orpheum theater.

TINY SLIPPER OF NEW CINDERELLA IS FOUND

Want Ad the Certain Medium Through Which It Returns to Its Charming Owner

Modern Cinderella has discovered her prince in Madison. She lost her slipper and the prince found it. Cinderella is Miss Violet MacMillan—the prince is a State Journal want ad.

It was one of the littlest, prettiest slippers imaginable for a woman to wear and there is no wonder she lost it. So little is it that it is a wonder the prince found it. A satin pump 12 1-2 child's size is an article not hard to lose from a package in a crowd, especially when one is paying slight attention to the bundle.

And that is what Miss MacMillan, a dainty princess of the footlights who is playing at the Orpheum theatre the first of the week, was doing yesterday—paying slight attention to the bundle of new, especially made slippers she was carrying with her when she went out walking.

She carried the package with her all the time to be sure she would not lose it. She must jealously guard her slippers; they are so small and difficult to obtain, because they are specially ordered and manufactured. But in the excitement of the day Cinderella became careless. And the drama of her good fortune began when she discovered the grievous fact that she had lost a slipper.

Miss MacMillan wore the slippers to the theatre. They were so pretty when she put them on that she could not resist the temptation of wearing them right away. So she carried her old ones. But when she got to the theatre she did not want to risk the beauty of the new treasures by stretching them. She changed to the old ones again and wrapped the new ones in the bundle and placing it under her arm, proceeded to go shopping.

Not until Cinderella reached the New Park Hotel did she notice that the string had become untied and one of her precious slippers had been lost. She and her friends retraced their steps but no avail.

The "princess upon this discovery took the first opportunity to set the most up-to-date agency at work in her behalf. The Wisconsin State Journal want ad columns were resorted to and lo, and behold! the want ad brought immediate response and it was not long before Miss MacMillan was again in possession of the pretty little satin pump. The Wisconsin State Journal want ad was the modern "prince to the modern "Cinderella."

CARUSO CHARGED WITH EMPLOYING FERRET TO HUNT

Italians Arrested On Middleton Road By Two Deputy Game Wardens

DENIED HAVING ANIMAL IN POSSESSION

Officials Say He Appeared At Wrong Moment And Incriminated Masters

Caruso was arraigned in the municipal court this morning charged with hunting rabbits with a ferrit. It was not Enrico, the opera singer, but Nicko, who is a resident of the Italian quarter, and he was not alone, for Frank Mazo, Stifi Dimaggio, Jack Napola and Joe Quinn were arrested with him for the same offense by Deputy Game Wardens Andrew Sampson and M. L. Berschens, who caught them halfway between Madison and Middleton Saturday.

The men denied having a ferret but, according to the wardens, the animal came out of a hole just then, contradicting their statements. The prisoners have entered pleas of not guilty and their case has been adjourned until next week.

FIVE MAY BE DEAD IN FIRE

THREE KNOWN TO DIE IN BLAZE IN NEWARK, OHIO, HOTEL EARLY TODAY

NEWARK, O., Jan. 6.—Three men are known to have perished and two others are believed to be dead in the fire which early today destroyed the Kearns hotel here. Three mn were badly hurt jumping from the upper windows of the hotel.

KINDLY YOUNG MAN TAKES AWAY POSSESSIONS

LA CROSSE, Wis., Jan. 6.—C. J. Helrud, Rushford, Minn., came to La Crosse and met a kindly stranger, who helped him carry his grips and offered to lend him his room. They went to find the room an dthe kind goung man knocked Helrud down and took his watch, ring, overcoat and suit. Helrud told the police.

WHO CAN WEAR IT—THE SLIPPER OF THE MODERN CINDERELLA?

Scores of Madison women today called at the Schumacher store and tried on the dainty slipper worn by Miss Violet MacMillan, who appears in the feature act at the Orpheum theater.

Not one foot was small enough to fit in the tiny bit of footwear.

When Miss Mac Millan called at the Schumacher store this morning she was greeted by several Madison women who wanted proof that even the Modern Cinderella could wear such a small slipper.

The demonstration was given, and Miss Mac Millan was able to fit on the slipper without the use of a shoe horn—it was a decidedly easy fit.

Madison women this afternoon continued to flock to the Schumacher store, bubt up to a late hour no one was abibe to wear the slipper of the Modern Cinderella.

CHARGE GOVERNMENT RANGER IN RIOTS

WASHINGTON, Jan. 6.—Charges that Henry Ratcliffe, superintendent of the United States forest reserve in Routt county, Colo., led a mob that on Jan. 2 interfered with court proceedings and deported leaders of the striking miners from Colorado were received by Representative Keating of Colorado in a telegram from Colorado union officials today. He referred them to Chief Forester Graves, who ordered an investigation.

ADVERTISING RATES

On account of the increased cost of publishing the Union the lowest advertising rate will hereafter be 20 cents per inch instead of 18 cents as heretofore. Eighteen cents per inch for a paper like the Union does not cover the cost of production as has been recently demonstrated by a rigid cost system investigation. The fact that surrounding newspapers are furnishing space at less rates than cost will have no influence on the Union. All we can say is that we will be pleased to see them finally wake up to a realization of what they are doing. Some of them are aware of the impossible situation into which they are drifting, but are too proud to acknowledge that they have made a mistake heretofore in estimating the cost of doing business. "Pride goeth before a fall—Jefferson, Wis. County Union

SIX LABOR MEN TO BE RETRIED IN DYNAMITE CASES

Federal Circuit Court of Appeals Grants Leaders New Trial

APPEALS OF TWENTY-FOUR ARE DENIED

Held That Evidence In Small Number of Case Insufficient

CHICAGO, Jan. 6.—The United States circuit court of appeals today granted the appeals of six of the men convicted in the Indianapolis dynamite trial for a new trial and denied new trials to twenty-four other appellants.

The convicted men granted new trials were: Olaf A. Tveitmeo, San Francisco; James E. Ray, Peoria, Ill.; Richard H. Houlihan, Chicago; William J. McCain, Kansas City; Fred Sherman, Indianapolis; William Bernhardt, Cincinnati.

In reversing the convictions of the six defendants, the court held that the evidence in their cases was insufficient, and remanded their cases to the district court for new trial. In the meantime, they will remain at liberty.

BOARD OF COMMERCE SCHEDULE IN EFFECT

The first days since the adoption of the new schedule by the Board of Commerce according to which there are representatives of the various committees in the office of the board to meet with people have been a decided success. Messrs. Burgess, Boissard, Swansen, Lighty and Teckemeyer of the committees of industry, conventions and publicity, legislation, educational and transportation were on hand during their scheduled hours and received visitors.

ARRANGE KERMIT'S MARRIAGE SOON

NEW YORK, Jan. 6.—Arrangements for th emarriage of Miss Belle Willard, daughter of Joseph E. Willard, ambassador at Madrid, to Kermit Roosevelt, son of Colonel Roosevelt, will be made immediately after Kermit's return to New York. Kermit is now touring South America with his father.

"Naturally, the bride's family will set the date and make the arrangements," said Archibald Roosevelt, Kermit's brother, today. "All I know is that the wedding will probably take place soon after Kermit returns."

HOLDS COMBINE OF PHYSICIANS TO BE ILLEGAL

Attorney General Owen Threatens to Prosecute Men Who Conspire Against Eugenic Law

INDIVIDUALS SAFE

Single Doctor Cannot be Prosecuted For Refusing to Make Required Examination

That Madison physicians and many others all over the state, who are trying to sit down on the new eugenics law, stand in danger of prosecution for conspiracy, was the announcement of Attorney General Owen Tuesday morning.

"Whenever two or more physicians," said Attorney General Owen "make a formal or informal agreement refusing to make examinations as specified by the new law they are treading on extremely hazardous ground."

The attorney general and his department are keeping a close lookout for such agreements among doctors throughout the state. If the movement grows to any extent and begins to take the for mof a united opposition to the law, action against such conspiracies may be expected. Individuals are, of course, safe. It is within their province to refuse to make examinations.

Throughout the state there have been indications lately of physicians organizing and refusing to comply with the law.

SOLDIERS TO REACH OAK CREEK TROUBLES

DENVER, Colo., Jan. 6.—A company of state militia from Trinidad passed through Denver early today enroute to Routt county, northern Colorado, where bloodshed has been threatened as the result of deportation of coal strike leaders by the Taxpayers' league. The soldiers will reach Oak Creek, scene of the strike, tonight or tomorrow. Routt county was quiet today.

UNSUBSTANTIAL, SAYS UNTERMEYER OF MORGAN

CHICAGO, Jan. 6.—Characterizing the recent retirement of J. P. Morgan and his associates from several directorates as "unsubstantial," Samuel Untermyer, counsel for the Pujo "money trust" committee, today declared for a national board to curb big corporations, in an address at a luncheon of the Illinois Manufacturers' association.

DENY STORY THAT CARDON WILL LEAVE

LONDON, Jan. 6.—The British foreign office today authorized a flat denial of fake stories published in the United States that Sir Lionel Carden is to be removed as minister at Mexico City and transferred to Rio de Janeiro.

JOHNNY COULON TO BATTLE ON JAN. 1

MILWAUKEE, Wis., Jan. 6.—George Chip, the Newcastle, Pa., miner who is laying claim to the middleweight championship, following his defeat on two occasiins of Frank Klaus, on Sunday was signed for a ten round go with Gus Christie of Milwaukee before the South Side A. C. here.

GEORGE CHIP WILL FIGHT IN MILWAUKEE

RACINE, Wis., Jan. 6.—Whether Johnny Coulon, who has been out of the game practically ever since the death of his father two years ago, can come back as a champion before the Belle City A. C. here Jan. 21, when he meets Young Sinnett of Rock Island, Ill., claimant to the bantamweight title.

THE WEATHER

FOR MADISON—Mostly cloudy tonight and Wednesday; not much change in temperature; brisk southwest to west winds.

TEMPERATURE

Yesterday—Noon, 20; 3 p. m., 22; 6 p. m., 21; 9 p. m., 18.

Today—Midnight, 20; 3 a. m., 22; 6 a. m. 24; 9 a. m., 25.

Maximum during 24 hours ending 9 a. m., 25; minimum during 24 hours, ending 9 a. m., 18; mean, 22; normal, 17.

RELATIVE HUMIDITY

7 p. m., 84; 7 a. m., 87.

PRECIPITATION

During 24 hours 7 a. m., none; normal, .50; accumulated departure since January 1, —28.

TODAY IN OTHER YEARS

Warmest in 1880, 58; coldest in 1834, —20; wettest in 1885, 1.30.

ODDITIES IN THE NEWS OF A DAY

BROKE MOTHER'S RIB

HAMMOND, Ind—Mrs. George Gannon's son squeezed her so hard he broke a rib.

STAMP FOR JURY WAIVERS

CHICAGO—William Wilhelms, 50, frequent defendant in police court, bought a rubber stamp bearing his signature to save him the trouble of signing jury waivers.

CHIMES WAKE NEIGHBORS

TENAFLY, N. J.—Because fifteen minute chimes in a memorial tower to her dead husband kept her neighbors awake, Mrs. Julia G. Lyle was enjoined by Vice Chancellor Lewis.

TRAILED BY GUM DROPS

HUNTINGTON, L. I.—Trailed by gum drops which stuck to a sleuth's feet, Harry English, 17, was arrested and confessed robbing a candy store.

SPOILED IT ALL

CALDWELL, N. J.—Seeking home and fireside and wife, James Baldwin advertised. "Must be educated and know music and have income," it read. But it was spoiled when he added, "Will watch other party."

SHOOT WHEN REFUSED

NEW YORK—Refused a drink, west side gunmen, six of them, shot and killed John Murphy, bartender, with one volley. All but two escaped.

TANGO TOO MODEST

LONDON—"So modest that it bores me to tears," was the verdict of one woman participating in a straw vote at a theater, which resulted 731 for the tango to 21 against.

SUFFRAGE FIGHT COSTS $2,500,000

LONDON—The publication that "arsonettes" did $2,500,000 damage in England in 1913 has alarmed the insurance companies, who contemplate raising the rates on suffragette risks.

NO MONEY LEFT

BERLIN—The committee soliciting funds for the next Olympic games was shocked to learn that military officers had exhausted the field raising money for the riding contests.

HAD LONG MEMORY

WASHINGTON, Pa.—Playing a fiddle he had not touched "nigh on to 30 year," Henry Fields, 96, took first honors at his birthday "fiddlin' bee." Six octogenarians fiddled for second place.

DIES ON STEAMER GOING TO NORWAY

R. M. LAMP RECEIVES WORD OF DEATH OF ANDREW J. EVERSON OF DEERFIELD

According to a dispatch received from the White Star line office at Southampton, Andrew Everson of Deerfield, en route to Bergen, Norway, died on board the Wilson line steamer crossing the North sea. The cause of the young man's death is unknown. His body has been landed at Christiana to await disposition.

Mr. Everson purchased a ticket from Madison to Bergen from R. M. Lamp, 126 South Pinckney street, Madison, and sailed from New York on the White Star line Olympic, early in December. It is understood that he has relatives in Deerfield and the surrounding farming districts.

EVER HANDLED $750 IN GOLD? START DOING IT!

This picture game is funny, but the money is serious gold coin

There is only one picture game —and The State Journal is about to start it. The $750 cash picture game does not in any way resemble the old style endurance tests in canvassing. It is a game —purely and only a recreation, to be played during your leisure hours at home.

It's the fairest and easiest sort of a picture solving entertainment. Each picture will represent the title of one book only. The pictures will not represent characters in books, or plots. They will simply represent book titles.

And to those who come closest to naming the 77 book titles that the 77 pictures were drawn to represent The State Journal will award 102 prizes, beginning with $300 in cash, $150 in cash and grading slowly down to smaller cash awards.

No book or literary knowledge will be required. It will be useless in this game, which will be won by those having plain, average shrewdness—and using it. For The State Journal will issue, upon the appearance of picture No. 3, a catalogue of book titles, arranged in alphabetical order.

This is the official list of titles from which the 77 titles to be represented by the 77 pictures were selected. Therefore the catalog contains each of the correct titles. All you will have to do will be to pick the correct titles from the catalog!

And picture No. 1 will appear next Monday. Watch for it, clip it out, save it and solve it. Then clip out picture No. 2 Tuesday. When you have secured all 77 pictures you will be notified when to send them in.

ALL EMPLOYES OF FORD COMPANY GET $5 PER DAY

Great Profit Sharing Plan Creates Sensation in Economic Circles and is Praised

CROWD AT GATES

Ten Thousand Unemployed Men Would Come Under Scheme And Secure Big Help

DETROIT, Mich., Jan. 6.—Ten thousand ragged and determined men, some ragged and unkempt, others seemingly prosperous, this morning fought for places in the line that stretched out from the employment window at the Ford Motor company in Highland Park —a line that continued for many blocks from the company's factory.

Each man sought to become one of the army of 22,000 workers who will benefit under the $10,000,000 profit-sharing plan, made public yesterday by Herny Ford, head of the big concern. The formation of the line had started at 3 o'clock this morning, when a small group of the city's unemployed took up their position before the big factory gates to await their opening at 7 o'clock. An hour later several hundred were waiting in the bitter cold. At 6 o'clock the crowd had become a shoving, jostling, mirthless mob of men, each with a sole aim to reach the employment window before all of the 4,000 jobs created by the Ford company's shift from a nine to eight-hour day, were portioned out. A squad of half a hundred police mantained a semblance of order.

Reduce Working Hours

"There," said Ford this morning, pointing to the struggling mob, "is probably the chief reason we have adopted this plan. We wanted to give employment to more men, so we reduced the working day from nine hours in two shifts to eigth hours in three shifts."

Each man of those who struggled before the factory gates this morning, who is hired by the Ford company, will be emplyoed at a wage of not less than $5 per day, whether he be floor sweeper, janitor or mechanic's helper. Until the details of the profit-sharing scheme were announced, the minimum wage had been $2.34. Henceforth, beginning with next Monday's payday—the first in 1914—no man in the employ of the Ford company who is over 22 years of age will receive less than $5 a day. This means 90 per cent of the 22,000 employees.

Justice at Home

James Couzens, secretary-treasurer of the company, who, with Ford, devised the details of the plan, today made public the motives that caused the seven Ford company stockholders to vote to permit their employes to share in approximately one-half of the concern's yearly profits.

"We believe that social justice begins at home," Couzens said. "We want those who have helped us to produce this great institution and are helping to maintain it to share our prosperity. We want them to have present profits and future prospects. Thrift, good service and sobriety will be encouraged and recognized.

"It is our hope to do still better by our employes in the future. We want them to be in reality partners in our enterprise. We do not agree with those employers who declare that 'the movement toward the bettering of society must be universal.' We think that our concern can make a start and create an example for other employers. That is our chief object."

Couzens announced that the public would not be expected to pay for the increased wages of the Ford employes, an that there would be no increased wages of the Ford employes, and that there would be no increase in the price of the Ford product.

Make Men Contented

Henry Ford today refused to aid to his simple statement of last night, when, in explaining his motive for creating the profit-sharing plan, he said:

"We believe in making 20,000 men prosperous and contented, rather than follow the plan of making a few slave drivers in our establishment multimillionaires."

Carnegie in Praise

NEW YORK, Jan. 6.—Reiterating his famous declaration that he would consider it a disgrace to die without distributing his millions, Andrew Carnegie, in an interview with the United Press this afternoon, asserted that the Ford profit-sharing plan forecasts a new era of more equal ristribution of wealth.

Social Advance—Redfield

WASHINGTON, Jan. 6.—A "social advance" and "a recognition of the man in industry," were Secretary of Commerce Redfield's character of the Ford Motor company's plan to distribute a $10,000,000 melon to employes.

License Committee

The license committee of the city council will hold a meeting Tuesday evening.

The Wisconsin State Journal

CITY EDITION

VOL. 123 NO. 76. MADISON, WIS., MONDAY AFTERNOON, JUNE 29, 1914 PRICE TWO CENTS

Archduke Francis Ferdinand and Wife Slain

INDUSTRIAL COMMISSION PLANS FOR END OF LONG STRIKE

Board of Arbitration Suggested as Means to Settle Carpenters' Trouble

MAY RESUME WORK

Attempted Mediation by Other Committees Unsatisfactory—Both Parties Agree to Consider Proposition

With a view to compromising the differences existing between the contractors and carpenters the state industrial commission, after conferences with both factions at which no agreement was reached, recommends the following plan of settling the trouble which now exists and for the adjustment of future controversies:

First—That all the matters under dispute shall be left to a Board of Arbitration, to be composed of five representatives elected by the carpenter contractors of Madison and five representatives selected by Local 314 Carpenters' Union.

Second—That the decision of this board shall be final, but in case the board cannot reach a decision on any point, they shall agree upon an umpire, and his decision shall be final.

Third—That both the contractors and the union agree that they accept as binding any decision that is arrived at by the board or the umpire.

Fourth—That pending this arbitration the men shall go back to work under the agreements existing heretofore, and any decision that is reached by the board or umpire in regard to wages, shall date from the time that work was resumed.

Fifth—That the decision of this Board of Arbitration shall contain a provision for making a permanent arbitration board, to which all matters under dispute between the carpenter contractors and the Carpenters' Union shall be referred before any strike takes place.

The Industrial Commission respectfully submits this proposition to the contractors and to the union, and urges each side to accept it and notify the commission by Wednesday morning.

Respectfully submitted,
Industrial Commission:
C. H. Crownhart,
J. D. Beck,
F. M. Wilcox,
Commissioners.

President Kenison of the local union announced today that the plan of the industrial commission would be given full consideration by the union. The contractors will meet Tuesday night to discuss the proposition.

The attitude of either side towards the proposed schedule of arbitration is not known. Attempted mediation by other committees and municipal bodies have so far failed.

GILBERTSON FUNERAL HELD THIS AFTERNOON

The funeral of Endre Gilbertson, whose death occurred in a Waukesha sanatorium last Friday, took place this afternoon. Services were held at the Powers parlors at 1:30 and from the Bethel Lutheran church at 2:00. The remains were taken to Stoughton at 3:55. A large number of the friends of the dead man went to Stoughton to attend the services, which were held in that city.

THE WEATHER

FOR MADISON—Fair tonight and Tuesday; slowly rising temperature; light to moderate winds becoming variable Tuesday.

FOR WISCONSIN—Fair tonight and Tuesday; slowly rising temperature.

TEMPERATURE

Yesterday—Noon 55; 3 p. m. 57; 6 p. m. 59; 9 p. m. 57.

Today—Midnight 56; 3 a. m. 54; 6 a. m. 53; 9 a. m. 59.

Maximum during 24 hours ending 9 a. m. 60 at 4 p. m. Minimum during 24 hours ending 9 a. m. 53 at 5 a. m. Mean 56; Normal 70.

RELATIVE HUMIDITY

7 p. m. 72; 7 a. m. 66.

PRECIPITATION

During 24 hours ending 7 a. m. 0. Normal .15. Accumulated departure since January 1 —1.17.

TODAY IN OTHER YEARS

Warmest in 1870-94; coldest in 1895-50; wettest I 1906-90.

RIOTING FOLLOWS DEATH OF ROYAL PAIR AT SERAJEVO

Slaughter of Serbs Feared When Bodies of Archduke And Wife Are Moved TO LIE TOGETHER

City Put Under Martial Law When Stores And Homes Are Broken Into Late Today

SERAJEVO, Bosnia, June 29.—Serious rioting by furious mobs occurred on the streets here this afternoon. Scores of Servian business places and dwellings were demolished by pro-Austrian mobs, while preparations were being made to remove the bodies of the assassinated Archduke Franz Ferdinand and his consort to Vienna tonight. Police and soldiers charged the rioters ineffectually in several quarters of teh city. It is reported that several Servians were killed.

Late this afternoon the fury of the mobs was increasing, and it was believed that when the bodies of the Servian assassin's victims are removed to mthe army hospital there is grave danger of a great slaughter of the Servs by the infuriates Austrians.

Officials today declared that after Ferdinand received Gavrio Prinzip's bullets through the neck as he lay in the arms of his wounded wife, his last wards today: "Sophie, you must live for the sake of our children." Then he immediately expired.

The bodies of the dead prince and his wife were embalmed today by Dr. Dynes, commander of the army hospital, assisted by Chief Surgeon Arenstein. It was because of the serious character of the anti-Serb demnostrations here today that the emperor decided to have the bodies leave for Vienna tonight. They will go on a special train to Mekovitsche, where they will be placed aboard an Austrian battleship and will be escorted by a squadron of warships to Trieste. The bodies will arrive at Vienna on Thursday.

While no arrangements have yet been made here for the royal funeral, it was stated unofficially that the ceremony would probably be held July 10. As yet the emperor and all his people are stunned by the shock of the tragedy.

It was announced today that the body of Franz Ferdinand will not lie in the imperial crypt in the Capuchin church in Vienna, but that the archduke and the countess of Hohenberg will be interred side by side in the private crypt of the picturesueq castle of Amstetten, which overlooks the Danube.

Martial law was proclaimed in the city late today and Austrian troops took possession of all strategic points after warning with drum and trumpet was sounded through the streets. This action was taken after the behavior of the mobs became particularly threatening. Reports were current that their activities were started by the explosion of a bomb by a Servian on a corner near the city's center. Two persons were said to have been injured by the explosion and a score of Serbs were badly battered by the furious mobs. Then its leaders formed into a long procession, with the portrait of Emperor Franz Joseph in the lead. Serb residences and stores along the line of march were broken into, looted and demolished, until a strong force of soldiers dispersed the rioters.

U. S. INCOME TAX LAW UPHELD

DETROIT FEDERAL COURT RENDERS DECISION—FIFTEEN LIKE CASES PENDING

DETROIT, Mich., June 29.—Constitutionality of the new federal income tax law was upheld today in a decision rendered by Judge Arthur J. Tuttle in the United States district court here. This is the first court ruling on the law. The validity of the act was questioned by John F. and Horace E. Dodge, Detroit manufacturers. Appeal will be made to the United States supreme court.

Fifteen other suits of identical nature are now pending in the United States.

Dodge brothers recently attempted to bring their case before th District of Columbia suprme court, but it was thrown out of court for lack of jurisdiction.

TRANSFER 1,016 PASSENGERS OFF STRANDED OCEAN LINER ON SUNDAY

Anchor Liner California Goes Ashore on North of Ireland in Fog

WIRELESS RESCUES

Three Hundred of Lists are Landed at London; Others Go to Glasgow

LONDONDERRY, Ireland, June 29—Hard and fast on the rocks of Tory island, off the coast of County Donegal, the Anchor liner California still hung today, surrounded by fog, while her 1,016 passengers, taken off by by British warships without loss of life, were landed here or are on their way to Glasgow aboard the Donaldson liner Cassandra. Three hundred of the passengers were landed here.

Wireless from the California this afternoon said that, while the forward part of the vessel was stove in by the crash, it is expected she will be floated within a few hours. Captain Coverly and his crew were still on board and several British torpedo boats which came to the rescue with the first "S O S" were still standing by.

The California left New York June 20 for Moville and Glasgow. If the vessel is gotten off the rocks, she will probably be taken to Glasgow for repairs.

The California was carried off her course by a dense fog early in the day. Her captain did not hear the fog horn signal of the Tory island lighthouse and his vessel was smashed on the rocky promintory of that island. There was absolutely no panic among the passengers.

The California's bows were badly stove in from the grounding, and two forward compartments were flooded. The vessel is in a dangerous position, but the sea is smoothed and it is believed she can be towed safely into port.

The California was bound from New York to Glasgow, via Moville. She is 470 feet long and her tonnage is over 8,000.

Three hundred passengers en route to Ireland were landed at Londonderry. The other passengers are proceeding on board the Cassandra to Glasgow.

MUNICIPAL STOCK CO. FOR LIGHTING DEERFIELD FAILS AT FIRST MEETING

The proposed formation, of a municipal stock company for the electric lighting of Deerfield has fallen through. At a recent meeting of the signers for stock in the company a vote showed that the majority were not in favor of standing by their signatures making the stock company impossible.

A movement to hold a special election for the purpose of bonding the village to provide lights is receiving favorable attention, however, and Deerfield stands a good chance of being electrically lighted in the near future.

LATEST

BULLETIN

ST. PAUL, Minn., June 29.—The coffer dam, partially completed and forming a portion of the big government dam across the Mississippi river here, broke at 2:35 this afternoon and twenty-foot wall of water is coursing down the river, sweeping everything before it.

Water Board Meets Friday

The board of water commissioners will hold the regular monthly meeting Friday night at the city hall.

AUSTRIAN CROWN PRINCE SLAIN AT WIFE'S SIDE

ARCHDUKE CHARLES FRANCIS FERDINAND, now heir to Austrian throne, and wife, Zita.

ARCHDUKE DIED IN ARMS OF MORTALLY WOUNDED WIFE HE BRAVED EVERYTHING TO MARRY

Was Warned By Her Not To Expose Self To Assassins—She Dies In Prayer

WAS MORGANATIC BRIDE

VIENNA, June 29.—Archduke Franz Ferdinand died, as he would probably have preferred to have died, in the arms of his beloved wife—the wife whom he married in the face of the most strenuous opposition.

The duchess pleaded with her husband after the bomb throwing not to expose himself again. He would not hear her warnings, and insisted on making his visit to the hospital to inquire concerning those whom the assassins' bomb had injured. His wife, not the less courageous, insisted that she go with him.

The assisin lay in wait at a spot where he knew the carriage would have to slow up because of a curve in the road. The presence of the duchess in the carriage made him hesitate momentarily. Then he fired. His bullet struck the duchess. Immediately his second shot lodged in the archduke's throat, severing the juglar vein. Herself almost unconscious, the duchess by superhuman endeavor raised the bleeding body of her royal husband in her arms. Her blood ran with his as she wept and pleaded for his life not to pass out with the bloody stream. He died as she held him. As his body stiffened, the mortally wounded wife fell on her knees, praying, and herself died in this position. The automobile, meanwhile, had been speeding to a physician. The royal couple were dead a few moments after the shots.

The duchess' devotion to her husband has always been marked in Vienna. Born Sophie, countess of Chotek, of an ancient family, the archduke married her despite the fact that he had to swear that he would never attempt to place her on the throne with him, and that his children by her would forfeit their right to the throne. Emperor Francis Joseph agreed to this morganatic marriage.

The hide-bound conventions of the Vienna court were never better illustrated today in publication in official organs of the details of the assassination here. The Vienna Gazette, official government paper, describing the death of the archduke in detail in its official section, with no mention of his consort. In another section, unofficially, the death of the wife was described.

ASK DEATH PENALTY FOR ANTHONY PETRAS

GENEVA, Ill., June 29.—Death for Anthony Petras, for the murder of Theresa Hollander, was the demand of State's Attorney Tyers, when he made his opening address today. Petras showed deep emotion and his young wife wept when she heard his life demanded.

STEVENS HEARS MANY MOTIONS THIS MORNING

An hour before the case of Conklin & Sons against the Gisholt Machine company was resumed in circuit court this morning, various motions were argued before Judge Stevens. The former case will probably last several days yet.

The Wisconsin State Journal

STATEMENT OF JUDGES ON RECENT PICTUREGAME

MADISON, WIS., June 24, 1914.

We, the undersigned, judges in the Wisconsin State Journal's Booklovers' Picturegame certify that the checking of the answers has been accurately and correctly done and the awards made strictly in accord with the correct findings of the checkers.

DONALD D. MACLAURIN,
JOSEPH M. BOYD,
CLARA WHITNEY.

HEIR TO AUSTRIAN THRONE SHOT TO DEATH IN STREET AFTER WARDING OFF BOMB

Servian Hatred for Rule of House of Hapsburg Blamed for Dual Tragedy

WIDE PLOT IS SEEN

Feared News Will Mean Death to Franz Joseph and Youth, 26, Will Ascend Dias

VIENNA, June 29—The map of Europe may be altered by two assassins' bullets that yesterday struck down to instant death at Sarajevo, Bosnia, Archduke Francis Ferdinand, heir to the throne of Austria-Hungary, and his morganatic wife, the duchess of Hohenberg. Gravest fears are entertained here that the octogenarian emperor, Franz Joseph, now en route here from his summer palace at Ischl, cannot recover from this latest of a long series of tragedies that have marked his life.

Reports here today said that Sarajevo was practically under martial law, while the government sought the details of the plot which they believe was responsible for the tragedy.

Two students, one of whom threw a bomb at the royal pair, which the archduke deflected from his carriage without injury, and another who later fired the shots which caused their death, are held. They disclaim in any plot, but police are cetrain the long smouldering hatred of the Servian part of th populace was behind the murders. The bomb thrower was a Servian compositor named Gabrinovics, who came to Sarajevo from Trebinje.

The murderer was Gavrio Princip, also a Servian, of Grahovo, a mere boy of 19 years of age, who said he was a student. Supporting the authorities' belief of a widespread plot was the discovery of a third bomb, unexploded, near where the tragedy occurred.

It is assumed that a third assassin stood ready to hurl this at the royal couple had Princip's bullets not found their mark. This bomb came from Belgrade, Servia, according to the police.

Rigid questioning of the two Servians failed to elicit any admission of a plot. Both were cyncally indifferent. The bomb thrower injured nearly a score of people. His missile, hurled at the royal carriage, was deflected by the archduke and exploded near the carriage which followed him, injuring two military aides and a number of townspeople.

It was while the archduke and his wife were en route to the hospital to visit Count von Boos-Waldeck and Colonel Morrizzi, injured by the bomb explosion, that they were assassinated.

Careworn and feeble, the aged Emperor Franz Joseph arrived here at 11 o'clock this morning. The populace massed at the station, gave him respectful greeting in a tremendous demonstration. Ministers Berchtold and Tisza met the monarch and on his arrival at the palace he immediately called a ministerial conference.

Black flags float from all public buildings today and from nearly all the houses. The greatest apprehension is felt that the emperor, weakened by his recent protracted illness, may not survive this latest tragedy in his life.

The heat here is terrific and debilitating in the extreme to the aged ruler.

The political situation created by Archduke Francis Ferdinand's assassination may be acute, especially if the aged emperor cannot withstand the shock of the tragedy. The new heir to the Austrian throne is Archduke Charles Francis Joseph, who is 26 years of age. He is popular with the people of the dual monarchy, but is believed to lack th forcefulness of character of the slain heir apparent.

It was the ambition and forcefulness of the Archduke Francis Ferdinand that caused Servia's hatred of the Hapsburgs, the family to which he melonged. Servia hated Austria-Hungary because that monarchy prevented realization of the Servian dream of a port on the Adriatic, following the division of land acquired in the latest Balkan war. In 1908, Herzegovia and Bosnia were absorbed by Austria, which sought further an dfurther to extend its boundary southward and to acquire more extensive Slav territory. Backed always by Russia, Servia has resented this onward march of the dual monarchy—and always has blamed Archduke Francis Ferdinand, the strong, the ambitious, for Austria's aggressive policy, rather than the aged Emperor Franz Joseph.

Dominant Austria-Hungary has long been hated by Servia, Montenegro and other small principalities who felt slowly but surely Francis Ferdinand was absorbing their territory.

EVENTS IN HOUSE OF HAPSBURG SINCE HEAD TOOK THRONE

Francis Joseph, at age of 18, put on the tottering throne in 1848.

Young emperor forced to make war on his own people during revolution in Hungary, which was put down with great bloodshed.

Italy revolted 1859; Austrian forces slaughtered at Solferino, Magenta and Novera, and emperor forced to flee and his brother, Maximilian, driven out of the country.

Maximilian sent to Mexico as emperor, where after short stormy reign he is executed by Mexican soldiers.

Carlotta, wife of Maximilian, goes insane as result of husband's execution.

Emperor's only son and heir, Crown Prince Rudolph, is murdered, together with his mistress, Baroness Vetsera, during drunken revel in 1889.

Archduke John Salvator, emperor's nephew, renounces his succession to thrown, assumes name of John Orth, sails for America; ship supposed to have been lost, as he was never heard from again.

Emperor's granddaughter elopes from her royal husband and lives with an army officer.

Francis Ferdinand, heir apparent, married beneath him and the humbled emperor had to acquiesce. The children of this match may mount the throne, bringing to an end the dynasty of Hapsburg.

His wife became estranged and lived in mediation or travel.

Empress Elizabeth is assassinated in Switzerland, Sept. 10, 1898.

Several attempts made to assassinate the emperor, who seems to bear a charmed life, as he has always escaped.

Francis Ferdinand, heir apparent, and his wife, the Countess Chotek, are assassinated.

"I'LL WATCH YOUR CAR," "GO AS FAR AS YOU LIKE," SAYS LEW SHANKS—HE DID

CHICAGO, June 29.—Former Mayor S. L. Shank of Indianapolis drove up in front of the Hotel Sherman with his $5,000 automobile.

"Let me watch it for you," asked a stranger as Shank got out.

"Go as far as you like. I can't stop you watching," was the genial reply of the famous potato mayor.

The stranger apparently took advantage of the permission, as the Chicago police are today looking for Shank's auto at Shank's request.

ELGIN BUTTER MARKET

Elgin, Ill., June 29.—Elgin sales today were at 26½c.

How Should "Forward" Face

Should "FORWARD," which is to stand on the capitol dome face State Street which would be facing west and the University?

Should she face Monona Avenue which will be facing the future city Plaza and water gate to the city and the ultimate park extension?

Should it face Wisconsin Avenue? Or should it face one of the eight thoroughfares radiating out from the capitol park?

European cities have been made beautiful because their builders had the vision to see their cities in the future.

Think ahead. How would you face "FORWARD?" Give us your vote by putting an X in the square of your choice.

I vote to have "FORWARD" face,—

☐ MONONA AVENUE.
☐ KING STREET.
☐ EAST WASHINGTON AVENUE.
☐ NORTH HAMILTON STREET.
☐ WISCONSIN AVENUE.
☐ STATE STREET.
☐ WEST WASHINGTON AVE.
☐ SOUTH HAMILTON STREET.

Signed, ...

Address ....

Mail your vote to "FORWARD," State Journal, the votes will be announced daily in the State Journal until the position is settled and the votes as they are received will be forwarded to the Capitol Commission.

E X T R A!

The Wisconsin State Journal

CITY EDITION

VOL. 125 NO. 32 MADISON, WIS., FRIDAY AFTERNOON, MAY 7, 1915. PRICE TWO CENTS

LUSITANIA IS SUNK

EXTRA!

CHINA AND JAPAN AT PEACE NOW

TOKIO, May 7.—Peace between Japan and China was assured today when Group 5 of the Japanese demanuds, most obnoxious to China and other powers, was officially withdrawn.

Group five, of the Japanese demands most obnoxious to China and the Chinese government in February contained seven articles providing for Japanese advisers in Chinese political, financial and military affairs and other comprehensive concessions.

With this important concession on the part of Japan and the reported acceptance by China of Japan's other demands, peace seemed certain. A cessation of Japan's warlike preparations was expected to follow today's official announcement.

The Japanese populace is very quiet today, apparently unconcerned with the momentous matters of state-craft.

NAVY DEPARTMENT NOT SURPRISED

Officials Believe Plan For "Inside Explosion" Has Been Carried Out

WASHINGTON, May 7.—Navy department officials expressed no surprise this afternoon when told of the Lusitania disaster. The suggestion that the explosion was "inside" the ship surprised them still less.

They said they had been discussing the probability of an inside explosion among themselves from the time the ship sailed.

They based their suspicions on the anonymous warnings circulated on the dock at the time of departure. These they said they took seriously.

Had a torpedo attack been planned they said they thought no warning would have been given.

The disaster confirmed them, they said, in their opinion that La Touraine disaster was similar in character.

CAMPBELL CASE NOT YET ENDED

Attorney Who Tried To Break Will Intends To Carry Case Farther

ST. LOUIS, Mo., May 7.—L. Frank Ottofy, chief counsel for the relatives of the late James Campbell, traction magnate, who sued to break Campbell's will disposing of his $16,000,000 estate to his wife and daughter and eventually St. Louis University, will go before the grand jury and seek indictments as a result of the methods of the defense in the trial ended last night, he said, after the verdict. The jurors found Mrs. Louis Ann Campbell Burkham to be the natural born daughter of Campbell. Her parentage was the prime issue and the decision in her favor threw the other counts out.

Mrs. Margaret C. Harrison, Mamie Spergo, James G. Campbell, Archie W. Campbell and Genevieve Baker, of Chicago and Cincinnati were the original plaintiffs, but later Mrs. Rose V. Curtis, a sister of Campbell, became a plaintiff.

GASOLINE EXPLODES; DAMAGE IS SLIGHT

EDGERTON, Wis., May 7.—A gasoline stove in the home of Willard Doty, yesterday afternoon exploded and caused slight damage to the interior of the kitchen. It was caused by overheating. The timely appearance of Mr. Doty probably saved other portions of the residence.

MEMORIAL EXERCISES

Announcement was made this morning by Mayor Kayser that Memorial Day exercises will be held on Monday, May 31, instead of May 30, as that date falls on Sunday.

Details of the program will be announced next week.

Great Ocean Liner Blown Up By German Submarine

EXTRA!

GIANT LINER CARRYING 1400 PASSENGERS LOST OFF COAST OF IRELAND

Think Infernal Machine Inside of Ship May Have Caused Sinking; Fishing Fleet Saves Passengers.

LONDON, May 7.—The steamer Lusitania, filled with passengers, many of whom were Americans, was either torpedoed or blown up by an infernal machine while off Old Head of Kinsale at 2:33 this afternoon. The latest reports received here say that all of the passengers were saved.

Sinking of the Lusitania was the hardest blow of the war to date so far as neutral commerce was concerned.

The reports received here are fragmentary but all agree that the big liner began calling for help by her wireless at 2:33. The first to pick her up was the wireless station at Lands End.

APPEAL URGENT

The appeal was urgent. "We have a big list, rush help" flashed through the air and immediately orders were sent to the nearest points to get every available craft to the scene.

The fishing fleet from Kinsale was early on the scene and immediately began the work of taking on board the passengers from the big liner. It is understood that the Lusitania's own boats were used to care for her passengers. On all of her recent trips these boats have been swung overside and their covers ready for any eventuality and it is possible that to this precaution may be due the salvation of the passengers.

BULLETINS ON EXPLOSION

LONDON, May 7.—Lloyds confirmed the report of the sinking of the Lusitania, but placed the time at 2:15 this afternoon.

BULLETIN

LIVERPOOL, May 7.—At 5:40 this afternoon the local offices of the Cunard line issued a statement confirming the report that the Lusitania had been sunk.

LIVERPOOL, May 7.—At 5:36 this afternoon the authorities declared that they were without any further details of the sinking of the Lusitania. They stated that it was not known how many had been saved.

WASHINGTON, May 7.—President Wilson had just finished lunch when Assistant Secretary Forster told him the Lusitania had been sunk. No comment was vouchsafed.

Official information was lacking.

WASHINGTON, May 7.—A state department despatch from Ambassador Page, London, received at 2:30 P. M., confirmed news of the Lusitania's loss. The message said:

"Lusitania torpedoed off Irish coast this morning. Sank in half hour. No passenger list given."

NEW YORK, May 7.—A cablegram received by the Cunard Line read:

"Liverpool—Following received by Admiralty Galley Head, 4:25 p. m. "'Several boats, apparently full of survivors seen southeast nine miles Greek steamer proceeding to assist.'"

Public Well Posted

The first word reaching London of the plight of the Lusitania, was an unconfirmed rumor received at the general offices or the Cunard Line. It said that the big steamer was in trouble. The line officials made it public and promised to keep the public informed of everything that happened.

There was much excitement. There had been grave doubt that the Germans were in earnest when they threatened to attack the passenger carrying liners. The sinking of the Falaba had been considered the final act of this kind and when it was realized that the biggest passenger liner in the world had fallen to the war, London was aghast.

Crowds Calm

Crowds were attracted to a big building on the Battery with the first whispering of the rumor. They grew in magnitude every moment. But officials of the company remained calm and receipt of word that probably all of the ship's passengers were saved averted such scenes as attended the receipt of the word of the Titanic's destruction.

The prophetic warnings received by passengers when the Lusitania sailed Saturday were recalled. Scores of the more prominent personages were handed telegrams when they boarded the vessel, signed "John Smith," "Henry Jones," "James Doe" and other patently fictitious names warning them to cancel passage. Some mentioned torpedoing as the fate which would befall the Lusitania; others merely hinted at mysterious danger. Mysterious strangers circulated among passengers and their friends on the pier who whispered warnings and predicted dire things would happen on the voyage. Their persistence led to

(Continued on Page 2, column 1)

2 MORE HOME RULE COMPLAINTS ARE THREATENED

District Attorney Sauthoff Serves Notice When Pierce Case Is Called

CONTINUANCE IS ASKED

County Official Announces That He Will Tolerate No More Delays

Two more complaints against members of the Home Rule and Taxpayers' league may be sworn out for violation of the corrupt practices act, according to a statement made yesterday by District Attorney Sauthoff. He threatens this action if another attempt to delay the case of Charles E. Pierce, president of the league is made.

Mr. Sauthoff declared it had been agreed to argue the case and file briefs in municipal court and that regardless of the outcome it should be taken to the supreme court.

The matter has been adjourned several times and had een set for hearing yesterday but was continued to May 14 on request of Attorney T. C. Richmond.

SKYLINE BILL ADVANCED BY UPPER HOUSE

Measure To Compel Madison To Supervise Building of State Street Engrossed

WEEK'S WORK FINISHED

Action On Bill To Repeal State Fair Appropriation Postponed

The Glenn resolution calling upon the city of Madison to properly supervise the erection of buildings on State street was this morning ordered to engrossment in the senate by a vote of 15 to 5.

Senator Glenn, in speaking of his resolution, deplored the manner in which commercialism has pressed closer and closer to the university.

"State street was once a beautiful thoroughfare but can now be said to be a blight upon the city. Commercialism has destroyed the beauty of the most important street in the capitol city."

"The city of Madison has received millions through the location of the university in the capital city, but so far nothing has been done to preserve the connecting link between the capitol and the university."

The only senators voting against the resolution were Ackley Albers, Huber, Potts, and Staudenmayer.

Put Through Two Calendars

The senate disposed of both Friday and Saturday calendars, putting over all measures of importance until next week.

The Bray bill giving the industrial commission power to pass upon the reasonableness of hospital and doctors' bills was ordered to engrossment without discussion.

After discussing the Bradley bill repealing the $255,000 appropriation to the state fair, passed by the last legislature, further action was postponed until next Thursday. The bill is recommended for indefinite postponement by the senate state affairs committee.

The Cunningham bill, providing a site for a hospital for crippled children was sent to engrossment.

The Stevens bill, permitting the granting of saloon licenses to hotels, was reconsidered and referred to the committee on state affairs.

The Monk bill raising the age of consent to 18 years was ordered to engrossment.

Bills Laid Over

Bills laid over until next week were:

Hanson—relating to abolition of election pamphlet; Richards—relating to sale of cigarettes; Tomkins—relating to powers of trust companies; Baxter—relating to Barbers board.

The Hart bill prohibiting fraudulent advertising for men in time of strike was recommended for killing by the judiciary committee.

The Weber bill relating to qualifications for deputy sheriffs was ordered to a third reading after the adoption of an amendment submitted by Senator Bray exempting intrastate as well as interstate railroads from the provisions of the act. The bill requires that deputy sheriffs must be citizens of the United States, and have resided a year in the state.

THE WEATHER

FOR MADISON—Generally fair tonight and Saturday, probably frost in exposed places tonight; westerly winds

TEMPERATURE

Yesterday—Noon, 64; 3 p. m., 57; 6 p. m., 55; 9 p m., 53.

Today—Midnight, 51; 3 a. m., 41; 6 a. m., 40; 9 a. m., 42.

Maximum during 24 hours ending 9 a. m., 65 at 1 p. m. Minimum during 24 hours ending 9 a. m., 40 at 6 a. m. Mean, 52. Normal, 54.

RELATIVE HUMIDITY

1 p. m., 55. 7 p. m., 77. 7 a. m., 78.

PRECIPITATION

During 24 hours ending 7 a. m., .20. Normal, .12. Accumulated departure since January 1, .64.

TODAY IN OTHER YEARS

Warmest in 1880, 86; coldest in 1885, 27; wettest in 1904, 1.19.

DOINGS OF THE DAY

Dr. J. C. Elsom will give an illustrated lecture tonight at 8 o'clock in assembly chamber on "Birds and Trees."

LONDON, May 7.—The determined opposition of the Irish nationalists and the independent Irish nationalists, who joined forces on Thursday to oppose the new liquor taxes of David Lloyd George, forced the government to postpone until next week the second reading of the bill embodying the chancellor's plan.

Madison Industries Make 152 Articles and Employ 4,800 Men

The Wisconsin State Journal

VOL. 129, NO. 2. 78th Year — Full Leased Wire Service of THE UNITED PRESS. — MADISON, WIS., TUESDAY AFTERNOON, APRIL 3, 1917 — Latest Edition — PRICE TWO CENTS

LA FOLLETTE BLOCKS WAR DECREE

TODAY'S VOTE LARGEST IN CITY'S HISTORY

BOTH SIDES CLAIM BIG VOTE IS AID

Indications Are That More Than 9,000 Will Cast Ballots; Women's Vote Is Light

A canvass of the polls at noon today predicates the information that Madison will at this election cast the largest vote in her history. An analysis of the votes cast in each ward up to 12 o'clock noon, one-third of the day, indicates that the total vote will be 9,000 or 9,500.

At noon the vote cast in all wards was 3,354, more by four or five hundred than the number of votes cast a year ago.

In the Sixth ward especially was the vote heavier than formerly. In the Ninth, Fifth, Fourth Seventh and Eighth ballots cast were on the increase over the same period a year ago.

Drys again assert that this heavy vote predicts victory. For the first time the real strength of the dry forces in this city is being registered, they claim. The wets made a similar claim.

The women's vote was light. Up to noon not more than twenty-five over the city had voted for the office of superintendent of schools.

The vote up to noon was:

Ward	Vote	Ward	Vote
First	250	Sixth	
Second	335	1st pct.	210
Third	200	2nd. pct.	210
Fourth	303	3rd. pct.	151
Fifth		Seventh	
1st pct.	305	1st. pct	307
2nd. pct.	241	2nd. pct.	61
		Eighth	307
		Ninth	235
		Tenth	250

In the Fifth ward considerable challenging was done. The booths were crowded continually and affidavits and oaths and sworn statements were the usual order. One student said he went thru more rigmarole than the president did when he took the oath.

Two years ago the vote was 4,310 to 4,066 in favor of the wets.

At 6:10 o'clock today, ten minutes after the polls had opened, three women voted in the Fifth ward. The inspectors were barely awake when Mrs. Ed Oakey, Miss Madeline Oakey and Miss Mabel McMurry registered their preference.

SEE BREAK WITH AUSTRIA POSSIBLE

Notice Served By President Dual Monarchy Must Keep Hands Off

WASHINGTON, April 3.—A break with Austria is by no means avoided, according to the general view here today. Instead, in postponing discussion of the situation President Wilson merely served notice that unless Austria keeps hands off in the war between the United States and Germany she too must come under the ban.

PAGE AND BALFOUR HOLD LENGTHY CONFERENCE TODAY

LONDON, April 3—American Ambassador Page held a lengthy conference with the British Secretary of State for Foreign Affairs, Arthur J. Balfour today.

CLEVELAND AND ST. PAUL BANKS IN RESERVE SYSTEM

WASHINGTON, Apr. 3—The Cleveland Trust company of Cleveland and the People's Bank of St. Paul, were admitted today to the federal reserve system.

PRESIDENT'S MESSAGE
The full text of the message President Wilson delivered to Congress last night will be found on Page 3 of this edition.

THE WEATHER

Unsettled weather with rain Wednesday.

TEMPERATURE

Yesterday—Noon, 38; 3 p. m., 44; 6 p. m., 45; 9 p. m., 37.
Today—Midnight, 38; 3 a. m., 36; 6 a. m., 37; 9 a. m., 42.
Maximum during 24 hours ending 9 a. m., 47 at 4:00 p. m. Minimum during 24 hours ending 9 a. m., 25 at 4 a. m. Mean, 41. Normal, 39.

RELATIVE HUMIDITY

1 p. m., 38. 7 p. m., 45. 7 a. m., 84.

PRECIPITATION

During 24 hours ending 7 a. m., .01. Normal, .06. Accumulated departure since Jan. 1, —1.05.

TODAY IN OTHER YEARS

Warmest 1882, 72; coldest 1856, 8; wettest 1907, .47.
Sun sets at 6:26.

F-L-A-S-H

Look for the FLASH!

The Madison Gas & Electric company thru arrangement with The State Journal, tonight will flash the result of today's election to every home in the city.

The State Journal will have men at every polling booth to get the returns the minute they are compiled. When these are compiled, which should be by 9 o'clock, the word will be passed to the power station of the lighting company and the result will flash over the city this way:

WET—1 Flash.
DRY—2 Flashes.

Watch for them. Keep your lights burning so you can get instantaneous information.

No attempt will be made to flash the results of the aldermen or other contests. Only the wet and dry election result will be given. But detailed information will be given on all angles of the city and state election in an early morning extra to be issued Wednesday morning.

Remember the signal, one flash if the city stays wet and two flashes if it goes dry.

ORDER CO. G. RECRUITED TO FULL SIZE

Captain Smith and 14 Others Start On U. S. Advice To Increase Ranks To 150

Orders from Washington last night advised all company commanders of national guard units to recruit their companies to war strength at once.

Company G needs 150 men. It has 93 men and three officers now.

Captain Smith, on receipt of the telegram, detailed himself, three non-commissioned officers and eleven privates to go on recruiting duty in the city and county today.

Capt. Smith will be in charge of the recruiting party. First Sergeant Clifton Brown, Supply Sergeant Robert Moore and Corporal Mike Lang are the non-commissioned officers. Others who make up the detail are Privates Maurice Carr, Schultz, Russel Agnew, Herbert Ward, Oswald Pressentin, Terassa, Clarence Kroseman, Mike Pankratz, Dempsey, Anderson and Gannon.

Officers will be on duty at the armory from 8 o'clock in the morning until 10 o'clock at night. Recruiters will also be sent out to towns in the county.

Headquarters company, Capt. Myron C. West, commanding, is also shy of full war strength and prospective recruits with a talent for band playing or who can ride horses are requested to communicate with headquarters armory at 307 West Johnson street.

Corporal Holmes and Privates Leo Olson and Mack were added today to the recruiting party.

Prospects of fight couldn't keep Leo Olson out of the ranks of the militia. Olson was a private in Company G on the border but was honorably discharged in San Antonio before the troops came home. He returned to Madison ten days ago and last night re-enlisted in Company G.

Private Glenn Adams, who was also discharged in the south, returned from San Antonio several days ago. Private Carnahan who stayed in the south will not come back here, it is reported. Carnahan is police reporter on the San Antonio Express.

MINNESOTA BOXING BOARD BARS KILBANE AND BROCK

MINNEAPOLIS, Minn., April 3.—Johnny Kilbane, featherweight champion, was today barred from boxing in Minnesota by the state boxing commission. The commission also barred Matt Brock, of Cleveland. Kilbane and Brock, the commission charged, signed for a bout in Cleveland after they had already agreed to stage the fight in Minneapolis.

ARMY OF 3 TO 5 MILLION MEN FOR AMERICA

WASHINGTON, April 3—Three million to five million men will probably be raised for America's armies.

At least one cabinet member wants three million as a minimum army men recommend up to five million.

The process will be to get them in increments—in groups—of 500,000 as rapidly as they can be officered.

Chairman Chamberlain of the senate military committee says the increments can be obtained at an annual expense of $156,000,000 each; the general staff, however, estimated a far higher amount.

The navy may be raised to 150,000 men, as against a present authorized war strength of 87,000.

U. S. SHIP IS TORPEDOED; NO WARNING

Sinking of Armed Freighter Aztec Confirmed: 28 Missing and Believed Dead; 19 Are Rescued

WASHINGTON, April 3.—Official confirmation of the sinking of the American armed freighter Aztec, was received in a cable from Paris this morning.

The Aztec was torpedoed far at sea off the Island of Ushan.

The cable reads:

"Foreign office informs me American steamer Aztec torpedoed 9 p. m. last night (Sunday) far out at sea off the Island of Ushan; that one boat from the steamer has been found with 19 survivors who were landed this afternoon at Brest. Twenty-eight still are missing and altho two patrol vessels are searching for them, the stormy conditions of sea and weather render their rescue doubtful.

"The foreign office is not informed of the names of survivors. Will cable further details as soon as possible."

Hope Wanes For 28

PARIS, April 3.—Twenty-eight of the crew of the armed American liner Aztec were still unaccounted for today and hope was fast being abandoned for their safety. Because the Aztec was torpedoed at night, and when a heavy sea was running, it is not believed any additional lifeboats survived the bad weather. Nineteen of those aboard the vessel, the first armed American merchantman to fall victim to a German submarine, were picked up by a French patrol boat.

Official reports today said the Aztec had no warning of the attack. The torpedo struck the ship squarely amidships inflicting a vital wound and immediately putting the wireless out of commission. Lifeboats were immediately cast off, but one of these was smashed at once. Eleven are believed thus to have perished. Lieut. Fuller Gresham and twelve bluejackets, the gun crew aboard the Aztec, were all saved, according to first reports here.

PITTSBURG RESORT FIRED BY WOMEN

Owners Declare "Nightriders" Responsible for Blaze During Revel of Society Members

PITTSBURG, Pa., April 3.—Owners of the famous roadhouse known as "The Mule's Ear" admitted today that they understood the place was burned down by a score of women "nightriders" who attacked it with torches early Sunday morning while revelry was at its height.

More than a score of members of Pittsburgs exclusive clubs an an equal number of women barely escaped with their lives.

BALTIMORE GUARDS CLASH WITH GERMAN SAILORS

TEUTONS ATTACK WHEN CHALLENGED BY GUARD: SUBDUED BY SOLDIERS

BALTIMORE, Md., April 3.—German sailors from the steamer Smyra were in a clash with men of the Fourth regiment early today, after two of their number were challenged by one of the guardsmen. The Germans immediately attacked the militia man. The guardsman shouted for help. The sailors also called to their comrades. Twelve sailors answered and other soldiers hastened to the pier. No shots were fired, the guardsmen finally subduing the sailors.

Two Germans were arrested.

KANSAS TOWN TO BE UNDER WOMEN'S RULE

VALLEY CENTER, Kas., April 3.—This city was believed today to have established a world precedent when it elected a woman mayor, a city council composed entirely of women and a woman police judge. Miss Avis Francis, young and pretty is the new mayor.

MINNESOTA SENATE VOTES FULL AID FOR PRESIDENT

ST. PAUL, Minn., April 3.—A resolution urging that every Minnesota representative and senator in congress vote to back President Wilson was adopted unanimously in the Minnesota senate today. The senate pledged itself to take necessary action to lay the resources of the state at the disposal of the nation.

COOPER IS RETURNED TO HOUSE FOREIGN COMMITTEE

WASHINGTON, April 3—The republican reassignment in the house returns Representative Cooper, Wisconsin, pronounced pacifist to the foreign committee.

E-X-T-R-A

Extra editions of The State Journal Wednesday morning will carry the news of the election and the war.

Watch for them!

The first extra will be issued early Wednesday morning. Complete information on the result of the wet and dry vote as well as the aldermanic races in Madison will be given, as well as interesting election news from over the entire state and the latest war news.

The next edition will be issued later in the morning and will carry the latest news on congress as well as complete election returns.

Watch for The State Journal extras.

The State Journal will answer telephone calls tonight and give the latest election returns. The State Journal telephone number is 6,000.

GERMANY TO SET NEUTRALS AGAINST U. S.?

Contemplates Protest On War Declaration With Hope of Influencing South America, Is Report

AMSTERDAM, April 3.—Germany is contemplating formal protest to neutral nations, against America's action in declaring war, Berlin advices this afternoon asserted.

By such an appeal, it was said Germany hopes particularly to influence South American nations in her favor.

New Peace Offer

AMSTERDAM, April 3.—The Central Powers are planning a new peace offer, the Berlin Lokal Anzeiger stated this afternoon.

There have been frequent and persistent rumors lately that the Teutonic powers were preparing to make another bid for peace. The nearest official of these reports came from Count Czernin, foreign minister of Austro-Hungary, who recently declared the central powers' desire for peace was still open to acceptance.

MRS. THOS. M. HATCH HEADS UNITED WOMAN'S CLUB

Mrs. Thomas M. Hatch is president of the United Woman's club, which was printed yesterday as the United Woman's clubs and reported as sending telegrams to President Wilson, Senator La Follette and Congressman Nelson. Mrs. Herman Gaertner is the vice-president of this organization while Mrs. Frank X. Scheen is the treasurer.

"The United Woman's club was organized with the idea of interesting the German women of this city in equal suffrage," was Mrs. John Hausmann's statement today.

The club held its first meeting in January and has a membership of 30 or 40 women.

CALLS POPULAR CONTROL ONLY PEACE BACKGROUND

WASHINGTON, April 3.—Universal manhood suffrage in Germany and a cabinet ministry under guidance of the people and not under the "thumb of the emperor" these are the foundations upon which Germany can establish a sound background for her peace offer if one is in contemplation.

This comment was made by one of the highest officials of the government this afternoon after reading a dispatch announcing that the Lokal Anzeiger of Berlin anticipated a new peace move by the central powers.

NAVY BRANCH TO EXPEND GIANT SUM

WASHINGTON, April 3—The navy department will immediately spend the $18,000,000 emergency appropriation for increased navy yard facilities as follows:

At Portsmouth, N. H., facilities for the immediate construction of ten submarines. One slip for the construction of a capital battleship and additional machine shops, $3,000,000.

Philadelphia, two slips and shops about $6,000,000.

Norfolk, one slip and shops, about $5,000,000.

Puget Sound and Mare Island ship ways (number and amount not stated).

Nothing was given out as to a station on the Great Lakes.

Wisconsin Senator, By Insisting On Rules, Delays Declaration

BULLETIN

WASHINGTON, April 3.—At the meeting of the senate steering committee, it was decided to hold a continuous session of the senate from 10 o'clock tomorrow until the "war bill" is acted upon and passed. It is the purpose of the committee to prevent any filibustering or delay to the war resolution, such as was caused today by Senator La Follette.

By CARL D. GROAT
(United Press Staff Correspondent)

WASHINGTON, April 3.—Pacifism, in the person of Senator La Follette today effectively blocked action on the "war resolution" in congress until tomorrow.

Thru a parliamentary maneuver—demanding the regular order—he halted senate action on the resolution. Heated words followed in which Senator Martin, floor leader, pointed out the "tremendous consequences" behind the resolution and La Follette retorted, objecting to being "lectured."

Martin declared the resolution must go thru before anything else and in view of La Follette's demand for the regular order of business, caused an adjournment until tomorrow.

House Delays Action

The house committee, expecting passage of the senate amended war resolution today, had postponed action until tomorrow, expecting to ratify the senate action.

The senate adjourned shortly after one o'clock.

Martin asked La Follette to withdraw his objection.

La Follette said Martin was trying to lecture him and said he had the right under the rules to ask for one day's time.

"I ask for the regular order, Mr. President," he said and sat down, grim determination on his face.

Martin jumped from his seat in a rage.

"I had no idea of delivering a lecture," he said. "I have the right to call attention of the senate and senators to the tremendous consequences of the resolution involved.

"It is quite unnecesary to call my attention to the consequences," La Follette retorted. "I insist on the regular order."

"The resolution of course, goes over under the rules," Martin said with resignation, "but I have the right to comment on the resolution."

"There can be no comment on the resolution," ruled Vice-President Marshall.

Holds Up Other Business

"I don't believe the senate ought to proceed to any other business while this resolution is pending," Martin shouted.

"I move that the senate adjourn until 10 a. m. tomorrow.

Galleries and senate broke into a storm of applause at Martin's words, a rare occurrence in the upper body of congress.

Senator Gallinger, New Hampshire, asked for order in the galleries which continued cheering.

Vice President Marshall threatened to clear the seats and dismiss the doorkeepers if there were any further outbreaks.

Senator McCumber, North Dakota, asked Martin to permit him to send to the clerk's desk, a resolution to be printed in the record.

Martin firmly objected.

"I move that the senate adjourn until 10 o'clock tomorrow," he repeated his lips drawn to a tight line.

Vice President Marshall put the question and with a chorus of ayes, and faint echo of "noes" the senate adjourned.

PLACE GUARD ON BRIDGES IN STATE

National Guard Companies Given Details; Holway Expects Calling of First

Wisconsin is rapidly taking precautions against war dangers. Guards, it was learned today, are being placed at practically every important bridge in the state. Several national guard companies from the Third Wisconsin infantry called out early last week, have already been sent out to patrol bridges, highways, factories, business buildings and shipping. The army censor prohibits the State Journal from stating the points to which the companies have been sent. Company F, Portage, departed for "somewhere in Wisconsin" last night.

Preparations continued today at Adjutant General Holway's office in the work of reorganization of the guard. Holway declared that the First and Second infantry regiments are ready to go out at a very few hours' notice. Holway believes it likely that these two regiments will be called out within the next two weeks.

Recruiting Growing

Recruiting for the guard is growing. According to General Holway, more than fifteen hundred men have been added to the ranks since the guardsmen returned from the border. In addition he declared that many guardsmen have received honorable discharges to enter the regular army and navy. Holway has no means of knowing what increase in recruiting the Third infantry has made. This regiment is now in the hands of the army officers and their activities are hidden under a heavy censorship.

A bill providing for a state council of defense, to act in co-operation with the national council of defense in event of war, will probably be introduced in the legislature this week. The bill has already been drafted and is in the hands of Gov. Philipp. It provides that committees representing labor, banking, farming, machinery, etc., shall be appointed to gather statistics as to Wisconsin's resources.

Would Exempt Farmers

These statistics will be compiled and the committees will also advise as to what industries would be desirable for the manufacturing of certain kinds of war supplies. Senator Wilcox, Eau Claire, was originator of the idea. It will also be proposed to Gov. Philipp shortly to exempt farmers and their sons from national guard duty. Men in favor of this idea declare that it will be just as important to grow the food as it will to have men on the firing line, who have to be fed. In the case of those farmers who are in the regiments already called out, a move is being started here to ask congress for legislation exempting them.

MAISSEMY TAKEN IN BRITISH PATH

Haig Forces Continue Enveloping Move: Threaten Lines To St. Quentin

BY PERRY ARNOLD
(United Press Foreign Editor)

NEW YORK, April 3—British forces thrust their northern enveloping movement around St. Quentin still further forward today. United Press dispatches from the front indicated the taking of Maissemy, five miles northwest of St. Quentin, but only a bare three miles distant from the main road from that city to Cambral.

The British therefore have established themselves where they seriously menace the communications between Cambrai, supposedly the main center of the Hindenburg line, and St. Quentin, as well as LaFere still further south.

The French statement detailed no important activity.

Claim Germans Repulsed

Petrograd's official report detailed violent German assaults on the northeastern front, which Russian troops repulsed, apparently in heavy fighting.

German troops still occupy all of Bigium, except a strip approximately twelves miles wide and forty miles long, they hold a zig zagging line embracing French land from beyond Lille to Lens to Cambrai, St. Quentin, and Laon and a few miles before Rheims along to a sweep around Verdun; then back to around St. Mihiel; up again to beyond Pont-a-Mousson, thence very close to the French border down to near Mt Donon. Below St. Die the line runs on German territory in Alsace.

Two Towns Taken

WITH THE BRITISH ARMIES AFIELD, April 3 The British forward movement around St. Quentin was reported today to have taken the town of Maissemy in its enveloping grip.

Northward around Arras, the town of Henin was occupied in other advances.

WAR STATE RESOLUTION IS FAVORED

Senate Foreign Relations Committee Reports Cut Amended Document With Only Senator Stone Objecting

WASHINGTON, April 3.—The senate foreign relations committee today reported out the administration state of war resolution amended so as to strengthen its entire text, with but one dissenting vote—that of Chairman Stone.

The house foreign affairs committee met informally during the forenoon. Chairman Flood announced that with the appointment of the republican members this afternoon, he would call the full committee and proceed to consideration of the war resolution.

House Meeting Wednesday

After obtaining a full membership, the house foreign committee this afternoon decided not to meet until tomorrow morning. It had been informed that the senate intended to stay in session until it passed its amended war resolution and the house body expected to adopt that.

"We are ready to do business," one member announced.

During the informal morning session the house body merely discussed the situation.

The house met at noon with scarcely more than one hundred members in their seats. Important conferences delayed most of them.

Blind Chaplain Couden in a prayer ringing with patriotism, invoked divine assistance "in the momentous days that are to follow."

The War Resolution

The president is directed to "employ the entire naval and military forces of the United States" against Germany and to "bring the conflict to a successful termination."

"All of the resources of the country," the resolution ends, "are hereby pledged by the congress of the United States."

The resolution as amended reads:

"WHEREAS: The Imperial German government has committed repeated acts of war against the government and the people of the United States of America, therefore be it,

"RESOLVED: By the senate and House of Representatives of the United States of America in congress assembled, that the state of war between the United States and the Imperial German government which has been thrust upon the United States is hereby formally declared; and that the president be, and he is hereby, authorized and directed to employ the entire naval and military forces of the United States and the reserves of the army to carry on the war against the imperial German government and to bring the conflict to a successful termination all the resources of the country are hereby pledged by the congress of the United States."

President Wilson's suggestion for a "pay as you go" war will meet opposition in the house.

This was clearly indicated today when Minority Leader Mann announced his belief that "we must immediately borrow money" and issue bonds.

He pointed out that the nation still is paying its civil war, Spanish-American and Panama canal debts.

Will Debate But Is United

Congress may debate considerably other phases of President Wilson's recommendations. But it will be a congress united on the central theme that war is here and that it must be waged to the last man and to the last dollar in order that democracy shall not perish from the earth.

The matter of extending credit to the allies will probably cause extensive discussion.

As for financial matters, congress will heed the advice of the chief executive, tho it may go thru some brief verbal gymnastics before passing the revenue bills. Moreover, congress will follow the president's lead in the matter of other vital matters.

Will Grant Wilson's Demands

On the whole the spirit of congress is unanimously behind the president. What he asks will be granted.

A canvass of congress today showed that it approved President Wilson's speech last night and his recommendations.

"The best speech he ever made," was the most frequent characterization on both sides of the capitol.

The problem of financing America's part in the world war today was directly before President Wilson and his cabinet.

The department heads await only action by congress on the "war resolution" introduced last night before submitting the first "war budget" calling for hundreds of millions of dollars.

Spy Bill In Senate

Senator Culberson, Texas, chairman of the judiciary committee, today introduced the administration's general spy bill.

A universal compulsory military training bill providing for immediate raising of an army of five hundred thousand men was introduced by Senator Chamberlain, chairman of the military affairs committee, today.

The Wisconsin  State Journal

VOL. 129, NO. 3. 78th Year | Full Leased Wire Service of THE UNITED PRESS. | MADISON, WIS., WEDNESDAY AFTERNOON, APRIL 4, 1917 | Latest Edition | PRICE TWO CENTS

MADISON VOTES OUT SALOONS BY 415

Owen And Marshall In Close Race For Bench

COUNT LATE TODAY IS FOR JUSTICE

Campaign Committee for Incumbent Claims His Election By More Than 20,000 On Fragmentary Returns

The race for justice of the supreme court between Attorney General Walter C. Owen and Justice R. D. Marshall promises to furnish another close finish, with the odds slightly favoring the return of Justice Marshall at 3 o'clock Wednesday afternoon.

Justice Marshall's campaign committee is claiming his re-election by over 20,000. Attorney General Owen says that the returns thus far are not sufficient to indicate what the final outcome will be.

Justice Marshall showed surprising strength in Milwaukee, his lead in that county being 3,686. On the other hand Owen gathered a lead of over 1,000 in Winnebago; an estimated lead of 1,500 in Brown county, with 900 of it coming from Green Bay, its leading city; a lead of over a thousand in Dane county; a majority of over 700 in Racine; a lead of 337 in the city of Beloit; and about 700 in Jackson county.

Justice Marshall carried Superior by about 800, La Crosse county by nearly a thousand, and ran well in his home city of Chippewa Falls.

Supporters of Attorney General Owen contend that the returns from the rural districts, and particularly from the northwestern part of the state will more than make up any apparent lead that Justice Marshall may have. Over half of the counties of the state have thus far not been heard from at all. Indications are that it may take several days before the contest is finally decided.

Telegrams to the State Journal from Milwaukee early this morning brought the following information

Janesville—In 21 out of 27 precincts Marshall leads by 502.

Shanowo—Marshall has 130 majority.

Alma—Twelve out of 26 precincts in Buffalo county give Owen 676, Marshall 462.

Chippewa Folls—Marshall led by 400.

Tomah—Marshall has a slight lead in the county.

Baraboo—Sauk county went for Marshall by 3 to 1.

Ladysmith—Owen 342, Marshall 279.

Whitewater—Marshall 555, Owen 277.

Ripon—Owen 330, Marshall 343.

Depere—Owen 191, Marshall 147.

Darlington—Owen 224, Marshall 171.

Antigo—Marshall is leading in the county, two to one.

Oshkosh—With Neenah and Menasha to hear from, and eight county precincts missing, Winnebago county voted 1,815 for Owen and 1,163 for Marshall.

Oconomowoc—Marshall leads by 69.

La Crosse—Returns from 17 out of 26 precincts give Marshall 2,007, and Owen 1 276.

Beaver Dam—Owen 581, Marshall 602.

Racine—Complete returns for the city give Owen 2,510 and Marshall 1,727.

Green Bay—Incomplete returns from the county give Owen a lead of 1,500.

Merrill—Marshall leads Owen in the county 3 to 2.

WETS REFUSE TO GIVE POSITION

Disclaim Knowledge of Report They Will Contest Election

Wet leaders interviewed today on the report that yesterday's election would be contested, declared they had taken no steps and knew nothing of the rumor. However, the report persistently goes over the city to the effect that the students' vote in the Fifth ward will be the subject of litigation and that in event of an adverse decision a bill to prohibit students from voting would be introduced into the legislature.

"That's the thanks we get for closing on Loyalty day," said a saloonkeeper on the Square today. The saloons closed two hours last Saturday.

THE WEATHER

Rain tonight followed by clearing Thursday.

TEMPERATURE

Yesterday—noon, 49; 3 p. m., 50; 6 p. m., 50; 9 p. m., 47.

Today—midnight, 45; 3 a. m., 42; 6 a. m., 40; 9 a. m., 42.

Maximum during 24 hours ending 9 a. m., 51; at 4 p. m. Minimum during 24 hours ending 9 a. m., 39; at 7 a. m.

Mean, 45; normal, 39.

RELATIVE HUMIDITY

1 p. m., 43; 7 p. m., 54; 7a. m., 67.

PRECIPITATION

During 24 hours ending 7 a. m., 0. Normal, .06. Accumulated departure since January 1, —1.58.

Wet and Dry Results in State

The changes in Wisconsin from wet to dry, dry to wet, and those remaining unchanged with the majorities where obtainable follow:

Wet Towns Go Dry

Abram, 35
Armstrong, 70
Baldwin, 36
Bayfield
Baraboo, 89
Belleville, 5
Belmont, 1
Brandon, 17
Cameron
Clinton, 10
Cobb
Delavan
Doylestown, 1
Elroy, 24
Ellsworth, 49
Fort Atkinson, 25
Galesville
Glenwood
Iron River
Ladysmith, 222
Linden
London, 40
Madison, 415
Markesan, 50
Mellen
Merrillan, 5
Mondovi
Nekoosa, 3
New Lisbon, 25
Osseo
Owen
Pelicam Lake, 1
Park Falls
Pleasant Prairie
Reedsburg, 90
Ridgeway, 11
Rosendale, 8
Schley (Town), 4
Sharon
Somers
Spooner
Spring Valley, 36
Stanley
Suamico, 32
Waupun, 156
Wausaukee, 4
Whitewater, 225
Wonewoc

Wet Towns Stay Wet

Alma Center, 13
Altoona, 9
Almena
Amherst, 15
Ashland
Bangor
Beaver Dam, 300
Beloit, 344
Bloomer
Brill
Burkhardt
Chaseburg
Cashton
Columbus, 22
Chippewa Falls, 339
Cuba City, 40
Crescent, 7
Darlington, 43
Delafield, 207
Eau Claire, 169
Edgerton, 70
Lavelle, 9
Lena, 75
Mineral Point, 4
Monroe, 169
Monroe (Town)
Monico, 13
Muscoda, 17
Newbold, 14
Norwalk
Oconomowoc (Town, 17
Oconomowoc City
Oconto, 339
Onalaska
Palmyra, 63
Pensaukee, 11
Pembine
Portage, 179
Rhinelander, 209
Ripon, 48
Rock
Elkhorn, 31
Fox Lake, 55
Gilett, 5
Genoa
Gordon, 19
Highland, 29
Horicon, 226
Independence
Janesville
Kenosha
Lake Geneva, 164
Waukesha
Washburn
Sarona
Shawano, 191
Spring Green, 15
Spruce, 4
St. Joseph
Stoddard
Three Lakes, 44
Tomah, 87
Underhill, 2
Wabeno, 4
Woodruff
Wheeler

Dry Towns Go Wet

Blanchardville, 53
Browntown, 15
Hudson, 52
Lime Ridge
Menomonie
Muscoda
New Richmond, 49
Platteville, 60
River Falls
Superior, 183
Westfield, 32

Dry Towns Stay Dry

Abbottsford
Almond
Augusta, 7
Argyle, 68
Arlington, 30
Black River Falls
Boscobel
Bruce, 39
Coloma
Darien
Draper, 5
Doylestown, 1
Ellsworth
Elmwood
Fall River, 25
Genesee
Gilmanson
Hancock, 7
Hammond, 20
Hollandale, 8
Hustlee
Janesville (Town), 29
Kendall
Kingston
Lake Mills (Town)
Lake Mills, 23
Lancaster, 240
Withee
Little River, 28
Lone Rock, 23
Lodi, 108
Milton
Mifflin, 100
Merrimac, 30
North Crandon, 9
Ogdensburg, 19
Oconto Falls, 14
Omro, 26
Oregon, 76
Pardeeville, 43
Radison, 30
Randolph, 39
Reedsville, 100
Rice Lake
Shell Lake
Sparta
Stiles, 78
Townsend, 11
Trempeleau
Troy
Turtle Lake
Viroqua
Wauwatosa
Waupaca, 98
Waupaca (Town), 62
Wautoma
Wilson, 64
Winneconne, 15

ELVER WINS IN ALDERMANIC RACE

Quinn Defeats Buergin and Stock, Barry, Gibbs and Prien Win

First Ward—George Gill.**
Second Ward—E. F. Gibbs.*
Third Ward—John C. Prien.*
Fourth Ward—D. C. Sullivan.**
Fifth Ward—Howard Piper.
Sixth Ward—Ruthwin Elver.
Seventh Ward—John Stock, Jr.*
Eighth Ward—Pat Barry.*
Tenth Ward—Frank Lucas.**
Ninth Ward—Thomas Quinn.*
**Uncontested. *Re-elected.

Ruthwin Elver defeated Martin Loftsgordon in the Sixth ward by 400 votes. Howard Piper defeated John Lewis in the Fifth in easy fashion, having a margin of 250 votes. Ald. Thomas Quinn disposed of former Ald. William Buergin by 80 votes in the Eighth. In the Second, E. F. Gibbs was returned over Peter Schmitz by 75 votes, and in the Seventh John Stock, Jr., won over Carl Johnson by 200 votes. John C. Prien walked away from Richard Poore, 326 to 78 in the Third. There were no contests in the First, Fourth or Tenth wards on alderman.

For supervisor, Schmelzer defeated Streber 362 to 296 in the Ninth ward. Louis Haak received more votes, 555, than either of the aldermanic candidates, while his opponent, Mahoney, received a scattering few. John Togstad was returned from the Sixth over George Sauthoff. In the Fifth, Fred Gratz was given a hot race by Hayes, winning out by ten votes.

In the Fifth ward women registered 35 votes for Mrs. Bradford of Kenosha, and in the Tentth ward they gave her 95 votes.

The vote by wards where there were contests for alderman:

SECOND—Gibbs, 425; Schmitz, 347.
THIRD—Prien, 326; Poore, 78.
FIFTH—Piper, 714; Lewis, 472.
SIXTH—Elver, 1,035; Loftsgordon, 614.
SEVENTH—Stock, 542; Johnson, 328.
EIGHTH—Barry, 402; Toellner, 360.
NINTH—Quinn, 378; Buergin, 298.

There were three contests for supervisor. They follow by wards:

FIFTH—Gratz, 598; Hayes, 588.
SIXTH—Sauthoff, 501; Togstad, 559.
NINTH—Schmelzer, 362; Streber, 296.

THIRD OF CO. G ON GUARD DUTY

First Regiment Mobilizing In Sections; Protect Bridge and Plants

The First Regiment is being mobilized in sections. One third of Company G is now doing guard duty and recruiting duty.

Yesterday eighteen members of Company A, Reedsburg, and Baraboo, were called out to guard the bridges at Kilbourn and Merrimac. It is believed that more local troops will be called out in Madison shortly to guard plants and bridges.

A guard detail from the Third regiment has been sent to Camp Douglas and for miles on each side of the camp are guarding the railroad tracks.

WET CITIES CUT BY BIG DRY VOTE

Madison Leads Prohibition Procession With Waupun, Baraboo and Others

Drys have strengthened their hold in Wisconsin as a result of yesterday's wet and dry contests, according to returns received by the STATE JOURNAL up to 3 o'clock this afternoon.

In only eight towns did the wets gain. They were Menominee, Superior, Platteville, River Falls, Hudson, New Richmond, Menomonie and Blanchardville. Superior, the second largest city in the state, went wet by the narrow margin of 180 votes. The drys gained Baraboo, Green Lake, Berlin, Waupun, Rosendale, Omro, Merillan, Elroy, Fort Atkinson Madison, Reedsburg, Brandon Fox Lake Township, Doylestown, Markesan, and London. Merrillan, which has been wet for seventeen years, went dry for the first time by five votes. Waupun, where the state prison is located, went dry by 156 votes.

Drys were especially jubilant today as a result of the vote here which placed Madison, the state capital, in the dry column. Prohibitionists claim this is especially significant, in that it will probably have its effect on the action of the state senate which next week will take up the state wide prohibition referendum bill, which has already been passed by the assembly.

The drys declare they are satisfied with the results thus far and are confident that the final returns will show they have practically swept the state in the "no license" contests.

The following show the result of yesterday's wet aid dry contests:

SAY BULGARIA IS SEEKING PEACE

Separate Negotiations Opened Thru Switzerland Says Swiss Paper

GENEVA, Switzerland, April 4.—The Lausanne Gazette declared this afternoon that negotiations by Bulgaria for a separate peace had been undertaken in Switzerland.

QUIT FIGHT ON THE REFERENDUM

Over the long distance phone last night Assemblyman John F. Donnelly of Milwaukee announced that he would withdraw his motion for reconsideration of his vote by which the Evjue bill passed last week. This means that the bill will go over to the senate without any opposition.

"The purpose for which the motion for reconsideration was offered has been served," declared Assemblyman Donnelly. "As soon as the legislature convened on Thursday I will ask that I be permitted to withdraw the motion. No further fight will be made on the bill in the house.

PACIFISM RUNS HIGH IN SENATE

Long Debate Permitted On War Resolution Which House Foreign Committee Favors for Passage

BULLETIN

WASHINGTON, April 4.—Senator La Follette entered the upper chamber for the first time today shortly before 4 o'clock and began speaking.

WASHINGTON, April 4.—Tho pacifism ran in a discordant undertone in congress today, support of a war to the finish was assured by both the upper and the lower houses.

The house foreign committee voted favorably upon the senate amended war resolution and leaders served notice that the measure would come up tomorrow for passage.

If objection arises it will be forced thru under a rule checking debate. Two pacifists, peace-at-any-price to the last, Cooper and Shackelford, voted against the resolution.

Senators Object to War

On the senate side, Stone and Vardamann, decried the war move, but stirred staid members and the galleries to the depths by declaring themselves ready personally to go to the utmost limit in making war against Germany a success.

Stone, however, will vote against the resolution.

Senator Hitchcock opened the senate debate. His speech and Senator Lodge's aroused an otherwise dignified body to the highest pitches of patriotism. The senate will act and act forcibly. Pacifist speeches may delay proceedings for a time but the congress sentiment as a whole is for war—and war it will be by tomorrow night unless plans go askew.

The house will take up the Martin war resolution at 10 tomorrow morning.

Would Postpone War

A resolution designed to postpone war with Germany and give her a chance to change her present methods was introduced in the senate between speeches by Senator McCumber, North Dakota, as a substitute for the senate foreign committee measure.

McCumber proposed that the United States recognize the right of any belligerent to establish and maintain a blockade by any means, but that any further sinking of American ships without notice or loss of American lives be regarded as an act of war.

"I am pausing long enough on the brink of war to allow Germany to withdraw her illegal submarine warfare," he said. "There can be no great war without violating the rights of neutrals. We ought to exercise a great deal of charitableness to the warring nations in this respect."

McCumber proposed that Americans be warned off ships while negotiations with settlement with Germany. He announced specifically that he did not condone Germany's submarine acts but held that the United States ought to remain neutral in order that it might better serve humanity later.

Norris to Oppose War

Senator Norris, Nebraska, one of the "willful twelve" who blocked passage of the armed neutrality bill, declared that he would oppose the war resolution.

"Urging that there be no faltering, no division, no weakness in the nation," Senator Hitchcock upon opening of the senate today, began his argument for passage of the resolution that will make war with Germany an open actuality.

The senate almost immediately went to work on the administration's state of war resolution when it convened.

Shortly after Senator Jones introduced a federal woman suffrage resolution and Senator Sheppard a federal prohibition measure, Senator Hitchcock, ranking democratic member of the foreign relations committee, moved consideration of the war measure.

Appeal Dramatic

Hitchcock's appeal was the more dramatic as he declared he had always been opposed to war and even in face of that former belief, asked congress to pledge the nation to a war that may last three years and cost much blood sacrifice; a war "that shall have no gethsemane."

"We want no more territory; demand no indemnity; have no historic grudges to settle and no racial antipathies," Hitchcock began.

"We alone of all nations will spend our treasure and lives without hope of material gain.

"While the vote has not been taken, we know the decision—it is war!" he shouted.

Senator Swanson, of Virginia, then began his address.

Senator La Follette, one of the "willful twelve" was not present when the senate began its patriotic program.

"Honor, wisdom and self-interest, demand that, in the language of our secretary of state, we should defend our rights upon the seas from whatever quarter violated without com-

(Turn to Page 7, column 3)

Wet and Dry Vote By Wards

Corrected returns, checked with those on file at the city hall today give the Dry forces a larger majority by four votes than reports early this morning credited. The actual majority is 415 against the saloon, a figure which must stand until the official canvass.

The vote cast for license was 4,145 and against license, 4,560. The corrected table:

	1917		1915	
	WET	DRY	WET	DRY
First	190	308	237	314
Second	405	415	444	335
Third	295	134	299	141
Fourth	393	291	433	271
Fifth—				
1st precinct	182	554	247	609
2nd precinct	158	412	157	422
Sixth—				
1st precinct	323	304	384	233
2nd precinct	388	281	387	219
3rd precinct	245	234	232	173
Seventh—				
1st precinct	403	409	386	406
2nd precinct	62	57		
Eighth	513	303	551	261
Ninth	435	278	387	223
Tenth	153	580	166	459
Total	4,145	4,560,	4,310	4,066

LONG FIGHT OF EDUCATION WINS

State Journal To Continue Campaign for Better Madison

For years The State Journal has been fighting in season and out of season, in campaigns and out of campaigns for a Dry Madison. It has been a long fight of education but at last the fight is won and with the people of Madison the State Journal rejoices in the victory.

When Richard Lloyd Jones, the editor of the State Journal, was asked this morning to comment on the victory he said:

"Every campaign is a spurt, a hurry dash to the goal. As soon as the pistol shot that announces the opening of the campaign is fired, the candidates are 'off,'—the race is on. So with the wet and dry fight,—the liquor forces were 'off' as soon as the Dry campaign managers got on the cinder path and put their toes to the tape. It was a fair race.

"The years of unyielding fight for the dry cause by The State Journal put 5,560 voters in the race. It was more than the wets could muster and that is the whole story. The wets lost and they have lost for good. That is the opinion of the 4,560 voters who carried the dry banner to victory and who are determined that the pennant of the better Madison will never again be surrendered.

To Continue Fight

"The dry forces will continue to carry on their fight; they have just begun. The State Journal will continue to fight for a dry Madison; it will continue to fight the insidious political power of the breweries. The liquor forces will unquestionably attempt to reopen the question at the spring election a year hence, but they will not find that the drys have been asleep at the switch; the drys will battle as persistently for decency in Madison as they have in the past. The State Journal will continue its fight vigorously and uncompromisingly. Every attempt at blind pigging in the city will be brought to the light of the public. Every attempt by the liquor forces to either violate or evade the law will be brought to the attention of the voting public.

"The liquor forces may attempt to play the old, out-worn game of holding saloon property empty as an exhibit of "the idle store" result of a dry town. But this will be so obvious as to result in a boomerang, as does every trick and device which the booze forces attempt to put across to justify their diabolical business.

Credit To 500 Citizens

"Great credit" Mr. Jones declared "must be given to the band of about 500 Madison citizens who composed the Madison Dry League of which Emerson Ela is president, Frank H. West, vice president; L. I. Oeland, secretary; M. H. Hovey, treasurer and A. Ivan Pelfer, campaign manager. This organization and these workers bore the burden of the campaign which was the grand final spurt that put the Dry Pennant over."

The campaign was well organized. The Drys made a detailed canvass of the poll lists in each ward and precinct. They had a complete registration of known dry votes and they got the dry vote out. They did the job in a real businesslike way. They circulated dry literature and put out truth telling and convincing literature and billboard posters.

This detailed work was a large factor in the result. Never before has Madison conducted so thoro a campaign. This time no stone was left unturned. Every dry voter was known and an effort was made to get every dry vote to the polls.

But there were other large elements in the campaign. The planning of the campaign so that public interest could be centered upon the wet and dry issue at the right time, and so that the climax would be reached on election day and not two or three days ahead of the time for voting, was of first importance.

The campaign for a dry Madison really opened with the Bryan speech at the stock pavilion in January. Then came addresses by the Rev. Father A. B. G. Dunn of Eau Claire, Senator Richard Jones of Duluth, Charles M. Sheldon of Topeka, Kan., Capt. Richmond P. Hobson and James Schermerhorn of Detroit. Also there was the business men's dinner in the basement of the capitol, at which addresses were made by B. S. Pearsal, Alexander Metz and S. Peget of Elgin, Henry Johnson of Superior, J. S. Scadden of Crystal Falls, Mich., and F. J. Vea of

MIDDLETON MAY NOT BE "OASIS"

Rumor Current Board Contemplates Refusal To Renew Saloon Licenses

Middleton may not be an oasis in the desert after Madison ousts the saloon June 30 of this year if rumors on the street this morning can be credited.

From one Middleton resident a statement came that that village, not desirous of catering to the rough element of Madison which may seek refreshing refuge in the bars of that village, had served notice on bars in that vicinity, particularly Frank Hoover's and Metz's at Pheasant Branch that no licenses would be issued to them if Madison went dry.

Several Middleton officials were called on the phone today to verify the statement but they were ignorant of such action, they said.

If it isn't true the rumor is at least valuable for the suggestion it carries and Middleton, having some regard for the morale of its patrons, may do officially what the residents have't done with the referendum.

RESERVE BANKS TO FINANCE WAR

Monthly Statement Says Con-Congress Will Be Asked for Special Legislation

WASHINGTON, April 4.—That the United States will be largely if not altogether financed in war with Germany thru the federal reserve banks was indicated today by the monthly statement which declared that in order to meet financial and banking problems growing out of the present crisis; congress will be immediately asked to pass legislation granting the federal reserve board additional rights.

J. P. MORGAN NOMINATED FOR STEEL DIRECTORSHIP

NEW YORK, April 4.—J. P. Morgan, H. P. Davison, Charless Steele and William H. Porter were nominated for directorships in the Bethelehem Steel corporation at the annual meeting today.

Directors Harry Bronner, C. A. Buck, Alan A. Ryan and Charles M. Schwab were renominated.

PACIFIST MEETING IN GUTHRIE ENDS IN PATRIOTIC SHOW

GUTHRIE, Okla., April 4.—It took the sheriff to stop the riot in the Auditorium when a peace meeting suddenly broke into a patriotic demonstration.

NO-LICENSE CARRIES BY BIG MARGIN

Sixty-Three Saloons To Go Out of Business At Midnight June 30; Wets Talk of Contest

Trammeled and badgered by the saloon element, Madison like the proverbial worm turned yesterday and asserted itself against the saloon by a majority larger by two hundred than any majority given the wets in past elections.

Madison went dry by 415 votes for one year. The city has 63 bars.

The total vote was 8,723 on the wet and dry question, of which 4,560 voted dry or against the saloon and 4,145 voted for the saloon.

Every saloon in the city will go out of existence at midnight on June 30 this year.

Defiant and confident the wet forces everywhere predicted victory by margins from 100 to 300. Th drys, equally confident, were the best guessers. Emerson Ela, president of the dry league, predicted a majority of 500 votes yesterday.

Almost in every ward in the city substantial gains were made by the anti-saloon campaigners. Even the Sixth ward, the pivot of past wet and dry elections gave the saloon yesterday a majority of 136 as against 378 two years ago.

The drys gained in the Second, Fourth, Seventh, Eighth, Ninth and Tenth wards. These wards and the Fifth gave splendid indorsements to the fight for a clean city.

Wets Talk of Contest

Rumors of a contest were afloat in the city last night but could not be verified. The object of the contest would be the student wards, particularly the Fifth. However there is plenty of material for the dry side from this ward if a contest arises. Cases were cited to The State Journal last night where students were permitted to register a week ago but not permitted to vote yesterday, being told they belonged in the First ward. Why this fact wasn't discovered when the men registered will be a point of information to be sought this week.

Students and faculty members and a good many residents who looked as tho they might have gone to school at one time were challenged right and left in the Fifth ward. The wets made frantic attempts to keep the vote in this ward down to a minimum. At least 340 votes were challenged in the entire ward and 105 of these were in the first precinct. If the wets succeed in throwing all of these challenges the drys would still have a majority of 71 votes.

Students and others challenged were compelled to answer five or more questions and then go thru devious processes to vote. Thruout the morning there was a line waiting to vote. A number, discouraged and compelled to make classes, left without voting and it is said, did not come back. One university professor, a resident of the ward for fifteen years, was challenged.

Lights Flash Results

The State Journal's system of signals, worked by the Madison Gas & Electric company, flashed the result over the city shortly after 9 o'clock. In one section of the downtown quarter the lights did not flash, due to a mechanical difficulty. However residents here were informed over the telephone of the outcome.

No word was more expressive expressing its appreciation of the dry victory than the first precinct of the first. Having gone wet a considerable majority, the watchers around the counters expected that the first flash would be the last.

"Wet," shouted the crowd as the State Journal flashed the first signal.

"Hell," was the next cry, as the second flash was given.

Efforts were made to get statements from men who managed the wet campaign last night but the wets had retired early—a few minutes after the result was flashed.

NATIONWIDE DRY BILL IN SENATE

Introduced As "Vital War Measure;" Immediate Action Is Demanded

WASHINGTON, April 4.—A national prohibition amendment was introduced in the senate today as "a vital war measure" and immediate action demanded by Senator Sheppard, of Texas.

The bill provides authority for congress to absolutely prohibit the manufacture, sale or transportation of intoxicating liquors.

As a war provision the senator declared temporary measures by statute are under consideration to make the restriction effective at once.

Washington was six feet two inches tall. He had brown hair, which became thin and gray.

The Wisconsin State Journal

VOL. 129, NO. 5. 78th Year | Full Leased Wire Service of THE UNITED PRESS. | MADISON, WIS., FRIDAY AFTERNOON, APRIL 6, 1917 | Latest Edition | PRICE TWO CENTS

WAR IS DECLARED

WASHINGTON, April 6---War was declared at 1:13 this afternoon.

At exactly that hour President Wilson signed the joint resolution passed by the house and senate, declaring a state of War between the United States and Germany.

An hour before the resolution was signed by Vice President Marshall at 12:13.

These were the last formalities necessary to make the United States an ally of England, France and Russia in the world war of democracies against autocracy.

WAR COUNCIL BILL TO PASS HOUSE TODAY

Home Defense and Mobilization of State's Resources To Be In Hands of Board of 12 Members

FULL TEXT OF BILL
The full text of the state council for defense bill will be found on Page 3.

The lower house of the Wisconsin legislature reconvened at two o'clock this afternoon to consider the first war measure, precipitated as a result of the declaration made today.

The bill which was offered with a recommendation for passage by the joint committee on finance, provides for a council of twelve members to assist the governor and the adjutant general in ascertaining the war resources of Wisconsin. The bill will be passed today.

At first Speaker Whittet sought to obtain unanimous consent for the consideration of the bill. Assemblyman Charles D. Rosa of Beloit then said that he yielded to no man in patriotism, but he would like to know what was the need of taking the bill up immediately.

Speaker Submits to Delay

"There are some things that can not be known to the public at this time in this crisis," declared Speaker Whittet. Speaker Whittet finally agreed that the bill go over until two o'clock this afternoon, and that the assembly then discuss the matter fully in a committee of the whole.

The council, under the terms of the bill, will be composed of twelve members to be appointed by the governor, including representatives of the manufacturers, labor, farmers, women engaged in Red Cross work or relief societies; physicians, bankers, representative of railroads, trained engineer, adjutant general, two citizens from the state at large and the governor as an ex-officio member. The members of the council shall be paid $5 a day and traveling expenses.

This board shall co-operate with auxilliary boards in cities, towns and villages and may employ expert help in gathering information on the resources of Wisconsin that can be used in waging war. After the members are appointed they shall assemble at Madison and elect one of their number as chairman and another as secretary.

Have Wide Powers

If at any time the investigations of the board shall show that there is distress in the state thru the lack of food or fuel, the council shall report this matter to the executive who shall call a special session of the legislature and have the government take charge of the food and fuel supply of the state and have it distributed so as to eliminate want. The state council is specifically directed to co-operate with the national council.

"All monies shall be paid out under the audit and supervision of the state, whether contributed by the state or by individuals as subscriptions. The bill appropriates an unlimited amount, but not more than $10,000 can be expended by the council at one time, except by the express

(Turn to Page 11, column 1)

THE WEATHER

Fair and warmer tonight. Saturday increasing cloudiness.

EXTRA!

OWEN WINS BENCH SEAT; LEAD IS 5,000

Election Claimed for Attorney General As Figures Are Received From Fifty Counties

Attorney General Walter C. Owen has been elected to succeed Justice R. D. Marshall as a member of the state supreme court. His lead will run over 5,000, and may exceed 10,000.

The result in the closest contest for the supreme bench in years became evident as the official returns began coming into The State Journal office from county clerks in all sections of the state today. At three o'clock this afternoon, the lead of the attorney general in 50 counties, twenty-one of which were official and the remainder practically complete, had mounted to over 5,000. The remaining 20 counties are in the majority of cases small, and a majority of them are claimed as certain for Owen.

Price county gave Owen a lead of 745 officially; Clark county complete gave him 1794; La Fayette 505; Outagamie 282. Marathon complete went to Marshall by 835; his home county, Chippewa, added 687; Marinette gave him 246; Trempealeau added 191.

The counties from which practically no returns have been received are:

Adams, Barron, Burnett, Calumet, Columbia, Dodge, Forest, Green Lake, Iowa, Juneau, Monroe, Oneida, Polk, Richland, St. Croix, Sawyer, Vernon, Vilas, Washburn.

OWEN-MARSHALL MAJORITIES

Counties Precincts	Owen	Marshall
Ashland	600	
Bayfield	430	
Brown	1,168	
Buffalo	214	
Chippewa		687
Clark (Official)	1,794	
Crawford		65
Dane	1,000	
Door	250	
Douglas (Complete)		555
Dunn (complete	681	
Eau Claire (Official)		786
Florence (Officiol)		67
Fond du Lac (all but 2)		198
Grant (all but 4		45
Green	500	
Iron (Official)	129	
Jackson	700	
Jefferson (Official)		1,518
Kewaunee (comp)		132
Kenosha (all but 1)	570	
La Crosse		800
LaFayette (Official)	505	
Langlade (all but 5)		519
Lincoln (all but 6)	182	
Manitowoc (all but 1)	297	
Marquette (Official)		75
Marathon (Official)		835
Marinette (Official)		246
Milwaukee		2,686
Oconto (all but 12)		27
Outagamie (Official)	283	
Ozaukee (comp)		381
Pierce (Official)	1,313	
Portage (Complete)	185	
Price (Official)	745	
Racine	900	
Rock (Official)		297
Rusk (est)	200	
Sauk (Official)		1,066
Shawano (est)		200
Sheboygan (est)	300	
Taylor (Official)	380	
Trempealeau (Official)		191
Walworth (est)		500
Washington (all but 2)	489	
Waukesha (Official	537	
Waupaca	1,000	
Waushara (all but 3)	719	
Winnebago	1,045	
Wood (all but 2)	425	
Total	17,718	12,881

President Wilson's Proclamation

WASHINGTON, April 6.—The President's proclamation reads:

"WHEREAS, the congress of the United States, in the exercise of the constitutional authority vested in them, have resolved, by joint resolution of the senate and house of representatives bearing date this day, that the state of war between the United States and the imperial German government which has been thrust upon the United States is hereby formally declared:

"WHEREAS, it is provided by Section 4067 of the revised statutes, as follows:

"'Whenever there is declared a war between the United States and any foreign nation or government or any invasion of predatory incursion is perpetrated, attempted or threatened against the territory of the United States by any foreign nation or government, and the president makes public proclamation of the event, all natives, citizens, denizens or subjects of the hostile nation or government being males of the age of 14 years and upwards, who shall be within the United States and not actually naturalized, shall be liable to be apprehended, restrained, secured and removed, as alien enemies.

"'The president is authorized in any such event by his proclamation thereof or any public acts to direct the conduct to be observed, or the part of the United States towards the aliens who become so liable; the manner and the degree of the restraint to which they shall be subject, and in what cases, and upon what security their residence shall be permitted and to provide for the removal of those who, not being permitted to reside within the United States, refuse or neglect to depart therefrom; and to establish any other regulations which are found necessary in the premises and for the public safety.'

"WHEREAS, by Sections 4068, 4069, and 4070 of the revised statutes, further provision is made relative to alien enemies:

"Now, therefore, I, Woodrow Wilson, president of the United States of America, do hereby proclaim to all whom it may concern that a state of war exists between the United States and the imperial German government and I do specifically direct all officers, civil or military of the United States that they exercise vigilance and zeal in the discharge of the duties incident to such a state of war; and I do, moreover, earnestly appeal to all American citizens that they, in loyal devotion to their country, dedicated from its foundation, declare the principles and justice, to uphold the laws and give undivided and willing support to those measures which may be adopted by the constitutional authorities in prosecuting the war to a successful issue and obtaining a secure and just peace:

"And, acting under by virtue of the authority vested in me by the constitution of the United States and the said sections of the Revised Statutes, I do hereby further proclaim and direct that the conduct to be observed on the part of the United States toward all natives, citizens, denizens or subjects of Germany, being males of the age of 14 years and upwards, who shall be within the United States and not actually naturalized, who for the purpose of this proclamation and under such sections of the revised statutes are termed alien enemies, shall be as follows:

"All alien enemies are enjoined to preserve the peace towards the United States and to refrain from crime against the public safety and from violating the laws of the United States and of the states and territories thereof, and to refrain from actual hostility or of giving information, aid or comfort to the enemies of the United States and to comply strictly with the regulations which are hereby or which may be from time to time promulgated by the president; and so long as they shall conduct themselves in accordance with law, they shall be undisturbed in the peaceful pursuit of their lives and occupations, and be accorded the consideration due all peaceful and law-abiding persons, except so far as restrictions may be necessary for their own protection and for the safety of the United States; and towards such alien enemies as conduct themselves in accordance with law, all citizens of the United States are enjoined to preserve the peace and to treat them with all such friendliness as may be compatible with loyalty and allegiance to the United States.

"And all alien enemies who fail to conduct themselves as so enjoined, in addition to all other penalties, prescribed by law, shall be liable to restraint, or to give security or to remove and depart from the United States in the manner prescribed by Sections Four Thousand and Sixty-Nine and Four Thousand and Seventy of the Revised Statutes, and as prescribed in the regulations duly promulgated by the president;

"And pursuant to the authority vested in me, I hereby declare and establish the following regulations, which I find necessary in the premises and for the public safety:

"(1) An alien enemy shall not have in his possession, at any time or place any fire arm, weapon or implement of war, or component part thereof, ammunition, maxim or other silencer, bomb or explosive or material used in the manufacture of explosives;

"(2) An alien enemy shall not have in his possession at any time or place or use or operate any aircraft or wireless apparatus, or any form of signalling device, or any form of cipher code, or any paper, document or book written or printed in cipher or in which there may be invisible writing.

"(3) All property found in the possession of an alien in violation of the foregoing regulations shall be subject to seizure by the United States;

"(4) An alien enemy shall not approach or be found within one half of a mile of any federal or state fort, camp, arsenal, aircraft station, government or naval vessel, navy yard, factory or work shop for the manufacture of munitions of war or of any products for the use of the army or navy;

"(5) An alien enemy shall not write, print, or publish any attack or threats against the government or congress of the United States or either branch thereof, or against the measures or policy of the United States or against the person or property of any person in the military naval or civil service of the United States, or of the states or the territory or of the District of Columbia or the municipal governmentship therein;

"(6) An alien enemy shall not commit or abet any hostile act against the United States, or give information, or comfort to its enemies,

"(7) An alien enemy shall not reside in or continue to reside in, to remain in, or enter any locality which the president may from time to time designate by executive order as a prohibited area in which residence by an alien enemy shall be found by him to constitute a danger to the public peace and safety of the United States, except by permit from the president and except under such limitation or restrictions as the president may prescribe;

"(8) An alien enemy whom the president shall have reasonable cause to believe to be aiding or about to aid the enemy, or to be at large to the danger of the public peace or safety of the United States, or to have violated or to be about to violate any of these regulations, shall remove to any location designated by the president by executive order and shall not remove therefrom without a permit, or shall depart from the United States if so required by the president;

(Turn to Page 11, column 3)

As the president affixed his signature to the document Lt. Commander Byron McCandless signalled across the street to the navy department that war was formally on and orders were flashed out from the government wireless to the ships at sea and to the forts of the United States.

Simultaneously every steam whistle in Washington and on the Potomac river nearby was opened wide and their screeches could be heard in every corner of the nation's capital.

While the ink was still wet on the historic war resolution, messages to all the countries of the earth were sent notifying them of this government's action.

The state department informed the Swiss minister here representing the German interests in the United States of this country's action. The minister will communicate the word formally to Berne by cable and thence to Berlin.

United States representatives in every foreign and South American capital should have the news within the next 24 hours.

President Wilson signed the war resolution while alone in the library of the white house two minutes after it had reached the executive mansion from the capitol.

President Wilson later this afternoon issued a proclamation to the people of the country declaring a state of war exists between the United States and the Imperial German government.

At the same time he especially directed all officers of the United States government, civil or military to exercise vigilance in the discharge of their duties incident to such a state of war.

At the same time he appealed to all American citizens to uphold the laws of the land and "give undivided and willing support to those measures which may be adopted by the constitutional authorities in prosecuting the war to a successful issue and in obtaining a secure and just peace."

8 SPY SUSPECTS TAKEN IN CHICAGO

Arrests Mark Beginning of Campaign To Protect Lives and Property

CHICAGO, April 6.—Eight German spy suspects were taken into custody by federal agents here today. The arrests, according to the department of justice investigators, marks the beginning of a campaign to comb the city thoroly to protect American lives and property.

Steps were also being taken by Captain J. C. Dillon, radio inspector, to dismantle 5,000 amateur wireless stations.

CO. G CALL DUE INSIDE 24 HOURS

Order Expected At Any Time In Office of Adjutant General Holway

At the office of Adjutant General Holway here today, it was stated that orders calling out the first and second Wisconsin infantry regiments are expected within the next twenty-four hours.

NO STEP AS YET TO RAISE FUNDS

Administration To Await Idea of Amount Needed for War Before Acting

WASHINGTON, April 6.—No steps toward raising revenue for the huge war budgets asked by the administration will be taken until some more definite idea is obtained of the amount to be raised, Representative Garner, of Texas, a leader on the ways and means committee, declared today, after a conference with Secretary McAdoo.

The following message was flashed by the navy department this afternoon directly after President Wilson signed the war resolution to all navy ships and stations:

"The president has signed an act of congress which declares that a state of war exists with Germany."

This notice, the navy said, is not an order to mobilize.

There were prospects that such an order would go thru shortly, however.

Sent to State Department

From the white house the engrossed resolution was sent to the state department, there to rest as one of the most important papers filed away in the government records.

It bears no outward mark of difference from hundreds of thousands of other state papers in the department files. But it marks the beginning of a new war of civilization, according to President Wilson—a war which must determine whether democracy or imperialism shall rule the world.

Immediately after signing the joint resolution for war the president issued a proclamation to the people of the country, declaring a state of war exists between the United States and the imperial German government.

He asks all American citizens "all devotion to their country, dedicated from its founding to the principles of liberty and justice," to uphold the laws of the land and "give undivided and willing support" to all measures adopted by the government" in prosecuting the war to a successful issue and in attaining a secure and just peace."

The president also asked all aliens to conform to the regulations which he outlined in the proclamation.

AGAIN THE LUCKY THIRTEEN
WASHINGTON, April 6—Vice President Marshall signed the war resolution at 12:13 p. m.
Exactly one hour later to the second President Wilson signed his name—at 1:13 p. m.
Thirteen is President Wilson's lucky number.

SUBMARINES HOVERING NEAR S. A. TRADE ROUTE

NEW YORK, April 6.—German submarines are near the Great Circle, trade route between New York and Cape San Roque and other South American ports, a warning sent out by wireless early today said. British and other allied ships were warned to be on the lookout for U boats in latitude 26 north, longitude 56.42 west.

THE SUNDAY  STATE JOURNAL

VOL. 6, NO. 36. 6th Year. Full Leased Wire Service of THE UNITED PRESS MADISON, WIS., SUNDAY MORNING, AUGUST 11, 1918. TWELVE PAGES PRICE FIVE CENTS

YANKS SMASH FORWARD

Battle Rages on 150-Mile Line

FOE IN MAD ROUT; BURNS SHELLS, GUNS

British, French and Americans Gain Ground on World's Largest Front; Take Many Towns

BY WILLIAM PHILIP SIMMS

WITH THE BRITISH ARMIES IN FRANCE, Aug. 10.—The great battle was surging onward in full tilt tonight. The eastern horizon glowed dull red where the 2nd and 18th German armies were burning their stores to prevent them from falling into the hands of the pursuers.

Occasionally a great flash lighted the clouds where an ammunition dump was going up.

Von Der Marwitz and Von Hutier were too hard pressed to destroy everything. As I walked on the battle-field there were evidences of tremendous hurry everywhere.

TAKE HUGE STORES INTACT

Huge stores of supplies and ammunition were taken intact. The Germans turned their own howitzers on abandoned dumps now well behind the British lines in the hope of setting them off. Roads were found mined ready to be blown up, but the Germans had no time. Advanced hospitals were discovered with lint, bandages and medicine strewn everywhere showing the astounding confusion that must have existed when some one cried, "The British are coming."

Guns, howitzers and field pieces up to eight inches and larger were taken intact, either still in position or overturned in the roadside gullies with their gun limbers nearby, because the allied cavalry, supported by whippets, tanks and armored cars, were at the Germans' heels. Lorries loaded with artillery maps and other headquarters' documents and material were left in the road, their drivers being killed or captured by the cavalry.

PENETRATE TOWN; BURN TRAIN

One car penetrated a town and set fire to a train. Another headed off and killed an aviation officer trying to escape in his automobile. The automobile was captured.

Airmen reported the roads in the region of Roye and Nesle packed with troops retiring eastward. It was learned from prisoners that German officers made desperate efforts to rally their men wherever they assembled, even in a handful, to make whatever resistance was possible, principally by fighting from machine gun nests. These were easy pickings for the whippets which bore down rapidly, firing their machine guns as they went. The men who ran were killed and those who resisted were ground into the earth, staining the sides of the whippets with blood. Surrender was the only alternative.

CAVALRY CHARGES GUNS

In places the Germans fought stubbornly. One battery of field guns, firing point blank and somewhat damaging the tanks, was charged by cavalry with drawn sabres. The gun crews were killed or captured. Cavalry charging past Beaufort encountered a German officer frantically waving his hands and shouting: "Don't enter the village. It's brigade headquarters." The officer was taken prisoner and the cavalry dashed into the village and killed some and captured others of the brigade staff officers, including the brigadier general.

Farther north armored cars penetrated huts which were serving as corps headquarters. Many staff officers were killed.

Vast quantities of ammunition on the ground—greater than the number of German guns warranted—indicated that some of the artillery was being used elsewhere, perhaps supporting the sorely pressed crown prince.

RUPPRECHT'S REPLY FEEBLE

Rupprecht's reply to Haig's artillery was rather feeble. The stiffest resistance was on the extreme flanks. The British had some difficulty north born opposition eastward of Moreuil and crossing of the river proved difficult. The Germans held Grenonville wood, atop the ridge, on the eastern bank between Moreuil and Plessier and they made the valley sizzle with machine gun bullets. The French attacked once and were forced back. Their second attempt won the ridge and wood. French cavalry poured thru the opening, quickly joining up with British cavalry operating down the Amiens-Roye road past Mezieres toward Lequensel, which held out for a day.

French and British troops are cooperating beautifully. Comparatively

(Turn to page 10, column 1)

THE WEATHER

WISCONSIN—Partly cloudy and cooler Sunday with thunder showers in east portion; Monday probably fair.

SPIRIT OF WAR GRIPS CHILDREN

—Photo by McKillop and Ruud

Left and right—Joseph Edwards, Henry Heim, Philip Smith, Philip Heim, Bernard Jordan, Herman Heim, Kendall White, Robert Wiedmann, Donald McKenna, Clara Marten, Jean McKenna, Betty Martin, Jack McKenna, Marcia McKenna, Esther Ripp, Mary Jane Ripp, Clara White, Lucian Hagk, Joseph Owens.

Gilman Street Youngsters Set Example of Loyalty; Kaiser Bagged; Armed Guard Before, Machine Gun Behind

By HARRIET M'CORMICK

Every day or so I see something that strikes my patriotic chord and sends the little shivers up and down my spine. But the biggest thrill of all came Friday afternoon when I met twenty or more neighborhood "kids" of the Gilman street district, staging a patriotic parade. Publicity for the Red Cross was their object. They that that it would be fun and at the same time would help along the sewing society that their mothers belonged to that makes bandages for the big American soldiers in France. At least that is the way little Jack McKenna, the "Y. M. C. A. director," explained the parade's origin.

"I heard mother say some people didn't know there was a Red Cross, so we wanted to have everybody know about it," divulged Jack. Everyone in the Gilman and State street districts did know that there was a Red Cross society when those children disbanded after an hour's procession.

Flag Heads Parade

About 2 o'clock on Friday afternoon the parade formed in the McKenna back yard, 219 West Gilman street. Jack had a lot of business about him and it wasn't long before the procession filed down Gilman street.

There was Joseph Edwards, carrying the American flag and honored by the leading position. (Everyone was requested to remove one's hat when the flag passed by. Joe spotted the unpatriotic offender at once.) Behind the flag bearer were Henry Heim and Philip Smith, forming the color guard.

The Kaiser bagged! Bagged he was by these children. They had him in a gunny sack, and the honors of carrying the kaiser were given to Philip Heim and Bernard Jordan.

Not even a Red Cross unit would dare enter France without a machine gun, so this Red Cross squad was equipped with one. It belonged to

(Turn to page 10, column 1)

LOYALTY TO BE KEYNOTE LABOR DAY

3,000 Madison Workers Will March in Great Parade; Prof. Commons to Be Speaker at Park

Madison will have a "win the war" Labor Day.

Plans are practically completed for the monster parade. Over 3,000 Madison workers will march. The twenty-five Madison unions will participate, each organization carrying the union service flag in honor of members now in the service of the nation. The service emblem of the Federation of Labor, with its 300 stars, is expected to be completed by Labor Day and will be carried in the parade.

Loyalty will be the keynote. The unions are coming out in force to show their unquestioned support of the government in winning the war. The program will be given at Vilas park following the parade. The relation of labor to winning the great struggle will be discussed by the speakers.

COMMONS CHIEF SPEAKER

Prof. John R. Commons, speaker of the day, will devote his address to a discussion of such problems as have confronted labor since war was declared. He probably will be introduced by President Joseph H. Brown of the Madison Federation of Labor.

A delegation of farmers is expected to participate in the parade. A committee of farmers has been appointed from the outlying rural districts to co-operate with Madison workers in making the celebration a success.

The parade will form in sections, with each union forming a section. The march probably will start from Wisconsin avenue and, going around the capitol square, will proceed to Vilas park.

LOYALTY PROGRAM PLANNED

Altho present plans are merely tentative, the committee of laborers is working hard to get matters in shape by Sept. 2. Every worker in Madison will be called upon to show his loyalty by assisting in the day's celebration. National labor men have said the time has come for organized labor to signify to the president its unwavering support in winning the war. Communications accordingly have been sent to every local in the nation requesting demonstrations on Labor Day in support of the program.

SOCIALISTS MAY ACT ON PLATFORM

ST. LOUIS STAND EXPECTED TO COME UP DURING CHICAGO CONVENTION

CHICAGO, Aug. 10.—Action regarding the St. Louis platform American socialists may be taken before the close of the annual national conference of that party, begun here today. A resolutions committee has been appointed.

Forty-seven delegates attended the opening session. More were expected Sunday when, it was believed, routine matters would be rushed through. No public statements were made as to campaign plans.

Louis Knollwolf has accepted a position in the laboratory of the Indiana Condensed Milk plant.

REVOLT IN BULGARIA MAY WEAKEN ENEMY

KAISER'S ALLY TO SEEK ARMISTICE WITH ALLIES, BELIEF; PEOPLE SEE KAISER'S DEFEAT

WASHINGTON, Aug. 10.—Revolt in Bulgaria and defection from the German alliance is believed possible and perhaps impending.

Events of extreme significance are transpiring behind the tight censorship. High entente officials here are daily expecting Bulgaria to snap the weakening strings that have tied her to the German alliance for four weary years with nothing but increasing prospects of defeat as compensation.

An armistice until the end of the war, rather than a separate peace between the Bulgaria and the allies, is likely, entente officials say. Difficulties in framing a separate peace in the Balkans which would satisfy Serbia, Greece and Italy and almost insurmountable until the general peace conference meets to remake the map of Europe.

Latest developments pointing toward Bulgaria's defection are:

1—German setbacks on the western front, foreshadowing ultimate defeat for the central powers.

2—Czar Ferdinand's hasty trip to Germany.

3—Wildest disorder and popular ill-feeling toward the war party in Bulgaria.

4—Hatred of Turkey lately revived over territorial differences.

5—Germany's non-committal attitude toward Bulgaria's demands for concessions against Turkey.

Germany's visible weakening on the western front is hastening Bulgaria's decision. Having little more to gain in the conflict, Bulgaria has been closely watching the turn of events since America entered the war. Now that Germany appears likely to be defeated, she wants to break away from the central powers before the crash comes.

Playing Germany's Game?

Bulgarian agents have recently visited Switzerland and other neutral nations on peace missions and to feel our sentiment toward Bulgaria. While the United States has made no official announcement of its attitude, President Wilson blocked an attempt in congress last winter to declare war on Bulgaria, evidently hoping to conciliate her and weaken Germany in southeastern Europe.

Serbia and Greece, however, warn the allies against Bulgarian attempts to involve them in peace discussions. In a joint official statement issued by the Serbian and Greek repesentatives here tonight, the allies are cautioned that Bulgaria is playing Germany's game by trying to open a discussion for peace between Bulgaria and the

(Turn to page 10, column 3)

KIDNAPPING GANG BELIEVED FOUND

PHILADELPHIA POLICE ARREST GIVE PERSONS; CHILDREN IMPRISONED; BONES IN CELLAR

PHILADELPHIA, Aug. 10.—With the arrest of four women and a man in connection with the alleged kidnaping of two children, the police believe they have behind the bars a syndicate which has been trafficking in children. All are held without bail.

The arrests were made in a house on south Fifteenth Street, believed by the police to have been a baby farm. Nine children, ranging from 18 months to 17 years of age, were found therein.

In a search of the cellar the police tonight dug up some bones. Until they are passed upon by anatomists, it will not be definitely known whether they are those of children.

CASUALTIES OF FOE NEAR 60 000, CLAIM

Horizon Glows Red Before Allied Advance; Hun Prisoners Seem Pleased At Being Captured

The new allied offensive has grown into the largest battle front in history.

The German war office indicated Sunday that the fighting now extends over a front of practically 150 miles from the Yser river to the Oise.

The main battle front is between the Oise and the Ancre, a distance of fifty miles. From the Ancre northward to the Yser, Berlin announced that the allies have launched "thrusts and partial attacks" at many points.

The battle thus includes all of the Picardy and Flanders salients, the intermediate territory around Lens, the Belgian sector as far north as Dixmude and the former Oise offensive front as far east as Ribecourt. A stretch of 35 miles—between the Oise and Soissons—is all that separates this great battle area from the Aisne-Vesle line.

MONTDIDIER IS CAPTURED

Substantial progress was reported all along the Picardy front Saturday by both the British and French war offices. Montdidier was outflanked and captured together with a large number of prisoners and great quantities of material.

Americans, making their first appearance in the battle, captured Morlancourt and the adjacent heights in co-operation with the British, thus removing the principal obstacles to the allies advance along the Somme. In the center, Australians and Canadians advanced from two to four miles, threatening Chaulnes and Roye. To the southward the French swept forward six miles on a 12 mile front, taking Ressons-sur-Matz and driving toward Lassigny.

German prisoners are estimated at more than 30,000 and over 400 guns are believed to have been captured. The total enemy casualties are estimated at from 50,000 to 60,000, while the allied casualties are believed to be not more than 6,000 to 7,500.

ALL ASSAULTS REPULSED

The Germans are retreating precipitately upon the line from Peronne to Noyon, formed by the Somme from Peronne to Nesle, and the canal from Nesle to Noyon. Enemy prisoners, however, express doubt that the Germans will be able to make any strong resistance on this line—so closely are they being pressed—and there is a probability that the retirement may continue to the old "Hindenburg line."

On the Vesle-Aisne line the Germans are fiercely counterattacking the Americans and a terrific battle is raging north of the Vesle, between Bazoches and Fismette. All assaults have been repulsed.

RAINCOAT ORDERS DROPPED BY U. S.

QUARTERMASTER GENERAL DROPS CONTRACTS HELD BY INDICTED MANUFACTURERS

WASHINGTON, Aug. 10.—All government contracts for raincoats held by firms whose officials were indicted, following investigatons by the department of justice, today were ordered cancelled by Brigadier General R. E. Wood, acting quartermaster general. New contracts willl be awarded to other firms.

PARIS SAFE; RHINE NOW IS IN PERIL

BY J. W. T. MASON

NEW YORK, Aug. 10.—America's decisive influence upon German strategy has been made plainly evident this week by the refusal of Hindenburg to accept Marshal Foch's challenge to a pitched battle for the mastery of the Montdidier salient and the highly important front southeast of Amiens.

Faced by a strong British attack, undertaken in conjunction with the French on the south and Americans on the north, Hindenburg has turned to the defensive, duplicating the tactics he employed in his retreat from the Marne. The importance of this week's progress by the three allies is not so much in the actual ground gained, but in the implied acknowledgment by Hindenburg that he must shorten his front to save his reserves.

Hindenburg Shortens Line

The military results that have fallen to Marshal Foch in three days include the removal of Amiens from any immediate danger of a new German offensive; the re-opening of the important Amiens-Paris railway which was previously under command of the German guns, and the elimination of the strategic value of the Montdidier salient as a possible base for a new German drive to Paris.

These highly important consequences of this week's victories are secondary, however, to the fact that Hindenburg has declined to permit his reserves to be used for counter attacks. The allies have had to meet strong defensive resistance by the Germans, but no evidence has been apparent that Hindenburg dares to engage in severe offensive combats to regain his former line between the Montdidier corner and the Somme.

Foe Has Shot His Bolt

The reason is unquestionably due to the character of the fighting shown by the Americans during the Marne engagements and the knowledge in Germany that an unlimited number of the same kind of troops are now being dispatched from the United States to France.

Hindenburg has shot his bolt. He can no longer hope to win. Henceforth, he must abandon the conflict or fight at most for a draw. The dominant pre-occupation at German headquarters is to build up a new reserve organization which must meet the forthcoming major offensive of the Americans. Hence, Hindenburg has revealed a new timidity in holding his enormously extended front in the west.

The allies have pushed into German positions this week with unprecedentedly slight casualties. Again the reason is Hindenburg's fear to resist when resistance means the depletion of his reserves. Hindenburg cannot tell how soon these same reserves will be needed to defend German territory against vast American armies advancing toward the Rhine.

Rhine Now in Peril

A few short weeks ago it was safety of Paris and the channel ports that dominated the military situation along the west front. Today, it is beginning to be the safety of the Rhine. The strain of defensive strategy is passing from the allies to the Germans.

There can be no question but that the kaiser knows his armies in the west must eventually fall back at least to the old Hindenburg line so that reserves may be taken from the shortened front. The beginning of that movement is visible in this week's developments between Montdidier and the Somme. The Rhine for the first time is influencing events in Picardy.

CLIMB VESLE PLATEAU IN FACE OF FIRE

Hun Counters Fail to Keep Our Boys Back; Terrific Close-Range Fighting Staged

BY FRANK J. TAYLOR

WITH THE AMERICAN ARMIES IN FRANCE, Aug. 10.—(Night)—American troops advanced in force from Fismes today and after capturing Fismette began pressing northward up the steep south slope of the Aisne-Vesle plateau.

Their advance was made in the face of enemy counter attacks of the most savage character and was accompanied by fierce close range fighting.

AMERICAN BLOW SURPRISES HUN

The American assault on Fismette surprised the enemy and 100 prisoners, including officers, fell into the hands of the Americans.

Germans are counter attacking fiercely in an attempt to hold back the American advance north of the Vesle. Close range fighting of a terrific nature is under way along the railroad on the north bank of the Vesle, through Bazoches and Fismette, where the American infantry is withstanding the German attacks.

DESTROY FOE DUGOUTS

The Americans, attempting to advance up the slope to the ridge position held by the boshes earlier in the day, concentrated the most intense barrage possible upon this area, partially destroying German dugouts, entrenchments and strong points. The remaining defenses were too strong for frontal assaults, however. They will have to be blasted away still more.

The entire American front is now a continual infero. Both artilleries are concentrating on the river valley and the highlands to the south and north.

BATTLE TO PROTECT MOVEMENTS

German airmen are exceptionally aggressive, trying to prevent all allied observation. While seeking out a particular German gun yesterday, American aviators brought down two boche battleplanes.

It is still believed that the German pressure here is not permanent and that they are simply fighting to protect more important movements.

GERMAN AMERICAN HURT BY SUSPICION

WARBURG SADLY QUITS RESERVE BOARD; WILSON ASSURES HIM OF CONFIDENCE

WASHINGTON, Aug. 10.—A strikingly dramatic example of suffering the kaiser has inflicted upon loyal Americans of German extraction in this country, was offered tonight in the publication of letters exchanged between Paul M. Warburg, member of the federal reserve board and President Wilson.

"These are sad time," said Warburg in his letter urging that he be excused from the board. "For all of us they bring sad duties, doubly hard for men of my extraction."

Warburg, a German by birth, and with two brothers now bankers in Germany asked relief because "certain persons have started an agitation to the effect that a naturalized citizen of German birth, having near relatives in German public life, should not hold a position of trust in the service of the United States."

The president in replying and consenting, "only because I read between the lines of your generous letter that you, yourself, feel more at ease if you are left to serve in other ways" declared Warburg carried with him "my sincere friendship, admiration and confidence."

WAR MOTHERS ASK 1-CENT FARE

WASHINGTON, D. C.

The War Mothers of America have appealed to Director General McAdoo for a one-cent a mile rate to their national convention to be held in Evansville, Ind., Sept. 18-20. This is the same rate given their soldier sons who go home on furloughs of 10 days or more.

The convention committee says the home of every War Mother in Evansville will be thrown open during the convention to visiting War Mothers, and that speakers of national prominence, including many noted War Mothers will deliver help-to-win-the-war speeches.

Already, according to the committee, delegates from 20 states have signified their intention of attending the convention, at which the national organization of War Mothers will be perfected. President wilson has been invited to address the War Mothers and it is believed if he cannot get away from Washington for the convention he will designate some member of the cabinet as his representative.

Mr. and Mrs. S. J. Morgan, Miss Rose Morgan and O. A. Bort motored

The Wisconsin  State Journal

VOL. 131, NO. 191. 79th Year. Full Leased Wire Service of THE UNITED PRESS MADISON, WIS., MONDAY AFTERNOON, NOV. 11, 1918. LATEST EDITION PRICE TWO CENTS

TRUCE TERMS REVEALED

WASHINGTON, D. C. Nov. 11–The Allied-American armistice terms, as announced by President Wilson in Congress today include:

Cessation of hostilities.

Evacuation of invaded territories, including Alsace-Lorraine and Luxemburg.

Surrender of vast amounts of guns and equipment.

Evacuation of left bank of Rhine.

Surrender of vast rolling stock in occupied territories.

Abandonment of Bucharest and Brest treaties.

Unconditional surrender of all German forces in East Africa.

Reparation of damage done.

Surrender of scores of submarines and larger war craft.

Concentration of aircraft at stipulated points.

Evacuation of all Black Sea ports.

Restoration of all Allied and United States merchant vessels.

Duration of the armistice to be 30 days.

Wilson Tells Crowder To Stop Draft

QUIT LEFT OF RHINE, EDICT TO GERMANY

Leave Invaded Lands; Give Up Enormous Supplies; Repatriate Captives; Neutral Zone Among Terms

BY CARL D. GROAT

WASHINGTON, D. C., Nov. 11.–President Wilson this afternoon told congress and the world terms Germany accepted when she signed the armistice.

These terms pictured Germany surrendering abjectly to Gen. Foch on the field, her armies beaten, her government overturned and her master in flight.

A small congress and a small crowd heard the president's burning words, but enthusiasm ran riot.

The president's address follows:

"Gentlemen of the congress:—

"In these anxious times of rapid and stupendous changes it will in some degree lighten my sense of responsibility to perform in person the duty of communicating to you some of the large circumstances of the situation with which it is necessary to deal. The German authorities who have at the invitation of the supreme war council been in communication with Marshal Foch, have accepted and signed the terms of armistice which he was authorized and instructed to communicate to them. These terms are as follows:

"Military clauses on the western front:

"1—Cessation of operations by land and in the air six hours after the signature of the armistice.

EVACUATION OF ALSACE-LORRAINE

"2—Immediate evacuation of invaded countries. Belgium, France, Alsace-Lorraine, Luxemburg, so ordered as to be completed within 14 days from the signature of the armistice. German troops who have not left the above mentioned territories within the period fixed will become prisoners of war. Occupation by the allies and United States forces jointly will keep pace with the evacuation in these areas. All movements of evacuation and occupation will be regulated in accordance with a note annexed to the stated terms.

"3—Repatriation beginning at once and to be completed within 14 days of all inhabitants of the countries above mentioned, including hostages and persons under trial or convicted.

"4—Surrender in good condition by the German armies of the following equipment:—Five thousand guns (two thousand five hundred heavy; two thousand five hundred field); 30,000 machine guns. Three thousand minenwerfer. Two thousand airplanes (fighters, bombers—firstly, D—seventy-threes and night bombing machines). The above to be delivertd in Simmstu to the allies and the United States troops in accordance with the detailed conditions laid down in the annexed note.

"5—Evacuation by the German armies of the countries on the left bank of the Rhine. These countries on the left bank of the Rhine shall be administered by the local authorities under the control of the allied and United States armies of occupation. The occupation of these territories will be determined by allied and United States garrisons holding the principal crossing of the Rhine, Mayence, Coblenz, Cologne, together with bridgeheads at these points in thirty kilometer radius on the right bank and by garrison similarly holding the strategic points of the region. A neutral zone shall be reserved on the right bank of the Rhine between the stream and a line drawn parallel to it forty kilometers to the east from the frontier of Holland to the parallel of Gernsheim and as far as practicable a distance of thirty kilometers from the east of the

(Turn to Page 3, column 2)

CITY CLOSES SHOP; CELEBRATES PEACE

S. A. T. C., UNIVERSITY AND TOWN IN JOYFUL UPROAR OVER VICTORY

VICTORY DAY IN MADISON

Factories—All shops and industrial plants closed for the day.

Stores—Employes to have morning for holiday. Stores reopen at 1 p. m.

School children—Assembled at grade buildings and then massed at Madison high school for parade. Dismissed for remainder of day.

Parade—Mayor Sayle proclaims holiday; directs citizens to celebrate as they wish; parade will organize itself.

Capitol employes—M. F. Blumenfeld, superintendent of public property, approves holiday for all state employes who wish to take it.

The S. A. T. C., the university and the city gave themselves joyoously and noisily to the victory celebration today.

After the clarion call thru the night, which heralded the great news story to Madison, the streets seethed with merrymakers up to the formation of the afternoon parade, which led from the capitol park out State street and University avenue to Camp Randall.

Here a program was staged, with Richard Lloyd Jones presiding. Chief Justice Winslow spoke for Wisconsin; Prof. W. H. Kiekhofer for the university; the Rev. W. J. McKay for the G. A. R.; Lieut. Cordoria of Italy for the Allies and Maj. Holloway, commandant at the university, for the United States army.

The Student Army Training corps gave an exhibition drill and community singing was conducted.

Whistles blowing, fire bells clanging, church towers chiming, mobs cheering, howling and shrieking for joy, hailed the glad tidings of peace in Madison this mornng at the same moment the magic flash carried the great news from one end of the world to the other.

At 1:45 a. m., when the first flash ticked its message to the tired operators who had kept steady vigil for the last 72 hours, Madison was slumbering peacefully in the quietest hour of the night.

A few minutes later the town was a bedlam of noise, factory whistles were blowing, crowds were thronging onto the streets. Every man, woman or child who could walk, ride, or borrow a crutch, was in the streets and about the square to celebrate peace on earth.

Beginning in two and threes, the crowd gradually grew in number. In a few moments out of the chaos of the night, an organized parade was marching about the square, crazy with joy. Songs, yells and auto horns resounded about the brilliantly lighted capitol dome.

Headed by Mayor Sayle, the chaotic mob, which already had gone around and around the square, started in a glorious parade at the city hall.

Miss Marion Felix, a university student from Chicago, holding high a liberty torch, led Scherer's military band. Already the Liberty Belle had placed a dozen or more red liberty torches about the capitol park. Marion had been keeping the torches, for she knew peace was coming soon and she has some one over there.

The old bell which has been in the city hall since 1855, came out of the basement, and was hoisted to a city truck loaded with city employes. Workmen from the Milwaukee road yards, the first to open up with whistles, followed next in the procession, shouting, weeping and dancing in the middle of the street.

Thousands of civilians and students fell into line where they could. In a separate body, the co-eds, protected by the military police, followed the great crowds. The French girl students marched in a group singing "La Marseillaise."

"On Wisconsin," "Skyrocket for Wilson," "Let's Go," resounded thru the cold, night air.

THE WEATHER

Fair and warmer tonight and Tuesday.

OUTSTANDING DRAFT CALLS CANCELLED

Boards Will Be Notified to Halt Entrainments Under Selective Service

WASHINGTON, D. C., Nov. 11.—President Wilson today authorized Provost Marshal General Crowder to notify all draft boards that calls now outstanding for military service be cancelled.

Pending further instructions no more inductions will be made into the army nor entrainment promoted under these calls, according to unofficial announcement today.

Crowder announced in his telegram to draft boards "merely to cancel outstanding calls and stop the entrainment thereunder of men for the army. All registrants released from induction under the provisions of this telegram are liable for immediate call in the usual manner at any time.

"The orderly process of classification, physical examination and other activities of the selective draft law will not be affected or interrupted as the result of this telegram."

Trains en route to camp now have been ordered back.

Decisions in regard to demobilization were being made in Secretary of War Baker's office today.

In the conference were Secretary of War Baker, Secretary of the Navy Daniels, Chief of Staff March, Chairman Hurley of the shipping board and Felix Frankfurter of the war labor policies board.

"Current calls are not cancelled. Local boards will entrain their quotas strictly in accordance with allotment circulars unless advice to the contrary by telegraph," read messages which Adjt. Gen. Orlando Holway wired to draft boards of Wisconsin today. About 3,000 men leave the state for camp today and word was expected from Provost Marshal General Crowder at Washington hourly that outstanding calls were cancelled. Without it, however, the state draft administration and adjutant general were constrained to act on yesterday's telegram from Washington, which said current calls would stand.

Fifteen thousand Wisconsin men are due for entrainment in the five-day period opening today.

From Madison today local board No. 2 for the eastern Dane county district sent 73 men for Camp Wadsworth, Spartansburg, S. C. Friday the Madison city board is to send 225 in two contingents; Board No. 2 has called 91; Board No. 1, 142.

Madison city board entrained five men for special service to Fort Ethan Allen, Vt., today. They are Robert Weaver, Edwin J. Longfield, Floyd E. Brickwell, Joseph Zoch and Joseph Neff.

DIES IN FRANCE

Roger J. Moore Victim of Bronchial Pneumonia

Private Roger J. Moore, son of Mr. and Mrs. William Moore, R. F. D. 1, [illegible] pneumonia in France, while enroute from the port of debarkation to camp.

He entered service in July, was trained at Camp Upton, N. Y., from which point he sailed for overseas Sept. 3 with the Blackhawk division.

Roger J. Moore

Mr. Moore was 24 years of age. He leaves his parents, three brothers and four sisters.

CITY GETS "FLASH" IN THREE MINUTES

STATE JOURNAL SCORES BIGGEST SCOOP EVER OBTAINED IN MADISON

Extra editions of The Wisconsin State Journal informed Madison of Germany's unconditional surrender and the end of the world war at 1:45 this morning, just three minutes after official announcement was made by the State Department in Washington.

With wires running direct into the State, Army and Navy building in the national capital; edtorial, mechanical and circulation forces that had "stood by" without a break since 7 a. m. Saturday, and a "trick of the trade" gave The Wisconsin State Journal the greatest scoop any Madison paper ever scored.

Hold Papers for "Flash"

At 6 o'clock last night three inside pages of The Wisconsin State Journal were placed on the press. Two first pages were made up, one heralding the signing of the truce by Germany's envoys at General Foch's headquarters, the other telling of the rejection of the terms by the enemy. Unconditional surrender was the best guess. Developments during the day indicated that Germany was seething with revolt; that her armies were no longer able to put up a semblance of defense before the great allied onrush.

The unconditional surrender page went on the press, and the big machine started grinding out extras to be held in The State Journal office until receipt of the "flash" that Germany had thrown up the sponge. The rejection page was moulded and ready to be put on the press in case The State Journal had guessed wrong.

Six automobiles and dozens of newsboys waited the release message.

Schedule of "Flash"

Here's the schedule of the "Truce is Signed" "flash" from the time it was announced by the State Department until it was on the streets of Madison:

1:42—State department makes announcement that Germany had signed truce.

1:42:15—United Press operator in The State Journal office receives "flash" over leased wire.

1:44—Newsboys released with extras.

1:45—First State Journal extra announcing end of conflict sold at entrance to State Journal building.

Newsboys were rushed to every section of the city in automobiles while members of The State Journal staff were phoning factories with the request that whistles be blown.

While crowds were gathering for the pre-dawn parade around the capitol, square, the second extra edition, much more complete than the first, was being sent broadcast thru the city.

The State Journal extras were on the streets at least fifteen minutes before those of its nearest competitor.

EXTRAS BRING $75 FOR RED CROSS

STATE JOURNAL PEACE EDITION AIDS MERCY CAUSE AT LODI

The Lodi branch of the Red Cross is $75 richer today by reason of the sale of 150 copies of The State Journal peace extra there this morning.

The papers were donated by The Journal agent there to the mercy cause, whereupon patriotic citizens, disdaining to "sponge," fell upon the news merchant and took his entire stack of papers in record time.

Sales ranged as high as $1 per copy.

HARLAN FRYE DIES SUNDAY IN CAMP

Private Harlan Frye, son of Taylor Frye, head of the child labor department of the Wisconsin Industrial commission, died yesterday at Camp Greenleaf, Ga., of pneumonia. The boy's parents, who now reside on a farm at Brooklyn, will have the body brought here for burial. It is expected to arrive tonight.

GENEVA OR BRUSSELS TO GET PEACE MEETING; QUIET GRIPS FRONT

Germany Deserted by Her Allies, Forced to Accept Unconditional Surrender; Truce Terms Make Renewal of Conflict by Hun Impossible.

BULLETIN

LONDON, Nov. 11.—The empire and its allies have won the greatest victory in history," declared Premier Lloyd-George today, in an address from the steps of his residence.

"You are well entitled to rejoice. It is you and your sons and daughters who have done it. Let us thank God."

BY ROBERT J. BENDER

WASHINGTON, D. C., Nov. 11—At 6 o'clock this morning (United States Eastern time) the greatest war in history came to an end.

The state department officially announced early today that German plenipotentiaries signed the United States-allied armistice terms at Foch's headquarters at 5 o'clock this morning and the hostilities ceased at 11 o'clock (both French time). While an armistice merely halts war and does not end it, the terms laid down by Foch are such as to prevent Germany from renewing hostilities. The war, therefore, may be regarded as definitely ended.

GENEVA AND BRUSSELS ARE CONSIDERED

There remains now the great problems of the peace conference and the gigantic work of returning the fighters to their home lands. As to the first, Geneva and Brussels are mentioned as the most likely points for the peace negotiations and as for the second, the general staff already has completed its plans for demobilization.

Thruout the nation today celebrations were held. President Wilson, aroused from his bed at an early hour, was told the news and prepared a statement for the country.

JOY BEGINS EVERYWHERE

From the white house to every land there was rejoicing. Thousands of telegrams poured in to Washington reflecting the great relief that the struggle was over and the anxiety of relatives for news of when their boys might return.

America, free from the ravages of war, unscathed by the destructive hand of the Hun hordes, looked across the seas to find the battlefields of France and Belgium silent for the first time in four years.

Where for 51 months, giant guns, poisonous gases and bursting bombs had wrought destruction, there was quiet today.

GERMANY ALONE AT END OF FRAY

At the close of the unprecedented strife Germany stood alone, before the wrath of 22 civilized nations. These twenty-two were in arms, five others had severed relations with her government and two others—Russia and Rumania—she had embittered by enforcement of a vicious peace. Her enemies had called to the colors over 23,000,000 men during the conflict, determined to crush forever the power that had upset the peace of the world.

Her allies, Bulgaria, Turkey and Austria-Hungary had left her when her strength began to weaken, and finally her own people, seeing at last the disaster their treacherous emperor and war lord had brought upon them, overthrew his reign and he has fled the country.

Badger Weather

Partly cloudy with local thunder-showers late tonight or Friday. Warmer, winds becoming south to southwest Friday.

The Wisconsin State Journal

City Edition

SIXTEEN PAGES

VOL. 135, NO. 111. 81st Year. MADISON, WIS., THURSDAY AFTERNOON, JULY 22, 1920. PRICE THREE CENTS

THRONGS HEAR HARDING ACCEPT

G. O. P. REPUDIATED BY "BOB"

OLD PARTIES FAILURES, HE CLAIMS

Senator Plans to Launch New Political Organization That Will Be "Aggressively Progressive", Belief

IN a signed editorial in his magazine today, Senator Robert M. La Follette repudiates the Republican party as a member of which he secured his election three times as governor of Wisconsin and twice as United States senator.

Interest in the editorial goes to the point of whether, when his term expires two years hence, Senator La Follette plans to retire, or whether he will seek re-election as a Republican, or as an independent.

It has been suggested that at that time La Follette may stand for election to the senate as the candidate of a new party of his own making, the presidential candidate of which he may aim to become in 1924.

WASHES HANDS OF PARTY

Senator La Follette seems fully to wash his hands of the "G. O. P." in the editorial, which begins with the declaration that "The two old parties have failed." If the old parties have failed, the only answer would seem to be a new party. That La Follette was ready to become the candidate of a new party this year had it been possible to form one on such broad lines and general principles as much underlie any successful national party, is sufficiently apparent.

For upwards of twenty years Senator La Follette has been holding before his followers the hope that eventually "representative government" would be restored through the agency of the Republican party. That he has abandoned this idea seems evident. That if health stays with him he will undertake the formation of a new party, if not in time for the congressional elections in 1922, at least before the presidential campaign four years hence, is the one reasonable deduction, for as one who believes in political parties the senator is undoubtedly awake to the inconsistency of seeking office under the label of a party which he has unconditionally repudiated.

WANTS AGGRESSIVE PARTY

"Popular government canont long endure in this country without an ag-

(Turn to page 4, column 3)

FIVE INJURED IN AUTO COLLISIONS

Two auto accidents in which 10 persons were either severly injured or badly shaken up occurred in Waunakee last night. As a result five of the participants are in the General hospital here today.

A car driven by Mike Silburn and son, William, of Wausau collided with a large machine containing five members of the family of Arthur Ellinson near the schoolhouse in Waunakee, demolishing both cars. B. Billig, Madison, who recently lost a limb here when he was struck by a train, and who had just been discharged from the General hospital, was in the Silburn car. He received severe bruises and was brought to Madison last night. Mrs. Ellinson and son, Arthur, received minor injuries and were also brought to the General hospital.

Oscar Simon, son of Mike Simon, and Lawrence Taylor joyrided into the iron bridge near the malt house in Waunakee last night. Simon is in the General hospital here suffering contusions of the chest, face and limb.

MINE WORKERS IN STRIKE THREAT

NEW YORK—A report is current here that the United Mine Workers of America have threatened a general strike unless the car assignment order of the Interstate Commerce commission is rescinded. Under the order, cars would be assigned to mines capable of greatest immediate production. The miners claim this would throw thousands of miners out of work at the mines discriminated against.

HARDING TO TALK IN BIGGER CITIES

COLUMBUS, O.—Senator Harding will speak in several of the larger cities of the country, but he will not make a "barn storming tour." Will H. Hays, chairman of the Republican national committee, said.

After a conference of the Republican campaign committee here, Hays indicated that Harding might speak both on the Pacific and Atlantic coasts.

The committee adopted a resolution urging Republicans in the Tennessee legislature to vote for suffrage ratification.

THREE KILLED IN BELFAST RIOTING

BELFAST—Rioting between unionists and Sinn Feiners was resumed here this afternoon.

The postoffice at Falls Road was wrecked during the fighting. Police fired on the rioters, wounding one soldier and several civilians.

Latest police advices said three persons have been killed, including one woman, more than 40 wounded dangerously and 50 wounded slightly. Property damage was estimated at $500,000.

Troops today erected barb wire barricades at different points in the city in an effort to restrict the rioting.

DUBLIN—Two officers and two soldiers were attacked by Sinn Feiners near Ennistimon today. Two of the attackers were shot dead and another fatally wounded.

REFERENDUM OF RAIL MEN SOUGHT

CONSERVATIVE UNION LEADERS WORK FOR UNANIMOUS AGREEMENT ON AWARDS

BULLETIN

WASHINGTON—Railroads presented today to the Interstate Commerce commission a schedule of rates aimed to raise $626,000,000 additional revenue to meet the wage award granted workers. The suggestions include: An increase of 20 per cent in passenger fares; an increase of 20 per cent on excess baggage rates and additional charges of 50 per cent for parlor and sleeping car privileges.

CHICAGO — Conservative railroad union leaders today worked to secure unanimous agreement of all unions to order a referendum vote on the acceptability of the awards announced Tuesday by the United States railroad labor wage board, as a compromise on the radical demand for flat rejection of the $600,000,000 increase.

Indications coming from the conferences of the three groups of railroad union leaders considering the award, were that the referendum would be ordered.

The three big groups meeting adjourned at noon, apparently as far from agreement as ever.

The men re-convened in 16 separate meetings to thresh out the referendum proposal.

The railroad labor board went into session today to consider demonds of expressmen.

SEVEN ACCEPT, REPORT

Seven railroad unions today were reported to have definitely accepted the wage award announced Tuesday by the United States railroad labor wage board.

The Order of Railway Telegraphers positively refused to consider the award, according to information today and an order for a strike vote was said to have been issued.

The Order of Railway Conductors early today had not determined its attitude.

Trainmen, Engineers, Switchmen, Shopmen, Locomotive Firemen and Enginemen and Mates and Pilots were the organizations said to have definitely accepted the award.

Rail union chiefs toay were confident sporadic strikes would not result. An unauthorized strike of employes of the Grand Trunk here last night was considered the result of local conditions.

HIGHER POSTAGE RATES?

WASHINGTON — The railroads may ask the interstate commerce commission for higher rates on mail transportation to help raise revenues to meet the $600,000,000 wages award, railroad executives meeting here said today.

At the postoffice department it was said that any increase in mail rates probably would result in higher postage charges.

SWITCHMEN STRIKE

DENVER, Colo.—About 50 Chicago, Burlington and Quincy switchmen here were on strike today in protest against the United States railroad labor board's wage award.

CIVIL POPULACE FLEEING WARSAW

BERLIN—The civil population of Warsaw has begun evacuation of the Polish capital, according to reports reaching here today. The Polish front wing apparently has crumpled and the bolshevik troops were reported pursuing the retreating Poles at a rate of 25 kilometers daily.

AMERICANS WARNED

PARIS—Upon the urgent advice of French military experts, all American relief workers have been ordered to hold themselves in readiness to quit Poland on an hour's notice.

HUNGARY OFFERS AID

PARIS—The Hungarian government has offered to extend military aid to the entente against the Russian bolshevik government, according to a dispatch from Budapest today.

GERMANY BARS TROOPS

BERLIN—Dr. Walter Von Simons, German foreign minister, today declared the German government would not consent to movement of allied troops through German territory for the assistance of Poland.

GOLF CHAMP ELIMINATED FOR TITLE

Madison Players Survive First Round of Championship Flight in Big State Tourney

FRIDAY'S PROGRAM

9 a. m.—Third round, championship, 8 players; semi-finals, President's trophy, 4 players; semi-finals, Vice President's trophy, 4 players; semi-finals, Director's trophy, 4 players.

10:30—Age limit (50)—18 holes, medal play, handicap.

11—Junior handicap—18 holes, medal play, handicap, for players under 18 years of age, open to sons of members of the Wisconsin State Golf association.

2 p. m.—Semi-finals, championship, 4 players.

3—Four-ball foursome, combined scores to court.

8—Annual meeting state golf association.

THE sensation of the state golf tourney here was the defeat of Ned Allis, III, of Milwaukee, 1919 state title holder, by W. D. Martin, Jr., of Kenosha, 18 years old, this morning in the first round for the championship flight by a score of two up. Martin has never participated in a championship contest before, his only appearance having been made in previous years in the father-and-son events. Allis is eliminated by his defeat from the second round which began at 2 this afternoon.

The morning was filled with surprises. One was the defeat by John S. Main, Madison, of H. S. Hadfield, Blue Mounds, three up and one to play. Main is matched this afternoon with Martin who defeated Allis. F. W. Jacobs and E. E. Parkinson are two Madison men who survived the championship flight this morning. For the Vice President's trophy, G. A. Bauman and Phil Sanborn susvived the morning's rounds.

Martin played splendid golf throughout. Allis was never in the lead although the score was even several times.

With the score one up in his favor, Martin, driving for the 17th hole, dropped the ball on the green 10 feet from the hole. Allis outdid him and dropped the ball four feet from the hole, but missed the putt and lost his chance to even the score.

Martin was two up at the end of the first eight holes. Allis took the ninth hole and finally evened the score at the 13th hole. Martin won the next and again was in the lead. After Allis failed to even at the 17th hole, Martin took the 18th, winning the match 2 up and eliminating the state champion from the contest.

Allis' medal score was 80, 41 out and 39 in. Martin's score was 79, 40 out and 39 in. Allis was slightly off color throughout the round.

The second round of the championship flight started at 2 this afternoon. The 32 contenders qualifying yesterday were reduced to 16 by the morning's events. The other events were participated in by 16 players this morning. The number in each event was reduced to eight for the second rounds this afternoon.

TODAY'S SCORES

The results of the first round of the championship flight were:

H. H. Rockwell, Beloit, defeated N. S. Lindsay, Milwaukee, by default.

W. D. Martin, Jr., Kenosha, defeated Ned Allis, Milwaukee, two up.

J. S. Main, Madison, defeated H. S. Hadfield, Blue Mound, three and one.

A. A. Jonas, Blue Mound, defeated K. L. Head, Michiwaukee, two and one.

Gordon Gilbert, Racine, defeated G. Lance, Kenosha, three and one.

R. Gelatt, La Crosse, defeated D. P. Wheeler, Madison, four and three.

Dave Foster, Beloit, defeated G. K. Carroll, Blue Mound, six and five.

A. M. Evans, Wausau, defeated K. Dickinson, Appleton, one up in 19 holes.

F. W. Jacobs, Madison, defeated P. M. Davis, Blue Mound, two and one.

C. Douglas, Green Lake, defeated V. A. C. Henmon, Madison, two up.

E. C. Parkinson, Madison, defeated J. B. Harris, Janesville, one up.

P. J. Dickinson, Appleton, defeated I. C. McLaughlin, Michiwaukee, one up.

C. C. Allen, Kenosha, defeated E. Niemeier, La Crosse, two and one.

R. Gordon, La Crosse, defeated G. W. Kent, Sheboygan, five and four.

George Van Auken, La Crosse, de-

(Turn to page 4, column 1)

SEAMAN TOSSES HAT INTO RING

MILWAUKEE—"In response to a generous call from Representative Republicans in all parts of the state, I hereby announce my candidacy for Republican nomination for governor at the September priamry," Col. Gilbert E. Seaman, endorsed by the "stalwart" Republican gathering recently at Madison and the "progressive" Republican gathering in Milwaukee, declared in a statement issued here today. Col. Seaman soon will announce the principles and purposes which, he said, will guide him in office.

REFORESTING NEED SEEN AS U. S. DUTY

Philipp Urges National Program at Laboratory Decennial; Birge Advocates Restricted Use of Wood

ADDRESSES by Gov. E. L. Philipp, president E. A. Birge of the university, and Director C. P. Winslow, opened the decennial celebration of the United States Forest Products laboratory at Agricultural hall today.

After luncheon at the gymnasium, the program continued with inspection of the laboratory and the exhibit of wood products and samples, followed by an automobile tour of the city, and boating and swimming.

Gov. Philipp related lumber history, showing the rapid deforestation of the country and the immediate need for reforestation.

NATIONAL OBLIGATION

"Private enterprise cannot be relied upon to replant our forests," he said. "The growth is too slow and substantial returns could not be expxecter for at least 50 years. As a state enterprise it is too costly and as the product will benefit the entire country it would be neither practical nor possible to tax the people of the state for a national benefit.

"The project of replanting our forests is essentially a national obligation and should be taken hold of in earnest by the national government.

"Lands not yet occupied by agriculture should be reserved for reforesting purposes, and replanting of cut over lands commenced. It should become a settled rule that wherever a tree is cut down a new tree be planted."

BIRGE URGES RESTRICTIONS

President Birge said the time is coming when the amount of timber we may use must be restricted to the annual increase. A program similar to that now applied to fish, whereby the fish supply is replenished by fish hatcheries must be put into practice with trees.

"The United States must very soon adopt the moral and legal restrictions placed on forests which Europe has followed for years," he said.

A quarter of a century from now the prosperity of the state will depend upon men trained in agricultural and forestry schools who dedicate the products of the human mind to development and preservation of nature and the world," he declared.

DEANS PLAN SCHOOL

Eight forestry deans of large universities are expected to attend a conference tomorrow afternoon to discuss plans for forming post graduate schools to train forestry graduates in use of wood products. The deans are C. C. Cory, California; R. S. Hosner, Cornell; E. G. Cheyney, Minnesota; F. F. Moon, Syracuse; H. Wrinkennerder, Washington; Prof. E. R. Mairrer, Wisconsin; J. W. Tomney, Yale, and Dr. J. E. Paul, Chicago.

Tonight there will be a banquet at the gymnasium, with talks by Burr W. Jones, C. F. Kettering, and Lieut. Col. W. B. Greeley.

NO OFFER MADE FOR STATE COURT

"No offer has been made to anyone," was the answer today from the executive office in reply to an inquiry regarding the statement in a Madison morning paper that U. S. Circuit Judge Martin L. Lueck was to be appointed by Gov. E. L. Philipp to the Wisconsin supreme court to fill the vacancy created by the death of Chief Justice J. B. Winslow. Judge Lueck's name has been presented to the governor, but no action has been taken.

CHILD HEIR TO 60 BARRELS BOOZE

CLEVELAND, O.—Sherman Goodfriend is only two years old and therefore can't realize what it means to be the owner of 60 barrels of 100 proof whisky. His fathers' will filed in the probate court here today, wills him the liquor. The will stipulates that the liquor shall be sold and the proceeds held in trust for Sherman until he reaches the age of 21. Attorneys said the law prevents the sale of whisky in its present state.

SOUTH ROCKFORD VENDETTA RAGES

ROCKFORD, Ill.—The murder of Joe Mascoli in South Rockford last night was called a vendetta killing today by Charlie Boscio, confessed murderer of Frank Ferrance, South Beloit. Boscio said both murders were vendetta affairs and asserted others were to follow. Masoli's body was found in front of a church with 17 stiletto wounds in it.

MUST SAFEGUARD U. S., IS STAND OF HARDING

MARION, O.—Following is a summary of Senator Harding's speech accepting the Republican presidential nomination:

LEAGUE OF NATIONS: The league covenant was conceived for world super government, negotiated in misunderstanding, and intolerantly demanded by its administration sponsors, who resisted every effort to safeguard America and rejected it when these safeguards were inserted. The party means to hold America unimpaired and unsurrendered, but not aloof. America aspires to and the Republican party is committed to an association of nations co-operating to preserve through justice rather than force. No surrender of rights to a world council or its military alliance or any assumed mandatory shall summon American youths to war, and the Republican party welcomes a referendum to the people.

FORMAL PEACE: Formal and effective peace *is* promised as quickly as a Republican congress can pass its declaration and a Republican executive sign.

INTERNATIONAL RELATIONS: With the senate advising, all nations would be approached with proposals for a new relationship to commit the moral forces of the world, America included, to peace and justice, still leaving America free and independent.

MEXICO: Relations with Mexico should be friendly and sympathetic with a plain and neighborly understanding about protecting the border and lives and property of Americans in Mexico. Without this understanding which must be faithfully kept, there can be no recognition.

MUST ENFORCE LAW

PROHIBITION: There is divided opinion respecting the Eighteenth amendment and the law making it operative, but there can be no difference of opinion about honest law enforcement. Modification or repeal is the right of a free people, but we cannot nullify because of divided opinion.

PARTY GOVERNMENT: Masterful leadership may becoming manifest its influence, but a people's will remains the supreme authority. No man is big enough to run the republic. Party sponsorship in government as distinguished from personal, individual, dictatorial or autocratic government. During the war autocracy was established in the name of Democracy and the first committal is for restoration of representative popular government under the constitution through the agency of the Republican party. A cabinet of the highest capacity with the vice president participating, and cordial co-ordination between the two houses of congress is promised.

UNREST: The world is in revolution and agents of discord hope to see America part of the great red conflagration. America must not only save herself, but must be the voice to sober the world. The individual must submit to the will of the majority. This movement is not to be halted through liberties and we must not abridge the freedom of speech, press or assembly which are as sacred as religious belief. But the right to crush sedition, stifle contempt for law, stamp out peril to the republic is insisted on as the first essential of liberty. American government contemplates orderly changes as the majority thinks best, but no authority shall abridge the rights of the minority and men have a right to question the system in the fullest freedom, always remembering that the rights of freedom impose the obligations which maintain it.

HUMAN ELEMENT FIRST

LABOR: Higher wages should continue, but the wage earner must give full value for the wage received. No conflict of interests in industry is recognized. The human element comes first. Employers should understand the yearnings of wage earners and wage earners should understand the problems of capital. Collective bargaining is approved as outstanding right but if exercised must not destroy the sacred right of the individual. Strikes against the government are properly denied, but any American has the right to quit his employment just as he has a right to seek it.

HIGH COST OF LIVING: No one remedy can be promised. Patriotic production, economy, denial and sacrifice are urged. An intelligent and courageous deflation of the currency is promised, together with sincere efforts to strike at government borrowing and the high cost of government. Prevention of unreasonable profits is promised and profiteering will be challenged with all the legal and moral powers of government and the people.

RAILROADS AND TRANSPORTATION: Present railroad inefficiencies due to the withering hand of government operation and opposition to government ownership is re-affirmed.

The government which must play its part in restoration. Returns must be so gauged to enlist necessary capital and we must foster as well as restrain. Development of highways with federal co-operation is indorsed and development of internal waterways as well as free use of the Panama canal for American shipping is urged.

NEW FARM PROGRAM

AGRICULTURE: A new and forward looking program is called for. Farmers should be encouraged to join co-operative organizations to market their products and agriculture should be encouraged. Reclamation and irrigation should go forward with federal aid.

TARIFF: Belief in protective tariff is asserted and its saving Americanism will be called for again.

BUDGET—The budget will affect a necessary and helpful reformation and federal departments should be more businesslike, and return thousands of employes back to productive work.

MERCHANT MARINE: America should be the leading maritime nation of the world and the government should aid in expanding trade abroad both in revealing markets and speeding cargoes.

PREPAREDNESS: The navy should be ample for protection and able to assure dependable defense. The army should be small, but the best in the world with a mindfulness for preparedness that will avoid the unutterable cost of our previous neglect.

IMMIGRATION: Standards should be with a view to future citizenship and every man who becomes a citizen must become an American heart and soul.

CHILD LABOR: Every forward step in unshackling child labor should be held and conditions of woman's employment be elevated.

EX SERVICE MEN: They have our gratitude which must have genuine expression. The sacrifices made should be requited and those still suffering disabilities should be abundantly aided.

SUFFRAGE: It is earnestly desired that the suffrage amendment be ratified. All women are urged to accept the responsibilities that suffrage will bring.

TAXATION: War taxes must be revised to meet peace needs and in the interest of equity and distribution of the burden.

LIBERTL BONDS: The government should make Liberty and Victory bonds worth all the citizens paid in purchasing them.

LYNCHING: The federal government should stamp out lynching, and negro citizens should be guaranteed enjoyment of rights.

U. S. TO ROUND UP DRAFT DODGERS

BY A. L. BRADFORD

WASHINGTON — A nation-wide round-up of more than 100,000 draft deserters will be started soon by the war department as a final effort to bring to justice men who failed to answer the call to America's draft army during the war, Adjutant General Peter O. Harris said today.

The war department has been preparing a mammoth list of names of men who can be classed as actual draft deserters. This list is estimated to contain names of 100,000.

The final list of draft deserters will be published as the first step.

Fifty dollars reward will be offered for delivery of a deserter.

Every man of the war department's "slacker list" will be subject to military court martial, General Harris said.

FOE ASKS LEAVE TO RESIST REDS

PARIS—Germany yesterday formally submitted a request to the allied governments for permission to mass troops at and around the Baltic port of Memel, to resist an invasion by the soviet forces which the note says is believed to be impending. The German note said the communist elements in Germany were becoming increasingly strong, and that a "barrier of bayonets" was necessary to prevent establishment of soviet rule in Germany.

MINNIE HAD TAKING WAYS

MEMPHIS—Minnie Cherry is a "champion clothes thief," the cops here allege. Minnie, so they say, hired out to four families within a month and each time left with a greatly enlarged wardrobe. She's awaiting trial.

NEW DEAL FOR PEACE IS KEYNOTE

League Covenant Is Scored by Republican Presidential Candidate as "Supreme Blunder"

Senator Harding's speech in full, accepting the Republican nomination, will be found on page 6.

By RAYMOND CLAPPER

MARION, Ohio—Immediate declaration of peace and a new effort to form an association of all nations, based on justice rather than force, was promised by Warren G. Harding, formally accepting the Republican presidential nomination here today.

Scoring the league of nations covenant as the "supreme blunder," he lauded the senators who opposed its unequalified ratification as "sentinels on the towers of constitutional government." The nominee was silent regarding ratification of the treaty or the league in case he is elected. However, he said, he welcomed a referendum.

Harding opened his address with a broadside at "personal, dictatorial and autocratic government." He said "no man is big enought to run this great republic."

"Our first committal," he continued, "is the restoration of representative popular government under the constitution through the agency of the Republican party."

THOUSANDS HEAR SPEECH

The speech, delivered at Garfield park here in the presence of thousands assembled from all corners of the nation, dealt with a multitude of questions.

As to formal peace, Senator Harding said:

"I promise you formal and effective peace so quickly as a Republican congress can pass its declaration for a Republican executive to sign."

LODGE PRAISES HARDING

Henry Cabot Lodge, in his speech notifying Senator Harding, denounced the League of Nations covenant as submitted by the president as "another name for the evil combination which was attempted a hundred years ago by the illomened Holy Alliance."

Lodge spoke at length on the league question, and praised Harding for his conspicuous part in the league as written.

After being serenaded by the Columbus Glee clug, Senator Harding introduced to its members Col Theodore Roosevelt, Jr., who has just arrived on the front porch. "We are going to roll it up bigger than ever before" shouted young Teddy at the conclusion of a brief speech.

The McKinley club of Canton following shortly thereafter, was the only delegation to appear in frock coats and black silk hats.

Just before noon some 2,000 members of various organizations from Cleveland, led by the Woman's Republican League of Cleveland, marched past the house. The senator and Mrs. Harding waved their greetings.

WOMEN CARRY OUT PROGRAM

Militant suffragists swooped down on Senator Harding today somewhat piqued because the candidate issued his appeal for action on suffrage by the Tennessee legislature on the eve of their arrival. Militants had not counted on this sudden move by Harding, but they went through with their program and asked the candidate to use his influence for ratification.

One hundred women, members of the national woman's party, representing 15 states, marched in procession to Harding's front porch. Mrs. Bertha C. Moller of Minneapolis was in charge.

Miss Sue White, Tennessee, state chairman of the national woman's party, and Mrs. H. O. Havemeyer, New York, were speakers.

CALLS G. O. P. SLOW

Mrs. Havemeyer scored the Republican party as being slow in securing ratification.

"We need a thirty-sixth state and it seems as if it as impossible for us to attain it as it was for the children of Israel to enter the promised land," she said.

The suffragists arrived shortly before ten o'clock dressed in white and carrying their purple, white and yellow banners. After they had formed a semi-circle at the steps of the front porch Senator Harding came out and listened attentively to the speeches. He declined to make extended reply, explaining that his attitude on suffrage would be set forth in his acceptance speech.

Anticipating the call of the woman's party delegation Senator Harding last night sent a telegram to Mrs. Carrie Chapman Catt, president of the national American woman's suffrage association now in Nashville, saying: "If any of the Republican members of the Tennessee assembly should ask my opinion, I would cordially recommend immediate favorable action."

It was a great day for Harding's home town. From all over Ohio, and from many districts outside of Ohio, the pilgrims came. They poured out of every train and moved in cheering detachments through gaily decorated streets toward the Harding home on Mount Vernon avenue for a glimpse of the candidate before going to to Garfield Park, where the formal notification ceremonies were to take place at 2 p. m.

FINAL EDITION

The Wisconsin State Journal

4 P.M. EXTRA

VOL. 126, NO. 36. 84th Year MADISON, WEDNESDAY, NOVEMBER 5, 1924 PRICE THREE CENTS

COOLIDGE IS GIVEN 379 VOTES

Daggett New Sheriff, Sachtjen Winner

LA FOLLETTE, BLAINE LEAD BY 50,000

Two Women Killed, One By Car, Other By Blast

Entire Ticket Wins Sweeping State Victory

Senator Sets Pace For Coolidge With 209,434 Votes; Receives Fewer Votes Than In 1922

MILWAUKEE—With more than half of the state's 2,681 precincts reported, Senator Robert M. La Follette was leading President Coolidge in Wisconsin by more than 50,000 votes.

The vote in 1,411 precincts of the state gave:

La Follette 209,434; Coolidge 156,522; Davis 33,409.

The vote for governor in 1,279 precincts: Blaine 156,544; Lueck, 117,891.

With La Follette's sweeping victory in Wisconsin, the entire state ticket which he had endorsed appears also to have been elected by a large majority.

Henry Huber, republican, was far out in front of his seven opponents for lieutenant governor, with Karl Mathie, democrat, running second.

Fred R. Zimmerman, republican, was well in the lead in his race with four opponents for secretary of state. John M. Callahan, democrat, was second.

Solomon Levitan, republican, apparently was having little trouble winning over his four opponents in the contest for state treasurer.

Herman L. Ekern, republican, was leading his four opponents in the attorney general race, with J. A. Simpson, second.

Both La Follette and Blaine ran far behind the majorities they piled up in the election two years ago. Senator La Follette in his last race for the senatorship received 379,494 votes against 63,818 for Mrs. Jessie Jack Hooper. Blaine at the same time received 367,929 votes against 51,929.

The present election will give both

(Turn to page 12, column 1)

GUILTY OF ASSAULT; FINE AND COSTS

Arnold De Vries was found guilty of assault and battery today in Judge O. A. Stolen's superior court, and was fined $10 and costs. The compainant, represented by Attorney Henry Casson, was R. Knoff, also of Madison.

WEATHER

Unsettled tonight and Thursday; probably rain turning to snow flurries. Much colder. Strong shifting winds becoming south west.

Official Report by U. S. Weather Bureau

City	Temperature Highest Yesterday	Temperature Lowest Last night	Precipitation 24 hours to 7 a. m.
Madison	50	39	
Milwaukee	46	42	
Chicago	48	48	
Green Bay	48	38	
Wausau	46	36	
Duluth	42	28	
Minneapolis	50	40	

MADISON WEATHER

Yesterday	Temperature	Relative Humidity	Wind Velocity	Cloudiness
Noon	42	50	3	20
7 p. m.	45	50	7	80
Today:				
7 a. m.	45	70	12	70

Highest temperature 50 at 2 p. m.

Lowest temperature 39 at 12 m.

Mean temperature yesterday 42; normal 41.

Total precipitation since Jan. 1. 28.63 in. Normal 28.42.

Sun rises at 6:35; sets 4:45.

TODAY IN OTHER YEARS

Warmest in 1895, 66.

Coldest in 1901, 16.

Wettest in 1882, 1.07 inches.

La Follette In Rally Cry, to New Fight

SENATOR Robert M. La Follette today called upon progressives to "close ranks and gird themselves for the next battle."

He declared they will not be dismayed by the landslide for Coolidge.

"We have not been defeated, but overwhelmed for the time being by the use of slush funds, intimidation, technical obstruction, and abuse of power in securing a place for independent electors on the ballot and in the count and return of votes," the Wisconsin senator said in his first comment upon the election.

"The election of Calvin Coolidge by a landslide is apparent from the returns now in. The American people have chosen to retain in power the reactionary republican administration with its record of corruption and subservience to the dictates of organized monopoly.

"The progressives will not be dismayed by this result. We have just begun to fight. There can be no compromise on the fundamental issues for which we stand. The loss of this one battle in the age-long struggle of the masses against the privileged few is but an incident.

"Until more complete returns are available, it is impossible to forecast what the reaction of this result will be upon the progressives with regard to the future. But insofar as I am personally concerned, I am enlisted for life in the struggle to break the combined power of the private monopoly system over government and to restore it to the people."

PLEAD NOT GUILTY TO SHOPLIFTING; DOPE TO COURT

The three alleged shop-lifters arrested Monday by police, entered pleas of not guilty when arraigned before Superior Judge O. A. Stolen.

Max Hernzon, Mrs. Fred Andrews and Mrs. Anna West were the names given police by the trio, who claim Green Bay as their home. Bail of $2,500 was required of each, and hearings will be held Thursday.

All of the evidence held by the police, including an opium pipe set, a quantity of the drug and several articles of clothing alleged to have been stolen from a local store, were ordered turned over to the court.

DETROIT RIOTS PUT TWO IN HOSPITAL

DETROIT—Two election rioe s just before the polls closed caused two men to go to the hospital and several to be placed under arrest. Police reserves were called to both riots. In one riot a patrolman and a bystander were both stabbed in the legs, while two persons fought n the streets. It was a fight between adherents of two mayorality factions, one of whom is said to have Ku Klux Klan backing.

SELL ENTIRE STOCK FOR CATHOLIC CLUB

Announcement of the sale of the entire subscription of stock for the new Catholic Community house was made at the meeting of the Knights of Columbus noon-day luncheon club today. The amount of the subscription totaled $125,000. The articles of incorporation were read, and plans are now being made for erection of the building in the Spring.

The plans for the entertainment of the Notre Dame team are being enlarged to include ceveral notable men.

Trigger of Gun Bumped on Step, Shell Exploded

Sun Prairie And Jim Town Women Victims Of Accidents; Probe Ordered

SUN PRAIRIE—Mrs. Katherine Kuhle, who was knocked down by a car just as she alighted from another, Monday afternoon, died early this morning at a Madison hospital.

Herman Hermanson was driving the car which ran into Mrs. Kuhle. His car was behind her machine and both were headed toward Madison. Mrs. Kuhle was stopping in front of the home of a sister, and Hermanson was apparently unable to stop when she got in the path of his car.

A son, about ten years old, and several brothers and sisters survive Mrs. Kuhle. Her husband died several years ago. She was 40 years old.

GUN KILLS WOMAN AIDING HUSBAND

By Staff Correspondent of The Journal

RICHLAND CENTER—Mrs. Hollie Chitwood was accidentally killed Tuesday afternoon when a shotgun she was carrying exploded as she set it down, and blew her head off.

Mr. Chitwood, working on the road near his father's farm at Jim Town, saw a squirrel and shouted to his wife to bring his gun. As she was returning it to the house she laid it upon the steps of the porch and the contact released the trigger.

Sheriff Zietzman and Coroner J. T. Bolto were summoned. An inquest will be held today. Mrs. Chitwood is survived by her husband and two children.

SAUTHOFF HIGHLY ENDORSED FOR POST

Although entiely unopposed, Harry Sauthoff, republican, was given a big endorsement for the state senate. Mr. Sauthoff was opposed early in the primary campaign by the Rev. O. H. J. Preus, De Forest, but shortly before election Mr. Preus withdrew from the race. Mr. Sauthoff will succeed Senator Henry A. Huber, Stoughton, who was elected lieutenant governor Tuesday.

OHIO CASTS LARGEST VOTE FOR PRESIDENT

COLUMBUS, O.—Ohio gave President Coolidge the largest vote accorded a presidential candidate, incomplete returns indicated today, but the Coolidge landslide was insufficient to carry Harry L. Davis, republican, into the governorship and Vic Donahey, democrat, appears to be reelected.

United Press reports from 5,191 of Ohio's 8,500 precincts gave Donahey 583,929 and Davis 516,645.

The presidential vote in 5,390 precincts was: Coolidge 701,902; Davis 284,929; La Follette 247,920.

ERICKSON FINED FOR DRIVING WHILE DRUNK

Melvin Erickson was fined $50 and costs today in superior court after pleading guilty to driving his car while drunk. In addition, Erickson was placed on probation and forbidden to drive his car for six months.

Burmeister Is Loser by 3,000, Count Reveals

G. O. P. Candidates For Sheriff And Assembly Easy Victors; McDonald Behind

BY HENRY NOLL

JOSEPH DAGGETT, republican candidate for sheriff, and Herman W. Sachtjen, republican candidate for member of the assembly in the first district, were swept into office by the largest pluralities ever given aspirants for those positions at the Tuesday election.

Seventy-one out of 77 precincts give Daggett a lear of 3,818 over Otto H. Burmeister, independent. Daggett polled a total of 17,763 votes while 13,945 votes were recorded for Burmeister. William P. Whalen, democrat, received 4,349 votes. Returns from the missing precincts probably will swell Daggett's majority to more than 4,000 votes.

Sachtjen made a surprisingly big run. Final returns place him in the lead with 4,937 votes to the good. Of the 20,075 cast for assemblyman in the first district Sachtjen received 11 219. James J. McDonald, independent, 6,282. J. H. Bowman, democrat, 2,574.

The overwhelming results have proved again what has been established before that it is impossible for an independent candidate for county or legislative office in Dane county to win.

Both Messrs. Burmeister and McDonald conducted vigorous campaigns.

In Stoughton Daggett led Burmeister by a small majority, the vote being 873 to 821. Whalen got 145 votes.

All of Daggett's associates on the republican county ticket went into office with big majorities over their democratic opponents.

May Be Speaker

Election of Mr. Sachtjen from the first assembly district for the third consecutive time makes him a formidable candidate for speaker of the lower house.

It is understood besides being the candidate of Gov. John J. Blaine, he is also the chief executive's choice for the speakership. Clinton G. Price, Wausau, is also a candidate for the speakership.

According to friends of Mr. Sachtjen he will resign as state prohibition commissioner the first of the year.

The wet and dry issue was an important factor in the campaign between Mr. Sachtjen and Mr. McDonald.

Although it had been predicted that

(Turn to page 12, column 7)

Buy Alcohol For Radiator Today; Bad Weather On Its Way

BUY alcohol for your radiator today in order to avoid the rush Thursday, for the following day will see real football weather, with snow flurries and everything, is the friendly tip the official weather predictor of the United States weather bureau gave the motor editor of The Wisconsin State Journal today. Fearing to break the news too abruptly, the weather man hinted that the cold weather would advance slowly, and it would not be unpleasantly cold until Friday.

The Smile of Victory

The Winners

President—Calvin Coolidge.
Vice President — Charles G. Dawes.
Governor—John J. Blaine.
Lieut. Gov.—Henry Huber.
Secy. of State—Fred R. Zimmerman.
State Treasurer—Sol Levitan.
Attorney General—Herman Ekern.
Congressman—John M. Nelson.
State Senator—Harry Sauthoff.
Assemblyman—Herman Sachtjen.
Sheriff—Joe Daggett.
District Attorney—Philip La Follette.

WOMEN TO FILL 2 STATE CHAIRS

Mrs. Rose Elected In Wyoming; "Ma" Ferguson's Foe Charges Ballots Ousted

CHEYENNE, Wyo.—Mrs. Nellie T. Ross has been elected governor of Wyoming by a majority of 5,000 votes over her republican opponent, Eugene J. Sullivan, according to claims of the democratic state committee on incomplete returns today.

AUSTIN, Tex.—Dr. George Butte, republican candidate for governor in Texas, in refusing to concede the election of Mrs. Miriam Ferguson, today charged that ballots had been thrown out at the polls. Butte declared today he would demand an investigation. Mrs. Ferguson continued to hold a lead of approximately 34,000 votes.

BROOKHART HITS POLITICAL SKIDS

Trails Democrat In Iowa Returns; Magnus Johnson Trailing In Minnesota

DES MOINES, Ia—Iowa was practically assured this afternoon of having a democratic member in the United States senate for the next six years.

Late returns failed to shake the early lead guarnered by Daniel Steck, democrat, who is running against Senator Smith W. Brookhart, republican.

Returns to the United Press from 1,771 precincts out of 2,418 in the state gave Seck 331,064; Brookhart 315,743.

Senator Brookhart, however, refused to concede the election to his democratic opponent. In a statement to the United Press over long distance telephone from Washington, Ia., Brookhart said he would hold out hope for reelection until the last precinct was heard from."

President Coolidge has the 13 electoral votes of Iowa. Returns from 1603 precincts give Coolidge 364,420; Davis 99,301; La Follette 178,821.

All of the republican congressional candidates were leading their opponents by comfortable majorities.

JOHNSON BEHIND

ST. PAUL—In 1,436 precincts, Thomas D. Schall was leading Magnus Johnson for United States senate. Schall had 187,701 and Johnson 175,307.

The driver honked to demand the whole of the road. "Now you're Teuton!" cried the passenger.

Missouri, Long Doubtful, Hops on G.O.P. Wagon

Landslide For President Fails To Check Election Of Al Smith And Gov. Donahey, Both Democrats

By ROBERT J. BENDER
United Press Staff Correspondent

NEW YORK—Coolidge 379; Davis 139; La Follette 13.

With the possible exception of a switch of New Mexico's three votes from Davis to Coolidge, this will be the standing of the presidential candidates in the electoral college when final tabulations are in.

New Mexico, where the count always is slow, the democrats waged a strong fight against "Fall rule" and the stigma imposed upon the former secretary of the interior by the oil scandal was expected on the face of early returns to defeat President Coolidge in the state.

Missouri For Coolidge

Of the other doubtful commonwealths, Missouri turned definitely into the Coolidge column today, after wavering throughout the night; and in Montana, where Senator La Follette was making a strong bid for the electoral votes, the day's tabulations showed steadily increasing margins for President Coolidge.

PROGRESSIVES CARRY DANE

Incomplete returns today showed that the La Follette-Wheeler ticket carried Dane county over Coolidge and Dawes two to one. Forty-six precincts out of 77 give the La Follette-Wheeler ticket 22,135 and Coolidge and Dawes 11,743, giving the former a lead of 10,392.

A poor showing was made by Davis and Bryan, democratic candidates, who only polled 2,009 votes in the same precincts.

With the presidency settled, chief interest centered in the complexion of the next congress. The house is assuredly safely in Coolidge's hands, with material republican gainn, three of them in Davis' home state of West Virginia.

The senate, however, is still in doubt.

"Al" Smith Wins

Great as were Coolidge's pluralities, however, he was unable to prevent the victory of two popular democratic state executives—Gov. Vic Donahey of Ohio and Gov. Al. Smith of New York. Coolidge failed to measure up to Warren G. Harding's landslide in New York four years ago, but it was an overwhelming victory nevertheless in the Empire state and that Smith should be returned by nearly 200,000 majority despite it, testified to the latter's tremendous popularity.

Donahey's reelection despite the Coolidge sweep in Ohio was less imposing, but equally striking.

In states where the democrats or independents sought to make the Ku Klux Klan an issue, they were beaten with apparently but one exception. Texas, according to late returns, has elected "Ma" Ferguson governor. She made her campaign against the klan. The fate of Ed Jackson, republican candidate for governor in Indiana, also is somewhat in doubt. Jackson was defined as the klan candidate during the Hoosier campaign.

Tennessee, Kentucky Flop

On the face of the tabulations early today, there were two flops in normally democratic states that dem-

(Turn to Page 14, Column 1)

The Wisconsin State Journal
A Fact-Finding Newspaper

VOL. 130, NO. 51. 88th Year. MADISON, SATURDAY, MAY 21, 1927 FOURTEEN PAGES PRICE THREE CENTS

Lindbergh Makes Hop to Paris

Lone Pilot Wings Way to Goal After Crossing Atlantic

By A. L. BRADFORD
United Press Staff Correspondent

LE BOURGET FIELD, France — Captain Charles Lindbergh, the flying mail man, arrived to day by air from New York at 10:21 Paris time.

He was the first man every to fly from New York to Paris and as the wheels of Lindberg's monoplane touched the ground the dream of airmen that the North American and European continents should be linked in non-stop in airplane flight was realized.

Lindberg arrived at 5:21 p. m. eastern daylight time after 33 1-2 hours in the air on the flight of approximately 3,600 miles by way of the New England coast, Nova Scotia and New Foundland.

By UNITED PRESS

CHERBOURG, France—At 3:30 p. m. Eastern daylight saving time, a monoplane believed to have been that of Capt. Charles Lindbergh flew over here at a great height in the direction of Paris.

PASSES OVER PLYMOUTH, ENGLAND

LONDON—(UP)—The admiralty tonight announced receipt of a message from Admiral Bentinck that an airplane passed over Plymouth, Eng., at 2:40 p. m., Eastern daylight saving time, flying south-southeast at an altitude of 6,000 to 8,000 feet. The message said "the nationality of the plane was unknown, but it was presumed to have been Lindbergh's".

ALL PARIS PRAYING HE'LL WIN

PARIS—(UP)—All Europe today awaited news that Charles Lindbergh, the lone flier, had won. It was expected Lindbergh would arrive here from New York between 7 and 9 p. m. tonight, French daylight time. That would be between 2 and 4 p. m. Eastern daylight time.

Having recovered from the first shock of amazement that any man would attempt what Lindbergh was expected to achieve today, American residents in Paris from Gen. John J. Pershing and Ambassador Myron T. Herrick down to the flapper tourists were rooting for him to win.

"Four sandwiches in his plane and only a couple hours sleep before he started," exclaimed a youth of unmistakably American environment. "My Gawd!"

That more or less suggests the attitude of Paris in general toward the unassuming daring of Lindbergh.

Log of Flight

Time given is eastern daylight saving:

7:51 1-5 a. m. Friday—Took off at Roosevelt Field, N. Y.

9:05 a. m.—Passed E[illegible] Greenwich, R. I.

9:15 a. m.—West Middleboro, Mass.

9:40 a. m.—Halifax, Mass.

12:45 p. m.—Cape St. Mary, Nova Scotia.

1:05 p. m.—Springfield, Annapolis county, Nova Scotia.

1:50 p. m.—Milford, Hants county, Nova Scotia.

4 p. m.—Main Adlen, Nova Scotia—l[illegible] time seen on North American mainland.

4:05 p. m.—Mulgrave, between mainland and Cape Breton Island.

7:15 p. m. [illegible] Johns, Newfoundland—last time seen over land in the western hemisphere.

12:40 a. m. Saturday—Empress of Scotland at latitude 49.24, longitude 43.72, reported it saw plane believed to be Lindbergh's.

6:30 a. m.—Reported from an unnamed ship that Lindbergh was sighted 200 miles off Ireland.

9:40 a. m. (Approximate)—Plane which might be Lindbergh's sighted over Valentia, Ireland.

12:20 P. M.—Plane reported sighted over Smerwich Harbor, Ireland.

12:50 P. M.—Report by way of London says plane passed over Golee, 60 miles from Smerwich Harbor.

2:40 P. M.—Reported seen at Plymouth, England.

8 P. M.—Reported as passing Star Point, England.

8:20 p. m.—Reported passing Cherbourg, France.

London Unable to Give Information

LONDON—(UP)—The British air ministry this afternoon said it had no reports of Charles Lindbergh's airplane being sighted, denying rumors that British airplanes were escorting him across the English channel. The air ministry said no orders had been given for such an escort.

Favorable Wind Blowing in France

LE [illegible] [illegible]nce—(UP)—A 30-mile an hour wind was blowing here today and the skies were cloudy, but conditions were not such as to deter Capt. Charles Lindbergh if he wants to enter France over this port. The wind was west-northwest and would help the flier toward Paris.

Pinedo Starts Hop to Azores Tonight

TREPASSEY, N. F.—(UP)—Francesco de Pinedo, Italian four-continent flyer, planned to depart at sunset tonight on a 1,600 mile flight over the Atlantic to the Azores Island.

Lenroot's Daughter Undergoes Operation

WASHINGTON, D. C.—Miss Katherine Lenroot, of Superior, assistant chief of the children's bureau, department of labor, and daughter of former Senator Irvine L. Lenroot, underwent an operation for appendicitis here Friday. Miss Lenroot today was reported doing well.

Two Deny Sun Prairie Charges of Larceny

Ernest Moen and Kenneth Moen, arrested in Sun Prairie by Cal Strohmenger, marshall, pleaded not guilty in superior court this morning of larceny. The pair is charged with stealing two tires from John Rene and Ernest Budich, both of Sun Prairie. They were held on $500 bail each for trial May 23.

Mob Beats Three In Building Row

Memorial Union Scene of Battle Between Workers

Structure Damaged, Contractors Claim; Ink Discolors Stones; Roberts to Investigate

BY ELGAR A. BROWN

FANNED by Contractor Jacob Pfeffer's flat rejections of compromise proposals in the Memorial Union building strike, flames of dissension between union men and strike breakers burst forth with renewed fury at the building site Friday night and left behind a tr[illegible] of wreckage.

By far the most furious and devastating demonstration yet recorded in the history of the present controversy occurred when 200 union men marched enmasse down Park street, deployed through the four-acre tract, routed 15 non-union carpenters from their quarters, drubbed and manhandled half a dozen of them and demolished their frame shack.

Ink Causes Damage

Bottles of ink, hurled against the Bedford sandstone front of the new Memorial Union building and penetrating to a depth of nearly an inch, caused most extensive damage. About 20 stones must be replaced to eradicate the stains, a sub-contractor said this morning, and workers expressed belief that two large sections of the front part of the structure must be torn down in order to take out these stones.

A pile of sandstone columns as yet unplaced, located at the rear of the building, was similarly damaged.

Plans Investigation

District Attorney Glenn Roberts will conduct a thorough investigation of the disturbances Friday night, he declared this morning. He indicated he would enlist the aid of police and would hold John Doe hearings if necessary to ascertain the facts and place the responsibility.

Mr. Roberts left the city at noon for a week-end trip without announcing whether he will take action against Mr. Pfeffer, as requested by union men, for alleged violation of a state law prohibiting transportation of workmen to a job without notifying them of the existence of a strike.

With black eyes and bruised faces, nearly all of the 21 non-union men chased from the grounds Friday night returned to the scene this morning, some of them intending to go to work. All activities had ceased, however, and it was declared probable construction would be held up pending an inspection of the damage by insurance appraisers.

Union pickets were watching the strike-breakers from the steps of the historical library building this

(Turn to Page 6, Col. 3)

Weather

(Official Report by U. S. Weather Bureau)

Local showers and thunderstorms probable in northern and extreme eastern Wisconsin tonight. Fresh to strong southerly winds.

City	Temperature Highest Yesterday	Lowest Last Night	Precipitation 24 hours to 7 a. m.
Madison ..	58	50	.45
Milwaukee	50	44	.16
Chicago...	62	50	.22
Green Bay	58	46	.20
Wausau...	50	42	.12
Duluth....	40	36	.92
Minn'polis	48	44	1.00
La Crosse.	54	50	.22
Dubuque..	60	56	.46

MADISON WEATHER

Yesterday	Temperature	Relative Humidity	Wind Velocity	Cloudiness
Noon ...	55	63	16	100
7 p. m...	50	85	20	90
Today:				
7 a. m...	64	84	10	30
Noon ...	79	59	22	10

Highest temperature: 58 at 11 a. m.
Lowest temperature: 50 at 7 p. m.
Mean temperature: 50. Normal: 59.
Total precipitation since Jan. 1: 10 inches. Normal 9.95 inches.
Sun rises at 4:28; sets 7:24.

TODAY IN OTHER YEARS
Warmest in 1921: 86.
Coldest in 1883: 32.
Wettest in 1917: .92 inches.

SPEEDER FINED $15

H. D. Dudley was fined $15 in superior court this morning for speeding. S. Blancoe and B. J. Miller were each fined $1 for violating traffic regulations.

Will's Praying for Lindbergh

CONCORD, N. H.—No attempt at jokes today.

A slim, tall, bashful, smiling American boy is somewhere out over the middle of the Atlantic ocean, where no lone human being has ever ventured before. He is being prayed for to every kind of Supreme Being that has a following. If he is lost, it will be the most universally regretted single loss we ever had.

But that kid ain't going to fail, and what could be better to celebrate his arrival tha[illegible] another donation [illegible] over 600,000 of our very own, who are not even fortunate enough to be flying over water, but have to stand huddled upon the banks and look into it as it washes away their lifetime's work. They didn't even have enough to buy a paper to know that he had gone.

Nothing would please him better than for you to help them in his honor, for he comes from the banks of the Mississippi and he knows what it can do.

**Yours,
WILL ROGERS.**

Wright Alimony Hearing Delayed

Goes Over to Thursday With Examination on Property Status

The adverse examination of Frank Lloyd Wright, scheduled to be held at 10 o'clock this morning before Court Commissioner William H. Spohn, was continued until May 26, according to a statement made today by Miss Tillie Levine, Bull and Biart, and A. J. Bieberstein, attorneys for Mrs. Wright.

he postponement was made in order that both of the attorneys for Mr. Wright, L. H. Bancroft, Milwaukee, and James Hill, Baraboo, could attend the hearing.

At the same time a hearing will be held on the petition for temporary alimony which Mrs. Wright is seeking. This hearing is being held or the same day so that Wright's attorneys would not be forced to make more than one trip to Madison.

Fire Kills Daughter; Farmer to Be Held

SAULTE STE. MARIE, Mich.—(UP)—When Otto Weyonen, 60, recovers from an epileptic spell, which he suffered while watching officials remove the body of his 14-year-old daughter, Esther, from the ruins of his farm home, police here say he will be held for questioning in connection with her death.

Officials, in removing the charred remains of the girl from the ruins of the burned home, declared they found a hole in the skull which resembles a bullet hole. They also declared a rifle found in the ruins contained a discharged cartridge.

Weyonen declared he was asleep when the fire started and that he was unable to save his daughter after he had made his way from the home.

Capital City of Chinese Extremists is Menaced

LONDON — (UP) — An Exchange Telegraph dispatch from Hongkong today said it was reported there that the army of General Yang Sen had captured Wuchang, a city of the southern bank of the Yangtze river directly across from Hankow, extremist nationalist capital.

Protest British Stand

WASHINGTON, D. C.—(UP)—More than 100 men and women belonging to the Hands of China committee, said to be composed of labor elements of Philadelphia, Baltimore and Washington, demonstrated before the British embassy here today carrying banners and protesting against "British imperialism" which they declared was driving the world into another war.

May Move District Telephone Offices

Because of the installation of new switchboards and the consequent c[illegible]ding in the Wisconsin Telephone company building, it was reported today that district headquarters of the company will be removed to another Madison building. There is no intention of increasing the size of the present structure, it is understood.

'See You in Paris', Says Daring Airman

Wiping his sleepy eyes, Capt. Charles A. Lindbergh, lone wolf of the New York to Paris flyers, shook hands with friends and stepped into the miniature cabin of his plane, the "Spirit of St. Louis," as friends and admirers burst into cheers. He enjoyed only two hours sleep on the night preceding his departure and flew alone. This picture, showing him as he said farewell, was rush to The State Journal by telephoto.

Editor Hits Governor In Scorching Reply

Zimmerman Called "Effervescing Gentleman"; Fails to Measure Up to Job, He Declares

GOV. FRED R. ZIMMERMAN in replying to the charges made by Senator Walter S. Goodland, Racine, deliberately evaded the issues involved, Senator Goodland declared today.

Senator Goodland in his "comments and criticisms" in the Racine Times-Call refers to the governor as an "effervescing gentleman" and declares no governor Wisconsin ever had "so utterly failed to measure up to the job and its responsibilities as the present encumbent." His editorial follows:

Mr. Goodland's statement follows:

"In Oshkosh the other day the governor of Wisconsin, when asked if he had any statement to make about the comments of the writer of this column about the doings at Madison, said: 'Nobody in Madison takes Goodland seriously; why should I do so?'

"His Failure Historic"

"What were the mental gyrations and gymnastics of the executive mind that led him, in less than a week, to devote a column and a half of explanations and expletives in reply to the very things he said no one took seriously?

"But the writer is not surprised at this. No one will be who has

(Turn to Page 6, Col. 1)

British-Soviet Break Likely, Seamen Told

ATHENS—(UP)—Unconfirmed dispatches from Constantinople today said the British consul had instructed captains of British ships to be alert for a possible rupture of Anglo-Russian diplomatic relations.

No British ship has crossed the Bosphorus headed for Russian harbors since May 12, it was understood.

A break in British-Soviet diplomatic relations has been considered a possible result of the recent raid by Scotland yard on the Russian trade delegation headquarters in London.

A. B. C. and Kiwanis Will Meet Jointly, May 30

The American Business club and the Madison Kiwanis club will combine in meeting on Memorial Day, May 30, at the Park hotel. Col. John G. Salsman is to address members of the two organizations.

F. J. Vea to Head Wagon Company

President for 19 Years Again Chosen by New Organization

STOUGHTON, Wis.—F. J. Vea, for 19 years president of the Stoughton wagon company which was recently reorganized into the Stoughton Company, was elected president of the new concern at a meeting of the board of directors Friday afternoon. Election of other officers was postponed until a future meeting of the directors. Two members of the executive committee also were named. They are Mr. Vea and Emerson Ela, Madison attorney. The third member of the committee will be selected at the next session of the board.

Clarence Dilley Freed on Abandonment Charge

Clarence Dilley, charged with abandonment, was dismissed in superior court this morning. Dilley was ordered to pay costs.

Coolidge May Accept South Dakota's Bid

WASHINGTON—(UP) — President Coolidge conferred today with Senator Norbeck Republican, South Dakota, on accommodations offered him for a summer White House in the Black Hills.

The president queried Norbeck on arrangements which could be made should he decide to spend his vacation there.

The site offered the President is the state game lodge, 14 miles from Custer and 30 miles from Rapid City. He would be lodged in a 35-room state-owned hotel, and his staff would live a mile away in a tent camp.

Mayers and Strehlow Held Oldest Merchants

Older merchants of Madison are asked who is the oldest among them in the weekly bulletin of the Madison Association of Commerce today. Andrew Mayers will be recorded as the oldest and H. Strehlow the second oldest unless new evidence is given, the bulletin says.

Dr. E. R. Schmidt Will Address ABC Monday

Dr. Erwin R. Schmidt, chief surgeon of the Wisconsin General hospital, will address members of the American Business club on the subject of "Progress in Surgery" Monday noon at the Loraine hotel.

Mother Keeps Nerve as Boy Dares Space

DETROIT—(UP)—Reports that Charles Lindbergh, youthful trans-atlantic flyer, had been seen over Valentia, Ireland, were hailed by his mother, Mrs. Evelyn Lodge Lindbergh as a "Godsent miracle."

"Oh, I do hope it's so," she gasped, when the United Press informed her of the report. "You can't tell how much this means to me. I don't believe my boy will fail.

"Was his plane working all right, —or was it—not working so well?" she asked, a quiver in her voice.

Informed that the plane was flying high and fast, he sighed in relief.

High School Teacher

Lindbergh's mother is a teacher in the chemistry department in Cass Technical High school here. She received her preliminary schooling in Detroit, then went to the University of Michigan at Ann Arbor, where she met the man she married.

They went to Minnesota in the nineties. Charles' father was a representative in congress from 1907 to 1917. Following his death, Mrs. Lindbergh moved back to Detroit in 1925 and took up her duties as a teacher.

"Cool as Cucumber"

Mrs. Lindbergh went to bed at 10 Friday night after hearing reports that her boy Charlie had left behind him the last bit of land.

"She was cool as a cucumber," her uncle, John C. Lodge, confided to the United Press. "Not a bit of nerves. But then, she's always like that and the boy's just like her."

Lindbergh's grandparents came to the United States from Sweden in 1860. His paternal grandfather was a member of the Swedish parliament.

Boy Hit By Truck Severely Injured

Lawrence Terasa Rushed to Hospital Following Street Accident

Lawrence Terasa, son of Mrs. Anna Terasa, 204 North Sixth street, was seriously injured when he was struck by a Ford truck this noon between Fifth and Sixth streets on East Johnson street.

The truck, driven by Frank Brown, was going east on Johnson street when the Terasa boy ran across the street in front of the truck. He was knocked unconscious.

Brown stopped his truck and assisted in placing the boy in a passing car in which he was rushed to the Methodist hospital. He was unconscious when he was returned from the operating room.

At the hospital this afternoon it was believed that the boy was suffering from possible internal injuries. The extent of the injuries had not been ascertained.

Brown immediately reported to the police station after the accident had occurred. He was not held by the police.

West Division Band at Track Meet Here

West Division High school, Milwaukee, sent its band to Madison for the interscholastic track meet today, and they paraded the capitol square at 1 p. m. on their way to Camp Randall, where the meet was held.

Y.M.C.A. Issues Second Call for Library Books

The second call for books to be used in building up a library at the Madison Y. M. C. A. was issued today. Four hundred volumes were received when the first call was made and the Y. M. C. A. authorities are endeavoring to build up a library of 1,000 volumes. Each book donated will have the donor's name on the inside cover.

Pleads Nolo Contendere to Charge of Forgery

John O'Brien, arrested Friday by Detective Romain York for forgery, pleaded nolo contendere in superior court this morning. Judge S. B. Schein deferred sentence. O'Brien is said to have passed a $10 check bearing the name of Bill Burke at the office of the Madison Fuel company.

Thistlethwaite Announces Open Drill Saturday

VOL. 130, NO. 173. 88th Year. MADISON, FRIDAY, SEPTEMBER 23, 1927 PART THREE

Tunney Wins Fierce Tilt From Dempsey

TUNNEY retained his title as heavyweight champion of the world Thursday night at Grant Park stadium and thereby demonstrated that he is much more of a battler than many of us have been conceding him. Fighting a well-planned battle, and holding his head even when the "Manassa Man Mauler" had beaten him to the floor, the blond from Greenwich Village proved that he was every inch a champion.

The affect of this fight in the writer's opinion will be to make Tunney a more popular champion. Not that he will ever be as popular a champion as Dempsey would have been had he won, but this fight should result in his being much more of a hero to the great mass of fight fans who have never seen him. Time after time during the course of the fight, the referee cautioned Dempsey for hitting low, and once one of the judges excitedly ruled a foul on one of the blows to the champion's body. Throughout it all, Tunney fought gamely and cooly, and never once during the course of the fight did he cry "Foul."

* * *

An interesting sidelight on the fight is furnished by an incident that occurred Thursday. While watching practice at Camp Randall, Les Gage, director of publicity at the University of Wisconsin, introduced the writer to Laurence Perry, one of the most authoritatice sport writers of the East. Perry said he had sent his assistant to the fight, that the mit game had no appeal for him any more, and that he would rather see a football game any time.

It is interesting and satisfying to reflect that a man, who has seen as much sport as Laurence Perry and whose word carries so much weight should choose to watch the workouts of a football team that is slated to finish low in the conference standings in preference to seeing a prize fight that had been labeled as the "Battle of the Century."

"Johnny" Parks, captain of the 1926 freshman team, loomed up as a formidable threat for a line berth on this year's team when he broke through the first team time after time Thursday afternoon. Parks is one of those quiet, unassuming boys that does not look like a terror, but who is bad business for opposing linemen. John rowed on the freshman crew last spring and he evinced the same qualities there that are making him a formidable contender for a line berth on this year's varsity eleven.

Football fans who have been clamoring for reports on the Badgers will be able to see for themselves Saturday afternoon when Coach Glenn Thistlethwaite will hold his first open practice of the year. These practices will be held from time to time and will allow fans to catch momentary glimpses of the Cardinal eleven throughout its training season.

Wisconsin's early fall schedule this year has been arranged with an eye to dropping Michigan. Cornell college plays here a week from Saturday, and the Iowa collegians are coached by "Dick" Barker who teaches the Yost system. That will be good training for the Michigan game, for when the Badgers train for the opening game of the season they are also putting in some licks for the opening conference game of the season, Oct. 15, with the Wolverines.

Then there is the game Oct. 8 with Kansas at Lawrence. This aggregation is also coached by a follower of the Yost system, Franklin Cappon, who, in his playing days, shoved his bald head over more yards of enemy territory than any fullback of his time in the conference. Here again, the Badgers can train for Kansas and still be putting in some work to beat Michigan. It is a well arranged schedule to beat Michigan and there are plenty of Cardinal supporters who would give the gold out of their teeth to see the Wolverines take a trouncing at old Randall field.

To those who sat in the stands one crisp October afternoon in 1925 and watched a youngster named Benny Friedman who was later to become one of the greatest quarterbacks of all time, score one touchdown and help score another within the space of a little less than two minutes against Wisconsin's homecoming crowd, it seems as though no greater satisfaction could come from a football season than to beat the Wolverines.

There are other scores that Wisconsin has to settle with Michigan. One year when the Badgers had what was probably the greatest football team in the Middle West, an underrated team from Ann Arbor hopped into town and battled the Badgers tooth and nail to a 7 to 7 decision. Then there was another year when it looked as though the Badger had the Wolverine by the throat after Doyle Harmon had kicked a field goal to give Wisconsin a 3 to 0 lead. Battling like Tigers instead of the little badgers that they are named after, the Cardinal warriors were tossing back the best that Yost's men had to offer until a lapse of watchfulness on the part of Wisconsin allowed Rockwell to score a touchdown on a play that the Badgers thought had been completed.

That is plenty of scores to settle with this old rival from Ann Arbor. They are all friendly scores, but that does not prevent the rivalry from being just as intense. Should Wisconsin be able to turn the tables on Michigan this year, there would be a ray of sunshine in the life of many a Wisconsin traveling salesman who has to make Michigan territory. Not that this is an appeal for justice to the traveling salesmen, but the poor fellows have taken it for quite awhile.

East Side High Loses Quarterback

Kitson Declared Ineligible Was on Regular Team

Schultz and Cirves Look Best of Morrow's Men in Long Scrimmage Thursday

BY "RED" MICH

THERE is moaning and groaning and rolling of the eye bail sin the camp of East Side high school's football team today, and little wonder it is, with the forces of disaster apparently working overtime to cut down the chance of the Purple and Gold.

Not yet over the shock of losing Francis Longfield through an injury, Coach Archie Morrow discovered Thursday night that Vincent Kitson, a sophomore youngster who was counted on to handle the quarterback position, is ineligible because of a "con" on his report card. It seems that Kitson's numerical grades for last semester never were checked up until Thursday, when the sad facts were revealed.

This leaves the East Side mentor in more or less of a predicament, because he has been working hard with the young pilot, expecting him to play the next three years for dear old East. Now he will make a choice between Bazan and Gilbert, both ambitious but young and inexperienced.

Hold Long Scrimmage

Morrow put about 50 men through a stiff scrimmage Thursday, shifting the lineups of both his teams and continuing the sod-socking for about an hour until every able bodied youth on the premises had had a chance to display his worth.

There were encouraging features, such as the performance of Schultz and Cirves in the backfield, but the line showed that it still has plenty to learn. With the exception of the Reque brothers, there are no real veterans on the forward wall, and the boys need polishing.

Norman Reque is being tried at center part of the time, and Schantz and Ruskauff are also making bids for the pivot berth, with nobody certain of it as yet. Al Reque has one guard job to himself, and that's about the only thing settled, so far as the line is concerned.

Prep Elevens Battle

While the Eastsiders were pounding each other over the turf Thursday, Coach Jacques was also sending his Wisconsin high hopefuls through a scrimmage, and he expressed himself as satisfied with the results of the workout. The Badger Prep second team is not strong enough to keep up the pace of the first stringers, and the veteran backs rode through for many a long gain Thursday.

Two men counted on as regulars, George Kelly and Novotny, were missing from the practice because of "charley horses" but Jacques expects them to be back next week. Kelly is a veteran back and Novotny a promising end candidate.

In the course of Thursday's melee about 35 men saw service, and nobody complained about a lack of exercise.

On his "first" team, Jacques started Laughborough at center, Coffman and Cool at the guards, Grabbert and Fuss at the tackles, Nelson and Smedal at the ends, Briggs at quarterback, "Petey" Nelson and Baskerville at the halves, and Haenzschel at fullback.

The other eleven had Sheely at center, Jasper and "Trash" at the guards, Hommel and Harris at the tackles, Behrend and Joe Kelley at the ends, Duncan at quarter, Rusch and Otis at the halves, and Lund at fullback.

Howard Johnson, the Central coach, did not give his charges any real scrimmage Thursday, and he doesn't expect to send them through any more until Saturday morning. Howard is more than slightly worried about his line, and he is concentrating on the charging machine and other nefarious devices to improve the forwards.

Mrs. Fraser Wins From French Star

By ROBERT A. HEREFORD
[Universal Service Correspondent]

GARDEN CITY, N. Y.—Habit is a peculiar thing.

Miss Alexa Stirling, one of Dixieland's many pretty girls, three times won the American women's golf title while a resident of Atlanta, Ga. She formed the habit there for Atlanta, who produced Bobby Jones and Watts Gunn, has a habit of turning out champions.

And Mrs. Alexa Stirling Fraser, although married, and become an adopted daughter of Canada, can't seem to get out of her winning ways. Thursday the former southern girl defeated Mlle. Simone Thion de la Chaume, champion of France and England, in the third round of the national women's golf classic in progress on the Cherry Valley links. Mrs. Fraser, whose experience has given her always brilliant game remarkable steadiness, defeated the temperamental French mam'selle 3 up and 2 to play, and now reigns as the top heavy favorite for the title.

Miss Ada MacKenzie, Canadian champion and medalist of the present tournament, trod a more difficult golf road than her adopted country woman. Miss Virginia Van Wie, the stout hearted Chicago girl, who drives with the power of a man, offered the severest sort of resistance, relinquishing to the Canadian champion only at the eighteenth green, one up.

Miss Maureen Orcutt, youthful Metropolitan champion, also had a close call, being taken to the twentieth green by Miss Marie Jenny, of the Hudson River club before triumphing. In the remaining match of the day Mrs. Miriam Burns Horn of Kansas City, defeated her western sister, Mrs. Harry Pressler of San Gabriel, Cal., the western champion, 2 up and 1 to play.

Mrs. Fraser meets Mrs. Horn in one of the semi-final matches for today and Miss Orcutt is bracketed against Miss MacKenzie.

The day was cool and crisp and clear and the gayly dressed women stood out against the green background of the links with the striking relief of a steriopticon view.

Tilden and Johnson Win Three Matches

CHICAGO—(LP)—Bill Tilden and Wallace Johnson, both of Philadelphia, playing as the Middle Atlantic States Tennis team, won three matches from the Missouri Valley team composed of Wray Brown, St. Louis, Junior Coen, Kansas City, and Harris Coggeshell, Des Moines, in the third annual intersectional team tennis tourney at the Chicago Town and Country club.

Tilden beat Brown 6-1, 7-5, Johnson elimited Coen easily, 6-3, 6-2.

Tilden and Johnson won the doubles match from Brown and Coggeshall 6-2, 6-4.

The big surprise of the day was the defeat of John Doeg, of Santa Monica, Calif., by Berkeley Bell, Austin, Texas school boy, 8-6, 3-6, 6-1. Louis Thalheimer, Dallas, lost his singles match to Edward Chandler, of San Francisco, 6-4, 6-3.

The Texas team, Bell and Thalheimer won the doubles match from the California team 21-19, 6-3, after a hard struggle.

Herb Schwarze Returns to School for Fall Semester

Wisconsin's track prospects took on a more brilliant aspect when it was learned that Herbert Schwarze had returned to college and was officially enrolled. The big Milwaukee boy was a pupil of Tom Jones, and during the year he was away from Wisconsin, set the world's record indoors in the shot put. Herb is also a good discus thrower, and can heave the hammer and javelin.

Team Shows Little in Scrimmage; Smith Eligible

Report Gains Circulation That Joe Kresky Has Chance of Becoming Eligible

By HENRY J. McCORMICK

YOU won't have to take our word for what goes on at Camp Randall for very long now; Coach Glenn Thistlethwaite has announced that Saturday afternoon's practice will be open to the public, the first open workout held to date.

Practice is scheduled to get underway at 4 o'clock Saturday afternoon and continue for two hours.

Football candidates received their second real scrimmage of the year Thursday afternoon at Randall field. To tell the truth, this session must have been excruciating to Coach Thistlethwaite if Tuesday's was disappointing.

Linemen Charge Fast

There is this much to say about Thursday's scrimmage, however; the linemen on both the first and second teams charged fast and low on defense, but the offensive linemen allowed the opposing wall to sift through without a great deal of opposition.

A ray of sunshine filtered through the drab air of Randall field Thursday afternoon when it was announced that Lewis Smith, one of the leading candidates for the fullback position, had been definitely declared eligible. At the same time, word was passed around that Joe Kresky would be eligible if he passed a condition examination Saturday.

Schuette is still ineligible, but it is expected that this case will be cleared up at any time now. His return to the line will be a big help as he was probably the most dependable lineman on the 1926 aggregation and his weight, fight, and punting ability are assets that are sorely needed by the present questors for Big 10 honors.

Should Kresky become eligible, the prospects for a hard-driving backfield would be increased about 50 per cent since the Marinette boy is a terrific plunger and the best blocker on the squad. Recently one who was close to the working powers "on the hill" asserted that Kresky had no chance of becoming eligible, but it is to be hoped that he has been mistaken.

The first team Thursday night lined up with Rose, Crofoot, Rebholz and Weigant in the backfield. "Jack" Wilson was at center, flanked by Schuette and VonBremer at guards, Ketelaar and Wagner at tackles, and Mansfield and Warren at ends. Opposing this outfit was one in which the backfield was made up of Clement, Arne, Ziebell, and Breckenfeldt. Conry was at center, the guards were McKaskle and Sykes, the tackles were Ritter and Parks, and Hotchkiss and Taylor were at ends.

Rose and Crofoot did some neat work for the first team and Rebholz sent a couple of neat spirals off his toe during the course of a scrimmage thta lasted about a half hour.

"Bob" Sykes looked good at one guard on the second team, and "Johnny" Parks, captain of the 1926 freshman team stood out at a tackle on the second team like a lighthouse in a fog. He broke up plays sent at him and opened good holes for the backs when the team was on offense.

Ends Poor on Defense

Warren, who had looked like a find while playing offensive end, betrayed woeful weaknesses on defense Thursday night and it will take a great deal of coaching before he will be able to meet the heavy attack sent against conference teams' ends. Mansfield also showed some defensive weaknesses and looked none too good at working on the opposing tackle when his team was carrying the ball.

McKaskle, the huge boy from Arkansas who walked all the way up here to enter school as a freshman last year, has been improving rapidly this year, and he is going to give everybody a battle for a tackle or guards position on the first eleven.

With Welch and Cameron nursing injuries that keep them away from practice, Coach "Stub" Allison is trying to develop a few ends who will be able to play conference caliber football. The material is none too promising but "Stub" will get the most out of it—he is that kind of a coach, a driver but one whom all the fellows feel a deep affection for.

John Cavosie Enrolls at University of Minnesota

THE following extract from the Minneapolis Daily Star of Tuesday, Sept. 20, under the signature of John Getchell seems to settle the much discussed question of where John Cavosie, former high school star at Ironwood, Mich., and the star of last year's freshman team at the University of Wisconsin, will cast his lot.

It is interesting, also, to note that William Maki came to Madison to register this fall but left when he learned that he was expected to work to earn his way and that no one was going to hand him a check book.

With Maki when he came to Madison were two other Ironwood boys and between them they had just $12 not enough for anyone of them to register. None of them were wrought up over the idea of earning their own way, yet they are entering at Minnesota,—one of the schools comprising the Big Ten and a traditional foe of Wisconsin.

Cavosie will have to remain at the Gopher institution for two years before becoming eligible in accordance with a conference ruling that states that any freshman who shall leave one conference school because of unsatisfactory scholastic work and enter another Big Ten school shall have to be in residence at the other school for two years before he shall be eligible for conference competition.

Here is the story:

John Cavosie, considered one of the best college football prospects in the country after his wonderful showing as fullback on the Ironwood, Mich., high school team, today enrolled at the University of Minnesota.

Along with Cavosie came William Maki and Oscar Vicklund, teammates. Along with Fred Lucksells, who registered Saturday, there are four members of the Ironwood team, which won the state championship last year, enrolled at the Gopher institute.

Cavosie played fullback while on the prep school team and weighs 204 pounds, standing six feet two inches. Cavosie had planned to enter Michigan or Notre Dame, but when his other teammates decided to come to Minnesota he changed his plans.

The fullback is the outstanding player on the squad but Maki, Vicklund and Lucksells were all heralded as good high school players and all will be welcomed to the frosh squad, which promises to be a strong one.

Milwaukee Wins, Holds League Lead

[By United Press]

ORDER of the three leading teams of the American association was unchanged by Milwaukee's 7 to 3 defeat of Minneapolis Thurdsay, Toledo and Kansas City both winning their contests and trailing the Brewers by a game and a game and a half, respectively.

Twenty hits gave Kansas City 17 runs while St. Paul was making a total of 4.

The Toledo-Louisville contest went 14 innings after the score was tied at six-all in the sixth. Three runs by the Mudhens ended the affair, 9 to 6.

Columbus and Indianapolis were idle.

Two Ohio Boys Aid Badger End Problem

A dearth of end candidates for the extremities of the Badger line this fall, which has been one of Coach Thistlethwaite's chief worries, has been replenished the last few days with the addition of a likely pair of Ohio boys to the squad of wingmen.

Ebert Warren of Akron and Art Mansfield of Cleveland are the boys who will make the two veterans, Welch and Cameron, step to be assured of steady employment again this fall. Just a week ago "Stub" Allison the popular new end coach at Wisconsin, was bemoaning the fact that he could see no one at first sight to relieve the above mentioned regulars.

Thistlethwaite shifted Mansfield from fullback to end as an experiment last week, mainly because the big Cleveland boy lacks the power and drive essential to line plugging. "Dynamite" went to work with a will, and now finds himself lining up on the first eleven in the absence of Welch, who is temporarily on the injured list.

Warren, who has been out of school a year, returned late this fall. The coaches had not counted upon him, but from the manner in which he has improved the last three days, he will be heard from in the Conference this year.

"Christy" Flanagan Makes Up Scholastic Deficencies

NOTRE DAME Ind.—(Special)—Six men worked off scholastic difficulties during the past summer and will be given a chance to make the Notre Dame football team as a result of successful attendance at summer school. Prominent among these was Christy Flanagan, famous half-back of the Irish team who buckled down to work and made up the three weeks that he missed last winter as the result of running afoul a disciplinary requirement.

Tony Bernardi Promises Demetral Rough Evening

TONIGHT promises to be a wild evening at Turner hall when Tony Bernardi, big, rough, burly, and confident, clashes with Jimmy Demetral, Madison Greek middleweight, in the second bout of a double windup card that will open the fall wrestling season in Madison.

Bernardi is to put Jimmy on his back twice in 90 minutes or go away with only 25 per cent of the gate, the 75 per cent going to the winner. Tony bears Jimmy no special good will since the time this summer when Demetral met Bernardi while the latter was traveling with a carnival and took away some of his money.

Bernardi will scale about 180 pounds and Demetral will enter the ring at approximately 158 pounds.

The other match on the card will be a finish match between "Bulldog" Brown of Madison and McIntosh of Antigo. Brown has never been known as a gentle man on the mat and his opponent is declared to be one of those wrestlers who love to butt heads, and otherwise disport themselves after the fashion of a couple of belligerent goats.

The first match between Brown and McIntosh will be called at 8:30 and will go to a finish. The main bout will go until Demetral takes a fall or for 90 minutes.

Advance ticket sales have been encouraging despite the fact that the match is being sandwiched in between the Dempsey-Tunney fight and one of the tightest baseball races the national league has ever seen.

However, there are a goodly share of mat fans in Madison who want their wrestling whether or not two pug uglys are battling for the heavyweight championship of the world and a slice of dough big enouh to choke an ox.

Demetral is working with the idea of obtaining a return match with "Johnny" Meyers, middleweight champion of the world, and he welcomes the opportunity of working against a big tough grappler like Bernardi.

Jimmy Smith Bowls Here

JIMMY SMITH, world famous bowler, will exhibit and give personal instructions Sunday afternoon and evening at the New Plaza alleys.

Smith is known for his record of bowling 16 perfect scores. In 1911 he made the world's tournament record score in the Canadian Bowling Association tournament, Toronto, Canada with games of 279—236—256—771. He also holds the world's record for 30 consecutive games at Denver, Colo., in September, 1925, and his average then was 243 21-30.

Smith will be lined up with some of Madison's champs, who have been selected from star teams of the city. This lineup will probably include Auby Ehrman, Tony Schwoegler, Roy Bowes, Joe Hackett and others.

Gene Goes Down For Count of 13 In the Seventh Round

[Pictures in the Peach]
By DAMON RUNYON
(Universal Service Correspondent)

SOLDIERS' FIELD, Chicago—Down on the canvass for a count for the first time in his boxing career, sniffing the resin dust there, with the murderous old Manassa Man Mauler glowering over him with evil intent, Gene Tunney, the fighting marine, got up and carried on to victory against Jack Dempsey Thursday night.

He got the decision of the judges, George Lytton and Sheldon Clark, Chicago business men, and of Referee Dave Barry, an old time boxer, at the end of 10 desperate rounds, with 150,000 men and women still fairly limp from the excitement of the seventh round.

It was in that round that Dempsey swarmed all over the big blond New Yorker, knocking him down—not with one punch, but with a wild rain of smashes, as Tunney's pale body hung over the ropes. Tunney fell flat on his back, then sat up, his pallid features pinched with the strangest expression of bewilderment, and it seemed to me, some embarrassment.

Tunney Rests on One Knee

A man who has never been on the floor before in a fight can not be expected to know just how to deport himself under the circumstances. Probably sheer instinct caused Tunney to get to one knee, and so he rested with Dave Barry, the referee, repeating the count of the timekeeper in Tunney's ear, Dempsey nearby, his dark, scowling countenance flecked with blood, his eyes gleaming fiercely, his soggy gloves raised as he set himself like an animal for the spring.

The count went to nine, with the great crowd spread out over Soldiers' field screaming hysterically in the wolf cry of the human pack scenting the kill. Some say it was a good 12, but that is something to be argued later in columns upon columns of comment. It seemed a long time even to a neutral.

Tunney Runs Away

Once he got on his feet, Tunney began running backward as only a skillful boxer in distress knows how to run. Back, back, back he went with the glowering Dempsey fairly grunting in anger as he pursued, Dempsey bobbing his body and swinging his hands in a wild effort to reach the fleeing Tunney.

"Stand still and fight," yelled the Dempsey adherents.

The entire crowd was standing up, the men with their heads jutted forward, their teeth bared, and their eyes glittering, the women with their hands clenched tightly.

The bell closing the seventh round found Tunney out of immediate danger. Then as calmly as a delicatessen dealer slicing up his bologna, he proceeded to cut Dempsey to pieces with his spearing left. It was a fairly even fight as I saw it going into the tenth, with the knockdown weighing strongly in Dempsey's favor.

As showing the wide difference of opinion over these pugilistic encounters, however, some of the spectators thought a draw would have been fair to both men, though they probably wouldn't have cared to have had much money invested in Dempsey's chances in a longer battle.

"Take a lead, take a lead," implored Bill Duffy and Leo Flynn from Dempsey's corner through the ninth, sensing how a fight that seemed to be surely won was slipping away from them as Tunney piled up point after point, while Dempsey was lumbering wearily at Tunney, the old legs beneath the bronzed body of the Manassa Mauler failing to respond to his call.

They meant for Dempsey to throw punches.

"Take a lead!" they clamored, more feebly, through the tenth. They seemed to realize that the victory and the title that gave $1,000,000 to Tunney Thursday night against $450,000 to Dempsey, had gone beyond recall.

Looked Sure in 7th

And it had appeared such a sure thing in the seventh, with Tunney groveling on the floor, and Dempsey apparently as strong as a bull.

Small wonder that they looked so downcast when the champion's gloved hand was lifted in token of triumph at the close of the tenth. Small wonder that even Dempsey also jerked away from the scene immediately after shaking hands with Tunney. Outside of the seventh round there was scarcely enough excitement to repay the 150,000 spectators for the $2,800,000 that George (Tex) Rickard, the "under cover" promoter of the event estimates was in the box office, an estimate that is probably high. George Getz, a Chicago business man, was supposed to be the promoter, but it was Rickard's show.

For three rounds they both were so cautious that had it been a preliminary they would have been booed by the crowd. Dempsey had dropped his old style of tearing in, and was trying to make Tunney do the leading. The latter is supposed to be strictly a counter puncher, waiting on the other fellow's leads, but he frequently took the aggressive.

Dempsey finally abandoned his waiting policy, and began bobbing and crowding Tunney. Oddly enough, at times he even outboxed the master boxer. Tunney kept missing him with his right hand smashes, though his left seldom failed to smear Dempsey's countenance.

Under the rules that prevail in Chicago when a man goes down, the official timekeeper at the ringside starts counting and the referee is supposed to pick up the count immediately. But a member of the boxing commission says that its rule is that the count does not start until the boxer who has knocked the other down is in the corner furthest from the fallen man.

Dempsey first went to his own corner, within a few feet of Tunney after the knockdown, then moved along the ropes over to a neutral corner as the referee, Barry, pointed it out to him.

He was a little slow in following up his advantage as Tunney got to his feet, no doubt of that.

As Tunney was running backward, Dempsey once motioned at him with his gloved hands as much as to say, "come on!" but Tunney is a cautious young man, and his only reply to the invitation was another retreat. He had made one mistake in getting within range of the punches of the greatest slugger of modern pugilistic times, and he was taking no more chances at that moment.

Not a Great Puncher

Tunney has never been accounted a great puncher. He is a stiff puncher, but there is no "kill" to his blows. He has fought Dempsey twenty rounds, and has failed to have him on the floor for a count. Dempsey dropped once as Tunney landed a blow, but it seemed more of a slip than a real knockdown, and the same thing happened later to Tunney.

I would say that for at least nine seconds Tunney was thoroughly befogged as he knelt on the floor. The punch that staggered him back to the ropes was a long left hook to the chin. He was assaulted with a volley of punches from both Dempsey's hands, but the one that put him on the floor as I saw it, was a right hand smash to the chin.

He was not unconscious, but he was certainly dizzy. Dempsey acted calmly enough as he moved into his own corner, scarcely looking at the man on the floor, but the second hand of the clock moves rapidly and those were precious seconds that Dempsey was losing. Perhaps Tunney could have gotten up just the same if the count had continued on from the four at which it was discontinued to the nine. That is not for me to say.

Then again the added four seconds may have been just the time he required to clear his befogged bean thoroughly. Who can tell?

"You admit that you counted 13 over Tunney?" Beeler, the official timekeeper, was asked in my hearing.

"Yes," he said.

And there you are.

But that gets the old Manassa Man Mauler nothing at the moment. The dignified Tunney remains the champion of the world, and no one who saw him in action Thursday night will say that he didn't fight a masterly battle to keep his title.

He proved his gameness. There always has been some doubt of that in the minds of those who do not like Tunney, but he has plenty of what they call "heart." He is no

(Continued on next page)

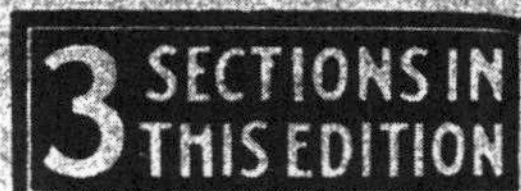

The Wisconsin State Journal

A Fact-Finding Newspaper

VOL. 133, NO. 134. 90th Year. MADISON, THURSDAY, FEBRUARY 14, 1929 TWENTY-FOUR PAGES PRICE THREE CENTS

Gangster Guns Kill 7 in Chicago Garage

Mother of Governor Dies at 72

Death Calls at Sheboygan Home; Was Daughter of Jacob Vollrath, Pioneer Manufacturer

GOVERNOR AND MRS. KOHLER left Madison Wednesday night for Sheboygan, called there by the death of Mrs. Minnie Vollrath Kohler, 72, mother of the governor.

Mrs. Kohler had been ill for several weeks. Governor Kohler visited with her last week, but he was in Madison when she died about 6 o'clock Wednesday night. Mrs. Kohler's other son, Herbert, and her three daughters, Evangeline, Marie, and Lilly, all of whom lived at the family home at Sheboygan, were present.

Mrs. Kohler was too ill to be present when her son was inaugurated governor, but she heard the ceremonies via the radio. The supreme wish of her life was to visit the governor in the executive office.

LEGISLATURE ADJOURNS

Out of respect to Governor Kohler, whose mother died Wednesday night, the Wisconsin legislature today passed a joint resolution making adjournment for the week fall earlier than is customary. The legislature, which customarily adjourns on Friday for the week-end, will reopen next Tuesday. The flag on the capitol flew at half mast today.

Mrs. Kohler was the daughter of Jacob J. Vollrath, pioneer manufacturer of Wisconsin. She lived in Sheboygan most of her life. Her husband, John M. Kohler, came to this country as a child of three with his parents from the Austrian Tyrol. The family settled on a farm.

John Kohler founded in 1873 the company of which the governor now is head. That was two years before Walter was born.

Besides her two sons and three daughters, Mrs. Kohler is survived by four grandsons, John, Walter, Jr., Carl and Robert, all sons of the governor. Also surviving her are two sisters, Mrs. John Riess and Mrs. Rudolph Weimer, and a brother A. W. Vollrath, all of Sheboygan, and Frank, a ward of the family.

Funeral services for Mrs. Kohler will be held from the Kohler home in Sheboygan at 2 p. m. Saturday.

The funeral will be conducted by the Rev. A. Parker Curtis of the Episcopal church.

Editors Here For State Convention

President Kuypers Opens Meeting at 2 P. M. Today

(Pictures on Page 1, Part 2, and page 15)

John A. Kuypers, De Pere, president of the Wisconsin Press association, opened its three-day convention at the Park hotel today (with an address of welcome at 2 p. m.

Speakers besides Mr. Kuypers will be A. A. Washburn, editor, Dairyman - Gazette, Clintonville; George Greene, editor, Waupun Leader; R. M. Smith, advertising department, Chicago Tribune; and Gordon Crump, editor, Cambridge

(Continued on page 8 column 8)

Weather

(Official Report by U. S. Weather Bureau)

Mostly cloudy tonight and Friday; no decided change in temperature; fresh west winds.

City	Temperature Highest Yesterday	Lowest Last night	Precipitation 24 hours to 1 a.m.
Madison	17	8	.01
Milwaukee	24	14	.06
Chicago	24	14	.06
Green Bay	14	0	
Wausau	14	0	.01
Duluth	12	8	.02
Minneapolis	16	6	.02
La Crosse	14	10	.01
Dubuque	18	8	

MADISON WEATHER

	Temperature	Relative Humidity	Wind Velocity	Cloudiness
Yesterday				
Noon	9	91	12	100
7 p. m.	9	88	5	100
Today:				
7 a. m.	8	91	10	100
Noon	13	88	10	10

Highest temperature 13 at 1 a. m.

Lowest temperature 8 at 7 a. m.

Mean temperature 9; normal 18.

Total precipitation since Jan. 1, 2.20 in. Normal 2.28.

Sun rises at 6:57; sets 5:28.

TODAY IN OTHER YEARS

Warmest in 1882, 49.

Coldest in 1905, -22.

Wettest in 1849, 1.30 inches.

2 Beer Bills Follow O.K. of Dry Poll

BULLETIN

Two bills to legalize the sale of beer in Wisconsin were introduced in the state senate this morning. Senator Walter Polakowski, Milwaukee, introduced one measure, providing for complete repeal of the Severson dry law enforcement act, and Senator Thomas Duncan, Milwaukee, presented another, providing for the legalization of the sale of 2.75 per cent beer in the state.

By HAROLD M. GRIFFIN

SENATOR THOMAS M. DUNCAN'S resolution providing for a referendum on the question of repealing or amending the Severson dry law to permit 2.75 per cent beer has just one more obstacle to hurdle before it can be placed on the ballot at the April election in the form of a referendum.

The assembly elections committee reported unanimously today for adoption of the resolution. It has already passed the senate and its friends say it will not encounter serious difficulty in the lower house. Then it goes on the April ballots in the form of a referendum and if the

(Continued on page 8 column 2)

Buyer Liable Under Dry Law Teasdale Says

THE present prohibition act provides that both the seller and buyer of liquor can be prosecuted through the prohibition of "sale," Senator Howard Teasdale, Sparta, told the senate committee on state and local government Wednesday afternoon in the hearing on his bill calling for penalties for those who buy or drink liquor.

Senator Teasdale explained that in a sale there is a buyer and a seller and inasmuch as the transaction is illegal both are guilty. He declared, however, that this interpretation has not been followed, so he introduced his bill to make such provisions more specific.

Although Senator Teasdale declared that he expected the committee to recommend the bill out for passage the committee practically told him that they would recommend it for killing.

"Do you realize, senator, that if this bill went through you'd have to get a new legislature?" Senator M. F. White, Wimmecone, asked.

"I don't want to besmirch the leg-

(Continued on page 8 column 1)

Mrs. A. F. Rosen Dies at Home Here

Mrs. Elizabeth Rosen, 54, wife of August F. Rosen, died at 1:30 p. m. today at her home, 26 North Hancock street. Her death came after a lingering illness.

She is survived by her husband, one daughter, Miss Eleanor Kathryne Rosen, living at home; her mother, three sisters and seven brothers. August F. Rosen is secretary and treasurer of the Rosen Heating company. His wife had been a resident of Madison for 34 years.

Funeral arrangements will be made later.

Bill Killing Grain, Cotton Exchange Defeated in Senate

WASHINGTON.—(U.P.)—The Caraway bill to prevent sale of cotton and grain in futures markets was defeated today in the senate. The Caraway bill would have done away with cotton and grain exchanges. The vote against it was 27 to 47.

Dream Comes True Friday

Frank Asks $11,500,000 for 1929-31

U. W. Wants $9,500,000 for Operation, $2,000,000 for Buildings in Next Biennium

THE budget amount of $9,581,990 for operation, maintenance and ordinary capital for the University of Wisconsin for the next two years was asked by President Glenn Frank before the joint finance committee of the legislature this afternoon.

President Frank has, in addition, listed new building needs totaling $2,340,316. He will confer with the committee to consider which of the projects included in this total building program may best be undertaken during the next two years.

He has said before that he advocates spending approximately $2,000,000 on the building program during the next biennium. The total, therefore, he would recommend that the legislature approve is more than $11,500,000.

Of the $9,581,990 total, $4,738,852 has been budgeted for use during the university year 1929-'30, and $4,843,138 during 1930-'31, President Frank said. This represents money to come from the state, after legislative approval.

"Broadly speaking, the total expenditures of the university are made for three major purposes: for running the university in Madison, for rendering various public services throughout the state, for erecting, equipping or remodeling buildings," said the president.

"For running the university in Madison the state is asked to provide $3,904,694 for 1929-'30 and $4,102,960 for 1930-'31," he continued.

(Continued on page 8 column 7)

Girl Refuses $70,000 Left by Milwaukeean

MILWAUKEE—(U.P.)—Miss Lillian Ziemer announced today that she will refuse a bequest of $70,000 left her under the terms of the will of John Holler.

Holler cut off his relatives with small sums and left Miss Zeimer the $70,000 for "her kindness and friendship." Miss Ziemer had cared for Holler during his last sickness, the will said.

Miss Ziemer gave no reason for renouncing the fortune, which will be divided among the relatives.

Seek to Rescue Man from "Worst Prison"

Belgian Unable to Escape From French Penal Colony Six Years After Finishing Term

By FRANK H. BARTHOLOMEW

[United Press Staff Correspondent]

(Copyright 1929 by United Press

LOS ANGELES — An effort to rescue a man buried alive for 46 years in the "worst prison on earth" was begun here today.

The man is Paul Lamont, a citizen of Belgium and a former master of languages at London university.

The prison is Devil's Island and its associated penal colony of St. Laurent de Maroni, in French Guiana.

Ended Term Six Years Ago

Six years ago Lamont, now 78 years of age, had finished a 40-year sentence for forgery and was a free man. Today he is more surely a prisoner than at any time during his 40 years of servitude, according to a report to the Belgian ambassador at Washington by W. E. Allison-Booth, American, who himself has just returned from the French penal settlements, one of the few men to come away alive.

Allison-Booth landed in Los Angeles after shipping half way around the globe in order to get back to the United States.

Left on Island

He was second officer on a supply steamer plying between New York and the tropic prison colonies. On his last trip from the United States to Devil's Island and St. Laurent he was left behind at the latter point, and spent three months awaiting

(Continued on page 8 column 1)

Lenroot Gets Nomination for Judicial Post

IRVINE L. LENROOT

[By United Press]

WASHINGTON — President Coolidge today sent to the senate the nomination of former Senator Irvine L. Lenroot, Wisconsin, to be associate judge of the United States court of customs appeal.

Death Toll in Europe Still Rising

[By United Press]

LONDON—Intense cold paralyzed Europe today, causing death and suffering over the whole continent, and fatalities from freezing and accidents, since Saturday, mounted to 121.

A serious fuel and food shortage occurred in several sections, transportation systems were hampered severely and it was feared the ratio of deaths would mount unless relief came.

Such widespread cold has never been known before. A temperature of 74 below zero was reported in Poland. Only once in history has a lower temperature been recorded on earth. That was in north central Siberia, where it was 90 below in 1917.

Fifty persons collapsed with frozen ears, hands and feet when 10,000 assembled to receive a small ration of free coal, a Central Radio dispatch from Budapest said. The remainder rushed the police cordon guarding the supply and helped themselves.

A supply of food and rum was dropped to the steamer Saym, frozen

(Continued on page 8 column 6)

Aunt Het

"A woman don't really crave kissin'. She just hates to think her husband don't care about kissin' her no more."

W. A. DEVINE

NEW MADISON POSTOFFICE

City Ready to Dedicate Postoffice

$1,000,000 Federal Building to Be Center of Elaborate Ceremony Friday

BY JOHN CULNAN

(History and Pictures on Page 24)

A CIVIC dream dating back to 1912 will be realized Friday when Madison's new $1,000,000 federal building fronting upon Monona avenue will be dedicated under the auspices of the Association of Commerce with appropriate ceremonies.

The presence of hundreds of school children, including the bands of Central and East Side high schools and union chorus, will feature the exercises, which are scheduled to open at 2 p. m. on the steps of the structure if the weather permits, otherwise in the lobby.

Meyers to Raise Colors

Jesse S. Meyers, commander of Lucius Fairchild post, Madison unit of the G. A. R., will be accorded the honor of raising the colors over the building for the first time. He will be escorted by Lyall T. Beggs, commander of William B. Cairns post, American Legion, and Marvin H. Levenick, commander of Marion C. Cranefield post, Veterans of Foreign Wars. The drum and bugle corps of the latter organization will also participate in the ceremonies.

Grant Miller, chief post office inspector of the national system, representing Postmaster General Harry S. New at the exercises, will formally accept the keys of the new building from C. W. Thomas, superintendent for Murch brothers, St. Louis firm which has held the general contract.

Schmedeman to Talk

Mayor Schmedeman will deliver a brief address, and Postmaster W. A. Devine will receive custodianship of the building from Mr. Miller. Thom-

(Continued on page 8 column 6)

School Site Move Vetoed by Mayor

Disapproves Resolution Directing Decision On South Side Site

BY HENRY NOLL

Mayor Schmedeman has withheld his approval of a resolution adopted at the last council meeting which directs the board of education to make a recommendation for the purchase of a school site for the south side at the next council meeting. It was learned today. The resolution was introduced by Ald. C. R. Parr, who contended that the old Franklin building is in an unfit condition and that a new school should be ready Sept. 1.

Mayor Schmedeman was out of the city today and his reasons for vetoing the resolution are not known definitely, but it is believed he deemed it unnecessary for the council to take such action.

At the school board meeting held four days prior to the council action, it was decided to make the south side school matter a special order of business for next Tuesday night.

Board for Richmond Site

As far as the school board is concerned, it has made a recommendation for the purchase of the Richmond site for the proposed new Franklin school. Until the board decides otherwise, this recommenda-

(Continued on page 8 column 4)

Grim Irony in Lindy's Romance

By KENNETH G. CRAWFORD

[United Press Staff Correspondent]

[Copyright, 1929, by United Press]

WASHINGTON — There is a grim irony behind the romance of Col. Charles A. Lindbergh and Anne Spencer Morrow.

The flying colonel is seeking her hand cast aside the heritage of political hatred from his father, the late anti-Wall street representative from Minnesota, the avowed enemy of big banking and the instigator of the 1911 "money trust" investigation.

An Old, Old Story

The story is old. It has been sung by wandering minstrels. Shakespeare told it in his Romeo and Juliet.

Now with the engagement of the daughter of Dwight Morrow, ambassador to Mexico, multi-millionaire, and former Wall street banker, to the son of the late Rep. Charles A. Lindbergh, non-partisan free thinker and enemy of the house of Morgan, fiction becomes a reality.

Anne Born to Purple

Lindbergh's father never missed an opportunity to sink oratorical barbs into Wall street, big bankers and the house of Morgan.

Anne Morrow was born to the

(Continued on page 8 column 5)

Rieder Resting More Comfortably

Although there has been no noticeable improvement in the condition of Charles T. "Chuck" Rieder, Madison tire dealer, he is resting more comfortably today, it was reported by St. Mary's hospital authorities this morning. Mr. Rieder is still in a critical condition with injuries received Sunday when he was attacked by an enraged bull on his farm on the Speedway road.

Senate Body Favors Summer White House

WASHINGTON—(U.P.)—The Fess bill proposing an executive commission to pick a summer White House near Washington was ordered favorably reported today by the senate public buildings and grounds committee. The action was taken following President Coolidge's message Wednesday to congress advising an appropriation of $48,000 for conditioning Mount Weather, Va., as a country White House.

Huber Doesn't Want to Appoint Probers

Lieutenant Governor Would Be "Embarrassed" After Charges Made by Barry, He Says

Lieut. Gov. Henry A. Huber today asked the state senate to relieve him of the duty of appointing the two senate members of the committee to investigate political activities in recent years. Huber's move came as a surprise. When the assembly passed the Prescott resolution last week for an investigation of campaign funds, it was urged that Huber should have the authority to appoint the senate members.

In asking the senate to make the appointments he referred to the recent charges against him as "wicked and biased."

"The freeing of every public act of any selfish motive is a necessary requisite if people are to have confidence in their government," Lieut. Gov. Huber said. "I say this in view of a situation that has arisen in our public affairs.

"There are a number of resolutions pending before the senate asking for an investigation of recent political campaigns. The resolution, already adopted by the assembly, now before the committee on corporation and taxation, provides for the appointment of the joint membership on that body by the presiding officer of each house. Ordinarily I would welcome this honor. But because of recent charges, wicked and biased as I feel they are as far as they touch upon my reputation and political conduct, it would greatly embarrass me to make appoint

(Continued on page 8 column 4)

Badger Eleven to Play Penn in '30, '31

AFTER months of negotiations, Wisconsin and Pennsylvania have signed for a home and home intersectional football series in 1930 and 1931, it was announced here today by Head Coach Glenn F. Thistlethwaite and Athletic Director George E. Little, both of whom worked to complete arrangements.

Though it is not certain that the first game will be played at Camp Randall, Ernest B. Cozens, athletic director at Pennsylvania, has indicated that it would be agreeable with him if the 1930 game were to be played at Madison, with the '31 game at Franklin Field.

Approval of the arrangements by the Wisconsin athletic council was not needed since that body authorized an intersectional football series early last fall.

Colgate This Year

Next fall, Wisconsin will meet Colgate at Camp Randall, but the Pennsylvania series will mark Wisconsin's first appearance in the east since 1899 when the Badgers lost to Yale, 6 to 0.

Scheduling of Pennsylvania culminates years of effort on the part of Mr. Little to land an advantageous series with some strong, representative eastern foe. Negotiations with Penn were started last summer when Mr. Little was in the east interviewing officials of several schools to sound out their ideas on an intersectional football series.

Other Competition Likely

"There will be further negotiations between the University of Pennsylvania and ourselves which may bring the two schools together in other varsity sports," said Mr. Little.

It is understood that there is a strong likelihood of Wisconsin and Pennsylvania meeting in a home and home series in at least two other major sports during the years of 1930-'31. The two sports mentioned most often are basketball and track, though there is a possibility of the Penn crews meeting Wisconsin in a regatta that may become an annual affair.

Coaches Lou Young and Glenn Thistlethwaite are enthusiastic over the success of the directors of the two schools in coming to an agreement.

$2,570,000 More Dry Fund Asked

Mellon Prepares Estimate of Extra Appropriation for Year

WASHINGTON — (U.P.) — Secretary Mellon announced today the treasury has prepared a supplemental estimate of $2,570,000 for prohibition enforcement which it will submit to the house appropriations committee. The extra appropriation, Mellon said, is asked in compliance with a request from the house committee for an estimate of what additional funds the treasury could use in this fiscal year.

Limit on Bus License Fees Proposed in Legislature

Two bills restricting the size of license fees which cities or towns may charge bus companies are pending before the legislature today.

One, offered by Assemblyman Oscar J. Schmiege, Appleton, limits the charge to $25 in villages, $35 in cities of the second, third or fourth class, and $50 in cities of the first class.

The other, proposed by Assemblyman John Rohan, Kaukauna, would limit the fee to not more than the company might be charged if it were taxed at the regular rate prevailing on city or town property.

Every Man in Building Shot Down

Beer War Flames Out as Two Auto Loads of Bandits Defy Police

[By United Press]

CHICAGO—Seven employees of a north side cartage company were murdered with sawed-off shotguns today when two automobile loads of bandits raided the garage in which the company had its headquarters.

Frank Gusenburg, the only man to be taken from the scene of the shooting alive, died a few hours later in a hospital.

Police construed the assassinations as an outgrowth of the Chicago beer war and said it was likely that some of the men working for the S. M. C. Cartage concern had been engaged in running beer.

Aiello Gang Rival Killed

One of the dead was said to have been identified as Pete Gusenburg, a lieutenant of George "Bugs" Moran, northside beer rival of the famous Aiello gang. Pete's brother, Frank, was wounded, and died later.

The raid was one of the most daring in the long history of Chicago gang feuds. The two carloads of raiders drew up in front of the garage shortly before noon, leaped out and entered the garage.

Came then the roar of sawed off shot guns. Persons in the neighborhood said they thought there had been an explosion in the building.

Given No Defense

A few minutes later half a dozen or more gangsters raced out of the garage, took their places in the two automobiles and sped away.

The victims were said to have been treated in the usual gang manner—shot down without a chance to defend themselves.

Every available squad car at the detective headquarters was pressed into action and raced north through the loop with screaming sirens.

Lined Up Along Wall

When police arrived on the scene they found everyone who was in the garage at the time of the raid had been shot, presumably lined up against the wall as though for execution by an official firing squad.

Act of Vengeance

On the bodies was found ample evidence that the crime was an act of vengeance with no thought of robbery. Wrist watches were left

(Continued on page 8 column 8)

Lindy's Mother to Wed Master of Ship, Rumor

NEW YORK — (U.P.) —The New York Times said today that an unverified report was current here that Mrs. Evangeline Lindbergh, mother of Col. Charles A. Lindbergh, would announce her engagement to Capt. F. E. Anderson, master of the S. S. President Wilson, shortly. The President Wilson is operated by the Dollar line.

Vatican Settlement to Be Ratified April 21

ROME. — (U.P.) — Both the senate and the Chamber of Deputies will convene April 21 to ratify the Vatican settlement, it was announced today. The settlement probably will be signed by the Pope and King Victor Emmanuel on the same day.

U. S. Takes $16,082,000 Bid for 11 Ships

WASHINGTON. — (U.P.) — The United States shipping board formally accepted the $16,082,000 bid of the Paul W. Chapman and company, Inc., New York, for 11 ships of the United States and American merchant line, this afternoon.

Poor Pa

"Our daughter Betty is goin' to our church again. She found out that the baritone she admired at that other church is engaged."

The Wisconsin State Journal

A Fact-Finding Newspaper

VOL. 135, NO. 29. 90th Year. MADISON, TUESDAY, OCTOBER 29, 1929 TWENTY-FOUR PAGES PRICE THREE CENTS

More Billions Slashed From Stock Values

8 Drowned, 66 Saved in Shipwreck

Heroic Coast Guards Save Many From Steamer Wisconsin Off Racine

[By United Press]

KENOSHA—The second big shipwreck on Lake Michigan within a week claimed eight lives today while coast guardsmen fought their way through mountanous waves to save 66 others from the 40-year-old steamer Wisconsin after it had floundered in a storm 13 miles off the coast.

Among the rescued brought to hospitals here, 20 were suffering from severe injuries.

Captain Stays With Ship

True to the traditions of the sea Capt. Hugo Morrison of the Wisconsin went down with his ship.

Only one person of the 75 who set out from Chicago Monday night was unaccounted for on the last checkup. Coast guardsmen told of seeing his body float out of reach on the crest of a high wave. They were rescuing the others.

The Wisconsin, her hold filled with water, her radio silenced and lights darkened, dived to the bottom early today just as the last life boat hung snarled in the davit.

Last Boatload Lost

Members of the crew said Captain Morrison stood on the starboard deck with his arms folded, as the cold gray waves folded over his ship.

The 15 men in the last life boat were dumped into the lake, some of them going to their deaths, the others struggling in the waves until coast guard boats, tugs and fishing craft, summoned by radio, came to their aid.

Several of the injured were crashed against the side of the Wisconsin when the life boat ropes snarled.

Near Milwaukee Wreck

A few miles north of the spot where the Wisconsin went down the car ferry Milwaukee was swamped last week with a loss of 53 lives. Only nine of the bodies have been recovered.

Fred Triever, a survivor of today's tragedy, said the Wisconsin ran safely through last week's storm

(Continued on page 6 column 1)

Grundy Hits Tariff Role of Midwest

By PAUL R. MALLON
[United Press Staff Correspondent]

WASHINGTON — The Western states, whose senators are re-writing the republican tariff bill "haven't any chips in the game at all," because they pay only a little more than 2 per cent of the income taxes, Joseph R. Grundy, legislative agent and raiser of republican campaign funds told the senate lobby investigating committee today.

"If it was not for the provision of the constitution that gives every state two senators, these states would never be heard of," Grundy said. "The income tax figures show the relationship of the states.

"We find these representatives of so little note are obstructing and destroying the great reserves of taxation to such an extent that it is a national tragedy and I think it ought to be pointed out to the country by some one."

Grundy's complaint he later explained was not against the fathers of the country in giving each state two senators but against "the kind of men they send here."

"If they sent senators like Vare, republican, Pennsylvania, or Charles L. Eyanson, agent of the Con-

(Continued on Page 6, Column 2)

Aunt Het

"I ain't seen Pa try to dance since the time he was tryin' to kill a mouse for me an' it run up his britches leg."

Stock Crash Aids Real Business, Assert Heads of Madison Firms

INTERVIEWS obtained by The State Journal show that Madison bankers and business men agree with President Hoover that the crash in the stock market is not an indication of bad business conditions, and in fact, that it will have a good influence by redirecting money now invested in inflated stocks into active business channels.

The public has pretty well outgrown the old idea that when the stock market went to pieces everybody would suffer. Years ago that was true, not because it should have been true for any sound reason, but because almost invariably a general business panic ensued.

CROWLEY

Banks called loans, and tightened up on new loans. Concerns about to launch new enterprises gave them up. People were afraid of banks, and current earnings went into stockings. Financial fear ruled the country, with the result that activity was greatly decreased, unemployment ensued, and out of a purely fictitious situation actual hard times came about. All this was cured in 1913 by the establishment of the federal reserve bank. It served two purposes: one, to maintain public confidence; the other, to actually provide cash where it was needed.

This present slump in stock prices merely amounts to taking the wind and water out of stock inflated far beyond their value. The stable stocks, prices of which were actually based upon resources and sustained earning power, will recover. There will be some losses on the part of those who invested unwisely in stocks that had been boomed beyond their reasonable value, but the bulk of the losses will be sustained by those who have been following the practice of buying on margin, and were sold out in the tremendous slumps of the past ten days.

An interesting feature of these losses is that while on the first break last week the losers were mostly the smaller dealers and speculators, in Monday's break it was the big financial speculators who were beaten.

Throughout the country business and banking leaders engaged in the actual work of production and distribution view the situation not only without alarm, but with general approval. They point out that a drastic remedy has come to heal an unhealthy situation in the stock market, and that while a momentary flutter may be felt, the inevitable result will be the return of a great supply of money to the ordinary and useful productive and commercial uses of the nation.

HOOVER

The following interviews with Madison bankers and business men sustain this view:

A general decline in stocks to the level of their earning power should be of benefit to the agricultural industry, stated Prof. B. H. Hibbard, agricultural economist at the university, in commenting this morning on the stock crash.

"Even though farmers have played little or none with stocks," he said, "the abnormal high prices of stocks have drained from the agricultural industry money that might well have been used in the industry.

"Relatively, agriculture will be in a better position with the decline of stock to normal values."

"The crash in the market came about because the folks who were playing it were doing so for speculation and not for investment," claims Leo T. Crowley, president of the Bank of Wisconsin.

"The downfall was inevitable and had to come. After the adjustments have been made it will be a great boon to Madison business and community development in general."

"For a community like Madison to take seriously the crash of the stock market seems very foolish to me," said Joseph Rothschild, manager of Baron's store.

"New York, of course, will feel it. As the center of the market gambling world it is natural to find people who live there playing the market and losing their earnings when it crashes. In Madison, however, the number who do so is negligible. In our store of 100 employes I doubt if there is one who plays the market, and they naturally are not concerned when it tumbles. In the same size store in New York, however, probably a fourth of the employes would be gambling on the market. I do not see how a Madison business man can be sensibly concerned over the situation."

"We feel that the new condition on the market will be beneficial to business rather than depressing," said J. Frank Kessenich, Jr., of Kessenich's store.

HIBBARD

"Most of the profits that have been made on the rise in the market have been paper profits, and have not given people any more money to spend than they had previously. Now that the crash has come and some have been 'burned' I anticipate a return to the normal conditions of buying and selling that are so important to any stable business."

"The change in the market eventually will react favorably for home builders and the organizations that finance home buildings," in the opinion of C. C. Collins, of the C. C. Collins and son Lumber company.

"Money which previously has been gambled on the market will be utilized for the building of homes. We are looking forward to a great building year."

"The market crash has not made the slightest impression on our business so far and we do not anticipate any," said Harry Dimond, manager of Hill's store.

"Our type of business is not affected by fluctuations on the market, and we are planning the biggest year in our store's history."

"The market crash is a move in the right direction and is of

(Continued on Page 6, Column 4)

T. E. Burton, Ohio G.O.P. Leader, Dies

(Picture in Peach)
[By United Press]

WASHINGTON — Senator Theodore E. Burton, Ohio, for years a republican leader and close personal friend of President Hoover, died at his home here Monday night.

He was 78 years old and had been in poor health for the past year. Although confined to his home for weeks he maintained his usual interest in legislative matters and kept in close touch with his office until only a few days before his death.

He suffered a seemingly mild attack of influenza about a month ago but, in his weakened condition, was unable to combat it and suffered a serious relapse last Wednesday.

Bishop William T. MacDowell of the Methodist Episcopal church is to officiate at formal funeral services at the senate chamber at 2:30 p. m. Wednesday. President Hoover will attend the rites. The body will be taken to Cleveland for burial.

The senate adjourned today out of respect for Burton, whose death was called to the attention of the senate by Senator Fess, Ohio, when that body convened today.

Fess presented a resolution expressing the senate's regret at the death of the Ohio legislator and instructing Vice President Curtis to name a committee of 13 senators to take charge of the funeral and accompany the body to Cleveland.

Union Needs Only $323 in Campaign

Total is Now $104,453; Final Meeting Will Be Held Friday

The Community Union fund climbed to a total of $104,453 with today's reports from volunteer workers of $2,017, and now stands within $323 of its goal of $104,776. William H. Spohn, president of the organization, is scheduling one last meeting for Friday noon, November 1, at the Park hotel, to bring in the remaining dollars.

Initial Gifts, under the chairmanship of A. H. Kramer, today made a report of $240, carrying that division over the top of its goal of $50,126. Second ward, under the chairmanship of John Bidwell, also went over the top today.

The University division, under Prof. F. H. Elwell and Prof. R. R. Aurner, now lacks but $25 of making its goal of $8,000, with today's reports of $207. Retail Business, under Paul and Arthur Towell, today reported $454, cutting its shortage down to but $229 to go.

Shortages reported in other divisions were $732.75 in the Capitol; $691.90 in the third ward; $300 in the fourth ward; $238.80 in the fifth ward; $377.03 in the sixth ward; and $45 in Nakoma. Chairmen in these divisions are still carrying on and promise additional reports for next Friday's meeting.

Senator Watson to Rest in Florida for 3 Weeks

WASHINGTON. — (U.P.) — Senator James E. Watson of Indiana, Republican floor leader, is retiring from party leadership in the senate, temporarily, and is leaving Thursday for Florida on order of physicians for a three-weeks' rest.

Dr. J. R. Straton, Noted Fundamentalist, Dies

Famed Baptist Minister, Backer of Bryan in Scopes Case Succumbs

[By United Press]

NEW YORK—Dr. John Roach Straton, noted fundamentalist minister, died at Clifton Springs, N. Y., according to word received at his residence here today.

Heart disease was given as the cause of death.

Straton, pastor of the Calvary Baptist church here, had been ill for some time. His wife was at the bedside.

Rise Was Sensational

The rise of Straton in the ministry was sensational and rapid. Born in Evansville, Ind., in 1875, he attended Mercer university, and later took a professorship at Baylor university. He accepted a call to a Chicago pulpit and from there came to the Calvary Baptist church, regarded by clergymen as the most influential fundamentalist pulpit in the denomination.

Straton rallied to the support of William Jennings Bryan in the Scopes' case at Dayton, Tenn., and was an incessant worker for stern censorship of the theater.

Fought Al Smith

In the 1928 presidential election, he came out against Alfred E. Smith because of the latter's stand on prohibition. His plans for a 29-story combination church and hotel aroused criticism from members of his congregation. Straton's belief in healing by prayer also gained him considerable publicity.

Besides his wife, Straton is survived by three children—Hillyer, a minister; Jack, a lawyer; and Douglas.

DR. JOHN ROACH STRATON

Peterson Guilty of Killing Sister

NEILLSVILLE — (U.P.) — Paul Peterson, Waukegan, Ill., who admitted to a jury that he killed his sister and brother-in-law near Greenwood, Wis., Aug. 26, was found guilty of first degree murder by a jury today. The jury, which was out for 15 hours, was given the case Monday night.

Peterson was on trial only for the killing of Mrs. Ernest Riggs, his sister, but during the trial he had admitted taking also the life of his brother-in-law during a fit of anger brought about by domestic difficulties.

The conviction carries with it a maximum sentence of life imprisonment.

Daladier Gives Up Cabinet Attempt

PARIS. — (U.P.) — Edouard Daladier, radical Socialist leader, abandoned today his efforts to form a cabinet to succeed that of Aristide Briand, who resigned last week.

Daladier's decision came soon after the Socialist party refused to participate in the new government.

It was understood Pres. Gaston Doumergue was unlikely to invite Briand or any other political leader to attempt to form a cabinet before Wednesday.

Now Is Time to Get That Doll, Children

HELLO, girls and boys!

How are you all today and how are the many beautiful Wisconsin State Journal dolls that have left my headquarters to make their home with you? I hope that all the children who have received dolls are being very kind to them; it would break my heart to know that one of my lovely children was being treated roughly.

It's almost the first of November! That month always makes me think of one thing—Thanksgiving! Just think of all the things you little boys and girls will have to be thankful for this year. So many of you have received your dolls already; and if the rest of you continue to work the way you have these past few weeks you'll soon have yours too.

And then, right at the heels of Thanksgiving comes Christmas—good old jolly Christmas time! That's when you just HAVE to own one of my glorious dolls.

I think it would only be fair to give you a little warning that I won't be in Madison forever, you know. There are thousands of little girls and boys in other parts of the country, too, and I must visit them.

I never can tell how long I will be in one city, so if I were you I'd work terribly hard these next three weeks or so to be sure that I'd have a dolly.

I'll be with you again tomorrow!

Plane Lost in Mountain Snow Storm

[By United Press]

LOS ANGELES—The southwest's second great air hunt within three months started at dawn today when planes took the air from Los Angeles and Albuquerque, N. M., to search for the Western Air express passenger liner feared lost near the rugged Arizona-New Mexico state line.

Two passengers and a crew of three were aboard the plane when it took off from Kingman, Ariz., at 7:24 a. m. Monday, after refueling on its flight from Los Angeles to Albuquerque.

The plane was seen over the Adamana and again over Navajo, Ariz., some 160 miles west of Albuquerque, but from Navajo its course remained a mystery.

Snowstorm Along Route

A snowstorm, reported raging along the route, might have sent the pilot off his course, fliers said.

George Rice, who found the wreckage of the T. A. T. plane which crashed three months ago on Mount Taylor with a loss of eight lives, was at the controls of the searching plane which took off at 3 a. m. from Albuquerque. Another ship left Los Angeles about the same hour. No passengers were carried in either because they were to fly low.

First Search Fruitless

The first airplane dash into the wild territory today proved fruitless.

Pilot George Rice, who left Albuquerque early today, returned to the Albuquerque airport shortly after 11 a. m. and reported no trace of the lost plane.

Rice got as far as Gallup, N. M., where a heavy snowstorm forced him to turn back. Visibility was poor, he said.

Airplanes were rendered virtually useless in the search for the missing liner today as brisk snowstorms prevailed at Albuquerque, Grants and Gallup.

Receive Two Clues

Two clues to the missing plane were revealed in dispatches from Albuquerque.

A storekeeper at Zuni, N. M., 20 miles south of Gallup, reported he saw a plane pass at 11 a. m. Monday. A big tri-motored ship was

(Continued on page 6 column 5)

Weather

(Official Report by U. S. Weather Bureau)

Snow or rain tonight and Wednesday. Not much change in temperature. Fresh easterly winds.

City	Temperature Highest Yesterday	Temperature Lowest Last night	Precipitation 24 hours to 7 a.m.
Madison	38	[illegible]	.05
Milwaukee	42	38	0
Chicago	46	42	.05
Green Bay	40	[illegible]	0
Wausau	36	[illegible]	0
Duluth	34	[illegible]	0
Minneapolis	36	[illegible]	.16
La Crosse	38	[illegible]	[illegible]
Dubuque	42	[illegible]	[illegible]

MADISON WEATHER

Yesterday	Temperature	Relative Humidity	Wind Velocity	Cloudiness
Noon	36	74	[illegible]	100
7 p. m.	38	[illegible]	16	100
Today—				
7 a. m.	38	[illegible]	[illegible]	100
Noon	39	[illegible]	12	100

Highest temperature 38 at 7 p. m.
Lowest temperature [illegible] at 7 a. m.
Mean temperature 37; normal 41.
Total precipitation since Jan. 1, [illegible] in. Normal [illegible].
Sun Rises at [illegible], sets [illegible].

TODAY IN OTHER YEARS
Warmest in 1901, 73.
Coldest in [illegible], 13.
Wettest in [illegible], 1.25.

Schmedeman Vetoes Mack Truck Purchase

Mayor Proposes That All Bids Be Submitted to Committee of Experts

MAYOR SCHMEDEMAN today vetoed the common council's action of last Friday night in voting the purchase of a Mack International fire pumper.

The mayor's message, presented at the special council session called this afternoon to act on snow removal equipment, proposed that all bids be submitted to a committee of experts for a recommendation.

The committee, providing the council approves the plan, would consist of university engineering college faculty members and members of the state engineering staff.

Discusses "Improper" Methods

The mayor also called attention to rumors of alleged improper methods employed by sales representatives and urged that in the future, when the city purchases such apparatus the competing companies be requested to send no salesmen to Madison.

Chances of over-riding the veto were considered slim as the council convened at 2 p. m. today, as the Mack purchase received a bare majority of 11 and a three-fourths vote, amounting to 15 ballots, is necessary to nullify the mayor's action.

Mr. Schmedeman's veto message follows:

"I am returning herewith without my approval a resolution for the purchase of the Mack fire equipment.

Has Confidence in Council

"It is only after very careful consideration of the entire situation that I take this action. For weeks the Council has wrestled with the

(Continued on page 6 column 5)

Budget Body Hears All Requests Tonight

A budget embodying all requests of the various city departments will be submitted to the board of estimates at its first meeting tonight by City Auditor George Nelson.

City Engineer E. E. Parker will be the first department head to appear before the board to explain the needs of his office and that of the street department, which he temporarily heads.

In the meantime the city board of education will meet tonight for final action on its own budget, which likewise must be presented to the board of estimates, which consists of the mayor and the finance committee of the council. The school board was scheduled to convene at 4 p. m. and will continue its session following supper at Central high school dining room.

West Point Head Talks Navy Game With Good

WASHINGTON—(U.P.)—Maj Gen William R. Smith, superintendent of the military academy at West Point, N. Y., conferred with Secretary of War Good today preliminary to a conference there later with Rear Admiral S. S. Robison, superintendent of the naval academy, in an attempt to arrange resumption of athletic relations between the two schools. Good expressed the opinion agreement would be reached.

Move to Rid Lake Mendota of Sewage

A DEFINITE step was taken today to rid Lake Mendota of sewage from the state insane asylum and soldiers' hospital.

After a conference with W. G. Kirchoffer, consulting sanitary engineer for the state, and T. L. McIntosh, assistant attorney general, the sanatorium and building committee of the Dane county board adopted a recommendation that the gravity sewer under construction from the city limits to the new county tuberculosis sanatorium be increased in size from 12 to 15 inches and that the state be allowed an equity in the extension.

This resolution, which paves the way for connection of the state hospital with the city system, probably will be presented to the county board at its November meeting.

One of Dane county's assemblymen, it was learned today, probably will be requested to introduce at the next session of the legislature a bill specifically appropriating funds to make the connection.

In the meantime, legal representatives of Madison, Middleton and Shorewood Hills decided at a conference this morning to draft a petition for the creation of a metropolitan sewerage district to be submitted at the second general conference to be held in the capitol with the state board of health over means to solve the Middleton sewage problem.

Whether or not this conference will be held Wednesday as planned, will depend upon the return of Dr. C. A. Harper, state health officer, who has been absent from the city this week. He is expected back tonight.

Mistrial Ends Case Against Ex-Governor

TAMPA, Fla. — (U.P.) — Former Gov. Sidney J. Catts' trial on a counterfeiting charge ended in a mistrial today.

The jury had been out more than 13 hours when its foreman, C. B. Dickens, reported to Federal Judge Alexander Akerman that the jurors were unable to agree.

The court then dismissed the jury and declared a mistrial.

Woman Lies in Car Wreck 2 Hours; Dies

PRAIRIE DU CHIEN—(U.P.)—After lying in the wreckage of an automobile for two hours, Mrs. N. S. Jennings was brought to a hospital here Monday so seriously injured that she died within a short time. Mrs. Jennings' husband was seriously injured when their car left the road, and neither could move until a passing motorist aided them two hours after the crash.

Bankers End Slump Just Before Close

50 Billion Lost in Last Few Days; Volume Sets New Record Today

By ELMER C. WALZER
United Press Financial Editor

NEW YORK—Millions of dollars in backing from bankers, and statements of confidence from financiers, applied brakes to the stock market at the close today and prices swung upward in the last three minutes of trading.

But the rally was ended by the gong which closed the greatest day in the markets history and the books were closed with additional staggering losses, marked against even the strongest issues.

Trading today was at the greatest volume in history—16,410,030 shares. The previous record was 12,848,650 last Thursday.

This is the third sales record today.

The first was made in the first half hour when business amounted to 3,259,800 shares and again in the first two hours when trading reached 8,378,200 shares.

Steel Leads Break

The final reversal in prices was an amazing recovery. During the day, quotations had shot down, down, down. Trading had been at its greatest rate, passing the 13,000,000 mark at 2:10 p. m.

In the last hour the down swing continued. United States Steel, leader in all good movements of late, had slumped off to 167 in a steady rout.

Three minutes before the close came the turn. Steel was bid up to 175—an eight point gain.

Steel Closes at 174

Steel's closing quotation was at 174, off 12 points on the day, but far higher than it had been only a few minutes earlier.

American Can closed at 120 with a loss of 15 points but 10 points higher than it was earlier this afternoon. New York Central closed at 189½ for a net 3½ point gain after being below 180 during the day.

All tickers were far behind the market.

Thousands Sold Out

No one tried to follow prices. Few had the pleasure of giving orders. Brokers sold out thousands of accounts. Many large operators felt the pinch.

The stock ticker at 2:50 p. m was nearly one and one-half hours late, and the curb 115 minutes.

Cities Service Falls

On the curb Cities Service featured with a sale of 117,000 shares at 21⅝ off 2⅞. Later the issue broke further and word was received that the company would withdraw rights to buy new stock at the original offering price of $45 for present holders. The down movement was aided by collapse of one curb brokerage house.

Sales of active stocks by periods calculated by the stock exchange were:

10:30—3,259,800.
12:00—8,378,200.
1:30—12,652,000.
2:10—13,838,000.

Most prices closed above their lows but were still 2 to 20 points or more below the previous close.

Prices seemed to have no bottom. Despite positive assurances from bankers and economists that the bottom had been reached Monday, the market tobogganed downward at wide drops.

Drop 1-50 Points

Shortly after 1 p. m. prices were down 1 to 50 points on both the big board and the curb exchange, with new lows for the year or longer established in many shares. The market value loss was tremendous, totaling upwards of $50,000,000,000

(Continued on page 6 column 6)

Poor Pa

"Ma got out our daughter Betty's baby clothes Sunday, an' we enjoyed lookin' at 'em an' thinkin' of the time when we could control Betty."

Badgers and Buckeyes Trip Purdue, Michigan, Title Favorites, in Upset Victories

Full Details of All Important Football Games in Journal Sports Section

Wisconsin 21	Ohio State 20	Janesville 14	Northwestern 19	Yale 27	Indiana 0	Harvard 14	Notre Dame 63
Purdue 14	Michigan 7	Madison Central 6	U.C.L.A. 0	Chicago 0	Iowa 0	Army 13	Drake 0

The Wisconsin State Journal

A Fact-Finding Newspaper

VOL. 139, NO. 18. 92nd Year. HOME EDITION MADISON, SUNDAY, OCTOBER 18, 1931 THIRTY PAGES PRICE FIVE CENTS

THE WEATHER

Wisconsin: Fair and somewhat warmer today; Monday, partly cloudy to cloudy, some likelihood of local showers.

Capone Found Guilty on Five Counts

ACTS 20:35

THE devil may find work for idle hands in some cities—but in Madison he's lost his job to the Y. M. C. A., the Y. W. C. A., the Boy Scouts, the Girls Scouts, and the Neighborhood House.

* * *

"The agencies which help to build health and character are especially necessary in these days and merit whole-hearted and generous support," says President Hoover.

* * *

Leopold Stokowski, famous conductor of the Philadelphia orchestra, hits the well known nail on its equally prominent head when he says that communities should not only feed and clothe families suffering as a result of unemployment, but it should provide generously for those institutions and facilities which enable the unemployed and their dependents to make profitable use of enforced leisure time.

* * *

"BY devoting this leisure to music and the other arts," Stokowski says, "and by reading about the amazing progress in science, the American people may emerge from the present period of discouragement with a finer, more spiritual culture."

* * *

Only 23 of the 2226 Madison children registered as members of one of the five recreational agencies (Y. M. C. A., Y. W. C. A., Boy Scouts, Girl Scouts, and Neighborhood House,) have been brought into juvenile court.

* * *

An analysis of the occupations of the fathers of the children who are members of the recreational agencies shows that 35 per cent of them are members of trades; 25 per cent are laboring men; 14 per cent are members of professions; 9 per cent are merchants; 8 per cent are salesmen; 6 per cent are city and

(Continued on page 7 column 1)

BadgerFights StateTaxLaw in High Court

WASHINGTON, (U.P.)—The plea of "Equal rights for men" as an echo to Wisconsin's advanced legislation on equal rights for women has been brought before the supreme court.

The plea was interjected by a husband who seeks to be freed from having his wife's income included with his own under the state income tax.

Wisconsin prohibits the husband from exercising any control over the property of his wife, gives her equal rights to sue or be sued, and allows her various other property rights. But it holds him responsible for her income tax.

Tax Rises

After Albert A. Hoeper, Marathon county, a widower, married Florence Rowley, a widow with a separate income, the state successfully collected not only the tax on his wife's income from him, but also a higher rate on his own income, for the lumping of the two sums forced the total into the higher brackets.

In appealing from this ruling by an attack on the constitutionality of such procedure, Hoeper, through his attorneys, opened up the whole equal rights question. The case was submited for the court's decision through filing of briefs.

Cites Ancient Case

The sum involved, he notes, is small, "But is more than John Hampden's twenty shilling ship tax." Hampden unsuccessfully resisted King Charles of England's levy of peace time ship taxes in 1636. They were later abolished.

Commenting on the allegedly uneven dealing with the men of the state on the subject of taxation, while allowing women many new privileges, Hoeper's attorney said:

Rescinds Old Law?

"By particular and definite declarations of policy and property rights, the state has wiped out every vestige of the old common law unity as to property rights.

"The union is a social, not a financial unity.

"Whether this policy of financial [illegible] will in time tend to weaken the social interdependence and unity is a social problem which does not concern us here. For weal or woe, financial seperation is established as the fundamental policy of the state."

Four Boys Crash Theater Via Coal Chute; Nabbed

Four boys, each about 14, were taken into custody temporarily Saturday night when police received complaint that they had gained entrance to the Capitol theater by the inexpensive means of a coal shut. They admitted they had used similar methods in previous visits and in entering the Orpheum. They were lectured and released.

Masked Bandits' Raid Nets $200 at Rockford

ROCKFORD, Ill.—(U.P.)—Masked bandits held up a branch office of the Forest City Wholesale Grocery company Saturday, forced two employes and a customer to lie on the floor and robbed the cash register of $200. Warning their victims, [illegible] Faye and William Bargren, joint managers, and Walter Misevich, a customer, to keep still, the robbers then ran down an alley, where they leaped into a waiting car and escaped.

150 U. S. Men Raid Oshkosh, Fondy Saloons

61 Arrested as Largest Squad Visits 47 Places; Evidence Seized; Bail Refused

MILWAUKEE — (U.P.) — Federal prohibition officers from South Bend, Ind., Chicago, Milwaukee and Madison, raided 47 saloons and night life places in Oshkosh and Fond du Lac late Saturday, taking 61 persons into custody.

The places were raided simultaneously by 150 officers, believed to constitute the largest squad ever assembled in Wisconsin. They stepped into appointed places at the same time, along the main streets of both cities, which have been unmolested by prohibition officers for many years.

The officers entered 18 places in Fond du Lac and 29 in Oshkosh, confiscating a large amount of alleged liquor. Groups of raiders were directed by M. G. Carmichael, Milwaukee; Ray J. Nye, Madison; Major Howard Long, South Bend; and Arthur C. Hamilton, Chicago.

None of the prisoners will be released until Monday, when they will be arraigned in their respective cities.

Although many friends of the prisoners presented bail, none was accepted and county jails in Fond du Lac and Oshkosh were crowded.

Among the prisoners at Fond du Lac was Roy Turner, former police lieutenant there.

Edison Faces Final Hours

BULLETIN

WEST ORANGE, N. J.—(U.P.)— Dr. Hubert S. Howe, Thomas A. Edison's physician, issued the following bulletin at midnight:

"Mr. Edson's respiration is rapid and shallow. His pulse is accelerated and is of poor quality. There has been no evidence of suffering at any time."

Dr. Howe said at 11:30 p.m. Saturday that there would be no further bulletins until today unless there was a decided change in his patient's condition. Two hours later the physician said "there has been no change in Mr. Edison's condition since the previous bulletin."

WEST ORANGE, N. J.—(U.P.)— Thomas A. Edison, deep in the stupor that precedes death, was losing ground so rapidly Saturday that doctors believed he might die at any moment.

It was only a question of how long his heart could hold out. He had not taken food for eight days, except for a few negligible spoonsful of stewed fruit.

The member of the family were within easy call, expecting the end to come at any time.

"This is the first time I have felt definitely the end is approaching" said Dr. Hubert S. Howe, the attending physician.

Lindberghs to Start Flight at Vancouver

Will Not Go to Seattle, Colonel Says

SEATTLE, Wash. —(U.P.)— Col. and Mrs. Charles A. Lindbergh returning from their vacation trip in China, will fly east from Victoria, B. C., when their ship, the American Mail liner President Jefferson, reaches that port late Tuesday.

In a radiogram to the American Mail line and Seattle chamber of commerce Saturday, Lindbergh said:

"Have just received information plane will meet U. S. Victoria. Regret very much circumstances our return make stopping at Seattle impossible."

A Lockheed plane, sent from the factory at Los Angeles to replace the Lindbergh plane, damaged in China, will be used to speed the couple to New York. It previously had been announced that the Lindberghs would come to Seattle and take off from here.

After The Ball Was Over

Wisconsin scorned no means of scoring Saturday afternoon in its sensational 21 to 14 victory over Purdue; the above picture shows John Schneller scoring Wisconsin's second touchdown by pounding straight through a wall of Purdue linemen. Schneller is on the ground in the fore part of the picture but he is safely over the line as the diagonal stripes indicate. Other pictures in sports section.

—Photo by Vinje-Russell.

Boyd Directors' Statement Says All Debts Will Be Paid

Districting for Congress Held Possible

Wylie Rules District Reshaping at Special Session Valid

Failure of the Wisconsin legislature to meet the requirements of Section 3 of Article IV of the constitution that demands that the legislature adopt a law reapportioning the assembly and senate districts of the state on a basis of the population shown in a federal census, does not prevent the passage of a reapportionment law at either a special or a regular session held later according to an opinion Saturday by Deputy Attorney-General Fred M. Wylie to Milton Murray, secretary of the interim legislative reapportionment committee. In the opinion, Mr. Wylie points out that the opinion of the Wisconsin supreme court holding the reapportionment law passed by the legislative session of 1891, — the famous democratic gerrymander — unconstitutional. The Wisconsin supreme court held:

1. Failure to pass a reapportionment act at the first session after enumeration does not result in a lapse of the power; but
2. That the duty continues until performed.
3. The power to reapportion does not lapse by the veto of an act, nor by there being an adjudication that it is unconstitutional.
4. The duty may be performed at a special session.
5. The duty may be performed at a subsequent session.
6. Legislators elected from districts prescribed by an unconstitutional apportionment act serve de facto.

In the opinion a ruling is also made as to the right of cities to annex property located in a different legislative district than that of the municipality, during the interim between the passage of reapportionment laws.

The opinion holds that the annexations can be made, but also decides that the annexed territory remains in the legislative districts in which they were located before the annexaton until a new reapportionment law is passed. This decision affects several annexations in Milwaukee county where portions of towns of Milwaukee county in other assembly districts were attached by annexation.

Four Officers Issue Plea for Confidence Which Asserts That No Constitutional Immunities Will Be Claimed

The following statement was brought to The State Journal office Saturday night by A. T. Rogers:

To the creditors of the Joseph M. Boyd company:

For the past two weeks the two local newspapers have been waging a caustic battle of words in an attempt to settle the question as to which paper has condemned the Joseph M. Boyd company, its officers and directors the most. The controversy has passed the point where it is educational or instructive to the public.

Neither paper has made any apparent effort to inform the creditors of the Joseph M. Boyd company and its associated companies, what they may expect by way of dividends on their claims although these people are no doubt primarily interested in what the possibilities and probabilities are of their having their money returned to them.

By innuendo attempts are being made to infer that the board of directors were derelict in their duties. This obviously involves a question of fact. But fragments of the true situation have been made public. We are entitled, we believe, that we be not prejudged until all of the facts are made known.

The undersigned directors desire to say to the district attorney and to all other public officials who have a right to know, that we, and each of us, welcome an opportunity to appear and testi-

(Continued on page 4 column 3)

Jobless Invited to Church Rally

Mrs. Diehl, Rev. Logan to Speak Tonight

Unemployed Madison people have been invited to a downtown rally at 7:30 tonight in the First Methodist Episcopal church to hear discussions of the slogan, "Not Charity but a Chance."

Speakers will be Mrs. Nannie E. Diehl, new executive secretary of the Public Welfare association, and the Rev. Harlan C. Logan, pastor of the First Methodist Episcopal church and president of the Madison Ministerial association.

"We hope to make this gathering of vital help to the Community Union," Dr. Hunt said.

TaxValuation in $4,890,150 Drop in City

Board Sharpens Pruning Knife to Keep Expenses Within Income

By HENRY NOLL

Repeal of several state laws on personal property and present economic conditions have resulted in a decrease of $4,890,150 in the assessed valuation of Madison's real and personal property, City Assessor John Stock announced Saturday.

According to the figures released by Mr. Stock the total valuation of all property is assessed at $146,378,070 as compared to $151,268,220 a year ago. The real estate has been assessed at $134,108,770, an increase of $833,745. A reduction of $5,723,895 has resulted in the personal property assessment which dropped from $17,993,195 in 1930 to $12,269,300 this year.

Mr. Stock explained that the reduction is due to repeal of the personal propery taxes on automobiles and on horses, wagons and sleighs, to the fact that merchants are not carrying as large stocks as they did last year and to the reduction in the amount of work turned out at the manufacturing plants. By the passage of the four cent gasoline tax the city will receive its share of the tax from the state but the exact amount will not be known until later in the year. Last year the assessments on autos alone aggregated $3,904,155, on motorcycles, $4,400;

(Continued on page 4 column 5)

100 Builders Here Toil For Hoover, Four For Phil

Herbert Clark Hoover has about 25 times as many men working in Madison construction jobs as has Philip Fox La Follette.

Put it another way. There are about 100 men employed on the newly started U. S. Forest Products laboratory job, a government project, which is expected to cost in the neighborhood of $900,000 and will be finished on Aug. 21, 1932, and an average of four men are employed on the new state office building which was started about the middle of April, 1930, and will not be finished until late next spring. The office building, or rather the portion now under construction, which is about one-fifth of the entire structure, will cost more than $400,000.

It's an interesting contrast, the speed and dispatch with which the Forest Products laboratory building project has been put under way as compared to the amazing slowness with which the state office building is being constructed.

The excavating work for the laboratory is nearly complete and

(Continued on page 4 column 1)

Woman Killed in Accident at Stoughton

Mrs. Ovren Run Down by Car Driven by Dr. Koch of Janesville

[State Journal News Service]

STOUGHTON—Mrs. Christine Alme Ovren, 73, Quam's Park, was fatally injured Saturday when she was struck by a car driven by Dr. Vincent Koch, Janesville, on highway 51, three miles north of Stoughton.

Mrs. Ovren died at 6:20 p. m., 20 minutes after the accident.

Dr. Koch and Ludwig K. Finsness, Stoughton, who saw the accident, said Mrs. Ovren was crossing the highway near Halvorson's store at Lake Kegonsa, going to the L. C. Quam farm to get milk.

Dr. Koch swerved in an effort to miss her, as she watched another car approach from the south. Dr. Koch was driving southward from Madison, where he had attended the Wisconsin-Purdue football game.

As the auto headed toward a ditch, a rear fender struck the woman, hurling her to the ground. An ambulance took her to a hospital here, where Dr. Koch aided in caring for her. She had suffered a fractured skull and arm. Dr. Koch was accompanied by Karl Kautlehner, Janesville.

Mrs. Ovren is survived by three daughters, Mrs. John Thompson, Racine; Mrs. J. M. Murphy, Madison, and Mrs. John Ritter, Los Angeles, Calif., and a son, Theodore Alme, Madison.

Japanese Regret U. S. Intervention

Country Sees Threat in Attitude, Representative Says

By SAMUEL DASHELL
[United Press Staff Correspondent]
[Copyright, 1931]

GENEVA.— Participation of the United States in the league council's deliberation on Manchuria was viewed as an "Unhappy event" Saturday by Kenkicki Yoshizawa, Japanese representative on the council.

"We have the greatest admiration and respect for the American people," he said in an interview with the United Press. "There are many close bonds of friendship. We deeply regret the incidents that led to American intervention on the council and consider it an unhappy event.

"American participation is regarded in the nature of a threat and a menace which is irritating the Japanese people. Although overruled by the council, Japan maintains the unconstitutionality of the American invitation also that it is contrary to procedure."

Yoshizawa was interviewed shortly before he visited Aristide Briand, France, president of the

(Continued on page 4 column 6)

Pilot Makes His Fourth Forced Parachute Leap

KANSAS CITY, Kans. — (U.P.) — Jack Ayers, pilot for the Branif Air Lines, made his fourth forced but successful parachute jump Saturday when the plane in which he was stunting crumpled and fell into the Missouri river.

U. S. Jury Convicts Gang Leader After Eight-Hour Session

AL CAPONE

"Big Shot" Freed From One Indictment; Promises Further Fight for Freedom

BY RAY BLACK
[United Press Staff Correspondent]

FEDERAL BUILDING CHICAGO—Al Capone, gangster chieftain, was found guilty Saturday night of income tax evasion by a jury in United States district court.

The verdict was returned at 11:13 p. m. after the jury had been out eight hours and 30 minutes.

Capone was found guilty of five counts on the second indictment charging tax evasion from 1925 to 1929. The jury found him not guilty on the first indictment, which charged income tax evasion in 1924.

Under the verdict Capone is subject to 17 years in federal penitentiary and $50,000 fine.

Judge Wilkerson deferred sentencing Capone until 10 a. m. Tuesday, and announced he would hear arguments on a motion for arrest of judgment at that time.

Rushed to Courtroom

Capone had been rushed from his headquarters in the Lexington hotel to the courtroom. The big gangster walked into the federal building with Defense Attorney Michael Ahern to the boom of news photographers' flashlights.

He was biting his lower lip as he strode up the corridor leading to the courtroom.

Three of the five counts charged tax evasion and were punishable as felonies. Two of the counts charged failure to make return on the income tax and were misdemeanor counts. The felony counts cover the years 1925, 1926 and 1927. The misdemeanor counts are for years 1928 and 1929.

Squirms in Chair

Capone squirmed in his chair as the verdict was read. His eyes filled with tears as Clerk of Court Sullivan read the verdict in a voice that carried to the corners of the courtroom.

"I'm not through fighting yet," Capone declared.

"My feeling through the whole trial was that I was up to bat with two strikes on me. But I'm not going to admit defeat until the higher court rules against me.

'I Won't Cry'

"I feel satisfied that my attorneys put up the best fight they could. There's no use crying now.

(Continued on page 7 column 4)

Hoover and Gifford on WIBA Today

President's Unemployment Program Featured on National Network

One of the greatest gatherings of outstanding personalities today will be heard over WIBA and an NBC network this afternoon at 5 o'clock when the National Broadcasting company features a one-hour broadcast on President Hoover's unemployment program.

Mr. Hoover

The president and Walter S. Gifford, chairman of Mr. Hoover's unemployment commission, will be the speakers. Mr. Hoover, who will speak from Fortress Monroe, Va., will be introduced by Mr. Gifford from New York City.

A scintillating array of radio and stage artists will enhance the program. Will Rogers, probably the country's most popular humorist; Lawrence Tibbett, noted stage and screen baritone; John Phillips Sousa and the U. S. Marine band; Leopold Stokowski and the Philadelphia orchestra; Lily Pons, famous soprano; and Sophie Braslau, noted contralto.

The broadcast will open with Graham McNamee announcing Sousa and the Marine band from Fortress Monroe, Va. Lawrence Tibbett will follow from San Francisco. Lily Pons will be heard from New York and then the program will be switched to Philadelphia for the orchestra selections under direction of the famous Stokowski.

Mr. Gifford

Mr. Gifford will be introduced at this stage by McNamee, and will in turn introduce the president.

Sophie Braslau, contralto, will follow the president's talk from New York and will be introduced by David Ross, NBC announcer. The program will be concluded with selections by the Philadelphia orchestra and the Marine band.

Badger Guard Cut 200 Men

Wisconsin's national guard units are being reduced by 200 men on orders from Washington on the ground that the state guard has more than its allottment of personel, Adjutant General Ralph M. Immell announced Saturday night.

National guard enlistments have been unusually popular, possibly because of the depression, General Immell said. A similar condition also prevails in other states, he declared.

As a result of the order from Washington, the tate guard s being cut to 4,680 men, the figure Washington, the state guard is belotted to the Wisconsin guard.

142 Mile-an-Hour Average Wins Patrick Trophy Race

GALVESTON, Tex—(U.P.)—Lieut. Don W. Mayhue, Palestine, Ill., a member of the eighth squadron, third attack group, won the national Mason M. Patrick air trophy race at Fort Crockett Saturday with an average speed of 142.59 miles an hour over the 60 mile course.

Lieut. Eric G. Danielson, eighth squadron, Spokane, Wash., was second with an average speed of 141.45 miles an hour.

Lieut. Richard A. Morehouse, Columbus, Ohio, was third, with a speed of 140.904 miles an hour.

The Wisconsin State Journal
A Fact-Finding Newspaper

THE WEATHER
Occasional rain or snow tonight and Thursday. Little change in temperature. Moderate variable winds. (Weather tables on page 4)

VOL. 139, NO. 151. 93rd Year. ★★★ HOME FINAL MADISON, WEDNESDAY, MARCH 2, 1932 TWENTY PAGES PRICE THREE CENTS

Lindbergh Ready to Pay $50,000 Ransom Demanded for Return of Kidnaped Baby

Son, Suffering With Cold, Taken From Crib in Home by Captors, One a Woman

Wife, Expecting Another Child, is Pale and Drawn as Police Seek Clues

BULLETIN
HOPEWELL, N. J.—(U.P.)—Douglas G. Thompson, former mayor of Englewood, N. J., arrived here this afternoon, and it was said he would take charge of arranging for payment of $50,000 to the kidnapers of Charles A. Lindbergh, Jr.

By BATES RANEY
[United Press Staff Correspondent]

HOPEWELL, N. J. — Feeling that the "main thing is to get the baby back," Col. Charles A. Lindbergh was preparing today to pay the kidnapers of his 20-month-old son, Charles A., Jr., $50,000 if he can get in touch with them.

Police advised this course and the anxious father was ready and willing to give the amount demanded by the persons who Tuesday night abducted the child, ill with a cold, from the Lindbergh nursery in the stone house in the Sourland mountains. One of the kidnapers was believed a woman.

There were reports, which the Lindberghs and their advisers would not verify, that the letter, left in the baby's crib, threatened the child with harm if the ransom demands were not met.

Plane Drops Message

Meantime, two occurrences with possible significance occurred, as thousands of police, state troopers and volunteers aided in a hunt for the kidnapers.

First, a mysterious plane this afternoon flew over the Lindbergh estate and dropped a streamer with a weight attached. It appeared to be a strip of canvas, and watchers suspected it might contain a note either from kidnapers' agents or from air searchers hunting for some clue from the vantage point of the skies. The Lindbergh home, however, denied any message had been received.

Second, a postcard to "Charles Lindberg Princeton N. J." was found in a mailbox at Newark this afternoon, with the following unsigned pencil message:

> **"Baby safe. Instructions later. Act accordingly.'**

With cold daring, the actual kidnaper crept up a short sectional ladder into the second floor nursery sometime between 7:30 and 10 p. m. Tuesday night, took the child down the ladder, and left behind the ransom demand.

> **FIRE ADDS TO TURMOIL**
> HOPEWELL, N. J.—(U.P.)—A fire on a farm about three miles from the Charles A. Lindbergh estate today caused sounding of the fire siren from the Lindbergh station. The fire call added excitement to the tense situation arising from kidnaping of the Lindbergh baby.

This note, demanding the $50,000 for the child's freedom, was reported to have said in substance:

> **"We will be back tomorrow (Wednesday) to talk business. Don't talk to the police or the papers."**

Meantime, the kidnaping created a worldwide sensation.

Thousands Hunt Child

Literally thousands of police and state troopers were put on alarm guard, watching highways, and state and national boundary lines. Over the teletype wires of the eastern states and up along the Canadian border flashed word that one of the nation's most famous babies had been stolen.

The kidnapers apparently had not realized the furore and resentment their deed would cause. Police everywhere went to work with a will to come up with the kidnapers, while the federal departments of justice, commerce and treasury in Washington, offered to do all within their power to track down the criminals.

$25,000 Rewards Cancelled

After Gov. A. Harry Moore, New Jersey, had announced a reward of $10,000 for the capture of the Lindbergh baby kidnapers and the state senate resolved to increase the amount to $25,000, the reward was cancelled out of consideration for Colonel Lindbergh.

Moore telephoned the distraught father and told him of the proposed state action. Lindbergh expressed the fear that the reward might endanger his child, whereupon the reward plans were cancelled.

President Hoover manifested his interest.

Aviators from many parts of the

Separated by Kidnapers

This is the first photo of Mrs. Charles A. Lindbergh and Charles Augustus Lindbergh taken together. The photo was especially posed at the Morrow home, Englewood, N. J.

Baby's Arrival Got Worldwide News Comment

Everything About Child Draws Interest

ENGLEWOOD, N. J.—(U.P.)—Arrival of the blue eyed 7 4-5 pound Lindbergh baby on the birthday of his mother here June 22, 1930, caused more worldwide newspaper comment than any other birth on the North American continent.

No royal child, for whose arrival a nation waited with anxious interest, ever attracted more public speculation before its birth or was watched more closely afterward.

Would it be a boy or a girl? Would he be a flier like his father? Numerologists, astrologers, and others wrote articles on the subject.

Birth Kept Secret

But despite all the ceaseless, 24-hour vigil by newspaper men at the Morrow estate, the newspapers did not learn of the birth until several hours after young Charles Augustus, Jr., uttered his first lusty howls.

He wasn't Charles Augustus, Jr., then—and that led to another wave of newspaper speculation. What would his famous parents name their first son?

Has Never Flown

The baby's first picture—his orange juice diet—any change of nurses: all were duly recorded in the press in greater detail than if the youngster had been heir to a throne.

The greatest interest seemed to

(Continued on page 2 column 4)

U.S. Justice Department Offers Help

Congress Hears Plea for Action to Stop Kidnapings

WASHINGTON — (U.P.) — The force of the federal government today was thrown into the search for the kidnaped baby of the Charles A. Lindbergh family.

The department of justice offered its complete cooperation in the search.

The coast guard of the New York and New Jersey divisions was instructed to offer its aid to the New Jersey police.

Watch Planes, Border

The department of commerce prepared a request to all commercial airport authorities to watch incoming and outgoing planes and for their pilots to report anything which might be of value.

Assistant Secretary of the Treasury Lowman in charge of customs announced customs agents at border points or elsewhere will give all possible aid.

President Hoover read accounts of the kidnaping early this morning and was deeply moved. He asked to be kept informed of developments during the day.

Congress Hears Pleas

Demands for prompt action by congress on bills empowering the federal government to act in kidnaping cases were made in both

(Continued on page 2 column 4)

Smith Charges Misconduct

Found Wife With Man in Hotel, Claim

Cruel and inhuman treatment and misconduct with persons known and unknown were alleged as causes of action in a complaint filed in circuit court today in the divorce suit of H. Bowen Smith, Maple Bluff, against his wife, Mrs. Ruth Smith.

The complaint, which asks custoy of the couple's four-year old son, alleges that Mrs. Smith has used intoxicants to excess and is unfit as custodian of the child.

Found With Man, Charge

The document, filed by Buell and Lucas as attorneys for Smith, charges that Mrs. Smith was found by her husband in a room at the Hotel Loraine with a man named Ray Hughes at 1:45 a. m. on the night of Feb. 12. It alleges misconduct with other men in Madison and West Palm Beach, Fla.

In the absence of her attorney Laurence Hall, who is out of the city, Mrs. Smith today declined to issue a statement. It is believed however, that the case will be contested. She is now occupying the home in Maple Bluff, following a brief stay at the Hotel Loraine after her return in January from a trip to Florida, while her husband and small son are living with his parents, Mr. and Mrs. Harrison A. Smith, also of Maple Bluff.

Met in Boston

The young couple, who met in Boston while Smith was a student and his wife hostess in a tea room, was married in Chicago, Nov. 19, 1927, and lived together until about Dec. 5, 1931, when Mrs. Smith went to West Palm Beach, Fla.

Upon her return, Jan. 23, summons was served upon her in the divorce action. Accommodations were obtained for her temporarily at the Hotel Loraine, the complaint states, but she later obtained a court order permitting her to occupy the home on Maple Bluff pending disposition of the case.

Denies Parents' Influence

An affidavit signed by Smith, filed with the complaint today, denies that his father had any part in the arrangements at the hotel, that his parents in any way influenced the divorce action, that they had forcibly kept the child from his wife, that they had notified her that she could not come on their premises or that they had "advised her to ge out of town immediately."

On about April 14, 1931, the husband's affidavit avers, Mrs. Smith, accompanied by her sister, "who passes under the name of Gracy Styles and Grace Baldwin," with the little boy and a maid, left on a trip, as he had previously supposed, to the home of Mrs. Smith's mother in Boston. But on the eve of the trip, he claims, he was notified that they were going to West Palm Beach where, the affidavit states, "that the husband of Grace Styles was in jail."

The trip was made in the Smith

(Continued on page 4 column 7)

Boyd Firm's Affairs Shifted to U.S. Court on Bankruptcy Plea

Beecroft Building Company Files Involuntary Petition Against Company; Summons Served on President

A move long anticipated to shift jurisdiction in disposal of the financial affairs of the Joseph M. Boyd company from circuit court to federal court, materialized today when an involuntary petition in bankruptcy was filed against the investment concern.

The petition, signed by the Beecroft Building company, Thomas Gordon and W. G. Beecroft as creditors, was presented in U. S. district court by Schubring, Ryan, Clarke and Peterson. Summons was served Tuesday upon Joseph M. Boyd, president of the suspended investment firm.

Transfer Case

The step, it was declared by Attorney William Ryan today, removes the case from the jurisdiction of Judge A. C. Hoppmann in Dane county circuit court. It follows the recent decision of Judge Robert S. Cowie, who held the assignment through circuit court invalid as an invasion of the field covered by the bankruptcy act.

Acts of bankruptcy by the Boyd company are alleged in the petition as justifying the proceedings in federal court.

It declares that the Boyd company, as agent for the Beecroft Building company, received $216,000 from the sale of Beecroft bonds between April, 1929, and August, 1930, which was never accounted for nor paid to the Beecroft company but was appropriated to the use of the Boyd company.

Neglected Pay, Charge

It alleges that the Boyd company, between August 18, 1930, and March 18, 1931, received $33 interest and $100 principal from Mattie Dorman on a mortgage owned by Thomas Gordon, of which Mattie Dorman was mortgagor; and that the Boyd company has neglected to pay the sum to Gordon or to account for it.

It declares William G. Beecroft advanced to the Boyd company $58.86 to apply on interest due on a mortgage debt of which Dr. Beecroft was mortgagor and that the Boyd company appropriated the sum and failed to account for it.

Charges Other Acts

It charges that on Jan. 28, 1932, the Boyd company committed an act of bankruptcy in allowing a creditor, Frank Hess, Madison, to obtain preference through legal proceedings and committeed another act of bankruptcy on Dec. 31, 1931, in suffering Fred Klein, Sr., another creditor to obtain a default judgment.

On March 31, 1931, the petition states, the directors of the Boyd company made an assignment of all its property to C. E. Karn, L. D. Atkinson and Leo T. Crowley as trustees and that on July 30 Frank Hess commenced an action in circuit court, where he obtained a lien by service of a garnishee summons on the trustees. On Dec. 31, it adds, a judgment of $6,723 was rendered in circuit court in favor of Hess and on Jan. 29 the judgment was rendered against the

(Continued on page 4 column 1)

Quash Indictment Against Benham

Widow Gave Draft, Court Finds

BELVIDERE, Ill.—(U.P.)—The indictment charging Albert W. "Fifty Per Cent" Benham with operating a confidence game was thrown out of court today by Circuit Judge Albert E. Fisher, midway in the trial.

Defense counsel late Tuesday filed a demurrer charging an error in the indictment and upon opening of court today Judge Fisher ordered the indictment quashed.

In this, the first of a series of cases against Benham, he was accused of obtaining $300 from Mrs. Marie Johnson, a middle-aged widow of Belvidere. The indictment, which charged she gave Benham cash, was quashed after she testified the investment was in the form of a draft. Benham again will be brought to trail March 14.

Cheese Body Cuts Salaries, Reduces Staff

Federation Accepts Corniea Resignation, Successor to Receive $7,000 Less; Vote 7 Point Plan

Nearly all officials of the National Cheese Producers' federation had their salaries slashed and some employes were dismissed as a result of a joint conference Tuesday afternoon in the capitol between representatives of the college of agriculture, the department of agriculture and markets, leading farm organizations and the cheese marketing cooperative.

Final decision not to reemploy Frank Corniea, resigned business manager, was made and it was agreed that some man with a background of Wisconsin's cheese marketing channels should be employed to replace Corniea at about $5,000 a year instead of $12,000 which was paid Corniea.

Discussions centered around applying the seven-point program of reform which had been suggested during a joint meeting of the same groups early this winter.

Elimination of William Hutter, Spring Green; Gus Brickbauer, Elkhart Lake, and R. R. Smith, Plymouth, as fieldmen was definitely decided upon, The State Journal learned. Hereafter, it was decid-

(Continued on page 14 column 7)

Chinese Quit Battle Area for New Line

Chapei, in Flames, Appears Doomed as Japs Fire Native City

BULLETIN
SHANHAI— (U.P.) —Japanese tanks entered war-torn Chapei today, the first move toward definite occupation of the zone. Simultaneously headquarters troops of the ninth division entered Tazang.

By HERBERT R. EKINS
[United Press Staff Correspondent]
[Copyright 1932, by United Press]

SHANGHAI (Thursday) — The native city of Shanghai was in flames today as the torch and incendiary bombs were applied to Chapei in the wake of the retreating Chinese army.

Chapei was burning along a mile front in the north station area. Huge cotton mills exploded with terrific detonations, the flames shooting high in the air.

American observers claimed the Japanese were setting the fires because of snipers and machine gun nests remaining after the general Chinese withdrawal to 12½ miles from the city.

Chapei Appears Doomed

Fortunately, there was no wind and the flames did not menace the international settlement.

The bulk of the Chapei area,

(Continued on page 4 columr 2)

Central Senior High to Close, Board Votes Over Parents' Protest

Reject Plans to Close Brayton School, Suspend Teachers' Salary Schedule

By HENRY NOLL

Transferring of all senior high school students from Central high to West and East side highs at the opening of the fall term in September was voted Tuesday night by the board of education, 4 to 3, in spite of petitions signed by more than 500 citizens who protested against the change. The petitions were presented by Ald. Albert J. Schwoegler, who was accompanied by Ald. W. H. Conlin and delegation of parents of children attending Central senior high.

The board rejected the recommendation of Supt. R. W. Bardwell that Brayton school be closed and that the teachers' salary schedule be suspended. Approval was given the recommendation to give all teachers, members of the clerical staff and officers of the schools a week's vacation without pay after the school house janitors had been eliminated.

In view of the $75,000 cut made in the budget by the common council, Bardwell recommended discontinuance of senior classes at Central high, closing of Brayton, suspension of the salary schedule and a week's vacation without sal-

(Continued on page 4 column 3)

Security Bank Offer May Be Sought Again

Capital City Creditors' Sales Committee Confers With Officers

Renewal of the Security State bank's offer for purchase of the assets of the Capital City bank may be sought by creditors, it was indicated today.

The same committee of the general creditors' group named at the meeting in Central High school last Thursday night conferred Tuesday afternoon with officers of the east side bank, it was learned.

Warren E. Hicks, chairman of the sub-committee, who today was studying the original offer made by the Security State bank, pointed out that the offer was made at the invitation of the state banking

(Continued on page 4 column 5)

Jobs to Fade in Frank Plan to Save Funds

President Tells Ways to Save $408,609 as State Emergency Hearings Continue

By MICHAEL GRIFFIN

By a sweeping reorganization and reassessment of its operation and administration, the University of Wisconsin can revert to the general fund $408,609 from Feb. 15 of this year to June 30, 1933, President Glenn Frank informed the state emergency board today when hearings were resumed on budgets of various state activities.

To save this money the university will have to make several retrenchments, Frank explained, but the officers are willing if the emergency board deems them necessary.

Although no mention of the possible dismissal of some professors, associate and assistant, was made, Frank and Dean Chris Christensen of the college of agriculture informed Governor La Follette privately that some faculty members would lose their jobs.

In his statement to the board, Frank listed 10 methods by which the $408,609 can be saved. They are by leaving vacancies unfilled wherever possible to redistribute the duties of the position vacated; by staff reductions through educational readjustments; by economies in staff replacements; by elimination or consolidation of services; by deferment of less vital maintenance; by stringent restriction of divisional expenditures; by postponement of minor improvements; by curtailment of expenditures for business items; by the return to the general fund of certain special capital appropriations and capital balances, and by a refund to the state of a

(Continued on page 14 column 1)

Woman, Life Prolonged With Rare Serum, Dies

CHICAGO— (U.P.) —Mrs. Andrew Nelson, 41, died today from Addison's disease. Seven months ago her life was prolonged when a supply of cortin, a rare serum, was brought from Buffalo by airplane to combat the disease. Although the serum had been available since, it failed to save her.

Atty. Sheldon Kills Self in Office

Lives Five Hours in Hospital After Bullet Passes Through Head

Henry T. Sheldon, of 102 North Spooner street, a Madison attorney, died in a Madison hospital Tuesday at 9:10 p. m., five hours after he had shot himself through the head with a revolver in his office in the Gay building.

SHELDON

Ill health and financial difficulties were blamed by Coroner William E. Campbell, who said the death was a suicide.

He was found by A. J. Bieberstein, attorney, who came to Sheldon's office to obtain assistance in a legal matter. Bieberstein found him sitting in his chair gasping for breath. He sought medical aid, thinking Sheldon had suffered a stroke. When he returned, he noticed

(Continued on page 4 column 5)

Invites Women to Two Republican Gatherings

SHEBOYGAN—(U.P.)—Mrs. Harry E. Thomas, Sheboyyan, national republican committeewoman, today invited Wisconsin women to attend two district meetings in the near future. Republicans of the second district will meet March 4 at Oconomowoc and women in the sixth district will gather March 10 at Fond du Lac. Candidates for delegates to the national convention will be present.

'Lame Duck' Amendment Started on Way to States

WASHINGTON — (U.P.) — The probable 20th amendment to the constitution, in the form of the Norris proposal to abolish "lame duck" sessions of congress, was started today on the way to the states for ratification. The senate adopted a compromise amendment already agreed to by the house. The amendment now goes to the department of state for submission to the states.

State Journal and 600 Other Newspapers to Conduct National Presidential Poll

The State Journal, in collaboration with 600 newspapers throughout the country, will conduct a presidential poll beginning Friday —exactly one year before the next inauguration of a United States chief executive.

Every day for a week, a ballot will be published in The State Journal. Readers will be asked to mail them to the Election Editor at The State Journal office.

While voters must sign their ballots in order for them to be counted, the names will remain secret. The names have been asked in order to avoid duplicate voting or ballot stuffing.

No suggestions will be made on the ballots. The voter may cast a ballot for any person he chooses, a member of any party.

The vote will be the most comprehensive and diversified ever attempted, aimed to give an indication even before nominations are made of the nation's popular choice for president.

The State Journal will conduct the trial vote in this area, and will announce the national totals each day as they are compiled by Central Press association, sponsor of the balloting throughout the country.

Anti-Hoarding Committees Lay Plans for Campaign

Committees of the Madison Anti-Hoarding campaign held meetings throughout today, Harry L. French, general chairman, said this afternoon.

He will present the first of 10 nightly broadcasts on WIBA at 7:30 p. m. Thursday. Others announced by Charles J. Birt, chairman of the speakers' committee, as indicating willingness to address groups and to broadcast messages against hoarding included the Rev. Joseph Lederer, Harry Dimond, Mrs. K. L. Hatch, John P. Butler, and Mrs. James A. Jackson, Jr.

Other radio talks will be made at 6:25 p. m. each day on WIBA, the committee has announced.

Merchants' aid in the drive against hoarded funds was pledged to L. M. Hanks, chairman of the

(Continued on page 4 column 5)

THE WEATHER
Snow or rain tonight and Thursday. Not much change in temperature. Strong shifting winds.

The Wisconsin State Journal

A Fact-Finding Newspaper

VOL. 141, NO. 40. 93rd Year. ★★★★ MADISON, WEDNESDAY, NOVEMBER 9, 1932 TWENTY-TWO PAGES PRICE THREE CENTS

ROOSEVELT WINS RECORD VOTE

Schmedeman, 89,969 Victor, Leads Democrats' Tidal Wave Over Four of State GOP Ticket

Dammann Only Republican to Survive Flood, First Since Peck's Reign 37 Years Ago

A sweep that tumbled republicans from the highest to the lowest offices in the state and set Albert G. Schmedeman, Madison's four-time mayor, in the governor's chair and F. Ryan Duffy, Fond du Lac, in Sen. John J. Blaine's U. S. senate seat, was recorded today with Wisconsin in the democratic columns nationally for only the fourth time in the history of its statehood.

Here and there the count gave some small consolation to the republicans, but those instances were rare among state and congressional offices.

First in 37 Years

For the first time since George W. Peck, the author of "Peck's Bad Boy," was governor of Wisconsin 37 years ago, the state today was promised a democratic administration.

With the democratic governor was assured a democratic senator at Washington.

Returns from 2,325 of the state's 2,900 precincts gave for president: Hoover, 292,907 Roosevelt, 583,103; Thomas, 38,658.

Returns from 2,168 precincts gave for senator: Chapple, rep., 296,176; Duffy, dem., 456,034; Seidel, soc., 45,151.

Returns from 2,245 precincts gave for governor: Kohler, rep., 358,378; Schmedeman, dem., 448,347; Metcalfe, soc., 40,789.

This democratic wave which rode the crest of the Roosevelt boom extended far out into the county offices, displacing republican incumbents of long standing in such hitherto republican strongholds as Marathon county. Dane county's republican incumbents, however, held their lines and were returned to office.

Regular republican incumbents in congress appeared displaced and even some of the La Follette progressive republican group bowed to democratic opponents.

The part played by members of the La Follette faction in their desertion of President Hoover and other republican candidates and their transfer of allegiance to the democratic party swung the victory for the followers of Franklin D. Roosevelt.

Dammann in Lead

While the democratic candidates for constitutional state offices below governor held a lead over their regular republican opponents, one notable exception remained the La Follette influence. That was the candidacy of Secretary of State Theodore Dammann, the only member of the La Follette

(Continued on page 6 column 8)

Republicans Carry Madison

Complete returns from Madison today showed that Kohler carried the city by 3,538 votes. The vote was: Kohler, 14,631; Schmedeman, 11,093; Metcalfe, 402; and Dean, 23. The entire republican state ticket carried Madison.

Big Day for O'Malleys

MILWAUKEE — (U.P.) — The O'Malleys went places in the Wisconsin election, as befits a railroad man and his son.

Thomas J. O'Malley, 65, conductor on the Chicago and North Western passenger train between Chicago and Green Bay, was elected lieutenant governor of Wisconsin.

His son, Thomas D. O'Malley, 31, is the new congressman from the fifth district. They're both democrats.

Lioness Crushes One of Her Triplets

PUEBLO, Col. (U.P.)—Lena, the lioness in the Pueblo Zoo, had triplets, but now she only has twins.

The three cubs were born to Lena, who tended them carefully. But somehow, whether through accident or design, no one save Lena knows, she sat down on one of them, crushing its life out.

State's First Family

Elated Friends Rush to Cheer Mayor and Wife

Since the moment Tuesday night the returns showed his victory was assured, Mayor A. G. Schmedeman and his wife have been stampeded with groups of well wishers, and messages of congratulations.

Celebrators shattered the peace of the mayor's home Tuesday night when returns showed he was governor-elect of Wisconsin. Nearly 50 ardent democrats and admirers marched into his Wisconsin avenue residence. They were heralded by a band, composed largely of University of Wisconsin students, which they had met as it was returning from an engagement.

"I'm Awfully Happy"

The governor-elect spoke to a radio audience from the dining room of his home Tuesday night. He expressed pride at being chosen governor. After the broadcast he was bundled into his overcoat and "kidnaped." A parade through Madison ended in the parlor of the Eagles' home, where another large group of admirers was awaiting him.

"I'm awfully happy, boys," he said.

Speaks Over Radio

From his home, the governor-elect spoke to the state over the radio. Schmedeman said:

"Incomplete returns from all sections of Wisconsin indicate that democracy in Wisconsin has followed the nation in calling upon the party of Jefferson to lead the country to sanity and out of the

(Continued on page 4 column 5)

—State Journal Photos

Wisconsin's governor-elect and the state's first lady-to-be, Mayor and Mrs. A[illegible] G. Schmedeman of Madison, are shown above in a photograph taken at their home this morning. Mr. and Mrs. Schmedeman, whose home for many years has been at 504 Wisconsin avenue, will be required to move little more than a block when they occupy the executive mansion in January. Below, the governor-elect is shown at the microphone as he gave his "speech of appreciation" Tuesday night when his election became a certainty.

Duffy Victory Over Chapple Hits 159,858

Fond du Lac Democrat Sails Into Blaine's U. S. Senate Seat by Big Vote

F. RYAN DUFFY

F. Ryan Duffy, Fond du Lac democratic lawyer, was swept into the U. S. senatorship over John B. Chapple, the young man who came out of the north to defeat John J. Blaine for the republican nomination to that office, by his party's landslide victory at the polls Tuesday.

Returns from 2,168 of the state's 2,900 precincts gave Duffy 456,034 votes; Chapple 296,176 and Emil Seidel, socialist, 45,151.

Chapple was the weakest candidate on the republican ticket, running considerably behind the republican vote for former Governor Kohler. Kohler trailed Schmedeman by 89,969 votes.

Dane county gave Chapple 16,763, and Duffy 26,549. In Dodge county,

(Continued on page 6 column 3)

Chapple Carries 10th Ward

Madison's tenth ward, home of many of the University of Wisconsin's faculty members, gave John B. Chapple a 846 vote majority over F. Ryan Duffy in the U. S. senatorial race. Chapple, republican, who campaigned on the radical issue at the university, polled 3,155 votes in the 10th ward to his opponent's 2209.

Cyclonic Wind Kills 10, Injures 50 Near Havana

HAVANA, Cuba — (U.P.) — A cyclonic wind damaged the Camajuani district today, messages received here said. Ten were killed and 50 injured.

Sam Insull, Jr., Returns to Chicago from Europe

CHICAGO—(U.P.)—Samuel Insull, Jr., returned to Chicago today from Europe, where he has spent several weeks with his mother and his father, Samuel Insull, the former utilities magnate now a prisoner in Greece.

Ald. Frank Alford May be City's New Mayor Within Two Months

Dane County Reelects All Incumbents

Finn Beats Schwoegler Five to Two; Risser Victor by 14,840

All republican incumbents of county offices were safely returned for the next two year term, although their democratic opponents polled a surprising number of votes, due to the Roosevelt landslide.

Sheriff Fred T. Finn was re-elected for his third term as sheriff by a vote of almost five to two over Al J. Schwoegler. Finn received 30,-

(Continued on page 4 column 1)

Schmedeman Won't Retire Until Work is Completed, He Says; Three Courses Open for Selection

By HENRY NOLL

Madison will have a new mayor within the next two months as the result of the election of Mayor Schmedeman as governor Tuesday.

Sentiment today appeared strong for the election of Ald. Frank Alford, chairman of the council finance committee, as successor to the mayor until next spring, when the voters will be asked to fill the unexpired term of Mayor Schmedeman.

Schmedeman broke all records last April by being elected mayor for the fourth consecutive term. His present term expires in April, 1934.

According to City Attorney Theo-

(Continued on page 4 column 3)

Henney Wins 2nd District from J. B. Gay

Wisconsin Elects Five Democrats to Congress; Republicans Probably Two

Dr. C. W. Henney, Portage democrat, will represent the second district in congress, it became certain today when tabulations showed his vote 48,254 and his opponent's, John B. Gay, Portage republican, 40,164.

Five of Wisconsin's newly elect-

(Continued on page 6 column 6)

The President-Elect

FRANKLIN D. ROOSEVELT

Democrats Win Senate, House; Watson, Moses, Smoot, Bingham Beaten

McAdoo, Tydings and Wagner Hold Leads Over Republican Opponents

By LYLE C. WILSON
[United Press Staff Correspondent]

NEW YORK—Democrats swept into undisputed control of the next senate today, maintained a better than two to one lead in the house and were assured of controlling a wet 73rd congress next year. Short session control of the senate still is in doubt but the democrats will remain in control of the house this winter.

The election appears to have been a political massacre. Democrats have elected 19 senators, seven of them in republican strongholds. Further democratic gains are likely.

Davis, Dale Wins

Republicans so far have elected two senators, James J. Davis, (repn., Pa.), and Porter H. Dale, (repn., Vt.) Davis is wet, Dale dry. Republicans are leading in five senate races: Colorado (short term) Nevada, Oregon, North Dakota and South Dakota.

Democrats are leading in Arizona, Colorado (long term) Idaho, Kansas, New Jersey, Washington, California and Ohio. James P. Pope, democratic candidate in Idaho, is a dry. The other democratic leaders are unsualifiedly wet or pledged to the national platform with its promise of immediate beer and repeal.

Democrats Win House

The North and South Dakota republicans are drys and the other three republican leaders are pledged to the republican platform which promises change in prohibition.

With more than half the house contests decided, democrats had won 187 seats and republicans 70. The wets had 147 seats divided between 46 republicans and 101 democrats. An aggregate of 59 winners were classed "doubtful" on prohibition. There were 48 drys among them of whom 15 were democrats and 33 were republican. The balance were pledged to the national platforms.

Democrats have defeated Senator Bingham, (repn., Conn.), Senator Glenn, (repn., Ill.), Senator Brookhart, (repn., Ia.), and the regular republican nominee in that state, Henry Field, Senator Moses, (repn., N. H.), the president pro tem of the senate; John B. Chapple, who defeated Senator Blaine, (repn., Wis.), in the primary; Senator Watson, (repn., Ind.), the senate majority leader; and Senator Smoot, (repn., Utah), chairman of the finance committee and dean of the senate.

Watson, Moses Lose

Republican Senate Leader Watson, in congress for 38 years, conceed defeat in Indiana to Frederick Van Nuys, democrat, and Sen-

(Continued on page 6 column 5)

Fred Nicholson Surrenders to Federal Court

Verona Man Pleads Not Guilty to U. S. Car Theft Charges

Fred Nicholson, formerly proprietor of the Eagles Nest restaurant at Verona, surrendered to arrest today on a federal warrant charging conspiracy to violate the motor vehicle theft law.

Nicholson was indicted by the grand jury which convened here last month. He was arraigned this morning before Commissioner Frank R. Bentley, pleaded not guilty and was released on $2,000 bond.

The indictment also names Dominick Nuccia, who has been confined in the Dane county jail several months. It consists of one count and charges overt acts of which 17 involve Nicholson.

The charges grew out of the arrest, on Sept. 11, 1931, of Tony Abene, Chicago, who was trapped by Sheriff Fred Finn, with Nicholson's co-operation, in the act of transporting a stolen car to Verona.

Admitting that he had bought cars from Abene and resold them, Nicholson declared at the time that he engaged in the business in good faith, not knowing that the cars were stolen, and thought the bills of sale presented to him were bona fide. When a stolen car was traced to his place of business in Verona he voluntarily assisted county officers in capturing Abene, who is now serving an 18-month

(Continued on page 4 column 4)

Rotary Comes to Hospital, Saves Hirsig's Record

Louis Hirsig's perfect record for Rotary club attendance during the past 20 years was still without a blemish today, although he is confined to the Madison General hospital, recovering from an operation.

Reluctant to see his unique record broken, members of the Stoughton Rotary club came to Madison today and held their weekly meeting in a hospital room so that Madison's star member could answer present to the roll call, just as he has every week since 1913.

Hirsig's failure to miss a single meeting in 20 years is unparalleled in Rotary annals, just as the club's action in bringing the meeting to him is without precedent in club history. A charter member of the Madison Rotary club, he served as one of the founders of the Stoughton chapter.

Every committee in the Rotary organization has at one time or another had Hirsig's services during the past two decades, and in 1917 and 1918 he served the Madison club as president.

New Yorker Takes 42 States to Get 472 College Votes

Hoover Plans to Attempt to Regain Riches

PALO ALTO, Cal.—(U.P.)—President Hoover announced today in his first public declaration since his defeat for reelection that he intended to return to private life, to recoup his personal fortune.

The president in an interview let it be known that he intended to return to Palo Alto to take up his permanent residence. The exact nature of his future private occupation he was unable to reveal.

President Hoover indicated that he had not the remotest idea what he would do after March 4, but that he intended going back to work as a private citizen.

The president also said that he planned now to depart from Palo Alto Saturday night for Washington. He will take the southern route, going by way of Los Angeles across Arizona, New Mexico and over the Santa Fe trail.

In the meantime, he said he would rest for the rest of the week, possibly taking occasional drives in the vicinity of his home here.

Reis Winner Over Riley for State Senate

Lamb Defeats Bieberstein for Assembly; Hanson Elected

Alvin C. Reis, progressive republican, was elected state senator from Dane county in Tuesday's election, defeating his democratic opponent, Miles Riley, by 3,431 votes.

REIS

Reis, a former assembly floor leader for the La Follette faction, received a total of 23,243 votes while Riley polled 19,812. Both Reis and Riley are Madison attorneys. Riley showed considerable strength in several county precincts where Reis was considered strong. The city race was practically neck and neck.

A regular republican will represent the Madison district in the assembly during the next session through the victory of Francis Lamb. Lamb defeated Adolph Bieberstein, democrat, by a total of 4,425 votes. Only one precinct in the ninth ward was missing from the total. Lamb polled 13,118 votes to 8,693 for Bieberstein.

For second district assemblyman, Jim Hanson, veteran Deerfield progressive, defeated J. M. Blaska, democrat, 5,538 to 3,926.

Albert J. Baker, Mt. Horeb, was a winner over Stanley S. Gordon, Verona, for third district assemblyman. With nearly all the returns reported, Baker had a 463 vote lead over his democratic opponent. Baker had a total vote of 4,400 to 3,937 for Gordon.

Name Geo. Sayle Receiver for Blied Apartments

George W. Sayle, Madison, realtor, has been appointed receiver for the Blied apartments on West Gilman street, it was announced today. Sayle is receiver representing the Central Wisconsin Trust company which is acting as trustee for the bondholders.

Hoover Wins 59 Electoral Ballots as Landslide Hits Him Harder Than Smith

By RAYMOND CLAPPER
[United Press Staff Correspondent]

NEW YORK — Franklin D. Roosevelt, governor of New York, has been elected president of the United States by one of the greatest landslides in history.

The same landslide which carried the democratic nominee to the White House swept a democratic majority into both houses of congress, and returned democratic governors in state after state.

A total of 25,883,535 votes were tabulated by the United Press today.

On the basis of this count, Governor Roosevelt had carried 42 state, with 472 electoral votes; President Hoover, six, with 59 electoral votes.

The division of popular votes was as follows:

Roosevelt 15,001,860.
Hoover 10,531,485.
Thomas 350,189.

If this proportion continues throughout the count is expected to reach 40,000,000, Roosevelt would have a clear majority in the popular vote.

The last democratic president to win an actual majority was Franklin Pierce in 1852. He polled a 51 per cent majority. Roosevelt was running with more than a 54 per cent majority.

Thomas Below Expectations

The vote of Norman Thomas fell sharply below earlier calculations, but in many districts the Thomas vote had not been reported. The previous highwater mark of socialist strength came in 1921. Eugene V. Debs polled 900,000 votes.

Governor Roosevelt surpassed the victory four years ago of Hoover over Alfred E. Smith. He was assured 461 electoral votes from 41 states with the probability he would add 11 more from Kentucky where the "honest election law" delayed the count. In 1928 Hoover carried 40 states with an electoral vote of 444.

Hoover Below Smith

President Hoover had carried only six states, four in New England—Maine, Vermont, New Hampshire and Connecticut—Delaware and Pennsylvania, which remained true to republican tradition despite a tremendous popular vote for Roosevelt. Not a state west of the Mississippi did he carry, despite his five trips into the farming country with fervent last-minute appeals for votes. He carried every one of them in 1928.

His electoral vote totaled only 59. Smith carried eight states, with an electoral vote of 87, in 1928.

Wisconsin, a state which has been democratic only twice since 1860, went for Roosevelt. It was an upset, and although it was expected to some extent, its size was unexpected. An indication of how the state felt could be seen in the Dane county vote. Complete precincts in the county gave Hoover 19,037 and Roosevelt 27,355. Dane county is traditionally republican. The county gave 16,736 votes to Chapple for United States senator and 26,549 to Duffy.

The presidential election was a national expression of liberal thought, President-elect Roosevelt said in his first statement to the country today following his unprecedented victory at the polls:

"My friends I am granted this opportunity to extend my deep appreciation to the electorate

(Continued on page 6 column 1)

Hoover Offers Best Wishes, Aid

HOOVER MANSION, PALO ALTO, Cal. — (U.P.) — President Hoover at 9:34 p. m., Tuesday, conceded the election to Gov. Franklin D. Roosevelt, his democratic opponent. He telegraphed congratulations to the New Yorker.

Hoover telegraphed Roosevelt:

"Hon. Franklin D. Roosevelt, Biltmore Hotel, N. York City: I congratulate you on the opportunity that has come to you to be of service to the country, and I wish for you a most successful administration.

"In the common purpose of all of us, I shall dedicate myself to every possible helpful effort.

"Signed,
Herbert Hoover."

The Wisconsin State Journal

A Fact-Finding Newspaper

VOL. 143, NO. 66. 94th Year. MADISON, WEDNE SDAY, DECEMBER 6, 1933 18 Pages ★★★★ Final Price Three Cents

THE WEATHER

Increasing cloudiness followed by snow Thursday. Warmer tonight, colder Thursday. Fresh to strong southwest winds shifting to northwest Thursday.

Dispensaries or Licensed Liquor Stores Seen Here

Pres. Roosevelt Proclaims Repeal, Transfers Taxes, Opposes Saloons

WASHINGTON—(U.P.)—The dikes were opened for the legal entry into the United States or foreign liquor today as officials moved to carry out a pledge by President Roosevelt to turn the tide of prohibition repeal against the bootlegger and saloon to the objective of temperance, law and order.

The president made his pledge in a formal proclamation of repeal. He issued it Tuesday night an hour after Utah ended constitutional prohibition. Simultaneously Chairman Joseph H. Choate, Jr., struck the first blow in the government's new battle against bootleggers with announcement of initial allotments of liquor import quotas.

Shifts Recovery Taxes

The president's proclamation contained a ponderous legal statement shifting part of the recovery taxes from business to liquor. Then he appealed, personally, to "the good sense of the American people not to bring upon themselves the curse of excessive use of intoxicating liquor."

Such a course would be "a living reproach to us all" and detrimental to the health, morals and social integrity of the nation, Mr. Roosevelt said.

After hailing repeal as "a return of individual freedom," the president sought the cooperation of all citizens to "remove forever from our midst the menace of the bootlegger."

"The policy of the government," Mr. Roosevelt said, "will be more to see to it that the social and political evils that have existed in the pre-prohibition era shall not be revived nor permitted again to exist."

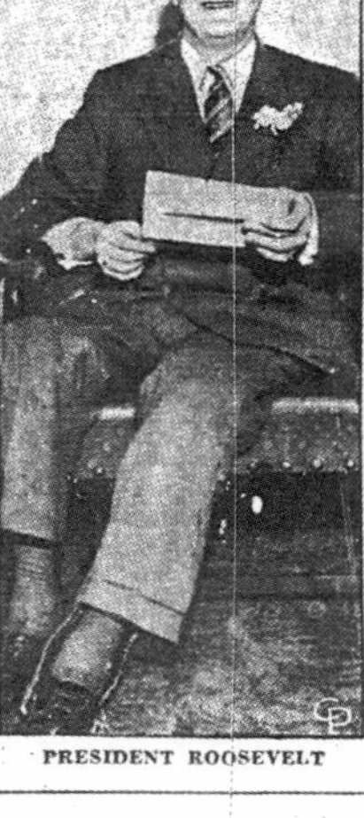

PRESIDENT ROOSEVELT

Choate immediately announced that first allotments of import quotas had been made on a basis of a four-month supply in the period from 1910 to 1914. If they are insufficient, they are "subject to additional allotments as trade negotiations are completed," Choate said. He revealed he had been working 16 hours a day with Ray C. Miller of the agricultural adjustment administration to make the allotments.

The president asked the country to confine its liquor purchases "to those dealers or agencies which have been duly licensed by state or federal license."

"Observance of this request will result in the consumption of alcoholic beverages which have passed federal inspection, in the break-up and eventual destruction of the notoriously evil illicit liquor traffic, and in the payment of reasonable taxes from the support of government and thereby in the superceding of other forms of taxation.

"I call specific attention to the authority given by the 21st amendment to the government to prohibit transportation or importation of intoxicating liquors into any state in violation

(Continued on page 6, col. 2)

Behind The News

By Paul Mallon

[Copyright, 1933, by Paul Mallon]

WASHINGTON—A little inside spat lies behind this current exaggerated talk about 20 to 100 liberals walking out on the new deal.

Spat Such quarrels happen in the best of families. The boys won't leave home in the end. They are merely growling because they are temperamental and uneasy.

There is something fundamental in the constitution of a liberal which makes him hate compromises. These new deal liberals are interested primarily in governmental reform. To them recovery is of secondary importance. They would resign rather than see recovery come without reform.

It probably will not come to that. Mr. Roosevelt wants reform as much as they do, but he has the responsibility also of promoting recovery. The prospects are that a little heart-to-heart talking between him and the liberals will quiet the present feeling of unrest.

◇ ◇ ◇

The liberals have been uneasy about the proposed revision of the securities bill for one thing.

Securities They noted that Earle Baillie, member of the firm of J. and W. Seligman (investment bankers) was made a special treasury assistant. They heard the story that he was going to do the rewriting of the securities act. It probably was not true, but that did not keep them from being disturbed.

Baillie organized half a dozen of the largest investment trusts in Wall street including the Tri-Continental Securities corp. and selected industries.

As chairman of the railroad securities committee he told the Investment Bankers' assn. (Oct. 31, 1933) that the securities act was a puzzle, stating "It is not apparent how future railroad financing can be done."

You can readily see where even an erroneous rumor that he was going to have anything to do with the securities act would set all liberal hearts aflutter.

◇ ◇ ◇

Every insider knows the securities act has not operated successfully. They differ about the reasons for its failure.

Failure The liberals say it is due to the fact that Wall streeters have conducted a filibuster against the law, refusing to do any capital financing under it. The Wall streeters say the law is so impractical that even legitimate financing cannot be undertaken. They probably are both half right.

But those in the know whisper that a new proposition has recently been put before the federal trade commission which may shed a new light on the whole matter.

A plan for financing $7,000,000 of new securities has been proposed. If the commission sanctions it, the way may be opened for breaking the deadlock.

◇ ◇ ◇

All the wise bees around the White House hive are buzzing now that you will see no important money policy action before the spring

Spring pickup is in sight. That is the time for money planning as well as for more romantic activities.

Every one expects a substantial business pickup then even if the present uncertainty is continued. All do not agree, however, that the president can play around with the present gold price policy that long. They know he will have to find some new artifices if he wants to keep away from stabilization and permanent devaluation.

Not a soul among the topmost stratum of insiders has an idea what artifices he could possibly use.

◇ ◇ ◇

Certain men at the right hand of the president are complaining about the stress being laid on the money policy.

Strategy They believe the public has been misled into believing that is the cure for all our ills. Actually, it is not nearly so important as the NRA, AAA, and PWA, in their opinion. They have advised a soft-pedaling of the money talk and some high pressure salesmanship on the regular recovery agencies.

The idea is that the opposition is using the money feature as a center of attack, obscuring the reform fundamentals. You may see administration publicity turn on that new tack shortly.

Frightened Burglar Loses His Flashlight

A burglar attempting to enter the home of Mrs. Laura Glover, 22 W. Wilson st., early today was frightened away, dropping a flashlight and screw-driver, police reported.

Burned Son's Hands With Matches, Claim

APPLETON, Wis. — (U.P.) —Mrs. Clara Vajko, Appleton, accused of burning her small son's hands with matches because she wanted to punish him, today was under $500 bond charged with mayhem.

Lindy, Anne Reach Brazil

Fly True Course Over Atlantic for 1,870 Miles

NATAL, Barzil —(U.P.)— Col. and Mrs. Charles A. Lindbergh, flying a true course for 1870 miles, arrived in their big seaplane over the Natal harbor at 11:55 a. m. CST today after a spectacular flight from Bathurst, British West Africa.

The Lindberghs had traversed the South Atlantic ocean, in a straight airline, landing at noon, 16 hours out of Bathurst.

The flight completed 19,000 miles of aerial touring since their departure from New York on July 9.

City Declares Holiday

The Lindberghs came down to a city that had declared an unofficial holiday in their honor. They were greeted by cheering thousands, swarming on every vantage point along the rocky shores.

Rowboats, motorboats and launches jammed the River Potengy where it sweeps into the ocean near the splendid new Pan-American naval airport.

All business had been suspended since noon, and the entire population joined to make the reception the most notable ever given a visiting celebrity.

Anne Takes Controls

The flying weather was splendid, and the radio land stations were in contact with the plane every 15 minutes throughout the night.

The first communication was established within six minutes of their takeoff.

Mrs. Lindbergh remained at the radio for several hours, but later relieved the colonel at the controls, while he took over the wireless "department."

Plane Is Stripped

They started from Bathurst at 2 a .m. Greenwich mean time (3 p. m. Tuesday CST).

Their plane was stripped of everything dispensable. Baggage, fuel, food, even water were reduced to what those at Bathurst thought to be a dangerous minimum.

Lindbergh was tall and coldly efficient as he gave the plane a final look over before he got into the pilot's cockpit. Mrs. Lindbergh, small and in jodhpurs that have become a uniform for her, looked fit and was supremely confident. They set 14 hours as the possible time.

No sooner had the plane, after a long run down the mouth of the Gambia river, been in the air sufficiently long for Mrs. Lindbergh to raise the wireless aerial than she began flashing her messages to the Pan American Airway stations along the jutting eastern coast of South America.

Injured

E. RANDALL SEARS

E. Randall Sears Injured as Auto Tips Into Ditch

Condition is Reported Much Improved

[State Journal News Service]

RICHLAND CENTER—E. Randall Sears, circulation manager of The Wisconsin State Journal, was reported resting comfortably in Richland hospital today after being injured in an auto accident near Blue River Tuesday.

Mr. Sears' condition was greatly improved this afternoon, and it was expected that he would be able to return to Madison Thursday. He was reported definitely out of danger.

The car was driven by George Rentschler, Madison florist, who was accompanying Mr. Sears on a business trip. The men were taken to Blue River and then to the hospital here. Mr. Sears suffered from loss of blood and was given a transfusion from Mr. Rentschler at the hospital Tuesday night.

The car overturned when Mr. Rentschler drove into a ditch to avoid another car which came around a sharp curve. Mr. Sears, who was thrown against the windshield, suffered cuts about the head and body bruises. Mr. Rentschler was not seriously injured.

Conscience-Stricken, Admits Dells Slaying

A 15-months effort to find a fourth member of a bandit gang which killed Ole Hanson, 40, proprietor of the Black Oaks resort at Wisconsin Dells ended today in Kansas City, Mo., when Richard L. Riley, 28, Chicago, walked into police headquarters and gave himself up, according to a United Press report.

Burdened by a guilty conscience, Riley confessed he participated in the robbery when Hanson was killed the night of Aug. 7, 1932.

Names Grippando

Two of the bandits were arrested in Chicago two days after the murder and it was their implication of a third party named "Riley" which started the long search that ended today.

They were James Grippando, 30, and John Paul White, 19, both of Chicago. Grippando confessed firing a shot, but not the fatal one.

Riley today named Grippando as the probable slayer.

Will Face Charge, Belief

After the robbery, Riley said, he went to California and obtained work. The crime preyed on his mind, he told police, and when he arrived in Kansas City he decided to give himself up. He indicated he was willing to return to Wisconsin to face charges.

Riley said the robbery and slaying were the aftermath of a party which

(Continued on page 6 column 6)

Boosts State's Job Allotment

U. S. Gives Increase of 5,000 Men

An increase of 5,000 men in the quota to be put to work on Wisconsin CWA projects was authorized in a telegram to the state central CWA office here Tuesday night. The allotment of this quota to the respective districts of the state will

(Continued on page 6, column 2)

May Change Boyd Charge

Risser Considers High Court Opinion

The charges of aiding embezzlement against R. H. Farness, A. T. Rogers, and R. R. Kropf, officers of the defunct Joseph M. Boyd co., may be changed as a result of the state supreme courts' decision, Dist. Atty. Fred Risser said today.

The defendants properly should be charged as principals and not "abettors" if they are to be charged at all, the supreme court ruled Tuesday in ordering trial for the men.

Mr. Risser said today some changes will be made in the charge in view of the decision, but no changes will be made in the "blue sky" securities law charge, basis for which the high court held was weak.

"The supreme court, as I understand its opinion, sustains my action in filing additional charges against the Boyd officers," the prosecutor said.

Attorneys for the three Boyd co.

(Continued on page 6, column 5)

'Day by Day' Yearbook to Be Available Soon

And 'Bertha' Will Be Seen in All Her Glory

—And the villain still pursued her!

Remember when those lines brought a thrill? Back in those good old days when a girl's reputation for modesty was shattered the moment an ankle peeked out from beneath the folds of her skirt?

Those days will be recreated next week when "Bertha, the Sewing Machine Girl" is presented at Turner hall for the benefit of the Empty Stocking club.

Set for Dec. 15, 16

The old melodrama from the times when one knew a villain by his bushy, black mustache and discerned the heroine by her matchless modesty and unblemished purity will be presented in all its glory

(Continued on page 6, col. 1)

Betty Cass' Annual Treat Going to Press

"Now, when I was a girl—"

Do you remember Betty Cass' little story about high school youths which started out that way? And do you recall her yarn about "Tippy", the dog—and those crackling comments when the democrats moved into the capitol—and that heart tugging "drammer" on the day the banks were all closed—and the fascinating tale of the geese on the Otto Toepfer farm—and The Brig and Steak—and the dozens of "wisecracks" that have kept "Madison Day by Day" sparkling through the year?

Here's Big News!

Whether you remember or not, you'll be interested in this announcement:

The 1933 Madison Day by Day yearbook is about ready to go to press. Betty Cass has hopes that it will be all printed and available for you by the end of the week.

Those stories mentioned above are only a few samples of the fascinating material that will appear on its 64 big pages. It is crammed

(Continued on page 6, column 6)

Paul Kelleter Ouster Bared

'Leave' Voted Nov. 22 by Board

The state conservation commission at its meeting Nov. 22 adopted a resolution effecting discharge of Conservation Director Paul D. Kelleter, notified him verbally last Saturday of its action, and Tuesday sent him a copy of the resolution, is was learned today.

Kelleter continued today his refusal to comment upon the circumstances of his leaving the department next Jan. 31 after a two-months leave with pay.

The commission resolution merely established that the director would be given the leave, that his "separation" from the department would occur Jan. 31, 1934, unless he were to re-enter the federal forest service before that time, and that Commissioner Ralph M. Immell be unpaid acting director until a new one were named.

Kelleter has no arrangement for nor immediate prospect of re-entering the federal forest service, it was learned, although members of the commission referred to such an intention when queried about his leaving his present post. He was in the forest service for many years before coming to Wisconsin.

Kills Woman, Stabs Daughter Slays Self

HOT SPRINGS, Ark.—(U.P.)—Jack Walton, 30, Chicago, fatally stabbed a woman, critically wounded her daughter, terrorized a hotel manager, and then killed himself here today.

A few minutes after Walton invaded a hotel room, Mrs. Stella Shattas, 30, and her daughter, Irene, 14, both of Chicago, ran out screaming and bleeding from stab wounds.

Mrs. Shattas dropped dead a few feet from the door.

Loses Life Savings in Bet, Kills Self

MINNEAPOLIS — (U.P.) — Albert R. Zeimer, 34, Minneapolis, was certain Army gridders would defeat the seemingly demoralized Notre Dame team last Saturday.

He backed his judgment with his life savings at 5 to 2 odds. Notre Dame broke a losing streak to beat Army 13-12.

Late Tuesday a bellhop heard two shots in a hotel room. Police broke in the door and found Zeimer's body with a note explaining the bet.

Physician Kills Self After Love Quarrel

LOS ANGELES, Cal. — (U.P.) — Dr. W. Dewey Wightman, 41, prominent Los Angeles physician, shot and killed himself as a tragic aftermath to a domestic quarrel over "another woman," police announced today as they released his attractive, titian-haired wife from custody.

Hearings Start Dec. 19 on U.W. Trade Charges

Hearings will start Dec. 19 before the department of agriculture and markets on the complaints that have been served in the name of that depatment upon various university corporations and officials to determine whether they are committing unfair trade practices in competing with Madison business concerns.

The hearings will be to determine whether there shall be an order issued by the department to the effect that the university activities

(Continued on page 6, column 3)

Arrest Bootleg Drinkers, Chief of Police Asks

After the sale of hard liquor has been legalized in Madison, all persons caught drinking or in possession of bootleg whisky should be arrested and prosecuted the same as the parties who sell it, in the opinion of Chief of Police William H. McCormick. "It would be a good idea for the common council to pass such an ordinance," the chief said. He claimed such an ordinance would be the mose effective weapon for wiping out illegal whisky. "With the return of legal liquor there is no excuse for anyone's buying or drinking bootleg liquor," he declared.

Oases Aren't; Thirsty 'Celebrate' on Suds

Liquor is Legal, But There is No Liquor, Ramblers Discover; 'Smart Money' Stays at Home

BY KENNETH R. KENNEDY

All the "smart money" stayed in Madison Tuesday night as the "noble experiment" ended and liquor became legal but remained scarce.

This reporter, at behest of the city editor, scraped together 83 very ignorant cents and toured the small towns which were supposed to be oases for Madisonians parched by failure of the common council to permit the sale of anything above seven per cent.

Home Is the Hunter

He returned with (a) a variety of beer, ranging from 3.2 to 5.5, (b) one illegal (or was it legal?) "shot," (c) one glimpse of a pint of real Golden Wedding whisky, and (d) 23 cents which will be sent out for cigars a soon as the office boy gets here.

This assignment looked so swell that four assistants immediately

(Continued on page 6, column 5)

Madison Takes It Quietly

With the city beer ordinance cramping the style of Madison drinkers, police here reported a quiet Tuesday night, the first after the end of national prohibition.

Seven men were arrested for drunkenness in the city, which was not unusual for prohibition days. One man today faced a charge of drunken driving after his car went into the Yahara river, the only mishap reported Tuesday night.

County highway police made no arrests and no accidents were reported. The sheriff's force brought in two men for drunkenness.

Four Go Wet in a Big Way

Car Takes Dive in Yahara River

Four Stoughton met "went wet" early today when their car plunged into the Yahara river at Jenifer st., police reported. They were arrested for drunkenness, then removed to Madison General hospital to be treated for cuts and bruises.

Police, answering a call, found Wilbur Snyder, 26, and Elmer Skavlen, 23, standing on the Yahara bridge. They were covered with blood. They told police their car went into the river, and they had waded out.

The pair was taken to the station, where another call was received from 629 Riverside dr. There William Hanson, 26, was found, suffering from lacerations about the face. The fourth man, Arnold Moe, 27, was discovered at the East Side cafe. He admitted he was the driver of the car.

He was booked on a charge of drunken driving.

Mrs. C. P. Norgord Dies in New York

Mrs. C. P. Norgord, Albany, N. Y., a former resident of Madison, died today after a brief illness. Her husband now assistant New York commissioner of agriculture, was formerly connected with the University of Wisconsin college of agriculture and was for a number of years state commissioner of agriculture. Surviving are her husband, three daughters, Mrs. Gladys Anderson, Duluth, Helen, and a third daughter at home, and one grand child.

Mother Loses Suit for Death of Son

MILWAUKEE— (U.P.) —The Milwaukee Electric co. today was victor in a $20,000 damage suit brought by Mrs. Mary Stengel, Milwaukee, for the death of her son, Frank.

Mrs. Stengel alleged her son was killed when he stuck his head out of an unscreened street car window and was struck by an iron beam when the vehicle passed over a trestle. The company contended, however, that he removed the screen after he had taken a chew of tobacco for the first time.

NRA Board Cites Factory

Madison Name Sent to Chicago Officials

A Madison manufacturer who has "violated the NRA code by failure to observe the hour and wage standards" and who has neglected to appear before the board here, has been reported to the Chicago district NRA compliance board, Jerome B. White, secretary of the Madison board, announced today. The decision was reached at a meeting of the board in the Hotel Loraine Tuesday night.

Rockford Romance Goes on the Rocks

Charging that her husband failed to support her and abused and insulted her, Mrs. Wilma Haak, 27, was granted a divorce today from Elmer Haak, 30, on grounds of cruel and inhuman treatment. The couple was married Dec. 15, 1924, in Rockford, and have three children which were awarded to Mrs. Haak.

Repeal Fails to Halt Trial

Gannon Changes Plea; Fined $25

BULLETIN

Emmett Gannon, changing his plea to guilty, was fined $5 on each of five counts today by Federal Judge Patrick Stone.

Penalties for prohibition law violations prior to its repeal can still be imposed, Judge Patrick T. Stone ruled in effect in federal court today.

Judge Stone is believed to be the first judge to be called upon to rule on the point, raised here within a day after repeal of the 18th amendment became effective.

The court denied a motion by Laurence Hall, attorney for Emmett Gannon, who sought to enter a plea in bar prior to an alternative motion to quash the charges against Gannon in three different cases. The cases, dating back to 1932, have been continued over several court sessions while Gannon was recuperating from injuries received in an

(Continued on page 6, column 4)

Scottsboro Negro Sentenced to Die

DECATUR, Ala.—(U.P.)—Clarence Norris, second of the Negro defendants to be retried in the Scottsboro assault case, was convicted by a Morgan county jury here today. The jury fixed penalty at death, the same as in the case of Haywood Patterson, first of the defendants to be retried and similarly reconvicted.

Perry Neighbors Back Glaeden's Pardon Plea

Henry K. Glaeden, 70-year-old former treasurer of the town of Perry who must otherwise stay in state prison until Sept. 23, 1935, on one to three year terms given him for embezzling $8,000 of town funds, today asked Gov. Schmedeman to pardon him so that he may use the few remaining years of his life in making restitution and atoning for the injustice to his neighbors of many years.

And the neighbors, 189 of them living in Mt. Horeb, Blue Mounds,

(Continued on page 6, column 6)

Council Vote May Favor Compromise

Booze Ordinance Up Again at Meeting Tonight

BY HENRY NOLL

Sale of liquor in city dispensaries or licensed liquor houses may be approved by the common council tonight as a compromise in the event an ordinance to permit whisky to be sold in taverns, hotels, clubs and drugstores fails to receive a sufficient number of votes.

At the special meeting Tuesday the council was unable to consider an amendment to the beer ordinance to permit the sale of whisky without additional license fees until the state legislature has passed a liquor control law owing to failure to muster enough votes to suspend the rules.

Suspension Needed

It will still be necessary to suspend the rules tonight on the ordinance which is being prepared today by the city attorney's office as the meeting of Tuesday was adjourned until tonight. If the council would postpone action on the ordinance until the regular meeting Friday, suspension of the rules would not be necessary.

It takes 14 votes to suspend the rules. Only 12 voted for suspension Tuesday. Ald. Elmer E. Mills was out of the city, but if he is present tonight supporters of the ordinance feel he will vote with them.

Opstedal May Switch

Ald. A. J. Opstedal voted against supension of the rules because he felt a reasonable license fee should be collected for sale of hard liquor or else a municipal dispensary should be operated. With the new ordinance providing that 25 taverns be licensed to sell whisky and that they be compelled to pay a $100 additional license until April, it is possible he may vote for suspension of the rules.

Some aldermen are opposed to picking out 25 tavern keepers from the 95 who are now selling beer. It is likely that the entire ordinance may be overthrown and another effort made to permit all taverns to sell hard liquor until the state has provided a regulation act.

60 Taverns Possible

There is also some sentiment in favor of an ordinance which would

(Continued on page 6, column 4)

Grove Adopts License Law

Permits Hard Liquor Sales

On the day the supreme court upheld its dry ordinance, the town board of Blooming Grove Tuesday unanimously passed an amendment providing for licensing taverns for sale of hard liquor.

The amendment placed the license fee at $100 a year, with a provision that a license to expire next June will cost $50, in addition to fees paid for licenses for the sale of beer.

It also provided that each hard liquor licensee must post a $500 bond for compliance with the town's zoning ordinance. It was explained that this provision was made partly to prevent applications by persons from outside the township.

No change was made in the closing hour of 1 a. m. for the taverns, but an article was included to forbid all kinds of gambling and gaming devices.

Beats Grandmother, Gets Maximum Fine

MILWAUKEE — (U.P.) — Frank Kelley, 32, pleaded self defense when araigned in district court today on a charge of beating his 76-year-old grandmother, Mrs. Dora Kelley. Judge A. J. Hedding fined Kelley $100, the maximum under the city ordinance for assault and battery. An 80-year-old neighbor testified he and other neighbors rescued Mrs Kelley from her grandson.

Home-Final Edition

The Wisconsin State Journal
A Fact-Finding Newspaper

The Weather
Fair tonight and Tuesday. Continued warm. Light southerly winds.

VOL. 144, NO. 112. 95th Year. MADISON, MONDAY, JULY 23, 1934 14 Pages ★★★★ Price Three Cents

Officers Kill Dillinger in Chicago

Gas, Electric Rate Cut of $181,900 Proposed for City

Behind The News

[Copyright, 1934, by Paul Mallon]

WASHINGTON — Reports from Berlin regarding the feelings of the German government when it received Secretary of State Hull's aide memoire about preferential treatment of creditors by Germany and her attempt to bargain over payment to Americans, said that the communication was something of a shock.

Easy

It was so disagreeable that it was not permitted to be published in Germany. But, if the paper as delivered caused the German officials so much pain, those on the inside in the state department are wondering what kind of colic would have seized them if it had been sent in the form in which it was first drafted.

According to credible information, Secretary Hull was very much in favor of using much stronger language and even wished to depart somewhat from the point at issue to reflect on policies of the nazi regime in general. In this, of course, he ran up against diplomacy of the traditional sort, which influences permanent officials trained on conventional lines. These advised against putting the case in such blunt terms as the secretary desired, and, after much discussion, they finally won out.

The secretary may have a chance later to use vigorous language, since the Germans are now negotiating with France as to Dawes and Young loan payments with the possibility of results like those in the case of Great Britain, which caused the United States to protest in the first place. This also would be disadvantageous to American bondholders and be ample ground for further representations.

Nevertheless, nearly everyone in the department concerned with the matter sees little good in calling names without having any stones to throw, which seems to be the situation of the United States. Germany buys about $62,000,000 more from us, and, hence, the weapon which Great Britain wielded is not available to us. It is conceded that, because of the vital necessity to

(Continued on page 5, col. 2)

State Would Make Rate Among Lowest

Reduction of Madison Gas and Electric Company rates to save about 20,500 customers in and near Madison $181,900 in the next 12 months alone was proposed by E. W. Morehouse, chief of the state public service commission's rates and research department, to the commission at a hearing in the capitol this afternoon.

A residential electric rate proposed by Morehouse would give customers of the Madison untility one of the lowest rates in Wisconsin for either municipal or privately-owned utilities, he said.

60c Fixed Charge

The residential electric schedule he suggested would be of the fixed charge type now in use by utilities serving nearly 40 per cent of Wisconsin's electric customers and would provide:

A fived net monthly charge of 60 cents.

For the first 50 kilowatt hours used each month, a rate of 2.25 cents net compared with six cents on the first 30 hours use of connected load provided in the existing schedule.

For the next 150 hours of monthly use, 2 cents net.

For all over 200 hours, 1.75 cents net.

Cut In 1932

The only change proposed in the residential gas rate schedule is reduction from 95 cents to 90 cents net of the charge per 1,000 cubic feet of gas for the 1,600 cubic feet used after the 400 feet covered by the 55 cents monthly minimum charge.

In 1932 the commission reduced rates of the Madison Gas and Electric co. $201,000.

Expenses Increased

Commissioners A. R. McDonald and Fred S. Hunt conducted this afternoon's hearing. Alvin C Reis, commission general counsel, examined Morehouse. The company was represented by Olin and Butler.

The Madison Gas and Electric co., even without a rate reduction would have its operating income reduced by $59,102 in the next 12 months, Morehouse estimated; due to an increase of $76,202 in operating expenses partly offset by an estimated increase in operating revenues of $17,100.

The rates and research chief figured the operating income of the company in the 12 months ending June 30, 1935, would be $591,786 compared with $650,888 in 1933.

Morehouse testified the company

(Continued on page 5, col. 3)

Butte Strike Battle Flares

Minneapolis Police Guard Trucks

[By United Press]

Butte, Mont., was center of the strike focus today as a two months walk out of copper workers flared into a wave of violence.

The dispute, long smouldering, swung attention away from the quieter scenes at Minneapolis and on the Pacific coast.

Authorities of the Anaconda Copper co. threatened to appeal to the governor for state troops to preserve order after a weekend marked by widespread destruction of property which they charged was instigated by strikers.

Strikers on the other hand raised the threat of a general strike.

Police Convoy Trucks

Shot gun-armed police squads convoyed trucks through Minneapolis today while angry pickets milled in the market district shouting threats but offering no resistance.

More than 4,000 national guardsmen were concentrated in the Twin Cities ready to spring into instant action on orders of Gov. Floyd B. Olson. The governor promised martial law at the first show of violence.

Pickets who halted movement of city garbage trucks for several hours were withdrawn at noon.

Longshoremen Vote

On the Pacific coast the outcome of a ballot by longshoremen on arbitration of all maritime workers differences was eagerly awaited.

A favorable vote is expected to

(Continued on page 5, col. 2)

Pfiffner, Democratic Leader, Succumbs

STEVENS POINT—(U.P.)—Funeral services will be held here Tuesday for J. R. Pfiffner, 49, Stevens Point attorney and prominent democrat, who died late Saturday after an eight months' illness.

A graduate of the University of Wisconsin, Pfiffner practiced law at Watertown and Tomahawk before returning to Stevens Point 19 years ago. He was a director of the First National bank here and had served two terms as district attorney of Portage county.

Pfiffner was the Wisconsin member of the resolutions committee at the democratic national convention in Chicago.

Miss Mahoney, House Mother at University, Dies

Miss Josephine Mahoney, 81, pioneer Madison resident and house mother for University of Wisconsin co-eds, died Saturday night at her home on Monona dr. after a long illness.

She came here from Fox Lake in 1874, and since then was interested in charity and civic work in the city. She was one of the first workers promoting improvement of Columbus park. Then in 1929 she and her sister, Margaret, donated their home on Monona dr. to the Norbertine Novitiate. Miss Mahoney was a member of the Norbertine Third order. For many years she directed a girls' rooming house in the university district.

Besides her sister, a brother, Daniel C. Mahoney, Juneau, survives.

Funeral services will be held at 9 a. m. Thursday at Fox Lake.

Burglars Take Safe, Miss $46

Despite the heat wave, burglars carried a 600-pound safe out of the Becker and Byrne garage, 2623 Monroe st., early today and carted it to a side road near Verona.

The burglars obtained between $50 and $60, but when the safe was found later this morning $46 was still in a folder which the burglars overlooked.

The burglars entered the garage after the closing hour at midnight by smashing the rear door. The safe was hauled out of the front office.

Detective John Arnold, investigating the burglary, located the safe near Verona.

Roosevelt to Reach Islands on Tuesday

ABOARD THE U. S. S. NEW ORLEANS — (U.P.) — The U. S. cruiser Houston, carrying President Roosevelt over smooth seas to the Hawaiian islands, drew close to its mid-Pacific destination today. Before noon Tuesday he will arrive at Kailua. A tremendous welcome awaited the first president to visit the picturesque insular possessions.

16 Cremated in Bus Fire After Crash

$225,000 Blaze Started by Wreckage of Accident

OSSINING, N. Y. — (U.P.)—Searchers of the charred hulk of a bus that was a flaming coffin for at least 16 persons, feared an even greater death list today as they sifted ashes for evidence of human cremation.

Fifty men, women, and children were in the blazing bus that careened down a steep hill within sight of Sing Sing prison, and plunged over a 40 foot embankment. It was an end to a Sunday holiday excursion so horrible that authorities feared many of the charred remains never would be identified.

Toll May Reach 17 or 18

Nearly a score of the surviving passengers were in hospitals. Two of these are not expected to live.

It was feared the death toll might reach 17 or 18.

All the victims were members or friends of the Brooklyn Democratic league. They were on their way to Sing Sing to see their baseball team play a convict nine. A gay Sunday excursion at its start, the party was transformed with tragic suddenness into a terror-stricken group watching relatives screaming and dying in the mobile pyre.

Fire Sweeps Yard, Boats

The fire spread from the bus to the lumber yard into which it fell, destroyed virtually the entire yard, then spread to a dock in the Hudson river and swept 19 boats.

Preliminary check showed that brakes on the antiquated bus were defective. Survivors said that several times on the journey from Brooklyn to Ossining the driver, Frank Imperatore, had difficulty in stopping.

Survivors said the bus approached the top of the descent leading to the prison with comparative high speed. Imperatore jammed the foot brake to the floor. He jerked up on the hand-brake. There was an odor of burning rubber but speed was unchecked.

Human Torches Jump

The mad descent started, the bus was out of control. Several forced open the doors and jumped.

At the bottom of the quarter-mile dash, the driver chose to plunge into the iron railing rather than crash directly into an obstruction. Obviously he did not know what lay beyond the railing.

There was a terrific roar as the bus hit the bottom and flames spurted from every side. Four human torches wriggled loose from the wreckage and dived into the river. They were rescued by yachtsmen.

Driver Feared Crash

Scores of persons were at the scene but none could approach the inferno. Screams of the dying and wails of spectators echoed above the roar of the fire.

Fire apparatus fought the blaze more than an hour before it was brought under control. Total damage to property was estimated at more than $225,000.

Bernard Campisi, 15, one of those who leaped from the bus, said he heard the driver remark that "we'll be lucky if we reach Ossining in this boat."

10 Injured in Crashes

Brodhead Man Near Death

Ten persons were injured, five seriously, in Madison and its trading area in weekend automobile accidents. They were:

Paul Schilling, 53, Brodhead; Wayne Robinson, 17, and Roy Curtis, 16, Richland Center; Donald Baljour, 17, Rochester, Minn.; Baird Markham, New York City, 18; Mrs. Frank Jaster, Milwaukee; Cecila Jaster, Milwaukee; Mrs. Nels Femrite, Blooming Grove; Sylvia Femrite, Blooming Grove; George Morrell's daughter, 5, of 142 N. Franklin st.

The two Milwaukee women were bruised and cut in a motor collision between cars driven by Mrs. Marie A. Coleman, Shorewood, and William C. Hinz, 419 N. Few st. The accident happened here Sunday.

Injured by Truck

Jumping from an ice truck in the path of a car driven by Norman Anderson, 3242 Milwaukee st., the Morrell girl was injured Saturday afternoon. The accident occurred near her home. She was taken to the

(Continued on page 5, col. 5)

Warden Devine is Named Chief

Appointment of Barney Devine, Webster, as Wisconsin's chief conservation warden to succeed Harley W. MacKenzie, new department director, was announced today by the latter.

The commission also has named Robert A. Gray, Milton, to head a new division on commercial and contract fishing. Both Divine and Gray are former conservation wardens.

Devine began service with the department Nov. 14, 1913 and Gray April 14, 1924.

Guns Settle the Score

Editors' Note: Normally The State Journal refuses to publish pictures of the dead; all such pictures received here go into the wastebasket. But as an object lesson to prove the trite but true quotation that "crime never pays", The State Journal publishes here the last photograph taken of John Dillinger, vain and ruthless criminal, as he lay in a Chicago alley after the guns of justice had ended his blood-marked career.

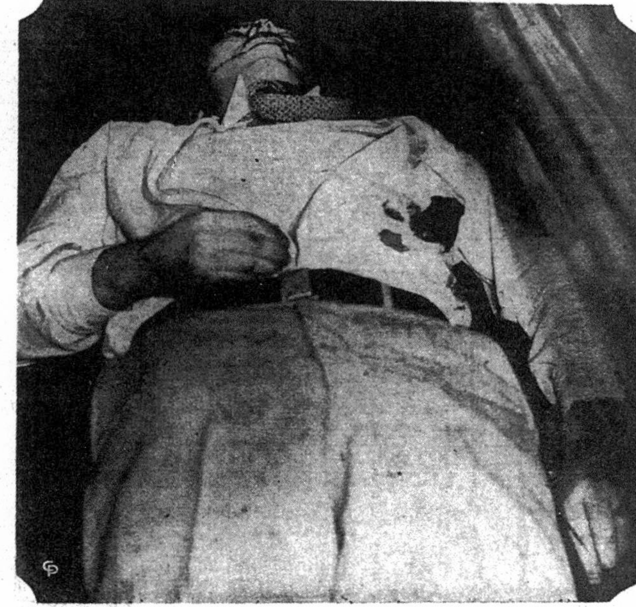

Mercury Hits 101, Record

Two Overcome Here by Sunday Heat

HOURLY TEMPERATURES

Sunday		Today	
7 a. m.	73	1 a. m.	76
8 a. m.	76	2 a. m.	75
9 a. m.	81	3 a. m.	75
10 a. m.	87	4 a. m.	74
11 a. m.	92	5 a. m.	73
Noon	93	6 a. m.	74
1 p. m.	95	7 a. m.	75
2 p. m.	96	8 a. m.	86
3 p. m.	99	9 a. m.	85
4 p. m.	99	10 a. m.	86
5 p. m.	100	11 a. m.	90
6 p. m.	98	Noon	96
7 p. m.	97	1 p. m.	99
8 p. m.	89	2 p. m.	100
9 p. m.	85	2:30 p. m.	101
10 p. m.	82	3 p. m.	100
11 p. m.	79		
Midnight	77		

After hitting 101 at 2:30 p. m., the mercury slipped back to 100 at 3 p. m. today. It was the second consecutive record-breaking day, with Sunday's high of 100 setting an all-time mark, too. Two persons were overcome by the heat here Sunday.

The previous record for today was 99, set in 1901.

While, the populace sought surcease from suffering by flocking to beaches, driving around the lakes, or attempting to cool off at home with fans and drinks, the mercury boiled up to the 100 mark, five degrees hotter than the previous record for July 22—95 in 1901.

A slight breeze Sunday night brought some relief, but early this morning another blast was on its way. Forebodings of another scorching day came in the five degree rise between 8 and 9 this morning, sending the mercury up to 85.

Although the weather bureau reported no immediate relief in sight, Eric Miller, government meteorologist, said that the outlook for today is more favorable than it was for Sunday. He saw a slight possibility of northwest winds from the Dakota plains bringing thundershowers, but added that was more of a hope than a prediction. Show-

(Continued on page 5, col. 3)

Three Dillinger Pals Still 'Wanted' Here

With the violent death of John Dillinger, only three members of his gang remained today to be brought to book under indictments returned by a Madison grand jury.

His career of crime has ended leaving Wisconsin's capital city in the role of interested and vigilant spectator, with nothing but rumor to indicate that he ever "favored" Madison with his attentions other than as a probable casual visitor.

Indicted Here

Had Dillinger lived, he still would have faced an indictment charging him with having harbored and concealed Tommy Carroll, member of his outlaw crew in the bloody "getaway" at the Little Bohemia resort in Northern Wisconsin on April 22, who later was killed by detectives at Waterloo, Ia. The death of Carroll would not have affected the charge against Dillinger, Stanley M. Ryan, United States attorney said today.

Six gangsters escaped the trap laid by federal officers at the Little Bohemia. Dillinger and Carroll are dead. "Pat" Reilly is in custody. "Baby Face" Nelson, Homer Van Meter and John Hamilton are still at large.

Two Sweethearts Jailed

Of the four "sweethearts" who spent the eventful weekend with them at Emil Wanatka's resort near Manitowish, two are in a federal prison and two, captured and released on probation, are sought again on bench warrants. Jean Crompton, alias Ann Sothern, who had changed from blonde to brunet when she was re-arrested as the terrified companion of Carroll at the scene of his slaying by Iowa detectives, and Patricia Cherrington, alias Patricia Young, are serving one and two-year terms in prison.

Two Girls Hunted

Helen Gillis, alias Marian Marr, wife of "Baby Face" Nelson, and Marie Conforti, alias Rose Ancker, will join them at Alderson, W. Va., when and if they are apprehended in company with their outlaw associates.

Madison's contact with the gang has been limited to its experience as "host" to the four women. Members of the crew doubtless have eaten at Madison restaurants and probably have bought gasoline at Madison filling stations, for one or more of the cars that took the gang from Chicago to the Little Bohemia resort in April is believed to have passed through the city, and one, driven by John Hamilton, was reported to have been disabled and stored in a garage at North Leeds, 18 miles north on Highway 51.

Madison Visits Hinted

Whether or not Dillinger ever contemplated one of his daring holdups in Madison may never be known unless one of his associates "talks," but there is evidence to warrant belief that members of the gang, if not Dillinger himself, have stayed over night in the city on one or more occasions.

When the three "Dillinger girls" were guests at the Dane county jail, one of them, Marie Conforti, it was learned today, remarked:

"As many times as I've been in Madison, I never thought I'd be locked up here."

The sweetheart of Homer Van Meter also revealed at the time

(Continued on page 2, col. 3)

Execution Awaits 187 Multiplied Rat 'Pets'

Sheriff Fred T. Finn prepared today for an execution by getting the lethal chambers ready.

Those who will pay the price to the state are 187 white rats who have made their home at 616 Williamson st., under the protection of John Harrison who "didn't have the heart to kill them."

They Bothered Appetites

City health officials investigated the case and found Harrison let the rats run at random about the house much to the disgust of five or six other tenants. The other tenants seemed to object particularly to the presence of rats while eating.

Harrison was ordered into superior court today on a charge of maintaining a nuisance and he told the story of his rats to Judge Roy H. Proctor.

Harrison explained that he was a "social revolutionist" and that his religion prevented him from killing the rats. It seems there were two white rats in the house back in December and they were male and female. Health department officials found 187 there this morning.

Wanted: Pied Piper

The judge ordered Harrison to gather up the rodents and deliver them to health department officials today and to report again Tuesday morning in superior court. The judge deferred sentence on Harrison.

And when the rats are delivered to the health officials, the sheriff will have to execute them, because he is the official executioner.

Halsey, Dean of Bar, Dies

Milwaukee Judge, 94, Succumbs

MILWAUKEE—(U.P.)—Death today had claimed Wisconsin's oldest and most colorful legal figure, Judge Lawrence Woodruff Halsey, 94, the oldest member of the Masonic order in the state and a charter member of the American, Wisconsin and Milwaukee Bar assn.

Judge Halsey died of age infirmities at his Lake drive home Sunday while his daughter, Mrs. Louise H. Darrow, stood at his bedside. He had been confined to his home and his bed a large part of the past three years.

He was graduated from the University of Wisconsin law school in 1865. Two years later he established a partnership with Col. H. B. Jackson at Oshkosh, Wis.

After moving to Milwaukee and entering the firm of Johnson, Rietbrock and Halsey, he was elected to the circuit court bench to succeed his senior partner, D. H. Johnson, in 1901. He retired in 1923 after holding the circuit court judgeship for four six year terms.

Judge Halsey was an officer in the Light Horse squadron, a member of the Old Settlers' and the Sunset clubs and oldest member of the board of trustees of the Knights of Phythias in Wisconsin.

Two Women Hit as 17 Feds, Police Slay Desperado

Bandit Led to Death by Gang Molls, Purvis Reveals at Inquest

By ROBERT T. LOUGHRAN
[United Press Staff Correspondent]

CHICAGO—John Dillinger's life history was ended today on the books of the law. In a drab coroner's office just removed from the ice-filled vault where Dillinger's body lay, a solemn jury wrote the last chapter.

It read:

"Justifiable homicide by officers of the federal government."

The man who ran him down was not present, the man whose bullet killed him was not named, and the informant who led him to his death was not mentioned.

The entire investigation of the life of the man who was sought for months lasted less than 20 minutes.

Bore Three Battle Scars

The coroner's jury was told that in addition to the three bullet wounds which brought about his death there were three scars of other battles.

One was in the calf of the left leg, another in his thigh and the third in the neck.

They probably were received in one of the outlaw's many clashes with the law—perhaps at Little Bohemia lodge in upper Wisconsin, at east Chicago, Ind., when he killed a policeman, or in his escape from a federal trap at St. Paul on March 31.

Received Tip Sunday

A few brief sentences by two federal agents told the entire official story of Dillinger's death Sunday night at the door of a motion picture theater just off the famous gold coast.

They told of a "tip" at 5 p. m. Sunday, hasty organization of an ambush outside the little Biograph theater, and then of the shooting in which Dillinger died the kind of death he had dealt to others.

Blame Woman for Death

Their guarded testimony seemed to confirm a startling fact already revealed by other investigators.

Dillinger was led to death by a woman.

Police and Melvin Purvis, chief of the federal bureau of investigation, refused to confirm reports that two women who attended the theater with him Sunday night were in custody.

Purvis said, however:

"It was women who led him to his grave."

For months Purvis had sought and questioned the women of Dillinger's gang. He concentrated on that quest almost to exclusion of an actual search for the ultimate quarry.

Quizzed Six Gang Molls

At one time, an informant said today, federal agents held six women known to have associated with

Additional pictures and stories on the infamous career of John Dillinger will be found on page 2 of this edition.

Dillinger, John Hamilton, Geeorge "Baby Face" Nelson and others of the killing crew that followed the ace desperado.

And finally the plan bore fruit.

Reports of the way the "tipster" made contact with the federal agents differed, but every fact available pointed inescapably to the fact that it was a woman.

Point to Woman's Escape

With Dillinger when he grabbed for a gun in the face of 17 threatening officers was a woman—some said two women. One, at least, was flashingly garbed in a red dress.

Despite her conspicuous dress and the fact that the agents were prewarned, she escaped without pursuit while Dillinger fell in a hail of bullets.

Purvis smiled knowingly but refused comment when it was suggested that the red dress may have been chosen deliberately. Dillinger might have been missed in the crowd entering and leaving the theater. A crimson dress was inescapable

Talked for Freedom, Belief

In two months the government arrested six women of the gang. Two are in federal prison, two are free on probation. Two more were arrested here and freed.

Underworld reports persisted that they had "talked" as the price of freedom.

It was by facts concealed, rather than those revealed, that the inquest witnesses told the true story of Dillinger's end.

Samuel P. Cowley, special agent and assistant to Purvis, gave the most detail to the jury of six men. He told of the first "tip" Sunday night that Dillinger would attend the Biograph, lured from hiding by a play of crime, "Manhattan Melodrama."

Keeps Tip Secret

"Who gave that tip?" asked Coroner Frank J. Walsh.

"I am unable to give that information," replied Cowley.

"Do you mean you do not know?"

"I know, but I cannot reveal it."

Cowley told then of hasty preparations for an ambush. Police of

(Continued on Page 2, Column 1)

Mysterious Girl Who Sold Bandit to U.S. Guarded

BULLETIN

CHICAGO—(U.P.)—Weary from a six-hour ride in a hearse from his farm home in Indiana, John W. Dillinger, sr., 73-year-old Quaker farmer, arrived here this afternoon to claim the body of his son.

CHICAGO — (U.P.) — A mysterious "girl in red" sat in a movie theater with John Dillinger Sunday night, knowing that she had pointed the treasonable finger of death at him and that he probably would die in a hail of bullets when they walked from the place, it was revealed today.

The girl who "sold" the nation's most murderous outlaw to the authorities—she was lured into the betrayal by a $15,000 reward—was reported to be under heavy guard in a Chicago hotel this afternoon.

Fears Gang Revenge

Federal department of justice agents, whose unerring guns barked a finis to Dillinger's bloody reign of terror Sunday night, feared that some survivor of his gang might make a bold effort to take her life.

An East Chicago, Ind., police officer whose buddy was shot to death by Dillinger in a bank raid several months ago persuaded her to lead the outlaw to his execution—in a welter of blood in a dark alley.

Purvis Keeps Secret

At the inquest today Melvin H. Purvis, the government's chief manhunter in the Chicago area, said he had received a tipoff that Dillinger and a girl would be at the theater, a neighborhood movie house on the near north side.

But never, he said, would he reveal the identity of his informant.

From other sources, however, it was learned that the East Chicago policeman, Martin Zarkovich, met the girl through a man whose acquaintance he made in a saloon several weeks ago.

Seek Dillinger's Hideout

While Dillinger's body lay on a slab in the county morgue awaiting arrival of his 73-year-old Quaker father from Mooresville, Ind., authorities turned to a hunt for the slain desperado's hideout.

They felt sure he had been living on the near north side in the neighborhood of the Biograph theater from which he emerged to find a waiting death much like that depicted by the gangland melodrama he had just witnessed.

Their only clues to the place were a pair of keys tied together with a soiled string.

Prisoner Slugs Richland Sheriff, Escapes at Jail

RICHLAND CENTER—Fred Turner, 23, Richland Center, returned here from Lansing, Mich., where he was arrested Friday on car theft charges, escaped today by slugging Sheriff Thomas Wait just as he was being taken into the county jail.

Turner was charged with taking a Ford coupe belonging to Carl Elliott, Richland Center, here Tuesday night.

With a club apparently concealed in his clothes, he struck Wait over the head at the entrance of the jail, and escaped in the darkness.

Wait received a partial concussion of the brain and a partial skull fracture, according to his physician, Dr. C. F. Dull. He was resting comfortably today at the hospital.

It was believed part of the injury was received when the sheriff fell to the walk after being struck.

Bishop's Body Found in Glacier Park

GLACIER PARK, Mont.—(U.P.)—Searchers today found the body of the Rev. William F. Faber, missing head of Montana's episcopal diocese. Bishop Faber, missing since Friday, had drowned.

The Wisconsin State Journal

A Fact-Finding Newspaper

Weather
Fair tonight. Saturday & thunder shower probable. Not much change in temperature. Light southeast winds shifting to northwest late Saturday.

VOL. 146, NO. 136. 96th Year. MADISON, FRIDAY, AUGUST 16, 1935 ★★★★ 22 Pages *Price Three Cents*

Crash Kills Post, Rogers

Senate Votes Tax on Rich, 57 to 22; Session Nears End

Two Amendments Expected to Be Killed

By H. O. THOMPSON
[United Press Staff Correspondent]

WASHINGTON — Adjournment of congress neared today with the record breaking, two day passage of the tax-the-rich bill by the senate. The eight-month-old session, marked by much bitterly disputed legislation, probably will end next week.

With the president's $250,000,000 tax-the-rich bill safely in the hands of friendly conferees, major obstacles to adjournment were half a dozen bills yet to be reported out of conference.

The senate broke all records for speedy consideration of a revenue measure in racing through two days of debate that ended in a 57 to 22 vote in favor of the bill Thursday night before half-filled galleries and an apathetic assemblage of senators.

Adjourn Next Thursday

Senators thought principally of adjournment. Republicans, realizing the futility of oppositioin, were content to let democrats take responsibility for a hastily drawn and speedily passed tax measure. Democrats wanted to get the business over with as quickly as possible.

New deal leaders set adjournment before the end of next week as their goal. Senate Majority Leader Joseph T. Robinson said he believed adjournment could be accomplished by Thursday, possibly before.

Besides the tax bill, principal measures in conference are the omnibus banking bill, gold clause amendments, and the federal alcohol control bill.

Ban Tax-Exempt Bonds

The speed with which the tax bill was passed by both houses amazed seasoned observers. When the task of writing a tax bill was first broached, three weeks was regarded as the least possible time that would be required.

Washington's summer heat and the overwhelming democratic majority accomplished the seemingly impossible.

Before passing the bill the senate added two amendments which probably will be killed in conference.

One was by Sen. William E. Bo-

(Continued on page 6, col. 8)

Legislature Gets Bi-Partisan Bill to Cut Oleo Tax

A bill to reduce Wisconsin's new 15 cent a pound tax on oleomargarine was introduced in the legislature today.

The measure, designed, its authors said, to answer retaliatory tactics taken in southern states against Wisconsin business, was recommended by the joint finance committee for passage by a vote of 7 to 4.

Assemblyman Donald P. Ryan (dem., Milwaukee) co-sponsor of the bill with Assemblyman John L. Sieb (prog., Racine) said he proposed to restore the six cents a pound tax on oleomargarine made from domestic fats and oils but leave the 15 cent levy on butter substitutes made from imported materials.

Ahead Behind

The Wisconsin legislature today had won the national legislative talkathon. Adjournment Thursday of the Massachusetts general assembly left the Badger lawmakers in sole possession of the field—the last legislature to remain in session. The Wisconsin legislators have been sitting here since Jan. 9.

Alive, Well

A. J. ALTMEYER

A. J. Altmeyer, Madison, assistant U. S. labor secretary, was alive and well today, despite rumors here that he had died. Unfortunate juxtaposition of his picture and the news of another man's death in a Milwaukee paper was blamed for the rumor. Altmeyer had been mentioned as a possible appointee to headship of the new federal social security agency.

Double Trouble

Ragweed doubled on the Wisconsin General hospital slides this morning. Out of 16 pollen grains to a cubic yard, 10 were ragweed. The report Thursday morning showed 16 pollen grains, five ragweed.

Lindy May Fly to Death Spot, Return Bodies

Colonel Plans Tragic Hop to Alaskan Scene

WASHINGTON — (U.P.) — Col. Charles A. Lindbergh may fly on a tragic mission to Alaska to supervise return of the bodies of Will Rogers and Wiley Post, killed in an airplane crash, advices today indicated.

While the capital mourned the deaths of the famous actor and the equally famous aviator, advices to Assistant Treasury Secretary Stephen B. Gibbons indicated that a telephone conversation this afternoon would decide whether America's premier flier would undertake the mission.

Gibbons planned to talk to Lindbergh, now at Northhaven, Me., by telephone. It was believed they might decide whether Lindbergh would fly the bodies back or whether they would be returned by the coast guard cutter Northland as had been previously suggested.

Coast guard officials reached a sister of Mrs. Rogers at Skowhegan, Maine, this morning, who told them that Mrs. Rogers was prostrated and grief stricken.

The sister told officials that Mrs. Rogers would be happy to have Lindbergh take charge of returning the body.

At the same time the coast guard said Pan-American Airways had offered its facilities in the return of the bodies.

The nation's most prominent official and public personages, led by President Roosevelt, paid tribute to

(Continued on page 6, col. 3)

Actor Humorist, Globe Flier Die in Alaskan Plane Crash

Last Flight

Rambling Tour Ends in Death for Pair as Craft Crashes Near Point Barrow on Hop to Farthest North Outpost of Territory

By FRANK DAUGHERTY
[United Press Staff Correspondent]
[Copyright, 1935, by United Press]

POINT BARROW, Alaska—Wiley Post and Will Rogers, famous air duo, were killed at 8:18 p. m. Thursday (12:18 a. m. today CST) when their plane crashed 15 miles south of here.

Lost in a fog and with the engine missing, Post nosed the plane into the tundra, striking hummocks of moss. The plane's right wing was broken, its nose and engine driven into the cabin. The crash instantly killed both occupants.

Lost in Fog, Land

They became lost in the fog about 5 p. m. and landed their Lockheed Orion low winged monoplane at Walkpi, an Eskimo village. Post made repairs to the plane's engine which had been missing badly and asked natives the way to Point Barrow.

The fog was lying almost to the tundra and they decided to wait for it to rise. Post and Rogers ate dinner with Eskimos camped on a river bank and after the meal decided to take off despite the fog.

Both Instantly Killed

Natives said the engine appeared to be running smoother as the big ship lifted from the river and took off in the blinding mantle which overhung the country.

It was not long after that the ship plumetted into the tundra, the motor being driven into the cabin by the force of the crash, killing Post, who made two successful trips around the world. Rogers was thrown clear of the plane which ground looped over onto its back. Rogers' death also was instantaneous, however.

Post Caught in Wreckage

Post's watch stopped at 8:18 p. m., Point Barrow time. The humorist's still was running when Sergt. Stanley Morgan of the U. S. signal corps Point Barrow station, and I reached the scene.

Morgan was notified in Point Barrow by excited natives and we reached the vicinity of the crash in a whale boat, manned by natives.

Post's body was pulled from the wreckage where it had been smashed among the controls and cabin.

Rogers' body was placed with that of Post in the whale boat and returned to Point Barrow. Here the bodies were turned over to Dr. Henry Griest, superintendent of the Presbyterian Mission hospital, where they were taken to await the arrival of the coast guard cutter Northland.

Both Badly Crushed

Both bodies were badly crushed. The plane was demolished. Gasoline spewed over the water between the moss hummocks, caught fire and blazed for several minutes.

Post, 'round-the-world record holder, and Rogers, the humorist, movie actor and famous air traveler, were on a leisurely trip around Alaska.

Originally intending to visit Point Barrow several days ago, instead they flew from Aklavik, N. W. T., to Fairbanks and spent the interval visiting central Alaskan points. They took off Thursday from Fairbanks and their arrival had been awaited at this farthest north outpost of civilization with keen anticipation by the few white persons here.

Daughter's Picture Falls

While natives and whites struggled to beach the boat carrying the bodies here, an ink-stained piece of

(Continued on page 6, col. 1)

Pictures, Stories

A full page of pictures relating to Wiley Post and Will Rogers will be found on Page 7 of this edition. Sidelights on their lives are published on Page 6.

Will Rogers (top) and Wiley Post (bottom) were killed early today when their plane crashed near Pt. Barrow, Alaska. Mrs. Post (below Rogers) abandoned plans to accompany the pair on the journey shortly before their takeoff from Seattle. At the right, below, is Post as he appeared in the costume he used on his attempts to break speed records in the stratosphere.

E. F. Appleby, Singer, Dies

Resident of 50 Years Succumbs at 77

Edward F. Appleby, 1139 Rutledge st., a resident of Madison for more than a half century and active in music affairs throughout that period, died at his home early today after an illness of nearly a year. He was 77.

APPLEBY

Funeral services will be held Saturday at 4 p. m. at the Fitch-Lawrence parlors, with the Rev. A. T. Wallace, of Pilgrim Congregational church, officiating. Pallbearers will be Jackson Reuter, H. O. Bigelow, J. W. Snell, J. W. Brown, Dr. E. P. Bridgman, and John Simpson. A quartet from the Mozart club will sing.

Mr. Appleby was born in Green Lake county, Wisconsin, Nov. 3, 1857, the son of Mr. and Mrs. William H. Appleby, of Dutchess county, New York. As a child, he went with his parents to Ripon, Wis., where he

(Continued on page 6, col. 7)

No - Balm Bill Dies in House

[By United Press]

The Shenners bill to ban heart balm suits in Wisconsin today was a dead issue of the 1935 legislature.

The assembly disposed of it late Thursday by killing it, 57 to 33, and then refusing to reconsider the adverse vote.

Assemblyman Marius Dueholm, (prog., Luck), Polk county farmer, denounced the measure, warning:

"If we pass this bill, we might as well turn our daughters out into the street for any playboy that might come along."

Before defeating the Shenners measure, the assembly adopted an amendment by Assmb. John O'Malley, (dem., Milwaukee), which would have permitted alienation of affection suits if couples had been married two or more years or had children, but barred all others.

O'Malley said his amendment would do away with "rackets" and at the same time "protect the home."

Genzmer Leads Attack

Assemblyman Elmer T. Genzmer, (dem., Mayville), led the attack on the bill, accusing the senate of not taking it seriously and warning that it "would take away balm from a person mistreated, lied to and de-

(Continued on page 6, col. 6)

Hopson Bares $350,000 Pay

May Have Received $550,000, He Says

WASHINGTON—(U.P.)—Howard C. Hopson defended his companies' expenditure of nearly $900,000 to fight the Wheeler-Rayburn utilities bill by charging today that the measure would destroy $6,000,000,000 worth of utilities securities.

"That is about one-half of all the utilities securities issues," the Associated Gas & Electric co. official told the house lobby investigating committee on his third appearance before it.

Hopson, who contends he isn't wealthy but wishes "it were true," told the committee under questioning that he received $300,000 to $500,000 last year from his "personal companies" plus $50,000 salary from A. G. & E.

Got $2,000,000, Charge

The rival senate committee has charged that Hopson received some $2,000,000 from A. G. & E., directly or indirectly, during the past five years, while dividends were being omitted. The senate group, having agreed to "divide" Hopson with the rival house committee, was waiting to question him again today.

Hopson said the A. G. & E. expenditures in fighting the bill in-

(Continued on page 8, col. 6)

U. W. Man

Howard C. Hopson was a man of military and literary ambitions when he attended the University of Wisconsin. The story of Hopson, the student, will be found on page 5.

New State Ad Bill Advanced

Assembly Engrosses $50,000 Fund

The assembly late Thursday engrossed the Staudenmaier bill to appropriate $50,000 to advertise Wisconsin's tourist attractions.

A similar appropriation was vetoed by Gov. La Follette and the new measure was advanced under agreement with progressive leaders that it would be approved if the legislature passes revenue raising [illegible]

La Follette said he vetoed the original appropriation because the [illegible] had failed to provide new [illegible]

[illegible] amendment by James T. Cav[illegible] (dem., Antigo) to increase [illegible] appropriation was rejected 71-18. [illegible] Paul Alfonsi, Pence, progressive leader, warned that if it [illegible] he would have to vote [illegible] the bill.

[illegible] perfectly willing to have this [illegible] and held by the enrol[illegible] clerk in the assembly until [illegible] time as enough money is [illegible] to take care of the normal [illegible] of the state," Alfonsi [illegible]

[illegible] that the administration [illegible] same opinion and that [illegible] appropriation was a [illegible] for the state.

[illegible] Alfonsi declared, [illegible] La Follette vetoed the ap[illegible] he said that we must [illegible] much money for the [illegible] old age and mothers'

[illegible] on page 6, col. 5)

They Say Today:

"Where's the Jew? Let's get him!" A Berlin mob. **Page 10.**

"Progressives will make a desperate effort to get the legislature away from Madison before Labor day." Winter Everett, **P 4.**

"Tuberculosis is losing its grip on the world." Dr. Logan Clendening. **Page 2.**

"It was a strange mixture of errors and double plays." Fred Graff covers the Blues-Red Sox game. **Page 1, Sports.**

"Anything worse in this land than trying to tell a football coach anything is to try and tell four of them. Roundy. **Page 19.**

Assembly Kills School Aid Bill

Griswold Measure Dies, 47 to 32

[By United Press]

The Wisconsin assembly today killed, 47 to 32, the Griswold bill to appropriate $2,000,000 yearly for high school aids. Madison would have received about $54,800 under terms of the bill.

Defeat was voted after Assemblyman Paul R. Alfonsi, Pence, progressive floor leader, said "as chairman of the peace conference committee Griswold had nerve sending this bill over here without taxation provisions. We ought to have nerve enough to kill it."

The assembly passed bills to plug income tax loopholes, to repeal business loss provisions of the present income tax law, and to raise income tax rates gradually from 7 per cent on the 13th $1,000 to 25 per cent on all income in excess of $25,000. It also provided a 50 per cent increase in the inheritance tax.

The Cashman bill to exempt cream and milk hauling trucks from commercial carrier regulations was killed, 43 to 40.

U. S. Will Speed La Crosse Bridge

Gov. La Follette this afternoon announced that the immediate rebuilding of the bridge across the Wisconsin channel of the Mississippi river at La Crosse had been taken up with the federal highway commission and that that department had promised to rush preliminary surveys for the improvement and to hasten not only the appropriation, but the rebuilding of the bridge as soon as possible. It was a span of this bridge that recently collapsed, killing two persons.

Rogers 'Sure Scared' of Madison; Post Couldn't Bear Noisy Welcome

But Humorist Liked the Folks, Globe Girdler Won Tribute in Visits Here

Death of Will Rogers and Wiley Post recalled to many Madisonians today how the city had played host to both of them during the last 10 years.

In 1925, they found Rogers a genial, amusing visitor who confessed he was "sure scared" when he looked over a crowd containing a number of university students and faculty members which he addressed.

Modest Souls

In 1931, after his famous 'round the world flight with Harold Gatty, Post visited Madison and its citizens found him and his partner a pair of modest souls who stopped a parade about the city in their honor and absolutely declined to make an appearance at a Madison theater.

Post was to have visited Madison again in the summer of 1933, but the visit had to be canceled when his world-circling plane, the Winnie Mae, crashed into a tree as he took off from Quincy, Ill. He suffered a basal skull fracture which kept him in a Quincy hospital for a short time.

Wrote for State Journal

Rogers was known to State Journal readers through a series of Sunday articles in 1927 commenting on current news events, always humorously and sometimes caustically.

Rogers appeared here on a program at the Central high auditorium with the De Reske singers on Oct. 22, 1925.

Will found that he liked Madison, but thought it was highbrow, he confided to a State Journal reporter.

"I sure like you folks," he said. "You didn't muff a single gag. I was sure scared when I looked the crowd over. I didn't come here to talk to college students or professors.

"I wanted to talk to business men, you know, Rotary and all that. That's where I get away.

Meets All Comers

"The university folks don't know what's going on in the world, and I don't know what's going on in these schools."

The Journal reported that Will

(Continued on page 6, col. 4)

Kohler Seen in Race for G. O. P. Presidential Vote

Intimations that former Gov. Walter Kohler may be a candidate for the republican nomination for president are construed from his name's being one of seven on a ballot sent out by Roy L. Brecke, secretary of the republican executive committee, to members of the republican state central committee, members of the state republican executive committee, and the republican county committee chairmen.

In a letter accompanying the ballots, Brecke said they are being sent out to obtain a reflection of the sentiment of Wisconsin republicans on the presidential situation. The letter said the selection of the recipient will not be made public.

Borah Favored

Other names on the ballot were former President Herbert Hoover, Sen. William H. Borah of Idaho, Rep. Hamilton Fish, Jr., of New York, Gov. Alfred M. Langdon of Kansas, Sen. Arthur Capper of Kansas, and Sen. Arthur H. Vandenberg of Michigan.

In an informal poll of the state central committee recently, a number of the committeemen indicated their preference for Borah.

Demands Meeting

Edward H. Bacon, Milwaukee, member of the republican state central committee from the fifth

(Continued on page 6, col. 1)

Youth, Father Held in Killing

Kenosha Boy Quizzed After Quarrel

KENOSHA—(U.P.)—Achille "Kelly" Derange, 41, operator of a bakery shop, was shot down in true gangland fashion today as he stood outside the door of the shop.

Just before he died, Derange gasped the name of a relative, charging him with the fatal shooting. Police apprehended Sam Covelli and his son.

Covelli denied any knowledge of the crime. Police later questioned Covelli's son, Richard, 22, following a report that on Saturday night he made a threat on Derange's life.

Police Inspector Charles Rock said Richard had been in a fight Saturday night and told the officer, "next time, instead of sending out the wagon, you can take your time because you'll need a hearse." The officer said he separated Derange and Covelli.

Richard Covelli likewise denied any knowledge of the slaying.

Racers' Car Inspection to Start at 9 Saturday

[illegible] entered in the Wisconsin State Journal's Soap Box [illegible] Sunday will be inspected at [illegible] garage, 13 S. Webster [illegible] 9 a. m. and noon Saturday. [illegible] Arthur Sandell of the city [illegible] department, announced [illegible]

[illegible] entire wing of the garage will [illegible] to inspect the 60 entries [illegible] Derby. Boys must have their [illegible] at the garage between the [illegible] hours and they are warned that the official inspectors will adhere rigidly to the rules.

Cars commercially built or not conforming to the rules regarding safety features, height, width, tread, etc., will be barred from the race. Although entries had mounted to 60 this morning, it was expected some cars would be disqualified. Further entries were expected during the day, but the list was to be officially

(Continued on page 6, col. 7)

Clipper Plane Off for Wilkes Island

SAND ISLAND, Midway Islands—(U.P.)—Pan American Airways' four-motored clipper ship took off from a coral-edged lagoon of this mid-Pacific island at 9:21 a. m. (P.S.T.) today, bound for Wilkes island of the Wake group, 1400 miles westward.

La Crosse City Attorney, Wounded by Wife, Dies

LA CROSSE, Wis. — (U.P.) — Oscar J. Swennes, 45, city attorney of La Crosse for 16 years, died today from bullet wounds inflicted by his wife.

Mrs. Swennes Thursday shot her husband and then committed suicide by opening the gas jets in the kitchen of their fashionable home.

When neighbors reported the Swennes had not been seen all day, detectives cut through a screen door and found Mrs. Swennes slumped over a kitchen chair, attired only in lounging pajamas. Swennes was found stretched across a bed, undressed and unconscious.

Near the body of the woman, Irene, about 44 years old, was found a newspaper clipping inferring the city attorney might have been leading a "double life."

Mrs. Swennes returned from a western trip Wednesday. Police believe she shot her husband early

(Continued on page 6, col. 8)

"... to renounce the throne ..."

'I Am Most Anxious That There Should Be No Delay'

LONDON — (U.P.) — Text of King Edward's announcement abdicating the throne of the British empire follows:

"After long and anxious consideration I have determined to renounce the throne to which I succeeded on the death of my father, and I am now communicating my final and irrevocable decision.

"I will not enter now into my private feeling but I would beg that it should be remembered that the burden which constantly rests upon the shoulders of a sovereign is so heavy that it can only be borne in circumstances different from those in which I now find myself.

"Realizing as I do the gravity of this step, I can only hope that I shall have the understanding of my peoples in the decision I have taken and the reasons which have led me to take it.

"I conceive that I am not overlooking the duty that rests on me to place in the forefront the public interest when I declare that I am conscious that I can no longer discharge this heavy task with efficiency or with satisfaction to myself.

"I have accordingly this morning executed an instrument of abdication in the terms following:

"I, Edward VIII of Great Britain, Ireland, the British Dominions beyond the seas, King Emperor of India, do hereby declare my irrevocable determination to renounce the throne for myself and my descendants. My desire is that effect should be given to this instrument of abdication immediately.

"In token thereof I have hereunto set my hand this 10th day of December, 1936, in the presence of the witnesses whose signatures are subscribed.

(Signed) "Edward R. I."

"My execution of this instrument has been witnessed by my three brothers, the royal highnesses, the Duke of York, the Duke of Gloucester, and the Duke of Kent.

"I deeply appreciate the spirit which has actuated the appeals which have been made to me to take a different decision and I have, before reaching my final determination, most fully pondred over them.

"But my mind is made up.

"Moreover, further delay cannot be but most injurious to the peoples whom I have tried to serve as Prince of Wales and as king, and whose future happiness and prosperity are the constant wish of my heart.

"I take my leave of them in the confident hope that the course which I have thought it right to follow is that which is best for the stability of the throne and empire and the happiness of my peoples.

"I am deeply sensible of the consideration which they have always extended to me both before and after my accession to the throne and which I know they will extend in full measure to my successor.

"I am most anxious that there should be no delay of any kind in giving effect to the instrument which I have executed and that all necessary steps should be taken immediately to secure that my lawful successor, my brother, his royal highness the Duke of York, should ascend the throne.

"Edward, R. I."

"... and the reasons ..."

Weather

Fair tonight and Friday. Colder tonight. Minimum near zero. Rising temperature Friday. Diminishing northwest wind.

The Wisconsin State Journal

A Fact-Finding Newspaper

Home-Final Edition

VOL. 149, NO. 71. 98th Year. MADISON, THURSDAY, DECEMBER 10, 1936 26 Pages ★★★ Price Three Cents

King Edward Abdicates to Go Into Exile, Marry Wally

"... for a few pitiful hours ..." Story on Page 1

"... the door is closed ..." Story on Page 8

"... a final farewell ..." Story on Page 8

"... just before the chime ..." Story on Page 1

"... the silence was uncanny ..." Story on Page 1

"... the flag dipped ..." Story on Page 1

"... demonstrations were futile ..." Story on Page 1

"... never again on its soil ..." Story on Page 8

Duke of York to Succeed to Throne Friday as Albert I

"... the crown was on the casket ..." Story on Page 8

"... I am going to marry ..." Story on Page 1

"... in a pink villa ..." Story on Page 8

"... the empire's sweethearts ..." Story on Page 8

"... it was a love match ..." Story on Page 8

"... although he proposed many times ..." Story on Page 8

Progressives Cry 'No,' But Confer Again on Frank

By MORRIS H. RUBIN

A routine and expected flurry of denials served only today to strengthen a State Journal report Wednesday that regent dismissal of Pres. Glenn Frank is imminent.

Harold M. Wilkie, regent president and spearhead of the "fire Frank" drive, said, as is his custom, that The State Journal story was "incorrect." But, added Wilkie with significance:

"When it comes to open meeting, you'll have your story. I don't want to discuss what the executive committee said in conference with the president. It will all come out."

The "it" to which he referred was the campaign to oust Frank and its background of bitter dispute over university financing and administration.

They Meet Again

Wilkie, who with Clough Gates, Superior regent, spent two hours in private conference with Gov. La Follette Monday, day before the regent meeting, was back in conference with the governor today. Gov. LaFollette left budget hearings to confer with Wilkie.

Frank remained silent, pointing out that it has always been his custom not to divulge the nature of conversation with individual regents. He was referring to a conference behind closed doors with Wilkie and Gates Wednesday.

That the axe job would be finished soon was reported by those who think that Wilkie is developing a distaste for assignment as leader of the bloc of progressives opposed to the president. Basis of the belief is the fact that Wilkie doesn't think he's helping his law business by taking a strong stand in so controversial a question.

Gates Gets Load

Evidence of this has been detected in the increasing load of "policy" work given Gates, a comparative newcomer to the board. Loading of responsibilities on Gates, particularly in the Frank ouster campaign, has been accomplished with considerable misgivings by high progressives, because Gates is not considered as well equipped as Wilkie in that kind of activity.

Meanwhile, the university administration and faculty remained tense with excitement, wondering whether the next move and the final, fateful one will come Wednesday when the regents meet in special session to listen to Wilkie's presentation of the budget situation to be offered Gov. La Follette Thursday quite apart from Frank's budget statement.

A Preliminary Step

The decision to have an independent regent presentation was believed to be a preliminary step in the drive for dismissal.

Discussion of possible successors to Frank, if and when the axe falls, still centers on two campus figures, Deans Lloyd K. Garrison of the law school, and E. B. Fred of the graduate school. Also mentioned now for the first time is Prof. John Gaus, university political scientist and close friend of Gov. La Follette.

The Daily Cardinal, undergraduate publication, rallied to Frank's defense today with a front-page editorial assailing the progressive party for **"choking a university administrator from office without making specific charges against him and allowing him to present a defense."**

Despite this and other evidences of growing support in Frank's favor, it was more than ever apparent that his cause is hopeless even though he should decide to fight it out. On the 15-member board he can hope for seven votes at the most, one short of a majority.

The Lineup

As they line up now, giving Frank every possible doubtful vote, the roll-call would be:

For dismissal: Robert V. Baker, Jr., Kenosha, Edward J. Brown, Milwaukee; Gates; Kenneth Hones, Colfax; A. M. Miller, Little Chute; Raymond Richards, Wisconsin Rapids; Mrs. Clara T. Runge, Baraboo, and Wilkie, all La Follette appointees—eight.

Against: A. C. Backus, Milwaukee; E. M. Christopherson, Pigeon Falls; Mrs. Jessie Coombs, Oshkosh; Daniel H. Grady, Portage; Gunnar Gunderson, La Crosse; George W. Mead, Wisconsin Rapids; and John Callahan, superintendent of public instruction and ex officio board member with a vote—seven.

Pope Sits in Chair, Then Returns to Bed

VATICAN CITY—(U.P.)—Pope Pius arose from his sick bed for 10 minutes today while attendants aired his bed room, trustworthy sources reported. With Dr. Arminta Milani and Cardinal Pacelli, papal secretary of state at his side, he was taken in a wheel chair to a nearby studio. It was understood that Dr. Milani convinced him that it would be wise to prolong his rest period until Christmas.

Young St. Nick

This is Cartier Blackburn, State Journal carrier salesman, showing an Empty Stocking club collection envelope. All The State Journal's Madison carriers will distribute these envelopes to their customers Friday, and on Saturday they will pick up the customers' contributions to the cause of a happy Christmas for the city's needy children.

Yeggs Smash Nelson's Window, Take Five Rings

Burglars smashed a window of the O. M. Nelson and Son Jewelry store, Capitol square, early today and stole five small diamond rings valued at $500, police said. Bertram Crary, 649 E. Johnson st., Western Union messenger passing the store, noticed a brick wrapped in paper at the door, part of one window shattered, and an empty plush ring box next to the brick.

$124 Added to Christmas Toy Fund

EMPTY STOCKING FUND	
Previously reported	$541.69
Bridge party (additional)	9.50
Kappa Delta Alumnae	5.00
Sons of American Veterans	2.00
Madison Garden Club	5.00
Madison Independent Retail Food Dealers	10.00
Merchants on north side of 500 block on State st.	16.00
Auxiliary of Nat'l Letter Carriers assn. No. 508	5.00
Ladies' Auxiliary of Brotherhood of Locomotive Engineers	2.00
Other contributions	69.61
Total	$665.80

Contributions of $124.11, as listed above, were reported by the Empty Stocking club today, bringing the official total to $665.80. The exact amount to be realized from last Sunday's basketball game is still undetermined, but this is expected to be about $1,000.

The additional $9.50 from the Empty Stocking club bridge party brings the total from this event to $191.50, the largest amount it has ever produced.

The contribution from the merchants on the north side of the 500 block on State st. resulted from their campaign to raise funds for Christmas lighting and decorations in the block. When they discovered that the fund was oversubscribed by $16, the merchants voted to contribute that sum to the worthy cause of making Christmas a happy occasion for needy children.

Those who participated in the gift were:

Wagner's College shop, the Chocolate shop, Tiffany's, Two Millers, Pantorium, Wehrman's leather goods store, Jones Typewriter co. Templin Jewelry shop, H and M Sales co., Snowdon's, Singer Sewing Machine co., Meuer art store, and Karl Thies.

The Empty Stocking club is still far from its goal of $3,000, the amount necessary to assure every needy child in Madison a stocking full of toys and candy on Christmas. Don't YOU want to help make this possible? If you do, send your check today to the Empty Stocking club, in care of The Wisconsin State Journal.

Cleveland's Property

NEW YORK—(U.P.)—Baseball Commissioner K. M. Landis today ruled that Bob Feller was the property of the Cleveland Indians and ordered that club to pay the Des Moines club $7,500 to relinquish its claim.

Up She Goes!

3000
2750
2500
2250
2000
1750
1500
1250
1000
750
500
250

Watch this thermometer in The State Journal every day. It will show the progress of the Empty Stocking club in its campaign to raise $3,000 with which to make Christmas happy for Madison's needy children. If you want to help keep the mercury in the thermometer climbing, send your check today to the Empty Stocking club, in care of the The State Journal.

Football Banquet Open to Women

Women will be admitted to the university football banquet at the field house tonight, it was announced today by the committee in charge, in refutation of the report that the affair is for men only. Tickets may be obtained at the field house up to 6:30, scheduled starting time.

By WEBB MILLER

[Copyright, 1936, by United Press]

LONDON—King Edward VIII abdicated today from the throne of Great Britain, renouncing for love the rulership over the world's greatest empire and one-quarter of the inhabitants of the globe.

He gave up his crown so that he could go into perpetual exile and marry Mrs. Wallis Warfield Simpson, twice-divorced American.

A breathless, stunned house of commons received from the king an historic document giving up the "heavy burden" of kingship because of the difficult personal situation in which he finds himself.

Duke of York to Be King

The Duke of York, his brother, will succeed to the throne, probably as Albert I after parliament passes necessary bills Friday.

The duke's daughter, imperious little 10½ year old Princess Elizabeth, becomes heir presumptive to the throne, Britain's next queen if her father dies without a son being born to him.

Wally Calls King "Boysy"

The woman for whom Edward gave up his throne apparently was moved by the tremendous import of the king's act, and sought to console him.

She talked cheeringly to the king after word of his formal abdication was first flashed to Herman L. Rogers, at whose villa she is a guest, at Cannes.

She affectionately called the king "boysy," on the telephone.

The scene in the house of commons was one of the most solemn in England's long history. Never before has a king voluntarily given up that mighty throne.

But his majesty's government was determined not to permit a divorcee and commoner to share it with Edward of the House of Windsor.

At 3:42 P. M.

The king was equally determined to make her queen or marry her in any case. He therefore decided against fighting his ministers and the constitution, a losing struggle.

The historic occasion came at 3:42 p. m. (9:42 a. m. CST) on Thursday, Dec. 10, 1936, after Edward had been on the throne 324 days.

Just before Big Ben, the voice of the empire, chimed the three-quarter hour, the speaker called on Baldwin.

The prime minister arose from his seat and walked to the bar of the house.

In a voice which by a mighty effort of will power he kept steady, the stocky country squire, the very epitome of conservative England, said:

"A message from his majesty the king, sir, signed by his majesty's own hand."

The silence was uncanny, painful. The throng which filled the small, gloomy chamber where centuries of history has been made, seemed to have suspended animation. There was not even the sound of loud breathing.

The speaker read the king's message.

The emotions of the assembly can only be imagined when he came to the solemn words:

"I, Edward VIII of Great Britain,

Police Guard Wally as Hundreds of Notes Threaten Her Life

CANNES, France. — (U.P.) — The next move of Mrs. Wallis Warfield Simpson, for whom Edward VIII of England today gave up his throne, was obscured today by a double guard of reticence and secret service men surrounding her.

The strong police reinforcements were sent because Mrs. Simpson has received hundreds of threatening letters, it was learned. She was permitted to taste no food that had not been tested before meals, it was asserted.

It was understood first that she planned to remain in the villa of Mr. and Mrs. Herman L. Rogers here until after Christmas. It was emphatically stated that Edward was not proceeding to Cannes.

But as the day wore on definite assertions in the Rogers household that their guest would remain until after the holidays were not so positive.

After word that the king had formally abdicated was flashed from London, Rogers was unwilling to say more than that "Mrs. Simpson will remain at least until Friday," although he did not say she was planning to leave.

From this it was deduced that Mrs. Simpson might not be wholly certain of her plans, or might even attempt to slip away quietly to escape the ring of reporters surrounding her.

News of Edward's act was telephoned to the villa, where Rogers received the call.

The United Press correspondent asked Rogers, an American, whether Mrs. Simpson would marry Edward.

"I cannot answer that," Rogers replied.

The correspondent urged:

"Can't you say either 'yes' or 'no'?"

Rogers answered:

"I cannot commit myself, but everything would indicate that is her idea."

It was learned that Mrs. Rogers was buying personally all food for the household and taking it in her own car to the villa.

All letter and packages were examined before they reached the villa.

Armed secret service men were in the villa, near Mrs. Simpson's bedroom, at all hours of the day and night, it was asserted.

It was to this unhappy plight that her romance with King Edward had brought the cheery Mrs. Simpson, the one-time Baltimore society woman who has taken her place with other women of history.

Edward Drinks as Throne Topples

FORT BELVEDERE, Eng.—(U.P.)—Edward VIII of England—who will be Mr. Windsor in a few hours—sat hunched deep in an armchair at his country residence today and toyed with a glass of whisky at the time that his own fateful words, read before parliament 20 miles away, were stripping him of his crown and everything that goes with it.

On the Inside:

◊ ◊ ◊

Weather

WISCONSIN: Local thundershowers Sunday; Monday generally fair, with somewhat cooler in extreme east.

The Wisconsin State Journal

A Fact-Finding Newspaper

Today Is: JULY 4

VOL. 150, NO. 94. 98th Year. MADISON, SUNDAY, JULY 4, 1937 20 Pages ★★★ Price Five Cents

Snow, Sleet Storm Hinders Amelia's Rescuers

Sit-Down Illegal—Perkins

"Jury to Probe Steel Violence." See Story, Page 18. "Dynamite Plot Discovered." Story on Page 18.

WASHINGTON — (U.P.) — Labor Secretary Frances Perkins asserted Saturday night that sit-down strikes are illegal and "unsuited to the temperaments and conditions of our modern life in this country."

Her statement, in an open letter to Rep. J. William Ditter (r., Pa.) was the first public declaration on legality of sit-downs by any ranking member of the administration.

Miss Perkins some time ago had stated her belief that the legal status of the sit-down had not yet been determined.

In response to a request by Ditter for clarification of the labor department's view on the issue, Miss Perkins wrote that she accepted the opinion of the third circuit court of appeals that sit-down strikers in the Apex hosiery plant at Philadelphia "were acting unlawfully."

"You ask if in view of this court order and opinion I will clarify my own and the department's position on this subject," she wrote.

"First, may I say that, of course, I accept this decision of the court as defining and applying the law to this particular type of strike. I deduce from the opinion that strikers may not lawfully use the sit-down method . . ."

Miss Perkin's letter to Ditter explained:

"It is not and never has been an official position of the department of labor or of the secretary that sit-down strikes are either lawful, desirable or appropriate.

"In fact the officers of the department and the secretary have urged union leaders and members not to use the method and to bend every effort to take the men out of a plant where used . . ."

"I note that you attach some blame to the federal government and in particular the department of labor for temporizing with this situation.

"I call your attention to the fact that the local and state agencies have all the police powers for maintaining order — enforcing local ordinances and the common law in regard to trespass, etc., and that the federal government has no authority in this respect.

"The governors of the states where this type of strike has occurred have used their best judgment in handling the situation. Knowing the people of their states and being closer to the facts and circumstances they have been in a position to exercise patience and to use explanation and educative persuasion if and when that was the best method of securing the proper behavior of their fellow citizens.

"I want to assure you, sir, that American wage earners — however unwise they may have been at times in the selection of method or their behavior during industrial disputes—are not revolutionary in thought or feeling and do not seek to impair civil government, ruin industry or change our conceptions of private property.

"They sometimes have been hard-pressed, treated with impatience, contempt and brutality when they were trying to improve their working conditions and status by collective bargaining.

"We all hope that that will soon be a thing of the past. I am opposed to the use of force and violence in labor disputes by the employers, as well as by the wage earners, and if public officials are obliged to use force it should be only after every effort at reasonable persuasion of both sides has broken down.

"Let me further assure you, sir, that no encouragement to the use of lawless methods flows from the department of labor nor will it under my administration."

Ohio Troops To Aid Plant Opening

COLUMBUS, O., — (U.P.) — Governor Martin L. Davey announced late Saturday he would comply with the request of Cleveland city and Cuyahoga county officials for aid of Ohio national guardsmen in reopening four struck Cleveland Republic Steel corp. plants Tuesday.

Miss Earhart Scores Long List of Air Triumphs

"Amelia Earhart Putnam

Finish of flight from Honolulu to California.

At completion of solo hop across Atlantic ocean.

In New York following non-stop flight from Mexico City.

Amelia with husband, George Putnam.

U.S. Ships, Planes Scour Pacific For Lost Fliers

HONOLULU, T. H.—(U.P.)—A snow and sleet storm almost unprecedented in the South Pacific late Saturday turned back a navy plane flying to the rescue of Amelia Earhart and her navigator, Capt. Frederick Noonan, who disappeared on a flight around the world.

This freakish storm caused consternation among naval authorities directing the search for America's foremost woman flier and reduced the chances that the fliers might be found either adrift in the trackless Pacific or down on some nameless atoll far off the shipping lanes.

When the naval headquarters here announced that the seaplane had been forced to turn back when only 500 miles from Howland island, which Miss Earhart overshot on the flight from New Guinea, hopes were running high that a rescue could be made. Throughout the day faint radio signals crackled across the Pacific from the plane's radio, KHAQQ. In a calm voice Miss Earhart was sending at frequent intervals "S. O. S.—S. O. S."

Thus, the immediate task of finding the tousle-haired flier and her navigator rested with the U. S. coast guard cutter Itasca which was plying about in the waters near Howland island, a tiny sand spit in the normally sunny and placid South Pacific just a few miles north of the equator.

Naval authorities said that there was no possibility of sending another plane toward Howland island before night because an earlier departure on the 1,800-mile flight would mean a hazardous landing on the island at night. Knowledge of weather between Hawaii and Howland island, authorities explained, is most uncertain because of the lack of reporting facilities.

No one had knowledge of this storm when Lieut. W. W. Harvey and seven companions took off at 9:53 p. m. PST Friday. This same storm raging over the one and one-half mile by one-half mile cigar shaped Howland island might have engulfed Miss Earhart while on the 2,550 mile flight from New Guinea.

The navy reported that the seaplane flew into the storm at dawn Saturday and battled its way through sleet for two hours, rising to the highest altitude it was capable of obtaining. But there electrical storms were encountered.

The U. S. navy Saturday night pressed its powerful wartime resources into the search for America's foremost woman flier, and the U. S. S. airplane carrier Lexington weighed anchor at Santa Barbara, Cal., at 6 p. m. (PST) and rushed under forced draft to San Diego preparatory to a dash across the Pacific to the vicinity of Howland island.

When the Lexington nears the cigar shaped coral and sandy isle in about six or seven days it will release a covey of the 72 seaplanes aboard her on a systematic hunt for the famous flier and her navigator, Frederick Noonan.

At San Diego's naval base the navy's radio broadcast orders to all enlisted personnel and officers attached to the Lexington to be prepared to board the aircraft carrier off the Coronado roads at 6:30 a. m. today and be ready for a month's cruise. Seventy-two officers and men comprise the crews of the eight squadrons of navy planes attached to the Lexington.

Meanwhile the U. S. S. Colorado was speeding from Honolulu toward Howland Island. The Colorado carried three seaplanes. Also en route to the island from a point between it and Honolulu was the U. S. S. Swan, a mine sweeper. The Swan was posted 900 miles from here to give any possible aid to Miss Earhart had her plane successfully reached Howland Island and taken off from this port.

While these spectacular rescue efforts were being launched the U. S. coast guard cutter Itasca cruised about in a freakish sleet and snow storm within a radius of 80 miles from the island which is just north of the equator. The Itasca radioed late in the day that it had sighted no trace of the silver and orange "Flying Laboratory" and that search was extremely difficult owing to the inclement weather.

It was this storm that forced back the navy's attempt to reach the area by air.

In Oakland, Cal., George Palmer Putnam, husband of the woman flier, asked a local radio station to broadcast hourly requests that his wife signal by radio whether she was on land or afloat and north or south of the equator.

Miss Earhart was scheduled to land at Howland island shortly after noon, Pacific standard time, Friday, after a 2,700 mile flight from New Guinea. The last word from the plane in

'I Don't Worry,' Amelia Said Here

Speaking in Madison in March, 1936, before a crowd of 700 at the Hotel Loraine, Amelia Earhart, world famous axiatrix, said:

"It is often less dangerous on a trans-ocean flight than in one's own backyard . . . . I dont worry until there is something to worry about and then it is often too late to worry."

Saturday night Miss Earhart was lost in the expanse of the South Pacific where her round-the-world plane was forced down sometime Friday.

State Gets $1,000,000 Pension Aids

Federal grant of more than $1,000,000 to Wisconsin for pension aids to the state's needy aged was announced Saturday by H. L. McCarthy, the U. S. social security board's regional director.

The actual amount, $1,077,007, will help finance 36,000 old age pensioners from July 1 to Sept. 30, McCarthy said. In addition to the grant for the three month period, the U. S. treasury released $279,067 to help cover the cost of a previous quarter.

"Besides being one of the first states to adopt all standards of public assistance set by the social security board," McCarthy said, Wisconsin was also one of the first states to adopt an old-age assistance law 10 years before the social security act was passed. It has had a state law for old-age assistance since 1925, only two years after Montana had enacted the first such law in the United States."

McCarthy reviewed provisions of the Wisconsin law, pointing out an applicant for old age assistance must be 65, a citizen of the United States and a resident of the state for about five years. Maximum pension is $30 but the average is $20, one dollar more than the national average.

Boy, 4, Drowns in Yahara Near Lake Waubesa

Child Falls from Pier Near Home

On the scum laden waters of the Yahara river Saturday afternoon, death snuffed out its second life in 24 hours time in Madison lake and river waters.

Four-year-old LaVerne Sprague, son Mr. and Mrs. E. W. Sprague, McFarland, drowned in the river a quarter of a mile east of Lake Waubesa when he tumbled off a pier in front of his home.

Fifteen minutes later he was dragged from four and one-half feet of water by a neighbor, Fred Yaeger, who happened by the pier and saw the lad's body in the water.

Madison police were called and arrived a few minutes later, but efforts to revive the boy with lung-motor and artificial respiration failed.

No one, apparently, saw the accident. Neither did anyone hear the lad scream for help. Neighbors did, however, recall that he had been playing on the pier for at least two hours after lunch.

His mother, hysterical and near collapse after the accident, only sobbed.

"I've lost my boy. I've lost my boy."

Little LaVerne could not swim. He very seldom went in bathing at all and only with one of his two older brothers or his parents. He often played down near the river, but was forbidden to play on the pier. His body was recovered only a few feet from the end of the pier, so neighbors who arrived at the scene shortly after Yaeger had dragged him from the mucky waters, judged he must have been playing on the forbidden pier.

Surviving the boy are his parents, his grandparents, Mr. and Mrs. Martin Vinje, McFarland, and two brothers, Willard of Edwards Park, and Floyd of McFarland. The body is at the Joyce funeral home here.

Funeral services for Lillian Ziegler, 16-year-old Pheasant Branch girl who was drowned off the west shore of Lake Mendota Friday afternoon, will be held Monday morning from St. Bernard's Catholic church at Middleton, the Rev. Peter Hildebrand officiating. Burial will be in St. Peter's church cemetery at Ashton.

Burgess CIO Votes Strike Continuance

Burgess Battery co. strikers in the fourth week of their quest for higher wages voted down a "back to work" proposal Saturday by a large majority.

The proposal, advanced by a small group, was to meet with company officials and if given the original offer made by the company, the union was to call off the strike and members were to go back to work.

Voting this proposal down, the CIO union committed itself to continue its strike until the company accedes to union demands for higher wages, one week's vacation with pay seniority rights, union recognition and the 40 hour week.

The company's first offer met these demands except for the 20 per cent wage boost asked. Since that time the company has limited the offer to seniority rights.

At a meeting between both sides, called by the labor relations board Friday, the company would not discuss the vital wage issue, union officials said Saturday. The flat stand taken by the company against wage boosts, criticized at the union meeting today, stiffened the determination of the majority to stay out on strike.

The union also decided to shut down the boiler in the Burgess Battery plant. Shut down by the strikers earlier, it was started going again by the strikers. Saturday, finding the company was adamant on the question of wages, they agreed to close the boiler down once more.

Another meeting will be held Thursday at 10 a. m., at the American Labor League hall, in response to a request by members that meetings be held regularly, besides those called in emergencies.

Sutter Leaves Estate of $4,500 to Widow

John Sutter, Madison, who died June 22, left an estate valued at $4,500 to his widow, according to his will filed in county court Saturday.

Jammed Highways Bring Crashes As City Plans 'Safe, Sane' Fourth

Thousands of cars crammed Madison area highways Saturday night, ramming open the way for an expected record-breaking motorist throng scooting over roads for the double holiday starting this morning.

Minor accidents, with few persons injured, prefaced something city and county officials feared, were powerless to prevent, fatal accidents.

Sol Epstein, Wife Hurt

Sol Epstein, distributor for The Wisconsin State Journal, and his wife were injured Saturday night when their car collided with another on highway 14 near Janesville.

Mrs. Epstein was taken to Mercy hospital, Janesville, with cuts and bruises and a possible broken leg. Mr. Epstein received minor cuts and bruises.

The accident happened when a car driven by John Krause, Chicago, got out of control and crossed the highway in the path of the Epstein car. Several in the Krause car were injured slightly.

Mr. and Mrs. Epstein were on their way to Chicago for the week-end.

Knocked down by a car as he was crossing a street Saturday night Omer Tow, 42, Fairfax, Ia. received a scalp laceration and a bruised leg. He was taken to the Methodist hospital. Tow told doctors that he dodged three cars but didn't see "the fourth one coming." He was visiting relatives here.

"Safe and Sane"

Except for a yacht race Monday, Madison's Fourth of July calendar is as bare as the proverbial cupboard. No parade, no fireworks display, not even a baseball game is scheduled for the week-end holiday.

The Mendota Yacht club will provide the only public activity with its 34th annual Liberty cup race on Lake Mendota at 2:15 p. m. Monday off the foot of Hancock st. Otherwise, Madison residents will spend the week-end on picnics or on the road to resorts. The city's "safe and sane" ordinance prohibits shooting of fireworks.

Firecrackers Start

Reports of illegal firecracker reports filtered into the police station Saturday night, as some youngsters began early celebration of their independence day.

Police were notified by Chief William H. McCormick of an ordinance prohibiting retail sale of firecrackers, told to take or order all offenders over 18 to the station, take more youthful offenders to their homes, warn parents of the firecracker rule.

If the weather is clear, highways will be jammed with motoring pleasure-seekers. Filling station operators will cash in while the going is good, but immediately after the holiday week-end will meet possibly to discuss reduction of prices to meet cuts inaugurated by four privately-owned Standard Oil co. stations.

The rush of cars began early Saturday, continued through the night. Early Saturday morning, one statistical observer out on the Middleton road, for example, counted 45 cars passing. Of those, 40 of them showed Illinois license plates as they tore northward away from the city.

Double Snapshot Contest Prizes for This Week

Due to unavoidable circumstances and the large number of entries in The Wisconsin State Journal's last week's snapshot contest, judges were unable to select winners and award prizes.

All entries made last week will be entered in next week's contest and the prizes will be increased. Announcement of the winners of chas and merchandize prizes in the two-week contest which ends this Thursday at midnight will be made in next Sunday's Wisconsin State Journal.

Watch Tuesday's Journal for a story giving the complete list of prizes. Here's your chance to make a double killing in prizes, two weeks in one. Get out that camera.

Chief Objects to Ambulance Control Shift

A "movement" is under way to remove the ambulances from the police department to the city board of health, Police Chief William H. McCormick revealed Saturday.

The chief, who expressed opposition to the idea, said the proposal was not discussed with him by city officials. He said he learned of the proposed change from a member of his department who heard of the plan from a city hall official.

McCormick said he understood the idea of placing the ambulances under jurisdiction of the board of health was based on economy. Medical students from the University of Wisconsin would be employed as ambulance drivers, the chief said he was informed.

If the proposal comes before the police and fire commission, the chief indicated he would vigorously oppose the plan on the grounds that the emergency ambulances are necessary police equipment. The police ambulance squad are trained in first-aid methods and have performed valuable services to the police department, McCormick contended.

City officials and police commission members could not be reached Saturday afternoon for comment on the proposal.

Child Falls from Window; Condition Critical

25-foot tumble from a third story window at her home Saturday night sent Barbara King, 4, daughter of Mr. and Mrs. Leo King, 1123 E. Dayton st. to Methodist hospital with a possible skull fracture and serious bruises.

Hospital attendants said her condition was critical.

The tot fell from the kitchen window of the King apartment when she climbed on to the sill to look out the window.

Woman Dies of Crash Injuries

TOMAH, Wis. — (U.P.) — Mrs. Petra Kohler, 59, Kenosha, died in a hospital here today of injuries she received when the automobile in which she and her daughter, Margaret, and Ray Booth, also of Kenosha, were riding overturned in a ditch seven miles east of here. Booth and Miss Kohler suffered minor injuries.

On The Inside:

◇ ◇ ◇

"...would collect thousands..."

Woman Explorer Rescues Friends

NEW YORK —(U.P.)— Mrs. Osa Johnson, the explorer, reported to her New York representatives today that she had rescued two friends who had been lost a week in the African jungle southwest of Nairobi, Kenya colony. The cable said that Mrs. Johnson led a party which found Phillip Whitmarsh, millionaire Canadian gold mine operator, and his wife in a jungle clearing uninjured but without food. The Whitmarsh's were forced down while flying to Nairobi to meet Mrs. Johnson.

Baraboo Unions Plan Council

(State Journal News Service)

BARABOO—Plans for formation of a central labor council were discussed here Friday night at a mass meeting of persons interested in the union movement. Herbert Hillebrandt, AFL, organizer from Madison, spoke. Two locals have been formed here recently one in the Island mill, the other among musicians.

Fire Menaces Film Stars' Homes

HOLLYWOOD—(U.P.)—Grass and brush in the hills above Dark Canyon road near First National studios caught fire late Saturday, menacing the homes of many motion picture personages, including that of Alan Dinehart, film character actor. Five fire companies and 45 men were sent to fight the blaze.

3,000 See Monroe Swiss Tourney Open

MONROE—Despite a wind, hail, and rain storm which broke over the city Saturday night approximately 3,000 persons crowded the business square for ceremonies opening the triennial national turnfests of the Swiss-American Gymnastic society.

Swiss athletes from 12 cities and spectators numbering several thousand from as many more cities in all parts of the United States were present.

Sen. Duffy opened the program with a short talk and then left immediately by plane for Milwaukee. Other speakers were Mayor Charles Kohli, Carl Marty Sr., and Bruce M. Blum.

A band concert, Swiss yodeling, singing and dancing and an exhibition of flag throwing by Franz Hug, Switzerland's world champion flag thrower, were on the program.

Monroe, Swiss cheese capital of the United States, and located in the heart of Wisconsin's famed "Little Switzerland" country is the smallest city ever to play host to this national tournament of gymnasts.

Athletes who will start competitoin Sunday came from 12 cities, Madison, Milwaukee, Chicago, New York, Hudson county, New Jersey; San Francisco, Detroit, Pittsburg, Philadelphia, Toledo, and Cleveland.

Pickpockets were reported in the crowds that milled about the old courthouse Saturday night. One man, Theodore Ammann, Philadelphia, reported he lost $300 to a pickpocket.

T. R. Hefty Ill With Pneumonia

Thomas R. Hefty, president of the First National bank, is confined to Wisconsin General hospital with pneumonia. Mr. Hefty entered the hospital Friday. His condition is satisfactory, attendants said.

Socialite Freed In Murder Case

LOS ANGELES, Cal. — (U.P.) — Henry Suydam Satterlee, said to be a member of a prominent and wealthy New York family, who was questioned during the hunt for the Inglewood murderer of three little girls, today was exonerated by police of all connection with the case.

They Say Today:

"It's too foolish to even think about." Yoo-Hoo, Mrs. Roosevelt! You split an infinitive in your flustration about another romance. Page 11.

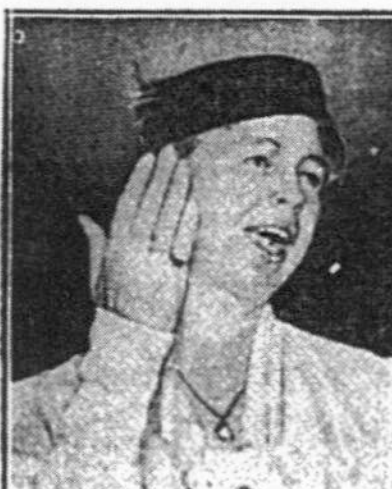

MRS. F. D. ROOSEVELT

"I think that the important thing is to stop wars and establish lasting peace in the world." For a lad of 15, Jerry McNutt thinks pretty thoughtfully. Page 17.

"I'll come by for you at 7:30 sharp Monday morning." These Longfellows don't want to miss a second of doings. Page 20.

"Losing those two men hurts us because our squad is so small, but there's nothing to be done about it." On the whole, Harry Stuhldreher is pretty well pleased. Page 1, sports.

"She will pull through." George Palmer Putnam is worried but confident in his wife's cool courage. Page 2.

"Maybe there isn't a new era in Wisconsin athletics unfolding before our eyes, but certainly there is a very definite change in the old order of things." And a very important one, too, Henry J. McCormick's convinced. Page 1, sports.

The Wisconsin State Journal

A fact-finding Newspaper

VOL. 151, NO. 161. 99th Year — MADISON, SATURDAY, MARCH 12, 1938 — 12 PAGES — PRICE THREE CENTS

Washington

By Harlan Miller

When babies get too big to kiss the best thing a senator can do in Washington is to take 'em for a ride on the 780-foot monorail subway between the capitol and the senate office building . . . As the tots scoot around the two curves, they swear undying fealty to their senator.

◊ ◊ ◊

MRS. PHIL SHERIDAN . . forgotten belle

This subway saves the elder statesmen many a precious step . . . But alas, some have to traverse two blocks of corridors before they reach their sanctums in the far corner . . . There's a bell beside the elevator which a senator can ring so the subway car will wait for him. (Representatives have to walk in THEIR tunnel.)

◊ ◊ ◊

An afternoon solitude will descend on the White House for a month. Mrs. Roosevelt is to be away lecturing . . . If she were here, another thousand or two would be sipping a cup of tea with her during March . . . Her engagement book is already made up till June. She probably has a reception scheduled to begin within an hour after she returns. She is away a lot, but makes up for it when she gets home.

"—inner huddle: behind the ropes."

One hot summer evening someone phoned Joe Kennedy at his estate near Washington and asked if he could bring out Jules Henry, the rugged, square-jawed French charge d'affaires. Joe rebelled.

"Hell," said Joe, "we'll probably all have to put on stiff collars."

But Monsieur Jules showed up minus collar, tie and coat, and Joe said:

"If this is diplomacy, I'll try some."

◊ ◊ ◊

Quaint American ethical note: Magnates who boil at the thought of the president syndicating his writings while in the White House would fall all over each other at the chance to sponsor his fireside radio chats at any price.

◊ ◊ ◊

POTOMAC TRIPE: One senator always musses his manicurist's hair when she finishes his nails . . Another senator always buys his toupes in Vienna, a laggard shade grayer each year . . . One vice president purloined a set of cut glass inkwells which had been in the senate 100 years.

"—better than senatorial kisses."

Washington forgets her belles and heroes quickly. No one connected the wrinkled little old lady who used to gaze (until a fortnight ago) at Phil Sheridan's statue near her house, with the great beauty of the seventies, daughter of a general, who married Gen. Sheridan . . . Great beauties should be remembered by the portraits of their heyday, like Widow Sheridan's above.

◊ ◊ ◊

YANKEE COURT: The nearest thing to a court scene at the White House is the resplendent crowd that gathers "behind the rope" in the Rose room at presidential receptions. A place behind the rope is gained only by specific invitation: that exalted square o. carpet is for cabinet members, diplomats, great personages.

◊ ◊ ◊

Pathetic and grotesque are the wiles and ruses used by the thirsty for glory to attain the hallowed enclosure i: the room beyond the Blue room, where the president greets his guests.

With a little imagination, a little gaudier costuming, it might almost be a chrome from Louis XIV's court . . . almost, but not quite . . . Occasionally a bold desperate courier or an indomitable dowager ducks under the velvet rope to join the elect, to be seen by the lesser elite on their way to the refreshments.

Boyle Continues Fight on Wives in City Service

Ald. William H. Boyle is determined that the common council bar married women from entering the city service. He introduced an ordinance to that effect last summer.

Several weeks ago he discovered that no action had been taken on it. At this request, it was referred to the board of personnel. At Friday night's council meeting the board tossed the ordinance back into the laps of the aldermen without any recommendation.

"I maintain that the board should act on this ordinance one way or another," Boyle said. "It is not fair for the board not to take action."

Weather

Partly cloudy tonight and Sunday. Colder Sunday. Fresh shifting winds. (Story,

Do You Know

when the pedestrian has the right-of-way at an intersection? When he has started to cross the highway with the green or "GO" signal. If the movement of traffic is not controlled by a traffic officer or traffic signal, the pedestrian has the right-of-way.

Austrian Nazis Cheer Hitler's Arrival; War Scare Sweeps Through Europe

'To Face the Music . . .'

Speed Bornstein Suspect to Cell Here

By LAWRENCE FITZPATRICK

Finally consenting to waive extradition, Roy Stevens, 40, ex-convict from California and suspect in the Bornstein murder case, was sped back to Madison by police detectives from Maquoketa, Ia., late Friday.

After changing his mind several times during a two-hour talk with Dect. Lieut. John R. Arnold and county, Iowa, in the Iowa jail, county, Iowa, in the the Iowa jail, the tall, slightly stooped suspect agreed to return to Wisconsin "to face the music."

Stevens had sought to bargain with Madison and Iowa officials. He said he "would gladly go back to Wisconsin if Iowa would drop the charges of robbery" against him.

May Return to Iowa

Dist. Atty. Lyall T. Beggs and County Atty. Arthur Janssen of Iowa after a conference announced they had agreed that Stevens should be returned to Madison and that in the event he is acquitted here in connection with the Bornstein murder he will be returned to Iowa to face robbery charges.

Convinced that he could not bargain with the two prosecutors, Stevens signed the waiver handed to him by Lieut. Arnold. The waiver was approved by Iowa District Judge Frank D. Kelsey and the Madison police car carrying the suspect quickly sped away.

Stevens was locked in a cell at police headquarters here where he will be held until police complete their investigation. Witnesses will view the suspect and more serious charges will be lodged against Stevens early next week, Beggs said.

Isadore Victor, 317 Huntington ct., attendant at the Sinaiko filling station, Murray and Regent sts., who witnessed the murder of his brother-in-law, Oscar Bornstein, by a green-hooded bandit-killer, told officials he was positive Stevens was the man after viewing him at the Iowa jail.

"I'll never forget that man," Victor said. "I knew he was the man the second he walked into that room in the jail . . . I looked at other men the police showed me, but that's the man," Victor repeated referring to the tall, sandy complexioned Stevens.

The filling station attendant who was slugged by the killer of his brother-in-law, pointed to the odd-sized, shawl collar overcoat as a mark of identification. Arnold and Detective Everett Mellor had made trips to La Crosse and Sparta to find the overcoat which Stevens sold for 25 cents to a vag he met in the Sparta jail. Stevens quickly admitted the coat was his when Arnold asked him to try it on at the Iowa jail.

In Jail Here Before

When Lieut. Arnold first talked with Stevens briefly at the Iowa jail Tuesday, the prisoner denied he was ever in Madison. While returning to Madison Friday night Stevens remarked to Arnold with a faint smile that he had slept in the Madison jail several months ago as a transient.

Apparently Stevens didn't intend to stay in the small Iowa jail because he had remarked to a fellow prisoner, "I can get out of this cracker-box any time I want to."

The prisoner, who knew Stevens when they were both inmates of Folsom prison in California, warned the Jackson county sheriff that Stevens might try to escape. Late the other night when the sheriff inspected the jail he found Stevens sitting in the "bullpen" with his hat and coat on. Taking no chances, the sheriff locked him in a solitary confinement cell.

When Madison police first asked Stevens to return to Wisconsin, the prisoner replied that "I like this jail and I plan to stay here."

Will Name Own Aide

Doran Elected Relief Director, Boyle Chairman

By HENRY NOLL

Thomas J. Doran, supervisor of the Lafayette county public welfare department, was elected relief director for Madison by unanimous vote of the common council Friday night.

He was given authority to appoint an assistant director and supervisor of case workers and also to employ a temporary staff of case workers and stenographers in order to be ready to administer relief April 1 when the county outdoor relief department passes out of existence.

THOMAS J. DORAN

Before the council voted on director it confirmed Mayor Law's appointment of Ald. William H. Boyle as chairman of the outdoor relief committee to succeed Ald. Patrick H. Barry, resigned. Law has yet to name a member of the committee as Barry also asked to be relieved of membership.

After Doran had been elected the question was raised as to whether he was a department head and under civil service. City Atty. Doris E. Lehner declared that although the ordinance classifies him as an employe he is in fact also a department head, and therefore comes under the merit system. In compliance with the civil service ordinance he will be on probation for six months after which he will serve for an indefinite period. He could be removed only for cause after six months.

It is believed that Doran will name Bjarne Romnes, relief director of Richland Center, as his assistant and supervisor of case work. Before the council decided to hold an examination for candidates for the position Romnes was selected by the outdoor relief committee as assistant director. Both Doran and Romnes were in Madison two days this week, making plans for the organization of the department.

Will Copy County Records

Before the council proceeded to the election of a director Ald. George E. Gill moved that the aldermen adjourn to the mayor's office for a caucus. His motion was voted down. Besides Doran, Romnes and Kenneth D. Morrow also appeared on the eligible list for director. Miss Frances L. Guggenheim and Romnes also were certified for assistant director and supervisor of case work but the council concluded that the director should name his assistant.

Mayor Law advised the council that Doran had recommended that the city employ five case workers now with the county department and five stenographers as of March 21 and direct them to copy the records of Madison relief clients so that the list will be available to the city April 1. The county board welfare committee has voted not to release the records on the ground that they are confidential and should not be taken out of the office.

Law, however, told the aldermen that Doran did not think the county committee would object to the plan outlined by him as in that case the records would not leave the county outdoor relief department until April 1. Doran suggested that the five case workers in charge of city relief clients be employed.

Plan More Exams

On motion of Ald. Norris E. Maloney, Doran was authorized to employ provisional help and directed the board of personnel to make plans at once for holding examinations for all positions in the department. Law said it was the plan to hire the case workers and stenographers needed at this time only for a temporary period and hold open competitive examinations in the near future.

Ald. Barry said he was pleased to see the council elect Doran who was the choice of the outdoor relief committee prior to the time the council insisted on holding examinations.

City Auditor George Forster as director of personnel presented an ordinance from the personnel board providing that all semi-skilled and unskilled labor be employed through the state employment office without being compelled to submit to a civil service examination but that all those recommended by the state office be first examined as to their physical fitness by the board of health. The ordinance was referred to the ordinance committee.

Residents Win Zone Change Fight. (Story on Page 2, Column 1).

Bride Takes Poison After Quarrel

A bride of six weeks, worried over a quarrel with her husband, took poison on the doorstep of a friend Friday night, and died shortly afterward in a Madison hospital, Coroner Edward Fischer said today.

The woman, Mrs. Casper Ripp, 22, who lives in the 1900 block of Winnebago st., took an ounce of carbolic acid, according to the coroner.

Fischer said that her husband, an employe of a Madison packing company, went to his brother's home in Waunakee Thursday night after a "difference" with his bride of six weeks.

Friday night, according to Fischer, the young woman went to the home of a friend, on the east side, and waited for him to return from a show. He met her at the steps, Fischer said, tried to persuade her to "go home, rest, and forget about it."

The man went inside, then heard the woman calling, Fischer said. He went outside, and she told him that she had taken poison and wanted some milk. He ran in, got the milk, then called police. An ambulance took her to the hospital, where she died at midnight.

Fischer said no further investigation would be made. The body was taken to the Frautschi funeral home.

Police notified her parents, Mr. and Mrs. John Hildebrandt, who live near Madison.

'The Net Result . . .'

Resign, Norris Asks TVA's Chairman

WASHINGTON —(U.P.)— Sen. George W. Norris, (Ind., Neb.), "father" of the Tennessee Valley authority, today demanded the resignation of TVA Chairman Arthur E. Morgan. If Morgan does not resign, Norris said he may introduce a resolution in the senate to remove him.

Norris made his statement soon after President Roosevelt released the transcript of his conversation Friday with Morgan and the two other TVA directors with whom the chairman is quarreling—David E. Lilienthal and Harcourt A. Morgan.

Mr. Roosevelt told the directors that they should reconcile their differences or resign.

rector would resign. Chairman Morgan said that he would not. His demand for a congressional investigation of TVA was supported by a congressional bloc led by Sen. H. Styles Bridges (r., N. H.), a consistent critic of TVA.

The net result of President Roosevelt's conference seemed to be an intensification of the bitter quarrel among the directors, and the apparent certainty that it could not be settled without a removal of one or all of its members.

The president asked the directors to meet with him again next Friday or to send him evidence in support of their charges against

Lou Gehrig Signs for Year at $39,000

LOU GEHRIG

ST. PETERSBURG, Fla.—(U.P.)—Lou Gehrig, New York Yankee first baseman, today signed a one-year contract for $39,000, the third highest salary ever paid a baseball player.

Alvis Jailed in $7,125 Fort Swindle

A Madison man, Maurice S. Alvis, 1018 Clymer pl., was held in Ft. Atkinson today, as Sheriff Harry O'Brien and other officers sought two other men for allegedly working a confidence game in which C. J. Braun, a Kokomo, Ind., contractor, lost $7,125.

Alvis was taken to Ft. Atkinson Friday night, and charged with being an accessory before the fact. Dist. Atty. Harold Dakin had not indicated when Alvis would be arraigned.

Picked Up Here

Inspector Leo J. Kinney of the Madison police, said that Alvis was picked up here after Madison police learned the description of the men allegedly involved in a "pinball game" at Ft. Atkinson.

Kinney said that Alvis, when he was taken to the station, admitted a part in the deal, and quoted Alvis as saying he got $100 for it.

Two other men, who have been around Madison, first named as "John Doe," and "Richard Roe," charged with obtaining money under false pretenses, were listed in amended warrants as George Ragan and William Cleland, Kokomo.

Friday a Beaver Dam resident was freed after questioning in connection with the case. Police Chief Harry Mueller of Ft. Atkinson said the man, whom he declined to name, admitted he had gone to a hotel in Beaver Dam to get the two men believed to have been the suspects to carry them to their automobile.

It was believed that the pair had become suspicious that they were being watched and were afraid to get their clothes.

Let Him Off Here

Kinney said that Alvis admitted that two men returned him to Madison and let him off at Park st.

According to the inspector, Alvis originally was to have received $500 for posing as a district attorney in the deal.

Kinney said that a friend of Alvis had appeared at the station and told about the proposed "deal," originally set for Beaver Dam, fearing that his friend would get into trouble.

Duncan to Be Called to Inquest

BULLETIN

MILWAUKEE—(U.P.)—Deputy Sheriff Pat Dickey was sent to Madison on a motorcycle today to serve Thomas M. Duncan, secretary to Gov. La Follette, with a subpena to appear at an inquest here into the death of Henry F. Schuette.

MILWAUKEE—(U.P.)—The Milwaukee county coroner's office announced that a subpena will be issued today for Thomas M. Duncan, secretary of Gov. La Follette, commanding him to appear March 14 at an inquest into the death of Henry F. Schuette, 69.

Duncan is at liberty under $5,000 bond pending preliminary hearing scheduled here March 31 on a first degree manslaughter warrant accusing him of being the hit and run driver of an automobile which struck and killed Schuette on the night of March 9. Coroner Frank J. Schultz announced plans to have a subpena served upon Duncan at the Wisconsin General hospital at Madison, where his physician said he was being treated for mental shock.

It was uncertain whether Duncan is in condition to appear.

Britain to Prevent Clash, Belief; Italy 'Approves' of Coup

[By United Press]

LINZ—Hitler enters Austrian city amid wild acclaim. Nazis ordered to mass for huge torchlight parade in der Fuehrer's honor. Hitler greeted by Seyss-Inquart.

BERLIN—Germany rejects British-French protests on Austria as "unwarranted." First German troops reached Italy's Brenner pass.

LONDON—Cabinet declares Britain feels Germany's action is bound to have disturbing effect on British-German relations and on public confidence in Europe. Cabinets all over Europe meet to discuss gravest crisis since 1914.

PARIS—Leon Blum seeks cabinet of all parties to face crisis but encounters difficulty over communists.

BRUSSELS—Stock exchange closed. Belgians gravely concerned over safety of small nations.

ROME—Disclosed Hitler wrote Mussolini outlining his plans in Austria.

VIENNA—German troops pour into Austria. Nazis take over. Schuschnigg in protective custody. Anti-Jewish incidents start.

PRAGUE—Cabinet in emergency session decides Czechoslovakia will fight if invaded.

VATICAN CITY—Vatican circles feel Hitler coup is blow to church.

By WEBB MILLER

[Copyright, 1938, by United Press]

LONDON — Europe, panic-stricken, faced today its gravest diplomatic crisis since the black days of July, 1914, which preceded the World war.

Adolf Hitler's lightning coup in Austria, in open and bold defiance of Great Britain and France, shook Europe's chancelleries with the greatest war scare since the armistice.

Cabinets and foreign office staffs in Great Britain, France, Italy, Czechoslovakia, Germany, and other countries worked at high tension most of the night. All over Europe, from London to the Black sea, cabinets met again today to quell a veritable diplomatic panic and to prevent missteps which could conceivably plunge Europe into a major war.

The opinion was that Great Britain, the key nation, would prevent war.

Throughout western and middle Europe, governments tried to gauge the far-reaching repercussions of Hitler's mailed-fist smashing of Austria's independence. But barring unforeseen developments observers have believed that despite the gravity of the situation, the danger that it might result in a major war was remote.

Il Duce Neutral

The chief reason for this confidence is the certainty that neither England nor France will go to war to prevent Germany's absorbing Austria and that Premier Benito Mussolini, although in a most embarrassing position, has, for practical purposes, declared his neutrality in the Austrian crisis.

But observers fear that unless the situation is handled with the utmost caution, Hitler's nazification of Austria may hasten the eventual European upheaval.

Hitler's coup altered the diplomatic equilibrium of Europe and is likely to have a number of far-reaching results. Coming just at the moment when Prime Minister Neville Chamberlain of Great Britain has embarked upon a policy of rapprochement with the dictatorial countries, Hitler's action deals a body blow to Chamberlain's scheme for continental appeasement.

Britain Bitter

The reaction in Britain was evidenced by the press in so bitter that Chamberlain will scarcely dare, even if he is so inclined after Hitler's defiance of Britain's protests against the ending of Austrian independence, to proceed with his "deal with dictators" policy.

Thus Britain and France are certain to be impelled to even closer cooperation in the diplomatic field.

Mussolini must be chagrined by Austrian developments. It is highly significant that the Italian press, always under the thumb of the government, fall today—for the first time since the formation of the Berlin-Rome axis—to endorse fully and promptly any international diplomatic action undertaken by Germany.

In view of this development, it's in the cards that Chamberlain will now make a strong effort to break the Berlin-Rome axis or badly bend it by seeking a broad rapproachement with Mussolini.

Therefore the next few months are likely to witness efforts toward a general reshuffling of diplomatic line-ups.

Despite the fact that Britain and France have, five separate times, reaffirmed the necessity of preserving Austria's independence and integrity, neither will go further than protests and peaceful pressure in trying to save the country from nazification.

As regards Czechoslovakia, in a confidential conversation I had last month in Prague with the Czechoslovakian foreign minister, he left no doubt of his country's precarious position once Hitler had absorbed Austria unless her allies, France, Russia, and the little entente, came to her rescue.

NEVILLE CHAMBERLAIN

". . . a general election . . ."

BULLETIN

LONDON—(U.P.)—The British government announced today that it felt that the action of the German government in Austria was bound to have a most disturbing effect on Anglo-German relations and upon public confidence throughout Europe.

This momentous statement was issued after a two-hour cabinet meeting at which members decided that the nation was faced with the definite issue of peace or war.

The situation was so urgently grave that it was reported that Prime Minister Neville Chamberlain might call a general election to obtain the attitude of the country toward Germany.

BULLETIN

BERLIN — (INS) — The Austrian city of Innsbruck was occupied by German troops at noon today, it was officially announced this afternoon.

Bulletins

BUDAPEST — (U.P.) — The Hungarian government today ordered reinforced control of the Austrian border to prevent an influx of socialists and Jews fleeing from the new nazi regime in Austria.

PARIS—(INS)—Dispatches received here today stated Prince Ernst Rudiger von Starhemberg, former leader of the disbanded Austrian heimwehr, has been arrested in Vienna. The report was taken to indicate von Starhemberg had made a hurried return to Austria. He was last reported in Italy with his bride, the former Nora Gregor.

PARIS—(INS)—By a vote of 6,565 to 1,644, the socialist national council agreed to support Premier-designate Leon Blum in his efforts to form a national union government with sweeping powers to deal by decree with any possible emergency arising from the Austrian crisis.

BRUSSELS— (U.P.) —Archduke Otto, pretender to the Hapsburg throne of Austria, plans to leave immediately for Paris, it was learned today. The revelation led to speculation as to whether Otto planned to make another bid for the throne to rally his followers against nazification of Austria by Adolf Hitler.

WASHINGTON— (U.P.) —A flag bearing the symbol of Adolf Hitler—the swastika—was raised over the Austrian legation here today.

PRAHA (PRAGUE) Czechoslovakia — (U.P.) — Czechoslovakia today reasserted that any attempt by Germany to encroach upon her borders would be met with armed resistance.

Hitler Flays Schuschnigg Rule as "Brutal." (Story on page 3, Column 3.)

VIENNA — Fuehrer Adolf Hitler, preceded by thousands of German troops, came to Austria today and was hailed by the now dominant nazis as a liberator.

The nazification of the country was accomplished and anti-Jewish agitation began.

The ousted chancellor, Kurt Schuschnigg, and other officials were in custody, guarded by storm troopers.

German mechanized troops were everywhere in the country and one detachment crossed to the Brenner pass, gateway to Italy.

The first tanks entered the suburbs of Vienna in late afternoon.

Parade in Vienna

A great torchlight parade will be held in Vienna tonight and Hitler will speak by radio from Linz. Government circles said the fuehrer would come here Sunday. Most businesses and many banks were suspended today in honor of the German coup and celebrations were held throughout the country.

Before going to Linz to review the German troops which had poured across the frontier in the morning, Hitler visited Braunau and inspected the room where he was born. Then he went to Leonding, five miles from Linz, where he bowed at the graves of his parents.

A crowd of 20,000 in the streets of Braunau cheered the native son who left Austria as a penniless youth and returned today as leader of the Germanic race.

Four hundred German army planes circled with a deafening roar over Hitler's car as the procession wound into the city. Cries of "heil Hitler!" and the nazi song, "We Go Marching On," rang through the air.

An official delegation headed by Acting Chancellor Arthur Seyss-Inquart and Heinrich Himmler, chief of the nazi gestapo, welcomed the fuehrer on his arrival in the Hauptplatz, where the city hall is located.

From Munich, the fuehrer issued a lengthy proclamation justifying his action on the grounds Schuschnigg had oppressed the nazis "by the most brutal means of terror."

As his proclamation was read over the radio by Dr. Paul Joseph Goebbels, propaganda minister, the fuehrer already was in Munich, birthplace of the nazi movement, 40 miles from the Austrian frontier.

Guards at Munich

He had secretly concentrated almost all of his 3,000 bodyguard troops at Munich during the night.

He had flown there this morning after appointing Field Marshal Hermann Goering, his right hand

'Only a Few Recognized Them'

Lindberghs Sail Secretly for England

NEW YORK — (U.P.) — Col. and Mrs. Charles A. Lindbergh sailed for England early today as secretly as they arrived for a holiday vacation last Dec. 5.

They boarded the North German Lloyd liner Bremen at precisely the hour of sailing.

Visitors had been sent ashore and the gangplanks on the upper level of the ship's pier were hauled in. Five minutes later an automobile sped through the entrance to the lower level, where no outsiders are permitted.

The flier and his wife dashed from the car to a baggage gangplank that had been left up for them, and went immediately to their cabin. Only a few persons recognized them. Their names were not on the passenger list.

WEATHER
Fair tonight and Friday. Rising temperature Friday. Diminishing northerly winds. (Tables on Page 2.)

The Wisconsin State Journal

A fact-finding Newspaper

The News Index will be found on Page 2 in this edition.

VOL. 152, NO. 165. 99th Year — MADISON, THURSDAY, SEPTEMBER 15, 1938 — 20 PAGES — PRICE THREE CENTS

Chamberlain, Hitler Temporarily End Parley; Prime Minister Hurries to London Friday

PWA Allots State $8,512,169; Five Grants to U. W.

Six Madison Projects Allowed $672,954; City Hall Plan Omitted

Dual Building Plea Sent by La Follette

Madison Area Shares in PWA Grants. (Story on Page 1, Part 2, Column 3).

Allotment of $8,512,169 to finance 45 per cent of the cost of 114 Wisconsin projects, including grant of $672,954 to pay the PWA share of $1,495,454 worth of Madison projects, was announced in Washington today by PWA Administrator Harold L. Ickes.

Five of the six Madison projects which won PWA approval are plans for University of Wisconsin construction, according to a report received today by Sen. La Follette.

Although the PWA failed to allot funds for construction of a new Madison city hall as part of a dual city-county building, Mayor Law today urged Madison voters to vote next Tuesday for bond issues for the proposed building and for three new schools.

Bob Sends Wire

In a telegram to Ickes today, Sen. La Follette pointed out that "people are extremely anxious to have the joint building" and urged that "this project may be considered despite delay on the county's part of the application."

Six Madison Projects

Madison projects for which funds were ordered released today were:

1. Erection of an addition to the Nine Springs Sewage disposal plant, at a total cost of $300,000, of which PWA is granting $135,000.

2. Remodeling of the University of Wisconsin heating plant with addition of boilers and new equipment, at a total cost of $270,000, of which PWA is furnishing $121,500.

3. Construction of a cancer research building on Charter st., at the east entrance of the Wisconsin General hospital, at a total cost of $340,000, of which $108,- will be provided by PWA.

4. Erection of an addition to the university law school building, mostly for library facilities, at a total cost of $175,000, of which PWA will pay $78,750.

5. Construction of a west wing to the university's home economics building, at a total cost of $225,000, of which PWA will put up $101,250.

6. Erection of a two-story addition to the university agricultural chemistry building, to be used for a greenhouse and laboratory, at a total cost of $285,454, of which WPA will pay $128,454.

Share Not Exhausted

Today's allotments, totaling $8,512,169, do not exhaust Wisconsin's share of the PWA fund, on the basis of Ickes' statement to Wisconsin newspaper men last week. At that time Ickes estimated that in addition to projects already approved, Wisconsin was entitled to about $10,000,000 more in PWA grants.

Approval of Wisconsin projects today again gave Madison the biggest chunk in the state with the exception of Milwaukee. Nevertheless, Madison failed to get allotment of funds on a number of city projects.

Hydro Project Doubtful

Discussing his failure to allot funds for the $26,000,000 Wisconsin and Fox rivers development program, Ickes said there was still some prospect that the project might be approved, although the chance was not too strong.

The money would be available, he said, in the unexpected contingency that there are some withdrawals in some states and failure to qualify for some projects in other states.

Madison had asked for funds for a city hall, schools on the new Marquette grounds, Burrows field and in the Washington school district, for repaving of State st. and other projects.

"Not Licked Yet"

City officials and others will make efforts to contact Sen. La Follette in the hope of getting funds for some of the projects.

City Atty. Harold E. Hanson said if the bond issues are approved next Tuesday they will remain in effect three years so in case congress makes another PWA appropriation in January or at a later session the action of the voters will still stand.

"We are not licked yet," Law said, although disappointed because of Madison's failure to be recognized. It is possible that some of the communities in the state may not take advantage of their allotment, or that some of the other states will not ask for the full share of the quota. In that case we may get something out of it. It is also possible that another PWA appropriation will be made at the next session of congress and that we will get favorable consideration.

Mayor Asks Bond Vote

"Therefore, I urge the citizens to vote for the bond issues so that if money is provided later we can proceed with the work at once and not be compelled to hold a special election. I am surprised that we did not even get some of our minor projects approved."

The city has been put to considerable effort and expense in preparing plans and making applications for funds. Tentative plans were prepared for the joint city-county building for which the council appropriated $500 for architect services. The board of education also had some expense in having tentative plans made of proposed new schools.

City officials pointed out that additions to Dudgeon and Longfellow schools were approved two and a half years after the application had been filed.

Including the Dudgeon and Longfellow school additions and the nurses home for the Madison General hospital, the city had planned projects at a total cost of $3,270,915. Of this amount the city's share was estimated at $1,510,225 and federal grants at $1,471,890. Funds for Dudgeon and Hawthorne and the nurses' home have been allowed from a previous PWA allotment and bids on the nurses' building will be opened Sept. 29.

After city officials had been advised that only about $8,500,000 was left for Wisconsin projects, they realized they would not get all they asked but hoped funds would be made available for some of the schools and the city hall.

Including Dudgeon and Longfellow schools and the nurses' home, the city had made application for the following projects:

Dudgeon school addition, gross $65,000; city, $35,750; grant, $29,250.

Longfellow, gross, $90,000; city, $49,500; grant, $40,500.

Nurses' home, gross, $202,000; city, $50,000; grant, $90,900; the balance of $61,000 to be taken from the hospital endowment fund.

Water mains, gross, $64,000; no city share, grant, $28,000, $35,200 to be provided by the water department.

State st. paving, gross, $97,000; city, $53,350; grant, $43,650.

Marquette school, including Harvey and Hawthorne districts, gross, $398,960; city, $219,428; grant, $179,532.

Burrows field school, including Lapham, Brayton and part of Lincoln districts, gross, $375,557; city, $206,557; grant, $169,000.

Washington-Doty-Draper school, gross, $578,182; city, $318,000; grant, $260,182.

East high school addition, gross, $85,000; city, $46,750; grant, $38,250.

City hall, gross, $836,000; city, $459,800; grant, $459,800; grant, $376,200.

Civic building and naval armory, gross, $350,000; no city share; grant, $157,000; loan from the government, $192,500.

Dredge, gross, $49,250; city, $27,088; grant, $22,160.

Widening of E. Washington ave. bridge, gross, $26,116; city, $14,364; grant, $11,752.

No. 7 fire station, gross, $53,850; city, $29,638; grant, $24,212.

Allotment of $8,512,169 for the 114 local Wisconsin projects does not mean that the La Follette administration's $26,000,000 hydro development of the Wisconsin river has been disapproved, Ickes said, but added he thought it would be a "shrewd" guess that the $11,700,000 grant sought for the project would not be forthcoming.

Eyston to Come Back

Cobb Zips 350 M.P.H. for Mark

JOHN COBB

BONNEVILLE SALT FLATS, Utah—(U.P.)—John Cobb, English sportsman, drove his 2,500 horsepower Railton racer today at an average speed of 350.20 miles an hour, a new world's record for speed on land.

Cobb's tremendous speed was attained shortly after dawn in a renewal of the friendly racing duel with a fellow countryman, Capt. George E. T. Eyston, holder of the previous record. Eyston said he would bring his seven-ton Thunderbolt back to the salt track tomorrow in an attempt to recapture the record.

Monday Cobb had failed by the slender margin of 2.97 miles an hour to equal Eyston's mark. Conditions at dawn today were perfect.

Cobb required only three minutes and 14 seconds to travel the full 13½ mile length of the world's fastest course on his north run. A plane that started out immediately overhead as Cobb headed south arrived several minutes after the Londoner brought his racer to a halt.

Cobb, 36, bachelor London fur broker, attained his speed, breaking Eyston's record of 345.49 miles an hour, by passing through the measured mile from south to north at 353.29 m. p. h. and at 347.11 m. p. h. on the south-bound run.

Cobb also established a new world's record for the kilometer at a speed of 350.07 miles per hour.

Cobb said he was uncertain about his future plans if Eyston should break his record tomorrow.

"I may stay and try and lift it again and then I may not. I don't know. The salt was just slightly moist and the car dragged some. So I believe it still has possibilities of reaching higher speed."

Hee Haw! Hee Haw! Mule Elected GOP Delegate

MILTON, Wash. — (U.P.) — Mayor Kenneth Simmons, a democrat, proved his point and laughed today at republicans who elected a long-eared brown mule as their city precinct committeeman.

The mule was entered as "Boston Curtis" on the ballot in the state primary just completed. Mayor Simmons wanted to prove that a certain percentage of the voting public pays no attention to the names of candidates.

He also thought it would be a good joke on the republicans who had made no nomination for the post.

"Let us bray," the mayor said when returns showed the mule had received 51 votes.

Bay Shore Paving Plan Revised to Meet Objections

Ald. Walter L. Plaenert today said plans for repaving and widening S. Shore and W. Shore drives from Vilas ave. to Gilson st. are being revised to meet objections made by property owners on the streets. At a recent meeting home owners objected to widening the pavement to 36 feet. Residents expressed fear the drive would be used as a speedway. Plaenert conferred with Ladislas Segoe, city planner who is making a survey of Madison, and Mayor Law, City Engineer T. F. Harrington, City Atty. Harold E. Hanson and City Forester James G. Marshall with the result that the plans are being revised. The width of the pavement probably will be 27 feet.

Australian Girl Beats Miss Lumb

FOREST HILLS, N. Y.—(U.P.)—Nancye Wynne, top-ranking player of Australia, led the way into the semi-final round of the national singles championships today with a three-set victory over Margot Lumb, of England, 6-4, 5-7, 6-1. Miss Lumb, conqueror of Helen Jacobs in the previous round, was buried under an avalanche of forehand drives which cut the lines and constantly pulled her out of position.

Moreland, Fischer Lose in Golf Meet

OAKMONT, Pa.—(U.P.)—The bigger they are the harder they fall, so today two of the great ones of amateur golf were knocked out of the national championship with a thud that could be heard all the way to downtown Pittsburgh.

Johnny Fischer, Cincinnati, one of the hot favorites here, lost an extra-hole match to Willie Turnesa, Briar Cliff Manor, N. Y., and Melvin Harbert, Clay, N. Y., defeated Gus Moreland, Peoria, Ill., who won the medal in the qualifying round and seemed to be on his way to great things.

Harbert, a kid who played golf with Chick Evans at the age of six, refused to be awed by Moreland's reputation and fought back like a tiger up to the 16th green where he calmly dropped the putt that bounced Moreland out of the tournament.

Johnny Goodman, defending champion, blazed around the first nine in a three-under-par 34 today to move into the quarter finals with a 4 and 2 victory over J. E. French, Jr., San Francisco.

Results of today's third round play:

Johnny Goodman, Omaha, defeated James French, San Francisco, 4 and 2.

Pat Abbott, Altadena, Cal., defeated James French, San Francisco, 4 and 2.

Pat Abbott, Altadena, Cal., defeated James Fraser, Absecon, N. J., 2 up.

Dick Chapman, Greenwich, Conn., defeated T. Suffern Tailer, Westbury, N. Y., 2 and 1.

Joseph Thompson, Hamilton, Ont., defeated Walter Blevins, Kansas City, 1 up, 19 holes.

Edwin Kingsley, Magna, Utah, defeated Wilfred Crossley, Dedham, Mass., 4 and 3.

Melvin Harbert, Clay, N. Y., defeated Gus Moreland, Peoria, Ill., 3 and 2.

Chris Brinke, Birmingham, Mich., defeated Frank Strafaci, Great Neck, N. Y., 3 and 2.

Willie Turnesa, Briar Cliff Manor, N. Y., defeated Johnny Fischer, Cincinnati, one up, 20 holes.

Chief of Weather Bureau Dies

CHICAGO — William R. Gregg, 58, chief of the U. S. weather bureau in Washington, died Wednesday night of coronary thrombosis. Gregg died in his hotel suite, where he had been confined since a heart attack last week as he attended an air transport meeting. At his bdside were Mrs. Gregg and a daughter, Ruth Chamberlayne Wall.

State Renews Buckman Investigation

State investigation into the affairs of B. E. Buckman and co., bankrupt Madison securities firm, was renewed today when Atty. Gen. Orland S. Loomis disclosed plans for a John Doe inquiry in Manitowoc, where the company maintained branch offices.

Nine witnesses have been subpenaed for the John Doe investigation, which is a sort of one-man grand jury probe in which witnesses testify secretly and without challenge by opposing counsel.

Purpose of the John Doe inquiry will be to determine whether additional warrants should be served in connection with collapse of the Buckman co. and its accompanying loss of hundreds of thousands of dollars to Wisconsin investors.

The company's three officers, B. E. Buckman, president; Louis C. George, vice-president, and E. C. Holt, secretary-treasurer, are now in the state prison serving terms for violation of the Wisconsin securities law.

The attorney-general's department did not indicate today whether they would take testimony from the three imprisoned officers.

Madison Girl Charges Fraud

MILWAUKEE— (U.P.) —U. S. Commissioner Floyd Jenkins today heard testimony of eight persons that they had been cheated by William J. Cressy, 32, who is charged with using the mails to defraud. Among witnesses who told of sending Cressy money for jobs they said never materialized was Sylvia Levin, Madison, an offive worker who testified she had sent Crissy a check for $3 in reply to an advertisement in a Madison newspaper.

Judge Proctor's Mother Dies

Mrs. May F. Proctor, mother of Superior Court Judge Roy H. Proctor, died today at her home at 925 Conklin pl., after an illness. Besides her son, Mrs. Proctor is survived by a daughter, Helen, and two grandchildren, Mary and John Proctor, all of Madison, and one sister, Mrs. Kate Brower of Rochester, Ind. The body is at the Fitch-Lawrence undertaking parlors.

Lloyds Stops War Risk Policies

LONDON — (U.P.) —Lloyd's underwriters decided today to exclude war risk insurance from all existing and future marine policies, effective at midnight Saturday.

Pollen Count

A sharp dip in total pollen count, 65 grains per cubic yard, all of which was ragweed, was reported by the Wisconsin General hospital for Wednesday. Count for Tuesday was 100 of which 96 grains were ragweed.

George Safe in Georgia 'Purge' Poll

BULLETIN

ATLANTA, Ga. —(U.P.)— Sen. Walter F. George, whom President Roosevelt asked the Georgia electorate to defeat in Wednesday's democratic primary, won renomination today on the basis of unofficial tabulations which gave him 208 county unit votes—two more than the required majority.

ATLANTA, Ga.— (U.P.) —U. S. Sen. Walter F. George, whose defeat was asked by President Roosevelt as a step toward liberalizing the democratic party, appeared headed today to victory in the Georgia democratic senatorial primary.

The chief executive's New Deal candidate was out of the race and a rabid anti-New Dealer was running second.

George generally was considered the president's chief object in his campaign to oust conservatives and elect liberal legislators as he was the only one mentioned by Mr. Roosevelt as the candidate to be defeated. In the South Carolina and Maryland primaries, in which the New Deal also lost, the President inferentially spoke of the candidates but did not call names.

Talmadge Real Threat

Lawrence S. Camp, whom the president personally endorsed as his favorite, carried only six of the 159 counties, according to incomplete returns.

Eugene Talmadge, ex-governor of Red Gallus fame and an anti-New Dealer, ran a close second to George.

With 206 county votes necessary for election—the statewide popular vote does not count—George was leading in sufficient counties to give him 216 units if he maintains the present pace.

Camp Far Behind

Talmadge, however, had the possibility of corralling 166 votes in the counties where he led and also the possibility of overtaking George in the incomplete precincts.

Camp had but 18 county unit votes.

Incomplete returns from each of the 159 counties gave the popular vote as follows:

George	124,216
Talmadge	90,211
Camp	67,211

The complete but unofficial county unit vote from 112 counties as divided follows:

George	178
Talmadge	104
Camp	18

Camp, the United States district attorney, said he "regretted that his fight for President Roosevelt's principles was not successful," but that he was sure it would be "carried on by others."

Win for 'Jefferson'

Roosevelt had singled out four democratic congressmen of lukewarm new deal convictions to oppose personally in state primaries, and George, if victorious, will be the third renominated over his opposition. South Carolina renominated Sen. Ellison D. Smith; Maryland renominated Sen. Millard Tydings, the first to face the test. The fourth is Rep. John J. O'Connor, New York, who is seeking both the democratic and republican nominations in the Sept. 20 primary there.

Before the polls closed George had given out a victory statement saying "it certainly looks like a clear cut victory for Jefferson democracy . . . I am confident that the voters are exercising their rights to the free ballot, without dictation, and vindicating the challenge to my democracy."

At the same time Camp had said: "Georgians are voting to uphold the best friend they ever had, Franklin D. Roosevelt."

May Resume Conference in Few Days

War or Peace?

Here are today's developments in the gravest crisis Europe has faced since 1914:

BERCHTESGADEN—Rushing to Adolf Hitler's alpine home by plane, train, and car, Prime Minister Chamberlain of Britain began his momentous conversation with the Fuehrer at 5 p. m.

PRAGUE—The Czechoslovak government instituted criminal proceedings against Konrad Henlein, Sudeten leader, accusing him of his treason.

EGER—The Sudeten German party issued a proclamation demanding nothing less than outright union with the Nazi reich.

PRAGUE—Renewed fighting occurred in Sudetenland as Sudeten leaders exhorted their followers to defend themselves from "murder". Reports were current that Viscount Runciman, British mediator, planned a first-hand tour of the disordered region.

ADOLF HITLER — NEVILLE CHAMBERLAIN

BERLIN—German officialdom expressed belief that a single hour of "honest discussion" between Chamberlain and Hitler would suffice to solve the crisis. A general strike was called throughout the Sudeten area of Czechoslovakia.

LONDON—Chamberlain's wife led prayers for peace in Westminister Abbey. Lloyds cancelled all war risk insurance. Acting Premier Sir John Simon consulted the speaker of the house to consider an emergency meeting of parliament.

WASHINGTON — America formulated a policy of "strict neutrality."

Test Hitler War Threat

BULLETIN

BERLIN—(U.P.)—Prime Minister Neville Chamberlain will return to London Friday, it was announced officially tonight, and will go back to Berchtesgaden for another conference with Adolf Hitler within a few days.

Chamberlain and Hitler, the announcement said, had "an open and extensive exchange of opinion at today's meeting in Berchtesgaden."

By WEBB MILLER
(Copyright 1938 by United Press)

BERCHTESGADEN — Neville Chamberlain and Adolf Hitler bargained face to face in the Bavarian alps today while a worried world waited to hear whether the result would mean peace or war in Europe.

After three hours, Chamberlain emerged from the villa and hurried to his hotel, serious but unworried.

The head of the British government and the leader of greater Germany, met in the great hall of Hitler's retreat within an hour of the end of Chamberlain's unprecedented 700-mile dash by air and train from London.

Chamberlain came for a showdown on what must be offered Hitler to satisfy his demand for self-determination for the Sudeten German minority in Czechoslovakia.

It was impossible to know what went on at the momentous meeting within the guarded precincts of Haus Wachenfeld. Before flying here from London, however, I was told by reliable diplomatic sources that Chamberlain would, in effect, ask Hitler point blank:

"Are you anxious for a military adventure, or seriously anxious to collaborate in working out a peace plan beginning with the Sudentens, and capable of being extended elsewhere in Europe, including the colonies question?"

The suggested question was prompted by information in diplomatic quarters indicating that the nazis wish to achieve a military triumph.

To Talk of Spain

If, on the contrary, Hitler is prepared to accept a diplomatic victory, the British and French are prepared to facilitate it on a basis of granting the Sudetens a degree of autonomy "exceeding their wildest hopes."

..Informed British sources believe that in exchange for concessions in the Sudentenland, Chamberlain wants Hitler's collaboration in solving the Spanish war problem.

It is known that Chamberlain does not intend to commit himself finally here, but to propose that since Viscount Runciman, British mediator, is acceptable to the nazis, Sudentens and Czechs, Runciman be allowed to work out a generous "fifth plan" to replace the four previously rejected.

Chamberlain's foremost object

La Follette to Rally Followers at Cedar Rapids

Phil Refuses Kraschel Plea to Pull NPA Out of Iowa Poll

Gov. La Follette replied with a blunt "no" Wednesday when emissaries for Gov. N. G. Kraschel of Iowa pleaded with him to withdraw National Progressives of America from the hot Iowa election fight, The State Journal learned today.

Three prominent Iowa officials, representing the corn state's democratic governor, pleaded in vain that the entrance of the La Follette party in the Iowa general election would greatly impair Kraschel's chances of reelection.

Gov. La Follette reportedly not only turned the request down cold, but told Kraschel's agents that he would go into Iowa a week from Saturday to rally his followers there at the first Iowa state convention at Cedar Rapids, where a full NPA slate is expected to be named.

Kraschel was in Madison Wednesday, but did not himself confer with the governor. Ostensible purpose of his Wisconsin visit was to take his son to St. John's Military academy at Delafield. Nevertheless, his personal envoys went into a huddle with the governor and were reported to have emerged empty-handed.

The trio were Robert Burlingame, former secretary to Kraschel; John Denniston, state librarian, and Byron Allen, Iowa social security administrator. Burlingame and Allen attended La Follette's NPA conference in Des Moines last spring.

Neither Gov. La Follette nor Kraschel's aides would comment formally on the conference, but the Wisconsin governor did indicate that he sent the Iowa delegation home empty-handed.

LA FOLLETTE — KRASCHEL

Kraschel and his lieutenants have been worried ever since the Iowa governor's erratic handling of the Maytag strike at Newton last month. They appeared concerned lest the La Follette party drain away the labor vote and leave Kraschel a prey to the republican ticket.

Gov. La Follette indicated that he held no particularly high hopes that NPA would elect any state officers in Iowa this fall. Chief objective, he said, will be to get two per cent of the total Iowa vote and thus qualify for a regular place on the ballot in the 1940 election.

Meanwhile, the governor's new party appeared to be planting seeds in other states, notably Idaho, California, and Oregon. Although there have been reported gestures from President Roosevelt and from NPA toward running Sen. James P. Pope of Idaho on the NPA ticket in Idaho, Gov. La Follette indicated Wednesday that it was quite unlikely that the present progressive senatorial nominee would withdraw in favor of Pope.

Unknown to most political observers, NPA has a ticket in Idaho and will make a strenuous fight in the general elections. Pope, defeated in the democratic primary last month despite new deal support, would have been a coalition NPA-new deal candidate if the original plan were carried to fruition.

Shoppers to Dine at Expense of Merchants Friday and Saturday, 'Fall Shopping Days'

'I shall conduct this fight, no matter against whom, until the security of the reich and our rights are guaranteed.

ADOLF HITLER

The Wisconsin State Journal
A fact-finding Newspaper
VOL. 154, NO. 152. 100th Year | MADISON, FRIDAY, SEPTEMBER 1, 1939 | 26 PAGES | • • • • | PRICE THREE CENTS

England's Ultimatum: Cease or We'll Start

Hitler's Danzig Grab Lights Powder Keg; Pole Cities Bombed

BERLIN—Adolf Hitler's Nazi war machine smashed into Poland tonight in new drives, despite the warning by France and Great Britain that failure to withdraw immediately means a European war.

BERLIN—Hitler annexes Danzig and sends his troops and bombers against Poland; Both sides claim victory in border warfare. Warsaw, other Polish towns bombed. Polish embassy staff leaving Berlin.

WARSAW—German planes bombs Warsaw and other Polish cities. German offensive started from southern Poland to Baltic.

ROME—Hitler notifies Mussolini that he does not require Italian military assistance in the present crisis. The council of ministers, meeting with Mussolini, decides that Italy refrain from taking any military action.

OTTAWA, Ont.—(UP)—Prime Minister Mackenzie King announced today after an emergency cabinet meeting that if Great Britain becomes actively involved in the conflict between Germany and Poland, Canada will stand by her side.

PARIS—"It's started", says Premier Daladier. Mussolini proposes five-power conference—France, Germany, Italy, and Russia; France orders general mobilization, evacuation of non-combatants from Paris.

PARIS—Polish sources report Berlin attacked by Polish bombers. Polish radio broadcast claims 16 German planes shot down near Danzig harbor.

Into the Fire!

NEVILLE CHAMBERLAIN

Bulletins!

(See Page 2)

BULLETINS

BERLIN—(U.P.)—Polish artillery bombarded the Beuthen railway station at 11:30 a. m. today, the DNB, official German news agency, announced.

BERLIN—(U.P.)—The Polish embassy today announced that its staff was departing from Berlin immediately.

BULLETIN:

WARSAW—(U.P.)—Air raid sirens screamed for the third time at 12:40 p. m., today and 10 minutes later the heavy thud of anti-aircraft guns sounded from the west. The air raiders were not sighted and apparently were driven off.

2 1-2 Billions Voted for War Credit

LONDON—(U.P.)—The house of commons without a record vote tonight approved a war credit of 500,000,000 pounds (roughly $2,250,000,000).

The bill for the war credit introduced by Chancellor of the Exchequer Sir John Simon established the huge credit for defense, for maintenance of public order and for efficient prosecution of any war in which Britain might be engaged.

WEATHER

Partly cloudy, not much change in temperature tonight and Saturday. Light south winds.

France Joins in Fatal Step; Chamberlain Fears Worst

By WEBB MILLER

LONDON—(UP)—Prime Minister Neville Chamberlain delivered what amounted to an ultimatum to Germany in the house of commons tonight when he declared that unless German troops were withdrawn from Poland, the British and French would have to fulfill their treaty obligations to fight for Poland.

Chamberain laid the blame for bringing Europe to the verge of a catastrophic war squarely on Adolf Hitler.

France tonight then joined Great Britain in the virtual ultimatum to Germany to withdraw troops from Poland.

The tenor of the Prime Minister's speech left little doubt he believed Germany would refuse to comply with what he termed his "last warning", and that a general war would follow.

There was an impressive silence when Chamberlain made his fateful pronouncement, although other parts of the speech were cheered loudly.

The prime minister indicated his lack of hope Hitler would recede from his military venture when he said:

"It now remains for us to set our teeth and enter upon this struggle which we so earnestly endeavored to avoid, with determination to see it through to the end.

While Chamberlain spoke, Britain proceeded with the evacuation of 3,000,000 women, children and helpless persons from the big cities to safer places in the country; the king signed a formal order of general mobilization by land, air and sea; Poland appealed to Britain and France to stand by their treaty obligtions, and it officially was indicated that there seems scarcely a chance of avoiding a general war.

There was a burst of deep-throated "hear, hears" when Chamberlain told commons:

"The German chancellor would plunge the world into misery to serve his own senseless ambition."

◊ ◊ ◊

Chamberlain spoke in a determined manner and his voice often verged on anger. The house membership sat on the edge of the seats and leaned forward tensely.

Chamberlain clenched his right fist into the palm of his left as he spoke of Hitler's 16-point demands on Poland, which he said had not been communicated to Britain and that the government knew of them only through a radio broadcast.

He castigated the Nazi government, declaring:

"As long as that government exists and pursues its motives of the last two years, there will be no peace in Europe."

Chamberlain was entirely in black, except for a white wing collar.

Britain, the prime minister said, will stand unhesitatingly behind her military obligations to aid Poland in case of aggression.

CHAMBERLAIN MADE HIS STATEMENT AS GERMAN TROOPS INVADED POLAND AND GERMAN PLANES WERE REPORTED BOMBING POLISH CITIES.

The prime minister laid the blame for the invasion of Poland on Germany, declaring that Poland had offered to negotiate the dispute and had been turned down.

◊ ◊ ◊

Before Chamberlain made his portentous statement to parliament, Poland had invoked the clause of her treaties with Britain and France, calling for their aid in case Poland is the victim of aggression.

BRITAIN, CHAMBERLAIN SAID, HAS INSTRUCTED ITS AMBASSADOR TO BERLIN TO ASK FOR HIS PASSPORT UNLESS GERMAN TROOPS ARE WITHDRAWN FROM POLISH SOIL.

The prime minister indicated the temper of the British government by announcing that a bill would be introduced making military service ages 18 to 41, which would vastly increase the heavy forces already called out under a general mobilization order signed by the king today.

There can be no peace in Europe, the prime minister said, as long as the Nazi government exists and continues to pursue its present methods.

"We are resolved these methods must come to an end," he declared.

Chamberlain revealed Sir Nevile Henderson, the British ambassador to Berlin, has been instructed to hand the German government what amounts to an ultimatum, saying that unless Germany suspends aggressive action and withdarws from Poland, the British government unhesitatingly will fulfill its treaty obligations to Poland.

BRITAIN, THE PRIME MINISTER REITERATED, WILL OPPOSE FORCE WITH FORCE.

Chamberlain described his present statement as a "last warning" to Germany. His speech was greeted with wild cheers from all parts of the house.

Chamberlain emphasized Britain had gone to the extreme limit to reach a peaceful settlement and Poland had done nothing to obstruct negotiations for such a settlement.

He said France as well as Britain had instructed embassadors to ask for their passports unless German troops are withdarwn from Poland.

◊ ◊ ◊

Britain and France, Chamberlain declared, have agreed that Germany has committed an aggressive act threatening the independence of Poland and therefore Britain and France must fulfill their treaty obligations to come to Poland's assistance.

The loudest burst of cheering heard in commons in years came when Chamberlain, pounding the dispatch box before him, declared:

"THE RESPONSIBILITY FOR THIS TERRIFIC CATASTROPHE LIES ON THE SHOULDERS OF ONE MAN"

Chamberlain had opened his speech in tones so low he was almost inaudible, but as he progressed, he warmed to his theme and increased in vehemence.

He declared he feared, because of Hitler's attitude, he could not avoid the repsonsibility of asking Britain to decide between peace or war.

Weather
Fair tonight. Wednesday partly cloudy and somewhat warmer, wind becoming fresh southeast Wednesday.

The Wisconsin State Journal

A fact-finding Newspaper

EXTRA!

VOL. 156, NO. 9. 101st Year — MADISON, TUESDAY, APRIL 9, 1940 — 20 PAGES — PRICE THREE CENTS

Berlin Draws 'Flying Curtain' Along Danish, Norse Coasts

Allies Rush 'Full Aid' to Norway as Hitler Seizes Denmark, Oslo

Ships, Planes Speed to North Sea Battleground

Bulletins

Drs. Quislings' Cousin Proclaims New Government

DR. A. A. QUISLING

BERLIN—(U.P.)—The official news agency reported from Oslo tonight that Vikdun Quisling, leader of the anti-Communistic national Union party, had declared himself head of a new Norwegian government.

(The German agency dispatch indicated a government was being set up under Quisling in opposition to the Norwegian government of Premier Johan Nygaardsvold, which fled to Hamar when the Germans occupied Oslo.)

Quisling was quoted as saying in his broadcast that Britain had violated Norway's neutrality by laying mines in Norwegian waters. He said the Nygaardsvold government had made only an "empty protest" against the British action.

Dr. Abraham A. Quizling, 1918 Rowley ave., member of the Madison Quisling clinic, said today Vikdun Quisling is a cousin, whom the Madison Quislings last saw in a visit to Norway in 1931.

Vikdun, Dr. Quisling said, was Norwegian minister of war then. He is about 40 years old.

FDR SPEEDS TO WASHINGTON

HYDE PARK, N. Y.—(U.P.)—President Roosevelt left by special train this afternoon for Washington where complete reports are awaiting him on the German invasion of Scandinavia. He received last minute reports by telephone from the state department.

GERMANS OCCUPY BERGEN, CLAIM

WASHINGTON—(U.P.)—The Norwegian legation today received word from the Norwegian foreign minister that the Germans have occupied Bergen, important Atlantic coastal city of 100,000 inhabitants.

HULL EXPECTS NEUTRALITY EXTENSION

WASHINGTON—(U.P.)—Secretary of State Hull indicated today that application of the neutrality law to the the new areas of conflict could be expected.

RADIO SAYS GOVERNMENT RESIGNS

STOCKHOLM—(U.P.)—The Oslo radio station reported tonight that the Norwegian government has resigned and that a government of national defense" would be formed. (With the occupation of Oslo by German troops, it was presumed that the radio announcement was German-sponsored.)

GERMANS BOMB SOUTHERN PORT

BERLIN—(U.P.)—An authoritative source said today the German air force bombed Kristiansand, Norwegian port at the southern tip of Norway, because it had resisted German occupation.

DUTCH HEAR BRITISH TO CLOSE WATERS

THE HAGUE, The Netherlands—(U.P.)—An extraordinary cabinet meeting was called late today to consider, some quarters said, reports that a large British fleet, carrying an expeditionary army, was steaming northward close to Dutch territorial waters.

BRITISH PLANE SHOT DOWN, CLAIM

STOCKHOLM—(U.P.)—A report from Oslo said tonight a four-motored British airplane had been shot down near the Oslo airport by two German pursuit planes. The British craft was said to have burst into flames when it crashed and its crew killed.

GERMANS IN SWEDEN, REPORT IN PARIS

PARIS—(U.P.)—The Swedish legation received unconfirmed reports today Germans had landed in Sweden as well as Norway. The legation also heard without confirmation Germans had mined Swedish west coast waters and ports.

The legation said the Swedish government had urged the population to evacuate the larger Swedish cities.

The Norwegian legation said the evacuation of Oslo and other Norwegian cities had been carried out successfully and the Norwegian government was sitting 15 miles outside Oslo.

COPENHAGEN QUIET, WASHINGTON HEARS

WASHINGTON—(U.P.)—The state department's first official information from Copenhagen today confirmed that the Danish capital was controlled by German soldiers. The dispatch added the city was quiet.

STEINLE WINS IN CANVASS

MILWAUKEE—(U.P.)—Circuit Judge Roland J. Steinle defeated Atty. Leonard C. Fons by 87 votes, the Milwaukee county election commission's official canvass showed today. The canvass gave Steinle 132,100 votes and Fons 132,013. The commission decided to summon election officials from some localities for questioning in the hope of untangling questioned counts.

They Say Today

TED WILLIAMS

Some day I'm gonna knock a pitch right down one of those wise guy's throats and don't think I won't." The tossers don't want to try tickling Ted Williams. Page 16.

"These petitions by show people may be for publicity purposes." Despite the razzberry, George Jessel and Li'l Lois aren't going to rush Judge Joseph Murphy. Page 6.

"The aggressive, dynamic Republicans were replaced about 1932." Paul McNutt aims some elaborate sarcasm at Glenn Frank and Tom Dewey. Page 17.

"The entire Milwaukee county Republican organization is for Heil." And Lansing Hoyt wants no survey silliness. Page 8.

"These things—Christian doctrines and a moral sense, which people call little and old fashioned—count the most." Washington, warns Prof. J. O. Christianson, can't fix everything. Page 5.

"I got more time in the air than I paid for." Henry Fonda and fellow fliers finally find a hole in the fog. Page 7.

"Omar Crocker's character has been built well, indeed, if it can withstand the shame of Sacramento." A father wonders about some of the builders. Page 4.

The Feature-Finder

Sea Fight Already Raging, Report

By WEBB MILLER

LONDON—(U.P.)—The Allied supreme war council was believed tonight to have agreed on swift retaliation against Germany's invasion of Norway and Denmark, and it was indicated operations already were in progress along the eastern shores of the North sea.

The supreme war council met in London shortly after Prime Minister Neville Chamberlain had announced Britain and France were sending full aid to Norway and that powerful navy units were at sea.

Official sources said important developments might be expected within the next 12 hours and there were many reports of naval and aerial fighting off the Norwegian coast.

British spokesmen said the Norwegian government was determined to resist.

(Official sources in Paris reported naval engagements already were in progress off Norway and dispatches from Oslo and Stockholm reported British planes had appeared over the Norwegian capital.)

Details of the sea battle were not immediately available. An official foreign office spokesman cautioned correspondents to be patient about naval developments in Scandinavian waters.

"When a warship is at sea, it has to keep its radio silent, unless it wants to reveal its whereabouts to the enemy," he said. "So we will not get the news ourselves. Very probably you will get a very good story within tthe next 12 hours."

◇ ◇ ◇

The Swedish radio, in a special broadcast late today reported a **"very bitter naval battle at present is going on between German and British naval forces off the Norwegian coast."** The weather was described as stormy and the sea heavy. Further details were lacking.

◇ ◇ ◇

The Columbia Broadcasting system said it had intercepted the following announcement by the British Broadcasting company:

"The latest news received on the war in northern Europe is a short message from Paris which states that a battle between the allied and German fleets is reported to have begun at several points off the western cast of Norway. The actions are proceeding in a heavy storm with rolling seas. No more than that is yet known."

◇ ◇ ◇

The British foreign office also announced Howard Smith, British minister to Denmark, had been taken a prisoner, along with his entire staff, by German troops. He said the arrest of Smith and his staff "undoubtedly was a breach of international custom," but expressed the hope the men might be released soon.

Announcing that the British government considered Denmark as an enemy-occupied country similar to Czechoslovakia and Belgium in the World war of 1914, the spokesman said the foreign office had received information from Oslo that the Norwegion government "is in good heart and bent on resistance."

The foreign office at the same time announced it had not been in communication with the British minister to Sweden, in Stockholm, for some hours.

Mrs. Koehler Breaks Back in Fall

Mrs. Arthur Koehler, 109 Chesnut st., wife of Arthur Koehler, wood expert at the Forest Products laboratory, suffered a fractured back when she slipped and fell on a rug in her home Monday.

She was rushed to the Methodist hospital where her condition today was reported as "satisfactory."

Warm Winds Will Speed Lake Opening

Warmer weather is in store for Wednesday to help speed the opening of Madison's tardy lakes, Eric R. Miller, government meteorologist, announced today.

A small "low" has developed in Wyoming preceded by snow in North Dakota and northern Montana, and probably will drift along the Canadian border to produce snow in northern Wisconsin Wednesday.

Only clouds were forecast for Madison, however, and southeast winds will cause a rise in temperature which ranged from 42 Monday to 33 early today.

Lake Wingra was about two-thirds open early today and Monona showed widening strips of open water along the shores while Mendota retained an almost unbroken expanse of white shell surface.

Roundy Gets Ahead Becomes a Greek With a Gold Key

Joseph Leo Roundy Sage of Mendota Lawnmower Pusher Coughlin now has a P. T. S. to add after his signature.

In a Memorial Union meeting fraternity, The Wisconsin State Journal sports columnist "explained" to the engineers "how to push a lawnmower."

He received an honorary membership and a gold plated key in return.

Woman Kills Self by Hanging, Coroner Finds

Mrs. Mary Olson, 33, of 1821 University ave., committed suicide by hanging at 1:45 p. m. today in the home of her friends, Mr. and Mrs. Albert Strommen, 2706 Center ave., Coroner Wayne Fisher said. Fisher said she had made her home with the Strammens since she suffered a nervous breakdown.

Prudence Gray, 3, Struck by Car

Prudence Gray, 3, daughter of Mr. and Mrs. K. D. Gray, 1106 Williamson st., was injured Monday when she was struck by a car driven by Paul Rouse, Arlington, police reported today.

She was taken to the Methodist hospital where officials said she is suffering from a concussion and possible skull fracture.

Police said Rouse was driving slowly when the girl ran out from behind a truck into the path of his car at Williamson and Ingersoll sts.

Thief Steals $26 from Apartment

A thief who crept into the first floor apartment of Irene Mackie, 130 Langdon st., escaped with $26 which he stole from Miss Mackie's purse, detectives reported today.

Patricia Donovan, Daughter of Attorney, Killed

FREDRICKSBURG, Va.—(U.P.)—Patricia Donovan, 22-year-old daughter of Col. William J. (Wild Bill) Donovan, prominent Buffalo and Washington attorney, died Monday night of injuries received when her automobile crashed into a tree 35 miles south of here.

Miss Donovan was known as "the daughter of the Fighting Sixty-ninth," the World war regiment which her father led. She was born in Buffalo, N. Y., the day her father joined the regiment and was christened by the Rev. Francis Duffy, celebrated war chaplain.

Donovan was chief defense attorney in the oil trials here.

Car Bruises Running Boy

Darrell Chard, 8, of 125 Division st., suffered slight bruises when he ran in front of a car driven by H. W. Luck, 913 Williamson st., at the intersection of Winnebago and Division sts., Monday police reported today. The youth was treated by a physician.

OSLO'S PRINCIPAL STREET
". . . German and Norwegian officers . . ."

Oslo Watches Air Skirmish; Quietly Greets Invaders

By OLAV MYRE

OSLO, Norway, (Via Telephone to Stockholm)—(U.P.)—German armed forces occupied the capital and south coast of Norway today, bombarded the outskirts of Oslo and battled defending aerial forces that included craft described as British planes.

◇ ◇ ◇

(Editor's Note: This dispatch, the first from Oslo in more than 15 hours, was telephoned planes were mentioned by Myre only at the beginning of the dispatch when he said they fought German craft over the capital at 5:30 p. m., But he also reported several encounters between German and Norwegian planes. He gave no explanation before being cut off of the presence of British planes over Oslo except to specify separate engagements in which British and German craft participated in addition to German battles with Norwegian planes.)

◇ ◇ ◇

Persistent rumors circulated that a vast allied aerial fleet was speeding toward the Norwegian capital.

A German destroyer, badly damaged, apparently by Norwegian coastal guns in Oslo fjord, steamed slowly into Oslo harbor where it anchored. (The Stockholm radio reported two German warships had been sunk by the Norwegians in Oslo fjord. Another report identified one of the sunken ships as the Gneisenau, German battle cruiser.)

Occupation of the capital was without serious resistance in the city itself, except for aerial operations.

I saw German airplanes dive low over the Oslo airfield and release bombs which scored direct hits on Norwegian planes but the Norwegian air force fought back valiantly.

I believe I saw four German planes crash and probably two Norwegian craft that went down.

The German bombing planes scored direct hits on six Norwegian planes on the Fornebo airfield, on the outskirts of Oslo, where they fought with the Norwegian craft.

There was no confirmation of reports that other Allied planes were en route to Oslo, but there were persistent rumors 600 to 700 British and French craft were en route.

The occupation of Oslo occurred without major incident in the city. The population generally stood by and watched the German soldiers in full war kit march along the central street.

About 300 to 400 German soldiers, some mounted and some with machine guns, participated in the march of the first units into the city.

Norwegian officers rode in automobiles with some of the German officers, spectators noted.

Royal Family Flees to Hamar

QUEEN MAUD — HAAKON

LONDON—(U.P.)—The Stockholm radio said tonight that the Norwegian royal family had fled with the government to Hamar.

Scandinavia Swings Toward Allies as Germany Strikes

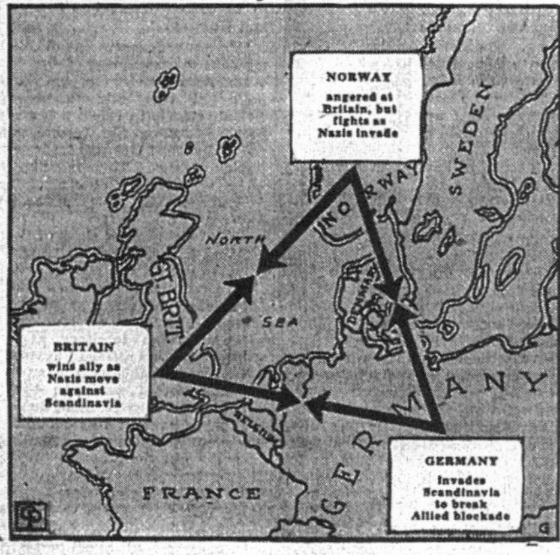

Sweden Mobilizes; Dutch on Lookout

The World Today

COPENHAGEN—First to fell the latest extension of Nazi might, this capital quickly and quietly submits to German troops.

OSLO—Norway, unlike Denmark, resists Hitler's legions. The government, however, flees to establish a provincial capital while German and Allied forces battle in the air, on the sea. The city was quiet as the troops entered.

STOCKHOLM—Sweden mobilizes its forces, awaits with uncertainty the extension of war.

LONDON—Promises of immediate Allied aid to Norway show results as British planes and ships battle those of Germany. Prime Minister Chamberlain predicts "ultimate defeat" of the reich.

BERLIN—Action against Scandinavia was necessary, says Germany, to protect the reich and to defend Denmark and Norway against Allied plans.

WASHINGTON—Special train speeds President Roosevelt to White House.

By JOE ALEX MORRIS
(United Press Foreign News Editor)

Europe reached zero hour today.

Adolf Hitler's armed forces occupied Denmark, fought their way into Norway, occupied Oslo, and faced the combined Allied forces along a vast new war front in Scandinavia.

Great Britain and France immediately accepted the challenge, announced they were rushing "full aid" to Norway (Denmark was not mentioned), promised the Nazis' "rash" aggression would lead to their ultimate defeat.

Powerful naval units, planes, and possibly expeditionary forces were mobilized by belligerents—and by the little neutrals—as the thrust into Scandinavia threatened to draw all of Europe into the conflict.

German and British planes were reported fighting off the Norwegian coast; rumors of a sea battle were broadcast; Sweden mobilized her defense forces; Holland cancelled military leaves after hearing reports (denied in London) of a British expeditionary force en route to Dutch waters; the British government declared the blockade of Germany was being tightened swiftly in the Balkans and the Far East.

But the real action was still to come.

Orders presumably already have been given for the Allied counter-action against the German invasion of Scandinavia, and somwhere at sea or somewhere in the skies over the North sea the test of power may already be in progress.

Nazi planes, it was announed in Berlin, are establishing a "flying curtain" along the Danish and Norwegian coasts to meet any Allied challenge. German naval and military units, after bombardment of Kristiansand and fighting around Oslo (where the big Nazi battle cruiser Gniesenau was reported sunk by Norse guns), were described as in complete command of the Skagerrak entrance from the North sea to the Baltic.

◇ ◇ ◇

Reports received via Stockholm said Nazi marines in sailor disguise had seized ports along Norway's North sea coast, including Bergen, Stravanger, and Narvik. In Berlin, Nazis said they had made sure Scandinavia would not see a British or French face for the duration of the war — and they alertly awaited the Allied counter-stroke.

Until that counter-stroke comes, the Nazis appeared to have improved vastly their ability to strike at the Allied shipping lines and naval forces in the North sea. Air and submarine bases in Denmark and Norway—which Berlin insisted would remain independent sovereign states— would greatly improve the German position for attacks as far as the British isles.

A press conference in London indicated the Allies already had struck with their naval and air forces. A spokesman said important news was to be expected "within the next 12 hours."

With clock-like speed and efficiency German troops moved over the Danish border and by 8 a. m. Copenhagen was in German hands. Simultaneously German troops landed in Norway, German warships blasted at Norwegian coast defenses, and German airships bombed Norwegian cities—but Norway fought back, and announced it was at war with Germany.

Quickly the Allies moved to aid Norway. Hasty telephone conferences between Paris and London and hasty war cabinet and war council sessions decided on immediate action.

◇ ◇ ◇

Every capital in Europe was on the alert. So was Washington and far-off Tokyo. The question on the lips of high officials and common citizens alike was: Does this mean long-dreaded total war will come?

Certain it was the Allies were preparing urgent and drastic counter-measures.

◇ ◇ ◇

Germany announced her action as "protective." Propaganda Minister Paul Joseph Goebbels went to the microphone of the German radio to announce Germany would not use Scandinavian nations as bases for operating against Great Britain unless the British "compel" such action.

German Foreign Minister Joachim von Ribbentrop told the press Germany's forces "will see to it that during this war no Englishman or Frenchman will get a glimpse into Norway or Denmark."

And in Berlin, too, it was said that assurance of "complete loyalty" had been obtained from the Danes, that the German occupation occurred without incident, and that life in Copenhagen was proceeding normally.

◇ ◇ ◇

But in Norway it was different. The Norwegians resisted the German assault. Coastal batteries beat off an

Weather
Fair, cooler, with frost tonight. Minimum temperature about 40. Saturday fair with rising temperature. Fresh northeast wind.

The Wisconsin State Journal
A fact-finding Newspaper

Home Final Edition

VOL. 156, NO. 40. 101st Year | MADISON, FRIDAY, MAY 10, 1940 | 32 PAGES | PRICE THREE CENTS

Nazi War Machine Swoops Into Lowlands

Belgians, Dutch Battle Blitzkrieg

Churchill Replaces Chamberlain

President 'Freezes' Dutch, Belgian Credits

FDR, Grieving for Holland, Repeats: U. S. Will Stay Out

WASHINGTON — (U.P.) — President Roosevelt said today he personally was in full sympathy with the views of Queen Wilhelmina in her proclamation rallying Holland to fight the German invasion.

At the same time the president declared in a press conference that he saw no change in the situation to warrant revision of his belief this country can stay out of war.

BULLETIN

WATCH FOR "CHUTE" INVASION, BRITONS WARNED

LONDON—(U.P.)—The home office tonight warned the British Isles "everyone should be on the lookout for German troops landing by parachute."

37 DIE IN ATTACK ON BRUSSELS

LONDON—(U.P.)—Thirty-seven persons were killed and 61 wounded in the German air attack on the Brussels airdrome district, it was said in authoritative quarters tonight. The Belgians were said to have held off the attack of German troops at all points.

BRITISH BOMB NAZIS ON WESTERN FRONT

ROYAL AIR FORCE HEADQUARTERS, FRANCE—(U.P.)—British bombing planes today bombed German troops on the western front and British fighters destroyed "numerous" enemy planes in aerial combat, it was reported tonight.

GIBRALTAR OPEN, BRITISH INSIST

GIBRALTAR—(U.P.)—British naval authorities officially denied today that the Straits of Gibraltar had been closed.

BRITISH ORDER: "SHOOT SUSPICIOUS"

LONDON—(U.P.)—The British war office in a move apparantly aimed at "fifth column" threats, announced today that sentries had been stationed at all vulnerable points in the British Isles with orders to shoot anyone who failed to answer their challenge.

He said he would not go into detail on that subject because it was speculative. He warned reporters not to interpret the word "speculative" under any conditions to mean this country may become involved in the European struggle.

◇ ◇ ◇

Authorizing direct quotation of his statement endorsing Wilhelmina's proclamation, Mr. Roosevelt said:

"I think I can say personally I am in full sympathy with the very excellent statement that was given out—the proclamation by the queen of the Netherlands—and let it go at that. It is worth reading."

The president indicated he is not yet ready to proclaim a state of war between Germany and the low countries, thereby invoking full force of the neutrality laws.

Mr. Roosevelt's press conference was held shortly after he had conferred with state, justice, navy, and army officials for 35 minutes on new problems of American neutrality.

He did not disclose any details of that meeting.

Other Washington developments:

ONE: Admiral Harold R. Stark, chief of naval operations, categorically denied reports the U. S. battle fleet would leave Hawaii for the Philippines, ostensibly in an attempt to head off any possible Japanese move toward the Dutch East Indies. The latter supplies all of this nation's rubber and most of its tin.

TWO: The Allies were disclosed to have ordered 4,000 latest-type pursuit, interceptor, and bombing planes from American manufacturers during the past month.

THREE: The war department announced it will ask Mr. Roosevelt to request an additional $80,000,000 for the purchase of 200 big four-engined bombers for long-range patrol duty in connection with the nation's western hemisphere defense policy.

FOUR: Chairman Norman H. Davis of the American Red Cross issued a nationwide appeal for a special $10,000,000 war relief fund to help alleviate suffering of Europe's civilian population.

FIVE: An executive order was issued freezing an estimated $1,372,000,000 in Dutch and Belgian credits and investments in this country in order to prevent the German invaders from cashing in on the holdings.

Asked whether the Dutch West and East Indies and their adjacent waters might possibly be included in combat area from which American ships are barred, Mr. Roosevelt replied flatly that no change now is contemplated in the present definition of such area.

• • • •

They Say Today

CROCKER

"I really didn't want them, but I hated to see them go to waste." With four large steaks under his belt, Omar Crocker thinks he might enter the Olympic tryouts as a heavyweight. **Page 25.**

"The highway committee never came out and asked for petitions." But you can't kid Alva Eighmy, who thinks "planted" road aid pleas are "damn poor practice." **Page 8.**

"This looks crazy to me, but it isn't." In 30 or 40 years, Prof. O. R. Zeasman believes, all the farms that need it will be terraced. **Page 8.**

"Both of these are mighty fine guns." Sen. Ernest Lundeen gets 27 bulls eyes at 300 yards with the new Garand and Johnson rifles, but will "leave it up to the army which one to buy." **Page 20.**

"There's a bachelor tax . . . I would have to pay if I don't get married." When Chavala Sukumalanandana gets back to Thailand he'll do better than seven dates in four years. **Page 1, part 2.**

"With the New York Yankees in last place anything can happen in the world." And Germany, Roundy observes, is grabbing everything but our left halfback. **Page 27.**

"Dawgone these people that call the minute you get into a bathtub." But if he leaves two dollars he owes you, that's different, according to Mr. Bumpstead. **Page 1, part 2.**

The Feature-Finder

If Hitler takes Holland, the U. S. is faced with defense of the Dutch possessions in the West Indies, a defense to which it already is committed. Dutch possessions include Dutch Guiana, the islands of Aruba and Curacao, and other smaller Caribbean islands.

Labor Wins Demands for Resignation

By FREDERICK KUH

LONDON — (U.P.) — Prime Minister Neville Chamberlain resigned tonight and Winston Churchill agreed to form a new government.

The new government — it was agreed without exception —shall be one of national unity in which labor, liberals and conservatives alike join, to meet the threat of the dread German blitzkrieg.

The change of government was being accomplished in record breaking speed for the ordinarily slow, and traditionally formbound British parliamentary system.

It is the first time in a career devoted to politics—most of it in the spotlight—that Churchill has headed a new government.

Technically, he is not yet head of a government but none in London doubted that he would be able to enlist the necessary support to achieve a cabinet of national unity.

What will be the make up of the new government was not yet known but it was expected to include David Lloyd George, Britain's war prime minister and veteran liberal.

For the time being—until all formalities are out of the way—the present ministers will remain at their posts.

Chamberlain was granted an audience just before 6 p. m. tonight by King George at Buckingham palace at which time he submitted his resignation and suggested Churchill be called in to form a cabinet.

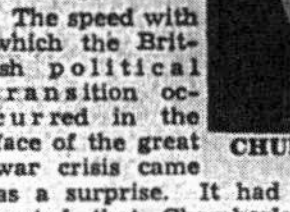

CHURCHILL

Immediately after Chamberlain returned to No. 10 Downing st., Churchill appeared at Buckingham Palace to receive the formal request from the king.

The speed with which the British political transition occurred in the face of the great war crisis came as a surprise. It had been expected that Chamberlain would continue on an interim basis for at least a few days while the preliminaries of constructing a national unity cabinet were being dealt with.

However, with unusual swiftness the labor party—long a stumbling block in attempts to obtain a coalition government—met at Bournemouth and announced it was ready to enter a new cabinet if Chamberlain stepped down.

◇ ◇ ◇

Later, Chamberlain in a radio broadcast tonight declared Churchill had accepted the task of forming a new government on a national basis.

Chamberlain declared when it became evident his resignation was essential to formation of a national government, he presented his resignation to King George tonight.

He said that his other cabinet colleagues had placed their resignations in Churchill's hands for his disposition as might prove necessary in the reconstruction of the government.

He declared he was perfectly willing to serve under Churchill in the new war cabinet and called on the British people to unite in support of the new prime minister.

Chamberlain spoke in a voice that sank almost to a whisper at the start of his broadcast. But when he reached the passages in which he denounced Hitler it was pitched in a key of indignation and power such as radio listeners had never before heard from him.

◇ ◇ ◇

Meanwhile in Paris, Premier Paul Reynaud issued a communique tonight announcing reorganization of the French cabinet as a broader coalition government.

The right-wing group brought into the government was headed by Louis Marin, president of the Nationalist Republican Federation party.

It included Jean Ybarnegary, vice-president of the ultra right wing group headed by Col. Jacques De La Roque, who at one time was charged with leading a French Fascist movement.

Both Marin and Ybarnegary were named ministers of state and members of the war council.

As the Battle Started

Fears of the "lowland neutrals" that German invasion was close at hand earlier this week, is described graphically by this map received only Thursday. These jitters became actualities early this morning when the Nazis war machine swung into action against Holland, Belgium and Luxembourg, almost exactly as anticipated.

Among the cities bombed by the Nazis were the Hague, Rotterdam and Nijmegen in Holland; Antwerp and Brussels in Belgium, and Calais and Lille along the French border.

Prepare! Prepare! Prepare!

(An Editorial)

Blitzkrieg has begun. The German ruse to decoy Great Britain and French forces to Norway failed, but being all set, Hitler took advantage of the political diversion in England relating to the Chamberlain dynasty, to make the move he had hoped to make when English and French forces were scattered in Scandinavia.

This presages a sudden attempt to conquer England, and as things stand now, it is quite within the cards.

Canada will be next, by way of Iceland and Alaska, one seven hours, the other four and a half hours from the American border, and we cannot defend these outposts.

Perhaps at long last the American people will awaken to the fact that this country must arm to the ultimate limit of its capacity, to defend itself on its own dunghill.

American mothers and young men who shrink at the idea of joining American expeditionary forces to foreign soil, can put away these cares. The fight for democracy and for American independence will be right here at home. We couldn't, were we to try, send an expeditionary army to aid the Allies, nor could we feed and munition those who actually arrived. When England, with its great battle fleet, couldn't land expeditionary forces in significant numbers in Norway, just across the channel, how could we go 3,000 miles to do the same job.

And so now that this worry about an expeditionary army is dissipated, may we not now expect Americans, mothers and sons, to prepare defense of the home fireside, which within six months is liable to be our task. Napoleon was smothered in the invasion of Russia. It is our hope that Hitler will be smothered in his invasion of America.

And the German plans for the invasion of Canada and the United States are just as thoroughly prepared as were those of Poland, Czechoslovakia, Norway, Belgium and Holland and the same inside machine is working. It is our estimate from various sources of information that there are 10,000 German spies in the United States and Canada, working from within in important governmental and industrial institutions.

We can't build battleships for this emergency, even were they important. But we should develop a factory capacity to turn out three airplanes a day for every one that Germany can produce. We should develop a tremendous manufacture of submarine and submarine destroyers. The fundamental importance is the factory capacity. Our only way to help the allies is to send them this sort of war equipment, including ordnance and ammunition, and the cheapest way out for the United States is to have the battle won over there if possible, so we needn't worry too much about extending credit for exportations.

The Wisconsin State Journal predicts that unless Germany is halted in Belgium and the Netherlands, the war will be in America within a year. That's not too much time to prepare.

The blitzkrieg which has come to seven peaceful countries will come to us unless it is stopped in Belgium and Holland. And at this moment that seems to us a remote chance.

"Strike, till the last armed foe expires!
Strike for your altars and your fires!
Strike for the green graves of your sires!
God, and your native land!"

Berlin Claims Swift Seizure of Key Bases

At a Glance

(By United Press)

BERLIN—Germany invades Holland, Belgium, Luxembourg; claims to have occupied The Hague, Dutch capital, bombed three French airdromes, captured all important Dutch, Belgian airports; Adolf Hitler exhorts troops that "hour has struck" for the fight in earnest.

AMSTERDAM—Dutch, aided by Allied men and planes, fight back against German invasion; defense forces reported resisting "desperately" German troops at three points; Dutch behind barricades attempt to hold off Germans seeking to occupy Rotterdam; Queen Wilhelmina calls upon her people to resist invaders as dikes are flooded and bridges are destroyed to halt invaders.

BRUSSELS—Belgians claim troops commanded by King Loepold halt invaders at frontier; terrific air battle reported over Mons area between Belgian-Allies craft and Germans. Government rejects German demands for non-resistance, advises Berlin that a state of war exists.

LONDON—Allies rush aid to invaded low countries; Britain's leaders strive for unity in face of anticipated blitzkreig on London; capital prepares to evacuate 400,000 to 500,000 children; Germans drop first bombs on British soil near Canterbury; Prime Minister Neville Chamberlain calls upon king, possibly to resign in face of opposition refusal to serve in his cabinet. Two members of Dutch cabinet arrive from The Hague by plane.

PARIS—German planes bomb Lyons airport and seven other towns; France warns of reprisals if open towns bombed; government in constant consultation.

BERNE—German planes bomb Berne—Jura Alpine district.

ROME—Pope confers with British and French ministers to Holy See on new war crisis; German ambassador calls upon Mussolini to outline the new German moves against low countries.

WASHINGTON—President Roosevelt says he is personally sympathetic with views of Holland's queen in rallying her forces against invasion; reports he still believes U. S. can stay out of war.

Hitler Guides 'Decisive Blow'

By JOE ALEX MORRIS
(United Press Foreign News Editor)

Holland and Belgium fought desperately tonight against a blitzkrieg invasion by Adolf Hitler's armed forces.

The German high command, seeking bases for a knockout blow against Great Britain, reported that German air, land and sea forces had broken enemy resistance in the first phase of a lightning invasion of Belgium, Holland and Luxembourg.

But from Amsterdam and Brussels came reports the Nazi troops had been checked along the frontier and the Allied powers were throwing their full strength into the conflict.

The Germans officially claimed to have crossed Luxembourg, to have smashed 15 miles into Belgium and taken Malmedy, to have advanced 20 miles in southern Holland to capture the Maastrich fort and to seize bridges leading over the Albert canal on the Dutch-Belgian border.

The Germans claimed to have destroyed almost 100 enemy planes while losing only seven or nine of their own in an advance to both the Maas and Ijsel rivers. They also claimed the capture of all important Dutch and Belgian airdromes.

The Dutch and Belgian military commands asserted, however, that their main defense lines were holding, that a German assault on the city of Rottendam was being beaten back and that German detachments landed by plane at strategic points in a campaign now familiar to Nazi foes had been surrounded and were being strongly attacked.

The Hague, which the German radio claimed had been occupied, remained in Dutch hands and tonight the Dutch high command broadcast a statement that the German surprise strategy had failed due to the determined defense by Dutch troops.

In swift succession, dispatches told the story of lightning

• • • • • • • •

KING LEOPOLD

QUEEN WILHELMINA

Weather

Thunderstorms tonight and Wednesday. Cooler Wednesday. Fresh southerly winds.

The Wisconsin State Journal

A fact-finding Newspaper

Home Final Edition

VOL. 156, NO. 64. 101st Year. MADISON, TUESDAY, JUNE 4, 1940 18 Pages ★★★★ Price Three Cents

Says If Britain Loses New World Will Come to Rescue

Churchill Admits 'Colossal Disaster'

'Barlow Acted Legally . . .'

Court Upholds State's Right to Fire 65

By LAWRENCE H. FITZPATRICK

The Heil administration won a thumping victory in the Wisconsin supreme court today over the Wisconsin State Employes assn., when the seven justices unanimously agreed that Elmer Barlow, commissioner of taxation, acted legally in dismissing some 65 employes in reorganization of the department of taxation.

The high court's opinion, written by Chief Justice Marvin B. Rosenberry, reversed an order of Circuit Judge A. C. Hoppmann and upheld throughout the contentions of J. Ward Rector, deputy attorney general, who represented the commisioner of taxation.

The decision upheld the state's contention that abolition of the old tax commission and departmental reorganization had separated the employes from state service and they were not to be considered as hired again by the state until they were reemployed by the new department of taxation.

Reorganization of the old tax commission by the 1939 legislature resulting in reduction of employes in the interests of economy and efficiency was one of the most important changes in state government sponsored by the Heil administration.

This particular reorganization move drew the fire of the State Employes assn., which retained counsel to fight the case to the highest state court on the contention that Commissioner Barlow acted illegally in violation of civil service laws.

◊ ◊ ◊

While some nine employes were named in the case, the decision will affect the status of some 65 employes who were divorced from the state's payroll as a result of the tax department reorganization, attorneys said.

◊ ◊ ◊

The case reached the supreme court when the state appealed the order of Judge Hopmann denying a motion to quash mandamus actions brought by the employes to force Barlow to reinstate them. The high court remanded the case to Hoppmann, who will quash the Mandamus action in compliance with the supreme court's decision.

◊ ◊ ◊

The controversy turned upon the construction to be given section of the statutes which read, **"the personnel of the present tax commission may be selected in whole or in part by the state department of taxation herein created, or the said department herein created may select its personnel in whole or in part from eligible civil service lists."**

"We reach the conclusion," the supreme court said, "that the section should be construed as to give the department of taxation a choice as to its personnel which might be taken from former employes of the tax commission or from 'eligible civil service lists.'"

The court held that the words "eligible civil service lists" did not mean departmental reempolyment lists, pointing out Barlow had a choice of lists as well as individauls.

"The tax commission having been completely abolished, its employes were by that act separated from state service and were not connected with state service until they were reemployed by the new department of taxation or in some other department of state government pursuant to law and the rules of civil service," the court explained.

The court's statement upheld the contention of Rector, who had argued the law passed by the 1939 legislature did not contemplate employes of the old tax commission should continue, without selection, by the new department of taxation as permanent employes.

◊ ◊ ◊

Answering the argument of Atty. A. J. Bieberstein, counsel for the employes, that Barlow in effect made a selection of employes when he certified payrolls of the department before the reorganization, the supreme court said:

"The legislature could not have intended that the commissioner of taxation should be compelled to exercise the power conferred upon him with reference to selection of personnel upon the very first day he took office.

"It must have been within the contemplation of the legislature," the court continued, "that the commissioner of taxation should have a reasonable time to familiarize himself with the work on the department, efficiency of employes and needs of the service which would affect reorganization of the department as contemplated by the act."

In reply to arguments advanced by counsel for the American Federation of Labor, who joined in the case to aid the state employes, the court denied the contention employes who have attained civil service must be regarded as having acquired a property right which could not be taken away "by the whim of a legislature or a department head."

"Rights under the civil service law are conferred by act of the legislature," the decision stated. "What the legislature may give it may take away. This court has nothing whatever to say with respect to the policy of the law. All questions of public policy are primarily for the legislature as this court has held many times. In this country there is no vested or contract right for an office."

Showers to Follow Record 86°

MONDAY			
Noon	84	7 p. m.	81
1 p. m.	84	8 p. m.	79
2 p. m.	84	9 p. m.	77
3 p. m.	86	10 p. m.	75
4 p. m.	85	11 p. m.	74
5 p. m.	84	Midnight	73
6 p. m.	83		
TODAY			
1 a. m.	71	9 a. m.	76
2 a. m.	69	10 a. m.	76
3 a. m.	68	11 a. m.	78
4 a. m.	67	Noon	81
5 a. m.	66	1 p. m.	82
6 a. m.	69	1:45 p. m.	83
7 a. m.	71	2 p. m.	82
8 a. m.	72		

Madison's relief from the season's warmest weather spell was delayed today by slow movement of the "setup" but thundershowers predicted for Monday night and today should arrive by tonight and Wednesday, said Eric R. Miller, government meteorologist.

The mercury reached the highest point of the year at 3 p. m. Monday when 86 was recorded. The previous maximum was 85.3 Sunday.

While the fluid dropped to 66 early this morning it had risen to 76 at 9 a. m., only one degree below the mark registered at the same hour Monday.

The cool air mass expected to bring a 10-degree drop here today remained in the west, but had moved slightly eastward, Miller reported, bringing drops to 50 at Pembina, Devils Lake and Jamestown, N. D., 37 at Lewiston, Mont., and 29 at Big Piney, Wyo.

Cities along the axis of the low pressure trough received heavy rains, Sioux City, Ia., having recorded 6.32 inches up to 7 a. m. today, while Minneapolis reported 1.62, Springfield, Minn., 1.54; Sioux Falls, S. D., 1.45; Huron, 1.32, and Durwell, Nebr., 1.43. In Wisconsin, Park Falls recorded .79 of an inch.

Swarsensky Speaks on 'Tolerance'

Rabbi Manfred Swarsensky, of the Beth-El Temple, will speak on "Tolerance" at the Baron's tea room meeting of the Madison Council of Christians and Jews at 6:30 tonight. It will be the group's last regular meeting of the season.

They Say Today

"He did not tolerate the best brains in industry and the economic life of the country." And that, Fritz Thyssen explains, is where Hitler blundered. Page 8.

"We don't want people to sit behind this movement to dodge the duties of citizenship." The church advances aid for conscientious objectors "with caution." Page 5.

"This is to advise that the dog license purchased by you expired May 31." So did the dog, G. W. Barrington replies to the city council. Page 3.

"The debt piled upon this country is just that much subtracted from our ability to defend ourselves." To Sen. James A. Reed it looks as if the United States defense is 30 to 45 billion dollars weaker than it was when Mr. Roosevelt took office. Page 3.

"Each year we are asked to do more and more on less and less." The Family Welfare and Children's Service assn. may have to limit its work, the Community Union is warned. Page 12.

FRITZ THYSSEN

The Feature-Finder

Paris . . . and Bombs

When the Nazi air force poured its load of bombs on Paris Monday, the city felt for the first time in World War II the real horrors of attack from the skies. This picture shows a seven story apartment house, the front of which has been smashed away by an exploding bomb.

Maxwell Loses Two Pay Cases

Frank Maxwell, former city treasurer who started out by sueing the city for back wages, ended up in the supreme court today with the city winning a counterclaim against him for an overpayment of salary.

The ex-treasurer was a double loser when the supreme court in an unanimous decision by Justice Chester A. Fowler, held Maxwell's claim for back salary was properly denied and that amounts paid him in excess of his salary can be recovered by the city.

◊ ◊ ◊

Maxwell had sued the city for $1,845 back pay from Jan. 1, 1933, to April 6, 1936. The city, represented by Doris E. Lehner, assistant city attorney, coutner-claimed that Maxwell allegedly had been overpaid $571.70 by taking a 5 per cent increase above the $2,400 salary set by the common council.

Circuit Judge Alvin C. Reis dismissed both claims and both sides appealed to the high court.

◊ ◊ ◊

In answer to the claim by James J. McDonald, counsel for Maxewell, that a city officer could not waive part of his salary during his term of office, the high court said:

"It seems manifest that a city officer, like any other person, may make a gift to the city, if he wants to, and that the gift may be made of a part of his salary as well as anything else. The officer cannot be coerced to waive his salary by threats of removal or refusal to reappoint. No threats of coercion were involved in this case."

The supreme court said the conceded facts clearly show an intent of Maxwell voluntarily to contribute to the city $50 a month of his salary in 1933 during a period of financial emergency, "and we conclude as a matter of law that upon those facts such contribution was made."

Justice Fowler's opinion further held that a 5 per cent increase voted by the common council in 1935 was void for the reason the law provides that salaries of officers shall not be increased or diminished during the term of office.

◊ ◊ ◊

In regard to the city's counterclaim against its former treasurer, the court made this comment:

"The excess payments of $12.50 per month during the second term and $37.50 per month during the third term being unlawful, can they be recovered? Apriori, it would seem that they can."

◊ ◊ ◊

Taking a neat slap at Judge Reis, "Mother Goose" principle as stated in his decision holding the city could not recover, the decision said:

"The trial court considered that 'what is sauce for the goose is sauce for the gander,' and that on that 'Mother Goose' principle the city could not recover salary unlawfully paid to the treasurer if the treasurer could not recover salary lawfully deducted," but the high court concluded, "a sum paid to a city officer in excess of his salary can be recovered."

FRANK MAXWELL

335,000 Allies Rescued as Dunkirk Falls to Nazis

At a Glance:

FRANCE—Battle of Dunkirk nears its end as remaining Allied troops embark for England under heavy bombardment. Germans reach outskirts and artillery shells departing troop transports. Allies block Zeebrugge harbor by sinking concrete ships there. French airplanes bomb German territory in reprisal for raids on Paris. Anti-aircraft guns in action today as German plane flies over capital. West front generally quiet.

GREAT BRITAIN—Churchill tells commons despite "colossal military disaster" in Flanders, 335,000 Allied troops were rescued. He hints Allies may take offensive against Germany. Allied air forces make apparently extensive raids into Germany in reprisal for German raid on Paris. Britain intensifies defense precautions, guarding roads and rounding up Fascists.

GERMANY—Germans say they have consolidated positions in Belgium and can strike at London and Paris "and the hearts of Britain and France" whenever they choose. Nazis proclaim capture of Dunkirk. Communique claims 79 French airplanes were shot down in raid on Paris, and 300 to 400 destroyed on ground. Report eight persons killed in Allied air raid on Munich suburb.

ITALY—Mussolini and council of ministers approve series of decrees completing Italy's preparedness for war.

THE AMERICAS—United States is target for "Fifth Column" activities in Latin America, reports from various capitals state. U. S. senate foreign relations committee considers resolution making Monroe doctrine more binding on 21 republics.

By UNITED PRESS

Prime Minister Winston Churchill, in terms of the "blood, tears, and sweat" he forecast lay ahead when he became leader of Britain on May 10, today told the house of commons a "colossal military disaster" had been suffered in Flanders but the empire would carry on until "the new world with all its power and might steps forth to the liberation and rescue of the old."

Even as Churchill revealed that 335,000 Allied troops had been rescued from Flanders the Nazi high command announced the city of Dunkirk and 40,000 Allied soldiers had fallen to Adolf Hitler's legions.

France announced her air force, acting with swiftness and determination, had carried out extensive bombing raids over Germany early today in retaliaton for the Nazi raid on Paris Monday in which 45 civilians were killed and 149 wounded.

Italy, armed to the teeth and on a full war footing, was still a belligerent neutral although the council of ministers told Premier Mussolini to "count on us" in any crisis.

◊ ◊ ◊

The prime minister spoke in straight - from - the-shoulder terms of the great battle of Flanders in which the British lost 30,000 killed, wounded, or missing. He warned the nation to be prepared for the Germans to strike at Paris or London because Hitler has "the whole of the channel ports in his hands and we have been told he has a plan for invading the British Isles."

In a dramatic passage of his speech, Churchill referred indirectly to America. He said that even in the unbelievable possibility the British Isles were subjugated the empire and the fleet would carry on until "in God's good time the new world with all its power and might steps forth to the liberation and rescue of the old."

There was a "victory inside the deliverance" of Allied troops from the German trap in Flanders and it was scored by the British air force, Churchill said, but he warned the nation against considering the deliverance a victory "because wars are not won by evacuations."

◊ ◊ ◊

Churchill, telling the story of what experts believe was the greatest single military operation in British history, said:

ONE: A total of 335,000 French and British were rescued from Flanders by the Allied navies and a fleet of a thousand boats, but the British alone lost 30,000 men, almost 1,000 guns and "all our transport and armored vehicles" in a "colossal military disaster" that weakened the French army and resulted in the loss of the Belgian army.

TWO: The Allied forces at Calais were given "an hour to surrender" but they fought on in the burning city for four days in an heroic episode that enabled the French to establish lines protecting Dunkirk and thus permit evacuation of the Allied armies. Only 30 unwounded men were rescued from Calais.

THREE: The British need no longer withhold opinion on the "pitiful" capitulation of King Leopold of the Belgians, which cut off the Allied line of retreat in the north. (Cries of "treachery" rang through the house after this statement.)

FOUR: The British Expeditionary force will be "reconstituted" and built up once again "under its gallant commander in chief" Gen. Viscount Gort, because "there is no reason why the losses cannot be repaired in a few months."

FIVE: Far heavier losses were inflicted on the Germans than were suffered by the Allies in the battle of Flanders and the German air force was "frustrated in its task" of destroying the retiring Allied forces.

SIX: The British empire and the French republic "will defend to the death their native soil, aiding each other like good comrades to the utmost of their strength . . . we shall never surrender."

SEVEN: Britain must expect "another blow to be struck almost immediately against us or France. We are told Hitler has a plan for invading the British isles but this has often been thought of before." He said, "We shall prove ourselves again able to defend our island home . . . if necessary alone."

EIGHT: British munitions are being supplied with greater rapidity than ever, there are now more powerful armed forces on the British isles than at any time in this war or the World war and "we

Bulletins

ZURICH, Switzerland—(U.P.) German air squadrons roared over Switzerland toward the Rhene valley again today and fragmentary reports indicated widespread aerial bombardment of France.

ROME — (U.P.) — An announcement today said telephone communications between Italy and France had been suspended.

LONDON— (U.P.) —Richard Butler, undersecretary for foreign affairs, told the house of commons today the government was prepared to enter into normal relations with the Soviet government.

U. S. Seeks Air Bases in SouthAmerica

WASHINGTON—(U.P.)—Fear of trouble in the western hemisphere hastened congressional action on President Roosevelt's $5,000,000,000 emergency defense program today as he submitted details on proposed expenditure of $1,277,741,170 he requested last week.

WASHINGTON—(U.P.) — Chairman David I. Walsh of the senate naval affairs committee told the senate today that the administration is negotiating for the establishment of United States air bases in South America.

Walsh did not elaborate on his statement, made as he explained provisions of the pending naval aircraft expansion bill.

Walsh was the first official to state negotiations actively were under way. The state department and other administration sources frequently have denied such reports.

Reports have been that the government started negotiating with several Latin American nations shortly after the outbreak of the European war. Recent Fifth Column activities in a number of American republics reportedly spurred the negotiations.

The army and navy have been anxious to obtain bases to protect the Panama Canal.

◊ ◊ ◊

Meanwhile, Director J. Edgar Hoover of the Federal Bureau of Investigation revealed top-ranking officials of four government departments have formulated a coordinated policy of defense against subsersive elements.

And Gen. George C. Marshall, chief of staff, urged congress to give President Roosevelt "a fire extinguisher" for preserving peace in the western hemisphere by granting him additional authority to call the national guard and reserves into active service in the absence of congress.

◊ ◊ ◊

Hoover said spokesmen for the army and navy intelligence services, the state department, and the FBI meet regularly to plan the attack against Fifth Columnists.

Hoover said the group, described as an internal defense council, was working closely with intelligence units of the treasury department, and had developed plans for pooling of information among government agencies and for cooperation of other law enforcement agencies in the nation.

Government officials depend on this network of enforcement to lessen the need for volunteer groups.

Seventy-seven armory robberies during nine months of the fiscal year resulted in loss of 124 firearms and 29,390 rounds of ammunition, bringing the total loss from 1933 to 1940 of 3,298 firearms and 425,459 rounds of ammunition, the FBI reported.

◊ ◊ ◊

Marshall urged the house military affairs committee to urge approval of a bill empowering the president to send militiamen into active service outside this country in event of emergency between the end of this congressional session and the beginning of the next.

He cited the rise of "indirect, subversive methods in the western hemisphere, and said such movements would be "dangerous to us, specifically to the Panama Canal."

He explained the program as one of using a "fire extinguisher rather than the entire fire department."

CALAIS GRAVELINES DUNKIRK NIEUPORT OSTEND ZEEBRUGGE YPRES LILLE CAMBRAI

Closer . . . Closer

Like giant hands, the powerful armies of Adolf Hitler have strangled Allied resistance in Flanders and now clutch the entire English channel coast from the mouth of Somme at Abbeville northward. The great ports of Calais, Gravelines, Nieuport, Ostend, Zeebrugge and today Dunkirk have fallen, one after another, into the Nazi grasp.

Whitbeck Wills $59,000 to U. W.

The University of Wisconsin, experiencing consistently decreased revenues, today saw a picture with a brighter side.

It was a check delivered to M. E. McCaffrey, secretary to the regents, from the executors of the estate of Prof. R. H. Whitbeck, former university geographer, who died July 27, 1939.

Approved in a board of regents meeting several months ago, the gift the professor had presented the university for fellowships never was officially appraised.

Today, instead of the $10,000, or $20,000 he thought he might get "if we are lucky," Secretary McCaffrey had a check for $59,443.65, and the promise of about $3,000 more.

"You bet we're happy," McCaffrey laughed.

Under terms of Prof. Witbeck's will, the money is to be placed in a trust fund, and two-thirds of the income from it is to be awarded annually by the geography department staff in two equal fellowships to meritorious graduate students doing major work in the department. Income will be available for awards in 1941-42.

The remaining one-third of the annual income shall be allowed to accumulate for periods of three or four years, and then shall be awarded by the geography staff to one of its members as a fellowship for foreign travel in the interests of geography. A portion of the income may also be used for financing geographical publications written by members of the geography staff, the bequest specifies.

Colloday Sentenced on Morals Count

Charles MacLain Colloday, 44, of 324 W. Washington ave., today was fined $250 and costs or six months in the county jail after pleading guilty to lewd and lascivious conduct with Mrs. Rae Marie Osgood, 31, whose bruised body was found in a bedroom in Colloday's house May 27.

In imposing sentence, Superior Judge Roy H. Proctor said:

"The charge might well have been more serious—adultery. However, I feel the defendant is entitled to some consideration since he has been in jail since May 27."

Colloday attributed his conduct to drink. His attorney, John Culbertson, said, "we all admit the unfortunate situation in which Mr. Colloday finds himself is true."

Alfonsi Seeks Progressive Nomination

PENCE, Wis. —(U.P.)— Paul R. Alfonsi, 32, assemblyman for Iron and Vilas counties since 1933, announced today he will run for the Progressive party nomination for governor in Wisconsin's September primary.

Alfonsi proposed to "inform the electorate of what has actually transpired in this state since the Republican administration took over in January of 1939."

OFFICIAL STATE PAPER

The Wisconsin State Journal

A fact-finding Newspaper

VOL. 157, NO. 179. 102nd Year — THIS PAPER CONSISTS OF FOUR SECTIONS—SECTION ONE — SUNDAY, MARCH 30, 1941 — MADISON — ★★★★ — Price Five Cents

WISCONSIN: Mostly cloudy and warmer today, followed by light rain north and west-central; Monday cloudy and colder with some light rain or snow flurries; fresh south or southeast winds today.

On Tuesday:

(An Editorial)

Here are some reflections on Tuesday's election, just last minute words upon which we can all reflect. Let's first have the ticket for election we think advisable:

For supreme court—Chester A. Fowler.

For superintendent of public instruction—John M. Callahan.

For alderman—

1st ward—Douglas Nelson.
3rd ward—Rodney Sperle.
5th ward—Harold A. Johnson.
7th ward—William E. Huntley.
9th ward—Franz G. Haas.
11th ward—John Coyne.
13th ward — Harrison L. Garner.
15th ward — Herbert J. Schmiege.
17th ward — William H. Boyle.
19th ward—M. Lee O'Brien.

◇ ◇ ◇

We believe that in Madison the public attention should first turn to the question of the auditorium. There has been submitted a referendum which, we believe, has been worked out broadly and soundly enough by Mayor Law and his associates to fill the bill. As a capital city, Madison has no longer-felt want than an auditorium, because obviously it is the natural convention city of Wisconsin. In today's paper on Page 18, Russell B. Pyre has thoroughly covered the questions of the advantages of an auditorium, and we believe the picture presented is a convincing one. To us it seems it would be a grave error not to vote for a Madison auditorium.

It goes without saying the referendum for installment tax payments should be passed.

◇ ◇ ◇

First in order of importance in the state poll is the supreme court election. You will find Justice Chester A. Fowler's name heading our list of candidates.

Early in the campaign a Milwaukee committee, admittedly a Reis organization, made "a non-partisan statement" in which it said Judge Reis, if elected, would be the judge of the common people."

Obviously the mine run of people wouldn't get much consideration.

On a postcard bearing Judge Reis' picture, and no doubt his consent, a group of veterans whose signatory authority is Lawrence A. Brown, Jr., appeals to another special group. The card says:

"We veterans should be represented on the supreme court by someone who understands our point of view. Al Reis is the man."

Were Judge Reis elected, this might embarrass him. What if his obligation to the "common people" and the to the veterans should conflict? Of course, it doesn't matter at all what his obligation to all the people of all parties and organizations might legitimately require.

The last tirade of the Capital Times was over a list of people who contributed $49.50 to Judge Fowler's campaign, according to law. The inference is that every contributor is a criminal, and Judge Fowler is a criminal to accept the money. Of course, had they contributed to Judge Reis, it would have been a glorious civic effort.

In the presence of the editor of this newspaper, Judge Reis recently deprecated the assault on Judge Fowler's ripened years, but the last Reis "folder" to appear entitled, under a picture of Judge Reis, "Elect Alvin C. Reis," winds up with a proud assertion that Reis is 30 years younger than Fowler.

The whole thing has been a perfect example of the conversion of a non-partisan election to a partisan field day. The Capital Times, which has stooped to every political subterfuge, from direct partisan appeal to assault upon the legitimate support and supporters of Judge Fowler, has not had the grace to acknowledge any one of several occasions on which, in an unguarded moment, they had credited Judge Fowler with judicial leadership on the bench.

Prior to this campaign we have admired Alvin C. Reis as a man, as a scholar, as a soldier, as a public servant, and as a jurist. But in permitting and subscribing to all the ordinary political technique of a political campaign in his own behalf, in an election which the laws says shall be non-partisan, he has left us with a feeling of regret.

Judge Fowler has permitted no political leader or organization to be his spokesman, or has he permitted politics to influence his campaign in any way.

◇ ◇ ◇

We are urging the reelection of John M. Callahan as state superintendent of schools. Previously, we have reviewed the excellent record of Superintendent Callahan over a period of years, but at this time we are particularly interested in his reelection because, of all the candidates, he alone is standing unqualifiedly for a very vital forward step in our rural educational program. We refer to rural school consolidation. Supt. Callahan is not shirking the fact that in many quarters there is local opposition to this idea. He is prepared to stand or fall with it. That's a man's way.

To the school board contest this year we welcome Elizabeth Brandeis Raushenbush. Three of the candidates, Dr. R. W. Huegel, Ray Felt, and Herbert C. Schenk, are already members of the board, and thus well known to the electorate, but Mrs. Raushenbush is running for public office for the first time.

Daughter of the distinguished retired supreme court justice, Louis D. Brandeis, Mrs. Raushenbush has made a noteworthy record in her own right as economist and as a teacher. But it is as a resident of Madison, which she has been for 18 years, and as the mother of a 12-year-old son, with the deep interests of a Madison resident and as a mother that Mrs. Raushenbush will bring her talents and her splendid background to Madison's educational problems.

We consider Mrs. Raushenbush eminently qualified and we believe Madison will not fail to take advantage of the outstanding service it has been offered in her candidacy.

39-34 Victory Gives Wisconsin National Basketball Championship

Badgers Bring Home Bacon

Victors Return at Midnight

Although the triumphant University of Wisconsin basketball team will arrive in Madison at the early hour of 12:50 a. m. Monday at the North Western station, plans formulated by Badger rooters as Wisconsin won Saturday night indicated several thousand fans will be on hand to greet the team.

Members of the university boxing team will return here at 10 p. m. today at the west side Milwaukee road station.

Mayor Law Saturday night urged all who could to "meet the team."

"There's nothing too good for that team in this town," the mayor said.

By HENRY J. McCORMICK (State Journal Sports Editor)

KANSAS CITY, Mo.— The end of the trail came here Saturday night for as gallant a team as ever wore the flaming cardinal of the University of Wisconsin, and at the end of the trail was a clear-cut national championship.

Wisconsin's great basketball team defeated Washington State, 39-34, and that marked the Badgers' 15th straight victory of the season, their 20th win in 23 games, and the first national championship that ever has been won by a Wisconsin quintet.

Kansas City hadn't expected to see Wisconsin handle the Washington State team as easily as it did. As a matter of fact, Kansas City hadn't expected to see Wisconsin win this game.

Coach Harold E. "Bud" Foster's Badgers won with poise that must have been amazing to both Washington State and the spectators. Wisconsin had the ability to win this game by a big margin, but the Badgers played it as they had played every other game all year when they figured they wore the big pants.

◇ ◇ ◇

And the Badgers definitely wore the big pants in this game. They were the tough ball club from start to finish, they were the team that never had the slightest doubt in its ultimate winning destiny.

◇ ◇ ◇

Not only did the Badgers win this game, but the player selected as the most valuable was Johnny Kotz of Wisconsin.

As Kotz toted back the trophy, you might guess who was the first one to slap him on the back. It

(Continued on Page 2, Col. 2)

'We Americans Have Risen Above Any Considerations of Party Politics

FDR Warns of Danger of Communists, Nazis, Defeatists; Proclaims U. S. Unity

By T. F. REYNOLDS

PORT EVERGLADES, Fla. — (U.P.) — President Roosevelt Saturday night warned America of peril from Communists, Nazis, defeatists and their dupes, but said Americans are transcending partisanship to defend democracy and to assist nations resisting the march of dictatorships towards world domination.

Lashing out at Communists, Nazis and the Berlin-Rome-Tokyo alliance alike, Mr. Roosevelt asserted enemies of democracy and their agents or dupes in this country are attempting to spread terror in America **"to shatter the confidence of Americans in their government and in one another."**

The president summoned all Americans, whether Democrats, Republicans, or independents, to rally to the defense of their way of life. But he warned the task entails sacrifice — **"You have to work overtime and work harder than ever before in your life."**

He set as the alternative:

"If our kind of civilization gets run over, the kind of peace we seek will become an unattainable hope."

Sun tanned and refreshed after eight days of sunshine at sea, Mr. Roosevelt spoke by radio to the world from the cabin of the presidential yacht Potomac, tied up at a dock here. He spoke as chieftain of the Democratic party and addressed his speech to a nation-wide series of dinners of party leaders observing Jackson day.

But his address went beyond the party celebration. The president made it obvious he was talking to all Americans. The two-party system remains as a basic principle of American political life, he said, but in the present grave national emergency **"we Americans—nearly all of us—have arisen above any considerations of party politics."**

Mr. Roosevelt promised his party and the nation action to meet the crisis arising from a world at war.

"I have become more than ever clear that the time calls for courage and more courage—action and more action," he said.

"In our own day the threat to our union and to our democracy is not a sectional one. It comes from a great part of the world which surrounds us and which draws more tightly around us day by day."

This threat, he said, is directed against the basic principles of American liberty — "freedom of speech, freedom of the press and the air, freedom of worship." **Then he carefully identified the source from which this threat originates.**

"These are the eternal principles which are now being threatened by the alliance of dictatorship nations," he said, in an unmistak-

(Continued on Page 2, Col. 6)

Journal Brings Holy Land Exhibit to Madison

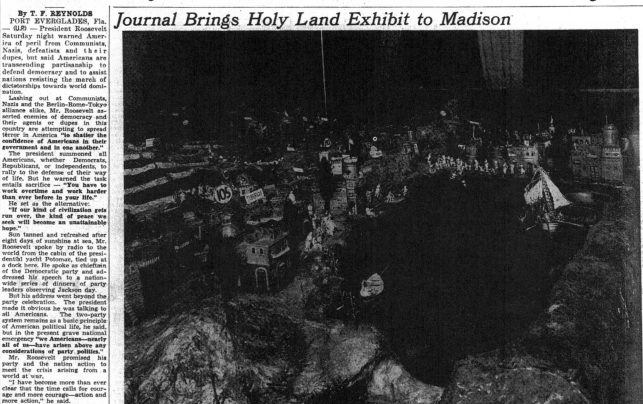

Some idea of the size of the Holy Land exhibit which will be shown in Madison during Holy Week is given by the above picture. The Sea of Galilee and the city of Tiberias are depicted, but this is only one section of the huge panorama.

The Wisconsin State Journal is bringing the reproduction of Palestine to the city for a limited stay starting April 7. The exhibition hall will be at 332 W. Johnson st. Proceeds will go to the Empty Stocking club.

Moving Figures Tell Ancient Story of Biblical Palestine

A Holy Land exhibit which reproduces the Palestine of Biblical times in faithful miniature will be shown at 332 W. Johnson st. April 7-15 as a feature of Madison's Holy week observance.

The unusual replica, only one of its kind in the world, is being brought to the city by The Wisconsin State Journay. Proceeds will go to the Empty Stocking club.

Complete in every detail, the exhibit reproduces the mountains, valleys, and plains of the Holy Land, the Sea of Galilee and River Jordan, Jerusalem, Bethlehem, and other towns, and many famous New Testament characters. Scenes from the life of Christ enacted by moving figures are an outstanding feature of the exhibit.

The model will be erected on an 18 by 44 foot platform in the exhibition hall, 332 W. Johnson st., where it may be seen by visitors. Exhibition hours will be from 11 a. m. to 4:30 p. m. and 7 to 9:30 p. m. on weekdays and from 1 to 4:30 and 7 to 9:30 p. m. on Sundays. Admission will be 30c for adults and 15c for children.

◇ ◇ ◇

The mammoth display weighs 20,000 pounds and contains 64,000 pieces. It was made by Joseph and Salvatore Gauci and required 10 years to build.

◇ ◇ ◇

The Gauci brothers, natives of the island of Malta, will arrive in Madison Monday and start setting up the Palestine panorama. It will require a week's labor on the part of six workmen to fit the 64,000 pieces together.

Religious leaders, historians, and craftsmen have paid the exhibit high praise in other cities where it has been shown. Its limited stay in Madison will coincide with the Easter season and serve as a vivid reminder of the life and crucifixion of Christ.

◇ ◇ ◇

Included in the panorama are 1,200 buldings and 740 animated figures, each minutely carved to scale. There are 124 scenes from the Bible, the most famous showing the Savior as he walked on the waters of Gallilee. Special lighting and the movement of the characters adds to the naturalness of the setting.

Among the more famous places reproduced are Solomon's temple, the Roman road to Damascus, Jacob's well, Jaffa gate, the stable where Christ was born, the hills of Nazareth, and the City of David.

The Gauci brothers gave 10 years to creating the Holy Land exhibition. They visited Palestine to study topographical features of the country and conducted extensive research in the architecture and life of Christ's time in preparing to make the 64,000 pieces.

Visitors will have a good view of the elaborate panorama when it is shown in Madison. Tiers of different heights are being erected in the exhibition hall, and observers will see the display from every angle as they walk around these. The Gauci brothers will tell the story as scenes are dramatized, and printed programs will provide a guide to the more famous places shown.

'Our Future at Stake . . .'

Avoid Defense Strikes, Green Warns AFL

WASHINGTON —(U.P.)— Pres. William Green of the American Federation of Labor Saturday night called on all American Federation of Labor unions to avoid strikes in defense industries.

"While we must insist upon fundamental principles," Green said, "when collective bargaining breaks down we should submit issues to mediation and arbitration, doing everything within our power to avoid strikes.

"The future of our nation, our democratic institutions and the very existence of a free labor movement are at stake. The American labor movement will as always give unreserved service to the cause of freedom."

Green's appeal to AFL unions not to strike was an editorial, "Labor's Obligation," in the April issue of the American Federation, official AFL monthly.

He said the "key issue" in the present war is "personal freedom" and he added this was "the goal which has inspired organized labor throughout the ages."

◇ ◇ ◇

Other actions on the labor front Saturday night included:

Telegrams sped to President Roosevelt and other officials stating the refusal of these CIO United Automobile Workers to return to work on vital defense contracts at the Allis-Chalmers plant at Milwaukee.

The 22-day strike by the CIO at the Federal Motor Truck co., which officials said had $5,000,000 in army and navy truck orders was settled, and men will return to work at Detroit Monday.

Striking workers at the Plainfield, N. J. plant of the Condenser Corporation of America agreed to return to work on the basis of a settlement arranged by the new defense mediation board. The strike had affected 25,000 men.

Twenty thousand members of the CIO United Mine Workers union were ordered to quit work in Illinois coal mines Monday at expiration of a UMW contract with the operators' association.

The federal government prepared to intervene in wage-hour negotiations for the Appalachian soft coal industry to prevent a threatened shutdown this week.

(Details on page 2)

Get Licenses by Tuesday, Police Warn

If you haven't your tag, you're "it."

City and county officers are prepared to arrest motorists who do not have proper licenses, they said Saturday night.

The deadline is April 1, Tuesday, and there'll be no fooling, the officers said.

The Madison branch of the state motor vehicle department did a landslide business in selling auto licenses Saturday, but the last minute rush is expected to continue Monday and Tuesday.

All motorists must have the 1941 plates by midnight Tuesday or be able to show proof that their licenses have been ordered.

More than 3,000 persons purchased licenses over the counter here Saturday, and 14,000 mail orders were handled in the "biggest day's" business, Commissioner Hugh M. Jones said.

There are still 100,000 car owners in the state who have not placed their orders, Jones said, but most of them will get their plates through the mail.

News Index

PSC Rips Edgerton Utility Ways

Sharp criticism of the city of Edgerton's management of its municipal water utility in bookkeeping, accounting, and diverting of funds to general city uses was voiced in an order signed Saturday by the Wisconsin public service commission.

The order, signed by all three commissioners, R. W. Peterson, Robert A. Nixon, and W. F. Whitney, declared that while records showed a total of 84,492,000 gallons of water pumped in 1939, only 38,051,000 gallons were metered, billed, and paid for.

The discrimination the commission found, resulted from free service to some agencies, pointing out that the city swimming pool, golf course, and street department never were billed for water.

The utility, managed by the city council, was credited with $60,000 reserve on the city's books, but this fund actually amounts only to $9,000, the commission found. Of this difference, $20,000 may have been taken by the city as return of advances and an additional $20,000 may have been used legally for other uses, the commissioners said.

The commission also pointed out the utilities equipment needed repair and its reservoir was being used only temporarily by permission of the state board of health.

After ordering a complete audit and notifying the council the commission will set up a bookkeeping system for the utility, the commissioners suggested a full-time manager for the system and a non-partisan commission to replace the city council in direction of the utility.

Russia Lauds Jugoslavia's Revolt

British Navy Pursues Crippled Italian Fleet

By HARRISON SALISBURY (United Press Staff Correspondent)

Great Britain hurled another crushing blow at Italy's already half-crippled naval fleet Saturday night and a Nazi military move against Jugoslavia appeared to be in preparation.

The British blow against Italian sea power was dealt in the eastern Mediterranean. No final report was available as the action was said to be still in progress with British warships speeding at forced draught in an attempt to deliver another fatal blow before the Fascist fleet could get within the protective shelter of shore batteries on the Italian mainland.

Thus far, however, London reports indicated that six Italian warships have been damaged badly and some of them sunk. One was a crack warship of the 35,000-ton Littorio class. Four were cruisers and one a destroyer.

Which of these vessels had been sunk was not known but First Lord of the Admiralty A. V. Alexander believed that two cruisers might now lie at the bottom of the Mediterranean.

The action started in the Ionian sea Friday when the British eastern Mediterranean fleet under Admiral Sir Andrew Cunningham came upon an Italian squadron which included battleships, cruisers, and destroyers.

The Italians apparently had left their customary anchorage under shore batteries to venture out for an attack upon the heavy convoys which the British and Greeks have been moving through the eastern Mediterranean.

The British said that the Italians dispersed but the British were able to bring some of the ships to battle and scored heavily on a Littorio battleship, two cruisers, and a destroyer.

The Royal Air Force then went into action and reported hits on two more cruisers and a destroyer. Other RAF units blasted at Italian air bases near Taranto, presumably to enable the British warships to work in close to the Italian coast without danger of air attack.

A Rome high command com-

City to Remove 30 Shacks from 'Hell's Half Acre'

A "cleanup program," to remove 30 or more dilapidated shacks in "Hell's Half Acre," between the Oregon road and the county fairgrounds, will be launched within a few weeks, A. O. Johnson, town of Madison building commissioner, announced Saturday.

The program will be under direction of Johnson and Dr. A. C. Stehr, town health officer, who already have conducted a joint investigation of the area.

"Efforts will be made to move occupants of the shacks into "decent homes," Johnson declared.

OFFICIAL STATE PAPER

The Wisconsin State Journal

A fact-finding Newspaper

VOL. 158, NO. 6. 102nd Year | THIS PAPER CONSISTS OF THREE SECTIONS—SECTION ONE | MADISON, SUNDAY, APRIL 6, 1941 | 32 Pages ★★★★ | Price Five Cents

Weather

WISCONSIN: Cloudy followed by rain Sunday night possibly beginning extreme west Sunday afternoon; Monday cloudy, rain east and south, warmer extreme south Sunday, colder Monday south and west central.

Nazis Attack Slavs, Greeks

Russia Signs Pact With Serbs

Look What Came In with Spring!

This little colt is a frisky, month-old Belgian, the only living one of three colts which have arrived at the University of Wisconsin farms this spring. He's mostly tan and white—and hungry.

With all the dignity of one of its elderly ancestors, this chick calmly surveys the world that has been revealed after she pecked her way into the open. She's awaiting a trip from a Madison hatchery to a private farmer.

Little lambykins here wants her mamma, because she's only a day old, and she'd much rather sleep or have lunch than stand up on scales which show she weighs only 7 lbs. She's also a university farm product.

Just call me "Big Ears," folks. I'm a two-week-old Guernsey calf, and from my stall at the university farms, I look out upon the world pretty curiously.

FDR Calls Murray in Steel Peril

BULLETIN

PITTSBURGH — (U.P.) — President Roosevelt has personally intervened in the threatened stoppage of work at the far-flung mills of U. S. Steel corp," and has summoned Philip Murray, Congress of Industrial Organizations president, to Washington for a conference, it was reported in steel circles here Saturday night.

(By Leased Wire)

A "work stoppage" of 250,000 employes of the United States Steel corp., called for Tuesday by Pres. Philip Murray of the Congress of Industrial Organizations, will be delayed at least a week, a source close to the management predicted Saturday night.

OTHER DEVELOPMENTS ON THE LABOR FRONT:

ONE: The defense mediation board took over three more disputes, while continuing its efforts to settle the Allis-Chalmers strike.

TWO: Michigan's Gov. Murray Van Wagoner and Labor Conciliator James Dewey announce they expect to bring Ford Motor co. and CIO-United Automobile workers into a joint conference Monday or Tuesday.

◇ ◇ ◇

In notices sent out to Steel Workers Organizing Committee members employed in 14 subsidiaries of the far-flung U. S. Steel plants, engaged in millions of dollars of defense work, Murray said:

"This notice is to advise you that there will be a cessation of work at the mills and plans of the subsidiary companies of the U. S. Steel corporation on midnight Tuesday, caused by the lock-out by these companies."

The management source said the company and the SWOC will reach an agreement Monday delaying for at least a week the "work stoppage" called by Murray.

Murray had charged that U. S. Steel had rejected Friday a proposal by the SWOC that work continue in the corporation's mills until midnight April 15, with any contract benefits to be applied retroactively to April 1.

The statement by his informed source indicated, therefore, that U. S. Steel now will accept the SWOC proposal in that matter.

Officials of the corporation refused comment on Murray's work-stoppage statement.

Van Wagoner and Dewey announced they "hope to reach a settlement Monday or Tuesday."

"Minor differences are rapidly disappearing so that now it will be possible to discuss issues of settlement," the statement said.

Getting both parties to sit down together at a conference table would be a major victory for conciliators. Never in Ford history has the automobile manufacturer consented to discuss issues with a CIO union.

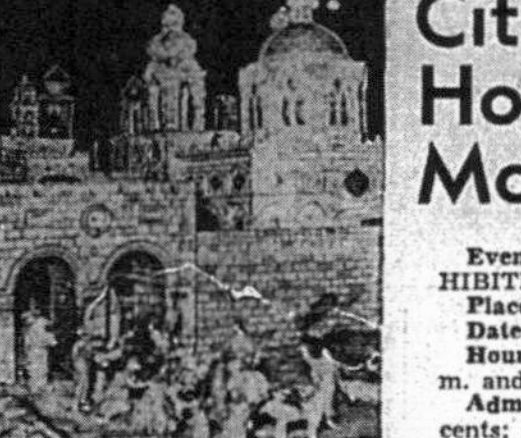

Palm Sunday

Inspiring for the Easter season, the Holy Land exhibit will open at 332 W. Johnson st. Monday under auspices of The Wisconsin State Journal. Christ's triumphal entry into Jerusalem through the Golden Gate, the Biblical incident being commemorated in Palm Sunday services today, is shown above. This is one of the many scenes from the life of Christ re-created in the exhibit.

Wild Land Goes Back to the Wild

By ROD VAN EVERY

The pheasants, rabbits, and ducks soon will have "The Jungles" all to themselves. They will be able to go about their animal ways and enjoy their home lives without disturbance from "shackers."

The shackers will be moved out. Saturday, Building Commissioner Gordon E. Nelson said he would serve notice on the Lake Forest co. early this week that shacks on the Fitchburg rd., north of Wingra (Murphy's) creek, must be razed in 30 days. Legal phraseology of the notice will mention "abatement of a nuisance."

The shacks, constructed on land belonging to the Lake Forest co., are slipped together of conglomerate materials from linoleum and tarpaper to metal signs. Litters of junk are islands in greasy mud surrounding the squatters' shacks.

◇ ◇ ◇

From it, a cock pheasant rises with a whir of wings to make any hunter catch his breath. Off Wingra creek, just across the road three mallards take off with frantic feet and glinting wings. A rabbit breaks from under a torn, rusty fender and scoots into the bush.

This was their home in the first place. And it will be theirs again.

◇ ◇ ◇

"We will be glad to have the squatters out, and we will cooperate with the city and the building commissioner in getting them out," Chandler B. Chapman, president of the Lake Forest co., said.

Nelson said the prospective city action would clean up one of the last squatters' settlements in the

(Continued on Page 2, Col. 3)

City to See Holy Land Monday

Event: HOLY LAND EXHIBITION.
Place: 332 W. Johnson St.
Dates: April 7-15.
Hours: 11 a. m. to 4:30 p. m. and 7 to 9:30 p. m. daily.
Admission: Adults, 30 cents; children under 12, 15 cents.
Sponsorship: The Wisconsin State Journal for benefit of the Empty Stocking club.

Starting at 11 a. m. Monday, residents of Madison and southern Wisconsin will have their first opportunity to see the animated Holy Land exhibit created by the Gauci brothers.

The authentic reproduction of Palestine as it was in Biblical times, with miniature figures dramatizing stirring scenes from the life of Christ, is world-famed. It will be on view at 332 W. Johnson st. during Holy Week, fitting in with the Easter observance and appealing to persons of all faiths.

Exhibition hours will be from 11 a. m. to 4:30 p. m. and 7 to 9:30 p. m. every day this week. On Easter Sunday, the schedule will be from 1 to 4:30 and 7 to 9:30 p. m.

Admission will be 30 cents for adults and 15 cents for children under 12. The Wisconsin State Journal is bringing the unusual display to the community, and proceeds will go to the Journal's Empty Stocking club.

Defying description, the exhibit shows in panorama the entire country of Palestine. Jerusalem, the walled city, is set on a high hill, its magnificent buildings bejeweled with lights. The River Jordan winds from the Sea of Galilee to the Dead sea. Outside Bethlehem is the stable where Jesus was born, and overhead the Star of the East burns brightly.

Nazareth, Joseph's home and workshop, Mt. Tabor, Jacob's well, the Plains of Rephaim, the brook from which Young David gathered pebbles, the Field of Boaz where Ruth gleaned corn, the Tower of Shiloh, the wilderness of Judea, the Decapolis desert, the small fishing village of Magdala—all are reproduced in their proper location.

The naturalness of the setting is enhanced by tiny olive trees actually brought from the Holy Land, by palms and other shrubbery, by windmills, and by sheep, cows, and camels in the fields.

Perhaps most fascinating of all are the animated scenes. Lazarus is raised from the dead and comes out of his grave at the command of Christ. At the scene of the Nativity the cattle kneel. A small boy catches fish, and boats rock to and fro on the Sea of Galilee.

There are 740 animated characters, and the way their lifelike movements are controlled has amazed electricians and craftsmen in other cities where the exhibit has been shown.

The exhibit runs continuously and may be seen at any time within the stated hours. Tiers have been erected in the exhibition hall so that everyone will have a good view.

Worth $8,000 and possibly as much as $25,000 is the chess set here being used by Naomi and David Showalter, daughter and son of Mrs. Norine Showalter, 2421 Center ave. Stolen from a southern plantation during a Civil war raid, the chess set is made of hand wrought ivory. The hollow pieces at one time may have been used by Chinese opium smugglers.

Madison Children Get Valuable Heirlooms

Dust of King James' Court, Old China Seeps From Gifts

Naomi and David Showalter, daughter and son of Mrs. Norine Showalter, 2421 Center ave., aren't quite sure, but they may possess a small fortune in two collector's items, steeped in romance and historical lore, recently given them by their paternal grandfather.

The two items are a chess set and a clarinet.

◇ ◇ ◇

Either of the articles may be worth enough to send David, 14, to the University of Wisconsin and his sister, Naomi, 19, to a Chicago commercial art school . . . with plenty left over.

The 70-year-old grandfather who last week made a gift of the chess set and clarinet to his grandchildren says, "Leave me out of this. I just wanted the children to have these things before I die."

The chess set, for which the grandfather two years ago refused $8,000, is surrounded by the romance and legend of the Civil war, old England, and perhaps mysterious, silent China. It looks the part.

The story is that Naomi and David's great grandfather acquired the hand carved ivory set from a Union soldier after a raid on a southern plantation during the Civil war.

"For all we know, maybe great grandfather himself lifted the set," says Naomi. "Anyway, great grandfather gave the set to grandfather, and now he has given it to us."

◇ ◇ ◇

Carefully and delicately carved, no two of the chess men are alike. Even the pawns differ minutely from each other. The entire set is

(Continued on Page 2, Col. 1)

'Teach Them a Lesson'

(By Leased Wire)

German Panzer divisions moved into Greece and Jugoslavia at dawn today.

Shortly before, Soviet Russia, whose agreement with Germany had touched off the present war in September, 1939, signed a friendship and non-aggression pact, effective immediately, with JUGOSLAVIA.

◇ ◇ ◇

The announcement of the German attack was made by Nazi Propaganda Minister Paul Joseph Goebbels over Radio Berlin, and was picked up in London.

Joachim von Ribbentrop, Nazi foreign minister, had announced the attack on Jugoslavia to the foreign press at the same time.

A Columbia Broadcasting System resume of Ribbentrop's announcement said:

"England has just prepared a new crime against Europe. England has landed troops in the Balkans after Dunkirk and they are attempting to create a new theater of war.

"A blind government had made a pact with Jugoslavia and has offered military aid against the Reich. Germany always tried to secure friendly relations with Greece and Jugoslavia but all in vain.

"Hitler has announced that since this morning (Sunday) German troops have been marching against the English to teach them a lesson. This will teach them a lesson."

◇ ◇ ◇

A Nazi order of the day, issued to the German army of the east at 5 a. m. (Berlin time), said:

BERLIN — April 6, 1941. —SOLDIERS OF THE SOUTHEAST FRONT—Since early this morning the German people are at war with the Belgrade government of intrigue. We shall only lay down arms when this band of ruffians has been definitely and most emphatically eliminated, and the last Briton has left this part of the European continent, and these misled people realize that they must thank Britain for this situation, they must thank England, the greatest warmonger of all time."

"The German people can enter into this new struggle with the inner satisfaction that its leaders have done everything to bring about a peaceful settlement."

THE ANNOUNCER THEN SAID, ACCORDING TO THE NATIONAL BROADCASTING CO.:

"We pray to God that he may lead our soldiers on the path and bless them as hitherto."

◇ ◇ ◇

Russian Treaty

The Russo-Jugoslav treaty binds the two for five years to pursue a policy of neutrality and "strictest friendship" in the event one of them is attacked, Moscow radio said.

A 5 a. m. Radio Moscow newscast said the treaty was signed in the Soviet capital Saturday "after negotiations which have been taking place in Moscow during the past few days."

The treaty stipulates that Russia and Jugoslavia agree to respect

(Continued on Page 2, Col. 5)

British Halt Axis Rush Into Libya

By WALTER COLLINS

CAIRO —(U.P.)— Britain's desert fighters were reported Saturday night to have stemmed the Axis threat in Libya, east of Benghazi, and pounding imperial columns smashed past Adowa and the vital line of the Awash river in a headlong race for Addis Ababa and complete domination of Italy's East African empire.

A military spokesman said Saturday night that the "remnants" of the forces commanded by Italian Gen. Dismones are falling back upon Addis Ababa after being driven from their defensive positions on the Awash river by a hard-hitting force of South Africans.

Operations in the Middle Eastern sector went forward at breakneck pace as Gen. Sir Archibald Wavell's staff rushed to mop up East Africa in order to turn their full attention to events in other portions of the vast sphere of desert, mountain, and jungle.

◇ ◇ ◇

SATURDAY'S DEVELOPMENTS:

ONE. Italo-German mechanized and armored forces have been halted east of Benghazi and the situation there is now "well in hand."

TWO. The British column which took Asmara has now dashed south, past Adowa, on the road to Addis Ababa. More Italian infantry were captured in addition to nearly 5,000 now held in Eritrea.

THREE. A South African column, hammering up the Addis Ababa railroad, has crossed the Awash river, 97 miles from the Ethiopian capital. This was the best defensive position the Italians had short of Addis Ababa.

The reported halting of the Axis column which has driven 190 miles up the Libyan coast past Benghazi in 10 days was regarded here as the day's most important news.

British forces have been withdrawn from Benghazi and concentrated further east while the Royal Air Force was turned loose in a series of smashing attacks designed to break up the tenuous line of Axis communications that stretches back more than 600 miles to Tripoli.

RAF bombers smashed at Axis troops and motor transport colums and reported that their attack had been most effective, causing a number of fires and explosions.

Other bombers carried out particularly heavy attacks upon Tripoli which is the main base of the new Italo German force.

It was thought here that the Middle East command's laconic statement that the situation was "well in hand" might indicate that Wavell has now chosen the battlefield on which he will meet the new Axis threat. If this is so, a fierce struggle can be expected since Germany is known to have a considerable panzer force in Libya, in addition to dive-bomber squadrons.

They Say Today

"It wouldn't hurt my teacher to come and listen to you." A 10-year-old listener at a geological story hour thinks his instructor "never saw a mastodon or heard of Archie, the earlybird. Page 11.

"We put a city on our approved list of the majority of the community gives our members square treatment." Madison has done that, the national president of the Rambling Hobo Fellowship of America reports. Page 11.

"Serbia is just a combination of a sniper's paradise, a schedule wrecker, and a quartermaster's nightmare." Prof. Robert L. Reynolds isn't surprised the Serbs thumbed their nose at the Axis. War features. Page 9.

"He doesn't know what he's talking about." Rep. Stephen Bolles, Secretary of War Henry Stimson notwithstanding, thinks Camp McCoy is capable of supporting the 32nd division the year-round. Page 6.

"Just as America began with the 13 states, so now may we begin with a nucleus of world democracies and spread to a universal government." Clarence Streit outlines his "union now" nightmare for the dictators. Page 3.

"Bridges a man over many a tight place when his pocketbook is lean." Newspapers of the 1890s found in a cabinet in the old Miner residence expound the benefits of Battle Axe plug. Page 28.

New War Service in Bow Today

In addition to a thorough daily coverage of the war news, The State Journal takes Madison behind the news in an exclusive feature page today.

An interesting, graphic picture service—Telefact — quickly answers war questions, Madison people are given a chance to tell their experiences. And recognized experts relate their inside information.

All on Page 9 today.

Feature Finder

'The Company Is to Blame,' But . . .

Perlman Rebukes Allis Union for 'Dirty Hands'

Strange it is some Americans won't act like Americans. Strange it is some minority groups persist in using tactics which keep them from gaining favorable public opinion and thereby growing into more power.

◇ ◇ ◇

So mused Selig Perlman, University of Wisconsin economist, in a quick glance over the country's labor situation for The State Journal Saturday.

◇ ◇ ◇

There is one big advantage English working men have over their United States brethren, the professor explained. He knows, too, because behind his opinions are years of study of labor, and a recent teaching year in South Wales, England.

"Over there," he declared, **"there is a spontaneous solidarity among working men. There aren't more than 40 or 50 per cent of the workers in unions, but if there is a strike, everyone goes out.**

"They figure they're all Englishmen, you see."

In this country, Perlman noted, there's a case of "all Americans aren't all America." The workers here come from all different sorts of backgrounds and nationalities and environments, and they're much more individualistic.

Now Perlman—frankly enough—is and has been pro-labor. But he doesn't like the way some of the anti-defense strikes have going

Madison Dooms 'The Jungles' and Its Palace

With curtains in its windows, this shack in "The Jungles," on the Fitchburg rd. near Wingra (Murphy's) creek, is above the average living quarters in a squatters' settlement which will be ordered razed by Building Commissioner Gordon E. Nelson.

Near this shack another shanty contained the bodies of William Power and his sister, Margaret, who died of starvation and exposure. The couple had been dead a month to six weeks when their bodies were found March 25.

(More Pictures on Page 2)

OFFICIAL STATE NEWSPAPER—OFFICIAL CITY NEWSPAPER

The Wisconsin State Journal

A fact-finding Newspaper

VOL. 159, NO. 69. 103rd Year | THIS PAPER CONSISTS OF TWO SECTIONS—SECTION ONE | MADISON, MONDAY, DECEMBER 8, 1941 | 22 Pages | Final | Price Three Cents

Weather

Partly cloudy, becoming fair and colder tonight. Minimum about 15 degrees. Tuesday fair, continued cold. Northwest winds tonight, diminishing Tuesday.

Congress Votes War on Japs; Woman Casts Lone 'No' Ballot

Japan Attacks on All Pacific Fronts

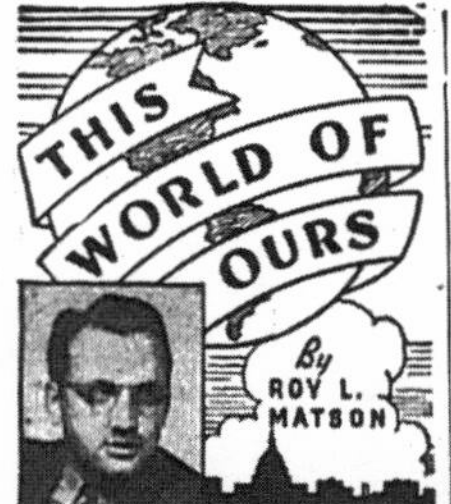

NOW IT IS DIFFERENT.

Now every moment of all your existence is going to be changed. Every word you hear, every word you speak will mean something more than it did before. Every thought in your head, every hope, every fear, will be sharper, strike deeper.

Everything you do, no matter how small, how insignificant it may seem, will be done in a new sense, with new expressions, new implications. Everything that is done to you and for you may be done in the same way, but in a spirit different from any you have known before this Sunday of terror, this Sabbath day the day on which the last flickering of human hopes died in the blinding rays of the rising sun.

You live now in an America at war. Your world from this day is a world of war and a world that can hold nothing more than war.

◇ ◇ ◇

YOU MUST NOT BE afraid.

To be afraid now will be to lose yourself, and, worse, to betray the people and the things for which you live and to which you are pledged.

Your president has told you there is nothing to fear but fear.

You must believe him.

You must have faith — in yourself, in the people, and in the systems sworn to save you and your things, and in something else in which this nation's faith must never be shaken.

◇ ◇ ◇

BUT YOU MUST NOT BE flip and foolishly assured about this thing. It cannot be easy. It will take longer than some people have told you. It will be harder to do and it will be harder to bear than you have imagined in all your months of worrying.

It will be hardest for those who have sons and fathers, husbands and sweethearts in the places of battleships and bombs. For those there must be an awful, nameless terror, a cold fear that is the worse because it challenges the courage and the bravery of those who must feel impotent and helpless in the face of it. The lot of these is heartaches and tears. You must remember these.

But for these and for all the rest of us, it won't all be in heartache and tears. It will be in our food, in our clothing, in our homes, in our pleasures, and in our desires. They will hurt, the big things and the little things, and they won't be any fun. It won't ever be easy to be noble about them. You must bear them, without tears, without a band on your sleeve, without sympathy.

◇ ◇ ◇

BE AS TOLERANT AS YOU can.

It will be difficult, almost impossible, for anyone to tell you where tolerance ends and comfort for the enemy begins. Remember only that your country is at war and that in war the values, the good and the evil you have always known, must change.

You will be taught to hate . . . and you must hate. You must love certain things more, but you must hate different things, bitterly and completely and enough to affirm your love of the others.

◇ ◇ ◇

YOU MUST LEARN TO pray, whether you have a religion, a church, a creed, a faith—or only yourself and a cold, confident certainty in the strength of humans alone.

But you must remember, as you pray, that other peoples have prayed, all around the world, and have made their soul-deep vows again and again. And yet, without common, earthly steel and iron, without guns and tanks and planes and shells, their prayers have turned to sobs, hopeless, empty, futile.

You must be realistic.

◇ ◇ ◇

ON THIS SUNDAY NIGHT, the capital of this nation—the proud, bright Washington of the United States of America—has been darkened and blotted in a blackout, last land of democracy, last land of the world where the lights have gone out.

This is sad, too. This is unbelievable, inconceivable. It cannot be true. And it shall not be true, it shall not be this way . . . if you keep the faith, if you can remember that this world is not yours, but that you are this world's.

If these are yours to do and to be done, the lights may shine again.

Help It Grow

EMPTY STOCKING CLUB

Previously Reported	$994.06
Middleton Woman's Club	2.00
Swan Creek Sewing Circle	5.00
Ruste School Mothers' Club	5.00
Individual Gifts	37.00
TOTALS	$1,043.06

Britain Enters; 1,500 Killed, U. S. Admits

By JOE ALEX MORRIS
(United Press Foreign News Editor)

The United States and Britain smashed back at Japan today on a 6,000-mile Pacific war front that flamed from Hawaii's coral beaches to the jungle shores of Malay and Thailand.

The American battle fleet was reported challenging the Japanese striking force which raided Hawaii with heavy loss of life and naval damage. A great naval engagement was rumored in the waters west of America's Pacific gibraltar.

Nine Nations Join U. S. in War

Besides the United States, these countries have made formal declarations of war against Japan:

Great Britain, Canada, Netherlands East Indies, Costa Rica, Australia, Nicaragua, China, Haiti, and Honduras.

◇ ◇ ◇

Here is the picture:

LONDON: Prime Minister Winston Churchill carries Britain into war against Japan with a formal declaration before parliament.

TOKYO: Japanese naval command claims sinking of U. S. battleships Oklahoma and West Virginia; damage to four other battleships; damage to four heavy cruisers; heavy destruction of U. S. planes; probable sinking of U. S. aircraft carrier (rumored to be the Langley); capture of "many" enemy ships; sinking of U. S. minesweeper Penguin at Guam.

HAWAII: White House reports 3,000 casualties, including 1,500 fatalities, in Japanese air attack; loss of "old" American battleship and destroyer.

WASHINGTON: American battle fleet carrying out sweeping operations and has destroyed "a number of" Japanese

(Continued on Page Two)

. . . Japan unleashes its fury . . .

'One and Indivisible'

(An Editorial)

It's a World war now.

The anticipation of army and navy authorities, the state department, and the White House that inevitably if we did not go to war, the war would come to us, has been fulfilled.

The administration's international policy of aid to Britain and domestic preparedness was almost an act of God. Japan would have struck its blow with less hesitancy and with tremendously greater effect had not the program of aiding democracies advanced our defense production to a point where it at least is becoming formidable.

The expectation of what happened on Sunday must have been in the minds of the men who, against serious opposition, started the two-ocean navy program. It was belated, but at least it is well under way. News from the east is very bad, and probably it will be worse before it gets better. The treacherous attack had been long and well planned, and while it had been feared, the element of surprise lent power to the Japanese arms. Probably damage already done will not be easily and quickly repaired.

That Mussolini and Hitler instigated the ambush goes without saying. It was the Hitler philosophy, the Hitler technique. Whether or not they or we declare war will make no difference in the inevitable sequence. They will strike us on sea and land wherever the opportunity exists.

The first essential is American solidarity. The vigorous and honest differences of opinion between administration leaders and the isolationists must be forgotten. It must be treated as though it had never existed. There should be no post mortems.

The beginning of this policy and the effectuation of this philosophy came from the right source to be effective. The Chicago Tribune, leading isolationist newspaper and champion of "America First," paved the way when it said in the front page editorial:

"America faces war through no volition of any American . . . . Recriminations are useless . . . . All of us, from this day forth, have only one task. That is to strike with all our might to protect and preserve the American freedom that we all hold dear."

Sen. Burton K. Wheeler, isolationist leader in congress, voices the same sentiments, emphasizing them with the declaration that our job is "to give them hell."

The American oath of allegiance will be every American's bible from this time on:

"I pledge allegiance to the flag of the United States of America,
And to the Republic for which it stands,
One nation indivisible, with liberty and justice for all."

Here's the A-B-C of Pacific WarStrength

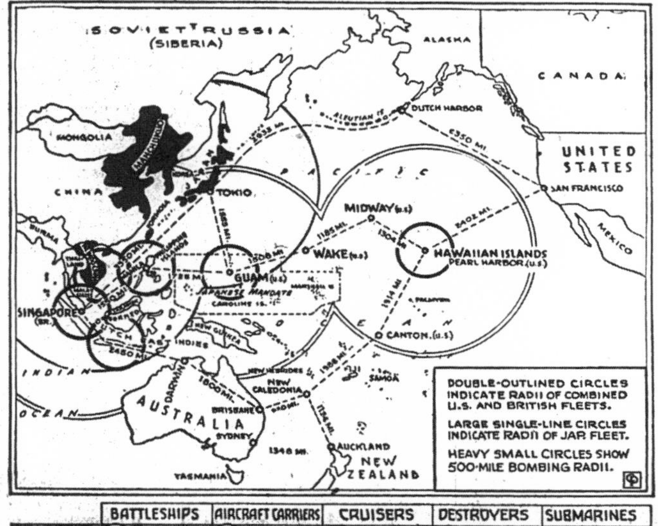

	BATTLESHIPS		AIRCRAFT CARRIERS		CRUISERS		DESTROYERS		SUBMARINES	
		BUILDING		BUILDING		BUILDING		BUILDING		BUILDING
UNITED STATES	17	15	7	11	37	54	170	192	113	73
IAPAN	10	8	8	2	46	10	125	11	71	7

The map above gives at a glance the military situation into which Japan sailed today with her bombers and battleships. Within these spheres she faces the A-B-C-D foes — Australian, British, Chinese, and Dutch. The chart beneath the map shows present and potential naval strengths of the United States and Japan.

First List of Casualties

BULLETIN

Mr. and Mrs. John L. Fletcher, Janesville, were advised by the United States war department today that their son, John, 32, was killed in the bombing and machine gunning of Wheeler field, Hawaii, Sunday. Mr. and Mrs. Thomas Plant, Wausau, learned that their son, Donald, 22, died of "gunshot wounds" at Ft. Shafter, Hawaii.

(By United Press)

The first United States casualties in the Japanese attacks were revealed today in word sent to the parents of the victims by the navy department.

The dead:

First Lt. Hans Christiansen, 21, Woodland, Calif.

Second Lt. George A. Whiteman, 21, Sedalia, Mo.

Private George C. Leslie, 20, Arnold, Pa.

Private Peter Niedzwiecki, Grand Rapids, Mich.

Private Dean W. Cebert, Galesburg, Ill.

Former Track Star Believed on Hit Ship

MILWAUKEE — (U.P.) — Joseph M. Doherty, 26, former Marquette university track star, and Richard Schulz, 18, Milwaukee, were believed by friends and relatives here to have been members of the crew of the U. S. West Virginia, which was reported sunk by Japanese war plan in their attack on Pearl Harbor Sunday.

MANILA BOMBARDED

NEW YORK — (U.P.) — The National Broadcasting co's correspondent at Manila reported today that "Manila is now under Japanese bombardment."

Stunned City Counts Men in Pacific Area; Prepares Defense

War in the Pacific today struck at Madison's heartstrings.

The city has men in the air, on the ground, and at sea in the far eastern area where the Japanese attacked Sunday.

It has men at home who will go in America's resistance of the Nipponese.

It has problems of defense within its own borders and city police and county sheriff departments redoubled efforts to protect Madison industry from sabotage.

On Pages 4, 5, and 7 of today's State Journal are reports of this city at war, gathered from all the Journal's widespread news sources. They include:

Police Chief William H. McCormick and Sheriff Edward Fischer promised extra protection for industrial plants, with perhaps no more men assigned to guard duty, but greater and more frequent checking than at any time since 1917-18. The Gisholt Machine co., Madison-Kipp corp., and the Scanlan-Morris co., especially, will be watched extra carefully. All are active in producing for defense.

Hospital Unit Ready

Japan's attack brought renewed readiness from the Wisconsin General hospital unit No. 44, an affiliate of the United States army medical corps. Its 37 members, from doctors to nurses, are ready to move immediately wherever ordered.

The unit has been organized here for about a year. Dr. F. L. Weston is in charge.

At least 83 Madison and Madison area men are with the United States navy in the Pacific, perhaps already afloat on their way toward the Philippines.

They left Dec. 17, 1940. Some of them were back in the city hardly more than a fortnight ago, on leave. Lt. D. B. Poupeney, Stoughton, headed the unit, which originally went on the U. S. S. Fox for patrol duty between Seattle and Alaska. Since then, members have been transferred to other cruisers and destroyers, whose locations now are official naval secrets.

Many Affected Here

When Japan struck, Secretary of War Henry L. Stimson ordered the entire United States army into uniform. That affected a score of

(Continued on Page 9)

Tell Us of Sabotage, Boyle Asks Citizens

U. S. Dist. Atty. John J. Boyle announced today his office would be open 24 hours a day and he urged Madison residents to be on the alert for any evidence of sabotage.

Boyle asked persons who are unable to contact the Federal Bureau of Investigation to call him at his office in the federal building with any reports of sabotage or acts against the government.

U. S. Censors Military News

Capital Speeds All-Out Plans

WASHINGTON — (U.P.) — The government today censored publication of military information in this country and all cable and radio messages originating in the United States and her outlying possessions.

The army, navy, Federal Communications Commission, treasury, and postoffice department suppressed information that might be

(Continued on Page Two)

Feature Finder

FDR Pledges Triumph Over Invaders

By LYLE C. WILSON

WASHINGTON —(U.P.)— Congress today proclaimed existence of a state of war between the United States and the Japanese empire 33 minutes after the dramatic moment when President Roosevelt stood before a joint session to pledge that "we will triumph—so help us, God."

Democracy was proving its right to a place in the sun with a split second shiftover from peace to all-out war.

The senate acted first, adopting the resolution by a unanimous roll call vote of 82 to 0, within 21 minutes after the president had concluded his address to a joint session of both houses.

The house voted immediately afterward and by 1:13 p. m. a majority of the house had voted "ayes."

The final house vote was announced as 388 to 1. The lone negative vote was cast by Rep. Jeannette Rankin, (R., Mont.), who also voted against entry into World War 1.

The resolution now has to be signed by Speaker Sam Rayburn and Vice President Henry A. Wallace before it is sent to the president at the White House. His signature will place the United States formally at war against the Japanese empire, already an accomplished fact.

Text of the war resolution:

"Declaring that a state of war exists between the Imperial Japanese government and the government and the people of the United States and making provision to prosecute the same:

"Whereas the Imperial Japanese government has committed unprovoked acts of war against the government and the people of the United States of America; therefore, be it

"Resolved by the senate and house of representatives of the United States of America in congress assembled, that the state of war between the United States and the Imperial Japanese government which has thus been thrust upon the United States is hereby formally declared; and the president is hereby authorized and directed to employ the entire naval and military forces of the United States and the resources of the government to carry on war against the Imperial Japanese government; and, to bring the conflict to a successful termination, all of the resources of the country are hereby pledged by the congress of the United States."

The resolution was before both

(Continued on Page Two)

BULLETIN

WASHINGTON — (U.P.) — Congressional leaders will take the war resolution to the White House for the president's signature at 4 p. m. today, the White House announced.

JEANNETTE RANKIN
. . . *she voted no* . . .

Bulletins

Nazis Quit Moscow Aim

BERLIN — (U.P.) — A Nazi military spokesman said today Germany had abandoned all attempts to capture Moscow for this winter.

The military spokesman said that large scale operations by Germany on the eastern front have been ended for this winter.

Moscow, he said flatly "will not be captured before spring."

He said the early start of the severe Russian winter caused the Germans to make this decision.

JAP TROOP SHIPS SUNK

SAN FRANCISCO —(U.P.)— The Singapore radio heard by a United Press listening post here today reported that two American-built Hudson bombers operating off the northern Malayan coast had scored direct hits on two Japanese troop ships and another bomber had scored a direct hit on a barge loaded with Japanese soldiers.

ALASKA ON WATCH

JUNEAU, Alaska —(U.P.)— Gov. Ernest Gruening today placed the entire territory of Alaska on 24-hour watch for protection of radio stations, telephone exchanges, oil tanks, public utilities, and docks. Naval forces in the area previously had been ordered to duty.

AEF CHANGE PLANNED

WASHINGTON — (U.P.) — Chairman Andrew May (Dem., Ky.) of the house military affairs committee, said today the committee will meet Tuesday to frame legislation to repeal restrictions of the selective service and national guard acts forbidding the use of those troops outside the western hemisphere.

FBI SEIZES 736 JAPS

WASHINGTON — (U.P.) — Atty. Gen. Francis Biddle announced today that Federal Bureau of Investigation agents had seized 736 Japanese nationals in the United States and in the Hawaiian islands Sunday night.

NETHERLANDS AT WAR

LONDON — (U.P.) — Queen Wilhelmina said today the kingdom of the Netherlands considers itself at war with Japan and puts all of its military and power resources at disposal of the common war effort.

HONDURAS WARS ON JAPS

TEGUCIGALPA, Honduras —(U.P.)—The congress of Honduras, by a unanimous vote, declared war on Japan today, and ordered martial law for the duration of the war.

NAVY WARNS AIRCRAFT

SAN FRANCISCO —(U.P.)— The navy announced Sunday night that effective at once, "all aircraft flying over navy stations other than naval air

(Continued on Page Two)

OFFICIAL STATE NEWSPAPER—OFFICIAL CITY NEWSPAPER

The Wisconsin State Journal

A fact-finding Newspaper

VOL. 159, NO. 72. 103rd Year | THIS PAPER CONSISTS OF TWO SECTIONS—SECTION ONE | MADISON, THURSDAY, DECEMBER 11, 1941 | 28 Pages | Final | Price Three Cents

Weather

Cloudy and warmer, occasional snow tonight and Friday. Increasing southeast winds.

U. S. at War With Nazis, Italy

Bomber Sinks Jap Warship

THE WOES OF WAR ARE so many, the burdens to bear so great that you want to seize and exploit the slightest item that may be called good and in any way attributable to the things that have made the woe as well.

Maybe it is ridiculous, but three or four times in the past two nights I've had to poke my eyeballs back into their sockets over a sight I haven't seen in years and which I have concluded may be credited to the attack o. Pearl Harbor.

That is the old and I thought perished practice of gentlemen arising to offer women their seats upon a crowded bus. I saw it happen, three or four times, and I was amazed .nd deeply impressed.

◊ ◊ ◊

NOW, OFFHAND AND EVEN with a little thought you might expect people to be even more preoccupied with heavy thoughts than ever before. You might express no wonder at finding them a little more sour, slightly snappier, increasingly inconsiderate toward their neighbors, more bitter and meaner to the whole world.

But, strangely, it hasn't worked out that way around here since last Sunday. I think you may see in a hundred ways how people suddenly have been drawn closer together, how they have forgotten their small complaints against someone else, their inclination to blame another for their own troubles and to take their worries out, in nasty little ways, on the rest of the world.

◊ ◊ ◊

THIS BIGGER WORRY, this tragedy that is everyone's has made a strong and broad bond. It has made almost everyone want to do something for somebody else as well as himself. It has made people open their eyes and look around for ways to be helpful and decent and kind.

That is one reason why there is going to be enough money for Herbie Strand's leg. That is one reason why, despite high taxes and defense bonds, the Empty Stocking club still figures it will get enough money to give every child here an honest Christmas.

And I think that is one reason, silly as it may sound, and awful as the price has been, why the gentlemen, whether they know it or no, again are arising and mumbling the unfamiliar, **"Seat, lady?"**

◊ ◊ ◊

WAR FOR AMERICA PROBably will change another national and annoying habit, too. Of course, someone ought to have changed it a long time ago with some sound whacking of the britches attached to the young and thoughtless smartalecks who boo and hiss every time the flag flies across the newsreel screen or the camera shows a shot of the U. S. navy ploughing the seas or the army on the march.

No, they never really meant it. But someone must have given them the idea that it was a smart thing to do. I trust someone or something will have given them another idea by now that it is a thing that would be twice as smart not to do.

◊ ◊ ◊

SOMEBODY SOUNDED some good advice yesterday, though, when he cautioned citizens not to let the war uproot them too severely from their daily lives and habits. It will be best for everyone concerned if all of us stick to our jobs, work hard and faithfully at them until we're told what better work we may do.

I have heard a great many people say they can't keep interested in the ordinary things about them any more. A woman said it was hard right now to imagine that just a few days ago she was thinking about the pretty things, the fluffy, luxurious things she had wanted for Christmas.

The lady has the right idea probably, but you can't let it carry you too far.

◊ ◊ ◊

YOU CAN'T FOR INSTANCE, let yourself forget entirely about parking meters, pinball machines and slot machines. The government is going to stop alloting materials for the last-named, Atty. Gen. John Martin has said the middle-mentioned are illegal **(and we'll soon see what happens about that)**, and the stuff that goes into the first-signified might better be turned to the materials of defense.

Those are :.nall items, too, but they look like good and bright possibilities—if not probabilities—from this distance, which, we still may hope, isn't far.

Luzon Situation Well in Hand, Stimson Declares

BULLETIN

WASHINGTON—(U.P.)—The navy announced today that the defending marine garrison on Wake island has sunk one Japanese light cruiser and one destroyer by air action.

The garrison has defended the island in the south Pacific against four separate attacks in the last 48 hours by enemy aircraft and one by light naval units.

The Japanese were expected to resume the attack and attempt a landing.

(By United Press)

Secretary of War Henry L. Stimson announced today that a United States bombing plane had sunk a 29,000-ton Japanese battleship and asserted that the situation was completely in hand in the fight against a Japanese attempt to invade the Philippines.

Later army communiques, indicating an increasingly favorable United States position, said a Japanese detachment which landed near Lingayen on the west coast of Luzon island was being disposed of in mopping up operations and that interceptor planes had driven off a Japanese bombing formation which brought a noon air raid alarm to Manila.

Stimson told a press conference that the office of naval

Scene of Most Action

intelligence had just "confirmed the sinking by army bombers of the 29,000-ton Japanese battleship Haruna off Luzon."

Launched in 1913

The Haruna was launched Dec. 14, 1913. Its standard displacement was 29,330 tons and it carried a crew of 980. Its overall length was 704 feet.

Its armament, according to Janes "Fighting Ships," included a main battery of eight 14-inch guns; 16 6-inch; eight 5-inch anti-aircraft, four machine guns, and four landing rifles. It has four submerged torpedo tubes.

The battleship, first major Japanese casualty, burst into flames and sunk after three direct bomb hits off the northern coast of Luzon island and was left blazing fiercely.

Besides the direct hits, the American bombing plane dropped two bombs close to its sides.

The Manila Tribune reported that an American tank ship was sunk during Wednesday's Japanese raids on Manila and that one American and one British freighter were damaged. Several seamen were killed and at least 24 wounded, the Tribune said.

The Tribune reported 15 Japanese planes shot down in Wednesday's raids, the Manila Bulletin nine.

The Tribune reported 30 civilians killed and 250 wounded in all. The Bulletin reported 37 killed and 46 wounded in the Pasay suburb alone and said at least 140 wounded were brought to Manila from the Cavite naval base.

The Bulletin reported that two Catholic priests had been arrested at San Fernando, in Pampanga province, for alleged fifth column activities.

The Bulletin asserted also

(Cont. on Page 2, Col. 5)

Carriers to Sell Defense Stamps

130 Journal Boys Join Drive Jan. 1

Beginning Jan. 1, an army of 130 Wisconsin State Journal carrier boys will act as official United States agents for the sale of defense stamps.

This announcement is being made by The State Journal in answer to a request received from the treasury department to enlist newspaper carriers as defense stamp agents. The nation wide campaign will start Jan. 1 when carrier boys will solicit their subscribers for defense stamps which the boys will deliver and collect for each Saturday.

This project is being conducted

(Cont. on Page 2, Col. 6)

Feature Finder

Tire Stores Here Have No Order to Halt Sales

Madison tire merchants reported to The State Journal late this afternoon that they had received no notice of the new tire sale prohibition issud Wednesday by Priorities Director Donald Nelson.

The sales ban prohibits all sales of new auto tires "except for top defense orders," between today and Dec. 22. The order is designed to stop a consumers' buying wave which broke out after the Japaneses attack on American territory, Nelson announced:

'Eternal Vigilance'

(An Editorial)

Rep. John D. Dingell (D., Mich.) is clamoring for a resolution which would order a court martial of naval officers in America's Pacific squadron.

We believe that Rep. Dingell should be court martialled, or perhaps the word is impeached.

This is no time for cheap political advertising, and no patriotic and level-headed member of congress would impose court martial with no information as to the facts.

Dingell's outburst occurred on Tuesday. Wednesday's news brought official information that the Prince of Wales and another capital British battleship had been sunk.

At least we had the excuse that as a nation long at peace, we had few if any members of any arm of the service experienced in actual combat.

But there is no such excuse for the British. They have been fighting long and hard, on land and sea and in the air, and their losses were more damaging than our own. We lost a capital ship, they lost two, and the consequences were the same as they would have been if all three had been line ships in the American navy.

If there was delinquency on the part of our Far Eastern admiralty, the matter should be taken in hand at once. But justice is as important as liberty in the American concept. We want a quick, thorough and competent investigation of what has happened, but we do not want to prejudge the matter. We American journalists, for the most part, can only assert those laymen's opinions formed from the sidelines, and the question that has been raised in our mind as most vital is whether we have been and are producing the right sort of weapons.

There has long been a conflict of opinion in the navy as between line battleships and fast, small cruisers and pocket battleships. If the lesson taught us so far is conclusive, our production should go into this type of warboat, and into airplanes, aircraft carriers, submarines, and destroyers.

Please note that we and the British have lost three capital ships, none of which was struck by a gun fired by an enemy ship. The air bombers and submarines did the job.

To reach a proper conclusion we must learn many things. Are the men actually in command of our navy the most competent the navy affords? Is our whole building program at variance with the practicabilities of modern warfare? Was our Eastern naval authority in readiness, in alertness for the attack which it might well have presumed might come at any moment?

We must draw, not only upon our best army and navy authorities, but upon our scientists. We have examples here at home. The smoke screen was devised by Prof. Burgess of the University of Wisconsin and of the Burgess Laboratories. The submarine detector was invented by Prof. Max Mason of the University of Wisconsin.

But out of it all one lesson seems to have been emphatically taught. There should be unified command. Another lesson is that there are no Sundays in war.

President Roosevelt should take the bull by the horns in this situation. Impulsive diatribes are out of order. A swift but deliberate and searching analysis of the whole situation is imperatively demanded. Only by such a step can the confidence of the American people in its armed forces be sustained, because the questions raised are on every tongue in the nation.

"Eternal vigilance is the price of liberty."

Lost to Badgers?

PAT HARDER

Harder, 3 Other Grid Stars Visit Recruiting Office

Recruiting activity continued lively at Madison army and marine stations in the federal building today when considerable numbers of university and high school students were among the applicants for enlistment or sought information.

Among the University of Wis-

(Cont. on Page 2, Col. 7)

Bulletins

British Far East Fleet Chief Lost

SINGAPORE— (U.P.) —Sir Tom Philips, commander-in-chief of Britain's Far Eastern fleet, is missing in the Prince of Wales-Repulse disaster, an official communique said today. Sir Geoffrey Layton was named temporary commander of the Far Eastern fleet.

U. S. Reporters Held in Nazi Reprisal

WASHINGTON—(U.P.)—The state department announced today that it has received word that American correspondents in Germany are being held in custody in a villa at Wannsee, a suburb of Berlin, and will be released coincident with the release of German correspondents held by United States officials.

AUTO QUOTAS CUT

WASHINGTON — (U.P.) — Civilian Supply Director Leon Henderson today announced new drastic reductions in passenger automobile production quotas for this month and January. The December quota is to be about 60 per cent below the corresponding production last year and the January quota 75 per cent less than in January, 1941.

BRITISH SAVE 2,330

LONDON —(U.P.)— The admiralty reported tonight that approximately 2,330 officers and men have been saved from the sunken battleships, Prince of Wales and Repulse.

Duce Wins Race to Tell World; Hitler Admits Africa Loss

(By Leased Wire)

Premier Benito Mussolini was the first to inform the American people they were at war with Germany and Italy as well as Japan.

His balcony speech to 100,000 cheering Italians wasted no time declaring war. It was heard in the United States shortly after 6 a. m. (CST). He promised his people victory and stated it was a privilege to fight beside Germany and Japan.

First official German notice of a war declaration came from Hans Thomsen, German charge d'affaires in Washington. He brought the report to the state department at 8:15 a. m. He had telephoned Secretary of State Cordell Hull of the developments during the night.

Meanwhile, Adolf Hitler, suffering from a cold and unable to arouse his voice to its full shrill pitch, was reviewing the entire war developments in a speech to his Reichstag.

Hitler's speech was still being recorded in the United States as Mussolini and Thomsen made their announcements.

Hitler admitted momentary defeat in Africa, a lull on the Russion front because of bitter cold, told of Europe's impregnable defenses and then launched into a comparison of himself and President Roosevelt, blaming Roosevelt and Woodrow Wilson for the troubles with Germany. He expressed no ill feeling toward the United States but promised Germany would deal out the first blow as it has done throughout its two years of hostilities.

Finally, Hitler got to the war declaration and announced he had ordered passports to be given the United States representative in Berlin.

Berlin then explained Foreign Minister Joachim von Ribbentrop made the formal declaration on behalf of Germany at noon (4 a. m. CST) in a note to the American charge d'affaires.

Hitler

ADOLF HITLER

BERLIN—(German Radio Recorded by United Press at New York)—Germany and her Axis partner, Italy today declared war on the United States.

Foreign Minister Joachim von Ribbentrop made the formal declaration on behalf of Germany at noon (4 a. m. CST) in a note handed to the American charge d'affairs in Berlin.

Adolf Hitler in a speech later before the Nazi reichstag announced that "I today gave the order that the passports shall be given to the American ambassador (sic) in Berlin."

Germany and Italy, Hitler told the reichstag, are honoring their obligations under the tri-power military alliance and coming to the aid of Japan "in the struggle forced upon her."

The association of Germany, Italy and Japan, proclaimed the fuehrer, will last "at least as long as the war lasts."

◊ ◊ ◊

Among the reasons Hitler listed for his declaration against America was that it planned to attack Ger-

(Cont. on Page 2, Col. 4)

Mussolini

BENITO MUSSOLINI

ROME— (U.P.) —(Radio Rome recorded in Bern by United Press) —Premier Benito Mussolini declared war on the United States today in a speech before a 100,000 cheering Italians from the balcony of his Venice palace.

"Fascist Italy and National Socialist Germany have allied themselves with Japan in a war against the United States of America," he said.

"We shall bring you victory."

"This is a great day in the history of the continent of Europe," Mussolini continued.

"Italy and her ally Germany together with Japan enter the war against the United States.

"One hundred and fifty million men are resolute to do everything to reach final victory.

"We shall wage war in order to conquer.

"After an infinite series of provocations the Japanese have struck in the Pacific and have achieved great victories.

"It is a privilege to fight at their sides.

"The tri-partite pact (the German - Italian - Japanese alliance,

(Cont. on Page 2, Col. 6)

Congress Votes AEF for FDR; Draft May Hit 18-64 Group

WASHINGTON — (U.P.) — The senate and house today swiftly passed legislation permitting President Roosevelt to use American troops anywhere in the world in prosecution of the war against the Axis.

The measure enables dispatch of United States armed forces to battle zones anywhere in the world and provides that terms of service shall extend until the end of the war and for six months thereafter.

Acting immediately after they had passed resolutions declaring a state of war exists with Germany and Italy, the two houses voted the measure which permits selectees to fight outside the western hemisphere.

The senate approved the guard bill 86 to 0, and shortly thereafter the house passed it by a voice vote.

Sen. Hiram W. Johnson, (R., California), who blocked passage of the bill Wednesday withdrew his objection in the light of "the two momentous events which have entirely changed my purpose," the existence of war with Germany and Italy.

Sen. David I. Walsh, (D., Mass.), announced that 50,000 selective service personnel soon would be taken into the navy.

Brig. Gen. Lewis, B. Hershey director of selective service, said today that it might be desirable eventually to register all men between the ages of 18 and 64, inclusive, for military service, civilian defense, and other purposes.

Hershey made it clear, however, that he did not expect any abrupt

(Cont. on Page 2, Col. 3)

Four Cherry Trees Cut Down at Capital

WASHINGTON — (U.P.) — The capital's famed Japanese cherry trees, mecca of tourists from all over the world, today were a casualty of the war in the far east.

Four were chopped down Tuesday night. The vandals attached to one stump a note saying:

"To hell with those Japanese."

Help! Help!

EMPTY STOCKING CLUB	
Previously Reported	$1,336.06
Henry L. Quentmeyer Auxiliary, USWV	3.00
Faustina Club	2.00
Silver Springs Community Club	2.00
Orton Park Christmas Tree Fund	3.00
Individual Gifts	2.00
Total	$1,348.06

Unanimously, Congress Votes 'Long Expected'

Nations May Race for Atlantic Islands; East Coast Guarded

BULLETIN

WASHINGTON — (U.P.) — President Roosevelt today signed declarations of war with Germany and Italy.

By LYLE C. WILSON

WASHINGTON —(U.P.)—The United States today went to war against Germany and Italy, making it an all-out battle against the Axis, including Japan.

President Roosevelt sent to congress his second war message within 70 hours and the legislators snapped through resolutions recognizing existence of hostilities with Germany and Italy.

Notification of German and Italian declarations of war against the United States reached the state department, respectively, at 9:25 and 9:50 a. m., EST, today.

Congress received Mr. Roosevelt's message at 12:24 p. m., and adopted appropriate war resolutions by 1:04 p. m.

"The long known and the long expected has thus taken place,"

The Lineups

THE ALLIES

United States, Great Britain, Canada, Australia, New Zealand, China, Costa Rica, Panama, Nicaragua, El Salvador, Honduras, Haiti, Dominican Republic, Guatemala, South Africa, Cuba, Free France, Greece, Netherlands East Indies, Belgium, and Poland.

THE AXIS

Germany, Japan, Italy, and Manchukuo.

the president told congress in a message read separately by clerks in each house.

"The forces endeavoring to enslave the entire world are now moving toward this hemisphere."

We went to war unanimously this time. There were no dissenting votes to either war resolution, although Rep. Jeannette Rankin (R., Mont.) voted "present" instead of

(Cont. on Page 2, Col. 1)

Drive Planned Against Pinballs

County Sets Friday Deadline

A drive against illegal pinball machines was planne. today by Sheriff Edward Fische Mayor Law, and Chief of Police William H. McCormick.

Fischer set Friday as the deadline for removal of all illegal pinball machines from Dane county.

An opinion by Atty. Gen. John E. Martin Wednesday declared that machines which pay off in free games were gambling devices and illegal.

Fischer warned:

"In view of an opinion by the attorney general that all pinball machines giving tokens or free games are gambling devices, I have ordered that they must be out of the county by Friday at Midnight. Otherwise the machines will be picked up and the owners prosecuted."

Ald. Harold A. Johnson, fifth ward announced today, that on Friday night he will introduce an ordinance in the common council to prohibit licensing of pinball machines in Madison.

Chief H. McCormick announced he had requested pinball machine owners to take off the mechanical device that gives players free plays.

According to the chief's order the machines can be retained in taverns, drugstores and other licensed business places if the free pay mechanism is eliminated.

They are 327 pinball machines licensed in Madison. The license year expires Jan. 1.

The Johnson ordinance will be referred to a committee and reported back to the council Dec. 26.

OFFICIAL STATE NEWSPAPER—OFFICIAL CITY NEWSPAPER

The Wisconsin State Journal

A fact-finding Newspaper

VOL. 159, NO. 76. 103rd Year | THIS PAPER CONSISTS OF TWO SECTIONS—SECTION ONE | MADISON, MONDAY, DECEMBER 15, 1941 | 16 Pages | Final | Price Three Cents

Weather

Cloudy tonight and Tues day. Rather mild Tuesday. Probable fog. Moderate southerly winds.

2,729 Killed in Hawaii, Knox Says

"Most earnestly I urge my countrymen to reject all rumors. These ugly little hints of complete disaster fly thick and fast in wartime. They have to be examined and appraised."

◇ ◇ ◇

THE PEOPLE OF AMERICA heard the president of the United States speak those words to them last Tuesday night . . . and then, I guess, they all promptly yawned and went to bed.

At least, they haven't paid much attention to his solemn pleading on any day since. The telephone bells in The State Journal news room are wearing thin and everybody who answers one has to guard against saying, before he's spoken to, **"No, ma'am, it isn't true."**

◇ ◇ ◇

No one can blame anyone for being anxious in these times. But our very anxiety and impatience is making things 10 times tougher for our nerves than we need make them and we're shagging ourselves into a situation that must make the Unhon. Hirohito rub his small yellow hands in unhon. satisfaction and the Unholy Hitler tweak his mustache in glee.

They like it that way. They want us to be wild-eyed and uncertain, panicky, alarmed, and alarming. They want us to believe the most awful, the most discouraging, and the most outlandish things about ourselves that the rumor factories can produce.

And they can produce some dandies.

◇ ◇ ◇

AND ALL LAST WEEK THEY turned them out . . . and all of them found a ready market here. The telephones rang incessantly.

"How many killed in New York?"

"None, madam."

"But I heard . . ."

"Do you know that the entire East high school senior class has marched down to the recruiting station in a body to enlist?"

"No, sir, we have checked on that. It isn't true . . ."

"But a fellow told me . . ."

"Is it true the government is going to start drafting girls next week?"

"No, ma'am, that is not true."

"Well, my neighbor said a friend told her . . ."

"Why don't you publish the facts about 10,000 soldier boys dying of scarlet fever (sometimes smallpox, sometimes diphtheria, sometimes hard drilling) **in Camp So-and-So. Every night they ship out 400 or 500 coffins. . . ."**

"Madam, that is an old, old war rumor. It comes up a dozen times in every war. If it were true, we would publish it, you may be assured. It is not true."

"Well, I know it is true. I know a lady in our club who had a letter from a friend in Iowa who heard . . ."

"Are they still bombing New York?"

"New York has not been bombed. We have received dozens of telephone calls in the past hour about this. Where did you hear it, sir?"

"Well, my wife called me. She said she heard it on the radio."

"It is not true."

"Well, why would they have it on the radio then?"

◇ ◇ ◇

Well, maybe it was on the radio . . . on short wave from Germany or Japan. And yet there are people who prefer to get themselves steamed up over the obvious lies of the enemy, put out to steam them up, rather than the careful reporting of American newsgatherers.

Don't for the sake of yourself and your country, give these things half a second's thought . . . but keep calling us if you're in any doubt.

◇ ◇ ◇

WE HAVE HEARD COMplaints, too, about the lack of specific information on certain events of last week. Believe us, these people are no more anxious to hear every shred of the news than we are to give it to them.

But on some things we shall have to wait. We must remember that this is war and that makes everything different. We want to know exactly what happened at Pearl Harbor last Sunday. But there are some people who want to know even more than we do . . . the Japanese and the Germans. If we were to tell the enemy every detail (which we would be doing if we made the details public), the enemy would know exactly what its next step should be. As long as the enemy is doubtful, he is uncertain and we have him at a disadvantage. Try to remember that when you get impatient and angry.

◇ ◇ ◇

MEANWHILE, DON'T ENcourage, don't keep alive the nasty rumors. One of our own correspondents sent us a confidential memo the other morning from a small city near Madison.

"You may want to check this

(Cont. on Page 2, Col. 5)

35 Register As County Defense Office Opens

Three Organizations Offer Help During First 90 Minutes

Dane county residents began lining up for home defense jobs today.

Thirty-five individuals registered for volunteer activities during the first hour and a half the recruiting center at 10 S. Webster st. was in operation. The office, located next to the police station in former quarters of the city relief department, will be open until 8 tonight and from 9 a. m. to 8 p. m. daily.

John T. Drechsler, 1632 Monroe st., and Mrs. Edith B. Fleeton, 804½ Chandler st., were the first persons to sign up. Three organizations, the Dane County Pharmaceutical assn., chapter 42 of the Wisconsin State Employes assn., and Sea Scout ship 501, registered their members as a body.

Returns 'Satisfactory'

Early returns were satisfactory, said Frank W. Starkweather, who is directing the recruiting bureau for the Dane County council of Defense. A. M. Lockard was assisting with registration today, and Starkweather plans to organize a governing body to help enroll volunteers and to assist in the office.

Most of those registered this morning expressed willingness to do any type of volunteer work "for which I'm needed." When the civilian defense program is completely organized, men and women will be needed in the city and county as firefighters, air raid wardens, spotters, radio assistants, first aid workers, clerical workers, and in many other capacities. The program to be followed here was outlined by the national Office of Civilian Defense for all American communities.

Chairmen Appointed

More men than women registered during the first 90 minutes, and the group included machinists, stenographers, housewives, business men, and a clergyman. A fifth of the first 35 volunteers were members of The Wisconsin State Journal staff.

Further progress was made in the city and county defense planning with the appointment of chairmen for planning protection, health and welfare, service and supplies, publicity, and aviation committees Saturday.

Meanwhile civilian programs were being organized rapidly throughout the state and nation. About 800 Milwaukee Boy Scouts pledged assistance, and Mayor Carl Zeidler planned to mobilize 11,000 city employes for civilian tasks in Milwaukee.

The Wisconsin Petroleum assn. suggested that the state's 7,000 filling stations be turned into headquarters for air raid spotters.

The first air raid drill in Illi-

(Cont. on Page 2, Col. 3)

They Say Today

"America can't expect to lick the Japs before breakfast." But we'll win by superior resources, Josephus Daniels believes. **Page 5.**

"I cannot and therefore will not use my ministry to bless, sanction, or support war." Dr. John Haynes Holmes resigns his pastorate. **Page 3.**

DANIELS

"Report to the draft, son, even if you have to bring the cow along." Mrs. Lulu Montgomery solves a problem. **Page 14.**

"Japan cannot fight a long war." Dr. Hu Shih sees danwar." Dr. Hu Shih sees danger for the little brown brothers. **Page 14.**

"Air raid warnings should be uniform throughout the country." Mrs. Roosevelt wants to make it easier for travelers. **Page 5.**

• • • •

Feature Finder

Arizona, Five Other Ships Lost, Secretary Tells FDR

EXTRA!

WASHINGTON — (U.P.) — Secretary of the Navy Frank Knox, declaring the navy was not on the alert against the surprise attack on Hawaii, revealed today that the Pacific fleet lost the battleship Arizona, three destroyers, and two lesser craft there Dec. 7.

Knox disclosed for the first time that the navy had suffered 3,385 casualties in the Hawaiian attack —2,729 officers and men killed and 656 wounded—fatalities in the sudden attack ranging 4 to 1 over the injured.

At the same time, he told a press conference that a formal investigation will be initiated immediately by the president to determine why the U. S. military services in Hawaii were not on guard against the sudden Japanese onslaught.

He summarized the results of the Hawaiian engagement as follows:

ONE. The navy lost the battleship Arizona by a direct bomb hit; the old target ship Utah which was being used as a training ship for anti-aircraft gunnery and experimental purposes; the destroyers Cassin, Downes, and Shaw; and the mine layer Ogalala.

TWO. Japanese losses included three submarine and 41 aircraft.

THREE. Navy personal losses on both ships and shore included 2,729 officers and men killed and 656 wounded.

FOUR. Army losses were severe in aircraft and some hangars, but replacements have arrived or are on the way.

Knox said the navy sustained damage to other vessels—damage varying from ships which already have been repaired and made ready for sea, or which have gone to sea, to a few ships which may require from a week to several months to repair.

The batleship Oklahoma, one of the older ones, was capsized but can be righted and repaired.

"The entire balance of the Pacific fleet with its aircraft carriers, its heavy cruisers, its light cruisers, its destroyers and submarines are uninjured, and are all at sea seeking contact with the enemy," Knox said.

Knox, who flew to Hawaii to see first hand what damage had been done to United States navy ships in the Japanese attacks, returned to the capital late Sunday night by plane.

He conferred with President Roosevelt for half an 'our after his arrival, saw him for two hours and 25 minutes this morning, and then returned to the White House after his press conference.

One essential fact stands out, Knox said, and that was that the Japanese strategy was to knock out the United States before the war began.

"This was made apparent by the deception practiced, by the preparations which had gone on for many weeks before the attack, and the attacks themselves which were made simultaneously throughout the Pacific. In this purpose the Japanese failed," he said.

In discussing the forthcoming formal investigation into the failure of the armed services to be on the alert, he said that further action would be dependent on facts and recommendations to be made by an investigating board.

"We are all entitled to know if (a) there was any error of judgment which contributed to the surprise, (b) if there was any dereliction of duty prior to the attack," he added.

His whirlwind inspection tour convinced him, Knox said, that after the initial attack the defense "by both services was conducted skillfully and bravely."

Knox was asked whether there was any Fifth Column activity in Hawaii which contributed to the Japanese surprise assault. He replied:

"It was the most effective Fifth Column work that's come out of this war except in Norway."

Knox said that allegations that U. S. ships took an intolerably long time to get steam up and get out of the way "not true."

He elaborated on this by saying that the Japanese had "most per-

(Cont. on Page 2, Col. 2)

President Opens Red Cross Drive

Pictured in the White House, President Roosevelt formally sets the war fund drive of the Red Cross into high gear by urging Americans to give a minimum of $50,000,000. With him are S. Sloan Colt, Red Cross war fund campaign chairman, and Norman Davis, chairman of the American Red Cross.

Roosevelt, Willkie Talk at White House

WASHINGTON— (U.P.) —President Roosevelt today called in Wendell L. Willkie, his Republican opponent in the 1940 presidential race, for a luncheon conference. The White House did not discuss reasons for the meeting.

Mrs. Frost Dies of Auto Injury

Wife of Professor Succumbs at 71

Mrs. W. D. Frost, 71, of 1010 Grant st., who was injured when an automobile skidded into her in the icy streets Friday, died Sunday at a Madison hospital.

She is survived by her widower, professor emeritus at the University of Wisconsin; two sons, Russell and Theodore, Madison, a brother, the Rev. Robert Elwell, Seattle, Wash., and five grandchildren.

Funeral services will be held at 2 p. m. Wednesday at the First Congregational church. The Rev. Alfred W. Swan will officiate, and burial will be in the Forest Hill cemetery.

The body was taken to the Fitch-Lawrence funeral home.

Miss Schwab to Wed Middleton RCAF Pilot Wednesday

Mary Anne Schwab, Middleton, and John E. Pritchard, Middleton, who is home on furlough from the Royal Canadian Air Force, will be married at St. Bernard's rectory in Middleton on Wednesday morning.

Pritchard obtained a special marriage license Saturday, and in his speedy action, it was inadvertently reported that he and Miss Schwab had been married by Superior Judge Roy H. Proctor.

Pritchard, a wireless operator and air gunner, must leave Saturday to be on coast patrol duty at Halifax by Christmas day. His bride-to-be will join him "when he is properly stationed and we can have some quarters in which to live."

Griffith to Head Indiana Powder Plant

WASHINGTON—(U.P.)—The war department today assigned Major George F. Griffith, ordnance officer on duty at the smokeless powder plant at Radford, Va., as commanding officer of the Wabash river ordnance works, Newport, Ind., effective Jan. 5.

Griffith had been scheduled to be the commanding officer of the projected Badger ordnance plant at Merrimac, Wis. The post there has not yet been filled, officials said.

Truck Tips, Kills Camp McCoy Soldier

CAMP McCOY, Sparta—(U.P.)—Pvt. Orville Connerily, 27, Orleans, Ind., a motor mechanic with the 50th anti-tank battalion in training here, was crushed to death today beneath a truck which skidded and tipped over.

Miller Warns Drivers of Fog

Cloudy and Mild Weather Predicted

The cloudy and "rather mild" weather the Madison area will experience tonight and Tuesday probably will be accompanied by fog, Eric R. Miller, government meteorologist, warned motorists today.

The mercury has been rising gradually since Sunday, with Sunday's high temperature of 24 degrees at midnight up to 29 degrees at 6 a. m. today. Lowest temperature Sunday was 13 at 6:30 p. m.

A cold, dry air mass covers most of the interior United States, Miller said, and a barometric low is approaching through the Dakotas, accompanied by fog but no precipitation as yet. A deep low on the north Pacific coast is causing heavy rains along the coast as far south as southern California.

Southern United States was blanketed by clear and cold weather, with freezing temperatures reported in northern Florida.

House Committee Backs Navy Boost of 150,000 Tons

WASHINGTON — (U.P.) — The house naval affairs committee today approved legislation authorizing a 150,000-ton increase in the size of the navy.

The navy had requested authorization for a 30 per cent expansion which would have amounted to 900,000 tons.

Rep. James W. Mott (R., Ore.), said that the amount of expansion was reduced by the committe because 150,000 tons was all that the nation's shipbuilding facilities can accommodate in 1942.

The navy's original request contemplated a three-year building program.

The naval affairs committee said the navy could come to congress periodically and ask for the rest of the proposed expansion as fast as shipyards became available to handle construction of more tonnage.

Dane Red Cross Starts Drive for War Funds

Workers Expected to Surpass Goal of $50,000

More than 70 civic leaders of Madison and Dane county rolled up their sleeves and went to work Sunday as the Red Cross war fund drive held its first organization meeting at Hotel Loraine.

Called to the colors of a drive which is expected to surpass the $50,000 goal set for the city and county, these key members of the Red Cross and scores of cooperating organizations heard the announcement of officers of the drive, as well as expressions of support.

"There are 2,000 boys from the city and county in service already," declared Mayor Law. "Already we have lost lads from our own homes and schools at Manila and Pearl Harbor. It is for these boys, for their comrades, and the boys who will go into the army and navy in the months to come that the Red Cross is asking this money. Madison and Dane county will do their part."

Offices Open Tuesday

Offices of the war fund drive will be opened Tuesday in the Park hotel, R. J. Neckerman, chairman, announced. Officers of the campaign follow: William H. Frederick, general secretary; Norman T. Gill, treasurer; Arthur Towell, promotion director; Mrs. Lohra Davies, county contact.

"We didn't select this time to have the war fund drive—Hitler and his Japanese cronies chose it for us," declared Neckerman. "But the coming of war has found the Red Cross with an excellent organization in the city and county, and this organization will be used.

"In order to continue the essential daily work of the Red Cross headquarters here, we are setting up an additional drive headquarters," he continued. "We believe that the people of Madison and Dane county will spontaneously bring their contributions to this office in the Park hotel."

Contributions also will be received at all banks and building and loan companies in the county, it was announced.

Chief Justice Marvin Rosenberry emphasized that this campaign is not a duplication of roll call efforts, and declared that the need for a larger sum of money for war relief makes it essential for individual givers to double their roll call contributions.

"The roll call committees have done a fine job in the work they have undertaken," declared L. M. Hanks, chairman of the Madison roll call. "I know I speak for all of them in pledging their support to this vital project."

"If we don't see actual service with the army and navy, we can

(Cont. on Page 2, Col. 4)

Voluntary Gifts 'Ante' $1,900

Voluntary gifts, received without solicitation already have given the Red Cross war fund a good start toward its $50,000 total, headquarters revealed today.

The first six gifts received totaled $1,900. Contributors included Baron Bros., George Boissard, Mr. and Mrs. L. M. Hanks, Sybil Anne Hanks, Harry S. Manchester, Inc., and the Rennebohm Drug stores.

Other contributors whose gifts had been received before noon today are the following:

Cecelia F. Abry, Brick Layers and Masons Union 13, Richard Fischer, Mrs. Robert Jenkins, Helen Johann, Mrs. K. Kogelmann, E. B. McGilvery, Mrs. Helene Miers, Mr. Snyder, Leah Welke, and an anonymous giver.

Play Bear Would Make One Little Madison Girl Happy

KEEP IT GROWING

Previously reported	$1,527.09
Badger Kennel Club Puppy Match	10.00
Individuals gifts	65.29
Total	$1,602.38

Dictated by a Madison girl, this letter reached The State Journal today:

"Dear Santa Claus:

"I am 3 years old, 3 and a half, and I have no sister and brother. But I have a nice daddy and mother and a grandmother.

"If you could find me a little polar bear and a lamb and a yearling, I shall be happy. I mean PLAY bears and lambs and yearlings, not real ones like those in the zoo, for I would not have anywhere to keep real ones. I want to sleep with them."

◇ ◇ ◇

While this little girl may not be one of those who needs the help of the Empty Stocking club, her request is typical of the modest demands of those who require its services if they are to have a merry Christmas.

It's up to Madison to see that its children — all its children — have their "polar bear and lamb and yearling," and their dolls and other toys and candy.

You can help guarantee it by sending your contribution today to:

"The Empty Stocking Club, in care of The State Journal, Madison, Wis."

U.S. Army Traps, Bombs Three Jap Forces in Luzon

By JOE ALEX MORRIS
(United Press Foreign News Editor)

American armed forces struck offensively against Japan in the Philippines—and possibly in Japanese waters—today as British armies battled in defense of Hong Kong and Singapore.

On the island of Luzon, United States aerial bombs blasted Japanese invaders penned in three isolated coastal sectors in an effort to cut them to pieces and other planes attacked enemy reinforcements moving by sea toward the islands.

American and British dispatches from the Far Eastern fighting fronts told of counter-blows by air and sea that boosted to 15 the total of Japanese transports sunk or damaged by United States and Dutch forces.

Unofficial reports this afternoon indicated that Japanese land operations have been brought to a virtual standstill by the powerful blows of American and Philippine air forces.

Failure of the enemy to better his positions on Luzon was indicated by a war communique at Washington saying that land operations against the Japanese were continuing in the northern sectors of Aparri and Vigan and in the southeast near Legaspi.

Tokyo Warns Ships

The Tokyo radio, meanwhile, warned its ships to be alert for American submarines in Japanese territorial waters, indicating that results might soon be expected in connection with the recent statement by U. S. Admiral Thomas C. Hart at Manila that the underwater fleet was striking.

The Japanese also reported enemy planes had flown near the island of Formosa but they were not definitely identified.

On other Far Eastern fronts, the British defenders of Hong Kong had withdrawn from the mainland area of Kowloon and were reported withstanding terrific Japanese aerial and artillery bombardment as the enemy sought to bridge a half-mile water gap in an assault on the beleaguered island. Latest dispatches indicated that all attacks were being turned back.

British headquarters reported that imperial forces have fallen back under heavy Japanese attacks in exposed northwestern Kedah, but Singapore's defenders appear to have broken the force of an attempted Japanese blitz sweep of the Malayan peninsula.

American defenders of Wake island still were holding out.

Claims broadcast by the official radio at Tokyo were vague but asserted that progress had been made toward the three prime objectives—Hong Kong, Singapore, and Manila.

The reports from both sides showed:

LUZON ISLAND — American defenders of the Philippines said that two more enemy transports were damaged heavily in the Legaspi sector, on the southwestern tip of Luzon island where the Japanese previously had landed.

The only other Japanese landings, according to U. S. communiques, were at Aparri in northern Luzon and Vigan, on the west coast, and these sectors were reported "in hand."

A Tokyo broadcast, quoting imperial headquarters, said that Japanese "units" had attacked the U. S. army barracks at Tarlac, only 70 miles northwest of Manila, and destroyed a military barracks. The attack apparently was by air, the subsequent developments in this sector—which was not mentioned in the American communique— were not disclosed and there was no other information to support the Japanese claim.

Claim 44 Planes

Tokyo also asserted that 44 American planes had been destroyed on Luzon and that a U. S. submarine had been sunk off the Philippines. The Japanese landing at Aparri was said in the Japanese propaganda broadcasts to be making progress toward establishing an air base for bombing attacks on the Manila area.

Japanese planes attacked U. S. military objectives on Luzon again today, causing an air alarm in Manila but dispatches said that effectiveness of enemy raids continued to decrease. At least 40 enemy planes have been shot down.

Philippine officials were taking drastic action against Fifth Columnist elements, arresting scores of suspects — especially members of the anarchistic Ganap organization — and putting down a native uprising in Pangasinan province.

HONG KONG: A Japanese offensive, launched Sunday, was reported pounding at the island defenses without important results so far. British dispatches said that defense of the 32-square-mile island was proceeding according to plan, with 2,000 civilian volunteers helping the armed forces protect a half-mile water gap which the enemy must cross. Japanese artillery and aerial bombardment continued and Tokyo claimed that a landing attempt has been made

• • • •

Bulletins

Nazis Attacked in Paris

VICHY—(U.P.)—Two new attacks against Germans took place in Paris today, it was reported, including the tossing of what was described as "a dynamite artichoke" into a restaurant requisitioned by the Nazis.

Rose Bowl Game Moved to Durham

PASADENA, CALIF.—(U.P.) — The Rose Bowl football game has been officially transferred to Durham, N. C., it was announced today.

Baraboo Man Killed in War

LeRoy Church, 26, Dies in Hawaii

BARABOO — Pvt. LeRoy E. Church, 26, son of Mr. and Mrs. William H. Church, Baraboo, was killed in action at Hickam Field, Hawaii, Sunday, Dec. 7, the war department notified the parents Sunday night.

The Baraboo man enlisted as a mechanic in the air corps Nov. 18, 1940, and sailed from San Francisco to Honolulu Dec. 12, 1940. He was with the base engineering department at Hickam Field.

Mr. Church had lived in Baraboo four years before enlisting in the army. He attended Lodi high school. The parents formerly resided on a farm between Lodi and Prairie du Sac.

Survivors besides the parents are three brothers, Theodore, Madison, and Kenneth and Howard, Milwaukee, and the maternal grandparents, Mr. and Mrs. Everett Gottschall, Baraboo.

Jap Raids Slay Kewaunee Man

KEWAUNEE —(U.P.)— Joseph A. Muhofski, 23, was killed in action with the United States fleet off Hawaii during Japanese raids, according to a telegram from the war department received by his parents, Mr. and Mrs. Joseph Muhofski, Kewanee.

A radio man, third class, Muhofski enlisted March 22, 1940. He had been stationed at Pearl Harbor since January, 1941. He was a member of the crew of a seaplane which operated from a battleship.

Besides his parents, Muhofski is survived by a brother and two sisters.

State Opposes U. S. Job Security Plan

A resolution opposing centralization of all state employment services and unemployment compensation laws under federal officials in Washington, signed by Gov. Heil and members of the state advisory committee on unemployment compensation, has been sent to Washington and officials of surrounding states, the executive offices announced today.

Wheeler, Norris Ask United Hemisphere

WASHINGTON —(U.P.)— Sens. Burton K. Wheeler, (D., Mont.) and George W. Norris, (Ind., Nebr.), today appealed for a "united front" by all western hemisphere republics in the war against the Axis powers.

Blackout Paint Advertised in N. Y.

NEW YORK —(U.P.)— Blackout paint—similar to blackout paint made and used successfully in Britain—was being advertised in New York papers today.

Tokio, Texas, Ready to 'K. O. Tokio'

TOKIO, Tex.—(U.P.)—The little west Texas town of Tokio—three stores, a school and a handful of houses—took as its slogan today: "K. O. Tokio."

Your Journal Carriers have sold
579,847
U. S. War Stamps
Since January 10

OFFICIAL STATE NEWSPAPER—OFFICIAL CITY NEWSPAPER

The Wisconsin State Journal

A fact-finding Newspaper

Weather
Warmer Sunday and Sunday night.

VOL. 161, NO. 39. 103rd Year | THIS PAPER CONSISTS OF TWO SECTIONS—SECTION ONE | MADISON, SUNDAY, NOVEMBER 8, 1942 | 30 Pages—★★★★—FINAL | Price Five Cents

2nd Front Opens

U.S. Invades Africa

COL. FAY O. DICE MADE A speech to the graduating classes at Truax Field Saturday morning. It was a simple, straightforward speech and I kept thinking about one of the boys I had come to know pretty well in that class. I wondered whether he was breathing, "Boloney!" while he listened, as he always did to me. I wanted to ask him about it when it was over, when Col. Dice had finished:

"Thank God for men like you."

◊ ◊ ◊

"WELL," HE SAID, "I'LL let you know when I get there . . . . wherever that is. I wonder where it is. I wonder where we're going."

"Nobody knows, huh?"

"Nobody knows. We won't know until we get there. We'll be sealed in the train and we won't know anything until they break us out. . . . Oh, we hear every place in the world. Some are going to gunnery school, a few wise guys to officers' training. A lot of us will go down south some place . . . . . You know, I got a hunch I'm going right smack across the water some place. I think I'm going to hear things right away. So does my mother. She cried last night, when I called her . . . ."

"Well," we said, "that's what you told me you wanted a long time ago, wasn't it?"

"Oh, sure," he said, "sure, of course . . . . Only . . . well . . ."

◊ ◊ ◊

HE STILL HAD HIS GAS mask strapped across his shoulder as we stopped in the mud out in front of his barracks to say goodbye. He had just marched from his graduation at Theater No. 2 and in a few hours he was to fall in for transport, a step nearer—or to—the combat that wins the war.

I had known him for quite a while and I always worried about him. He was a bitter man, older than most, mean and sour and cynical. All the time he had gone to school here he had sneered at it, hated it, cursed the day he had been drafted and torn from a well-paying job and his family.

Every time I saw him he would have a tough word for his post, his officers, the town, the buses, the weather.

And who, if you please, was I to argue with him and tell him he was wrong?

◊ ◊ ◊

NOW HE STOOD, SHIVERing a little, at the soggy squadron roadside, between the monotonous rows of drab barracks, watching the hundreds of others coming from the exercises, other hundreds marching off in fatigue clothes, another squad piking to classes, some to mess.

"Mess," he said. "Mess. . . . . Say, it's a mess trying to get anything to eat in your town . . . But you know," he scratched his chin, "you know the people in Madison are pretty wonderful. I remember some picnics and parties and I've been to a lot of dinners . . . . People have been pretty swell."

"Sure," I said. "Why not?"

"Well," he said, tightening his lips again, "I was surprised they were. I didn't think they would be . . . . Say, see this fat guy coming? He's the guy who gave me the black eye the first week here. Man, did I hate that guy. A big stiff . . . Hello . . . Hello, Stuffy . . . . How's boy? . . O. K., Stuff, O. K., boy . . . . ."

That fat guy—Stuffy—slogged by with a grin and beat the mud

(Continued on Page 2, Column 4)

Army Accepts 86 Dane Men

Boards 3, 4 Group Will Report Monday

Names of 86 Dane county men accepted for military service in the second October call were announced Saturday by selective service Boards 3 and 4.

Most of the new soldiers will start army life Monday at Ft. Sheridan, Ill. Two from Board 3 will report for duty Tuesday, and two went to camp immediately after passing physical examinations Oct. 26.

Alvin R. Thaden, clerk of the village of Dane, is among the Board 4 men scheduled to leave this week.

Board 3 will send the following persons Monday:

Anderson, Ball

Thorbjen Anderson, 522 E. Wilson st.; George Ball, 409 S. Livingston st.; Donald Myron Biederman, Marshall; Vernon Raymond Brickson, Route 1, Sun Prairie; Gilbert Seneca Deakin, Sun Prairie; Herbert Wolfgang Dermody, DeForest; Stanley Theodore Donstad, 306 Reindahl ave., Madison; Henry Melvin Edwardson, Route 2, Edgerton; LeRoy Mathias Ellis, Windsor;

Nathaniel Horning Evers, West Allis; Roy Edward Flint, McFarland; Francis Joseph Freidel, Sun Prairie; Howard Edward Grinde,

(Continued on Page 2, Column 5)

We Hit Your Enemy Don't Obstruct Us, FDR Tells France

PRESIDENT ROOSEVELT

WASHINGTON —(U.P.)— In connection with current military operations in French north Africa, the president Saturday night broadcast by radio to the French people, the following message in French:

"My friends, who suffer day and night, under the crushing yoke of the Nazis, I speak to you as one who was with your army and navy in France in 1918. I have held all my life the deepest friendship for the French people—for the entire French people. I retain and cherish the friendship of hundreds of French people in France and outside of France. I know your farms, your villages, and your cities. I know your soldiers, professors and workmen. I know what a precious heritage of the French people are your homes, your culture, and the principles of democracy in France. I salute again and reiterate my faith in liberty, equality, and fraternity. No two nations exist which are more united by historic and mutually friendly ties than the people of France and the United States.

"Americans, with the assistance of the United Nations, are striv-

(Continued on Page 2, Column 1)

Nazis Reel Back on Russ Fronts

North, South Invaders' Attacks Are Stopped

MOSCOW —(U.P.)— The Soviet high command announced Sunday that the Russian army had shattered new enemy attacks in Stalingrad and inflicted heavy losses in tanks and planes on Axis forces in the Caucasus, where the German drive toward the rich Russian oil fields had been stalled for five days.

The Germans were bringing up reserves to replace their enormous losses in the Caucasus area northeast of Tuapse, provisional Soviet Black sea base, and Russian artillery shelled reinforcements heading for the front. A battalion of enemy infantry was wiped out, the midnight command asserted.

On all fronts the Russians said they killed more than 1,100 Axis troops, downed 16 planes, smashed or captured more than 68 tanks, and wiped out German defenses and guns on the front northwest of Stalingrad, where a Russian relief army continued to hammer at enemy lines between the Don and the Volga.

The Russian army blasted German siege troops out of their crumbling fortifications in and on both sides of Stalingrad Saturday and its armored trains shattered a tank-led Nazi shock force in the

(Continued on Page 2, Column 3)

Truax Graduates Largest Class

Officers See Allies on Road to Victory

By MATT-MOORE TAYLOR
(State Journal Staff Writer)

Assured by officers that the United Nations are "on the road to victory," several hundred radio operators and mechanics received certificates from the army air forces technical training command Saturday at graduation exercises at Truax Field.

The contingent was the largest completing training at the Madi-

See page 8 for pictures of typical moments in life of Truax field soldiers.

son post and included operators for the first time. Radio mechanics were from the school's third class.

Military and civilian officials participated in the program at the post theater, which was filled with

(Continued on Page 2, Column 6)

Americans, British Squeeze Axis in Africa

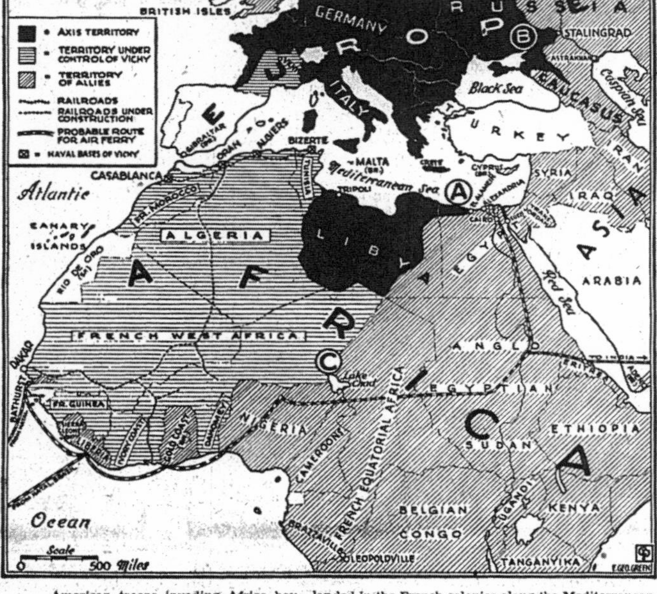

American troops invading Africa have landed in the French colonies along the Mediterranean and Atlantic coasts of Africa. Meanwhile the British 8th army races after Axis forces fleeing beyond the El Alamein line (A) and Europe reports rumors of a British, Fighting French, and American drive northward from the Lake Chad region (C) toward Tripoli. American and British offensives are a second front relieving Axis pressure on Stalingrad (B), Pres. Roosevelt points out.

Count of Bodies Incomplete, Navy Notes

Japs Lose 5,188 Men in Solomons Battles

WASHINGTON —(U.P.)— At least 5,188 Japanese troops have been killed in land fighting in the Solomons since U. S. forces invaded that area Aug. 7, the navy announced late Saturday, indicating that American troop losses are under 1,000.

The navy set Japanese losses at this figure in a communique issued a few hours after disclosure that American army forces on Guadalcanal advanced several miles against enemy forces east of Henderson field on Friday. The earlier communique also disclosed that marines had repulsed light enemy attacks from west of the field.

The first communique said army troops crossed the Malimbu river, encountering only light resistance. The Malimbu stretches inland about four miles southward of Koli point, near the scene of enemy landings Tuesday and Wednesday nights.

The navy said its figure for enemy losses was based "on an actual count of enemy killed in actions ashore and does not include estimates of those killed in enemy-controlled areas where no

(Continued on Page 2, Column 2)

'Remove Germans from North Africa,' Montgomery Orders

CAIRO—(U.P.)—Liuet. Gen. Bernard L. Montgomery ordered his eighth army Saturday night to finish the job of "removing the Germans from north Africa" as it pressed hot on the heels of the wrecked Afrika korps now striving to brace for a stand on the Libyan frontier.

"There is much to be done yet, and it will call for a supreme effort and great hardship on the part of every officer and man," the British general warned.

"Forward, then, to our task of removing the Germans from north Africa! The Germans began this trouble, and they must now take the consequences."

As Gen. Montgomery's message sped through the desert outposts, the imperials hurled armored forces, motorized infantry, and swarms of planes at the remnants of Marshal Erwin Rommel's once vaunted force, now possibly whittled to 25,000 of its original 140,000 men.

U. S. Flyers Praised

The westward surge was believed to have carried the main imperial striking force well beyond Mersa Matruh, 110 miles west of the crumpled Alamein line, and advance units were thought to be nearing the Libyan frontier, where the routed Axis forces apparently hoped to snatch a foothold in rugged Halfaya (Hellfire) pass.

As the battle moved westward, Maj. Gen. Lewis H. Brereton's United States army air force of the Middle East was credited with a major contribution to the Allied victory in Egypt.

The American airmen shot down 45 Axis planes, sank or badly damaged an uncalculated number of tons of enemy shipping, and knocked out many tanks and motor vehicles between Oct. 1 and

(Continued on Page 14, Col. 6)

Feature Finder

Football Scores

Iowa 6, Wisconsin 0
Illinois 14, Northwestern 7
Indiana 7, Minnesota 0
Notre Dame 13, Army 0
Ohio State 59, Pittsburgh 19
Michigan 35, Harvard 7
Georgia 75, Florida 0

(More scores on Page 19)
(More Scores on Page 22)

Raiders Swoop on Brest, Genoa

RAF, Yankees Make Big-Scale Attacks

LONDON—(U.P.)—American and British planes plastered the port area of Brest Saturday in a raid on the German-held French coast after the Royal Air Force had struck powerfully at Italy Friday night, heavily bombing Genoa and leaving the port aglow with flames visible for 120 miles.

Air raid alarms sounded in Switzerland Saturday night, indicating that the RAF for the second straight night was taking the air war to Italy.

Submarine Base Attacked

American Flying Fortresses and Liberators escorted by Allied fighters attacked the German docks and submarine pens at Brest with heavy bombs in an afternoon sortie from which all bombers returned, a joint British and United States communique revealed.

From dawn to dusk RAF fighters ranged the continental coast

(Continued on Page 2, Column 1)

The Dates: Nov. 12, 13, 14

Bring Three Things to Gas Registration Ration Board Warns

Registration for gasoline rationing will take place Thursday, Friday, and Saturday, Nov. 12, 13, and 14 in schools throughout Madison and Dane county, Vern G. Zeller, Dane county ration board chairman, announced Saturday.

Only passenger cars and motorcycles will be registered this week, Zeller said. Vehicles having truck licenses will obtain certificates of war necessity from the Office of Defense Transportation, and will register for gasoline later.

Automobile dealers will register for cars with dealer licenses at the ration board at a later date also, Zeller said.

Application forms will be available Monday morning at gasoline stations throughout the city, he said, but these forms must be taken to the registration stations to be filled out. They can not be mailed to the board.

When motorists register for their basic gasoline ration book, they must have:

ONE—The certificate of registration or certificate of title of the motor vehicle.

TWO—A list of the tire serial numbers of all five tires for the automobile or three for the motorcycle.

THREE—A certificate of disposal of all tires in excess of five for each automobile or three for each motorcycle.

The serial numbers of tires, the Office of Price Administration

(Continued on Page 2, Column 7)

Powerful Units On 2 Coasts, FDR Reveals

By LYLE C. WILSON

WASHINGTON —(U.P.)— American army, navy, and air forces, equipped with the most modern armored weapons, are landing now on the Mediterranean and Atlantic coasts of French African colonies in the opening of the long heralded second-front against the Axis, the White House announced Saturday night.

The White House and the war department announced the landing operations simultaneously shortly after 9 p. m. (8 o'clock Madison time.) The invasion of Africa evidently is on a tremendous scale. It is commanded by Lieut. Gen. Dwight Eisenhower, commander of United States forces in the European theater.

The White House also issued the text of a message broadcast by Mr. Roosevelt to the French people informing them in their own language of the purpose of the expedition and assuring that the Allies seek no territory and have no intention of interfering with friendly French authorities in Africa.

The announcements did not precisely locate the American landings. But it appeared possible that the maneuver could develop into the western end of a pincers strategy designed to crush German Field Marshal Erwin Rommel's Axis legions once and for all in North Africa.

GEN. D. D. EISENHOWER

The White House said the invasion was undertaken to:

ONE. Prevent Axis military occupation of any part of northern or western Africa.

TWO. Deny the Axis any African springboard from which to launch an attack against the Americas.

THREE. Provide second front assistance to our heroic allies in Russia."

"The landing of this American army is being assisted by the British navy and air forces and it will, in the immediate future, be reinforced by a considerable number of divisions of the British army," the White House announcement said.

"This expedition will develop into a major effort by the Allied nations and there is every expectation that it will be successful in repelling the planned German and Italian invasion of Africa and prove the first historic step in the liberation and restoration of France."

The statement emphasized that the "French government" as well as the French people had been informed of the United Nation's intentions to move into French colonial Africa but there was no intimation that Vichy had agreed to the high strategy.

A war department communique, issued simultaneously,

(Continued on Page 14, Col. 1)

Today's War Score

	Allies	Axis
Africa	X	
Solomons	X	
Pacific	X	
Russia	X	
Air War	X	

Score based on all available war news of last 24 hours.

The Reasons

AFRICA—U. S. invades Africa as British relentlessly pursue Rommel's remnants toward Libyan border.

SOLOMONS—American forces push ahead on Guadalcanal; count of bodies shows Jap losses heavy.

PACIFIC — Australian troops penetrate Papua, near Buna, Jap base on New Guinea.

RUSSIA—Soviets repel Nazis on all fronts.

AIR WAR — Royal Air Force and Americans blast at Genoa, Italy, and Brest, France, and at Axis installations in Holland and Belgium.

Yanks Launch Biggest Attack, Witness Says

By C. R. CUNNINGHAM

ALLIED HEADQUARTERS, North Africa —(U.P.)— Scores of thousands of American troops, led by amphibious landing parties and air borne shock troops, landed Sunday in numerous areas of French West and North Africa.

It is the opening of offensive action in the European theater by Yankee doughboys who are slogging into action on this side of the Atlantic for the first time since 1917-18.

The operation, launched under the cover of huge fleets of naval warships and airplanes, was described as the largest single American offensive action in history.

American land, air, and sea forces with the cooperation of British naval and air forces and a small number of British infantry are carrying out landings in French West and North Africa.

American troops have landed simultaneously in numerous areas of Africa.

Now We Start Real Action, Army Warns

LONDON—(U.P.)— A United States army spokesman declared Sunday that the invasion of French African colonies is "the start of the real American war in the European theater of operations."

"The action far overshadows any American action in this hemisphere previously," the spokesman said.

Asked if the move could be described as a pincers, he said:

"A pincers has only two parts—this has many parts."

Your Journal Carriers have sold 598,804 U. S. War Stamps Since January 10

OFFICIAL STATE NEWSPAPER—OFFICIAL CITY NEWSPAPER

The Wisconsin State Journal

A fact-finding Newspaper

Weather: Slowly rising temperature Sunday and Sunday night.

VOL. 161, NO. 53. 103rd Year — THIS PAPER CONSISTS OF TWO SECTIONS—SECTION ONE — MADISON, SUNDAY, NOVEMBER 22, 1942 — 32 Pages—★★★★—FINAL — Price Five Cents

Allies Open New Attack

THUS ENDS A PAGE OF glory.

Thus, in the chill twilight across Camp Randall, it ends, and the thousands in the concrete tiers stand and cry the old, old words again, **"Varsity! . . . . Varsity!"** and a little kid on the cinders behind the sidelines jumps and whirls and whoops to all about him:

"We won! We won! We beat the Gophers! We won!! We won! We beat Minnesota!"

Ah, sonny, sonny, the children who have grown old in these parts, waiting to say those words! Keep shouting them, sonny, keep singing, sing them out . . . . .

◊ ◊ ◊

IT ENDS THAT WAY OUTside, around the soggy, cleat-ripped field, and high inside the eastern stands, up in the dressing room, Elroy Hirsch, the sick boy, the pale, wan ghost with the blood caked under his nose and around his lips, makes a big grin at a slim little man coming up to him in a long overcoat and a new blue hat.

"Hi, Pop," says Elroy, and it gets quiet around them and nobody says anything. Then Elroy says, **"How are you, Pop?"** and grabs the new blue hat and crunches and smashes it all around his father's head.

His Pop can't say anything either. He can only put his arms out and pull his boy to him with all the mud and the blood and the dirt upon his shirt of red and his pants of gold.

"Ah, Pop," then Elroy says, **"Ah, Pop . . . Hey, Pop, you better fix your hat. They want to take your picture."** And Elroy takes the hat and smooths it out and puts a crease across the middle.

◊ ◊ ◊

IT ENDS WITH A BIG MAN named Schreiner coming into the locker room and pushing through the booming crowd and crying, **"Davey! Davey! . . . . Oh, Davey, what a game! Good, Davey, good!"**

And Capt. Schreiner, the greatest end you or anyone else saw in all your lives, the captain with the ball hugged under his arm, says, **"Thanks, Dad,"** and squeezes his father's arm and forgets everybody around him, everybody trying to slap his back and grab his hand.

For this is Dad's day and here is Mr. Harder, looking anxiously into his great son's beaten face and then at his twisted, limping leg, and here is Mr. Calligaro and Mr. Wink and Mr. Hoskins. For this, the program says, is Dad's day.

But the program is wrong. Within this dressing room, maybe, it is right. But outside, this day belongs to the thousands still singing in the crowded streets and to those who will be cheering all across this country . . . . and to those who must wait to hear, this year, in the far, strange places of the world.

It is the day of all these and it ends with the little guy, the tired and weary-eyed Harry Stuhldreher, standing in the midst of his men, the men who were sick and injured and full of flu and grippe and colds, the men the experts said could never hope, possibly, to lick the mighty Minnesota.

He stands there and he looks around once and he says, **"I have never been so proud of any boys,"** and then he has to turn and go away and the boys duck their heads and start unbuckling blocking pads and shoulder guards and ripping off the miles of torturing tape around their arms and feet and legs.

◊ ◊ ◊

HOW IT BEGAN I CAN'T tell you. You have to go far back for that, years back when the boys who have fought across this page of glory were little kids, like the one jumping on the cinders. You have to go back farther than that, I suppose, to consider Harry Stuhldreher and Russ Rippe and Guy Sundt, George Fox and Bob Reagan and Dynie Mansfield and Frank Jordan.

But I can tell you how it began and how it was all the way along from the bench today.

◊ ◊ ◊

IT IS COLD ON THE BENCH and it is colder when Minnesota comes out. Minnesota is big and always terrifying. The mighty legend of Minnesota is maddening and frightening, and here is Wisconsin, sick and battered and short-handed.

Here is Jack Wink, a symbol for today, brave and fine in a uniform, but with one leg stiff, one leg crippled so badly he can't walk. He can't play. It is only a nice gesture to let him get out here in a uniform.

And here comes Wasserbach, another who has been in the hospital all week.

"How's the cold?" a teammate asks him as he trots to the bench.

"Oh, fine," says Wasserbach, **"fine, fine, fine,"** and then coughs so hard and so long he has to lean over to get his breath.

Oh, sure, fine, fine, fine.

◊ ◊ ◊

HERE'S THE BAND AND the band is the world champion, anyway. The band plays "Praise the Lord and Pass the Ammu-

(Continued on Page 10, Column 1.)

Wisconsin Beats Minnesota, 20-6, to Finish Best Season Since 1912

Five Plays, and Badgers Start on Victory Road

Wisconsin's football team struck with the speed of lightning Saturday afternoon in Camp Randall stadium when it scored its first touchdown in the first five plays of the game, and in the above picture Fullback Marlin (Pat) Harder is shown driving to the three-yard line. Halfback Dick Luckemeyer (70) is screening Harder from view. Two plays latter Harder scored from the three-yard stripe. Halfback Elroy Hirsch (40) is sprawled on the ground and End Bill Baumgartner of Minnesota is on one knee while Ashley Anderson, (22) Wisconsin offensive quarterback, is in the background.

46,000 Watch Golden Gophers Lose Their Shine

Scoring in 3 Periods, Badgers Whirlwind Over Ancient Rivals

By WILLARD R. SMITH

Page Gardner Wilson, the circus press agent, to help write the story of Wisconsin's 20-6 defeat of Minnesota before a record crowd of 46,000 Saturday, completing the greatest football season the Badgers have enjoyed since they were conference champions in 1912.

Only a man who knows all the superlatives and fancy adjectives can do justice to this 1942 Wisconsin team which won eight games, tied Notre Dame, lost only to Iowa, and counted among its victims Ohio State, the team that has a slight mathematical edge on the conference title.

Whirlwind!

Because against Minnesota Saturday the Badgers were, to borrow those circus phrases, "marvels," "peerless," "inconceivably impressive." and the "radiant new super-spectacle" they offered was "the greatest show on earth" to loyal Wisconsin fans.

The fact that Ohio State played six conference games while Wisconsin played only five gave the former their mathematical advantage in final standings. Each lost only one conference game but Wisconsin points with pride to its 17-7 victory over Ohio State and does not need to bow to the Buckeyes.

Minnesota's mighty Golden Gophers were humbled in whirlwind fashion by Wisconsin, even without the quarterbacking of Sophomore Jack Wink, who has called signals all season. Ashley Anderson, reserve quarter, replaced Wink on offense and Len Calligaro, a converted fullback,

(Continued on Page 23, Column 3.)

Grid Scores

WISCONSIN 20, Minnesota 6
Ohio State 21, Michigan 7
Indiana 20, Purdue 0
Great Lakes 6, Illinois 0
Notre Dame 27, Northwestern 20
Auburn 27, Georgia 13
Iowa Seahawks 46, Nebraska 0
Yale 7, Harvard 3
(Complete scores on Page 25)

French Hurl Troops into Tunisia Battle; Major Fight Coming

By C. R. CUNNINGHAM

ALLIED NORTH AFRICAN HEADQUARTERS—(U.P.)—French forces launched a new counter-attack against Axis troops in the interior of Tunisia Saturday while American and British reinforcements and supplies were rushed forward by land, sea, and air for a major battle expected to develop momentarily.

The French struck at the Germans near the point where American forces had sent Adolf Hitler's troops reeling back Thursday in the first clash between American and German ground forces since 1918.

Sharp fighting was reported under way for a bridge, the key to the most vital crossroads in the vicinity. Its possession would be invaluable to either side and front reports said it now was held by the Allies.

French sources said the Germans were on continuous patrol behind their own lines in that sector, about 30 miles southwest of Tunis.

They were bringing up supplies constantly although Royal Air Force planes harassed them relentlessly.

The American and British columns continued their advance across Tunisia at several points. Front reports said bad weather prevented the Germans, fighting with their backs to the Mediterranean, from attacking the Allies in a last-ditch effort to avert a "desert Dunkirk."

From the force cutting across the waist of Tunisia, the Americans were sending forward ace fighter pilots, flying British Spitfire planes and new long-range American fighter planes.

U. S. Armored Units Advance

From the American force in the west, Maj. Gen. George S. Patton was sending light armored units to join the mass sweep across Tunisia.

The Americans were training French troops in the use of United States army equipment, all of which was the most modern.

Headquarters established that in the initial clash between the Americans and the Germans, the

(Continued on Page 2, Column 1)

Italians Cry 'Peace,' Reports to London Say

(By United Press)

Italian morale has sunk so low, said advices reaching London Saturday that King Victor Emmanuel, visiting Genoa, was greeted with cries of "Peace!" from the Italian populace. The advices said the situation was so intense that Benito Mussolini dared not accompany the king.

Japanese Ships Approach Buna

Enemy Forces Begin Last Ditch Stand

GEN. MacARTHUR'S HEADQUARTERS, Australia — (U.P.) — Japanese naval forces again are approaching Buna beleagured enemy base on the north shore of New Guinea, where American and Australian troops are driving steadily ahead in the bitterest fighting of the campaign, Gen. Douglas MacArthur announced today.

A headquarters spokesman said an Australian column, descending the main jungle trail from Kokoda, had occupied the village of Soputa, 8 miles inland from the Buna-Gona area.

He said they were pressing their advance toward Buna and Gona, and were threatening Sanananda, the port of Buna located 4 miles north of the big base.

Japanese forces were making a desperate last-ditch stand in a triangular area between Buna and Gona, 10 miles apart on the coast, and Soputa.

Zeros Attack

The Allied forces, reports from the front said, were maintaining pressure on the two landward sides of the triangle despite heavy aerial assaults by Zero planes and inadequate support from Allied aircraft.

The Japanese were making their defense from trenches and fixed positions they had time to prepare in front of their main New Guinea base at Buna.

While official reports failed to mention Allied casualties, the references to extremely heavy fighting indicated that the cost of this climactic battle can be expected to be high.

Front reports indicated that the Japanese were hurling greater numbers of Zero fighters into the battle. They also were taking full advantage of bad weather conditions on the Port Moresby side of

(Continued on Page 2, Column 1)

Today's War Score

	Allies	Axis
Africa	X	
Pacific	X	
Russia	X	
Italy	X	
Burma	X	

The Reasons

AFRICA — "Second Front" — French open new attack as Allies hem in Axis troops in Bizerte-Tunis area and control Mediterranean.

AFRICA — Rommel — British begin to catch up with fast-fleeing Afrika korps.

PACIFIC — Solomons—Marines make 6-mile advance on Guadalcanal.

PACIFIC—New Guinea —Allies close in on Japs in Buna-Gona area.

RUSSIA — Soviets hold initiative all along the front.

ITALY — RAF pounds Turin, industrial city, as Italian morale sags.

BURMA—U. S. bombers sucessfully raid Lungling, highway base held by Japs.

They'll Mark Holiday, but Not as Usual

The thousands of soldiers, sailors, and WAVES in Madison won't get home for Thanksgiving, but they'll feast on the king of birds at mess halls.

All military men and women will go to classes as usual Thursday. The reminder of Thanksgiving will come at noon when they get a meal featuring turkey and all the trimmings of holiday dinner at home.

Hudreds of turkeys will be browning long before daylight in huge ovens at Truax Field. The army is allowing a pound of turkey to each man, Capt. Philip J. Teusink, general mess officer, said.

25 Items on Menu

Twenty-five different items make up the Thanksgiving menu at the army air force post. Mess stewards expect no difficulty in stuffing and roasting the birds and baking pumpkin pie for the city's largest military group.

"The cooking is no trouble," Teusink said. "What's worrying us is where we're going to put everything. The plates aren't big enough to hold all we're going to serve that day."

The five-course meal will start with oyster stew and crackers and get down to business with roast young turkey, dressing, and giblet gravy, candied sweet and snowflake Irish potatoes, whole kernel corn, buttered peas, cranberry sauce, bread and butter, and lettuce and tomato salad.

Both Coffee and Sugar

The dessert menu consists of pumpkin or mince pie, fruit cake, and ice cream, and the feast will be topped off with assorted nuts, grapes, oranges, and apples, and chocolate bars, Apple cider, coffee (with sugar), and milk will be on the drink counter.

Soldiers may have a chance to gnaw cold turkey legs for supper, but, the mess officer said, "We

(Continued on Page 2, Column 3)

Kenneth Rufi Pales at Jury's Verdict: 1st Degree Murder

MONROE — Kenneth Rufi, 19, paled slightly as a jury of four women and eight men found him guilty Saturday night of first degree murder of Ned Hartwig, Monroe cattle buyer, after about three hours and 28 minutes deliberation.

The 19 - year - old defendant maintained the same calm he had shown throughout the four-day trial when the jury filed in at 7:45 p. m. Saturday and announced the verdict which carries a penalty of mandatory life imprisonment.

Circuit Judge Jesse Earle, Janesville, who presided at the trial, will hear defense arguments for a new trial Wednesday.

The courtroom crowd remained silent when the court announced the jury's verdict. One woman juror, whose daughter, about the same age as Rufi, was killed in an accident about a year ago, wept.

Three Verdicts Possible

Mrs. Ned Hartwig, widow of the Monroe cattle buyer who was slain by a shotgun blast on the night of Mar. 2, was present in the courtroom and took the news calmly. Mrs. Hartwig, who was with her husband in the Hartwig home on the night of the murder, sighed as defense counsel moved for a new trial. "now we may have to go through it all again."

The case went to the jury at 4:17 p. m. and the group deliberated until recessing for dinner at 6. The jurors returned at 7:25 and apparently reached a decision almost immediately, for the attorneys were sent for, and the foreman announced the verdict at 7:45.

Judge Earle's instructions to the jury, after the summing up arguments of the attorneys for the state and the defense, permitted a verdict of first degree murder,

(Continued on Page 2, Column 6)

Milwaukeean Killed in Deer Season's First Fatality

WISCONSIN RAPIDS —(U.P.)— Curtis Hill, 39, Milwaukee, is the state's first hunting fatality this season.

Hill died Saturday afternoon at a Wisconsin Rapids hospital of a rifle bullet wound in his abdomen. He was shot early Saturday morning near Necedah, Juneau county, by an unidentified hunter.

Juneau county authorities are investigating.

Well-Behaved, Happy Crowds Cheer Victory

Wisconsin football fans who waited 10 long years to cheer a victory over Minnesota were doing it in the small hours this morning and Madison police were cheering, too, because the happy Badger football throngs in the night spots were well behaved.

Downtown hotels, restaurants and bars were jammed to capacity. traffic before and after the Wisconsin-Minnesota game was the heaviest in years, but only five accidents were reported to city and county police and few "drunk and disorderly" calls were received late Saturday night.

Released from the gloom of Minnesota defeats, Badger fans lined up three-deep at the bars and vied with one another for the attention of the bartenders.

There were so many people that few could get the attention of the bartender often enough to get too much to drink.

Crowds Chant Score

Wisconsin's 20 points were scored over and over, and at one place the count from one to 20 was chanted repeatedly by the crowd.

Only one fan missed the game by being in police custody while it was played. He woke up at the station about 5 p. m. His first question was:

"How did Wisconsin come out?"

His second question was:

(Continued on Page 10, Column 6.)

Russians Open Winter Offensive

2,000 Axis Troops Killed in One Day

MOSCOW — (U.P.) — Russian forces, driving back weary Axis troops on four fronts and killing upwards of 2,000 in one day's fighting, appeared today to have initiated the first stages of their winter offensive.

The Soviet midnight communique reported successes at Stalingrad, southeast of Nalchik in the Caucasus, northeast of the enemy-held Caucasian port of Tuapse, and in the Mozdok area at the entrance to the Grozny oil fields.

(Radio Berlin referred to the operations as "the first Soviet winter offensive with its center of gravity in the area of the big Don bend." Today's Russian communique did not mention activity in the Don bend area.)

The initiative appeared to be passing to the Russian army

(Continued on Page 2, Column 3)

Mrs. Otjen Earns $300 Monthly from State Council of Defense

Mrs. Maud Neprud Otjen, wife of Col. C. J. Otjen, Milwaukee, once director of women's activities in the Wisconsin Republican party, has been appointed to a $300-a-month job as staff member for the Wisconsin Council of Defense, The State Journal learned Saturday.

Mrs. Otjen went on the Council of Defense pay roll in October, The State Journal learned, and received $300 for her October work and another $300 for November. Mrs. Otjen has been prominent in Republican circles since the days of Gov. Blaine, when she was active in the party machine.

A survey of the Council of Defense pay roll, besides revealing that Mrs. Otjen had been employed, revealed Saturday that Seth Pollard, executive secretary of the organization, has been receiving $400 a month, and that at least five members of the council have been receiving salaries in excess of $250 monthly.

They are Al Reeke, staff member, $250 a month; L. F. Thurwacher, commander of the citizens defense corps, $275; H. A. Friedman, publicity director, $250 a month; Harold Shadd, staff member, $250 a month; and Mrs. Otjen, $300.

There are also 11 employes at the Council offices who are receiving $150 or less.

The figures also showed that the Council was paying $496.16 monthly for rent—a sum paid to the Wisconsin Bankshares Corp. for rent in the 110 E. Wisconsin bldg., Milwaukee.

MRS. MAUD NEPRUD OTJEN

Feature Finder

Flying 9 Miles High, Spitfire Wins Battle

LONDON — (U.P.) — A British Spitfire has risen to almost 50,000 feet—more than 9 miles high—over the western desert to shoot down a German reconnaissance plane of special high altitude design, the air ministry disclosed today.

Two other pilots of the Middle East command have reached only slightly lesser heights in a perilous fight against bitter cold and lack of oxygen to intercept Junkers-86 planes, long range German reconnaissance ships which have been equipped with two powerful engines and an enormous wing-span designed to lift them above the ceiling of any existing fighter. When they appeared over England this summer, possibly with light bomb loads, they were able to fly away with photographs unchallenged.

The Middle East command gave the three pilots permission to take up Spitfires in an attempt to intercept the Ju-86. The first to go was Flying Officer Reynolds, Kenya, whose age, 35, made him decidedly an "old man" for such an exploit.

Crews Work Fiercely

Reynolds went well over 40,000 feet, closed with the enemy and gave him a cannon burst. The starboard engine of the Junkers

(Continued on P. 12, Col. 1)

Crackerjack War Map on Page 4

On Page 4 of this edition The Wisconsin State Journal presents a large background map of the vital war area to help its readers follow the news from the front.

You'll find this map valuable for daily reference in following developments from the war area as reported by United Press staff reporters direct from the front lines.

THIS PAPER CONSISTS OF TWO SECTIONS—SECTION ONE
18 Pages—★★★★—FINAL
Price Five Cents

OFFICIAL CITY NEWSPAPER
OFFICIAL STATE NEWSPAPER

The Wisconsin State Journal

VOL. 152, NO. 154 104th Year. A fact-finding Newspaper MADISON, FRIDAY, SEPTEMBER 3, 1943

Weather
Scattered thunderstorms tonight and Saturday forenoon. Cooler Saturday forenoon.

Battle of Europe Opens, Allies Swarm into Italy

Yankee Fliers Hit Paris Area, Blast Brenner Pass Rail Line

Paris

LONDON—(U.P.)—American Flying Fortresses flew over the Eiffel tower to attack an aircraft factory on the edge of Paris today while other Fortresses raided an airplane assembly plant near the French capital and five airfields in one of the heaviest daylight assaults of the war.

The big bombers blasted the Caudron-Renault aircraft factory in the Paris suburbs and left a 5,000-foot column of black smoke rising into the cloudless sky from the west bank of the Seine. It marked the first time American bombers had crossed the heart of Paris.

Other Plants Bombed

The second Fortress formation bombed the Potez plant at Meulan-les-Mureaux, 20 miles outside Paris, and others smashed an Axis fighter plant dispersal area five miles south of Dieppe on the channel coast.

It was believed that up to 1,000 Allied planes may have taken part in all the day's operations over western Europe.

The Fortresses also attacked the airdrome at Romilly sur Seine, a replacement and supply center for the German air force.

Fortress crew members, most of whom were seeing Paris for the first time, said the Eiffel tower looked like "a little oil derrick" far below. Their view was somewhat hampered by thousands of black and white flak bursts and they were kept busy by German fighter planes.

Twenty-nine enemy planes were shot down and the day's operations cost the Allies eight heavy bombers and two fighters.

Paris Itself Hit, Axis Says

There were indications that the raids on France may have been the greatest daylight attacks of the war. The Axis radio claimed a heavy assault on Paris which caused great damage and struck

(Continued on Page 2, Column 1)

Nazi Lifeline Hit

The Brenner pass, which military observers have regarded as a main German defense against Allied invasion thrusts up from Italy, was attacked today in the first stages of the invasion of Italy. American bombers wrecked a railroad bridge just south of the pass and also cut the railroad line 30 miles below the pass.

Brenner Pass

ALLIED HEADQUARTERS, North Africa —(U.P.)— American Flying Fortresses, in their longest raid of the war from North African bases, have smashed the German lifeline into Italy by wrecking a railway bridge just south of the Brenner pass, a communique announced today.

Apparently flying more than 1,300 miles round trip, the Fortresses blasted the railway bridge at Bolzano, 40 miles south of the German border, only a few hours before British and Canadian invasion troops landed in southern Italy.

Another contingent of Flying Fortresses cut the Brenner pass railway at Trento, 30 miles farther south, and a third formation bombed the northern industrial center of Bologna, 200 miles north of Rome.

The raids on Bolzano and Trento obviously were timed to deprive the Axis high command of its most important route of reinforcement and supply between Germany and Italy at a moment when the greatest demands were about to be made upon it to combat the Allied invasion.

"The Bolzano railroad bridge carrying the line from the Brenner pass has been hit and broken," the Northwest African air forces communique said. "Hits also were made on the yards and adjacent tracks.

"At Trento, also on the route from the Brenner pass, the rail-

(Continued on Page 2, Column 2)

Planes Blast Italy, Then Troops Land

Early today the battle of Europe began when Allied troops crossed the 2-mile Messina straits separating Sicily and Italy and landed at Reggio Calabria and nearby Scilla. The black plane shown on the map is a reminder of the intense "softening up" process with which Allied bombers preceded the land invasion.

Nazis Desert Italians, Swiss Reports Say

BERN, Switzerland –(UP)– Advices from the Italian frontier late today said German troops are hurriedly evacuating the tip of the Italian boot in fear that they will be cut off by further Allied landings on the peninsula.

If the report proved true, it evidently would shatter the remaining hopes of the Italian command that the Nazis might be willing to cooperate in the defense of southern Italy.

The advices said the Germans abandoned the poorly equipped Italian soldiers, seized all available trucks, tanks, and armored cars, and left the scene of battle in such orderly fashion that it appeared the evacuation of Calabria had long been planned.

By REYNOLDS PACKARD
(United Press Staff Correspondent)

ALLIED HEADQUARTERS, North Africa – (UP) – Gen. Sir Bernard L. Montgomery sent his British Eighth army across Messina straits today with orders to "knock Italy out of the war" and it landed on the toe of the Italian boot against ground opposition but unchallenged by air or sea.

Hundreds of invasion craft carried the war-tempered veterans of Africa and Sicily across the water gap to open the second fighting front on the continent of Europe.

(Military sources in London said the invasion force established a bridgehead on the extreme southwest coast of Italy in the first few hours of fighting, but warned that heavy Axis resistance still was to be expected.)

Gen. Sir Bernard L. Montgomery's veterans of the African and Sicilian campaigns blazed the Allied trail, opening the battle of Europe with a landing, which, a dispatch from Sicily said, was made "not without difficulty."

The amphibious assault was carried out under cover of a tremendous land, sea, and air bombardment. It was made across the narrow straits against the Italian beach in the regions of Reggio Calabria and Scilla.

American Flying Fortresses, ranging far out ahead of the fleets mustered to support the invasion of Europe, smashed Axis comunications at the south end of the Brenner pass bottleneck between Germany and Italy, in what appeared to be a blow aimed at blocking any Nazi reinforcements of the Italian peninsula.

(First Axis radio reports of the invasion said the Allies had landed on both sides of Reggio Calabria; that the situation "cannot be estimated" at the moment; and that the landing force was about a division strong.)

Although a dispatch from Eighth army headquarters in Sicily said that "our first foothold in Europe has been established," a spokesman emphasized the difficult nature of the landings and urged against any feeling that the attack would be a walkover.

Axis Gunners Confused

Searchlights on the Italian coast tried to pick out targets for the Axis guns as the invasion fleet moved across the straits, but they were dealt with quickly by the British navy.

Mortars in the first wave of assault boats carpeted the landing zones with smoke shells, making the dark night even blacker and turning the Axis fire into a confusion of blasts instead of precision gunnery.

The monitors kept all their guns in action, maintaining a deadly fire which had knocked out some mainland guns before the first landing boats crammed with hel-

(Continued on Page 2, Column 4)

ALLIED HEADQUARTERS, North Africa— (U.P.) —A pilot who flew over the straits of Messina said today that neither sea nor air forces of the Axis challenged the British and Canadian amphibious landings on the Italian mainland.

New Russ Drive Told by Berlin

Artillery, Infantry Open Donets Attack

LONDON —(U.P.)— The German DNB news agency reported today that the Russian army had launched a powerful offensive on the middle Donets front southeast of Kharkov.

A broadcast DNB dispatch said the "anticipated" attack of the Soviets had been under way since early morning. It evidently was made in concert with the Russian drives below Kharkov and above the sea of Azov, which bracketed the area.

The Russians used hundreds of batteries of heavy artillery and strong air support in an effort to wear down the German front before the infantry struck, DNB said.

"Detailed reports on the progress of this new, large scale battle are not yet available," the agency added.

Soviets Advance in Donets Basin

MOSCOW — (U.P.) — Russian armies drove six miles past the newly captured German stronghold Sumy today and to the south threatened to engulf the whole

(Continued on Page 2, Column 1)

Atchoo Chart

	Total pollen	Rag-weed	Mold spore
For 24 hours ending 9 a. m. today	506	496	17
Previous 24 hours	442	437	20

Japs Lose Third of Cargo Tonnage

WASHINGTON—(U.P.)—Secretary of Navy Frank Knox declared today that more than one-third of Japanese cargo tonnage in existence at the outbreak of war and acquired since then has been sunk.

Knox met reporters who were awaiting word of new blows against the Japanese by the American task force which blasted Marcus island. Vice-Admiral John S. McCain, deputy chief of naval operations, warned the uneasy enemy Thursday night that the recent Marcus attack was but a "token" prelude to the destruction of Japan itself.

According to figures released by Knox, more than 2,539,630 tons of Japanese cargo shipping have been sent to the bottom of the Pacific by the Allies.

Loss Hampers Japs

Knox said this loss undoubtedly is making it difficult for the Japanese to exploit profitably their war-gained territories.

He said that at the start of the war the Japanese had 6,358,891 tons of cargo shipping.

Since that time, he added, it is estimated "by those assumed to know" that the Japanese have acquired 1,250,000 tons through new construction and seizures. A considerable portion of the new construction, he said, is wooden ships.

Subs Win Praise

He said that 77 per cent of the total sunk were through submarine actions. The overall estimate of losses included sinkings by all of the United Nations, but the predominant proportion of the losses were inflicted by U. S. forces.

Knox took occasion to laud the American submarine service which he said has "done an outstanding job—a perfectly splendid job for which too high praise can't be given."

Knox said he had no information on the Marcus island raid by the American carrier task force, which

(Continued on Page 2, Column 3)

Board to Ask Dismissal of Rennebohm

Dismissal of Fred Rennebohm, city milk inspector for the past seven years, will be recommended to the city personnel board by the board of health, it was learned today.

The board's action Thursday night followed a series of hearings at which Rennebohm was questioned on alleged violations of department rules and "insubordination."

Rennebohm, now on vacation, has been called before the board on previous occasions.

One of the principal charges, board mmebers reported, was that he released information, without authority, on the results of milk tests.

Rennebohm, under city civil service rules, is entitled to a hearing before the bureau of personnel if he requests it.

Religion Grows in England, Coleman Says

By MAT-MOORE TAYLOR
(State Journal Staff Writer)

Religion is stronger in England than ever before and the people look to the church for leadership in the post-war world, the Rev. Michael Coleman, vicar of All Hallows church, London, said here today.

"The war has brought about an enormous revival of interest in religion (in Great Britain)," said the priest whose church was destroyed in the bombing of London, "but not necessarily a tremendous return to church-going."

Clergymen are going to the people, he explained, telling of chaplains speaking at munitions plants during lunch hours, visiting homes and community centers, and holding services "anywhere" when their churches were destroyed by bombs.

Fr. Coleman came to Madison from Victoria, Canada, where he is on a mission to the British Columbia diocese of the Church of England. As chaplain in the Canadian merchant navy he has made several trips in the Pacific re-

(Continued on Page 2, Column 2)

U.S. Waits Word of Other Blows

Yankees Expected to Be in Action Soon

WASHINGTON — (U.P.) — Pres. Roosevelt and Prime Minister Winston Churchill today followed reports of the Allied drive into Italy with close attention, examining official dispatches from the new front between conferences with high Allied war experts.

Mr. Roosevelt and the prime minister conferred after dinner Thursday night and waited until 1 o'clock this morning for the official flash that the Italian invasion had begun. But when it did not come by that time, both men—tired

(Continued on Page 2, Column 1)

Feature Finder

Italy Gloomy as Allies Strike

Nation Near Chaos, Travellers Report

LONDON — (U.P.) — Italy was reported shaken by a chaotic tangle of military and political troubles today as the British Eighth army invaded her southern boot.

The long-expected attack came as speculation in London on how long Italy could stay in the war reached its height.

Rico Avello, a Spanish engineer, arrived in Barcelona from Rome Thursday night and told newsmen that all Italy was caught in a wave of deep depression. A passenger on the same plane said the country was "moving rapidly toward political chaos."

The Daily Express reported in a Bern dispatch that Premier Marshal Pietro Badoglio, successor to the fallen Mussolini, had arrested

(Continued on Page 2, Column 7)

Eberhardt, Beauty Shop Owner, Dies

Leonard Eberhardt, 53, owner of the Cardinal Beauty shop, 631 State st., died at the shop today after a heart attack. His home was at 616 W. Shore dr.

The police ambulance was called, but Mr. Eberhardt was dead when it reached the shop. The body was taken to the Frautschi funeral home.

Survivors are his wife, Marie; three sons, Lieut. Leo H., with the U. S. army in Iceland, and Herbert and Siegfried, at home; two brothers in this country, Henry, Madison, and John, Dubuque, Ia., and his father, two brothers, and two sisters in Germany.

A Madison resident for 20 years, Mr. Eberhardt was known to hundreds of women residents. He was born at Stuttgart, Germany, and operated a beauty shop there before coming to this country in 1923.

He served three years in the German army during World War I, most of the time on the Russian front. He had been associated with the Madison and Wisconsin foundation, the Mannerchor, and the Optimist club.

Hansen New Head of Army School

Lieut. Col. William R. Young, commanding officer of the U. S. Armed Forces institute, has been transferred from Madison and Lieut. Col. Carl W. Hansen appointed commandant of the army education school.

Hansen's home is at Quincy, Ill. He came here from Ft. Washington, Md., where he had been with the adjutant general's school.

Col. Young had been director of the institute since it was organized in April, 1942. He was ordered to report to the special services replacement pool, Lexington, Va.

Bi-Monthly Tin Can Collection to Continue

The bi-monthly schedule of tin can collection, adopted early this summer, will be continued at least through the fall, City Engineer T. F. Harrington announced today. The next collection will be set for the last two days in October.

Troops Hunt for Baraboo Flier Who Bails Out of Blazing Ship

NEW YORK —(U.P.)— Search for a missing army pilot, Second Lieut. Charles J. Collins, who bailed out of his fighter plane before it crashed and burned Wednesday night, was intensified today when army pilots spotted a large "SOS" outlined in the clay in the wooded, rolling hills near Brimfield, Mass., the army air force at Westover Field, Mass., announced through the eastern defense command here. Collins is from Baraboo, Wis.

More than 600 troops from Westover Field who had been searching for the pilot were notified of the discovery and continued the search in widening circles from the point where the message was inscribed. Early reports that his parachute had been found proved erroneous when officers reaching the scene examined the remnants and learned it was not parachute material.

Army authorities set up a command post southwest of Brimfield and are maintaining radio com-

LIEUT. CHARLES COLLINS

munications with the planes and ground searchers.

Collins is the son of Mrs. Jeanette M. Lindsay, Baraboo.

'Hot' Wire Kills Man Near Sparta

SPARTA—Alfred C. Taylor was fatally injured and his brother severely burned when they came in contact with a live wire at Camp McCoy late Thursday. They are sons of Mrs. Minnie Taylor, Route 2, Tomah..

The brothers were working on a pole near the post headquarters when a live wire broke, falling across Alfred, who was knocked 30 feet to the ground. Walter attempted to rescue him and was severely burned. He was rescued by Pvt. Roland E. Kornfuehre, Camp McCoy.

Alfred died at the Camp McCoy Station hospital, where Walter also was taken.

Under Cover of Moonless Night, Allied Fleet Puts Out for Italy

By ALAN MOORHEAD
(Representing the Combined British Press)

AN INVASION PORT, Sicily—(U.P.)—Many hundreds of Allied ships and barges set out for the Italian coast Thursday night with only the light of the stars to guide them to the enemy beaches.

There was no moon to betray them and the sea had been consistently calm for more than a week.

Extraordinary scenes led up to the moment when the first wave of the expedition got under way.

For the past 10 days, vast numbers of men and vehicles have been feeding the invasion ports. If you can imagine a pre-war London traffic jam magnified 100 times, then you can guess what the roads have been like.

Storm Hampered Preparations

Once I watched a battery of heavy guns being drawn foot by foot with winches across the sheer face of a precipice.

One night an unseasonable and violent storm swept the beach embarkation area. In the night, bridges were washed away and where there had been heavy dust, bulldozers struggled through mud to make new roads and detours.

It was hot by day. Perched half-naked on top of their guns and tanks, the men kept sucking grapes and melons bought from Italian peasants along the way.

Sometimes traffic halted for an hour and infantry jumped down and brewed sticky tea in the vineyards.

New and complex road signs sprang up all over the country to guide the columns down to their right coves and beaches.

Meanwhile, invasion barges — that same mosquito fleet that made

(Continued on Page 2, Column 2)

More and More Troops Land

By C. R. CUNNINGHAM
(United Press Staff Correspondent)

ADVANCE ALLIED PHOTOGRAPHIC RECONNAISSANCE FIELD, North Africa, Sept. 3, 1:30 p. m. —(U.P.)— The first pilot returning from the Italian mainland battlefront said today that he saw Allied warships streaming toward the coast at 10 a. m., their guns spitting fire against the shore as they snaked back and forth around invasion barges.

Flying Officer George Craig, a Spitfire pilot from Edinburgh, Scotland, brought the first report of the situation at midmorning which revealed that troops still were pouring onto the toe of Italy.

A steady stream of invasion barges was flowing to Italy, Craig said, under a protecting screen maintained by the warships.

Craig, a tall, 24-year-old former policeman was the first photo reconnaissance pilot to come back from the front.

"There were absolutely no other planes around me while I was flying in perfect weather from far up in Italy down the western coast over the straits of Messina," Craig said.

"We could look down and see all those invasion craft. They looked like a school of fish, and they were moving fast.

"Apparently a lot of fire was being directed at the landing troops from up in the hills. And of course the ships kept firing constantly, probably hitting enemy guns back in the hills."

Louis A. Geffert Dies at Home

Louis A. Geffert, 75, retired harness maker, died today at his home, 1047 E. Johnson st.

Mr. Geffert operated a harness shop in the first block of E. Washington ave., for many years and was well known among early residents.

Survivors are his wife; a son, Clarence, Beaver Dam, and two daughters, Mrs. J. B. Williams, Ottumwa, Ia., and Mrs. Frank R. Dentz, Jr., Lebanon, Pa.

The body was taken to the Frautschi funeral home.

The Wisconsin State Journal

A fact-finding Newspaper

MADISON, TUESDAY, JUNE 6, 1944

HOME FINAL
PRICE FIVE CENTS
22 Pages—★★★★
VOL. 154. NO. 65 105th Year

Allies Smash Ahead in Normandy

♦ ♦ ♦ ♦ ♦ ♦ ♦ ♦ ♦

Drive Covers All Peninsula, Nazis Say

Where Allies Land on Normandy Coast, Seize Footholds, Fight Inland

Prime Minister Churchill revealed today that Allied invasion troops were fighting in Caen, 9½ miles inside northwest France, shown in the "Low Shores" sector of the above map, a sector covering the Cherbourg-to-Le Havre coast line, where Germans said Allies had landed. Churchill said invasion penetrations had reached several miles depth in some cases, and that footholds had been established. An Allied spokesman said the invaders had "gotten over the first five or six hurdles," and Germans admitted invasion landing barges had penetrated two estuaries behind the Atlantic Wall.

Allied invaders are trying to capture important railway junctions, such as shown along heavy lines above, after inland landings in France, German reports declared today, after admitting invasion from Cherbourg to Le Havre. Allied reports said the invaders threatened to take a railroad leading straight to Paris.

Allies Drive Germans North of Rome on 17-Mile Front

ALLIED HEADQUARTERS, Naples—(U.P.)—The Allied Fifth army drove the battered Germans in disorderly retreat across the Tiber river on a 17-mile front from Rome to the Tyrrhenian sea today and sent powerful armored columns 5 miles beyond the river under orders to destroy the fleeing enemy.

Front dispatches said German Field Marshal Albert Kesslering's broken 14th army was offering only the feeblest sort of rear guard resistance as Allied tanks and riflemen burst across the winding Tiber at a score of points north and west of Rome.

At many points the enemy retreat had turned into a disorganized rout under the raking fire of Allied planes and tanks, and 2,000 Germans threw down their arms and surrendered to a fast-rolling British column that trapped them on the east bank of the river.

Every bridge across the Tiber below Rome had been blown up by the fleeing Germans, but 11 of the 14 main spans inside the capital were intact and Allied troops were crossing in a steady stream.

Only in the northeastern outskirts of Rome did the Germans offer any determined resistance. A force of enemy tanks was reported battling desperately around the Littoria airport in an attempt to stem the swift Allied advance long enough for the main body of Kesselring's troops to escape.

Official sources said the Vatican had been by-passed in all Allied operation.

French troops on the Fifth army's right knifed deep into the hills east of Rome, seizing the highway junction of Tivoli, 16 miles outside the capital.

The French thrust threatened the line of retreat for tens of thousands of German 10th army troops falling back slowly before the British Eighth army in the mountainous country and east of the Via Casilina.

The Eighth and Fifth army fronts were linked in a continuous front winding 70 miles inland from the Tyrrhenian coast, through Rome and down into the Sacco valley, and the almost pocketed German 10th army appeared to be fighting only a desperate rear-guard action in an effort to extricate the bulk of its forces.

Thy Will Be Done

◆ ◆ ◆

Our Father which art in Heaven, hallowed be thy name.

Thy kingdom come. Thy will be done, on earth as it is in Heaven.

Give us this day our daily bread.

And forgive us our trespasses as we forgive those who trespass against us.

And lead us not into temptation, but deliver us from evil: For Thine is the kingdom, and the power, and the glory, forever. Amen.

Here's Scene from Bomber 5,000 Feet Up

By COLLIE SMALL
(United Press War Correspondent)

WITH A MARAUDER FORMATION OVER THE INVASION COAST —(U.P.)— No-man's land is 5,000 feet below.

It's somewhere between the grey, channel-washed beaches on which Allied troops are swarming from their landing barges and the brown fields beyond. The wink of gunflashes in the half-light of dawn in those fields came from Germans fighting the invasion.

My aerial grand-stand seat is in a Marauder piloted by First Lieut. Carl Oliver of Sacramento, Calif., a part of an unending stream of Allied aircraft, ranging from fighters to heavies, which is streaming across the channel to support the infantry assault

Five thousand feet is one of the lowest altitudes the medium bombers ever have bombed from in this theater, but we chance the German flak to pinpoint our targets.

We weave through flak that bursts all around us and then go into our bomb run. Hundreds of fragmentation. bombs tumbled through the bomb bay doors upon the German gun emplacements below Great columns of smoke and dust spiral up among the formations.

"That will teach those so and so's to shoot at us!" bellows the bombardier, First Lieut. Eldon Le

(Continued on Page 2, Column 4)

Bulletins

LONDON —(U.P.)— The German-controlled Vichy radio said today that violent fighting was taking place on the islands of Guernsey and Jersey, west of the Norman peninsula, and that the Allies were suffering heavy losses.

LONDON —(U.P.)— The German Transocean news agency said today that about 80 medium-sized Allied warships were approaching the town of Ouistreham in the estuary of the Orne river.

LONDON —(U.P.)— DNB, German news agency, acknowledged today that Allied tanks had penetrated several kilometers between the towns of Caen and Isigny on the Normandy peninsula.

LONDON —(U.P.)— More than 640 naval guns, ranging from 4-inch to 16-inch, are bombarding the French beaches and enemy strong points in support of the Allied armies, Allied supreme headquarters announced today.

LONDON —(U.P.)— German coastal artillery in France opened up with salvoes across the channel soon after noon today, shaking towns in southeast England.

WASHINGTON—(U.P.)—Headquarters of the European theater of operations reported to the war department today that Allied aircraft covering the invasion "are hitting any target that has a bearing on the strength of the armies at the front."

WASHINGTON —(U.P.)— The house today approved a resolution which would require institution of courtmartial proceedings against Maj. Gen. Walter C. Short and Rear Admiral Husband E. Kimmel before Sept. 7.

FDR Writes Prayer —Asks All to Join Him

WASHINGTON—(U.P.)—Following is Pres. Roosevelt's prayer for success of our arms in their task—a prayer in which he asks all to join when he utters it by radio at 9 tonight over WIBA and all network stations:

My fellow Americans:

In this poignant hour, I ask you to join me in prayer:

Almighty God: Our sons, pride of our nation, this day have set upon a mighty endeavor, a struggle to preserve our republic, our religion, and our civilization, and to set free a suffering humanity.

Lead them straight and true; give strength to their arms, stoutness to their hearts, steadfastness to their faith.

They will need Thy blessings. Their road will be long and hard. The enemy is strong. "e may hurl back our forces. Success may not come with rushing speed, but we shall return again and again; and we know that by Thy grace, and by the righteousness of our cause, our sons will triumph.

They will be sore tried, by night and by day, without rest—'til the victory is won. The darkness will be rent by noise and flame. Men's souls will be shaken with the violences of war.

These are men lately drawn from the ways of peace. They fight not for the lust of conquest. They fight to end conquest. They fight to liberate. They fight to let justice arise, and tolerance and good will among all thy people. They yearn but for the end of battle,

(Continued on Page 2, Column 5)

Patricia Mich Plans to Divorce Editor

Daniel D. Mich, executive editor of Look magazine and former Wisconsin State Journal managing editor, confirmed from New York today the report that his wife, the former Patricia Leary, of Boscobel, had gone to Florida to establish three-month residence preparatory to beginning suit for divorce.

Affirming an observation in Walter Winchell's column, written for publication Wednesday, that "the wife of Look's executive editor is in Florida, but not for the climate," Mich said that the agreement for the divorce had been a friendly one and that the terms and settlements had been amicably reached.

Mrs. Mich, at present taking a course at Daytona Beach in care of returning disabled service men, will return to New York to live after granting of the divorce.

The pair was married in Chicago on Nov. 18, 1927.

Invaders Fighting 10 Miles in France

BULLETIN

LONDON —(U.P.)— The German Transocean news agency said tonight that the Allied "offensive area" had been extended to the entire Norman peninsula.

LONDON —(U.P.)— Radio France at Algiers quoted a German broadcast today as saying that Allied parachutists had occupied an airdrome in the Boulogne-Calais area of the French coast along the straits of Dover.

By VIRGIL PINKLEY
(United Press War Correspondent)

SUPREME HEADQUARTERS, Allied Expeditionary Force, London—American, British, and Canadian invasion forces landed in northwestern France today, established beachheads in Normandy, and by evening had "gotten over the first five or six hurdles" in the greatest amphibious assault of all time.

Prime Minister Winston Churchill revealed that Allied troops were fighting inside Caen, 9½ miles inside northwest France, that the invasion penetrations had reached several miles in depth in some cases, and that footholds had been established on a broad front as the operation proceeded "in a thoroughly satisfactory manner."

Gen. Dwight D. Eisenhower's supreme headquarters revealed that the Allied armies, carried and supported by 4,000 ships and 11,000 planes, encountered considerably less resistance than had been expected in the storming of Adolf Hitler's vaunted west wall.

German broadcasts reported Allied troops pouring ashore most of the day along a broad reach of the Norman coast and to the east, and admitted that invasion landing barges had penetrated two estuaries behind the Atlantic wall.

The apparent key to the lightness of the German opposition to invasion forces opening the battle of Europe was contained in a disclosure that thousands of Allied planes dropped more than 11,200 tons of bombs on German coastal fortifications in eight and a half hours Monday night and early today.

Luftwaffe to Fight to Death

As massive Allied air fleets took over complete command of the skies over the invasion zone, Reichmarshal Hermann Goering issued an order of the day to his air force declaring that the invasion "must be fought off, even if it means the death of the luftwaffe."

Late in the day Churchill, making his second statement of the day to commons, said the invasion was proceeding "in a thoroughly satisfactory manner." Earlier he told commons it was going "according to plan—and what a plan!"

Simultaneously the German DNB news agency reported that the invasion front "has been further widened." German broadcasts throughout the day told of the amphibious assault developing on a grand scale, with fighting as deep as 10 miles inland—a figure apparently extended by the last enemy report.

The Allied command gave the go-ahead order Monday night despite strong northwest winds and rain squalls when weather experts forecast improving conditions today. The weather still was somewhat unfavorable, however,

(Continued on Page 2, Column 1)

BEACHHEAD ESTABLISHED

Invasion Scheduled for Monday, Delayed

LONDON—(U.P.)— The Allied high command revealed today that the invasion of western Europe originally was scheduled to take place Monday but had to be postponed for 24 hours because of bad weather.

D-Day in Madison

A picture of Madison and its surrounding communities at their work and their prayers on invasion day, gathered by State Journal reporters and photographers, is presented on Pages 3 and 8 in this edition, designed for a permanent reminder of this historic day and as a handy letter from home to the men and women making the news on the fighting fronts.

To Father of All for Sons of Many

A reverent mother and daughter, Adelaide and Mrs. August Knoche, Sr., 427 W. Dayton st,. knelt in the dimness of Holy Redeemer Catholic church early today, repeating prayers for the soldiers who are invading Europe's new front. Mrs. Knoche's son, Pvt. Richard, is serving with the army medical corps at Camp Bowie, Tex., and a grand-nephew, Pvt. Robert Knoche, is with the marines at San Diego, Calif.

Russian Attack Seen Within 48 Hours

LONDON —(U.P.)— Military observers said today that a general Russian offensive coordinated with the Anglo-American attack from the west may be launched within the next 48 hours and almost certainly will begin before the week-end.

The United Press informants said a crushing two-way attack from the east and west was laid down by the American, British, and Russian leaders at the Tehran conference last year, envisaging the complete destruction of German military power before the close of 1944.

Both the German radio and other reports reaching London indicate that Soviet artillery has been increasingly active all along the lower Dnestr front, where huge Russian armies are believed to have completed their regrouping in preparation for a new drive to the west.

Henry Resigns, Files for Congressional Post

Robert K. Henry, Jefferson, today filed his papers as a candidate for the Republican nomination for congress in the second district and announced his resignation as a member of the state banking commission effective July 1.

Henry, former state treasurer, said he was resigning from the banking commission to make the race for congress in this district.

Feature Finder

Weather

Clearing and diminishing winds tonight with scattered light frost in lowest places. Wednesday fair and warmer.

Weather
Cloudy and cooler tonight with occasional light rain. Thursday cloudy and cooler. The low, 40; the high, 50.

The Wisconsin State Journal
A fact-finding Newspaper

Don't Burn This Paper . . . Paper Fights for Victory — MADISON, WEDNESDAY, NOVEMBER 8, 1944 ★★★

HOME FINAL
PRICE FIVE CENTS
20 PAGES
VOL. 155, NO. 39 105th Year

FDR's Lead Grows to 2,630,384

State Voters Reelect Wiley, Support Dewey

The Winners

PRES. ROOSEVELT GOV. GOODLAND

Tables on Pages 2, 10, and 11

President
Franklin D. Roosevelt (D)
Vice-President
Harry S. Truman (D)
United States Senator
Alexander Wiley (R)
Governor
Walter S. Goodland (R)
Lieutenant Governor
Oscar Rennebohm (R)
Secretary of State
Fred R. Zimmerman (R)
State Treasurer
John M. Smith (R)
Attorney General
John E. Martin (R)
Congress, First District
Lawrence Smith (R)
Congress, Second District
Robert K. Henry (R)
Congress, Third District
William H. Stevenson (R)
Congress, Fourth District
Thad Wasielewski (D)
Congress, Fifth District
Andrew J. Biemiller (D)
Congress, Sixth District
Frank B. Keefe (R)
Congress, Seventh District
Reid Murray (R)
Congress, Eighth District
John W. Byrnes (R)
Congress, Ninth District
Merlin Hull (P)
Congress, Tenth District
Alvin E. O'Konski (R)
Assembly, First District
Lyall T. Beggs (P)
Assembly, Second District
Earl Mullen (P)
Assembly, Third District
R. W. Roethlisberger (R)
District Attorney
Norris E. Maloney (P)
Sheriff
John R. Arnold (P)
Coroner
Edward Fischer (P)
County Clerk
Austin Johnson (P)
Register of Deeds
Albert O. Barton (P)
County Treasurer
Clarence Femrite (P)
Clerk, Circuit Court
Myrtle Hansen (P)
Surveyor
Andrew Dahlen (P)

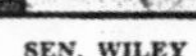

SEN. WILEY ROBERT K. HENRY

Third Army Opens New Drive Near Metz

BULLETIN

WITH THE U. S. THIRD ARMY IN FRANCE— (U.P.) — American troops have captured at least 13 towns in the first 12 hours of a new offensive along a 27-mile front between Nancy and Metz.

By J. EDWARD MURRAY
(United Press Staff Correspondent)

PARIS — Lieut. Gen. George S. Patton's American Third army made a new attack between Metz and Nancy in eastern France today and advanced up to 1 mile in the first few hours, capturing at least four villages and crossing the Seille river.

The doughboys forced the Seille, and tributary of the Moselle, at several places approximately 13 miles south of Metz and already had outflanked that enemy bastion from the south, United Press War Correspondent Collie Small reported.

On the southwestern approaches to Cologne, a German counter-attack drove American First army troops out of the hamlet of Kommerscheidt, some 13 miles southeast of Aachen, but the doughboys held firmly to high ground 500 yards to the northwest and edged closer to Schmidt, a mile to the southeast.

Kommerscheidt was the third town to be won and lost in the period of a few days at the tip of the deepest Allied salient in Germany. The swaying street

(Continued on Page 2, Column 7)

Budapest Radio Says Reds Land on Nearby Isle

LONDON — (U.P.) — Radio Budapest said today that Soviet troops, outflanking the Hungarian capital from the south, had landed on a small island in the middle of the Danube, river 4 miles away.

"Fighting is going on not far from Budapest," the broadcast said, adding that Soviet artillery and anti-aircraft guns already were firing from Dunaharaszti, suburban town on the east bank of the Danube also within 4 miles of the capital.

The Hungarian broadcast said the attack apparently was designed to build up a base for an assault on 30-mile-long Csepel island, an industrial center between the eastern and western arms of the Danube below Budapest.

The Soviet high command for the second straight day made no mention of the fighting around Budapest in its communiques.

Senator Ahead of McMurray by 100,043

Dewey, Leading FDR by 26,945, Wins State Electoral Votes

Wisconsin voters returned Republican Alexander Wiley to the United States senate in Tuesday's election.

Wisconsin, which started the "draft Dewey" boom in the state delegate election last April, stuck with the Republican presidential nominee. Though Dewey's campaign ended in disaster on a nationwide scale, he won the 12 electoral votes of Wisconsin Tuesday.

Returns from 2,969 of Wisconsin's 3,098 precincts gave:

Dewey	**646,117**
Roosevelt	**619,172**
Thomas	**9,403**
Teichert	**689**

Wiley survived a bitter attack by his Democratic opponents as one of eight "willful men" who voted against all important administration defense measures before Pearl Harbor.

Wiley, a Republican, was followed by his Democratic opponent, Rep. Howard J. McMurray, a 100 per cent New Dealer, and Madison's Progressive Harry Sauthoff who ran a poor third.

Returns for 2,931 of the state's 3,098 precincts:

Wiley (R)	**592,399**
McMurray (D)	**492,356**
Sauthoff (P)	**55,812**
Uphoff (S)	**6,661**

The incumbent, a 60-year-old small town lawyer of Norwegian parentage from Chippewa Falls, thus will return to the senate for his second six-year term. McMurray based his campaign on an attack against Wiley's record of having voted before Pearl Harbor against lend-lease, extension of selective military service, repeal of the neutrality act, and permitting U. S. vessels to enter combat zones to deliver lend-lease cargo. Both Vice-Pres. Henry A. Wallace and his successor-elect, Harry Truman, campaigned in this state against Wiley.

Wiley countered criticism of his voting record by assailing the Roosevelt administration's domestic policies. His campaign won vindication in the rejection of Pres. Roosevelt and administration supporters by Wisconsin voters. It was the president's first defeat at the Wisconsin polls since he was elected president in 1932, but it failed to hinder his reelection.

Voters Elect Roethlisberger, Beggs, Mullen

Dane county Republicans captured one of this county's three seats in the assembly from Progressives Tuesday in general election voting that was marked by improvement of GOP strength in this traditional stronghold of the LaFollette party.

Republican winner was R. W. Roethlisberger, Verona farmer and county board member, who defeated Progressive Cornelius Sorenson, Mt. Horeb, for the third district assembly seat vacated by retirement of Albert Baker, Mt. Horeb Progressive.

Beggs Defeats Becker

In Dane county's two other assembly districts, Progressives continued to hold their offices. In the Madison district, Progressive Lyall T. Beggs, incumbent, defeated Stuart Becker, Republican nominee and first ward alderman. In the second (eastern) district, Progressive Earl Mullen, Blooming Grove, was reelected to defeat Sverre O. Braathen, Republican from the town of Dunn.

Returns showed:

Third District (Complete)	
Roethlisberger (R)	**6,111**
Sorenson (P)	**5,095**
First District (Complete)	
Beggs (P)	**14,721**
Becker (R)	**12,431**
Mintz (Soc.)	**215**
Second District (Complete)	
Mullen (P)	**6,023**
Braathen (R)	**4,561**

In 1940, Progressives captured the district won Tuesday by Republican Roethlisberger when they

(Continued on Page 2, Column 3)

Goodland Leads GOP to Triumph

Party Wins Easily as Democrats Gain, Progressives Falter

Walter Samuel Goodland, 81, today led Wisconsin's state constitutional officers in a successful drive for reelection in a Republican victory that saw Madison's Oscar Rennebohm added to the list of GOP state officials as lieutenant governor.

Goodland and his companion candidates—Secretary of State Fred R. Zimmerman, Atty. Gen. John E. Martin, and State Treasurer John M. Smith—all were reelected easily in state voting in which the rise of Democratic strength and virtual disappearance of Progressive power were the outstanding developments.

Tops State Vote

Goodland, who for the past two years has served as "acting" governor since the death of Progressive Gov. Elect Orland S. Loomis, had asked for election as governor in fact on the basis of his record.

Wisconsin voters' in Tuesday's general election, paid the aged but vigorous chief executive a smashing tribute by awardng him more votes than any other candidate on the state ticket.

GOVERNOR

Returns from 2,934 of the state's 3,098 precincts gave:

Goodland (R)	653,300
Hoan (D)	489,206
Benz (P)	61,084
Nelson (S)	6,351

LIEUTENANT GOVERNOR

Returns from 2,665 precincts gave:

Rennebohm (R)	566,945
Whaling (D)	375,781
Gates (P)	64,342
Helberg (S)	8,370

SECRETARY OF STATE

Returns from 2,658 precincts:

Zimmerman (R)	648,608
Joyce (D)	339,506
Woelfel (P)	10,587
Kirst (S)	9,976

STATE TREASURER

Returns from 2,658 precincts:

Smith (R)	587,385
King (D)	346,681
Johnson (P)	50,043
Benson (S)	13,744

ATTORNEY GENERAL

Returns from 2,658 precincts:

Martin (R)	543,647
Keller (D)	367,401
Dieterich (P)	70,593
Davis (S)	10,840

Goodland, by his victory, becomes the oldest man ever to be elected to the governorship of any state.

Outstanding aspect of the state election Tuesday was the potential power displayed by Democratic candidates for the state constitutional offices. For the first time in many years, the Democratic state ticket ran ahead of the Progressive nominees.

Two years ago Wisconsin Progressives elected a governor in

(Continued on Page 2, Column 6)

The Long, Hard Road

The shortest distances to Berlin from advanced Allied lines today:

Western Front—296 miles (from point near Nijmegen. Unchanged in week.)

Russia—315 miles (from Warsaw. Unchanged in week.)

Italy—535 miles from point south of Ravenna. Unchanged in week.)

The Electoral Vote:

ROOSEVELT	
Alabama	11
Arizona	4
Arkansas	9
California	25
Connecticut	8
Delaware	3
Florida	8
Georgia	12
Idaho	4
Illinois	28
Kentucky	11
Louisiana	10
Maryland	8
Massachusetts	16
Minnesota	11
Mississippi	9
Missouri	15
Montana	4
Nevada	3
New Hampshire	4
New Jersey	16
New Mexico	4
New York	47
North Carolina	14
Oklahoma	10
Pennsylvania	35
Rhode Island	4
South Carolina	8
Tennessee	12
Texas	23
Utah	4
Virginia	11
Washington	8
West Virginia	8
Total	407

DEWEY	
Colorado	6
Indiana	13
Iowa	10
Kansas	8
Maine	5
Michigan	19
Nebraska	6
North Dakota	4
Ohio	25
Oregon	6
South Dakota	4
Vermont	3
Wisconsin	12
Wyoming	3
Total	124

Again, Perseverance Wins for Rennebohm

Oscar Rennebohm, Wisconsin's lieutenant governor-elect, is an outstanding example of persevering youth rewarded by success in business and politics.

The former Leeds farm boy who worked his way through school and built a business which he developed from one to 13 drug stores in Madison in 32 years won success in his initial political venture, the lieutenant governorship.

Meeting people and making new acquaintances is one of Oscar Rennebohm's happiest diversions from business, and his campaign this year in the primary and general election gave him wide opportunity to combine that activity with practical results.

As lieutenant governor, Rennebohm will preside over the state senate and serve as acting governor in the absence of Gov. Walter S. Goodland, a long advance since young Oscar Rennebohm was a member of the debating team at East Division high school in Milwaukee.

Rennebohm literally hammered his way into school at the age of four years. The rural school teacher got tired of having him follow his brothers and sisters to school and pound on the door with a stick for admission and so she eventually let him in and put him to work with the other beginners.

There were five boys and four girls in the Rennebohm family, and when Oscar was 10 years old, they moved to Milwaukee. He had a job as a newspaper carrier boy there, earning 15 cents a week and saving 10. When he amassed $4 he paid it to another boy for a newspaper route which did not belong to the seller and which Oscar therefore did not get, a deal which doubtless influenced many later Rennebohm business transactions. Soon, however, the boy had his

(Continued on Page 2, Column 4)

OSCAR RENNEBOHM

MRS. OSCAR RENNEBOHM

Entire Progressive Slate Wins in Race for Dane County Posts

Defeating one of the biggest Republican threats in 10 years, the Progressive party clinched its hold on Dane county offices by reelecting its entire slate in Tuesday's election.

Reelected were Sheriff John R. Arnold, Treasurer Clarence L. Femrite, Register of Deeds Albert O. Barton, Clerk of Circuit Court Myrtle L. Hansen, Surveyor Andrew Dahlen, Coroner Edward A. Fischer, County Clerk Austin N. Johnson, and Dist. Atty. Norris E. Maloney.

The Republican vote was stronger in Tuesday's election than in any other race for county offices since before the Progressives moved into the courthouse in 1934. Most of the Progressives were elected by less than half of the majority they carried in the last election.

Closest battle was the district attorney's race which ended in Maloney defeating Atty. Edward J. Owens by only 3,342 votes. Maloney was low man in votes received on his party's slate, while Owens carried top honors for the Republican ticket. In the 1942 election, Maloney polled 73 per cent of the total votes cast, as compared to the less than 52 per cent he received in this election.

High man of the opposed candidates on the Progressive ticket

(Continued on Page 2, Column 5)

Train Wreck Kills 10

COLFAX, Calif.—(U.P.)—At least 10 persons were killed and a score injured early today when a 14-car section of the southern Pacific Challenger, bound for San Francisco, was derailed 3 miles west of here, plunging the engine, the baggage car, and one coach into a ditch.

2,600 of 4,147 Service Ballots Return

City Clerk A. W. Bareis today reported that of 4,147 men and women in the armed service to whom ballots were mailed, 2,600 voted.

Electoral Count: 407; Dewey Concedes; Record Vote Forecast

New Deal Tide Assures Democrats Control of Both Houses of Congress

By LYLE C. WILSON
(United Press Staff Correspondent)

NEW YORK—The election of Pres. Roosevelt to a fourth term was conceded today by Gov. Thomas E. Dewey as steadily mounting returns from a potential record vote also guaranteed the Democrats numerical control of the house and bolstered the party's strength in the senate.

The count of the ballot in this first wartime election in 80 years continues, and at 1:30 p. m., CWT, a United Press tabulation showed the following popular vote in the 48 states:

Roosevelt	**20,864,847**
Dewey	**18,234,463**

The national returns continued to show Mr. Roosevelt had won or was leading in 34 states. Later returns might switch a few of those states, but not enough to affect the verdict.

Gov. Dewey had won or was leading in 14 states with 124 electoral votes. Necessary to win are 266 electoral votes. Mr. Roosevelt's 34 states totalled 407.

The president's percentage of the vote was 53.3; Dewey's 46.7.

At the same hour four years ago it was Roosevelt 55.1, and Willkie 44.9.

Dewey Failed in East

Dewey lost this 1944 election because he failed to break through Roosevelt defenses in the East. The big cities and most of the big states went for a fourth term. Big New York put its 47 electoral votes solidly behind the president. He exceeded his 1940 vote margin of 224,440 piling up a plurality of 391,000 on the basis of tabulations so far.

But he would have lost the state to Dewey but for the aid of the American Labor party, which allegedly is controlled or influenced by the Communists, and the new Liberal party, an anti-Communist labor organization, making its political debut this election.

The returns in mid-day showed that 351 house members had been elected. The breakdown was:

Democrats	204
Republicans	145
American Labor party	1
Progressive	1
Contests undecided	84

4 GOP Senators Elected

At the same hour, 17 candidates, had been elected to the senate. The breakdown was:

Democrats	13
Republicans	4

Undecided contests 18. Democrats led in 9 and Republicans in 9.

Senate holdovers who did not

(Continued on Page 2, Column 1)

Henry Wins 2nd District Congress Seat

Second congressional district voters Tuesday decided to send a Republican to the seat in the house of representatives that for 10 years has been occupied by a Progressive.

Winner of the position vacated by retirement of Harry Sauthoff, (P-Madison) is Robert K. Henry, Jefferson banker and former state treasurer and member of the state banking commission. Henry was an easy winner over John Nash, Pewaukee Democrat, Herbert C. Schenk, Madison Progressive, and Margaret Gray, Middleton Socialist.

Complete results:

Henry (R)	**74,981**
Nash (D)	**33,732**
Schenk (P)	**21,934**
Gray (Soc)	**786**

In winning, Henry carried every county including Dane, traditional Progressive stronghold where in past elections Satuhoff had built up enough of a lead to overcome narrow defeats in the other four counties in the second district.

The general collapse of Progressive party strength notable in the statewide voting haunted Schenk's campaign. Four year ago, Democratic strength surpassed Progressive in only one county in the second district—Jefferson. Tuesday, the Democratic congressional nominee ran ahead of the Progressive nominee in every county except Dane.

Henry, twice elected state treasurer and once nominated for governor, was a member of the banking commission until he decided to seek the congressional post.

The vote by counties:

Columbia: Nash, 3,057; Schenk, 843; Henry, 8,788, and Gray, 29.

Dodge: Nash, 5,430; Schenk 843; Henry, 13,678, and Gray, 56.

Jefferson: Nash, 5,248; Schenk, 753; Henry, 10,095, and Gray, 59.

Waukesha: Nash, 9,078; Schenk, 754; Henry, 18,625, and Gray, 180.

Dane: Nash, 10,919; Schenk, 18,770; Henry 23,795, and Gray, 462.

FR Foreign Policy Wins, Ball Says

WASHINGTON—(U.P.)—Sen. Joseph H. Ball, young Minnesota Republican who broke with Gov. Thomas E. Dewey on the foreign policy issue, said early today that Pres. Roosevelt's reelection endorses his conduct of the war and his plans for United States participation in a strong international peace organization.

Ball's statement:

"Pres. Roosevelt's reelection Tuesday was a strong endorsement by the people, cutting across party lines, of his administration's conduct of the war and its plans for United States participation in a strong international organization to prevent future wars. Those objectives transcend party lines and our task is to seek national unity in achieving them."

Risser Wins by 5,563

Fred Risser (P-Madison) Tuesday won reelection to a third term in the state senate in a four-cornered race with Republican, Democratic, and Socialist opposition.

Returns from all of Dane county's 82 precincts gave:

Risser (P)	**25,430**
Fiore (R)	**19,867**
Schlotthauer (D)	**9,816**
Sikkema (Soc.)	**219**

Closest challenger to the veteran Progressive campaigner was A. J. Fiore, Madison fuel dealer making his first venture into the political field. Third was George Schlotthauer, Madison attorney who failed to carry a single county precinct but who did surpass Fiore in a few. John Sikkema, Socialist, also failed to carry a precinct.

In the city of Madison, Fiore carried the first, 10th, 13th, 19th, and 20th wards, and scored heavy advantages in surrounding suburbs and in rural areas where it was obvious that the tendency to vote the straight Republican ticket was having effect. Risser carried the remainder of the city wards, and counted heavy advantages in the towns of Blooming Grove and Madison.

In 1940, Progressives won 61 per cent of the total votes cast in Dane county for the senate seat, Republicans got 31 per cent, and Democrats 8.

Feature Finder

Madison Weather
Cloudy and windy tonight and Sunday with occasional light showers. Continued mild temperature. Low tonight 51, high Sunday 68.

The Wisconsin State Journal

A fact-finding Newspaper

Don't Burn This Paper . . . Paper Fights for Victory — MADISON, SATURDAY, MARCH 24, 1945 ★★

HOME FINAL
PRICE FIVE CENTS
8 PAGES
VOL. 155, NO. 173 105th Year

Five Allied Armies Cross Rhine

Yanks, British, Canadians Push 3 Miles in North

EYEWITNESS REPORTS:

3rd, 9th Army Men Find Little Resistance

By ROBERT RICHARDS
(United Press War Correspondent)

WITH THIRD ARMY, ACROSS THE RHINE, Mar. 23—(Delayed)—Lieut. Gen. George S. Patton's Third army troops surged across the Rhine in assault boats Friday night against only a few scattered rifle shots.

And by today not a single Nazi soldier could be found around the American bridgehead on the east bank of Germany's great river barrier.

About 150 Germans were quickly rounded up in the first few hours after the crossing, but that apparently was the end of the opposition.

Neither airplane spotters who flew over the bridgehead nor doughboys streaming along both sides of a dirt road from the river saw one German soldier today. The German army had just vanished.

It was obvious that Patton's blinding speed again had thrown the Nazis into turmoil. The German First army, which undoubtedly had been expected to combat the crossing, was virtually destroyed west of the Rhine and the Nazis may have been unable to cope with the situation.

"Like Midnight Mass"

Both American officers and troops were plainly bewildered by the lack of German reaction. They used such words as "easy" and "holiday" in describing the crossing and one lieutenant said it was "like going to midnight mass."

Only a scattering of rifle fire burst around Patton's men as they started across the Rhine in hand-paddled assault boats about 10 p. m. Friday.

The crossing was made where the Rhine is extremely wide, but its current is not swift. Rather, it moves along with a lazy, green sluggish pace.

Within 25 minutes, the majority of an entire company was across the great river. And behind them came an endless stream of troops who hopped ashore in eager pursuit of the elusive enemy.

During the night, German artillery sent over several bursts and one of the assault boats was seriously damaged. Another of the small craft was sunk just after dawn when nine ME-109s zoomed down close to the water and strafed the boats. But even this didn't shake the troops' composure. They just kept paddling until they reached shore.

Busy Ferrying Point

Today the crossing place is rapidly assuming the aspects of a busy ferrying point on any American river. Boats are moving in every direction and only the smoke from a nearby town is giving evidence of war.

Our artillery stood by during the crossing, prepared to blast the Germans at the slightest provocation, but it never arose and they did little shelling.

While Patton's feat was accomplished with about no opposition, some of the officers cautioned against over-optimism.

One battle-seasoned veteran, First Lieut. Frank E. Bailey, 26, Portland, Ore., believed that "things won't remain so nice."

"It takes some time for old Jerry to get his artillery back and get up where he can let fly at us," Bailey said. "Then we will catch plenty."

No Signs Yet

But there were no signs of it yet.

Maj. Charles E. Strunk, Topeka, Kas., who flew over the bridgehead early today, said all he saw was "our own GIs walking along without opposition. I had expected to come out and find our fellows fighting it out with the Germans right along the water's edge."

By CLINTON B. CONGER
(United Press Staff Correspondent)

ACROSS THE RHINE WITH AMERICAN NINTH ARMY—The American Ninth army stormed the Rhine en route to Berlin in the darkness early Saturday and achieved its initial objectives against surprisingly light opposition.

I came across the Rhine with our infantry and after two hours on the east bank of the great river not a single casualty had been reported by the group which I accompanied.

Opposition was so light that hopes were running high among the American men and officers that they were engaged in the war's last campaign in Europe.

Battalion after battalion of our forces are pouring across the broad Rhine, which is slow-flowing at this crossing point.

Our assault boats are chugging back and forth across the river, spilling troops on the "Berlin bank" as fast as they can be shuttled across.

We hopped off at 2 a. m.

Airborne Moves In

Ahead of us American and British glider and parachutists of the First Allied airborne army already had landed well beyond the river.

And in our area British commandos had silently slipped across the river about four hours before the general H-hour.

The main German forces on the east bank of the river have not yet engaged us. They are known to include the remnants of the crack German First paratroop army. Possibly they are being held back while the Nazi command tries to figure out where the main weight of our attack will fall.

Anti-Climax

My crossing of the river was almost an anti-climax after the days and hours of tense waiting. In the hours before the kick-off possibly the world's greatest artillery barrage had crashed down on the Nazi positions across the river, flattening their strongpoints around the defenders' hads.

But as we crossed the Rhine it was deathly still. Only the quiet lap of the water against the sides of our boat could be heard. Later

(Continued on Page 2, Column 5)

Red Offensive Increases Along Oder Front

Six Divisions Smash to Golzow on Berlin Road

BULLETIN

LONDON —(U.P.)— Marshal Stalin announced tonight that the Red army has advanced 43 miles in a new offensive in Hungary. The assault was opened after counter-attacks by 11 German tank divisions were repelled.

BULLETIN

LONDON — (U.P.) — A German military commentator reported today that Nazi troops have evacuated Szekesfehervar, 34 miles southwest of Budapest and key to the Lake Balaton defenses of Austria.

LONDON—(U.P.)—Nazi broadcasts said at least 90,000 Red army troops, already 6 miles beyond the Oder river, were storming German defenses 32 miles east of Berlin today in what may be the first stages of the climactic battle for the capital.

Six Soviet rifle divisions, supported by 100 or more tanks, cracked through the Oder river line opposite Kuestrin and smashed down the shortest road to Berlin as far as Golzow, 32 miles from the capital, before being halted Friday, German broadcasts admitted.

Other German broadcasts said Soviet pressure was increasing all along the Oder front between Kuestrin and Frankfurt, 16 miles to the south.

The Russians have been attacking Klessin, 33½ miles east of Berlin and 9 miles south of Kuestrin, fiercely "from all sides" for nine days, the Germans said.

While Moscow did not immediately confirm the thrust, both Russian and Nazi dispatches for the past few weeks have reported preparations for a resumption of the Soviet march on Berlin almost complete.

Allied observers have speculated that the Russians would strike toward Berlin simultaneously with an Allied smash across the Rhine in the west in coordinated win-the-war offensives.

Far to the northeast, Second White Russian army forces drove into the outskirts of blazing Danzig and Gdynia after a break-through to the sea midway between the two Baltic ports and isolating the respective garrisons.

Moscow dispatches said it appeared that the final battle to clear Gdynia and Danzig was under way. The Danzig garrison was hemmed into a pocket of 300 square miles and that at Gdynia, 75 square miles.

Second army troops wedged through to the Baltic between the two ports at Zoppot, 6 miles northwest of Danzig. Zoppot itself was captured, along with a 3-mile stretch of the Baltic coast line.

In upper Silesia, the Russians advanced to the Moravian border on a 45-mile front and virtually isolated Leobschuetz, one of the main fortresses protecting the entrance to the Moravian gap through the Sudeten mountains to Prague and Vienna.

Patton's Army Breaches River Near Ludwigshafen

It's 'Final Assault,' Montgomery Says

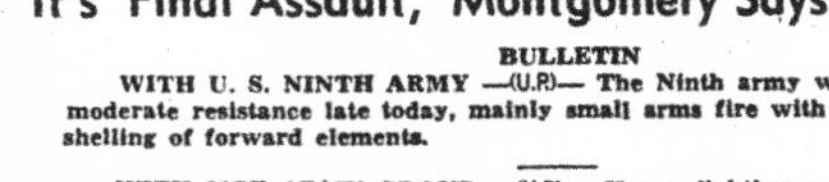

BULLETIN

WITH U. S. NINTH ARMY —(U.P.)— The Ninth army was meeting light to moderate resistance late today, mainly small arms fire with increasing artillery shelling of forward elements.

WITH 21ST ARMY GROUP —(U.P.)— Heavy fighting was going on tonight in the Wesel-Rees area along the east bank of the Rhine. The British Second army had taken more than 1,500 prisoners.

By BOYD D. LEWIS
(United Press War Correspondent)

PARIS—Four Allied land and air borne armies exploded across the Rhine on a broad front north of the Ruhr today and swept east for 3 miles or more in the "last battle of the European war.

In the south, another army—the American Third—crossed the river.

The broad Rhine barrier was breached at four or more points along a front of perhaps 40 miles extending south from the Rees-Wesel sector to Duesseldorf in the Ruhr basin.

Massive armored and infantry forces of the American Ninth, British Second, and Canadian First army were smashing eastward across the burning Westphalian plain against amazingly weak opposition.

Field dispatches indicated they were close to a junction with paratroops and glider-borne infantrymen of the Allied First Airborne army who dropped behind the German lines some miles east of the Rhine.

Veteran amphibious assault teams of the United States navy were working side by side with the ground troops, manning hundreds of big invasion craft massed secretly behind the Rhine for the spectacular crossing.

Twenty hours after the first British shock troops plunged across the river into Wesel, the stunned Germans had failed to mount a single major counter-attack.

Their boasted battle screen along the east bank of the Rhine was shattered beyond repair, and a decisive Allied break-through that could knock Germany out of the war appeared a definite possibility.

Headquarters spokesmen said the Germans' main reserves had not yet joined the battle, and it was indicated the tremendous Allied aerial bombardment of the past three days had crippled the enemy's main communications lines.

The Germans' last hope of averting an immediate breakthrough on the northern high road to Berlin lay now in rushing in their reserves over an area already partially controlled by the Allied airborne forces.

Almost 40,000 veteran American and British sky troopers were reported running riot through the German rear, slashing communications, knocking out gun positions, and clearing the way for a lightning armored sweep into the German heartland.

Front correspondents said Field Marshal Sir Bernard L. Montgomery, commander of the three ground armies, was rushing armored columns through the bridgeheads in great strength. Long lines of tanks and armored troop carriers were rolling up in the wake of the trail-blazing doughboys, ready to swing through and exploit any crack in the Germans' main defenses east of the Rhine.

Sixty-odd miles to the south, the American First army was crowding up against the southern flank of the Ruhr from its expanding Remagen bridgehead east of the Rhine.

Ninety miles south of the First army, Lieut. Gen. George S. Patton's American Third army raised a new threat to the Germans with a surprise crossing of the Rhine near Ludwigshafen. Patton's blazing tank columns there were less than 270 miles southeast of Berlin—closer than Montgomery's men.

Hundreds Surrender

Hundreds of beaten Germans were reported surrendering to the Allied infantrymen along the east bank of the Rhine as the advance

(Continued on Page 2, Column 1)

Today's major assault by four Allied armies breached the Rhine at four points between Rees, at the top of the map, and Duesseldorf, at the bottom.

Air Fleets Pour Supplies Over Rhine

BULLETIN

ROME —(U.P.)— Italy-based American heavy bombers today bombed Berlin for the first time.

LONDON — (U.P.) — American airmen back from the pre-offensive bombardment of the Ruhr said today that a "colossal ground battle" was raging just east of the Rhine near Wesel on the 21st army group front.

More than 200 Liberators dropped supplies to the First Allied airborne army east of the Rhine in the first aerial provisioning of the advanced forces.

Coastal observers who had observed the trans-channel air traffic throughout the war said they never had seen such a spectacular display of aerial might. Bombers, fighters, gliders, and transport planes by the thousands swarmed toward the Rhine front and back again.

One of the day's first operations reported was an assault by more than 1,050 Eighth air force heaviest on 12 German air fields north of the Ruhr.

Returning crewmen said the fields east of the Rhine in the Wesel area were dotted with Allied gliders.

Front dispatches said Allied planes blasted 30 targets in and north of the Ruhr Friday, and dozens of towns and villages blazed like torches all night.

In the day's first announced strike by the American heavies, more than 850 fighters went along on escort duty and to patrol over northwest Germany.

Most of the air fields attacked were jet-propelled fighter bases. The fields were at Hopsten, Achmer, Vechta, Vechtel, Rheine, Hesepe, Nordhorn, Ateenwijk, Zwischenhahn, Plantlunne, Vaarelbusch, and Varrell.

It was the fourth straight day of aerial assault on the Ruhr and its environs which were being softened for the Rhine drive.

American Flying Fortresses and Liberators with strong escorts of fighters led the parade at dawn, followed by squadron after squadron of RAF Spitfires.

During the night, RAF heavy bombers smashed at German troops and fortified positions on the east bank of the Rhine north of the Ruhr valley. Smaller formations of Mosquitos dropped two-ton block-busters on Berlin for the 32nd straight night.

U. S. Carrier Sunk Off Iwo

300 Men Lost With Bismarck Sea

GUAM—(U.P.)—Survivors of the U. S. escort carrier Bismarck Sea, sunk by enemy aerial attack off Iwo Jima Feb. 21, said today that Japanese machine gunners strafed and killed 100 of their shipmates as they struggled helplessly in icy, mountainous seas.

(The Japanese Domei agency said today that two American aircraft carriers which it identified as the "Randolph" and the "Coupens" had been "seriously damaged" at Ulithi in the western Carolines in a surprise raid by Japanese navy planes the night of Mar. 13. The dispatch was reported by the FCC.)

Loss of the 10,200-ton Bismarck Sea with more than 300 casualties, including those shot in the water, was announced today by Admiral Chester W. Nimitz.

The commander, Capt. John Lockwood Pratt, Milford, Del., and Coronado, Calif., and about three-fourths of the ship's personnel were rescued by a destroyer and destroyer escorts.

Among the survivors were six aerial observers of the Fourth marine division.

They had come aboard after a scouting mission over Iwo. Just five minutes before the Bismarck Sea received two mortal hits 30 miles offshore.

Two of the observers, Lieut. Col. Charles F. Duchlein, Baton Rouge, La., and Capt. Norman Goulet, South Milwaukee, Wis., went over the side near the anchor when the "abandon ship" order was given. They were about 1,000 yards away when the Bismarck Sea sank from sight.

Novick's Car Stolen? Chicago Says 'Yes,' Detective Says 'Baloney'

When a detective captain's car is stolen it's front page news.

But Detective Capt. David S. Novick today vehemently denied that it was his car that was stolen this week by two 21-year-old Madison men and driven to Chicago on stolen gasoline.

A Chicago newspaper reported that the two men Fred W. Hunt and Rodney Ruggins, both on parole from the state reformatory at Green Bay, had confessed to Chicago police that they stole Novick's car.

"It's a lot of baloney," Novick claimed. "My car isn't worth stealing." The detective captain said the car was stolen from the Keyes and Walker used car lot on E. Washington ave., and that his name must have been placed on the stolen car report because he telephoned Chicago police about the theft.

Lloyd K. Garrison Named Vice-Chairman of WLB

LLOYD GARRISON

WASHINGTON—(U.P.) — Lloyd K. Garrison, on leave from his post as dean of the University of Wisconsin law school was named today to succeed George W. Taylor as vice-chairman of the War Labor Board (WLB).

Taylor recently was made chairman of the board. Garrison has been with the WLB since 1942 when he joined the agency as general counsel. At the time of his appointment he was one of the public members of the board.

Kraege Urges Quick Action on Car Lots

By RUSSELL B. PYRE
(State Journal Staff Writer)

Immediate action to acquire a limited area near the capitol square as an experimental off-street parking venture was urged by Mayor Kraege Friday night at an informal session with common council members after the regular council meeting.

Kraege submitted a report by the appraisal committee of the Madison board of realtors, which has been working several months on a revaluation of properties in three blocks recommended as sites by the city plan commission. The report showed values slightly higher in most cases and slightly lower in a few instances compared with an appraisal made two years ago.

Members of three standing committees—finance, property and municipal service—comprising a majority of the council membership, authorized the mayor and other city officials to sound out property owners on their "asking prices."

The report on 14 properties in Block 66, facing Fairchild, W. Mifflin, and Henry sts., showed a total appraised value of $152,175 compared with an assessed value of $128,475. The properties, including the Buick garage, appraised at $28,250, would accommodate 262 cars, and without the garage property 200 cars, City Engineer T. F. Harrington estimated.

In Block 107, between Webster, E. Main, and Butler sts., 17 properties, with estimated capacity for 278 cars, were appraised at $147,950 compared with an assessed value of $145,600.

Block 105, between Doty, S. Pinckney and W. Wilson sts., excluding the American Legion clubhouse and a nearby filling station, was appraised in two sections, with a total valuation of $59,800 against an assessed value of $49,250. The Kentzler garage and Starkweather parking lot properties were given a combined value of $41,600 and three smaller properties $18,200. The total area appraised would accommodate 157 cars, while the Kentzler and Starkweather sites would accommodate 127, Harrington said.

Fugitive Driver, Found at Home, Fined on 8 Counts

James Thomas Stormer, the 19-year-old driver who eluded police in a half-hour chase over west side streets Thursday and then escaped from the hospital where he had been taken after colliding with an oil truck, was located today at his home and arraigned in superior court on charges of eight traffic violations.

Superior Judge Roy H. Proctor fined Stormer $100 and costs for reckless driving, and incorporated in that charge the complaints against the youth for driving against traffic failure to yield the right of way, running three arterials, and two counts of speeding.

Stormer pleaded guilty to all of the charges, explaining that he "didn't remember a thing after driving off capitol square." He had escaped from a squad car by traveling as fast as 65 mph in the Highland ave. area, police said, but was captured when his car hit a Struck and Irwin Fuel Oil Co. truck at Commonwealth and Fox aves. Four hours later he "walked out" of Methodist hospital where he had received treatment for multiple cuts and a head injury.

Only two weeks ago, Stormer was released from probation by Dane county authorities. He had been under supervision for nearly a year for repeated disorderly conduct and drunkenness arrests.

Judge Reis, 53 Today, Will Take Dip---If

Circuit Judge Alvin C. Reis today observed his 53rd birthday with the usual business until noon i nthe courthouse. The judge said he planned a birthday swim in Lake Mendota "if the su comes out this afternoon."

Sylvester, Mt. Horeb, Killed Over China

MT. HOREB — First Lieut. William A. Sylvester, 25, air transport command flier, was killed over China Mar. 16, the war department today notified his parents, Mr. and Mrs. S. A. Sylvester, Mt. Horeb.

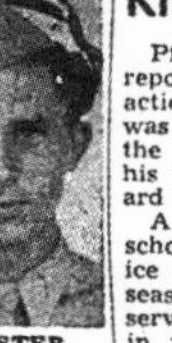

SYLVESTER

The pilot received his wings in 1943 and had been flying "the Hump" delivering supplies to China.

He is survived by his wife in Milwaukee, his parents, and a sister, Mrs. G. A. Davison, a Stoughton teacher.

Lieut. Sylvester graduated from West Salem high school and attended the University of Wisconsin.

James Hammond Killed in Action

Pfc. James Hammond, who was reported on Feb. 19 as missing in action in France since Jan. 16, was killed in action on that date, the war department has notified his parents, Mr. and Mrs. Howard Hammond, 539 W. Main st.

A graduate of Central high school in 1943, he entered service July 9, 1943, and went overseas in September, 1944. He served with the armored infantry in the Seventh army, and had received the expert infantryman and combat infantryman badges.

Survivors include his parents; two sisters, Jean and Alice, and two brothers, John and Jerome, all at home.

A memorial mass will be sung at St. Raphael's Catholic church at 8 a. m. Wednesday.

Ernie Pyle in the Pacific

Without Landing Prerequisite Carrier Bakers Toss In Cake

By ERNIE PYLE

IN THE WESTERN PACIFIC—The second day I was aboard our carrier, the chief steward came up to my cabin and happily announced that he had a cake for me, but it was so big he didn't know how to handle it.

For a while I couldn't get what he was driving at, but finally he made it clear.

It seemed the night bakers had baked a huge cake for me, and it was to be served at dinner that evening. The steward was worried because the cake was so big they didn't have a board big enough to put it on, and therefore couldn't put it on the table where everybody could see it.

ERNIE PYLE

But that evening when we went down to dinner, here was the cake in front of my chair, right in the middle of the table, almost filling it up. They had solved the problem by getting the carpenters to make a board.

Written in pink icing on top of the white cake were the words "Welcome Aboard, Mr. Pyle," and as somebody suggested, I was so taken aback at being called "Mr. Pyle" that I didn't recognize it at first.

I was very pleased and embarrassed by this first official cake of my lifetime, and of course I had to take a lot of ribbing from my friends. They said they'd been slaving on that damn ship for a year and nobody had ever baked a special cake for them.

Then one of the ship's photographers came and took pictures of me ostensibly cutting the cake when I wasn't cutting it at all. And then we ate it.

After supper I groped my way through the labyrinth of passages below, and finally tracked down

(Continued on Page 2, Column 5)

Tipple Gets Bronze Star for Saar Feat

(Special to The State Journal)

WITH THE 95TH INFANTRY DIVISION, Germany—Pfc. Richard E. Tipple, son of Deputy Sheriff and Mrs. John E. Tipple, 2414 Chamberlin ave., Madison, has been awarded the Bronze Star medal for heroic achievement in connection with military operations against the enemy during hard fighting in the 95th "Victory" division's bridgehead across the Saar river from Saarlautern.

Pfc. Tipple is a member of Company L, 379 infantry regiment of Gen. George Patton's famed Third army. In the face of heavy machine gun and sniper fire Tipple fired his rocket launcher from an exposed position with devastating effect on enemy troops entrenched in houses in the cross-river suburb of Saarlautern-Roden.

As his platoon moved into the buildings to rout the remaining Germans, Pfc. Tipple entered one of the houses alone. Inside he captured eight German soldiers who had been servicing a machine gun.

Tipple was graduated from Madison West high school.

Subject to Change

(By United Press)

The nearest distances to Berlin from advanced Allied lines today:

Eastern Front—31 miles (from Zaecherick).

Western Front—268 miles (from Mainz).

Italy—524 miles (from Po di Primaro river.)

Madison Weather
Cloudy and cooler tonight. Saturday mostly cloudy and continued cool. The low tonight, 33; the high Saturday, 50.

The Wisconsin State Journal

A fact-finding Newspaper

Don't Burn This Paper . . . Paper Fights for Victory

MADISON, FRIDAY, APRIL 13, 1945 ★★★

HOME FINAL
PRICE FIVE CENTS
30 PAGES
VOL. 156, NO. 13 106th Year

Weeping Crowds See FR Start Home

Here Is Mr. Roosevelt's Last Picture

PRESIDENT ROOSEVELT

This is the latest news picture of Pres. Roosevelt taken at Washington a few days before his departure for Warm Springs, Ga., where he died suddenly at the Warm Spring foundation.

City Services Planned Saturday for Roosevelt

Madison will join the rest of the nation Saturday in a day of mourning for the man who led the United States for 12 years.

Citywide memorial services will be held at the University of Wisconsin field house at 11 a. m. under sponsorship of the state, city, churches, armed forces in the community, university, and civic and business groups. The university concert band will play.

Business life will come to a standstill during the hours of the funeral in Washington, and retail stores on Capitol square and State st. will remain closed all day. All weekend events on the campus have been cancelled.

Thousands of civilians and servicemen and women will honor Pres. Roosevelt at the memorial services in the field house. Speakers will represent the state, city, university, armed forces, and the Madison Council of Churches. All university classes will be dismissed to permit students and faculty members to join the rest of Madison at the solemn rites.

The Madison Business assn. announced that downtown retail stores will not open their doors Saturday. Food stores expected to close from 2 to 4 p. m. while the funeral is being held in Washington, and taverns planned to cease business for the same hours. Dairies will deliver and process milk as usual, but will close as soon as the essential work is finished.

Mrs. Helen Klingelhofer, president of the Madison Hairdressers and Cosmetologists assn., asked beauty shops to close all day "if arrangements can be made."

Plans for the joint service were made today at a meeting of city, state, religious, business, and university representatives.

Madison's main postoffice, and the University and East Side stations will close at noon Saturday, except that one stamp window and the general delivery window will remain open at the main office. Postmaster W. J. Hyland announced today.

The capitol, city hall and most offices in the courthouse will be closed Saturday. Some courthouse offices, which are required by law to be open, will operate in the morning.

News of Death Leaves City Stunned

The news of the death of Pres. Roosevelt hit Madison hard, striking with an intensity the death of no other man in the world could have evoked.

To thousands it came when the wailing cry of, "Extra! Pres. Roosevelt Dies!" came up with heart pounding suddeness from all corners of the Capitol square, then went out to the side streets as newsboys carried the chant to the far corners of the city.

Populace Stunned

To thousands it came via the spoken word over the radio that brought a sudden deathlike silence in homes of the city, a silence broken only by voice of the announcer as a stunned populace listened.

To thousands, working in war plants, the news was brought by loud speaker, or, coming by phone, was carried with prairie fire speed from worker to worker.

There were two general reactions, one following upon the heels of the other.

The first was that the news could not be true.

The second was a stabbing feeling of personal concern, a wonder what would happen to the country and the world now that the deft hand at the helm had been removed at a time when it was most needed.

Telephones Jammed

The telephone office was flooded with calls, and the blaze of lights on the switchboard of The State Journal continued for more than an hour, as Madisonians concerned with what they hoped were rumors, called for official information.

The news of the death of Pres. Roosevelt was not announced in Madison theaters, but patrons were told of the death of the chief executive by attendants when they left the theaters.

Some thought the news was a

(Continued on Page 2, Column 4)

Big B-29 Fleet Attacks Tokyo

WASHINGTON—(U.P.)—The war department today confirmed Japanese reports of a Super-Fortress attack on Tokyo. The announcement said a fleet of Super-Forts in "very great strength" dropped incendiary bombs on military and industrial targets in the Japanese capital today.

Tornado Toll Set at 81 in Oklahoma

OKLAHOMA CITY — (U.P.) — Death toll in a series of tornadoes which slashed destructive paths across Oklahoma was revised today to 81 and was expected to mount.

More than 500 were reported injured by tempestuous winds which heavily damaged half a dozen communities Thursday night, centering in the southeastern part of the state.

Rescue crews, including 300 soldiers, searched frantically through smashed homes and other buildings for many persons still unaccounted for.

The greatest loss of life was reported at Antlers, a town of 3,200 population which was almost entirely laid waste by the terrific force of the tornado. At least 51 bodies were recovered and more were being found "every few minutes." More than 200 other persons were reported injured at Antlers.

Nine persons, including five students of the demolished Oklahoma School for the Blind, were

(Continued on Page 2, Column 8)

Reds Take Vienna; Report Puts Yanks 15-16 Miles from Berlin

Nazi Defenses Seem Collapsed, Dispatches Say

1st, 3rd Armies' Drive Almost Splits Reich, Menaces Leipzig

(By United Press)

Russian troops today captured Vienna, capital of Austria, while American forces were reported 15 to 16 miles from Berlin, capital of Germany.

BULLETIN

JENA, Germany — (U.P.) — This historic university town is in American hands, except for stray nests of snipers. The town gave up with hardly a struggle.

BULLETIN

WITH THE UNITED STATES FIRST ARMY IN GERMANY—(U.P.)—American First army troops rolled ahead as much as 25 miles today and drove to within 7 miles of Leipzig.

BULLETIN

WITH THE U. S. THIRD ARMY — (U.P.) — American troops today reached the Weisse river. The river is roughly parallel to the Saale and 15 to 25 miles beyond it.

By BOYD LEWIS
(United Press War Correspondent)

PARIS—American troops were reported unofficially only 15 to 16 miles from Berlin today and field dispatches said German resistance appeared to have collapsed even on the last approaches to the wrecked capital.

Far to the south, the American First and Third armies virtualy cut Germany in two with parallel advances that carried almost two-thirds of the way across the Reich and brought the great military base of Leipzig within artillery range.

First army troops reached and perhaps entered Leipzig's companion stronghold of Halle, 15 miles to the northwest, and German spokesmen said other Yank columns were about 10 miles west and southwest of Leipzig at Merseburg and Pegau.

Paratroop Landing Report

Flying tank columns of the Second Armored division officially were out in front of the U. S. Ninth army drive on Berlin after crossing the Elba river near Magdeburg and pushing ahead more than 5 miles to positions 55 miles or less southwest of the capital this morning.

• Unconfirmed Radio Paris reports said, however, that American paratroops had dropped into Brandenburg province only 15 to 16 miles west of Berlin and linked up with the Second Armored division at an undisclosed point.

At the same time, United Press War Correspondent Robert Vermillion reported that the German defenders east of the Elba were fighting no harder than those overwhelmed by the Americans west of the river—where resistance for three days has been almost negligible.

Strong Units Are Across

Vermillion disclosed that strong infantry reinforcements already were over the Elbe and moving up to join the battle for Berlin, with three more divisions at the west bank on a 75-mile front looping to within 45 miles of the city.

To the south, two other American armies—the First and the Third—smashed nearly two-thirds of the way across Germany to

(Continued on Page 2, Column 3)

'Frisco Parley Will Be Held as Scheduled

WASHINGTON — (U.P.) — The United Nations will meet in San Francisco as scheduled on Apr. 25, determined now to create as a memorial to Franklin D. Roosevelt a world organization capable of keeping the peace.

Mr. Roosevelt was one of the major architects of the new peace structure.

His great collaborators — Premier Marshall Josef Stalin and Prime Minister Winston Churchill —described him on his death as the world leader in the cause of ensuring security for the whole world.

Mr. Roosevelt, who has done so much to prepare the United States this time to take its proper place in the new organization and to avoid the mistakes of 1920, had

(Continued on Page 2, Column 4)

Stone Administers Oath to Truman

With the sudden death of Pres. Roosevelt, Vice-Pres. Harry S. Truman was sworn in as president of the United States in a ceremony at the White House. Present were (left to right) Atty. Gen. Francis Biddle, Secretary of State Edward R. Stettinius, Jr.; Pres. Truman; Supreme Court Justice Harlan Fiske Stone, administering the oath of office; War Mobilization Director Fred M. Vinson, and Rep. Joseph W. Martin of Massachusetts, minority leader of the house of representatives.

Truman Takes Helm, Vows to Follow Course of FDR

Through the death of Franklin Delano Roosevelt, Vice-Pres. Harry S. Truman of Missouri has become president of the United States.

Truman was elected with Mr. Roosevelt in 1944. He formerly was U. S. senator from Missouri, and succeeded Henry A. Wallace in the vice-presidency.

HARRY S. TRUMAN

By LYLE C. WILSON
(State Journal Staff Correspondent)

WASHINGTON — Pres. Harry S. Truman today took the nation's helm, and congress, chiefs of the fighting forces and foreign policy leaders closed ranks behind his pledge of quick victory and firm peace as a memorial to Franklin D. Roosevelt.

Within a few hours of taking over the White House he had gone to capitol hill and arranged to make a formal declaration of his objectives before a joint congressional session at noon CWT Monday. He may speak by radio to the armed forces Tuesday night.

Mr. Truman wants Americans to stay on the job Saturday in deference to our late president. But he also believes that "wherever they are" they will want to "share in spirit" in the White House funeral services.

He received pledges of unity and support by the Republicans of the senate and by leaders of all political persuasions.

The leaders of the nation and of its war effort rallied in a massive demonstration of their unity of purpose with the new president.

James F. Byrnes, "assistant president" under Mr. Roosevelt until a few days ago, hurried to the White House to offer its new occupant his intimate knowledge of Mr. Roosevelt's vital discussions with Prime Minister Churchill and Marshal Stalin at Yalta.

There was immediate speculation that Byrnes, who recently resigned as war mobilization director, would return to the White—House to assist Mr. Truman at least for the period of the emergency.

Those who met with Mr. Truman were Senate Democratic Leader Alben W. Barkley (Ky), Senate Republican Leader Wallace H. White, Chairman Tom Connally (D-Tex.) of the senate foreign relations committee, Sen. Warren R. Austin (R-Vt.), Democratic Whip Lister Hill (D-Ala.), Sen. Arthur H. Vandenberg (R-Mich.), Sen. Robert M. La Follette (P-Wis), Sen. Burton K. Wheeler (D-Mont.), House Speaker Sam Rayburn (D-Tex.), House Democratic Leader John W. McCormack (Mass.), House Republican Leader Joseph Martin (R-Mass.), and House Democratic Whip Robert Ramspeck (D-Ga.).

His first official act was to is-

(Continued on Page 2, Column 5)

Solemn Leaders See Truman Sworn In on Roosevelt Bible

By ROBERT J. MANNING and SANDOR S. KLEIN
(United Press Staff Correspondents)

WASHINGTON — The gray-haired man with the gold-rimmed spectacles walked into the awesome confusion that was the White House and into the most momentous hour of his life.

He came in as Vice-Pres. Harry S. Truman and he walked out again as the 32nd president of the United States. He stepped around reporters eager for more news of the death of Franklin D. Roosevelt. He walked past red-eyed secretaries and stenographers who couldn't believe the news. He moved quickly through the glare of photographers' flashlight bulbs.

He made his way into the apple-green cabinet room of the White House. Cabinet members were seated there, solemn-faced. Leaders of congress were there, too. They stood in groups, talking quietly.

Uses Roosevelt Bible

Harry S. Truman sat down in an overstuffed leather chair. It was understandable that he was not completely at ease. Then up stepped Chief Justice Harlan F. Stone of the United States supreme court. The vice-president got to his feet. Someone gave him a Bible from Mr. Roosevelt's office.

He held it reverently on his left palm. His right hand was on the cover. The clock on the mantlepiece pointed to 6:05 p. m. CWT. Three minutes later, the chief justice began administering the oath of office:

"I, Harry Shippe Truman, do solemnly swear that I will faithfully execute the office of president of the United States and will, to the best of my ability, preserve, protect and defend the Constitution of the United States."

'No Middle Name'

The chief justice recited the oath from memory. The new president repeated the words after him, phrase by phrase. But when he came to his name, he said, "Harry S. Truman." He did not use the name "Shippe," and persons who know him well said that was because he really has no middle name; that he was christened

(Continued on Page 2, Column 7)

Movie Theaters Asked to Close

NEW YORK — (U.P.) — All motion picture theaters in the United States have been asked to close Saturday until 6 p. m. in respect for Pres. Roosevelt, the war activities committee of the motion picture industry announced today.

3 U. S. Columns Converge on La Spezia

ROME — (U.P.) — Three Fifth army columns converged today on the Italian naval base of La Spezia, where reports of heavy explosions indicated the Germans were blasting the city.

In eastern Italy, Eighth army troops went across the Santerno river in considerable strength and were steadily expanding three bridgeheads against strong German counter-attacks. The Germans were reported using Tiger tanks.

Pope Pius Wires Personal Condolences

ROME —(U.P.)— Pope Pius XII cabled his personal condolences to Mrs. Roosevelt and Pres. Truman early today immediately after he learned of Mr. Roosevelt's death.

900 Walk Out at Gisholt Over Flag Rule

Because they thought the company's failure to fly a flag at half-mast was disrespectful to the late president, 900 employes of the Gisholt Machine Co. left their jobs for an hour today.

Company officials said the flag was not up because of the rainy weather and said the incident was due to "a misunderstanding on the part of the men and lack of knowledge of flag-flying regulations." The banner was raised at noon, and the men returned to work.

The group walked out at 11 a. m., before consulting George Donner, grievance committee chairman of the CIO union at the plant. Donner got in touch with Stanley Johnson, company vice-president, and the latter said he had called Truax Field on the propriety of displaying a flag in bad weather. Military officials told him plants handling government contracts did not fly a banner in rain unless they had a battle flag.

The ruling was read to the workers, and at the same time the skies showed sign of clearing. The Stars and Stripes were raised by Fred T. Finn, chief of guards at the plant, and employes resumed their tasks.

Affable Man Keeps Humility in Biggest Job

By CHARLES B. DEGGES
(United Press Staff Correspondent)

WASHINGTON — An affable little man who didn't even want to be vice-president and who demands that he remain "Harry" to folks who know him—that's the 32nd president of the United States.

When Harry S. Truman left his seat in the senate to become vice-president, he made it plain to newspapermen that he didn't want his new job to "make any difference." And those who know him say that still goes, even though he now is president of the United States.

The story of Harry Truman is cae that could have taken place only in this country. His path from a Missouri farm to the White House led him through various commonplace jobs and then into politics.

Among Most Respected Senators

He was elected to the senate with the aid of the Pendergast political machine in Kansas City. But he remained free of the stigma that marked many Pendergast men. When that political machine collapsed, he emerged unscathed and was one of the most respected men in the senate.

His fearless conduct as chairman of the senate war investigating committee—long known as the Truman committee — proved clearly his high sense of responsibility in public office. His committee spared no one, not even high administration figures, if it thought their war leadership deserved public criticism.

Under his leadership, the committee made government savings estimated at upwards of $1,000,000,000.

Vowed to Follow FR

Thursday night at 6:08 Harry Truman kept a vow he made 11 years ago to follow Pres. Roosevelt "to the end." He stood in the White House to take the oath of chief executive and pick up the burdens laid down just 2 hours and 35 minutes earlier by his friend. He indicated that he would carry on as Mr. Roosevelt would have wished it.

Mr. Truman was born on a Lamar, Mo., farm on May 8, 1884—60 years ago. He graduated from the Independence, Mo., high school and later studied two years at the Kansas City Law school. Defective vision kept him out of West Point.

He drew $3 a week in his first job—dusting bottles in a drug store. He tried being a railroad timekeeper, bank clerk, and

(Continued on Page 2, Column 2)

Cardinal Extra First on Streets; Journal's Second

The Daily Cardinal, student publication, was the first Madison newspaper to reach the streets with an "extra" telling of the death of Pres. Roosevelt. First in the Madison business section was The Wisconsin State Journal, whose presses started to roll at 5:40 p. m. The State Journal sold more than 8,000 copies of its "extra" in the business and residential areas to citizens who sought confirmation of the radio reports.

Soldier, Sailors Escort Hearse to Train

Muffled Drums, Black-Hung Colors Precede Cortege

BULLETIN

WASHINGTON— (U.P.) —If Franklin D. Roosevelt had lived to address the Jefferson day dinner here tonight, he would have told his listeners that all of the peoples of the world must learn to live together in peace if civilization is to survive, it was revealed late today.

TWO FULL PAGES OF PICTURES—See Pages 10 and 11

WARM SPRINGS, Ga.—(U.P.)—The body of Franklin D. Roosevelt today was borne from the "Little White House" of Georgia to the roll of muffled drums, starting the long, last journey to Washington.

The special train left at 10:13 a. m. CWT.

The hot southern sun shone in a blue sky as the funeral cortege left the green hills the president loved so well. The procession slowly moved down the winding mile-long road to Warm Springs station.

In the distance a church bell pealed from some country steeple.

Along the road stood hundreds of residents of the president's "other home." They bared their heads and stood in silence as the cortege passed.

First came the U. S. army band from Ft. Benning, Ga. The roll of its muffled drums carried softly over the countryside in the still, warm air.

Behind the band marched 1,000 infantrymen, led by three companies of carbine-carrying troops, followed by riflemen. Their colors flew black streamers to signify the mourning of the nation.

Then came the hearse bearing the president's body in a copper-lined, flag-draped mahogany casket.

Mrs. Roosevelt Calm

As the troops reached the little station across the tracks from the Warm Springs hotel and the little row of stores and business buildings, they deployed into company front and presented their arms at the salute.

Behind the hearse and at each flank was the honor guard of high naval officers, afoot. Next came Mrs. Franklin D. Roosevelt, dressed in black with a fur cape. She sat stiffly upright, outwardly composed as she had been throughout.

With Mrs. Roosevelt rode Fala. He sat quietly at Mrs. Roosevelt's feet, apparently sensing that something was wrong.

Veterans Weep

Along the route, troops—overseas veterans—stood at attention. Many of them cried openly as they stood rigidly presenting their arms.

The cortege wound through the pleasant grounds of the Warm Springs foundation. Some two

(Continued on Page 2, Column 1)

Funeral Services to Be Saturday at White House

(By Leased Wire)

Funeral services for Mr. Roosevelt will be held in the East room of the White House at 3 p. m. CWT Saturday. The Rt. Rev. Angus Dun, Episcopal bishop of Washington; the Rev. Howard S. Wilkinson of St. Thomas' church; and the Rev. John G. McGee of St. John's church will conduct the services. Two hundred of the highest-ranking Washington officials and international representatives will attend.

The Roosevelt family was being summoned to Washington. Two sons now overseas will not be able to attend the funeral—Lieut. John and Lieut. Comdr. Franklin, Jr., both in the navy—but their wives will be there. Other family members at the services will include Col. and Mrs. James Roosevelt and Brig. Gen. and Mrs. Elliott Roosevelt. Elliott is coming from Europe.

Until the burial, the president's body will be guarded 24 hours a day by four sentries chosen from enlisted men of the navy, the army, and the marine corps. The sentries were posted at each of the four corners of the coffin and will be rotated in regular shifts.

This was the only guard of honor planned now. There were no plans for the president to lie in state in Washington.

At 9 p. m., Saturday, the funeral party will leave Washington by train for the Roosevelt estate at Hyde Park, N. Y. It will arrive there at 8 a. m. CWT Sunday.

The president will be buried at 9 a. m. Sunday in the sunlit garden between his Hyde Park home and the Franklin Roosevelt library—a garden bordered by a hemlock hedge and a profusion of rose bushes.

The Rev. W. George Anthony of St. James church will conduct the simple burial services.

Madison Weather
Partly cloudy, strong winds this afternoon. Fair tonight. Wednesday partly cloudy and not quite so windy; continued cool with freezing temperatures late tonight. Low expected tonight, 31; high expected Wednesday, 55.

The Wisconsin State Journal

A fact-finding Newspaper

Don't Burn This Paper . . . Paper Fights for Victory

MADISON, TUESDAY, MAY 8, 1945 ★★★

HOME FINAL
PRICE FIVE CENTS
26 PAGES
VOL. 156, NO. 38 106th Year

European War Ends at 5:01 P.M.; U. S., Britain Turn Fury on Japanese

Lips Move in Prayers, Not Cheers

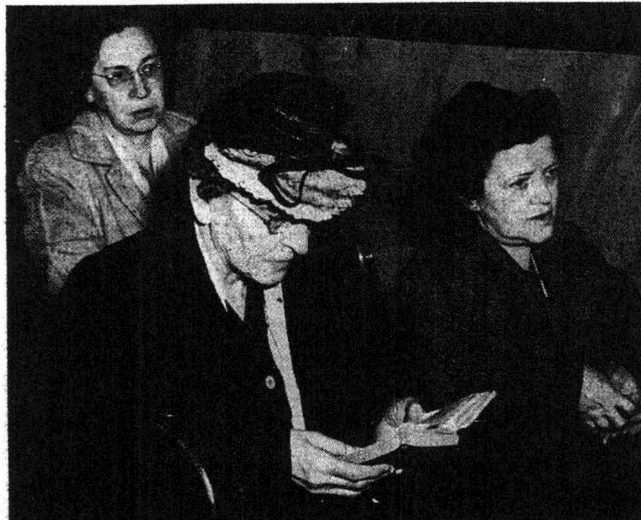

Prayers of thanksgiving that one phase of the war had ended mingled with prayers that the war in the Pacific would come to an early end when worshippers went to their churches this morning with the official announcement that the war in Europe had come to end. Shown in the above picture at St. Raphael's—typical in churches of Madison—are, left to right in the front row, Mrs. Joseph Geier, 326 W. Doty st., and Mrs. Frank Ripp, 351 W. Washington ave. In the back row is Mrs. Margaret Kalscheur, 545 W. Washington ave.

Glorious Victory Only Half Complete, President Warns

(Text on Page 26)

WASHINGTON —(U.P.)— Pres. Truman, announcing the "unconditional surrender" of Germany, today told the country that the war was only half over and warned the Japanese that they can expect nothing but complete destruction unless they, too, surrender.

Mr. Truman proclaimed the end of the war in what he called a "solemn but a glorious hour" and called on the nation to pray for strength to bring about the end "of treacherous tyranny of the Japanese."

He coupled this, however, in what seemed to be an effort to encourage unconditional Japanese surrender—with a statement that "unconditional surrender does not mean the extermination or enslavement of the Japanese people."

'Stick to Your Post'

Before going on the air Mr. Truman, surrounded by the leaders of his government, told a crowded news conference that the watchword of the nation now should be "work, work, and more work."

"I call upon every American to stick to his post until the last battle is won," he said. "Until that day, let no man abandon his post or slacken his efforts."

Declaring that he wanted it emphasized repeatedly that much work remained before final victory, he said "our victory is but half-won."

"The West is free," he added. "But the East is still in bondage to the treacherous tyranny of the Japanese. When the last Japanese division has surrendered unconditionally, then only will our fighting job be done."

Congratulates Leaders

He also pointed to the need for hard, toilsome, painstaking work to achieve "an abiding peace, a peace routed in justice and in law."

The president sent his congratulations and thanks to Prime Minister Winston Churchill, Premier Josef Stalin, Gen. Charles de Gaulle.

To Gen. Dwight D. Eisenhower he said:

"All of us owe to you and to your men of many nations a debt beyond appraisal for their high contribution to the conquest of Naziism."

Mr. Truman counted the cost of victory. He did not forget "the terrible price we have paid to rid the world of Hitler and his evil band."

He called upon the nation to observe Sunday, May 13, as a national day of prayerful thanksgiving.

He gave no details of the surrender except to say in his proclamation that "the Allied armies, through sacrifice and devotion and with God's help, have wrung from Germany a final and unconditional surrender."

"The victory won in the West must now be won in the

(Continued on Page 2, Column 1)

Writers Rap 'Disgraceful Double Cross'

PARIS—(U.P.)—Supreme Allied headquarters today enforced disciplinary action against Edward Kennedy, chief of Associated Press (AP) correspondents on the Western front, for filing an unauthorized dispatch describing the German surrender at Reims.

Kennedy was one of seven American correspondents assigned to fly from supreme headquarters to Reims to witness the capitulation. He alone sent out a Reims dispatch Monday despite a group pledge on the part of the correspondents that their copy would not be released for publication until authorized by supreme headquarters. Such authorization did not come until today.

Although the original action against the AP suspended all its filing privileges throughout the European theater, this order later was amended to apply only to Kennedy.

Fifty-nine of Kennedy's colleagues assigned to SHAEF—all except those representing the AP—signed a letter to Gen. Dwight D. Eisenhower today, describing Kennedy's action as the "most disgraceful, deliberate, and unethical double cross in the history of journalism."

The correspondents asked Eisenhower to reinstate his suspension of the facilities of the AP in the European theater, but the general rejected this request, explaining that any decision to punish an entire American organization would have to come from the war department.

(Commenting Monday on the suspension of all AP filing facilities in the European theater of operations, Paul Mickelson, general news editor of the AP in New York, said: "The suspension is like being thrown out of Wahoo, Neb., after the whole thing is over.")

The United Press (UP) man assigned to the Reims trip was Boyd D. Lewis, European news manager, who filed dispatch No. 1 with the SHAEF censor when he returned to SHAEF. That dispatch was released for publication at 8 a. m. CWT today.

Pledged 'On Their Honor'

Lewis and the other correspondents assigned to Reims were put under this pledge by Brig.-Gen. Frank Allen, SHAEF press relations officer:

"This story is off the record until the respective heads of the Allied governments announce the fact to the world. I, therefore, pledge each an every one of you on your honor not to communicate the results of this conference or the fact of its existence until it is released by SHAEF."

(In a dispatch from Paris today, United Press War Correspondent Boyd Lewis, who was pres-

(Continued on Page 2, Column 7)

Reds Take Dresden; Fighting Ends in Prague, Czechs Say

BULLETIN

LONDON—(U.P.)—The Partisan-controlled Czech radio said today that hostilities have ended by agreement in Prague, one of the last German pockets of resistance in Czechoslovakia.

BULLETIN

LONDON—(U.P.)—Gen. Dwight D. Eisenhower, in a V-E Day order of the day, thanked the men and women of the Allied expeditionary force and said they had "taken in stride the military tasks so difficult as to be classed by many doubters as impossible."

BULLETIN

LONDON—(U.P.)—Soviet troops have captured Dresden after a two-day battle, Premier Stalin announced in an order of the day today.

By VIRGIL PINKLEY
(United Press Staff Correspondent)

PARIS — The bloodiest war in European history will come to its official end at 12:01 a. m. Wednesday, European time, (5:01 p. m., today CWT) with the formal end of hostilities on a continent desolated by more than five years of conflict.

The agreement formalizing the unconditional surrender will be ratified in Berlin today, with Field Marshal Wilhelm Keitel, chief of the German high command, officially acknowledging that Germany is beaten.

Sitting around the table with Keitel in Berlin will be:

For the western Allies: Air Chief Marshal Sir Arthur W. Tedder, deputy supreme commander.

For Russia: Marshal Gregory K. Zhukov, commander of the First White Russian army.

For France: Gen. Jean de Lattre de Tassigny, commander of the French First army.

To save lives, the cease fire order already has sounded. But the fighting went on today in some small and scattered sectors.

Fanatical Nazis, defying the big command's unconditional surrender, held out in some parts of Czechoslovakia, in French Atlantic ports, in the Channel islands, and in some pinpoints in the Aegean.

And on the Russian front resistance continued in some considerable strength. But Prime Minister Churchill warned in London that if the Germans held out after the 12:01 a. m. deadline, they would become outlaws under the rules of war, and would be attacked from all sides by the Allies.

In his address, Churchill promised that Britain now would concentrate all her force against Japan.

The German "peace" government of Grand Admiral Karl Doenitz, successor of Adolf Hitler, was carrying on a semblance of official functions at Flensburg on the Danish frontier.

Reichsmarshal Hermann Goering, ousted in the last days of organized resistance from the command of the German air force, was believed to be with the Doenitz government. So was Heinrich Himmler, gestapo chief and interior minister.

Churchill said the unconditional surrender of Germany was signed at 2:41 a. m. Monday at Reims.

Doenitz and Gen. Jodl, representing the German high command, signed for Germany. Lieut. Gen. Walter Bedell Smith, Eisenhower's chief of staff, and Gen. Francois Sevez signed for the western Allies, and Gen. Ivan Susloparov for Russia.

A German high command communique, presumably referring to Monday's events as usual, said big guns of the German garrisons in the western coastal pockets—La Rochelle, St. Nazaire, Lorient, Dunkerque—"shelled enemy batteries and troop movements."

Evidently this was the last communique the high command would issue, since it now was committed to stop fighting.

The high command announced that the greeting "Heil Hitler" no longer would be used in the German army.

The Allied proclamation of victory in Europe was made simultaneously in London, Washington, and Paris. No word came immediately from Moscow. It appeared that the Russians might be waiting until Zhukov has signed the surrender document in Berlin later today.

Supreme headquarters released a statement by Gen. Dwight D. Eisenhower after the signing of the surrender document at his headquarters.

He said:

"In January, 1943, the late Pres. Roosevelt and Premier Chur-

(Continued on Page 2, Column 8)

B-29s Again Raid Suicide Plane Bases

(By United Press)

U. S. First division marines pressed within slightly more than a mile of Naha, capital of Okinawa, today to pace a general 10th army advance as nearly 50 more Super-Fortresses again attacked Japanese suicide plane bases on Kyushu.

Four airfields on Kyushu were picked out by the big bombers in a follow-up of Monday's assault in which crewmen reported eight hangars at Usa "blasted right off the map."

Meanwhile Allied troops were poised for a thrust into Tarakan's rich Paomesian oil fields just east of liberated Tarakan town. Australian officials announced that Tarakan town had been captured.

Gen. Douglas MacArthur disclosed that Allied planes already were operating from the newly-captured airfield, 3 miles northwest of Tarakan town, adding another base for the growing aerial offensive.

A Tokyo broadcast said the Super-Fortresses also raided the Kochi district of nearby Shikoku island, and that 70 Mustang fighters attacked airfields on Boso peninsula south of Tokyo.

In other fighting on Okinawa the 77th division neared Shuri, the island's second city, while the

(Continued on Page 2, Column 1)

Madison's Reaction: Let's Get at Japs

Madison received Pres. Truman's announcement of victory in Europe soberly and thoughtfully today, its joy tempered with the realization that unconditional surrender of Japan remains to be achieved through hard fighting and bloodshed.

There were few outward signs of celebration, but war plants had brief observances, schools and the University of Wisconsin had special assemblies, some people took the day off, and clergymen prepared for solemn worship tonight.

Everywhere the emphasis was on "the job is only half done." The man on the street, workers on production lines, soldiers and sailors, city and state leaders expressed the same grim thought—"now let's get at the Japs and get it over with."

Pray in Last Hours

Families with men in the European theater remembered that the "cease firing" order would not be effective until 5 p. m. today and prayed that their loved ones would be spared death and injury during the last few hours. Some went to church to kneel at altars.

V-E Day brought new casualty lists to The Wisconsin State Journal. It was apparent that the days, weeks, and months ahead would bring many more sad telegrams to Madison and area homes and additional lists of dead, wounded, and missing to The State Journal office—from Germany as well as the Pacific. It was likely, too, that false peace rumors would mark the battle against the Japs just as untrue reports had confused the European situation, starting as long ago as last October.

Taverns Close

Tavern and liquor stores in city and county were closed all day in keeping with the request that celebration be avoided and production of needed war supplies continued without letup. War plants reported little absenteeism. Business continued in most stores.

Streets were less crowded than on an ordinary weekday since Truax Field soldiers living on the post were kept in camp and naval radio schools gave no holiday.

The end of the brownout tonight was expected to bring larger crowds to the downtown area. Lights on theater marquees and in store windows will be permitted for the first time in four months. The capitol dome was spotlighted Monday night.

Although riotous celebration was reported in some neighboring counties Monday night, police and sheriff's officials said all was quiet in Madison and Dane county.

Go to Work Calmly

A State Journal reporter touring the city between 6:30 and 8 a. m. found men and women going to work calmly and in as large numbers as usual, although a number carried portable radios. The strict ban on radios at the U. S. Armed Forces institute was lifted for the day to permit service men and women to listen to the president's message.

Young people were more excited than their parents and big brothers and sisters. State Journal newsboys began calling before 6 a. m. to ask when they should report for duty, and a dozen assembled watchfully around teletype machines as they waited for the extra to roll.

The city's reaction was a contrast to Nov. 11, 1918, but at that time the Allies didn't have Japan to lick.

"Everybody went crazy then,"

(Continued on Page 2, Column 5)

Churches Will Hold Rites of Thanksgiving Tonight

Solemn services of thanksgiving will be held in Madison churches tonight in observance of V-E day, and songs of joy will be combined with prayers for a complete victory and a lasting peace.

The Te Deum will be sung in all Catholic churches at 7:30 p. m. A joint Protestant service will be conducted at 8 p. m. in the First Methodist church under sponsorship of the Madison Ministerial assn.

A number of Protestant congregations will meet at their own churches for worship.

William B. Cairnes post, 65, American Legion, will hold religious services at the clubhouse at 8 tonight. They will be open to the public.

A V-E worship service will be held at 7:30 tonight at the Bashford Methodist church, N. Seventh st., and E. Washington ave.

Members of the First Church of Christ Scientist will meet at 8 p. m.

Singing of the Te Deum, the church's hymn of joy, will be combined with sermons at some Catholic churches. Priests will carry out Archbishop Moses Kiley's request that V-E day be observed "in a spirit of thanksgiving to God and prayer for a speedy and complete ending of the war and an enduring peace."

At Blessed Sacrament, the Te Deum will be by the school choir which is especially trained in Gregorian music.

The order of worship of the Federal Council of Churches will be used at the joint services at the First Methodist church. Rabbi Manfred Swarsensky of Beth El temple will talk on "We Remember Before Thee," and the Rev. A. T. Wallace of Pilgrim Congregational church on "We Dedicate Ourselves to Thee." Music will be by the Methodist choir.

Other churches holding services tonight:

East Side English Lutheran, 7:45.
Immanuel Lutheran, 8.
Our Saviour's Lutheran, 8.
Holy Cross Lutheran, 8.
Monona Lutheran, 8.
Luther Memorial, 8.
Calvary Lutheran, 7.
St. Paul's Lutheran, 8.
Mt. Olive Lutheran, 8.
Parkside Presbyterian, 8.
St. John's Lutheran, 8.
First Congregational, 8.
Memorial Evangelical and Reformed, 7:45.
Bethany Evangelical Free church, 8.

Paper From 4 Wards Picked Up Wednesday

Paper will be collected in four Madison wards Wednesday. Residents are urged to have their paper in bundles at the curb for the collectors.

The organizations responsible for collections follow:

Ward 2 — St. Vincent de Paul society (G-1017).
Ward 3 — Boy Scouts (B-2).
Ward 6 — Volunteers of America (B-6792).
Ward 7 — Salvation Army (B-6468).

Meet in Berlin

MARSHAL ZHUKOV

TASSIGNY TEDDER

MARSHAL KEITEL

Next: Japan, Churchill Tells Joyful Britain

LONDON—(U.P.)—Prime Minister Churchill today proclaimed the end of the war in Europe and pledged that Britain now would concentrate all her forces against Japan.

Britain may allow herself a "brief moment of enjoyment," he told his countrymen in a brief radio speech, but added:

"Japan with all her treachery and greed remains unsubdued. Her despicable cruelties call for justice and retribution. We must now concentrate all forces for the task ahead.

"Long live the cause of freedom! God save the king!"

Churchill broadcast from the cabinet room at his official residence, 10 Downing st., at 3 p. m. (8 a. m. CWT), then proceeded to commons.

The house gave him an uproarious welcome. When the cheers had died down, he read to the members the same speech he had broadcast a half-hour earlier.

He reviewed briefly the signing of the original unconditional surrender pact of Gen. Dwight D. Eisenhower's headquarters at Reims Monday and the arrangements for its ratification in Berlin today.

Despite the capitulation, he said,

(Continued on Page 2, Column 2)

Our Fighting Men Still Need Plasma

Although the war in Europe officially ended today, the need for blood donations continued without letup.

Red Cross officials asked for a 10 per cent increase in donors during the four-day period the blood bank will be in the city this week. Appointments may be made with Badger 2159 after 11 a. m.

Improved methods make it possible for the bank to handle 10 more contributors each hour than were handled on previous visits.

The blood bank was to be at Turner hall from 2 to 6 p. m. today, from noon to 6 p. m. Wednesday and Thursday, and from 10 a. m. to 3 p. m. Friday.

House Passes Highway Bill; Veto Expected

With only two dissenting votes, the assembly today gave final legislative approval to the highway segregation bill, clearing the way for the controversial legislation to be sent to the governor who is reported ready to veto it.

Assemblyman Walter Cook (R-Unity) accused Gov. Goodland of "pernicious lobbying" in connection with the bill.

The vote was on concurrence in a senate amendment earmarking ton mile tax revenues to be used for improvement of city streets connecting state trunk highways. The bill puts income from gas, motor carrier, and other highway taxes in a separate fund to be used for road purposes only.

Only lawmakers voting against the amendment were Assemblymen Rudy Roethlisberger (R-Verona) and Randolph Runden (R-Union Grove). Earl Mullen (P-Blooming Grove) was paired against concurrence with Guy Benson (R-Spooner) joining the 88 legislators favoring the amended bill.

Cook pleaded with the assembly not to take final action on segregation before the legislature has acted on the building improvement bill which the governor favors. Pointing out that Goodland has indicated he will veto the segregation measure unless steps are taken to improve educational and welfare institutions, Cook declared, "If that's not pernicious lobbying, I never heard of it."

The lawmaker, only person speaking on the measure, said he favored both bills and warned that "the boys who feel keenly about building needs" may not "go along with the rest of us" to override the governor's veto.

Eyewitness Describes Surrender of Germans

(EDITORS NOTES: Here is an eyewitness account of Sunday's surrender at Reims by one of the seven American news and radio reporters who saw it take place. This story was filed at 8 a. m. Monday (1 a. m. CWT) with censorship at supreme Allied headquarters in Paris for transmission as soon as the official embargo was lifted.)

By BOYD D. LEWIS
(United Press War Correspondent)

REIMS, France, May 7.—(Delayed by Censor)—Representatives of four Allied powers and vanquished Germany scrawled their names on a sheet of foolscap in a map-lined 30 by 30 foot room at 2:41 a. m. European time today and ended World War II in Europe.

I witnessed this historic scene.

Effective at 5:01 P. M.

In a ceremony exactly 20 minutes long, Col. Gen. Gustav Jodl, chief of staff of Admiral Doenitz' government and long-time close friend of Adolf Hitler, surrendered all German armed forces on land, sea, and in the air.

The surrender is effective one minute after midnight Wednesday, British double summer time (5:01 p. m., CWT).

A high officer said almost all firing had ceased on the remaining fronts.

The actual signing took five minutes. There are four copies of the surrender document, and in addition the naval disarmament order which was signed by Admiral Sir Harold Burroughs, Allied naval chief.

Immediately after signing the last document with a bold "Jodl," the Nazi arose, bowed and in a broken voice pleaded for generosity "for the German people, the German armed forces" who, he said, "both have achieved and suffered more perhaps than any other people in the world."

Ike Smiling, Restrained

Gen. Dwight D. Eisenhower, smiling, confident, and restrained, sat with his deputy, Britain's air chief, Marshal Sir Arthur Tedder,

(Continued on Page 2, Column 3)

Madison Weather
Cloudy, with showers and thunderstorms today. Partly cloudy tonight and Monday. Continued mild. High today, 72; low tonight, 52.

The Wisconsin State Journal

A fact-finding Newspaper

Don't Burn This Paper . . . Paper Fights for Victory — MADISON; SUNDAY, JUNE 10, 1945 ★★

HOME FINAL
PRICE FIVE CENTS
26 PAGES
VOL. 156, NO. 70 106th Year

U. S. Raids City Black Market

Allies Strike Rich Jap Borneo Empire

Land, Sea, and Air Units Hit Labuan Island

Tokyo Radio Tells of Whole Division Being Put Ashore

By DON CASWELL
(United Press War Correspondent)

MANILA — Gen. Douglas MacArthur today reported widespread air and naval attacks against the eastern and northwestern coasts of Borneo and Japanese broadcasts said Allied troops had landed on Labuan island off the northwest Borneo coast.

MacArthur's Sunday communique gave no confirmation of the Tokyo reports, which said the landings occurred Friday.

Heavy, medium and fighter bombers attacked Borneo airdromes and installations along the east and northwest coast, destroying many buildings and sinking a coastal freighter and two river steamers, the communique said. The raids were a continuation of those which have been growing in intensity in recent weeks.

Light naval units blew up a Japanese fuel dump at Sandakan, some 200 miles northeast of Labuan island, the communique disclosed.

Presumably MacArthur would direct any new landing operations in the Borneo area. Australians who landed May 1 on oil-rich Tarakan island, off the northeastern coast of Borneo, were under his over-all command.

Tokyo said that the landings on Labuan, at the entrance of Brunei Bay, came after a heavy naval bombardment and that about a division of troops came ashore. A landing on Labuan would extend about 250 miles to the south the grip which Allied forces already hold on the islands along the eastern edge of the South China sea.

The only ground operations covered by MacArthur's Sunday communique were those in the Philippines, where American and Filipino forces are pressing a cleanup campaign against the Japanese, and in the New Guinea and northern Solomons area, where Australian and New Zealand forces are engaged in simi- studying the records in detail, lar tasks.

Maj. Gen. Robert S. Beightler's 37th infantry division spearheads liberated Solano and advanced to within four miles of Bagabag in an eight-mile drive along the Cagayan valley road.

Airmen covered the Cagayan

(Continued on Page 2, Column 1)

Journal Photographer Accompanies Federal Agents On Cleanup

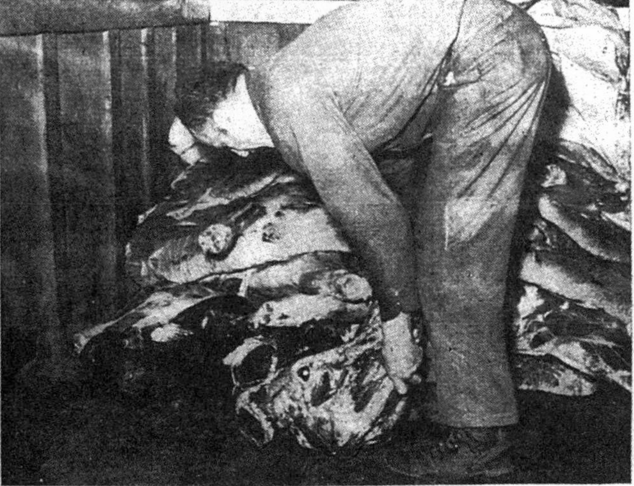

—State Journal Staff Photo

Shown in the picture at the left, Morris Lipsen, Middleton slaughterer and cattle buyer, is shown reading the federal warrant which has been handed him by U. S. Marshal John Comeford.

The picture was taken by a State Journal photographer in Lipsen's shop at 824 Mound st. an instant after it had been handed him by Comeford.

In the picture at the right, Frank Kowing, employed by Lipsen as the driver of an unmarked truck, is shown unloading a part of a truck load of meat.

(Another picture on page 2)

Lipsen Charged With Illicit Meat Deals

Middleton Cattle Slaughterer Held; Another Arrested

By JOHN NEWHOUSE
(State Journal Staff Writer)

Striking swiftly to crush black market operations in meat in Madison, federal officers and investigators of the Office of Price Administration working with a staff of State Journal reporters and photographers Saturday night moved against sellers of illicit meat in the city.

In a night raid, officials burst into the butcher shop of Morris Lipsen, Middleton cattle buyer and slaughterer whose outlet is in Madison, arresting him on a federal warrant.

Lipsen was arrested on two charges, one of acquiring rationed meat without the surrender of ration points and the other of the slaughter of cattle and calves as a Class II slaughterer without having qualified for an interim quota.

Thor Jacobson, farmer-slaughterer who operates a meat market at 22 North st., also was arrested on a federal warrant late Saturday night at his home on Highway 18, 11 miles east of Madison.

Immediately after the warrant had been read to Jacobson, his wife, standing at his side, turned on the officers with:

"Why don't you get Morris Lipsen, too?"

She was advised that Lipsen already was in custody.

Jacobsen, charged with selling and transferring rationed meats as a "primary" distributor without receiving ration points and for slaughtering cattle without a permit, told OPA officials and State Journal reporters how both he and Lipsen had slaughtered in the Jacobson slaughter barn.

This, small, dirty and bloody structure over the hill from the Lipsen home was flanked by a lean-to, approximately 6 by 20 feet, in which were huddled seven cattle, one trampled into the deep mud, the others stuck up to their middles in the muck.

" . . . $2 a head . . ."

Jacobson insisted "somebody must have put those cattle in there while we were gone today." He admitted, however, that he had been slaughtering cattle which Lipsen brought him for a fee of $2 a head and that since he had told Lipsen he couldn't do it for him longer, Lipsen and men he hired were doing their own slaughtering in the Jacobson barn, paying Jacobson $1 a head.

Jacobson said he did his own slaughtering to supply his North st. shop, but had ceased even this since May 15. He said he had told Lipsen "not to bring any more cattle here." Lipsen brought them in his own unmarked truck and removed the carcasses in another truck. Some, he said, Lipsen brought from a Lipsen-owned yard near Middleton and some "from other places."

Confronted at his shop at 824 Mound st. with a federal warrant issued Saturday night Lipsen's only comment was:

"I've got to call my lawyer."

With the permission of U. S. Marshal John Comeford, who had served the warrant, the meat dealer, with stolid face, put in a long distance call to his lawyer and talked long and earnestly, frequently referring to the federal warrant before him.

Curious people congregated about the front of the shop, windows blazing with light in the dark streets and intermittently brightening with the flare of flashbulbs.

While the meat dealer, short, stocky, and partially bald, talked with his lawyer, an unmarked truck drifted up to the curb.

"What the hell?" asked the surprised driver, and then jammed his truck into gear and roared off.

An OPA investigator grinned to himself, set off behind the truck. He chased it around the block and forced it to the curb.

"Who the hell are you?" asked the driver.

"The OPA has caught up with you, son," said the OPA official.

Returned to the shop by the shepherding car of the investigator, the driver, Frank Kowing, began to unload the truck.

He posed willingly for a picture by a State Journal photographer.

"I wouldn't have driven away if I knew you wanted to see me," he told the OPA investigator.

"We got nothing to be ashamed of. Just stick around and you'll see it."

There were between 15 and 20 fore quarters of beef along with bloody heads and pieces of liver, heart, and other parts on the bare floor of the truck.

The meat was not wrapped. To unload it, Kowing walked into the truck. He did not bother to clean his shoes.

While he was still unloading

16 Poles Freed by Russians, Paris Reports

LONDON — (U.P.) — The Paris radio said Saturday night that 16 Polish leaders, arrested by the Russians, had been released through the efforts of Harry Hopkins, special envoy of President Truman who recently left Moscow after conferring with Soviet chiefs.

There was no confirmation from other sources of the broadcast, which was recorded by the BBC. The arrest of the Polish leaders was announced by Moscow several weeks ago. They were charged with diversionary activity in the rear of Red army lines.

The London Polish government asserted they had been sent to Poland with the full knowledge of Russia to confer on the problem of setting up a Polish government of national unity as envisaged at the Yalta conference.

NEW LAWS OF WISCONSIN

CHAPTER 270, An act to amend 27.06 of the statutes, relating to mill tax for county parks and powers of the county board.

CHAPTER 271, An act to repeal 97.02 (5) (eighth paragraph); to renumber 97.02 (5) (respective unnumbered paragraphs exclusive of the eighth paragrapn) to be 97.02 (5) (a), (b), (c), (g), (h), (i), (j), (k), (n), (o) and (p); and to create 97.02 (5) (d), (e), (f), (l) and (m) of the statutes, relating to standards for powdered skim milk, powdered buttermilk and other milk products.

CHAPTER 272, An act to create 247.28 of the statutes, relating to support and maintenance of wife and children.

CHAPTER 273, An act to repeal and recreate 100.07 of the statutes, relating to audit of payments to milk producers, and providing a penalty.

CHAPTER 274, An act to repeal 25.17 (8), (9) (f) and (h), 42.32 (last paragraph after (4)); to repeal and recreate 25.28 (1) and 42.47; to amend 25.17 (1) and (4), 42.24, 42.32 (Introductory paragraph) and (4), 42.33 (1) (c), 42.34, 42.40, 42.41 (1), 42.29 (1) (Introductory paragraph) and (2) (Introductory paragraph) and (b), 42.50 (1), (2) (b) (d) and (3); to create 25.17 (1a) and 42.23, relating to the teachers' state retirement system.

CHAPTER 275, An act to create 60.29 (18m) of the statutes, relating to fire protection to towns and liability of towns for fire fighting service.

CHAPTER 276, An act to create 41.375 of the statutes, relating to university extension courses for county normal school students.

CHAPTER 277, An act to create 206.34 (1) (m) of the statutes, relating to investments od domestic life insurance companies.

(Text on Page 24).

WOW!

Cow-Milking Catfish Speared In the Act

BLENCOE, Ia. — (U.P.) — Milk fed catfish was on the menu today at Leo Delanty's cafe.

Delanty bought the fish from Marion Sweesy, who said he speared it with a pitchfork as it hung to a cow's udder. The cow was standing belly deep in water which had flooded Sweesy's pasture when the Little Sioux river overflowed.

The catfish, Sweesy said, had milked the cow dry.

Col. La Follette Arrives in Madison

Col. Philip F. La Follette arrived in Madison Saturday from the Philippines where he has been on Gen. MacArthur's staff. The former governor, who flew from Manila to San Francisco and from San Francisco to Chicago, is in the city on a 30-day leave. Press reports from Manila have said La Follette was receiving an army discharge.

U. W.'s Pres. Fred to Get Marquette Honorary Degree

MILWAUKEE—(U.P.) — Honorary degrees will be conferred by Marquette university at its commencement July 1 upon Pres. Fred of the University of Wisconsin and Archbishop Francis J. Spellman, New York.

FRED

The Rev. Peter A. Brooks, S. J., president of Marquette, announced that Archbishop Spellman will deliver the commencement address and receive the honorary degree of doctor of letters. An honorary degree of doctor of science will be conferred upon Pres. Fred.

Marquette's senior class was said to be the largest since the first year of the war, with about 450 candidates for degrees.

Rep. O'Konski's Wife Will Christen Ship

SUPERIOR—(U.P.)—Mrs. Veronica O'Konski, Mercer, wife of Rep. Alvin E. O'Konski (R-Wis.), will christen the Hawser Eye, ocean-going cargo vessel, at launching ceremonies Monday at the Walter Butler shipyard.

W. A. Marriott, Fair Manager, Dies Suddenly

W. A. Marriott, 58, Milwaukee, state fair manager, died late Saturday night at a Harrisburg, Pa., hospital where he was taken Friday after suffering a cerebral hemorrhage while on a train returning from Washington.

He died without regaining consciousness and before his family, who were en route to Harrisburg by plane, could reach his bedside. En route were his wife and his son-in-law and daughter, Mr. and Mrs. Arthur O. Schroeder, 1501 Morrison st.

Marriott had attended a conference in the national capitol with Office of Defense Transportation (ODT) officials and with fair officials from other states on whether a state fair should be held this year. He was stricken while conversing with Raymond Lee, secretary of the Minnesota state fair.

Mr. Marriott formerly was in the hardware business in Baraboo and was prominent in Elks and Masonic circles. He lived with his wife on the state fair grounds in Milwaukee.

Besides his wife and daughter, survivors include one son who is on his way to the Pacific with the armed forces.

Lawmakers Face Hot Issues in Final Week

By REX KARNEY
(State Journal Staff Writer)

With friendly ties between Gov. Goodland and the Republican party finally and apparently irrevocably severed, the Wisconsin legislature Monday will head into the final hectic week of its 1945 session.

Tempers will be short and debate undoubtedly will be violent and acrimonious as the lawmakers, most of whom are Republican, tangle over major issues which will be settled one way or another before the recess Friday.

Gov. Goodland last week gave concrete indication that he did not care whether amicable relations were maintained between the executive office and the Republican majority in the senate and assembly.

Berates Lawmakers

Early last week he berated lawmakers, in a special message, for refusing to carry out the program he had outlined to them in January. Friday, he made 10 appointments to high state office without even consulting or informing legislators and other officials of his own party.

Friday also, he vetoed a Republican-supported bill that would have restricted political candidates from jumping from one party to another, a measure he had promised GOP leaders he would sign. That veto message, expected to be a "hot one" will be read to members of the senate Monday.

Consequently, verbal shrapnel is expected to be cutting and heavy this week as lawmakers come to grips with the major items still facing the 1945 session.

The sharpshooting undoubtedly will be particularly vicious as lawmakers consider three of the governor's pet programs—the state postwar building program, Goodland's anti-gambling bill, and his veto of the bill segregating highway funds.

There is a chance that the governor may win the highway segregation fight, for reasons that will be apparent later in the week. The assembly already has overridden his veto of the highway segregation bill, and the issue will be finally determined in the senate Tuesday at 10:15 a. m., when the measure is scheduled as a special order of business.

(Continued on Page 2, Column 2)

Square Off

CONNALLY — EVATT

Sen. Connally, Evatt Debate Veto Issue

SAN FRANCISCO—(U.P.)—Sen. Tom Connally (D.-Tex.) and Australian Foreign Minister Herbert V. Evatt squared off Saturday night for the last major debate of the United Nations conference—on the veto issue.

The long-awaited official debate between the big and the little nations over the right of the Big Five to veto, if they wish, virtually any action or decision of the proposed world security council, began in a closed subcommittee meeting Saturday morning. It was continued at an extraordinary Saturday night session of the full committee, called to speed action on this explosive question.

Connally is the ranking representative of the Big Five on the committee and must carry the hod for those powers on this vital issue until the Yalta voting formula finally is approved by the whole conference.

His opponent is Evatt, who has won for himself here considerable fame for his caustic criticism of the big powers and for his leadership of the little and middle powers.

It was Evatt who Friday fought a Big Five attempt to streamline debate on the veto issue by dismissing the subcommittee.

The Connally-Evatt verbal duel was certain to produce a final flourish for this nearly completed conference which is aiming toward adjournment between June 16 and 20.

The final decision on the veto issue and the whole Yalta voting formula is almost foregone. No one expects the little powers to oppose its incorporation in the charter as it now stands, although they are expected to express dis-

(Continued on Page 2, Column 5)

Aerial Attacks Hit Japs Hard

Navy Carrier Planes Raise Havoc

BULLETIN

WASHINGTON —(U.P.)— A large B-29 force struck at targets today on the mainland Japanese island of Honshu for the second time in 24 hours, the war department reported.

GUAM—Adm. William F. Halsey's third fleet carrier planes and long-range army fighters from Iwo blasted airdromes and key installations on Japan's home islands of Kyushu and Honshu Friday and Saturday in the growing aerial offensive to bomb Japan nearer defeat.

Striking in coordination with Saturday's three-way B-29 raid on aircraft plants which obtained "excellent results," the carrier and land-based fighter bombers spread fires and explosions through the Japanese installations at Kanoya airfield on Kyushu and Kagimigahara airfield.

Halsey's rampaging third fleet aircraft destroyed at least 30 en-

(Continued on Page 2, Column 2)

Bus Knocks Down Light, Mail Box

A Sherman park bus, driven by Robert J. Jeffry, 26, of 505 Maple ave., Saturday traveled too close to the curb in front of the Belmont hotel and knocked down an ornamental light and mail box. No one was injured.

Yank Bayonets, Grenades Cut Foe's Lines; 67,703 Nips Die in 71 Days

After 10 Weeks on Okinawa

OKINAWA
Makiminato
AIRFIELD
Kuba
Nakagusuku
NAKAGUSUKU BAY
Naha
Shuri
AIRFIELD
6th MARINES MOPPING UP ORUKU
AIRFIELD
Yonabaru
ORUKU PENINSULA
1st MARINES DRIVING ON ITOMAN
CHINEN PENINSULA
AIRFIELD
Koya
Sashiki
96th INFANTRY EXTENDING HOLD ON SOUTHEAST COAST
Itoman
7th INFANTRY KNIFING INTO JAP DEFENSES
YAEJU-DAKE ESCARPMENT
Gushichan
Makabe
Kiyan
0 5 Miles
ROADS RAILROADS

By WILLIAM F. TYREE
(United Press War Correspondent)

GUAM—American infantrymen, driving into a hail of machine gun fire and routing the enemy with hand grenades and the cold steel of bayonets, Saturday broke through the outer defense ring of cliff-studded Yaeju-Dake plateau where the last big pocket of Japanese troops on southern Okinawa was fighting to the death.

Total Japanese dead were estimated at 67,703 as the battle blazed through its 71st day.

Tokyo said that scores of American warships and landing craft were massed around the southern end of Okinawa, possibly indicating the Americans were preparing for a major amphibious landing behind the last enemy line to bring the 10-week-old campaign to a smashing conclusion.

Troops of the seventh division's 17th regiment unleashed a savage frontal attack on the northeastern end of the cave-

(Continued on Page 2, Column 3)

Four American Soldiers Killed in Bremen Blast

PARIS —(U.P.)— Twenty German police officers and four civilians were killed and four American soldiers are dead or missing as a result of the explosions in the Bremen police station last Tuesday, an official report disclosed Saturday.

Supreme headquarters also said four Americans were injured severely. Thirty German police officers also were badly hurt and 61 officers were injured slightly.

According to the official version, two explosions of undetermined origin almost leveled the headquarters, located in the heart of Bremen, at 11 a. m. on June 5.

The building, a four-story stone structure built on a quadrangle, had walls two-feet thick and it was estimated that 1,500 pounds of TNT would be necessary to cause the damage wrought in the explosion.

Wife Claims Bridges Had Child by Dancer

SAN FRANCISCO —(U.P.)—Mrs. Agnes Bridges filed a divorce cross-complaint today charging her husband, labor leader Harry Bridges, of being the father of a child assertedly born in New York city two years ago to another woman, identified as a night club dancer.

Madison Weather
Sunny and warmer today. Partly cloudy tonight and mostly cloudy Monday. Showers late tonight and Monday, with little change in temperature tonight and Monday. Low tonight 59. High today 82.

The Wisconsin State Journal

A fact-finding Newspaper

Don't Burn This Paper . . . Paper Fights for Victory

MADISON, SUNDAY, JULY 15, 1945

HOME FINAL
PRICE FIVE CENTS
20 PAGES
Vol. 156, No. 104 106th Year

U. S. Fleet Bombards Jap Steel City

Battleship Wisconsin Joins in Attack on Muroran

Butter Cut By 8 Points

WASHINGTON—(U.P.)—The red point value of creamery butter was cut from 24 to 16 points a pound at midnight.

The Office of Price Administration (OPA), announcing the cut, said the point value of farm or country butter and process butter would remain unchanged at 12 points a pound.

The reduction in the creamery butter point value was decided upon, OPA said, because of reduced military requirements for August and to prevent accumulations of butter in cold storage houses. The OPA warned that if supplies are exhausted too fast the ration value will have to be increased.

Originally OPA planned to cut the butter point value on July 29 by 4, instead of 8, points.

The OPA said, however, that the movement of civilian purchasing has slowed down somewhat in the past two or three weeks, particularly in metropolitan areas.

Top-Ranking Heroes Serve Among 300,000 State Has Sent to War

A skinny little fellow, whose wizened face looks more natural under a baseball cap than a hat bearing the three stars of a vice admiral, drove his dusty car into Hillsboro last week to focus the eyes of the nation upon Wisconsin as a state which—in that instance alone—has made a considerable contribution to the prosecution of the war.

But there are others besides Mitscher, the daring little guy whose Task Force 58 jabbed and slugged the Japs back on their naval heels.

MITSCHER

There's Gen. Douglas MacArthur.

And Admiral William D. Leahy, presidential chief of staff.

And Maj. Richard Bong, ace of aces.

And Maj. Gen. Nathan F. Twining, boss of the 15th Air Forces in Italy.

And Capt. Earl E. Stone, commander of the U. S. S. Wisconsin, mighty battlewagon of the fleet.

To say nothing of the 300,000 men the state has sent to war and the efforts of those who stayed at home.

MacArthur was just another of the pupils in a Milwaukee high school back in the 1890s. But he went to West Point from Wisconsin, graduating in 1903, and rose rapidly.

MACARTHUR

In 1918 he was a brigadier general, was placed in command of the famed 42nd (Rainbow) division, and had a lot of his fellow and higher officers worried when he conducted night raids in person.

In 1931 he was made a full general and became chief in staff of the army. After organization of the defense of the Philippines, he retired in 1937. But on July 26, 1941, he was appointed commanding general of all forces in the Far East.

The world knows his brilliant, though losing, battle of the Philippines; the dark Apr. 9, 1942, when he left Bataan vowing to return, and his fighting through the South Pacific on the comeback trail.

Recall His Words

They remember that he said, a year later:

"Our flag lies crumpled, its proud pinions spat upon in the gutter, the wrecks of what were once our men and women groan and sweat in prison toil.

"I was the leader of that lost cause and from the bottom of my stricken heart I pray that a merciful God may not too long delay their redemption."

They remember, also, another date: Oct. 20, 1944, when MacArthur strode from a landing craft to the shore of Leyte in the Philippines at the head of 250,000 men, brought there by a 600-ship flotilla.

LEAHY

And now, as commander of all army forces in the Pacific areas, the former Milwaukee schoolboy is leading the way to Tokyo.

Then there's another Wisconsin schoolboy—this time from Ashland: Admiral Leahy.

Appointed to Annapolis

The admiral was appointed to Annapolis from Wisconsin in 1893. He was a young ensign during the Spanish-American war when he was on the U. S. S. Oregon when that ship made its celebrated run around the Horn to Santiago, Cuba, in time to play a decisive part in the battle with the Spanish fleet there in 1898.

BONG

He went on to see active service in the Philippine insurrection, the Boxer rebellion in China, and World War I. From January, 1937, to August, 1939, he was chief of naval operations and, after his retirement, was twice called upon by Pres. Roosevelt as his personal troubleshooter—first as governor of Puerto Rico and later as ambassador to Vichy, France.

Then, in July, 1942, Pres. Roosevelt found a new assignment for the Wisconsin man, that of chief of staff to the president to aid Roosevelt in his dual role as president and commander in chief of the armed forces.

Now he is on his way as ad-

(Continued on Page 2, Column 3)

Food Poisoning Sweeps Hospital

800 Vets, Civilians Ill at Mayo General

GALESBURG, Ill.—(U.P.)—More than a third of the soldier patients at Mayo General hospital were stricken Saturday by an epidemic of food poisoning described as "moderately severe," Col. Henry L. Krafft, commanding officer, said Saturday night.

No fatalities had resulted at a late hour Saturday night, Col. Krafft said. The food poisoning, traced to a ham salad served at noon, struck down more than 800 of the hospital's 2,400 patients and civilian workers.

The poisoning hit less than an hour after the meal. The emergency wards of the hospital were quickly filled to overflowing and the services of all available doctors, nurses, and orderlies were ordered.

Two of the three general mess halls were affected.

"Many are now improving but they will be kept under observance for the next 24 hours," Col. Krafft said.

Stanley Hanks Critically Ill

STANLEY C. HANKS

Stanley C. Hanks, 50 Fuller dr., Maple Bluff, president of the Stanley C. Hanks Co., Madison realtors, was critically ill Saturday night at Wisconsin General hospital.

Johnson Votes Against Charter in Committee

Decision Offset as Millikin, Bushfield Drop Reservation Plan

WASHINGTON — (U.P.) — Sen. Hiram W. Johnson (R-Calif.) Saturday night placed himself on record as the only member of the senate foreign relations committee opposed to the United Nations peace charter, but its prompt ratification appeared certain.

Johnson, 77-year-old veteran legislator who was a leader of the fight against the League of Nations 25 years ago, made a special trip to the capitol to record his "no" vote against the committee recommendation that the charter be ratified. He was not present Friday when the committee voted 20 to 0 for ratification.

The "aye" votes were raised Saturday when Sen. James C. Murray (D-Mont.) had his vote recorded in a telephone conversation with Committee Chairman Tom Connally (D-Tex.). The committee vote now stands 21 to 1.

Johnson's opposition was more than offset by formal announcements by two Republicans that they would support the charter.

Sen. Eugene D. Millikin (R-Colo.) said his fears of certain points in the document had been dispelled, and he now planned to vote for it without change. Sen. Harlan J. Bushfield (R-S. D.) revealed that he had abandoned his original plan to offer—and fight for adoption of—certain reservations.

(Millikin, however, Saturday

(Continued on Page 2, Column 5)

Italy Declares War on Japan

Hopes to Join United Nations

ROME —(U.P.)— Italy declared war against Japan today and the foreign office stated frankly that it hoped Italy's entrance into the Far Eastern war would help her become a member of the United Nations.

Italy has been seeking full status as an ally instead of co-belligerent.

The foreign office said Italy considered her relations with Japan broken since September, 1943, when the Japanese "in full violation of international law interned all Italian diplomats in concentration camps both in Japan and temporarily occupied territories."

The foreign office pointed out that Italian diplomats still were interned under "extremely severe conditions."

The declaration of war was voted unanimously by the cabinet Friday, the foreign office said.

An Italian foreign office announcement said that the Swedish government had been asked to take over Italian interests in Japan and to notify the Japanese government of the declaration of war.

The United States, British, Russian, Chinese, and French governments already have been informed, the statement said.

16,700 Return to Work at Akron Plant

AKRON, O.—(U.P.)—Four classes of workers among the 16,700 United Rubber Workers (CIO) strikers at the Firestone Tire and Rubber Co., Saturday night were ordered to return to work immediately to prepare the plant for full production by 2 p. m. today.

I. H. Watson, local president, ordered powerhouse attendants, maintenance men, mechanics, and janitors to ready the plant for full operations to be resumed today.

Contract negotiations with Firestone officials will be resumed at 10 a. m. Monday, he said.

(The move to return at Akron leaves an estimated 20,000 workers still idle throughout the nation. A major walkout in southern Illinois of 11,000 Progressive Mine Workers members, however, loomed when the miners threatened to join 3,000 fellow miners on strike because of the meat shortage.)

Members of the union voted nearly three to one late Saturday to end their 14-day strike. Watson said 1,220 of the 16,700 striking employes attending a four and a half hour session voted to return.

German POWs Help Save Columbus Pea Crop

Some 500 German prisoners of war at the newly-established camp in Columbus are working 8 to 14 hour shifts in nearby pea factories and a condensery, saving the crop for American consumption.

At top a shift is leaving the camp to enter trucks and be driven to work. Shifts leave every few hours and work almost around the clock.

The prisoners do the hardest labor at nearby factories. At bottom (left) one pitches peas into the viner as part of his daily stint, for which he is paid 80 cents a day.

Capt. Huldreich M. Stienecker, (bottom, right) Battle Creek, Mich., electrical contractor, is in charge of the camp. Here he inspects a load of peas at a Columbus cannery where prisoners will process the food. (Other pictures on State Page).

Big Three to Meet in Kaiser's Palace

WITH PRES. TRUMAN ABOARD U.S.S. AUGUSTA —(U.P.)— The Big Three conference will begin Monday in the former Potsdam palace of Kaiser Wilhelm, Germany's World War I leader, it was learned Saturday night as Pres. Truman and his party neared Antwerp, Belgium.

Mr. Truman will step ashore at Antwerp at 10 a. m. British time (3 a. m. CWT) Sunday, ending his eight day trans-Atlantic trip. Then he will make a one-hour motor trip to Brussels, where he will board a plane for Potsdam.

At Potsdam, a suburb of Berlin, Mr. Truman will live in an American compound about 10 minutes away by car from the site of the formal conference sessions.

He will sit down in the Kaiser's palace Monday for his first historic meeting with British Prime Minister Winston Churchill and Marshal Josef Stalin—a conference which the president hopes will promote an early end to the Pacific war and mold the foundation of a lasting peace.

As advanced guards of the three top men of the three nations arrived at Potsdam, all precautions were taken to safeguard members of the 10-day conference.

Russian troops stood guard at 50-yard intervals along the highways leading to the conference grounds. All visitors, including newspapermen, were forbidden to

(Continued on Page 2, Column 4)

Stalin, Molotov Leave

LONDON — (U.P.) — Exchange Telegraph reported from Moscow today that Premier Josef Stalin and Foreign Minister V. M. Molotov have left Moscow for Berlin.

Heavy Toll Expected in Jutland Explosion

LONDON —(U.P.)— A heavy death toll was expected from the explosion of a carload of ammunition in a freightyard near Aarhaus, Jutland, an Exchange Telegraph dispatch from Copenhagen said today.

Soldiers' Cars Collide, Injuring Three

Three persons were injured Saturday when an Appleton soldier's car crashed into the rear of a car driven by a Madison soldier on the Middleton rd. at the entrance to Shorewood Hills.

The injured were:

Mrs. Beda Nyberg, 324 Dow ct., wrenched neck, treated at Madison General hospital and released.

Sgt. Alvar F. Nyberg, 324 Dow ct., sprains and bruises, treated at Methodist and released.

Lloyd DeNoble, Appleton, chest bruises.

DeNoble, an army veteran recently returned from Europe, told police he failed to see the Nyberg car stop. Sgt. Nyberg was driving, with his mother in the front seat. The accident happened about 5 p. m.

Captives' Work Proves Good

Men Work Hard, Gripe About Food

By HAROLD E. McCLELLAND
(State Journal State Editor)

COLUMBUS — German prisoners of war at the newly-established camp at Columbus are saving the pea crop and helping can it to feed American civilians and American soldiers fighting Japan, former ally of the Germans.

Nearly 500 prisoners working in four pea factories and a condensery in and near Columbus are giving good service and are not displacing civilian workers, The State Journal learned during a tour of their barracks and the factories last week.

The 9,000 Germans working in the state's pea factories are producing $40,000 a day cash income for the federal government besides saving the crop.

They now total 50 per cent of all male labor in Wisconsin pea factories, and the armed forces will get about 43 per cent of the total pack.

"Gripe" About Food

The German prisoners are paid 80 cents a day in canteen coupons and apparently their only "gripe" is about the food.

"Better go in the mess hall and take a picture of what we eat," one prisoner told a guide to tell the State Journal photographer.

"We're hungry all the time," he grumbled.

But their menu the day of the tour indicated they eat pretty well, certainly better than American prisoners in German camps.

The German breakfast on the day of the tour included milk, pancakes, an egg, thin marmalade, and coffee. The American enlisted men at the camp ate oranges, dry cereal, fresh milk, two fried eggs, two strips of bacon, toast, butter, and coffee.

Spare Ribs for Dinner

For dinner the Germans ate spare ribs and potatoes, stewed rhubarb, rye bread, and water, while Americans ate roast chick-

(Continued on page 7, column 4)

Allies Open Harbor at Balikpapan; Extend Hold in Area

Rush Machinery to Borneo to Utilize Rich Pandansari Oil Refineries

(By Leased Wire)

A U. S. Pacific fleet force including the battleship Wisconsin and other powerful warships is now bombarding the Japanese steel city of Muroran on Hokkaido island in the second successive day of a thundering sea and air assault that has not yet been opposed by the enemy.

Swarms of carrier aircraft, possibly more than 1,000, joined the warships in blows at northern Honshu and Hokkaido and any other worthwhile target.

Meanwhile, Gen. Douglas MacArthur announced that Allied naval and engineer units have opened the harbor facilities of Balikpapan bay to Allied shipping and amphibious patrols have extended their control of the huge bay to a point 14 miles north of Balikpapan. He also reported that American troops battling the last resisting Japs in the Philippines captured three important enemy-held towns in mountainous north Luzon, made a new landing on Southern Mindanao, and advanced 17 miles against light resistance.

Borneo's Oil to Aid Drive

Patrols Take Jap Seaplane Base

MANILA — (U.P.) — With the Balikpapan harbor now open, the Allies are in a position to rush in new machinery to rebuild the shattered Pandansari refineries, which before the war had an output of more than 1,000,000 tons of gasoline and petroleum products a year.

They may also land more supplies to complete the conquest of Borneo and prepare its rich oilfields for new production to power the final drive on Japan.

Allied control of the bay was extended to a depth of 14 miles from its mouth when an amphibious patrol penetrated far up the eastern shore and destroyed a Japanese seaplane base. The base was undefended by the enemy.

Meanwhile, the battle of 200-foot high Mt. Bataochampar continued to rage north of Balikpapan, with heavy Australian artillery barrages supporting the attack of ground troops driving to outflank the height.

The Australians made slight advances both east and west of the enemy stronghold after cleaning out a barrier of minefields.

Other Seventh division units pushing up the pipeline northeast

(Continued on Page 2, Column 7)

Outagamie Attorney Withholds Prosecution Under Thomson Law

APPLETON —(U.P.)— Dist. Atty. Elmer R. Honkamp, Appleton, said here Saturday that he would not prosecute alleged violators of the new Thomson anti-gambling law until he had an interpretative opinion from the attorney general.

State beverage tax agents in a statewide search for gambling violators had picked up six Outagamie county residents in whose places of business they had discovered gambling devices. Honkamp said that in each of the places the devices were not in operation but were stored in rooms not open to the public.

The Thomson law provides that district attorneys start circuit court actions against alleged violators or report to the attorney general within 10 days as to why they have not complied with the law. The penalty for violators is license revocation or restraining injunction.

Raids Continue, Nimitz Reports

Enemy Powerless to Oppose

GUAM —(U.P.)— Throwing another punch into the Japanese homeland, the Pacific fleet bombardment group swung around the fog-shrouded northern islands to train heavy guns on the key industrial center today.

The battleships Wisconsin, Iowa and Missouri are among the warships plastering Japan mainland for the second time in 21 hours.

The attack opened at 9:26 a. m. today (Tokyo time—6:26 p. m. CWT) and was still continuing when Fleet Admiral Chester W. Nimitz reported the bombardment in his sixth communique in 28 hours.

More than 1,000 carrier aircraft were attacking Honshu and Hokkaido at the same time in a continuation of the latest Third fleet blow against Japan which opened Saturday at dawn and was being pressed without a respite for the enemy.

Lose 429 Planes

The Japanese already have lost 429 planes destroyed or damaged—all but three wrecked on the ground—and 43 vessels sunk or damaged in the fleet attacks which began at Tokyo last Tuesday.

The world's most powerful naval force still prowled off northern Japan, prepared to throw tons of bombs and shells into every worthwhile target in a naval and aerial assault which the Japanese appeared incapable of preventing.

The bombardment force struck Hokkaido through the heavy mists covering the northern islands in a rapid follow-up to Saturday's assault against the Kam-

(Continued on Page 2, Column 6)

Feature Finder

Schmale's Shot Saved Buddy Treed by Jap

(Special to The Journal)

OKINAWA (Delayed)—A shot by Marine Corp. Wilburt W. Schmale, Madison, Wis., saved the life of a fellow marine who was attacked by a Jap when he was, literally, up a tree.

Pfc. Myrl V. Pifer, Wadsworth, O., was on a lofty perch completing a telephone connection when the Jap charged him.

"I wished I had wings when I saw that Jap come out of the cane field I had just come through," Pifer said.

The enemy was throwing grenades at the treed marine when Schmale's shot killed him.

Schmale's wife and his parents, Mr. and Mrs. William Schmale, live at Mendota Beach. He has been in the marines three years and overseas about a year.

CORP. WILBURT SCHMALE

Madison Weather
Cloudy and cool this afternoon. Clearing late tonight. Sunday partly cloudy and warmer. Low tonight 63, high Sunday 85.

The Wisconsin State Journal

A fact-finding Newspaper

Don't Burn This Paper . . . Paper Fights for Victory

MADISON, SATURDAY, JULY 28, 1945 ★★

HOME FINAL
PRICE FIVE CENTS
EIGHT PAGES
VOL. 156, NO. 117 106th Year

Bomber, Lost in Fog, Hits Empire State Bldg.; 13 Die

2,000 Planes Blast Wrecked Nip Fleet

Former Journal Man Describes Crash Into Empire State Bldg.

EDITOR'S NOTE: The author of the following dispatch is president of the James W. Irwin company, management consultants, and former managing editor of the Wisconsin State Journal.

BY JAMES W. IRWIN
(Written for the United Press)

NEW YORK—At about 10 a. m. today I was sitting alone in my office on the 75th floor of the Empire State bldg.

Outside the windows there was a dense fog.

The roar of airplanes going overhead is a familiar sound to those of us who have offices in this giant structure.

But this morning I heard one coming that seemed to be headed right my way.

I ran into the hall as the roar increased. Just as I hit the hall the plane struck.

A girl elevator operator had just opened the door of the elevator shaft on my floor. The blast blew her all the way across the hall.

She is in the next office as I dictate this to the United Press. No first aid has reached us yet. We are isolated.

There are at least 11 other casualties on this floor alone, mostly women, some of them badly burned.

I am told that the plane struck

JAMES W. IRWIN

the building several floors above my office. That would be hard to tell from here. The halls are

(Continued on Page 2, Column 4)

Domengeaux Calls Mendota 'Excellent'

A congressman investigating the manner in which the nation cares for its returned servicemen today came to the conclusion that the Veterans Administration hospital at Mendota is an "excellent" institution that is doing "an outstanding job."

Rep. James Domengeaux (D-La.), member of a congressional investigating committee probing charges that the veterans hospitals and hospital care are inadequate, said that the Mendota unit was "one of the best" he had seen during his inspection tour.

A medically-discharged World War II veteran himself, Domengeaux will leave Sunday for Minnesota to continue his investigation of federal veterans facilities.

'Beautifully' Equipped

He said his investigations so far indicated that Veterans Administration hospitals were "beautifully equipped" places, but that in many cases Veterans Administration physicians "still are practicing horse and buggy medicine." He blamed the situation on the fact that "obviously, we aren't attracting the best personnel into the service."

Domengeaux had no criticism, however, either for Lieut. Col. L. E. Trent, manager, or Lieut. Col. Claude Tompkins, clinical director, of the Mendota facility. During an inspection trip Friday, the congressman frequently expressed praise for the two men and said he was "amazed" that 50 per cent of the World War II veterans who have been treated for neuropsychiatric disorders here are discharged as cured.

169 There

At the present time, there are 97 World War I and 72 World War II veterans being cared for at Mendota. (The Mendota veterans facility is a federal facility. It has no connection with Mendota State hospital, which is a state mental hospital.)

Tompkins pointed out that the Mendota facility is receiving patients both directly from the army and from the soldiers' own homes. Domengeaux discovered that a few service men resent being sent to Mendota because the public confuses that place with the state mental hospital which is nearby.

"A few of the boys feel that there is a stigma attached to treatment in a mental hospital," Tompkins pointed out. "It's the same old problem, that can be solved only by lay education. People sometime must realize that they can become mentally sick as well as physically sick."

Lauds Physical Plant

Domengeaux found that the physical plant at the Mendota vet-

(Continued on Page 2, Column 4)

Eugene Burns, Riding Bike, Killed by Car

Eugene Burns, who would have marked his 15th birthday today, died en route to Methodist hospital about 8 p. m. Friday shortly after being struck by a car as he was riding a bicycle on Highway 113, a short distance from his home at Route 1.

The youth, son of Mrs. Esther Burns, was struck by a car driven by Edgar Landl, 47, of 1212 Vilas ave., while he was playing with several other children on the lawn of the Chester Olson residence, about one-half mile from the Mendota railroad station.

Young Burns rode his bicycle down the Olson lawn, across a small ditch, onto the highway directly in the path of the Landl car. Deputy Coroner Leo J. Kinney said. The car, traveling about 35 miles an hour, topped a rise in the road and struck the bike near dead-center, Kinney said. The youth was thrown against the windshield, fracturing his skull and his left leg.

Kinney called the death unavoidable and accidental.

The boy, who had returned to his home several weeks ago after working in Northern Wisconsin, was taken to Methodist hospital by Olson, who had witnessed the accident.

The boy is survived by his mother, Mrs. Esther Burns, and two brothers, Marine Sgt. Robert Burns, at Camp Lejeune, N. C., and Charles at home.

Funeral services have been tentatively set for Monday afternoon at St. John's Lutheran church, Westport, with the Rev. Otto J. Wilke officiating. Burial will be in the church cemetery. The body was taken to the Frautschi funeral home.

Cole Circus Goes On Despite Derailment

BRAINERD, Minn.—(U.P.)—The Cole Brothers circus went on today despite the derailment Friday of five flat cars of the circus train near Belle Prairie.

Two men were injured in the accident which was caused by a broken journal. The men, Reuben Schalow and William Burns, were brought to the hospital here.

The train, en route from St. Cloud to Brainerd, was on the Minnesota and International line of the Northern Pacific. After the wreck, the balance of the train was routed via Staples to Brainerd.

YM to Spend $65,000 Fund for Building

The Madison YMCA will spend $65,000 for post-war remodeling of its W. Washington ave. building, Pres. Walter H. Ebling announced today.

Plans call for rebuilding of locker and shower rooms and the athletic club, enlarging and sound-proofing of the swimming pool room, and re-arrangement of first floor lobbies, club rooms, and offices. A snack bar will be installed on the first floor to serve members and dormitory residents.

Ebling said that the 25 YMCAs in Wisconsin would spend more than $1,600,000 in the post-war period for construction of new buildings and remodeling of present structures to meet changed community needs and demand for more co-educational facilities.

Construction slated in Wisconsin is part of a $50,000,000 nationwide Y building program. Ninety per cent of the institutions plan to install swimming pools.

Johnson, Who Enlisted at 15, Wins Bronze Star for Bravery

A Madison man who enlisted in the army at 15 today held the Bronze Star for the skill and bravery with which he gave medical aid to 12 wounded soldiers in the second week of the invasion of Hitler's "impregnable fortress."

He is Pfc. Sidney P. Johnson, son of Mr. and Mrs. Sidney S. Johnson, 709 W. Olin ave., and he also has the Purple Heart.

JOHNSON

A company aid man, the medical soldier was awarded the Bronze Star for an action at La Poterie, France, on June 19, 1944, when he was attached to the 401st glider infantry.

While his company was attacking a strong enemy position, five men in the front lines were wounded, the citation said. Johnson went forward under rifle and artillery fire to give first aid and evacuate the injured and stayed "alone and without covering fire" when the company withdrew to attack from another position.

He made improvised litters, took the five men out, then rejoined the company in the new attack and cared for another seven casualties "with such skill as to save the lives of men with wounds involving arterial bleeding."

Johnson went into service with the national guard "when he was 15½," his mother said. On discovering his age while he was at Camp Shelby, Miss., the army gave him an honorable discharge, and he reenlisted when he was 18.

The soldier, who has been overseas since September, 1943, is expected to return to the United States in about seven weeks. He is now in France.

Nip Armada Knocked Out, Reports Say

30,000-Ton Battleship Spotted on Bottom of Harbor Near Kure

GUAM — (U.P.) — The greatest carrier strike in history turned Nippon's inland sea into a graveyard of wrecked and burning Japanese ships today as some 2,000 warplanes of Admiral William F. Halsey's Third fleet resumed the attack on the Kure naval base.

Slamming in at dawn through a skyful of flak and fighters, Halsey's American and British fliers blazed a new trail of death and ruin across waters still dotted with hulks of 308 enemy ships smashed in their first onslaught last Tuesday and Wednesday.

'Out for Duration'

United Press Correspondent Richard Johnston reported from a warship off Japan that on the basis or reports from many carriers, "the enemy battle fleets have suffered such blows from this week's three-day assault that it probably will be out of action for the duration. This means forever."

United Press Correspondent Ernest Hoberecht reported from Vice-Admiral John S. McCain's flagship that a pilot said Kure harbor was "covered with burning ships."

One warship damaged in earlier attacks was a mass of explosions and flames, Hoberecht said the airmen reported. Other warships were shattered similarly. One was seen to take four or five hits with heavy bombs. Another had two raging fires astern and on the bow.

Spot Battleship

The first wave of attacking dive bombers spotted the 30,000-ton battleship Hyuga lying on the sandy bottom of Nasaka Jimi harbor, outside Kure, her decks awash and her superstructure burned out.

The great ship and 22 other warships, the last major fighting force in the imperial navy, were holed by Allied bombs and rocket fire Tuesday.

Japanese broadcasts said about 670 carrier planes attacked wide areas of southern Honshu and northern Shokoku today, concentrating on Kure and the inland sea region. They said the targets

(Continued on Page 2, Column 5)

Chinese Take Kweilin

CHUNGKING—(U.P.)—The Chinese communique tonight reported that Kweilin, the former great American airbase city in Kwangsi province, has been recaptured by Chinese forces.

The reoccupation of the city was completed at 10 p. m. Friday, the communique reported, by troops under the command of Gen. Tang En-Po.

Japanese forces were reported fleeing to the northwest with Chinese in hot pursuit.

Council Votes Pay Boost for City Workers

By HENRY NOLL
(State Journal Staff Writer)

Emergency pay increases of $5 per month for the lower salaried city workers and $3 for those in the higher brackets were voted by the common council Friday night after the aldermen had debated for an hour in caucus whether to grant requests of $15 per month for the general city workers and $10 for policemen and firemen.

In caucus a motion was made that the city employes be informed that it is not possible to grant their request at the present time, but this was overwhelmingly defeated. Mayor Kraege then recommended the $5 and $3 raises, which action was approved.

Kraege estimated that the increases given will require about $68,000 additional funds for the year.

The roll call:

For the $5 and $3 increases: Ald. Brown, Campbell, Coyne, Garner, Harbort, Hastings, Heisig, Huntley, Lerdahl, McNulty, Morhoff, Nelson, Reynolds, Schmelzer, Smith, Straus, Walsh, Watson—18.

Against the increase: Ald. Becker and Lucas—2.

"Further increases of salaries at this time are not justifiable," Ald. Stuart H. Becker contended. "The present salaries paid city workers are on a comparable level with those of state and county governments and industries. We are not justified in increasing salaries with surplus funds which accumulated as the result of the tax boost last spring."

Ald. Warren D. Lucas said that the only way to solve the problem is to find a formula which would justify itself as the cost of living prices change. He advocated doing away with the index

(Continued on Page 2, Column 6)

Petain Asked Aid to Nazis, Doyen Says

PARIS—(U.P.)—Gen. Paul Andre Doyen testified today that Marshal Henri Philippe Petain urged French collaboration with the Nazis even after the sensational arrest of Pierre Laval in December, 1940.

Doyen was head of the French armistice commission delegation in 1940-41. He testified at Petain's treason trial that after the arrest of Laval for his temporary banishment from the Vichy regime, he received a letter signed by the old marshal which said:

"Laval's departure does not mean the end of collaboration with the Germans. This will continue as before."

Bald, 72-year-old Michel Clemenceau, son of France's first World war "Tiger," opened the sixth day of testimony as the state's ninth witness. Doyen followed him.

Petain sat slumped impassively in his chair.

Clemenceau by inference accused Petain of guilt in the imprisonment of former Premier Paul Reynaud and the assassination of Georges Mandel, Reynaud's interior minister.

He told of visiting Reynaud and Mandel in their Portalet fortress prison before "Alas for them, they were handed over to the Germans by Petain and sent to a German prison. Reynaud escaped German 'justice,' but you all know what happened to Mandel.

"Who is to blame in this horrible affair? He who guided the criminals' hand. These men told me, 'We only want justice'."

Clemenceau said he went to see Petain in Vichy and asked him to take steps to prevent crimes, but never received an answer.

City Council Approves V-J Day Ordinance

By unanimous vote, the common council Friday night approved the V-J day ordinance. It provides that if the war with Japan ends before 1 p. m. all beer and liquor establishments must close for the rest of the day. If the news of the end of the conflict comes after 1 p. m. they must remain closed until noon the following day. If the war ends on a Sunday or legal holiday, no beer or liquor can be sold during the entire day.

Congress to Act on Arms Use, Truman Pledges

President Radios Senate, on Verge of Charter Vote

WASHINGTON — (U.P.) — The senate, driving to a vote within a few hours on the United Nations charter, received presidential assurances today that military agreements with the new world organization must be approved by congress.

A special message from Pres. Truman, aimed at one of the few controversial points of the week-long debate, was laid before the senate by its president pro tempore, Kenneth D. McKellar, (D—Tenn.)

It was transmitted from Potsdam, where Mr. Truman is engaged in Big Three meetings.

He'll Ask Congress

The charter provides in article 43 that member nations shall make armed contingents available to the security council for use in suppressing future aggression. It provides that member nations shall negotiate special agreements with the security council on the amount and terms under which such forces shall be available.

"When any such agreement or agreements are negotiated it will be my purpose to ask the congress by appropriate legislation to approve them," the president's message said.

Senate debate had centered on the question of whether such agreements could be put into force by executive action, a joint resolution of congress, or by a treaty requiring a two-thirds senate vote for ratification.

Notes Arguments

Mr. Truman took note of those arguments in his special message. He definitely ruled out the possibility of ratification by presidential decree only.

Administration leaders in the senate interpreted his language as ruling out the treaty theory also, and assuring that the agreements would be submitted to both houses of congress as a joint resolution.

The president's message:

"During the debate in the senate upon the matter of the senate's giving its advice and consent to the charter of the United Nations, the question rose as to the method to be followed in obtaining approval of the special agreements with the security council referred to in Article 43 of the charter.

Senators Object

"It was stated by many senators that this might be done in the United States either by treaty or by the approval of a majority of both houses of the congress.

"It was also stated that the initiative in this matter rested with the president and that it was most important to know before action was taken on the charter which course was to be pursued.

"When any such agreements are negotiated it will be my purpose to ask the congress by approriate legisaltion to approve them."

Calls Senate Back

The way for charter ratification at the end of six days of debate was cleared Friday night in a session which lasted until 7:14 p. m.

Democratic Leader Alben W. Barkley of Kentucky called the senate back into session at 10 a. m. today to make certain that the few remaining speeches could be completed and a vote taken before the weekend recess.

Chairman Tom Connally (D-Tex.) of the foreign relations committee field the ratification resolution, which, under senate rules, cannot be acted upon until the day after its introduction.

During Friday's debate, the senate heard a moving appeal for ratification by Sen. Walter F. George (D-Ga.), whose son, Marcus, was lost while flying submarine patrol duty over the Atlantic two years ago.

In a voice choked with emotion the grey-haired southerner urged the senate to accept the charter so that, in the words of Lincoln at Gettysburg, "These honored dead shall not have died in vain."

Forget-Me-Not Sale Approved by Council

American Disabled veterans were authorized by the common council Friday night to hold a forget-me-not sale Sept. 8.

EMPIRE STAT) BLDG.

Attlee, Bevin Go to Potsdam for Parley

LONDON— (U.P.) —Prime Minister Clement Attlee and Foreign Secretary Ernest Bevin left for Potsdam today to resume Big Three discussions after Attlee told a cheering assembly of his supporters that there would be no pussyfooting in his administration "and the battle will be a tough one."

Attlee and Bevin left by plane for Potsdam shortly after formally assuming office. Before they left, Atlee addressed a gathering of the 393 newly elected Labor members of commons.

"Our honeymoon will be a short one," Attlee said, "and then, make no mistake about it, the fighting will start.

"We now have the clearest mandate from the people and we are going straight ahead."

Attlee said he was picking the strongest possible cabinet and would not hesitate to change ministers who do not succeed at their jobs.

"We may be forced to pass over colleagues who have done long and distinguished fighting," he said, "but I trust they will understand and not take offense."

As he concluded, he said, "Now Bevin and I must buzz off to Berlin."

It was a hectic day for normally shy and retiring Attlee. He and the six key members of his government already picked were sworn in at a privy council con-

(Continued on Page 2, Column 7)

Blast Rocks Midtown Manhattan

NEW YORK—(U.P.)—A B-25 bomber crashed and exploded in the 78th floor of the Empire State bldg. today and the upper part of the tallest building in the world instantly became a blazing inferno for hundreds of office workers perched 1,000 feet above the street.

The plane was lost in a fog when it struck. It broke into a giant, spectacular burst of flame. The explosion rocked midtown Manhattan.

Nearly four hours after the disaster, the death toll was in doubt. A police captain in the building said at 1:30 p. m. that 13 bodies had been found in the structure, 11 on the 79th floor, one on the 78th, and one on the 72th. Earlier police headquarters said 19 had been killed. Many of the bodies were so mangled that it may be days before the death list is completed.

Of the 13 bodies, 12 were unidentified.

The only body identified was that of Paul Deering, identified by police as living in Tarrytown, N. Y. Earlier he was identified as a reporter for the Buffalo, N. Y., Courier-Express. Deering's body was recovered from a window ledge on the 72nd floor. Police believed he died trying to escape from a higher level.

Flames raged out of control in six floors of the building for 40 minutes. Three elevators crashed from the 80th floor to the ground. Glass and debris rained into the street.

Penetrates Wing

The plane struck the north side of the building, penetrated a wing of the floor, destroyed everything in its path, and went out the south wing of the building. Part of it landed on the roof of the 12-story Waldorf bldg. on 33rd st.

Six the dead were reported to be soldiers, some of whom presumably were members of the plane's crew of five.

Only the fact that it was Saturday morning, when many offices are closed, prevented a far greater disaster.

The 78th floor was unoccupied. On the 79th floor, occupied by offices of the war relief service of the National Catholic Welfare council, several persons were killed. Nine bodies were reported found on the 79th floor. Three bodies were taken from two of the fallen elevators. The third was empty.

Apparatus Sets Record

An enormous crowd gathered in the street and the largest amount of firefighting apparatus ever assembled in New York City was rushed out in four fire alarms. Glass and debris continued to shower down for almost an hour. The 34th st. foyer of the building was converted into an emergency receiving station. Bellevue hospital sent all available doctors, nurses and disaster equipment.

First reporters to fight their way up past the smoke-clouded 69th floor found the cowling of the plane still stuck to the side of the building. The point where the plane struck was near a bank of 10 elevators. All floors from the 69th to the 79th were littered with debris.

About 20 feet inside the window nearest where the plane struck lay one of the B-25's engines and half a propellor. A fragment of a propellor was imbedded in a wall.

Office windows were shattered 10 floors up and 10 floors below the 78th story. A stream of firemen, police, priests, doctors, and nurses moved up and down the stairs. Six charred bodies lay in and near the Catholic Welfare offices.

Oven, LaGuardia Says

Mayor F. H. LaGuardia, quickly at the scene, inspected the 78th floor and said:

"It was just an oven."

He said the plane was "flying too low." City regulations forbid flying fewer than 5,000 feet over the city, he said.

Eye-witnesses said the plane zoomed down Fifth ave., apparently in trouble.

Nanette Morrison, typist in the office of Carl Byor Associates, publicists, was gazing out the window as the plane approached. Not realizing her peril at first, she leaned from the window and started to wave to the crew members, she said.

The army said the bomber left

(Continued on Page 2, Column 1)

OPA Suspends Sauk Station

J. E. Pifer Charged With Violations

J. E. Pifer, operator of a Sauk City gasoline station, was suspended from dealing in gasoline for the duration of rationing Friday when he appeared before Thomas Fairchild, hearing commissioner of the Office of Price Administration (OPA) in answer to charges of accepting coupons for which he did not surrender gasoline, transferring 733 gallons of gasoline upon coupon credit, and not maintaining a balanced ration account.

In other actions:

ONE. Allan Thompson, operator of Thompson's Service station, Elroy, received a 30-day suspension upon charges of accepting unendorsed certificates for tires. The entire sentence was stayed.

TWO. William Bonhotel, operator of Bonhotel and White service station, LaValle, was suspended from dealing in gas at his station for 30 days, with all but the initial 6 days stayed. The order exempted all deliveries made by tank truck to farmers.

An OPA investigator, the first witness against Pifer, testified his investigation had shown the dealer had stamps or debits for a total of 2,829 gallons, above the 2,000 he could legally possess.

Notations upon salesbooks and notebooks showed that the operator had sold 733 gallons of gasoline on ration point credit, the investigator said.

Called adversely, Pifer heard Ellis Hughes, OPA attorney, claim that he had driven 20,000 miles when his gas rations would

(Continued on Page 2, Column 6)

Used Tire Racket Lands Two Men in Dane County Jail

A used tire racket Friday landed two Chicago men in Dane county jail after they pleaded guilty to federal charges of selling automobile tires at above-ceiling prices.

The Chicagoans, Manny J. Oren, 31, and Isadore Weinstein, 24, were arrested at the O. C. Harris Co. garage on Highway 18-51 by the sheriff's department, which had been informed by Milwaukee headquarters of the Office of Price Administration (OPA) that they were headed toward Madison.

Arraigned by the federal district attorney's office before Court Commissioner J. J. McManamy, the men pleaded guilty to two counts and were sent to jail when they failed to provide $2,000 bond each.

The two admitted selling 31 used tires at above-ceiling prices at Ft. Atkinson July 1 and attempting to sell 32 tires to Harris. They were talking to Harris when authorities spotted their truck and recognized the license number.

The Ft. Atkinson purchaser was the Fox super service station.

OPA investigators said the pair had been working out from Chicago, picking up junk tires worth about 75 cents each and selling them as "sound" at prices in excess of the ceiling. They will be sentenced later by Federal Judge Patrick Stone.

Chief Deputy Paul Lappley and Deputy Russell Williams made the arrests. The office of U. S. Dist. Atty. Charles Cashin prosecuted the men on complaint of OPA.

Madison Weather

Partly cloudy and warmer this afternoon. Fair and cool tonight. Tuesday partly cloudy with little change in temperature. Low tonight, 59, high Tuesday 83.

The Wisconsin State Journal

A fact-finding Newspaper

Don't Burn This Paper . . . Paper Fights for Victory

MADISON, MONDAY, AUGUST 6, 1945 ★★★

HOME FINAL

PRICE FIVE CENTS

14 PAGES

VOL. 156, NO. 126 106th Year

Atomic Bomb, 2,000 Times Mightier Than Biggest Blockbuster, Hits Japan

580 B-29s Batter Five Nip Targets

Hiram Johnson, Who Fought League, Charter, Dies at 78

SEN. HIRAM W. JOHNSON

WASHINGTON — (U.P.) — Sen. Hiram Warren Johnson, California's Republican elder statesman, died in his sleep at Bethesda naval hospital here today. He would have been 79 on Sept. 2.

The life-long isolationist, who helped prevent United States' entry into the League of Nations more than two decades ago, and who opposed the United Nations charter recently approved by the senate, had been in the hospital since July 18.

Wife With Him

He had been in poor health for several years.

Johnson's secretary said death was due to cerebral thrombosis. Mrs. Johnson was with him when he died and his son, Lieut. Col. Hiram W. Johnson, Jr., was reported flying here from San Francisco.

Death came at 6:45 a. m. Johnson had entered the hospital last month reportedly for a physical checkup.

He was the second ranking member of the senate in terms of continuous service. He had been a senator continuously since Mar. 16, 1917, being outranked only by Sen. Kenneth McKellar, (D-Tenn.).

His death leaves vacancies on five senate committees. Most important was his position on the foreign relations committee of which he was the ranking Republican member and, in event of a change of administration of which he would have been chairman.

On Other Committees

Other important committees of which Johnson was a member were the commerce and naval affairs committees. He also served on the irrigation and reclamation, and the immigration committees—both vital to west coast interests.

In the foreign affairs committee, Johnson cast his vote against the United Nations charter. When the vote was taken in the senate itself, however, he was unable to be present because of his weakened condition. His vote was paired against approval of the charter.

Johnson, who was born in Sacramento, Calif. Sept. 2, 1866, first

(Continued on Page 2, Column 4)

Underground Busy in Reich, Rally Told

Cancerous Fascism still is flourishing in Europe, a Madison Anti-Fascist Refugee rally audience was told Sunday night by speakers who asserted that:

ONE. "Our leaders at Potsdam have given us the signal" to "lick Franco Spain" by encouraging resistance among the Spanish people and caring for Spanish Republican refugees.

TWO. A Nazi underground, sparked by Hitler Youth fanatics, is at work in Germany preparing to obstruct the Allied occupation actively and to strike again for world domination.

"A bridgehead of Fascism stretches from Madrid to Buenos Aires right here to Madison, Wis.," charged Louis "Studs" Terkel, Chicago writer, producer, actor, and radio commentator. During the war that bridgehead was based in Berlin, he said, asserting that now "Fascism has moved to Spain."

Spanish People Ready

"We here can lick Spain, not by fighting but because the Spanish people are ready, willing, and able to knock off Franco . . . The Potsdam declaration is our cue. Our job is to help Spain join the United Nations," he added.

(Pres. Truman, Prime Minister Attlee, and Premier Stalin declared in their report on the Big Three Potsdam conference that Spain would not be eligible to the United Nations as long as Gen-

(Continued on Page 2, Column 4)

44 Called to Service

Thirty-four Madison and Dane county men reported for induction into the armed forces today, and 10 more will report Tuesday.

Madison men inducted from Board 3 were:

George E. Donner, Route 64; Sanford S. Hustad, 2645 E. Johnson st.; Dale F. Phillips, Route 50; Anthony C. Zingsheim, 1915 Spohn ave.; Leonard S. Lochner, 1742 Sheridan st.; Gerald S. Osborn, 2610 Coolidge st.; Wilmer A. Gallagher, 520 Johnson st.; LeRoy E. Payne; Earl C. Adams; Clarmont A. Redders, Guy Blakely, Jr., and Buro N. Hosoume.

Others included:

Clifford J. Karas, Wayne, Mich.; Robert L. Miller, Route 1, Basco; Elmer L. Moungey, Route 1, Marshall; Edward J. Bedner, Route 1, Sun Prairie; James V. Benesch, Route 2, Marshall; Leo Bakke, Sun Prairie; Arnold H. Iligen, Sun Prairie; Charles A. Knight, Stoughton; Paul F. Austin, Sun Prairie; Edgar H. Strohbusch, Cambridge; Clarence K. Seils, Route 1, Stoughton; Wilbur H. Noltemeyer, DeForest; Obie R. Offerdahl, McFarland; Johnas O. Larson, Cottage Grove; Lawrence M. Bailey, Stoughton; Harold R. Splittgerber, Helenville; Bernard G. Wagner, Sun Prairie; Jerome E. Speth, Waunakee; Lyle D. Ziegler, Sun Prairie; Byron V. Nelson, Stoughton; Loren E. Shelhamer, Sun Prairie, and Earl T. Gausmann, Cottage Grove.

Members from Board 4 who will report Tuesday are:

Glenn L. Wills, 702 Eugenia ave.; Vernon L. Anderson, 318 Main st.; Robert C. Haak, 2032 Fisher st.; Lorin H. Crawmer, Jr., 3917 Paunack ave.; Milo D. Froh, Milwaukee; Vincent E. Prehn, Kenosha; Burnett V. Severson, Route 2, Cross Plains; Delmar H. Solberg, Route 1, Verona; George Rowe, Route 1, Oregon, and Daniel R. Morhoff, Middleton.

First Polio Victim Reported Here

Madison's first poliomyelitis victim of the 1945 season was admitted to Wisconsin General hospital Saturday, the city board of health reported today. The patient is a 17-year-old West side youth who had been employed this summer on a railroad section crew.

F. J. Meyer Buys Kelsey Residence

The Fenton Kelsey, Jr., home at 825 Farwell dr., Maple Bluff, has been sold to Frederick J. Meyer, president of the Red Dot Foods Co. Mr. and Mrs. Meyer, whose present home is at 3853 Nakoma rd., will not take possession until September, 1946.

The house, which has a large lakefront footage on the Maple Bluff shore of Lake Mendota, was once owned by Mrs. William O'Neil, and before that by the William Balderstons.

130 Mustangs Raid Tokyo, Enemy Reports

Super-Forts Strike 1st Simultaneous Blow at 3 Home Islands

B-29 Named for Madison Plasters Tokyo. (Story on Page 12.)

GUAM—(U.P.)—Towering fires visible 150 miles swept through four Japanese cities after a 580-plane Super-Fortress raid today and Tokyo reported that a "small number" of B-29s struck at Hiroshima, an important Japanese army base 20 miles northwest of Kure.

(There was no immediate reaction from 20th U. S. air force headquarters to Pres. Truman's disclosure of the existence of the atomic bomb.

(Tokyo said both incendiary and explosive bombs were dropped on Hiroshima, but beyond Pres. Truman's reference to it as the first atomic bomb target, there was no information available on the raid from official Allied sources.)

Report Huge Fires

Veteran B-29 crewmen returning from their 3,850-ton pre-dawn raid said they started tremendous fires at the industrial centers of Maebashi and Nishinomiya-Mikage on Honshu, Saga on Kyushu, Ibari on Shikoku, and at the synthetic gasoline plant at Ube.

Tokyo reported U. S. fighter-bombers hit Tokyo and five surrounding prefectures a few hours after the Super-Fortress smash. Attackers included 130 Iwo-based Mustangs, which reportedly struck in two waves for an hour shortly before 9 a. m., Tokyo time, bombing and strafing military and transport objectives.

The first wave raided Saitama, Gumma, and Tochigi prefectures, all north of Tokyo, the enemy broadcast said. The second wave struck northern Tokyo itself and Chiba, Ibaraki, and Tochigi prefectures.

Claim 7 Down

The enemy claimed seven Mustangs had been shot down and three others badly damaged.

Radio Tokyo said some of the B-29 bombs also fell in the big Honshu war production center of Osaka, Japan's second largest city.

Maebashi was raided for about two hours and suffered a "considerable loss," Tokyo said.

Only light fighter opposition and meager to moderate anti-

(Continued on Page 2, Column 6)

Hartshorne Returning to U. W. After Map Duty

WASHINGTON — Richard Hartshorne, University of Wisconsin professor of geography, will return in September to his post here after serving as chief of the geography division of the Office of Strategic Services (OSS) since September, 1941.

He provided a large share of the maps for the entire European campaign from the invasion of North Africa to V-E day and put together many of the much photographed maps in Gen. George C. Marshall's office.

Mrs. Hartshorne and their children are expected in Madison this week.

Mrs. Bull, Active in Fraternal, Church, Patriotic Groups, Dies

MRS. MARGARET J. BULL

Mrs. Margaret Jane Hammond Bull, 71, of 310 Clemons ave., prominent in fraternal, religious and patriotic organizations, died Sunday at a Madison hospital after a long illness. She had been active at the USO club since it opened.

Born Jan. 21, 1874, at Edgerton, Mrs. Bull was married to George R. Bull, Feb. 6, 1890, at Edgerton. In the same year Mr. and Mrs. Bull moved to Sun Prairie where he became publisher and editor of the Sun Prairie Countryman. After a residence of 31 years in Sun Prairie they moved to Madison in 1921. In 1940 Mr. and Mrs. Bull observed their golden wedding anniversary. Eight children, two of whom preceded their parents in death, were born to them. Mr. Bull died Dec. 7, 1943.

At the time of her death Mrs. Bull was president of the H. W.

(Continued on Page 2, Column 8)

Hawaii Mars, Largest Airplane, Sinks After Emergency Landing

LAUNCHING OF THE HAWAII MARS

LOVE POINT, Md. — (U.P.) — Glenn L. Martin Co. engineers began preparations today to raise the Hawaii Mars, world's largest airplane, from the Chesapeake bay where it sank Sunday during a high-speed emergency landing.

None of the 10 men aboard the 72½-ton flying boat was injured seriously when loss of a vertical stabilizer interrupted a test flight and forced her down near Love Point, across the bay from the Naval academy at Annapolis.

The impact of the 120-mile an hour landing cracked open the hull and the big ship began sinking. The water was only 25 feet deep and the tail and tip of one wing remained above the surface.

The Hawaii Mars was launched only two weeks ago as the first of 20 such transports being constructed for the navy. The Martin Co. said it would be taken back to its Baltimore plant for overhauling.

Veteran Test Pilot William E. Coney, who was at the controls, told the United Press that the landing speed was far too great for the under-structure to withstand. It was his first crackup in 18 years of flying.

Coney, who flew the ship on its first flight two weeks ago, said it would be examined for structural weaknesses. The next plane of the Mars type, he said, "will be structurally perfect."

The injured crewman was R. S. Noble, flight test engineer, who was taken to a Baltimore hospital for treatment of cuts and contusions.

33 Gambling Devices Seized at 12 Places in Five Counties

Thirty-three more gambling devices, including 13 slot machines, have been confiscated by state agents who are continuing to find taverns and other establishments violating Gov. Goodland's new anti-gambling law, Chief Clyde S. Tutton of the beverage tax division announced today.

In the most recent inspections, state agents found 12 establishments in five counties to be violating the law.

The seizures brought to the number of gambling devices confiscated since the law became effective to 1,093.

At the same time, Tutton emphasized that his department is continuing to enforce other state laws relative to tavern and cigaret tax regulation, and pointed out that during July, 17 taverns or other establishments were charged with violating either the liquor laws or regulations affecting the sale of cigarets.

Counties and places in which gambling devices were discovered in the latest raids:

Clark — Robert Benzcschawel, Bob's tavern, Thorpe, one 5-cent ticket gambling machine and one large jar of 25 cent number tickets. J. Arthur and Pearl Johnson, Lucky Twelve tavern, Homburg, one 25-cent money punch board and cigar box of numbers tickets.

La Crosse — Hugh L. Goodenouch, the Arches, near Onalaska, two 5-cent slot machines. Frank Niesen, Log Cabin, Bangor, one sidearm slot machine.

Marinette — Louis and Clement Benzie, BBB tavern, Niagara, one bingo tumbler with balls and glass and one chuckaluck cage. Charles Paulos, the Y club, town of Peshtigo, one 10-cent Mills slot machine. Henry Schumacher, Sailor's inn, Marinette, one ticket jar with tickets, six bags of tickets, and five punch boards.

Marquette — James Roberts, Montello, one 1-cent slot machine.

Waushara — Otto Lietz, near Coloma, one pinball machine, one large Owl slot machine which plays coins ranging from 10 cents to $1, and one 5-cent slot machine. Herman Piller, Tustin hotel, near Fremont, two 5-cent slot machines, two numbered raffle wheels. Robert M. Stahl, Lakeside Lodge tavern, near Hancock, one 1-cent slot machine. Walter Ernst, Silver Crest resort, near Wautoma, one 1-cent slot machine and two 5-cent machines.

McIlhattan Dies in Sinking of Nip Ship

Capt. Vernald Graves McIlhattan, 28, whose widow and daughter live at 1632 Monroe st., died in the sinking of a Japanese prisoner ship last Dec. 15, the war department has notified his family.

The Madison officer, a University of Wisconsin graduate, was a defender of Bataan and Corregidor and was captured by the Japanese on May 7, 1942. The last letter from him was written July 15, 1944, from Camp Cabanatuan, Luzon, and was received by his wife Jan. 11, four weeks after his death.

Survivors are the wife and daughter, Nancy Jo, 4; the parents, Mr. and Mrs. F. V. McIlhattan, Spencer, and the grandparents, Mr. and Mrs. J. D. Graves, Long Beach, Calif.

Capt. McIlhattan was in the ROTC unit at the university and became a second lieutenant in the infantry reserve on graduation in 1938. He served at Ft. Wayne, Mich., Ft. Benning, Ga., and Ft. Ord, Calif., before he was sent to the Philippines on Sept. 8, 1941.

The captain majored in zoology at the university. He was a member of Alpha Sigma Chi and Scabbard and Blade, was president of the House council for two years, coached the rifle team, and was captain of the advanced drill team.

City Opens First Parking Lot

Madison's first municipal parking lot, between Doty, Pinckney and E. Wilson st., opened for business today after completion of oil surfacing. First customer was Frank Weston, Madison insurance man, who also was the first patron of the lot under private ownership.

Col. Middleton, Medical Adviser to SHAEF, Returns

COL. WILLIAM S. MIDDLETON

Col. William S. Middleton, dean of the U. W. Medical school, has returned to Madison on leave, and was visiting friends at Wisconsin General hospital this morning.

Col. Middleton was chief medical consultant for the Supreme Headquarters Allied Expeditionary Forces (SHAEF).

During his service in London, Col. Middleton was named a fellow of the Royal College of Physicians, an honor bestowed on only two other American physicians. In January he was given the Alumni Award of Merit by the University of Pennsylvania.

He entered military service May 1, 1942.

Aces' Baby Drowns at Farm

Sharon Ace, 16-month-old daughter of Mr. and Mrs. John Ace, Basco, drowned early today in a fall into a horse tank at the farm home south of Paoli.

Nobody witnessed the accident, Coroner Edward Fischer said. The little girl was playing in the yard while her mother was in the house and the father and two older children were working on a fence. Fischer said she apparently stumbled and fell into the low watering tank for animals, where she was discovered later.

NEW LAWS OF WISCONSIN

CHAPTER 526. An Act—To establish a municipal court of Dane county, to be known as the "Small Claims Court for Dane County," and to prescribe its jurisdiction and powers.

CHAPTER 527. An Act—To amend 85.01 (4) (d) of the statutes, to the issuance of licenses and permits for motor vehicles and taxation of such vehicles.

CHAPTER 528. An Act—To amend 241.28 (3) and (4); and to create 220.08 (20a) of the statutes, relating to assignment of accounts receivable and assets of delinquent banks.

CHAPTER 529. An Act—To repeal and recreate 95.48 (1) (g) of the statutes, relating to Bang's disease.

CHAPTER 530. An Act—To create 14.42 (17) of the statutes, relating to authorizing the state treasurer to accept safekeeping receipts of federal securities purchased of which he is custodian.

CHAPTER 331. An Act—To amend 48.17 (1), 48.20 (4) and 48.22 (2) and to repeal and recreate 48.18 of the statutes relating to charges for care at industrial schools.

CHAPTER 331. An Act—To repeal 361.24 and to amend 361.23 of the statutes, relating to security for witnesses appearance on trial of criminal proceedings.

(Text on Page —)

Americans Unleash Weapon Exceeding 20,000 Tons of TNT

Truman Reveals 1st Use of Missile, 'Harnessing Basic Power of Universe'

By CHILES COLEMAN
(United Press Staff Correspondent)

WASHINGTON — The United States has unleashed against Japan the terror of an atomic bomb 2,000 times more powerful than the biggest blockbusters ever used in warfare.

Pres. Truman revealed this great scientific achievement today and warned the Japanese that they now face "a rain of ruin from the air the like of which has never been seen on this earth."

More and more of these devastating bombs, unlocking the vast hidden energy that lies within the atom, will tumble on Japan if they continue to reject the Potsdam surrender ultimatum.

Used 1st Time Sunday

The new atomic bomb was used for the first time Sunday. An American plane dropped one on the Japanese army base at Hiroshima.

Its use marked victory for the Allies in the greatest scientific race in history. We put $2,000,000,000 and the work of 125,000 persons into the project.

A single bomb has more power than 20,000 tons of TNT. It has more than 2,000 times the blast power of the British "Grand Slam" bomb, the largest ever used previously in the history of warfare.

Secretary of War Henry L. Stimson disclosed that an improved bomb would be forthcoming shortly that would increase "by several fold" the present effectiveness of the new weapon.

The war department said that it was not yet able to make an accurate report of the damage caused by the first bomb.

"Reconnaissance planes state that an impenetrable cloud of dust and smoke covered the target area," an announcement said. "As soon as accurate details of the result of the bombing become available, they will be released by the secretary of war."

Development of the bomb, a victory of American scientists in a desperate race with Germany, is "the greatest achievement of organized science in history," Mr. Truman said in a statement released at the White House.

Ready for 'Obliteration'

The United States, he added, is now prepared "to obliterate more rapidly and completely every productive enterprise the Japanese have above ground in any city."

He revealed that the July 26 ultimatum issued to Japan at Potsdam was made "to spare the Japanese people from utter destruction."

When the ultimatum was rejected, the atomic bomb was sent into action.

Mr. Truman revealed that "two great plants and many lesser works" employing more than 65,000 workers are producing the new atomic bomb. Even more destructive bombs are being developed, he said.

Most Closely Guarded Secret

Production centers are located at Oak Ridge, near Knoxville, Tenn., at Richland, near Pasco, Wash., and near Santa Fe, N. M.

Mr. Truman's statement, released while he still was en route home by cruiser from Potsdam, lifted the secrecy from one of the most closely-guarded enterprises of the war. No mention of atomic power or any possible use of it in warfare has been allowed under the newspaper and radio code of the office of censorship.

'It is an atomic bomb," he said. "It is a harnessing of the basic power of the universe.

Japs 'Won't Use One'

"The force from which the sun draws its power has been loosed against those who brought war to the Far East."

Stimson revealed that Uranium is the essential ore in the production of the bombs. He added that steps have been taken and will continue to be taken to insure adequate supplies of this mineral."

Stimson said that "we are convinced that Japan will not be in a position to use an atomic bomb in this war."

"It is abundantly clear that the aircraft fire were encountered. One B-29 was lost.

Other B-29s mined enemy wat-posession of this weapon by the United States even in its present form should prove a tremendous aid in the shortening of the war against Japan," Stimson said.

Stimson praised highly the sci-

(Continued on Page 2, Column 1)

U. W. Men Helped Create Atomic Bomb

University of Wisconsin physicists, working in deep secrecy in laboratories at Sterling hall, contributed to the development of the atomic bomb, existence of which was made known to the Japs in deadly manner Sunday.

Although Pres. Truman gave the world some of the facts on the powerful new weapon today, the full story of the part university scientists contributed to successful experimentation cannot yet be told.

It was learned, however, that five members of the physics department were doing hush-hush work connected with the atomic bomb up to two years ago. Then all five were taken by the government and removed from the campus, with their apparatus, to "another place" where the projects were continued.

Names Are Secret

It was disclosed, too, that "at least 30" former members of the department have contributed and are contributing to the making of the most powerful bomb the world has ever known.

None of the names of the Wisconsin physicists connected with the work can be revealed, Prof. L. R. Ingersoll, physics department chairman, said.

Scientists have known for 20 years or longer that the enormous amount of energy in the atom could be put to effective use "if

(Continued on Page 2, Column 5)

Feature Finder

Madison Weather
Partly cloudy today, fair tonight and Monday. Continued pleasantly cool. High today, 79; low tonight, 55.

The Wisconsin State Journal

A fact-finding Newspaper

MADISON, SUNDAY, SEPTEMBER 2, 1945 ★★

HOME FINAL
PRICE FIVE CENTS
20 PAGES
VOL. 156, NO. 153 106th Year

Silent Japs Sign Surrender Papers as MacArthur Pledges Rule of Justice

Truman Foresees Era of Peace, Prosperity

Gee! Won't School Ever Open?

NANCY FRAILING AND BILLY WILLIAMS

When a kid has lived through five whole years of life without being permitted to go to school, the last few days before one enters kindergarten pass very, very slowly. So that, naturally, a kid is not to be blamed for going over to sit on the kindergarten steps.

That's what Nancy Frailing, daughter of Mr. and Mrs. Charles Frailing, 2525 Oakridge ave., and Billy Williams, son of Mr. and Mrs. W. E. Williams, 2901 Atwood ave., are doing.

The steps are those of Lowell school, and the kindergarten doors behind them will swing open Wednesday (Story on Page 20).

War Chest Goal Set at $400,000

A minimum of $400,000 will be needed to cover the "transition" budget of the Madison War Chest, Frank A. Ross, president of the War Chest, said Saturday in announcing that there will be a fourth War Chest campaign Oct. 15 to 25.

"Locally," Ross emphasized, "the work of the agencies included in the Community Union, and the local war service agencies will be greater than ever. Madison will be serving the soldiers at Truax as long as the need continues. Within the next year veterans will be coming back with questions about jobs, a place to live, benefits and insurance, and guidance in many other problems. Veterans' Information headquarters is ready for them."

Welfare and recreation services are being stressed because during the reconversion period families will be faced with additional problems of readjustment, he said.

Nationally, USO and USO camp shows will carry on until demobilization is an actuality. United Seamen's service will have to continue its work while the merchant ships are engaged in bringing men and material home.

"Relief in the Pacific," Ross went on, "is naturally up because of the necessity for sharply increasing American aid to the Philippines, China, and reconquered areas.

"The trend in European civilian relief," Ross said, "is to do a fast, immediate job. It is necessary to face the fact, however, that the coming winter will present a serious condition and it will be impossible to terminate assistance in liberated areas abruptly."

Lasting Peace Set as Theme of Holy Hour

The complete program for the fourth annual public Holy Hour, to be held next Sunday, Sept. 9, at 7:30 p. m. at Breese Stevens field, was announced today.

The ceremony, first public Holy Hour to be held in Madison since the war ended, will be dedicated to a lasting peace. It is sponsored by the Madison and Dane county Holy Name societies.

The Most Rev. Moses E. Kiley, archbishop of Milwaukee, will be the celebrant at the solemn benediction which will close the hour of prayer and hymns, and also will be the speaker and will deliver the meditations.

A processional again will open the program. Altar boys from

(Continued on Page 2, Column 4)

President Proclaims Today V-J Day; Pays Honor to War Dead

By ROBERT J. MANNING
(United Press Staff Correspondent)

WASHINGTON — Pres. Truman Saturday night proclaimed the end of mankind's bloodiest war and the beginning of an era of world peace and prosperity assured of fruition by the same free skill and energy which produced the atomic bomb.

In a broadcast following Japan's unconditional surrender aboard the U.S.S. Missouri—"That small piece of American soil anchored in Tokyo harbor"—Mr. Truman said:

"As president of the United States, I proclaim Sunday, Sept. 2, 1945, to be VJ-Day—the day of formal surrender by Japan. It is not yet the day for the formal proclamation of the end of the war or of the cessation of hostilities."

Day of Retribution

"But it is a day which we Americans shall always remember as a day of retribution—as we remember that other day, the day of infamy."

The president made his broadcast at the White House surrounded by members of his cabinet. Tonight, as he did after VE-Day, he will broadcast a brief message of congratulations and thanks to America's fighting men.

Mr. Truman declared that "the evil done by the Japanese war lords can never be repaired or forgotten." But he added that "their power to destroy and kill has been taken from them" by the "strongest and toughest and most enduring forces in all the world"—the forces of liberty.

Honors War Dead

The president said that the thoughts and hopes of all America go out, first of all, to "those of our loved ones who have been killed or maimed in this terrible war."

And, he added, "we think of our departed gallant leader, Franklin D. Roosevelt, defender of democracy, architect of world peace and cooperation."

But though the dead can never come back and "no victory can make good their loss," Mr. Truman held out to the bereaved and to the living victims of war this

(Continued on Page 2, Column 3)

Japanese Doctor at POW Camp Admits Tortures

ABOARD THE HOSPITAL SHIP BENEVOLENCE, Tokyo Bay —(U.P.)— The Japanese medical officer in charge of the Shinagawa prison camp Saturday confirmed some of the worst charges of barbaric mistreatment of Allied prisoners.

Capt. Hisikichi Tokoda admitted: (1) patiens were sometimes given the barbaric "mochasa" or burning treatmen; (2) they sometimes were slapped by Japanese guards; (3) they suffered from malnutrition due to insufficient food; (4) the patients were required to do "light" work; (5) those too sick to work sometimes were placed on reduced rations.

He denied: (1) that Red Cross supplies were withheld; (2) that Allied doctors in the hospital ever were prevented from attending patients; (3) that patients were ever kicked or beaten.

All these types of "treatment" he steadfastly defended as "standard practice."

Jap Premier Promises End of Militarism

Nip Leader to Tell People Full Story of Their Defeat

TOKYO—(U.P.)—Premier Prince Naruhiko Higashi-Kuni indicated today that the two-day extraordinary session of the Japanese parliament beginning Tuesday will mark the end of ruthless military domination in Japan and the beginning of a new policy of "friendship" with the rest of the world.

The premier said he hoped to restore Japan's place in world leadership and economy. He said there was evidence that Japan's defeat and her position as a conquered and hated country would be treated with utmost frankness and realism by the present government.

Prince Naruhiko, 58, who is greatly loved by the people and regarded as one of the most democratic members of the imperial family, told Japanese newspapermen bluntly that the defeat of Japan was caused by the sudden collapse of her fighting strength and said, "I intend to reveal everything without hindrance at the diet session so the people will fully understand the facts." He said he wanted the people to realize how thoroughly they had been defeated.

The premier called for the entire nation to "repent fully" as the first step toward reconstruction, announced that freedom of speech and of the press would be revived, and said he hoped a general election would be called so that the people could properly express their thoughts.

The emperor will open the diet session Tuesday by personally reading an imperial rescript. The premier will outline his policies to the house of peers in the morning and the house of representatives in the afternoon Wednesday.

Motorists Clog State Highways

Family Cars Hit 'The Open Road'

Wisconsin highways this weekend vividly tell the story of what happens when the American public combines the end of a long war, a Labor day holiday, and vacation weather with a natural resort area.

The family car, considerably depreciated and, in many cases, running on dangerously thin tires, was to be found headed "for the open road" Saturday and today.

Observers reported seeing out-of-state auto licenses "just like before the war." This tied in with resort and hotel owners' reports that their establishments were filled to capacity and that in many instances they had to turn away would-be guests.

The end of gas rationing, the closing down of war plants or curtailment of schedules, and the first peacetime Labor Day holiday since 1941, sent thousands of families out on the highways with the obvious consequences—an increase in the number of accidents.

At the same time that the na-

(Continued on Page 2, Column 4)

Pleasantly Cool, Forecaster's Wish

The Madison weather forecast calls for partly cloudy today, fair tonight and continued pleasantly cool. The high expected today is 79, and the low expected tonight is 55.

Two City Men Helped U. S. Achieve War's Greatest Scientific Victories

Two Madison men, neither in uniform but each a frontline "soldier of science," contributed heavily to the development of radar and the atomic bomb, The State Journal has learned.

Each of these men has been doing tightly-hidden research since a few weeks after Pearl Harbor. Only the surrender of Japan allowed them to acknowledge their connection with the two greatest scientific successes of World War II.

Davies Perfected Radar Device for Bombing Control

The radar expert is Robert Davies, 28, son of Mrs. Losia Davies, 1615 Hoyt st.

A 1939 graduate of the University of Wisconsin, Davies has worked since early 1942 at the radiation laboratory of the Massachusetts Institute of Technology (MIT), in Boston.

More than 3,800 of the nation's top physicists and high-frequency radio technicians have been at MIT on this project.

The Madisonian's particular task was the perfection of an airborne bombing control, the amazing radar device that enabled Allied aviators to "see" through overcast and clouds and bomb accurately military targets on the ground, miles below.

Davies majored in physics at the university, and did a senior thesis on "An All-Electric Thermostat," under Prof. J. R. Roebuck. He studied another year toward his master of science degree, and left in 1940 after completing all his academic work toward the higher degree, but still lacking a few weeks of the residence requirements.

He went to work for a thermometer manufacturing concern, but in February, 1942, received a letter from MIT. It offered him a position in "research work on high freqnency electronics."

It also offered something like a 20 per cent pay cut, but the opportunities and challenge were so much greater, Davies left his commercial work and went to Boston.

Since then, he has been working

(Continued on Page 3, Column 1)

ROBERT DAVIES

DR. DONALD W. KERST

Dr. Kerst Made Major Contributions to Atomic Bomb

The atomic bomb worker is Dr. Donald W. Kerst, University of Wisconsin graduate who is considered one of the leading young physicists of the nation.

The son of Mr. and Mrs. Herman S. Kerst, 428 N. Murray st., Dr. Kerst began his "atom-smashing" work in a Wisconsin laboratory in Sterling hall on The Hill. He earned his first degree in 1934, and won doctor of philosophy rank (never stopping for a master's degree) in 1937.

Now only 33, Dr. Kerst in 1941 invented a machine called the "betatron," an electron-hurling machine called the "weightiest contribution to atomic physics" in 10 years. For his work in this he won an honorary degree from Lawrence college, Appleton, in 1942.

After teaching at the University of Illinois, and doing research in Schenectady, N. Y., laboratories, Dr. Kerst was called early in 1942 to apply his knowledge of atoms and how to harness them to what eventually became the atomic bomb.

He moved to a desert station near Santa Fe, N. M., and worked there, in comparative isolation, for more than three years. Results of his work rained down as atomic bombs on Hiroshima and Nagasaki in early August to convince the Japanese they should surrender.

That, of course, meant that Kerst could have no qualms about working on the greatest destructive weapon the world ever has seen.

(Continued on Page 3, Column 2)

Rules Japan

GEN. DOUGLAS MacARTHUR

22-Minute Ceremony Ends Six Years of Bloodiest War

Allies Offer 80 Million Defeated Nips Hope of Eventual Freedom, Dignity

(Text of Surrender on Page 3)

By WILLIAM B. DICKINSON
(United Press Staff Correspondent)

ABOARD THE U. S. BATTLESHIP MISSOURI, In Tokyo Bay, — Two silent Japanese officials today surrendered their empire unconditionally to the United Nations in a rapid ceremony aboard this mighty American warship.

Without a single word, Foreign Minister Mamoru Shigemitsu, on behalf of Emperor Hirohito and the Japanese government, stepped to the broad table holding the duplicate copies in Japanese and English of the surrender terms. After several moments of fumbling with his watch and pen, he signed the surrender document which made 80,000,000 people from Emperor Hirohito down subject to the authority of Gen. Douglas MacArthur, the supreme Allied commander.

Jap Empire Collapsed

At the moment of signing, Japan was reduced to her four main islands and such minor islands as the Allies grant her. Her people, her government, her demi-god emperor, her industry, her very life came under Allied military rule and will remain there until the day when she is deemed to have for the first time in her 2,605 years of history a democratic, peacefully inclined government and thus is worthy of rejoining the family of nations.

A heavy overcast covered the skies over Tokyo bay as the surrender ceremony was completed in approximately 22 minutes, formally ending history's bloodiest war six years to the day after Germany's invasion of Poland on Sept. 1, 1939.

More than 800 warplanes—parading in one final display of Allied aerial might over the battered Japanese homeland—dipped and turned over the great Allied armada jamming Tokyo bay.

Gen. Douglas MacArthur, Supreme Allied commander, was tense and expressionless as he began the surrender ceremony and invited Shigemitsu to affix the first signature to the surrender documents—one bound in gold and one bound in black, the latter the Japanese copy.

"May Peace Return . . ."

Following Shigemitsu, came Gen. Yoshijiro Umezu, signing for Japanese imperial general headquarters.

Shigemitsu's fumbling and delay of several moments before signing was the only departure from the efficient, smoothly-working procedure prepared by the Allies.

When he took his seat at the table, Shigemitsu carefully removed his top hat and gloves and then anxiously searched through his pockets, apparently seeking a pen. Lieut. Gen. Richard K. Sutherland, MacArthur's chief of staff, stepped up to help Shigemitsu gain composure.

The Japanese foreign minister then carefully studied a watch. When MacArthur suddenly appeared irritated by the delay, Shigemitsu drew another watch and considered it. Then he dipped his pen in the ink, leaned over the paper, and began the signature that brought Japan's dreams of

(Continued on Page 2, Column 1)

92 Houston Survivors Returned to Calcutta

WASHINGTON — (U.P.) — The navy announced Saturday night that 92 officers and men of the old cruiser Houston, missing since the Battle of the Java Sea in February, 1942, have been returned to Calcutta from a Japanese prisoner of war camp in Thailand.

It had been disclosed earlier this week that 300 survivors in all were found in the Thailand camp.

One other officer and one crew member have been liberated in Thailand, the navy said.

The navy said that word received from the senior naval officer of the American legation in New Delhi was that all the officers liberated were in "good" condition.

The navy said that of the 932 men believed to have been aboard the Houston, 108 still are listed as dead, 594 missing, and seven status unknown. No Wisconsin men were listed among the survivors.

The Houston, one of our fightingest ships in the war's early days, disappeared without a trace on the night of Feb. 28, 1942, after a three-day running fight with a superior Japanese force.

Painters' Plea in WLB Hands

Union, 'Recessed,' Demands Wage Boost

The long-standing demand for wage increases from $1.25 to $1.50 an hour by the Madison Painters and Decorators union was left in the hands of the War Labor Board (WLB) Saturday night after union members had voted a "recess" until Tuesday on further action on the WLB's delay.

The WLB refused the union's demand for higher wages early this summer and the union appealed for a reversal. A meeting was held by the Madison group Friday night in Labor temple to discuss steps to be taken and it was there, according to George A. Nelson, business agent for the union, that the group representing approximately 210 painters, voted the "recess."

Meanwhile, Frank Dickert of Klein-Dickert Co. said that employers had signed an agreement with the union last April in which they agreed to increase wages if and when the WLB so directed.

"That's all we know about it," he told The State Journal. "We received no notice of what decisions were made at Friday night's meeting.

"It doesn't look as if much can be done about it here in Madison. It's all up to the War Labor Board."

Kenneth Fish Dies in Enemy Blast

RICHLAND CENTER — Kenneth Fish, 36, fireman first class, Richland Center, was killed Aug. 21 "in an enemy ordnance explosion," the navy department Saturday informed his wife and his parents, Mr. and Mrs. Ray Fish, Richland Center.

His wife, the former Waiva Emshoff, Richland Center telephone operator, had been informed he was working in an acetylene gas plant on Okinawa. He entered service in July, 1944, and went overseas July 29, 1945.

Survivors include his wife; a son, Richard, 13, and a daughter, Lorraine, all in Richland Center; his parents, and five sisters, Mrs. Myron Clark, Menasha, and Mrs. Coral Miller, Mrs. Virgil Sheafor, Mrs. Gerald Meeker, and Sally Fish, all of Richland Center.

No Paper Monday

So its employes may be free to celebrate Labor day, The Wisconsin State Journal will publish no regular editions Monday. Regular publication will be resumed Tuesday.

Feature Finder

Employment at Pre-War Level, Madison Kipp Plans for Future

EDITOR'S NOTE: The following article is one of a series designed to give a true picture of employment in Madison as the city enters the post-war period.

The Madison Kipp Corp. was at peak war production when the war with Japan came to an end, turning out products so vital to the war that production had to be maintained until the news of surrender.

Then, overnight, $3,000,000 in war contracts were cut off.

The immediate result was that Madison Kipp had scores of machines in its plant tooled to jobs which could no longer be continued and workers whose services could no longer be used.

Reconversion is now well under way at the plant, and the amazing thing is this:

Above 1940 Period

Employment today is above that during the 1940 period which was considered normal for the civilian business which was a major part of the plant activity.

The reason for this is threefold.

For one, work is being rushed upon products made by the plant in its regular civilian business, such as mechanical lubricators and high speed drills.

For another, many of the pre-war customers have recently ordered substantial amounts of die castings which can be—and some of which are now being—produced from dies that were in production before the war.

Retooling Done

And for a third, a large amount of retooling is being done to accommodate a large number of orders for die castings which have come to the plant.

Increasing the production potential at the plant has been the addition of several hundreds of thousands of dollars worth of

(Continued on Page 3, Column 3)

Madison Weather
Cloudy with occasional rain this afternoon. Rain or snow tonight and Wednesday morning. Partly cloudy Wednesday afternoon. Little change in temperature. Low tonight, 28; high Wednesday, 35. Sun rose 6:27; sets 5:52.

The Wisconsin State Journal

A fact-finding Newspaper

MADISON, TUESDAY, MARCH 5, 1946 ★★★

HOME FINAL
PRICE FIVE CENTS
18 PAGES
VOL. 157, NO. 153 107th Year

Churchill Warns of Russian Expansion

Workers Reject Gisholt's Offer

Striking steelworkers of the Gisholt Machine Co. voted unanimously today at a meeting at the Eagles clubhouse to reject an offer of the company in settlement of the 13-day old strike.

Terming the offer of the company provisional as well as inadequate, 900 of the 1,100 steelworkers out on strike voted to turn down the company offer after they had been told that the company was well able to pay the 18½ cent increase per hour which has been under negotiation since last fall.

The company offered a straight 10 cent per hour increase in pay upon resumption of work, but with the increase not to be effective until it was approved by the "appropriate" federal agency when and if such approval should be necessary.

Notes Tax Refund Outlook

As evidence of the company's ability to pay the increase, George Reger, vice-president of Local 1404 of the CIO United Steelworker's of America (USW), told the members that the company will be eligible for a tax refund of $1,097,311 in the event that certain profit levels are not met. The figures, he said, were taken from Standard and Poor, national rating agency.

"Assets of the company have increased from $4,290,000 in 1939 to $12,310,000 in 1944," Reger told members of the union.

"The inventory for the same years increased from $1,520,000 to $3,530,000. The assets receivable increased from $460,000 to $1,650,000 and the book value of the firm increased from $13,440,000 to $33,490,000."

Says Productivity Rises

He said that the company "saves 16¼ cents per hour on the work of every employe due to the shift from the 50 to the 40 hour week and the resultant non-payment of overtime. Despite this," he said, the company gets the same price for its product as it did in 1941.

A further saving of the management, which he claimed was saving nearly the total amount of the requested increase, comes in the increased productivity of the worker on the shorter week, Reger said. A worker necessarily must pace himself slower to work the longer hours, he said, slowing production.

"During the war years, the company had nearly trebled its operations and its value," Reger said, "and all of this has been done under the OPA.

"All the way down the line, the company has been able to make money under the OPA and make more than it ever did."

Outlines CIO Policy

Emil Costello, field representative of the United Steelworkers from Milwaukee, outlined national federal and CIO policy in settling steel strikes, pointing out that recent developments so new they have not been analyzed by the union further complicate wage settlement problems.

He pointed out, however, that the national policy of the CIO was against helping management procure price relief because of increases in wages under the 18½ cent level at which strikes were

(Continued on Page 2, Column 3)

As Steelworkers Rose to Register Votes

Nine hundred of the 1,100 striking steelworkers of the Gisholt Machine Co. rose to a man this morning to register their votes against acceptance of an offer by the company which would have ended the 13-day old strike. Shown above is a portion of the crowd, with George Reger, vice-president of Local 1404 of the steelworkers, in the foreground. William C. Stighham, president of the union, is the man at the far right at the speaker's rostrum. —State Journal Staff Photo

Senate Confirms Krug Without Controversy

WASHINGTON — (U.P.) — The senate without controversy today confirmed power expert J. A. Krug as secretary of interior, succeeding Harold L. Ickes.

Senate action on the nomination was requested by Democratic Leader Alben W. Barkley, (D-Ky.), a few hours after the senate lands committee had approved it.

Barkley told the senate that the nomination was "non-political" and, because the position was vacant, it should be approved as soon as possible.

Republican Leader Wallace H. White, Jr., (Me.), joined Barkley in urging prompt confirmation, and the senate did so without debate or roll call.

Krug, 38, will become the youngest member of Pres. Truman's cabinet. He will succeed Harold L. Ickes, 71, who resigned recently after a stormy protest against the nomination of Edwin W. Pauley to be undersecretary of navy.

The public lands committee voted its approval of Krug in a brief executive session after questioning him for less than an hour on his knowledge and views concerning western problems under interior department jurisdiction.

Krug assured the senators he would follow the policies laid down by congress. He said he is a firm believer in the theory that the best government is the one which governs the least.

He said his chief qualifications for the job probably were his interest in public service, a profound respect for democracy, and "a certain amount of energy and vitality."

He reminded the committee that as last chairman of the War Production Board he lifted governmental controls of materials as rapidly as supplies became plentiful.

Krug acknowledged an intense enthusiasm for public power development. He recalled he formerly was chief power engineer and power manager for the Tennessee Valley authority.

But, he said, he was not convinced that the authority setup is the soundest way to develop waterways of every section of the country.

"I think there might be some cases where the need for water for irrigation is so great that the power development must be sacrificed," Krug said.

He said public power should be distributed to retail consumers by local communities, either through cooperatives or existing privately owned systems, but not by the federal government.

KRUG

House Mangles Patman Bill

Supporters Rally to Save 'Something'

WASHINGTON — (U.P.) — House supporters of the Patman housing bill, shaken by two straight setbacks, rallied today for an effort to salvage something from the president's housing program for veterans.

A triumphant coalition of Republicans and southern Democrats joined Monday in eliminating what Mr. Truman called "the heart" of his program—federal subsidies to encourage production of scarce building materials.

Backers of the Patman bill said they would try today to push through the controversial issue of putting price controls on new homes. If they succeed, they will make another attempt to put used homes under price ceilings.

They conceded, however, that their chances of success were slim. Rep. A. S. Mike Monroney, (D-Okla.), who had such an amendment ready, predicted that the substitute Wolcott bill would be introduced in the house at once.

The substitute bill, prepared by Rep. Jesse P. Wolcott (R-Mich.), would attempt to control prices on new homes by limiting the amount of mortgage insurance the National Housing administration would be permitted to write.

Patman's camp contended that this merely would result in contractors' requiring would-be purchasers to have a larger down payment, resulting in no price control at all.

The proposal to turn over $600,000,000 to the Reconstruction Finance Corp. for subsidy purposes was defeated by a teller vote of 161 to 92, despite the president's plea that it was vital to his program.

More Pupils Demonstrate at Theaters

The second teen-age demonstration against present theater prices was held by about 35 high school pupils in front of the Orpheum and Capitol theaters Monday night.

The demonstration, termed a "nuisance" by Police Chief William H. McCormick, and marked by a chanting of "We want lower prices," was broken up when about seven of the youngsters were taken to the police station. The rest of the group soon followed, demanding the release of those apprehended.

The group, according to McCormick, carried out the "picketing" as part of initiation ceremonies into a Central high school organization. The matter was to be turned over to school authorities today.

Meanwhile, representatives of the Madison Youth council announced that they would meet with theater managers "within a few days" to see what could be done. They emphasized, however, that they were an "impartial party" and that the demonstrators were "on their own." Chosen to meet with the theater managers were Harlan Shaw, 17, East high school, and Lyman Bixby, 17, West.

The first demonstration was Friday night, when about 50 teen-agers picketed the theaters with placards.

Canning Sugar to Be Issued Beginning Monday

WASHINGTON — (U.P.) — First 1946 canning sugar will be available next Monday, the Office of Price Administration (OPA) announced today.

Sparfe Stamp 9 in Ration Book 4 becomes good for 5 pounds of sugar on that date. It will be valid through Oct. 31.

Another canning sugar stamp will be validated later, possibly in late June or early July, OPA said. It was unlikely that the canning allotment this year will be more than 10 pounds per person.

OPA cautioned that no increase in the regular sugar ration can be foreseen now, and urged housewives to continue to budget home sugar use according to the present rate of rationing.

The next regular sugar stamp becomes valid May 1.

Church Council Plans to Ask End to A-Bomb Output

COLUMBUS, O. — (U.P.) — The Federal Council of Churches will be asked Wednesday to request the U. S. government to stop manufacture of atomic bombs and affirm publicly, with suitable guaranties, that it will not be the first to use atomic weapons in any possible future war.

The recommendation will be presented to the council, which is meeting in Columbus, in a commission report on the relation of the church to war in the light of the Christian faith during a plenary session Wednesday morning.

Production of the bombs should be stopped pending development of effective international controls that should be assigned ultimately to civilian agencies. The commission recommended.

Briton Admits 'Leak' of Secrets

Atomic Researcher Charged in London

LONDON — (U.P.) — A British crown prosecutor announced in Bow st. police court today that Dr. Alan Nunn May, 34-year-old scientist who did government atomic research in Canada, had admitted communicating official secrets to an unidentified person.

May was arrested Monday as he finished a lecture on atomic energy to a class in King's college of the University of London. He was charged with violation of the official secrets act.

The court postponed further hearings on his case until Mar. 19 when he appeared today.

The prosecutor told the court that May had admitted "communicating certain information within the meaning of the official secrets act" to an unknown person.

May was not asked to plead guilty or not guilty, and the prosecutor said he did not wish to present any evidence at this time. May refused to disclose the identification or nationality of the person to whom he gave atomic energy information, the prosecutor said.

He also refused to answer other questions.

Egyptian Police Fire on Rioters

CAIRO — (U.P.) — Egyptian police fired on anti-British demonstrators in Alexandria today in a renewal of rioting in which more than 17 persons were killed and more than 300 wounded Monday.

An undetermined number of casualties were caused when police opened fire at Alexandria. Victims were taken to hospitals in ambulances.

Two Cardinals Land at Chicago

CHICAGO — (U.P.) — The TWA Constellation "Star of Lisbon," carrying Samuel Cardinal Stritch of Chicago and Edward Cardinal Mooney of Detroit, landed at noon today at the municipal airport.

The big plane landed on the fog-shrouded field after a nonstop flight from Gander, Newfoundland. The fog prevented a scheduled stop at Detroit to discharge Cardinal Mooney.

CARDINAL GLENNON ILL

DUBLIN — (U.P.) — John Cardinal Glennon, archbishop of St. Louis, was taken seriously ill tonight at the residence of Eire's president, Sean O'Kelly, and first reports said the 82-year-old prelate had suffered a heart attack.

Hughes' Plane Sets New Record

CULVER CITY, Calif. — (U.P.) — An east-west commercial speed record of 10 hours and 15 minutes was held today by Howard Hughes, millionaire movie producer who flew a half dozen movie stars here from New York in a TWA Constellation plane.

The plane left La Guardia Field, New York, at 4:48 a. m. (EST) Monday and landed at Hughes' aircraft plant here at 12:04 p. m. (PST). The previous record, set by another Constellation last Feb. 1, was 10 hours 49 minutes.

City Acts to Spur Building at Truax

By RUSSELL B. PYRE
(State Journal Staff Writer)

The Madison city council adopted three resolutions at a special meeting Monday night to facilitate development of 99 temporary housing units at Truax Field in "the quickest and most economical way."

One resolution appropriated $24,000 to the Madison Housing Authority as an outright grant to finance "preparation of the site and installation of utilities to the building line."

Another authorized the housing authority to enter into an agreement with the Federal Public Housing Authority (FPHA) under which FPHA will remodel Truax barracks in one block and part of another and turn the completed units over to the Madison authority for operation.

The third was a required indemnity agreement pledging the city to pay any deficit between revenues and operating expense.

Larger by $4,000

The $24,000 grant, a "required contribution" not recoverable by the city, is $4,000 larger than the original estimate, but will finance site preparation and utilities in two entire blocks of barracks in the area near the Sun Prairie road.

Barracks in the remainder of the second block may be remodeled later, Mayor Kraege told the council. The site will be prepared for 120 units.

The FPHA expects to spend about $200,000 on the 99 units (three units to a building), employing its own contractors on a "cost plus" basis, Kraege and Finance Chairman H. L. Garner explained.

While the cost of about $2,000 a unit is larger than the city's estimate of $1,400, the result probably will be a better quality of dwelling units than the city could have produced, the council was told.

Eliminates Zone Change

Federal development of the housing project will eliminate legal complications involving Dane county zoning regulations and town of Burke objections, Kraege explained, as the government will be building on its own property and is not affected by local regulations.

While the FPHA program is designed to have a life of only two years after the war emergency period ends, it provides for year-to-year extensions in some circumstances, he said.

The council received and referred to the housing authority two resolutions by Ald. Richard A. Smith affecting the housing situation.

One directed the housing authority to cooperate with the FPHA in establishing an agency here to coordinate distribution of building materials.

The other provides that the housing authority, in cooperation with the Office of Price Administration (OPA) sponsor a "city-wide publication" clarifying the

(Continued on Page 2, Column 4)

Spain Rejected 3-Power Plea in Advance

WASHINGTON — (U.P.) — Spain repudiated the American-British-French appeal for the overthrow of the Franco regime 24 hours before the appeal was issued, it was revealed today.

The views of the present Spanish regime were communicated to the United States on Sunday in a short note anticipating the three-power declaration. The note was made available through authoritative sources to correspondents today.

"The Spanish government wishes to inform the government of the United States in advance," the Spanish note said, "That Spain repudiates any foreign pressure put upon her, since it considers that the question of its interior regime is a matter concerning exclusively its own sovereignty."

The three-power declaration was announced late Monday.

The declaration was addressed to the Spanish people—specifically to "leading patriotic and liberal-minded Spaniards." It expressed the hope that they soon would find means to bring about the "peaceful withdrawal" of Franco and establish an interim or caretaker government. This temporary regime would remain in power until free national elections could be held.

It got a mixed reception in the United States congress where reaction ranged from "great stuff" to charges of American intervention in Spain. Critics also rapped the tri-power move as "further Russian appeasement."

Franco's reaction was anticipated. In fact, there were indica-

(Continued on Page 2, Column 5)

U. S. Tax Office Opens at 8:30 a. m.

Office hours at the Madison office of the internal revenue bureau, on the third floor of the federal building, are 8:30 a. m. to 5:15 p. m., R. W. Roloff, chief deputy, announced today. Crowds, waiting to file returns before the Mar. 15 deadline, have been gathering in the corridors early, Roloff said, in the mistaken impression that the office opens at 8 a. m.

Gen. Lee Censors GI 'Gripe' Letters

ROME — (U.P.) — Lieut. Gen. John C. H. Lee, American commander in the Mediterranean theater, confirmed today that he was censoring all GI "gripe letters" to the army newspaper Stars and Stripes, and threatened to dismiss any Communists found on the paper's staff.

Lee told a press conference, at which three GI's from the Stars and Stripes staff participated, that he already had signed the censorship directive and intended to enforce it.

Lee acknowledged under questioning that he had seen no harmful letters published in the service newspaper's "mail call column," but he intimated strongly that he regarded it as potentially dangerous to army morale.

Dutch Girl Thanks Clothes Donor

Stanley C. Bran, 1726 Commercial ave., is taking a just pride these days in the response he made to the Victory Clothing collection drive, which terminated about two weeks ago.

His badge of good will is a letter he received several days ago from a little Dutch girl in Amsterdam, Holland. The gist of her message was that a pair of Bran's trousers are now the property of her father—who was mighty glad to get them.

The little girl, straying here and there in her letter from the precise rules of grammer and punctuation, began, "Dear Mr. Bran, my name is Mia Herrendorf, and I am a Dutch girl and lived in Amsterdam, Holland. I will thank you very much for the trousers you gave for they Dutchmans. We in Holland have enough money to buy clothes ourself, but we don't have the materials to make them.

"You will know that Holland is poor now and cannot buy anything.

"I found your address in the pocket of the trousers you gave, and that was very nice. Then now I can thank you myself for it.

"My father was very glad to get this trousers.

"I hope you can read this letter then. I never write English and it is a long time ago I learned it at school a little. Now I close this letter and I hope you get him okay.

"I say you now goodbye from my father, mother, and me."

When he first received Mia's letter of gratitude, Bran was puzzled as to how his name and address came to be in the trousers' pocket. His wife cleared up that mystery, saying she had slipped the note in just before her husband set off for the Madison clothing depot.

Bran has been able to secure information about the Herrendorf family from Evert Rot, a native Dutchman now in this area for six months on a tulip bulb-selling tour. The two men met recently, and Rot said he was from the same neighborhood in Amsterdam. He said he thought he knew the family, and that he believed Mia to be about 12 years old.

Feature Finder

Byrnes Says Reds Violated Pact on Iran

BULLETIN

WASHINGTON — (U.P.) — The United States has notified both Russia and China that negotiations between them alone for disposition of Manchurian industries would be contrary to the American open-door policy in the Far East.

The state department released today the text of a note sent to Chungking and Moscow which revealed the Russians had claimed that Japanese enterprises in Manchuria were legitimate war booty. Russia proposed that enterprises remaining in Manchuria after removal of war booty be jointly operated by China and the Soviet Union.

WASHINGTON — (U.P.) — Secretary of State James F. Byrnes made it clear today that this country feels that Russia violated its agreement by failing to withdraw its troops from Iran by Saturday.

He was asked at a press conference whether there was any question in his mind about Saturday having been the deadline for withdrawal of all foreign troops from Iran.

Byrnes replied emphatically that there was no question in his mind.

The press conference was devoted almost entirely to questions and statements on problems of American-Russian relations. These included:

ONE. Revelation that the Iranian ambassador here received this morning a communication from his government for delivery later today to the state department.

TWO. Byrnes' statement that the Potsdam declaration pledged the Allies to allow Japanese troops to return to their homes after surrender. This was indirectly linked with unconfirmed reports that the Russians have removed some Japanese troops to Siberia. Byrnes had no comment on the specific case.

THREE. Byrnes' assertion that the geographical limits of Gen. Douglas MacArthur's command in the Far East extend wherever there is enemy territory or enemy troops. Byrnes said his understanding was that MacArthur's

(Continued on Page 2, Column 5)

Yoder 'Resigns' as Whitewater College Head

Robert C. Williams, 51-year-old assistant to the president of Superior State Teachers college, will succeed C. M. Yoder as president of Whitewater State Teachers college. Yoder's "resignation" was accepted at a secret meeting of the board of teacher college regents today.

The board also accepted the resignation of J. H. Ames as president of River Falls Teachers college. Ames' resignation will be effective July 1. The president of the board will appoint a committee of five to recommend a successor. The board gave no public explanation why either Ames or Yoder "resigned."

Yoder's resignation was accepted, The State Journal learned, because of the governing board's dissatisfaction with his administrative procedures and because the Whitewater president has had repeated difficulty with his faculty. His letter of resignation, read to the board in closed session this morning, said he would leave "immediately."

The board in executive session then agreed to give Yoder's post to Williams. Formal action on Yoder's resignation and Williams' election were to take place at an open board meeting this afternoon.

Williams now is serving as assistant to Pres. Jim Dan Hill at Superior Teachers, and served as acting president during Jim Dan Hill's service in the nation's military forces. A native of Iowa, Williams is described by board members as "an extremely capable man."

Before newspaper reporters were expelled from the board session this morning by Board Pres. Edward J. Dempsey, several minor matters were discussed but laid over until this afternoon's meeting.

A letter from Joseph R. Cotton, Milwaukee State Teachers instructor who was dismissed in September, was read. Cotton demanded a rehearing in his case, and charged that Board Members Dempsey and Mrs. Dorris Marks had represented "business interests" who had sought his discharge.

Board members were warned, in a communication from the As-

(Continued on Page 2, Column 2)

Woman Accused of $16,200 Jewel Theft

MILWAUKEE — (U.P.) — Charged with the theft of $16,200 worth of jewels from the home of her employer, William Pabst, Mrs. Anna Mae Bailey, cleaning woman, waived preliminary hearing in district court Monday and was bound over to municipal court for trial.

Wants U. S., Britain to Be Permanent Allies

Urges UNO to Set Up World Armed Force at Once

FULTON, Mo. — (U.P.) — Winston Churchill said today that Russia seeks "indefinite expansion" of her "power and doctrines," and called for a permanent Anglo-American military alliance which might some day include common citizenship.

Pointing to the Soviet "shadow" upon "scenes so lately lighted by the Allied victory," the former British prime minister called for firm and immediate steps, including establishment of an international armed force by the United Nations Organization (UNO), to prevent another war.

Great Britain's wartime leader was introduced by Pres. Truman as he spoke at little Westminster college here, and the president had seen the prepared text before it was delivered.

This small Missouri town and its sedate college campus provided an incongruous setting for Churchill's thundering denunciation of the manner in which Communists in Europe have obtained "power far beyond their numbers, and are seeking everywhere to obtain totalitarian control."

At the outset, Churchill told his audience of college students and rural Missourians that he spoke without any official standing, that he was speaking only for himself.

Then he got down to international cases, making these points in rapid succession:

ONE. The UNO must "immediately" begin an "international armed force" with each participating nation providing air force units.

TWO. It would be wrong to give the atomic bomb secrets to UNO. They should be held for the time being by this country, Great Britain, and Canada.

THREE. The people of any nation should be given the right of "free, unfettered elections, with secret ballot . . ."

FOUR. There should be cooperative Anglo-American use of sea and air bases. This would be in continuance of wartime "mutual security."

FIVE. A "special relationship" between this country and the British commonwealth would be consistent with overriding loyalties to UNO.

SIX. "Nobody knows what Soviet Russia or its Communist International organization intends to do in the immediate future, or what are the limits if any to their expansive and proselytizing tendencies."

SEVEN. The "Russian dominated" Polish government has made "enormous and wrongful inroads upon Germany . . ."

EIGHT. One of the more "somber facts . . . on the morrow of a victory" is the "growing challenge and peril to Christian civilization" caused by "Communist

(Continued on Page 2, Column 3)

Mrs. Conner 'Ill;' Hearing Postponed

Because of her "physical illness," preliminary hearing in superior court for Mrs. LaVera V. Conner on charges of killing her husband in the heat of passion, was postponed today until Mar. 14.

Mrs. Conner's attorney, Darrell MacIntyre, asked for the postponement, declaring that his client was under a doctor's care for shock and a heart ailment, and that he had been able to confer with her only once since her husband was shot Feb. 23 in the E. Dayton st. apartment of Mrs. Marion Aasen, 32-year-old divorcee.

MacIntyre said he was going south Mar. 15, and asked the court to set a hearing before that date, at which time he would request that a date for Mrs. Conner's preliminary hearing be scheduled.

Dist. Atty. Norris E. Maloney objected vehemently, declaring that "it's all right for Mr. MacIntyre to take a vacation, but this is a serious enough case to have it brought to trial immediately." MacIntyre said he was considering entering a plea of present insanity for his client, and if granted, the plea would postpone Mrs. Conner's trial until doctors declare that she is fit to stand trial.

Superior Judge Roy H. Proctor sternly told Maloney he would not "force an ill woman to come into court," and postponed Mrs. Conner's preliminary hearing until Mar. 14. The judge told MacIntyre the court would make no inquiry into Mrs. Conner's sanity until requested by the defense counsel, but that if her "physical condition" prevented her from appearing in court for hearing Mar. 14, MacIntyre should inform him "a day in advance," with doctors' certificates to prove her illness.

After Landslide, Rain

MADISON WEATHER

Partly cloudy this afternoon becoming cloudy tonight and Thursday with rain beginning late tonight and continuing Thursday. Little change in temperature this afternoon. Warmer tonight. Colder Thursday. Lowest temperature expected today—42 degrees; highest, Thursday—50.

The Wisconsin State Journal

A fact-finding Newspaper

MADISON, WEDNESDAY, NOVEMBER 6, 1946 ★★★

HOME FINAL

PRICE FIVE CENTS

24 PAGES

VOL. 169, NO. 37 107th Year

City Manager Plan Favored by Margin of 3,508 Votes

System Becomes Effective in April; Journal Backed Set-Up 20 Years

Table on Page 5

Madison, governed by a mayor and council since it was incorporated as a city 90 years ago, voted Tuesday, by a margin of 3,508, to change its form of government.

By a count of 14,937 to 11,429, the citizens decided to place its administration in the hands of a city manager and a council of seven members, elected at large.

The new system becomes effective next April, when the voters will elect the seven aldermen replacing the present council of 20, and the new council will choose the city manager.

Backed by Journal

The change represents a crystallization of public sentiment fostered nearly 20 years by The State Journal and the League of Women Voters of Madison, and brought to a head last June 3, when a meeting was held in the Community Center to organize the Madison Citizens Association on Municipal Government.

Tuesday's referendum was made mandatory by a petition, signed by more than 5,000 voters and filed in August by the citizens association.

Only seven of the city's 41 precincts voted against the city manager plan. They were the second precinct of the sixth ward, 291 to 227; the second of the 14th, 213 to 177; the second of the 15th, 380 to 314; the first and second of the 17th, 260 to 173 and 307 to 199; and the first and second of the 18th, 551 to 412, and 420 to 312.

Trend Shown Early

The trend in favor of the change was presaged at 8:25 p. m. by the vote from the first precinct to report—the second of the second, which registered 388 to 303 for a city manager.

The biggest vote was cast in the 20th ward, and the biggest margin for the city manager plan was turned in by the first precinct of that ward (Nakoma)—709 to 224; the second precinct went 689 to 393.

Heavy margins in favor of the change also were recorded in the first, tenth, 13th, and 19th wards.

Henry Beats Rice; Carries All 5 Counties

ROBERT K. HENRY

GOP Wins Every Wisconsin District. (Story on Page 4.)

Robert K. Henry, former Jefferson banker and a one-time member of the state banking commission, won a second term as the Wisconsin second district's representative in congress Tuesday.

Henry turned back the challenge by William Gorham Rice, professor of law at the University of Wisconsin, who was the Democratic nominee. The total vote was 68,402 for Henry to 39,523 for Rice. The Rev. A. T. Wallace, retired Madison minister who was the Socialist candidate, drew only 882 votes.

Henry carried all of the five counties in the second district, including Dane county. He won his healthiest margin in Waukesha, where he ran ahead of Rice by a count of 17,576 to 5,549. In Dane county the count was close—26,413 for Henry to 23,419 for the Democratic candidate.

The Republican nominee's victory in all five counties was an unexpectedly strong showing. Henry has been ill and unable to campaign, while Rice had carried on an aggressive campaign in all five counties in the district.

The county by county totals:

County	Henry (R)	Rice (D)	Wallace (S)
Dane	24,613	23,419	645
Dodge	10,654	3,724	47
Columbia	6,869	2,975	27
Jefferson	8,699	3,856	—
Waukesha	17,567	5,549	163
Totals	68,402	39,523	882

Burke's Race So 'Hot' Town Hall Catches Fire

The election race in the town of Burke was so hot, the town hall caught fire, officials reported today.

The blaze Tuesday, due to an overheated pipe, was unnoticed by election officials and was spotted first by a citizen coming in to vote.

Voters and officials formed a bucket brigade and put out the fire before the Sun Prairie fire department could arrive. Damage was slight.

Victors in Top Races

—State Journal Staff Photo

JOSEPH R. McCARTHY

GOV. GOODLAND

Matson Urges Steps to Compel Moving Switch Yards from City

By RUSSELL B. PYRE
(State Journal Staff Writer)

Five effective steps to compel removal of the Milwaukee railroad's switch yards from the city were suggested to the West Side Business Men's assn. Tuesday night by Roy L. Matson, editor of The State Journal.

Explaining why The State Journal opposes the W. Washington ave. underpass, Matson also answered the challenge of J. P. Woolsey, association past president, now chairman of its civic affairs committee, to tell how he would go about getting the yards out of the city as an alternative to the underpass.

Matson debated the subject with Woolsey at a meeting of the business men's organization in Moose hall.

Quit "asking" the railroad to move its tracks, he proposed, and "TELL" it to move, with these measures as a club to enforce the demand:

ONE. Have Mayor Kraege inform the railroad company that public opinion insists upon removal of the yards.

TWO. Make operation of the railroad roundhouse and switch engines impossible within the city limits by strict enforcement of the smoke ordinance, supplemented by:

THREE. Revision or reenactment of a reasonable but forceful ordinance prohibiting the blocking of crossings by trains.

FOUR. Request the Wisconsin legislature to enact a law empowering the public service commission (PSC) to order removal of railroad blights from the cities on grounds of health, safety, and city progress.

FIVE. Request the next legislature to enact on enabling law which would permit cities to help pay for removal of railroad yards.

Matson predicted that other Wisconsin cities would join Madison in urging the state lawmakers to enact these measures.

He summarized The State Journal's reasons for opposing the underpass as follows:

ONE. It will not solve the traffic problem.

TWO. The underpass would spike down the railroad yards in the city forever, and thus:

A. Destroy important property values.

B. Drive citizens and businesses out of Madison as others cities have learned.

C. Insure continued traffic hazards on 92 other grade crossings scattered throughout the city.

D. Insure more and longer traffic delays all over the city.

E. Deprive Madison of deserved railroad service and efficiency through continuance of inefficient and insufficient facilities, duplication of facilities and excessive operation costs.

F. Block development of the University of Wisconsin with a

(Continued on Page 4, Column 1)

• • •

Need Underpass Now, Woolsey Says, Denying 'Freeze' Peril

Madison, facing an acute traffic problem, can't force the Milwaukee railroad to remove its switch yards under present laws and can't afford to wait enough years for "public opinion" to compel their removal.

This contention, as the primary rea[illegible]n why the W. Washington ave. underpass "must be built now," was emphasized repeatedly by J. P. Woolsey, past president of the West Side Business Men's assn., in his debate with Roy L. Matson, editor of The State Journal, before a crowd of more than 200 men and women who filled the Moose lodge hall Tuesday night.

Woolsey also repeatedly denied that the underpass, once built, would "freeze" the railroad yards forever inside the city, as predicted by Matson.

'Let's Fight'

Both speakers drew long applause, and both drew barrages of questions from the floor in a heated discussion that followed their arguments, along with the suggestion, also from the floor, that this meeting may have represented "the crystalization of public opinion for which Madison has waited many years."

"Let's fight," proposed Col. J. W. Jackson, as Joe Rothschild, manager of Baron Brothers store, renewed his application for the "carp fishing privilege" in the subway—if it is built.

Matson found another strong ally in Sidney Pritzert, University of Wisconsin student from Philadelphia.

Cites Philadelphia

The Pennsylvania road, for 100 years held a strangling grip on his city which reduced "magnificent mansions to hovels," but is now "getting out of Philadelphia" because the people of the city "finally got up enough gumption" to force it out, Pritzert declared.

"And Madison," he predicted, "can do the same thing."

Woolsey, president-treasurer of the Heilman Baking Co., and chairman of the West Side association's civic affairs committee, insisted that he, too, would like to see the railroad yards removed, but, he demanded:

"Is Madison so much more powerful than Chicago or Milwaukee that it can force the railroads to do something these much larger cities have been unable to do? I doubt it."

Chicago for more than 50 years, has been complaining that the Illinois Central tracks, along the lakeshore, have "stifled" the city, but has not been able to do anything about it, he claimed, and Milwaukee's experience has been similar.

Protests Criticism

Woolsey also charged that the newspapers had been unable to exert enough influence upon public opinion to force action for solution of the railroad problem "after all these years," and objected to the criticism heaped upon his association for its "successful" fight to obtain the underpass.

"I didn't hear a d--- thing from any of you about what you were going to do to get the railroads out until the West Side Business Men's assn. started to fight for the underpass," he said. "Where have you been all that time?"

"Right in there, fighting," Matson replied.

"We've gotten results, and now

(Continued on Page 4, Column 3)

Banner Year, All Right

SAN FRANCISCO—(U.P.)—Below a banner headline "GOP Wins Congress", the San Francisco News' first edition today carried the sub-banner:

"California Does What Comes Nationally."

Traffic Cases

GOOD MORNING, JUDGE!—(Superior Court)—Driving under the influence of liquor—Henry O. Eickhoff, 24, of 1914 E. Dayton st., $100 bail forfeited.

Speeding — Isadore Schwartz, 440 State st., $10 bail forfeited; Maynard R. Figy, Route 1, New Glarus, $15 bail forfeited; F. A. Hoerner, Beaver Dam, $15 bail forfeited; Willis E. Gifford, 245 Standish ct., $8 bail forfeited; Richard C. Johnson, 1013 Seminole highway, $8 bail forfeited.

Arterial — Theodore R. Hulet, 619 Mendota ct., $5 bail forfeited; Anton DeVas, 1805 Keyes ave., $5 bail forfeited; Norbert Kerl, Mazomanie, $5 bail forfeited.

Passing on hill—F. A. Hoerner, Beaver Dam, $5 bail forfeited.

Failure to yield right of way—Helen A. Hohlfeld, 1911 Vilas ave., $5 bail forfeited.

Passing at intersection—Patrick E. Mooney, 2038 E. Mifflin st., $10 bail forfeited.

Driving on left side—David D. Coward, 123 N. Butler st., $3 bail forfeited.

Driving truck on restricted—G. L. Potter, 460 N. Few st., $2 bail forfeited; George L. Tuschel, Sun Prairie, $2 bail forfeited.

Deathless Days

(Since Last Fatal Traffic Accident)

Madison 26

Dane county 1

Goodland, McCarthy Lead GOP Landslide

Republicans Win Control of Both Congress Houses

Get 50 Senate Seats, Four Above Majority Among Representatives

By LYLE C. WILSON
(United Press Staff Correspondent)

NEW YORK—Republicans won control of congress today in a countrywide election swing to the right after 16 years of Democratic rule.

The GOP captured the senate on the basis of incomplete returns with a total of at least 50 seats. Latest reports showed it had elected 222 members to the house of representatives — four more than needed for a majority.

Four senate contests remained in doubt—in Arizona, Montana, New Mexico, and West Virginia.

The Republican sweep in a great turnout of voters throughout the country thrust upon Pres. Truman the difficult task of dealing with an opposition congress during the remaining two years of his present White House term.

The 80th congress, convening next Jan. 3, will have Joseph W. Martin, Jr., veteran Massachusetts Republican, as speaker of the house.

Sen. Arthur H. Vandenberg, who has been the Republicans' chief adviser to Secretary of State James F. Byrnes, probably will be president of the senate.

Overhaul Promised

Republicans have promised that the new congress will overhaul the government. They have pledged reduced taxes and sharp cuts in federal spending in an effort to balance the national budget.

The election victory, which stripped Democrats of their power in many of the country's big cities where they had been unbeatable during the regime of the late Pres. Roosevelt, resulted in early speculation on a possible GOP triumph in the 1948 presidential race.

Dewey Wins Easily

Gov. Thomas E. Dewey of New York, who unsuccessfully opposed Mr. Roosevelt for a fourth term, was reelected in New York by a thumping majority over Sen. James M. Mead, Democratic New Dealer who until recently conducted the senate's war profits investigation.

The drums are now beating again for Dewey in talk of 1948 Republican presidential possibilities.

The latest returns showed that, in addition to their senate victory, the Republicans had captured 41 house seats formerly held by Democrats. But they lost one in Massachusetts, which meant a net gain of 40 over their present strength.

GOP Jubilant

At the same hour, Democrats had elected 10 senators and were leading in Arizona and West Virginia, which they now hold. Republicans had elected 22 senators, and were ahead in Montana and New Mexico, now Democratic.

The Republicans were jubilant

(Continued on Page 2, Column 3)

Dane County Assemblymen Win Reelection

Table on Page 5
(Picture on Page 2)

All three of Dane county's representatives in the state assembly won reelection in Tuesday's voting. They are Rudy Roethlisberger, Republican Regular from Verona, and Lyall T. Beggs, Madison, and Earl Mullen, Blooming Grove. Beggs and Mullen are former Progressives.

Roethlisberger was the easiest victor, while the Democratic challengers of both Beggs and Mullen drew unexpectedly heavy support.

Beggs, running in the city of Madison district, won over Dorothy Rall, Democrat, the wife of a University of Wisconsin instructor, by a count of 15,238 to 11,087. Mrs. Rall carried nine of the city's 41 voting precincts in her unsuccessful race.

John Blaska, member of the Dane county board, carried five of the 29 precincts of the county's eastern district against Mullen, who was a pre-balloting favorite.

Voting by districts follows:

First District

Beggs (R) 15,238
Rall (D) 11,087
Bergenske (S) 424

Second District

Mullen (R) 5,776
Blaska (D) 3,870

Third District

Roethlisberger (R) 7,229
Sebert (D) 4,231
Uphoff (S) 164

Bus Plan Rejected; Audit Change Voted

Controversial Transportation Amendment Loses by 4 to 3 Edge

MILWAUKEE—(U.P.)— Wisconsin voters answered "no" in a firm voice Tuesday to the question of whether state money should be spent for transporting parochial and private school children from their homes to their schools.

Voters decisively turned down the hotly debated "school bus" amendment to the state constitution, but approved a second amendment transferring responsibility for auditing state accounts from the secretary of state to the legislature.

Latest returns on the two constitutional amendment proposals placed before the voters were:

SCHOOL BUS AMENDMENT: 3,111 out of 3,147 precincts, 445,353 votes for, 507,262 against.

AUDITING AMENDMENT: 3,111 precincts, 414,598 votes for, 278,319 against.

The school bus amendment, which had been approved by the 1943 and 1945 legislatures, provoked such a heated political and religious argument throughout the state that many observers credited it for the heavy turnout of voters in Tuesday's election.

The brunt of the fight against it was waged by the Wisconsin Council of Churches, an organization of 11 Protestant groups.

Catholics generally supported it. Both Protestants and Catholics organized special campaign committees to get their views before the public. The campaign on this measure was one of the most bitter in the state's history.

Protestants argued that spending money for the benefit of parochial schools would be a step towards ending the historic separation of church and state. Catholics replied that parochial students were being discriminated against because they could not ride on public buses although their parents paid taxes which paid for the buses.

The less-publicized auditing amendment was supported by numerous civic and taxpayers' groups. It repeals the constitutional provision making the secretary of state the state auditor and allows the legislature to decide how auditing work should be handled. The legislature could create a separate auditing department or give the job to the present state budget bureau.

Backers of the amendment say it will modernize the state's financial setup by coordinating controls over state spending.

How City, County Voted

Here is the city of Madison's vote on the two state referendum questions:

To allow legislature to provide for transportation of children to parochial and private schools:

In Favor—9,300
Opposed—17,479

To allow legislature to establish bureau to audit state expenditures, rather than have secretary of state do it:

In Favor—13,383
Opposed—9,705

Here is the total Dane county vote on the two state referendums:

To allow legislature to provide for transportation of children to parochial and private schools:

In favor 16,123
Opposed 32,621

To allow legislature to establish bureau to audit state expenditures, rather than have secretary of state do it:

In Favor 22,149
Opposed 19,075

Table on Page 5

The Winners

U. S. SENATOR
Joseph R. McCarthy (R)

GOVERNOR
Walter S. Goodland (R)

LIEUTENANT GOVERNOR
Oscar Rennebohm (R)

SECRETARY OF STATE
Fred R. Zimmerman (R)

STATE TREASURER
John M. Smith

ATTORNEY GENERAL
John E. Martin (R)

CONGRESS
First—Lawrence Smith (R)
Second—Robert K. Henry (R)
Third—William Stevenson (R)
Fourth—John Brophy (R)
Fifth—Charles Kersten (R)
Sixth—Frank Keefe (R)
Seventh—Reid Murray (R)
Eighth—John Byrnes (R)
Ninth—Herlin Hull (R)
Tenth—Alvin O'Konski (R)

COUNTY CLERK
Austin Johnson (R)

COUNTY TREASURER
Clarence Femrite (R)

SHERIFF
Edward A. Fischer (R)

CORONER
David C. Atwood (R)

CLERK OF COURT
Myrtle Hanson (R)

DISTRICT ATTORNEY
Edwin Wilkie (R)

REGISTER OF DEEDS
A. O. Barton (R)

COUNTY SURVEYOR
Andrew Dahlen (R)

Suspected Butler St. Polio Victim Treated

A 7-year-old N. Butler st. boy, a pupil at Lincoln school, was admitted to Wisconsin General hospital Tuesday with an illness suspected to be polomyelitis but not yet definitely diagnosed: There were no other new polio cases in the city or at the hospital and the hospital reported no deaths or discharges.

Six new polio cases, including two in Dane county, were reported to the state board of health today, bringing the total for the year to 1,249. The county cases, at Cross Plains and Sun Prairie, had been announced previously. The other victims included two in Wood River township, Burnett county; one at Prairie du Chien, Crawford county, and one at North Bend township, Jackson county.

Dana Hails Victory, Urges Unity Now

Commenting upon the defeat of the referendum to permit state-supported buses to transport parochial school children, Ellis H. Dana, Madison, executive vice-president of the Wisconsin Council of Churches and one of the leading opponents of the plan, said today, "As Americans, the citizens of Wisconsin have spoken and the nation has heard. A great American principle which guarantees equality and liberty for all faiths has been upheld. Understanding each other better, now let us close ranks and work together."

County GOP Slate, Including 6 Ex-Progressives, Wins Easily

All eight Republican candidates for county offices, six of them former Progressives now waving the GOP banner, won easy victories in Tuesday's election over weak opposition from one Democratic and six Socialist candidates.

Coroner Edward A. Fischer, former Progressive sheriff for two terms and coroner for four terms, rode back into the sheriff's office on the Republican ticket by defeating the Democratic candidate, Deputy Sheriff Herman P. Kerl, 34,676 to 12,727.

In all his 12 years of Progressive politics, Fischer had never carried the perennially Republican village of Maple Bluff until Tuesday when the village gave him a majority of 507 to Kerl's 68.

The only precinct to mar the GOP county candidates' clean sweep of all 103 county precincts, was the village of Cross Plains, Kerl's birthplace which gave him a 109 to 65 vote margin over Fischer.

Dr. David C. Atwood, the only county candidate endorsed by the Republican party who won against opposition in the primary election, was elected coroner by Tuesday's voters with a 35,083 majority over Socialist candidate, Verl M. Smith.

Deputy Dist. Atty. Edwin M. Wilkie moved into the district attorney's post with no opposition, and Surveyor Andrew O. Dahlen, former Progressive, retained his job without opposition.

The other former Progressive candidates, each of whom polled more than 35,000 votes as Republicans, were Clerk of Circuit Court Myrtle L. Hansen, County Clerk Austin N. Johnson, Treasurer Clarence L. Femrite, and Registrar Albert O. Barton.

The defeated Socialist candidates, none of whom won more than 1,900 votes, were Ramona First, August J. Plath, Edwin D. Richards, Miriam Bright, and Robert C. Saucerman.

Governor Victor by 3 to 2 Margin; Joe by 2 to 1

Democrat Candidates for State, Congress Seats Snowed Under

State wide Charts on Pages 1 and 10.
Dane County Chart on Page 5.

By WILLIAM H. MEYERS
(United Press Staff Correspondent)

The state of Wisconsin belonged to the Republicans today.

Every Democratic candidate for state and congressional offices was snowed under by a landslide of GOP votes. Even in Milwaukee county the Republicans were "in" by slim — but definite — margins.

The Democrats ran close only in one of the two congressional districts they had held during recent years in the metropolitan area.

Almost complete returns from the fourth showed Republican John Brophy beating the Democratic nominee, Edmund V. Bobrowicz, 49,060 to 44,409. A third candidate, Incumbent Thaddeus Wasielewski, who ran as an independent, took 38,578 votes.

In the fifth district, with only a few precincts missing, Charles J. Kersten defeated Rep. Andrew J. Biemiller by a vote of 75,536 to 59,174.

Throughout the state it appeared voters had "had enough."

Voters gave Gov. Goodland an advance 84th birthday present by handing him a 3 to 2 margin over his Democratic opponent, former Milwaukee Mayor Daniel W. Hoan.

The seat which the LaFollette family held for more than 41 years in the senate went to "young Bob's" victor in the primaries, Joseph R. McCarthy, the 37-year-old dynamic circuit court judge from Appleton. McCarthy, a former marine air gunner, whipped the veteran campaigner, Howard J. McMurray, by nearly 2 to 1.

Throughout the night, as returns rolled in from all sections of the state, the Republicans never were threatened.

The vote:

U. S. SENATOR

Returns from 3,111 out of 3,147 precincts gave:

McCarthy (R) 616,126
McMurray (D) 373,418
Knappe (S) 3,974

GOVERNOR

Returns from 3,111 out of 3,147 precincts gave:

Goodland (R) 672,776
Hoan (D) 404,501
Uphoff (S) 3,888

LIEUTENANT GOVERNOR

Returns from 3,118 out of 3,147 precincts gave:

Rennebohm (R) 592,773
Nelson (D) 364,211
Roach (S) 4,412

SECRETARY OF STATE

Returns from 3,065 out of 3,147 precincts gave:

Zimmerman (R) 667,058
Kaiser (D) 306,787
Kirst (S) 3,089

STATE TREASURER

Returns from 3,058 out of 3,147 precincts gave:

Smith (R) 644,067
Kamper (D) 293,873
Benson (S) 4,565

ATTORNEY GENERAL

Returns from 3,097 precincts out of 3,147 precincts gave:

Martin (R) 665,838
Hawkes (D) 274,118
Davis (S) 443

The other state offices — lieu-

(Continued on Page 2, Column 1)

Madison Vote

Here is the way the 20 wards in Madison voted for the two offices:

GOVERNOR
Goodland (R)—15,495.
Hoan (D)—11,917.
Uphoff (S)—356.
Eisenscher (Com)—18.
Kenyon (Soc-Labor)—4.

U. S. SENATOR
McCarthy (R)—13,000.
McMurray (D)—13,580.
Knappe (S)—359.
Cozzini (Soc-Labor)—19.

Table on Page 5

Coal Talks Resume; Krug, Lewis Absent

WASHINGTON — (U.P.) — Coal contract negotiations were resumed today after a one-day layoff for the elections.

Neither Secretary of Interior J. A. Krug nor Pres. John L. Lewis of the AFL United Mine Workers (UMW) attended the negotiating session.

Krug is scheduled to end his western tour at Los Angeles tonight. He may be here in time to attend Thursday's negotiations. Lewis is expected to join the conference when Krug does.

Government and union negotiators are discussing Lewis' demand that his contract with the government be revised.

Feature Finder

Warmer Tonight
MADISON WEATHER
Mostly cloudy this afternoon through Saturday. Snow flurries and slightly colder this afternoon, warmer tonight. Little change in temperature Saturday. Low tonight, 15; high Saturday, 24. Sun rose, 7:15, sets, 5:08.

The Wisconsin State Journal

A fact-finding Newspaper

MADISON, FRIDAY, JANUARY 30, 1948

Home Final
22 PAGES
PRICE FIVE CENTS
VOL. 171, NO. 119 109th YEAR

Gandhi Assassinated in New Delhi; Hindu-Moslem Outbreak Threatens

Crashes, Search Kill 42

Sparta Family Believed Aboard Wrecked Plane

(By Leased Wire)

Semi-official reports on the search for a missing American plane said today it had been found wrecked in the French Alps, that a Flying Fortress engaged in the search crashed and killed 10 crewmen, and that the wreckage of still another transport was found.

Report said the C-47 which disappeared Tuesday with five American children, three women, and four crewmen had been spotted on a mountain slope near Digne, France.

Forty-two lives would be accounted for if the reports of the three crashes were borne out.

Dispatches from Grenoble reported the crash of the Flying Fortress against the mountainside near Digne, in the region where wreckage believe to be that of the missing plane had been sighted.

Sparta Family on It, Belief

A former Sparta woman and her three children, en route to join their husband and father at Trieste, were believed aboard the C-47 missing since Tuesday on a flight from France to Italy.

The woman was Mrs. Gifford Moak, daughter of Mrs. Carl Smith, Sparta. The children were Gifford, Jr., 5; a girl, 3, and another girl, Verna, 18 months. They lived in Worcester, N. Y.

The family was to join Warrant Officer Moak at Trieste.

Find Wreckage

Ground parties moving through the mountains of southeastern France toward the crashed Flying Fortress found wreckage believed to be that of a C-47 transport which disappeared with 20 persons aboard while flying from Pisa, Italy, to Frankfurt last month.

The Milan air traffic control center, in reporting the discovery of the third wrecked plane, said that according to the ground party, all aboard the Flying Fortress—four officers and six enlisted men—were killed

Air War Chief, 28 Others on Lost Plane

LONDON—(U.P.)— Air Marshal Sir Arthur Coningham, wartime commander of Allied tactical air forces, and 28 other persons were missing today aboard a transatlantic plane believed down about 400 miles east of Bermuda, the British South American Airways (BSAA) announced.

The BSAA, operators of the Tudor transport, said Coningham was among the 23 passengers and six crewmen aboard the plane. It last was heard from at 11 p. m. (5 p. m. CST) Thursday.

The passenger complement was made up of 16 Britons, one Swiss, two Czechs, and four "stateless" persons, according to the records of the line. The transport was piloted by Capt. D. Colby.

Coningham was the only prominent Briton aboard. He commanded the first tactical air force in French North Africa in 1943, and the second tactical air force in 1944-45. He was made air marshal in 1946.

Ten American Super-Fortresses from Bermuda were shuttling over the area east of Bermuda where the transport was feared down, the BSAA reported.

Markets at a Glance

Stocks lower in quiet trading.
Bonds irregular; U. S. governments steady.
Curb stocks irregularly higher.
Futures closed off 3 to 3½ cents; corn off ⅞ to 3⅝ cents; Oats off ⅝ to 1¼ cents; soy beans off 1½ to 5 cents; and lard futures off 28 to 50 points.
Cattle slow and dull, hogs and sheep higher.

Dow-Jones Stock Averages
By Thomson & McKinnon

30 Industrials	174.71	up .24
20 Rails	51.65	dn. .03
20 Utilities	32.62	dn. .02

Volume, 890,000 shares.

Feature Finder

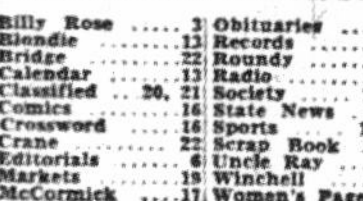

To Start New Air Service

—State Journal Staff Photo

The twin-engined plane shown above dropped into the Municipal airport at Truax Field Thursday on its inaugural flight to the city.

Heralding the beginning of service from Madison to a network of cities in Wisconsin and two other states, the Wisconsin Central Airlines ship taxied to the administration building for a brief ceremony.

Mrs. Howard Morey, wife of the chairman of the state aeronautics commission, is shown above as she snipped the ribbon which symbolized the freeing of the plane for service to the city. Helping her is Francis M. Higgins, Clintonville, airline president.

The ship was welcomed to the city by City Manager Howell, William C. Sachtjen, council president, and representatives of various clubs and organizations.

Others present included Robert Skuldt, airport manager; Howard Morey and Tom Jordan, of the aeronautics commission; Ed Konkol; Jesse Zimmerman, of the Civil Aeronautics Commission; Frank Swoboda, of the Lions club; Marshall Straus and Ray Messner, of the Optimist club; J. W. Jackson of the Madison and Wisconsin foundation, and W. H. Harris, of the Kiwanis club.

The Boy Scout Drum and Bugle corps provided music, and a banquet at Hotel Loraine at night climaxed the inaugural.

Service to Madison will begin Feb. 15, postponed from the scheduled opening Sunday because of bad flying weather which has made completion of the required number of proving runs impossible.

Governor Backs New Building Over Fireproofing at Mendota

MILWAUKEE — A recommendation that a new hospital building be constructed at Mendota State hospital rather than fireproofing the existing structure may be made to the 1949 legislature by Gov. Rennebohm, it was indicated today.

The governor was a speaker Thursday night before a gathering of the Wisconsin chapter of the Associated General Contractors of America.

'Better Business'

"Some time ago," Rennebohm said, "I inspected the state hospital at Mendota for a substantial appropriation had been made to fireproof the upper floors of this building.

"As a businessman it seems like better business to me to put that money into a new structure rather than to spend it on a building entirely obsolete, and at the moment it seems to me that is the recommendation that should be made."

Rennebohm pointed out that the state now has in the treasury about 23,500,000 to be spent for public buildings and said that "while even that amount is not adequate for our steadily increasing needs it is a substantial sum."

Delay in Building

The chief executive indicated that state money would be released for public buildings when the need for them is critical.

He added that in other cases the construction probably would be delayed until prices had levelled off, there was a more adequate supply of labor, and materials were in better supply.

Through that system, Rennebohm indicated, the state would be able to get more for its money and the construction industry and the labor it employs would also benefit by having state business to fall back on when private business fell off.

Milwaukee Road's Net Doubled in Year

Net income of the Milwaukee road for December, 1947, after all charges, was $1,511,201 compared with a net of $595,213 for the same month of 1946, C. H. Buford, president, reported today.

The net for the full year of 1947 was $6,655,272, equal to $5.93 per share of Series "A" preferred stock, compared with 12 months' net of $3,176,068 for the previous year, he said.

December net railway operating income was $2,393,784, an increase of $1,091,804 over December, 1946. Gross for the system was $21,729,316, an increase over December, 1946, of $4,690,670.

Herb Pennock, Former Yank Pitcher, Dies

NEW YORK—(U.P.)— Herb Pennock, general manager of the Philadelphia Phillies, died today at Midtown hospital of a cerebral hemorrhage.

Pennock, 53, a former star southpaw pitcher with the New York Yankees, collapsed in the lobby of the Waldorf-Astoria hotel as he prepared to attend a National league meeting. He was pronounced dead upon his arrival at the hospital at 1:05 p. m.

2 Boards of Regents Map Unity

U. W., Teachers' Groups Admit 'Over-Lapping'

By REX KARNEY
(State Journal Staff Writer)

Stirred by legislative and public discussion of the over-lapping in Wisconsin's system of higher education, the regent boards governing the state university and teacher colleges met today to begin setting up machinery to coordinate the work of their institutions.

Meeting in joint session at the Memorial Union, regents moved toward appointment of a joint committee that will probably make a study to see exactly where Wisconsin's post-high school educational institutions duplicate their efforts.

Agree There's Over-lapping

The teacher college regents came to this morning's session supported by their individual college presidents. University regents had refrained from summoning their deans to the discussions.

After two hours of talk at which U. W. Regent John Jones and Teacher College Regent Helen Eby failed in the effort to stir up a debate on the subject of who should be promoting extension work, it appeared that regents agreed there was "over-lapping" in about a half-dozen fields.

These fields were:

ONE. The university now operates an extension program, and the teacher colleges are going to enter that field.

TWO. The systems have a similar problem in how much to pay their instructors.

THREE. The university has an extensive graduate program. Should the teacher colleges go into that field?

FOUR. The university and teacher colleges apparently have a different system of teacher-tenure.

FIVE. Both the university and the teacher colleges train teachers.

SIX. Both compete for funds from the legislature, both for operational and building budgets.

SEVEN. Both the university and the colleges have the problem of "mass-production" — in other words, how big should regents permit the institutions to become?

U. W. Regent Charles Gellatt suggested that "this group is much too big to go into the details of these problems," and he suggested that the actual work of the survey be referred to a committee of two university and two teacher college regents.

Jones complained that "a committee too often is a convenient way of burying things that don't smell too well."

Says Plan Needed

But C. M. Newlun, Platteville State Teachers president, warned that "there has been a lot of talk about consolidating higher education" and that therefor the managers of the state's several systems had better have a plan ready for the next legislature.

"What we should have is a plan supported by all the educational units — the university, teacher colleges, and the vocational

(Continued on page 2, column 6)

Nearly Million Raised Toward U.W. Centennial Gift, Boosters Here Told

Nearly $1,000,000 already has been raised toward the $5,000,000 the University of Wisconsin foundation plans to give the university as a centennial gift, it was revealed here Thursday by F. J. Sensenbrenner, president of the board of regents.

Sensenbrenner

He also disclosed that:

ONE. Oscar Mayer and Co. has pledged a contribution of $25,000, and

TWO. "Substantial" gifts have been made by Gov. Rennebohm and by the George Johnson family of Madison, and both have pledged further "substantial" contributions during the next several years.

For Several Uses

The money is to be used for scholarships, fellowships, and professorships; for special equipment for research, and for "the Wisconsin Idea building," a center for university institutes.

Sensenbrenner and a group of the campaign leaders addressed 50 "outstanding leaders of Madison and Dane county" at a Park hotel luncheon meeting called by the Madison and Wisconsin foundation to discuss organization of the drive in this area.

Speakers included Herbert Kohler, national campaign chairman; Howard Potter, president of the university foundation; Justice Elmer Barlow of the state supreme court, honorary campaign chairman for Dane county, and F. Halsey Kraege, president of the Madison and Wisconsin foundation.

Pledge Support

The 50 at the meeting—mostly Madison area businessmen — unanimously adopted a resolution pledging support to the drive and to the county chairman who will be named to work with Barlow in raising Dane county's $507,000 quota.

While praising county residents for their "unfailing loyalty" to the university, several speakers described themselves as "embarrassed" that so far no Dane county chairman has been found.

Barlow is prevented by professional considerations from actively directing the drive here.

The officials outlined plans for the campaign — "which is just

(Continued on Page 2, Column 3)

Highlights in Career of India's Fasting 'Saint'

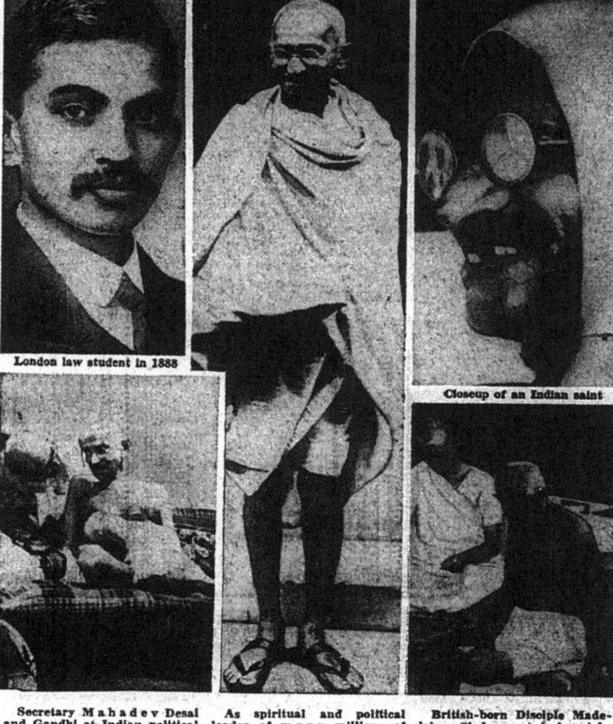

London law student in 1888

Closeup of an Indian saint

Secretary Mahadev Desai and Gandhi at Indian political meet.

As spiritual and political leader of many millions of Hindus.

British-born Disciple Madeleine Slade seated beside Gandhi.

'Overhaul' Districts, School Group Told

(Another Story, Page 13)

The county committees set up by the 1947 legislature to reorganize school districts should give the districts a thorough overhauling, Michael Kies, Milwaukee county school superintendent, said today.

Kies told a discussion group at the University of Wisconsin's conference for county school committeemen that the committees should not "tinker" piecemeal with school district boundaries.

Major Reshuffle Needed

"That's been going on for 100 years. What we need now is a major reorganization," he said.

Kies advised county committeemen to make complete plans first for consolidating and changing school districts and then hold hearings on their plans before issuing any orders altering districts.

Assemblyman W. W. Clark (R-Vesper) cautioned them to be sure your reorganization plan is right before taking action on it so it won't have to be undone later."

Clark said the state school study committee, of which he is a member, will issue some general principles soon to guide county committees.

Improve Rural Schools

Some 375 county committeemen, city school superintendents and principals, school board members and representatives of teachers colleges, county normal schools, tax and education groups are attending the conference. Sixty-five counties are represented.

In a speech to the entire group, Dr. Shirley Cooper of the National Education Assn's. rural service department said better educational opportunities for rural children, rather than saving money, should be the aim of school transportation programs.

Good Drivers Stressed

He said school boards should use "great care" in selecting competent school bus drivers and should require all of them to pass strict physical examinations. In general, he said, it's better for shall boards to own their buses instead of contracting with a bus company to carry the children.

Dr. Julian Butterworth of Cornell university said rural schools are not doing enough to help handicapped children.

He explained a school reorganization system that is being proposed in New York which would enlarge school districts and enable them to hold special classes for handicapped youngsters.

Daughter Born to Shirley Temple

SANTA MONICA, Calif.—(U.P.) —Shirley Temple, the screen's most famous little girl star, gave birth to a baby girl today in Santa Monica hospital.

SHIRLEY

Both mother and daughter were "doing" well," the hospital reported.

Shirley's mother said the child probably would be named Linda Susan.

Shirley's husband, John Agar, accompanied Shirley to the hospital at 2:30 a. m. and was pacing the floor when the baby arrived.

Helen Keller Sees Beyond War to Peace

By HELEN MATHESON
(State Journal Staff Writer)

There would never be another war, Helen Keller believes, "if women of the world could see the things I have seen."

Miss Keller is blind and deaf and for many years she was unable to speak, but she talks naturally of "seeing" war-ruined Europe and the only tragedy she thinks of is the world's.

'There Would Be No War'

"If people could only see the things I have seen — the men in the hospitals . . . the blind, maimed children . . . the tremendous, bottomless pit of tragedy — there would be no war," she tells you, her painfully expressed words stumbling a little in her earnestness.

Miss Keller came to Madison late Thursday to address a group of young people at Central high school this afternoon on behalf of the children of Europe and Asia who were crippled and blinded in the war.

She is making a nationwide tour to plead for American children's help for "the poor little ones."

To Visit More

She saw those pitiful youngsters last winter when she visited Britain, France, Italy, and Greece.

She will visit more this spring and summer when she starts a world trip by way of the Orient—**"to visit my blind fellows and to plead with governments and people to rise above ignorance and beggary to useful, happy lives."**

If Miss Keller thinks of herself as a child as one of "the poor little ones," it is without self-pity.

Stricken with a fever when she was a baby of 19 months, she was left deaf, blind, and mute and

(Continued on page 2, column 7)

Burmeister Quits as Madison Town Clerk

George W. Burmeister, Madison town clerk for many years, announced today that he has resigned to enter the selling field.

Burmeister said he has accepted a position in Milwaukee.

Mrs. Arelene Johnson, deputy town clerk, has been named acting clerk until the vacancy is filled at the spring election.

The Madison town board will meet with City Manager Howell in his office Monday at 11 a. m., it was announced today, to discuss mutual fire protection problems.

All India Stunned by Death

Extremist of His Group Fires Shots; Bombay Riots Start

BULLETIN

BOMBAY — (U.P.) — Rioting broke out in Bombay tonight on receipt of word that Mohandas K. Gandhi had been assassinated, and shortly before midnight six persons had been killed and 26 injured.

By JAMES MICHAELS
(United Press Staff Correspondent)

NEW DELHI — Mohandas K. Gandhi, "saint of India," was shot and killed today in an assassination which may set the whole subcontinent of India ablaze with warfare between Hindus and Moslems.

Riots started in Bombay the moment the news of the assassination arrived.

The 78-year-old Indian whose people had christened him the "great soul of India" died at 6:15 a. m. CST with his head cradled in the lap of his 16-year-old granddaughter, Mani.

Midst 1,000 Followers

Just half an hour previous a Hindu fanatic, Ram Naturam, had pumped three bullets from a small caliber revolver into Gandhi's frail body, emaciated by years of fasting and asceticism.

Gandhi was shot in the luxurious gardens of Birla house in the presence of 1,000 of his followers whom he was leading to the little summer pagoda where it was his habit to make his evening devotions.

Dressed as always in his homespun, sack-like dhoti, and leaning heavily on a staff of stout wood, Gandhi was a few feet from the pagoda when the shots were fired.

Gandhi crumpled to the ground instantly, putting his hand to his forehead in the Hindu gesture of forgiveness to his assassin.

Three bullets penetrated him, one in the upper right thigh, one in the abdomen, and one in the chest.

He spoke no word before he died. A moment before he was shot he said—some witnesses believed he was speaking to the assassin—**"you are late."**

Shot at Close Range

The assassin had been standing beside the garden path, his hands folded palms together before him in the Hindu gesture of greeting.

But between his palms he had concealed a revolver with which he shot Gandhi at a range of a few feet. He fired a fourth shot in an attempt at suicide but the bullet merely creased his scalp.

The shots from the pistol sounded like a string of firecrackers going off and it was a moment before Gandhi's devotees realized what had happened.

Then they turned on the assassin savagely and would have torn him to bits had not strong police guards intervened with rifles and drawn bayonets.

Gandhi quickly was borne back to Birla house and placed on a couch with his head in his granddaughter's lap. Within a few moments she spoke to the stricken throng:

"Bapu (Father) is finished."

Then Mani rose and sat cross-

(Continued on Page 2, Column 1)

Madison Will Get $73,975 Share on State Liquor Taxes

The city of Madison will receive $73,975 as its share of the $3,577,705 that was collected by the state in liquor taxes during the last six months of 1947, figures on file with the secretary of state showed today.

The money is distributed to to towns, cities, and villages, on the basis of population, and each governmental unit will receive $1.14127 for each person enumerated within those governmental boundaries in the 1940 census.

Units in Dane county will receive a total of $148,954.

Next to Madison, the largest allocation in Dane county will go to the city of Stoughton which will receive $5,413.

Sun for Sunday
MADISON WEATHER
Clearing this afternoon, fair and cooler tonight. Sunday fair with moderate temperatures. Low tonight, 45; high Sunday, 65. Sun rose, 4:34; sets, 7:16.

The Wisconsin State Journal
A fact-finding Newspaper

MADISON, SATURDAY, MAY 15, 1948

Home Final
PRICE FIVE CENTS
10 PAGES
VOL. 172, NO. 45 109th YEAR

U. S. Recognizes New Jew State; May Lift Arms Ban

CIO Meat Strikers Attack National Guard With Fists

Soldiers With Rifles, Pistols Escort Non-Strikers Into Swift Plant

SOUTH ST. PAUL —(U.P.)— Bitter, cursing CIO pickets fought a brief battle with heavily-armed national guardsmen today, then stepped aside reluctantly as non-strikers entered the Swift and Co. packing plant here.

Fist-fighting flared for several minutes before the guard rushed in reinforcements with fixed bayonets to hold back an angry crowd that shouted its support of the defiant pickets.

Strikers Flail Guards

Strikers flailed away at the guards, who did not strike back with rifle butts but merely used arms to fend off the pickets' blows. No one was injured in the skirmishes.

Three pickets were arrested. There was no shooting.

Soldiers with rifles and pistols escorted non-strikers through the picket lines to the boos and jeers of onlookers.

Sullen pickets joined in the taunts, but made no attempt to interfere after the first brief flareup.

Guardsmen also were stationed at the smaller Armour and Co. plant.

There was no violence at that plant but non-strikers were not going through the lines despite presence of guardsmen behind a small line of pickets.

Quiet at Newport Today

All was quiet also at nearby Newport, scene of bloody fighting Friday between a band of 200 men and workers at the Cudahy Packing Co. plant.

Embittered pickets grappled with officers and enlisted men who sought to place them under arrest for ignoring orders to clear a road to traffic.

Fist-fighting broke out and it was not until the guard rushed in reinforcements that they were able to subdue three pickets arrested on the spot.

Guard officers ordered immediate reinforcements and within a matter of minutes 40 truckloads of troops from nearby bivouacs thundered into the Swift area.

Guards Fix Bayonets

There were about 20 men in each truck. Fifteen jeeps and several ambulances also sped to the scene.

Guards with fixed bayonets guarded the crowd closely after the first flareup of fighting.

Pickets at first indicated they would obey guard orders to respect a court injunction prohibiting them from keeping non-strikers from their jobs.

With machineguns leveled at them, they fell back and opened their lines.

"Are you going to let those scabs in?" a workman shouted to a lieutenant on a halftrack cruising the area. The lieutenant nodded.

Pickets Stop Car

When the halftrack moved away from the plant gates, three pickets stepped in front of a car attempting to pass through the gates.

The halftrack rushed back to the gates. A captain joined the lieutenant.

"Step aside," the captain ordered.

The pickets refused to budge. A lieutenant colonel ran from a nearby gatehouse. He conferred briefly with the captain, then ordered him to arrest the three strikers.

The captain, flanked by the lieutenant and four enlisted men with rifles, walked up to the pickets and started to place them under arrest.

Fighting broke out and other strikers rushed from a crowd near the scene to help their fellows.

On orders from the colonel, there was no firing.

Other soldiers rushed forward and pointed their rifles at the crowd to keep others from joining the fray.

Governor Raps State Institutions

Admits He Withheld Building Approval

Gov. Rennebohm deplored the conditions in which many of the state's wards must live, at the same time admitting that he had withheld approval for badly-needed buildings, in a talk in Milwaukee Thursday.

RENNEBOHM

Speaking before the Marquette University Alumni club, the governor pointed out, rather ruefully, that Milwaukee county is doing "a much better job" in caring for its unfortunates than the state.

"In a tour of state institutions I found 1,575 overcrowded humans at the Chippewa Falls hospital," he said. "Facilities are bad. The attendants were good.

'Don't Know Why . . .'

"At the home for delinquent children at Sparta I found 366 children literallly packed together. I honestly don't know why we can't do better."

Turning briefly to segregation of highway funds, "which I have never been in favor of," the governor added that highway expenditures could not be blamed for lack of welfare construction.

"There are sufficient funds available for building," he declared. "Frankly, I have withheld approval of such building because so many private builders need the materials and labor."

Spending Pace Hit

(This week, the state legislative council charged that the welfare department "isn't spending" its near-$11,000,000 postwar building fund fast enough, although the week before the department and Gov. Rennebohm decided to build a $2,000,000 hospital at Mendota.)

In spite of its shortcomings in the field of welfare, the governor said, Wisconsin has "the finest state government in the United States."

"I believe we are unique among state governments inasmuch as we have no graft," he told the alumni group, adding that stories of lobbying are "greatly exaggerated" and that most lobbyists are of a very high type.

Clearing Skies Due Today, and Sun Sunday

The Madison area can look forward to a sunny Sunday after absorbing another half-inch of rain Friday night, the weatherman assured us today.

By noon the sun was breaking through the heavy morning overcast, and the temperature was up to 65.

It will be somewhat cooler, but clear, tonight, with a low of 45 forecast.

Sunday will be fair with moderate temperatures, with a high of 65.

Showers Friday and early today put the rainfall in Madison since Jan. 1 almost three inches above normal.

The Madison office measured .57 inches of rainfall in the 24 hours ending this morning, and .54 inch fell at the airport. La Crosse and Wausau had .25 inch apiece, but up in Canada they really had a shower—Winnipeg reported 1.44 inches.

Street Renamed; It's All So Confusing

The city council changed the name of a street in Sherman Park Friday night at the suggestion of the Madison postoffice, to eliminate conflict with another street of the same name on the South side, but succeeded in removing only part of the confusion.

Sherman Park's Fisher st. was rechristened Sheridan st. But the South side's Fisher st. isn't far from O'Sheridan st.

19 Arrested in Siam in Gold Robbery Case

BANGKOK, Siam — (U.P.) — Nineteen suspects, including five Siamese army men and two goldsmiths, have been arrested for last Wednesday's $2,000,000 gold robbery, police announced today.

About 1,200 ounces of the total of 43,000 ounces of gold stolen was recovered by police in a goldsmith's shop. Part of it was already in a melting pot when found.

Hit on Mail Fraud

ISADORE GINSBERG

Ginsberg, 'Gray Marketeer,' Son Indicted

NEW YORK — Isadore Ginsberg, 52-year-old lawyer turned lumber merchant, who was denounced by Sen. Joseph R. McCarthy (R-Wis.) as "the most vicious of gray marketeers" was indicted on charges of mail fraud here Friday.

The 300-pound Ginsberg was named in a federal grand jury indictment with his son, Maurice, 20, a student at Syracuse university.

Got Money, No Delivery

The Ginsbergs were charged with advertising in midwestern and southern newspapers that they had scarce building materials for speedy shipment.

The indictments said the Ginsbergs received $15,921 from contractors and builders in advance for materials that were never delivered.

From 1945 to this year, according to the indictment, the Ginsbergs changed the name of their firm from the East and West Building Materials Co., to the Transcontinental Lumber Corp., keeping the same office in Queens.

In March, a Queens grand jury indicted the elder Ginsberg of a grand larceny charge involving the sale of gypsum lath.

He was charged with accepting $1.575 from the Crystal Lumber Co., of Winston-Salem, N. C., for 1.260 bundles of the lath, which the company said were never delivered.

Clashed With McCarthy

Ginsberg is the man with whom Sen. McCarthy tangled violently during the senator's investigation of materials shortages that were plaguing the building industry.

McCarthy found that although the wholesale price of plaster board was about $20 around New York, Ginsberg had been buying it up at a higher price and then selling it to desperate contractors in other parts of the country for prices ranging up to $60.

While Ginsberg insisted he merely had been taking a "legitimate profit" the Wisconsin senator denounced him as a "vicious, grey market racketeer."

Bennett Meyers Indicted on Tax Evasion Charge

DAYTON, O.—(U.P.)—A federal grand jury today indicted Bennett E. Meyers, former air force major general, for income tax evasion.

The indictment followed the charge brought this spring by internal revenue department agents that Meyers "wilfully and knowingly attempted to defeat and evade a large part of the taxes due and owing by the Aviation Electric Corp. . . ."

The corporation was the ill-fated Vandalia, O., firm founded by Meyers.

Bleriot Lamarre, one-time puppet president of the corporation, and his wife, Mildred, were among the 54 witnesses who testified before the grand jury here.

Others were Dayton internal revenue agents who brought the charge against Meyers.

District Atty. Ray O'Donnell said it had not yet been determined whether the former high army officer would be brought here for trial. A perjury charge is stilll pending against him in Washington.

Specifically, Meyers was charged in the indictment today with filing, on March 16, 1942, "false and fraudulent" statements about Aviation Electric's net income and the taxes owed on it for 1941.

Meyers filed a return reporting the income as $22,717.11, the tax $9.423.60. Actually, the grand jury charged, the income was $65,027.51, the tax $36,132.58.

Markets at a Glance

Stocks strong in active trading.
Bonds higher; U. S. governments did not trade.
Curb stocks higher.
Chicago stocks higher.
Wheat, corn, oats, and barley futures steady.

Dow-Jones Stock Averages
By Thomson & McKinnon

30 Industrials	190.25	up	1.65
20 Rails	62.18	dn.	.06
20 Utilities	35.79	up	.25

Volume, 2,590,000 shares.

West Allis Man Elected Head of CUNA Supply Directors

Elmer Christoph, West Allis, was elected president of the Credit Union National assn. (CUNA) supply directors Friday night at the Hotel Loraine.

Other newly elected members of the board include J. L. Bammerlin, Phoenix, Ariz., and B. B. Humphries, Asheville, N. C.

Thomas A. Kelleher, Utica, N. Y., was elected vice-president, and W. O. Knight, Jr., was elected treasurer. Both were former members of the board. Karl S. Little, Salt Lake City, Utah, last year's president, was reelected to the board.

Mutual Aides Reelected

Other members reelected were M. A. Pottiger, Harrisburg, Pa.; J. D. MacDonald, Dratmouth, Nov. Scotia; and John Suominen, Fitchburg, Mass.

All officers of the CUNA Mutual board of directors were reelected Friday. They are Joseph S. DeRamus, Chicago, president; W. W. Pratt, Philadelphia, Pa., vice-president; Gurden P. Farr, Detroit, Mich., secretary; and Harry C. Lash, Council Bluffs, Ia., treasurer.

Leonard Mitchell, Toronto, Canada, was the only new member elected to the Mutual board. Members reelected include John L. Moore, Oakland, Calif.; Moses C. Davis, Atlanta, Ga.; William Reid, Brooklyn, N. Y.; Harold Moses, New Orleans, La.; and Thomas M. Molloy, Saskatchewan, Canada.

..The CUNA group, including representatives from each of the 48 states, all dominions in Canada, and from Hawaii, continued its annual meeting at the Loraine today.

An American flag was presented to the group by the Canadian representatives early today. President Farr accepted the flag on behalf of the executive committee.

Officers' reports and discussion of the budget for the coming year were heard this morning and action on the proposed new headquarters in Madison and the annual election of CUNA officers were expected later today or Sunday, when the annual meeting will adjourn.

Tel Aviv Bombed by Arabs

Palestine Invaded from Three Sides

BULLETIN

TEL AVIV —(U.P.)—Egyptian planes attacked Tel Aviv late this afternoon for the fourth time today as Arab nations struck hard against the new-born Jewish state of Israel.

TEL AVIV — (U.P.) — Arab planes bombed Tel Aviv three times today and one Egyptian air force pilot was taken prisoner when his plane was forced down just north of the new Jewish capital.

The Egyptian government in Cairo announced officially that Egyptian planes raided the new-born state of Israel in the forefront of an Arab attack from all sides, including one raid on a Jewish airdrome outside Tel Aviv.

Egyptians Cross Border

The Cairo communique also confirmed that two columns of Egyptian troops crossed the southern Palestine frontier this morning.

Planes bombed ahead of one column striking for Gaza, important settlement on the coast 42 miles south of Tel Aviv.

Advance contingents were reported holding a height east of Gaza, 20 miles north of the Egyptian frontier, and waiting reinforcements.

The second column, striking 30 miles inland, was reported to have captured the Jewish settlement of Auja after an artillery barrage.

Jewish sources said direct Arab-Jewish negotiations for a truce in Jerusalem were started after Jews captured virtually all strong points abandoned by the British in the Holy City.

Egyptian troops spearheaded the assault, attempting an amphibious landing 21 miles south fo Tel Aviv and crashing across the southern Palestine border at two points.

Syrian and Lebanese troops roared down across the northern frontier several hours before the midnight deadline, riding into battle in 150 armored trucks.

Attack from East

King Abdullah of Trans-Jordan sent his Arab legion and Iraqi regulars slicing across the eastern frontier "to liberate the Holy Land from Zionism."

Jewish forces met the attack on their frontiers by fighting for footroom within Palestine. In swift thrusts they captured Acre, most of Jerusalem and took over Haifa and Jaffa.

Other attacks were launched to clear the highway to Jerusalem and against the Arab triangle pointed to Tulkarm in the north, which threatens the coastal plain.

Conciliator Hints Brewers Union to Ease Pay Demands

MILWAUKEE— (U.P.) —Federal Conciliator Clement J. Murphy said today the 20-day-old strike against the city's six breweries might be settled Monday.

Murphy, who has attended meetings between Brewers and the CIO union, indicated the union has dropped its demand from 30 to 22 cents an hour over the present scale. Union leaders denied this.

The management has offered the 5,600 striking brewery workers an increase of 13¾ cents an hour.

"Both sides are anxious to settle the strike," Murphy said. "I wouldn't be surprised if the strike were settled by Monday when negotiations will be resumed."

Fr. Flanagan, Head of Boys Town, Dies of Heart Attack in Germany

BERLIN—(U.P.)—The Rev. Msgr. Edward J. Flanagan, the famed "Father Flanagan" of Boys Town, Neb., died here early today following a heart attack. He was 61. a heart attack. He was 61.

The priest, who came here last Sunday for a two-week study of youth conditions, died at the 279th army station hospital at 2:05 a. m. (Berlin time), a few hours before he was scheduled to pitch the first ball in an army baseball game.

Col. F. T. Chamberlain, of the hospital staff, said the priest died of coronary occlusion.

Stricken at Dinner

He was stricken Thursday night during dinner at Harnach house, the army's guest house, and was rushed immediately to the hospital. Attendants were instructed to give out no information concerning him.

With the priest when he died were Patrick Norton, his assistant at Boys Town, his nephew, Sgt. Patrick Moriarty, the army's top youth organizer in Europe, and several doctors and nurses.

In a telephone conversation with priests at Boys Town after Fr. Flanagan's death, Norton told them:

'A Beautiful Death'

"He died a beautiful death, if death can be beautiful."

The priest's body will be flown to Boys Town within the next two days, probably by military aircraft.

Norton said funeral arrangements would be announced later after telephone consultation with Boys Town officials.

MSGR. E. J. FLANAGAN

In Frankfurt, Gen. Lucius D. Clay, American commander in Germany, said he was "shocked" to hear of Fr. Flanagan's death, and regretted that he had failed to see him.

Clay personally had obtained some clerical collars the priest wanted, and had planned to take them to him on his return to Berlin today.

The Rev. Edmond Walsh will continue as acting director there until Archbishop Gerald T. Bergan, head of the board of directors of Boys Town, returns from a tour of the orient.

Fr. Flanagan's death left hundreds of residents and alumni of Boys Town orphans. His view was that there was "no such thing as a bad boy" and his treatment of them was kindness and plenty of food and care.

Suffered Earlier Attack

Friends said Fr. Flanagan suffered a previous heart attack last week in Vienna, where he made a month-long study of youth conditions in Austria.

Hospital Chaplain Fr. Emmet L. Walso said: "He died peacefully. He apparently knew that he was going to die."

The priest was named a monsignor in the Catholic church in 1937, but he remained "Father Flanagan," the name he loved. He borrowed $90 and established Boys Town on Dec. 10, 1917, in a ramshackle building in a poor section of town.

Boys Govern Selves

As donations came in, slowly at first, Fr. Flanagan purchased 160 acres of land 10 miles west of Omaha and eventually built Boys Town. It was for boys of every race, creed, color, and religion. In 1937 it became an incorporated community with its own postoffice and a government by the boys themselves.

In 1947 Fr. Flanagan served as an expert consultant to the Japanese government at the request of Gen. Douglas MacArthur.

Council Votes Action to Get Lands for School, Hospital Use

By RUSSELL B. PYRE
(State Journal Staff Writer)

Two condemnation actions to acquire properties for school and hospital purposes were authorized Friday night by the city council.

City Manager Howell and City Atty. Harold E. Hanson were empowered to start proceedings against 4½ acres of the Rentschler greenhouse property at Regent st. and Highland ave., needed for expansion of West High school.

Also to be acquired by court action are three lots in the 900 block on Mound st., near Madison General hospital, as part of the site for the Jackson Reuter home for aged and chronically ill.

They are owned by Henry Deitelhof, Sam Paley, and the Pure Oil Co.

Warns of Costs

While Councilman H. L. Garner voted with the rest of the councilmen for the Rentschler action, he warned that "we must reconcile ourselves to the fact that this step is going to cost us a lot of money."

The map of the Rentschler holdings to be taken over, as submitted by Howell as director of public works, excludes the Rentschler residence and greenhouse buildings.

In other actions the council:

ONE. Dropped plans for paving of Capital ct., between Orchard and Charter sts., when Howell reported 6 out of 7 property owners had objected to assessments. Howell told the council the court may be improved temporarily with gravel and oil surfacing.

TWO. Adopted a resolution, recommended by the committee of the whole, requesting the city clerk to provide voter registration facilities in newly annexed areas.

THREE. Adopted an amendment to the building code permitting installation of "dispose-all" units in sinks of city homes for grinding and disposal of garbage through sewer drains. The action will necessitate changes in

(Continued on Page 2, Column 5)

Tavern Zoning Plea Opposed

Marlborough Heights Residents Hit Petition

Opposition of Marlborough Heights residents to any change in the addition's Residence "A" zoning was renewed Friday night at a public hearing before the city council.

Wayne W. Johnson, George Orsech, and Mrs. Lionel Moore, vice-president of the Nakoma Parent Teachers assn., appeared against an ordinance to change the "Tony" Frank tavern site at Warwick Way and Oxford rd., formerly Seminole highway, to Commercial "B".

Supplementing two petitions filed against the change, they held the rezoning would depreciate value of the entire residence area and pointed out that the new Crawford Heights plat, nearby, provides ample commercial space, plus parking facilities.

Sent to Plan Group

Atty. George F. Lange appeared for the tavern property owner, declaring the county zoning board had listed the corner as a natural commercial district. The ordinance was referred to the plan commission.

The council approved a report of the commission recommending adoption of two zoning changes and non-adoption of two others.

Oppsition was registered on only one of the four recommendations. The council approved, 5 to 2, with Councilmen Coyne and Sachtjen dissenting, an ordinance changing a parking and storage building site owned by the Bancroft Dairy Co. at Fitchburg and High sts. from Residence "A" to Commercial "B".

Adoption Unanimous

Action was unanimous in adoption of an ordinance changing the Elsener property at Lakeside st. and Lake ct. from Residence "A" to Residence "B" and in non-adoption of measures changing the Halperin Auto Parts Co. property at 205-207 S. Park st. from Commercial "B"; and the proposed Whalen Transfer Co. truck storage site at W. Johnson and N. Frances sts. from Commercial "A" to Commercial "B".

Public hearings were scheduled for June 11 on three proposed zoning amendments to change the property opposite the Bancroft Dairy parking lot site on Fitchburg st. from Residence "A" to Commercial "B"; properties in the triangular Woodlawn addition between Olin ave., Gilson and S. Park sts. from Residence "A" to Residence "B" and from Residence "C" to Commercial "B"; and property on University ave., at the rear of frontage opposite Shorewood Hills entrance, from Residence "A" to Residence "B".

Speculation Fever Booms Stock Market

NEW YORK —(U.P.)— American speculative fever boomed the stock market today to its heaviest Saturday trading in 15 years. Sales totaled 2,590,000 shares, best since May 27, 1933.

Chart followers hailed the market as a new bull movement. They plunged into the list with huge buying orders late Friday, and sales in that session reached 3,840,000 shares, a new eight-year high.

This buying attracted the outside public and gave Wall Street the appearance of the big days of 1926 when the post-World War I bull market was gathering momentum.

The small traders, who make the big bull markets, crowded the brokerage board rooms as they did in 1929. Women fainted in some of the crowds.

The little fellows bought all sections of the list and professional Wall Streeters who make it a point to "sell when everybody wants 'em" furnished the stocks for sale.

Dealings were so heavy that the tape fell behind the market in the first few minutes of trading. It never caught up.

At the peak of lateness the tickers were 13 minutes behind actual transactions.

The market closed 12 minutes after the final gong had sounded. Today's lateness also set a new record since 1933.

Motor Carriers Rate Boost Denied by PSC

The state public service commission today denied a request by the Wisconsin Motor Carriers assn. to raise minimum rates on contract freight shipments within the state by 20 per cent.

The PSC also turned down the association's application to substitute airline distances for highway mileages as a basis for rates. The PSC said the need for such a change had not been shown.

The minimum rate boost sought would have affected only a small fraction of motor carriers in Wisconsin.

F. S. Brandenburg Elected District Governor of Rotary

Frederick S. Brandenburg, president of the Democrat Printing Co., 114 S. Carroll st., was elected governor of the 144th district of Rotary International, at Rotary's 39th annual convention being held in Rio de Janeiro, Brazil.

Brandenburg has been president of the Vilas Park Zoological society since 1922 and is a past president of the Community Union. A member of the Madison Rotary club since 1914, he is a past president of that club.

As a district governor of Rotary International, he will visit 44 of the Rotary clubs in Wisconsin, comprising the 144th Rotary district, to advise and assist officers of those clubs on matters pertaining to Rotary service activities and club administration.

F. S. BRANDENBURG

Embargo in Effect 5 Months

President Maps Diplomatic Talks With New Country

(Austin to Resign Over Palestine Issue, UN Hears—Story, Page 2).

By R. H. SHACKFORD
(United Press Staff Correspondent)

WASHINGTON — (U.P.) — Pres. Truman is considering a proposal to lift the embargo on shipment of arms to Palestine, an informed White House source said today.

Such action would follow this government's recognition of the new Jewish state of Israel in Palestine.

Embargo on 5 Months

The embargo on arms shipments to the Middle East has been in effect for five months.

The White House, meanwhile, let it be known that Mr. Truman is considering the establishment of diplomatic negotiations with the provisional government of Israel.

White House Press Secretary Charles G. Doss told a news conference that reaction this far to the administration's recognition of Israel as an independent state has been overwhelmingly favorable.

Action Studied for Days

Ross also told reporters that Mr. Truman had been considering the action for several days before he made the surprise move Friday night.

Mr. Truman's action was taken a few minutes after a request for recognition came from Eliahu Epstein, agent for the provisional government of Israel.

The British government, Ross said, also was notified before the action was taken that Mr. Truman had it under consideration.

Ross said he knew nothing about a report that United Nations Delegate Warren Austin contemplated resigning as a result of the action.

On the question of removing the embargo on arms shipments to Palestine, it could not be learned whether the proposition under study pertained only to Palestine or to the entire Middle East.

Truman Urges Truce

In that statement the president urged a truce to work out a peaceful settlement of the Palestine dispute.

The letter of request for recognition of the provision government of Israel was less than 200 words and was brought to the White House by messenger at 6 p. m. EDT Friday, Ross said.

Meanwhile, Secretary of State George C. Marshall sternly forbade state department officials—

(Continued on Page 2, Column 3)

Minneapolis Times to Quit Publication

MINNEAPOLIS — (U.P.) — The tabloid Minneapolis Times will merge with the Minneapolis Star and morning Tribune on Monday, it was announced today.

The Minneapolis Star and Tribune Co., which owns all three papers, said the Times would cease separate publication after its final afternoon edition today.

The company gave rising costs, particularly in wages and newsprint, as reason for the merger.

The Times was started in 1939 as an evening edition of the Minneapolis Tribune, which had been a 24-hour newspaper. It began publication as a separate evening paper in 1941.

The announcement said that a majority of employes of the Times would be offered positions with the Star and Tribune without interruption or reduction in pay.

Door County Cherry Trees to Bloom Soon

STURGEON BAY — (U.P.) — Cherry blossoms on Door county's 8,000,000 trees will make their appearance next weekend.

W. L. Thenell, head of the largest cherry orchards in the world, said this year's blossoming is about average. In the 25 years Thenell has kept records, the trees bloomed their earliest May 5 1942.

The latest date came when no blooms were recorded until June 14, 1924.

About two months after blossoming the trees are loaded with an estimated 40,000.000 pounds of cherries. Thousands of Jamaicans, Mexicans, and Indians pick the fruit.

The Door county area, Thenell said, is now third in the country in cherry production. Most cherries are Montmorencies, with a few early Richmonds also grown.

Dark Outlook
MADISON WEATHER
Cloudy with rain tonight. Thursday, cloudy and slightly warmer.
Low tonight 48; high Thursday, 63. Sun rose, 6:36; sets, 4:38.

The Wisconsin State Journal
A fact-finding Newspaper

Call 6-3111 · MADISON, WEDNESDAY, NOVEMBER 3, 1948 · Dial 6-3111

Home Final
PRICE: FIVE CENTS
24 PAGES
VOL. 173, NO. 34 · 109th YEAR

Dewey Concedes to Pres. Truman

Gov. Rennebohm Beats Thompson

But Split-Tickets in State Give Big Margin to Truman

Zim Reelected; Both Smiths Lead; Fairchild Over Martin

By REX KARNEY
(State Journal Staff Writer)

Wisconsin citizens split their votes Tuesday to support Democrat Harry S. Truman for president and Republican Oscar Rennebohm for governor.

Completely confusing all the "experts" and political pollsters, Badger voters—on the bisis of almost complete returns—deserted Republican Presidential Candidate Thomas E. Dewey of New York, long a Wisconsin favorite and the conquerer of Franklin D. Roosevelt in this state two years ago.

52,000 Lead for Truman

Returns from 3,071 of Wisconsin's 3,143 precincts gave:

Truman (D)	628,860
Dewey (R)	576,441
Wallace (P)	23,726
Thomas (S)	11,597

But while voting for a Democratic president, Wisconsin voters favored Republican Rennebohm over his 35-year-old Democratic challenger, Carl Thompson of Stoughton.

Returns from 2,823 of Wisconsin's 3,143 precincts gave:

Rennebohm (R)	744,565
Thompson (D)	523,351
Berquist (P)	13,012
Uphoff (S)	8,441

On the basis of these returns, Mr. Truman had carried 39 Wisconsin counties while Gov. Dewey led in 32. Gov. Rennebohm walked away with 66 counties, while Democrat Thompson could win in only five.

Wisconsin Democrats did steal one state constitutional office, however, that of attorney general.

Democrat Thomas E. Fairchild, Milwaukee, had a comfortable lead over Republican Donald J. Martin also of Milwaukee.

Fairchild had 586,446 votes and Martin 533,844. Socialist Anna Mae Davis had 10,461 votes for attorney general while Progressive Michael Essin had 11,025.

There still is a slight chance that Democrat Antony Gawronski, Milwaukee, might catch up with George Smith, Milwaukee political Cinderella who unexpectedly captured the Republican nomination for lieutenant governor.

With four-fifths of the vote in, Gawronski could count 561,442 while Smith's total was 566,677. Alex Wallace, Progressive, had 13,549, while Socialist William Osborne Hart had 11,564.

Zim Wins Again

Republicans copped the secretary of state and treasury posts easily.

Veteran Republican Fred R. Zimmerman led the GOP ticket with 737,505 votes for secretary of state, compared to 465,900 for Erle Stoneman, his Democratic opponent.

Republican George Smith won the treasury post from Democrat Miles McNally, 603,749 votes to 526,397.

Socialist Archie Oliver had 10,516 votes for state treasurer, while Roy Samp, Progressive, won 12,757 votes for that job. Socialist Walter Benson attracted

(Continued on Page 2, Column 5)

County Offices Go Democratic

Only Myrtle Hansen, Dahlen Hold Posts

(Pictures, Page 10)
By JUNE DIECKMANN
(State Journal Staff Writer)

The dam broke!

And the wave of Democratic votes which inundated the Dane county courthouse washed out all but two of the eight Republican county office-holders.

The two GOP incumbents who managed to stay afloat were Clerk of Circuit Court Myrtle L. Hansen, who nosed out her Democratic opposition, Maxine Anderson, by only 520 votes, and Surveyor Andrew Dahlen, the only candidate who had no opposition for reelection.

Democrats Win

The victorious Democrats were Herman P. Kerl, sheriff; Atty. Robert W. Arthur, district attorney; Keith A. Schwartz, county clerk; Dr. A. L. Olson, coroner; Marvin E. Smithback, treasurer, and Miles C. Riley, Jr., register of deeds.

It was the first time in nearly four decades that the majority of county offices were filled by Democrats, and it was the first near-clean sweep by new county officers since the Progressive landslide of 1934.

The courthouse was filled Tuesday night and early today with old-fashioned election night excitement, as scores of spectators crowded with the candidates to watch the leads change in the seesaw county races.

Three Votes Close

Three of the incumbent Republicans were defeated by less than 700 votes. Sheriff Edward A. Fischer was beaten by Kerl by

(Continued on Page 2, Column 3)

Woman's Body Found at Stoughton

STOUGHTON — The body of an unidentified woman, about 50 years old, barefoot and clad only in black pajamas was found floating here in the Yahara river near the Fourth st., power plant bridge shortly before noon today.

The woman was wearing a wedding ring, Dr. R. F. Schoenbeck said. Dr. Schoenbeck was called to the scene after the body was discovered by a group of children who were walking along the mill race sidewalk after schools had been dismissed for the noon hour.

Dr. Schoenbeck pronounced the woman dead shortly after his arrival but gave no further details pending investigation by Dr. David C. Atwood, coroner.

The Stoughton police department is investigating.

Feature Finder

The Winners in Tuesday's Election

PRES. TRUMAN

GOV. RENNEBOHM

President
Harry S. Truman
Governor
Oscar Rennebohm (R)
Lieutenant Governor
George M. Smith (R)
State Treasurer
Warren Smith (R)
Attorney General
Thomas Fairchild (D)
Congress, 2nd District
Glenn Davis (R)
State Senator
Gaylord Nelson (D)
Assembly, 1st District
Ruth Doyle (D)
Assembly, 2nd district
John Blaska (D)
Assembly, 3rd District
Herman Eisner (D)
County Clerk
Keith A. Schwartz (D)
District Attorney
Robert W. Arthur (D)
Sheriff
Herman Kerl (D)
County Treasurer
Marvin E. Smithback (D)
Coroner
A. L. Olson (D)
Clerk of Courts
Myrtle Hansen (R)
Register of Deeds
Miles C. Riley, Jr., (D)
Truax Veterans Housing
For 15,353
Against 14,201
Veterans Bonus
For 275,203
Against 839,160

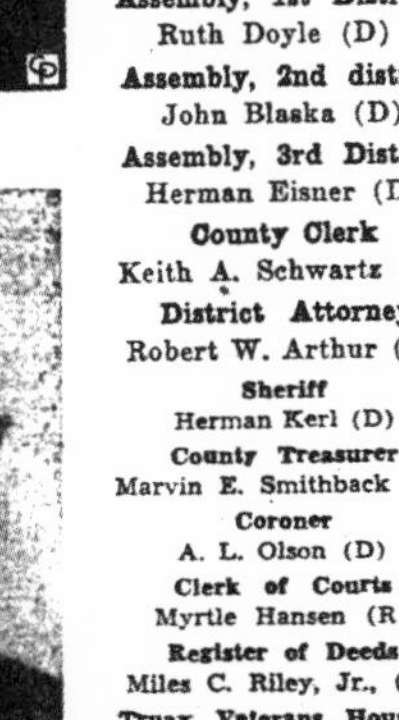

ROBERT ARTHUR
District Attorney

HERMAN KERL
Sheriff

Elected in Congressional Races in Wisconsin

First District
Lawrence Smith (R)
Third District
Gardner R. Withrow (R)
Fourth District
Clement J. Zablocki (D)
Fifth District
Andrew J. Biemiller (D)
Sixth District
Frank B. Keefe (R)
Seventh District
Reid F. Murray (R)
Eighth District
John W. Byrnes (R)
Ninth District
Merlin W. Hull (R)
Tenth District
Alvin E. O'Konski (R)

OKd, Truax Bond Issue Faces New Hurdle, Possible 3rd Vote

By RUSSELL B. PYRE
(State Journal Staff Writer)

Madison's $289,000 veterans' housing subsidy bond issue, approved by voters Tuesday by a narrow margin of 1,152, still faced another hurdle today, and possibly a third referendum.

Tuesday's referendum vote was 15,353 to 14,201.

A petition filed by the Madison board of realtors Monday, bearing names of 4,630 electors, and calling for an amendment limiting the city's contribution to moneys received from sale of the bonds, will be presented to the city council at a special meeting Thursday night, City Manager Howell said this morning.

Can't Foretell Action

Neither Howell, City Atty. Harold E. Hanson, nor officials of the Madison Housing Authority (MHA) were prepared to state today whether the council could adopt the petitioners' resolution without jeopardizing the MHA commitment with its financing company.

Howell's said he would make no statement until Hansen has studied the petition and Hanson declared he hadn't studied the resolution.

A letter from Stuart H. Becker, attorney for the board of realtors, accompanying the petition, said the signers represented more than the required 15 per cent of all voters at the 1946 gubernatorial election and that a referendum would be mandatory if the council did not adopt the resolution.

Passes in 20 Precincts

The bond issue referendum was given a favorable vote Tuesday in all but nine of the city's 29 precincts. Seven of the unfavorable precincts were on the West side and the eighth an East side—the first precinct of the 16th ward.

One precinct, the 6th, came up with a tie vote, 618 to 618.

Those voting adversely to the bond issue were the 10th ward, 769 to 698; both precincts of the 13th, 428 to 417 and 333 to 295; the first of the 16th, 376 to 334; all three precincts of the 19th, 562 to 479, 498 to 323, and 591 to 467; and both precincts of the 20th, 809 to 451 and 647 to 413.

Margins were narrow in several favorable wards, and the biggest majorities in support of the bond issue were in the fifth ward, 844 to 488, and the eighth ward, 819 to 494.

Vote Up, Margin Down

While the vote total of 29,554 on the bond issue was nearly twice as large as the 16,829 ballots cast in the Sept. 21 advisory referendum, the margin favoring the bonds was smaller than the 2,305 edge recorded in the September, when the tabulation was 9,567 for the bonds and 7,262 against.

While Thursday night's special council meeting is planned primarily to consider the proposed new pay plan for police and firemen, City Manager Howell said

(Continued on Page 2, Column 8)

State Kills Sales Tax for Bonus

MILWAUKEE — (U.P.) — Wisconsin voters told the legislature positively today that they don't want a sales tax to pay World War II veterans a bonus.

Returns from 2,887 out of Wisconsin's 3,143 precincts gave: 839,160 against the tax to 275,203 for it.

The advisory referendum asked voters whether the state should levy a 3 per cent retail sales tax to raise a maximum of $200,000,000 for a veterans' bonus.

The legislature had held that a sales tax was the only revenue measure that would bring in enough money to pay a bonus.

Voters also rejected decisively a constitutional amendment to allow cities and villages to condemn property for public use without first having a jury establish that it was necessary to take the property.

Returns from 2,523 precincts gave 613,344 votes against the amendment to 163,611 for it.

The amendment was sought by the League of Wisconsin Municipalities. The state, counties, and towns now have power to condemn property without a jury determination and the League sought the same authority for municipalities.

35,804 City Voters Set All-Time Record

Madison's vote in Tuesday's election totaled 35,804, an all-time record as predicted, City Clerk A. W. Bareis reported today.

It exceeded the previous high mark of 34,102, set in the 1940 presidential election, by 1,702.

The tabulation disclosed that 5,250 voters did not ballot on the $289,000 housing bond issue, the referendum vote having totaled 29,554.

Airlift Plane Crashes; 5 Killed, 5 Injured

FRANKFURT —(U.P.)— At least five army men were killed and five others critically injured late Tuesday when a C-47 transport plane crashed in a heavy fog near Wiesbaden, Germany, air force officials said today.

The plane was on a return flight from Northolt, England.

Officials said the plane overshot the runway on its first attempt to land. On the second attempt it plowed into the ground before reaching the runway.

GOP, Experts Upset by 'Political Miracle'

President Never Gives Up Lead, Puts Party in Congress' Saddle

By LYLE C. WILSON
(United Press Staff Correspondent)

Gov. Thomas E. Dewey conceded today that Pres. Truman had been elected in the closest presidential race in 32 years.

It was one of the greatest upsets in American political history. Mr. Truman had been given no chance in pre-election polls and forecasts. But he seized the lead with the first returns Tuesday night and never lost it.

He swept a Democratic congress into office with him. Republicans lost control of both the house and senate.

The presidential popular vote early this afternoon was:

Truman	20,559,397
Dewey	19,023,981
Wallace	956,360
Thurmond	807,035

Mr. Truman was leading in 28 states with 304 electoral voted.

Dewey was ahead in 16 states with a total of 189 electoral votes.

Thurmond was leading in four states with 38 electoral votes.

A total of 266 electoral votes is necessary to elect.

Congratulates Victor

Dewey, who had been mulling over cabinet selections and preparing to move to Washington in January, gave up shortly after 10 a. m. today.

In a crowded suite at the Roosevelt hotel in New York, James Hagerty, Dewey's press secretary, called in reporters and said:

"The governor has just sent the following telegram: **'My heartiest congratulations on your election and every good wish for a successful administration.**

"'I urge all Americans to unite behind you in support of every effort to keep our nation strong and free and to establish peace in the world.'"

Democrats already had claimed the victory.

Sen. J. Howard McGrath, Democratic national chairman, walked into party headquarters at the Biltmore hotel in New York and said it was all over.

Champagne Waiting

"We have possesson of sufficient facts," McGrath added, "to say that Pres. Harry S. Truman and Sen. Alben Barkley have swept into a Democratic victory."

Dewey not only conceded defeat in his second try for the White House, but announced at a press conference later that he never would seek the presidency again.

He said he had "no plans for the future," but denied that he would resign as New York governor. Dewey said he had no plans for reelection as governor.

He predicted Mr. Truman's

(Continued on Page 2, Column 1)

The Electoral Vote

As of 1:30 P. M. (CST)

TRUMAN	
Arizona	4
Arkansas	9
California	25
Colorado	6
Florida	8
Georgia	12
Idaho	4
Illinois	28
Iowa	10
Kentucky	11
Massachusetts	16
Minnesota	11
Missouri	15
Montana	4
Nevada	3
New Mexico	4
North Carolina	14
Ohio	25
Oklohoma	10
Rhode Island	4
Tennessee	12
Texas	23
Utah	4
Virginia	11
Washington	8
West Virginia	8
Wisconsin	12
Wyoming	3
Total	304

DEWEY	
Connecticut	8
Delaware	3
Indiana	13
Kansas	8
Maine	5
Maryland	8
Michigan	19
Nebraska	6
New Hampshire	4
New Jersey	16
New York	47
North Dakota	4
Oregon	6
Pennsylvania	35
South Dakota	4
Vermont	3
Total	189

THURMOND	
Alabama	11
Louisiana	10
Missisippi	9
South Carolina	8
Total	38

Democrats Will Control Both House and Senate

By RAYMOND LAHR
(United Press Staff Correspondent)

Democrats today captured control of both houses of congress.

The United Press tabulation showed the Democrats had elected 19 candidates in contests for the 32 senate seats involved in Tuesday's election.

With 30 holdover Democrats in the senate, they were assured of the 49 seats needed for a majority of the 96-member senate.

Democratic nominees also were leading in five of the unsettled senate races. Victory in all of those would run their senate total up to 54.

Democratic control of the house had been assured earlier.

The house tabulation showed 235 Democrats had been elected to the house, 17 more than the required majority of 218.

The Republican count showed that eight of their senate candidates had been elected and one other was leading. In the house, the Republicans were elected in 138 districts and leading in 34.

If the present trends in both parties continues, the senate will be composed of 54 Democrats and 42 Republicans.

The house lineup would be 262 Democrats, 172 Republicans, and one American Labor party member.

The Democrats went over the hump in the senate—assuring

(Continued on Page 2, Column 7)

Harry Olson, 83, Hit by Car, Dies in Hospital

Harry Olson, 83, of 109 N. Baldwin st., died this afternoon at a Madison hospital as a result of injuries suffered when he was struck by a car in the 300 block of W. Washington ave, Saturday.

All Four County Democrats Win in Races for State Legislature

(Pictures on Page 9)

Four Democrats, two of them in their first try for public office, ousted State Sen. Fred Risser and Assemblymen Rudy Roethlisberger and Earl Mullen and rolled over William C. Sachtjen, assembly aspirant from Madison on the Republican ticket, Tuesday.

Winners were Atty. Gaylord Nelson, Madison, new state senator for Dane county; Mrs. Ruth Doyle, Madison housewife, in the first (Madison) assembly district; John M. Blaska, town of Sun Prairie farmer, in the second assembly district; and Hermann Eisner, town of Berry farmer, third assembly district.

Blaska Wins Easily

Handiest winner was Blaska, who had bowed to Mullen by almost 2,000 votes in a try for the assembly two years ago.

The vote follows:

STATE SENATOR	
Nelson (D)	30,388
Risser (R)	28,736
Sadowsky (S)	352
1st ASSEMBLY DISTRICT	
Mrs. Doyle (D)	17,056
Sachtjen (R)	16,702
Doran (S)	257
Havenor (PP)	213
2nd ASSEMBLY DISTRICT	
Blaska (D)	7,838
Mullen (R)	5,117
3rd ASSEMBLY DISTRICT	
Eisner (D)	6,276
Roethlisberger (R)	6,180
Anderson (S)	75
Shipman (PP)	48

Risser, in the senate since 1936, got 28,736 votes to 30,388 for Nelson.

Mullen failed even to win in his home town of Blooming Grove, where the voters favored Blaska 910 to 721. Blaska carried the town of Sun Prairie, 291 to 79.

Former Progressive

Nelson, 31, is a graduate of the University of Wisconsin law school. He served in the army in the Pacific theater in World War II. He was active in the Progressive party during his school days.

In 1946, Nelson brought suit to force reapportionment of legislative seats on the basis of the 1940 census, a test case which finally went to defeat in the su-

(Continued on Page 2, Column 4)

Rep. Davis Reelected Over Wilkie; Carries Four Out of Five Counties

Glenn R. Davis, 34-year-old Waukesha Republican, earned a second term in congress Tuesday by carrying four out of five counties in the second district and turning back the challenge of Horace Wilkie, Madison Democrat.

With only three precincts in Dodge county unreported, the totals were:

Davis (R)	73,559
Wilkie (D)	62,514
Mrs. Uphoff (S)	614

Wilkie, who is chairman of the Madison Housing Authority, carried Dane county by a 10,357-vote margin, but Davis offset that by a victory in his own county of Waukesha, which gave him a 9,278-vote edge.

Carries Other Counties

Davis also carried Dodge, Jefferson, and Columbia counties which with Dane and Waukesha make up the second district.

Mrs. Mary Jo Uphoff, Oregon farm wife, the Socialist candidate, made her best showing in Dane county, where she attracted 433 votes.

GLENN R. DAVIS

The county-by-county totals:

County	Davis	Wilkie	Uphoff
Dane	24,629	34,986	433
Dodge*	11,500	6,245	
Jefferson	9,581	6,098	37
Columbia	7,677	4,291	10
Waukesha	20,172	10,894	134
Totals	73,559	62,514	614

*64 of 67 precincts.

In Dane county, Wilkie carried 72 precincts while Davis ran ahead in 20. Wilkie carried 21 of the city of Madison's precincts, while Davis won eight.

Wilkie Takes Stoughton

Wilkie carried all four wards in the city o Stoughton.

In Dane county outside of Madison, Wilkie had the lead in 51 voting precincts, while Davis captured 12.

But Wilkie's heavy Dane county vote was not sufficient to turn the tide. Davis' strength in the other four counties in the district pulled him through and earned him another term in the U. S. house of representatives.

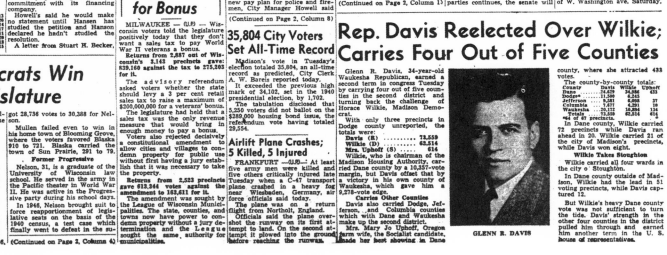

Humid, with Rain
MADISON WEATHER
Partly cloudy, warm, and humid, with thundershowers this afternoon and tonight. Thundershowers Friday and continued warm and humid. High today, 86; low tonight, 64. Sun rose, 4:18; sets, 7:38.

Wisconsin State Journal

Dial 6-3111 SECTION 1. MADISON, THURSDAY, JUNE 15, 1950 ★★★ Dial 6-3111

Morning Final
PRICE FIVE CENTS
30 PAGES, TWO SECTIONS
Vol. 172, No. 75 111th Year

New Vets Hospital to Employ 650

Tight Security Urged for Foreign Missions

Don't Act So Tough, Big Boy

Head high with indifference, Nancy Ann, a Yorkshire terrier, gives the brushoff to Czar II, a St. Bernard, at Pasadena, Calif., Kennel club show. Both look as if they could use a good brushoff. (International)

Fire All Aliens at U. S. Outposts, Senate Unit Asks

WASHINGTON — (U.P.) — A senate foreign relations subcommittee Wednesday called for a speedy tightening of security regulations at American diplomatic missions abroad to fight a "constantly growing" Communist spy effort.

Sens. Theodore F. Green (D-R.I.) and Henry Cabot Lodge, Jr., (R-Mass.), who investigated state department security precautions abroad, recommended the firing of all aliens employed at this country's foreign outposts because they are "the most likely means of foreign penetration."

Fifty Fired

The senators said that in Germany alone 50 of 2,000 American employes screened since Dec. 1 have been fired for "various security reasons."

Of 1,000 aliens screened, they said, 100 have been discharged.

Green and Lodge are members of the foreign relations subcommittee investigating Wisconsin Sen. Joseph R. McCarthy's Communist charges against the state department. They held hearings in Paris, Frankfort, Germany, Washington, and New York.

Tydings Goes Ahead

Meantime, the subcommittee, headed by Sen. Millward E. Tydings (D-Md.) went ahead with its plans to continue the investigation of the 1945 Amerasia stolen documents case despite Republican demands for a separate inquiry.

Edward P. Morgan, subcommittee counsel, said Far Eastern Diplomat John S. Service probably will be called for questioning early next week.

Service was one of those arrested in the case, but the grand jury did not indict him.

Lodge and Green called for replacement "as rapidly as possible" of all aliens employed for clerical work by U. S. missions abroad. They said that in the Paris embassy alone, 50 per cent of the employes were aliens.

"In many instances, aliens have access to classified material and these aliens have not had a full field investigation," they said.

Lodge and Green reported:

Aliens were the most likely sources of security breaches because their low pay makes them "a prey to bribery and to pres-

(Continued on Page 2, Column 5)

U.W. Commencement, Reunion Events Open

By ROBERT BJORKLUND
(State Journal Staff Writer)

Today opens a contrasting, but happy weekend of departure and reunion at the University of Wisconsin.

Parents and friends of members of the largest single class to graduate from the university began arriving Wednesday night and thousands more will take up temporary residence in Madison today in preparation for the 97th annual commencement which starts at 8:30 a. m. Friday in the fieldhouse.

Reunions Set

To complete the commencement-reunion picture, university alumni began arriving for their back-to-the-campus visits, class reunions, and Wisconsin Alumni assn. activities. Eleven classes from 1900 to 1945 have scheduled reunions.

When the 3,706 graduates receive their diplomas Friday, it will mark the end of the classroom bulge caused by World War II veterans studying under the GI Bill.

Veterans make up 63 per cent (2,500) of those receiving degrees.

Honors Meet Today

The commencement - reunion weekend will open at 4 p. m. today with the honors convocation in

(Continued on Page 2, Column 1)

Commencement at a Glance

TODAY

4:00 P. M.—Honors Convocation, Union Theater
7:00 P. M.—Twilight Concert, University Concert Band, Union Terrace.
8:00 P. M. —President's Reception, Great Hall
9:00 P. M.—Alumni Dance, Great Hall.

FRIDAY

8:30 A. M.—Commencement ceremony, Fieldhouse.
8:30 a. m.—Alumni registration, Union
12 Noon—Half Century club luncheon, Great hall, Union
12 noon—Home economics luncheon, Tripp Commons
4:30 p. m.—Birge hall dedication, former biology building.
3:00 P. M.—Board of directors, Wisconsin Alumni assn., Top Flight.
6:00 P. M.—Class of 1910 dinner, Black Hawk Country club.
6:00 P. M.—Class of 1915 dinner, Memorial Union.
6:00 P. M.—Class of 1920 dinner, Top Hat.
6 P. M.—Wisconsin Alumni past-presidents assn. Madison Club.
6:00 P. M.—Union Terrace night, sponsored by Wisconsin Union—Dance on the Starbeck, during the dinner and afterwards. Selections by the Medichoir, composed of freshmen, sophomores, and juniors in the medical school.

SATURDAY

8:30 A. M.—Alumni registration, Union
10:00 A. M.—Wisconsin Alumni assn. meeting, Play Circle.
11:30 A. M.—Rededication of Bascom Plaque, Class of 1910, Bascom hall
12 Noon—Class Luncheons:
1900—Alpha Phi house, 28 Langdon st.
1905—Madison club, 5 E. Wilson st.
1910—Picnic, Prof. Henry A. Schuette's, 719 Farwell dr.
1915—Georgian Grill, Union.
1917—Picnic, Mrs. W. H. Conlin's, 739 Farwell dr.
1920—Beefeaters Room, Union.
1925—Tripp Commons, Memorial Union.
1930—Old Madison West, Union, 12:30.
1935—Reception, 12:30, Old Madison East, Union, Luncheon, 1:00, Old Madison East, Union.
1940—Round Table Room, Union.
2:00 P. M.—Boat ride, Class of 1915.
4:15 P. M.—Boat ride, Class of 1945, Picnic supper on Union Terrace.
6:00 P. M.—Alumni dinner, GREAT HALL; Class of '25 in Tripp Commons.
8 P. M.—Alumni Day program, Union theater, Presentation of Steinway Grand Piano by Class of 1925, followed by short concert by Gunnar Johansen; presentation of awards; state of the university address by Pres. Fred.

SUNDAY

8:30 A. M.—Alumni breakfasts, Union Terrace.

A Sick Boy's Dream Comes True

Cleveland Ball Team Scores a Hit

BY JEAN BEHLING
(State Journal Staff Writer)

Bob Feller, Lou Boudreau, Gene Bearden, Bob Lemon, Larry Doby, Allie Clark, Luke Easter, Al Rosen. . .

Signatures on a letter that mean a dream come true to a Cleveland Indians baseball team fan.

Not only signatures on a personal letter, but an autographed baseball, too, are on their way to 10-year-old David Heydon.

David has been a very sick little boy for 11 weeks. He is the only son of Mr. and Mrs. O. S. Heydon, 2711 Kendall ave.

First it was nephritis, an inflammation of the kidneys, and then the pint-sized Indians' fan got pneumonia.

"How'd the Indians make out?" is consistently his first query when his father visits David in his St. Mary's hospital room.

And that is what led to the letter.

The idea was batted out late Wednesday by H. Ralph Allen,

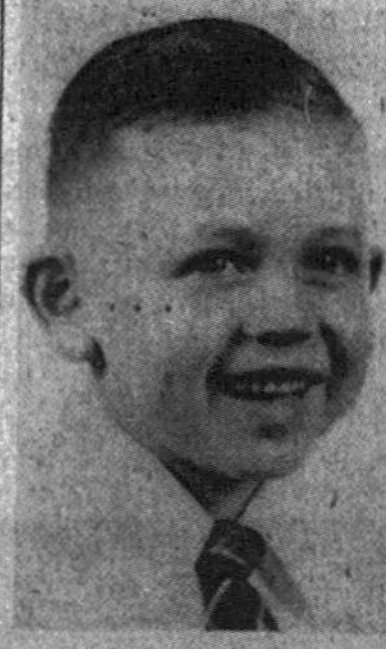

DAVID HEYDON

principal of Randall school, where David is a fourth grader. Allen thought a letter from one of the players might supply the psychological lift that would help bring the boy home more quickly.

On the receiving end of the idea was Henry J. McCormick, State Journal sports editor. Allen enlisted McCormick's aid in investigating the possibilities of getting the boy a letter from one of his heroes.

But McCormick went Allen one better.

He called Rudy Schaffer, Indians business manager. Schaffer was formerly with the Milwaukee Brewers baseball club.

And Schaffer promised quick service on a personal letter to David from members of the team—and the autographed baseball.

David is interested in all sports, and although baseball is a special favorite of his, he captained the winning basketball team at Randall school during the winter months this year.

Building Permits Again Top Millio

For a second straight month, May building permits passed the million dollar mark in valuation, according to the monthly report of Building Inspection Supt. Ray F. Burt, released Wednesday.

Last month's permits numbered 385, with a total value of $1,005,876, compared with 279 issued in May, 1949, a value of $432,490.

May business included 94 single-family homes, $65,900; three 2-family houses, $35,500; three 3- and 4-family units, $37,000; one residence of five or more units, $35,000; two amusement and recreation buildings, $77,000; one factory, $20,000; two public garages, $18,000; one filling station, $19,000; 33 private garages, $13,645; one fire escape, $190; and three television towers, $275.

Council Majority Shuns Initiative for Referendum

Denies Intent to Seek Vote on Manager Plan by Own Resolution

By RUSSELL B. PYRE
(State Journal Staff Writer)

A majority of the city council does not favor "pushing an early referendum" on its own initiative over retention or abandonment of city manager government, The Wisconsin State Journal learned late Wednesday.

Contrary to a statement in the Capital Times that the council would seek a vote "by its own resolution," Councilmen H. L. Garner, Henry E. Reynolds, John E. Coyne, and H. C. Schenk denied that any such intent had been expressed by the council.

Only Councilman William C. Sachtjen was quoted as saying the council might vote for a referendum "as early as the September primary."

Petitions Ready

Meantime Darrell D. MacIntyre, one of the sponsors of a public petition calling for a referendum in November, said he did not believe City Manager Howell's acceptance of a $20,000 offer for transfer to Des Moines, Ia., would affect the petition.

The petitions are "practically filled up," MacIntyre declared, but whether they will be filed will await conferences with Oswald Neesvig, the other sponsor, when Neesvig returns from Norway, he said.

Neesvig may not return until September, The State Journal was informed.

Kraege Hinted

Report was current Wednesday that several citizens had sounded F. Halsey Kraege, former mayor and acting city manager preceding Howell's arrival here, on his willingness to serve again if asked.

Some expressed belief that Kraege might be receptive to an offer "as a civic duty," but one councilman, who said he talked with Kraege, declared the former

(Continued on Page 2, Column 2)

'Do-Gooder' Has Too Many Friends, and Now Too Few

MILWAUKEE — (U.P.) — Carlos Garcia, 30, Milwaukee, Wednesday said he collected thousands of dollars from friends because he wanted to do them a favor.

His friends' only comment was "We want our money back."

Garcia, an engineer, told Deputy Dist. Atty. Aladin De Brozzo he was offered a 30 per cent discount on electrical appliances several months ago by a Southside distributor.

He cut his friends in on his good fortune, but as the orders piled up he lost his discount privilege.

Rather than disappoint his friends, he went to retailers. He got discounts of only 15 per cent or less from them, but he bought the appliances anyhow. He paid the difference in price by taking money from advance payments on future deliveries.

Finally he couldn't keep it up any longer. The district attorney's office received about 40 complaints and Garcia admitted he could not account for at least $9,000.

By late Wedensday Garcia had been charged with larceny as bailee in six warrants.

Schools Take Spanking as Pupils Apply Rule

SECAUCUS, N. J. — (AP) — Teen-agers took over the town administration Wednesday for a one-day rule celebrating Secaucus' golden jubilee.

The first act of the youngsters? All schools closed at noon.

Wake Up With a Smile
From Roundy

I see where they want to give City Manager Howell $16,000 if he would stay.

If the Journal would give me that I would stay and I'd climb up the State Journal flag pole every morning even with ice on it.

Read Roundy's Column on today's Sports Page

New Type Hay Rake Shown on U.W. Fields

A new type hay rake was demonstrated at the University of Wisconsin's Farm Field Day Wednesday.

The wheels with the rake teeth around their edges work independently of each other.

As the tractor moves forward, the wheels turn, rolling the hay into windrows with little or no disturbance, compared to the conventional side-delivery hay rakes.

Because the wheels operate independently, moving up or down with the roughness of the land, they would be especially suited to farms with terraces, observers were told.

—State Journal Staff photos

15,000 Farm Field Day Visitors Get Harvesting, Barn Ideas

BY ED MERCER
(State Journal Farm Editor)

New ideas in crop harvesting, particularly of hay crops, were shown to the more than 15,000 farmers who attended the annual spring Farm Field Day at the University of Wisconsin Hill farms Wednesday.

Despite heat and humidity, the visitors stayed until about 4 p.m. before leaving the farms.

They congregated around the various hay strips which were being cut and harvested by forage choppers, processed by hay crushers, and raked up by conventional and new type rakes.

See New Barn

They saw a portion of a pole barn being built, using telephone-type poles of pine impregnated with creosote under high pressure which forces the preservative material right into the heart of the poles.

These poles, as foundations for low-cost loose-housing barns, will last for 70 years.

The sinking of each of the brace poles 5 feet into the ground helps provide rigidity, doing away with the need of overhead truss construction for strength.

The cost of building a pole barn varies, depending on whether home-sawed and raised lumber is used, and on whether home labor is used. The cost is estimated at from $100 to $300 per cow in the herd.

Advantages Seen

For such a barn, the construction costs for a 30-cow herd would amount to $9,000, but that would include a good milk house, the barn itself, a 100-square foot cement pavement in front of the barn, and a raised platform milking parlor.

The platform not only speeds up milking but saves labor to the milker.

The cost is very little more than that of a conventional type barn,

(Continued on Page 2, Column 3)

The University of Wisconsin agricultural engineering department is working on refinements of the old hay crushers and have developed what they call a "kinker."

It "kinks" or breaks the stems, causing them to crack open and dry faster.

The machine makes it possible to put cured hay, with all the leaves remaining on it, into the barn.

Weather Unsettled; Humidity Rides High

Unsettled weather was the Truax field weatherman's prediction for the start of Madison's commencement weekend.

The thundershowers will be of short duration, but there'll be plenty of heat and humidity. The humidity early today was up to 92 per cent, equalling that of 8 a. m. Wednesday.

The thundershowers in the south and west portions of the state will spread out over the entire state on Friday.

The high temperature today will be 86.

Cafe Man Tips Help with State Vacation

PEKIN, Ill.—(AP)—Harry Sarnes left for a Wisconsin vacation with 11 women—one of them his wife.

The other 10 are waitresses, cooks, or helpers in the restaurant he operates here.

Sarnes said he will be picking up all checks during a week's vacation at a Webb lake Wisconsin resort in Burnett county.

"I'm just trying to show them a good time," Sarnes said. "Only one of them ever has been out of Illinois."

Price Index Reports 1st Drop Since Apr. 18

NEW YORK—(U.P.)— Dun and Bradstreet wholesale price index Wednesday reported the first decline since Apr. 18.

The index fell to $5.94 the week ended June 13 from $6 the week before.

The same week in 1949, the index stood at $5.68.

LATEST
2nd French Plane Hits; 42 Missing; Sabotage Hinted

PARIS, Thursday — (U.P.) — An Air France Skymaster carrying 53 passengers and crewmen crashed into the Persian gulf off Bahrein island today, two days after another Skymaster of the same line crashed in the same area with the loss of 46 lives.

Eleven persons were rescued from the wreckage of today's crash, according to first reports, and 42 were missing.

Air France officials said both planes may have been sabotaged by agents of Communist Leader Ho Chin Minh before leaving Saigon, Indo-China, currently torn by civil war.

The similarity of the crashes "opens up the possibility of sabotage on the Saigon-Paris run," Air France officials said.

Air France headquarters here reported that the four-engined plane crashed into the sea as it was coming in for a landing. Like the Skymaster which crashed Tuesday, the plane was enroute to Paris from Saigon.

New Zealand Reports Only 21 Unemployed

GENEVA, Switzerland — (U.P.)— New Zealand has only 21 registered persons unemployed, a New Zealand delegate told the annual conference of the International Labor organization here Wednesday.

Herbert L. Brockett, government representative at the conference, said that of a population of almost 2,000,000 the figure for registered unemployment dropped from 207 in July, 1949, to 21 last March.

Journal Features

6 Americans Rescued After Ethiopia Crash

ADDIS ABABA, Ethiopia —(AP) —Rescue parties driving powerful armored cars fought their way through roadless jungles Wednesday and brought out six Americans, including a woman and child, whose plane crashed Sunday.

Brief radio advices received here said they were taken to Belet Uen, about 35 miles from the scene of the crash near the Somaliland border.

The plane, a single-engined Norseman type, was piloted by K. L. Horton, who managed to get the craft's radio working after the accident. Names of the passengers were not known.

Ingvald Hembre Named State Masonic Officer

MILWAUKEE — (U.P.) — Walter Helwig, Wauwatosa, was elected grand master of the Masons in Wisconsin Wednesday.

He was chosen at the 106th annual communication of the Wisconsin Masons, which attracted more than 600 members from 306 lodges in the state.

Robert Varnum, Hudson, was elected deputy grand master, and Ingvald O. Hembre, Madison, senior grand master.

No Applications Wanted Before Spring of 1951

Davis Tells Plans for Professional, Civil Service Jobs

By MARY JAMES COTTRELL
(State Journal Washington Bureau)

WASHINGTON — Jobs for about 650 persons will become available when the Veterans hospital at Madison is completed in June, 1951, but no applications are wanted before next spring, the Veterans Administration (VA) late Wednesday informed Rep. Glenn Davis (R-Waukesha).

Doctors, dentists, and nurses will be selected by the hospital manager upon the recommendations of the professional standards boards of the profession concerned.

Apply to Medical Director

Applicants for these positions should apply to the chief medical director, Veterans Administration, Washington 25, D. C.

All other positions will be filled by persons with civil service status. Applicants lacking that status should watch the bulletin boards of their postoffices for announcements of civil service examinations and arrange to take the necessary tests.

Hospital staff jobs to be filled through civil service include those of: medical and dental technician, X-ray technician, librarian, social worker, chaplain, dietitian, cook, baker, meat cutter, physical medicine therapist, recreation technician, storekeeper, guard, laborer, hospital attendant, kitchen helper, clerical and administrative workers and a limited number of trades and crafts men, such as electricians, plumbers, and carpenters.

To Show Training

The VA advised potential applicants to submit their applications no sooner than next spring so that they can show any additional training or experience which they may acquire in the meantime.

Even if the 500-bed hospital is finished on schedule next June, an extra 60 to 90 days will be required to install equipment and prepare for the opening, the VA informed Davis.

Judge Says He'll Call Grand Jury on Lustron

COLUMBUS, O.—(U.P.)—A federal grand jury will be summoned "to fully and completely investigate" the transactions of Lustron Corp., manufacturer of enamel steel prefabricated houses, if the justice department takes no action, Federal Judge Mell G. Underwood said Wednesday.

The judge asked Atty. Gen. J. Howard McGrath on May 25 to look into the activities of the huge firm which he put into receivership Mar. 6 and turned over Wednesday to the Reconstruction Finance Corp. (RFC) for $6,000,000.

Lustron owed RFC $36,500,000 on loans granted in the four years of its existence.

'Inch-by-Inch' Search for Pair in Lake Fails

An inch-by-inch search Wednesday of that area of Lake Mendota where two Madison men are believed to have drowned May 24 failed to reveal any sign of their bodies, according to police.

Because the lake was "glass smooth" Wednesday, Officer Fred C. Williams went over the entire area in a boat.

William Maly, 51, of 2458 Hoard st., and Earl Williams, 32, of 2330 Lakeland ave., are presumed to have perished in the lake during a storm which came up while they were fishing.

The 22nd consecutive day of search for the pair was to start today.

Peru Rebels, Military Clash; 50 Reported Dead, 200 Hurt

AREQUIPA, Peru—(U.P.)—(By telephone to New York)—A revolutionary movement against the military government at Lima was in control of this second largest Peruvian city Wednesday night.

Fifty persons were reported killed and 200 wounded in clashes between the rebels and government forces.

Students Killed

An aroused citizenry overthrew the local authorities after the police killed several striking students who barricaded themselves in the campus of the American Independence college.

Dr. Juan Francisco Mostajo, a physician, was named president of a civilian revolutionary junta pledged to end "the tyranny of the Lima military junta."

Mostajo was opposition candidate to the vice-president of Peru on the same ticket with presidential candidate Ernesto Montagne whom Lima electoral authorities ruled out this week.

They charged that his nomination was fraudulent.

Remain in Barracks

Government forces remained in their barracks at the nearby resort town of Tingo, apparently awaiting orders from Lima.

Thus far there had been no organized reaction against the revolution.

Short Showers
MADISON WEATHER
Mostly cloudy with occasional showers or thundershowers ending by this noon. Fair and continued cool tonight and Thursday. High today, 80; low tonight, 52. Sun rose, 4:21; sets, 7:41.

Wisconsin State Journal

Dial 6-3111 SECTION 1. MADISON, WEDNESDAY, JUNE 28, 1950 ★★★ Dial 6-3111

Morning Final
PRICE FIVE CENTS
24 PAGES, TWO SECTIONS
Vol. 172, No. 88 111th Year

HALT WAR, U.S. TELLS RUSSIA

UN Votes Sanctions

World Group's First Military Step OKd, 7-1

Only Yugoslavia Opposes Arms Aid to South Korea

LAKE SUCCESS, N. Y. —(U.P.)— The Soviet-boycotted United Nations (UN) security council late Tuesday called on all UN members to join the United States in sending arms to hurl back the Communist invasion of South Korea.

It was the first time in history that a world organization has imposed military sanctions — against an aggressor.

Yugoslavia Against

The vote was 7 to 1 in favor.

Yugoslavia was against. Egypt and India did not take part in the voting because they had not received instructions from their governments.

The key clause of the American-proposed council resolution **"recommends that the members of the UN furnish such assistance to the Republic of Korea as may be necessary to repel the armed attack and to restore international peace and security in the area."**

The closest the League of Nations ever came to taking such extreme measures to keep the peace was in voting economic sanctions against Italy for invading Ethiopia.

First by UN

Never before has the 5-year-old UN imposed sanctions of any sort —diplomatic, economic, or military.

After adjournment, American Delegate Warren R. Austin issued a statement saying the action was **"regarded in the UN as of momentous importance in the history of the organized effort to stop war and apply the principles of peace."**

"The immediate effect of this historic action," he added, "should be to stop bloodshed and aggression in Korea. **The larger effect should be to discourage aggression everywhere.**

"This action should be hailed as encouraging faith in the U. S. support of the peace-making functions of the UN."

The vote came after a nerve-

(Continued on Page 2, Column 5)

Chinese Nationalists Order Attacks Halted

TAPEI, Formosa, Wednesday—(AP)—The Chinese Nationalists today ordered their air force and navy to cease attacks on the Communist mainland in accordance with a U. S. request.

Pres. Truman had ordered U. S. warships to protect Formosa against Red attack and at the same time asked the Nationalists to cease offensive operations.

Nationalist Foreign Minister George Yeh welcomed the president's order for warship protection as "a most welcome sign of comradeship in the fight against Communism."

It may be taken for granted that Chiang, while probably agreeing to a temporary halt in the Nationalist air and sea operations against the Communist China mainland, will not bind himself to forego his plans for an invasion attempt to win back China.

U.S. Leaders Solemn as Korean Crisis Mounts

Solemn looks mark the faces of Pres. Truman and two cabinet members as they walked from Blair House to the White House Tuesday as the Korean crisis placed a heavy responsibility on their shoulders. Atty. Gen. J. Howard McGrath (left) stares blankly ahead as Defense Sec. Louis Johnson closes his eyes and holds his head. (AP Wirephoto)

Sewage Deadline Set June 1, 1951

State Group's Order Clears Way for Test

The state committee on water pollution decided Tuesday to stand firm on its 1949 Madison sewage effluent diversion order, clearing the way for a court test on the constitutionality of the law on which the order was based.

In its Tuesday order, the committee reaffirmed its order of Oct. 19, 1949, requiring the Madison Metropolitan Sewerage district to pipe its effluent around the Madison lakes and into the Yahara river below the Lake Kegonsa locks by June 1, 1951.

The district appealed the 1949 order, and was given a new hearing before the water pollution committee last spring.

Prof. James G. Woodburn, president of the district's three-man governing commission, said Tuesday afternoon that the commission would study the order July 2.

The commission is expected to appeal the order to Dane circuit court, challenging the constitutionality of the 1949 law on which it is based.

If the order is sustained there, the commission undoubtedly will appeal to the supreme court; if it is reversed, the water pollution committee is expected to appeal to the high court.

The appeal must be filed within 30 days, but could not be heard by

(Continued on Page 2, Column 3)

South Korea Claims Reds Retreat 12 Miles

BULLETIN

TOKYO (Wednesday)—(U.P.)—Gen. Douglas MacArthur announced in a statement this afternoon that the forces of South Korea now are holding the Communist North Korean invaders.

(From United Press, Associated Press)

TOKYO (Wednesday)—The South Korean army reported today it had driven the Communist invaders out of Seoul and back to the edge of a key city 12 miles north, informed sources said.

The report came as U. S. air and sea forces sprang into action against the Korean Communist invaders on Pres. Truman's orders.

Moscow radio asserted, however, the Northerners had entered Seoul at four points.

Claims Red Retreat

But an American source which said the information came from South Korean army forces in the Seoul area reported that the Red invaders had been hurled back.

The source said the North Korean troops were turned back to the edge of Uijongbu, guardian city of the invasion valley 12 miles to the north.

He declared the Northerners were driven out of Seoul at about 11:30 a. m., Korean time (7 p. m., Tuesday CST).

Earlier reports had said the Northerners entered Seoul at 7 a. m. Korean time.

A Moscow broadcast had asserted Pres. Syngman Rhee and his government had fled Seoul and there was rioting in the streets.

Communications Out

A blackout of all communications with Seoul tended to confirm that the invaders had occupied part of the city at least for a time.

American jet fighter planes and attack bombers, meanwhile, strafed and bombed North Korean positions today.

An air force spokesman at the Itazuke air base, new advanced

(Continued on Page 2, Column 1)

Ralph E. Larson, 51, Insurance Man, Dies

Ralph E. Larson, 51, of 407 W. Main st., Madison insurance and real estate man, died suddenly late Tuesday night at his home.

Mr. Larson was a graduate of the University of Wisconsin and was a member of Phi Kappa Sigma fraternity.

A 32nd degree Mason, he belonged to Madison Masonic lodge No. 50, the Madison Consistory, and Zor Shrine. He was a member of the First Congregational church.

Surviving are his parents, Mr. and Mrs. A. C. Larson; a daughter, Jane, and a son, Ralph, Jr.; and a sister, Mrs. Harry Thoma, all of Madison.

The body was taken to the Frautschi funeral home.

House Approves Draft Extension

Votes Truman Power to Mobilize Reserves

WASHINGTON —(U.P.)— The house, spurred by the Korean crisis, overwhelmingly approved a one-year extension of the present draft law Tuesday but similar action was blocked in the senate until today.

The house voted 315 to 4 in favor of a compromise agreed to by senate-house conferees in less than an hour.

In addition to continuing the present draft law until July 9, 1951, it gives Pres. Truman new power to order the reserves and national guard to immediate active duty.

Sen. Democratic Leader Scott W. Lucas, Illinois, sought immediate senate action to send the bill to the White House, but was headed off by Sen. James P. Kem (R-Mo.), who objected to giving the president power to induct youths when congress is not in session.

The senate then agreed instead to vote on the compromise at noon, CST, today.

The compromise does not give Mr. Truman the three-year extension of the existing law he sought. But it removes restrictions on his power to induct men which both houses voted.

The conferees substituted a one-year extension of the existing law

(Continued on Page 2, Column 8)

Reds Call Truman's Move 'Aggression'

President Orders American Planes, Ships into Defense of South Korea

BULLETIN

LONDON, Wednesday —(UP)— Radio Moscow, quoting Pravda, official organ of the Communist party, today branded Pres. Truman's declaration sending military assistance to the embattled South Koreans a "direct act of aggression" against the Communist North Korean government and the Chinese Communist regime.

The broadcast was Russia's first official reaction to Mr. Truman's order.

(From United Press, Associated Press)

WASHINGTON — Pres. Truman late Tuesday sent a stiff note to Moscow demanding that Russia stop the Korean war shortly after he had ordered American combat planes and warships into the battle to save South Korea.

The state department dispatched the note as American forces under command of Gen. Douglas MacArthur went into shooting action to rescue South Korea from invasion by Russian-controlled North Korea.

Contains Warning

The note made it plain the United States believes Moscow has power to halt the invasion and was said to have added a warning that unless the Kremlin acts at once, Russia must take full responsibility for what happens in Korea.

Mr. Truman also ordered more American troops rushed to the strategic Philippines and more aid for Red-menaced Indo-China.

Tuesday night the Soviet-boycotted United Nations (UN) security council followed up the American action by calling on all UN members to join the United States in sending arms to hurl back the Red invasion of South Korea.

First Time in History

It was the first time in history that a world organization has imposed military sanctions against an aggressor.

The president moved swiftly and dramatically under Sunday's UN mandate to all UN members to come to the rescue of South Korea if Russian-controlled North Korean troops refused to pull back behind their own border.

"This they have not done, but on the contrary have pressed the attack," Mr. Truman said in a bluntly-phrased, 400-word statement. **"In these circumstances I have ordered United States air and sea forces to give the Korean government troops cover and support."**

'Beyond Subversion'

He said he took the far-reaching action because "Communism has passed beyond the use of subversion to conquer independent nations and will now use armed invasion and war."

After the president's orders had gone out the state department dispatched the note to the Russian government urg-

(Continued on Page 2, Column 6)

War News at a Glance

WASHINGTON — U. S. sends stiff note to Moscow demanding Russia stop war in Korea; Truman orders U. S. planes, ships to defense of South Korea. **(Story, Page 1.)**

LAKE SUCCESS — United Nations security council, in its first military sanctions, votes 7 to 1 to support U. S. plan to give military aid for defense of South Korea. **(Story, Page 1.)**

TOKYO — South Korean army reports it has driven Communist invaders out of Seoul. **(Story, Page 1.)**

WASHINGTON — House votes overwhelmingly to extend draft law for another year; gives Truman new power to order national guard and all reserves to immediate active duty. **(Story, Page 1.)**

LONDON — Truman's decision to meet force with force in Korea brings first reaction of approval from non-Communist Europe. **(Story, Page 1.)**

WASHINGTON — Draft of sweeping war powers law authorizing Truman to clamp freeze on prices, wages, manpower, and materials reported in readiness for war emergency. **(Story, Page 1.)**

WASHINGTON — Truman's decision to throw planes and ships into defense of South Korea wins swift approval in congress. **(Story, Page 2.)**

NEW YORK—"War scare" trading gives stock market busiest day since 1939. **(Story, Page 8, Sec. II.)**

Truman's Decision Wins Applause in Western Europe

LONDON —(AP)— Pres. Truman's decision to meet force with force in Korea brought a first reaction of applause from non-Communist Europe Tuesday night.

Prime Minister Clement Attlee announced that Britain would support in the United Nations (UN) security council the United States policy of firmness against Communism in the Far East.

The announcement in the packed house of commons drew gasps, a few seconds of stunned silence and then a roar of approval—from both the Labor and opposition benches.

In Rome an Italian foreign ministery spokesman said the Washington action was "timely and necessary."

Draft of Sweeping War Powers Law Reported Ready

WASHINGTON —(AP)— The draft of a sweeping war powers law, authorizing Pres. Truman to clamp a sudden freeze on prices, wages, manpower, and materials, is in readiness for any war emergency.

A spokesman said the National Security Resources Board (NSRB), charged with the planning of industrial mobilization, believes the standby "master plan" is up to date and ready for any demands.

Upon the declaration of a national emergency, Mr. Truman would hand the 20-title bill to congress.

The actual language of the act is confidential, but its general terms are known. The manpower title has been called "very extreme."

U. S. Evacuation Ship Reported in Distress

TOKYO, Wednesday—(U.P.)—The Japanese maritime security board reported today that an American ship with 600 evacuees from South Korea was in distress in heavy seas.

No other information was immediately available.

Boyle's, Sachtjen's Action in Zone Changes 'Questioned' by Attorneys

Propriety of recent action by two city councilmen in pressing zoning ordinance changes sought by relatives or clients was questioned unofficially Tuesday by several members of the Madison bar.

Both Councilmen William C. Sachtjen and Ted C. Boyle are lawyers. And a cardinal principle in the lawyers' code, according to fellow attorneys, is that **"you can't represent both sides of an issue."**

As councilmen, they pointed out, the two lawyers represent the city, and lawyer members of the city council, boards and commissions, often in the past have refused to vote on issues in which they or their firms had any possible interest.

On two recent zoning ordinances before the city council, however, Boyle in one case and Sachtjen in the other, neither disqualified him-

SACHTJEN BOYLE

initiative in favor of the change.

Two weeks ago the council, on Sachtjen's motion, rejected a non-favorable recommendation by the plan commission and adopted an ordinance changing property on Packers' ave., owned by Carl Sachtjen, uncle of the councilman, from Residence "A" to Commercial-"B".

in relation to the property, but took responsibility for the assurance that "a suitable planting strip" would be developed between the intensive commercial zone and the highly restricted residential lots immediately adjoining.

The plan commission, in its report, had restated its policy opposing abrupt transitions from restricted residential to intensive commercial zones unless they are separated by a protective barrier.

Boyle took the "advocate" role in another zoning action last Friday night.

The ordinance provided for two zoning changes.

One section would rezone a lot in the 2900 block on University ave., just east of the Home Lumber and Improvement Co. The other would change a lot on

Wherry Blocks Quick Vote on Arms Aid Bill

WASHINGTON —(AP)— Senate Republican Leader Kenneth Wherry of Nebraska Tuesday blocked administration efforts to speed action on the $1,222,500,000 arms aid bill which contains a $16,000,000 allotment for Communist-invaded Korea.

Wherry objected when the Democratic chieftains tried to win an agreement to set the showdown vote today.

After a conference with his GOP colleagues, Wherry said later that he had no objection to setting a voting time for Thursday or Friday.

Besides the Korean arms share, the bill will provide $1,000,000,000 for the Atlantic pact nations, $131,500,000 for Greece, Turkey,

France Rushes Move to Form New Cabinet

PARIS—(AP)—Pres. Truman's orders for active military aid to Korea shoved domestic issues in the French political crisis into the background Tuesday night.

Deputies of the Radical Socialist party adopted a resolution urging former Premier Henri Queuille, one of their number, to form a "government of public safety."

The phrase carries implications of great emergency.

Only an hour before, Queuille had given up his attempt to form a government when the Socialists refused to join a cabinet headed by him.

JOURNAL FEATURES

Some See Threat, Others Do Not

City Hopes It Won't Mean War

By JOHN R. PRINDLE
(State Journal Staff Writer)

News of the Korean crisis was received by Madison residents with different reactions.

Some saw in the United States support of Southern Korea a definite threat of war.

Others saw no such threat.

All agreed on one point — the hope that the action taken by American forces would not mean another war.

A housewife, Mrs. Elizabeth Woods, 3908 Paunack ave., probably voiced the fear of all mothers who have sons of draft age.

Asked her reactions to the Korean crisis, her

MRS. WOODS

much about the developments as yet.

"I hate to think about it," she said.

"I hate to think about all the boys of draft age, and of all those who just came back from the last war."

Asked if she saw a threat of another war, she said:

"No, I don't think so. But the news scared me. And of course I hope there will be no more war."

T. B. Peterman, realtor, was emphatic in his criticism of the handling of the whole Far Eastern situation.

"Another case of too little, too late," he said of the Korean situation.

He said "we just weren't on the job in Korea. A regiment of marines could have stopped the whole thing."

"On a recent trip to Washington state, he said, "I saw 22 aircraft carriers and I don't know how many other naval vessels tied up

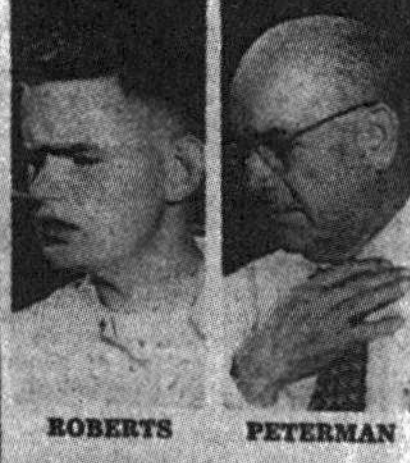

ROBERTS PETERMAN

should be. But they're not worth a damn where they are."

Mrs. Jerome Bartelme, 2910 Hauk st., housewife and native of Australia, said she felt America "did not have much option but to send aid to Korea," since it is obligated to do so under the UN.

Getting Cool Again
MADISON WEATHER
Cloudy and cool today. Sunday partly cloudy and continued cool. High today, 65; low tonight, 50. Sun rose, 5:29; sets, 6:07.

Wisconsin State Journal

Dial 6-3111 SECTION 1, MADISON, SATURDAY, SEPTEMBER 16, 1950 ★ ★ ★ Dial 6-3111

Morning Final
PRICE FIVE CENTS
16 PAGES, TWO SECTIONS
Vol. 178, No. 65 111th Year

8TH ARMY OPENS OFFENSIVE; GIs HIT INLAND FROM INCHON

Speed Unified West Defense, Use Reich Forces, U.S. Urges

Pact Members Get Revolutionary Plan to Defend Europe Against Aggression

NEW YORK—(U.P.)—Secretary of State Dean Acheson late Friday asked the 12-nation North Atlantic treaty council to approve a revolutionary "single package" plan for a powerful combined European defense force, including Western Germany.

Acheson called on the Western European powers to designate national contingents to be integrated into an international force to defend Europe against aggression.

Soon as Possible

The plan calls for a single supreme commander. The military force would be equipped at the earliest possible moment.

The secretary of state at a secret meeting of the 12 foreign ministers who constitute the treaty council argued that he saw no alternative but to use West German troops in the total defense force.

Authoritative sources said Acheson put the plan on the conference table for approval without reservation on any point.

Not As Ultimatum

But it was said he did not present the "single package" as an ultimatum.

Details of the American plan were being sent to foreign ministers representing Canada and 10 Western European nations.

Acheson pointed out to the first day's meeting that the American proposal constituted a complete revolution in American foreign policy.

He told the council that Pres. Truman's commitment for "substantial" American troops increases in Europe would be followed by the earmarking of addi-

(Continued on Page 2, Column 4)

Congress Clears Marshall's Move

GOP Loses Fight for Civil Control

(From Associated Press, United Press)

WASHINGTON — Congress overrode stormy Republican protests Friday night to approve a special law permitting Gen. George C. Marshall, a lifelong soldier, to take over the civilian post of secretary of defense.

Both house and senate passed a special bill waiving—for Marshall only—a provision of the 1947 unification law which forbids appointment of a military man to the defense secretaryship.

The house acted first by a vote of 220 to 105. The senate followed suit a few hours later, 47 to 21.

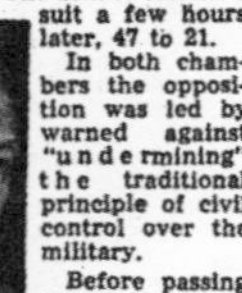

MARSHALL

In both chambers the opposition was led by warned against "undermining" the traditional principle of civil control over the military.

Before passing the bill, the house by voice vote adopted an amendment saying the appointment should not be a precedent for naming military officers to the cabinet post.

While the measure now goes to the White House, the senate still must confirm Marshall to succeed Louis A. Johnson, who resigned under pressure Tuesday.

Johnson's resignation is effective next Tuesday and, barring a hitch, Marshall should be con-

(Continued on Page 2, Column 1)

Hailstone Barrage Rips at Million Dollar Clip

JOPLIN, Mo. — (AP) — A barrage of large hailstones ripped through rooftops and windows, causing an estimated $1,000,000 damage early Friday.

The storm lasted about 10 minutes, hitting the city in two waves.

Allied Attacks Put Korean Front Ablaze

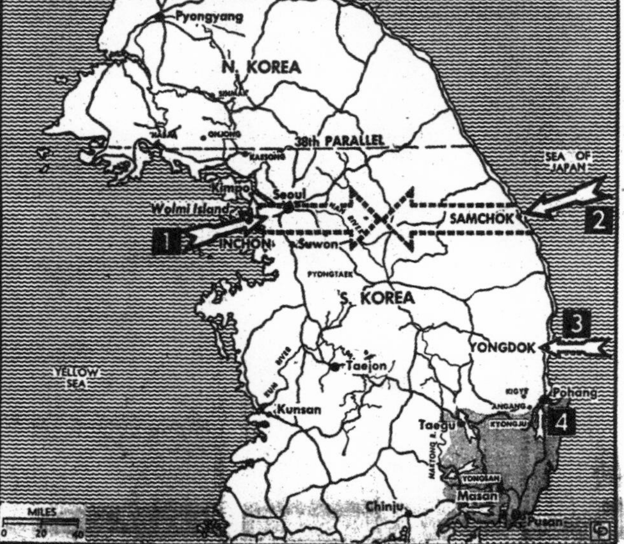

Allied troops struck out from their southeastern Korean beachhead lines (shaded) today in a general offensive timed with the big amphibious assault at Inchon (1), only 22 miles from Seoul, Red-held South Korean capital.

At Inchon the 10th army corps was driving inland in an attack aimed at slicing across the enemy's deep rear (broken arrows).

The massive amphibious assault coincided with the shelling of the Eastern port of Samchok (2) by the U.S. battleship Missouri and other Allied landings at Yongdok (3) and at a point only a few miles north of Pohang (4). International).

The giant U.S. battleship Missouri got into the Korean fighting for the first time Friday, uncovering her 16-inch guns to blast the Communists at Samchok (see map above), 95 miles north of Pohang.

The Mighty Mo sped secretly 11,000 miles from Norfolk, Va., to hit the East coast of Korea in a blow timed with the American landing at Inchon on the West coast. (International.)

Hollister Firm Sold; To Leave City Soon

Hollister, Inc., 303 E. Wilson st., one of Madison's oldest specialized industries, will discontinue its operation in Madison soon, company officials revealed Friday night.

Stuart J. Myers, president of the Meyers Laboratories, Warren, Pa., has purchased the controlling stock of the medicine-manufacturing firm.

The business will be moved to Warren.

Before the change in ownership Joseph L. Starr was president and secretary of the company and James D. Starr was vice-president and treasurer.

The business became widely known for its product—Hollister Rocky Mountain tea.

The firm was named after A. H. Hollister, its founder, who started in Madison in 1867. Joseph D. Downing and C. Henry Bernhard were later brought in as partners.

Governor Calls Big-City Heads for Civil Defense Plans Meeting

For speedy development of municipal defense plans of Wisconsin's larger cities, Gov. Rennebohm Friday invited mayors and city managers to attend a civil defense planning conference at the capitol Friday, Sept. 29.

The top city officials and their defense deputies or future deputies will meet with Col. Ralph J. Olson, state director of civil defense, at 10 a.m. in the assembly chamber.

Acting City Manager George Forster said that he will attend the conference, but that he had no idea of who would be chosen as defense assistant for Madison.

RENNEBOHM

Gov. Rennebohm sent his invitation to the officials through Col. Olson.

"The meeting is designed as a springboard guide for speedy development of municipal defense plans," according to the governor.

Col. Olson's letter acknowledged that municipal officials are "generally waiting for further instructions" in development of defense plans, and said that Gov. Rennebohm recognizes "the necessity for immediate planning action with all possible assistance from the state director."

Olson will present a suggested outline for development of plans, coordinating state policy with that to be announced by the National Security Resources board during the week of Sept. 25.

The meeting will be for officials of communities having 10,000 or more population. Smaller municipal areas will be similarly assisted as soon as possible, Rennebohm said.

City, 2 Railroads Sign Agreement on Law Park Crossing

Acting City Manager George Forster announced Friday that he has signed, together with executive officials of the North Western and Milwaukee railroads, an agreement authorized by the city council for establishment and protection of a crossing into Law park at Broom st.

The agreement, signed by C. H. Buford, president, for the Milwaukee road, and R. W. Carlton, assistant to the president of North Western, also calls for closing and barricading of the present S. Hamilton st. temporary crossing.

The two railroads also pledged to join the city in a petition to the state Public Service Commission (PSC) to order automatic crossing protection and to apportion the cost, 50 per cent to state funds and 50 per cent to the railroads.

Under the mutual plan, the city will install a 40-foot bituminous pavement across the tracks. The Milwaukee road will provide a flash signal on the west side of S. Broom st. and the North Western another on the east side.

JOURNAL FEATURES

14,261 Register at U.W.—10% Less Than Last Year

A total of 14,261 students had registered for classes at the University of Wisconsin late Friday afternoon, Registrar Kenneth Little reported.

He said the figure is about 10 per cent less than the number registered at the same time last year.

The major drop was in the number of undergraduates. Graduate registration was 200 over last year's mark.

Little estimated that the total university registration figure will be about 15,500 students on the Madison campus.

About 1,025 are expected to enroll in extension centers throughout the state and another 1,800 are expected at the center in Milwaukee.

Hickenlooper Delays O'Dwyer Confirmation

WASHINGTON —(AP)— An objection by Sen. Burke Hickenlooper (R-Ia.) Friday delayed senate action on the appointment of former Mayor William O'Dwyer of New York City as ambassador to Mexico.

Sen. Scott Lucas of Illinois, the Democratic leader, served notice he will bring up the nomination Monday.

Hickenlooper objected to approval of the nomination by unanimous consent, although he said he was ready to go ahead with consideration of it. However, the necessary motion to bring it up Friday night was not made, and his single objection was enough to hold up action.

4 Big, New Ships to Be Fitted as Troop Transports

WASHINGTON — (U.P.) — Four passenger vessels, including the 48,000-ton luxury liner SS United States, will be fitted out as troop transports, the maritime board disclosed Friday.

The other three are 13,000-ton combination passenger-cargo vessels — the Presidents Jackson, Hayes, and Adams — being built for American President lines.

The United States, being built with the other ships under government supervision, will be equipped to carry 12,000 troops and the smaller vessels from 2500 to 3000 each.

The announcement said the change in plans was made on request of the defense department on recommendation of the joint chiefs of staff

Two other vessels being built for American Export lines will be finished as commercial passenger ships as originally planned.

Wake Up With a Smile

From Roundy

Traffic officers in Madison should get a raise.

Standing on the corners in Madison and ducking cars is a dangerous occupation.

(Read Roundy's Column on today's Sport Page.)

Allies Start Giant 'Nutcracker' Attack

UN Drive Out of Southern Beachhead Begins Closing Huge Pincers on Reds

(From United Press, Associated Press)

TOKYO, Saturday — American forces swung the second blow of their one-two punch against Communist Korea today.

In a general attack perfectly coordinated with the 10th army corps' amphibious assault on Inchon and Seoul to the north, Allied troops smashed out of their southeastern Korean beachhead lines to carry out their part of the gigantic "nutcracker" offensive.

American and South Korean troops, backed by tanks, planes, and artillery, struck the Reds from the south end of the beachhead for more than 70 miles up to and beyond Taegu.

Aim for Seoul

Swinging over to the offensive a day after Gen. Douglas MacArthur personally directed amphibious landings at Inchon, the ground forces sought to tear the line to pieces and send spearheads 165 miles northwestward toward Seoul.

A late dispatch from Taegu in the northwest corner of the beachhead said American troops had gained 3 miles in that sector.

MacArthur's 10th corps assault landing quickly penetrated the port of Inchon, 22 miles west of Seoul. The general's aim was to seize supply routes there and clamp a vice on the Reds.

A flagship dispatch this morning said reinforcements were pouring into the scene of Friday's landings after the first waves quickly seized all objectives and swept east of Inchon ahead of schedule.

(A naval spokesman in Washington estimated the total force involved at upwards of 40,000.)

The marines hit their first major resistance near Sogam-Ni, 4 miles east of Inchon, and called up Pershing tanks to break up the North Korean strongpoint.

By noon today the leathernecks had captured all but the small southeastern flank of the 7-mile-long Inchon peninsula while a South Korean marine brigade cleaned out Communist stragglers.

Directs Operations

Tanks and artillery were put ashore to support the operations under personal direction of Gen. MacArthur.

By 6:48 p.m. Friday, a little more than an hour after

(Continued on Page 2, Column 2)

War News at a Glance

TOKYO — Allied troops smash out of southeastern Korean beachhead lines in general attack coordinated with amphibious assault on Inchon; MacArthur begins fashioning gigantic "nutcracker" offensive to crush Reds. (Story, Page 1.)

NEW YORK—Atlantic pact members receive revolutionary U.S. plan for speedy unified defense of Western Europe using Western German forces. (Story, Page 1.)

WASHINGTON — Congress overrides GOP protests to approve special law permitting Gen. George C. Marshall to take over civilian post of secretary of defense. (Story, Page 1.)

MADISON — Gov. Rennebohm calls mayors and managers of Wisconsin's larger cities to civil defense planning conference Sept. 29. (Story, Page 1.)

WITH U. S. SECOND DIVISION—Two U. S. sergeants tell how Communist soldiers threw at least three wounded, screaming American prisoners into roaring bonfire. (Story, Page 1.)

WASHINGTON — Mobilizer W. Stuart Symington threatens to seize stocks and publicize names of "unpatriotic chiselers and profit hogs" who are hoarding rubber and other vital commodities. (Story, Page 2.)

Britain Uncovers Red Sabotage Plot

LONDON — (AP) — The Labor government declared Friday it has uncovered a developing Communist plot to sabotage Britain's defense build-up with a series of lightning strikes.

Labor Minister George Isaacs said British Reds are aiming their first blows at the docks, the transport system, and the nation's meat supplies.

Shaw Has Setback; Specialists Worried

LUTON, England—(U.P.)—George Bernard Shaw, recuperating from surgery to reduce a broken left thigh, Friday suffered a setback caused by an old kidney ailment.

Specialists were said to be anxious about his condition.

Shaw, 94, had been progressing remarkably from the operation, performed Monday, the day after he fell in his garden at nearby Ayot St. Lawrence.

U.S. Sergeants Tell How Reds Threw 3 Wounded, Screaming GIs in Fire

WITH THE SECOND DIVISION, IN KOREA—(U.P.)—Two U.S. sergeants said Friday that they saw Communist soldiers throw at least three wounded, screaming American prisoners into a roaring bonfire.

Sgt. Lester Marcum, Vaughns Mill, Ky., and Sgt. Max H. Stephan, Greeley, Colo., were among the defenders of a command post overrun by the Reds Aug. 31.

They witnessed the atrocity from different points, but their stories were essentially the same.

They saw the Communists heap up some captured American blankets and pup tents. Gasoline or some other fuel apparently was used to make the fire hotter, and soon the flames were leaping 20 feet in the air

The Reds threw the pleading prisoners into the fire and then pushed on after the main body of retreating American troops.

Marcum was in command of a crew of nine Americans and four South Koreans manning a gun 200 to 300 feet from the command post.

He and his men lay low in their partly-concealed position when the Reds poured in. They were not seen But Marcum had a clear view of what was going on.

He watched the Communists start the fire.

"It appeared gasoline was used to make the blaze bigger," he said. "It was a helluva big blaze.

"The enemy then took up the wounded GIs who couldn't withdraw, and threw them into the fire," he added.

"I personally saw them throw three American soldiers into the fire. I know they were Americans because they were screaming 'don't do it! don't do it!'

"I am positive from the screams I heard that more than three soldiers were thrown into the fire," Marcum said.

Stephan led an infantry squad in the defense of the command post. He and his men were forced to withdraw.

About 150 feet from the post, Stephan's feet became tangled in some wire. While trying to get free, he saw the Communists start the fire.

"The fire was about 10 feet wide, but the flames went 20 feet in the air," he said.

"Two North Koreans carried the first American up to the fire, where a third joined them to help throw him in."

"Two more North Koreans, holding a GI upright between them, walked up to the fire," he added. "I heard the GI scream, 'don't!'

"One Korean slugged the GI with something and he sagged between the two Communists. Then he was thrown in the fire," Stephan said.

He saw a third American being carried toward the fire, but he had seen all he could stand and he turned away without seeing if the third man was thrown into the flames.

The Season's Here

MADISON WEATHER

Partly cloudy and much colder tonight through Thursday. Mostly cloudy and continued cool Friday. High today 50, low tonight 35. Sun rose 6:34, sets 4:49.

Wisconsin State Journal

Dial 6-3111 SECTION 1. MADISON, THURSDAY, NOVEMBER 2, 1950 ★ ★ ★ Dial 6-3111

Morning Final

PRICE FIVE CENTS

32 PAGES, TWO SECTIONS

Vol. 179, No. 133 111th Year

TRUMAN ESCAPES ASSASSINS; GUNMAN, GUARD DIE IN BATTLE

Here Are First Pictures of Attempted Murder of President

Shots Stop Gunman on Steps; Wounded Officer Removed

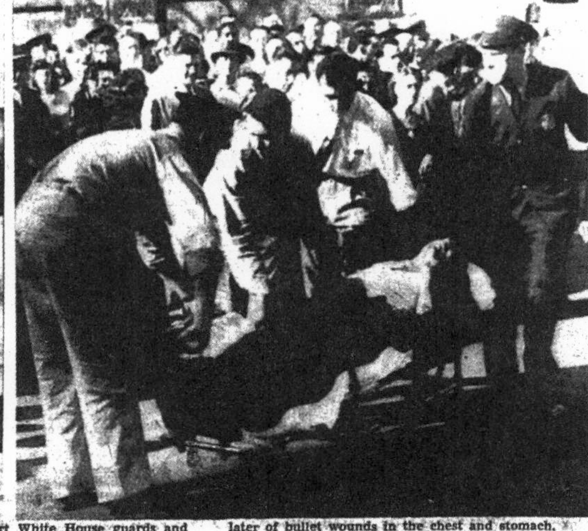

Wounded in Wednesday's furious gun battle, Oscar Collazo, would-be presidential assassin, is shown at the left, crumpled at the bottom of the steps leading to Blair House, Pres. Truman's temporary residence.

Collazo's Puerto Rican companion, Grisselio Torresola, was killed as alert White House guards and secret service agents turned blazing guns on the pair.

At the right, Leslie Coffelt, one of the guards, is shown being removed from the shooting scene on an ambulance stretcher as spectators watch. Coffelt died later of bullet wounds in the chest and stomach.

Two other guards were wounded in the fight.

Mr. Truman was awakened by the shots and saw part of the battle from an upstairs window. (AP Wirephotos). (More pictures, Page 2).

Alert Agents Shoot Puerto Rican Pair

President Witnesses Part of Fight; Two Officers Wounded at Blair House

(From United Press, Associated Press)

WASHINGTON—Pres. Truman escaped possible assassination by minutes Wednesday when two Puerto Rican revolutionaries were brought down in a wild gun battle on the president's Blair House doorstep.

One of the would-be assassins and a White House guard were killed in the shooting. The other assailant was wounded but was expected to live.

One gunman went down stretched out across the bottom of the mansion's steps. The other fell amid shrubbery nearby.

Thus Mr. Truman escaped the fate of Presidents Lincoln, Garfield, and McKinley, all of whom died of assassin's bullets.

Two other guards were wounded in the shooting affray, but both were expected to live.

Under Heavy Guard

The wounded Puerto Rican, Oscar Collazo, 37, of New York, was under heavy police guard at a hospital and will face a murder charge.

Killed in the maniacal attempt to storm the doors of the president's home was Collazo's friend and fellow New Yorker, Grisselio Torresola, alias Lorenzo Angelina Torresola, reputed American leader of the rabid Puerto Rican Nationalist splinter movement.

White House Guard Leslie Coffelt, who heroically stood his ground in the path of the gun-brandishing assailants, died at 5:19 p. m. (CST) while undergoing emergency surgery for bullet wounds in the chest and stomach.

Guard Joseph Downs was in critical condition with a bullet wound in the neck, and Guard Donald T. Birdzell was in fair condition with wounds in both legs.

Both to Recover

But Brig. Gen. Wallace Graham, the president's personal physician who supervised their treatment, said both "are going to pull through."

There was a report Washington police were seeking a third man identified tentatively as "Francisco Alonzo" in connection with the attempt.

He was believed to have tried to see Mrs. Truman earlier this summer and uttered a threat when ejected by police.

The secret service admitted only that they were "checking" on the

(Continued on Page 2, Column 2)

Assailant's 'Pleased' Wife, 12 Others Held

MRS. ROSA COLLAZO

(AP Wirephoto)

(From United Press, Associated Press)

NEW YORK—Officers with guns drawn Wednesday night arrested two men trying to enter the apartment of one of Pres. Truman's would-be assassins, raising to 13 the number of persons picked up here since the shooting in Washington Wednesday afternoon.

Eleven Puerto Ricans, including the wife of one of the assailants, already had been arrested on charges connected with the attempt to kill the president.

Wife Not Sorry

Mrs. Rosa Collazo, 40, whose husband Oscar lay wounded and under police guard in Washington, told secret service agents that she was not ashamed of what her husband had done, or sorry for it.

She was held under $50,000 bail.

Two detectives and a secret service man were inside the apartment of Oscar Collazo when the two callers knocked on the door. Guns leveled, the officers arrested the callers.

One of the men had in his pocket a letter written on stationery of the Puerto Rican Nationalist party, the officers said.

Another Shooting Solved

While agents rounded up the 13 persons, a shotgun blast in the East Bronx wounded four Puerto

(Continued on Page 2, Column 6)

Officers Step Up Security Plans for Saturday Talk

ST. LOUIS, Mo., —(UP)—Police and secret service agents late Wednesday began revising security plans for Pres. Truman's visit Saturday in the light of the Blair House shooting.

Mr. Truman is scheduled to make his only political address on behalf of Democratic candidates before next Tuesday's election.

Police Chief Jeremiah O'Connell said he would meet with secret service men today to discuss what additional security measures were needed

Police of East St. Louis, Ill., and military authorities at Scott Field, Ill., where the president's plane will land, were making similar plans. Mr. Truman will reach Scott Field late Saturday.

CARE Office Aid to Reuss Charged

Democrat Challenged on Story by Thomson

MILWAUKEE — Henry S. Reuss, Democratic candidate for attorney general, is "shamelessly using the facilities of the CARE organization in Milwaukee in his political campaign," Vernon W. Thomson, his Republican opponent declared here Wednesday night.

Speaking to a South Side armory audience here, Thomson charged that the Milwaukee office of CARE, a nation-wide charitable organization which sends relief packages overseas "has been operating as a political headquarters" for Reuss.

"The lights have burned in the CARE office far into the night while workers prepare, bundle, and mail out campaign literature in behalf of the Democratic candidate," Thomson said.

"Thus have the contributions of public-spirited citizens, concerned with the welfare of poverty-stricken war victims in Europe and Asia, been used for political purposes by the Democratic candidate for attorney general," Thomson charged.

Thomson challenged Reuss to deny that he knew the facilities of the CARE office were being used in his behalf. He said there was "no question" that they were being used with Reuss' "knowledge and consent."

"The people of Wisconsin are entitled to know how Henry Reuss has been able to divert the facilities of CARE to his own political ends," Thomson declared.

"They have a right to know whether the local and national officials of CARE sanction this sort of activity.

"CARE is an organization supported by public donations — contributions which come from citizens of every national origin, every religious creed, and every political party.

"It is disgraceful that the standards of political morality of Henry Reuss are so low that he would turn the CARE office into a political headquarters."

Thomson said he hoped **"this disgusting exploitation of an extremely worthy organization"** would not hurt its usefulness in Wisconsin.

To City, the Machine Doesn't Make Cents

BELLINGHAM, Wash. —(AP)— City employes hoped Wednesday they had stopped one inflationary trend.

A coin-wrapping machine was being repaired. It was putting 55 pennies into a 50-cent roll.

Where President Viewed Scene

Blair House Entrance

Police Booth

Path Of Torresola, Slain Gunman

Path Of Collazzo, Wounded Gunman

A

B

Dotted lines mark routes of two Puerto Rican revolutionaries who tried to storm Blair House in an attempt to assassinate Pres. Truman Wednesday.

One of the gunmen, Grisselio Torresola, was killed as he approached (A) from the west by gunfire from booth at right.

The other gunman (B) Oscar Collazo, fell wounded at foot of stairs (cross).

Pres. Truman peered out of the window to see what the shooting was all about but was quickly waved back by guards.

One guard was killed and two were injured during the melee. (AP Wirephoto)

'That's Real Shooting,' Cabby Says

(From United Press, Associated Press)

WASHINGTON — Persons who were near the scene of the Blair House gun battle Wednesday saw the action this way:

Mae E. Hayes, Arlington, Va., an official of the Association of American Railroads, was in a taxi that has just stopped at 17th st. and Pennsylvania ave.

"Suddenly I heard what I thought was a backfire," she said.

"That's no backfire, lady," her driver said. **"It ain't movies, either. That's shooting for real."**

Charles Corte, an Acme news photographer:

"I was leaving the White House in an automobile with other photographers when I heard the firing.

"I saw one officer kneeling in the middle of Pennsylvania ave., shooting toward the Blair House. After about 10 or 12 shots were fired, the shooting stopped. The policeman was lying on his back in the street when it was over.

"Pennsylvania ave. was a madhouse. Hundreds of people were scattering for safety in every direction."

Archie B. Davis, owner of the White-Way Sightseeing Co., who said he was walking in front of the White House when it started:

"I saw a policeman run into the middle of Pennsylvania ave., flop flat on top of the car tracks, and begin shooting at a civilian in front of Blair House.

"The civilian was running from the center of the house toward a patrol box at the west corner of the building. As he ran he fired at another White House policeman.

"As the civilian tried to jump a hedge in front of Blair House, he was caught by slugs and sprawled over the hedge."

Grover Ensley, staff director of the house-senate economic committee, who said he saw part of the battle from a window in the old state department building directly across Pennsylvania ave.:

"I saw one of the guards back away from the front of the house, firing as he went at one of the gunmen who seemed to be part way up the steps of Blair House when he was dropped.

United Givers' Fund Hits 89% of Goal

A total of $313,265 or 89 per cent of the United Givers' Fund goal of $346,642 has been collected or pledged so far in the drive, it was reported Wednesday night.

Campaign Chairman Oscar G. Mayer, Jr., said Wednesday night that pledges are coming into the givers' fund office in such large numbers that there is a very strong possibility that the goal will be reached.

"We cannot over-emphasize the fact that if our goal is not reached, the services of the 21 Fund member agencies will have to be cut," Mayer said.

With less than one day remaining in the drive, volunteers are urged to complete their solicitations and get all reports to the campaign headquarters, 16 S. Carroll st., by 4 p. m. today.

The final campaign dinner will be held tonight at Hotel Loraine. All campaign workers are urged to attend and may make reservations by calling the fund office, 7-2228.

Shooting Pictured as 'Revenge' Move

SAN JUAN, P. R. — (U.P.) — Grisselio Torresola, would-be presidential assassin killed by secret service men, may have sought personal revenge for injuries suffered by his sister and brother here during this week's revolt, it was learned Wednesday night.

Police identified Torresola as a brother of Doris Torresola, personal secretary to National party leader Pedro Albizu Campos. She was wounded during Nationalist party rebellion here on Monday and Tuesday.

JOURNAL FEATURES

Puerto Rican Chief Sees Link to Reds

SAN JUAN, Puerto Rico — Gov. Luis Munoz Marin declared Wednesday night that the assassination attempt on Pres. Truman makes him more certain Communists are taking part in Nationalist party revolutionary actions here.

He telephoned Pres. Truman to express personally the "joy of the Puerto Rican people" that the president was unharmed in Wednesday's assassination attempt, the governor's office announced.

The announcement said Mr. Truman told the governor the facts of the situation in Puerto Rico were well undestood in Washington and that the island would in no way suffer in the eye of the American people.

Munoz said that the people of Puerto Rico are "profoundly indignant of this criminal attempt" and that "we would feel highly shamed if we did not know that those carrying out these acts constitute a very small minority of our people."

LATEST

Puerto Rico 'Rebels' Leader Captured

SAN JUAN, Puerto Rico, Thursday — (UP) — National policemen poured five heavy volleys of rifle and pistol fire into the home of Pedro Albizu Campos early today and captured the Nationalist party leader when he fled into the street.

Law in Hospital After Heart Attack

James R. Law, 2011 University ave., chairman of the state highway commission, is in "good" condition at Methodist hospital, officials there reported Wednesday night.

He was taken there about a week ago after a heart attack.

George Bernard Shaw, Famed Irish Playwright, Dies at Age of 94

(From United Press, Associated Press)

AYOT ST. LAWRENCE, England, Thursday—George Bernard Shaw, one of the greatest playwrights of all time, died early today at the age of 94.

The long and incredible drama of his life came to its close in his red brick Victorian mansion "Shaw's Corners" some seven weeks after he slipped on the pebbly border of his garden and fractured h's thigh.

His housekeeper Mrs. Alice Laden came to the gate and told waiting newsmen "Shaw is dead."

She said death came at 4:59 a. m. (10:59 p. m. Wednesday CST.)

Ironically it was not the fracture that caused his death. Astounding his doctors, the Irish wit's "brittle bones," as he called them, knit perfectly after an operation despite his great age.

But the shock of his fall stirred into fatal activity a latent kidney bladder infection that might otherwise have lain dormant for years.

Last Sept. 11, Shaw was taken from this tiny village—where he wrote many of the plays, essays, and ideas that stirred the whole world—to Luton Dustable hospital.

After an operation on his thigh he underwent two operations for his kidney bladder. With the infection and its discomfort went

GEORGE BERNARD SHAW

(Continued on Page 2, Column 8)

Wisconsin State Journal

Morning Final
PRICE 5 CENTS
26 PAGES, TWO SECTIONS

Dial 6-3111 SECTION 1. MADISON, WEDNESDAY, APRIL 11, 1951 ★★★ Dial 6-3111

Vol. 180 No. 11 112th Year

TRUMAN FIRES MacARTHUR; RIDGWAY NAMED SUCCESSOR

House Places UMT Plan on Stand-By Base

Marshall Appeal for Setup Ignored; New Quota Starts

(From United Press, Associated Press)

WASHINGTON—The house ignored an 11th hour appeal from Defense Secretary George C. Marshall late Tuesday and voted against setting up a universal military training (UMT) program at this time.

On a series of voice votes, the chamber approved amendments to its UMT-draft bill which would put the training program on a stand-by basis and require passage of another law when, and if, congress decides UMT should go into effect.

Outright Kill Asked

A proposal by Rep. Graham A. Barden (D-N.C.), which would kill UMT outright may come up for a vote today.

The Barden bill would keep the draft alive another three years—as would the administration bill—but would make no mention of UMT.

The Barden bill also parts company with the administration measure on two other points; it would keep the draft age at 19 instead of lowering it to 18½, and would raise the term of service from 21 to 24 months, instead of 26.

Agree to Commission

At the end of the day, with all actions tentative, the expressed attitude of the house was this:

Pending a chance to vote outright against UMT in any form, it will agree to setting up a five-man commission to draft a UMT plan which would be meaningless until implemented by a subsequent law; it favors providing for a national security training corps but won't approve inducting any youths into it until another law is enacted.

MARSHALL

Shortly before the vote, Marshall urged congress to give the administration a free hand in setting up UMT whenever it thinks the world situation calls for it. He told a news conference he was afraid congress would "emasculate" the training program.

Simultaneously, the defense department set up a new quota system for assigning recruits to the

(Continued on Page 2, Column 2)

8 Die as Plane Trying to Pick Up Glider Falls

FAIRBANKS, Alaska —(U.P.)— An air force C-54 Skymaster attempting to pick up a glider on a training mission crashed and exploded on Ladd field here Tuesday, killing the eight crewmen aboard.

Capt. Joe Worthington, Ladd field public information officer, said the four-engined plane swooped down to snatch up the glider and that the nylon cable attached to the plane wound itself around the "elevator" to which the glider was attached.

The big plane then smashed into the ground and burst into flames, sending up a giant cloud of black smoke.

Names of the victims were withheld pending notification of next of kin.

Wake Up With a Smile

From Roundy

If the Indians ever have a reunion in Madison they'll come up Williamson street for sure.

That street ain't been fixed since they left.

(Read Roundy's Column on Today's Sport Page).

Tobey Recording Quotes Truman's 'Threat,' Withdrawal on RFC Fees

(From Associated Press, United Press)

WASHINGTON — Sen. Charles W. Tobey (R-N.H.) was quoted Tuesday night as saying Pres. Truman called him up and tried to intimidate him by saying the White House "had the goods" on various congress members in connection with Reconstruction Finance Corp. (RFC) loans.

Later, however, the president was reported to have talked to Tobey a second time and to have withdrawn the charges he had made against the legislators.

Highly placed congressional sources said Tobey told a senate subcommittee that he had made recordings of both conversations with the chief executive.

Tobey made the disclosures at a secret meeting of the RFC investigating subcommittee headed by Sen. J. William Fulbright (D-Ark.), it was learned.

Meanwhile, White House Aide David K. Niles and former Sen. Burton K. Wheeler identified themselves Tuesday as the men who made moves interpreted by Sen. Tobey as an effort to interfere in the RFC investigation.

Each of the two, interviewed separately, said that word went to Tobey through Wheeler that Donald Dawson, another White House official, is a "good guy" and the senatorial investigators ought to "go easy" on him.

SEN. CHARLES W. TOBEY

BURTON K. WHEELER

Both denied there was any effort to apply pressure.

Sen. Tobey said at a news conference Tuesday night, however, that the way he interpreted it, **"the White House palace guard"** tried to interfere in a senate inves-

(Continued on Page 2, Column 3)

Sidewalks Voted in Midvale Area

Council Committee Endorses Proposal

By RUSSELL B. PYRE
(State Journal Staff Writer)

A recommendation that sidewalks be ordered "as needed," throughout the Sunset Village-Westmorland area, was voted unanimously Tuesday night by the city council committee of the whole.

The resolution was offered by Councilman Henry E. Reynolds after a heat-charged hearing, which packed the council chamber

(Other Council Stories, Page 12)

to overflowing, showed an almost equal division of sentiment among property owners in the new Midvale school neighborhood.

The recommendation which will go to the council for final approval Friday night provides that work proceed as soon as possible on the "grid pattern" sidewalk program proposed by 500 petitioners.

And, at the suggestion of Councilman Franz Haas, it specifies that walks be constructed on both sides of S. Owen dr. this year.

Under the plan as approved, the

(Continued on Page 2, Column 4)

Still Wet Outlook

MADISON WEATHER

Mostly cloudy and cooler with occasional showers today. Partly cloudy and cooler tonight and Thursday. High today 44; low tonight 28. Sun rose 5:23! sets 6:35.

Veterans' Leaders Urge Adoption of Bonus Bill

Leaders of veterans' groups urged adoption of a veterans' bonus bill but some individual veterans and members of taxpayer groups opposed it at a hearing in the assembly chambers Tuesday afternoon.

Veterans' leaders said the pay-as-you-go bonus would not call for new taxes, and would not require a new administration agency. They said the bonus would be paid in 20 years when veterans would be at an age when they might need help.

Opponents Call It 'Insult'

Opponents of the bill charged it was "an insult to veterans to buy their patriotism," and that the plan was "inflationary" and would reduce the veterans' housing fund.

The bonus bill would give 350,000 World War II veterans $10 for each month of domestic and $15 for each month of foreign service, with payments ranging from $50 to $500.

The bonus would be paid in 1971 but heirs of veterans who died would be paid sooner.

The bill would be financed by one-quarter of the state liquor tax, repayments of veterans housing loans, and all funds over $5,000,000 in the veterans housing fund. It would end the housing loan program by 1971.

Roang Estimates Cost

Sverre Roang, Edgerton, said the bill satisfied all veterans' groups. Roang spoke for the Wisconsin Veterans council representing nine veterans organizations.

Roang told the assembly veterans and military affairs committee the bill would cost $113,000,000 if it covered veterans in service between Sept. 16, 1940, and Sept. 3, 1945. If the coverage were extended to June 30, 1946, he said it

(Continued on Page 2, Column 5)

News Strike Ends at Sheboygan Press

SHEBOYGAN —(U.P.)— The Sheboygan Press and the American Newspaper Guild signed a new contract Tuesday afternoon, ending a brief strike by some 33 Guild members in the newspaper's editorial, advertising, and circulation departments.

The new contract continues the union shop, A. Matt Werner, associate editor, said. A dispute over the union shop provision precipitated the walkout. Some workers walked out Monday and others joined them Tuesday and picketed the plant.

The newspaper continued publication during the strike.

The new contract, retroactive to Feb 1, includes a wage increase.

Judge Gives Lecture to Suit the Occasion

VICKSBURG, Mich.—(AP)—Circuit Judge Raymond W. Fox addressed a student audience at Vicksburg high school Tuesday on "Crime and Punishment."

While he was speaking in the auditorium, a thief broke into the principal's office and made off with cash and bonds valued at $100.

Ex-Policeman Held for Trial in Death After Tavern Fight

William Ott, 24, of 115 S. Bassett st., Tuesday afternoon was bound over to circuit court for trial on fourth degree manslaughter charges growing out of the Mar. 25 death of Martin A. Parkinson, 59, of 330 W. Wilson st.

His $750 cash bail was continued.

Superior Judge Roy H. Proctor ordered the ex-policeman held for trial after hearing an eye-witness account of the tavern scuffle in which Parkinson was fatally injured.

Thomas H. Burke, 424 N. Paterson st., a restaurant employe, testified at Ott's preliminary hearing that he was in the men's room of the Shamrock bar, 117 W. Main st. on the night of Mar. 18 and saw Ott strike Parkinson "a rather terrific blow on the head with his right fist." (Parkinson died at a Madison hospital a week later.)

He said that Parkinson was floored as a result of the blow and that Ott looked down at him and said "I guess he's out."

In response to questioning by Don Morris, assistant district attorney, Burke said that Parkinson had not appeared argumentative prior to being struck and that there was "no hostility in his voice" as he spoke to Ott.

Burke said that both men appeared to have been drinking rather heavily.

Defense Atty. William J. Coyne asked Burke how much he (Burke) had had to drink. Burke answered that he had drunk "no more than eight beers."

Dr. John T. F. Gallagher, 4049 Cherokee dr., physician who attended Parkinson during the week he remained unconscious in the hospital, testified that death was due to "hemorrhage and laceration of the brain substance."

He said that Parkinson suffered a skull fracture, but that the fracture was of significance "only in that it indicated that a blow had been struck."

Dr. Gallagher said that a blow on the head could have caused the injuries from which Parkinson died. He said that the autopsy performed after Parkinson's death "proved conclusively that death was due to the head injuries."

County Republicans to Elect Monday

Dane county Republicans will hold their annual meeting and election of officers at 8 p. m. Monday at the Hotel Loraine, Chairman R. W. Peterson, Madison, announced Tuesday afternoon.

Peterson, who has headed the Dane county club for the last two years, said he "definitely" is not a candidate for another term.

The meeting will elect a slate of officers to serve for the next two years, and name delegates and alternates from this county to the state GOP convention at Wisconsin Rapids July 7.

House Votes Startling 44% Cut in Spending

WASHINGTON—(AP)—The house voted a startling 44 per cent $370,298,211 cut Tuesday in the funds Pres. Truman had asked to operate a group of government agencies for the next three months.

He requested $843,463,579. The house approved only $473,165,368. The bill passed on a voice vote and was sent to the senate.

The state department got less than a tenth of the money it asked to build up physical facilities of the "Voice of America" program—$9,533,939 instead of $97,500,000,

UN Air, Artillery Attacks Wreck City of Chorwon

Fanatical Enemy Stems UN Drive on Hwachon Dam

TOKYO, Wednesday — (U.P.) —Allied air and artillery attacks have "completely destroyed" the Chinese Communist headquarters town of Chorwon, but a fanatical stand at the Hwachon reservoir stalled the Allied drive there, front dispatches reported today.

Chorwon, 17 miles north of the 38th parallel, was one of the southern anchors of the enemy's triangular buildup area from which the Reds have been expected to launch a mighty counter-offensive.

Launch 3 Attacks

Hwachon, 29 miles to the southeast, was the other. It was abandoned Monday.

The Communists counterattacked at three points along the front in an effort to stop the Allied drive while heavy resistance slowed Allied efforts to seize the Hwachon reservoir.

A diehard band of Chinese, working within rifle shot of Allied forces less than a mile distant kept open 10 of the 18 Hwachon floodgates Tuesday night, but the Pukhan river carried off the torrent.

Perhaps the biggest battle of the current campaign was in progress below the reservoir and North Koreans launched three counter-attacks to halt the Allied efforts to seize the enormous dam. All three were thrown back.

'Sacrificial Troops'

Chief resistance came from North Korean "sacrificial" troops, however, and the main Chinese force, which abandoned the town of Hwachon Monday, played no role in defense of the dam.

The Communists also abandoned the town of Inje, 11 miles south-

(Continued on Page 2, Column 5)

Girl Dies While Family Attends Brother's Rites

WAUKESHA—(U.P.)—A 2-year-old Waukesha girl died Tuesday afternoon of burns while her family was attending the funeral of the girl's brother, who had drowned.

Rose Washbish, daughter of Mr. and Mrs. William Washbish, was burned when a kettle of boiling water tipped on her last week. Her brother, Raymond, drowned last Friday.

Washbish is being treated at the veterans hospital here.

Panama High Court Voids Banning of Reds

PANAMA, Panama—(AP) — The supreme court of Panama ruled Tuesday in a three-to-two decision that an executive decree banning Communists from public office in Panama is unconstitutional.

Charges He Failed to Back U.S. Policy

Relief of Far East Commands a Climax to General's Outspoken Views on War

WASHINGTON—(UP)—(Wednesday)—Gen. Douglas MacArthur, soldier-hero of two world wars, was fired from all of his Far East commands by Pres. Truman today for not giving his "whole-hearted support" to administration policies.

The 71-year-old warrior who "came back from Bataan" was relieved of his commands in the climax to his outspoken differences on how to wage the Korean war and where and when to meet Communist aggression—on the battlefields of the Far East or in Europe.

Lieut. Gen. Matthew Ridgway, who took over the Eighth army as it was reeling in defeat after the Chinese Communist intervention in November, was designated by Mr. Truman as MacArthur's successor.

Lieut. Gen. James A. Van Fleet, was named to succeed Ridgway as commander of the Eighth army.

No Prior Indication

Mr. Truman's announcement was given to reporters hastily called to the White House at 1 a. m. (EST) this morning. There had been no prior indication from any responsible quarter before that Mr. Truman contemplated firing the illustrious general who commanded the gigantic effort which broke and defeated Japan in World War II.

In relieving the five-star general, Pres. Truman said:

"With deep regret I have concluded that General of the Army Douglas MacArthur is unable to give his wholehearted support to the policies of the United States government and of the United Nations in matters pertaining to his official duties."

The president told the general to turn over his command to Ridgway at once and "travel to such place as you select." Presumably, MacArthur would now return to the United States, on whose continental soil he has not set foot since 1937.

MacArthur was commander of the U. S. forces in the Far Pacific when the Japanese asked for surrender terms.

On Aug. 14, 1945, Pres. Truman designated him supreme commander of the Allied powers to receive the Japanese surrender aboard the Battleship Missouri in Tokyo Bay.

And in that role he continued until this day as the all-powerful head of allied occupation forces in Japan.

Additional Commands

Later he was given additional commands and responsibilities. In

GEN. MATTHEW RIDGWAY

GEN. DOUGLAS MacARTHUR

January, 1947, he was designated commander-in-chief of the American Far Eastern command in addition to his other duties.

When the Korean aggression broke out, Pres. Truman appointed him supreme commander of the United Nations forces in the Far East while retaining at the same time his previous positions.

Then he began the bitter struggle to wrest South Korea from the North Koreans and Chinese Communists, much as he freed the Philippines after those islands had been taken over by the Japanese.

In relieving MacArthur, Pres. Truman said that in view of his responsibilities under the United States constitution and the Unted Nations, "I have decided that I must make a change of command in the Far East."

"I have, therefore, relieved Gen. MacArthur of his commands and have designated Lieut. Gen. Mathew B. Ridgway as his successor," the president said.

Ridgway Named

Lieut. Gen. James A. Van Fleet was named to succeed Ridgway in command of the Eighth army in Korea.

White House release of the announcement was timed with delivery of the president's orders to MacArthur in Tokyo. The orders were transmitted through regular military communications channels.

In addition to the brief orders to MacArthur and Ridgway, the White House released a hitherto secret file of communications between the joint chiefs of staff and MacArthur which, according to Press Secretary Joseph Short, proved that MacArthur "on several instances recently" made statements publicly and privately which made it "questionable" in the president's mind whether MacArthur was in full sympathy with the policies of this government.

President Regrets

The president, in a brief statement accompanying his action, said he regretted having to relieve MacArthur because the general's place in history "as one of our greatest commanders is fully established."

"The nation owes him a debt of gratitude for the distinguished and exceptional service which he has rendered his country in posts of great responsibility," the president said.

"For that reason I repeat my regret at the necessity for the action I feel compelled to take in his case."

'Must Follow Orders'

Mr. Truman supported the idea of "full and vigorous debate on matters of national policy," but he said it was "fundamental" that military commanders follow orders.

Mr. Truman sent a personal order to MacArthur relieving him as "supreme commander, Allied powers; commander-in-chief, United Nations command; commander-in-chief, Far East; and com-

(Continued on Page 2, Column 6)

Tokyo Dumbfounded by Truman's Action

TOKYO, Wednesday — (U.P.) — Pres. Truman's announcement that he had fired Gen. Douglas MacArthur dumbfounded Tokyo today.

"Not now, not not now," Gen. Douglas MacArthur said today when questioned about his discharge from his far eastern command by Pres. Truman.

The announcement came shortly after 3 p. m. when MacArthur and most of his top staff members were absent from their offices.

Telephone circuits to Eighth army headquarters in Korea were jammed and there was no comment immediately available from Lieut. Gen. Matthew Ridgway, MacArthur's successor.

Sickened by Administration Mess, Democrat Walks Out on OPS, Party

WASHINGTON—(AP)— Former Gov. M. E. Thompson of Georgia Tuesday quit as a consultant with the Office of Price Stabilization, (OPS), charging that "official Washington is drifting in a sea of confusion, inefficiency, waste, and extravagance."

Thompson, a Democrat, said that he came to Washington as co-director for territories for OPS.

"Knowing that it was impossible to have two directors for the same job," Thompson said, "I offered to resign and accept another assignment."

But, he added:

"For 12 weeks I have been carried on the payroll as a consultant at a salary plus expense account of $53.48 per day. Yet, during this time, I have been consulted about nothing. I have had no assignment to do anything.

"On Feb. 19 at the White House, I told the president the story up until them. He called Don Dawson (presidential assistant) and instructed him to see that the mess was straightened out immediately. It hasn't been done.

"I am resigning and returning to my home in Valdosta, Ga. I refuse to be a parasite on the American taxpayers."

M. E. THOMPSON
(Acme Telephoto)

Thompson said that there are **"thousands upon thousands of others rendering no service but are on the public payroll, not only in Washington but throughout the United States."**

He charged that no real effort has been made to stabilize prices.

"Even those charged with this responsibility have contributed to the upward surge of prices by deliberately predicting higher prices," he said.

He continued that "thousands of loyal Americans are giving unselfishly of their time to defense work, but their efforts are being nullified by the indecision, bungling, and interference of schem-

(Continued on Page 2, Column 1)

JOURNAL FEATURES

Up to 42 Today
MADISON WEATHER
Partly cloudy and warmer today and tonight. Friday mostly cloudy and mild. High today, 42; low tonight, 23. Sun rose, 7:06; sets, 5:18.

Wisconsin State Journal

Dial 6-3111 SECTION 1. MADISON, THURSDAY, FEBRUARY 7, 1952 ★★★ Dial 6-3111

Morning Final
PRICE FIVE CENTS
24 PAGES, TWO SECTIONS
Vol. 181, No. 121 113th Year

Full Page of Pictures of George VI on Page 3

BRITAIN MOURNS BELOVED KING

New Queen Proclaimed

Elizabeth II Named as She Flies Home to Succeed Father

LONDON, Thursday—(UP)—Britain's Princess Elizabeth today was proclaimed officially Queen Elizabeth II.

The solemn proclamation was drafted by the Privy Council in the tradition-steeped, crimson and gilt salons of St. James palace.

As the council acted, the grief-stricken, 25-year-old daughter of King George VI, who died Wednesday, was flying from Africa en route home from a tragically interrupted holiday near Nairobi, Kenya.

'Queen of This Realm'

The proclamation referred to the new queen as "the high and **mighty Princess Elizabeth Alexandra Mary.**"

She had become, it said, "**Queen Elizabeth the second, by the grace of God queen of this realm and all her other realms and territories, head of the commonwealth, defender of the faith.**"

The proclamation was approved "with one voice and consent of tongue and heart," by members of Lords, the Privy Council, and "other principal gentlemen of quality."

It ended:

"God save the queen."

Approximately 250 notables were present in the banqueting hall of St. James palace — where the first Queen Elizabeth often supped—when the accession council was convened. After the proclamation was read to them, each signed.

To be Read Friday

It was directed that the proclamation should be read on Friday morning first from the balcony of St. James palace, then at Charing Cross.

The colorful procession of heralds and messengers from the College of Arms, escorted by household cavalry with burnished breastplates and helmets, then will proceed to Templar Bar, the boun-

(Continued on Page 2, Column 1)

History Eyes a Boy Ruling Over Nursery

LONDON — (AP) — A chubby little prince scrambled over the nursery floor Wednesday, unaware that the death of his grandfather has made him one of Britain's richest boys — with a legacy of grave responsibility.

Three-year-old Prince Charles, now heir-apparent to the British throne, spent the day much as usual, playing with his small sister Anne in hushed, grief-stricken Sandringham House, the Norfolk mansion where King George VI died.

CHARLES

Court officials could not say whether Charles has been told his grandfather is dead. The prince automatically became the Duke of Cornwall, entitled to the full revenues of the Duchy of Cornwall.

Mostly rents, they probably total around $500,000, but Charles won't see the money. The estates are administered by officials who look after crown property. He eventually will get a fixed allowance instead.

At this stage the little boy's life will not be changed much by his step toward the British throne. It will mean, eventually, that he will be moving with his family from Clarence house, their London home, across the street to Buckingham palace.

One of the immediate effects for him will be to bring his moth-

(Continued on Page 2, Column 3)

King Is Dead; Long Live the Queen

HER MAJESTY, QUEEN ELIZABETH II, NEW RULER OF BRITAIN

His Subjects' Tribute: 'He Was Good Man'

World Expresses Regret as Death Comes to Reluctant Monarch While He Sleeps

(From Associated Press, United Press)

LONDON—Britain's steady, beloved monarch, King George VI, who never had wanted the throne, died quietly Wednesday in his sleep.

It was a price the ailing king, 56, had known he might have to pay for shunning the wheel chair his physicians had recommended, and for continuing to shoulder the cares and duties of government.

With his death, his eldest daughter became Queen Elizabeth II, Britain's first woman ruler since Victoria reigned 51 years ago.

'He Was a Good Man'

She sobbed when she heard the unexpected news in Kenya, East Africa, one of the remnants of the once mighty British empire, but set out at once for home and the responsibilities of the throne.

The king's death plunged Britain and the Commonwealth into mourning.

His passing was a profound shock to 50,000,000 Britons and 560,000,000 subjects elsewhere.

Britons the length and breadth of the islands wept and paid their monarch tribute in five simple words: "**He was a good man.**"

Flags all over the world dipped to half staff. Even the Russians made this gesture of respect in Berlin.

15 Turbulent Years

George's reign spanned 15 years of turbulent history. He saw Britain lose much of the empire upon which, it had once been said, the sun never set. He saw it come to austerity, privation, and near bankruptcy.

He saw his countrymen stand against and help to conquer the bloody thrusts of Hitler and Hirohito.

For his own part, he refused to leave embattled England with his gracious queen, Elizabeth, and their two daughters, Elizabeth and Margaret.

Worn and wearied by persistent illness, he died at the royal estate of Sandringham where he was born 56 years ago.

His valet, John MacDonald, discovered the body when he took the king his usual early morning tea.

Queen Elizabeth and Princess Margaret were immediately awakened and told the news, and a radio message was dispatched to Princess Elizabeth in Kenya on a royal tour. The news was given to the world some three hours later.

It came as a shock, even though it was widely known that he was not in good health. Only Tuesday he had been rabbit hunting on the Sandringham estate, and there was no hint that his condition was any worse than usual.

Blood Clot Blamed

Coronary thrombosis—a blood clot—was believed to have been the immediate cause of death. Last September surgeons removed the king's cancerous left lung. Two years before that, he underwent an operation to relieve a circulatory ailment in one of his legs. His face was haggard and lined in recent months, and his condition had caused concern to his subjects.

The king, chafing at enforced inactivity, refused to adhere to the slow, steady walking paces suggested by his doctors.

He kept his schedule of appointments and insisted on

(Continued on Page 4, Col. 1)

KING GEORGE VI

World Flags Fly at Half Staff for King

(From Associated Press, United Press)

Much of the civilized world joined Britain Wednesday in mourning for gallant King George VI.

Men and women of every color and creed paid tribute to the modest monarch whose simple devotion to duty through 15 troubled years won him the respect and admiration of millions.

President Truman expressed the feelings of many in a message of sympathy to the British people. He termed the king "**a world personage who maintained the highest traditions of the English constitutional monarch.**"

He asked God's blessing on the new queen, Elizabeth, who was a guest of the Trumans in Washington only last fall.

"God bless Queen Elizabeth and may her father's exemplary memory provide the courage and inspiration she will need in the great responsibilities that lie before her," Mr. Truman said in a public statement.

The President also sent private message of condolence to the new queen, her mother, and her grandmother, Queen Mary.

The Russians limited their reaction to the king's death to a broadcast report that said only: "King George VI died."

On Washington's Capitol hill, the House adjourned early out of

(Continued on Page 2, Column 4)

Picadilly Darkened as Mourning Symbol

LONDON —(UP)— The blazing lights of London's Picadilly Circus were turned off Wednesday night as a symbol of mourning for King George VI.

Slag Blast at Gisholt Burns Crane Operator

LeRoy Poole, 1437 E. Main st., crane operator at the Gisholt Machine Co., suffered several second and third degree burns on his arms and legs in an accident at the plant late Wednesday afternoon.

He was taken to St. Mary's hospital where his physician reported he was in "excellent condition" Wednesday night.

Poole was injured when moist said, used to cool the bottom doors of a huge boiler plate melting pot, exploded slag and coke residue.

The sand evidently contained some moisture which ignited the slag, blowing coals into the crane cab, some 35 feet high, where Poole was sitting.

Fire Inspector Joseph Tisserand, who was near the plant at the time, said the accident was "just one of those things" and that no one was to blame.

JOURNAL FEATURES

Broadcast Leads Nation in Prayers

LONDON —(UP)— The British Broadcasting Corp. (BBC), Britain's government radio network, broadcast a short service for King George VI Wednesday night.

Listeners were invited to join in prayers for the late monarch and the royal family.

Bogus Check Artist Picks Perfect Dupe

HOUSTON—(AP)—A liquor store dealer reported to police Wednesday he was $75 loser to a man who passed a phony cashier's check.

The victim's name: Joe Loser.

'Nervous' Gunmen Rob Dodge County Bank, Get $1,000

ASHIPPUN, Wis. —(UP)— Two nervous young men, possibly the same ones who robbed a bank seven miles from this Dodge county village last year, brandished pistols at employes of the Ashippun bank and fled with about $1,000 they scooped from a cash drawer Wednesday.

The armed robbery was the sixth bank stickup in Wisconsin since last October. It was the fifth rural bank held up during the same period.

The robbers, between 18 and 20 years old according to Sheriff Herbert Schwantes, hastily cleaned out the cash drawer but avoided the safe where there was "much more" money.

The sheriff said the robbers fit the description of a pair who held up the Neosho State bank of about $500 Dec. 12. They, too, cleaned out the cash drawer and left before tackling the vault. And in both robberies, the men had the same type guns, Schwantes said.

The official said he believed the bandits were the same pair that held up a grocery store and tavern at Lomira about 31 miles southwest of here Tuesday night. That robbery netted $138.

The last Wisconsin bank robbery was nine days ago at Edmund, about 95 miles southwest of here.

Arson Suspected as Boy Tied to Bed Is Saved from Fire

FOND DU LAC —(AP)— A fire which destroyed a Fond du Lac county farm home and barn "definitely is a case of arson," Dist. Atty. Eugene McEssey said Wednesday night.

Eddie Blake, 4, who McEssy said was tied with a rope to a bed on the first floor of the house, was carried out unconscious by his father, Charles Blake. The mother, 30, was rescued by a neighbor.

The blaze occurred Wednesday morning on the farm rented by the Blakes near Campbellsport. The boy was revived at a hospital after being overcome by smoke. His mother also was hospitalized for treatment of smoke inhalation.

Both are guarded by a sheriff's deputy.

McEssey said the boy told him "mommy tied me." McEssey said Mrs. Blake related she could not remember what had happened before or during the fire.

Blake told authorities he was doing chores outside when a neighbor shouted that the house and barn were afire. Blake said he ran to the house, found his son tied to a bed and carried him outside.

Another neighbor, Francis Schulteis, found Mrs. Blake unconscious on the first floor and took her to safety.

Ex-Madison Newsman, T. M. Reay, Dies at 48

Thomas Morgan Reay Sr., 48, former Madison newsman, died Wednesday of a heart attack at his desk in the office of the LaSalle, Ill., Daily News-Tribune where he was managing editor.

Reay, who attended Wisconsin State college at La Crosse and the University of Wisconsin, was employed on the Madison staff of the United Press several years ago. He covered the famous oil trials for the United Press in Madison. He was editor of the Jefferson County Union, Ft. Atkinson.

Reay is survived by his widow, the former Elvira Allen, who was formerly of Madison, a son, Thomas Reay, Jr., a daughter, Jane Elizabeth; his father, Dr. George R. Reay, and a brother, Dr. G. D. Reay, both of La Crosse.

3,115 Enroll as U.W. Registration Opens

More than 3,000 graduate students, seniors, and juniors were enrolled in the University of Wisconsin Wednesday as registration for the second semester got under way, the registrar's office announced Wednesday night.

A total of 2,640 juniors and seniors enrolled, the office said, along with 425 graduate students.

Enrolment for the new term is "better than expected," an official said, running almost even with the same period last year.

Today the remaining juniors will register, along with portions of the sophomore class. Freshmen will register later in the week.

Total enrolment for the new term is expected to go over 12,500, the official said.

U. W. Awards Honorary Citations to 6 for Agricultural Leadership

BY ROBERT C. BJORKLUND
(State Journal Staff Writer)

For their leadership in American agriculture, six persons, including two from the Madison area, were awarded the University of Wisconsin's honorary recognition citations Wednesday night.

At the recognition banquet, attended by 500 persons in the Memorial Union, Pres. E. B. Fred awarded the citations after they were read by R. K. Froker, dean of the college of agriculture.

The banquet was a feature of the 1952 Farm and Home Week program.

The citations went to:

Arthur J. Gafke, Ft. Atkinson, as an outstanding farmer and rural leader.

Fred A. Stare, Columbus, for his contributions to the canning industry in Wisconsin.

Mrs. Emma Mathis Engel, Fountain City, as an outstanding homemaker and youth leader.

W. H. McNeight, Unity, for his activities as a farmer, service in community development, and leadership in civic improvement.

F. E. McGillivray, Milwaukee, president of the Milwaukee stock yards, for work in live stock marketing, education, and finance.

Ezra Taft Benson, Salt Lake City, Utah, nationally recognized leader in the field of farmer cooperatives.

Benson, who was main speaker at the banquet, called rural people

(Continued on Page 2, Column 6)

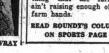

McNEIGHT STARE BENSON MRS. ENGEL GAFKE McGILLIVRAY

Wake Up With a Smile
From Roundy

From the shortage of help on the farms one thing that the farmer ain't raising enough of is farm hands.

READ ROUNDY'S COLUMN ON SPORTS PAGE

FAT BOY'S DIET
Have Fun Losing Weight!
By Elmer Wheeler

Better hurry and send for your Calorie Chart! They're going fast. Elmer shed 40 pounds after he started using his slide rule calorie chart—and you can too.

Turn to the women's page for the next installment of this hilarious series and find out how you can get one of the Fat Boy's Calorie Charts. It's in . . .

Today's Wisconsin State Journal

Trays, Questions Loaded

You Go to Yugo Press Conference

(Twentieth of a Series)

By ROY L. MATSON
(State Journal Editor)

BELGRADE, Yugoslavia—The Yugoslavians—black-booted, red-striped panted, epauleted generals, drably-dressed Communist party-leaders, and government functionaries—filed in along one side of the room.

We — 14 visiting American editors and writers — were herded down the other.

We stared at each other.

Then suddenly a battery of Klieg lights flared up, we blinked, and the newsreel cameras started to grind, sweeping along our ranks, then pushing right up to the noses on our faces. I wonder what the subtitles will say in the movie-houses next week.

Then, at 10 o'clock in the morning, the white-coated waiters swept in, huge trays loaded. Yes, you guessed it, with the inevitable slivovitz.

Oh, no, not again!

Not now!

Oh, yes, and the Yugos grasp the glasses eagerly, motion us to do likewise, and toss them off, bottoms up.

More waiters rolled in, laden with sandwiches, ham, pickles, cake, slugs of hard cheese, and big bottles of almost-black beer.

The press conference, Yugo style, is about to begin.

A pretty female translator called upon each of us to introduce himself and identify his home. She explained that we might take a choice of method, either moving about informally, drinking slivovitz, or taking chairs and conducting a formal question-an-answer period.

We hastily chose the latter.

Mostly to relieve an embarrassed and confused silence, I put the first question.

The leading general sputtered out an answer accompanied by a dirty look, both of which, translated, meant that he considered my

(Continued on Page 2, Column 2)

California, Here We Come!

Smell Those Roses!!! *Blue Streak Edition* Smell Those Roses!!!

From Rain to Snow
MADISON WEATHER
Rain today, snow tonight and Wednesday, with a possibility of 6 inches of snow by Wednesday night. High today 40, low tonight 35. Sun rose 7:03, sets 4:27.

Wisconsin State Journal

DIAL 6-3111 SECTION 1. MADISON, TUESDAY, NOVEMBER 25, 1952 ★★★ DIAL 6-3111

Morning Final
PRICE FIVE CENTS
30 PAGES, THREE SECTIONS
Vol. 183, No. 55 113th Year

ROSES' SCENT BOWLS OVER CITY

Kohler, Students Sing Praise to Thee, Wisconsin

Gov. Walter Kohler Joins 1,000 Rallying University Students in Singing [illegible] 'Varsity' at Capitol Monday —Gary [illegible] photo

6-Inch Snowfall May Cloak City

Pileup Possible by Wednesday

(Seven Injured in Mishaps, Story Page 2.)

What the weatherman called "typical winter storm" began moving into the Madison area Monday night and he said the rain and snow mixture would continue all day today with a possibility of an accumulation of 6 inches of snow by Wednesday.

The high forecast today was 40 and the low tonight 35.

A cold snap pulling temperatures down Wednesday was predicted by the weatherman who "cautiously" estimated that by that time the storm would have dumped 6 inches of snow over this area.

Statewide, the forecast called for rain or snow today with up to 10 inches falling in the southeast Wednesday.

Charts at the Truax Field weather bureau indicated the center of the storm, which formed in Texas,

(Continued on Page 2, Column 6)

'We'll Be Underdogs' in Rose Bowl, Ivy Says

"I definitely think we'll be underdogs," but "we can play the kind of a game that won't discredit the Big Ten."

That was the word Monday afternoon from Coach Ivy Williamson after his University of Wisconsin football team, co-champion of the Big Ten, was named to face undefeated Southern California in the Rose Bowl Jan. 1.

IVY WILLIAMSON —AP Photo

We'll "Slug It Out"

Williamson, who hit the [illegible] in his fourth year as Badger mentor, told the final 1952 meeting of the Herald-American's Quarterback club in Chicago that Wisconsin would "stay in there and try to slug it out" with the Pacific Coast conference champions.

"Southern California is a very sound and well-drilled team," Williamson said. "I'd like to see them and we'll have scouts on their game with Notre Dame."

Williamson returned to Madison Monday [illegible] to "rest a while" before beginning preparations for the post-season classic.

Meet Saturday

The Trojans play Notre Dame at South Bend Saturday, but Williamson said he didn't know whether he would see the game personally. He said scouting the game would not violate any agreement between the conferences.

Southern California has had Mel

(Continued on Page 2, Column 5)

Transit Offices Swamped Here

Special Trains, Flights Planned

Anxious Badger football fans by the hundreds plagued Madison transportation officials with requests for reservations to the West Coast Monday long before the announcement came that the University of Wisconsin got the Rose Bowl bid.

And by Monday night harried train and airline officials here were wondering if they would be able to get enough equipment to handle the expected mass exodus of Rose Bowl bound fans out of Madison.

One thing was sure. Railroad passenger agents in Madison announced at least four special trains will be made up in Madison to take care of the Badger rooters.

"Reasonable assurance" was given that special airline flights also would be made to Los Angeles.

Several business, civic, and fraternal organizations were planning to organize special trips and rail and airline officials were awaiting word on meetings before making final requests for special equipment.

H. G. Marsh, Madison ticket agent for [illegible] Western Road, said [illegible] definitely have at least two special trains leaving from Madison and maybe three." He said "it will depend on how many Madison organizations set up trips."

More than 50 individuals made reservations through Marsh [illegible] day and these were [illegible] for

(Continued on Page 2, Column 1)

Madison, UW Join Hands to Celebrate Badgers' Bid

Big 10 Vote Reported as 7 to 3

CHICAGO (AP) — Wisconsin became the Big Ten conference choice Monday to face Southern California in the Rose Bowl New Year's Day—reportedly by a 7-3 vote of the conference athletic directors.

The split, contested vote between two teams—tied for the championship and both eligible for bowl participation—was unprecedented.

The directors, whose decision in the past has been announced as unanimous, Monday selected Wisconsin over co-champion Purdue for the Pasadena classic.

Wisconsin, winding [illegible] a 21-21 tie against Minnesota, and Purdue, with a closing 21-16 victory over Indiana, [illegible] posted league records of winning four games, losing one and tying one.

It was the wildest wind-up in Big Ten history after a season of tremendous upsets. [illegible] teams were bidding for the title on the final day.

Kenneth L. (Tug) Wilson announced Wisconsin as choice of the [illegible] Monday after tabulating [illegible] votes [illegible] "what team best would represent the Big Ten in the Rose Bowl."

The voting margin was not revealed but there was strong speculation that Wisconsin had at least a 7-3 edge.

Wisconsin's co-championship with Purdue [illegible] the Badgers first title taste in [illegible] years.

Wisconsin, with an overall season record of 6-2-1 compared with Purdue's 4-3-2, will carry the Big Ten's hope of remaining all-victorious in the Rose Bowl.

It was believed that the Badgers' better overall record was an important factor in the selection.

Wisconsin beat Marquette, 42 [illegible], Illinois 20 to 6, Iowa 42 to 13, Rice 21 to 7, Northwestern 24 to [illegible] and Indiana 37 to 14, lost to Ohio State 23 to 14 and UCLA 20 to [illegible] and tied Minnesota 21 to 21.

In the six games played since

(Continued on Page 2, Column 7)

Don't Order Your Tickets Yet, U.W.'s Aspinwall Pleads

Don't order your Rose Bowl tickets yet!

That was the plea Monday of William Aspinwall, University of Wisconsin athletic ticket director, whose office was flooded with hundreds—yes, hundreds—of calls after news of Wisconsin's Rose Bowl selection "leaked out" about [illegible] Monday morning.

"We haven't had time to get things in order," Aspinwall said, "and when machinery for filling orders is set up in about a week, an announcement will be made as to when orders will be accepted."

Several phones in the ticket office were ringing steadily from Monday morning until 4:30 p.m. it was reported, and all callers wanted Rose Bowl information.

Aspinwall said students would be allowed tickets at half price, but added that "they will have to be picked up in Pasadena on New Year's Day."

He said priorities for other persons with university connections will be announced when everything is ready, "but not until."

"We'll let you know when," he [illegible]

New Year's Day News Kicks Off Parade, Rally

By WARREN [illegible] JOLLIMORE (State Journal Staff Writer)

The sky was red (for Wisconsin and roses) over Madison Monday night as the city and university joined hands to celebrate the selection of the Wisconsin Badgers as the Big Ten representative in the New Year's Day Rose Bowl football classic against Southern California in Pasadena.

The biggest celebration in Wisconsin athletic history [illegible] touched off Monday morning when news "leaked out" [illegible] Western Conference athletic directors named Wisconsin on the first ba[illegible]

Kenneth (Tug) Wilson, Big Ten commissioner, announced the decision, but did not reveal the margin by which the Badgers gained the bowl [illegible]

By the time the decision was made official at noon [illegible] ticket offices of Madison railroads already were being besieged with phone calls from anxious fans a[illegible] reservations to Pasadena.

Parade Starts

A giant — but orderly — parade of university students started up State St. from the campus about 10:30 a.m. Monday, a few minutes after the news had leaked out. It started out with Stan [illegible]itgen, drum major of the university football band, and some 30 band members leading a handful of cheering students.

By the time the parade reached the capitol and the [illegible] had induced Gov. Walter Kohler to leave a budget [illegible] a Rose Bowl victory for Wisconsin, the number had increased to almost a thousand.

And the band played on.

It was the happiest crowd that ever graced the steps of the Capitol, the one that stopped there Monday and chanted "We want Kohler, we want Kohler."

The students chanted and they sang and they waited—and Kohler didn't disappoint them.

Gives Victory Sign

He stepped to the first floor balcony above the excited throng and waved a familiar "V for Victory" with his fingers.

"We're all very happy today," he said, smiling. "Purdue's

(Continued on Page 2, Column 2)

Happy Team Also Makes a Resolution

Members of Wisconsin's bruising football team turned "college kids" for a few hours Monday after learning that they had been selected to represent the Big Ten in the Rose Bowl game at Pasadena, Calif., on Jan. 1.

But they took time out from their rejoicing to reflect soberly on the responsibilities which accompanies their honor.

[illegible] Simkowski, strapping [illegible] center, seemed to express the feelings of his team mates.

"Boy, I was right in the middle of that parade all over town to-

SIMKOWSKI BURKS

day," Simkowski said, "and I was cheering the Badgers same as everyone else. That's how I feel about it and that's how we all feel."

Then he paused a minute to think about the game that will be played by the Badgers against Southern California on New Year's day.

"Milt Bruhn will have his line ready for the game, don't worry about that," he said. "They (Southern Cal) will have a heavier line than us, but we'll have 'em on speed."

Other Badger players who were around long enough to comment seemed to feel about the same way.

Archie Roy Burks, stocky senior defensive back, was still nursing a grudge against himself over last Saturday's tie with Minnesota.

"It's a terrific honor for us to go out there," he said, "but it would be a lot nicer if we were

(Continued on Page 2, Column 1)

More News, Photos in Peach

Details on Wisconsin's Rose Bowl Trip Expected at Dinner Honoring Team Tonight, Henry McCormick Writes in Today's Sports Peach.

A Full Page of Pictures of Student, City Reaction to Rose Bowl Selection, Sports Peach.

Southern California Officials, Including Coach Jess Hill, "Happy" with Choice of Badgers, Story, Sports Peach.

A Picture of Coach Ivy Williamson Whiffing Roses at Wisconsin Freshman Football Banquet, Sports Peach.

Purdue, Edged for Bowl Bid, Wires Badgers Congratulations

Scores of congratulatory messages flooded the offices of the University of Wisconsin athletic department after the Rose Bowl announcement Monday.

But one of the most appreciated was a wire from the football players, coaches, and athletic department of Purdue university, co-champions of the Big Ten with Wisconsin and the team over which the Badgers were selected for the Jan. 1 classic.

MACKEY

The wire, signed by Guy Mackey, athletic director at Purdue.

"Congratulations on your Big Ten co-championship and Rose Bowl selection," the wire read. **"We'll be pulling for you at Pasadena on Jan. 1."**

That, from the players, coaches, and officials who had hoped for the coveted Rose Bowl nomination as hard as the Badgers had hoped for it, was a heartwarming message.

Wes Fesler, coach of the Minnesota team which tied the Wisconsin champs last Saturday, also [illegible] congratulations to the Badgers.

"Most sincere and hearty congratulations to you and your champions on their appointment as representatives to the Rose Bowl," Fesler's wire read. **"Our good wishes go to you."**

While players on other Big Ten teams and many Badger fans sent wires to Coach Ivy Williamson's office in Camp Randall stadium, the Badger mentor was not around to read them.

Williamson and Guy Sundt, Wisconsin athletic director, had gone to Chicago to a conference meeting, where they were to learn that Wisconsin was the Western conference's choice to meet Southern California in the Rose Bowl on New Year's Day.

U.W. Band Will Go, Professor Predicts

Hopes of the University of Wisconsin marching band for making the trip to the Rose Bowl were given a big boost Monday night when Prof. Kurt Wendt, Badger faculty representative to the Western conference, predicted that the bandsmen would be in Pasadena New Year's Day.

Wendt made his prediction at the annual "Band-quet" of the Wisconsin football band in the Memorial Union. The event was attended by about 200 persons.

"Although I do not know how such a trip will be financed," Wendt said, "I am willing to go way out on a limb and say that I'm certain that a way will be found to send you to California."

The bandsmen, 150 strong, whooped and cheered at the statement.

It has been estimated that it would take $45,000 or more to send the band to the Rose Bowl. Big Ten bands have made every trip since the pact was signed, always with private financing.

Price Director Resigns with Blast at Congress

WASHINGTON (AP)—[illegible] Woods resigned Monday as price director with a blast at Congress for providing what he termed a weak control law.

Woods said a news conference he had submitted his resignation to President Truman effective at the end of November.

He declined to make his letter of resignation public, saying it was up to the President whether it should be released.

However, he said he had been dissatisfied for some time and decided to quit rather than attempt to administer the price control law as it exists.

"I think the law needs a thorough overhauling," he said. "I think we have a weak law."

FEATURE FINDER

Parade Throws a Block into State St. Traffic

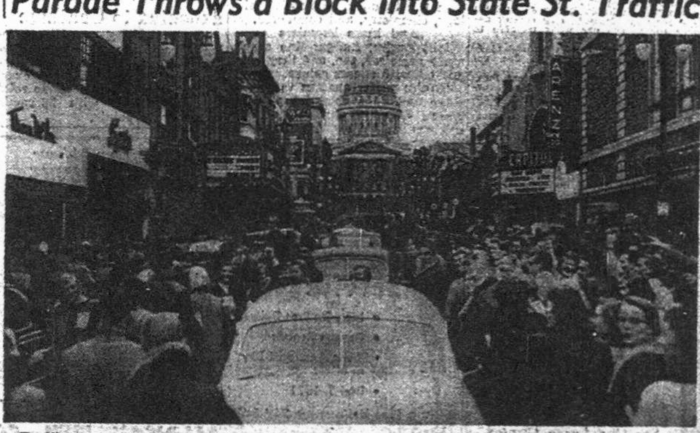

Traffic comes to a standstill on State st. Monday morning as parading university students shout their joy at the choice of Wisconsin as Big Ten Rose Bowl representative.

The jubilant throngs of students are shown as they marched toward the Capitol, where they coaxed Gov. Kohler out of a budget session and into a prediction of Badger Rose Bowl victory.

The photo was taken from the Johnson st. corner of State st. —Associated Press photo

Robinson Injured

BROOKLYN (UP)—Jackie Robinson, Brooklyn third baseman, suffered a pulled muscle in the groin in the seventh inning of Tuesday's game with Pittsburgh and although he had to leave the game, he was expected to return to the lineup today. Billy Cox replaced Robinson.

DIAL 6-3111 MADISON, WEDNESDAY APRIL 15, 1953 SECTION 2, PAGE 7

Games Today in Major Leagues

NATIONAL LEAGUE
St. Louis at Milwaukee
Pittsburgh at Brooklyn
New York at Philadelphia
Cincinnati at Chicago

AMERICAN LEAGUE
Philadelphia at New York
Detroit at St. Louis
Washington at Boston, postponed
(Only games scheduled)

Milwaukee Gets Sizzling Major League Opener

Lemon's 1-Hitter Blanks White Sox

Playing the Game

with HENRY J. McCORMICK

MILWAUKEE — The Milwaukee Braves opened their home big league season here Tuesday afternoon with a game that the capacity crowd will remember for a long time.

The capacity crowd that saw this game will remember it because it is the first home big league game Milwaukee has played in 52 years.

The spectator will remember this game for other reasons, too. They'll remember it because Milwaukee's first big league team since the ill-fated American League entry of 1901 defeated the doughty St. Louis Cardinals, 3-2, in 10 innings.

This was a memorable game for many reasons, and not the least of these is the performance put on by a lanky, fast-moving Negro youngster from Wilmington, Del., named William (Bill) Haron Bruton.

This Bruton is only 23 years old, and this is only his fourth season of professional baseball, but he looks like the goods. That may be too optimistic an appraisal of a boy who has played only two Major league baseball games, but optimism can be excused in the light of what he did in his first two games.

BILL BRUTON
looked even better

At this point, let it be pointed out that Bruton is the fellow who broke up this Milwaukee home opener in the 10th inning with a home run that skimmed out of reach of Enos (Country) Slaughter as he backed up against the fence in right field.

Bruton also hit a single and a triple in this game; he made a brilliant catch of Stan Musial's outfield smash in the eighth to retire the side at a time when the Cardinals had runners on second and third.

Don't get the idea that Bruton was the whole show. But there's no question but that he was the most brilliant part of it.

There was some outstanding work by Sid Gordon in left field for the Braves, and there was some excellent pitching by Warren Spahn.

There were misplays in this game, but it was an intensely interesting game. It had to be to hold most of the capacity crowd right down to the finish, for it was a wind-swept 42 degrees at the start, and it was colder than that at the finish.

The Milwaukee Braves now have played two games and won two games in the National League. They opened at Cincinnati on Monday with a 2-0 triumph, then tacked on the 3-2 victory here Tuesday in Milwaukee's home opener.

Bruton has made five hits in nine times at bat during those two games. He had a single and double in four trips to the plate at Cincinnati, then improved on that here with a single, triple and home run in five times at bat.

The game drew a flock of dignitaries, including Pres. Warren Giles of the National League, Baseball Commissioner Ford Frick, Governor Walter J. Kohler of Wisconsin and Milwaukee Mayor Frank P. Zeidler. Also on hand was Pres. Lou Perini of the Milwaukee Braves.

Gov. Kohler threw out the first ball, his effort being one that will not dim the memory of Christy Mathewson. Then the game got underway.

The dignitaries held the spotlight before "Play Ball" sounded, although there were some coarse remarks from spectators who seemed to be deriving no pleasure from the remarks of the speakers, but once the action began, the players were the center of attention.

Spahn's first pitch to Solly Hemus was called a "ball," and Spahn proceeded to walk him on five pitches. The Cardinals didn't get their first hit until Ray Jablonski hammered a single to right in the fifth inning. Spahn had faced only 13 batters in the first four innings.

Spahn wound up allowing six hits. Jerry Staley of the Cardinals allowed the same number.

There were two unusual double plays that didn't hurt the Braves' chances. The first came in the fifth. Slaughter led off with a walk, first St. Louis batter to get on base since the first man up in the first inning. He went to second when Spahn was charged with an error trying to pick Slaughter off first.

Jablonski crashed a single to right that scored Slaughter. Rip Repulski singled to left with Jablonski moving to second. Del Rice then sent Gordon back almost to the fence in left field for a drive, and Jablonski took off for third. Gordon nailed him there with a perfect peg to complete an unusual and thrilling double play.

The other Milwaukee twin-killing with an unusual twist happened in the sixth inning. Hemus led off with a walk, and took second on Red Schoendienst's sacrifice. Musial's roller then was converted into a double play when Hemus was trapped between second and third and Musial was tagged out trying for second. The double killing was made principally because Hemus fell down and made it possible to the Braves to catch Musial trying to move into second.

Whatever fate may hold in store for Milwaukee in the the National League, fans here never will forget that the Braves moved into first place on opening day and stayed right there the next day.

This was an historic opening day, representing as it did the evidence of baseball's first change of major league alignment in 52 years.

It would be memorable for that reason alone, but it also was memorable for some exceptional pitching and defensive play and for the all-around performance of that wing-footed, strong-armed youngster named Bruton.

Milwaukeeans appreciated Bruton's performance all the more because he played with the championship Milwaukee Brewers of a year ago in the American Association.

Fans will testify that he looked even better as a major leaguer Tuesday than he did last year as a minor leaguer.

And that was pretty good. Bruton's performance had to be exceptional to stand out as it did in an unusually fine game against a background of history.

Hurler Also Homers in 6-0 Cleveland Win

Minoso's Line Single in First is Lone Chicago Safety

CLEVELAND (AP)—Bob Lemon, the highest priced pitcher in baseball, hurled a one-hitter Tuesday as the Cleveland Indians won their opener from the Chicago White Sox, 6-0. Lemon helped put the frosting on the cake with a homer of his own, giving 53,698 fans an extra thrill.

Minnie Minoso's line single to left field in the first inning prevented the Indians' righthander from becoming the first pitcher to hurl an opening day no-hitter since teammate Bob Feller turned the trick against the White Sox in 1940.

Lemon, a 22-game winner last season, hit his home run off Saul Rogovin in the fourth inning. Bob Avila also homered for the Indians in an 11-hit assault against Rogovin, the loser, Mike Fornieles and Gene Bearden.

Only two runners got to third base and only three got as far as second against Lemon, who walked four, struck out three and retired 12 batters in succession between the third and seventh innings.

LEMON

In the second inning, Jim Rivera drew a walk, stole second, went to third on a grounder and was caught in an attempt to steal home. That was the closest the Sox came to scoring.

The Indians bagged a pair of runs in the first inning on four singles off Rogovin.

A pair of homers brought the count to 5-0 in the fourth. Lemon sent one over the right field fence and Avila drove one into the left field seats after Ray Boone had singled.

The Indians' final run was off Fornieles in the fifth.

Box score:

CHICAGO	AB	R	H	CLEVELAND	AB	R	H
Rox,2b	4	0	0	Boone,ss	4	1	2
Fain,1b	3	0	0	Avila,2b	4	2	2
Minoso,lf	4	0	1	Doby,cf	4	1	1
Stephens,3b	4	0	0	Easter,1b	3	0	2
Rivera,cf	3	0	0	Rosen,3b	3	0	1
Mele,rf	2	0	0	Mitchell,lf	4	0	1
Carr'squel,ss	3	0	0	Simpson,rf	4	0	1
Wilson,c	2	0	0	Hegan,c	3	0	0
Rogovin,p	1	0	0	Lemon,p	4	1	1
*-Boyd	1	0	0				
Brearden,p	1	0	0				
Fornieles,p	0	0	0				
Totals	28	0	1	Totals	34	6	11

*-Grounded out for Rogovin in 5th.

Score by Innings

Chicago ....000 000 000—0 1 2
Cleveland ......200 310 00x—6 11 2

E—Wilson, Boone, Fornieles. RBI—Easter, Rosen, Lemon, Avila 2, Simpson. 2B—Rosen. 3B—Boone. HR—Lemon, Avila. SB—Rivera. DP—Carrasquel-Fox-Fain, Avila-Boone-Glyn. Left—Chicago 5, Cleveland 6. BB—Fornieles 1, Bearden 1, Lemon 4. SO—Rogovin 3, Lemon 3. HO—Rogovin 9 in 4, Fornieles 2 in 2, Bearden 0 in 2. R and ER—Rogovin 5-5, Fornieles 1-1. U—Summers, Stevens, Robb, Froese. T—2:23. A—53,698.

Honor Badger Boxing Squad Here Tonight

The annual banquet honoring the University of Wisconsin boxing team will be held tonight at 6:30 in the Crystal ballroom of the Loraine hotel and one of the highlights of the night's program will be the showing of movies of Badgers in action in the National Intercollegiate Athletic assn. (NCAA) tournament last weekend at Pocatello, Idaho.

There will be no principal speaker. Fred Gage, a former Wisconsin football star, will serve as master of ceremonies and will introduce the Badger boxers and Coach Johnny Walsh, each of whom will speak. Walsh will announce the 1954 Wisconsin captain and also will name the winner of the "most improved freshman" award annually presented to a Badger boxer.

The winner of the "Chin Up President" award will also be made known at the banquet. Last year Bob Morgan received the honor.

Tickets for the banquet are priced at $3.50 each and are on sale at the Wisconsin - Felton Sporting Goods and the Ray Nelson Jewelry stores, and also will be available at the door tonight. Ladies are invited to the fete, which again is sponsored by the Downtown Boxing Seconds club.

Pro Hockey Score

STANLEY CUP

Montreal 7, Boston 3 (Montreal leads best-of-seven championship series, 3-1)

More than 36,000 baseball fans jammed the Milwaukee County Stadium Tuesday to watch the Milwaukee Braves open their 1953 home season. The attendance was the largest of the day in the National League and was exceeded in the American League only at Cleveland. The above picture shows a general view of the new stadium in its first official use. United Press-State Journal Telephotos

Happy Braves Hail Rookie Hero Bruton

MILWAUKEE (UP)—It was cold and windy in the Milwaukee County Stadium Tuesday, but red hot in the Milwaukee Braves' dressing room after their win over the St. Louis Cardinals.

Hero of the day was gangling, modest William Bruton, rookie center fielder whose freak home run in the 10th inning gave the Braves their first win before hometown fans.

Bruton's drive out to right field bounced off Enos Slaughter's glove and over the fence for a homer.

"I didn't look to see what the ball was doing," Bruton said afterwards. **"I just kept on running."**

Bruton said he got his four-bagger by hitting a knuckle ball.

Braves Manager Charlie Grimm raced out toward right field when Umpire Lon Warneke first indicated Bruton hit only a double. But "Jolly Cholly" calmed down when the umpire finally ruled the home run.

Cardinals' Manager Eddie Stanky just sat in the dugout.

"I don't argue about home runs," he said.

Cheering teammates pummelled Bruton as they rushed off the field and ran yelling into the dressing room. While players pounded Bruton on the back, Grimm and Braves' President Lou Perini beamed at them from a corner of the room.

"He's a great kid," Grimm said, looking at Bruton. Perini said:

"He's just what we've been needing in center field."

Then Perini jumped up and yelled at the players: **"You fellows were wonderful. This is just the beginning."**

In the subdued Cardinal dressing room, Stanky praised the Braves' performance and predicted the Braves would do much better this year than they had done as Boston's National League representative in 1952.

Slaughter said he missed Bruton's drive because his elbow hit the top of the fence, jarring his arm so he could not make the catch.

Warren Spahn, who pitched all the way for Milwaukee, summed up his teammates feelings about Bruton:

"A great team player."

Solly Hemus Dives Back Safely

Solly Hemus, St. Louis Cardinals shortstop, dives for the base as Milwaukee Braves Pitcher Warren Spahn attempts a pickoff with a snap throw to First Baseman Joe Adcock. The action took place in the first inning of the Braves-Cardinal game at Milwaukee Tuesday. United Press-State Journal Telephoto

Braves Attract Madison Fans to Home Debut

It was a warm, spring day in Milwaukee a couple of hours before Tuesday's baseball home opener started, but by game time the weather had cooled off considerably. These four Madison fans, however, stuck with their straw hats in helping to celebrate Milwaukee's return to the major leagues. They are, left to right, Tom McLaughlin, Bill Wendt, Dick Wilson and Norm Mago.

Canadiens Win, 7-3; Near Puck Crown

BOSTON (UP) — Maurice "Rocket" Richard tallied three goals Tuesday night as Montreal beat the Bruins 7-3 before 13,909 Boston Garden fans to give the Canadiens a 3-1 lead in the best-of-seven Stanley Cup hockey finals.

Boston must now take the last three games to win, two of which will be played on Montreal ice.

By their victory Tuesday night the Canadiens threatened to sweep the series in five games, just as they had in 1946 when these same two clubs met in the finals.

Scoring for Montreal Tuesday besides Richard were Lorne Davis, Dickie Moore, Bernie Geoffrion and Calum Mackay. Boston's goals were credited to Dave Creighton, Milt Schmidt and Jack McIntyre.

Cubs Trip Redlegs on Jackson's Double

CHICAGO (AP)—Ransom Jackson's double off the left centerfield wall in the eighth inning accounted for two unearned runs Tuesday and provided the Chicago Cubs with a 3-2 season opening victory over the Cincinnati Redlegs.

Ken Raffensberger, 35-year-old lefty, had scattered seven hits up to that time and looked as if he could keep the Cubs from their fourth successive opening day triumph.

Sauer Fails

Then third baseman Bobby Adams made a bad throw to second baseman Johnny Temple with Bill Serena's sharp hit. Serena was safe at first and Dee Fondy, who had belted his third single of the game ahead of him, pulled up at second.

The Wrigley Field crowd of 21,222 fans went wild when Hank Sauer, benched with a fracture of the little finger, was sent in to pinch hit. But Raffensberger made him pop out on the first pitch.

Then came Jackson with his winning double that scored Serena and Fondy.

Reds Score on Homers

Bob Rush, the Cubs' righthanded ace who won 17 games last season, and had a 2-1 record over Cincinnati, was the winner, matching Raffensberger's eight-hitter. He was backed up by three double plays.

The Redlegs collected all their hits off Rush in the first six frames, taking a 2-1 lead on a first inning homer by Willard Marshall and another homer hit into the right centerfield bleachers by Ted Kluszewski in the sixth.

The Cubs' other run came in the sixth when Frankie Baumholtz doubled. He went to second on Fondy's single and scored when Serena forced Fondy at second.

CINCINNATI	AB	R	H	CHICAGO	AB	R	H
Temple,2b	4	0	2	Miksis,ss	4	0	1
Adams,3b	4	0	1	Banlholtz,rf	3	1	1
Marshall,rf	4	1	1	Fondy,1b	4	1	3
Klusze'ki,1b	4	1	1	Serena,2b	4	1	0
Greengl'ss,lf	4	0	0	Ward,cf	2	0	0
Bell,cf	4	0	1	**-Sauer	1	0	0
McMillian,ss	3	0	0	Jeffcoat,vf	0	0	0
Seminick,c	2	0	2	Jackson,3b	4	0	2
Raf'berger,p	3	0	1	McCull'ugh,c	3	0	1
				*-Schramka	0	0	0
				Aatwell,c	1	0	0
				Herm'nski,lf	2	0	0
				Rush,p	3	0	0
Totals	32	2	8	Totals	31	3	8

*-Ran into force pla yfor McCullough in 7th.
**-Popped up for Ward in 8th.

Score by Innings:

Cincinnati .... 100 001 000—2
Chicago .... 000 001 02x—3

E—Adams. RBI—Marshall, Jackson 2. 2B — Temple, Jackson. HR—Marshall, Kluszewski. DP — Rush-Fondy; Adams-Temple-Kluszewski; Serena-Miksis-Fondy; Temple-McMillan-Kluszewski; McCullough-Miksis-Fondy. Left — Cincinnati 4, Chicago 7. BB — Raffensberger 3, Rush 1. SO—Raffensberger 5, Rush 5. R and ER—Raffensberger -1, Rush 2-2. U—Barlick, Gore, Jacksoski, Ballanfant. T—2:04. A—21,222.

Glenway, Monona Golf Courses Open

Madison's two municipal golf courses, Glenway and Monona, opened "officially" Tuesday with Mrs. Edna Grant and Mrs. Ruth Clinard purchasing the first two playing tickets. The duo played at Glenway.

Bob Odell Speaker at ESBMA Sports Banquet Thursday

Bob Odell, an assistant football coach at the University of Wisconsin, will be the principal speaker and four members of the 1952 Badger squad that tied for the Big 10 championship and played in the Rose Bowl will be special guests at the East Side Business Men's assn. (ESBMA) banquet for East high school athletes Thursday night. The fete will be staged in the ESBMA club house.

Coaches at each of Madison's five schools also will be guests along with Supt. Phil Falk. The banquet will start at 6:30.

The Wisconsin gridders who will attend are Gary Messner, Wendell Gulseth, Roger Dornburg and Jerry Wuhrman. Gulseth and Messner are East high graduates.

Fathers of East athletes wishing to purchase tickets can do so at East high school or Thursday night at the ESBMA club house.

College Baseball

Notre Dame 8, Iowa 2
Monmouth 5, Augustana (Ill.) 2

Braves Edge Cardinals, 3-2, in 10 Innings

Bruton's Home Run Breaks Up Tight Pitchers' Battle

By MONTE McCORMICK
(State Journal Staff Writer)

MILWAUKEE — A cold, bleak day ushered in the first major league baseball held in Milwaukee in more than half a century, but the wintry blasts off Lake Michigan were tempered by the sizzling battle in County Stadium which saw the Braves win their second straight National League game in as many starts with a 3-2 victory Tuesday over the St. Louis Cardinals in the last half of the 10th.

This was no ordinary major league baseball game for the 34,357 customers who paid their way into the beautiful new stadium; it was the beginning of a new era, and Bill Bruton made it a great day for the Milwaukee rooters when he blasted a home run over the distant right field fence with one out in the 10th inning to decide the game.

Team Opened at Cincinnati

The game was the season opener for the Cardinals, but the Braves made their National League debut on Monday when they played at Cincinnati and defeated the Redlegs, 2-0, on Max Surkont's three-hitter.

Bruton, a spindly-legged Negro with the speed of a gazelle, was the standout player on the field. Bill robbed the Cardinals of hits time and again, once gathering in a hard smash off Stan Musial's bat with men on second and third ready to score.

Bruton collected three of Milwaukee's six hits and scored the last two runs. He put the Braves ahead in the last of the eighth when he tripled over Enos Slaughter's head in right field with two out, and scored later on Sid Gordon's infield hit.

Bruton's home run in the 10th was almost a duplicate of his triple but it carried a little farther. Slaughter raced back fast and got a hand on the drive but couldn't hold it as the ball dropped over the fence for the blast that decided a tight battle and a red-hot pitching duel.

At first Umpire Lon Werneke called the blow a ground-rule double, but after Charley Grimm, the Braves' manager, stormed up to him in protest, Warneke waved Bruton across home plate with the winning run.

First Since 1901

The game marked the first regular major league game in Milwaukee since the city belonged to the American League for one season in 1901.

Milwaukee may not finish high up in this year's National League campaign, but now the Braves are in first place with a record of two victories and no defeats. This was a novel occasion for these Braves in another way; home in Boston last year the Braves never played before a crowd of more than 13,000.

The Milwaukee club took the lead in the second when Joe Adcock scored from first on an infield hit and an error. Joe had just singled when Del Crandall hit a slow roller down the third base line. Ray Jablonski got a slow jump on the ball and threw wild to first, Adcock scoring on the play, but a good throw by big Steve Bilko could have had Adcock at the plate.

The Braves hung tight to that one-run lead until the first of the fifth. Enos (Country) Slaughter walked and took second when Southpaw Warren Spahn tried to nip him off first and threw wild. Jablonski smashed a hard single to center, scoring Slaughter. Rip Repulski lined a singled to cen-

(Continued on Page 2, Sports)

A Great Start

MILWAUKEE—3

	AB	R	H	O	A	E
Bruton, cf	5	2	3	5	0	0
Logan, ss	2	0	0	3	2	0
Mathews, 3b	3	0	0	2	6	0
Gordon, lf	4	0	1	4	1	0
Pafko, rf	4	0	0	4	0	0
Adcock, 1b	3	1	1	8	1	0
Crandall, c	3	0	1	3	2	0
Dittmer, 2b	4	0	0	1	1	1
Spahn, p	4	0	0	0	2	1
Totals	32	3	6	30	15	2

ST. LOUIS—2

	AB	R	H	O	A	E
Hemus, ss	3	0	0	1	2	0
Schoendienst, 2b	4	0	0	4	2	0
Musial, lf-cf	5	0	0	1	0	0
Bilko, 1b	4	0	0	12	0	0
Slaughter, rf	3	1	0	1	0	0
Jablonski, 3b	4	0	2	0	2	1
*-Haddix	0	1	0	0	0	0
B. Johnson, 3b	0	0	0	0	0	0
Repulski, cf	3	0	1	2	0	0
**-Lowrey, lf	1	0	1	0	0	0
D. Rice, c	3	0	1	7	0	0
†-Benson	0	0	0	0	0	0
Fusselman, c	1	0	0	0	0	0
Staley, p	4	0	1	0	5	0
Totals	35	2	6	28	11	1

St. Louis .... 000 010 001 0—2
Milwaukee .... 010 000 010 1—3

*-Ran for Jablonski in 9th.
**-Doubled for Repulski in 9th.
†-Ran for D. Rice in 8th.
‡-One out when winning run scored.

RBI—Jablonski, Lowrey, Gordon, Bruton. 2B—D. Rice, Lowrey. 3B — Bruton. HR—Britton. S—Schoendienst, Crandall, Logan. DP — Gordon-Matthews; Logan-Matthews-Dittmer. Left — St. Louis 7, Milwaukee 6. BB — Staley 2, Spahn 3. SO — Staley 6, Spahn 2. HBP —Logan by Staley. U—Conlan, Warneke, Donatelli, Gorman. T—2:29. A—34,357.

Cloudy and Cool
MADISON WEATHER
Partly cloudy and continued cool today. Tuesday fair. High today, 83; low tonight, 60. Sun rose, 4:41; sets, 7:25.

Wisconsin State Journal

DIAL 6-3111 | SECTION 1 | MADISON, MONDAY, JULY 27, 1953 | ★★★ | PRICE 5 CENTS

Blue Streak Morning Final
20 PAGES, THREE SECTIONS
Vol. 184, No. 117 114th Year

TRUCE SIGNED

Ike Says We Give Thanks for Armistice

(From United Press, Associated Press)

WASHINGTON—President Eisenhower said Sunday night the nation greets with "prayers of thanksgiving" the signing of an armistice in Korea.

In a five-minute speech broadcast on all radio and television networks he said that in the Korean War the United Nations (UN) had met the challenge of aggression "with deeds of decision."

Must Not Relax

But he warned the American people that "we must not relax our guard," and reminded them that "only courage and sacrifice can keep freedom alive on the earth."

And while reviewing the military efforts of the UN in Korea he called on all nations to "see the wisdom" of the newly-signed truce and settle their differences without more "brutal" strife.

He noted that the "cost of repelling aggression has been high" and has been "paid in terms of tragedy."

The President expressed "solemn gratitude for those who gave up their lives in a foreign land" and assured the veterans and those widowed and orphaned that they have America's "pledge of lasting devotion and care."

Praises ROKs

He praised the fighting men of 15 Allied nations under the UN command and paid special tribute to the "valorous" army of South Korea.

In fighting side by side with U. S. soldiers, Mr. Eisenhower said, the South Koreans "demonstrated that men of the West and East can live and work together . . . in the pursuit of justice."

But in this hour of thanksgiving, he added, Americans must "discipline our emotions" and prepare for the forthcoming post-armistice political talks.

"Throughout the coming months," the President said,

(Continued on Page 2, Column 7)

UN Chief Calls Truce Session

Assembly to Set Up Post-War Conference

UNITED NATIONS, N. Y. (AP)—Lester B. Pearson of Canada, president of the United Nations (UN) General Assembly, Saturday night summoned the world parliament for a post-Korean truce session on Aug. 17.

Pearson issued the call from UN headquarters moments after he had been officially notified by Henry Cabot Lodge Jr., chief of the United States delegation, that the armistice had been signed at Panmunjom.

Tackle Unification

The assembly will meet to set up the Far Eastern political conference which the armistice terms specify must follow a truce signing within 90 days. It will tackle such thorny problems as Korean unification and withdrawal of foreign troops

PEARSON

The Assembly will set the actual date and pick the site for the conference. It also was expected to decide which countries will participate and to set up a general agenda.

Lodge, who relayed the news officially to the UN, said, **"Let us thank God and fervently pray that this armistice heralds a lasting peace."**

'Way Is Now Clear'

Sir Gladwyn Jebb, chief of the British delegation declared that the significance of the armistice was that the UN had defeated aggression and shown that it does not pay.

"We must never let this plain

(Continued on Page 2, Column 1)

Moscow Has No Comment on Truce

LONDON (AP)—The Moscow Radio Sunday night broadcast without comment the technical details of arrangements for the signing of the Korean armistice.

Rhee to Go Along for Limited Time

SEOUL, Monday (AP)—President Syngman Rhee promised today to observe the armistice for "a limited time" while a political conference tries to unify Korea peacefully.

In a statement, Rhee said:

"I have opposed the signing of the truce because of my conviction that it will prove to be the prelude to more war, not less; to more suffering and ruin; to further Communist advances by war and by subversion.

"Now that it is signed, I pray that my judgment of its effect may turn out to be wrong."

"We shall not disturb the armistice while a political conference undertakes within a limited time to solve peacefully the problem of the liberation and unification of Korea."

Here's 1st Photo of Armistice Signing

Here is the first photo received in the United States showing Lt. Gen. William K. Harrison, center, sign the Armistice document for the United Nations at Panmunjom, Korea.

Gen. Harrison, who represented the Allied nations, is flanked by two unidentified officers. This exclusive photograph was received in Madison late Sunday night by The Wisconsin State Journal.

The photograph was taken 45 feet away from the actual signing table. Flash cameras were not permitted at the signing. Both restrictions were at the insistence of Communist negotiators.

United Press-State Journal Radiophoto

Like Raindrops, City Lightly Shrugs off Truce

By WILLIAM CRAWFORD
(State Journal Staff Writer)

The announcement of truce in Korea Sunday night seemed to have about as much emotional impact on citizens in rain-washed downtown Madison as a lecture on the end of the War of 1812.

The end of more than three years of fighting and dying brought no dancing in the street, nor particular gayiety around Capital Square.

Those who spoke of it at all did so in passing, casually. There was no spirit of triumph, or even of climax.

It was a far cry from the frenzied hilarity of V-J Day—when Madison and the nation went wild in August, 1945.

A busboy standing in the back doorway of Hotel Loraine just out of the sloshing rain seemed to sum up the way most of Madison took the news. When told the truce had been signed, he said:

"Oh, did they? I hope it helps."

In a tavern a bartender told a customer. "The truce was signed."

The customer, one of three, playing a bowling machine, said: **'Oh yah? Say ya know that dime I lost in here came back just now."**

The opinion of some was that the truce was just another step, hardly more important, in the progress of the cold war.

One man said,**"I don't like it—I don't trust the Reds."**

One man seeking shelter under the port cochere of a hotel was more interested in discussing the leak in the top of his new convertible Cadillac than the truce.

Another bartender in a normally busy bar, with no customers and listening to the news

(Continued on Page 2, Column 8)

Prof. C. L. Huskins Genetics Expert, Dies at Age of 55

Prof. C. Leonard Huskins, 55, of 957 University Bay dr., died Sunday night at a Madison hospital after a long illness.

Prof. Huskins

Prof. Huskins was a member of the botany department at the University of Wisconsin, coming here in 1945 from McGill University, Montreal, Canada.

He was a member of the First Unitarian society of Madison.

A native of England, he was head of the department of genetics at McGill, having gone there to teach in 1930 after studies abroad.

He received his doctor of philosophy degree at Kings college, London, in 1925.

Surviving are two daughters, Mrs. Sheila Hori, Chicago, and Olwen, Madison; a son, John N., Madison; two sisters, a brother, and his father. Mrs. Huskins died Mar. 1, 1953.

The body was taken to the Frautschi funeral home. The family requested that flowers be omitted.

Provisions of Korean Truce Listed

MUNSAN, Monday (AP) — Here are the major provisions of the Korean armistice document signed today:

ONE. All hostilities on land, sea, and in the air cease within 12 hours.

TWO. All troops withdraw with their equipment within 72 hours from the demarcation line drawn along the battleline.

The Communist and United Nations armies both must pull back two kilometers (about 1¼ miles) from the line to form the buffer zone which will separate Allied troops from the North Korean and Communist Chinese forces.

THREE. Allies withdraw within five days from islands held off the North Korean coasts.

FOUR. No blockade of Korea is allowed.

FIVE. A freeze immediately takes effect on reinforcement of troops or equipment in both North and South Korea.

Each side may rotate up to 35,000 men a month on a man-for-man basis, but neither may raise the level of men or arms they had in Korea at the time of the armistice.

SIX. A military armistice commission takes control of supervising the truce and settling any violations. The commission is composed of five UN and five Communist officers, at least three from each side of general or admiral rank.

SEVEN. Ten joint Allied - Communist observer teams are organized for the commission to police the buffer zone and the Han River estuary.

EIGHT. Five ports of entry are designated in North Korea and five in South Korea through which men and arms may enter

(Continued on Page 2, Column 1)

10-Minute Session Halts 3-Year War

(From Associated Press, United Press)

PANMUNJOM, Monday—United Nations (UN) and Communist senior truce delegates signed the long-awaited Korean armistice in a crisp 10-minute ceremony today, halting three years and one month of undeclared war.

Scheduled for 10 a.m. (7 p.m. Sunday CST), the signing began at 10:01 a.m. and was over at 10:11 a.m. Eighteen copies of the historic document were signed.

All shooting along the 155-mile battlefront was to stop 12 hours from the signing at Panmunjom.

Three hours after the chief Allied and Communist negotiators had signed the agreement at Panmunjom, Gen. Mark W. Clark put his signature to the document at Munsan.

Chinese and North Korean commanders are to sign at their headquarters, but this will not affect the cease fire.

Harrison, Nam Il Sign Documents

Lt. Gen. William K. Harrison Jr., signed for the UN Command. North Korean Gen. Nam Il signed for the North Koreans and Chinese Communists.

The signing went like clockwork, in contrast with more than two years of bitter debate that led up to it.

Minutes after the historic document was signed and blotted, an authoritative source announced that the Communists had promised to return 3,500 American prisoners of war in a POW exchange to begin in a week or less.

The Republic of Korea, which opposes a truce that leaves Korea divided with Chinese Red troops in the north, was not represented at the signing.

The armistice was signed in a pagoda-like structure hastily built by the Communists in this wide place in the road near the 38th Parallel.

It was that historic parallel which the North Korean Communist Army crossed at dawn on June 25, 1950, in a surprise assault aimed at unifying Korea by force under the Red flag.

Delegates Sign 18 Copies

When the representatives of the warring sides entered the building the 18 copies of the truce document were placed on an empty table in the middle of the large room.

Gen. Harrison signed in a businesslike manner, with Col. C. Murray, veteran UN command liaison officer, handing him the drafts.

Gen. Nam and Harrison signed at the same time, alternating the documents.

Each chief delegate used only one pen on each document.

Neither showed any emotion.

Harrison questioned one of the copies. After a brief consultation of subordinates he signed it. The UN Command interpreter for Chinese said later Harrison simply wanted to make sure what was the proper place to sign.

A ripple of laughter broke out at one point among North Koreans in the hall, but the Chinese watched impassively.

Newsreel and television cameras hummed steadily and still cameras clicked at intervals throughout the ceremony.

Radio Networks Describe Ceremony

Combined radio networks broadcast a description of the

(Continued on Page 2, Column 2)

Korean War Draws to Close

Fighting to Halt at 7 a.m. Today

From United Press, Associated Press

SEOUL—Three years of war that has shattered this tiny Asian land, claimed 1,500,000 casualties, and threatened to touch off World War III, drew to a close today.

All fighting was due to stop at 10 p.m. (7 a.m. today CST), 12 hours after the signing of an armistice at Panmunjom.

Still, only hours before the signing, the Communists attacked in the early morning dark on the western front.

Elsewhere the battle lines were quiet. Only sporadic artillery and mortar fire lit the sky. And Gen. Mark W. Clark ordered his troops not to pick an unnecessary fight.

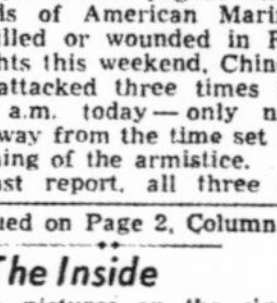

CLARK

Tension swept the trenches and bunkers from which dug-in Allied troops — knowing a cease-fire was near—peered into the blacness, alert for last-minute Communist attacks.

On the western front near Panmunjom's truce pagoda where hundreds of American Marines were killed or wounded in Red onslaughts this weekend, Chinese troops attacked three times before 1 a.m. today—only nine hours away from the time set for the signing of the armistice.

At last report, all three as-

(Continued on Page 2, Column 5)

On The Inside

More pictures on the signing of the Korean armistice will be found on Pages 2, 3, and 5, Sec. I, and Page 2, Sec. II.

Background and interpretative stories of the historic event will be found on Pages 3, 5, and 6, Sec. I.

Read The Wisconsin State Journal daily and Sunday, — first with the latest news and sports stories and pictures.

POWs to Be Home Soon, Clark Says

MUNSAN, Korea, Monday (U.P.) — Gen. Mark W. Clark said today the exchange of Korean war prisoners will start within a week if the Communists cooperate and that the first American prisoners should be "home in two or three weeks."

More than 3,000 American prisoners awaited release as the result of the armistice signing at Panmunjom, including Maj. Gen. William F. Dean, commander of the U. S. 24th Infantry division.

American prisoners in good physical condition will be sent home by ship.

Clark said the Allies will start moving prisoners "within a week if the Communist cooperate."

Sick and wounded American prisoners handed over at Panmunjom will be flown promptly to Japan, Clark said. Those who are in good condition will go from Inchon by ship to the United States.

MacArthur Has No Comment on Truce

NEW YORK (AP) — Maj. Gen. Courtney Whitney, aide to Gen. Douglas MacArthur, said Sunday night the former Far Eastern commander would have no comment on the signing of the Korean armistice.

U.S. Is No Closer to Peace, 5 U.W. Faculty Members Say

By FORREST FISCHER
(State Journal Staff Writer)

Five University of Wisconsin educators who have traveled in Communist dominated countries or have closely studied Communist policies Sunday unanimously expressed doubt that a truce in Korea closer to peace.

States ay closer to peace.

The general reaction of the group quizzed by The Wisconsin State Journal, which included two natives of Russia and a Czechoslovakian refugee, was skepticism over the sincerity of the Communists in signing the truce.

Dimitri Pronin, instructor in agricultural engineering, who was a second lieutenant in the Czar's Army and fought the Bolshevists for 2½ years during the World War I

MAYDA

era stated the truce was merely an "interruption of the entire struggle."

"I don't believe the struggle with Communism is finished," he added. "It is a timely interruption in the general struggle. I don't believe Russia will change her policy. The goals will remain the same."

Like Pronin the others were outspoken in their opinion that the Communists are using the truce as an instrument to further their cause.

Jaro Mayda, a Czechoslavakian refugee who is an assistant professor of political science and law at the university, felt that the "signature of the truce simply means that this is more advantageous to the Communists

(Continued on Page 2, Column 6)

Madison Police Assist, Prevent Oshkosh Fire

Madison police prevented a fire in Oshkosh Sunday.

Robert Lunder, Oshkosh, came into the Madison police station with a worried expression on his face.

"I left the fire burning under a pot of potatoes in my apartment in Oshkosh," he said, "and I'm afraid there'll be a fire there if it isn't turned off. Can you people do anything about it?"

Police radioed Oshkosh police with Lunder's instructions for entering the apartment, and authorities there entered and turned off the fire.

"Done just right," Oshkosh police radioed back.

Braves Lose 2 More, Fall 7½ Games Behind

The Milwaukee Braves dropped a doubleheader to Brooklyn Sunday, 3-2 and 2-1, falling to 7½ games behind the Dodgers current National League leaders.

The Braves return to Milwaukee for a make-up game with the New York Giants today. **(Full Details in the Sports Peach.)**

6 Milwaukee Brewers, Union Reach Agreement, End Strike

MILWAUKEE (AP)—Agreement was reached Sunday night in Milwaukee's 74-day-old brewery strike.

The Milwaukee Brewer's Association announced that its members had accepted the latest counter contract proposal by Local 9 of the CIO United Brewery Workers union.

The proposal was the one offered—and accepted by the union Sunday afternoon — by the Blatz Brewing Co., one of the six struck breweries.

The union in turn offered the same settlement to the other five breweries.

With the breweries' acceptance, the only step remaining before the strike, which has altered the flow of 15 per cent of the nation's beer output, is over union ratification of the agreement.

The proposal is expected to be submitted to the union's 7,000 members for ratification Tuesday.

Frank Verbest, president of Blatz, declined to divulge terms of the offer submitted to the union.

The main stumbling block to settlement of the strike had been the union's demand for a 35 hour work week.

James C. Paradise, union attorney, said the settlement proposal "makes provision for each one of the union's basic demands —a substantial wage increase, a comprehensive health and welfare plan, pensions and a reduction in hours of work."

Besides Blatz, the breweries struck were Pabst, Schlitz, Miller, Gettlemann, and Independent.

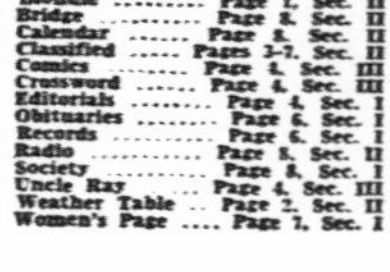

FEATURE FINDER

Bill's a Lot Closer to Madison Today--Even If He's in Korea

By JAMES ROBINSON
(State Journal Staff Writer)

An end to the Korean fighting at 7 a. m. today (Madison time) will mean many things to many people.

But to the family of Sgt. William D. Woodard, 256 Waubesa st., the day has special significance.

There's the matter of a dresser drawer, two cans of beer, several anniversaries, and a dog — not necessarily in that order, however.

Most important, the truce means that "Bill" really is coming home — perhaps sooner than expected. And everyone here anticipates Bill's first meeting with little Gloria, who was born about the time her daddy arrived in Korea.

WOODARD

Bill is the son of Mr. and Mrs. Ray Woodard, and the husband of the former Barbara Davis, 417 North st. The sergeant entered the Army 2½ years ago, and has been in Korea for nearly a year, including in his service the bitter battle for Sniper Ridge.

Bill left home enroute for the

(Pictures, Page 2)

fighting on July 12, 1952.

"Mom, you just leave my dresser drawer as it is," he ordered. "I can find anything I want in the dark, but nobody else could find a thing.

"I really am coming back, Mom," he assured his mother. "Just to prove it I'll put these two cans of beer in the refrigerator. You, leave 'em there,

(Continued on Page 2, Column 4)

Blowing Colder
Mostly cloudy with cold northerly winds today. Clearing and considerably colder tonight. Wednesday partly cloudy and cold. High today, 30. Low tonight, 10. Sun rose, 6:32; sets, 5:47.

Wisconsin State Journal

DIAL 6-3111 SECTION 1 MADISON, TUESDAY, MARCH 2, 1954 ★★★ PRICE 5 CENTS

Blue Streak Morning Final
24 PAGES, THREE SECTIONS
Vol. 185, No. 153 115th Year

FIVE CONGRESSMEN WOUNDED BY PUERTO RICAN FANATICS

Diagram Shows Lines of Fire in House Affray

This is a diagrammed general view of the House chamber, where Puerto Rican nationalists shot down five congressmen Monday.

Firing from the visitors' gallery, the attackers, pictured in this diagram, wounded Reps. Ben. F. Jensen (A); Kenneth A. Roberts (B); George H. Fallon (C); Alvin M. Bentley (D); and Clifford Davis (E).

A fourth confederate also was stationed in the balcony, apparently to reload the guns.

—United Press-State Journal Telephoto Diagram

Police are shown holding three Puerto Ricans who staged a shooting spree in the House chamber Monday, wounding five congressmen, and sending more than 200 lawmakers to cover.

The three, Mrs. Lilita Lebron, 34, Rafael C. Miranda, 25, Andres F. Cordero, 29, all of New York City, were said by police to be members of the "same gang" that tried to kill former President Truman in 1950.

A fourth man, Irving Fores, 27, New York City, (inset) also was seized. Police said his job was to reload the guns.

United Press-State Journal Telephoto

Bentley Given '50-50' Chance After Shooting

Band That Aimed at Truman Grabbed in Chamber Melee

(From United Press, Associated Press)

WASHINGTON—Three Puerto Rican fanatics, led by a 34-year-old woman, fired a fusillade of bullets into the unsuspecting House of Representatives Monday and wounded five congressmen, one critically.

The assailants, shouting for a "free" Puerto Rico, raked the chamber from an overhanging visitors' gallery with wild fire, from a dozen to 30 shots, while a fourth confederate stood by to reload the guns.

Some of the 243 lawmakers stood too stunned to move. Others threw themselves to the floor. Some crawled from the chambers or scurried behind desks.

Five fell wounded, one critically. Three raced upstairs to help subdue their assailants.

Reps. James E. Van Zandt (R-Pa.), Wingate Lucas (D-Tex.) and Joe Holtz (R-Calif.) and a handful of courageous spectators and House employes overpowered the gunmen.

Police called them members of the "same gang" that **tried to kill former President Truman in 1950 and said the attack was planned in New York on Feb. 22, the birthday of George Washington who led this country's fight for independence.**

The most seriously wounded was 35-year-old Rep. Alvin M. Bentley (R-Mich.). He was struck by two bullets, one piercing his body and puncturing his lung, liver and stomach, the other hitting his leg.

'50-50 Chance'

Bentley underwent an exploratory operation at Casualty hospital about five hours after the shooting. Dr. Clarence Stanley White, who performed the surgery, said at 8:30 p. m. he "is over the operation" and has a "50-50 chance" to live.

"He's in the hands of the Lord now," the surgeon told reporters.

Bentley's wife is expecting a baby in about two months.

Less seriously wounded were:

Rep. Ben F. Jensen (R-Ia.), shot in the back and taken to Bethesda (Md.) Naval Medical Center. The hospital said his condition was "good."

Rep. Kenneth A. Roberts (D-Ala.), wounded in the left thigh and knee. Surgeons ordered an exploratory operation on his leg, fearing serious injuries to his "nerves and blood vessels."

Rep. Clifford Davis (D-Tenn.), shot through the calf of the leg.

Rep. George H. Fallon (D-Md.), shot in the hip and removed to Casualty hospital. His condition was satisfactory.

Two noted Washington surgeons—Drs. J. Ross Veal and O. Hugh Fulcher—were called in to examine Bentley and Roberts.

Four Arrested

Police Chief Robert Murray said four Puerto Ricans charged with assault with intent to kill. He identified them as:

Mrs. Lilita Lebron, 34, of New York City, the "leader" of the group and a friend of the wife of one of the two men who tried to kill Mr. Truman.

Rafael C. Miranda, 25, New York City.

Andres F. Cordero, 29, New York City.

Irving Fores, 27, New York City.

The shooting was first ever to

(Continued on Page 2, Column 1)

REP. ALVIN M. BENTLEY
Shot in chest, leg

REP. GEORGE H. FALLON
Shot in the hip

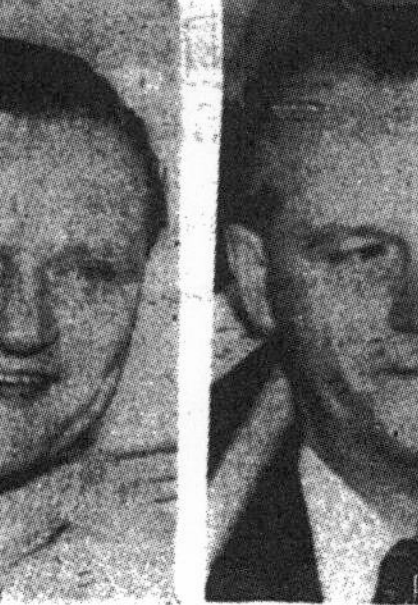

REP. CLIFFORD DAVIS
Wounded in right leg

REP. BEN. F. JENSEN
Shot in the back

REP. KENNETH A. ROBERTS
Wounded in the leg

Shots Stun Wisconsin Slate, Too

By FRANCES McKUSICK
(State Journal Washington Bureau)

WASHINGTON—"It was unbelievable. God, it was unbelievable."

These words were repeated over and over again by stunned members of the Wisconsin House delegation who were on the floor when "it" happened Monday.

Rep. Glenn R. Davis (R-Waukesha) said the first bullets sounded like firecrackers.

"Then I felt some plaster fall on my head and I realized it was real shooting. I made a dive for the floor and tried to get under cover. Lying in the aisle close enough for me to touch was Congressman Alvin Bentley. He was bleeding and his groans were terrible. But I couldn't help him.

DAVIS

"I looked up to the galleries and saw two men and a woman with guns.

"No one was doing anything to stop them. They walked around leisurely putting more bullets in

(Continued on Page 2, Column 3)

Van Zandt Tells How He Aided in Capture

By REP. JAMES E. VAN ZANDT
(As Told To The United Press)

WASHINGTON—I was sitting about four or five rows from the back of the House chamber and I heard what appeared to be fireworks.

I saw a group up in the gallery waving guns and firing and I heard a whistle.

I immediately hit the floor in the aisle on my stomach and crawled to the Republican cloakroom door on my hands and knees and ran from the door up the steps to the galleries.

As I ran by the radio room, a girl was just coming out of the gallery and several people grabbed her.

A six-foot Puerto Rican came out next and I grabbed him and took a Luger (pistol) away from him.

A spectator was wrestling with the other man out into the hallway from the gallery.

Someone took the big Puerto Rican away from me and I ran to help the spectator. We took a Luger from him, too.

VAN ZANDT

There were new magazines in both pistols indicating they had reloaded. A clip holds 10 bullets, I think. There were more bullets in their pockets.

The girl did not resist and the six-footer didn't either. But the little one kept fighting.

The girl had a flag and she shouted **"My country is entitled to independence."** I asked the six-footer where he was from and he said, **"Puerto Rico."**

I think there were four or five of them all together because I passed two or three people running. I brushed by them and went after the man with the gun.

Rep. Wingate Lucas of Texas (Democrat) pointed a finger at one of the fellows and said "I know that fellow." The woman didn't have a gun when she came out. She dropped it in the gallery.

The little Puerto-Rican wouldn't let go of the gun. Some one stepped on his wrist when he had him on the floor and another pulled his fingers and I yanked his thumb. That's how we got the gun away from him.

McCormick to Cover NCAA Boxing, Too, as Roundy 'Catches' Braves on Vacation

Journal Readers to Get the Pitch from Roundy

By ROUNDY

See by Monday Journal that McCormick's going to Florida to watch the Braves, leaving me in Madison to do all the work for the state basketball tournament. What a racket. Me with 47 days vacation still coming.

So I told Don Anderson I'll make a deal. I'll stay in Madison for the high school kids when they come to town on March 18, 19, and 20, but after that I'm on my way to catch the Braves coming north.

First I'll have to stop in Chicago to see the Bobo Olson championship middleweight fight on April 2.

Now McCormick can get some time off, too.

Instead of watching th: Braves every day, he's going to leave team at Atlanta, Ga., and head for State College, Pa., for the National Collegiate Athletic Association (NCAA) Boxing Championship.

Now you sports fans are really going to get somethin'.

McCormick following the Braves. Me and the rest of the staff in town for the State Basketball Tournament. Then I'm leaving to go catch the Braves on the road while McCormick follows Wisconsin boxers at NCAA meet.

Man alive, if that isn't nice dish for Sports Peach. No wonder The Wisconsin State Journal is "First in Sports."

FEATURE FINDER

White House Guards Given Special Alert

WASHINGTON (UP) — Secret Service agents and White House police flashed a special alert around the executive mansion Monday in the wake of the shooting in the House of Representatives by Puerto Rican gunmen.

The memory of the attempted assassination of former President Truman by two Puerto Rican Nationalists in November, 1950, was still fresh in the minds of President Eisenhower's protectors and they were taking no chances.

Press Secretary James C. Hagerty said there was no need to strengthen the guard at the gates to the White House because the security detail is kept at top strength and effectiveness at all times. Any other added precautions were kept secret.

Mr. Eisenhower was in his office when he heard of the shooting at the Capitol. Hagerty gave him the news and shortly afterwards the chief executive telephoned an offer of help to House Speaker Joseph W. Martin Jr.

Then the President sent one of his legislative liaison officers, Homer Gruenther, to the offices of each of the wounded congressmen, offering any possible assistance by the White House.

Almost as soon as the President received the news, the White House police switchboard flashed an alert to each of the guard booths stationed along the iron fence enclosing the executive mansion grounds.

Cool But Fair
MADISON WEATHER
Fair and continued cool, today, tonight and Wednesday. High today, 68. Low tonight, 42. Sun rose, 4:31, sets, 7:16.

Wisconsin State Journal

DIAL 6-3111 | SECTION 1 | MADISON, TUESDAY, MAY 18, 1954 | ★★★ | PRICE 5 CENTS

Blue Streak Morning Final
32 PAGES, FOUR SECTIONS
Vol. 175, No. 48 115th Year

Hearings Halt for Week at Least

Supreme Court Rules School Segregation Unconstitutional

Justices Vote Unanimously; Delay Step to Enforce Rule

(From Associated Press, United Press)

WASHINGTON — The Supreme Court ruled Monday that the states of the nation do not have the right to separate Negro and white pupils in different public schools.

By a unanimous 9-0 vote, the high court held that such segregation of the races is unconstitutional.

It was the most sweeping action of its kind since Abraham Lincoln's Emancipation Proclamation.

Chief Justice Earl Warren read the historic decision to a packed but hushed gallery of spectators nearly two years after Negro residents of four states and the District of Columbia went before the court to challenge the principle of segregation.

Won't End Now

The ruling does not end segregation at once.

Further hearings were set for this fall to decide how and when to end the practice of segregation. Thus a lengthy delay is likely before the decision is carried out.

The decision requires no immediate changes in segregated school systems prescribed by law in 17 states and the District of Columbia and in four where it is permitted but not required.

It may be a year or more before the court rules finally on methods of ending school segregation and additional years before its rulings are carried down to local school districts.

For years 17 Southern and "border" states have imposed compulsory segregation on approximately two-thirds of the nation's Negroes. Officials of some states already are on record as saying they will close the schools rather than permit them to be operated with Negro and white pupils in the same classrooms.

Decision Quoted

In its decision, the high court struck down the long-standing "separate but equal" doctrine first laid down by the Supreme Court in 1896 when it maintained that segregation was all right if equal facilities were made available for Negroes and whites.

Here is the heart of Monday's decision as it deals with this hotly controverted doctrine:

"We come then to the question presented: Does segregation of children in public schools solely on the basis of race, even though the physical facilities and other 'tangible' factors may be equal, deprive the children of the minority group of equal education opportunities?

"We believe that it does."

James C. Hagerty, presidential press secretary, told a news con-

(Continued on Page 2, Column 1)

Reaction Depends on The Region

From United Press, Associated Press

Georgia, South Carolina, Mississippi, and Louisiana expressed firm and sometimes bitter opposition Monday to the Supreme Court decision which wipes out the cherished Southern tradition of separation of the races in public schools.

Kansas, Oklahoma, Texas, and Maryland said they would obey the ruling and sentiment in the other states affected varied from "disappointment" to pleas for "calmness" in this, the most critical issue to face the South since Reconstruction days.

Reaction to the Supreme Court decision ran generally along regional lines.

In the South, white political leaders reacted all the way from bitter criticism and near-defiance through milder anger and on to quiet caution. In Washington, Southern congressmen were generally not quite so defiant as their respective state governors, but they were bitter.

RUSSELL

Sen. Richard Russell (D-Ga.), a leader among Southern Democrats, said for example, that the opinion was a **"flagrant abuse of judicial power"** which strikes down the rights of the states as guaranteed by the Constitution."

But in the North, there was praise from Negro spokesmen, educators, and public officials. In Washington, Northern congressmen were almost unanimous in their praise of the court's decision.

Gov. Herman Talmadge of Georgia led off the Southern embittered reaction to the decision, charging that it reduced the Constitution to "a mere scrap of paper." He said he would do all within his power to preserve segregation in Georgia "without violence."

Gov. James F. Byrnes of South Carolina said he was "shocked" and that the ruling violated the Constitution.

The Georgia governor said the ruling **"blatantly ignored all law and precedent and usurped from**

(Continued on Page 2, Column 2)

Gov. Herman Talmadge of Georgia reads his statement over the telephone at Atlanta Monday shortly after the Supreme Court ruled that segregation in schools is unconstitutional. Talmadge said the decision reduced the Constitution to a "scrap of paper" and said he would work for "permanent segregation in Georgia's schools—though "without violence."

United Press-State Journal Telephotos

The attorneys who argued the case against segregation in schools are shown wearing their victory smiles as they pose in front of the U. S. Supreme Court building in Washington Monday. Left to right are George E. C. Hayes, Washington, D. C.; Thurgood Marshall, special counsel for the National Association for the Advancement of Colored People; and James Nabrit, Jr., professor and attorney at Howard University.

Ike Tells Army Not to Testify About Meeting

WASHINGTON (AP) — The McCarthy-Army hearings bumped into a presidential order Monday and the result was that they came to an unexpected, dramatic halt—for a week at least, maybe forever.

Taking a personal hand, President Eisenhower issued a directive forbidding Army witnesses to testify about the role of White House and other high officials in the televised controversy between Sen. Joseph R. McCarthy (R-Wis.) and civilian Pentagon chiefs.

They Protest

McCarthy cried **"Iron Curtain!"** Democrats raised a protest of "whitewash."

And in the end the Senate investigations subcomimtiee voted to recess the public inquiry until next Monday to see if Mr. Eisenhower would withdraw or modify his secrecy clampdown.

Acting Chairman Karl Mundt (R-S.D.) declared there is nothing about the recess which "even remotely implies a discontinuation of these hearings" for good.

EISENHOWER

The Democrats, however, said it looked to them as if the hearings may well have blown sky high—unless the President should change his mind.

The chances of Mr. Eisenhower's doing this appeared pretty slim.

Order Quoted

The President said in Monday's secrecy order, issued to Secretary of Defense Charles E. Wilson, that his stand was taken **"to maintain the proper separation of powers between the executive and legislative branches of the government in accordance with my responsibilities and duties under the Constitution."**

And he said, too, in language that left little if any room for backtracking:

"This separation is vital to preclude the exercise of arbitrary power by any branch of the government."

To support his stand, Mr. Eisenhower cited 26 precedents ranging back to George Washington's administration, in which chief executives have refused information to Congress.

He said that the separation of powers principle "must be maintained regardless of who would be benefitted by such disclosures."

Hearings End

And so ended—for the time being, at least—18 days of unprecedented, nationally televised hearings that brought day after day of testimony from Secretary of the Army Robert T. Stevens and Army Counselor John G. Adams—but only brief, incidental trips to the witness stand by their main antagonists, McCarthy and his chief counsel, Roy M. Cohn.

Specifically, Mr. Eisenhower's order forbade Adams—who was still on the witness stand when the breakup came—to give any further details of a Jan. 21 meeting of White House and other top level officials which led to the Army's head-on collision with McCarthy.

At the Jan. 21 meeting, in addition to Army lawyer Adams, were Sherman Adams, assistant to President Eisenhower; Atty. Gen. Herbert Brownell; Deputy Atty. Gen. William P. Rogers; Henry Cabot Lodge Jr., chief U. S. delegate to the United Nations and a part-time White House aide; and Gerald Morgan of the

(Continued on Page 2, Column 5)

U.S. History Gives Ike a Big Stick

WASHINGTON (UP) — President Eisenhower reached deep into American history Monday to cite 26 precedents for his refusal to reveal certain information to senators investigating the Army-McCarthy dispute.

The list, prepared for the President by Atty. Gen. Herbert Brownell Jr., dated back to the first term of President George Washington and continued through the administration of President Truman.

It summarized the outstanding examples in which a chief executive, believing the demands of Congress to be an encroachment on the executive branch, had refused to give up documents or information.

In one famous incident, President Theodore Roosevelt locked up the papers in the White House and told the Senate, in effect, to come and get them if it could.

Ten of the 26 cases occurred when Mr. Truman was in office. Five of "many instances" were taken from the Franklin D. Roosevelt administration. Presidents Jefferson, Jackson, Tyler, Buchanan, Grant, Cleveland, Coolidge and Hoover also were included.

◆ ◆ ◆

WASHINGTON (UP) — Federal Judge David A. Pine ruled Monday that a recorded telephone conversation is not legal evidence unless both parties to the conversation consent.

Judge Pine's ruling concerned conversations recorded mechanically. A similar issue in the Army-McCarthy hearings concerns conversations taken down in shorthand.

Pine made the ruling in the case of Warren L. Stephenson, prominent Washington Republican. Stephenson is charged with perjury in connection with testimony before a congressional committee investigating "four percenters."

Stephenson's defense asked the court to suppress a recording of a conversation between him and a California industrialist.

(Continued on Page 2, Column 6)

And it All Adds Up to Another Nice Day

Coolish, but generally nice weather will extend through today and Wednesday, the Truax Field weatherman said Monday night.

Today's high will be 2 degrees shy of reaching Monday's peak of 70, but the low was expected to equal Monday's 42, the forecaster said.

Fair skies were predicted for both days.

No rain was in sight, and the total precipitation again was ranging almost an inch below the average.

Total precipitation this year is 7.59 inches. The average is 8.49 inches.

With Spirit and Song, Madison Norsemen Celebrate Big Holiday

By ROBERT C. BJORKLUND
(State Journal Staff Writer)

Norway's independence day — Syttende Mai — was celebrated with all the spirit and song the Norsemen and their ladies of Madison could muster Monday night.

At the Blackhawk Country club, 115 members and guests of Ygdrasil Literary Society presented a transplanted bit of Norway echoing the day of celebration that burst throughout all of the Norwegian countryside.

In the American adaptation of the events of May 17, the Madison group took time to honor Herman L. Ekern, 2809 Columbia rd., for his long period of service to the society, state, and nation.

Mendez Hanson, 37 Sherman terrace, who read the tribute to Ekern, recalled his notable contributions as an attorney, public administrator, and counselor in the field of social legislation.

Ekern, who served in the state assembly, was attorney general of Wisconsin, and leader in the field of insurance, responded:

"I have found the public very generous and particularly, my good friends here."

The 81-year-old attorney twice served as president of the society and has a near-perfect attendance record for his 44 years of membership, according to Hanson.

In the program led by R. O. Christoffersen, 2635 Kendall ave., the group combined an unique bit of old Norway and Norwegian-Americana.

To the tune of "On, Wisconsin" they sang one line of a song that went:

"Vikinganden er for handen"—"the Viking spirit is a hand."

And it was.

The songs hailed Haugen, Lerdahl, Nereim, Reppen — "gode Norske navn," and when it got down to the last line that read: **"Hell at Wisconsin slike menn kan ha,"** Songleader Einar Haugen explained that **"it doesn't mean what you think it means."**

Translated, "hell" means fortunate.

And the lyric reads: **"Wisconsin is fortunate to have such**

(Continued on Page 2, Column 4)

Guatemala Gets Red Arms Load

State Department Denounces Action

WASHINGTON (UP)—The State Department reported Monday night that a shipment of arms has been sent from "Soviet-controlled territory" to Guatemala in Central America.

A special announcement called the action a "development of gravity" because of "the origin of these arms, the point, their destination, and the quantity of arms involved."

The department did not say what steps it planned to take.

U. S officials long have been critical of Guatemala because of reports that its government is strongly influenced by Communists.

The department said the ship Alfhelm arrived at Puerto Barrios, Guatemala, last Saturday "carrying a large shipment of armament consigned to the Guatemala government."

It said this country has been advised the arms were shipped from the Communist-administered port of Stettin in Poland. The shipment is now being unloaded at Puerto Barrios, it added.

State Department spokesman Lincoln White, who read the brief announcement, refused to make any comment or answer any questions.

The growing Communist influence in Guatemala, and to a lesser extent in some other Latin-American countries, led this country to sponsor an anti-Communist resolution which was overwhelmingly adopted at the recent inter-American conference at Caracas, Venezuela.

Gas Blast in Home Severely Burns Man

A gas stove explosion Monday afternoon burned Charles McCann, 28, of 2673 Milwaukee st., and caused his recently-hospitalized 22-year-old wife to lapse into shock.

Both were taken by police ambulance to Madison General hospital and returned home Monday night after emergency treatment. McCann was burned on his head.

The explosion happened about 2 p.m. in the kitchen of an unoccupied upstairs apartment in the two-flat building where the McCanns live.

Asst. Fire Chief Edward Durkin said the natural gas stove in the vacant flat apparently had been leaking for about two days. When McCann opened the kitchen to reach a storage room, the accumulated gas fumes ignited from the stove's pilot light, Durkin said.

The explosion, accompanied by a flash fire, knocked McCann and the kitchen door into a hallway, smashed the kitchen windows, and blew a hole in the ceiling above the stove.

The flash fire had nearly burned itself out when firemen from Nos. 5 and 8 companies arrived.

Mrs. McCann, who returned home Sunday after major surgery at Madison General, was in bed in the downstairs apartment. She was not injured in the blast, but suffered shock.

TV's 'Atomic Attack' to Be Pure Fiction

NEW YORK (AP)—An "atomic attack" on television tonight will be pure fiction, ABC said Monday night.

The network said the dramatic show to be put on at 7:30 tonight CST over the entire network will be realistic and authentic, thanks to the help of civil defense authorities.

But it won't be real, and viewers should not be excited by it, the network said.

The hour-long dramatization is to show what would happen in nearby Westchester County after a hydrogen bomb practically wiped out Manhattan Island.

Grove and Monona Taverns Close Today

All taverns in Blooming Grove and Monona must be closed during election hours today regardless of whether they are located in the school district where residents will be voting on a $750,000 high school bond issue, Dist. Atty. Richard W. Bardwell said Monday afternoon.

The polls are open, and the taverns must be closed, from 7 a. m. to 8 p. m.

Far East Military Persons Dock in U.S.

SAN FRANCISCO (AP) — The transport Gen. Hugh Gaffey arrived Monday from Japan with 1,694 military passengers.

Puppy Jumps, Shoots His Master's Friend

OMAHA, Neb. (UP) — A cocker spaniel puppy shot his master's friend Monday.

The puppy jumped into the lap of his master, Jerry Danahy, and kicked the trigger of a .17-caliber air rifle. The gun discharged, inflicting a two-inch gash on the jaw of Jerry Doula, 15.

The boy was treated at a hospital and released.

State Lake Dragged for Body of W. O. Perdue, Dairy Leader

MANITOWISH WATERS, Wis. (UP)—Vilas county authorities dragged Island Lake near here Monday for the body of William O. Perdue, one of the dairy producers' best known spokesmen.

The 56-year-old Perdue was missing and believed drowned in the lake near his summer home. He was last seen at 7:30 p. m. Saturday while fishing alone in a small motor boat.

The empty boat was found late Sunday, with its fuel exhausted.

PERDUE

Coroner P. J. Gaffney who aided in the search for Perdue, said "evidence indicates the probability that a burst of speed from the high-powered motor on the small boat may have thrown Mr. Perdue from it."

Perdue was general manager of the Pure Milk Products Cooperative with headquarters at Fond du Lac. The organization is the largest dairy producers' cooperative in the nation with some 18,000 members.

The cooperative had only 1,500 members when Perdue went to work for it in 1941. Since then he has worked vigorously to expand the organization and has become a familiar figure in Washington as he appeared before numerous congressional committees to testify in behalf of the dairy farmers.

He was born in Texas and was the first Federal Milk Marketing administrator appointed by the secretary of agriculture in the 1930s.

Since the Apr. 1 reduction in federal dairy price supports, Perdue has been promoting a five-point program among agriculture leaders which would restore the old price props at 90 per cent of parity.

Rattler Wastes Time Biting This Man's Leg

FERRIDAY, La. (UP) — Vernon Traxler stepped on a rattlesnake and held it with his foot while it bit his leg repeatedly.

A friend finally killed the snake, which had been wasting its time. Traxler has an artificial leg.

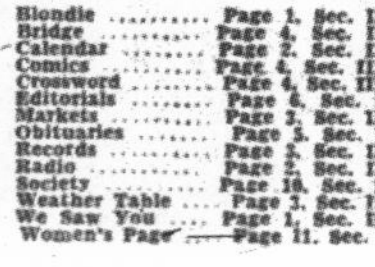

FEATURE FINDER

Wonewoc and Area Turn Out to Tour New Battery Plant

By JOHN PRINDLE
(Assistant State Editor)

WONEWOC—An estimated 1,000 persons from 17 southern and central Wisconsin communities who had heard about the new Ray-O-Vac plant in Wonewoc, visited the factory Monday to see for themselves.

The new building is the one that Wonewoc raised $150,000 to rebuild after the old factory burned to the ground in April, 1953. Residents of the five surrounding counties that supply labor for the plant were invited to an open house Monday.

Schools were out to allow grade and high school pupils to tour the factory where many of their parents are employed. The company furnished guides to take groups through and explain the making of dozens of specialized battery products.

The Wonewoc plant, called Ray-O-Vac's Special Products Division, makes none of the familiar flashlight batteries that are sold throughout the world, but manufactures specialty batteries, many of which are used by the armed forces.

Visitors Monday saw how the plant's 125 employes, most of them women, assemble hundreds of tiny parts into such things as fingerprint batteries, movie camera batteries, and weather observation batteries.

On display was one of the firm's newest products, a life jacket light designed for use by Navy and Air Force men who find themselves in the middle of an ocean. The special light uses sea water as the battery's electrolite, and is attached to a lifebelt.

When the sea water begins to activate the battery, the light will burn for 60 hours. It's a small light, but it can be seen for great distances at sea.

Leslie K. Pollard, 301 Newcastle way, Madison, a Ray-O-Vac vice-president, said he likes to think of the new factory as the "Phoenix of Wonewoc," after the famous Egyptian bird that burned itself up whenever it got old, and then emerged young again from the flames.

The village lost its only industry in the big fire a year ago, and some residents were ready to call it quits. But almost immediately the village formed the Wonewoc Development Corp. and raised $150,000.

The company, which considered moving the industry somewhere else after the fire, was persuaded by this showing of community spirit to remain, and work began on a new plant.

The old factory was a partly-remodeled brewery that never was meant for a battery factory. The new one, built on the site of the burned brewery, is a modern, efficient plant that the village is proud of.

Monday was visitors' day at the Wonewoc Ray-O-Vac Co. plant, and hundreds of residents of five surrounding counties toured the plant where specialized batteries are made.

Clarence Degner, above, right, was one of several guides who took tours through the factory. He points out to visitors how tiny parts for batteries are assembled, as three women employes do the assembling.

—State Journal Staff Photo

Still Chill

MADISON WEATHER

Partly cloudy and cold today. Friday partly cloudy, not quite so cold. High today 30. Low tonight 8. Sun rose, 7:08; sets, 4:23.

DIAL 6-3111 SECTION 1 MADISON, THURSDAY, DECEMBER 2, 1954 ★★★ PRICE 5 CENTS

Blue Streak Morning Final

46 PAGES, FIVE SECTIONS Vol. 187, No. 63 116th Year

SENATE CENSURES McCARTHY ON ONE COUNT; OTHERS TODAY

If Peaceful Means Fail

U.S. May Blockade China, Dulles Says

WASHINGTON (AP)—Secretary of State John Foster Dulles said Wednesday the United States might blockade Red China if peaceful means fail to protect the rights of citizens like the 13 Americans jailed by Peiping on spy charges.

He said he was confident, but not certain, that peaceful means would be sufficient.

Dulles made the statement during a news conference which he opened by announcing agreement with Nationalist China on a mutual defense treaty pledging the United States to retaliate, probably against the Communist-held China mainland, if the Reds attack the Nationalist stronghold of Formosa.

To Be Signed Soon

The treaty, Dulles said, would be signed sometime this week. He said it is "another link in the system of collective security" against Communist aggression in the Western Pacific.

Dulles' remarks about blockading Red China came when reporters sought clarification of his statements in a speech Monday night at Chicago.

DULLES

The secretary said then the United States would "exhaust peaceful means of sustaining our international rights and those of our citizens." He ruled out for the present any blockade of Red China such as Senate Republican Leader William F. Knowland, of California, has called for.

Dulles said that would be a "war action" and the White House issued a statement Tuesday agreeing with him.

Knowland, however, stuck to his guns. He said he had a difference of opinion and remained unconvinced measures short of a blockade would win relief for the 13 Americans.

Knowland Backed

Sen. Joseph R. McCarthy (R-Wis.) Wednesday declared himself "in complete sympathy" with Knowland's blockade proposal. Sen. William Jenner (R-Ind.) did likewise, terming the jailing of the 13 "perilously close to an act of war."

The 11 U. S. airmen and two civilian employes of the U. S. Army were captured after plane crashes two years ago. Radio Peiping announced last week they had been sentenced to jail terms as "spies," a charge denounced by the United States as

(Continued on Page 2, Column 4)

Susan Testifies on Illicit Affair

Admits Intimacies with Dr. Sheppard

CLEVELAND, O. (UP)—Freckle-faced Susan Hayes, the "motive" witness in Dr. Samuel H. Sheppard's wife murder trial, testified Wednesday she and the osteopath kept love trysts for 16 months during which he told her twice he was thinking of getting a divorce.

SUSAN

The prosecution rested its case with 24-year-old Miss Hayes' testimony, in which she said she and Sheppard once shared the same bed in the California home of friends for seven nights, while his wife visited elsewhere in the state.

She said he told her he loved his wife **"very much, but not so much as a wife."**

The slim, pretty laboratory technician told unfalteringly how Sheppard had been her lover from December, 1952, until March, 1954.

During the course of their illicit affair he gave her a ring and a watch, she said.

The ring and watch were the final exhibits presented in evidence by the state before it announced at 1:25 p. m. that it was resting its case, in the seventh week of the trial.

Miss Hayes said Sheppard told her several times he loved her, but she admitted that the only endearing word he used in his letters was written in closing, "Love, Sam." Her testimony did not bring out whether he had ever asked her to marry him.

The state contends Miss Hayes was only one of several women with whom the handsome, 30-year-old Sheppard had affairs. It charges Sheppard beat his pregnant wife, Marilyn, 31, to

(Continued on Page 2, Column 5)

2 Prominent Fort Women Die in Crash

FT. ATKINSON—Two prominent Ft. Atkinson women were fatally injured when their auto slid into a cattle truck on Highway 30 near here early Wednesday.

Mrs. Lillian Strommen, 54, was killed instantly.

Mrs. Nancy Keating, 50, died Wednesday night in a hospital here.

Four Others Hurt

Four others, also passengers in the auto, were injured:

Mrs. Strommen's husband, J. A. (Jack) Strommen, 53, a druggist, broken ribs, deep leg cuts, bruises.

Mrs. Keating's husband, Glenn, 56, Route 1, Ft. Atkinson, a cattle dealer, fractured nose, severe bruises to face and left side of chest.

Mr. and Mrs. Frank Gilbert, also of Ft. Atkinson,

Gilbert, 50, a state internal revenue department employe, suffered a brain concussion and fractured shoulder. His wife suffered minor bruises.

All four injured were reported in "satisfactory" condition at Ft. Atkinson hospital late Wednesday night.

Car Skids on Grade

The Strommen car, driven by Keating, skidded going down a slight grade and smashed into a

(Continued on Page 2, Column 3)

2 Die as Car Leaves Road, Smashes House

RACINE (AP)—A car skidded off icy Highway 41 in Racine County Wednesday and smashed into a house, killing two Marines stationed at Great Lakes, Ill., and critically injuring a third.

Deputies identified the dead as Oliver J. Keller Jr., 21, of Dubuque, Ia., and Frank J. Szabo, 19, of Tovey, Ill.

Ervin H. Sears, 22, of Cincinnati, O., was taken to St. Luke's Hospital here with a fractured spine.

The accident happened about 12 miles northwest of here.

Mrs. Louis Bauer was just four feet away from a window in the living room of her home when the car crashed into it. She was unhurt, but the force of the impact did considerable damage to the home.

Radio Clue Points--but Nothing's Found

A faint and fading radio message indicated that a plane missing in New Hampshire's White mountains was down just east of Berlin, N. H. (arrow), but a search for the wreckage Wednesday found nothing.

United Press-State Journal Telephoto

Slim Hopes Dim for 7 Down in Plane in White Mountains

MILAN, N. H. (AP)—Slim hopes dimmed Wednesday night for the survival of seven persons missing more than 30 hours in a Northeast Airlines plane downed in sub-freezing temperatures in the rugged, snow-covered White mountains.

While ground and air searchers combed the hilly, wooded terrain along the aircraft's Laconia-to-Berlin route without success, an expert mountaineer termed the survival chances of the six men and a woman "very slim."

Searchers were called off at nightfall, but Northeast Airlines President George E. Gardner said that a plane will be flown over the area from time to time during the night to watch for a possibility any survivor might have a fire to keep from freezing.

With temperatures sliding toward zero in the high elevations, Joe Dodge, manager of the Appalachian Mountain Club's Pinkham Notch Camp, said any survivors of the landing could not live another night without proper equipment and clothing.

The slim hope that spurred weary searchers was a faint and fading radio message, "presumably from the pilot," that said: **"Emergency—down 5 miles northeast of field . . . hill, but . . ."**

The message initiated a close air combing of the Bald mountain area, about 5 miles northeast of Berlin airport in Milan. However, the search by helicopter, private plane, and service aircraft failed to turn up the missing airplane.

Two reports of wreckage sightings—one in the early morning, the other in late afternoon—were checked out without confirmation. The early report had wreckage on Bald mountain, the other report had it on Double Head mountain, about 35 miles southeast of Berlin.

A slow helicopter, piloted by Lt. Kenneth M. Richardson of Westover, Mass., Air Force Base, flew the missing plane's scheduled route from Laconia to Berlin airport and reported no trace of the vanished craft.

Cmdr. Robert Gould, of the Salem, Mass., Coast Guard station, in another helicopter, covered some 95 per cent of a three-mile radius of the Berlin airport, also without success.

The plane disappeared Tuesday on a 68-mile run from Laconia to Berlin.

Mercury Dips to 9, Then Rises

Madison's fluctuating temperature kept the mercury busy in official thermometers Wednesday night.

The temperature dropped to a seasonal low of 9 degrees at 9:15 p.m., and appeared headed toward a further drop to 5 degrees.

But then it bounced back, sending the mercury up to 17 degrees early today.

The Truax Field Weatherman predicted the mercury would get up to 30 degrees later today, equalling Wednesday's high, but he said it would drop to 8 degrees tonight.

The previous low for the season was 19, recorded Tuesday, during the first heavy snowfall of the season which finally measured off at 7 inches.

After Wednesday's high the mercury dropped steadily.

Today was expected to be partly cloudy, the weatherman said, but Friday will not be quite so cold.

The frigid air, originating in central Canada, chilled the Plains states, sending the mercury to 8 below at Scottsbluff, Neb.

Meanwhile weather forecasters said a new storm front that could hit the nation with more snow was developing off the California coast.

Snow flurries pelted most of the northern Great Lakes region and extended eastward into central Pennsylvania.

Elsewhere in the nation clear skies prevailed with afternoon temperature extremes ranging from 5 above at Helena, Mont., to a mild 82 degrees at Brownsville, Tex.

You Can Buy Kitten and Help Stocking Club

(Latest Gifts, Page 18)

Anybody want a part-Persian kitten?

You can have one—or more—and help The Wisconsin State Journal Empty Stocking Club at the same time.

Mrs. S. N. Thomson, 3614 Odana rd., has offered to sell the kittens to help the club buy toys and other Christmas gifts for worthy children. She will sell them at $2 each, and give all the money to the Empty Stocking club.

"They are ready to leave their mother," she said, "and they are house-broken—I think.

"If you want a kitten, call at 3614 Odana rd. any morning after 8 or all day Saturday and have your check made to the Empty Stocking Club."

Mrs. Thompson's telephone number during the same hours is 3-6151.

You can help the club, too, by mailing your check, money order, or cash to "The Empty Stocking Club, in care of The Wisconsin State Journal, Madison 1, Wis."

Paris Airports Start Using Take-Off Tax

PARIS (AP)—Paris airports Wednesday began collecting a take-off tax of 1,200 francs ($3.42) on each passenger bound for the United States and elsewhere overseas.

For those bound for other European countries, or North Africa, the tax is 400 francs ($1.14).

The tax is to pay for airport maintenance.

TV Viewer Interrupts Movie to Shoot Wife

PANAMA CITY, Fla. (AP)—Chet Ferris, 55, told officers he interrupted a western television movie Tuesday night to shoot his wife and then returned to watch the western again until the police arrived, police chief George McCall said Wednesday.

He was still engrossed in the thriller when officers arrived.

Investigators said Ferris fired two shots into the chest of his wife as she cooked supper. She staggered to the front door before she died.

Ferris told police the couple had not quarreled immediately before the shooting. But officers quoted him as saying, "you would have done it too if you had the troubles on your mind that I have had for a long time."

He did not elaborate.

The Ferris family moved here five years ago from Riverdale, Md., near Washington, D.C.

He is a civilian machinist at the navy mines countermeasures station here.

Vote of 67-20 Finds Senator Guilty of Abuse

WASHINGTON (AP)—The Senate Wednesday night by a vote of 67-20 condemned the conduct of Sen. Joseph R. McCarthy on the first of three censure charges against him and cleared the way for final action on two other counts today.

The action amounted to a vote of guilty on the charge McCarthy obstructed the Senate and acted contrary to its traditions in failing to help a subcommittee which investigated him in 1951 and 1952, and in "abusing" the group's members.

He Fails to Vote

McCarthy himself did not vote on the censure resolution but denounced it as **"a foul job"** and said the American people know **"I am being censured because I dared to do the 'dishonorable' thing of exposing Communists in government."**

He vowed to continue his investigation of Communist infiltration. **(Story, Page 14)**

McCARTHY

The Wisconsin Republican also got a wholly new investigation started by charging that forgery and suppression of evidence have been used against him. In an outgrowth of this charge, Sen. William F. Knowland of California, the Republican leader, named a special committee to look into the alleged checking of senators' incoming mail by unauthorized persons. **(Story, Column 8).**

All the Democrats present and 23 Republicans joined in voting to "condemn" McCarthy's behavior toward the Hennings-Hayden-Hendrickson subcommittee which investigated his financial and other affairs in 1951 and 1952.

20 Republicans Back Him

Knowland and 19 other Republicans backed McCarthy. The vote came after a series of attempts to spare the Wisconsin senator from censure were defeated by similar lopsided margins.

Still to be disposed of are charges that McCarthy:

ONE. Abused Brig. Gen. Ralph W. Zwicker when the general appeared as a witness before McCarthy's Permanent Investigations subcommittee. He's likely to get more than 20 votes on that count.

TWO. Abused the Watkins committee which recommended he be censured on two other counts. McCarthy has called the committee an "unwitting handmaiden of the Communist party."

Sen. Bourke B. Hickenlooper (R-Ia.), one of the 20 Republicans who voted for McCarthy on the

(Continued on Page 2, Column 2)

Senate Probes 'Mail Checks'

Votes McCarthy Charge Inquiry

WASHINGTON (AP) — The Senate voted Wednesday night for an immediate overnight investigation of Sen. Joseph R. McCarthy's charges that "forgeries" were involved in a "mail check" made on his correspondence during the 1951-52 investigation of his finances.

Senate Republican Leader William F. Knowland (Calif.) called for the inquiry after McCarthy charged that Sen. Guy M. Gillette's name was forged to letters requesting the so-called mail cover.

2 Senators Named

The Senate then unanimously voted to name a two-man subcommittee to investigate the mail cover on McCarthy and any such checks on the mail of any other senators. Sens. Homer Ferguson (R-Mich.) and Walter F. George (D-Ga.) were named as investigators.

The action came after Sen. Carl Hayden (D-Ariz.) had disclosed that an elections subcommittee which investigated McCarthy's finances in 1951-52 ran a mail check in an effort to determine if he had used anti-Communist contributions to play the stock market.

McCarthy promptly charged that "important" evidence relating to the incident had been "suppressed" by staff members of the special committee which recently recommended that he be censured.

Background Told

The elections subcommittee was headed by Gillette, but the Iowa Democrat denied he knew anything about a mail cover. McCarthy told the Senate Gillette's name was "forged" to letters to the postoffice requesting the mail cover.

The mail cover did not involve opening or reading McCarthy's mail. Rather, the addresses on the envelopes were recorded to show with whom he was corresponding.

Knowland said he hoped the two-man subcommittee could go

(Continued on Page 2, Column 1)

Journal Begins 116th Year of Publication

The Wisconsin State Journal today begins its 116th year of publication.

The paper was founded Dec. 2, 1839, as a weekly by W. W. Wyman. In 1848 its name was changed to The Wisconsin State Journal and the paper became Madison's first daily.

The Wisconsin State Journal was published as an afternoon newspaper until Feb. 1, 1949. On that date it became a morning paper and publishes every day of the year.

Record Shows Mailman Carried, Not Carrier

ARMSTRONG, Mo. (AP)—W. T. Wallace retired Wednesday after 45 years on the job, during which he said he wore out a two-wheel cart, a buggy, a sleigh, six horses, three used cars, and 14 new ones.

He was a rural mail carrier here.

Actress Whose Hit-Run Car Killed Boy, 9, Gets 60 Days

LOS ANGELES (U.P.)—Blonde Actress Lynn Baggett was sent to county jail for 60 days Wednesday as a condition of her three years probation for felony hit-run driving in connection with the death of a 9-year-old boy.

The 27-year-old actress was acquitted of manslaughter charges in the death of Joel Watnick last July 6 but was convicted of hit-run driving for fleeing from the scene of a traffic accident.

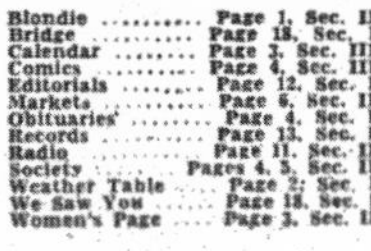

BAGGETT

"I am convinced of her attempt to evade responsibility of the law in leaving the scene of the accident," Superior Judge Mildred L. Lillie said in ordering the actress to jail.

Miss Baggett was driving a car borrowed from Actor George Tobias when she rammed a station wagon in which the Watnick boy and several other youngsters were riding.

The actress fled from the scene and her identity was not established until police located the borrowed car in a garage undergoing repairs. She then was surrendered by an attorney to police.

In stressing the necessity of some punishment, Judge Lillie told Miss Baggett that she had done "everything in her power" to evade detection.

The judge said he was convinced Miss Baggett was motivated by a feeling of irresponsibility rather than fear or panic in fleeing from the scene.

Miss Baggett is the estranged wife of movie producer Sam Spiegel. After hearing the verdict, Miss Baggett's mother, Mrs. Ruth Simmons, collapsed in court.

Feature Finder

25 Speeders Arrested in City on First Day of Radar's Use

Twenty-five speeders were caught by Madison police Wednesday during the first day's use of radar to arrest speeders in the city.

Thirteen drivers were arrested in school zones and the rest for exceeding the 25-mile-an-hour maximum speed in the city.

Officers in charge of operating the radar system said none of the drivers arrested offered much of a protest but were surprised at being stopped by the flashing red light at the end of the radar speed zone.

Patrolman James Schwarz, who was one of the night radar operators, said, **"I didn't get a single argument out of the five arrested"** Wednesday night. **"They just had a lot of faith in the machine."**

Sgt. Hiram Wilson of the department's traffic division said Wednesday night **"we've been warning drivers in the city for about four and one-half months about radar and I guess it's paying off. Traffic was moving along as it should Wednesday night in spite of the weather."**

The five speeders arrested Wednesday night were caught in the 3300 block of Sherman ave. and the 1200 block of Williamson st.

Between 11:15 a.m. and 1 p.m. police caught 13 speeders in the 3900 block of Nakoma rd. where the speed limit is 15 miles per hour past Nakoma school.

Eight other speeders were arrested by radar between 9:50 and 10:50 a.m. just two blocks from the school where the limit is 25 miles per hour in the 4100 block of Nakoma rd.

From now on radar checks will be made in alternate locations daily throughout the city.

Frost Likely Tonight
Continued cool today, with frost likely tonight. Continued cool Saturday. High today about 60; low tonight 32. Sun rose, 5:49 (DST); sets, 8 (DST).

Wisconsin State Journal

MORNING FINAL | SECTION 1 | MADISON, FRIDAY, MAY 3, 1957 | 5 CENTS | 40 PAGES, THREE SECTIONS Vol. 191, No. 33 118th Year

SEN. McCARTHY DIES AT AGE 47

Appointment Not Permitted

Election Expected for Senate Vacancy

By LEW ROBERTS
(State Journal Staff Writer)

Wisconsin law provides that Gov. Vernon W. Thomson will have to call a special election to fill the seat of Sen. Joseph McCarthy or leave the post vacant until the 1958 general election.

Wisconsin law does not permit the governor to appoint a successor to such a vacancy, although the laws of most states do.

Thomson was en route to a speaking engagement at New Holstein in Calumet county when the news of McCarthy's death reached Wisconsin late Thursday.

Expresses Sympathy

Leroy Luberg, executive secretary to the governor, talked to Thomson by telephone after the governor reached New Holstein. The governor expressed his condolences to the McCarthy family.

THOMSON

Thomson did not comment immediately on whether he would call the special election which he may by law. The chief executive declined to discuss that possibility "in deference to the senator's family."

Wisconsin law provides that the governor can order a special election in the case of a vacancy in the Senate or House of Representatives.

Governor Sets Date

If he so chooses, the special election must be held within 55 to 70 days after the governor issues the order. And a primary election must be held four weeks

(Continued on Page 2, Column 8)

News Shocks State Leaders

Wisconsin Republican leaders in legion expressed grief Thursday night at the death of Wisconsin's junior senator, Joseph R. McCarthy, a Republican from Appleton.

State GOP leaders were more "shocked" than "surprised." Reports had been circulating for weeks among the Republican party workers that McCarthy was in poor health.

Gov. and Mrs. Vernon W. Thomson expressed their "**deepest sympathy to Mrs. McCarthy and her baby daughter.**"

"Thousands of McCarthy's devoted followers will be grief stricken with the news of the senator's passing," Thomson said.

Philip G. Kuehn, Milwaukee, state GOP chairman, called McCarthy's death a "great shock."

"He was one of the most courageous and outspoken senators of all time," Kuehn said. **"He awakened America to the horrible inroads communism has made in our country. Many times he stood alone but he carried on his fight to the bitter end."**

A Wisconsin Republican who probably knew McCarthy as intimately as any made no reference to the senator's actions in Congress in paying his final tribute to McCarthy.

He was Sen. Gerald Lorge (R-Bear Creek), a 34-year-old lawyer from McCarthy's home county of Outagamie who had been a captain on McCarthy's team since 1946. That was the year McCarthy was elected to the Senate, and Lorge, fresh out of service, breakfasted with him in Washington the day McCarthy got there.

"Sen. McCarthy was the most fascinating and interesting political personage I have ever known," Lorge said Thursday night, visibly affected by the news of McCarthy's death.

"He was a person who liked people and who wanted people to like him, Lorge said. **"He was always willing and ready to offer assistance to any person who needed help."**

Kuehn said that McCarthy's death "shall be recorded as one of the most tragic casualties in

(Continued on Page 2, Column 5)

Gen. Zwicker Won't Comment on Death

TOKYO, Friday (AP)—A spokesman for Maj. Gen. Ralph W. Zwicker, long a target of the late Sen. Joseph McCarthy, said today the general will have "absolutely no comment whatsoever" on the Wisconsin lawmaker's death.

Zwicker, who takes command of the U. S. 24th division in Korea later this month, clashed with McCarthy only recently when the senator attempted to block his promotion to major general.

Zwicker currently is an assistant chief of staff at U. S. Far East Army headquarters.

Braves Defeat Pirates, 8-5

See the Sports Peach

SEN. JOSEPH R. McCARTHY
1909 — 1957

His Political Career Started as Democrat

By ARTHUR BYSTROM
(Associated Press Staff Writer)

Sen. Joseph R. McCarthy, who made his first bid for public office as a Democrat in 1936, became a Republican senator 10 years later and then went on to establish himself as one of the most controversial figures in modern American political history.

Death ended his colorful career Thursday.

He became a circuit judge four years after he finished law school following a house-to-house campaign in three north-central Wisconsin counties, challenged Sen. Alexander Wiley (R-Wis.) in 1944, and then went on in 1946 to beat the late Robert M. La Follette Jr., son of the famous "Fighting Bob."

His self-confidence that approached brashness in challenging La Follette, a three-term senator and one of the most respected men in Washington, set a pattern for his aggressive conduct in a turbulent career in the years to come.

Shortly after finishing law school at Marquette University, McCarthy went to work in the law office of Mike Eberlein, a prominent Republican of Shawano, Wis.

A year later, in 1936, he became president of the Seventh district Young Democratic clubs and made his first bid for public office by running for Shawano county district attorney. He was beaten by the Republican candidate.

He remained with the Young Democratic clubs for some time after that but gradually became less active and continued to practice law with Eberlein.

Becomes a Judge

In 1939 he entered the race for circuit judge against the incumbent, Edgar V. Werner. Eberlein also had planned to run

(Continued on Page 2, Column 3)

Frank Costello Wounded; No One Hears Shot

NEW YORK (AP) — Gambler Frank Costello suffered a grazing bullet wound of the scalp Thursday night in what police called "an apparent attempt at assassination."

The shooting occurred in the lobby of Costello's apartment house at 115 Central Park West, a plush Manhattan area, police said.

Costello was treated at Roosevelt hospital, and was scheduled for quick discharge.

Officers said Costello's wife and William Kennedy, a theatrical agent, were with him at the time of the shooting. They said they had just come by taxi from a restaurant on E. 55th st., where they had had dinner with Generoso Pope, publisher of an Italian-language paper, when the shooting occurred.

Detectives quoted Costello as saying that he, his wife and Kennedy were just passing through the building's street door into the lobby when he felt a sting above his right ear, then a quick flow of blood.

All three told police they heard no shot and did not see the gunman. After a few moments they went to Roosevelt hospital by taxi.

Costello, who has been described as one of the most powerful figures in national gambling and racketeering circles, was convicted in 1954 of evading $28,532 in federal income taxes. He began a five-year prison term last May, but was released on $25,000 bond.

He was freed by the Supreme Court pending a ruling on whether the law under which he was convicted provides a maximum sentence of only one year.

Feature Finder

Illness Closes Stormy Career

WASHINGTON (UP) — Sen. Joseph R. McCarthy, the Wisconsin farm boy who streaked across the U. S. political scene like a fiery comet, died at Bethesda Naval hospital late Thursday of acute hepatitis at the age of 47.

With his wife of less than four years, the former Jean Kerr, at his bedside, McCarthy succumbed at 6:02 p.m., EDT., after receiving Holy Communion and the last rites of the Roman Catholic Church.

He had been admitted to the hospital Sunday in serious condition.

Ill for Several Weeks

The hospital said he was "seriously ill at the time of admission and his condition progressively failed." It also said he had been ill at his home for "several weeks" before going to the hospital.

An aide said burial probably would be in Wisconsin. Messages of condolence poured into the senator's office and home throughout the evening.

The senator's body was taken to the Joseph Gawler's Sons, Inc., funeral home. A spokesman at the funeral home said he has received no instructions on arrangements.

Friends and foes alike in Congress expressed shock at his death. Some who had disagreed sharply with his political views and investigating tactics said he was "a fine fellow" and gracious in his private life.

Special Election Planned

McCarthy's second term in the Senate was due to expire in January, 1959. Wisconsin Gov. Vernon Thomson, a Republican like McCarthy, was expected to call a special election to fill the Senate vacancy.

Democratic control of the Senate would not be affected since the present political lineup is 49 Democrats and 47 Republicans.

McCarthy, who suffered various illnesses in the past, was fatally stricken by acute hepatitis, an inflammation of the liver which results in digestive disturbances and brings on acute exhaustion.

A spokesman for the Naval hospital said the senator took a turn for the worse between 4 and 5 p. m. The spokesman said it was apparent McCarthy was "slipping" and that about 5:30 p. m., "it became obvious he couldn't be saved."

The last rites of the Catholic Church were administered

(Continued on Page 2, Column 1)

Ike, Others Tell Widow of Sympathy

WASHINGTON (AP)—The President and Mrs. Eisenhower extended "profound sympathy" to the widow of Sen. Joseph R. McCarthy (R-Wis.) Thursday night on the death of her husband.

Mr. Eisenhower issued this statement through his press secretary, James Hagerty:

"I have just been informed of the sudden passing of Sen. Joseph R. McCarthy.

"Mrs. Eisenhower joins me in extending our profound sympathy to Mrs. McCarthy in the grievous personal loss she has sustained."

EISENHOWER

Hagerty said the President had sent a personal telegram to Mrs. McCarthy phrased in similar terms. This was not made public.

News of McCarthy's death shocked his colleagues on Capitol hill.

Sen. Karl Mundt (R-S. D.) who presided over the stormy McCarthy-Army hearings three years ago, said he had no idea that McCarthy's illness was "terminal in any way."

"I am greatly shocked at the tragic news of the unexpected passing of Joe McCarthy," Mundt said. **"His passing takes out of the American political arena a courageous fighter against communism and a stal-**

(Continued on Page 2, Column 6)

Full Page of Pictures on Sen. McCarthy, Page 3

For History: Figure of Controversy, a Biography, Page 7

City Murder Suspect Surrenders in Texas After Phoning Wife

(Another Picture, Sec. 2, Page 1)

Ralph O'Dell, wanted for the murder of a Madison bowling alley pinsetter, was convinced by his wife in a telephone call to surrender Thursday afternoon to El Paso, Tex., police.

Law enforcement officials left here at 6:20 p. m. by plane to return O'Dell here to face charges of slaying Joseph Knock, also known as Joseph Knox, 57, resident pinsetter at the Lark Lanes, 2550 University ave.

Dist. Atty. Joseph W. Bloodgood said that O'Dell would be charged with first degree murder.

Mrs. O'Dell, 23, of 1845 Fisher st., told The Wisconsin State Journal that her husband telephoned about 3 p. m. from El Paso wanting to know what had happened since he fled after Knock was shot about 3 a. m.

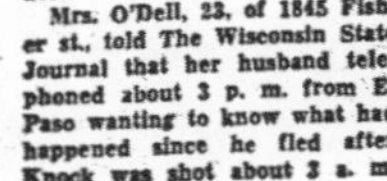

RALPH O'DELL

Saturday in a burglary attempt by O'Dell with two other men at the Lark.

O'Dell, 25, a foundry worker, formerly set pins with Knock at the Lark.

"He hadn't seen a paper or heard a news broadcast and didn't even know the other two had been picked up," Mrs. O'Dell said.

The "other two" are Edward Krueger, 25, of 1916 Fisher st., and Robert Otteson, 22, of 606 S. Brearly st., who were caught hiding in a boiler room at the Lark after O'Dell fled. They have pleaded innocent to first degree murder charges and identified O'Dell as the slayer.

Mrs. O'Dell's account of her telephone call continued.

"When I told him what had

(Continued on Page 2, Column 4)

Four Prominent State Republicans May Contend for McCarthy's Seat

At least four prominent Wisconsin Republicans were regarded as possible contenders for the late Sen. Joseph McCarthy's seat in the United States Senate.

The foremost possibility is former governor Walter J. Kohler, 53, three times governor of Wisconsin, who announced previous to McCarthy's illness that he was considering making the race.

Other possible Republican candidates include Glenn R. Davis, 42, Waukesha, a former Second district congressman and unsuccessful candidate for the GOP nomination last year against Sen. Alexander Wiley.

Lt. Gov. Warren Knowles, 48, New Richmond, who has been particularly active in party campaign work, is another possible GOP candidate.

Two Republican congressmen also are considered as possible timber for the senate. They are Rep. John W. Byrnes, 43, Green Bay, and Rep. Melvin Laird, 34, Marshfield. Both are former state senators and are well thought of among Republican party people.

KOHLER DAVIS KNOWLES BYRNES

It is unlikely that Gov. Vernon Thomson will enter the race. He long aspired to the gubernatorial post before he won election last year and is not expected to leave it now.

Leonard F. Schmitt, a Merrill attorney, also might be interested in making the race for the GOP nomination. He ran against McCarthy, in 1952 when six men were in the field and finished

(Continued on Page 2, Column 1)

Cloudy and Cool
Cloudy and cool with occasional rain today. Thursday mostly cloudy and a little warmer. High today, upper 60s; low tonight, 50-55. Sun rose, 6:17; sets, 7:39.

Wisconsin State Journal

MORNING FINAL | SECTION 1 | MADISON, WEDNESDAY, AUGUST 28, 1957 | ★★★ | 5 CENTS | 24 PAGES, THREE SECTIONS Vol. 191, No. 149 118th Year

PROXMIRE DEFEATS KOHLER IN SMASHING UPSET VOTE

Senate Passes Aid Bill of $3.7 Billion

WASHINGTON (UP) — The Senate passed its beefed-up $3.7 billion foreign aid money bill late Tuesday, and President Eisenhower promptly appealed to the House to follow suit "quickly."

The 62-to-25 roll call vote sent the bill to a House-Senate Conference committee, which must reconcile the Senate version with the smaller $2.5 billion program approved by the economy-bent House.

Coalition Vote

A bipartisan coalition of 32 Republicans and 30 Democrats voted for the bill. It was opposed by 15 Democrats and 10 Republicans.

The foreign aid and civil rights bills are the only remaining major roadblocks to adjournment of Congress late this week.

House-Senate conferees on the aid bill scheduled a meeting for 10:30 a. m. today in an attempt to hammer out a bill.

Ike's 'Pleased'

Mr. Eisenhower, who was "greatly pleased" by the Senate foreign aid vote, said its action in restoring some half-billion dollars trimmed from the bill by the House was "a substantial step in the right direction."

GOP leaders had warned him in advance that the House-Senate committee probably would trim the Senate figure.

The President's statement for quick House action was issued by the White House while he was at the Walter Reed Army Medical center visiting Mrs. Eisenhower, who is convalescing from her operation.

Below Request

The Senate total fell far below the President's original aid request in his January budget message and also was about $300 million less than his revised request which he had labeled an absolute minimum.

However, GOP congressional leaders reported after a White House conference which preceded the Senate vote that he was "well satisfied" with the Senate total. At the same time, Senate GOP Leader William F. Knowland (Calif.) cautioned him that the House - Senate Conference committee probably would cut it.

Mr. Eisenhower had appealed to the Senate to vote all of the $3.4 billion authorized in a bill passed earlier by Congress.

Besides $3 billion in new funds, the Senate bill called for reappropriation of $667 million in "carry-over" funds from previous years.

Young Man Admits 'Heiress Death' Hoax

By JUNE DIECKMANN
(State Journal Staff Writer)

A young farm man, posing as a wealthy sophisticate, admitted Tuesday that a story of his heiress wife's death from Asiatic flu was his "screwballish hoax" to gain himself publicity.

Trapped by his own extended pretense, Jerald Richard Jorstad, 24, Rt. 1, Newark, Ill., told police and Dist. Atty. Joseph W. Bloodgood that he had telephoned the death story of his non-existent wife to The Wisconsin State Journal last Saturday night.

JORSTAD

He was held in jail to be charged this morning in Superior Court with giving false information to a newspaper. He will also be charged with cashing two worthless checks, for $5 and $6.50, at the University YMCA, Bloodgood said.

The charge of giving false information carries a maximum penalty of six months in jail, $200 fine, or both. He faces up to a year's jail sentence and $1,000 fine on the check charges.

Jorstad admitted posing as "Richard Elton-Quincey Adams," son of a New York stock broker, since he came to Madison three weeks ago.

He said he had plans of using false records to "con" his way onto the University of Wisconsin journalism school staff as a teaching assistant and post-graduate student. Actually, he did not graduate from high school and got a high school diploma by taking extension courses while in the Army, he said Tuesday.

'End of Line'

His plans were progressing, but not fast enough for him to continue because of "a lack of immediate funds," so he devised the idea of an heiress wife and her death to give him "quick recognition to obtain credit and employment," he said.

Jorstad said he was "reaching the end of the line," so that he was not concerned with the probability that he would be discovered and arrested.

"I even felt that physical detention and becoming accustomed to routine and disciplinary action might do me good," he said.

Jorstad said he did not want to commit a felony, so he studied the Wisconsin statutes at the Madison free library and learned that giving false information to a newspaper was classified as a misdemeanor.

Admits Making Call

"It was just the thing for me because I couldn't select an every-day-routine-type misdemean-

(Continued on Page 2, Column 1)

WIBA Knocked Out as Cables Are Cut

Street repair crews of the L. S. Lunder Construction Co., working at Glenway ave. and Regent st., Tuesday dug up a main trunk cable leading into radio station WIBA and knocked out network, broadcast, and news lines.

The break occurred at 1:45 p.m. One hour later the station was back on the air, relaying programs to the main transmitter on the Fish Hatchery rd. via a mobile transmitter.

Phone company workers re-established network service at 3:45 p.m., and the Associated Press news wire went back into operation at 4:25 after more than three hours.

Smiles Tell Story of Sweet Victory

William Proxmire and his wife, Ellen, who managed his campaign, flashed big victory smiles at his Milwaukee headquarters Tuesday night as they learned he had been elected to Wisconsin's vacant U. S. Senate seat. Proxmire, who said he was "overwhelmed" at the size of his victory margin, will become the first Democratic U. S. senator from Wisconsin in 25 years. —AP Wirephoto

Size of Victory Vote 'Overwhelms' Winner

By JACK HARNED
(State Journal Staff Writer)

William Proxmire said Tuesday night he was "overwhelmed" by the size of the vote which brought him the personal triumph of election to the U. S. Senate.

Proxmire said in Milwaukee, where he heard the returns, that the special election was "the most emphatic way that farmers and small businessmen have of protesting against the Eisenhower Administration."

His election offers "a chance for the clean, young, and vigorous Democratic party of Wisconsin to show what it can do in the U. S. Senate and in the state capitol in 1958," he declared.

Returns Today

The senator-elect said he plans to make two plant gate appearances in Milwaukee early today before returning to his home in Blooming Grove. Such appearances, made by the hundreds, have been his major campaign weapon. He expected to be in Madison before noon today.

Then, Proxmire said, "I want to get to Washington as soon as possible." He said also that he would begin immediately his campaign for reelection in November, 1958.

Proxmire's defeated opponent, former Gov. Walter J. Kohler, was apparently so stunned by his upset defeat that he went into seclusion and couldn't be reached by newsmen.

No Kohler Statement

Kohler followed the results at his home in Kohler village. A spokesman said he would issue a

(Continued on Page 2, Column 4)

Hillsboro Tallies Its 269 Votes Quickly

HILLSBORO—It took only 20 minutes to tally the 269 votes cast here Tuesday.

This was record time, according to veteran Hillsboro poll workers, who attributed the speed to the fact that only 10 independent votes were cast. Walter Kohler received 142 of the other votes, and William Proxmire 117.

New State Laws

Chapters 604 to 612, new state laws.
(Texts, Sec. 2, Page 4)

$7\frac{1}{2}$c Pay Hike Set at Oscar Mayer

Some 3,500 plant employes of Oscar Mayer and Co. will receive a $7\frac{1}{2}$-cent per hour wage increase starting Sept. 1 under a three-year union contract signed in October, 1956.

The contract also called for increases in night premium pay fom $9\frac{1}{2}$ to 10 cents per hour.

It will raise minimum rates for male employes to $\$1.91\frac{1}{2}$ per hour, and for female workers to $1.90.

Announcement of the Sept. 1 pay boost was made jointly Tuesday by P. Goff Beach Jr., vice-president of operations, and Frank Davis, secretary-treasurer and business manager of Local 538, Amalgamated Meat Cutters and Butcher Workmen of North America AFL-CIO.

Red Cross Man Sent to Reedsburg to Help

REEDSBURG—A national Red Cross representative, David Curnock, Edgerton, has been assigned to the fire disaster area here and will handle requests for disaster aid.

He is the Red Cross field representative of southwestern Wisconsin.

All the immediate emergency needs have been met by the Reedsburg community and the Sauk county Red Cross, headed by Mrs. Dennis Clossey Sr.

Feature Finder

State Picks 1st Democrat Since '32 for Senate

By LEW ROBERTS
(State Journal Staff Writer)

Democrat William Proxmire bolted to a smashing upset victory Tuesday night over three-time Republican Gov. Walter J. Kohler to succeed the late Sen. Joseph R. McCarthy.

The vote in 3,359 of Wisconsin's 3,361 precincts, according to United Press tabulations, was:

Proxmire	435,462
Kohler	318,894

The balding, tireless, athletic Proxmire moved to Wisconsin 10 years ago with the express purpose of entering into politics.

He becomes the first Democrat sent to the U. S. Senate from Wisconsin since F. Ryan Duffy, Fond du Lac, smothered John Chapple, Ashland, in the Roosevelt landslide of 1932.

Takes Early Lead

The 41-year-old Proxmire took the lead with the first precinct reporting and quickly built up a commanding lead with returns from scattered rural precincts which normally vote Republican.

Kohler, 53, won only 16 of the state's 71 counties. Proxmire carried 33 counties that Kohler had won in both 1952 and 1954 gubernatorial races against Proxmire.

Kohler lost such Republican strongholds as Sauk, Richland, Jefferson, Lincoln, Waukesha, Columbia, and Green counties.

Three independent candidates trailed far behind, and their votes had no effect whatsoever on the Proxmire-Kohler contest.

Howard H. Boyle, Milwaukee attorney and a McCarthy Republican, had 20,231 votes; Douglas Wheaton, an "Always America First" Winneconne steamfitter, 2,242; and Mrs. Georgia Cozzini, Milwaukee Socialist Labor candidate, 749, all in 3,318 precincts.

Wins Dane County

Proxmire won Dane county, carrying all but 11 of the 94 precincts in building up a margin of 29,607 to 18,466 over Kohler. Proxmire's edge in the city of Madison was 16,507 to 11,912.

Proxmire tied Kohler in Brooklyn and lost to him only in Maple Bluff, Shorewood Hills, and eight Madison precincts. Proxmire won the two precincts of his home township of Blooming Grove by a four-to-one majority.

Counties won by Kohler were Walworth, Waushara, Green Lake, Vilas, Rock, Door, Shawano, Marquette, Ozaukee, Waupaca, Grant, Fond du Lac, Sheboygan, Washington, Outagamie, and Calumet.

The total vote, when all votes were counted, apparently was going to be nearly 800,000, a figure predicted earlier in the week by campaign aides of both major candidates. Only 460,000 votes had been cast in the primary for the special election four weeks earlier.

Swear-In Waits

Proxmire will not be sworn into office (by Vice President Richard M. Nixon) until after the canvass of votes by the secretary of state's office. This is expected to take about a week.

He will serve the 16 months of McCarthy's unexpired term. A senator to a full six-year term will be elected in November.

(Continued on Page 2, Column 6)

Braves Nip Giants, 4-3

Yanks Beat Sox; Cardinals Split; Cubs Beat Brooks

See the Sports Peach

Dr. Ganser Suffers Stroke in Canada

Dr. W. J. Ganser, 1030 Vilas ave., a staff physician at Madison General hospital, was reported in "fair" condition Tuesday night at hospital after returning here from Canada where he suffered a stroke.

He returned here Tuesday night flying by chartered plane from Duluth, Minn., to the municipal airport. He was on vacation in Canada when he suffered the stroke, authorities reported.

From the airport, he was taken by Bilsie ambulance with police assistance to Madison General.

Dr. Ganser has offices at 119 Monona ave. with Dr. E. G. Welke.

Reedsburg Fire Burns 7 Businesses

REEDSBURG — Seven business places were destroyed by an estimated $2 million fire which burned more than half a city block in downtown Reedsburg early Tuesday morning.

More than a hundred persons were put out of work.

As yet the cause of the fire was undetermined.

The fire started under the grocery and meat department of the Helms-Quinlan department store, located on N. Walnut st., at 2:10 a.m.

Seven fire departments from nearby cities and towns helped the Reedsburg department fight the blaze, which was brought under control seven hours later. Trucks came from Loganville, Rock Springs, Lake Delton, LaValle, Baraboo, Portage, and the Badger Ordnance Works.

The fire destroyed buildings on Main st., which runs perpendicular to Walnut, and on Second st., which runs paralled to Main was first noticed by the department store's night watchman, Paul Schrank, 40, who reported that he was cleaning the front of the

(Continued on Page 2, Column 1)

The Century-Old Helms-Quinlan Department Store at Reedsburg Goes Up in Flames. —Emery G. Gregory Photo

Wilking Wins Alderman's Seat; Marks, Hanson Named to Board

By STANLEY WILLIAMS
(State Journal Staff Writer)

Werner A. Wilking won bysix votes Tuesday over Mrs. Barbara J. Fraser to become the first alderman from the still-disputed 21st ward.

HANSON

Wilking, counsel for the State Department of Securities, lives at 5105 Spring ct.

He ran second to Mrs. Fraser in the July 30 primary.

The final vote was:

Fraser	92
Wilking	98

Mrs. Fraser has led the current campaign for signatures on new annexation petitions in a second attempt to bring the ward into the city. The first annexation is still being contested by the town of Madison.

MARKS WILKING

She led Wilking in the primary by a vote of 67 to 46. The wife of a University of Wisconsin professor, she lives at 5741 Elder pl.

James A. Marks, a university engineering instructor and head of the engineering job placement service, was elected supervisor from the new far West side ward.

He defeated James O. Campbell, 5521 Gettle ave., an accountant. Marks lives at 1733 Capital ave.

The final vote was:

Marks	133
Campbell	54

In the 16th ward election for supervisor, Lars M. Hanson won a 22-vote victory over Marvin Brickson, president of the Madison Federation of Labor.

It was a come-back in city politics for Hanson, who was alderman from the 16th ward until his defeat in the April, 1956, election by Ald. Glenn L. Henry.

The final vote was:

Hanson	602
Brickson	580

Hanson, who operates the Vogue Cleaners at 705 State st., lives at 413 Welch ave. Brickson, secretary of the Painters union, Local 802, lives at 2310 Willard ave.

The total vote in Madison was 28,861, which was about 58 per cent of the total registration. Pre-

(Continued on Page 2, Column 7)

A Little Cooler
Partly cloudy and a little cooler today. Fair and cooler Thursday. High today, about 65; low tonight, about 40. Sun rose, 6:47; sets, 6:50.

Wisconsin State Journal

MORNING FINAL | SECTION 1 | MADISON, WEDNESDAY, SEPTEMBER 25, 1957 | ★★★ | 28 PAGES, THREE SECTIONS Vol. 191, No. 175 119th Year | 5c

PRESIDENT EISENHOWER
'. . . enemies are gloating . . .'

IKE TELLS LITTLE ROCK: END ANARCHY, OBEY LAW

U. S. Troops Surround School

1,000 Paratroopers Arrive; Crowd Quiet

LITTLE ROCK, Ark. (AP)—Strapping paratroopers armed with live ammunition rolled into Little Rock Tuesday night representing President Eisenhower's historic decision to back a Federal Court integration order with force.

Hundreds of Little Rock citizens watched without a murmur as the force of about 500 men of the famed 101st Airborne division split, one group going to the Central High school grounds and another to the National Guard armory.

A number of Negro troops was among them.

500 More Arrive

Late Tuesday night a second 500 paratroopers arrived at Little Rock Air Force base, making a total of 1,000 soldiers. The new arrivals also separated into two groups and proceeded to the school and the armory.

BRUCKER

A newsman at the air base said he heard that even more paratroopers were on the way.

A few minutes later Adj. Gen. Sherman T. Clinger, who commanded the Guard that kept the Negro students out of Central High for more than two weeks, ordered all members of the Army and Air National Guard to "mobilize immediately" and await instructions.

Brucker Orders Guard

The federal troops are under the command of Maj. Gen. Edwin A. Walker, decorated combat soldier, who is commander of the Arkansas military district.

Army Secretary Wilber Brucker said all Arkansas Guardsmen were being ordered to report to their armories. He said probably only selected Guard units will be needed for immediate duty in Little Rock. An Army spokesman said Walker has authority to decide which troops to employ, and how and when to use them.

President Eisenhower, who expressed sadness at the "action I was compelled to take today," explained his reasons for ordering the troops and federalizing the Arkansas National Guard and Air National Guard in a nationwide television-radio address. **(Story, Column 7)**

The nine Negro students who were taken out of Central High Monday noon because of the danger of the explosive crowd probably will try to enter again today, this time under the protection of the armed troops. Mrs. L. C. Bates, Arkansas NAACP president, said "If federal troops are there to protect the children, the Negro children will go to school tomorrow."

Gov. Orval Faubus, who claims the President sent the troops in without proper authority, declined

(Continued on Page 2, Column 1)

Troops of 101st Airborne Division Roll Toward Duty at Central High School. —AP Wirephoto

Merchants Plan Use of New Shoplift Law

Armed with a new state shoplifting law, Madison merchants and law enforcement officials met Tuesday to find new ways to prevent what was termed a "major social and economic problem in the city."

Meeting at the Park hotel, the group, headed by the detail division of the Madison Chamber of Commerce, discussed methods of publicizing a new state law which protects the merchant or employe in his right to detain by force a shoplifter without fear of legal reprisal.

To Acquaint Merchants

Wisconsin is one of the first states to enact the law and Tuesday's planning meeting was called to acquaint merchants with ways of applying the new right, without abusing it.

The chamber expects to set up meetings with individual merchants and their employes to train them on how to handle shoplifters.

According to Richard Johnston, head of the retail division of the chamber, Madison merchants lose an estimated $1,200,000 a year from shoplifters.

Over the state, it's a $30 million crime.

More important, according to law officials at the meeting, it has become a growing social problem with the average age of shoplifters getting lower each year.

Both the city police and the Dane county sheriff's office, merchants were told, are keeping card files on all offenses, regardless of the value of the merchandise stolen, so parents, when called before a judge or juvenile officer, can see how far their children have gone in defying the law.

Before the 1957 Legislature's action, a merchant was hesitant to lay hands on a shoplifter to detain him for fear of being sued. The new law allows a "reasonable" amount of force in preventing shoplifting.

Parents Unaware

Circuit Judge Richard W. Bardwell Jr. pointed out that many parents, when confronted with the fact that their youngsters have been shoplifting, are ignorant of what their children have been doing.

Others at the meeting claimed the offense, even if small, "is the primary breeding ground for crime."

Among those attending were Deputy Atty. Gen. John Winner, Circuit Court Judges Bardwell and Edwin M. Wilkie, Superior Judge Roy H. Proctor, Dist. Atty. Joseph Bloodgood, Jerome Foy, Dane county probation officer; Sheriff Fred Goff, Detective Capt. Harry L. Milsted, Robert Carnes of the division of children and youth of the state Department of Public Welfare; George W. Foster, professor of law at the University of Wisconsin; I. W. Lackore, secretary of the Madison Chamber of Commerce, Johnston, and several Madison merchants.

Then I'll Pull Out Troops, He Promises

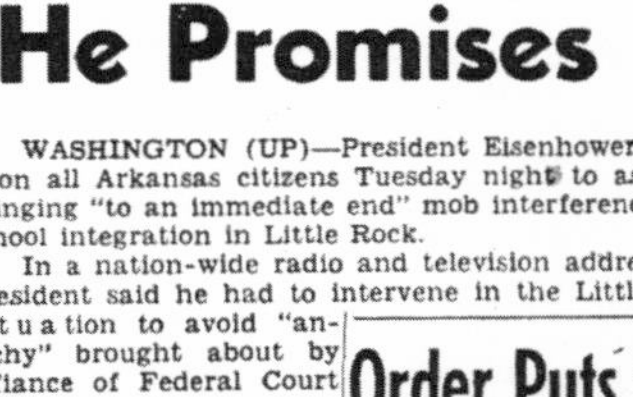

WASHINGTON (UP)—President Eisenhower called upon all Arkansas citizens Tuesday night to assist in bringing "to an immediate end" mob interference with school integration in Little Rock.

In a nation-wide radio and television address, the President said he had to intervene in the Little Rock situation to avoid "anarchy" brought about by defiance of Federal Court decisions.

The President said that federal troops will not be necessary if there is an immediate end to resistance to the Federal Court order to integrate Central High school.

He Explains

Mr. Eisenhower said he was saddened by the fact that he had to order the Arkansas National Guard into federal service and authorize use of regular Army troops to enforce integration at Little Rock.

"In that city, under the leadership of demagogic extremists, disorderly mobs have deliberately prevented the carrying out of the proper orders from a Federal Court," the President said.

Mr. Eisenhower noted that he issued a proclamation Monday calling upon the mob to disperse.

When "the mob" again gathered in front of Central High school Tuesday morning to keep Negro children from entering the school, he said, his duty was "inescapable."

"Mob rule cannot be allowed to override the decisions of the courts," the President declared.

'Enemies Gloat'

He said America's enemies are "gloating over this incident and using it everywhere to misrepresent our nation."

Mr. Eisenhower said these enemies are picturing this country as a violator of United Nations standards opposing discrimination because of race, sex, language or religion.

"And so, with confidence, I call upon citizens of the state of Arkansas to assist in bringing to an immediate end all interference with the law and its processes," he said.

"If resistance to the Federal Court orders ceases at once, the further presence of federal troops will be unnecessary and the city

(Continued on Page 2, Column 4)

Order Puts GIs in Little Rock

Guard Federalized; Other Troops OKd

NEWPORT, R. I. (UP) — President Eisenhower ordered federal troops into Little Rock, Ark., Tuesday to force compliance with court-ordered integration of the city's Central High school.

Moving swiftly to carry out the President's orders, the Army rushed 500 paratroopers from the elite 101st Airborne division from Ft. Campbell, Ky., to Little Rock. They were flown in Air Force transports to the scene of the integration disorders.

Calls the Guard

Mr. Eisenhower authorized use of the regular Army troops in an order that called the Arkansas National Guard into federal service to quell riotous obstruction of the school desegregation order handed down by a federal judge at Little Rock.

WILSON

Defense Secretary Charles E. Wilson drew up the necessary orders carrying out the President's mandate, and Army Secretary Wilber M. Brucker was given full authority to act in the integration crisis.

The President issued his historic order at Newport before flying to Washington to deliver a nation-wide radio-television report explaining his drastic action. **(Story above.)**

Arrives in Capital

The chief executive arrived at the capital at 4:50 p. m. and was driven immediately to the White House. There the chief executive promptly conferred with Atty. Gen. Herbert Brownell, who had

(Continued on Page 2, Column 8)

24 Vetoes Sustained; 8 Put Off

The Legislature Tuesday sustained 24 of Gov. Vernon W. Thomson's vetoes and delayed action on eight others.

The Assembly voted 69 to 25 to override the governor's veto of a bill permitting defendants in certain justice court actions to transfer their cases to courts of record for a $1 fee.

The Senate will act on that veto later this week. A bill vetoed by the governor must be repassed by both houses of the Legislature by a two-thirds vote in each in order to become law.

Another bill requiring no more than a five-day work week for policemen in cities of 10,000 to 150,000 population won a 62 to 34 vote in the Assembly, but was short of the necessary two-thirds.

The vetoes in both houses were sustained with little discussion. The more controversial vetoes, including an item veto in a raise bill which would have given legislators casual expense money of $75 a month when the Legislature is not in session, will be dealt with today and Thursday.

Vetoes sustained in the Senate included the governor's disapproval of the following bills:

Affecting speed limits in the city of Milwaukee; relating to special assessments against state

(Continued on Page 2, Column 3)

Report of More German Ship Survivors Denied

SANTA MARIA, Azores (AP)—A Portuguese news agency reported Tuesday night that 40 more survivors from the hurricane-wrecked German sailing ship Pamir had been rescued, but the report was later denied.

The news agency Ani said the U. S. Navy transport Geiger had picked up 25 survivors from a drifting lifeboat and 15 others from a life raft in mid-Atlantic. The Ani dispatch was received in Lisbon.

A few hours later the captain of the Geiger, in a radio message picked up by a German coastal radio station, denied that he had rescued 40 more men.

The Coast Guard in New York announced that a sixth survivor had been rescued from a lifeboat. Five survivors were picked up Monday night.

The Ani report could not be confirmed immediately because senior Portuguese officials here were not available. The U. S. Navy in London said it had been unable to maintain radio contact with the Geiger because of poor atmospheric conditions.

Braves Congratulated by State Legislature

The Legislature hustled through a joint resolution Tuesday congratulating the Milwaukee Braves on winning the National League pennant.

Copies of the resolution will be sent to all members of the Braves organization.

Gov. Vernon W. Thomson Tuesday sent a telegram to President and Mrs. Eisenhower inviting them "to attend the first World Series game ever to be played in Wisconsin" on Oct. 5.

"We would enjoy the opportunity to show you the unmatched spirit and ability of our Milwaukee Braves," Thomson wired the President.

A similar telegram was sent to Vice-President and Mrs. Richard M. Nixon.

Boat on Mendota Sinks; Pair Rescued

Perry Hibma, 49, resident caretaker at the Four Lakes Marine Service, 425 S. Blount st., and his fishing companion, Russell Stukel, 35, were rescued Tuesday from Lake Mendota after their boat sunk.

Unidentified fishermen in another boat saw the two men clinging to cushion-type life preservers just off Picnic Point shortly before noon. They fished them from the water and took them to the University of Wisconsin life-saving station.

Hibma said a repaired area in the bottom of their 20-foot inboard launch apparently was punched open by choppy waves. The boat sank in less than five minutes, he said.

Both men were in the 60-degree water for about 10 minutes but were in good condition after being rescued.

Crowd of 15,000 Opens Annual State Farm Progress Field Days

By ROBERT C. BJORKLUND
(State Journal Farm Writer)

MAUSTON—A crowd estimated at more than 15,000 persons — all as bright and shiny as the day itself — opened the annual Wisconsin Farm Progress Field Days near Mauston Tuesday.

It really was a picnic, a trip, and an education wrapped in one package.

Practical Show

Over the 900-acre site folks found the practical kind of agriculture demonstration that could be an important part of the operation on every Wisconsin farm.

The women enjoyed it, too, as they packed one of the largest tents on the grounds for sessions on home art, fashions, and appliances.

The program will be continued today and, along with the senior state plowing matches, will feature talks by Gov. Vernon Thomson, Sen. William Proxmire (D-Wis.), and Rep. Gardner R. Withrow (R-La Crosse).

BOSVELD SCHULTZ

Junior Titles

In the junior plowing events Tuesday, the state titles went to Ervin Schultz, 16, Elroy, who triumphed in the contour match, and to Bobbie Bosveld, 17, Markesan, winner of the junior level land event.

Both champions have been helping with the plowing job on their home farms since they were 12 years old, and the careful jobs they learned from their fathers really paid off.

Schultz, the son of Mr. and Mrs. Harold Schultz, used a 14-inch two bottom plow. He said the plot looked good after he turned the final furrow, but he didn't think that he had won.

Competed in '56

Bosveld, who competed in the 1956 event at Ft. Atkinson last year, found the going much easier this year. Recent rains had made the land almost too wet for plowing.

In the contour event, David Dehnke, Fall Creek, was second and Elmer Zuehls Jr., Princeton, third. Harold Seebecker, 18, Mau-

(Continued on Page 2, Column 5)

Falling Tree Blamed for Driver's Death

(By Associated Press)

A falling tree was blamed for the death of a Watertown motorist whose auto veered off a highway and crashed in a ditch Tuesday.

The death raised Wisconsin's 1957 traffic fatality count to 633, compared with 702 on the same date last year.

Edgar Kuenzi, 64, Watertown, died in a hospital of injuries suffered when his auto crashed beside Highway 109, 3 miles northeast of Watertown. Dodge county traffic officers said that Kuenzi's auto apparently veered off the highway when gusty winds snapped a tree, knocking it onto the right-of-way.

Feature Finder

The Wisconsin Legislative News

(Turn to Page 3)

Noon Bandit Gets $1,720 at Largest Bank in State

MILWAUKEE (AP) — Wisconsin's biggest bank—the First Wisconsin National bank in downtown Milwaukee — was the scene of a bold daylight robbery Tuesday.

The lone, apparently unarmed bandit, walked off with $1,720, handed him by a frightened young woman teller who said she was "too scared" to push the alarm bell.

The holdup took place in the busy lobby of the big financial institution during the noon hour.

Police said the thief pushed a note under the grating in the teller's cage occupied by Mrs. Judith Huebner, 20, a bride of three weeks. The note read:

"Don't get excited. Make up $2,000 in $20 bills and don't sound the alarm."

Mrs. Huebner, visibly shaken by her experience, said she took the tall, stern-vesaged holdup man at his word, although she saw no gun.

'Just Withdrawal Program, Ma'am'

"I knew he wasn't kidding," said Mrs. Huebner. "I thought about pushing the alarm bell but I was too scared to push it."

Mrs. Huebner said she told the robber she didn't have $2,000 but that she would have to go to the back and get it. He told her to give him whatever she had.

Then, she related, she stacked two $500 piles of $20 bills and $300 in assorted other currency and pushed it out. He took it and walked quickly through the lobby and out into the downtown district.

Braves Win 8th in Row, Spahn's 21st

See the Sports Peach

Doings of the Day in the Legislature

(Tuesday, Sept. 24)

SENATE

Passed a bill integrating Milwaukee county employes retirement system with social security.

Adopted a resolution in memory of Sen. Louis Prange (R-Plymouth), who died last month.

Concurred in an Assembly resolution congratulating the Milwaukee Braves.

Sustained eight vetoes of Gov. Vernon Thomson, delayed action on six others.

Adjourned to 10 a.m. today.

ASSEMBLY

Overrode, 69 to 25 a governor's veto of a bill permitting defendants to transfer certain cases from justice courts to courts of record upon payment of a $1 fee.

Sustained governor's vetoes of 18 bills.

Concurred, 92 to 0, in a Senate bill to combine the Milwaukee county employes' retirement system with federal social security coverage.

Concurred in a Senate resolution congratulating the Milwaukee Braves for winning the National League pennant.

Adjourned to 10 a.m. today.

ON, WISCONSIN

Braves Ready to Badger Yankees as Badgers Brave Mountaineers

Nice But Windy

Fair and pleasant today through Sunday. Rather windy today, warmer Sunday. High today, about 70; low tonight, near 40. Sun rose, 5:58; sets, 5:32.

Wisconsin State Journal

MORNING FINAL | SECTION 1 | MADISON, SATURDAY, OCTOBER 5, 1957 | ★★★ | 22 PAGES THREE SECTIONS Vol. 192, No. 5 119th Year | 5c

8 Column Photo of Your Braves in Sports Peach

REDS LAUNCH FIRST ARTIFICIAL SATELLITE

Stand for Standing Room

World Series "early birds," those unlucky ones without tickets, stand in line outside Milwaukee county stadium Friday in hopes of buying standing room tickets for three games in Milwaukee. Most stood, but many brought folding chairs and box lunches.

For anyone with tickets, the weatherman gladdened their hearts with a promise of sunny and cloudless skies with temperatures in the mid-60s at game time (1 p.m. CST) today.

A pair of fast-ball pitchers, Brave Bob Buhl and Yankee Bob Turley will be on the mound before a capacity crowd of 47,000.

—AP Wirephoto

To Detect, Track Sphere
World's Moonwatch Stations Alerted

CAMBRIDGE, Mass. (AP)—Astronomer J. Allen Hynek activated 150 Operation Moonwatch observation stations around the globe Friday night to detect and track the earth satellite launched by Soviet Russia.

Dr. Hynek and his staff prepared to receive at the Smithsonian observatory headquarters here reports from the specially equipped observation points around the world.

The more than 40 Operation Moonwatch observatories west of the Mississippi river were activated first because they were the nearest American points in the band of twilight. The satellite is most easily observed in the reflected light of the setting or rising sun.

Thirty stations in Japan next were alerted in advance of the twilight zone's approach in the Orient.

Hynek said the satellite, if at all visible in the United States Friday night, most likely would be seen near the Rocky mountain zone where bright twilight remained after the announced launching.

"The chances of our picking up the satellite (Friday night) depend on what time the satellite was launched," Hynek said. "This is the single most important piece of information we need to have."

Clouds partly obscured the skies along the East Coast of North America, but it was hoped clearing would occur in time for sunrise detection of the satellite.

Because of their extremely small size, man-made moons must be detected visually by binoculars or telescopes rather than by radar, an observatory spokesman said.

An observatory spokesman said Minitrak radio stations on the East Coast of North America and the West Coast of South America probably would be rather ineffective in receiving signals from the satellite because the devices are set for different frequencies than those used by the Soviets.

Another problem, he said, was that the weak satellite signals would bounce away from the top of the heaviside layer. Commercial radio signals bounce earthward from beneath the same layer.

Orbit of Russia's Earth Satellite

—AP Wirephoto Map

'Moon' Speeds Around Earth at 18,000 MPH

MOSCOW (UP)—Russia Friday night announced the first successful launching of an earth satellite.

Soviet scientists hurled the satellite into space earlier Friday and sent it spinning around the earth at a speed of 18,000 miles an hour and at an altitude of 560 miles, the announcement said. The sphere-shaped man-made "moon" was equipped with a radio transmitter sending signals to earth stations, the announcement said.

Beats U. S. by Months

The launching beat the United States by at least several months in the program to hurl an artificial moon into space during the current International Geophysical Year (IGY).

The Soviet announcement made by the Tass news agency called the launching a "tremendous contribution to the treasure house of world science and culture."

The Soviets said their satellite is 22 inches in diameter, or about twice the size of a basketball. It weighs 184 pounds—more than eight times the weight of the projected U. S. satellite—and it is expected to have a life of about three weeks.

Transmitters Sending Signals

According to the announcement, the satellite has two radio transmitters sending signals at 20.005 and 40.002 megacycles or 15 and 7.5 meter wavelengths, which were reported strong enough to be picked up by amateur shortwave radio operators around the world.

U. S. experts in Washington were amazed at the reported size of the Soviet moon. Dr. Joseph Kaplan, chairman of the U. S. national committee for the IGY, said its 184-pound weight and 22-inch span "is really fantastic. If they can launch that, they can launch much heavier ones."

The U. S. experts figured the first U. S. launching attempt would be made early next spring after an attempt to put some 6.4-inch, 4-pound objects into the earth's orbit for a short time in November.

'Pave the Way for Space Travel'

The Russian announcement said the satellite may be seen in the light of the rising and setting sun through binoculars and telescopes.

Completing its announcement, the Tass agency said, "Artificial earth satellites will pave the way for space travel . . ."

At dawn today, the satellite will be visible to watchers in Russia using only binoculars or small telescopes, the announcement said.

A dispatch from Tass late Friday broke the news of the mo-

(Continued on Page 2, Column 1)

Warsaw Sees New Uprising

Police, Militia Battle Rioters

WARSAW (UP) — An estimated 20,000 Poles battled club-swinging police and militia Friday night in central Warsaw.

Many of the rioters shouted for the downfall of Wladyslaw Gomulka, Communist party chief.

Two separate clashes left several injured, including some women. It was the second straight night of rioting in the tense Polish capital.

Mob Fights Back

An estimated 1,000 steel-helmeted police and "workers militia" charged with clubs and fired teargas bombs to try to break up the rioting. The mobs fought back with their fists, rocks, and paving blocks.

A United Press correspondent said members of the "workers militia" pulled passengers from streetcars and "beat" them during the height of the riots. He said he was among those beaten.

Protest Rally Held

Rioting flared viciously for three hours and was still underway late Friday. Students surged into the streets and were joined by adults.

Pent-up fury burst after police

(Continued on Page 2, Column 6)

Flu Strikes 189 Jefferson High Students

JEFFERSON — A flu epidemic in the Jefferson High school resulted in 189 student absentees Friday afternoon, according to Carl Hager, principal.

He said that the absentees represented about 29 per cent of the total enrolment of 479. Three teachers also were ill.

Hager said that after talking to medical authorities, he believed that the epidemic might have reached its peak Friday, although it was impossible to tell. Friday's absentee total was almost double Thursday's.

The closing of the school has not been discussed, and won't be unless about 50 per cent of the students become ill, he said.

Although some pupils were suffering from flu in the elementary schools, it was not in the epidemic stage.

The high school football team also suffered from the epidemic. Friday afternoon, eight of the 11 first stringers were ill. A game at Stoughton Friday night could not be called off because of Stoughton's advanced preparations, Coach Don Yahr reported.

Beloit Inoculations

BELOIT — Beloit police and fire department personnel Friday were inoculated against Asian flu by

(Continued on Page 2, Column 3)

Officials Hail 'New Era in Science'

WASHINGTON (AP) — The United States Friday night termed Russia's launching of an earth satellite "of great scientific interest" and urged the Soviets to supply details of their scientific experiments.

Hugh Odishaw, executive director of the U. S. committee for the International Geophysical Year (IGY) and official spokesman on American satellite affairs, also said this country awaited "with interest the definition of a specific orbit" for the man-made moon.

'A New Era'

Other distinguished American scientists attending an international rockets-satellite conference here said the Russian feat opened "a new era in science" and was the "most interesting experience" of their lives.

The White House had no comment on the Russian feat of beating the U. S. by at least several months in catapulting an artificial moon into space. President Eisenhower was spending the weekend at his Gettysburg, Pa., farm.

One expert close to the U. S. program for launching a satellite sometime during the IGY ending Dec. 31, 1957, said he wanted to know whether the Soviet satellite was a fully instrumented vehicle or "just a hunk of metal."

Accepted Word

Most American scientists quickly accepted the Soviet announcement. L. V. Berkner, vice-president and reporter for satellite programs for IGY, said:

"This opens a new era in science."

The Russian announcement may come up when Secretary of State John Foster Dulles meets at his home this afternoon with Soviet Foreign Minister Andrei A. Gro-

(Continued on Page 2, Column 5)

BBC Listens, Too, to Russian 'Moon'

LONDON, Saturday (AP) — The British Broadcasting Corp., BBC, said today it had picked up radio signals which may be from the Soviet satellite.

Luck Plays Role in Spotting Here

Prof. A. E. Whitford, chairman of the University of Wisconsin astronomy department, said Friday night that for the moment it would be pure luck if anyone sees the Russian satellite.

He said when observers determine its orbit, there probably will be places in the world where it will be visible through binoculars and low-powered telescopes and perhaps with the naked eye. These could be determined earlier if the Russian were to announce the orbit, he said.

Whitford said the satellite will be quite comparable to a jet plane in the speed of its short flight from horizon to horizon in areas where it will be visible. It will come slowly into view, he said, pass swiftly overhead, and settle out of sight.

The satellite will be visible only by reflected sunlight, he said. This means that it will be seen only when it is within view in an area during twilight hours, either before sunrise or after sunset.

He said no attempt was being made to search for the sphere Friday night at the university's Washburn observatory. If it is to pass within view of Madison during twilight, he said, he would be interested in trying to have a look at it.

An amateur group organized here to help track the American satellite when it is launched also is expected to be active in respect to the Russian satellite.

Diogenes Needs No Lantern in Madison

Within an hour Friday afternoon, two honest residents turned over to Madison police money which they found on sidewalks.

Mrs. Francis Tyler, 3834 Margaret st., gave police $6 and a billfold containing no identification which she found adjacent to the Block 53 parking lot.

The Rev. J. Laing Burns, 1205 Sherman ave., pastor of Parkside Presbyterian Church, gave police two $1 bills which he found in the 400 block of E. Washington ave.

Police will attempt to locate the persons who lost the money.

Pictures Salute News Boy Day

Today is National Newspaper Boy day and The Wisconsin State Journal salutes America's young businessmen with a page of pictures.

Turn to Page 4 for a look at an average week for the three Bourne boys, all Madison newspaper carriers. State Journal Photographer Edwin Stein's camera covers the subject from alarm clock to savings account.

Feature Finder

Networks Broadcast Signals From Satellite

NEW YORK (AP) — NBC said Friday night Radio Corporation of America (RCA) communications had picked up the sound of the Russian earth satellite.

NBC interrupted its regularly scheduled radio and television programs at 7 p.m. to broadcast the satellite's radio transmission, which sounded like a steady series of morse wireless sendings.

Reception of the satellite's transmission was the first announced since Russia told the world of the launching earlier today.

CBS also broadcast the signal which it picked up from RCA.

Higher Education Unit Outlines Plans for a New Student 'Flood'

By JACK HARNED
(State Journal Staff Writer)

Planners of Wisconsin's future university and college programs came up with six points of guiding philosophy for the future of higher education at a Friday night meeting here.

The Coordinating Committee on Higher Education, meeting on the University of Wisconsin campus, will expand and formalize their statement of educational philosophy later, but agreed on important foundations for the state's plans to educate a doubled number of college - age youth within 20 years.

RENK

Generally, the committee said it believes:

ONE. That the state's future interests require it to meet the demand of increasing numbers of youth for education beyond high school.

TWO. That diverse types of post-high school education are necessary to meet diverse needs of youth in modern society, but all types must be of highest possible quality.

THREE. Each young person must have wise counsel in the choice of an educational course.

Private Colleges Vital

FOUR. Adequate support by citizens of private colleges is vital to a strong program of higher education.

FIVE. Educational opportunities should be offered as widely over the state as is consistent with sound educational and financial principles.

SIX. Citizens of the state will have the desire and resources to meet large expenses of expanded educational programs, but they must demand that the programs be effective, efficient, and economical.

The Coordinating committee includes Regents of the university and the state college system and makes a continuing survey of state-supported higher education programs.

Students Must Pay

How much of public higher education should be tax-supported and how much should be student-paid was also discussed by the committee, with a conclusion that students should pay a share, but a low one, and fees should not be a means of controlling enrollment.

"We'd all like to make education free, but we have to have a realistic proposition to take to the Legislature and historically the students share has been about

(Continued on Page 2, Column 5)

Auditorium Unit to Seek Public Views on Alternative Locations

The city auditorium committee Friday afternoon voted to re-examine alternative sites for a civic auditorium and the facilities that should go into it.

To begin the re-examination, it set public hearings for Oct. 14 and Oct. 30 at which all citizens and organizations will be invited to give their views on both subjects.

Suggested by Mayor

The action was suggested by Mayor Ivan A. Nestingen, chairman of the committee.

He said he still feels that the Metzner law, which forbids construction of the Frank Lloyd Wright auditorium on Monona Terrace, should be tested in the courts.

He pointed out that the Legislature has blocked the city from bringing suit, but he expressed the hope that a proposed suit by the Citizens for Monona Terrace committee would be successful.

NESTINGEN JACKSON

The mayor and committee members indicated they felt the two hearings would be only the first of many which will be required to hear everyone who wants to be heard on sites and facilities.

Seeks Public Sentiment

While he expressed his personal opposition to any change in the facilities planned for the Terrace structure, Nestingen said it would be well "to see if public sentiment has changed in the past three years."

Nestingen and Ald. Robert Nuckles, 18th ward, reacted sharply to a statement from the audience that the committee has not been open-minded on the subject of site.

Prof. James G. Woodburn, 211 N. Prospect ave., declared:

"There is a feeling that the

(Continued on Page 2, Column 7)

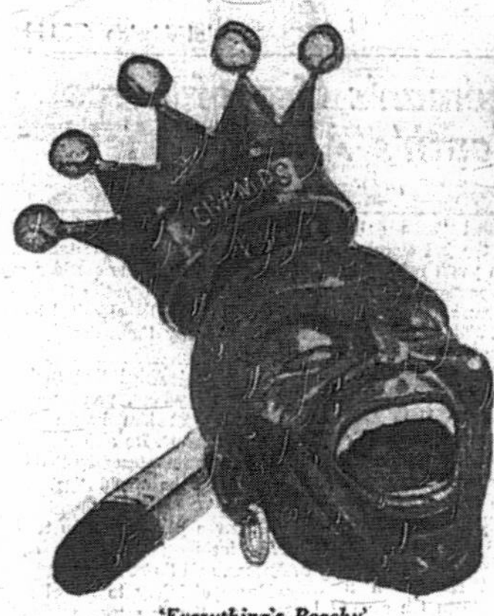
'Everything's Peachy'

BRAVO, BRAVES

ROOT JOHNSON BRUTON RIDDLE PIZARRO KEELY BUHL McMAHON SAWATSKI ADCOCK RYAN WICK* CONLEY PHILLIPS LOGAN TROWBRIDGE AARON ROACH CRANDALL HAZLE PAFKO DeMERIT RICE COVINGTON BURDETTE TORRE HANEY SCHOENDIENST MANTILLA JOLLY JONES MATHEWS SPAHN

*He's the Bat Boy

Burdette Stuff: Can't Be Beat
Mostly fair through Saturday. Somewhat warmer Saturday. High today, 60; low tonight, 35. Sun rose, 6:05; sets, 5:22.

Wisconsin State Journal

Series Stories, Page of Pictures in Sports Peach

MORNING FINAL | SECTION 1 | MADISON, FRIDAY, OCTOBER 11, 1957 | ★★★ | 40 PAGES, THREE SECTIONS Vol. 192, No. 11 119th Year | 5c

Yankees Doodled Dandily

MILWAUKEE GOES WILD

There Was Dancing in the Streets Thursday as Milwaukee Celebrated Braves World Series Victory. —AP Wirephoto

Biggest Blowout Since V-J Day

MILWAUKEE, Wis., Baseball Capital of the World (AP) — When Eddie Mathews stepped on third base in Yankee Stadium Thursday for the final out of the 1957 World Series, he also touched off the wildest celebration Milwaukee has seen since V-J Day.

The old city on the west shore of Lake Michigan which had been as quiet as a mouse while its million inhabitants sat indoors for two **hours and 34 minutes with eyes and ears glued to radio and television sets, suddenly erupted at 1:35 p.m. Thursday with a piercing shriek of unbounded joy.**

City Goes Wild

In short, Milwaukee lost no time in living up to its claim of being the "Baseball Capital of the World."

A crowd of 750,000 persons—with 250,000 of them in the downtown area—lined the parade route Thursday night.

Police Inspector Rudolph Miller, who made the estimate, said the demonstration was uncanny.

The 30-car caravan of convertibles taking the team to County Stadium had to be turned away from the original planned route through the city. Police said it would have been impossible to open the crowd to let the cars through.

Buses Pushed

Trolley buses that were stalled when their electric power pickup poles left the overhead wires while making sharp turns were pushed through the throng like toys.

Fans refused to budge for motorcycle policemen trying to clear a path.

And when the crowd learned the parade was taking a new route, every vehicle with a driver was put into use. They rode on bumpers and fenders, the tops, and hung through open windows for the ride to the stadium.

Normal two-way traffic on Wisconsin ave. for a brief period was turned into a one-way thoroughfare until police brought things under control.

Meanwhile, the merrymaking continued in downtown hotels and bars.

Fun Starts

But even though it brought out greater numbers of people, the night-time celebration could not match the spontaneous burst of joy that came when the game ended in the afternoon. Then:

Factory whistles blew!

Church bells clanged!

Men, women, and children poured out of towntown buildings like marbles being dumped out of a bag.

Streets were suddenly filled with automobiles, their horns blaring.

Pedestrians overflowed the sidewalks and swarmed into the streets, stopping traffic at some spots.

A long line of girls snake-danced down Wisconsin ave., the city's main street. One policeman directed traffic with a tomahawk given him by the crowd.

Taxis were rocked. Men did jigs on their hoods.

The mayor rang the old tower bell in the city hall, which normally sounds only for the Fourth of July—five times for each of the Braves runs, and then five times more for good measure. Then he gave city employes the rest of the day off.

'They Did It'

"They did it!" shouted nearly everyone at once.

"The Braves showed those Yankees who's bush."

Perfect strangers pounded each other on the back or shook hands—or both.

Windows in office buildings along Wisconsin ave., were flung open as if some strange power had released them simultaneously.

Somebody started dumping torn bits of paper from one high window. Then the confetti shower spread rapidly all long the city's

(Continued on Page 2, Column 1)

Our Own Series Record: 50,000-Plus

Sharing a "first," along with the Champion Milwaukee Braves, is your morning Wisconsin State Journal.

During the World Series, the net paid circulation of this newspaper has exceeded 50,000 copies each day. This is a new record in the growth of your favorite morning newspaper.

To the Braves: Hats off!

To our hundreds of new customers: "Good Morning!" And for many a morning to come.

State Democrats' Contests Set

By LEW ROBERTS
(State Journal Staff Writer)

A heated contest for state chairman and the problem of party endorsement of candidates will highlight the annual convention of the Democratic party of Wisconsin beginning here today.

About 2,000 party members are expected to fill hotels and spill over into motels for the convention, which ends Sunday afternoon.

Delegates—1,701 strong—will register from 2 to 8:30 p. m. All sessions will be held at Hotel Loraine except an opening session rally at 6:30 tonight in the Capitol theater.

The main speaker at the Capitol theater rally will be Sen. William Proxmire (D-Wis.), who scored an upset victory in the U. S. Senate special election Aug. 27 to become the state's first U. S. senator from the Democratic party in 25 years.

Proxmire will also be guest of honor at a reception in the Hotel Loraine Crystal ballroom at 9:30 tonight, with members of the Dane County Democratic club acting as hosts.

Battling for the state chairmanship of the Democratic party in a vote Saturday afternoon will be the incumbent, Philleo Nash, a Wisconsin Rapids cranberry grower, and Patrick J. Lucey, a Madison real estate man.

Nash, a White House staffer during the regimes of Presidents Roosevelt and Truman, is regarded as a slight favorite. He and his supporters point out that the Proxmire upset victory came during his office.

Lucey, a former assemblyman, has the tacit support of Proxmire himself and has been building support in the state, most of it outside Milwaukee and little of it within the state administrative committee.

Both Lucey and Nash will set up headquarters in the Loraine.

Another rhubarb is expected to develop Sunday afternoon, when delegates vote on a resolution to require the state Democratic party convention to endorse candidates for state-wide office in even-numbered years.

This is a recurring saddle-sore in the party and a similar move was defeated at the state convention at Green Bay in 1955. Proxmire is dead set against en-

(Continued on Page 2, Column 3)

Today's Program for Convention

11 a.m.—Meeting of Credentials committee, Hotel Loraine.

2-8:30 p.m.—Registration of delegates, lobby of Hotel Loraine,

2 p.m.—Meeting of principal convention committees—constitution, resolutions, rules, statement of principles.

6:30 p.m.—Opening session of convention at Capitol theater. Speakers to include Sen. William Proxmire (D-Wis.) and Dan Hoan, former mayor of Milwaukee.

9:30 p.m.—Dane County Democratic club reception for Proxmire, Crystal ballroom, Hotel Loraine.

Policeman's Use of Force in Youth's Arrest Upheld

By WILLIAM C. ROBBINS
(State Journal Staff Writer)

The police and fire commission early today ruled that the use of force by Patrolman Clarence O. Liebscher against Richard L. Bethel, 18, Oregon, during a July 20 arrest was "justified."

The commission said that Bethel's action before and after the arrest at Millard's Bar, 504 E. Wilson st., was "provocative in the extreme" and that Bethel was guilty of disorderly conduct.

Verbal Reprimand

The commission, however, gave Liebscher an official verbal reprimand for "departing from proper police procedure" by earlier asking Bethel if he wanted to carry out his own threat of violence against the policeman by fighting him.

Thomas J. Doran, commission president, announced the findings at 12:50 a.m., 5 hours and 35 minutes after the hearing was opened at the police department's commission room. The commission was in executive session for 30 minutes reaching its decision.

15 Witnesses Called

Fifteen witnesses were called, 13 by Atty. Jack McManus, Bethel's counsel. Atty. John T. Harrington, representative for Liebscher who was the first witness called by McManus.

Liebscher testified that he

(Continued on Page 2, Column 7)

Thomson Hits Talk of More Farm Income

WEST SALEM (AP)—Gov. Vernon Thomson Thursday night criticized "those who go about the state promising farmers greater income."

Thomson said that those who make promises "are guilty of deceit" and said that "we must find some gaps in the production-construction cycle which can be filled" before solving the problems.

He told a meeting of the Farm Bureau here that extensive efforts were being made by the state agriculture department and the university to improve marketing techniques and expand markets for state dairy products.

Wausau Board Backs Zoning for TV Tower

WAUSAU (AP)—The city Board of Appeals Thursday approved waiver of a Wausau Airport zoning ordinance in order to permit construction of a 648 - foot television tower by Station WSAU - TV atop Rib Mountain.

The final preliminary step to actual construction will be considered in Madison Friday when the state Conservation Commission meets to ratify a leave on space on the mountain.

The station will pay a nominal rental of $100 a year for the space.

NLRB Aide Puts Blame on Kohler Co.

WASHINGTON (AP)— A trial examiner for the National Labor Relations Board (NLRB) held Thursday that the Kohler Co. prolonged the 3½-year strike at its Kohler, Wis., plant by a series of unfair labor practices.

Examiner George A. Downing recommended that nearly all rank and file strikers whose jobs had not been filled by June 1, 1954, should be reinstated upon application or when the strike ends.

At the same time, however, Downing found that the company lawfully discharged the 13 members of the union's strike committee for their control and direction of mass picketing at the plant. Included were all principal officers of the union.

Downing said that the company should be required, if necessary, to discharge all employes hired as replacements since June 1, 1954. He said the company had failed and refused to bargain in good faith most of the time after that date.

Downing's findings and recommendations went to the full five-member board for action. They may be appealed within 20 days.

The strike was called by Local 833 of the United Auto Workers (UAW) union on Apr. 5, 1954 and is still in progress. The plant has kept in operation, manufacturing plumbing fixtures, heating equipment, electrical appliances, air-cooled engines and precision parts

In Detroit, Emil Mazey, UAW secretary-treasurer, said the finding confirms the union position and said the union is ready to resume negotiations.

Company officials could not be reached for comment.

Feature Finder

Farmers Throw Eggs at Benson; Listen to Ag Speech in Silence

SIOUX FALLS, S. D. (AP)—A band of embittered farmers splattered Agriculture Secretary Ezra T. Benson with eggs Thursday at a mass, open-air meeting.

A half dozen eggs crashed around Benson as he rose to defend his flexible farm price support policies before 7,500 farmers at the South Dakota Mechanical Corn Picking contest.

None of the eggs hit Benson, but one splashed his hat and another the suit of Republican Gov. Joe Foss, World War II Marine flying ace, who was on the speaker's stand.

BENSON

State troopers shoved their way through the crowd and collared five farmers who admitted lobbing the eggs from 40 yards away. Four of the farmers were in their 50s and the fifth, who still carried two eggs, was in his 20s.

The policemen took the farmers' names, but made no immediate arrests. They quoted the farmers as saying they had written letters to Benson and "never got any satisfaction."

However, Foss announced Tuesday night he would demand that the egg-throwers be prosecuted to fullest extent of the law.

"The next time they might throw bricks," Foss said.

Benson ignored the barrage during his 20-minute speech, which was received in almost absolute silence.

Afterward, he revealed it was the first such attack upon him during his many appearances before hostile farm audiences around the nation.

"It's un-American, certainly, and I don't think anything is ever gained by that sort of practices," he told newsmen. "Nothing like this has ever happened to me before."

Benson refused to let photographers take his picture wearing his egg-spattered hat.

"It's nothing — let's forget about it," he said as he hurried off to catch a plane back to Washington.

Foss commented "there weren't too many when you analyze the size of the crowd. In every group you find people who refuse to think. It disappoints your faith in your fellow man."

Ray Loftesness, Sioux Falls, vice-president of the National Cornpicking contest and master of ceremonies at the rally, offered a public apology to Benson after his speech.

Bright Outlook
Fair and little change in temperatures today through Thursday. High today, about 55; low tonight, near 30.

Wisconsin State Journal

SECTION 1 MORNING FINAL MADISON, WEDNESDAY, OCTOBER 29, 1958 ★★★ 44 PAGES, THREE SECTIONS Vol. 200, No. 29 119th Year 5c

VATICAN DIPLOMAT CHOSEN AS NEW POPE, JOHN XXIII

Pope John XXIII Raises Hand and Blesses Thousands in Rome After His Election as Pontiff Tuesday
—AP Wirephoto by Radio From Rome

Italian Prelate, 76, Will Lead Catholics

(Compiled From Wire Services)

VATICAN CITY — Angelo Giuseppe Cardinal Roncalli, an Italian skilled in Vatican diplomacy, was elected Pope Tuesday.

He chose the name John XXIII.

The bells of St. Peter's and 500 Rome churches rang out a carol of triumph. Hundreds of thousands in St. Peter's Square roared an ovation as the patriarch of Venice became Pope at the age of 76.

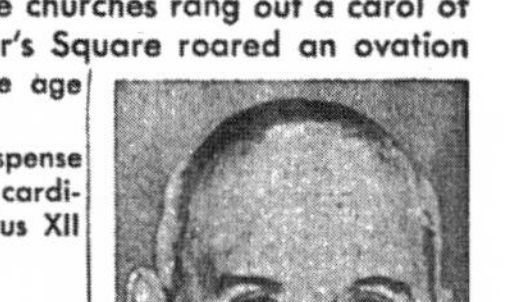

POPE JOHN XXIII

His election ended three days of intense suspense centering about a deadlocked conclave of the 51 cardinals, gathered to choose a successor to Pope Pius XII as head of the Roman Catholic church.

Crowd Roars

Disappointed in five other vigils—through 11 unsuccessful ballots in the past three days—the crowd broke into a joyous frenzy as John XXIII made his first appearance on the balcony overlooking St. Peter's square.

They roared "Viva Il Papa!"—Long Live the Pope!—over and over as the new pontiff slowly raised his arms in benediction.

The new pontiff, Italian like his predecessors for 436 years, is regarded by Catholics as the 262nd vicar of Christ on earth and a direct successor to St. Peter.

The selection of Cardinal Roncalli—19 days after Pius XII died—bore out predictions that the Pope would be chosen from among the older Italian members of the College of Cardinals.

Experienced Diplomat

Some might regard John XXIII as a "transition pope," not destined to institute any notable changes in church policy. But John XXIII, like his celebrated predecessor, has been a diplomat of many years experience.

Though his policies may prove conservative, he is expected to follow the general direction laid down in the 19 years of Pius XII's reign and to be a militant defender of the church's interests in world affairs.

The election ended a conclave which had seemed headed for a long deadlock. It was presumed he was elected on the 12th ballot of the 51 cardinals in the sealed-off, guarded conclave.

The balloting began Sunday morning. By Sunday night false reports on the selection of a pope had circled the globe, adding greatly to the suspense.

Drama Heightens

The drama of the conclave's last day was the sort of spectacle Romans love. Faithfully, day after day, huge crowds had assembled in the great square to await the news. Five times before, each forenoon and evening, smoke had puffed from a little grey chimney, indicating failure, and the crowd had turned away.

But hundreds of thousands were on hand again to await the sixth signal. It came in the form of a tiny wisp of smoke. None could say for sure whether it was white, indicating a new pope, or black, showing another failure. But there was just a little smoke. It was a favorable sign. The crowd stood stock still, and waited.

Something Different

Soon it became evident that this time, something different had happened. There was activity inside the Basilica. A light went on behind the glass doors of the central balcony facing the square. The low murmur of the crowd burgeoned into a rumble. There was scarcely room to turn around in the square by now, and Ro-

(Continued on Page 2, Column 1)

New Pope Speaks 7 Languages

VATICAN CITY (UP) — The travels and work of Pope John XXIII have given him seven languages.

In addition to Italian and Latin, he is fluent in Turkish, Greek, Bulgarian, and French and is acquainted with Russian.

The new Pope's full name is Angelo Giuseppe Roncalli. His last name is pronounced Rohn-kah-lee.

VATICAN CITY (UPI) — Vatican sources said Tuesday that Pope John XXIII probably would be crowned at ceremonies in St. Peter's Basilica on Nov. 9.

MOSCOW, Wednesday (UP) — The election of the new Pope went unreported by the official Tass news agency and Moscow radio all through Tuesday.

VATICAN CITY (UP)—Pope John XXIII, in one of the first acts of his pontificate, Tuesday night elevated Msgr. Alberto di Iorio to cardinal.

He thus followed the tradition that the prelate who serves as secretary of a papal conclave is immediately named a cardinal at its conclusion.

The appointment means the College of Cardinals stays at its strength of 51, since Cardinal di Iorio numerically takes the place of the new Pope. It also leaves at 17 the Italian representation in the college.

VENICE (AP)— The city of

(Continued on Page 2, Column 1)

Jasper Hits Out-State Funds for Proxmire

Claude J. Jasper Tuesday asked all Wisconsin citizen "to join me in preventing our state from being sold at bargain rates on a political auction block to absentee ownership."

Jasper, state GOP chairman, sent a special chairman's memo to all county Republican leaders reporting on the flood of out-of-state money to the major club promoting the reelection of Sen. William Proxmire (D-Wis.).

Poses Question

"Why is a senator from the great state of Wisconsin so unable to sell himself to the people of his own state that he was forced to go outside its borders for 80 per cent of his campaign funds?" Jasper asked.

The Proxmire for Senator club Monday reported to the secretary of state that it has received $47,724 and spent $57,000 since the primary election. The report showed that all but $9,088 of the contributions came from out of state.

The report also disclosed that the club has paid $54,414 to Dayton, Johnson, and Hacker, a Milwaukee advertising firm, for radio and television broadcasts and a small amount of newspaper advertising.

A Lavish Scale

"What is the interest of the out-of-state people in the election of Mr. Proxmire?" Jasper asked.

"What prompts the Eastern internationalists, the radical left wingers, the out-of-state unions and Texas cotton kings to finance more than 80 per cent of Mr. Proxmire's campaign?" Jasper asked.

The state GOP chairman said such financing enabled Proxmire to be on television, radio, and other media of advertising on a lavish scale never before matched in the history of the state.

"Whose interest will he serve?" Jasper asked. "Will he represent Wisconsin citizens or out-of-state benefactors who suddenly and with no announced reason purport to feel so deeply for us in Wisconsin?"

Pratt Identified

One $2,000 contributor to the committee, George Pratt Jr., Bridgewater, Conn., was identified Tuesday as country squire

(Continued on Page 2, Column 5)

Judge's Pick Quite Logical

Federal Judge Patrick T. Stone appointed a new Federal Court jury commissioner Tuesday.

At first glance the judge's choice seemed to be as logical as General Custer appointing Sitting Bull as a cavalry scout.

The judge, you see, was an active Democrat before his appointment to the federal bench, and his appointee is Thomas E. Coleman, 735 Farwell dr., Maple Bluff, for many years the state's No. 1 Republican.

COLEMAN

But all is not what it seems.

Federal law requires that the jury commissioner be a "well known member of the principal political party in the district opposite that to which the clerk may belong."

The clerk, Mrs. Lucille Alstad, is a Democrat. So, the judge went out and found the best known member he could find of "the principal political party opposite."

Coleman succeeds William G. McKay, 111 W. Wilson st., who has resigned because of ill health.

Judge Stone said the law originated right after the Civil War, when jury-fixing got to be a problem.

The salary, $5 per day of actual service, apparently dates from the 1860s, too.

Different Answers Totaled in Byrnes-Proxmire Debate

GREEN BAY (AP) — Sen. William Proxmire and Rep. John Byrnes (R-Green Bay) Tuesday night debated the senator's program, and as they have all through the campaign, came up with widely different answers.

PROXMIRE BYRNES

An audience of 700 persons attended the televised debate and were warned several times by the moderator, Circuit Judge Andrew Parnell of Appleton, that interruptions were deducted from the time of the speakers, but several times the principals were halted by cheers or catcalls.

Both speakers were armed with charts designed to establish their positions as they went over Proxmire's program bill-by-bill.

Byrnes insisted that bills sponsored by Proxmire would add 30 billion dollars to the federal debt, but Proxmire maintained they would mean a saving of 728 million dollars.

Byrnes' estimate of the cost of the bills was five billion dollars higher than his earlier claims. He said that not included in the earlier attack on the senator's

(Continued on Page 2, Column 3)

On the Candidate's Trail

Kastenmeier Believes Hard Work Paying Off

By LEW ROBERTS
(State Journal Staff Writer)

Robert W. Kastenmeier, Watertown, is leaving no voter intentionally unsought, no hand unshaken in his quest to unseat Rep. Don Tewes (R-Waukesha) in Wisconsin's Second Congressional district.

About as much as any candidate can be, the 33-year-old Democratic attorney is "satisfied" with his campaign.

EDITOR'S NOTE: Lew Roberts, Wisconsin State Journal political reporter, has been assigned to spend a day with each of the major candidates. "On the Candidate's Trail" gives an interpretative account of a day in Democratic Candidate Robert Kastenmeier's campaign for election as representative for the Second Congressional district.

Sees 2,000 Margin

"If I lose, I'll be able to say that it wasn't because I didn't work for it," he said Tuesday during a long day of campaigning in Madison and northeastern Dane county.

Kastenmeier

But he doesn't figure he'll lose. He figures to win by between 2,000 to 3,000 votes.

The contest is a rematch. In 1956, Tewes defeated Kastenmeier, 101,444 to 81,922. The district includes Dane, Dodge, Columbia, Jefferson, and Waukesha counties.

Wife's Smile Helps

"If there's a big swing (to the Democrats) we'll all go in," Kastenmeier said earnestly. "I think I'll win in either case."

Kastenmeier is a slender six-footer, serious-minded and articulate. In his approach to the man on the street, to whom he introduces himself and hands out lit-

(Continued on Page 2, Column 6)

Another Blast Kills 13 Miners

SUMMERSVILLE, W. Va. (AP)—An explosion in a coal mine killed 13 miners Tuesday and injured four others, two of them critically.

Thirty-seven others working nearer the entrance escaped unharmed.

It was the second mine explosion in two days in the West Virginia coal fields and brought the total dead to 35. Monday, 22 miners died when trapped gas ignited in a mine on the Virginia-West Virginia border.

A similar blast at the operation in 1957 killed 37 men.

Thursday a cave-in at a mine near Springhill, Nova Scotia, trapped 93 men. By Tuesday 21 bodies had been recovered and hope was all but gone for the others.

Both Sides, Opinion Given on Road Issue

How are you going to vote on the Mineral Point - Speedway rd. referendum?

To help Madison voters make up their minds on this confused and highly controversial question, The Wisconsin State Journal prints the arguments on both sides on Page 8 today.

It also gives the background on the proposal and counterproposal and the opinions of both sides on the consequences of a "Yes" and a "No" vote Nov. 4.

And, in summary, it gives The State Journal's own opinion and recommendation on the issue.

Body of Missing Oshkosh Girl Found

OSHKOSH (AP) — The body of an attractive 17-year-old Oshkosh girl missing for more than two months was found in a ditch Tuesday by two hunters.

The cause of death was not learned immediately.

The girl was identified as Ruth Schmidt, a blue-eyed blonde. She had been missing since Aug. 15.

Today's Chuckle

It may be true that it is never too late to mend our ways, but most people feel it is too early.

Feature Finder

More Stories on Inside

Nobel Prize Hinted for U.W's Dr. Lederberg

Prof. Joshua Lederberg, one of the University of Wisconsin's outstanding scientists, was reported Tuesday to be one of three Americans who may share the 1958 Nobel prize in medicine and physiology.

The Associated Press reported from Stockholm, Sweden, that word circulating in scientific circles there indicated that Dr. George W. Beadle, California Institute of Technology; Dr. Edward L. Tatum, of the Rockefeller Institute, New York City; and Dr. Lederberg would share the prize for their work in the fundamental basis of heredity.

All three are geneticists of world fame.

The preliminary report of potential prize winners is without precedent. The names of candidates for the award never are revealed, and the only official announcement made is of the actual winner. The final decision on the award will be made Thursday.

Dr. Lederberg declined to comment Tuesday on the report and refused to speak to reporters about the matter.

The report could be of considerable embarrassment to him in the event he does not receive the award, and he apparently feels it best to remain silent.

Dr. Lederberg, 33, has attained world recognition as a leader on the field of genetics. His contributions in the heredity of bacteria have been of great significance in

(Continued on Page 2, Column 8)

PROF. JOSHUA LEDERBERG

Pope Crowned-Story, Pictures, Page 7

Not So Nice
Cloudy, windy, and turning cool with a few light showers. Partly cloudy and cool tonight and Thursday. High today, between 55 and 60. Low tonight, near 30.

Wisconsin State Journal Election EXTRA

5c SECTION 1 MORNING FINAL MADISON, WEDNESDAY, NOVEMBER 5, 1958 ★★★ 38 PAGES, FOUR SECTIONS Vol. 200, No. 36 119th Year

Winners, Leaders

GOVERNOR
Gaylord A. Nelson, Democrat

LIEUTENANT GOVERNOR
*Philleo Nash, Democrat

SECRETARY OF STATE
Robert C. Zimmerman, Republican

ATTORNEY GENERAL
John W. Reynolds, Democrat

STATE TREASURER
Eugene M. Lamb, Democrat

U. S. SENATOR
William Proxmire, Democrat

HOUSE OF REPRESENTATIVES
(First District)
Gerald T. Flynn, Democrat
(Second District)
Robert W. Kastenmeier, Democrat
(THIRD DISTRICT)
Gardner Withrow, Republican

DANE COUNTY ASSEMBLY DISTRICTS
(First District)
Glenn L. Henry, Democrat
(Second District)
Fred A. Risser, Democrat
(Third District)
Richard L. Cates, Democrat
(Fourth District)
Carl W. Thompson, Democrat
(Fifth District)
David D. O'Malley, Democrat

COUNTY CANDIDATES
CLERK
Otto Festge, Democrat
TREASURER
Walter N. Smithback, Democrat
SHERIFF
Franz Haas, Democrat
CORONER
Michael Malloy, Democrat
CLERK OF CIRCUIT COURT
Jean E. Johnson, Democrat
DISTRICT ATTORNEY
Joseph W. Bloodgood, Democrat
REGISTER OF DEEDS
Harold K. Hill, Democrat
SURVEYOR
Alex W. Ely, Democrat
*Denotes candidate leading; returns incomplete.

NELSON RIDES CREST TO DEFEAT THOMSON

Democrats Win Firm Control of Congress

(By Associated Press)

A political landslide crunched the Republicans into defeat in Tuesday's election and assured the Democratic party of strengthened control of the next Congress.

Quickly and easily, the Democrats wrapped up control of Senate and House and marched on toward expanding their hold on both chambers.

Ike, Nixon Fail

President Eisenhower's own Republican congressman, S. Walter Stauffer, was swamped by the undertow in the 19th Pennsylvania district.

In a futile, almost frenzied attempt to halt the sweep, both Nixon and Mr. Eisenhower, himself, had thrown their power and influence into the great political war of 1958.

They warned that bigger Democratic majorities in Congress would mean spendthrift government by political radicals. They joined in a GOP prediction that the result would be socialism.

But the American electorate thundered out disbelief from thousands of voting booths around the nation.

Even so, the GOP defeat carried with it no clearcut rejection of Mr. Eisenhower's programs and policies. For these policies never became great, burning issues in an election decided pretty much on personalities and local problems.

No Mandate

Similarly, there was no explicit mandate for the Democrats to do anything other than what they have been doing — cooperating in large measure with the White House in putting through compromise legislation.

Democrats swept past their high marks of the last two years. They apparently were headed for crushing majorities.

Early today, Democrats had elected 236 House members—one more than the greatest number they had in the retiring Congress. And they obviously weren't stopping there—Democratic candidates led in 47 more races, including 28 for seats now held by the GOP. No Republicans were leading in races for seats now Democratic, either in the House

(Continued on Page 2, Column 1)

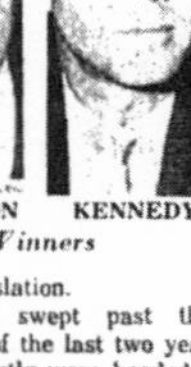

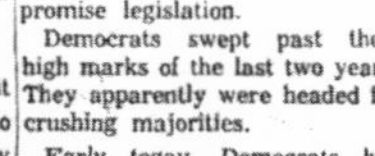

SYMINGTON KENNEDY HANDLEY BRICKER
Winners *Losing*

Zimmerman GOP Winner

BULLETIN

Philleo Nash pulled ahead of Lt. Gov. Knowles, 551,333 to 524,578 in late returns and was certain of victory.

By LEW ROBERTS
(State Journal Staff Writer)

Gaylord Nelson, riding the crest of a distinct state and national Democratic trend, Tuesday unseated Republican Vernon W. Thomson as governor of Wisconsin.

Nelson, a 42-year-old state senator from Madison, carried with him at least two of the four Democratic candidates for the other state constitutional offices now held by Republicans.

The vote for governor in 3,040 of Wisconsin's 3,403 precincts, according to Associated Press tabulations, was:

Nelson (D) **542,465**
Thomson (R) **434,429**

The late vote tally early this morning included nearly 650 of Milwaukee county's 671 precincts.

Thomson conceded victory to Nelson early today, blaming the national trend favoring the Democratic party for his failure to win reelection.

Thomson offered his "sincere good wishes to my successor in his task of maintaining the progress made by Republican state government during the past 20 years in establishing a way of (good) life."

Thomson urged all Wisconsin residents to assist Nelson but urged his own supporters to continue to work unceasingly for the preservation of the Republican principles of government and home rule.

He said he was proud that his administration had "fulfilled its obligation" with what he called "an unprecedented amount of state aids to local units of government" without increasing state income taxes.

Nelson becomes Wisconsin's first Democratic governor since Albert Schmedeman was elected in the Roosevelt landslide of 1932.

He is only the second Wisconsin Democratic governor in the 20th century.

NELSON ZIMMERMAN

His contest with Thomson had been regarded as a close one, with most observers giving the incumbent governor a slight edge.

Nelson battled Thomson neck and neck in the first scattered outstate returns from areas where Thomson had been expected to build up a lead to carry into Democratic Milwaukee county.

One of the two possible Republican survivors on the state ticket, with more than two-thirds of the vote counted, was Secretary of State Robert C. Zimmerman, who was opposed by Jerome Reinke, Kewaunee.

In 2,783 of the state's 3,403 precincts, the vote was:

Zimmerman (R) **316,618**
Reinke (D) **303,853**

Lt. Gov. Warren P. Knowles was leading Philleo Nash,

(Continued on Page 2, Column 1)

Sen. Proxmire Easily Defeats Roland Steinle

Sen. William Proxmire (D-Wis.) was reelected Tuesday, easily routing his Republican challenger, Roland J. Steinle.

The vote in 3,128 of the state's 3,403 precincts, according to United Press International tabulations, was:

Proxmire (D) ... **598,232**
Steinle (R) **448,802**

Steinle Concedes

Steinle conceded defeat at midnight in Milwaukee.

"Naturally I am disappointed that the voters of Wisconsin did not see fit to endorse the political convictions which I represent," Steinle said.

"There are fights that have to be fought regardless of the outcome and my principals remain the same and I shall always continue to fight for them," he added.

PROXMIRE STEINLE

Proxmire assumed the lead in the contest when the first few scattered precincts reported.

Lead Keeps Growing

He increased his lead steadily as the outlying returns came in and held a commanding lead going into traditionally Democratic Milwaukee county.

Steinle, 62-year-old former circuit judge, resigned from the Wisconsin Supreme Court early this year to run against Proxmire.

Proxmire, by dint of his incumbency and his vigorous campaigning, had been expected to lead the state-wide Democratic ticket, and he did.

Proxmire is the first Democratic senator to be reelected in Wisconsin this century. He will be 43 years old next Tuesday.

First Since 1932

When he was elected to the Senate in a special election last year, he was the first Democrat elected to the Senate from Wisconsin since 1932.

In the Roosevelt landslide of 1932, F. Ryan Duffy, a Fond du Lac Democrat and now a federal judge, was elected to the Senate.

After one term in the Assembly, where he represented eastern Dane county in the 1951 session, Proxmire set his sights on bigger political game.

He won the Democratic nomination for governor in 1952 by what amounted to default when no other major Democrat relished the task of taking on Walter Kohler Jr., the Republican incumbent seeking a second term.

Keeps on Running

Proxmire was routed by Kohler, as expected, but Proxmire had made the big start of shaking one million hands in the state. He ran again for governor, in 1954 again against Kohler, and in 1956 against Vernon Thomson. His

(Continued on Page 2, Column 6)

Brown Defeats Knowland in California

SAN FRANCISCO (AP) — Atty. Gen. Edmund G. (Pat) Brown Tuesday was elected California's second Democratic governor of this century.

The tide of Democratic votes upset the political career of his Republican opponent, Sen. William F. Knowland, who conceded at 10:32 p.m. PST. Apparently also swept Democratic Rep. Clair Engle into the U. S. Senate over Gov. Goodwin J. Knight.

Brown, a self-styled political moderate, claimed victory at 10:08. He then held a growing lead of more than 100,000 votes.

Brown jumped ahead of Knowland at the start of the counting of more than five million votes. The Republican senator at no point challenged the Democratic surge.

Returns from 5,698 of 28,896 precincts gave Brown 345,394, Knowland 235,658.

In the Senate contest, the vote from 5,676 precincts showed Engle 276,071, Knight 228,801.

It would mark the first defeat for both Knowland and Knight in long public careers.

Kastenmeier Defeats Tewes for Congress

Atty. Robert W. Kastenmeier, 34, Watertown Democrat, Tuesday spoiled the reelection bid of Rep. Don Tewes (R-Waukesha).

Kastenmeier won by a 7,000 vote margin over Tewes, who had beaten him in the Congressional race in 1956, with almost two-thirds of the precincts in the five-county district reporting.

The vote in 317 of the district's 330 precincts, according to Associated Press tabulations, was:

Kastenmeier (D) **73,937**
Tewes (R) **66,920**

Also riding the Democratic wave inundating the state and nation was Norman Clapp, Lancaster, publisher, who was trailing only slightly in his bid to unseat Rep. Gardner Withrow (R-La Crosse).

Withrow had been regarded as a prohibitive favorite to retain his seat. The vote in 392 of the Third district's 402 precincts was:

Withrow (R) **45,204**
Clapp (D) **43,314**

WITHROW KASTENMEIER

In the First Congressional district, Mrs. Eleanor Smith, Racine Republican, was losing a determined bid to become the first woman ever elected to Congress from Wisconsin.

She opposed Gerald T. Flynn, Racine Democrat, in an effort to accede to the House post held for several terms by her late husband, Rep. Lawrence H.

(Continued on Page 2, Column 8)

Democrats Take It All in County

By JUNE DIECKMANN
(State Journal Staff Writer)

Democratic candidates steamrolled into all eight Dane county offices Tuesday, most of them by near two-to-one majorities, complete election returns showed early today.

It was the third consecutive election that Democrats made a clean sweep of courthouse offices, and they did it with an avalanche of votes that never left their victories in doubt from the time the first of 97 precincts reported.

Republicans had pinned their main hopes on Sheriff Fred Goff, who has been in office since January, 1957, by gubernatorial appointment to replace the elected Democrat, the late Stanley Larson.

Goff polled strongest for his

(Continued on Page 2, Column 3)

Teachers' Convention to Close Schools

A two-day vacation awaits the thousands of public school pupils in Wisconsin this week.

Administrators and teachers will vacate classrooms Thursday and Friday to attend the annual convention of the Wisconsin Education Assn. in Milwaukee Thursday through Saturday.

Street Bonds Lose; Triangle's Approved

Madison voters approved a $1 million redevelopment bond issue for the Triangle area Tuesday, but rejected a $690,000 street improvement bond issue for the Speedway and Mineral Point rd. area.

The Triangle vote was 16,784 for, to 11,165 against.

The street bond vote was 16,832 against, 11,794 in favor.

(Story Sec. 2, Page 1.)

Democrats Gain 10 Seats in Assembly

(Another Story, Page 3)

MILWAUKEE — Democrats gained at least 10 seats in the Assembly and stood an outside chance of gaining control there, incomplete returns filed with the Associated Press showed early today.

Democrats picked up Assembly seats in Ashland, Dunn, Clark, La Crosse, Sheboygan, Vernon, and Milwaukee counties, the AP reported. The AP said returns on the state Senate races were also incomplete but that Democrats picked up some seats.

In 1956 there were 67 Republicans and 33 Democrats elected to the Assembly. The Senate composition in the 1957 session was 23 Republicans and 10 Democrats.

More Election News— City, State, National

—on Pages 2, 3, 4, 5, and Sec. 2, Page 1

Rockefeller Defeats Harriman, Gains GOP Spotlight for 1960

NEW YORK (AP)—Republican Nelson A. Rockefeller won the New York governorship Tuesday and became a key figure in speculation on the 1960 GOP presidential nomination.

Rockefeller's emphatic triumph over Democratic Gov. Averell Harriman, a fellow millionaire, attracted all the more attention because of the number of Republicans who were being defeated in other states.

Rockefeller, 50, led by more than 500,000 votes with the bulk of the returns in.

Further, he pulled his running mate, Republican Rep. Kenneth B. Keating, candidate for the U.S. Senate, to victory with him.

Shortly before midnight, Keating gained a 3,000 vote lead over Manhattan Dist. Atty. Frank S. Hogan, after trailing all evening.

But the vote-getting ability of Rockefeller in "a Democratic year" means he will have his backers for the nomination.

Conversely, Harriman's defeat was a blow to any 1960 ambitions he had for the Democratic presidential nomination, an honor he sought unsuccessfully in 1952 and 1956 against Adlai E. Stevenson.

ROCKEFELLER KEATING

For governor, returns from 11,346 of the state's 11,525 election districts gave:

Rockefeller 3,055,182; Harriman 2,513,735.

For senator, 10,342 districts gave:

Keating 2,482,390; Hogan 2,403,991.

GOP State Chairman L. Judson Morhouse predicted Rockefeller's victory margin might go as high as a half million votes.

Harriman conceded defeat at 10:45 p. m.

Harriman issued a statement congratulating Rockefeller and extending best wishes.

The governor said his administration would cooperate fully in transfering responsibilities of the state government to the Rockefeller administration which will take over in January.

Harriman had the backing of the Liberal party as well as the Democrats in his reelection bid.

Newsmen asked GOP Chairman Morhouse how he could explain the triumph in the face of Democratic victories in other states. He attributed it to progressiveness of the GOP in New York.

"The unity of our party here and the progressive record of the Dewey administration and the four years of progressive legislation enacted by a Republican state legislature — all these, I believe, are the reason we are winning here."

Harriman was seeking his second four-year term and Rockefeller his first try for elective office.

Metzner Loses as Democrats Win All 5 Seats in Assembly

By WILLIAM C. ROBBINS
(State Journal Staff Writer)

All five Democratic candidates were victorious in Dane county's Assembly races with Richard L. Cates, first assistant district attorney, scoring an upset victory over Republican incumbent Carroll E. Metzner, complete returns showed early today.

All the winners piled impressive vote totals in the record county turnout for a non-presidential election year.

Collectively, the five Democrats outdistanced their opponents by a 2 to 1 margin. In winning 90 of the county's 97 precincts, they totaled 40,204 to 19,602 for the four Republicans.

Cates actually outdistanced the rest of his Democratic ticket in scoring a narrow 295-vote win over Metzner, who was seeking his third term as Western Madison

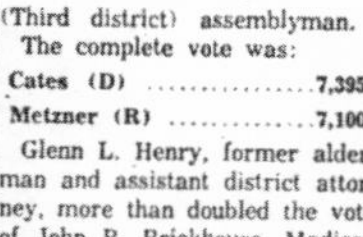

CATES HENRY

(Third district) assemblyman. The complete vote was:

Cates (D) **7,395**
Metzner (R) **7,100**

Glenn L. Henry, former alderman and assistant district attorney, more than doubled the vote of John B. Brickhouse, Madison attorney, to win the Eastern Madison (First district) election.

The comlete vote was:

Henry (D) **7,791**
Brickhouse (R) **3,402**

Henry, in gaining his 4,339 vote lead, carried all 10 precincts.

Cates' triumph was considered the most significant for the Democrats as other candidates were

(Continued on Page 2, Column 5)

Haas to Name Undersheriff Soon

Franz Haas, the Democratic sheriff-elect, said early today he will announce within 48 hours whom he will appoint to be his undersheriff when he returns to the sheriff's office in January.

Haas said, "It could be," when asked if his choice would be Vernon (Jack) Leslie, a former Madison policeman who was his undersheriff from 1952 through 1956.

Today's Chuckle

It's not so hard to make money these days. It's making a living that's so difficult.

Feature Finder

Still Cool

Partly cloudy and cool today and Saturday. High today, about 45; low tonight, about 25.

Wisconsin State Journal

SECTION 1 | MORNING FINAL | MADISON, FRIDAY, APRIL 10, 1959 | ★★★ | 44 PAGES, THREE SECTIONS Vol. 201, No. 10 120th Year · 5c

FRANK LLOYD WRIGHT, NOTED ARCHITECT, DIES

Wright: A Force of Nature

By HELEN MATHESON
(Assistant Managing Editor)

Frank Lloyd Wright once said "the safety of the soul depends on its courage."

He saw his organic architecture—"the architecture of democracy"—treated both as America's greatest creative achievement and as a bad joke.

He heard his private life described sometimes as a "circus," sometimes as "the most outstanding 20th century revolt against Victorianism."

'Truth Against World'

He chose as his crest a Druid symbol that means "truth against the world."

And in late years, he wrote that he had experienced "the best and the worst of everything."

At his death, Wright was probably the world's most celebrated architect. His work was known abroad as "the American expression in architecture." He was decorated by eight nations and awarded gold medals by the King of England and the American Institute of Architecture which pronounced him—at 80—a "titanic force."

He left behind him more than 700 structures, including some of the most famous buildings on earth: the nearly-completed Guggenheim museum in New York City, the Imperial hotel in Tokyo, his home, Taliesin, near Spring Green—and plans for others: a civic center on Madison's Monona Terrace and a mile-high skyscraper for Chicago.

Often Attacked

Yet throughout his life, his buildings were attacked as "monstrosities of material and form." His ideas were called half-baked, visionary, egotistical.

And his private life was marked by strife, by revolt against social mores, by debt so baffling he finally incorporated himself and sold shares, and by four great romances — all shadowed with grief and one, with ghastly tragedy.

Wright's defiance of convention attracted merciless publicity, but as he grew older public attitudes toward him became more kind. And as an old man he explained to one of his sons:

"The faith that is in me may be unable to go with laws, but it is never lawless."

Recently he had lived most of the year at his celebrated Taliesin near Spring Green, an 1,800-acre farm estate he valued at $2,500,000 and center of his architectural fellowship.

A Striking Figure

He was often seen in Madison, an erect, fragile figure wearing a jaunty pork pie hat on his white head, sports slacks, jacket, and flowing tie, gesturing with a cane, his conversation crisp and pungent.

As an architect, Wright believed that buildings must be "natural"—"native in spirit and making." Taliesin—Welch for "shining brow"—he built out of native materials on his family homestead.

"You don't spend your lives in insensitive, ugly buildings and still respect yourselves, for only beauty dignifies the soul of man," he told an audience in Madison's Unitarian Meeting House which he designed with a great glass prow to let in the outdoors.

On another occasion, he explained that he and his followers "only build for people we like. They get our houses as some get religion . . . for houses affect living—spiritual living. Architecture

(Continued on Page 6, Column 1)

Frank Lloyd Wright

Model of Proposed Monona Terrace

Death at Age 89 Ends His Lively Career

(Compiled From Wire Services)

PHOENIX, Ariz. — Frank Lloyd Wright, 89, the rebellious titanic force of modern architecture, died early Thursday.

Mr. Wright died before dawn in St. Joseph's hospital, his fame finally secure after more than 50 years of artistic and personal controversy with caustic critics.

Advancing age was largely responsible for the death of the colorful, white-haired founder of modern architecture. Mr. Wright had undergone an emergency operation Monday for removal of an obstruction in the intestinal tract.

Planning 90th Birthday

He had come through the operation successfully. The last hospital report Wednesday night listed his condition as satisfactory.

He himself had had no inkling of poor health and already had issued instructions just before his death that invitations for a party at Taliesin, near Spring Green, Wis., on his 90th birthday—June 8—be delivered.

One of the first to receive that invitation was William T. Evjue, editor and publisher of the Capital Times, Madison, Wis., who recently had visited the Wrights at Taliesin West near here.

'Just Sighed, Died'

Mr. Wright died at 4:45 a.m. (5:45 a.m. CST).

"He just sighed—and died," reported his night nurse, Mrs. Jessie Boganno, Glendale, Ariz. She said he appeared to be resting comfortably but did not speak during the last few hours of life.

With Mr. Wright at the hospital were his third wife, Olgivanna, and Wesley Peters, husband of Olgivanna's daughter whom Wright legally adopted. Mrs. Peters died 12 years ago.

Other survivors included two daughters, Mrs. Charles Gardner of Phoenix, and Mrs. Catherine Baxter of Menlo Park, Calif., mother of motion picture star Anne Baxter; four sons, Lloyd—who made his own career in architecture—and John of Del Mar, Calif.; David of Phoenix; and Robert of Washington, D. C.; nine grandchildren, six great-grandchildren, and a sister, Mrs. Maginal Barney of New York City.

'He Was a Great Man'

At Menlo Park, Miss Baxter said of her noted grandfather that the world would mourn the "passing of a great individual. His was a full life in which he certainly contributed more to others than most individuals are gifted to do. He was a great man."

All his life he fought for "natural housing," homes that would give a "sense of shelter and a sense of space," and functional, individualistic buildings that blended precision machine-age lines with nature's own living forms in stone and steel, wood, and glass.

His streamline technique or "Wrightisms" stirred controversy at home and abroad, leading him to professional victories and defeats, disappointments, and sometimes personal disaster.

But there was nothing small about him, except his neat, impeccably dressed little figure. Even his worst critics conceded his genius, and his followers considered him a giant in artistic building design.

Acclaimed at Home

Although he gained his first fame overseas, Wright at long last in 1950 won the reluctant acclaim of the American Institute of Architects which presented him with its gold medal—the profession's highest award—

(Continued on Page 2, Column 1)

If Not Withholding Tax —What? Nelson Asks

Gov. Gaylord Nelson Thursday challenged a split Legislature to adopt his income tax withholding plane or come up with something else to replace it.

NELSON

Nelson spoke to a joint session, his fourth personal appearance before the lawmakers since mid-January.

He pleaded for support for his withholding plan and ticked off his rebuttal against arguments which have been advanced in opposition to it.

Sees Surtax Rise

Nelson said if the plan isn't approved, the Legislature will have to increase the surtax on income tax from 20 to 40 per cent to finance the governor's proposed building program, or produce another alternative.

Passage of the withholding bill providing for speeded-up collection of income taxes would offer a "windfall" of $78 million.

Nelson has recommended that all of the state's $24 million share of the windfall be allocated for projects in the first year of his suggested $52-million, three-year state building program.

He said $4 million would be left over for application on the $16.5 million, second year phase of his building program.

He recommended that the other $54 million of the windfall be returned to local units of government to minimize the effect needed construction projects in localities have on the property tax.

'Easy to Criticize'

"It is simple enough to criticize any program," Nelson said. "But . . . with your criticism goes the responsibility of proposing an alternative you are willing to support and stand by."

He said his statement applied with equal force to the Democratic

(Assembly GOP Bristles at Nelson Bid, but Senators Are More Reserved. Reaction Story, Sec. 1, Page 12.)

majority in the Assembly and the Republican majority in the Senate.

"It is a fundamental rule in any democratic society that those who have the power to successfully oppose have the responsibility to constructively propose," Nelson said.

Republicans in control of the Senate have indicated strong opposition to the withholding plan.

Not a New Tax

The governor said the withholding system was not a new tax but was a better method of collecting the present income tax obligation. He said it would not change the present tax structure.

Nelson said Wisconsin's financial problem in buildings is due to delays in the past 22 years because of depression, World War II, and the Korean War. He said it was magnified by population growth.

"It makes sense to use the windfall now to help the state and its municipalities catch up," Nelson said.

He said the state has been borrowing from the future by failing

(Continued on Page 2, Column 5)

Upstate Man Killed as Auto Overturns

MARSHFIELD (AP)—Alois Newman, 45, of Edgar, Marathon county, was killed Thursday when the car in which he was riding went out of control on Highway 97 about 2 miles north of Marshfield and overturned.

On the Inside

Dulles Enters Hospital for X-Ray Studies

JUPITER ISLAND, Fla. (AP) — Secretary of State John Foster Dulles went to the Palm Beach Air Force base hospital Thursday for X-ray studies for the first time since his arrival at this resort 11 days ago.

The secretary, who is recovering from a hernia operation and treatment for cancer, was away from his vacation retreat — the home of Undersecretary C. Douglas Dillon—for three hours.

Today's Chuckle

A henpecked weatherman claims: "My wife speaks 150 words a minute with gusts up to 180."

'Some Delay' Seen on Terrace Project

The death of Frank Lloyd Wright will cause "some delay" in the Wright-designed Monona Terrace project, Mayor Ivan A. Nestingen said Thursday afternoon.

He added, however, that Mr. Wright's death "should by no means prevent the city from completing" the project.

Group Confident

Reaction of city auditorium committee members was varied, but none of them seemed to think that the auditorium cannot be built.

NESTINGEN

"The plans have been developed to a point where it is my feeling that we can complete the final plans and specifications with the talents and capabilities of the staff of the Frank Lloyd Wright foundation," Nestingen said.

The auditorium committee received preliminary plans from Mr. Wright several weeks ago, but delayed recommending their approval to the City Council until some basic questions of building materials and specific features to be included are settled.

To Clear Up Points

Nestingen said that the committee should confer with Wesley Peters, Mr. Wright's son-in-law, or some other representative of the foundation as soon as possible to clear up some technical points.

One of them, he said, is to determine who can represent the foundation in signing a stipulation dismissing the foundation's suit against the city.

The suit was to compel the city to go ahead with the terrace project despite the Metzner law which banned it. The law has since been repealed. City Atty. Harold E. Hanson has advised the auditorium committee that th suit should be dismissed before the prelimi-

(Continued on Page 2, Column 1)

U.W. Fee Hike Trimmed to $50

Fees for out of state students at the University of Wisconsin would be raised $50 a year instead of $100 under an action Thursday by the joint finance committee.

The committee reconsidered its previous action and voted, 9 to 4, in favor of raising out of state fees to $600 a year instead of $650 a year as voted earlier.

Assemblyman Fred Risser (D-Madison) said he favored only a $50 increase because the higher figure would give Wisconsin the top tuition in the Big Ten. He agreed with Assemblyman Richard Cates (D-Madison) that the university needs out of state students.

The committee defeated a motion that would have cut out the 4 per cent merit salary increase for faculty at the university and state colleges. Sen. Chester Dempsey (R-Waukesha) said the trend was away from tax increases and that the salaries of "one segment of the society should not be raised without raises for other segments."

Also defeated was a motion to cut the merit increase to 2 per cent.

Kennedy to Wait on Primary Bid

MILWAUKEE (AP) — Sen. John F. Kennedy (D-Mass.) who reportedly may lay his presidential aspirations on the line in the 1960 Wisconsin Presidential Primary, said Thursday that he regards the primary as of great significance but his current visit to Wisconsin doesn't commit him to enter it.

"It will be a significant and important primary," Kennedy told a news conference. "In fact, your state may be as crowded as a college campus phone booth next year. But I will not decide until the end of this year or early in 1960 whether I am going to be a candidate."

Kennedy held the news conference shortly after his arrival to address the annual Gridiron Dinner of The Milwaukee Press club. After this appearance he travels to seven state cities to make six speeches in the next three days.

Kennedy is scheduled to make three talks in Madison Saturday. At 9 a.m., he will speak at a breakfast in Hotel Loraine; at 12:45 p.m., to a Junior Chamber of Commerce meeting at the Wisconsin Center, and at 1:30 to University of Wisconsin students in Music hall.

A press conference also is planned in Madison.

Other Wright News

More Stories, Pictures, Sidelights on Frank Lloyd Wright Will Be Found on Page 6.

On Page 7 Is a Full Picture Page on Highlights of His Life.

See Editorial, Page 10.

Chief's Defense Set to Start Tonight as Hearing Resumes

By JUNE DIECKMANN
(State Journal Staff Writer)

Police Chief Bruce Weatherly's defense testimony is scheduled to start tonight when the police and fire commission resumes its hearing at 7 p.m. in Circuit Court on five misconduct charges filed against the chief.

Atty. Jack R. DeWitt, Weatherly's counsel, said he may call the chief as a witness in his own defense either tonight or Saturday, depending on how other testimony progresses.

DEWITT

Commission Pres. Albert A. Taubert said the hearings will be held tonight and all day Saturday in an attempt to complete testimony before Sunday. If not, he said the commission will decide late Saturday afternoon when the next session will be held.

DeWitt said he has 15 defense witnesses subpenaed and there "may be a few more."

DeWitt declined to name all of the witnesses he has subpenaed, but he said some will be medical men, to testify about Weatherly's crash injuries and resulting condition; character witnesses; and "others who saw Chief Weatherly at the Hoffman House where he is alleged to have been drinking."

DeWitt said among the Hoffman House witnesses will be Jack Stevenson, 4230 Esch lane, deputy Dane county coroner and a former Madison policeman; Atty. Albert J. McGinnis, 1940 Winnebago st.; Cosmas (Coz) Hoffman, co-owner of the Hoffman House; and Kenneth Zerwick, 212 S. Mills st., president of the Wisconsin Brick Corp.

The commission did not hold Weatherly's hearing Thursday night because of the absence of the last prosecution witness, Charles (Chuck) Hoffman, co-owner of the Hoffman House, 514 E. Wilson st.

Instead, it held its belated monthly meeting. No mention of Chief Weatherly's misconduct-charge hearing was made by the commissioners or the police chief.

Chief Weatherly reported in person on the March police business; Fire Chief Edward J. Page gave a report on his department's work during March, and the commission approved the one-year renewal of private detective

(Continued on Page 2, Column 3)

Proxmire to Close Milwaukee Office

WASHINGTON (AP) — Sen. William Proxmire (D-Wis) said Thursday he was closing his office in Milwaukee because the increasing heavy load of legislative work and correspondence "has compelled us to concentrate all of our staff in order to get the job done in Washington."

His home secretary, Jerry Bruno, will be assigned to the Washington staff, Proxmire said.

Feature Finder

The Wisconsin Legislative News

(Turn to Pages 3 and 5)

Spring Green Rites Pending; Body to Arrive on Saturday

(Special to The State Journal)

PHOENIX — The body of Frank Lloyd Wright, world-famed Madison area architect who died in a Phoenix, Ariz., hospital Thursday, will arrive in Spring Green Saturday.

The body will lie in state in the living room of his winter home at Taliesin West outside of Scottsdale, Ariz., until Friday. Only close friends of the renowned architect are being admitted.

Spring Green funeral service arrangements are still pending for Sunday or Monday. Burial will be in the Hillside Unitarian chapel cemetery just east of Taliesin East, the Wrights' resident grounds south of Spring Green.

Most of Mr. Wright's relatives on his mother's side are buried at the chapel cemetery. The chapel was constructed more than 80 years ago as a wayside place for prayer and was formerly known as the Wyoming Valley Unitarian Church.

Mr. Wright, as a boy, attended services at the chapel on those occasions when traveling Unitarian ministers stopped there.

Mr. Wright was often quoted as saying that he heard some of the greatest voices of Unitarianism in the chapel in his boyhood.

His uncle, the Rev. Jenkin Lloyd Jones, regarded as the most important single figure in the growth of Unitarianism in the Midwest, often preached at the chapel.

Funeral arrangements for the rites at Spring Green will be made by the Richardson funeral home, Spring Green.

Sunny, Warmer

Sunny and warmer today. Partly cloudy and continued warm Wednesday. High today mid-60s; low tonight 40. Winds southwesterly 10 to 15 miles an hour.

Wisconsin State Journal

SECTION 1 | MORNING FINAL | MADISON, TUESDAY, APRIL 14, 1959 | ★★★ | 22 PAGES, THREE SECTIONS Vol. 201, No. 14 120th Year | 5c

EXIT—Police Chief Bruce Weatherly (walking below clock with hand in pocket) leaves Circuit Courtroom No. 3 at 9:40 Monday morning after the police and fire commission announced he was fired. State Journal Photos by Edwin Stein

OUSTED WEATHERLY TO APPEAL FIRING

TENSE MOMENT—Mrs. Bruce Weatherly, left, clasps her husband's arm as she and the police chief listened to the police and fire commission announce it had found him guilty on four misconduct charges.

CHIEF STOIC—Weatherly didn't move a muscle, blink an eye or change his expression as the verdict was read. The picture shows Mrs. Weatherly as she turned her head away and closed her eyes after the verdict was read.

Acting Chief Gruber Takes Over Control

Commission Votes, 4-1, for Conviction on Four Charges

By JUNE DIECKMANN (State Journal Staff Writer)

Chief Bruce Weatherly's 20-year police career ended at noon Monday with his dismissal by the police and fire commission on misconduct charges.

Richard F. Gruber, the senior-ranking police inspector, immediately took over as acting chief in accordance with city ordinance. He said he planned "no changes for the present" in police operations.

4 to 1 Vote

The commissioners, by a 4 to 1 vote, found Weatherly guilty of drinking on duty, driving under

(See Editorial, Page 4)

the influence of liquor, driving his secretary home in a police car, and of conduct unbecoming an officer.

They acquitted him of suppressing evidence from Mayor Ivan A. Nestingen on the basis of medical testimony concerning a brain injury he received in his Jan. 8 traffic accident.

GRUBER

Weatherly's attorneys served notice they will appeal the conviction to Circuit Court. The judge has 25 days (until May 8) to schedule hearing, without a jury, on the appeal. According to state law, the court has authority to rule only on whether the commission's verdict was "reasonable."

Doesn't Bat an Eye

Weatherly didn't bat an eye when Commission Sec. James E. Doyle read the verdict which fired him from the $10,512-per-year chief's job he had held here since Jan. 1, 1949.

He stared at the commission bench and didn't even move when his wife, Inez, slipped into an attorney's chair alongside him, clasped his arm, and whispered consoling words to him.

Commission Pres. Albert A. Taubert said the commission will decide at its next monthly meeting, May 13, what procedure will be followed to name a new chief.

Commissioner Marshall Browne, publisher of the East Side News, cast the dissenting vote against the dismissal. Votes in favor of

(Continued on Page 2, Column 1)

Discoverer Up; Vanguard Isn't

Discoverer II was launched Monday from the West coast and went into a polar orbit, setting the stage for a gigantic game of aerial catch.

At Cape Canaveral, Fla., however, an attempt to put two Vanguard satellites into orbit on a single launching vehicle failed when the second stage did not ignite.

Stories on the unprecedented attempt for double-barreled shots follow.

Unique Double Effort Fizzles With 2nd Stage

CAPE CANAVERAL, Fla. (UPI)—A Vanguard rocket failed Monday night in an attempt to launch two United States satellites in one firing in a unique two-in-one experiment.

The second stage of the Vanguard's three-stage launching vehicle failed to function. The remaining portion of the rocket—including the two satellites—fell into the Atlantic.

2 Unique Moonlets

The Air Force earlier launched a Discoverer satellite into polar orbit from Vandenberg Air Force base, Calif.

Second-stage malfunction caused Vanguard failures on three previous occasions.

It was the first U.S. attempt to fire two satellites in one launching.

Nestled in the Vanguard's nose were two unique moonlets.

Plastic Sphere

The first moonlet was a device to explore the earth's unpredictable magnetic field. It was made up of an 18-inch cylinder containing a magnetometer, attached to a 13-inch fiberglass-resin sphere.

The second satellite was an inflatable plastic sphere coated with aluminum. This was to be blown up to its 30-inch diameter by nitrogen after the magnetometer was ejected from the Vanguard's third stage by a spring device. It weighed only three-tenths of a pound.

The magnetometer satellite was christened Vanguard III-A and the inflatable sphere Vanguard III-B.

Most Economical

The National Aeronautics and Space Administration (NASA), in charge of the Vanguard firing, said that "without a doubt, Vanguard III-B will be the most economical satellite ever attempted. The aluminum foil and plastic that form the skin cost only 65 cents."

It was the ninth try for the Vanguard, which made good in only two of its attempts. The rocket put the 6.4-inch Vanguard I on Mar. 17, 1958, into an orbit expected to last 2,000 years. Vanguard II, the seeing-eye weather satellite, was fired Feb. 17.

Planes to Try to Nab Satellite's 'Chuting Capsule

VANDENBERG AIR FORCE BASE, Calif. (AP)—The second United States Discoverer satellite roared southward into polar orbit Monday, setting the stage for a gigantic game of aerial catch in which planes may try to snatch its parachuting nose cone from the air.

Two hours after the launching, an Advanced Research Projects Agency (ARPA) spokesman said tracking stations in Alaska, Hawaii, and at this West Coast missile base had established that Discoverer II is in orbit.

'We Are Exultant'

The 1,600-pound satellite is whirling around the earth in a nearly north-south orbit every 94 minutes. At its high point, it is 445 miles from earth, at its closest, 158.

William H. Godel, director of planning for ARPA, said, "We are exultant over the second success in the Discoverer series."

The orbit would allow the satellite a life expectancy of about 30 days, he said.

Within 12 hours, he said, they will be able to determine if the orbit meets requirements for an attempt to recover the satellite's instrumented nose cone.

1 Chance in 1,000

If all goes well, the nose cone

(Continued on Page 2, Column 5)

Feature Finder

Criticism Misleading, Judge Flom Charges

By STANLEY WILLIAMS (State Journal Staff Writer)

Criticism of Dane County Court's public administrator has been slanted to mislead the public, Judge Carl Flom said in announcing that he plans no changes in the court staff.

Flom was elected to his first full six-year term on the bench in last Tuesday's election. He was appointed to the post by former Gov. Vernon W. Thomson to succeed Judge George H. Kroncke Jr., who resigned.

Required by Law

Use of the public administrator and fee system of reimbursement for his services dominated criticism of Flom in the campaign.

The criticism was misleading in two important ways, the judge said. First, he pointed out, Dane County Court, like all other Wisconsin county courts, is required by law to have a public administrator.

Second, he stressed, the public has been led to believe that the fees are paid by heirs out of their shares of estates. In fact, he said, the fees, which are set by law, are paid out of state inheritance taxes.

Regardless of what system is followed or who the administrator is, Flom emphasized, the heirs would not get the money now paid in fees for the administrator's services unless the state law were changed.

His Responsibilities

The public administrator is a lawyer in private practice appointed by the county judge. Among his duties are acting as administrator in estates where there are no heirs and computing the inheritance in any estates.

He is responsible to the judge to see that a fair value is placed on all property in an estate. Similarly, he is responsible for the accuracy and legality of the accounting for expenses in all estates. He must check and approve the evaluation, accounting, and tax computation of every estate before it passes through the court to the heirs.

Atty. Lyall T. Beggs has held

(Continued on Page 2, Column 6)

Oscar Toebaas, 71, Noted Madison Trial Lawyer, Dies

Oscar T. Toebaas, 71, Madison, one of the state's best known trial lawyers, died Monday while vacationing at Palm Beach, Fla.

He and his wife, Inez, had gone there in March. Mr. Toebaas had suffered a heart attack and virus infection last fall and winter.

A member of the Madison law firm of Toebaas, Hart, Kraege, and Jackman, 111 S. Hamilton st., he had been president of the Wisconsin Bar Assn. and at one time has been asked to serve on the Wisconsin state Supreme Court, which he reluctantly turned down.

He had also been president of the Madison Club and was active in several Madison community functions.

Funeral services will be at 10 a. m. Friday in Bethel Lutheran Church, 312 Wisconsin ave., the Rev. Morris Wee officiating.

Burial will be in Forest Hill cemetery. Friends may call at the Fitch-Lawrence funeral home, 626 University ave., after 7 p. m. Thursday.

Born in Iola, Wis., he had been a Madison resident since 1910 when he came here to study law. He was graduated from the Law School in 1912.

OSCAR T. TOEBAAS

He was married to the former

(Continued on Page 2, Column 8)

Middleton Bus Rates Increased

The Central Wisconsin Transportation Co. (Middleton Bus Co.) will increase its fare rates 5 cents a ride effective Wednesday.

The cash fare between Madison and Middleton will go up from 30 cents to 35 cents. Between Madison and Crestwood, Mendota Beach, Mohawk Park, and Blackhawk Park, the rates will be increased from 20 cents to 25 cents.

All ticket books which are good for 10 rides will be raised 50 cents.

The Madison-Middleton 10-ride ticket book will be increased from $2.70 to $3.20. The present $1.75 book for 10 rides between Madison and Crestwood will sell for $2.25 and the $2.20 book for 10 rides between Madison and points between the White grocery store and the new Piggly Wiggly store near Middleton will be $2.70.

Fares for children between 2 and 12 years will remain at 15 cents. The rate increase was recently approved by the Public Service Commission (PSC).

Wagner Case Suspect Held at La Crosse

MILWAUKEE (UPI) — Police announced late Monday night that authorities at La Crosse are holding a new suspect, a 25-year-old Racine man, in the murder of Ben Wagner, 6, nine days ago.

Police said he has admitted being in both Milwaukee and Ozaukee counties on the day the boy was abducted.

Detective Capt. Leo Woeffel said he was told the man owned a blue and white colored car, similar in description to the one described by Ben's playmate as the vehicle which carried the child to his death. (Earlier Story, Page 3.)

Today's Chuckle

Living a double life gets you nowhere twice as fast.

Mauston Girl Held for Trial in 2 Murders

MAUSTON — Elizabeth Jane Dakin, 17, was bound over to Circuit Court Monday afternoon on charges of first degree murder in the shooting of her mother and father on Dec. 1, 1958.

Her arraignment was scheduled for 10 a.m. Saturday.

Five Witnesses

Five witnesses appeared for the state at the preliminary hearing before Sauk County Judge Robert Gollmar Monday. Two of the witnesses, Mrs. Gunnar Johnson, Lyndon Station, and Derwood Staples, operator of the Cliff House resort near here, testified that the girl told them she had shot and killed her parents.

MISS DAKIN

Mrs. Johnson quoted the girl as saying:

"I shot my mother, and my father came home, and I had to shoot him, too."

Staples said the girl told him substantially the same thing. He added that she said:

"I don't know why I killed my father, because I loved him."

Insanity Plea Expected

The girl's attorney, Arlo McKinnon, Milwaukee, twice tried to introduce her mental state on the night of the shooting into evidence. But objections by Dist. Atty. Roland Vieth kept such evidence out.

It is expected that McKinnon will enter a plea of not guilty by reason of insanity at the arraignment.

The other three witnesses at Monday's hearing in Juneau County Court described events on the night Mr. and Mrs. Thomas Dakin were shot. There were no defense witnesses.

McKinnon twice tried to have

(Continued on Page 2, Column 4)

Wright Associates Confer With Mayor

Mayor Ivan A. Nestingen lunched at the Madison Club Monday with Wesley Peters, Frank Lloyd Wright's son-in-law; Eugene Masselink, secretary of the Taliesin Fellowship; William T. Evjue, editor and publisher of the Capital Times; and Prof. Harold M. Groves, University of Wisconsin economist who is a member of the city auditorium committee.

It was Nestingen's last chance to confer with Peters and Masselink on problems connected with the Monona Terrace project before the pair returned to Arizona after Mr. Wright's funeral. No decisions were announced on questions remaining to be settled concerning the Wright-designed Terrace project.

Officials See Dulles Resigning Post Soon

WASHINGTON (UP) — President Eisenhower delayed a decision Monday on John Foster Dulles' future as secretary of state.

Doctors, meanwhile, will make an effort to check Dulles' cancer by new medical treatment.

Most Administration leaders were gloomy about the prospects that Dulles could win his fight. They expected he would resign soon.

Dulles' condition aroused immediate concern in Congress about who will represent the United States at the foreign ministers' meeting in Geneva May 11.

Not Equal Footing

Sen. George Aiken (R-Vt.) said that unless Dulles is able to resume full-time work by that date, "I would expect he would resign."

"I don't think the country can go on and on without an active head of the State Department," Aiken said.

Aiken meant that an acting secretary could not stand on an equal footing with the ministers of the Soviet Union and the Western Allies.

Mr. Eisenhower gave no clue to the future after a 45-minute visit with Dulles at Walter Reed Army hospital Monday.

Observation, Treatment

Dulles, 71, returned to the hospital Sunday after cutting short a rest stay in Florida.

The White House announced that Dulles would undergo additional medical observation and new treatment—what kind was not reported.

Mr. Eisenhower went directly to the hospital after he interrupted his Augusta, Ga., golfing vacation for a quick visit to the capital. The break in the vacation had been planned previously.

He Looks 'Fine'

The White House said the two men talked alone most of the time about Dulles' health and "matters relating to world affairs."

On leaving, Mr. Eisenhower said Dulles looked "fine."

James C. Hagerty, White House press secretary, emphasized that Dulles has not resigned, despite some recurring rumors that he had decided to quit.

"I can say there has been no resignation submitted," Hagerty said.

June 15 Legislature Adjournment Sought

MILWAUKEE (UPI) — State Sen. Henry Maier (D-Milwaukee), Democratic floor leader, said Monday that he will ask the Democratic Joint Policy committee to set June 15 as the end of the present session of the Legislature.

The Legislature usually ends in July, but this year a special session will be needed in the fall to take up financial matters such as the governor's report from his Tax Impact Study committee.

Maier said the June 15 deadline could be met if the Democratic-controlled Assembly and the Republican-controlled Senate do not become stalemated on major legislation.

Elected as a 'Joke,' Student JP, 21, Takes His New Job Seriously

By JOHN CREIGHTON (State Journal Staff Writer)

Robert Mixson, 21, of 641 Anthony lane, who says he's "always good for a laugh," was quite serious when sworn in Monday as justice of the peace in the 19th ward.

The senior at the University of Wisconsin ran as a write-in candidate as a joke hatched by the Theta Delta Chi fraternity. His four votes defeated the nearest opponent by a 2 to 1 margin.

"I thought it was a big joke, when first asked to run," he said, "but I was almost shocked to speechlessness after learning I had won."

MIXSON

He probably will go down as the youngest justice of the peace in the ward's history and his election as one of the neatest stunts ever pulled by a university fraternity.

To members of his fraternity, and those of the Chi Omega sorority at the swearing-in ceremonies, the joke apparently carried more weight than the office. None was able to hold back giggles and outbursts of laughter during the oath in the Circuit Court clerk's office in the City-County building.

It was strictly business, though, for the slim, dark-haired JP, who is a mathematics and psychology major. "Now that the joke turned out to be the real thing, I hope to take the job seriously and be a credit to the office," he said.

He apparently means it. He bought a manual for the justice of the peace from the League of Wisconsin Municipalities. He said he's already been boning up on it.

His duties will include performing marriages, handling civil cases involving less than $200, and other tasks.

Mixson said he never had any political aspirations and, in fact, never took a political science course at the university. His chief aim is to be a statistician.

The credit for his election goes to Fred Kessler, 19, of Wauwatosa, where he is chairman of the Young Democrats.

Kessler, a sophomore majoring in political science, said he hatched the write-in campaign at 11 p.m. last Monday, the eve of the election.

He saw the election less as a joke than a means to make a

(Continued on Page 2, Column 3)

Warmer
Considerable cloudiness and warmer today. Chance of shower by evening. Thursday partly cloudy and little colder. High today, mid-50s; low tonight, low 30s.

Wisconsin State Journal

SECTION 1 MORNING FINAL MADISON, WEDNESDAY, APRIL 6, 1960 ★ ★ ★ 32 PAGES, THREE SECTIONS Vol. 203, No. 6 121st Year 5c

WINNER KENNEDY POCKETS SIX OF 10 STATE DISTRICTS

Bloodgood Wins Race for Judge

WILLIAM SACHTJEN JOSEPH BLOODGOOD

Tops Sachtjen by 1,400 Votes for New Court

By JUNE DIECKMANN
(State Journal Staff Writer)

Dist. Atty. Joseph W. Bloodgood won the new Superior Court "family" judgeship of Dane county Tuesday with a 1,439-vote majority over Atty. William C. Sachtjen, Madison's 12th ward alderman, complete election returns showed early today.

The vote from Madison's and Dane county's 97 precincts was:

Bloodgood	30,267
Sachtjen	28,828

Bloodgood, who was badly beaten by Sachtjen in the March primary six-man field for the judgeship nominations, rebounded strongly Tuesday.

Takes Early Lead

He took an early lead of about 550 votes with the first 30 rural precincts reporting; held his own when the city of Madison's 30 precincts reported, and then increased his lead to nearly 1,500 with the later reporting precincts from heavier populated Madison suburbs and Stoughton and Sun Prairie.

Sachtjen carried the city vote by a vote of 16,797 to 16,551, but Bloodgood's strong majority in rural areas cinched his victory.

To Resign D. A. Post

Bloodgood will resign his district attorney's post, which he has held since January, 1957, and become the county's new judge when the Superior Court Branch No. 2 begins operation May 2.

State law provides that Gov. Gaylord Nelson appoints a successor to Bloodgood as district attorney to serve out the remaining eight months of his term as the county's chief presecutor.

His salary as district attorney was $9,600 yearly, and as judge it will be $12,000.

'Clean Campaign'

"I am deeply grateful to the voters of Dane county for this most gratifying victory," Bloodgood said early today. "I could not have won without the wonderful support of my many friends

(Continued on Page 2, Column 3)

Maier Elected Milwaukee Mayor by Beating Reuss

MILWAUKEE (AP) — Henry W. Maier, 42, a Democratic state senator for the past 10 years, was chosen mayor of Milwaukee Tuesday in the city's nonpartisan election.

Rep. Henry S. Reuss, 48, also a Democrat, conceded that Maier won the election after less than one-half the votes were counted. With 264 of the 558 precincts reporting, Maier had 61,375 votes to 45,686 for Reuss.

MAIER

Maier has been in the state Senate since 1950 and the Democratic floor leader for the past four sessions. He was defeated for the United States Senate in 1956 and also lost when he sought the mayor's post in 1948.

Maier will succeed Frank P. Zeidler, a Socialist, who did not seek reelection. Zeidler has served 12 years.

Reuss was elected to Congress in 1954 and reelected in 1956 and 1958. He still can run for the fifth Congressional post this fall.

Apr. 18 Postmark on State Tax OK

The commissioner of the State Department of Taxation said Tuesday individual state income tax returns will be considered filed on time if they are postmarked or delivered on Monday, Apr. 18.

Commissioner John A. Gronouski said the exception to the statutory Apr. 15 filing date was being made because offices will not be open to the public that afternoon in observation of Good Friday, a legal half-day holiday.

Gronouski also announced that the department's assessor of incomes offices will furnish assistance to taxpayers in preparation of their income tax returns during regular office hours through Apr. 18. They will also be open on Saturday morning, Apr. 9.

Assessor of incomes offices are located in Madison, Appleton, Eau Claire, and Milwaukee.

County Judge Wins Manitowoc Reelection

MANITOWOC (UPI) — Incumbent County Judge Leon Jones of Manitowoc county won reelection Tuesday over Atty. Francis Yindra.

With 43 of Manitowoc county's 50 precincts reporting, Jones led Yindra, 12,527 to 7,619.

Manitowoc Defeats Fluoridation Proposal

MANITOWOC (UPI)—Fluoridation of this city's water supply was defeated in a referendum Tuesday.

The proposal to fluoridate the water supply lost by 7,396 to 2,591.

Sports Peach Has Baseball Schedules

Attention baseball fans:

The complete schedules of all games in the National and American Leagues will be found today in the Sports Peach.

You will want to clip them for handy reference.

Today's Chuckle

Money may talk, but today's dollar doesn't have cents enough to say very much.

Election Winners

Presidential Primary
Democratic
JOHN F. KENNEDY
Republican
RICHARD M. NIXON

Superior Court Judge
JOSEPH BLOODGOOD

County Board
10th Ward
DAVID J. OHNSTAD
12th Ward
HAROLD SPRINGER
14th Ward
JOHN KASIMATIS
16th Ward
CLYDE CHAMBERLAIN
21st Ward
JOSEPH C. GALE

School Board
RAY SENNETT
ARTHUR MANSFIELD

City Council
Sixth Ward
GEORGE ELDER
Eighth Ward
WENDELL M. PHILLIPS
12th Ward
LEONARD PORTER
14th Ward
HAROLD ROHR
16th Ward
LLOYD FOUST
18th Ward
RICHARD KOPP
20th Ward
BRUCE DAVIDSON
21st Ward
JAMES A. MARKS

School Bonds
YES

Harbor Funds
YES

Kopp Wins in 18th; 3 Incumbents Slip In

By STANLEY WILLIAMS
(State Journal Staff Writer)

A newcomer to politics, Richard D. Kopp, 30, toppled Ald. Howard Soderholm in the 18th ward and three other aldermen barely held their seats as city voters broke all records for an April election Tuesday.

Kopp outdistanced Soderholm by more than 300 votes, riding a wave of discontent with the alderman which climaxed in his attempt to change a number of street names in his ward.

Slim Margins

In a photo-finish, Lloyd Foust, East side building contractor, eked out a 14-vote victory over Vincent J. Phelan for the 16th ward seat.

Ald. Harold E. Rohr, 14th ward, managed a 34-vote span over his challenger on the South side, Clifford S. Roberts. Ald. James A. Marks clung to his 21st ward seat with a 30-vote margin over Ray J. Stanley.

Leonard Porter, 31, scoring his first victory in politics, racked up a 200-vote lead over 12th ward opponent, Arthur Dunham.

Limits Opponent

Ald. George Elder, Sixth ward, won another term on the council with an 81-vote margin over Peter F. Schmidt. Ald. Bruce Davidson, 20th ward, had the healthiest lead over his challenger, Donald S. Eisenberg, more than doubling his vote with a margin of some 1,000 votes.

Wendell M. Phillips, Eighth ward alderman, also won a new term, defeating Thomas Mair by nearly 250 votes.

Kopp, an insurance firm supervisor, succeeded in limiting Soderholm to a single term on the council. The only challenger to unseat an incumbent, he led the alderman by almost 400 votes in one precinct and trailed by 50 votes in the other although his other opponent, James W. Haraughty, threw his support to Soderholm afterward.

The final vote was:

Kopp	1,168
Soderholm	834

Rohr, a bitter opponent of the Capital Times and especially of the Monona Terrace auditorium project, survived a last-minute attempt of the Times to swamp him by unauthorized publication of new plans for the civic center.

The final vote was:

Rohr	943
Roberts	909

Marks, the 21st ward's County Board representative since it

(Continued on Page 2 Column 5)

Port Development Referendum Leads by Large Margin

A referendum to amend the Wisconsin Constitution to permit legistive appropriation for port development was carrying the state in returns early today.

The vote in 2,638 of Wisconsin's 3,460 precincts on the port development referendum was:

Yes	332,440
No	284,373

The amendment had been approved by the 1957 and 1959 Legislatures.

Its passage in Tuesday's referendum was the third and final step necessary to let the state make such expenditures. The proposal stemmed from the development of the St. Lawrence Seaway.

In past years, Wisconsin's constitutional ban on state spending for "works of internal improvement" had been amended to let the state spend money for highways, forestry, an airport program, and veterans' housing.

Port cities were divided on the referendum. The opposition was led by Milwaukee, which spent its own money building up the Milwaukee harbor.

Wisconsin has 22 ports on the Great Lakes, 12 of them rated major.

Marinette Votes Return to Mayor

MARINETTE (AP) — Voters of Marinette decided Tuesday to have the city return to a mayor form of government.

The vote was 2,449 to 2,106.

The city, which has been under a city manager with five councilmen elected at large, will be replaced by a mayor and 10 aldermen who will be elected a year from now.

Robert Levik is acting manager, who has been filling in since Manager K. W. Gardiner resigned a month ago. Levik will serve until a mayor is elected.

Steve Allen to End Regular TV Schedule

NEW YORK (AP) — Steve Allen's weekly television show will go off a regular schedule next season and appear instead from time to time.

Affiliates of NBC have been told by the network that Allen does not want to continue under the pressures of a weekly show.

His present time slot on other than Allen's appearances Monday nights will be filled by special shows.

4 A.M. EXTRA Vote Gives Him 20 of Delegates

By LLEWELLYN G. ROBERTS
(State Journal Staff Writer)

Sen. John F. Kennedy shook off stubborn early return rural support for Sen. Hubert Humphrey and swept to an impressive victory in Wisconsin's crucial presidential primary Tuesday.

The 42-year-old senator from Massachusetts took the popular vote on the Democratic side of the ballot and defeated Humphrey in six of the state's 10 Congressional districts.

The result is 20 delegates pledged to Kennedy and 10 **to Humphrey at the Democratic party nomination convention at Los Angeles in July. The state's 31st authorized vote will be split between the two men.**

SEN. HUBERT HUMPHREY

SEN. JOHN KENNEDY

Nixon Runs Strong

Vice-President Richard M. Nixon, unopposed on the Republican side of the ballot, had been expected to finish third but that finish was a strong third. At one time in the balloting he forged ahead of the vote total of Humphrey.

The vote in 3,039 of 3,446 precincts, as tabulated by the Associated Press at 4 a. m. today, was:

Kennedy (D)	389,417
Humphrey (D)	318,890
Nixon (R)	305,375

With the 3,039 precincts reporting, Kennedy had about 55 per cent of the Democratic ballot vote, Humphrey about 45 per cent. Nixon's percentage of the total state vote in those 3,039 precincts was a little more than 30 per cent.

Republican party leaders had said that in view of the Democratic contest and probable crossovers they would be satisfied with a Nixon percentage of 25 per cent or more.

Major Hurdle

The hotly contested Wisconsin primary was a major hurdle in Kennedy's bid for an early ballot nomination for the presidency at his party's national convention.

Kennedy picked up five convention votes by winning the popular vote and 15 more at the rate of 2½ each from the six Congressional districts he won. Humphrey's 10 votes represent 2½ delegate votes for the four districts he won.

The voting clearly showed that a substantial number of Republicans and independent voters who vote Republican most of the time crossed over to vote in the con-

(Continued on Page 2, Column 1)

Record Vote Totals Set in City, County

By WILLIAM C. ROBBINS
(State Journal Staff Writer)

Vote records for an April primary were set in both Madison and Dane county Tuesday as voters were drawn by the magic of the presidential campaign.

Voters flocked to the polls in such large proportions in the Madison area that several of the rural towns and villages actually ran out of ballots and were forced to use samples to complete the balloting.

The Madison area turnout reflected the statewide interest in the bitter Democratic battle between Sen. John F. Kennedy (D-Mass.) and Sen. Hubert H. Humphrey (D-Minn.) and the Republican attempt to keep their supporters on the GOP side of Vice-President Richard M. Nixon.

At Blooming Grove, there was such a long line of residents waiting at 8 p.m. closing time that they were shepherded inside the voting place and then permitted to cast their vote as much as 30 minutes later.

The record county vote was demonstrated dramatically as the village of Middleton and the towns of Madison and Westport ran short of presidential ballots and had to order more from the county clerk's office. Westport used up the 100 additional ones and then was forced to use sample ballots when they were gone.

The Madison total was 36,173, topping the previous comparable

(Continued on Page 2, Column 7)

Election News on the Inside

More election news will be found in Sec. 1, Pages 2, 4, 5, 6, and 9, and in Sec. 2, Page 1.

Gamble Benedict, Romania-Born Suitor Seek Quickie Marriage

DILLON, S. C. (UPI) — New York heiress Gamble Benedict and her sweetheart, Andre Porumbeanu, applied for a quickie South Carolina marriage license Tuesday and planned to be wed after a 24-hour waiting period.

It promised to be a stormy battle all the way to the altar for the society girl and her Romanian-born suitor.

They defied a New York court in running away, and Gamble, 19, ward of her grandmother, has been forbidden to marry without court permission. Porumbeanu, 35, whose Mexican divorce became effective Tuesday, faced a possible jail sentence for contempt of court.

The elusive pair were principals in an international love story when they fled to Paris together last winter. Their elopement plans

ANDRE GAMBLE

then were blocked because Porumbeanu's 1948 marriage had not been dissolved legally. Gamble's grandmother, Mrs. Henry Harper Benedict, dispatched relatives and lawyers to Paris to bring her back.

Mrs. Benedict, widow of a former president of the Remington Typewriter Co., initiated court action in Paris and in New York to break up the romance, and Gamble was placed under a court order to appear once a week in Girl's Term Court in New York to report on her activities.

But Gamble and Porumbeanu met secretly Monday — Gamble slipping away from her grandmother's town house on the eve of Porumbeanu's Mexican divorce becoming final. They went to Philadelphia by train, then headed South.

They applied for the marriage license just before closing time—5 p.m. — before Probate Judge Walker Allen at the county courthouse. South Carolina law provides that the applicants pick up the license any time after 5 p.m.

(Continued on Page 2, Column 4)

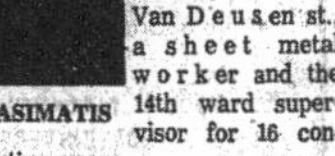

Feature Finder

Kasimatis, Gale, and Chamberlain Elected New County Supervisors

Three new Madison supervisors were elected to the 86-member County Board Tuesday, two of them defeating incumbents and the third replacing an incumbent who switched to the City Council, complete election returns showed early today.

KASIMATIS

The new board members are:

Atty. John Kasimatis, 31, of 531 W. Olin ave., who defeated Sherman Karnes, 55, of 230 Van Deusen st., a sheet metal worker and the 14th ward supervisor for 16 consecutive years.

Joseph C. Gale, 5713 Forsythia pl., an agent for the New York Life Insurance Co., who won over the one-year incumbent in the 21st ward, James H. Binger, 5706 Forsythia pl., a Johnson Plumbing Service steamfitter and mechanic.

GALE

CHAMBERLAIN

OHNSTAD

SPRINGER

Clyde Chamberlain, 3316 Ivy st., past president of the IVY Investment Assn. and operator of the Fair Oaks bar and grill, who nosed out Lars M. Hanson, 413 Welch ave., owner of the Vogue cleaners, to fill the 16th ward supervisor post vacated when

(Continued on Page 2, Column 6)

U.W. Faculty Kills Boxing

Stories, Photos in Sports Peach

Rain--Plus Snow
Light rain occasionally mixed with snow today. Wednesday mostly cloudy and continued cold. High today, 40; low tonight, 32.

Wisconsin State Journal

SECTION 1 | MORNING FINAL | MADISON, TUESDAY, MAY 10, 1960 | ★ ★ ★ | 26 PAGES, THREE SECTIONS Vol. 203, No. 40 121st Year | 5c

U.S. ADMITS SENDING SPY PLANES UNDER IKE'S ORDER

Hotel Robbed of $5,500

Edgewater Clerk Taped by Gunmen

Two black-masked gunmen strolled unnoticed out of Madison's plushiest hotel, the Edgewater, about 3:30 a.m. Monday with $5,500 of the hotel's receipts, $2,880 in cash, and left police holding nothing but empty bank bags.

"We don't even have a good description of the bandits. In fact, the only thing we're sure of is that the place was robbed," one of the city detectives said early today after nearly 24 hours of investigation.

No Link Seen

The holdup was "probably not" committed by the same men who stole at least $8,500 in cash, checks, and merchandise this weekend in burglaries at Lombardino's Garden restaurant, 2500 University ave., and the Schwartz, Inc., jewelry store, 440 State st., detectives said. "The stickup was a different type of operation," Detective Capt. Thomas Nee said.

Donald Patrick, 48, of 10 W. Gorham st., a Beloit native who has been on the midnight to 8 a.m. desk clerk shift at the hotel, 666 Wisconsin ave., since last September, was the bandits' victim.

He said he was alone in the well-lighted lobby office of the Lake Mendota shoreline hotel, sorting cash and checks, when the two masked men "popped up" from the customer's side of the reservation desk.

"They told me to 'hit the floor' with my face down and I did," Patrick told detectives.

Give Clerk 'Break'

The robbers bound Patrick's legs and arms with rolls of white adhesive tape which they took from their topcoat pockets, Patrick said.

"They were going to tape my mouth, too, but I have a cold and coughed and asked them not to put the stuff over my face. One of them said they wouldn't if I didn't cough too loud or say anything," Patrick told the investigators.

"The other one said it would be too bad for me if I did make any noise because they had a friend outside who would 'plug

(Continued on Page 2, Column 6)

WHERE GUNMEN HID—James Fiscus, left, and Douglas Schwerma, bellhops at the Edgewater hotel, pose Monday afternoon in front of the reservations desk to illustrate where two masked gunmen crouched until the opportune time to hold up the night desk clerk, Donald Patrick. Kenneth Forsmo, the day desk clerk, is standing behind the desk where Patrick said he was when surprised by the bandits.

CONTAINERS UNLOCKED—Janyce Thomas, secretary to the hotel manager, Austin Faulkner, checks the lobby-office safe and money cabinets from which masked bandits stole $5,500 about 3:30 a.m. Monday. The money containers, behind the lobby reservation desk, were unlocked when the robbers entered because Donald Patrick, night clerk, was preparing bank deposits.

State Journal Photos

Flights to Deter Surprise Attack

By JOHN SCALI
(Associated Press Writer)

WASHINGTON — The United States acknowledged Monday that it has sent spy flights into Russia — under President Eisenhower's general orders.

The State Department did not discourage a deduction that such flights may continue until Soviet leaders open their borders to inspection.

Refers to Summit

Secretary of State Christian A. Herter, in making the acknowledgement, strongly defended intelli-

Spying Isn't a One-Way Street. Story, Photos, Page 9.

gence flights by unarmed civilian planes as urgently necessary to guard the non-Communist world against surprise Soviet attack.

Herter suggested that next week's summit conference make an earnest attempt to agree on safeguards which would end the threat that either side could suddenly launch a nuclear onslaught.

With the approval of Mr. Eisenhower, Herter frankly admitted that U. S. planes have carried out "extensive aerial surveillance" of Communist territory under directives issued by the President as part of his national security duties.

HERTER

Here, there was mention of the National Security act of 1947, but the wording made it clear that Herter was speaking only of Mr. Eisenhower, who went into office in 1953.

'No Authorization'

"Specific missions of these unarmed civilian aircraft have not been subject to presidential authorization," Herter said.

After Soviet Premier Nikita S. Khrushchev reported the capture of American flier Francis G. Powers, 30, deep inside Russia, the State Department acknowledged an intelligence flight over Soviet territory probably was un-

(Continued on Page 2, Column 3)

Khrushchev Warns Allies of Reprisals

MOSCOW (UPI)—Soviet Premier Nikita S. Khrushchev warned Monday night that the Soviet Union will take reprisals against countries which permit United States reconnaissance planes to take off from their bases to carry out spy missions over Russia.

Khrushchev sounded the warning to an audience which included U.S. Ambassador Llewellyn Thompson and the envoys of Norway, Pakistan, and Turkey at a Czech embassy reception.

If Flights Repeated

He told the NATO envoys that if the May Day incident, when a U.S.U-2 plane was shot down over Russia, happens again and it is proven that the plane came from a foreign base, the Soviet Union will undertake reprisals against those bases.

"If someone intends to fly over our territory, reconnoitering objectives, and gleaning state secrets, we shall bring down such planes, just bring them down," Khrushchev said.

"More, if such flights are repeated, we shall take appropriate counter measures."

Khrushchev's speech at the reception commemorating the 15th anniversary of V-E Day was punctuated with applause, laughter, and cheers by the majority of his audience.

Loud Laughter

He said the spy plane flight was a "provocation deliberately timed for the summit meeting" scheduled to open in Paris Monday.

He told his audience, amid loud laughter, that the U.S. is in a "mess" because it was caught red-handed trying to spy on Russia.

Khrushchev ridiculed the U.S. statement on the incident. He said, "Moreover, the statement

KHRUSHCHEV

THOMPSON

blames us for not allowing to fly over and travel across our country those who want to study defenses, to discover secrets.

"This is a very dangerous explanation because it does not denounce, but tries to justify such a flight and seems to say that such flights are possible in the future, too, because the Soviet Union does not see fit to reveal its secrets to countries that pursue unfriendly policy towards us.

"I should say this: Those countries that have bases on their territories should note most carefully the following: If they allow others to fly from their bases to our territory, we shall hit at those bases because we assess such actions as provocations against our country."

Prolonged applause followed

(Continued on Page 2, Column 5)

New Social Rules, ROTC Trial Voted by Faculty

By SAMUEL C. REYNOLDS
(State Journal Staff Writer)

Revised student social regulations and a two-year trial period for the voluntary ROTC program were approved Monday afternoon by the University of Wisconsin faculty.

The social regulations, which will go into effect in September, 1961, provide that men and women over 21 years old may live in apartments and hold unchaperoned parties, but that no student of either sex may live in an apartment until reaching 21.

All but one of several motions made to alter or postpone adopting the new social regulations were beaten down. The faculty did delete one paragraph that stated in part: "The individual member of this university community is . . . responsible to the university for the conduct at gatherings at which he is present."

Prof. William G. Rice of the Law School suggested the deletion since it implied guilt by association.

"Would you, the members of the faculty, like to be held responsible for 'the conduct' of all people at gatherings you attend?" he asked.

His colleagues concurred in his doubts over the paragraph.

The new social regulations were approved by the Student Life and Interests committee and first reported to the faculty in April.

Dean of Women Martha E. Peterson pleaded that they be given at least a chance.

She said she was "unhappy over our present circumstances, in which we are not dealing honestly with the parents and not dealing honestly with the students."

Dean of Students LeRoy E. Lu-

(Continued on Page 2, Column 1)

Buending Fired Pistol, Tests Show

John Buending, 24-year-old county highway engineering aide and an expectant father, fired the pistol which killed his wife and himself Saturday night in their home at 4609 Windigo trail, Dist. Atty. William D. Byrne said late Monday afternoon.

Powder-burn tests and others made at the State Crime Laboratory showed that Buending fired one bullet at the base of his wife's skull, which killed her, and then killed himself with a shot into his right temple, Byrne reported.

An alcoholic blood test on Buending registered 2.12, the laboratory experts reported. Wisconsin courts considered a 1.5 test borderline intoxication for driving, and a 3.0 test indicative of being "passed out."

Byrne said no inquest will be held. The deaths were officially ruled a murder and suicide. The Buendings were expecting their child in about a month. Doctors were unable to save the unborn child.

109 Aboard, Jet Makes Belly Landing

NEW YORK (AP)—A Boeing 707 transcontinental airliner with 109 persons aboard skidded safely into Idlewild airport amid smoke and flames Monday after a landing gear collapsed as it hit the runway.

There were no injuries.

Smoke from a minor fire filled the cabin of Trans-World Airlines Flight 100 as it touched down nonstop from Los Angeles. A momentary streak of apprehension swept the passengers.

As the big plane ground to a halt on its belly, hostesses assisted the 100 passengers through emergency exits and down escape chutes.

The spectacular and fiery landing of the jet airliner triggered a disaster alert on the field. The fire department at first thought the plane had crashed and burned.

Later, TWA dismissed the incident as a frozen brake that had created a small blaze.

However, Capt. Henry Campbell of Los Angeles, pilot of the plane, said he was coming in for a normal landing when the nose wheel collapsed.

He hit the brakes and a shower of sparks spewed from the underside of the plane as it skidded along. These touched off the quickly extinguished fire.

TWA said the landing gear buckled and two of the plane's four engines scraped along the runway, catching fire.

Mitby Accepts School Post Here

Norman P. T. Mitby secured his release Monday night as director of the Green Bay Vocational and Adult school, and formally accepted the same post in Madison.

Mitby, who will become director here on July 1, was offered the Madison job last week but had to wait until the Green Bay board released him from his contract.

Fred M. Mason, president of the Madison vocational school board, said Mitby called him Monday night with confirmation of his release.

GOP in Third District Endorses Thomson Over Bosshard, 111-105

By LLEWELLYN ROBERTS
(State Journal Staff Writer)

RICHLAND CENTER—Former Gov. Vernon W. Thomson, 51, was endorsed for the Republican nomination for Congress from the Third district Monday night over John Bosshard, 39, former La Crosse county district attorney, 111 to 105.

Immediately after the balloting Bosshard told reporters he had reached no immediate decision on whether he would oppose Thomson, three-term state attorney general and one-term governor, in the September primary.

THOMSON

The district caucus endorsement carries with it organizational and party support.

Before the caucus Bosshard had told newsmen that if he lost the endorsement by a narrow margin he expected to make the primary race anyway.

As expected, Bosshard drew the bulk of his support from the northern end of the district, polling all of La Crosse county's 46 votes.

Thomson supporters from La Crosse county had previously protested they were without representation on the delegate list. In the other nine counties of the district the vote was:

Crawford — Thomson, 9; Bosshard, 4; Grant — Thomson, 33; Bosshard, 3; Iowa — Thomson, 11; Bosshard, 3; Juneau — Thomson, 2; Bosshard, 13; Lafayette — Thomson, 11½; Bosshard, 1½; Monroe — Thomson, 4; Bosshard, 15; Richland — Thomson, 16; Bosshard, 0; Sauk — Thomson, 14½; Bosshard, 12½; and Vernon — Thomson, 10; Bosshard, 7.

Earlier Thomson himself resolved what would probably have been a test vote on endorsement. A majority report of the rules committee would have required that any candidate submitting his name for the congressional endorsement abide by the caucus decision. A minority report opposed that provision. Thomson asked unanimous consent that the minority report be adopted. That carried.

After Bosshard addressed the caucus, however, he was asked by Gordon Roseleip, Darlington, if he would abide by the caucus endorsement decision.

"If we feel a candidate is en-

(Continued on Page 2, Column 7)

Today's Chuckle

Overheard in a jammed nightclub: "I'm so full of penicillin that if I sneeze in here I'm sure going to cure somebody."

Feature Finder

Kennedy and Humphrey Clash in West Virginia Primary Today

CHARLESTON, W. Va. (AP) — West Virginia's Democratic presidential campaign churned into its final hours Monday with Sens. John F. Kennedy (D-Mass) and Hubert H. Humphrey (D-Minn.) blazing away at each other as "can't win" candidates.

With fair skies and cool weather predicted, a little more than half of the state's 670,000 registered Democrats are expected to turn out today for a primary that might have a decisive effect on Kennedy's chances of getting his party's presidential nomination.

Humphrey Edge

In the last stage of their battle, Humphrey was generally credited with holding an edge over Kennedy.

Humphrey has been stung by Kennedy's contention that almost nobody gives the Minnesota senator a chance to win the nomination — that if he wins here other candidates who are not on the ballot will be the benficiaries.

Humphrey blasted back with an assertion at Nitro, where he was campaigning on this cold bleak

KENNEDY

HUMPHREY

day, that Kennedy couldn't win in November if he got the Democratic nomination.

Blasts Kennedy

"If people will look at the voting record, instead of clever advertising propaganda, they will see it is Kennedy, not I, who can't win for the Democrats in November," he said in a statement.

Humphrey said Kennedy "turned his back on President Truman . . . favors special privileges and tax policies against the average taxpayer . . . played 'footsie' with the big money interests . . . joined the Republicans to slow down housing construction . . . refused to provide jobs by needed public works programs."

Kennedy Replies

Kennedy fired back with the statement in a Huntington news conference that he is the only Democrat who can defeat Vice President Richard M. Nixon, the prospective GOP nominee. He said it doesn't make sense for persons to vote for Humphrey "when they really favor someone else."

"If I'm defeated, it'll be a wide open race (for the nomination)," he said. "If Mr. Humphrey wins, the chances of somebody being nominated who doesn't understand the problems of West Virginia would be greatly enhanced."

Kennedy said he can't believe that "West Virginia, with its great tradition, is going to make its judgment on the basis of religion."

Colder
Cloudy, windy, and colder with snow flurries today. Partly cloudy and cold tonight. Highs ranging from 25 to 33. See Weather Vane, Page 2.

Wisconsin State Journal

SECTION 1 · MORNING FINAL · MADISON, WEDNESDAY, NOVEMBER 9, 1960 · ★★★ · 28 PAGES, THREE SECTIONS · Vol. 204, No. 40 · 121st Year · 5c

JACK WINS

Nelson 'Squeezing In;' Kuehn Won't Concede

NELSON KNOWLES ZIMMERMAN MRS. SMITH

Zimmerman, Mrs. Smith, Knowles Win

By LLEWELLYN ROBERTS
(State Journal Staff Writer)

Gov. Gaylord Nelson early today shook off a persistent early lead of his GOP challenger, Philip Kuehn, and on incomplete returns appeared safely headed toward his second term as Wisconsin's chief executive.

Nelson, a 44-year-old Madison attorney, was behind Kuehn in the ballot counting until early this morning when a heavy Milwaukee county vote nudged him increasingly into the lead.

The vote in 3,064 of the state's 3,476 precincts, according to tabulations by Associated Press, was:

Nelson (D)	753,794
Kuehn (R)	723,053

The count included 510 of Milwaukee county's 693 precincts, where the vote is normally heavily Democratic.

Won't Concede

At 3 a.m. today neither Kuehn, in Milwaukee, nor Republican headquarters in Madison, was conceding the election to Nelson.

Kuehn's headquarters at the Knickerbocker hotel in Milwaukee said some of the missing precincts were in areas which might poll substantially for Kuehn.

Nelson was unable to carry at least three and perhaps all four of the Democratic candidates for state constitutional office along with him.

Secretary of State Robert C. Zimmerman, the only GOP survivor in the 1958 Democratic sweep, won handily but nervously from his Democratic challenger, William H. Evans.

Former Lt. Gov. Warren P. Knowles unseated Lt. Gov. Philleo Nash, Democratic incumbent, in a rematch, and Mrs. Dena Smith, won easily over the incumbent state treasurer, Eugene Lamb.

Reynolds Has Chance

At 3 a.m. today, with final returns coming in, only incumbent Democratic Atty. Gen. John W. Reynolds appeared to have a chance of going into office in January with Nelson. And Reynolds was trailing his Republican

(Continued on Page 2, Column 6)

2nd Term Won by Kastenmeier

By RICHARD W. VESEY
(State Journal Staff Writer)

Rep. Robert Kastenmeier, Watertown Democrat, won his second term in Congress, defeating Republican Don Tewes, Waukesha, by at least 14,000 votes in Tuesday's race for the Second district seat.

With 336 of the populous five-county district's 349 precincts reported the vote was:

Kastenmeier (D)	107,076
Tewes (R)	92,624

KASTENMEIER THOMSON

The totals included all of Dane county's 102 precincts and 74 of Waukesha county's 82 precincts.

There was one upset — a Republican victory — in the First Congressional race. It added one seat to the Wisconsin Republican power in the House when the Rev. Henry C. Schadeberg, Burlington, won over Rep. Gerald Flynn (D-Racine).

SCHADEBERG

With 209 of the five-county district's 258 precincts reported, Mr. Schadeberg, a political newcomer and Congregational minister, was leading Flynn with the following vote:

Schadeberg (R)	69,567
Flynn (D)	65,077

Returns included all but two Democratic wards in Kenosha. The balance of the returns, expected to favor Schadeberg heavily, included those from his home city and Burlington township.

Also not tabulated were rural votes in Kenosha county and Walworth county where returns were 3 to 1 in favor of GOP candidates.

Former Gov. Vernon W. Thomson, Richland Center, a veteran

(Continued on Page 2, Column 8)

Manitowoc County Swings to Kennedy

MILWAUKEE (AP) — Manitowoc county, making Wisconsin's first complete county report of Tuesday's voting, swung from its Republican position to give John F. Kennedy 17,499 votes to 14,541 for Richard M. Nixon, with returns in from all 51 precincts.

The mixed industrial and agricultural county on Lake Michigan gave Dwight Eisenhower 18,078 to 10,800 for Adlai Stevenson in 1956.

Winners, Leaders

PRESIDENT
John F. Kennedy (D)
VICE-PRESIDENT
Lyndon B. Johnson
GOVERNOR
*Gaylord Nelson (D)
LIEUTENANT GOVERNOR
Warren P. Knowles (R)
SECRETARY OF STATE
Robert C. Zimmerman (R)
STATE TREASURER
Mrs. Dena Smith (R)
ATTORNEY GENERAL
*George W. Thompson (R)
STATE SENATOR
26th District (Madison)
Horace W. Wilkie (D)
16th District
(Rural Dane County)
Carl W. Thompson (D)
STATE ASSEMBLY
First District
(East Madison)
Norman C. Anderson (D)
Second District
(Central Madison)
Fred A. Risser (D)
Third District
(West Madison)
Robert O. Uehling (R)
Fourth District
(East Dane County)
Jerome L. Blaska (D)
Fifth District
(West Dane County)
David D. O'Malley (D)
COUNTY CLERK
Otto Festge (D)
SHERIFF
Franz G. Haas (D)
COUNTY TREASURER
Walter N. Smithback (D)
CORONER
Michael Malloy (D)
DISTRICT ATTORNEY
William D. Byrne (D)
REGISTER OF DEEDS
Harold K. Hill (D)
CIRCUIT COURT CLERK
Jean E. Johnson (D)
COUNTY SURVEYOR
Alex W. Ely (D)
CONGRESS
First District
*Rev. Henry C. Schadeberg (R)
Second District
Robert W. Kastenmeier (D)
Third District
Vernon W. Thomson (R)
Fourth District
Clement J. Zablocki (D)
Fifth District
Henry Reuss (D)
Sixth District
William Van Pelt (R)
Seventh District
Melvin Laird (R)
Eighth District
John Byrnes (R)
Ninth District
Lester Johnson (D)
Tenth District
Alvin O'Konski (R)
REFERENDA
Madison Street Bonds—Yes
Madison Sewer Bonds—Yes
Milwaukee Debt Limitation—Yes

*—Asterisk denotes candidate leading but not certain winner.

Gov. Nunoz Wins Victory in Puerto Rican Election

SAN JUAN, P.R. (UPI) — Gov. Luis Munoz Marin Tuesday won victory for his Popular Democratic party and said his margin was greater because of the "dramatic pace" given the campaign by a Catholic church drive to defeat him.

He won by a margin of 121,000 votes over three opponents.

Munoz said the returns made him "feel proud to be a Puerto Rican and a member of a people that knows how to take political decisions without subjecting itself to any kind of pressure."

He said the election campaign was "apathetic" before the church-state conflict, but it then gave him a chance to fight.

Ike Goes to Bed Before Race Is Decided

WASHINGTON (UPI) — President Eisenhower went to bed at 10:30 Tuesday night with the outcome of the presidential race still undecided.

James C. Hagerty, White House news secretary, said the President authorized him to send a congratulatory telegram to the winner.

When Mr. Eisenhower went to bed Sen. John F. Kennedy was leading.

Today's Chuckle

As the X-ray specialist walked down the aisle to say the marriage vows with a former patient, someone whispered: "I wonder what he saw in her?"

Nixon Receives Wisconsin's 12 Electoral Votes

MILWAUKEE — Vice-President Richard M. Nixon Tuesday won Wisconsin's 12 electoral votes.

Nixon took the lead when the first returns began coming in, and lost it only twice to Sen. John F. Kennedy, the Democratic candidate. He piled up a good-sized lead in the outstate area, and held his own, although trailing in populous Milwaukee county.

The vote in 3,131 of 3,476 precincts gave

Nixon	807,914
Kennedy	745,601

Police Call a Halt to Ram's Capitol Tour

A real, live, fleecy white ram, large curving horns and all, was caught by police in the Capitol park Tuesday night.

The ram had the initials "L. A." painted in red on each side of its back. The Los Angeles Rams professional football team is in Madison this week, but team officials said the ram was not owned by the team.

Patrolman Charles Campbell and Inspector Herman Thomas corralled the ram under the auto turn-around at the Monona ave. entrance to the Capitol.

The animal was taken to the Pet Shelter, 202 Wingra dr.

Feature Finder

EXTRA

Nixon Virtually Concedes Race

WASHINGTON, Wednesday (UPI) — Sen. John F. Kennedy won the presidency of the United States today—the first Catholic and youngest man ever to be elected to the White House.

Vice-President Richard M. Nixon, his Republican rival, conditionally conceded defeat in an appearance at his Los Angeles headquarters shortly before 2:30 a.m. CST.

If Trend Continues

Smiling but sounding like a beaten man, Nixon said Kennedy would be the next President "if the present trend continues."

Kennedy waited on further word from Nixon—an outright concession—before making a statement.

Nixon went to bed without sending the customary telegram of congratulations to the presumptive winner. Nixon, however, did "congratulate Mr. Kennedy for the fine race in the campaign" and said he wanted Kennedy to know that, "if this trend continues and he becomes President, he will have my full support."

At that point, Kennedy's count on the United Press International board was 264 electoral votes, five short of the needed majority. But victory was assured by then. He had no runaway majority of the popular vote, however, and won by the closest margin in any presidential election at least since 1948.

JOHN F. KENNEDY

Count Reported

Campaigning with the manner and personality pull of Franklin D. Roosevelt, Kennedy won the same way by piling up massive majorities in big cities which gave him the prized blocs of electoral votes in the big states.

The count at 2:30 a.m. gave:

Kennedy	26,218,320
Nixon	25,268,336

Kennedy had only 50.92 per cent of the two-party vote.

Kennedy had won 19 states with 264 electoral votes and led in four others with 73 electoral votes for an indicated total of 337.

Nixon had won 21 states with 166 electoral votes and led in five with 26 electoral votes for an indicated total of 192.

In the big battleground states, Kennedy won New York, Penn-

(Continued on Page 2, Column 3)

More Election News Pages 2, 3, 4, 5, 6, 9, 11

Democrats Win Senate, House

WASHINGTON, Wednesday (AP)—The Democrats clinched control of Congress early today as mounting congressional returns gave them majorities in both the House and Senate.

Given a bulge of 43 holdover seats in the Senate, the Democrats quickly sealed their victory by picking up 18 of the 34 seats up for election with five still undecided. Democrats lead in three of those. They had a 66 to 34 edge in the last Senate.

Slight Inroads

In the House, the Republicans made slight inroads into the big Democratic majority of the last session, but were unable to mount a serious threat to take over the leadership.

The Democrats won the 219th seat needed to control the 437-member House at 3 a.m. and seemed certain to add to the total as the vote count progressed. At that point the Republicans had 107 seats.

Upsets Few

Upsets were few in the Senate races. Of the incumbents seeking reelection only Sen. J. Allen Frear (D-Del.), was toppled, losing out to Gov. Caleb Boggs, a

(Continued on Page 2, Column 1)

County Democrat Candidates Steamroll Way Back to Office

By JUNE DIECKMANN
(State Journal Staff Writer)

Democratic incumbent candidates steamrolled back into all eight Dane county offices, with near two-to-one majorities, complete returns from the county's 102 precincts showed early today.

It was the fourth consecutive election that Democrats made a clean sweep of courthouse offices, and they did it with an avalanche of votes that never left their victories in doubt from the time the first precinct reported at 6:40 p. m.

Republicans had hoped that the presidential vote for Vice-President Richard M. Nixon might turn the Democratic tide to their course on the county level here, but their expectations waterlogged badly.

HAAS BYRNE MALLOY SMITHBACK

It was a record vote in Madison and Dane county, with 91,944 of the estimated eligible 135,000 voters going to the polls.

In Madison, where there was a record 63,020 voters registered, 54,337 of them, or 86.221 of the total eligible, cast their ballots.

The Democratic balloting in Dane county Tuesday for county and state offices was 61.558 per cent of the total vote, while the

(Continued on Page 2, Column 4)

Uehling Is Lone GOP Winner for Assembly; Wilkie Victor

By WILLIAM C. ROBBINS
(State Journal Staff Writer)

Challenger Robert O. Uehling recaptured Madison's West side Assembly seat for the Republicans as Democrats retained the other six of Dane County's positions in the Legislature, final returns showed today.

Uehling, Madison's 19th ward alderman, defeated Mrs. Ruth B. Doyle, two-time former assemblywoman, by a 788-vote margin.

Making his first try for the Legislature, Uehling, 45, of 4330 Keating terrace, an attorney, won back the district which Democrat Richard Cates took from then-Republican incumbent Carroll Metzner two years ago.

UEHLING WILKIE BLASKA O'MALLEY

The rest of the county was a Democratic sweep, giving the party both of the Senate seats and four of the five Assembly seats.

In the other city tussle, Sen. Horace W. Wilkie, Democratic in-

(Continued on Page 2, Column 7)

Partly cloudy and warmer today through Thursday. High today, in the upper 20s; low tonight, 10 to 15. See Weather Vane, Page 2.

Wisconsin State Journal

SECTION 1 MORNING FINAL MADISON, WEDNESDAY, JANUARY 4, 1961 ★ ★ ★ 24 PAGES, THREE SECTIONS Vol. 204, No. 95 122nd Year 5c

After Castro Ultimatum

U.S. CUTS DIPLOMATIC RELATION WITH CUBA

The Final Blow: Embassy Staff Limited to 11

WASHINGTON (AP) — The United States Tuesday night broke off diplomatic relations with the Cuban government of Fidel Castro.

President Eisenhower at 7:30 p.m. CST issued a statement saying, "There is a limit to what the United States in self respect can endure. That limit has now been reached."

Reason: Ultimatum

The U. S. has asked Switzerland to handle all its diplomatic and consular duties in Cuba.

Mr. Eisenhower gave as his reason the ultimatum delivered by Cuba Tuesday morning which demanded that the U.S. limit the personnel in its embassy and consulate in Havana to 11 persons.

Mr. Eisenhower, in reciting what he called "harassments, baseless accusations, and vilification" by Castro, said U.S. friendship with the Cuban people was not affected by the break.

"It is my hope and my conviction that in the not-too-distant future it will be possible for the historic friendship between us once again to find its reflection in normal relations of every sort," he said.

Nothing On Base

"Meanwhile, our sympathy goes to the people of Cuba now suffering under the yoke of a dictator."

James C. Hagerty, White House press secretary, declined to answer any questions about what the U.S. intends to do with the naval base it operates in Guantanamo.

He was asked whether the U.S. still intends to defend the base by force if necessary against any attack by Castro and whether the U.S. intended to keep its naval personnel at the base.

To both questions, Hagerty said he could not go beyond the President's statement, which did not mention Guantanamo.

The U.S. has maintained that its rights to the base are guaranteed by a treaty of long standing.

No Effect at All

State Department Press Officer Joseph Reap said the U.S. intends to keep its naval base to which it has treaty rights for an indefinite time.

"This has no effect at all on the base," Reap said.

Other officials said that a break in diplomatic relations has no effect on treaty obligations.

CASTRO EISENHOWER

U.S.-Cuban relations have been deteriorating steadily since Castro's accession to power two years ago, when his revolution overthrew the former regime of Fulgencio Batista.

The last straw came Tuesday.

Follows Charges

Castro ordered the U.S. embassy staff cut to 11, declaring that the embassy harbored spies directing counterrevolutionary activities. The staff has recently numbered 87, having been cut in the past six months from about 120, but it has some 200 Cuban nationals who are needed to maintain the 10-story office building.

Castro's action was a followup to his charges last weekend that President Eisenhower had ordered U. S. marines to invade Cuba before Jan. 18. Castro-controlled newspapers said the Cuban government had learned of such a plot from reliable sources.

At the time, Hagerty described the charges as ridiculous.

Six Latin American governments have broken off relations with the Castro regime. They are the Dominican Republic, Paraguay, Nicaragua, Haiti, Guatemala, and Peru.

The U.S. break came two years and two days after Castro came to power in Cuba.

Halted Imports

Although the U.S. adopted what it called a policy of patience toward his regime, relations worsened as Castro began seizing American property without com-

(Continued on Page 2, Column 3)

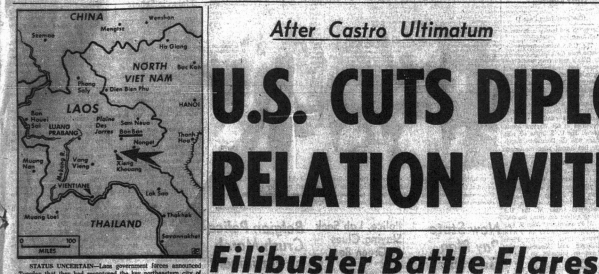

STATUS UNCERTAIN—Laos government forces announced Tuesday that they had recaptured the key northeastern city of Xieng Khouang from pro-Communist rebels, but the rebels claim they had reoccupied the city. The arrow shows the direction the rebels were driving on the city from Communist North Viet Nam, according to the Laos government. Underlined is Ban Ban, where loyal troops were reported holding out against the rebels. —AP Wirephoto Map

As East, West Wrangle

Laos Repeats Invasion Claim

(By Associated Press)

The jungle-shrouded war of Laos touched off East and West charges and counter-charges Tuesday of intervention in the Red-menaced Asian kingdom.

While facts and propagandist efforts were weighed, the government of Laos repeated at the United Nations its weekend charge that several Red battalions had moved in from neighboring North Viet Nam. It made only a minor change, saying now that there were six battalions rather than seven.

Authentic Information

In Washington, the United States accused the Soviet Union and Red North Viet Nam of carrying out at least 218 airlifts of weapons and Vietnamese soldiers to pro-Communist forces in Laos since Dec. 3.

OUM

The State Department based the charge on what it called "first class, absolutely authenticated information." The department did not specify how many North Vietnamese troops the U.S. believes were sent into Laos.

In Moscow, the Soviet government newspaper Izvestia called the intervention charge a lie put out by the Eisenhower Administration.

No Call for Action

The pro-Western Laotian government of Premier-Prince Boun Oum formally accused North Viet Nam of unprovoked aggression.

A notice filed with the UN claimed that six battalions of North Vietnamese soldiers have crossed into Laotian territory. There still was no call from Laos for Security Council action—only the request that its notice should be circulated to the 99 UN members.

The search for a peaceful solution to the crisis continued. In Bangkok, members of the Southeast Asia Treaty Organization (SEATO) emphasized that they want a political settlement of the Laotian conflict.

Withdraws Opposition

SEATO Secretary-General Pote Sarasin said members feel that military intervention in Laos to counter Communist aid may spread the war outside the kingdom.

Washington, under pressure from allies, conditionally withdrew its opposition to reviving a watchdog commission for Laos.

The evidence of Communist intervention issued by the State Department already has been known and to some extent discounted by U. S. allies concerned with Southeast Asian affairs.

Conditional Views

Britain favors a Russian proposal to revive the International Control Commission (ICC) first established for Laos after the Indo-China war ended in 1954.

A State Department spokesman said, "Our views on the usefulness of the ICC have been conditional upon the position taken by the royal Lao (Boun Oum) government."

Thomson Introduces Milk Flow Measure

(State Journal Washington Bureau)

WASHINGTON — Rep. Vernon W. Thomson of the third Wisconsin congressional district celebrated his first day in Congress Tuesday by introducing a bill permitting the free flow of fluid milk in interstate commerce.

The former Wisconsin governor expressed the hope that this measure which last year was sponsored by all members of the Wisconsin delegation, but never approved, might meet a more favorable fate in this Congress.

Filibuster Battle Flares as Congress Convenes

Liberal Forces, Conservatives Clash on Rules

More Congressional News, Sec. 1, Page 9

WASHINGTON (UPI) — The Democratic-controlled 87th Congress formally convened Tuesday and promptly plunged into a liberal-conservative battle over potential barriers to President-elect John F. Kennedy's legislative program.

Shortly after the House and Senate opened for business at noon, Senate liberals won a favorable ruling from Vice-President Richard M. Nixon, the presiding officer, and launched two drives to strengthen the Senate's anti-filibuster rule.

Action Blocked

But action was blocked at least until today by Sen. Richard B. Russell (D-Ga.), leader of Southern senators who have used the filibuster to head off civil rights bills. The maneuvering produced a sharp exchange between Russell and Nixon, the first of the fledgling session.

RUSSELL

Hanging fire in the House was a liberal move to purge conservative Rep. William M. Colmer (D-Miss.) from the powerful rules commitee. The aim is to make it easier to pry Kennedy's economic-welfare bills out of the committee, now dominated by a group of conservative Republicans and Democrats.

Democratic leaders indicated they planned to press ahead with the Colmer purge. Without objecting, they allowed the House to adopt rules of procedure that left Colmer's ouster as the only solution to liberalizing the rules committee.

Kennedy Bill

One of the first measures introduced in the House was a bill embodying Kennedy's proposals for aiding economically depressed areas. Rep. Kenneth J. Gray (D-Ill.) said he and Sen. Paul H. Douglas (D-Ill.) had agreed to sponsor the priority legislation.

The filibuster fight flared in

(Continued on Page 2, Column 7)

Members of the House Take Oaths as 87th Congress Convenes. —AP Wirephoto

Ex-Mental Patient Admits Shootings

MENOMINEE, Mich. (UPI)—A "gun crazy" former mental patient from Peshtigo, Wis., Tuesday night admitted he lied when he claimed he could not remember shooting a young Milwaukee couple last Friday night, and signed a full confession, authorities said.

Terrence Donovan admitted the slaying of Mrs. Mary Jane Degnan, Milwaukee bride of four months, only hours after a requiem high Mass was celebrated for her at St. Joseph's Catholic Church, Escanaba, Mich., were she was married last Aug. 20.

Her husband, Robert, 23, was unable to attend the funeral service. He was undergoing surgery at nearby St. Francis hospital in Escanaba for removal of a bullet fired into his chest by Donovan.

The Degnans were shot Friday night when a man flagged down their car on a road near Menominee while the young couple was driving to Escanaba for a New Year's holiday visit with their parents.

Many Taxpayers Mail Payments to City Treasurer

A stack of mailed tax payments — enough to fill three cardboard boxes — was received by the city treasurer's office postmarked before Dec. 31.

Treasurer Walter Hunter said no one in the office has had time to open or count them yet. But he said the stack looked about as big as last year's, despite the delay in getting them out.

Many taxpayers like to pay taxes before the end of the year and claim them as a deduction for income taxes on that year. Though the bills were sent out a little later than usual this season, most of them were mailed last Wednesday.

Mailed payments postmarked on Dec. 31 or before will be receipted as of Dec. 31, Hunter said. He had one small carton of mail segregated which he said did not make the deadline and could not be receipted with a 1960 date.

Hunter said the rush at the counter slacked off considerably Tuesday. He said his staff should have most of the mailed payments processed by the end of the week.

At -6, Mercury Tries for 10 Below

The lowest temperatures of the young new year were expected to chill Madison before dawn today.

At 1 a. m. today the mercury stood at 6 below zero and was expected to drop as low as 10 below early this morning.

The remainder of the day is supposed to bring partly cloudy skies and daytime temperatures warmer than Tuesday's. Snow flurries are predicted only for the extreme northern portions of the state.

Tuesday's high temperature was 16 at 2:40 p.m. The mean was a frigid 10, or 10 degrees below the norm for the date. The sporatic snow flurries Tuesday amounted to .01 of an inch of precipitation.

Today's Chuckle

A perfect wife is one who is willing to help her husband with the housework.

Pertinent Questions, Answers on Laos Crisis

VIENTIANE, Laos (UPI)—Here are some pertinent questions and answers on the current crisis in Laos:

Q—What and where is Laos?

A—Laos is one of the three former French Indochinese states in the heart of Southeast Asia. It became a completely sovereign state within the French union in 1949, but its relationship was not clearly defined. It was recognized by Communist forces in Indo-China and the United States in 1954 with the signing of the Geneva agreements ending the French Indo-China war. It joined the United Nations in 1955.

Laos is an under-developed jungle country slightly larger than the state of Minnesota, hemmed in on all sides by Communist China, Communist North Viet Nam, Cambodia, Thailand, Burma, and South Viet Nam. It is a constitutional monarchy with a royal capital at Luang Prabang and an administrative capital at Vientiane. It has an estimated 3 million inhabitants made up of dozens of different tribes of Chinese, Tibetan, Thai, and Malaya racial origin, speaking a multitude of different dialects and each having different customs.

Q—Why is Laos important?

A—Laos has symbolic and strategic importance for the free world.

Strategically, it is one of the key areas in the free world's defense perimeter designed to contain communism in Asia. It forms a sort of buffer zone between Communist China and Communist North Viet Nam and the staunch pro-American allies, Thailand and South Viet Nam. If Laos should come under Communist control, it would not only mean that millions of U. S. aid dollars would have gone down the drain, but it also would give the Communists a good base of operations for stepping up their widespread guerrilla warfare in South Viet Nam and launching a similar campaign in Thailand.

Symbolically, it can be likened to Korea to a certain extent because it is a spot where the U. S. and its allies have moved to check Communist aggression at the risk of war.

A high-ranking U. S. State Department official who visited Laos earlier this year summed up its importance with these words, some borrowed from Sir Winston Churchill:

"The loss of Laos would expose the soft underbelly of Southeast Asia to direct Communist aggression. It would be a terrific psychological blow to South Viet Nam and Thailand and other free nations in Asia if it should come under Communist control. It certainly would make Thailand and South Viet Nam take a second look at their close relations with the U. S."

Q—Who are the principals involved in the current Laotian crisis?

A—There are roughly three factions in Laos struggling for control, the rightists, the leftists, and the neutralists.

Heading the leftists is Prince Souphanouvong, so-called "Red Prince of Laos" and chairman of the Neo Lao Naksat (Communist) party, outlawed in 1959. The military arm of the party is Pathet Lao. Other key figures in the leftist group are Quinim

(Continued on Page 2, Column 1)

Henry A. Raemisch Taken to Hospital

Henry A. Raemisch, 60, 2104 Elmwood ave., Middleton, was reported in satisfactory condition Tuesday night in Madison General hospital, where he was taken early Monday after a light heart attack.

His physician said no visitors were allowed at present. Raemisch is the owner of a ready-mix concrete company in Middleton and a well-known businessman in western Dane county.

Feature Finder

Directors Back New State Pay Plan, but Kubista Asks Study

By LLEWELLYN G. ROBERTS
(State Journal Staff Writer)

A sweeping plan to revise the method and level of paying 16,000 state employes got substantial approval Tuesday from state department heads and scattershot opposition from an employes' union spokesman.

Roy E. Kubista, executive secretary of the Wisconsin State Employes Assn., asked the State Personel Board at a statutory public hearing for more time to study the plan and make recommendations.

KUBISTA

The association's membership is about 7,000.

The plan was endorsed in substance by Motor Vehicle Commissioner James E. Karns, speaking as chairman of the personnel advisory board to the Board of Personnel. The group headed by Karns is composed of heads of most of the biggest state departments.

"We want time to study it (the entire pay revision proposal) so we can do a proper sales job with the 16,000 people on the receiving end," Kubista said.

He proposed a second hearing after the personnel board studies suggested modifications to the plan, but there was no indication such a hearing will be held.

Carl K. Wettengel, director of the Bureau of Personnel, said state department heads and any other interested persons have until Friday of this week to file with his department changes they wish to suggest in the new pay plan.

Wettengel said all the recommendations for alterations will be studied and the Bureau of Personnel will present its final recommendation to the Board of Personnel in about three weeks.

The board itself may make additional changes before having the plan put into bill form and sent to the Legislature.

The estimated cost of the proposed plan, along with regular merit increases, would be $9.[illegible] million for the 1961-63 biennium. That would be an average salary increase of 12 per cent over the next two years.

A major feature of the plan provides three separate salary schedules — one for professional-managerial, one for general employes, one for crafts-labor-domestic. The state now operates with a single salary schedule.

The proposal, put together after

(Continued on Page 2, Column 4)

Rain to Snow
Rain this morning, becoming mixed with snow this afternoon and ending. Windy and colder today. High today, in low 40s; low tonight, in 20s. Weather Vane, Page 2.

Wisconsin State Journal EXTRA

SECTION 1 MORNING FINAL MADISON, WEDNESDAY, APRIL 12, 1961 MORNING FINAL 38 PAGES, FOUR SECTIONS. Vol. 201, No. 12 122nd Year 5c

1ST MAN IN SPACE ORBITS EARTH, RUSSIA ANNOUNCES

Nazi Challenges Israel Trial

Eichmann Shows Traces of Former SS Arrogance

By JOSEPH W. GRIGG
(United Press International)

JERUSALEM—Adolf Eichmann, a greying and worn out man but showing occasional traces of Nazi arrogance, challenged at the start of his trial Tuesday the right of Israel to bring him into court for the greatest mass murder in history.

The plea was presented forcibly by his attorney, Robert Servatius, a German who defended Nazi war criminals at Nuernberg. It was denounced by Israeli Chief Prosecutor Gideon Hausner as "irrelevant."

Hitler's Chief Instrument

Hausner's defense of the legality of Israel's position and its determination to hang the man accused of murdering six million Jews was still going on when court adjourned for the day. Court is to resume this morning.

The technicality of the arguments failed to obscure the drama of the first Jewish nation in 2,000 years seeking to bring to justice a man it calls Adolf Hitler's chief instrument in the extermination of the Jews.

For 75 minutes Tuesday, Eichmann, 54, tried to be the Nazi SS lieutenant colonel of old. He stood at attention while the indictment was read, first in Hebrew and then in German. His back was ramrod stiff, his face impassive behind the bullet proof glass of the prisoner's dock.

Before Legal Court

He appeared to be suffering from a cold and occasionally broke the parade ground rigidity to dab at his nose. Later, when the indictment was finished, he slumped in his chair, coughing occasionally and blowing his nose.

Hausner, who became Israel's prosecutor July 1 told the three-judge court that Eichmann "is here legally before a legal court to answer an indictment drawn up according to the law against Nazi criminals."

"He has been given a chance to defend himself and will be given full opportunity to defend himself if he so chooses," Hausner said.

He called on the court to try Eichmann as planned on the 15-count indictment. Twelve of the counts carry the death penalty.

Listens Raptly

Eichmann's bold opening bid was that the court declare itself incompetent. The wrangling over the question of legality took up almost all of the first day's session.

During the argument, Eichmann sat in his chair, a pale,

(Continued on Page 2, Column 3)

15-Count Indictment Summarized

JERUSALEM (UPI) — A digest of the 15-count indictment filed by Israel against Adolf Eichmann:

ONE. Eichmann with others, from 1939 to 1945 caused the killing of millions of Jews in his capacity as the person responsible for the execution of the Nazi plan for the physicial extermination of the Jews, known as "the final solution of the Jewish problem."

TWO. From 1939 to 1945, Eichmann and others placed many millions of Jews in living conditions which were calculated to bring about their physical destruction. These included putting Jews to work in forced labor camps, sending them to ghettos and detaining them there, driving them into transit camps and other concentration points, and deporting them and conveying them by mass transportation under inhuman conditions.

THREE. Eichmann and others caused the serious harm of millions of Jews by their enslavement, starvation, deportation, and persecution. He also caused them inhuman suffering and torture.

FOUR. Eichmann and others devised measures to prevent child-bearing among the Jews of Germany and countries occupied by her. This included sterilization of the off-spring of mixed marriages.

FIVE. Eichmann caused the murder, extermination, enslavement, and starvation of the civilian Jewish population in those countries and areas controlled by Germany and other axis countries.

SIX. Eichmann, in carrying out the acts described in counts 1 to 5, persecuted Jews on national, racial, religious, and political grounds.

SEVEN. Eichmann and others caused the spoliation of the property of millions of Jews in countries occupied by Germany by means of inhuman measures involving compulsion, theft, terrorism, and torture.

EIGHT. Eichmann, during World War II, committed acts constituting a war crime for causing the ill-treatment deportation and murder of Jews.

NINE. Between 1940 and 1942, in Poland, Eichmann committed acts constituting a crime against humanity for causing the deporta-

(Continued on Page 2, Column 5)

Guards Flank Adolf Eichmann in Bullet-Proof Glass Box at Opening of Trial in Jerusalem
—AP Wirephoto Via Radio From Jerusalem

Radio Contact Kept, Moscow Report Says

By HENRY SHAPIRO
(United Press International)

MOSCOW, Wednesday—Russia announced a successful launching of a man into space today.

The astronaut is still in orbit, the Tass news agency said, and radio contact is being maintained.

A Moscow radio announcer broke into a program and said in emotional tones:

"Russia has successfully launched a man into space. His name is Yuri Gagarin. He was launched in a Sputnik named Vostok which means 'East'."

Five-Ton Vehicle

The radio announcer said the Sputnik reached a minimum altitude of 175 kilometers (109½ miles) and a maximum altitude of 302 kilometers (187¾ miles).

The annuoncer said the weight of the Sputnik was 10,395 pounds,

White House Confirms It

WASHINGTON, Wednesday (UPI) — The White House announced today that American tracking stations have confirmed that Russia has launched "an object into space."

White House Press Secretary Pierre Salinger said "American tracking stations confirm the Soviet Union has launched an object into space. It is now orbiting the earth."

James Webb, administrator of the National Aeronautics and Space Agency, said "I think this is a splendid achievement."

or slightly over five tons.

The announcement came at 10 a.m. (2 a.m. EST).

It said everything functioned normally during the flight.

Constant radio contact is being maintained between earth and the Sputnik, Moscow radio said.

89.1-Minute Revolution

The announcer said the duration of each revolution around the earth is 89.1 minutes.

The title of the announcement, as aired over Moscow radio, was "The First Human Flight into the Cosmos."

The first space navigator was identified as Maj. Yuri Alekseyevich Gagarin.

'I Feel Well'

Tass said Gagarin radioed back at 9:22 a.m. (2:22 a.m. EST): "The flight is proceeding normally. I feel well." At that moment Gagarin was reported over South America.

The first space flight came almost three years and six months to the day since the Russians, on Oct. 4, 1957, launched Sputnik I, the first artificial earth satellite.

Since then the Russians have successfully launched 12 satellites. The United States has put up 38 satellites, but the Russians' have been much bigger, indicating their rocket boosters are far more advanced than those used by the United States.

The first astronaut is a major in the Soviet Air Force and is believed to be a test pilot.

The Tass announcement said the launching of the multi-stage space rocket which carried the Sputnik into orbit was successful.

After attaining the first escape velocity, it said, and the separation of the last stage of the carrier rocket, the space ship went into free flight on a round-the-earth orbit.

Reported Earlier

Reports of the launching of a Soviet space man had been reported repeatedly in Moscow for the past 24 hours.

The London Daily Worker and other sources had said the Soviets sent a man into space last Friday and brought him back alive.

Many persons in Moscow were convinced after today's announce-

(Continued on Page 2, Column 1)

U. S. Pushes Laotian Cease-Fire

WASHINGTON (AP) — Any further delay in a Laotian cease-fire agreement, a State Department spokesman said Tuesday, "would be a matter of very serious concern."

This assessment came from Press Officer Lincoln White after Secretary of State Dean Rusk told reporters he expects a Soviet reply "within a very few days" to a British proposal for an immediate cease-fire in Laos.

'Still Delicate'

Senate Democratic leader Mike Mansfield of Montana called the situation "still delicate, dangerous, and a long way from settled."

Mansfield spoke in the wake of overnight reports, confirmed by the State Department, that the Russians had increased their flow of arms and other supplies to rebel forces in Laos.

The British proposed several weeks ago, with U. S. backing, that the civil war in Laos be halted immediately and that an international conference be called to work out a permanent settlement.

Rusk Comment

A Russian reply had been expected momentarily during last week's Washington talks between British Prime Minister Harold Macmillan and President Kennedy. It never came.

Rusk emerged from a closed-door session with the Senate Foreign Relations committee Tuesday and told newsmen:

"I don't know, in view of all the circumstances, that there has been undue delay."

Asked whether the United States had stepped up its supplies to the Laos government, Rusk replied:

"To a degree."

Chinese Hand

At the State Department, White said the United States is concerned about the stepup in Soviet

(Continued on Page 2, Column 6)

Rain-Snow Mixture to Continue Today

The rain-and-snow mixture that began falling in some sections of the Madison area shortly after midnight Tuesday and was to continue sporadically throughout the night will keep on most of today, the Municipal airport weatherman said.

The precipitation started as showers early Tuesday night and was joined by snow coming from northwestern Wisconsin early today. The rain is expected to cease this afternoon, leaving a brief period of snow flurries before the moisture stops altogether.

Brisk winds and a high temperature reading in the low 40s, slightly lower than Tuesday, also were forecast for today.

Tonight's outlook is for partly cloudy skies and a low reading in the 20s.

Tuesday the mercury peaked at 52 at 1:30 p.m. The low was 26 at 5:50 a.m.

Fill 'Er Up, Check Tires--and the Kids

EVANSVILLE — If you happen to be a 4-year-old in a vacationing family of 10, you had better be fast at rest stops.

Little Peter Moore found this out when his parents stopped their station wagon full of children at an Evansville service station.

With the eight children apparently taken care of, the Rev. and Mrs. Moore, St. Paul, Minn., continued on their way. A short time later the station attendant felt a tug on his trouser leg.

"Where's my daddy?" Peter asked.

The attendant notified the State Traffic Patrol who stopped the Moore's near Madison. They hadn't missed Peter.

Mr. Moore vowed he would count his passengers before and after future stops.

New State Laws
Chapters 19 and 20, new state laws, texts. Sec. 2, Page 5.

Mayor-Elect Reynolds Will Skip Naming an Assistant for While

Mayor-elect Henry E. Reynolds said Tuesday that he does not intend to make an immediate appointment to the post of administrative assistant to the mayor.

"I expect to go along without one for a while," he said. "I'll just feel my way, to find out what I need and what I want."

REYNOLDS

Robert E. Nuckles, Reynolds' opponent in the mayoralty race and the present administrative assistant to the mayor, has resigned from the post effective next Tuesday, the day that Reynolds takes office. The post pays $10,125 a year.

Reynolds informed city department heads Tuesday that he will deliver an annual message at the noon organizational meeting of the City Council next Tuesday. He invited any suggestions on matters of over-all policy or on specific projects which the department heads think should be included in the annual message.

Reynolds also said Tuesday that he has decided on many of his committee appointments, but will not announce them at least until he has notified the people involved. He said he has not yet completed his selections for the membership of the auditorium committee, which will have charge of any auditorium-civic center project.

Reynolds is expected to replace the three citizen members of the committee, all of whom have been supporters of the Monona Terrace project.

But there have been reports that the mayor-elect is thinking of retaining several aldermen on the committee, including some who have been supporters of the Monona Terrace project in the past.

There are currently nine members on the committee, including five aldermen and Mayor Harold Hanson. Citizen members of the group are Prof. Harold Groves, Robert Cashin, and William Bazan.

Aldermen on the committee include George Elder, Sixth ward; Harrison L. Garner, 13th ward; Lloyd Foust, 16th ward; Richard Kopp, 18th ward; and Thomas Fitzpatrick, Fifth ward alderman who did not run for re-election this year.

Mrs. Ritchie Lewis Taken Ill at Home

Mrs. Ritchie Lewis, 74, of 4005 Hegg ave., suffered a heart attack at home Tuesday night and was in serious condition early today at St. Mary's hospital.

City Police administered oxygen to Mrs. Lewis at home before she was taken to the hospital by ambulance.

Mrs. Lewis is the wife of the retired Circuit Court clerk.

Driving Hint of the Day

Safety is a moral obligation.

Today's Chuckle

Filing cabinet: Where papers get lost alphabetically.

Feature Finder

Braves Lose in 10th, 2-1

- Read Monte McCormick's Story of the Game
- Roundy Has Some Comments on the Game
- Plus Box Scores of all the Games

in the Big Sports Peach Section

Audit Report Charges Extension Official With Getting 'Kickbacks'

By SAMUEL C. REYNOLDS
(State Journal Staff Writer)

A state audit report made public Tuesday afternoon charged that Marvin R. Foster, director of the University of Wisconsin Extension division's bureau of lectures and concerts, received "kickbacks" from performers he signed.

Foster, reached at his home at 2842 Regent st. Tuesday night, said "that language is a little bit strong" to apply to what he did.

L. H. Adolfson, dean of the Extension division, said that "there was a certain amount of indiscretion here, but no dishonesty."

A member of the attorney general's staff, who declined use of his name, said "I don't know if

MARVIN R. FOSTER

any legal action is being taken or not." He said any word on that would have to come from Atty. Gen. John W. Reynolds, who was in Washington, D. C., Tuesday.

The report, submitted to the governor's office by State Auditor J. Jay Keliher, said "this investigation disclosed that Mr. Marvin R. Foster received 'kickbacks' of a weekly 'salary' paid (dancer) Marta Becket while she was on tour for the bureau.

"Mr. Foster contended that monies he received were for services rendered as part of the artist's (Miss Becket's) act, and Marta Becket confirmed the fact that he served as narrator at most performances."

Foster said he did receive $1,88[illegible]

(Continued on Page 2, Column 7)

Cooler
Partly cloudy, cooler today. Clear, cool tonight. Partly cloudy Tuesday. High today, near 50; low tonight, 30 to 35. See Weather Vane, Page 2.

Wisconsin State Journal

SECTION 1 | MORNING FINAL | MADISON, MONDAY, MAY 1, 1961 | MORNING FINAL | 36 PAGES, THREE SECTIONS Vol. 201, No. 31 122nd Year | 5c

$2.9 MILLION GRANT APPROVED FOR U.W.

The Ducks Prefer to Walk

Things are pretty bad when ducks have to walk.
But this mallard couple, "grounded" by the Seattle Yacht club's annual skirmishes in Lake Washington, takes to the tennis courts until the water regains its calm. —AP Wirephoto

Proxy Fight Today

Financial Giants Plan Showdown

BALTIMORE (UPI)—A small army of lawyers, proxy clerks, and Wall st. agents began deploying here Sunday for the Alleghany Corp. annual meeting today that will decide the outcome of the biggest proxy battle in history.

Both the Allen P. Kirby management and the insurgent Murchisons of Texas are publicly exuding confidence in victory in the fight to control Alleghany, which directs the destinies of companies with assets of more than $6 billion.

Starts at Noon

Alleghany President Charles T. Ireland Jr. will preside at the meeting, scheduled to start at 1 p.m. CDT, but all eyes will be focussed on millionaire financier Kirby and John C. and Clint W. Murchison Jr., sons of Texas oil magnate Clint Murchison Sr. Although Kirby boasts a slight edge in the number of proxy votes he will carry into the meeting, both sides hint that they have powerful support that has not shown up in the reported figures.

ALLEN KIRBY

CLINT MURCHISON JR. JOHN MURCHISON

John D. Murchison said Sunday night that he doubts whether the outcome will be decided within the next two weeks.

Tally Proxies

Murchison said that it probably would take that much time to tally the proxies that will be cast at today's meeting.

He indicated that if he and his brother, Clint Jr., lose their bid to topple the management of Kirby, they might still retain their big holdings in the corporation.

A sidelight to the encounter was the arrival earlier Sunday of an armored car bearing the proxies of the Kirby forces.

Both warring factions have spent nearly $70 million in a stock-buying spree in the seven months of maneuvering for advantage. The Kirby forces already have pocketed upwards of 33 per cent of the total stock vote against more than 29 per cent by the Murchisons.

First Appearance

The importance Kirby attaches to the fight to retain his 24-year

(Continued on Page 2, Column 4)

Kennedy, Rusk Confer on Laos

President Interrupts Weekend in Virginia

WASHINGTON (UPI) — President Kennedy cut short a Virginia weekend late Sunday to fly back to Washington for top-level conferences on the growing Communist threat to the Western-supported government of Laos.

The President, apparently getting closer to some urgent decisions on U. S. policy toward Southeast Asia, met for about 90 minutes with Secretary of State Dean Rusk, Defense Secretary Robert S. McNamara, and other aides.

Point of Crisis

Rusk, who spent much of the day at the State Department conferring with his aides, told reporters as he left the White House only that the session with Mr. Kennedy concerned Laos "and other matters."

But it was increasingly obvious that the United States and its SEATO Allies were approaching the point where they must make some basic decisions unless the Communist-backed Pathet Lao rebels heeded a British-Soviet appeal for a cease-fire.

Most of the public discussion here centered on the possibility of some form of military intervention by the SEATO Allies. They are pledged to protect the integrity of Laos if the little Southeast Asian kingdom requests help.

UN Action

However, there also was a possibility of some action in the United Nations, perhaps a request for a joint police action such as was conducted in Korea. Although such a move would be subject to Soviet veto in the Security Council, it could be approved by the General Assembly.

Questioned about the meeting, Associate White House Press Secretary Andrew Hatcher said only that it was designed to "get an early start" on today's meeting of the National Security Council (3 p.m. CDT).

Other participants, besides Rusk and McNamara, included Paul Nitze, assistant defense secretary for international security affairs; State Department Political Officer Alexis Johnson, and Harlan Cleveland, assistant secretary of state for international organization affairs.

Sudden Return

Rusk, who remained on for a few minutes afterward to talk to Mr. Kennedy privately, was asked if Cleveland's presence indicated the United States was considering action through the UN.

The secretary said no, that

(Continued on Page 2, Column 3)

Spring Scenery Enchants U.W. Students

Sunday was a good day to sit back, relax, and enjoy the scenery. These seven University of Wisconsin students find that the weather is just right for sitting in front of Kronshage hall. And the scenery is improved by a pretty co-ed. —State Journal Photo by Rodney Sweet

Funds to Aid Cancer Work

Federal Health Unit Allocates Award

WASHINGTON—The University of Wisconsin has been awarded a $2.9 million federal grant to build a cancer research facility, Rep. Melvin R. Laird (R-Marshfield) announced Sunday.

The Cancer Research Council of the National Cancer Institute approved the university's application for the grant Sunday at a meeting in Washington, according to Frances McKusik, State Journal Washington correspondent.

Recognizes Work

The funds, granted the university on a non-matching basis, were provided for under an amendment to the Health, Education and Welfare (HEW) appropriations bill of 1961.

The amendment, introduced by Laird, provide a total of $3 million for emergency construction of facilities for cancer research.

The grant is seen as a recognition of the clinical work being done at University Hospitals, under the direction of Dr. Anthony R. Curreri, and the basic research being done at McArdle Research Institute here.

Laird said that 30 institutions applied for the money made available under his amendment with requests totaling $22 million.

"The University of Wisconsin has top priority for cancer research construction according to Sunday's decision of the Cancer Research Council," Laird said.

Build Laboratory

The $2.9 million grant which will be available immediately, will take care of the total cost of construction of the laboratory which will be devoted to basic research, he said.

Dr. Harold P. Rusch, director of McArdle Memorial Laboratories, said present plans for the center indicate that it will be built west of the University Infirmary building on the Medical School campus.

Rusch said that Laird's role in getting this appropriation for the university "illustrates clearly his genuine interest in the problems of public health and welfare," and that his intense interest in this area "led him to rally support in

(Continued on Page 2, Column 7)

CURRERRI LAIRD

Astronaut Shot Due on Tuesday

CAPE CANAVERAL, Fla. (AP)—Astronaut X—his identity masked from the outside world—tapered off in seclusion Sunday less than 48 hours before making history as the first American to try to penetrate space.

Expectancy and excitement gripped the nearby resort town of Cocoa Beach where some 450 U. S. and foreign newsmen concentrated for the man-in-space launch,, expected shortly after dawn Tuesday.

Own Favorites

Just about everybody had his own hunch as to which of the three "finalists" among the U.S. astronauts would step out of hangar "S" on Tuesday, revealed for the first time as the pioneer Yank to ride a rocket-boosted capsule into near space and back.

Many seemed to be betting on Lt. Col. John H. Glenn Jr., a green-eyed, red-haired Marine from New Concord, O. At 39, he is the oldest of the group.

But there were plenty of backers for 37-year-old Navy Cmdr. Alan B. Shepard Jr. of East Derry N. H., and 35-year-old Air Force Capt. Virgil L. Grissom of Mitchell, Ind.

Some "guessers" eliminated Grissom after he was seen eating in a Cocoa Beach restaurant Saturday night. The astronauts in the final days before launch are supposed to eat a carefully-controlled diet served in the spaceman "ready room" at the Cape.

Missile Ready

On the flat, virtually treeless expanse of this missile test center, the Redstone ballistic missile and the 3,000-pound cone-shaped space capsule stood locked in the gantry, a red steel tower which will be rolled away shortly before launch.

Final work was being done on the capsule, hidden behind green fiberglass paneling.

Some 3½ miles away, the chosen astronaut and his alternate—who would make the 115-mile-high journey if the principal became ill—rested in their special aqua-tinted quarters on the second floor of hangar "S."

There may be another rehearsal today of the impending short range space mission.

They're Ready

But to all intents and purposes, they are about as ready as technical ingenuity and foresight and their two years of almost-incredibly detailed training could make them.

The scientists and technicians who gave birth to Project Mercury and helped it grow since October 1958 say the every possible safeguard has been provided to assure that the astronaut comes through well and sound.

This 15-minute suborbital flight—which will carry the capsule and space pilot on a steep arc

(Continued on Page 2, Column 8)

Troops Land for Play at Guantanamo Base

GUANTANAMO BAY, Cuba (AP)—Thousands of United States sailors and Marines swarmed ashore at this naval base Sunday for play and relaxation.

But the regular Marine detachment here stepped up vigilance along prepared defense positions and along the fence surrounding the base, as Cuba celebrates May Day today.

The Navy has called for a normal work schedule today, but it is extremely doubtful that many of the base's 3,200 Cuban employes will show up for work.

Navy officials expect no trouble from Premier Fidel Castro, but should it come, the base is well prepared.

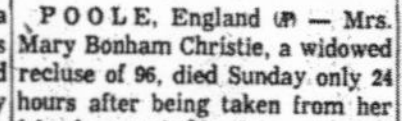

Uncrowned Queen Dies After Leaving Island

POOLE, England (AP) — Mrs. Mary Bonham Christie, a widowed recluse of 96, died Sunday only 24 hours after being taken from her island stronghold where she had lived alone in an 80-room castle for 34 years.

Known as the uncrowned queen of Brownsea Island, Mrs. Christie had been ailing for some time. She was removed from the island under doctor's orders and transferred to a mainland nursing home.

Standing in Poole harbor, the mile-square island and its castle were purchased by Mrs. Christie in 1927. She turned Brownsea into a wild life sanctuary and barred sightseers.

Today's Chuckle

It finally has been figured out how the Egyptians, with no heavy machinery, built the pyramids. They cut out coffee breaks.

Giants Bomb Braves, 14-4

Willie Mays Belts 4 Home Runs

See the Sports Peach

Hospitals Report Increase in Rates

CHICAGO (UPI) — The American Hospital Assn. Sunday reported a "general increase" in the average daily rates charged for hospital rooms throughout the nation.

The association said the increase "probably reflects not only rising hospital costs but also a trend toward a more realistic balance between charges for routine daily services and unit charges for special services."

The study showed that charges for basic services — room, board, routine nursing care, and minor supplies —average between $15 and $20 a day throughout the U. S.

Fifty-four per cent of the hospital beds in the nation were available at between $12 and $20 a day. Some 27 per cent were priced at $20 to $28 daily, while 15 per cent were less than $12 and 4 per cent over $28.

The association based its figures on reports from 4,692 hospitals.

Citizen Whines About Rifle Range Whiz; Erects Tent in Line of Fire

WEST MILFORD, N.J. (UPI)—Herman Kimble sat in a tent listening to the bullets whiz by and admitted that he had lost another round in his efforts to force a ceasefire on the nextdoor rifle range.

Kimble, 55, erected the tent in the line of fire to protest publicly the nerve-jangling situation in which, he said, bullets from the range ricochet into his backyard.

But his efforts were to no avail, Kimble said, reporting that as he and members of his family sat in their tent, they could hear the whine of rifle bullets overhead.

Kimble put up the tent Saturday as the latest move in a five-year protest against the range. He claimed bullets had ricocheted into his backyard, endangering the lives of his family and neighbors.

'I Never Thought I'd See Combat at Home'

He said that at first he had been only mildly annoyed when the range opened for skeet shooting only.

"But then when they switched to high-powered rifles three years ago, it was no longer funny," he said.

Originally, he had planned to sit in the open Saturday but he was forced to erect the tent because of rain.

Kimble's son-in-law, Richard Boyer, who lives nearby in the Macopin section of the township, spent part of the day in the tent, about 400 yards from the firing line in a heavily wooded area.

The range operator, Walter Fahlon, knew Kimble had erected the tent, Boyer said, but he didn't

(Continued on Page 2, Column 1)

On the Inside

Don't Miss...

Trouble in Brazil —President Kennedy's New Latin American policy has been badly gashed on the Cuban reef, according to Eric Sevareid on today's Page of Opinion. Recent events, he writes, have made Castro even more the hero, the U. S. even more the villain in Brazil.

Dating Older Men—How old a man should a girl date? What is a fair age difference? These and other questions are answered in Enid Haupt's column "Young Living" in The Woman's Journal, Sec. 2, Page 1.

The Sports Scene — Arnold Palmer bounced back in the winners circle Sunday by winning the Texas Open golf tournament. Read the details in The Sports Peach — plus stories of all the baseball games and the sidelights.

Feature Finder

Space Medics Prepare Treatment They Hope Will Be Unnecessary

CAPE CANAVERAL, Fla. (AP)—The petite blonde nurse carefully packed bundles of sterilized instruments into a metal box, part of a "portable hospital" being readied in case of emergency on America's first manned space flight, expected Tuesday.

"This package has been checked and double-checked to make certain nothing is left out," she said. "One missing item could mean the difference between life and death for the astronaut."

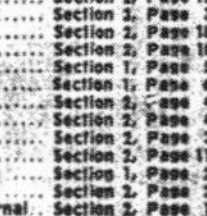

LT. SINEATH

The nurse, Air Force 1st Lt. Shirley Sineath, had the important task of preparing nine kits, each of which is made up of several cartons strapped together in a 1,933-pound packet.

Seven of the packs were placed aboard recovery ships which will be stationed under the astronaut's intended flight path. One is at a forward medical facility at Cape Canaveral, and the ninth was flown to Grand Bahama Island, where the space pilot is scheduled to be taken after the 115-mile high suborbital flight.

Shirley, a 23-year-old native of Sanford, N. C., is one of 55 medical personnel who will be on duty when the Redstone rocket blasts off with its human passenger.

At launch time, she will be stationed at the Cape forward medical facility. This is the emergency area where the astronaut will be taken in case of a rocket malfunction early in flight sends the capsule parachuting into the Atlantic ocean off the Cape.

"The portable hospital contains everything from bandages to anesthesia machines and resuscitators," Shirley explained. "They carry everything necessary for an emergency operation on a ship or one of the land medical areas.

Col. George Knauf, staff surgeon at nearby Patrick Air Force base, directs the overall medical operation for Project Mercury.

For more than a year, Knauf has conducted a school for space surgeons who will participate in the upcoming suborbital flight and later manned orbit tests. More than 200 military medical doctors each have received two or more weeks of training in space medicine at the school.

A team of medics headed by Air Force Col. William Douglas has worked closely with the astronauts for several months. In the final days before the flight they have run numerous physical and psychological tests on the man chosen for the mission.

Large staffs of doctors from all services will be at both the Cape and Grand Bahama facilities.

(Continued on Page 2, Column 2)

Church's $1,000 Investment Nets Return of 250%

DeKALB, Ill. (UPI) — A $1,000 investment in ingenuity has returned more than double that figure to the First Methodist Church.

The Rev. Mr. William White told his parishioners Sunday that a little more than $2,500 had been raised for charitable causes through their efforts.

On the first Sunday after Easter, Mr. White distributed $1,000 in $1 bills. Church members were urged to take the dollars and make them grow.

To date, Dr. Martin Bartels earned $32 by waxing cars. Other parishioners devised varied means to raise money, with one boy renting a trampoline and charging his friends so much a bounce.

Mr. White believed profits might reach $3,000.

Occasional Rain
Cloudy with occasional rain and chance of thundershowers tonight. High today, 60; low tonight, 50. Weather Vane, Page 2.

Wisconsin State Journal

SECTION 1 — MORNING FINAL — MADISON, SATURDAY, MAY 6, 1961 — MORNING FINAL — 24 PAGES, THREE SECTIONS, Vol. 201, No. 38, 122nd Year — 5c

'Man! What a Ride!'

U.S. ASTRONAUT'S LEAP IS 'OUT OF THIS WORLD'

The Nation's First Spaceman, Alan Shepard, Is Congrotulated After Historic Flight —AP Wirephoto

Shepard Returns Safely to Earth

2 Full Pages of Photos on 4, 5

CAPE CANAVERAL, Fla. (AP)—Beaming "Man, what a ride!" Astronaut Alan B. Shepard returned safely to earth Friday after blasting 115 miles into space—a perfect flight that gave the United States a mighty stride forward in the space race with Russia.

"What a beautiful sight," the 37-year-old test pilot exulted at the top of his 15 minute hop into space and back.

5,100 Miles an Hour

His 6-by-9-foot space capsule reached speeds of 5,100 miles an hour before plunging back down into the Atlantic 302 miles southeast, where it was plucked from the waves by a helicopter.

Shepard was flown immediately to the carrier Lake Champlain, where physicians began checking him over for any ill effects.

"I don't think there's much you'll have to do to me, Doc," he told one of the medicos.

From the carrier Shepard was flown to a hospital on nearby Grand Bahama island, where a doctor pronounced him "in excellent shape and health."

The physician who monitored his condition by radio during the flight—which subjected him to stresses up to 11 times that of normal gravity—reported the lean, muscular astronaut was probably the calmest man in the whole operation.

President Telephones

President Kennedy telephoned his congratulations to Shepard within minutes after the astronaut's arrival on the carrier and told him of a hero's welcome awaiting him in Washington.

The President said "this is an historic milestone in our own exploration into space."

A U.S. space agency official said Shepard's feat is only the beginning of America's exploration of space. Deputy Administrator Hugh Dryden said the National Aeronautics and Space Administration is planning to send an astronaut into orbit around the earth soon. Later, he said, one of them will travel to the moon and back.

The Redstone rocket used as a booster for Friday's flight blasted away from its pad here at 9:34 a.m. (CDT). Nineteen minutes later Shepard climbed out of the capsule's escape hatch and was picked up by helicopter.

'A Beautiful Day'

"It's a beautiful day," he told the 'copter crewmen. "Man, what a ride!"

Exciting as it was, the flight was still secondary to the feat of Russia's Yuri Gagarin, who last Apr. 12 was hurled into a 188-mile-high orbit around the globe. He returned to earth safely 108 minutes after being launched by a rocket much more powerful than that fired Friday.

A test of the only American rocket believed capable

(Continued on Page 2, Column 3)

Kennedy Asks More Funds

A Hero's Welcome Awaits Spaceman

WASHINGTON (UPI)—President Kennedy Friday pledged his Administration to follow up Cmdr. Alan B. Shepard's historic rocket flight with a request to Congress for funds for a "substantially larger" space program.

The President joined all Americans in rejoicing at the success of the flight and arranged to pay tribute to Shepard — and America's six other astronauts — at a special White House ceremony Monday.

KENNEDY

The ceremony with Shepard will be carried live on radio and television, probably about noon, as will a news conference which Shepard will hold (at noon CDT) in the State Department auditorium.

The President extended his personal congratulations to Shepard in a telephone call to the astronaut shortly after he completed his successful flight down the Atlantic missile range. Later Mr. Kennedy elaborated at a mid-afternoon news conference.

At the same time, the President warned the United States still was behind Russia and had "a long way to go in the field of space." But he declared that the nation was working hard and "we are going to increase our effort."

He got a prompt promise of congressional support from Chairman Richard B. Russell (D-Ga.) of the Senate Armed Services committee. Russell said "we must press forward . . . until we have achieved preeminence in space. Congress stands ready to support fully such a program."

Several members of Congress said they expected the President to award the Medal of Honor to Shepard, and they sponsored resolutions to that effect. The White House was silent on that point for the moment at least.

The President will take part in

(Continued on Page 2, Column 5)

Oklahoma Twister Kills 13, Hurts 40

POTEAU, Okla. (AP)—Thirteen persons were killed and at least 40 were injured Friday when a tornado smashed two small eastern Oklahoma villages near here.

The death toll could go higher as rescue workers dug into debris at the community of Howe, a town of 500 persons that reportedly was half-blown away. Nine were known dead there. Four were killed at Richeart.

Free World Has Praise for 'Public' Space Shot

LONDON (AP)—Alan B. Shepard's rocketing flight into space and safe return set pulses racing Friday in Western Europe and other parts of the non-Communist world.

Government leaders, scientists, and the man in the street seemed agreed generally that the United States boosted its prestige by allowing the public to share fully in the suspense of the historic blastoff.

'The Right Way'

The feeling ran through public comment that Shepard's flight was a shot in the arm not only for the United States but also for the whole non-Communist world.

Leonard J. Carter, secretary of the British Interplanetary Society, expressed apparent feelings of millions who clustered around their radios and heard direct relays from Cape Canaveral.

"The Americans had the right way of doing it," he said. "Unlike the Russians, they allowed us all to take part in the fantastic adventure. I was pretty well right up there in the capsule with him."

But while there was a stream of congratulations to the United States from friendly governments and scientists, there was some derision from beyond the Iron Curtain.

Red Derision

Prague Radio, a mouthpiece of the Red Czechoslovak regime, called the feat "scientifically primitive."

Moscow radio told Soviet listeners about the dramatic events at Cape Canaveral an hour and a half after they took place. In London, a Soviet embassy spokesman said: "This stage of development was reached several years ago in the Soviet Union."

But a benevolent attitude toward the United States seeped through in some smug places in Moscow.

American correspondents at a reception there were congratulated by a group of Soviet newsmen.

"It is a good start," said one

(Continued on Page 2, Column 8)

Calm, Cool Alan Was at His Best

CAPE CANAVERAL (UPI) — Alan B. Shepard is a tough and determined man.

He is tough enough to stand the crushing G-forces of a rocket blast-off. His brain and coordination are so sharp that he can control his own flight 115 miles into the heavens and 302 miles down range into the sea.

Jaunty, Human

He is determined enough to decide what he wants, and get it.

He is a jaunty man who can laugh on the way to a space ride, and he is human enough to reach into his capsule on the deck of a carrier and retrieve his helmet.

First as a test pilot and then as a volunteer astronaut, he is a man who seeks out danger and thrives on it as others seek pleasure or money. He didn't become by chance the first American to ride a rocket.

Those who know him say he was at his best Friday.

"I never saw Al operate more calmly, coolly, and precisely," said Astronaut Information Officer Lt. Col. John Powers after the flight.

Jolly, Joking

"He is a calm, cool and precise guy all the way anyway. While on the flight Friday he acted just like he was flying a T-bird (a comparatively slow jet trainer) from the cape back to Memphis."

After seeing him, fellow Astronaut Virgil Grissom said Shepard "looks just like he did before he got into his suit during the night.

(Continued on Page 2, Column 2)

Driving Hint of the Day

When approaching schools, use your eyes and save the pupils.

Today's Chuckle

Alarm clock: A small mechanical device to wake up people who have no children.

People Here Proudly Look Up to Shepard as a New Pioneer

By WILLIAM C. ROBBINS
(State Journal Staff Writer)

Madison reacted to the news of America's man-in-space triumph flight with quiet happiness Friday, but said it was not time to break out the champagne.

There was no shouting or backslapping, but national pride did show through.

There was also a definite reaction of genuine relief that Astronaut Alan B. Shepard survived the flight 115 miles above the earth and back without death or injury. Others compared Shepard to heroes who pioneered other frontiers for America.

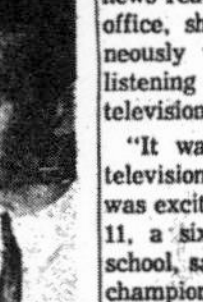
MARGARET EDWARDS — PROF. CODE

"I am very happy it came off so successfully, but it is nothing to have a great celebration about," Prof. Arthur D. Code, 4206 Mandan Crescent, professor of astronomy at the University of Wisconsin, said.

"I guess we won't be happy until we have a big booster going, but we should be happy that there is progress," he said.

Other residents in the Capitol Square area generally agreed with Code and thought the Mercury Project flight helped close the distance between the U. S. and Russia in the space race. The news reached almost every home, office, shop, and school instantaneously with many watching or listening to the historical event on television or radio.

"It was great. We saw it on television at school and it really was exciting," Margaret Edwards, 11, a sixth grade pupil at Hoyt school, said. She was the 1961 city champion in The Wisconsin State Journal spelling bee.

Many showed relief that the astronaut was safe and that the U. S. prestige didn't suffer a severe blow by a failure.

"I think I express the viewpoint of most Americans when I say I have a feeling not only of elation, but one of relief that it was successful," Jim Ingebritsen, 319 N. Blair st., said.

"I am happy that the maxi-

(Continued on Page 2, Column 1)

Braves Beaten, 6-5, in Twelfth

Story in Sports Peach

Feature Finder

'Just a Baby Step,' Mrs. Shepard Says

VIRGINIA BEACH, Va. (AP)—A beaming Louise Shepard said Friday her husband's journey to the fringe of space was "just a baby step" compared to new challenges ahead.

Radiating confidence in her astronaut husband, Alan B. Shepard Jr., she said Friday's feat helped soothe her disappointment over Yuri Gagarin's head start into space.

"They (the astronauts) knew they were so close. They knew like everybody else that they could do it," the 34-year-old brunette said after she had time to collect her thoughts.

Over and over she said, "It's wonderful. This will go down in history."

"Would you like to see your husband in orbit around the earth?" she was asked. She hesitated.

"Well," she said, drawing the word out, "it is a hard question, but," she sighed, "yes, since he wants it so very badly."

Poised, and obviously delighted with the space program, Mrs. Shepard said, "This is just a baby step, I guess, to what we will see."

Mrs. Shepard is a glowingly beautiful woman, tanned, with a sparkling white smile and deep-set eyes.

She faced a curious world Friday in a simple chocolate brown linen dress, topped with an embroidered pink cardigan sweater. On her feet were low heeled brown and white spectator pumps.

"She always looks like she stepped out of a bandbox no matter when you drop in," a neighbor, Mrs. John Matthews, commented. "Her house is just as immaculate as she is."

Louise Shepard's figure stays trim, probably because she, with her two daughters, Laura, 13, and Julianna, 10, shares her husband's enthusiasm for sports. She often goes bicycling along the rustic roads in the bay colony area here.

Alan, who is a golf enthsusiast, has tried to teach "his girl" the game, too.

Although all the astronauts have been invited to visit President Kennedy on Monday, Louise Shepard will continue to do what she has always felt is the right thing—stay home and keep things as normal as possible.

'Wonderful,' Mrs. Shepard Says After Flight —AP Wirephoto

Wisconsin State Journal

WEATHER: Considerable Cloudiness With a Chance of Showers Today. Partly Cloudy Tonight.

GOOD MORNING | SECTION 1 | MADISON, TUESDAY, AUGUST 22, 1961 | 22 PAGES, THREE SECTIONS Vol. 201, No. 141 122nd year | MORNING FINAL | 5c

500 SEARCH FOR SLAYERS OF POLICEMAN AT DELTON

VICTIM'S WIFE, CHILD — Mrs. James C. (Barbara) Jantz, 22, widowed by a fugitive gunman early Monday, cuddles her 5-month-old son, Timothy, in their Baraboo home.

—State Journal Photos by Rodney Sweet

AND HIS PARENTS — Mr. and Mrs. Clarence Jantz tried to console each other Monday on the back steps of their Baraboo farm home, still unable to believe that their only child, James, a Sauk county policeman, was dead.

2nd Gun Victim Little Improved

By JUNE DIECKMANN
(State Journal Staff Writer)

WISCONSIN DELLS — A posse of nearly 500 lawmen, National Guardsmen, and civilian volunteers continued their 'round-the-clock search of the rugged Baraboo bluffs and Wisconsin Dells area early today for two of three gunmen who killed one Sauk county policeman and seriously wounded another.

County Traffic Policeman James C. Jantz, 25, Baraboo, was killed in the street gunfight about 1:30 a. m. Monday in front of the Lake Delton town hall.

Injured by the same gunmen was Lake Delton Police Chief Robert E. Kohl, 46. He suffered bullet wounds in the lung, liver, and spleen. He was reported in "serious" condition at University hospital in Madison where he underwent lengthy surgery to stop internal bleeding.

His condition was reported as improved early today.

The hunted fugitives are William Joseph Welter, about 23, Franklin Park, Ill., and George Kristovich, about 30, Chicago.

Both Dangerous

Officials warned that they probably are armed and are considered dangerous.

NICKL

The third gunman, Richard Nickl, 22, Prospect Heights, Ill., was captured when he was thrown from the gunmen's car as it struck the ditch when they made a U-turn to avoid a roadblock on Highway 12 near Mauston about 10 minutes after the shooting.

He received fractures of both legs and is confined under guard at Mauston hospital where his condition was reported as "good."

Welter was described as being 5-feet 9-inches tall, weighing about 140 pounds, with short, wavy, possibly-dyed light brown hair, blue eyes, and a square jaw, and "fairly good looking."

Kristovich is "rougher looking," about 5-feet-10, weighing near 185 pounds, with dark hair and two missing or chipped front teeth on the right side.

Both Might Be Hurt

Sauk Deputy Sheriff Mike Spencer, who is heading the search,

Turn to Page 2, Col. 4

Wanted in Slaying

WILLIAM J. WELTER

GEORGE KRISTOVICH

These two men are being sought in the slaying of a Sauk county traffic policeman. If seen, notify law enforcement officers immediately. They are armed and dangerous. —AP Wirephotos

Their Dreams Broken, Mothers Share Grief

BARABOO—A young mother, with tear-reddened eyes and her 5-month-old son clutched in her arms, prayed Monday afternoon that the men who killed her policeman husband will be found soon.

"I pray that they are captured before they spoil somebody else's dreams, plans, and life," Mrs. James C. Jantz, 22, said.

About 2 miles north, in a homey farm house, another mother, some 30 years older, was also trying bravely to stop crying. She was Mrs. Clarence Jantz, whose policeman son—Barbara's husband—was her only child.

"You know, he was born Feb. 12, 1936, and I always told him he could grow up to be president like Abraham Lincoln," the elder Mrs. Jantz said.

A little farther north on Highway 12, at Lake Delton, there was another wife and mother unable to control her worry-caused tears. She was Mrs. Robert E. Kohl, wife of the Lake Delton police chief who was seriously wounded by the same gunmen who killed Officer Jantz.

And with Mrs. Kohl was her 18-year-old daughter, Sandra, most of the time a grownup lady, but not ashamed to cry like a child with the knowledge that her father was wounded severely.

All the women said they have lived in constant fear that the danger of their men's police work might result in something like the midtown gunfight in Lake Delton early Monday.

"I've known this could happen anytime," Mrs. Kohl said. "But when Bob asked me what I thought about his taking the chief's job seven years ago, I told him that if that was what he wanted, I wanted him to have it."

She even served as his radio dispatcher, with equipment in

Turn to Page 2, Col. 3

'I Saw the Gun Flash'

Witness Counts 30 Shots in 30 Seconds

LAKE DELTON — "There must have been 30 shots fired in about 30 seconds," James Agan, an eyewitness to the fatal shooting of Sauk County Policeman James Jantz and wounding of Lake Delton Police Chief Robert Kohl, told The Wisconsin State Journal Monday.

Agan, 27, formerly of Madison, is vacationing at Lake Delton from Ft. Collins, Colo., where he is a salesman of school jewelry. He was entering the C-Der-Del motel, about 30 yards from the street death scene, when the shooting happened.

AGAN

"It was about 1:30 a. m. when I saw the squad car with its flashing red light stop the black 1960 Oldsmobile. I looked to see if it was anyone I knew, and just that quick I saw the gun flash and heard the report," Agan said.

"Bob (Kohl) spun to the street and I knew he was hit. As the other officer (Jantz) ran toward the squad car to take cover, the three men came out both sides of their car shooting.

"One of them fired over the roof of the squad car and got the officer. Then they picked up the policemen's guns from the street and sped away just as another county officer, Fred Bayer, drove up and started shooting at them," Agan said.

Agan put in a 20-hour day Monday helping in the search for

Turn to Page 2, Col. 1

Gunmen's Victims: 2 Dedicated Policemen

BARABOO — Sauk County Policeman James C. Jantz, 25, Baraboo, and Lake Delton Police Chief Robert E. Kohl, 46, were "dedicated policemen who never shirked duty even knowing the danger it entailed," Deputy Sheriff Mike Spencer, former longtime Sauk sheriff, said Monday.

Jantz, who was killed by gunmen early Monday, joined the Sauk traffic police force three years ago. During the previous year he had worked as a part-time deputy on Spencer's sheriff's staff while also employed at the Northern Engineers firm in Baraboo.

Born in Pontiac, Ill., Jantz attended Sacred Hearts Catholic school in Lockport, Ill., before moving with his parents, Mr. and Mrs. Clarence Jantz, to a farm just north of Baraboo in 1950.

At Baraboo High school, where he graduated in 1954, he was an excellent student and star basket-

Turn to Page 2, Col. 7

JANTZ KOHL

U.S. Rejects Pact for Russ Flights

WASHINGTON (AP)—The United States announced Monday night that it has decided not to sign a U. S.-Soviet air route agreement now "in view of the international situation."

The Russians charged that by not going through on the agreement, the United States is failing to take a step which would improve currently tense East-West relations.

The U. S. decision not to sign was made with President Kennedy's approval after a month of negotiations had virtually cleared up the technical agreements needed to be worked out.

Instead of signing, so that the planned commercial air flights could be started between New York and Moscow, however, the U. S. negotiators insisted only on "initialing" the agreement that had been tentatively worked out.

U. S. officials said this means that when the international situation improves the government may, if they wish, go ahead with full signing of the agreement and the flights can begin.

After Johnson Reports, Kennedy Pledges Freedom of West Berlin

WASHINGTON (AP) — President Kennedy pledged Monday to maintain the freedom of West Berlin.

He renewed this pledge after receiving a firsthand report from Vice-President Lyndon B. Johnson on his flying mission to Germany.

Mr. Kennedy met with Johnson for almost an hour immediately after returning to the White House from an abbreviated weekend in Hyannis Port, Mass.

Johnson, who arrived in Washington before noon, went to Mr. Kennedy's office shortly after the President's return to report on his observations and meetings during his two-day journey to Bonn and West Berlin.

After their conference, Mr. Kennedy expressed gratitude to Johnson for his "remarkably successful and important" mission.

Mr. Kennedy said Johnson's report added to the government's

KENNEDY JOHNSON

recognition that "we are going to pass through difficult weeks and months to maintain the freedom of West Berlin."

"But maintain it we will," he said.

Johnson had said earlier that he was confident his journey had produced tighter links between West Germany and the other Western Allies.

Secretary of State Dean Rusk also participated in the conference, as did Johnson's traveling companions—Gen. Lucius D. Clay (Ret.), former United States military commander in Germany, and Charles E. Bohlen, special assistant to Rusk and an expert in Russian affairs.

Mr. Kennedy said Johnson's report emphasized the confidence and trust the people of West Berlin place in the U. S. and the heavy responsibilities that relationship places upon the U. S.

Johnson said his trip was a "most stimulating and inspiring experience." He described his talks with West German Chancel-

Turn to Page 3, Col. 1

Today's Chuckle

One secretary to another: "You'll love it here—once you accept the fact that there's absolutely no chance for advancement, raises or marriage."

On the Inside . . .

MUSCLE FLEXING — The Western Big Three Allies in West Berlin plan to counter every Communist East Germany military muscle-flexing on the border of the divided city, and the British did just that Monday. **Story, Page 2.**

FEATURE FINDER

New State Laws

Chapters 401 to 412, new state laws, texts, Sec. 2, Page 3

State Journal Gives Quick Assist to Lawmen

The Wisconsin State Journal Monday night gave a quick assist to the army of lawmen searching for two gunmen who killed a Sauk county traffic policeman and wounded the Lake Delton police chief.

Capt. Earl O. Sorenson of the Dane county sheriff's department asked for The State Journal's help at 5:50 p.m.

He received it at 6:30 p.m. —in the form of 100 leaflets bearing pictures of the gunmen being hunted. The leaflets were rushed to law enforcement officers at the scene by county deputies.

The search had been hampered by the fact that the huge posse did not have any means of identifying the gunmen.

The pictures arrived in The State Journal office via Associated Press Wirephoto after they were released by Chicago police. They were engraved in The State Journal plant—and the leaflets were printed through the fast cooperation of the night-time employes of the Journal composing room.

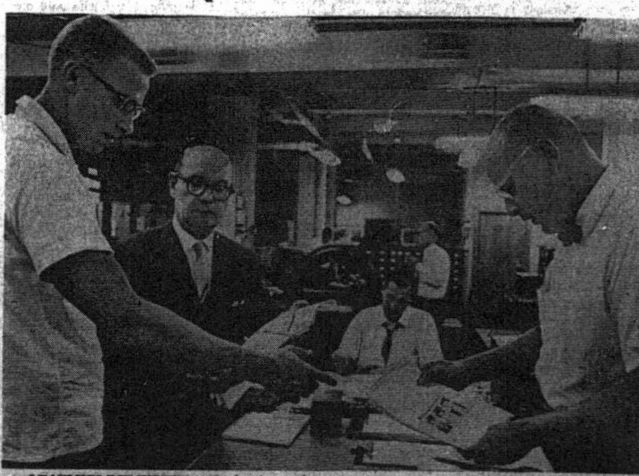

LEAFLETS DELIVERED — Richard Josephson, left, Dane county sheriff's deputy, receives delivery of leaflets bearing pictures of gunmen being hunted in Sauk and Juneau counties from Lawrence H. Fitzpatrick, center, Wisconsin State Journal managing editor, and Glenn Miller, right, city editor.

—State Journal Photo by Edwin Stein

Packers Trample Giants, 37-0, Nail Down Seventh NFL Crown

Camera Catches Usually Grim Lombardi in Rare During-Game Smile as Packers Return NFL Title to Green Bay —AP Wirephoto

Experience, Desire Pay

GREEN BAY (AP)—Coach Vince Lombardi and his Green Bay Packers agreed unanimously that experience and desire hoisted the Packers to their lop-sided 37-0 victory over the New York Giants in Sunday's National Football League title game.

"We didn't do anything special, but we were the greatest team in the league today," Lombardi said in the noisy Packer dressing room.

Lombardi said the championship victory was the greatest in his career. He added that size of the score was bigger than he expected.

"I don't know what was wrong with the Giants," Lombardi said.

"This was a team effort," Lombardi went on. "It's hard to single out individuals. But the defense was outstanding and Paul Hornung was a tremendous competitor.

"The bigger the game the better Hornung plays," Lombardi said.

Hornung, the NFL's scoring leader in the regular season and voted the league's outstanding player, said the Packers knew they were going to win "five minutes before the kickoff."

"We were confident and it turned out to be our day. We couldn't do anything wrong and the Giants couldn't do anything right," Hornung said.

'Up the Middle'

Lombardi and Hornung both said the Packer offense was the same as always, but the coach added: "We knew we had to feature Hornung because of injuires to fullback Jim Taylor."

"We knew the Giants could stop us on the weak side, so we went to the strong side and up the middle," Hornung said. "And it worked. And we gained on a couple of wide sweeps around the end. That's something you dont do very often against the Giants."

Hornung, a private in the army, was playing while on leave from Ft. Riley, Kans. He said he "wasn't far out of shape" when he joined the team for drills. "If anything, I was a little stronger."

Packer quarterback Bart Starr said he had room to operate "because of the blocking of the line. They did a spectacular job. They didn't miss a thing.

Taylor Slowed

"Hornung never looked better than he did in practice this week," Starr said, "and I decided I'd go with him every chance I could. He sure was great.' Hornung gained 89 yards in 20 carries.

Taylor, whose play was ham-

Turn to Page 3, Sports

Minnesota Battles UCLA

Scene Set, Cast Ready for Rose Bowl Spectacle

PASADENA, Calif. (AP) — The scene is set, the cast is ready, and Minnesota is still the favorite today to trim UCLA in the 48th edition of the famed Rose Bowl football extravaganza.

The show goes on before an expected 100,000, with the kickoff set for 4 p.m. (CST) .The nation's football fans can watch it on national television (WMTV).

Seek Revenge

The Golden Gophers, runner-up to Ohio State in the Big 10 title campaign, won seven and lost two games during the regular season. They vow they want revenge for their 17-7 defeat in this same big bowl a year ago to the Washington Huskies.

Coach Bill Barnes' Bruins of UCLA won seven and lost three games in 1961. In four previous appearances here, UCLA has never won.

This present UCLA squad is quick to point out that none of its members was around for any of the defeats. The last one was in 1956 and Michigan State came up with a last-minute field goal to win, 17-14.

All-Americans On Display

Two All-American stars will be on display.

The more prominent will be the Minnesota quarterback, Sandy Stephens. Coach Murray Warmath dislikes to have his team known as a one-man affair, but Stephens does most of the running, passing, and kicking.

The All-American Bruin is the team captain and field inspiration, 205-pound Ron Hull, their chunky, spunky center. Hull may not be too much in evidence because the fellows up front, the blockers, aren't so easy to distinguish from the stands.

But Hull summed up the UCLA game plan in just two words, and if they prove true, Minnesota may be in for real trouble.

Superb Blocking

How does UCLA expect to win, Hull was asked?

"Block and tackle."

It was superb blocking all season by the big Bruin line that brought them to the Rose Bowl, paving the way for a collection of fine backs to operate.

Employed in the single wing offense, tailbacks Bobby Smith and Mike Haffner were the key ground gainers and passers, and both will see about equal time today.

Stephens was the show-player for Minnesota. But credit must be extended to his supporting backs, such as the starters in this one, Dave Mulholland, Bill Munsey, and fullback Judge Dickson.

Rosters on Page 2

Television rosters and season statistics on all eight of today's bowl teams are on Page 2, Sports.

WARMATH BARNES
ready for big show

Weather Fit for a Queen at Pasadena

PASADENA, Calif. (AP) — The weatherman, who once had the ill humor to predict rain, now says Pasadena will enjoy New Year's Day weather fit for a queen — a Rose queen.

The Tournament of Roses parade is expected to run its brilliant course under clear, sunny skies, with temperatures in the mid-70s.

A comparatively balmy 50 degrees was the predicted minimum in the pre-dawn hours. That's when perhaps a million spectators will take their places along the six-mile parade route — while bands and beauties gather among the floats behind the starting mark.

Rain predicted last week didn't materialize, the forecaster said. Even fog — a problem here recently — isn't expected to reach Pasadena.

A blast of trumpets is to launch the parade at 10:40 a. m. (CST). The grand marshal will be Washington's Gov. Albert D. Rosellini.

The parade will be telecast nationally by CBS and NBC.

In the first of 57 floats will be Martha Sissell, the rose queen, and her court of six princesses.

Burleson Captures Sugar Bowl Mile

NEW ORLEANS (AP) — Dyrol Burleson slushed through a driving rainstorm to an easy mile victory Sunday in the annual Sugar Bowl track and field meet.

Burleson, 21-year-old senior at the University of Oregon and America's top miler, finished 30 yards ahead of Ernie Cunliffe of the Air Force in the slow time of 4:22.2. They ran over a track turned into a quagmire by a sudden rain.

John Uelses of the Marine Corps stole the show by vaulting to a meet record of 15 feet 6¼ inches over a board-covered runway.

Pro Basketball

NATIONAL

EASTERN	W	L	WESTERN	W	L
Boston	29	5	Los Angeles	30	11
Philadelphia	22	14	Cincinnati	20	18
Syracuse	14	22	Detroit	15	20
New York	12	25	St. Louis	13	24

Results Sunday
No games scheduled

AMERICAN

EASTERN	W	L	WESTERN	W	L
Pittsburgh	19	16	Kansas City	21	10
Cleveland	19	17	Los Angeles	19	13
Chicago	13	21	San Francisco	16	14
Washington	13	22	Hawaii	10	21

Results Sunday
Kansas City 91, San Francisco 90
Los Angeles 119, Pittsburgh 109

Wisconsin State Journal Sports

Monday, January 1, 1962
Section 3 ALpine 6-3111

NFL's Payoff Richest Ever

GREEN BAY (UPI) — The payoff for each player in Sunday's National Football League title game was the richest ever.

Each member of the winning Green Bay Packers received $5,195.44, and each member of the losing New York Giants got $3,339.99.

The total take was $1,013,792, with $300,000 trimmed from the top for the NFL Player Benefit Fund before the proceeds were divided.

A slice of $42,333.25 was set aside for the winner of the Detroit-Philadelphia second-place game in Miami next Saturday.

Hornung Wins Sports Car for Great Play

GREEN BAY (AP)—Paul Hornung of the Green Bay Packers was named the winner of a sports car given by a magazine (Sport) to the outstanding player Sunday in the National Football Leagues championship game.

Hornung was selected by the editors of the magazine. He will receive the car Wednesday in New York.

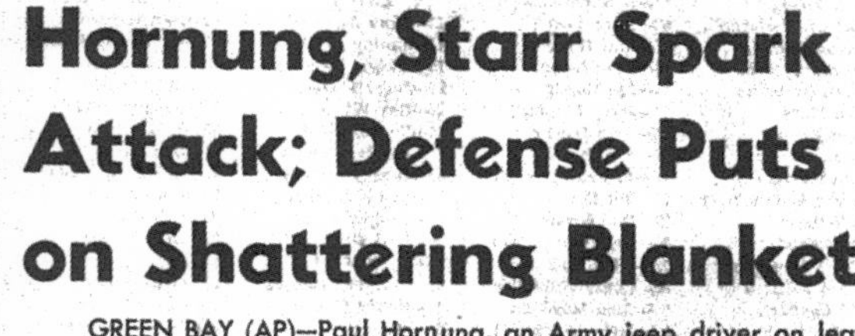

Hornung, Starr Spark Attack; Defense Puts on Shattering Blanket

GREEN BAY (AP)—Paul Hornung, an Army jeep driver on leave from Ft. Riley, Kans., scored 19 points Sunday in the Green Bay Packers' humiliating 37-0 victory over the New York Giants for their seventh National Football League title.

Hornung, voted the most valuable player in the league, smashed home for a six-yard touchdown, added four extra points, and kicked field goals of 17, 22, and 19 yards before 39,029 delirious fans who immediately started a wild New Year's Eve celebration.

Kramer Grabs Two

Bart Starr, Coach Vince Lombardi's fine but unsung quarterback, threw three touchdown passes in the rout as the Packer line manhandled the Giants on offense and completely bottled up New York's attack.

Ron Kramer, the "tight" end, caught two of Starr's TD passes of 14 and 13 yards, and Boyd Dowler, another Army man on leave from Ft. Lewis, Wash., nabbed the other for a 13-yard scoring play.

STATISTICS

	NY	GB
First downs	6	19
Rushing yardage	31	181
Passing yardage	99	164
Passes	10-29	10-19
Passes intercepted by	0	4
Punts	5-39	5-42
Fumbles lost	1	0
Yards penalized	38	16

This frosty day belonged to Hornung, former quarterback at Notre Dame who became a halfback at Green Bay under Lombardi.

Four Interceptions

While Hornung galloped and Starr hit his targets, the alert defenders intercepted four of Y.A. Tittle's passes. The only Giant threat came late in the second period when, trailing 21-0, Bob Gaiters' six-yard fourth down pass intended for Kyle Rote fell incomplete in the end zone.

The smashing victory by the Packers, who had been favored at slim odds of less than a touchdown, was worth $5,195.44 to each Green Bay player.

Each losing Giant collected $3,339.99 from the huge money pool, including $315,000 of the $615,000 paid for the network radio and TV rights. The total receipts were $713,792.

The other $300,000 from TV went to the Player Benefit Fund.

Tops Graham Record

Green Bay broke the game wide open in a 24-point second period after a socreless opening session on the frozen field. That awesome burst of power and passing skill put the Packers beyond reach of the sputtering Giant offense.

Hornung's scoring efforts smashed the old championship game record of 18 points set by Cleveland's Otto Graham in 1954 against the Detroit Lions. Al-

Turn to Page 2, Sports

Happy New Year

Green Bay	0	24	10	3	—37
New York	0	0	0	0	— 0

GB—Hornung, 6, run (Hornung kick)
GB—Dowler, 13, pass from Starr (Hornung kick)
GB—Kramer, 14, pass from Starr (Hornung kick)
GB—FG, Hornung, 17
GB—FG, Hornung, 22
GB—Kramer, 13, pass from Starr (Hornung kick)
GB—FG, Hornung, 19

Kramer Takes Perfect Starr Pass in End Zone —AP Wirephoto

'Nothing Wrong But Us'

No Alibis by Giants

GREEN BAY (AP)—"We met a solid ball club, a very good football team, and we don't have any alibis."

That was Coach Allie Sherman's comment shortly after his New York Giants absorbed a 37-0 licking from the Green Bay Packers in the National Football League championship game Sunday.

Then he said: "It was just one of those days. They were too good a football team for us to let the things happen that went on out there.

"Too Much For Us"

"Dropped passes, fumbles, and the like were too much for us," he added while his glum players peeled off pads and tape in the dressing room.

He was asked right away if the 21-degree weather or the hard field could be in any way considered reasons for the Eastern champions' dismal showing.

"No, there was nothing wrong out there but us," he said. "I don't want to make an alibi because we don't have any. I just wish we could have made the score respectable and stayed in the ball game."

Sherman said the Packers were the best team his Giants had

Turn to Page 2, Sports

Dowler Gets Behind Barnes, Grabs Starr Pass for Touchdown —AP Wirephoto

Statistics

RUSHING

GREEN BAY

	Att.	Yds.
Hornung	20	89
Taylor	14	69
Moore	6	25

NEW YORK

	Att.	Yds.
Webster	7	19
Wells	3	9
King	2	5

PASSING

GREEN BAY

	A	C	Yds	Int.	TD
Starr	17	10	164	0	3

NEW YORK

	A	C	Yds	Int.	TD
Tittle	20	6	65	4	0
Conerly	8	4	54	0	0

PASS RECEIVING

GREEN BAY

	No.	Yds	TD
Dowler	3	37	1
Kramer	4	80	2
Hornung	3	47	0

NEW YORK

	No.	Yds	TD
Rote	3	54	0
Shofner	3	41	0
Webster	3	5	0
Walton	1	19	0

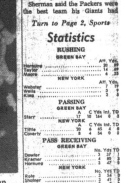

Wisconsin State Journal

WEATHER: Mostly Cloudy and Continued Cold. Low Tonight 5 to 10.

GOOD MORNING 38 PAGES, THREE SECTIONS Vol. 203, No. 122 123rd Year MADISON, THURSDAY, FEBRUARY 1, 1962 ★ ★ ★ MORNING FINAL 5c

GIRL PLUNGES—Jana Schepp, 17, a member of the Wallenda circus aerial act, falls from a high wire Tuesday night during an accident in which two members of the seven-person troupe were killed. Above Miss Schepp are three male members, who clung to her until a net was placed under her. She was injured.

This dramatic picture was taken during the tragedy in Detroit by an amateur photographer, O. C. Hansen, who attended the circus. —AP Wirephoto

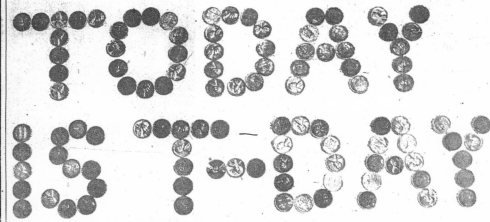

TODAY IS T-DAY

'The Show Must Go On'

Death of Pair Doesn't Stop Circus Family

DETROIT (AP)—Herman Wallenda and his son, Gunther, performed Wednesday night on the same high wire from which two aerialists of the Great Wallendas' troupe fell to their death Tuesday night.

Herman, 60, and Gunther, 30, teamed with aerialist Jean Mendez, who was flown in to fill the Shrine Circus gap left by the tragedy which befell the Wallendas.

First on High Wire

Besides the two killed, three others of the Wallenda troupe, which dates its beginning back to 1780, were hospitalized, one of them near death.

KARL WALLENDA

Mendez was first Wednesday night on the high wire three-stories above the concrete floor of the Fairgrounds Coliseum. He was followed by Herman and then Gunther.

Gunther rode a bike across the wire and teamed with Mendez to carry Herman standing on a cross bar between them. In their finale, Herman stood on his head on the bar.

But They Persist

As usual, the performers did not use a net.

A crowd of 5,000 gave the trio a howling ovation.

The Wallendas were a part of the matinee performance. At first, Producer Al Dobritch said they couldn't go on the high wire. But they persisted, and Dobritch finally agreed they could go on Wednesday night.

They had shown up on time for the matinee, both intent on "throwing something together on the wire," because, as Herman put it:

"The show must go on. We must act. I don't know why, but we must."

Balanced in Chair

It was on the high wire that the human pyramid of the Great Wallendas collapsed Tuesday night, dashing three of the seven performers to the floor, which was four stories below Jana Schepp, 17, who was at the top of the pyramid balanced in a chair.

Richard Faughnan, 29, and Dieter Schepp, 23, Jana's brother, fell to their deaths. Mario Wallenda, 22, sufefred a fractured skull and was in "very, very critical condition" Wednesday.

Jana, caught by Karl Wallenda, 56, and his nephew, Gunther, as they clung to the wire, was dropped finally to an improvised net quickly rigged from a blanket by performers on the floor. She bounced from the net, however, and suffered a concussion when she hit the floor.

Come From Hospital

Herman, whose nose was torn apart at the bridge; Gunther, who wasn't hurt; and Karl, who suffered a possible fractured pelvis and internal injuries, made their way to their platforms 36 feet above the floor.

Wallendas Brushed Death Before. Story, Photo of Pyramid, Page 8

Herman and Gunther were on hand Wednesday, coming from visiting those in a hospital, "to get something together."

Gunther, in Arab dress, took part in the circus spectacular at the opening, and both he and Herman "stood web," as usual, in "the aerial ballet."

Twirling high above Herman as he twirled his rope was Helen Baade, 22, who has adopted the name Marty Wallenda and who watched Tuesday night's tragedy.

Above Gunther twirled red-

Turn to Page 2, Col. 1

Wife of High-Wire Victim Sees Slip Start Tragic Chain of Events

DETROIT (UPI) — The wife of a circus high-wire performer who witnessed her husband's death plunge during a performance of the Shrine Circus said Wednesday she saw the slip that began the tragic chain of events.

Mrs. Jenny Faughnan, wife of Richard Faughnan, 29, killed with Dieter Schepp, 23, said she was watching the act when the tragedy struck.

"I saw Dieter was having trouble holding his balancing pole," she said. "He was the lead man in the human pyramid."

Mrs. Faughnan said Schepp was holding the pole "with the tips of his fingers instead of the palms of his hands. He was getting tired."

She said Schepp tossed the pole into the air to get a better grip. "When he did that, he lost his balance."

"I screamed and climbed down the platform ladder," she said. "They wouldn't let me near the men on the ground."

She followed the ambulance to the hospital. When told her husband was dead, she collapsed.

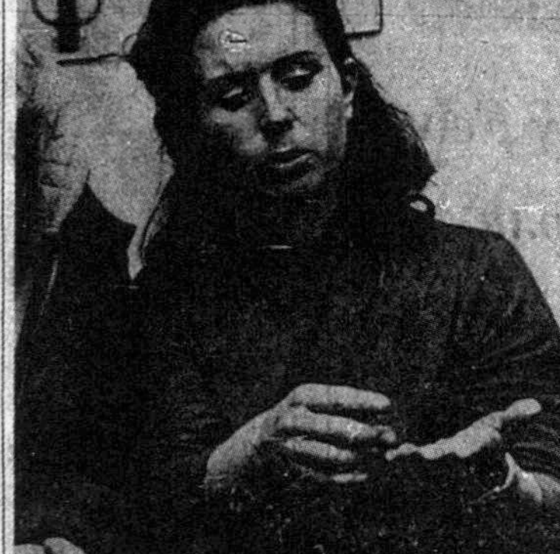

Mrs. Faughnan Describes Accident Which Killed Her Husband, Richard —AP Wirephoto

Kennedy Starts Stockpile Probe

Strategic Material at $7.7 Billion

WASHINGTON (AP)—President Kennedy welcomed two Soviet visitors to his news conference Wednesday, promptly slapped at communism—and announced an investigation of government stockpiling and potentially "unconscionable profits."

Mr. Kennedy volunteered word on those three items right at the outset of what was an unusual sort of session, with 420 newsmen.

The President had to share the attention of reporters straining to watch and hear him while they tried also to keep tab on Mr. and Mrs. Alexei I. Adzhubei, the son-in-law and daughter of Soviet Premier Nikita S. Khrushchev, and Texas Correspondent Sarah McClendon.

Plan Investigation

The chief news announcement was that a Senate subcommittee, with the cooperation of the Administration, is going to investigate what Mr. Kennedy termed excessive stockpiling of costly materials for emergency defense use. He called them "a potential source of excessive and unconscionable profits."

KENNEDY

Mr. Kennedy said the stockpile of strategic materials was started under contracts negotiated before his Administration took office, that it has soared to the $7.7-billion level, and that this is nearly $3.4 billion more than the amount required for a possible emergency.

'Cold Facts'

"No," Mr. Kennedy said, "I am not making any implication" — of wrong doing by an individual. But he said the whole matter calls for careful scrutiny to bring out the cold facts, at a Senate investigation to be headed by Sen. Stuart Symington (D-Mo.).

Nine rows back in the State Department auditorium sat Adzhubei, his wife, Rada, Georgi Bolshakov, editor of a Soviet magazine, and Mrs. Pierre Salinger, wife of Mr. Kennedy's press secretary. Adzhubei is editor of the Russian newspaper Izvestia, which printed his interview with Mr. Kennedy last November

Mr. Kennedy at one point said there is evidence of a desire of both Russia and the United States to come to an agreement over troubled Laos.

In a new twist to presidential

Turn to Page 2, Col. 6

Scandinavians Agree to Buy UN Bonds

UNITED NATIONS, N.Y. (UPI)—Denmark, Norway, and Sweden agreed Wednesday to buy $10.1 million worth of the $200 million bond issue voted by the General Assembly last month to keep the United Nations financially afloat.

Final action by the respective national legislatures will be required.

Sweden planned to buy $5.8 million worth, Denmark $2.5 million, and Norway $1.8.

Britain announced its intention of buying up to $12 million worth.

President Kennedy sent to Congress Tuesday a request for authorization for purchase by the United States of $100 million worth.

PENNIES FROM HAVEN—The banks are ready for the penny parade. Two employes of the First National Bank, 1 S. Pinckney st., have been packaging pennies for several days in preparation of T-day. At the coin-packaging machines are Mrs. Donald K. West, 407G Eagle Heights, left, and Mrs. Kenneth H. Scharmer, 318 Oriole lane.

No penny shortage is anticipated in Wisconsin because banks have built up their supplies. The First National Bank alone has about $10,000 in pennies on hand in Madison. —State Journal Photo by John Kreissler

Argentine Top Military Demands Castro Break

BUENOS AIRES, Argentina, Thursday, (AP) — Argentina's military chiefs were reported today to have handed President Arturo Frondizi an ultimatum demanding a break in diplomatic relations with Communist Cuba.

The threat of a new politico-military crisis flared overnight in the aftermath of Argentina's abstention at Punta del Este from the Organization of American States' majority vote to oust the Castro regime from OAS functions.

Round of Meetings

Reports of the ultimatum came from informed sources and the influential newspaper, La Nacion.

Informants said the military leaders presented their demands after a round of meetings with the interior and civil defense ministers and with Frondizi.

The three armed forces chiefs were reported furious over Argentina's refusal to go along with the 14-nation majority at Punta del Este.

Ask Ouster

Informants said they had demanded that in addition to ending ties with Havana, Frondizi dismiss Foreign Minister Miguel Angel Carcano and others who took a soft-line approach for Cuba at the hemisphere foreign ministers conference.

The reports of brewing crisis came less than three weeks after Argentina underwent major cabinet shifts in the economic and public works departments.

Informants refused to speculate on what the military's next move would be if President Arturo Frondizi refuses the demands.

The first indication of military unrest came in a communique issued by the air force secretariat expressing its stand regarding

Turn to Page 2, Col. 4

Cedric Parker Booked on Driving Charge

Cedric Parker, Waubesa Beach, city editor of the Capital Times, was booked by police early today on a charge of operating a motor vehicle while intoxicated after the car he was driving struck a parked car in the 900 block of W. Johnson st.

The owner of the car which Parker admitted hitting saw the license number of Parker's car and called police. Patrolman Charles Frank stopped Parker's car in the first block of N. Park st.

Waunakee Chief Joins His Wife at Hospital

George Manthey, 63, veteran Waunakee police chief, was taken by county police ambulance to Methodist hospital Wednesday night when he became ill at home.

His wife, Rosina, is in the same hospital recovering from surgery she underwent Jan. 24. Chief Manthey, who has been treated for diabetes for several years, was reported in "fairly good" condition by hospital officials.

Today's Chuckle

An average man is one who isn't so good as his wife thinks he is before she marries him, and not so bad as she thinks he is afterward.

On the Inside . . .

10-Cent Beer Goes Way of Free Lunch

MONROE—The 10-cent glass of beer and the free second cup of coffee become things of the past here today as the state sales tax goes into effect.

At a meeting Tuesday night, Monroe tavern owners decided to raise the price of a small glass of beer from 10 to 15 cents and increase its size from seven to 10 ounces. The tavern owners said the 5-cent increase also was influenced by an anticipated price boost by beer distributors.

Monroe restaurant owners, meeting Tuesday night, made the free second cup of coffee another tax casualty. The second cup now will cost 10 cents, the same price as the initial cup.

3% Sales Tax Now in Effect

And Withholding Trims Pay Checks

By WILLIAM C. ROBBINS
(State Journal Staff Writer)

Your new tax life in Wisconsin started today, TAX DAY.

The first major overhaul of the state's tax structure in a half-century was initiated with the start of Thursday, Feb. 1, 1962, making it an historic day in the job of financing state and local governments.

This is the T-Day story:

WHO: You.

WHAT: Will pay a 3 per cent sales tax.

WHERE: In Wisconsin business places.

WHEN: Starting today.

WHY: In order to accomplish a needed tax revision program. (See Story Below)

Tax Boost, Withholding

The other tax-collecting highlights of the new law involve the state income tax, including a tax increase of about $10 per $1,000 of taxable income during 1962. Also effective today is the withholding method of collecting state taxes from payrolls.

On the other side of the ledger, the tax program will accomplish some positive results.

It will provide enough money to balance the state budget which had a deficit of $56 million before the 1961 Legislature passed the measure. It wiped out the highly-probable necessity of enacting a 45 per cent annual surtax in order to balance the current state budget of $500,000.

Surtax Eliminated

The state surtax, which is 20 per cent on the 1961 income taxes, is eliminated this year.

There is 65 per cent forgiveness of your tax bill on 1961 income because withholding is now in effect.

The "take" from the sales tax and income tax increase will also

Turn to Page 2, Col. 3

The Tax and You on the Inside . . .

Summaries of the withholding and sales tax provisions of the new state tax law appear on SEC. 1, PAGE 17.

Stories on new ticket prices for Milwaukee Braves baseball games and a new cost policy for bowlers appear in the SPORTS PEACH.

Behind Sales Tax, Withholding: State Budget Balance, Revision

By LLEWELLYN G. ROBERTS
(State Journal Staff Writer)

Today is the day consumers in Wisconsin start shelling out pennies and dollars in the state's first massive sales tax.

This is the month when employers start withholding for state income taxes on paychecks, although increased income tax rates actually went into effect Jan. 1.

Why?

There are three reasons for the increased taxes—to balance the state budget, to cut in half the personal property tax on manufacturers and merchants inventories and on farm livestock, and to provide some relief for the real estate property taxpayer.

NELSON

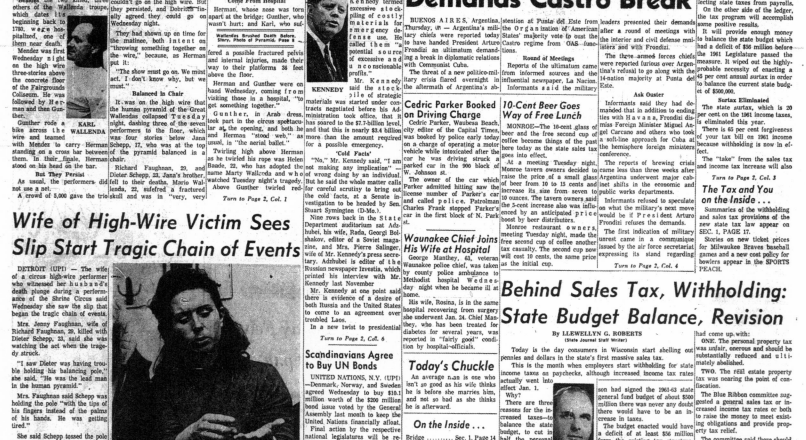

Once the 1961 Legislature had passed and Gov. Gaylord Nelson had signed the 1961-63 state general fund budget of about $500 million there was never any doubt there would have to be an increase in taxes.

The budget enacted would have a deficit of at least $56 million from the existing tax structure.

There had been an increasing clamor for tax revision. Nelson had twice campaigned with a promise of tax revision a predominant issue. His 1960 GOP opponent, Philip Kuehn, also pledged tax revision.

Nelson appointed a long-studying Blue Ribbon committee on revenue sources. It came up with answers previous study groups had come up with:

ONE. The personal property tax was unfair, onerous and should be substantially reduced and ultimately abolished.

TWO. The real estate property tax was nearing the point of confiscation.

The Blue Ribbon committee suggested a general sales tax or increased income tax rates or both to raise the money to meet existing obligations and provide property tax relief.

The committee said there should be no income tax increase without enactment of withholding as the federal income tax has operated for about 20 years.

Much of the revenue collected by the state is returned to local communities, either directly or in the form of state aids for education and welfare.

Welfare and education get most

Turn to Page 2, Col. 7

Page of Pictures, Page 3

ASTRONAUT GLENN DISPLAYS ICY COURAGE DURING ORBIT

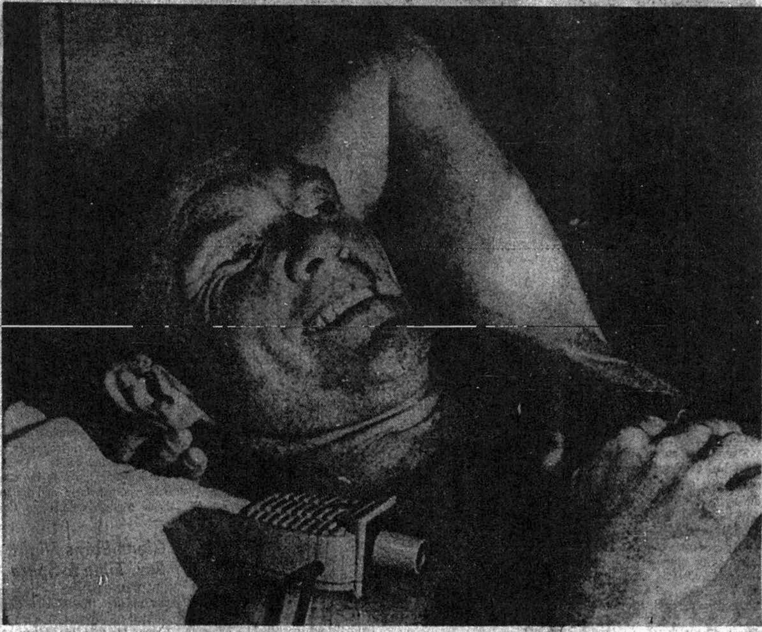

John H. Glenn Smiles as He Rests Aboard Destroyer Noa After Recovery From Orbit. Microphone to Record His Reactions Rests on Astronaut's Shoulder
—NASA Photo Via AP Wirephoto

Marine Circles Earth 3 Times

By BEM PRICE
(Associated Press Writer)

CAPE CANAVERAL — Astronaut John H. Glenn Jr. rocketed around the world three times Tuesday in a magnificent display of icy courage.

The 40-year-old Marine Corps lieutenant colonel's flight ended at 1:43 p.m. CST, in the Atlantic Ocean near Grand Turk island in the Bahamas, about 700 miles southeast of here.

Though the United States achievement lagged some 10 months behind that of the Russians, there was no doubt that Glenn's flight was a tremendous boost to the morale of the Western world and raised hopes that the U. S. would really catch up.

Glenn and his capsule were plucked from the sparkling blue seas by the destroyer USS Noa at 2:01 p.m., and Glenn reported, "My condition is excellent."

After taking a shower aboard the Noa, Glenn talked to his wife and then to President Kennedy by radio telephone.

At 4:44 p.m., he was transferred by helicopter to the anti-submarine carrier Randolph for a brief physical examination and at 7:04 p.m. was sent by whirlybird to Grand Turk island, arriving about 8 p.m. There he will stay for 48 hours and undergo a more exhaustive physical examination and questioning about the flight by a team of scientists and doctors.

As he left the Randolph for Grand Turk in a Navy plane, Glenn remarked, "I'm gonna sit back and let somebody else do the flying this trip."

He had suffered a minor injury on his flight. As he left the space craft, he skinned his knuckles. He arrived aboard the aircraft carrier wearing two little pieces of adhesive bandages on his right hand and asked for a glass of iced tea.

Upon arrival at Grand Turk at 8:11 p.m., Glenn saw his fourth sunset of the day. He was met by fellow Astronaut M. Scott Carpenter, who helped him out of the aircraft and butted his head against Glenn's chest playfully.

Glenn will undergo a thorough physical examination and talk for a couple of days into a tape recorder, covering every phase of his flight in minute detail.

Before the year is out, the U. S. plans to make four more flights similar to the one by Glenn and then wind up 1962 with an 18-orbit flight.

Selected for the next trip into space and around the world is Air Force Maj. Donald Kent Slayton of Sparta, Wis. His rocket is already here and undergoing tests.

Glenn's first comment as his capsule, Friendship 7, descended toward the gentle and tepid waters was contained in a radio message to Project Mercury control here:

"Boy, that was a real fireball of a ride!"

The decision to make that third orbit, after some minor technical difficulties had developed on the first two, was Glenn's.

When asked if he wanted to try for three, Glenn

Turn to Page 2, Col. 3

Glenn's on Top

The Wisconsin State Journal proudly places its masthead at the bottom of Page One today in humble tribute to John H. Glenn Jr.'s successful orbits around the earth.

We feel that nothing should be placed above the news of this all-American team accomplishment.

Diary of Historic Day in Space

CAPE CANAVERAL (UPI)—Diary of John H. Glenn's historic day in space (all times CST):

1:20 a.m.—Awakened at Hangar S by doctor for hefty breakfast of filet mignon, two scrambled eggs, orange juice, toast, jelly, and a coffee substitute.

2 a.m.—Given complete physical exam. Sensors attached to his body for up-to-the-minute checkups during flight.

3:30 a.m.—Put on his 20-pound, silvery space suit and joked with fellow Astronaut Donald Slayton while technicians gave space suit pressure check.

4:02 a.m.—Left Hangar S, flashed a grin with three quick waves at small crowd. Walked 14 steps to transfer van, gave security officer a friendly clap on the back, and climbed in van for ride to Launching Pad 14.

5:03 a.m.—Wedged into Friendship 7 space capsule after an elevator ride up the triangular-shaped gantry at Pad 14.

7:25 a.m.—Gantry pulled back. Gleaming white missile stood alone like Washington monument, and crews started touchy job of fueling the Atlas 109-D.

8:47 a.m.—The Atlas, shining in the sun, lifted slowly from its pad atop an orange ball of flame. It rose straight up into the sky and arched gracefully toward the east. Glenn said, "It's a little bumpy along about here."

8:53 a.m.—Glenn, 100 miles up and weightless: "I feel fine. The view is tremendous."

9 a.m.—Became free world's first man in orbit. Soared 100 to 160 miles above earth at about 17,545 miles an hour.

9:25 a.m.—First snack in space. Squirted food into his mouth from a tube.

9:38 a.m.—On pitch-black, "night side" of globe, spotted "bright lights" of Perth, Australia, and told ground stations to

Turn to Page 2, Col. 1

Baby Boy Shares 8:47 A.M. Spotlight

OSBORNE, Kans. (UPI)—A boy, born at the same moment Astronaut John Glenn began his historic flight Tuesday, has been named in honor of America's foremost spaceman.

Mrs. LeRoy Eller of Gaylord, Kans., gave birth to a 9-pound, 7-ounce boy at 8:47 a.m. in a hospital here. Mrs. Eller and her husband agreed to name the boy John Glenn Eller.

He'll See Glenn Friday

'You Did Wonderful Job,' Kennedy Says

WASHINGTON (AP) — President Kennedy congratulated Astronaut John H. Glenn Jr. Tuesday and told the first American to orbit the globe he would see him at Cape Canaveral on Friday.

"We are really proud of you, and I must say you did a wonderful job," Mr. Kennedy told Glenn in a short radio conversation.

Plans for Meeting

And Glenn, speaking from the destroyer Noa, replied, "It was a wonderful trip—almost unbelievable, thinking back on it right now. But it was really tremendous."

As to the plans for meeting with the President, Glenn commented, "I will certainly look forward to it."

Mr. Kennedy plans to fly to Palm Beach, Fla., late Thursday and shuttle by plane to the cape Friday morning to participate in a ceremony honoring Glenn.

The White House said Mr. Kennedy also would greet Glenn at the White House Monday or Tuesday morning.

That White House meeting likely will touch off a mammoth celebration. The White House said there would be a parade through the city streets and a reception at the Capitol.

Washington turned out thousands of spectators when Alan B. Shepard, the first United States man in space, was welcomed by the President last May.

Vice-President Lyndon B. Johnson will fly to the Bahamas—or wherever Glenn spends the next 48 hours with space agency officials, scientists, and physicians—and accompany the astronaut to Cape Canaveral Friday morning.

Chat for Minute

Mr. Kennedy spoke with Glenn late Tuesday afternoon via Navy communications. What is known as a single side band radio system linked Mr. Kennedy at his desk in the White House with Glenn aboard the Noa.

Press Secretary Pierre Salinger said they chatted for about a minute.

Even before Mr. Kennedy had talked with Glenn, he had publicly saluted the astronaut and declared that in space America must "be in a position second to none."

Speaking from the White House rose garden soon after the marine officer safely completed a three-

Turn to Page 2, Col. 8

President Kennedy Salutes Astronaut Glenn
—AP Wirephoto

Other Space Orbit Stories

Snow Expected to Top 4 Inches

More than 4 inches of snow and winds up to 25 miles an hour were predicted to hit southern Wisconsin early today.

Snow began falling in Madison shortly after midnight, and city street crews again started their sanding chores.

The snow was expected to diminish to flurries late today.

City Council Agrees in Praise of Glenn

The City Council Tuesday unanimously extended its congratulations to Astronaut John H. Glenn Jr. for being the first American to orbit the earth.

The resolution introduced by Ald. Richard Kopp, 18th ward, extended to Glenn and all members of project Mercury the council's heartiest congratulations in behalf of the people of Madison.

The resolution was the council's last order of business, and brought unanimous agreement among aldermen who had been battling on the Monona Terrace issue for more than two hours previously. (See Sec. 2, Page 1.)

On the Inside . . .

Today's Chuckle

Alimony: Bounty on the mutiny.

Overjoyed Family Utters Prayer of Thanks

ARLINGTON, Va. (UPI)—John Glenn's overjoyed wife and children uttered a prayer of thanksgiving Tuesday for the astronaut's successful space flight and then arranged a family celebration.

Mrs. Glenn said she had faith all along in her husband's safety.

Stepping out on the front porch of her brick and redwood rambler home after hours before three TV sets, Mrs. Annie Glenn told reporters she was "very happy" over her husband's historic flight.

Glenn's daughter, Lyn, 14, said she was "very happy, very excited." The astronaut's son, David, 16, well-versed in space lore, said Tuesday was "the biggest day of my life."

The children skipped school to watch their father's flight on TV with their mother, Mrs. Glenn's parents, a small group of friends, and the family pastor, the Rev. Frank Erwin.

The first lights in the Glenn home near Washington went on at 5:45 a. m. EST. Just 45 minutes before he was blasted into

Turn to Page 2, Col. 7

Mrs. John H. Glenn Jr., Daughter Carolyn, and Son David
—AP Wirephoto

Wisconsin  State Journal

WEATHER: Four or More Inches of Snow. Windy. Colder Tonight. High Mid-20s.

GOOD MORNING | 26 PAGES, THREE SECTIONS Vol. 203, No. 142 123rd Year | MADISON, WEDNESDAY, FEBRUARY 21, 1962 | ★ ★ ★ | MORNING FINAL 5c

Wisconsin State Journal

WEATHER: Partly Cloudy and Cooler. High in the Upper 40s. Low Near 25.

GOOD MORNING 28 PAGES, THREE SECTIONS Vol. 205, No. 23 123rd Year MADISON, TUESDAY, OCTOBER 23, 1962 Second-class postage paid at Madison, Wis. ★ ★ ★ MORNING FINAL 7c

Full Text of Speech, Page 3

JFK ORDERS CUBA BLOCKADE TO STOP MISSILE BUILD-UP

U.S. Ready To Shoot To Halt Soviet Ships

Navy Men Will Search Cargo for Banned Arms

WASHINGTON (AP) — The United States is ready to sink every Communist bloc ship headed for Cuba which refuses to stop and be searched under the blockade, a defense spokesman said Monday night.

He said this country's blockade fleet, now being deployed, will order any ship of any nation obviously bound for Cuban ports to stop and undergo search by a boarding party if necessary.

Procedure Outlined

(United Press International reported that the spokesman said there are Russian ships now en route to Cuba and "we propose to search them." He did not indicate how soon it would be before U.S. forces might intercept the Soviet vessels.)

The spokesman, under a barrage of questions, made it clear that force would be used if necessary in any case.

In discussing the big force of blockade ships now steaming toward intercept position, the spokesman outlined the procedure this way:

Forced to Stop

Air and sea patrols will be watching vessels move toward Cuba. Their positions will be reported by observation planes and ships. Warships will move in to intercept. They will hail the Cuba-bound ship. If it stops, a boarding party will be sent aboard to look over the manifest.

If offensive weapons or long range missiles or strategic-type aircraft, for instance, are found, the captain of the ship will be told he can head for any port other than Cuba.

If he reufses to change his course, "we will use force to compel him." Force also will be used

Turn to Page 2, Col. 3

Navy Orders 40 Vessels To Blockade

(Compiled from Wire Services)

SAN JUAN, Puerto Rico—The U. S. Navy announced Monday night that more than 40 ships and 20,000 men originally scheduled to participate in maneuvers near here now are "sustaining the blockade" of Cuba.

The men and ships were assembled in the Puerto Rican area under the announced intention of participating in annual Navy-marine maneuvers. They included 6,000 marines who were to have made a practice amphibious landing Monday at the island of Vieques.

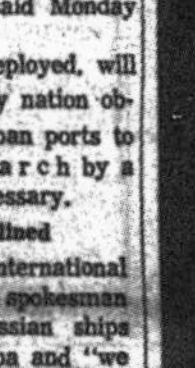

RIVERO

The announcement that the ships and men were diverted to the Cuban arms quarantine was made to newsmen by Lt. Cmdr. John Mackercher shortly after President Kennedy addressed the nation. Mackercher is spokesman for Vice-Adm. Horacio Rivero, under whose command the maneuvers were to have been carried out.

Throughout the Eastern seaboard, military moves were reported during the day. Among the reports:

ONE. Thirteen submarines and

Turn to Page 2, Col. 7

Grim President Kennedy Tells of Cuban Crisis —AP Wirephoto

Today's Chuckle

A bachelor is a rolling stone that has gathered no boss.

Cuba Mobilizes All Its Forces

KEY WEST, Fla. (Tuesday)—(AP)— All of Cuba's military forces have been mobilized as a result "of the news from the United States," Havana Radio said today.

The broadcast said the order was issued by Prime Minister Fidel Castro.

"Our combat units rapidly placed themselves on a fighting basis," said the radio.

The announcement, monitored in Key West, came a few hours after President Kennedy proclaimed a naval blockade against Cuba.

First Dependents From Cuba Base Arrive in U.S.

NORFOLK, Va. (AP) — The first two plane loads of dependents of military and civilian personnel at the Guantanamo naval base in Cuba arrived at Norfolk Monday night aboard Marine Corps turbo jet troop transports.

The Navy said two more transports were expected to arrive later Monday night.

The first plane, carrying 71 passengers, arrived at 6:10 p.m. (EST) after a four-hour flight from Cuba. The second, with 59 passengers, arrived at 7:30 p.m.

The dependents were taken from the Norfolk Naval Air Station to the Little Creek naval amphibious base where they were provided overnight accommodations in barracks buildings.

Mrs. Mary Chapman of Washington, D. C., wife of a navy lieutenant commander, and her teen-aged daughter were among the passengers. She said she had 15 minutes notice to get aboard the plane.

The passengers wore a varied assortment of clothing. Many of the women and children were in shorts.

A navy spokesman said 400 persons were expected to be evacuated by air from Guantanamo. Others will be brought from Cuba by ship.

Castro Slates TV Talk Today

KEY WEST, Fla. Tuesday (AP)— Prime Minister Fidel Castro will address Cuba on radio and television today, a Havana broadcast said this morning.

The radio said Castro "will make important declarations." No other details were given. The hour of the Prime Minister's address was not announced.

There has been no government reaction to the U.S. blockade, but a semi-official Havana television commentator described it as an "act of war" Monday night.

Luis Gomez Wanguemert, editor of the newspaper El Mundo, added that the U.S. appeared not to be heeding Soviet guarantees to defend Cuba.

Offensive Bases Cause Decision

WASHINGTON (AP) — President Kennedy ordered a United States "quarantine" blockade of Cuba Monday night, saying the Soviets are sending Prime Minister Fidel Castro missiles able to rain nuclear destruction on all the Americas.

Mr. Kennedy spoke in a grim emergency nationwide radio-television address in which he disclosed that, despite past Soviet assurances to the contrary, offensive atomic missile sites are being built in Cuba and Soviet jet bombers capable of carrying nuclear weapons have arrived there.

Mr. Kennedy outlined a program for fast military and diplomatic action to stop Cuba from being built up as a Communist launching base against the hemisphere and sent a letter to Soviet Premier Nikita Khrushchev calling for a halt.

Series of Swift Developments

Speedy developments amid an atmosphere of deep crisis followed the President's somber announcement:

ONE. A Defense Department spokesman said the U. S. is ready to sink every Communist-bloc ship headed for Cuba which refuses to stop for a search. The blockade, which could apply against planes later, applies against offensive weapons but not non-military necessities like food or medicine. **(See Story, Col. 1).**

TWO. The Navy said at San Juan, Puerto Rico, that the more than 40 ships and 20,000 men assembled for announced annual Caribbean exercises now are "sustaining the blockade" of Cuba. **(See Story, Col. 1).**

In Washington, the San Juan announcement was denied by Defense Department spokesmen. But the Pentagon would not say what was being done in the area.

THREE. The U. S. summoned the Organization of American States (OAS) to an emergency session here at 9 a. m. CST today in expectation that the inter-American group will approve the U. S. program, thereby giving it international legal standing. **(See Story, Page 3).**

FOUR. Canada said it has stopped Soviet planes bound for Cuba and the Caribbean from landing at Canadian air bases, such as the one at Gander, Nfld.

Soviets Man Missile Bases

State Department officials prepared a formal proclamation to be issued today after the OAS action.

Mr. Kennedy used the word "quarantine" to describe the naval ring around Cuba, since "blockade" implies an act of war. State Department authorities said, however, that the U. S. act included the essential elements of a blockade — inspection, visit, and search.

At the United Nations, U. S. Ambassador Adlai E. Stevenson called for an emergency meeting of the UN Security Council, which is expected to take place this afternoon. He sought a Security Council order for "immediate dismantling and withdrawal" of all offensive weapons in Cuba. **(See Story, Page 2).**

A Defense Department spokesman said Soviet missilemen are manning 1,200-mile range rockets in Cuba on mobile launch pads aimed at key American cities including Washington.

Plea Aimed at Khrushchev

Mr. Kennedy warned in his speech that any atomic attack against any nation in the Western hemisphere would bring full retaliation against the Soviet Union.

He coupled with this an invitation to Khrushchev

Turn to Page 2, Col. 4

JFK, Johnson Cancel All Political Trips

WASHINGTON (UPI) — President Kennedy and Vice-President Lyndon B. Johnson Monday night cancelled all further 1962 congressional campaign appearances due to the gravity of the Cuban situation.

This was announced by the White House shortly after Mr. Kennedy went on radio and television to tell the nation that he was clamping a blockade on arms shipments to Cuba.

JOHNSON

The campaign decision means that the President was dropping plans to visit nearly a dozen states between now and the Nov. 6 election.

Mr. Kennedy suddenly cancelled a trip to seven Midwestern and Western states Saturday and returned to Washington.

"He is definitely not going to participate any further in the campaign of 1962," said White House Press Secretary Pierre Salinger. "He plans to remain here in Washington at least for the foreseeable future."

Other Cuba Stories, Pages 2, 3, 4, 8, and Sec. 2, P. 1

Kuehn, Reynolds Clash Sharply Over Finances in Debate on TV

MILWAUKEE (UPI) — Republican Philip G. Kuehn and Democrat John Reynolds clashed on state financing Monday night in their first face-to-face showdown of the 1962 campaign for governor.

They accused each other of trying to fool the taxpayer who foots the bill.

The two major gubernatorial candidates appeared on an hour-long debate televised and broadcast in Milwaukee and Madison to deal with the question of state fiscal and tax policy. Kuehn and Reynolds both said they would let the home audience decide who had "won" in the Nov. 6 election.

It was the only scheduled meeting of the two candidates during the campaign.

Kuehn said the income tax plan Reynolds proposed to pay for state government operations would give Wisconsin the highest income tax of any in the nation. He said Reynolds' plan would send Wisconsin backwards and "business and industry will shy away."

KUEHN REYNOLDS

Reynolds said Kuehn was advocating a tax policy as part of a "drive of reactionaries for the rich to tax the poor."

Basically, Kuehn repeated his stand to freeze the state income tax while instituting a 3 per cent general sales tax with a credit refund feature.

Reynolds repeated his call for repeal of the state's current 3 per cent selective sales tax and reliance on an income tax for the needed state revenue. Reynolds, however, would keep a 3 per cent excise tax on liquor, tobacco, and automobiles.

Kuehn charged Reynolds, who has campaigned the past six years on a "beat-the-sales-tax" motto had, in fact, "accepted the sales tax concept" with his excise tax proposals for the three items.

The candidates charged each other with "fraud" for the claims that each of their plans would raise the needed revenue for Wisconsin's increased state spending.

Kuehn and Reynolds remained fairly calm during the periods in which they made their opening and closing statements, but during a question period, which lasted about 25 minutes in the middle of the program, they had exchanges and rebuttals which showed emotion.

Both agreed at the outset the program was probably "anti-

Turn to Page 2, Col. 1

On the Inside . . .

World Reacts Cautiously to U.S. Action

(By Associated Press)

The British Foreign Office commented today that President Kennedy's disclosure of a Soviet build-up in Cuba "will come as a shock to the whole civilized world."

A spokesman said Prime Minister Harold Macmillan was told in advance of the contents of the President's speech when U.S. Ambassador David Bruce called on him Monday.

The spokesman reported the Prime Minister would call a cabinet meeting for later today to consider the new Cuban situation in the light of Mr. Kennedy's speech.

In Ottawa, Canada has stopped Soviet planes en route to Cuba and the Caribbean from landing at Canadian air bases such as Gander, Nfld., Foreign Secretary Howard Green said Monday night.

In Moscow, Mr. Kennedy's speech came through on news

KHRUSHCHEV MACMILLAN GREEN ADENAUER

services two hours after midnight and found the city asleep.

But violent Soviet reaction to the stop-and-search blockade of aggressive arms headed for Cuba seemed inevitable.

The Soviet radio and official press agency Tass Monday carried reports of the American operations in the Caribbean.

"Washington is once again raising its armed fist over Cuba and once again threatening the peace and tranquility of the people," said a Moscow Radio commentator some hours before the Kennedy speech.

This paralleled statements made by Tass earlier in the day which had given a detailed outline of the building on Key West airfield of the movement of the various air carriers and other vessels.

In West Germany, a spokesman said Chancellor Konrad Adenauer's government "welcomes the determination of the U.S. government to counter the dangers arising from this situation."

The spokesman said his government already has made sure no war material reached Cuba aboard German vessels.

Mr. Kennedy's speech was relayed by radio direct to most European countries. Most radio stations extended their program time to carry his words, since European time is five hours and more ahead of Eastern time in the U.S.

West Berlin radio stations worked quickly on a translation to put out a report of the speech both to West and to Communist East Germany.

U.S. troops in Germany heard

Turn to Page 2, Col. 4

Wisconsin State Journal

WEATHER: Sunny, Windy, Warmer Today; High Near 50. Low Tonight 40. Fair Saturday.

GOOD MORNING 50 PAGES, FOUR SECTIONS Vol. 205, No. 40 123rd Year · MADISON, FRIDAY, NOVEMBER 9, 1962 Second-class postage paid at Madison, Wis. ★ ★ ★ MORNING FINAL 7c

Red Ship Inspection Today

ALL CUBA ROCKETS LEAVE

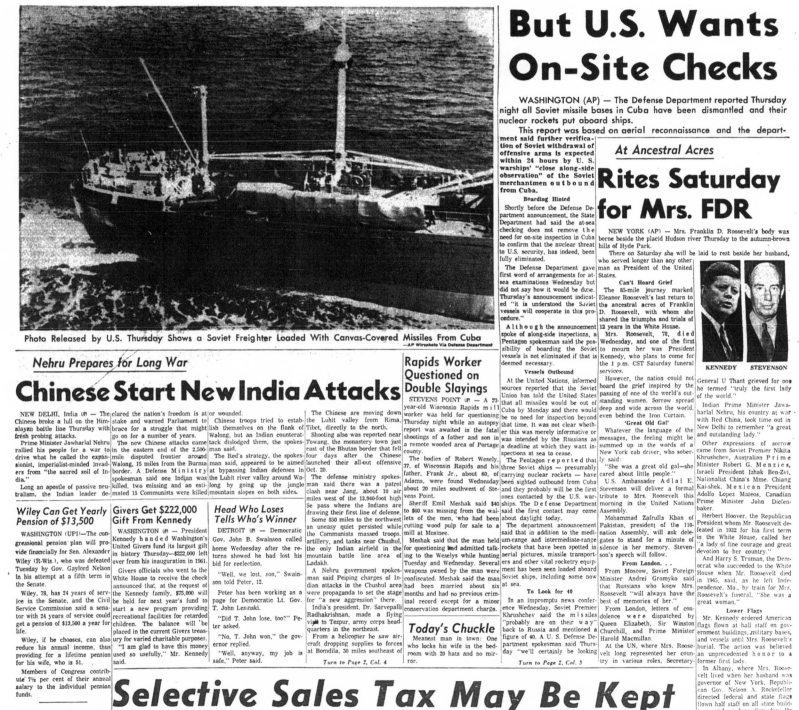

Photo Released by U.S. Thursday Shows a Soviet Freighter Loaded With Canvas-Covered Missiles From Cuba
—AP Wirephoto Via Defense Department

But U.S. Wants On-Site Checks

WASHINGTON (AP) — The Defense Department reported Thursday night all Soviet missile bases in Cuba have been dismantled and their nuclear rockets put aboard ships.

This report was based on aerial reconnaissance and the department said further verification of Soviet withdrawal of offensive arms is expected within 24 hours by U. S. warships' "close along-side observation" of the Soviet merchantmen outbound from Cuba.

Boarding Hinted

Shortly before the Defense Department announcement, the State Department had said the at-sea checking does not remove the need for on-site inspection in Cuba to confirm that the nuclear threat to U.S. security, has indeed, been fully eliminated.

The Defense Department gave first word of arrangements for at-sea examinations Wednesday but did not say how it would be done. Thursday's announcement indicated "it is understood the Soviet vessels will cooperate in this procedure."

Although the announcement spoke of along-side inspections, a Pentagon spokesman said the possibility of boarding the Soviet vessels is not eliminated if that is deemed necessary.

Vessels Outbound

At the United Nations, informed sources reported that the Soviet Union has told the United States that all missiles would be out of Cuba by Monday and there would be no need for inspection beyond that time. It was not clear whether this was merely informative or was intended by the Russians as a deadline at which they want inspections at sea to cease.

The Pentagon reported that three Soviet ships — presumably carrying nuclear rockets — have been sighted outbound from Cuba and they probably will be the first ones contacted by the U.S. warships. The Defense Department said the first contact may come about daylight today.

The department announcement said that in addition to the medium-range and intermediate-range rockets that have been spotted in aerial pictures, missile transporters and other vital rocketry equipment has been seen loaded aboard Soviet ships, including some now at sea.

To Look for 40

In an impromptu news conference Wednesday, Soviet Premier Khrushchev said the missiles "probably are on their way" back to Russia and mentioned a figure of 40. A U. S. Defense Department spokesman said Thursday "we'll certainly be looking

Turn to Page 2, Col. 3

At Ancestral Acres

Rites Saturday for Mrs. FDR

NEW YORK (AP) — Mrs. Franklin D. Roosevelt's body was borne beside the placid Hudson river Thursday to the autumn-brown hills of Hyde Park.

There on Saturday she will be laid to rest beside her husband, who served longer than any other man as President of the United States.

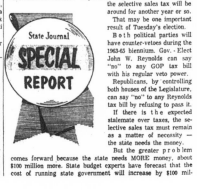

KENNEDY STEVENSON

Can't Hoard Grief

The 85-mile journey marked Eleanor Roosevelt's last return to the ancestral acres of Franklin D. Roosevelt, with whom she shared the triumphs and trials of 12 years in the White House.

Mrs. Roosevelt, 78, died Wednesday, and one of the first to mourn her was President Kennedy, who plans to come for the 1 p.m. CST Saturday funeral services.

However, the nation could not hoard the grief inspired by the passing of one of the world's outstanding women. Sorrow spread deep and wide across the world, even behind the Iron Curtain.

'Great Old Gal'

Whatever the language of the messages, the feeling might be summed up in the words of a New York cab driver, who soberly said:

"She was a great old gal—she cared about little people."

U.S. Ambassador Adlai E. Stevenson will deliver a formal tribute to Mrs. Roosevelt this morning in the United Nations Assembly.

Mohammad Zafrulla Khan of Pakistan, president of the 110-nation Assembly, will ask delegates to stand for a minute of silence in her memory. Stevenson's speech will follow.

From London. . .

From Moscow, Soviet Foreign Minister Andrei Gromyko said that Russians who knew Mrs. Roosevelt "will always have the best of memories of her."

From London, letters of condolence were dispatched by Queen Elizabeth, Sir Winston Churchill, and Prime Minister Harold Macmillan.

At the UN, where Mrs. Roosevelt long represented her country in various roles, Secretary-General U Thant grieved for one he termed "truly the first lady of the world."

Indian Prime Minister Jawaharlal Nehru, his country at war with Red China, took time out in New Delhi to remember "a great and outstanding lady."

Other expressions of sorrow came from Soviet Premier Nikita Khrushchev, Australian Prime Minister Robert G. Menzies, Israeli President Izhak Ben-Zvi, Nationalist China's Mme. Chiang Kai-shek, Mexican President Adolfo Lopez Mateos, Canadian Prime Minister John Diefenbaker.

Herbert Hoover, the Republican President whom Mr. Roosevelt defeated in 1932 for his first term in the White House, called her "a lady of fine courage and great devotion to her country."

And Harry S. Truman, the Democrat who succeeded to the White House when Mr. Roosevelt died in 1945, said, as he left Independence, Mo., by train for Mrs. Roosevelt's funeral, "She was a great woman."

Lower Flags

Mr. Kennedy ordered American flags flown at half staff on government buildings, military bases, and vessels until Mrs. Roosevelt's burial. The action was believed an unprecedented honor to a former first lady.

In Albany, where Mrs. Roosevelt lived when her husband was governor of New York, Republican Gov. Nelson A. Rockefeller directed federal and state flags flown half staff on all state buildings until sundown Saturday. He

Turn to Page 2, Col. 5

Nehru Prepares for Long War

Chinese Start New India Attacks

NEW DELHI, India (AP) — The Chinese broke a lull on the Himalayan battle line Thursday with fresh probing attacks.

Prime Minister Jawharlal Nehru rallied his people for a war to drive what he called the expansionist, imperialist-minded invaders from "the sacred soil of India."

Long an apostle of passive neutralism, the Indian leader declared the nation's freedom is at stake and warned Parliament to brace for a struggle that might go on for a number of years.

The new Chinese attacks came in the eastern end of the 2,500-mile disputed frontier around Walong, 15 miles from the Burma border. A Defense Ministry spokesman said one Indian was killed, two missing and an estimated 15 Communists were killed or wounded.

Chinese troops tried to establish themselves on the flank of Walong, but an Indian counterattack dislodged them, the spokesman said.

The Red's strategy, the spokesman said, appeared to be aimed at bypassing Indian defenses in the Luhit river valley around Walong by going up the jungle mountain slopes on both sides.

The Chinese are moving down the Luhit valley from Rima, Tibet, directly to the north.

Shooting also was reported near Towang, the monastery town just east of the Bhutan border that fell four days after the Chinese launched their all-out offensive Oct. 20.

The defense ministry spokesman said there was a patrol clash near Jang, about 10 air miles west of the 13,940-foot high Se pass where the Indians are drawing their first line of defense.

Some 850 miles to the northwest an uneasy quiet persisted while the Communists massed troops, artillery, and tanks near Chushul, the only Indian airfield in the mountain battle line area of Ladakh.

A Nehru government spokesman said Peiping charges of Indian attacks in the Chushul area were propaganda to set the stage for "a new aggression" there.

India's president, Dr. Sarvepalli Radhakrishnan, made a flying visit to Tezpur, army corps headquarters in the northeast.

From a helicopter he saw aircraft dropping supplies to forces at Bomdila, 30 miles southeast of

Turn to Page 2, Col. 4

Rapids Worker Questioned on Double Slayings

STEVENS POINT (UPI) — A 23-year-old Wisconsin Rapids mill worker was held for questioning Thursday night while an autopsy report was awaited in the fatal shootings of a father and son in a remote wooded area of Portage county.

The bodies of Robert Wesely, 37, of Wisconsin Rapids and his father, Frank Jr., about 60, of Adams, were found Wednesday about 20 miles southwest of Stevens Point.

Sheriff Emil Meshak said $40 to $60 was missing from the wallets of the men, who had been cutting wood pulp for sale to a mill at Mosinee.

Meshak said that the man held for questioning had admitted talking to the Weselys while hunting Tuesday and Wednesday. Several weapons owned by the man were confiscated. Meshak said the man had been married about six months and had no previous criminal record except for a minor conservation department charge.

Today's Chuckle

Meanest man in town: One who locks his wife in the bedroom with 20 hats and no mirror.

Wiley Can Get Yearly Pension of $13,500

WASHINGTON (UPI)—The congressional pension plan will provide financially for Sen. Alexander Wiley (R-Wis.), who was defeated Tuesday by Gov. Gaylord Nelson in his attempt at a fifth term in the Senate.

Wiley, 78, has 24 years of service in the Senate, and the Civil Service Commission said a senator with 24 years of service could get a pension of $13,500 a year for life.

Wiley, if he chooses, can also reduce his annual income, thus providing for a lifetime pension for his wife, who is 51.

Members of Congress contribute 7½ per cent of their annual salary to the individual pension funds.

Givers Get $222,000 Gift From Kennedy

WASHINGTON (AP) — President Kennedy handed Washington's United Givers fund its largest gift in history Thursday—$222,000 left over from his inauguration in 1961.

Givers officials who went to the White House to receive the check announced that, at the request of the Kennedy family, $75,000 will be held for next year's fund to start a new program providing recreational facilities for retarded children. The balance will be placed in the current Givers treasury for varied charitable purposes.

"I am glad to have this money used so usefully," Mr. Kennedy said.

Head Who Loses Tells Who's Winner

DETROIT (AP) — Democratic Gov. John B. Swainson called home Wednesday after the returns showed he had lost his bid for reelection.

"Well, we lost, son," Swainson told Peter, 12.

Peter has been working as a page for Democratic Lt. Gov. T. John Lesinski.

"Did T. John lose, too?" Peter asked.

"No, T. John won," the governor replied.

"Well, anyway, my job is safe," Peter said.

Art Carney Arrested for Drunken Driving

NEW YORK (UPI)—Actor Art Carney, long known for his second banana role to Jackie Gleason, was arrested Thursday on a charge of driving while drunk after his car collided with a taxi in Manhattan.

Police said neither Carney nor the cab driver was injured.

On the Inside . . .

Selective Sales Tax May Be Kept

By WILLIAM C. ROBBINS
(State Journal Staff Writer)

State Journal SPECIAL REPORT

With a "no-general-sales-tax" Democratic governor and a no-income-tax-increase" Republican Legislature, it looks as if the selective sales tax will be around for another year or so.

That may be one important result of Tuesday's election.

Both political parties will have counter-vetoes during the 1963-65 biennium. Gov.-Elect John W. Reynolds can say "no" to any GOP tax bill with his regular veto power.

Republicans, by controlling both houses of the Legislature, can say "no" to any Reynolds tax bill by refusing to pass it.

If there is the expected stalemate over taxes, the selective sales tax must remain as a matter of necessity — the state needs the money.

But the greater problem comes forward because the state needs MORE money, about $100 million more. State budget experts have forecast that the cost of running state government will increase by $100 million during the next two years — without any new spending programs. The present programs of public welfare, education, and the rest will cost about 20 per cent more, mainly because of population increases and cost-of-living increases.

The new governor and the new Legislature will do its most important wrangling over raising that $100 million.

The selective sales tax brings in about $120 million over a two-year period. During his campaign, however, Reynolds proposed to continue the tax on cigarets, liquor, and autos. The repeal of any part of the selective sales tax will increase the amount of new taxes needed to balance the budget.

Following traditional legislative procedure, the Republican lawmakers will wait for Reynolds to bring forward his executive budget and his tax program in bill form. After the budget is amended and passed, the Legislature will then take up the tax bills.

Legislators' Choice

The legislators have the choice of amending the governor's bill or passing a new one of their own. If the Republican lawmakers follow their election program, they will not pass a big income tax increase bill because they say that the rate is as high as it can go for the good of the state's business economy.

If the Democratic governor follows through on his campaign promises, he will veto any bill which expands the present selective sales tax. Apparently there isn't any question on that point.

"I'll keep my promise on that. You can bet your life I will," Reynolds said the morning after the election.

The Republicans do not have the two-thirds vote majority in the Assembly required to override a veto.

Reynolds has until about the first day of Spring to make his final decisions on his tax program, as the governor usually introduces his tax bill in late March, sometimes in early April. Reynolds is expected to make his first proposal anticipating defeat or severe amendment of the bill.

May Add Items

It seems highly unlikely that the Republicans will attempt to pass a general sales tax bill as they did in 1961, knowing that Reynolds would certainly veto it. They might propose to add a few more items to the selective sales tax list.

The time for compromise — or stalemate — will come after the preliminary skirmishes, including the likely defeat of the Reynolds tax bill and/or veto of a Republican substitute.

Passage of another surtax as the final solution can not be ruled out, as distasteful as it would be to legislators of both parties.

Reynolds has proposed to increase the tax on banks and other savings institutions, closing tax "loopholes," and eliminating the state income tax deduction for federal income taxes. This, while it will raise some revenue, will not balance the budget. It will nevertheless be the subject of many news stories out of the State Capitol.

Until one political party gains control of both houses of the Legislature and the governorship, it is likely that Wisconsin will continue to stagger from one side of Tax street to the other.

Minnesota Vote Margin 5 Ballots

MINNEAPOLIS (AP) — Republican Gov. Elmer L. Anderson Thursday night moved to within five votes of Lt. Gov. Karl Rolvaag, his Democratic challenger, on the basis of revised figures from Otter Tail county, one of 87 in the state.

With two small northwoods precincts still unreported, Associated Press figures gave Rolvaag 619,724, Andersen 619,719.

Observers said any firm, final result probably would have to wait the Nov. 20 meeting of the state canvassing board. Even then, on the basis of a predictable thin margin for whoever wins, a recount was regarded as a possibility. (Earlier story, Page 3)

Wisconsin State Journal

WEATHER: Cloudy and Warmer Today, Clearing Tonight Highs, in Upper 70s.

GOOD MORNING | 56 PAGES, THREE SECTIONS Vol. 203, No. 179 125th Year | MADISON, THURSDAY, AUGUST 29, 1963 | Second-Class Postage paid at Madison, Wis. | ★ ★ ★ MORNING FINAL | 7c

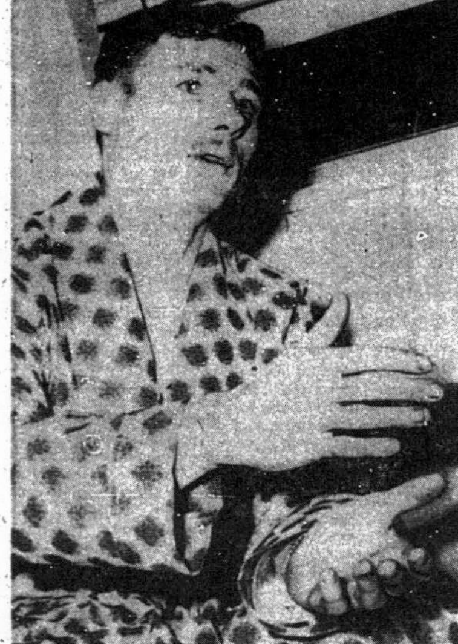

HENRY THRONE

'The ceiling kept getting closer and closer.'

A Miner's Story of the Will To Live

(Copyright, 1963, by the Associated Press)

By HENRY TERONE
(As Told to the Associated Press)

Miners Henry Throne and David Fellin suffered pain, hunger, and thirst while trapped for two weeks more than 300 feet underground in a Pennsylvania mine.

Throne tells how they were haunted by wild hallucinations. He credits man's will to live and constant prayer as factors that helped them to survive. Throne relates his personal story in this exclusive Associated Press article.

HAZLETON, Pa.—There were times when we saw people that weren't there and lights that weren't there and doors that weren't there.

Imagine seeing a door like a regular house door down in the bottom of a mine!

There was a time we heard rain and it really was rain coming down the drainage pipes and we thought the water would back up and flood the mine and drown us.

And while it was raining, I got mad—I must've been off my rocker a little—and I yelled at Davey, "Davey, I'm going home. I'm going alone if you don't want to come."

But, of course, I wasn't going anywhere. Not then. We were still more than 300 feet down. We still had a week to go before we could stand and walk again, not just sit and crawl, before we could breathe clear air again and see real light again.

But maybe I better start at the beginning. That's the only way I can get it clear in my own mind. So much got so mixed up later we couldn't tell day from the night or Monday from Sunday.

That first day, that Tuesday, Aug. 13, I went to work about 7:15 in the morning. It was a nice sunny day. I had no special thoughts, no hunches about something bad. It was just an ordinary working day.

We—that's David Fellin, Louis Bova, and me—we got down in the hole about 7:30 and by 8 we had filled the first buggy (a small wagon carrying coal to the surface). We were on the bottom of the mine, in a tunnel, where the sump water collects. Davey and me were on the right side of the shaft and Louis was on the left, separated by the buggy tracks.

Louis rapped three times for the buggy to go up and it went up and dumped the coal. Coming

(Turn to Page 8)

Speedy Capitol Moves Avert Railroad Strike

8 Bodies Found at Mine in Utah

MOAB, Utah (AP) — The bodies of eight dead miners were reported found Wednesday night after two of seven known survivors were brought up safely from a mine where an explosion had trapped 25 miners more than 2,700 feet underground.

A state official said rescue teams found the bodies about one-half mile into one of the tunnels which extend laterally and downward from the bottom of the mine shaft.

There also was a report the water level was rising rapidly in the tunnel.

There was no word whether the eight included the three dead reported earlier.

Rescuers were still searching for the five miners reported to have survived the initial blast.

The fate of the other men remained a mystery.

Rescuers, who themselves were trapped for up to an hour in the shaft by mechanical failures of the "lift bucket", almost reached the bottom of the main shaft again about 6 p.m., then lost communications with teams at the top.

"We had to bring them back up, it's cost us more time," said Hugh Crawford, chief engineer.

Air Is Good

"But the air is good where the five men are and it's getting better. We aren't too worried about them. They're still behind a lot of debris. They piled up some of it themselves to keep out the gas. That might have saved their lives."

He didn't speculate on the other 15. There has been no sign of them.

No one could guess when the rescuers might reach the five, let alone the other 15.

The main shaft of the mine reaches to a depth of 2,712 feet, but the trapped men are actually farther down than that, caught in two lateral tunnels that reach to 3,200 feet.

No Voice Contact

There has been no voice contact with the five men still down in the shaft who are known to

Turn to Page 2, Col. 1

HEADFRAME AND HOIST
SURFACE
NORTH
SHAFT 2,712 FT.
Men Working at 3,000 ft.
SALT
2,400 FT. DRIFT
3,200 FT. DRIFT
LIMESTONE
POTASH

X Locates Area Where Miners Were Found
—AP Wirephoto Sketch

Washington Needle Cleared After Scare

WASHINGTON (AP) — A brief bomb scare led police to clear the Washington Monument of visitors Wednesday as civil rights demonstrators marched away from the structure.

A quick check showed there was no bomb, however.

Park police who closed the monument said it was only as a "security move," without further details.

The disclosure that there was a bomb report and that it had proved unfounded came from downtown police headquarters a few minutes later.

Spectators at the march had been permitted to go up the monument elevators and view the civil rights march all through the morning. At about 1 p.m., park police cleared everybody from the monument and even refunded money to those who had paid for the ride to the top. They did not clear the area around the base of the monument.

Oscar Rennebohm To Have Checkup

Former Gov. Oscar Rennebohm, 201 Fairwell dr., was admitted Wednesday to University hospital for a medical checkup, hospital officials said.

Today's Chuckle

The best proof that apprearances are deceiving is the fact that the dollar looks just the same as it did ten years ago.

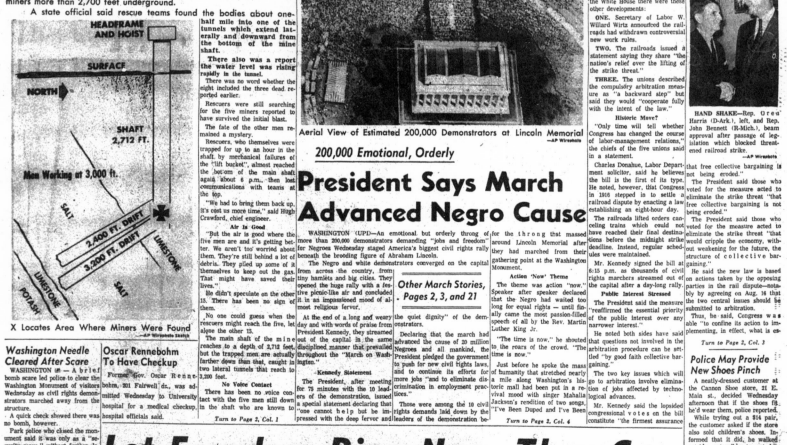

Aerial View of Estimated 200,000 Demonstrators at Lincoln Memorial
—AP Wirephoto

200,000 Emotional, Orderly

President Says March Advanced Negro Cause

WASHINGTON (UPI)—An emotional but orderly throng of more than 200,000 demonstrators demanding "jobs and freedom" for Negroes Wednesday staged America's biggest civil rights rally beneath the brooding figure of Abraham Lincoln.

The Negro and white demonstrators converged on the capital from across the country, from tiny hamlets and big cities. They opened the huge rally with a festive picnic-like air and concluded it in an impassioned mood of almost religious fervor.

At the end of a long and weary day and with words of praise from President Kennedy, they streamed out of the capital in the same disciplined manner that prevailed throughout the "March on Washington."

Kennedy Statement

The President, after meeting for 75 minutes with the 10 leaders of the demonstration, issued a special statement declaring that "one cannot help but be impressed with the deep fervor and the quiet dignity" of the demonstrators.

Other March Stories, Pages 2, 3, and 21

Declaring that the march had advanced the cause of 20 million Negroes and all mankind, the President pledged the government to push for new civil rights laws, and to continue its efforts for more jobs "and to eliminate discrimination in employment practices."

Those were among the 10 civil rights demands laid down by the leaders of the demonstration before the throng that massed around Lincoln Memorial after they had marched from their gathering point at the Washington Monument.

Action 'Now' Theme

The theme was action "now." Speaker after speaker declared that the Negro had waited too long for equal rights — until finally came the most passion-filled speech of all by the Rev. Martin Luther King Jr.

"The time is now," he shouted to the roars of the crowd. "The time is now."

Just before he spoke the mass of humanity that stretched nearly a mile along Washington's historic mall had been put in a revival mood with singer Mahalia Jackson's rendition of two songs, "I've Been Duped and I've Been

Turn to Page 2, Col. 4

Arbitration Set Under New Law

WASHINGTON (AP)—There will be no railroad strike.

Congress passed and President Kennedy signed legislation Wednesday night requiring arbitration of the dispute that threatened to shut down the nation's rail lines at midnight.

Even as the measure was being hurried from the Capitol to the White House there were these other developments:

ONE. Secretary of Labor W. Willard Wirtz announced the railroads had withdrawn controversial new work rules.

TWO. The railroads issued a statement saying they share "the nation's relief over the lifting of the strike threat."

THREE. The unions described the compulsory arbitration measure as "a backward step" but said they would "cooperate fully with the intent of the law."

Historic Move?

"Only time will tell whether Congress has changed the course of labor-management relations," the chiefs of the five unions said in a statement.

Charles Donahue, Labor Department solicitor, said he believes the bill is the first of its type. He noted, however, that Congress in 1916 stepped in to settle a railroad dispute by enacting a law establishing an eight-hour day.

The railroads lifted orders canceling trains which could not have reached their final destinations before the midnight strike deadline. Instead, regular schedules were maintained.

Mr. Kennedy signed the bill at 6:15 p.m. as thousands of civil rights marchers streamed out of the capital after a day-long rally.

Public Interest Stressed

The President said the measure "reaffirmed the essential priority of the public interest over any narrower interest."

He noted both sides have said that questions not involved in the arbitration procedure can be settled "by good faith collective bargaining."

The two key issues which will go to arbitration involve elimination of jobs affected by technological advances.

Mr. Kennedy said the lopsided congressional votes on the bill constitute "the firmest assurance that free collective bargaining is not being eroded."

HAND SHAKE—Rep. Oren Harris (D-Ark.), left, and Rep. John Bennett (R-Mich.), beam approval after passage of legislation which blocked threatened railroad strike.
—AP Wirephoto

The President said those who voted for the measure acted to eliminate the strike threat "that free collective bargaining is not being eroded."

The President said those who voted for the measure acted to eliminate the strike threat "that would cripple the economy, without weakening for the future, the structure of collective bargaining."

He said the new law is based on actions taken by the opposing parties in the rail dispute—notably by agreeing on Aug. 16 that the two central issues should be submitted to arbitration.

Thus, he said, Congress was able "to confine its action to implementing, in effect, what is es-

Turn to Page 2, Col. 3

Police May Provide New Shoes Pinch

A neatly-dressed customer at the Cannon Shoe store, 21 E. Main st., decided Wednesday afternoon that if the shoes fit he'd wear them, police reported.

While trying out a $14 pair, the customer asked if the store also sold children's shoes. Informed that it did, he walked outside, ostensibly to get his youngsters.

He and the new $14 shoes didn't return. He left his old shoes behind.

Let Freedom Ring Now, They Cry

By JEFF GREENFIELD
(Special to The State Journal)

WASHINGTON—"All of my life, I have waited for this to come to pass."

This joyous shout of an aged Negro marcher could well stand as the battle cry of 200,000 persons who jammed Washington Wednesday for the largest such demonstration in the capital's history.

They lined the pool at the Lincoln Memorial clear back to the Washington Monument; they spilled over into parks and clearings; they downed hundreds of gallons of soft drinks. Above all, they sang, cheered, shouted their conviction that racial discrimination must come to an end, and come to an end now.

White and Negro, men and women, they came. From New York alone came 40,000, forming a steady stream down the East coast from midnight until well into the afternoon.

They came up from Alabama and Mississippi; they came from the Midwest (Madison sent 35 participants); and they came from the West coast, too.

They came from Hollywood and Broadway, from the folk music centers, from the suburbs, and from the slums.

Marlon Brando, Burt Lancaster and Sammy Davis Jr., were there. But so were men from the ghettoes of Harlem and the teeming jungle that is Chicago's South side.

It was an orderly demonstration, but an awesome one. Under a blazing Washington sun, 200,000 of them stood in silence for the National Anthem, and listened to the speakers call for an end to racial bias "now—not tomorrow, not next week—but now."

The buses formed lines blocks long; hundreds of them poured out their cargo of demonstrators. They marched in an endless stream to the Lincoln Memorial, waving signs and singing.

It could not be called an organized march; there were too many. The Lincoln mall could not hold them all, and the attractions of shade and refreshments took their share of interest and enthusiasm.

But it was an unforgetable sight; it fulfilled the march leaders' hopes for a "living petition." For it brought tens of thousands of people hundreds and thousands of miles from their homes to stand up for a principle of equality.

It brought black and white down Washington's hot streets together, marching in suit jackets and work clothes, with professionally painted signs and crude, hand-lettered cardboard slogans; but all with the same message:

"Freedom, now."

There were congressmen there, and civil rights officials, glamorous Hollywood stars and famous names. But the main attraction, unquestionably, was the sea of humanity that turned out this hot August day in Washington to demonstrate—peacefully, but passionately—their demands for an equal society.

On the Inside . . .

Braves Trample Colts, 9-1

See the Sports Peach

Wisconsin State Journal

WEATHER: Cloudy and Windy Today. Colder Tonight. High, Near 30. Low, Around 20.

GOOD MORNING | 28 PAGES, THREE SECTIONS Vol. 204, No. 54 125 Year | MADISON, SATURDAY, NOVEMBER 23, 1963 | Second-Class Postage paid at Madison, Wis. | ★ ★ ★ | MORNING FINAL 7c

Johnson Now President

SNIPER MURDERS KENNEDY AS HE RIDES THROUGH DALLAS

JOHNSON SWORN IN—Vice-President Lyndon B. Johnson, flanked by his wife, Ladybird, left, and the widow of assassinated President Kennedy, right, is sworn in Friday as President of the United States by Federal District Judge Sarah T. Hughes of Dallas aboard the presidential plane before returning to Washington.

—Photo From UPI Telephoto by Capt. Cecil Stoughton, Official White House Photographer

Shots Wound Texas Governor

By FRANK CORMIER
(Associated Press Writer)

DALLAS—A hidden gunman shot President Kennedy to death with a high-powered rifle Friday.

Three shots reverberated and blood sprang from the President's face. He fell face downward. His wife clutched his head, crying, "Oh, no!"

Within half an hour, John F. Kennedy was dead and the United States had a new President, Lyndon B. Johnson.

And within the hour, police had arrested a man following the fatal shooting of the President and a Dallas policeman. He was identified as Lee Harvey Oswald, 24, of Ft. Worth. (Story, Column 1.)

The assassination occurred just as the President's motorcade was leaving downtown Dallas at the end of a triumphal tour through the city's streets.

His special car—with the protective bubble down—was en route to the Dallas Trade Mart, where he was to speak.

Governor Not Critical

Witnesses heard three shots. One hit the President in the head and the neck.

The third shot wounded Gov. John B. Connally of Texas in the side, but his condition was reported as "satisfactory" late Friday.

As the gunfire rang in the street, a reporter in the caravan screamed, "My God! They're shooting at the President!"

The motorcade slowed and then sped forward to Parkland hospital.

Onlookers, terrified at the sight and sound of the assassination, dived face forward for protection, fearing more shots. Police swarmed into the scene.

Helped From Car

At the hospital emergency entrance, AP Reporter Jack Bell saw the President stretched out face-down at full length, motionless on the back seat of the car. His suit still looked neat—but there was blood on the floor.

Secret Service men helped Mrs. Kennedy away from the car. Hospital attendants aided Connally and his wife.

It seemed clear that the assassination was carefully planned. In the Texas School Book Depository building, overlooking the overpass, officers found the rifle. They described it as a bolt-action, 6.5 mm. weapon, apparently of Italian make, with a telescopic sight.

Along with the rifle, partly hidden behind books on the fifth floor of the six-story building, were spent cartridges and scraps of fried chicken. The bullets had come from a 45-degree angle as the presidential car passed the building, which has a clear view of the underpass.

Sees Rifle Disappear

The shots were fired at 12:30 p.m. CST, and the President died at 1 p.m. He was 46 and the youngest man ever elected President.

Bob Jackson, a Dallas Times Herald photographer, said he looked around as he heard the shots and saw the rifle barrel disappearing into the fifth-floor window. He did not see the gunman.

Mrs. Kennedy, who was touring the Lone Star state with her husband, sat just ahead of him in the car when a rifle slug ripped a gaping wound in the back of his head and sent him sprawling forward.

Mrs. Kennedy tried to cradle the dying President's head in her arms as the driver sped toward the nearest hospital.

When the President was carried into the emergency room, Mrs. Kennedy walked behind—parts of her clothing drenched with blood.

Never Had Hope

The First Lady remained composed but, inside the emergency room, grasped hands with Mr. Johnson and his wife, Ladybird, in a reflex display of deep anguish.

Shortly after Mr. Kennedy's death—"We never had any hope of saving his life," one doctor said—Mr. Johnson was driven to Dallas' Love field, where he boarded the presidential jet transport, Air Force 1.

(Maj. Ted Clifton, Mr. Kennedy's military aide, was

Turn to Page 2, Col. 3

GOV. JOHN CONNALLY

President John F. Kennedy

Swore Allegiance to Soviet

Suspect Charged With Murder

DALLAS, Tex. (UPI)— Lee Harvey Oswald, 24, a man who once tried to renounce his American citizenship and swore allegiance to the Soviet Union, Friday night was tagged as the hidden assassin who killed President Kennedy.

A murder charge was filed against Oswald shortly before midnight, some 10 hours after he had been arrest on another charge — of slaying a policeman who stopped him for questioning on a suburban Oak Cliff street.

Police dragged Oswald from a movie theater after a fight.

Faces Grand Jury

"I did not kill the President. I did not kill anyone," Oswald told newsmen.

Dist. Atty. Henry Wade said the case against Oswald in the slaying of the President probably would go to a grand jury next week.

Wade refused to say whether fingerprints found on the murder weapon matched those of Oswald.

"I don't want to go into that," he said.

Calculating Killer

Police figured the man who slew the President had to be calculating.

The shots that killed the President and wounded Texas' Gov. John B. Connally came from a preselected spot, with a clear view of the motorcade. And there was evidence the gunman sat and calmly gnawed fried chicken waiting for the moment to shoot.

Police had one suspect, a man with ties to the scene of the shooting. But Oswald after hours of questioning held fast to this contention: I didn't do it.

100 Yards Away

The fatal shots came from the fifth floor from the top of the Texas Schoolbook Depository building, at a 45-degree angle, 100 yards away.

Police know this. They found the rifle, partly hidden behind some books. It was a bolt-action model with telescopic sights. They found spent cartridges and scraps of a meal.

Thousands were in the vicinity. The route of the President had been well-publicized and maps in the newspapers here pinpointed the route the President's car would take.

Policeman Slain

Forty-five minutes after the President was shot, a Dallas policeman was slain and this led to the arrest of Oswald.

The suspect was taken from a small theater and put up a fight—firing once from a pistol and cutting Patrolman M. M. McDonald in a scuffle.

Murder charges were filed against him in the death of the patrolman. Capt. Will Fritz of the Dallas Police Homicide Department said it had been established the man had been in the building from which the shots that felled the President came at the time they were fired.

Oswald, about 5 feet 9 and weighing about 160 pounds, answered the description of a young man sighted at the book depository building just after the President was shot.

Raises Clinched Fist

He was arrogant as he was brought in for questioning. When he saw a crowd of newsmen, he raised his handcuffed hands in a clinched fist.

Police said Oswald worked at the book depository building; had lived in the Soviet Union and married a Russian woman. On Nov. 1, 1959, he had said he was applying for Soviet citizenship.

Someone telephoned police just before 2 p.m. that a suspicious character had been seen entering the theater, a short distance from where Patrolman J. D. Tippett had been slain.

Police Tight Lipped

Just what caused the slaying of Tippett was not immediately clear.

Police said the slaying didn't make sense at first look.

By the time police had brought Oswald from the theater, a large crowd had gathered. It was in an ugly mood and had to be held back.

Police were tight-lipped if they

Turn to Page 2, Col. 6

Mrs. Kennedy Clings to Husband in Death

By PRESTON McGRAW
(United Press International)

DALLAS—Blood spattered her stocking, unnoticed.

She clung to her husband and helped to lift him tenderly to a stretcher.

She watched her husband's vice-president take the oath of office as chief executive, and she embraced him.

Mrs. Jacqueline Kennedy somehow managed to maintain her composure. She seemed almost in a state of shock. Tears came later.

Just minutes before a bullet crashed into her husband's head, she heard Mrs. John Connally tell him, "You can't say Dallas wasn't friendly to you."

As her husband toppled forward in the rear seat of the limousine, Mrs. Kennedy instinctively fell to the floor to hold him.

She stroked his brow. At the hospital, she helped carry him onto a litter brought out of the emergency ward.

Mrs. Kennedy walked into the hospital at the side of her dying husband.

Even in sorrow, she was a striking figure in her bright pink wool suit and pink pillbox hat over her dark hair.

She did not speak. Her husband died as she waited outside the room where he lay. Inside, surgeons were taking desperate measures.

Her thought was to return to Washington to her children, Caroline, 6, and John Jr., who will be 3 next week.

This was Mrs. Kennedy's first political tour with her husband since the 1960 campaign and the

Turn to Page 2, Col. 5

Lee H. Oswald, 24, Center, Prime Suspect in Kennedy Assassination
—AP Wirephoto

On the Inside . . .

Game Postponed

Badger-Gopher Match Reset for Thursday

Details, Sec. 3, Page 1

TV Networks Stick to News

Details, Sec. 2, Page 9

Other Kennedy News

Wisconsin State Journal

WEATHER: Rain Mixed With Snow This Afternoon. Colder. High, Near 40; Low, Near 30.

GOOD MORNING | 32 PAGES, THREE SECTIONS Vol. 204, No. 56 125th Year | MADISON, MONDAY, NOVEMBER 25, 1963 | Second-Class Postage paid at Madison, Wis. | ★ ★ ★ | MORNING FINAL | 7c

NIGHTCLUB OPERATOR KILLS ACCUSED ASSASSIN OSWALD

Lee H. Oswald Begins To Collapse as Bullet From Jack Ruby's Gun, Fired at Point-Blank Range, Smashes Into Him
—Copyright, 1963, by the Dallas Times-Herald and Photographer Bob Jackson, Via AP Wirephoto

Millions Watch Murder on TV

DALLAS (UPI)—Lee Harvey Oswald, accused assassin of President John F. Kennedy, was shot to death at point-blank range Sunday by a self-appointed executioner who pulled the trigger while millions watched on television.

Jack Ruby, 52, operator of a Dallas nightclub and an admirer of **President Kennedy, pierced a massive police security ring that had been set up in Dallas city jail to foil just such an attempt.**

Ruby said nothing to the manacled Oswald as he stepped up to him. He fired once with a .38-caliber snub-nosed pistol held four inches from Oswald's chest.

Ruby, struck while the accused assassin of the 35th President, handcuffed to a policeman, was being transferred to a maximum-security cell. Oswald fell to the floor writhing, and was dead within two hours.

Sunday night, Dist. Atty. Henry Wade said the state would seek the death penalty for Ruby.

"A second assassination doesn't help (justify) the first one," Wade said.

Palm Print Found

Wade disclosed that the "cinch" case against Oswald included a palm print found on the rifle that fired two bullets into Mr. Kennedy's throat and brain Friday while the President rode in a motorcade with his wife.

"As far as Oswald is concerned,

JACK RUBY
when arraigned for murder
—AP Wirephoto

the case is closed," Wade said.

The FBI announced, however, that its investigation was continuing.

Wade added that another Oswald palm print had been found on a box in the fifth-floor room of the building from which the assassin had framed the President in the telescopic sights of an Italian military rifle.

Wade said there was "no concrete evidence" that the pro-Communist Oswald had been assisted by anyone in the assassination.

It was disclosed that Oswald made a trip to Mexico Sept. 26 and stayed for a week. Purpose of the trip was unknown.

Oswald, who steadily denied firing the bullets that killed Mr. Kennedy, died at 12:07 p.m. on an operating table at Parkland Memorial hospital, a few yards from where President Kennedy died 47 hours and 7 minutes before.

Slips By Guards

The shooting of Oswald unfolded before millions of Americans watching on television who saw Ruby, in a snap-brim hat and brown suit, slip through police guards and kill a man whose name will live in infamy.

Ruby, described as "hot tempered," later told his sister, Mrs. Eva L. Grant: "I couldn't help it." Tom Howard, one of four attorneys who volunteered to defend Ruby, said he might plead temporary insanity, on the basis that Ruby was too distrought at the moment to know what he was doing.

Wade said that a man who shoots another in handcuffs "deserves the death penalty."

Subdued by Police

Ruby quickly was subdued by eight police officers after the shooting. He was whisked to a fifth-floor jail cell in the City hall building. An ambulance rushed Oswald, a pro-Communist, pro-Castro ex-Marine, to Parkland Memorial.

There, 12 physicians went to work trying to keep the accused assassin alive. One of them, Dr. Malcolm O. Perry, said Oswald was "lethally injured" when he arrived at the emergency room.

The single bullet passed through his spleen, pancreas, aorta, kidney, and liver, causing what the doctors said was "a massive injury to organs and massive loss of blood."

Said Absolutely Nothing

Oswald was first taken to a room in the hospital called "Trauma No. 2," just 10 feet from Trauma No. 1," in which Mr. Kennedy succumbed after being shot from ambush with Texas Gov. John Connally — who is recovering from chest and shoulder wounds in the same hospital.

Oswald said "absolutely nothing before or after he was shot," said Will Fritz, Dallas homicide chief.

Saturday, speaking to reporters and watched by Ruby, Fritz said flatly that "Oswald killed President Kennedy." The evidence against the former Marine misfit was said to be irrefutable.

Ruby, a onetime Chicago street brawler, operates the Carousel Club, a dimly-lit walkup strip joint complete with runway. He

Turn to Page 2, Col. 3

Widow Returns to Rotunda

Thousands View Kennedy Casket

WASHINGTON, Monday (UPI) — Thousands upon thousands of Americans filed past the coffin of John Fitzgerald Kennedy throughout the night in an outpouring of national grief.

Twice — once in the afternoon and then later during the night his widow was at the bier.

The vast throngs waited for hours in the chill night in patient lines that at times stretched more than two miles. By midnight — when the temperature outside was 38 degrees—more than 100,000 persons had filed into the Capitol Rotunda where the body of the late President lay in state. Police said the line seemed to be growing.

Dignitaries from more than 50 countries flew into Washington to join the tribute to the President at the Mass at 11 a.m. CST today and at the burial in Arlington National cemetery.

Astronaut Pays Tribute

It was nearly 11 p.m. CST when Astronaut John Glenn and his wife paid tribute. Shortly afterward Sen. Edward Kennedy (D-Mass.), the President's youngest brother, arrived and knelt for a prayer. His mother, Rose, had been there earlier. President Eamon De Valera of Ireland also was there.

On her second visit, Mrs. Jacqueline Kennedy again knelt and kissed the flag-draped casket as she had done earlier when the body of her husband was placed in the Rotunda.

She appeared unexpectely at 8:07 p.m. CST as thousands still waited in somber silence to share her grief. Then, accompanied by the President's brother, Atty. Gen. Robert F. Kennedy, she walked for several blocks only when she was recognized by passers-by did she step into a car which had been following her.

A little later, the President's mother, Mrs. Rose Kennedy, recently arrived from Massachusets, knelt with other family members beside the bier. At that time, 60,000 already had paid their respects.

It was the first time the mother had been in her son's presence since he fell before the sniper's bullet in Dallas Friday. A few hours before had come word that the President's assassin, Lee Oswald had been slain.

Mrs. Jacqueline Kennedy, veiled in black, personally relinquished her slain husband to the people at the conclusion of ceremonies that began with a procession to Capitol Hill and ended with her first kiss on the closed casket.

Moving Eulogies

After brief but moving eulogies Mrs. Kennedy, with Caroline, 6 Wednesday, at her side, walked to the bier, knelt with the child and placed her lips on the covering flag.

John F. Kennedy Jr., who is 3 today, had been standing quietly with his mother. But shortly before she walked forward he became restless and tried to make friends with those nearby. A naval aide led him away.

Then some seven hours later she suddenly appeared in the Rotunda from the night with Robert Kennedy at her side. Again she knelt and kissed the casket. After a moment she rose and looked dazedly about, until the attorney general took her arm and led her outside.

Procession Route

The people paying their respects at the Capital — and police were certain all could not possibly be admitted before the funeral — came from Washington and its

Turn to Page 2, Col. 4

Related Stories

BEREAVED FAMILY — Mrs. John F. Kennedy stands at a White House entrance with her children, John Jr. and Caroline, Sunday before joining the procession in which her husband's body was borne from the Executive Mansion to the Capitol.
—AP Wirephoto

On the Inside . . .

Wisconsin State Journal

WEATHER: Fair and Sunny Today. Highs in the Upper 80s. Low, 65.

GOOD MORNING | 30 PAGES, THREE SECTIONS Vol. 202, No. 94 125th Year | MADISON, FRIDAY, JULY 3, 1964 | Second-Class Postage paid at Madison, Wis. | ★ ★ ★ | MORNING FINAL | 7c

PRESIDENT JOHNSON
'we must not fail'

LBJ SIGNS STRONGEST RIGHTS LAW IN CENTURY

Where To Go, What To Do

Good morning!

A happy Fourth of July weekend to you.

The state will be humming with activity today through Sunday, with all the parades, races, ball games, and other assorted celebrations going on.

The biggest, most colorful Fourth of July program in all Wisconsin will be Milwaukee's circus parade. The spectacular is well worth the 70-odd mile trip to Milwaukee.

But if you don't feel like fighting the holiday traffic, the East Side Business Men's Assn. (ESBMA) Fesival will make it worth your while to stay in Madison. And an assortment of concerts and the Vilas park fireworks display nicely rounds out the weekend.

'Milwaukee, Madison, Mineral Point—Where? Where?'

In Milwaukee

CIRCUS — The Ringling Brothers and Barnum and Bailey circus will give its final performances in Milwaukee at 2 and 8 p. m. today at the Arena. Tickets are still available and may be purchased at the door.

PARADE — The "Day in Old Milwaukee" circus parade begins at 2 p. m. Saturday. (See map on Page 2 for route.) Leading off the parade will be 100 antique cars, followed by 34 parade wagons, four calliopes, a hundred clowns, horses, elephants, hippopotami, lions, tigers, camels, llamas, and 30 musical units. The parade will take 3 hours to pass a given spot.

AND FIREWORKS — A one-hour fireworks display, with 3,000 aerial shells, will begin at 9:45 p. m. on a carferry in Milwaukee harbor.

HOW TO GET THERE — Highway travel to Milwaukee Saturday is expected to be heavy, so come early, park far outside the congested downtown district, and take city buses downtown to the 5-mile parade route. Take Highway 30 to Milwaukee, turn onto the expressway (it merges with Highway 30 at the edge of Milwaukee county), and continue downtown to the 35th or 27th street viaducts. Park the car, and then take a downtown bus (they come along every five minutes or oftener) to a good viewing spot.

Or if you prefer, you can park at Mayfair shopping center, Highway 100 and North ave. Special buses will operate from Mayfair to downtown.

In Madison

EAST SIDE FESTIVAL — Tops on the list of Madison activities this weekend is the ESBMA Festival at Voit Field, 3400 block Milwaukee st. The Festival will be open from 6 p. m. to midnight today, and from noon to midnight Saturday and Sunday. The Festival includes rides, 4-H displays, band concerts, and exhibits.

FIREWORKS FOR THE FOURTH — The Madison Central Lions club will join the new Madison West Lions club to co-sponsor the annual Fourth of July fireworks display at Vilas park at dusk Saturday. The Madison City Band will play from 7 p. m. until the fireworks begin.

MUSIC — Two concerts Saturday, at 10 a. m. and 2 p. m. in the University of Wisconsin field house, will climax the junior high school session of the university's 35th anniversary summer music clinic. The morning concert will feature two bands and a chorus. Massed bands and chorus and an orchestra will perform in the afternoon.

The Madison City Band will open its Vilas park concert series with concerts at 3 and 7 p. m. Saturday and 3 p. m. Sunday.

The Madison Summer Symphony will hold a concert at 8

Turn to Page 2, Col. 3

It's Written in the Wind That Luci's 17

Luci Johnson, the teen-ager who sparkles around the White House, huffs and she puffs and she blows out the candles on her birthday cake Thursday as she observes her 17th birthday.

The long-time Johnson family cook, Zephyr Wright, whipped up the lemon cake, which is Luci's favorite. Clothes-conscious, like many a teen-ager, Luci received mostly clothes as presents. —AP Wirephoto

He Asks End to All Trace of Injustice

WASHINGTON (AP) — President Johnson signed the strongest civil rights law in nearly a century Thursday night, only three hours after Congress approved it, and called on Americans to "eliminate the last vestiges of injustice in America."

In an historic ceremony in the East room of the White House, Mr. Johnson pledged himself to "faithful execution" of the statute and announced immediate steps to insure its enforcement.

'Kind of Testing'

Mr. Johnson delivered a conciliatory statement to the nation, by radio and television, and to more than 200 lawmakers, civil rights leaders, and government officials on the spot who helped bring the sweeping legislation to enactment.

"We have come now to a kind of testing," Mr. Johnson said. "We must not fail.

"Let us close the springs of racial poison. Let us pray for wise and understanding hearts. Let us lay aside irrelevant differences and make our nation whole.

"Let us hasten that day when our unmeasured strength and our unbounded spirit will be free to do the great works ordained for this nation by the just and wise God Who is the Father of all."

What's Right

Then dignitaries clustered around him, each to claim one of the 72 pens with which he put his signature to the bill delivered from the Capitol with extraordinary speed after the 289-to-126 House vote which ended long and bitter congressional debate.

He appealed for voluntary compliance and predicted it will be given "because most Americans are law - abiding citizens who want to do what is right."

All provisions of the bill go into effect immediately except that barring discrimination in employment. That equal opportunities section takes effect in one year.

National Authority

In what was clearly an effort to calm the indignation of many Southerners and refute the objections of those who have denounced the measure as an invasion of states rights, Mr. Johnson told the country:

"It provides for the national

Turn to Page 2, Col. 1

Reaction: Compliance to Defiance

ATLANTA (AP) — Passage of the civil rights bill by Congress brought a variety of reaction in the South ranging from ready compliance to outright defiance.

Lester Maddox, operator of a segregated restaurant in Atlanta, said he would go to jail before he would serve Negro customers. Charles Lebedin, who said demonstrators had ruined his restaurant business, displayed a huge sign in a window offering to sell out at a reasonable figure.

Refuse To Comply

Gov. Paul Johnson of Mississippi said "there are tremendous dangers in the enforcement" of the law.

GOV. JOHNSON

He said he felt businessmen should refuse to comply with the law until it had been tested in the courts because "many people feel it is unconstitutional."

Integrationists, he said, should move "with caution, or we're going to have some chaotic days."

Urges Compliance

Directors of the Georgia Restaurant Assn. urged members to abide by the civil rights act. The association vigorously opposed the bill but said with its passage "we have no alternative but to comply."

The Fulton (Atlanta) county grand jury urged compliance with the new law "in fact and in spirit, for where law ends tyranny begins."

A number of Atlanta hotels, motels, and restaurants voluntarily dropped racial bars even before passage of the civil rights bill became certain.

In South Carolina, most hotel, motel, and restaurant owners who would comment indicated that they would abide by the law. But one, who declined to be quoted, said he had no intention of serving Negroes.

Not Much Change

Hugh Smith, manager of the Wade Hampton hotel in Columbia, S.C., said he believed there would be so little business for major hotels from Negro customers "that it won't be noticed."

Another South Carolina hotel manager who declined use of his name said he expected hotels,

Turn to Page 2, Col. 5

Congressmen Get $7,500 More

Senate Gives Pay Raise to 1.7 Million Workers

WASHINGTON (AP)—The Senate pased, 58 to 21, Thursday a $564-million pay raise bill boosting salaries for federal executives and judges, members of Congress, and 1.7 million rank-and-file workers.

(Wisconsin's two Democratic senators, William Proxmire and Gaylord Nelson, voted with the majority in approving the pay raise bill.)

The legislation, strongly urged by President Johnson as essential to keep talented people in government, goes back to the House, which passed a $533-million version last month.

Just before passage, however, the Senate took a crack at the nine Supreme Court justices by voting 46 to 40 to cut their raises to $2,500 a year.

(Proxmire and Nelson also joined the majority in voting to cut the increase provided for Supreme Court justices.)

The Administration, the House, and the Senate Postoffice and Civil Service committee had proposed the same $7,500 hike for the justices as awarded all other federal jurists.

In two days of debate, the Senate resisted all efforts to cut out, or defer until the federal budget is balanced, the $7,500 raises for senators and representatives. They now receive $22,500.

The measure carries increases of $10,000 for cabinet members, boosting them to $35,000, and $7,000 or more for 367 other government executives.

A total of 477 federal judges, including those who retired, would get $7,500 increases, with only the members of the Supreme Court limited to $2,500.

The 1.1 million classified civil service workers would get raises averaging 4.3 per cent, but these

Turn to Page 2, Col. 8

It'll Be Warm Through Holiday, and Maybe Rain

Temperatures will reamain in the upper 80s today and through the July 4 holiday, according to predictions from the Municipal airport weather bureau.

The prediction for today is for fair skies. Saturday should see partly cloudy skies and a chance of scattered thundershowers, the weatherman says.

The low tonight should be around 65.

Wednesday's storm dropped a half inch of rain (.53 of an inch) on Madison and dropped temperatures even more. The mercury fell from 84 degrees at 6 p.m. to 67 at 8 p.m.

Rainfall in Milwaukee was the heaviest since 1961 and the city bailed out from 2.12 inches of rain.

Reynolds Declares Road Emergency

Gov. John Reynolds Thursday officially declared a state of emergency to exist in Wisconsin from noon today until midnight Sunday in an effort to minimize Fourth of July traffic casualties.

He ordered into state service sufficient men and equipment of the Wisconsin National Guard as are necessary to aid members of the State Traffic Patrol.

Reynolds also urged all motorists travelling Wisconsin highways to exercise extreme caution during the period to assist in reducing accidents.

Cards Clip Braves, 4-3

Story in the Peach

Of State's Delegation, Only Van Pelt Against

WASHINGTON (AP) — William Van Pelt (R-Fond du Lac) was the only member of the Wisconsin delegation voting against the civil rights bill when it was passed by the House and sent to President Johnson Thursday.

Boy Candidate's Fate Uncertain

BOSTON (AP) — A 16-year-old boy's candidacy for the Massachusetts House of Representatives hinged Thursday on the fate of a bill setting a minimum age of 21 for holding a seat in the Legislature.

The problem arose when Leonard Tagg, a Weymouth High school student, discovered in the course of a history project that there is no apparent age qualification for holding a seat in the Legislature.

Tagg circulated petitions and obtained more than enough signatures to place his name on the November ballot as an independent candidate for a House seat.

When Tagg's candidacy came to the attention of Secretary of State Kevin H. White, he proposed in a bill to set a minimum wage.

But such a measure requires a four-fifths vote to be admitted for consideration.

The bill now is in the House Rules committte with the legislative leadership still undecided as to whether to act on it on the last day of the session or let White challenge the legality of Tagg's candidacy in the courts.

Today's Chuckle

A man can usually tell what kind of a time he is having at a party by the look on his wife's face.

GOP Leaders Snipe Over Issues

(By United Press International)

Republican leaders sniped at each other Thursday over campaign issues and the struggle of the two leading GOP candidates, Gov. William W. Scranton and Sen. Barry Goldwater, for the nomination.

On Capitol hill, Senate GOP Leader Everett M. Dirksen (Ill.), a Goldwater supporter, criticized the way Henry Cabot Lodge, a Scranton backer, performed in past campaigns.

Assertions, Denials

And GOP spokesmen in Pennsylvania differed publicly over inroads Goldwater has made in the Republican convention delegation in Scranton's home state.

Assertions and denials also surrounded the question of whether former President Dwight D. Eisenhower would come out openly in favor of Scranton at the convention starting July 13 in San Francisco.

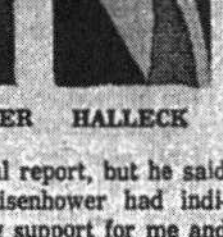

SCRANTON GOLDWATER DIRKSEN LODGE EISENHOWER LANDON ROCKEFELLER HALLECK

Some reports had said that Gen. Eisenhower, at Lodge's request, had agreed to put Scranton's name in nomination at San Francisco. But ABC reported Thursday that Gen. Eisenhower, in a telephone interview from his Gettysburg, Pa., farm, said he had no such plans.

According to ABC, Lodge did make the request at his hour-long meeting with Gen. Eisenhower at Walter Reed Army Medical Center Tuesday but Lodge left the hospital with no assurance one way or the other.

Scranton said he knows nothing of the original report, but he said that Gen. Eisenhower had indicated "strong support for me and is sympathetic to my presidential campaign."

In Topeka, Kans., Alf M. Landon predicted victory for Goldwater in his bid for the nomination.

Filling Ticket

Landon, who has been uncommitted in the struggle for the nomination, said, "It's all over. Sen. Goldwater has it."

He said the party should now turn its attention to filling the rest of the ticket.

Landon, who was the unsuccessful 1936 GOP nominee, suggested that Scranton accept the vice-presidential nomination to balance the ticket.

While the intraparty strife heated up, Scranton met in Eugene, Ore., with members of Oregon's 18-person delegation, which legally is bound to support New York Gov. Nelson A. Rockefeller

Turn to Page 2, Col. 6

On the Inside . . .

Wisconsin State Journal

WEATHER: Sunny and Warm Today. Warmer Thursday. High Near 90. Low Near 70.

GOOD MORNING | 32 PAGES, THREE SECTIONS Vol. 202, No. 127 125th Year | MADISON, WEDNESDAY, AUGUST 5, 1964 ★★★ | Second-Class Postage paid at Madison, Wis. | MORNING FINAL

7c

PRESIDENT JOHNSON
"all necessary measures"
—AP Wirephoto

LBJ ORDERS AIR ACTION AGAINST RED VIET NAM

3 Bodies Found by FBI; Believed Rights Aides

Identifying Waits Tests at Hospital

PHILADELPHIA, Miss. (UPI) —Three bodies believed to be those of three civil rights workers who vanished June 21 were found near here Tuesday in shallow graves.

Authorities were almost certain the male bodies were those of the three young men who disappeared six weeks ago. The bodies were sent by ambulance to Jackson, 70 miles away where doctors were waiting to make positive identification.

Found by FBI

An FBI search party digging in thick underbrush found the bodies about 5 miles southwest of here, a few hundred yards off Highway 21.

The scene was about 20 miles from where the burned-out station wagon used by the workers was found June 22. The vehicle was also found a few hundred yards off Highway 21—a moderately traveled blacktop road.

FBI agents and state highway patrolmen immediately cordoned off the heavily wooded area and investigators began an intensive search for other evidence.

Authorities had planned to fly the bodies to Jackson by helicopter for examination, but high winds in the area prevented this.

Mississippi Gov. Paul B. Johnson issued a statement Tuesday night saying the discovery had been made on a farm near where a new dam had been built.

Governor Pledges Aid

He said his information was that FBI agents who had been searching in the area decided to take a closer look after noting that the dam had collected no water although there had been several showers in the area.

"If these are the bodies of the three civil rights workers the investigating forces of the state of Mississippi will exert every effort to apprehend those who have been responsible for their deaths," Johnson said.

The three workers — Andrew Goodman, 20, New York; Michael Schwerner, 24, Brooklyn;

Turn to Page 2, Col. 8

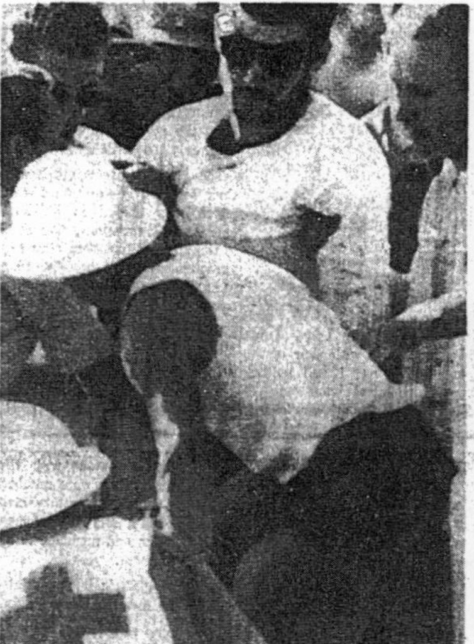

First One Out, Miner Michel Jacques Puts on Sun Glasses as Glare Shield

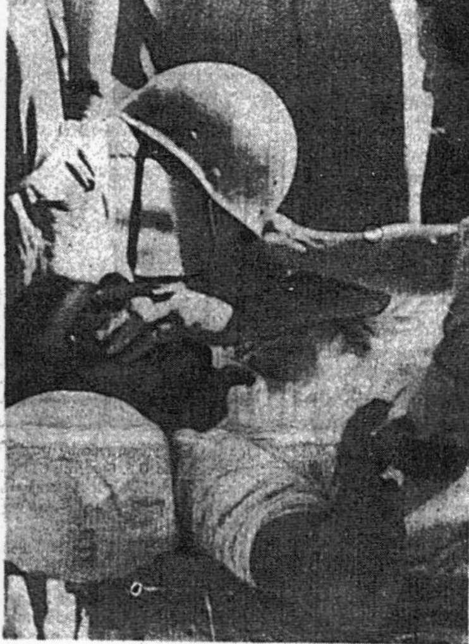

Later, on Stretcher, Even Glasses Weren't Enough, So Helmet Was Used
—AP Wirephotos by Cable from Paris

Frenchmen Ask for Wine

Trapped for 8 Days, Nine Miners Rescued

CHAMPAGNOLE, France (AP) — Nine French miners imprisoned eight days in the collapsed chambers of a deep limestone mine were hauled safely up a rescue shaft Tuesday, ready for a party with red wine and champagne.

Military ambulances sped them to a Champagnole hospital for checkups and any treatment they might need. The miners appeared to be in relatively good condition, though all but two had to be lifted into the ambulances.

Andre Martinet, the mine foreman, was among those who walked from the special aluminum capsule which hauled the men, one at a time, from their prison 270 feet below.

Even those placed on stretchers managed smiles and weak waves to the hundreds of relatives and villagers clustered around the rescue site.

Martinet had been a tower of strength to his men during the uncertainties of their ordeal. Shortly before the drill chewed gingerly through the last crust of rock in the ceiling of the mine, Martinet joked with a doctor on the surface over a telephone.

"I've talked with you quite a lot," Martinet said. "I'd like to see you. And when I come up we will have a party with red wine and champagne."

The only doubt over the fate of five other men who had been down in the Mt. Rivel mine when it collapsed dimmed the otherwise festive air which spread through the village in eastern France near the Swiss border.

Weary drilling teams continued work toward another section of the mine where tapping sounds have been heard. Men and equipment involved in rescuing the nine reinforced the crews probing for additional survivors.

Dust poured from a big drill spinning its bit into the mountainside.

Mayor Andre Socie of Champagnole said soundings provided sufficient reason for a "gigantic new effort" in drilling toward a

Turn to Page 2, Col. 7

Hearnes Leads in Missouri Vote

ST. LOUIS (AP) — Secretary of State Warren E. Hearnes clung to a nearrow lead over Lt. Gov. Hilary A. Bush Tuesday night in their hot battle for the Democratic gubernatorial nomination as counting passed the halfway mark in Missouri's primary election.

Bush stacked up a margin of more than 50,000 votes in his home area of Jackson county (Kansas City) but Hearnes more than made up for that in the St. Louis metropolitan area and in outstate Missouri.

Three other candidates got only token votes.

With 2,672 of 4,332 precincts tabulated, Hearnes had 216,215, Bush 201,805.

Rep. Richard Bolling, Kansas City, faced a stiff challenge in his bid for the Democratic nomination in the Fifth Congressional district but finally won out over County Judge Hunter Phillips.

Forecasters Match Par With High of 90

The Municipal airport weathermen were right on the nose in their prediction Tuesday, with a high of 90 recorded at 4:30 p.m., a low of 66 recorded at 6 a.m., and a decline in that oppressive humidity.

The forecast for today calls for fair weather, with a high in near 90. The low should be near 70.

The average temperature Tuesday was 78, only 6 degrees above the normal 72 for that date.

University of Wisconsin lifeguards reported Tuesday that water temperatures on Lake Mendota reached a warm 80 degrees.

PT Boats Attack 2 U.S. Warships

WASHINGTON (UPI) — Communist North Vietnamese torpedo boats again fired on American warships Tuesday, and President Johnson promptly told the nation that United States warplanes were responding with air strikes Tuesday night against the Red gunboats and their bases.

The Chief Executive, speaking as commander-in-chief of the nation's armed forces, also announced he had asked Ambassador Adlai Stevenson to take the U. S. case to the United Nations Security Council on an urgent basis.

In a dramatic, six-minute statement read on nation-wide television and radio, the President said his was a "solemn responsibility" but that "it is my considered conviction that firmness in the right is indispensable today for peace."

Mr. Johnson also said he had informed leaders of both parties "That firmness will always be measured," he added. "Its mission is peace." in Congress that he would immediately request a resolution "making it clear that our government is united in its determination to take all necessary measures in support of freedom, and in defense of peace, in Southeast Asia.

Assaults Called Outrage

He said the leaders assured him that such a resolution "will be promptly introduced, freely and expeditiously debated, and passed with overwhelming support."

Mr. Johnson described as an "outrage" the Communist assaults in the Gulf of Tonkin off the North Vietnamese coast — two in three days. But at the same time, he stressed that the U.S. retaliation would be "limited and fitting" for the present.

Obviously speaking to the Communists, he said: **"We Americans know, although others appear to forget, the risk of spreading conflict. We still seek no wider war."**

The President's announcement came at 10:35 p.m. CDT, about 13 hours after North Vietnamese PT boats attacked the U.S. destroyers Maddox and C. Turner Joy in international waters of the stormed-tossed gulf.

Destroyers Repulse Attack

The destroyers repulsed the attack after a three-hour battle in which two of the six PT boats were believed to have been sunk and two others damaged. There were no American casualties or damage.

Sunday, the Maddox was attacked in the same waters by three Soviet-built North Vietnamese PT boats. One of the Red vessel was believed sunk and the other two were crippled under fire from the Maddox and jet fighters from the carrier Ticonderoga.

NORTH VIET NAM · CHINA · HANOI · HAINAN · Gulf of Tonkin · LAOS · SOUTH VIET NAM · CAMBODIA · Phnom Penh · SAIGON · 0 100 Miles

Gulf of Tonkin where U.S. ships were attacked
AP Wirephoto Map

Shortly before Tuesday's attack, the State Department announced it had sent a stern diplomatic protest to the Hanoi government warning of "grave consequences" if any new assaults were mounted.

Series of Crisis Talks

The President's statement, coming after a series of crisis talks with high military, diplomatic, and legislative leaders, won the approval of Republican Presidential candidate Sen. Barry M. Goldwater (Ariz.).

In his statement, the President signaled a heavy diplomatic campaign to impress the world with the seriousness with which he considered "repeated acts of violence" against U.S. armed forces.

Make Position Clear

Besides his instructions to Stevenson at the UN, he also directed Secretary of State Dean Rusk to make the American position "totally clear to friends, to adversaries and indeed to all."

The President said it was for him "a solemn responsibility to have to order even limited military action by forces whose overall strength is as vast and as

Turn to Page 2, Col. 3

Barry Backs LBJ's Action

BALBOA, Calif. (UPI) — Republican presidential nominee Sen. Barry M. Goldwater (Ariz.) Tuesday night expressed strong support of President Johnson's course of action in the Southeast Asia crisis, including use of direct military air action against North Viet Nam gunboats and supporting facilities.

"I believe it is the only thing he can do under the circumstances," Goldwater said in a brief prepared statement issued after a personal telephone call from the President outlining his policy.

"We cannot allow the American flag to be shot at anywhere on earth if we are to retain our respect and prestige," said Goldwater, who long has been an advocate of a firmer policy in Southeast Asia.

"I am sure that every American will subscribe to the actions outlined in the President's statement," Goldwater said.

Negroes Toss Molotov Cocktails as New Violence Hits Jersey City

JERSEY CITY, N.J. (UPI)—Hit-and-run Negro raiders Tuesday night hurled dozens of Molotov cocktails and rocks into the streets and set fire to the exterior of an abandoned tenement in sporadic outbursts of violence in a strife-torn Negro neighborhood.

At one point, helmeted police fired a volley of gunshots into the air to disperse a mob of about 60 Negroes. At least three Negro men were arrested on disorderly persons charges in separate incidents.

Police Chief Joseph Smith said there were no injuries from the new disturbances. He said a cache of Molotov cocktails was found in a field near the Booker T. Washington housing project where the rioting first erupted Sunday night.

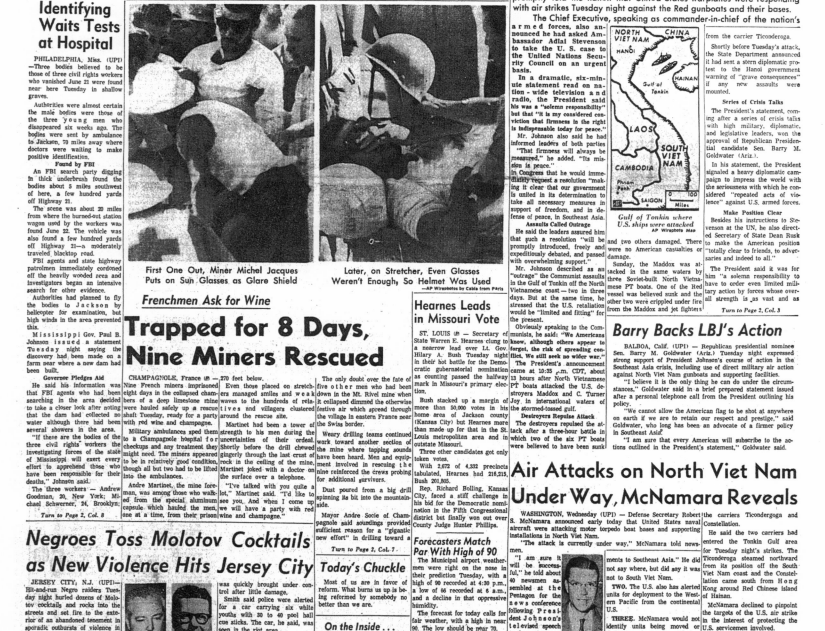

WHELAN HUGHES

The fire in the vacant tenement was quickly brought under control after little damage.

Smith said police were alerted for a car carrying six white youths with 30 to 40 pool hall cue sticks. The car, he said, was seen in the riot area.

Two of the gasoline bombs were thrown from the roof of a four-story tenement where earlier Tuesday two of the same type were tossed at a police car. Negroes also threw rocks at passing cars and exploded dozens of Molotov cocktails on scattered streets.

The Rev. James Trevillion rode the streets using a loudspeaker exhorting residents to stay calm and informing them that addition-

Turn to Page 2, Col. 6

Today's Chuckle

Most of us are in favor of reform. What burns us up is being reformed by somebody no better than we are.

On the Inside . . .

Reds Defeat Braves Twice
Story in the Peach

Air Attacks on North Viet Nam Under Way, McNamara Reveals

WASHINGTON, Wednesday (UPI) — Defense Secretary Robert S. McNamara announced early today that United States naval aircraft were attacking motor torpedo boat bases and supporting installations in North Viet Nam.

"The attack is currently under way," McNamara told newsmen.

"I am sure it will be successful," he told about 40 newsmen assembled at the Pentagon for the news conference following President Johnson's televised speech to the nation.

McNAMARA

McNamara indicated that results of the strike, launched by aircraft from two carriers in the Gulf of Tonkin, probably would not be known before daybreak here.

At the same time he announced these actions:

ONE. The U.S., as a precautionary measure, has moved "substantial military reinforcements to Southeast Asia." He did not say where, but did say it was not to South Viet Nam.

TWO. The U.S. also has alerted units for deployment to the Western Pacific from the continental U.S.

THREE. McNamara would not identify units being moved or their strength. But he said they were from all the services and were "appropriate to the provocation."

In a recital of the naval engagement in the Tonkin Gulf Tuesday, McNamara said it was all but certain that two of the North Vietnamese torpedo boats were sunk, and was probable that a third went to the bottom under the counter-attack of the two U.S. destroyers—Maddox and C. Turner Joy—aided by aircraft from the carriers Ticondergoga and Constellation.

He said the two carriers had entered the Tonkin Gulf area for Tuesday night's strikes. The Ticonderoga steamed northward from its position off the South Viet Nam coast and the Constellation came south from Hong Kong around Red Chinese island of Hainan.

McNamara declined to pinpoint the targets of the U.S. air strike in the interest of protecting the U.S. servicemen involved.

He emphasized that the air strikes were in progress as he met with newsmen and said the targets would be identified "at a time appropriate to the security of our forces."

He did make it clear, however, that the North Vietnamese capital of Hanoi was not being attacked.

The targets were patrol craft bases and "associated facilities"

Turn to Page 2, Col. 1

KC-Shrine Benefit at 7 Tonight at Breese Stevens Field

Wisconsin State Journal

WEATHER: Fair, Warmer Today, Not So Cold Tonight, High In 60s.

GOOD MORNING | 30 PAGES, THREE SECTIONS Vol. 202, No. 180 125th Year | MADISON, MONDAY, SEPTEMBER 28, 1964 ★ ★ ★ | Second-Class Postage paid at Madison, Wis. | MORNING FINAL | 7c

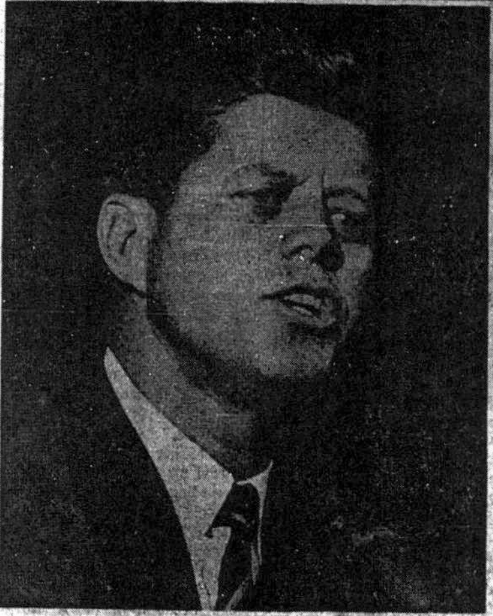

PRESIDENT JOHN F. KENNEDY

'Nightmare' in Dallas Remembered

The author of the following dispatch was in the presidential motorcade when President Kennedy was shot in Dallas last November. He later received the 1964 Pulitzer prize in journalism for national reporting for his eye-witness coverage of the tragedy.

By MERRIMAN SMITH
(United Press International)

WASHINGTON—Reading the Warren Commission report on President Kennedy's assassination was like ripping the bandage from a still-fresh wound.

Or staring into an awful nightmare being played back in painful slow motion on a mottled gray screen.

It was almost a hypnotic experience for one who was riding along Elm st. in Dallas in the fourth car behind the President when he was shot—the hypnosis of re-living through the report's 888 pages a dreadful but still historic happening.

Read Hungrily

A group of my UPI colleagues and I have been closeted on the seventh floor of the National Press building now for most of three days, studying the report line by line and writing a massive layout of news stories.

Skimming through the report for the first time when we received it from the White House early last Friday morning, I found myself reading hungrily.

I was soaking up hundreds of tiny details that I knew for the first time; not particularly important things but such aspects of the case as the pin-point medical record and the way ordinarily stable persons gave widely divergent accounts of how many shots were fired, what Mrs. Kennedy did immediately after her husband was hit (she isn't quite sure), and the thin-lipped city officials who did not want to release the President's body without an autopsy.

'Uneasy Chill'

Then in more careful re-reading, the raw drama began to emerge more clearly—the warped mind of Lee Harvey Oswald, the assassin, and the sleazy, crawling nature of Jack Ruby, the strip-joint loudmouth who exploded into permanent prominence of an evil sort by killing Oswald in the Dallas city jail.

While examining the dry language of reports on the Kennedy autopsy performed after his body was returned to Washington, I felt an uneasy chill of remembrance.

When the Kennedy car stopped at the emergency entrance of Parkland hospital that sunny afternoon, I ran to the side of the vehicle. The President was face down on the back seat, inert, and by all practical measurements, dead at that moment.

'He Didn't Hear'

Mrs. Kennedy cradled her arms around his head and I reported at the time she seemed to be whispering to him. From the Warren commission, I learned she was saying, "I love you Jack." But he didn't hear her. He had heard nothing since Oswald's second bullet blew away part of his head. The autopsy said the head wound measured five inches at its greatest diameter.

As we pored over the report in these recent hours, I recalled how the impact of the assassination, the flight home on the White House plane with the new President, somber and in control, the dead President in his casket and then the moving funeral—how all of these things did not crash down upon me until later.

After the funeral, I dragged home, pulled off my formal clothes and fell into bed. There began night after night of the most horrible dreams I have ever endured.

Scream of Sirens

Over a period of weeks—perhaps months, for I lost count—not a night passed without my hearing in troubled sleep those three sharp rifle shots from the Texas State Book Depository building . . . the scream of sirens . . . the skidding stop in the hospital driveway . . . brown bubbles coming from the chest wound of Gov. John Connally of Texas who also was shot but survived . . . the dark stain spreading down the suit of the face-down Kennedy.

For weeks I seldom slept for more than an hour at a time. There was no effective opiate. At the White House, I discovered Secret Service agents who had been on duty in the motorcade were suffering the same symptoms.

This awful nightmarish period passed eventually, but it comes back again occasionally. And now the Warren report. Dear God, may I never dream again. At least, not this dream.

Warren Commission Rules

OSWALD ALONE KILLED JFK

President, Mrs. Kennedy Smile and Wave in Dallas Parade Just Before He Was Assassinated —AP Wirephoto

No Conspiracy Evidence Found

By SAUL PETT
(AP Special Correspondent)

WASHINGTON — Lee Harvey Oswald — and Lee Harvey Oswald alone — murdered John F. Kennedy.

This was the long-awaited verdict Sunday from the presidential commission headed by Chief Justice Earl Warren of the United States, which also concluded:

ONE. There was no evidence of any conspiracy — foreign or domestic, from the left or the right — involved in the shooting in Dallas on Nov. 22, 1963, in which the U. S. lost its 35th President.

TWO. There was no evidence of any plot or connection between Oswald and the man who killed him two days later—Jack Ruby. Each man, independent of the other, evidently killed for his own emotional reasons.

Three Shots Fired

THREE. The Secret Service precautions for protection of the President were inadequate and did not even include, "as a matter of practice," the checking out of any building along the route of Mr. Kennedy's last motorcade. The FBI failed to alert the Secret Service to the presence in Dallas of Oswald, a known Marxist and one-time defector to Russia.

FOUR. The methods now used for the protection of the President require drastic over-hauling and modernizing.

FIVE. Three shots evidently were fired at the presidential limousine in Dallas in a time lapse ranging between about 4.8 seconds to more than 7. One shot probably missed.

Cause Wounds

Two bullets probably caused all the wounds suffered by

Turn to Page 2, Col. 3

Four Agents Drank a Few Night Before

WASHINGTON (AP)—Four Secret Service men riding behind President John F. Kennedy's car when he was killed had taken a few drinks in violation of rules in the early hours of that day, the Warren Commission said Sunday.

But the commission emphasized that the men did all they humanly could when the fatal bullets struck. The response of some of them "was in the finest tradition of goverment service," it said in its report on the assassination.

The commission gave this account:

Nine agents went off duty about midnight Nov. 21 in Ft. Worth. Hoping for a bite to eat, they stopped in at the Ft. Worth press club. No food was available, but they stayed at the club for periods varying from 30 to 90 minutes. Some drank beer — but no more than three glasses — and some drank mixed drinks—but no more than 1½ drinks each. No agent was intoxicated or act-

Turn to Page 2, Col. 5

Pictures, Page 6; Text of Report, Page 5

Mother Claims Case Not Shut

Can Tear It Apart, She Says of Report

FT. WORTH, Tex. (AP) — The mother of Lee Harvey Oswald slammed her fist down on a bound copy of the Warren Commission report Sunday and declared:

"I can break this whole thing apart—I'm going to make fools of them."

Mrs. Marguerite Oswald said the commission report — which concluded that her son was the assassin of President John F. Kennedy—was "ridiculous . . . I can tear this book apart." She was not specific.

MRS. OSWALD

"I am not bitter, I am indignant. This is not justice," she said.

She said she had been "conditioned" by published accounts of what the report

Turn to Page 2, Col. 8

On the Inside . . .

Braves Topple Phils From First

See the Sports Peach

MAGIC Report Lashed

Atty. Gen. George Thompson Sunday lashed out at State Insurance Commissioner Charles Manson for his tardy report which accused the Madison American Guaranty Insurance Corp. (MAGIC) of violating state laws.

Thompson's blast followed the report by Manson Saturday which cited 11 "comments and recommendations" concerning MAGIC's financial operations. Manson sent a letter with the report to Thompson promising the cooperation of his office.

To which Thompson said Sunday: "In this connection I cannot overlook your public declaration on Aug. 27 that the operations of this company (MAGIC) and its officers were apparently satisfactory and your department was no longer concerned about the financial structure of the company."

"Neither can I ignore the fact," Thompson continued, "that until I demanded your removal and threatened court action, in the absence of assistance from the governor, you not only refused to cooperate with my office and the Department of Securities, but actually withheld (MAGIC's) books after the Department of Securities, at my request, had made authorized arrangements for their availability."

Thompson, a Republican, demanded Manson's resignation on Sept. 2 in a letter to Gov. John W. Reynolds, a Democrat. The governor has not made any of-

Turn to Page 2, Col. 6

4 Die, Dozens Hurt as Trains Crash in Illinois

MONTGOMERY, Ill. (AP) — At least four persons were killed and dozens injured when a Burlington route passenger train crashed head-on with a Rock Island line passenger train standing still on a siding in Montgomery just before midnight Sunday.

A Burlington spokesman said the two-man engine crew of the Rock Island train was killed along with a railroad pilot on the Burlington train.

The pilot is a company official who accompanies an engine crew not familiar with the route. It was not immediately learned who the other fatality was.

Fire department units from at least 10 surrounding communities converged on the scene.

The Montgomery fire department spokesman described the crash as "very, very bad."

Montgomery is located about 40 miles west of Chicago.

At least 24 persons were taken to Copley hospital in Aurora. Others were taken to St. Joseph and St. Charles hospitals, also in Aurora.

Quick Action by Agent Credited With Saving Mrs. Kennedy's Life

WASHINGTON (UPI) — Jacqueline Kennedy's stunned first reaction to the sight of her mortally wounded husband in Dallas might have caused her own death but for the quick action of a Secret Service agent.

This was disclosed Sunday in the Warren Commission's report. Its pages recalled again the former First Lady's day of horror on Nov. 22, 1963.

MRS. KENNEDY

Photographs taken seconds after John F. Kennedy's assassination showed Mrs. Kennedy climbing over the back seat of their limousine and onto the trunk. Agent Clinton J. Hill was struggling to hop aboard the rear of the accelerating car.

In the commission's report, Hill recalled:

"Mrs. Kennedy had jumped up from the seat and was, it appeared to me, reaching for something coming off the right rear bumper of the car. She turned toward me and I grabbed her and put her back in the back seat, crawled up on top of the back seat, and lay there."

Presidential assistant David F. Powers, a close friend of the Kennedys, saw the scene from a followup car in the motorcade.

Powers said that "Mrs. Kennedy probably would have fallen off the rear end of the car and been killed if Hill had not pushed her back into the presidential automobile."

Mrs. Kennedy later could not remember climbing onto the back of the car.

Hill, who is still Mrs. Kennedy's Secret Service guardian, received a special citation from President Johnson.

Passes Depository

The presidential tour of Texas had been one of happy triumph for the First Lady.

When the President asked Powers the first night what he thought of their reception in San Antonio and Houston, Powers replied:

"The crowd was about the same as the one which came to see him before but there were about 100,000 extra people on hand who

Turn to Page 2, Col. 7

Warren Report Copies Available

A summary of the Warren Commission report on the assassination of President John F. Kennedy last Nov. 22 will be found in Sec. 1, Page 5 of today's Wisconsin State Journal.

In cooperation with the Associated Press and newspapers throughout the nation, The State Journal will distribute the complete report in book form by mail for $1.50 per copy.

For copies of the "Warren Commission Report", please use coupon on Sec. 1, Page 5, and mail your order directly to AP-Wisconsin State Journal, Box 66, Poughkeepsie, N.Y. Allow three weeks for delivery.

President Returns by Plane to Capitol

AUSTIN, Tex. (AP) — President Johnson arrived by plane in Washington Sunday night after a brief weekend visit to his ranch at Johnson City, Tex.

Today's Chuckle

Architect of ultra-modern church to minister: "Know what would be nice? Bucket pews."

Oswald Lived in Fantasy, Never Felt That He Belonged Anyplace

WASHINGTON (UPI) — Lee Harvey Oswald "never found anything to which he felt he could belong."

He imagined himself to be a big shot—"the commander." But most of those who knew him considered him meek and harmless. He needed to be admired. But not even his mother felt much affection for him. In school the other kids teased him. In the Marine Corps he was known as "Ozzie the rabbit."

In Russia, to which he defected, the Communists put him to work instead of lionizing him. Fidel Castro's Cuba refused to receive him. His wife, Marina, laughed at his political notions and complained publicly about his inadequacies as a husband.

She thought he could be happy "only on the Moon, perhaps."

LEE HARVEY OSWALD
'kids teased him'

Why did Lee Harvey Oswald kill John F. Kennedy in Dallas, Tex., on Nov. 22, 1963?

Was there ever a time in Oswald's career up to then when someone should have been able to predict: Some day this man will do murder?

The Warren Commission searched for possible motives. Were they political, personal, or simply a desire "to go down in history as a well publicized assassin?"

It found none which "satisfactorily explains Oswald's act if it is judged by the standards of reasonable men."

It discovered no place in Oswald's past where authorities at

Turn to Page 2, Col. 1

Wisconsin State Journal

WEATHER: Sunny, Cool Today. High 50 to 55. Low Tonight in Mid 30s.

GOOD MORNING — 58 Pages, Four Sections — Vol. 210, No. 19 — 127th Year — MADISON, THURSDAY, OCTOBER 19, 1967 — ★ ★ ★ — 10¢

76 HURT IN UW RIOTING; CAMPUS STRIKE RESULTS

Anti-Dow Protesters Fall Back in the Face of Charging Policemen Wielding Nightsticks Outside UW Commerce Building
—State Journal Photo by Norman Lenburg

Police Hemmed; No One Jailed

By JUNE DIECKMANN
(Of The State Journal Staff)

At least 63 protesters and 13 lawmen were injured Wednesday on the Bascom Hill heart of the University of Wisconsin campus where an anti-war sit-in demonstration raged to rioting.

No one was jailed during the afternoon mob action.

"We were too woefully outnumbered to make arrests," Police Chief Wilbur H. Emery said.

Emery said, however, that names of "probably 20 leaders" were taken and will be referred to University and city legal authorities for possible later court action.

Using tear gas and nightsticks, police routed the crowd of nearly 3,000 protesters and onlookers by 5 p.m.

RE - ENFORCED police crews, with dogs, had the campus under control Wednesday night, despite a re-grouping meeting at 7 p.m. on Bascom Hill of about 200 of the war-protest backers and some 4,000 other students and sympathizers objecting to the afternoon police action and University solicitation of it.

Sheriff's men also sealed off the downtown City-County Building with armed guards Wednesday night after receiving reports the protesters planned to "storm" the ground-floor Madison police headquarters in retaliation for the earlier police use of tear gas and nightsticks

Turn to Page 2, Col. 3

No Injury List

A list of students injured during the protests could not be released Wednesday night because it was not yet "verified," according to Paul Van Nevel, director of public information for the University of Wisconsin Medical Center.

"We want to make sure the list is completely accurate and plan to release it later," he said.

Protesting Police Action

Students, Faculty Vote Strike Today

By JAMES OSET
(Of The State Journal Staff)

University of Wisconsin students and faculty members — voted Wednesday night to call a strike today to protest police action in Wednesday's rioting here.

The students at a rally gave enthusiastic support to a proposal to boycott classes today and hold another rally at 8:30 a.m.

AFTER THE student rally at the Memorial Library steps, 157 faculty members voted at an "unofficial" meeting to join the strike to "condemn the use of police in force today on this campus and as action to emphasize our feelings."

Then a statement was issued by Michael Fullwood, Madison, president of the Wisconsin Student Assn. (WSA) calling for "a complete student and faculty strike today.

The statement also insists that "no academic sanctions be taken against students who have violated civil law."

University officials have said they will discipline students who disrupt University operations, whether or not they are arrested for their actions.

ABOUT 5,000 students, faculty members and onlookers attended Wednesday night's rally. The disorganized assembly took on form when William Simons, a history graduate student, grabbed a microphone and began speaking and acting like a moderator.

About 300 faculty members at the rally formed an unbroken chain around the students. Maurice Zeitlin, associate professor of sociology, said into the microphone, "Faculty members protest with you today's police brutality."

Percy Julian, a Madison attorney who has handled recent cases for demonstrators, told students involved in the demonstration to make statements on exactly what they saw when police entered University grounds.

A SPOKESMAN for the faculty group meeting Wednesday night said it was called on the initiative of several faculty

Turn to Page 2, Col. 4

More on Rioting, P. 6; Sec. 4, P. 1

Today's News on the Inside

Dow Co. Interviews Suspended

UW to Charge Riot Leaders

By ROGER A. GRIBBLE
(Of The State Journal Staff)

Madison Chancellor William H. Sewell Wednesday night suspended campus interviews by Dow Chemical Co. pending the outcome of a special faculty meeting today and said he will prefer charges against Wednesday's blockade leaders.

Sewell's statement, issued after a 2½-hour meeting with other University officials, was seen as a move to head off another confrontation between police and demonstrators.

"To guard the safety of our campus, we are suspending further interviews pending a special meeting of the faculty" (at 3:30 p.m. today), Sewell said.

"MEANTIME, we are preferring charges against leaders of the blockade, suspending them from the University, and referring their cases to the student conduct committee," Sewell declared.

A University spokesman said more than just the students arrested Wednesday would be involved in the suspensions, but he did not know the names of those to be suspended.

He said that at least six students apparently were arrested.

SEWELL SAID he conferred with student demonstrators Wednesday morning after the interviews were blockaded "in an effort to end the disruption. In all, we allowed the protesters more than two hours to comply with our warnings."

He added that before police were asked to clear the building "we declared the blockade an unlawful assembly and warned protesters to leave or face arrests.

"I deeply regret that it was necessary to bring police onto the campus to maintain the operations of the University," Sewell said. "This was done only after our (University) officers and staff found it impossible to maintain order. I regret that students and police

Turn to Page 2, Col. 2

On the Inside . . .

Flu Hospitalizes Treasurer Smith

State Treasurer Dena M. Smith, 67, was recovering Wednesday in Madison General Hospital from an attack of flu and a bronchial infection.

Today's Chuckle

Television shows have gotten so bad this season that many kids have gone back to doing their homework.

Protesters Carry One of Their Injured From Scene of Clash With Police
—State Journal Photo by Norman Lenburg

Police Carry One of Their Injured From Scene of Clash With Protesters
—State Journal Photo by Ira Block

Wisconsin State Journal

WEATHER: Sunny and Cool. High 40 to 45. Fair and Warmer Tonight. Low Near 30.

GOOD MORNING — 44 Pages, Three Sections — Vol. 211, No. 5 — 127th Year — MADISON, FRIDAY MORNING, APRIL 5, 1968 — ★ ★ ★ — MORNING FINAL 10¢

MARTIN LUTHER KING
assassination victim

MEMPHIS HUNTS KILLER OF MARTIN LUTHER KING

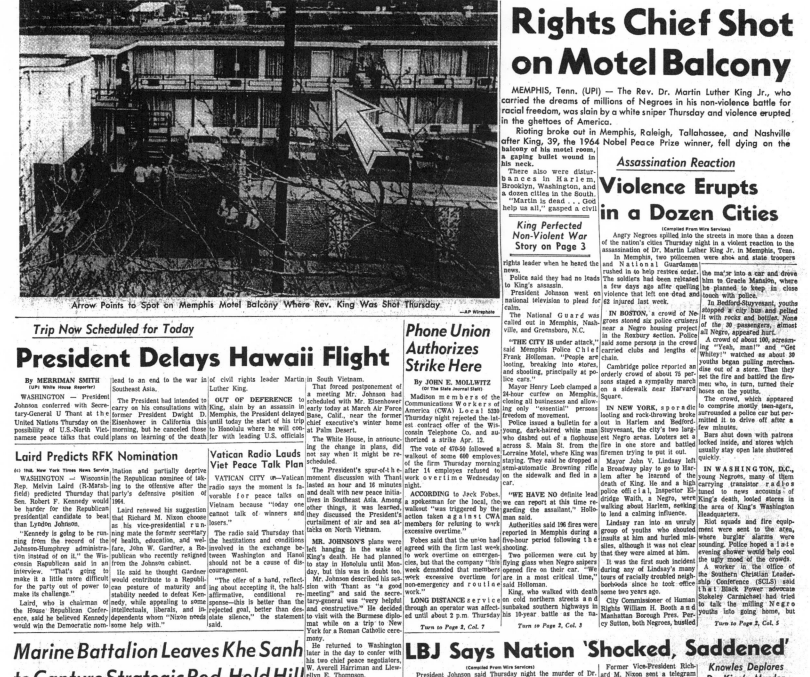

Arrow Points to Spot on Memphis Motel Balcony Where Rev. King Was Shot Thursday —AP Wirephoto

Rights Chief Shot on Motel Balcony

MEMPHIS, Tenn. (UPI) — The Rev. Dr. Martin Luther King Jr., who carried the dreams of millions of Negroes in his non-violence battle for racial freedom, was slain by a white sniper Thursday and violence erupted in the ghettoes of America.

Rioting broke out in Memphis, Raleigh, Tallahassee, and Nashville after King, 39, the 1964 Nobel Peace Prize winner, fell dying on the balcony of his motel room, a gaping bullet wound in his neck.

There also were disturbances in Harlem, Brooklyn, Washington, and a dozen cities in the South.

"Martin is dead . . . God help us all," gasped a civil rights leader when he heard the news.

Police said they had no leads to King's assassin.

President Johnson went on national television to plead for calm.

The National Guard was called out in Memphis, Nashville, and Greensboro, N.C.

"THE CITY IS under attack," said Memphis Police Chief Frank Holloman. "People are looting, breaking into stores, and shooting, principally at police cars."

Mayor Henry Loeb clamped a 24-hour curfew on Memphis, closing all businesses and allowing only "essential" persons freedom of movement.

Police issued a bulletin for a young, dark-haired white man who dashed out of a flophouse across S. Main St. from the Lorraine Motel, where King was staying. They said he dropped a semi-automatic Browning rifle on the sidewalk and fled in a car.

"WE HAVE NO definite lead we can report at this time regarding the assailant," Holloman said.

Authorities said 196 fires were reported in Memphis during a five-hour period following the shooting.

Two policemen were cut by flying glass when Negro snipers opened fire on their car. "We are in a most critical time," said Holloman.

King, who walked with death on cold northern streets and sunbaked southern highways in his 10-year battle as the na-

Turn to Page 2, Col. 3

King Perfected Non-Violent War
Story on Page 3

Assassination Reaction

Violence Erupts in a Dozen Cities

(Compiled From Wire Services)

Angry Negroes spilled into the streets in more than a dozen of the nation's cities Thursday night in a violent reaction to the assassination of Dr. Martin Luther King Jr. in Memphis, Tenn.

In Memphis, two policemen were shot and state troopers and National Guardsmen rushed in to help restore order. The soldiers had been released a few days ago after quelling violence that left one dead and 62 injured last week.

IN BOSTON, a crowd of Negroes stoned six police cruisers near a Negro housing project in the Roxbury section. Police said some persons in the crowd carried clubs and lengths of chain.

Cambridge police reported an orderly crowd of about 75 persons staged a sympathy march on a sidewalk near Harvard Square.

IN NEW YORK, sporadic looting and rock-throwing broke out in Harlem and Bedford-Stuyvesant, the city's two largest Negro areas. Looters set a fire in one store and battled firemen trying to put it out.

Mayor John V. Lindsay left a Broadway play to go to Harlem after he learned of the death of King. He and a high police official, Inspector Eldridge Waith, a Negro, were walking about Harlem, seeking to lend a calming influence.

Lindsay ran into an unruly group of youths who shouted insults at him and hurled missiles, although it was not clear that they were aimed at him.

It was the first such incident during any of Lindsay's many tours of racially troubled neighborhoods since he took office some two years ago.

City Commissioner of Human Rights William H. Booth and Manhattan Borough Pres. Percy Sutton, both Negroes, hustled the ma'or into a car and drove him to Gracie Mansion, where he planned to keep in close touch with police.

In Bedford-Stuyvesant, youths stopped a city bus and pelted it with rocks and bottles. None of the 30 passengers, almost all Negro, appeared hurt.

A crowd of about 100, screaming "Yeah, man!" and "Get Whitey!" watched as about 30 youths began pulling merchandise out of a store. Then they set the fire and battled the firemen who, in turn, turned their hoses on the youths.

The crowd, which appeared to comprise mostly teen-agers, surrounded a police car but permitted it to drive off after a few minutes.

Bars shut down with patrons locked inside, and stores which usually stay open late shuttered quickly.

IN WASHINGTON, D.C., young Negroes, many of them carrying transistor radios tuned to news accounts of King's death, looted stores in the area of King's Washington Headquarters.

Riot squads and fire equipment were sent to the area, where burglar alarms were sounding. Police hoped a late evening shower would help cool the ugly mood of the crowds.

A worker in the office of the Southern Christian Leadership Conference (SCLS) said that Black Power advocate Stokeley Carmichael had tried to talk the milling Negro youths into going home, but

Turn to Page 2, Col. 5

Trip Now Scheduled for Today

President Delays Hawaii Flight

By MERRIMAN SMITH
(UPI White House Reporter)

WASHINGTON — President Johnson conferred with Secretary-General U Thant at the United Nations Thursday on the possibility of U.S.-North Vietnamese peace talks that could lead to an end to the war in Southeast Asia.

The President had intended to carry on his consultations with former President Dwight D. Eisenhower in California this morning, but he canceled those plans on learning of the death of civil rights leader Martin Luther King.

OUT OF DEFERENCE to King, slain by an assassin in Memphis, the President delayed until today the start of his trip to Honolulu where he will confer with leading U.S. officials in South Vietnam.

That forced postponement of a meeting Mr. Johnson had scheduled with Mr. Eisenhower early today at March Air Force Base, Calif., near the former chief executive's winter home at Palm Desert.

The White House, in announcing the change in plans, did not say when it might be rescheduled.

The President's spur-of-the-moment discussion with Thant lasted an hour and 16 minutes and dealt with new peace initiatives in Southeast Asia. Among other things, it was learned, they discussed the President's curtailment of air and sea attacks on North Vietnam.

MR. JOHNSON'S plans were left hanging in the wake of King's death. He had planned to stay in Honolulu until Monday, but this was in doubt too.

Mr. Johnson described his session with Thant as "a good meeting" and said the secretary-general was "very helpful and constructive." He decided to visit with the Burmese diplomat while on a trip to New York for a Roman Catholic ceremony.

He returned to Washington later in the day to confer with his two chief peace negotiators, W. Averell Harriman and Llewellyn E. Thompson.

The President had been expected to discuss with Mr. Ei-

Turn to Page 2, Col. 4

Laird Predicts RFK Nomination

(c) 1968, New York Times News Service

WASHINGTON — Wisconsin Rep. Melvin Laird (R-Marshfield) predicted Thursday that Sen. Robert F. Kennedy would be harder for the Republican presidential candidate to beat than Lyndon Johnson.

"Kennedy is going to be running from the record of the Johnson-Humphrey administration instead of on it," the Wisconsin Republican said in an interview. "That's going to make it a little more difficult for the party out of power to make its challenge."

Laird, who is chairman of the House Republican Conference, said he believed Kennedy would win the Democratic nomination and partially deprive the Republican nominee of taking to the offensive after the party's defensive position of 1964.

Laird renewed his suggestion that Richard M. Nixon choose as his vice-presidential running mate the former secretary of health, education, and welfare, John W. Gardner, a Republican who recently resigned from the Johnson cabinet.

He said he thought Gardner would contribute to a Republican posture of maturity and stability needed to defeat Kennedy, while appealing to some intellectuals, liberals, and independents whom "Nixon needs some help with."

Vatican Radio Lauds Viet Peace Talk Plan

VATICAN CITY (AP)—Vatican radio says the moment is favorable for peace talks on Vietnam because "today one cannot talk of winners and losers."

The radio said Thursday that the hestitations and conditions involved in the exchange between Washington and Hanoi should not be a cause of discouragement.

"The offer of a hand, reflecting about accepting it, the half-affirmative, conditional response—this is better than the rejected goal, better than desolate silence," the statement said.

Phone Union Authorizes Strike Here

By JOHN E. MOLLWITZ
(Of The State Journal Staff)

Madison members of the Communications Workers of America (CWA) Local 5330 Thursday night rejected the latest contract offer of the Wisconsin Telephone Co. and authorized a strike Apr. 12.

The vote of 470-50 followed a walkout of some 600 employes of the firm Thursday morning after 14 employes refused to work overtime Wednesday night.

ACCORDING to Jack Fobes, a spokesman for the local, the walkout "was triggered by the action taken against CWA members for refusing to work excessive overtime."

Fobes said that the union had agreed with the firm last week to work overtime on emergencies, but that the company "this week demanded that members work excessive overtime for non-emergency and routine work."

LONG DISTANCE service through an operator was affected until about 2 p.m. Thursday

Turn to Page 2, Col. 7

Marine Battalion Leaves Khe Sanh to Capture Strategic Red-Held Hill

SAIGON (UPI)—A battalion of United States Marines pushed 1.5 miles out of Khe Sanh Thursday and seized Hill 471 to the south in the increasingly bloody campaign to lift a North Vietnamese siege of the isolated American position.

Hanoi radio said "American planes" bombed North Vietnam's extreme northwest corner near Laos, an area far above the U.S. raid limit line, but the Communists did not make a major issue of the charge

The raiders may have been U.S.-built Laotian planes which strayed off course.

The Marine battalion, up to 1,500 men, reported finding 30 North Vietnamese bodies as they pushed up Hill 471 overlooking the Khe Sanh valley. Most were believed killed by U.S. artillery strikes supporting the drive to clear the area of Communist forces.

TROOPS OF THE U.S. First Cavalry Division occupied another part of the high ground commanding firing positions into Khe Sanh. Fog and a murderous North Vietnamese artillery barrage inflicted casualties and stalled the big Allied push along Highway 9.

The Allied infantry-tank juggernaut was reported only two miles from the base Thursday in Operation Pegasus, code name for the relief operation.

The U.S. Command said Pegasus, which began last Monday, had killed at least 57 North Vietnamese at a cost of nine Americans killed and 78 wounded, most of them by Communist artillery.

The Hanoi radio report on the air raid said three waves hit a populated area 30 miles west of the North Vietnamese province capital of Lai Chau. This is 10 miles east of the Laotian border and about 20 miles south of the Red Chinese frontier.

The Communist report did not identify the planes by type, saying only that they dropped more than 50 bombs in raids Thursday between 8:40 and 10:40 a.m. The mountainous area near the ill-defined frontier is near zones hit in the past by American-built planes of the Laotian air force attempting to knock out Communist supply routes into Laos.

The U.S. Command said no

Turn to Page 2, Col. 8

On the Inside . . .

Ousted Czech Leader Recants
Story on Page 12

LBJ Says Nation 'Shocked, Saddened'

(Compiled From Wire Services)

President Johnson said Thursday night the murder of Dr. Martin Luther King had "shocked and saddened" the nation.

The President appeared in the doorway of his White House office, stern-faced, as he spoke on all television and radio networks.

"I'll ask every American citizen," he said, "to reject the blind violence that has struck down Dr. King, who lived by non-violence."

The President urged prayers for peace and understanding in the land and said:

"WE CAN achieve nothing by lawlessness and divisiveness among the American people."

He said he hopes all Americans would search their hearts.

At that point he said he was canceling all plans for the evening and postponing until today his planned takeoff for Hawaii and conferences there on problems of war and peace in Vietnam.

He was to have attended a Democratic fund-raising dinner at a Washington hotel Thursday night and was only minutes from leaving the White House when the tragic news came from Memphis.

THE WHITE HOUSE said Mr. Johnson had telephoned Mrs. King at her home in Atlanta and expressed his sympathy.

The nation's civil rights and political leaders reacted with anguish, shock, and grief, and there was fear the slaying could lead to more violence.

Vice-President Hubert H. Humphrey said the murder "brings shame to our country."

"An apostle of non-violence has been the victim of violence," Humphrey said.

Former Vice-President Richard M. Nixon sent a telegram to Mrs. King which said: "Dr. King's death is a great personal tragedy for everyone who knew him and a great tragedy for the nation."

SEN. ROBERT F. Kennedy (D-N.Y.) told a predominantly Negro audience in Indianapolis to pray for King's family, "but more important, say a prayer for our own country which all of us love."

Kennedy was informed of King's murder when he arrived at the Indianapolis airport on the last leg of a three-city campaign swing through Indiana.

Sen. Eugene McCarthy (D-Minn.) called the assassination a "tragedy for all Americans . . . not only have his people lost a noble and great leader, but all people, especially Americans, have lost a man of peace. We can only grieve."

Sen. Edward W. Brooke (R-Mass.), the only Negro in the Senate, said: "The crime is un-

Turn to Page 2, Col. 1

UW Memorial Set; No P.M. Classes

University of Wisconsin Chancellor William H. Sewell Thursday announced that a mass memorial service for Dr. Martin Luther King will be held at noon today on Bascom Hill at the University.

Sewell also said that after the noon memorial all afternoon classes today will be canceled "as an expression of the grief and concern the University community feels at this tragic event."

Knowles Deplores Dr. King's Murder
Sec. 2, Page 1

Wisconsin State Journal

WEATHER: Mostly Sunny and Warm Today, High Around 90. Low Tonight in 60s.

GOOD MORNING | 50 Pages, Four Sections Vol. 211, No. 66 127th Year | MADISON, WEDNESDAY MORNING, JUNE 5, 1968 | ★ ★ ★ | MORNING FINAL 10¢

KENNEDY SHOT!

LOS ANGELES, Wednesday (AP)—Robert F. Kennedy, brother of the assassinated President John F. Kennedy, was shot early today in a moment of political triumph.

Press secretary Frank Mankiewicz told newsmen Kennedy was wounded twice in the head — in the front of the forehead and near the right ear.

Dr. Ross Miller, who attended Kennedy immediately after the senator was shot, said Kennedy had a head wound but a "good heart beat."

It was a "cursory examination," Miller said, but on its basis "I would be forced to describe his condition as critical."

Miller said Kennedy's pulse was "rapid but strong and full."

Kennedy had just made a victory statement on the California Democratic presidential primary.

At least two other persons were reported hit by the gunman.

The apparent assailant, a man about 25 years old, curly haired, and of Latin appearance, was captured by Kennedy supporters. He was rushed through the Ambassador Hotel lobby by police.

The scene of shock and turmoil was nationally televised, for the shooting came moments after Kennedy had gone before the cameras with his primary victory statement.

A television reporter said the man who fired the shot was about 10 feet from Kennedy.

An early report said Kennedy's brother-in-law, Stephen Smith, also had been shot, but a short time later Smith was at a microphone asking that the room be cleared and did not appear to have been harmed.

The American Broadcasting Co. said its unit manager, William Wiesel, also was shot.

Kennedy was taken to Los Angeles Central Receiving Hospital.

Before he was removed from the hotel, a priest said he attempted to give the senator final rites of the Roman Catholic Church but the surging crowd pushed him away.

The priest said: "I gave him the rosary and he clenched it tightly and I was pushed away. There was blood on his head."

The Rev. Thomas Peacha then administered

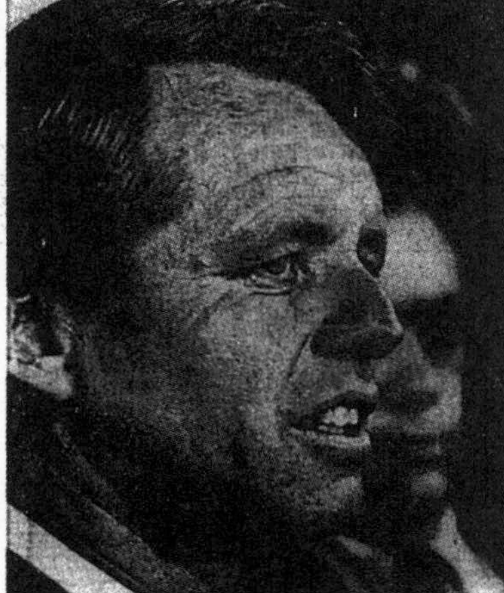

SEN. ROBERT F. KENNEDY

the rites in the emergency room of the hospital.

The priest said he did not talk to the senator directly and the senator did not talk to him.

An unidentified person in the emergency room said the senator appeared to be unconscious.

Kennedy later was moved to nearby Good Samaritan Hospital in the downtown Los Angeles area.

Kennedy was taken from the emergency room at Central Receiving on a stretcher. A reporter on the scene said a bottle resembling a blood plasma bottle was suspended over the stretcher.

The arrested man was hurried through a lobby throng still yelling and screaming at the news of the shooting.

"Kill him! Lynch him!" many in the crowd shouted. Many tried to reach the man, but police hustled him out of the lobby and down the stairs to an exit.

David Esquith, Michael Agron, and Ron Udell, all of Los Angeles, brought in a friend whom they said was also wounded in the shooting.

They identified him as Irwin Stroll, 17, Los Angeles. They said he didn't appear to be seriously injured.

The apparent gunman was pinned against a dish rack by Rafer Johnson, the former Olympic decathlon champion, and other Kennedy aides including pro football star Rossevelt Grier.

The shooting occurred in a small anteroom off the main ballroom.

Only those near the door knew at first there was a shooting.

Five doctors treated the senator before removal to the hospital.

Several Kennedy supporters called for towels immediately after the shooting. A news reporter hastily stripped off a velvet tablecloth and rushed into the kitchen area, jammed with shouting political supporters of the senator.

The scene was complete confusion. Television cameramen and men carrying tape recorders stood on serving tables and tried to hold their equipment close to where first aid was being applied to the wounded.

All the men were bleeding.

A tablecloth was used to stem the flow of blood from a blond man who was stretched over a chair. His shirt was up and he was bleeding profusely around the body.

Kennedy's eyes were reported to be open. He was licking the blood on his lips.

Kennedy's wife, Ethel, was at his side during his victory talk. He mentioned his dog, Freckles, and said the pet had been maligned during the campaign.

Turn to Page 2, Col. 4

Three Leads in Co-ed Slaying at UW Fade

By JUNE DIECKMANN
(Of The State Journal Staff)

Three more hopeful leads in the 10-day unsolved slaying of University of Wisconsin co-ed Christine Rothschild faded Tuesday, leaving lawmen still without a suspect, motive, or murder weapon, Undersheriff Vernon (Jack) Leslie reported.

Investigation by University, Madison, and Dane County lawmen left them with:

ONE. A 29-year-old hospital-confined mental patient, who confessed Miss Rothschild's murder last week, but whose hospital records obtained by court order Tuesday, plus other police investigation, discounted his confession.

TWO. A 24-year-old married Kenosha man jailed Monday night by Kenosha police as the suspected attacker of three Kenosha Carthage College co-eds on the Lutheran school's campus there last weekend.

"The probability is zero" that he was in Madison Sunday, May 26, when Miss Rothschild was slain here, Detective Charles Lulling and Sheriff's Sgt. Richard Josephson said.

THREE. A more conclusive FBI laboratory report which seemed to rule out the theory that Miss Rothschild's slayer may have been a man with whom she had breakfast during her early Sunday morning walk.

The report revealed that she had eaten only spinach. A partly-consumed can of diet spinich was found in her room at Ann Emery Hall on Langdon St.

"WE NEED a break," University Police Chief Ralph Hanson, head of the investigation, repeated.

Hanson's requested $5,000 reward money for information he hopes will produce the "break" needed leading to 18-year-old Miss Rothschild's slayer, was provided Tuesday by University Pres. Fred Harvey Harrington from the University's gift fund from private and corporate contributors.

THE MENTAL patient, picked up by police last Thursday night in the Memorial Union Rathskeller where he was bragging about committing Miss Rothschild's murder, was rechecked Tuesday after it was learned that he may have been absent on the murder Sunday from his confinement in the University Hospital psychiatric ward, near the murder scene.

Dist. Atty. James C. Boll, who obtained the patients' records with a court order from Circuit Judge William C. Sachtjen, said "the records showed nothing to confirm the patient's confession to the murder." The patient is now at Mendota State Hospital.

THE KENOSHA man was in-

Turn to Page 2, Col. 6

State Traffic Toll 85 Ahead of 1967

The death of a Milwaukee teenager Tuesday brought Wisconsin's 1968 highway fatality toll to 455, compared to 370 on the same date in record 1967.

Shiela Dadzinski, 16, Milwaukee, was killed when the car she was in hit a guard rail on the S. 27th St. viaduct and overturned, police said. She was thrown out.

On the Inside . . .

Argentine Heart Transplant Dies

BUENOS AIRES (UPI) — Antonio Enrique Serrano, 54, died Tuesday four days after he became Argentina's first heart transplant patient.

Serrano died in Model Clinic in the Buenos Aires suburb of Lanus of what Dr. Hector Ruggiereo described as "neurological" causes.

Serrano, a noodle salesman, has been in a coma since shortly after the operation Friday.

Ohio Medical Products Buys 160-Acre Site for a Building

Ohio Medical Products Division of Air Reduction Co. has purchased a 160-acre site for a new office building on Madison's East Side, W. A. Lunger, president, said Tuesday.

The property is located just east of Interstate 90 on Femritt Dr., the old Highway 12-18. The firm is presently located at 1400 E. Washington Ave.

Lunger said the firm will construct the new office and other facilities to allow for expansion. Mead and Hunt Inc., of Madison, has been selected as consulting engineers, he said.

The property was purchased May 31 from Henry, Christ, and Anna Weissinger, all of Madison.

Ohio Medical Products, formerly Ohio Chemical Co., is the largest manufacturer in the country of a combined line of anesthesia equipment, infant incubators, resuscitation equipment, and a highly sophisticated hospital pipeline system for oxygen, compressed air, and suction.

In 1965 the firm remodeled its present buildings and included a 50,000-square foot addition increasing floor space 26 per cent. By last year the firm's office staff was crowded.

The firm employs about 450 persons and is one of Madison's largest employers.

Gisholt Denies Deal With Ohio

Officials of Gisholt Machine Co., a division of Giddings and Lewis Inc., Tuesday denied rumors that it would acquire the Ohio Medical Products facilities across E. Washington Ave.

Louis Preysz, executive vice-president, said, "We're not going into that property."

Preysz said that Gisholt, however, was calling a press conference for 4 p.m. Thursday at the firm's offices, 1245 E. Washington Ave., to make an announcement. The subject of the press conference was not disclosed.

Ulcer Sidelines Mrs. Knowles

The governor's office Tuesday announced that Mrs. Warren P. Knowles has been ordered by her physician to cancel her public appearances for the next few weeks because of an ulcer.

Dr. Anthony Curreri, of University Hospitals, said that the governor's wife has an "acute duodenal ulcer." He told her to get several weeks of rest.

Paul Hassett, the governor's executive secretary, said that several public officials and friends have offered to represent her at public functions which Mrs. Knowles had originally been scheduled to attend.

Hassett said that Mrs. Knowles would take a vacation with friends. The destination was not announced.

Current Laws Don't Cover It

Synthetic Marijuana Leaves a Poser Here

A shipment of synthetic marijuana, valued at $20,000 on the user's market, has been confiscated by Madison police from a University of Wisconsin student dropout who flew it in from San Francisco, The State Journal learned Tuesday.

The ex-student, jailed overnight for questioning, has been released without charges.

WISCONSIN and United States narcotics laws apparently do not cover the new synthetic "pot," Asst. Dist. Atty. Michael Zaleski said.

The confiscated cache of synthetic marijuana is at the State Crime Laboratory, where expert analysts reported that it contains all the marijuana compounds.

Marijuana is a narcotic derivative of the hemp plant.

THE SYNTHETIC substance, white and powdery looking much like confectioner's sugar, has even more potency than the weed-grown narcotic, Detective Lt. Stanley Davenport said.

Several known marijuana smokers in the campus district here said they were "afraid" of the new synthetic powder because of its greater potency, Davenport reported.

This is the first known large shipment of the new synthetic narcotic to Madison, Davenport said. It originated in West Coast cities, and has been reported in use there only the last four or five months, he said.

THREE BREAD-sized plastic bags of the snythetic marijuana were confiscated by Davenport and Detective James McFarlane from the ex-student's suitcase as he left an inbound plane from San Francisco at Madison's municipal airport.

The traveler, and a University student friend meeting him

Turn to Page 2, Col. 8

Israel, Jordan Trade Gunfire

(By Associated Press)

Israeli jet fighters swooped on attack Tuesday against Jordan while ground gunners of both nations traded thunderous artillery barrages like those of the six-day Middle East war that began a year ago today.

Jordanian and Israeli accounts of casualties, damage, and how the fighting started varied widely. With the shooting dragging on past nightfall, ambassadors of the two countries took up an exchange of charges at the United Nations in New York.

Officials in Jordan said the Israelis fired first in "a surprise attack." Israeli spokesmen said the attack across the Jordan River was in reply to the shelling of four Israeli farm cooperatives.

Muhammad H. El-Farra, Jordan's UN ambassador, said 30 persons were killed, 60 wounded, and raging forest fires set off near the Jordanian city of Irbid, south of the Sea of Galilee.

Evans to Keynote GOP Convention

PORTLAND, Ore. (UPI) — Gov. Dan Evans of Washington state was named Tuesday to keynote the Republican National Convention in August.

Sen. Everett Dirksen's appointment as chairman of the platform committee also was confirmed. Dirksen, of Illinois, is the Republican leader in the Senate.

Rep. Gerald Ford of Michigan was named permanent convention chairman and Sen. Edward Brooke of Massachusetts temporary convention chairman.

Today's Chuckle

Definition of a tough town: It's one where nobody asks you what time it is. They just take your watch.

Carrier-Salesmen Collect This Week

Wisconsin State Journal carrier-salesmen will be making their bi-weekly collections Friday.

Payments on the first call will eliminate "call-backs" that require additional time and effort. Thank you.

McCarthy's Early Lead Falls Off

LOS ANGELES (AP) — Eugene J. McCarthy held a dwindling lead Tuesday night in California's climactic presidential primary, but talked like a man reconciled to seeing Robert F. Kennedy capture the final prize in their Democratic battle.

The Columbia Broadcasting Co. said its projection showed Kennedy would win the election and capture his second victory of the day.

With it, the New York senator would gain a major boost in his nomination race against the man he sees as the real opponent — Vice-President Hubert H. Humphrey.

KENNEDY MADE a carefully hedged claim of victory in a television interview.

"It would appear that I,' according to what you say with your machines, would be successful," he said on CBS

Once again, Kennedy said he hopes McCarthy and his followers will join with him in an effort to overcome Humphrey. Once again, McCarthy rejected the idea of an alliance and said he would continue his own campaign.

WITH 1,837 of 21,301 precincts

Turn to Page 2, Col. 3

Stockholders Vote Bus Company Sale to City With Subsidy Deal

By RAYMOND MERLE
(Of The State Journal Staff)

Madison Bus Co. stockholders Tuesday voted to sell the company to the city and to enter a subsidized operating agreement until the city makes the purchase.

City Council approval is now the only remaining major step toward a city-operated bus business. A public hearing on the proposed transaction and interim agreement is scheduled for Tuesday night's Committee of the Whole meeting.

Madison voters Apr. 2 approved two referenda questions giving the city authority to own, operate, or buy a bus business, and to borrow up to $1 million for that purpose.

THE OPERATING agreement would run from July 1, 1968, to Nov. 10, 1969, and the city could make the purchase anytime during that period.

The city would subsidize the company about $22,000 per month, or an amount to give the company a 5 per cent profit, until the purchase time.

WILLIAM STRAUB SR., bus company president, said after the special stockholder meeting that the company will revoke its dissolution proceedings, and dismiss its abandonment petition pending before the State Public Service Commission.

Mayor Otto Fesige said he was "very pleased' by the stockholder's action.

"This brings us one step closer toward a solution to the bus problem, and assures us of a continuation of bus service in Madison," he said.

THE PURCHASE option and subsidy arrangement were worked out during a series of recent meetings between city and company officials, and announced May 21.

Purchase price of the company has been set at $910,000 plus the cost of inventory and sup-

Turn to Page 2, Col. 2

Wisconsin State Journal

WEATHER: Variable Clouds, Warm, Humid, Thundershowers Likely. High Near 80, Low Near 50.

GOOD MORNING — 36 Pages, Three Sections, Vol. 213, No. 35, 129th Year — MADISON, TUESDAY MORNING, MAY 6, 1969 — ★ ★ ★ — MORNING FINAL — 10¢

Mayor's Truce Bid Fails

UW FIGHT ERUPTS ANEW

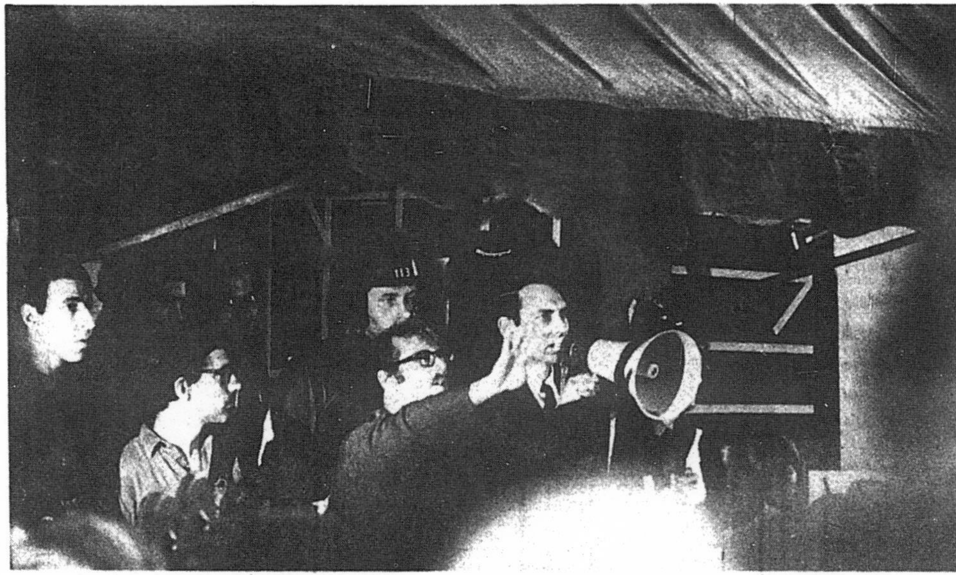

Mayor William D. Dyke Makes Futile Attempt to Appease Hippie Gathering Before New Outbreak Monday Night.

—State Journal Photo by A. Craig Benson

Street-Permit Proposal Spurned

By GEORGE MITCHELL and JON WEGGE
(Of The State Journal Staff)

For the third straight night, police and hippie student groups clashed in the W. Mifflin-Bassett Sts. area Monday night, after Mayor William D. Dyke had made a futile attempt to end the long struggle.

Riot-equipped police moved in again with tear gas to clear the area, which had been blocked off during the mayor's attempt to establish a truce by backing a proposal for street-closing permits, an issue over which the clashes originally began.

AS POLICE approached, they were greeted with a barricade on Mifflin St. which the hippie groups set afire.

From then on, it was one confrontation after another. City and Dane County police, augmented by enforcements from surrounding counties converged on the area.

More on Fracas: See Sec. 2, P. 1

The students scattered into hit and run groups, and the violence increased.

It continued early today, and a police official reported, "They're breaking windows all up and down State St." Among windows shattered were those at Rennebohm's, the University Book Store, and the Meuer Photoart House.

ONE CASE of arson by fire-bombing was reported at the Wisconsin State Insurance Building, 212 N. Bassett St.

Up to 1:30 a.m. today nine arrests were reported. The number of injured could not be determined.

The new action followed two nights of fights, arrests, injurie[s] and fire-setting which developed after police broke up a block party in the area on Saturday.

AND MONDAY night the group heard the mayor offer support of an ordinance which would provide street-closing permits "for parties, such as you wanted last weekend."

"I would expect to support it," the mayor said.

The group, which had greeted

Turn to Page 2, Col. 7

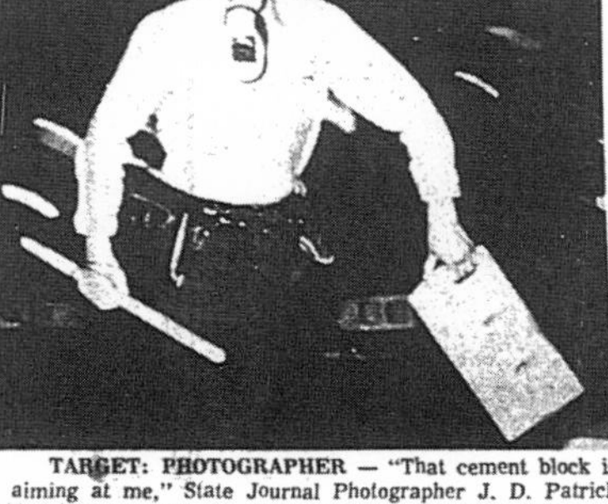

TARGET: PHOTOGRAPHER — "That cement block is aiming at me," State Journal Photographer J. D. Patrick said Monday night he was covering activity at State and Gorham Sts. The block shattered on the sidewalk beside him. Patrick said the Madison policeman also swore at him, grabbed him, and threw him against a building. "I got his badge number — 115," Patrick said.

—State Journal Photo by J. D. Patrick

'City Capitulation' Sought, Mayor Says

Only "total (city) capitulation" would satisfy the rebellious student leaders, Mayor William D. Dyke said late Monday night after his unsuccessful attempt to restore calm to the troubled University of Wisconsin campus.

The mayor made his statement after his hour-long meeting with about 1,200 University students in the student residential district.

"AFTER TALKING to them for almost an hour, it was obvious there was no negotiations possible," Dyke said. "It appeared to me that the only response acceptable to them was total capitulation and adoption of their terms." He said that among the disrupters was a group "whose only purpose is disruption. How many I can't say, perhaps 50."

"Clearly this is a group which wants to have its own community, its own standards, its own laws, its own territory," Dyke said after returning to the City-County building. "In a limited sense it is a rebellious act to frustrate the city and set up an island in the city which can be

Turn to Page 2, Col. 2

Louisiana Guard Called to Duty

Negroes Leave Southern U. Buildings

(By United Press International)

Negro students abandoned an occupation of Southern University offices in New Orleans Monday after Gov. John J. McKeithen called out the National Guard, vowing "We're not going to have a Cornell in Louisiana."

Some 300 black militants dispersed after a short-lived takeover of the administration building, registrar's office, business office, personnel office, and university switchboard.

They drifted away—some to softball fields—after their leaders told them to "split." The guard never arrived on campus.

There was no violence, and no immediate indication where the guardsmen ordered out by McKeithen would remain on standby duty.

At Alabama State

Montgomery police arrested 365 Negro students Monday after they refused to break up a demonstration in front of the Alabama capitol.

The students, most of them involved in nearly six weeks of protests at Alabama State College, were hauled off in three trucks and charged with failing to obey a police order.

Officers reported a special court session had been called in an effort to try most of the arrested students.

The students were demanding the resignation of the president of Alabama State.

At Long Beach State

About 500 militants trying to break up a military careers day program clashed Monday with 300 members of a conservative group at Long Beach State College.

Fistfights and namecalling broke out between the militants and 300 members of Young Americans for Freedom, a conservative group, who stood arm in arm around recruiting booths to hold off the demonstrators.

Police were not called to the campus, and the half-hour melee broke up only after the recruiters left the campus.

At CCNY

About 200 Negro and Puerto Rican students marched out of the South Campus of City College of New York (CCNY) Monday night after a two-week-long occupation that shut down the 20,000-student institution.

The occupation force marched into surrounding Harlem.

They withdrew from the campus after being served with a court injunction to end their takeover, which was begun

Turn to Page 2, Col. 3

A Salute From the Top

By HOLLY DUNLOP
(Of The State Journal Staff)

President Richard M. Nixon receives thousands of letters each day.

That's why Virginia Brendemuehl, 3009 University Ave., a music teacher at Shorewood Hills Elementary school, was amazed when she went to her mailbox Saturday and found a letter from the President.

Miss Brendemuehl had typed out a letter to President Nixon in early April. It wasn't about Vietnam, ABM, civil ri[ghts], inflation, or any of the other pressing problems facing this country.

INSTEAD, it was a short, folksy (she wrote that she includes the President in her prayers night and morning) letter about patriotism.

It seems that Miss Brendemuehl, a petite redhead, was having trouble teaching her second and third graders to stand up straight when they practiced nine patriotic songs for a "Spring Sing" they are giving at 5 p.m. Thursday at the school.

SHE WROTE: "At the time of President Ike's funeral you showed the country and my children what it meant to stand at attention when in the presence of the flag. Your example had an unbelievable affect on my children and now, they too, are beginning to stand as they should in the presence of the colors.

"Thank you for being what the country needs."

She received a reply from President Nixon Saturday, and an autographed photo she requested is on the way.

PRESIDENT Nixon wrote:

"Dear Miss Brendemuehl:

"I want you to know how pleased I was to receive your letter and to know that I was able to contribute to your students' understanding of patriotism.

"We have every reason to stand with respect as our flag goes by and as we raise our voices in patriotic songs. As you have taught your children, we pay respect to our flag as a symbol of our great national values — individual freedom under the law, equality of opportunity in all walks of life, justice and protection of the law for all.

"As children we memorize the songs. Experience in life teaches us to appreciate the meaning of the words.

"Congratulations to you for giving your students a great lesson. I know you have touched their lives and the future of our nation by taking this special interest.

"With every good wish. Sincerely, Richard Nixon."

MISS BRENDEMUEHL is convinced that the second and third graders will stand as erect

Turn to Page 2, Col. 6

UW Chancellor Praises Mayor

University of Wisconsin Chancellor Edwin Young Monday night complimented Mayor William Dyke for a "very real and sincere attempt to resolve a real and troublesome problem."

Dyke went into the area of student unrest Monday night and met with students.

The chancellor said, "I admire the mayor for his efforts. I wish students would disperse and go back to their living quarters."

Young said University officials had no immediate plans for formal meetings to discuss the outbreaks.

"I wish to emphasize, however, that although this is outside our jurisdiction, it is not outside our concern. We are trying to get information on students involved. Our University police have cooperated with city police under our mutual aid pact.

"This is a very deplorable situation and I hope that it ends soon."

Disruption Halts City Bus Service

All bus service in the city was halted at 10 p.m. Monday because of the student disruptions in the west-central portion.

Taxis avoided that area but continued to provide service elsewhere.

According to an unconfirmed report, the buses were stopped after at least one tire was slashed.

Taxi dispatchers said no cabs were going into the trouble area, but one dispatcher said a young driver equipped with a rag and bottle of vinegar for a crude gas mask sometimes ventured near the scene of the action.

The spokesman for the Madison Bus Co. said he presumed service would resume again this morning at the regular time.

Today's Chuckle

A girl no longer marries a man for better or worse. She marries him for more or less.

On the Inside . . .

News Quiz Notes History in Making

See Sec. 2, Page 2

Letter Perfect—That's What These Shorewood Hills Third Graders Are After Noting Music Teacher Virginia Brendemuehl's Letters To and From President Nixon.

—State Journal Photos

Wisconsin State Journal

WEATHER: Sunny With a High of 80 to 85. No Chance of Rain. Low 55-60.

GOOD MORNING | 36 Pages. Three Sections Vol. 212, No. 110 129th Year | MADISON, MONDAY MORNING, JULY 21, 1969 | ★ ★ ★ | MORNING FINAL | 10¢

ON THE MOON!

'A Giant Leap' for All of Mankind

—AP Color Photo

In Practice Session at Manned Space Center, Astronauts Aldrin, Right, and Armstrong Practice Lunar Surface Activities

Americans First to Walk on Dead Lunar Surface

By JOHN BARBOUR

SPACE CENTER, Houston (AP) — Two Americans landed on the Moon and explored its surface for some two hours Sunday, planting the first human footprints in its dusty soil.

They raised their nation's flag and talked to their President on Earth 240,000 miles away.

CIVILIAN NEIL ARMSTRONG and Air Force Col. Edwin Aldrin Jr. reported that they were back in their spacecraft at 12:11 a.m. CDT today. "The hatch is closed and locked," Armstrong reported.

Millions on their home planet watched on television as the pair saluted their flag and scoured the rocky, rugged surface.

The first to step on the moon was Armstrong, 38. His foot touched the surface at 9:56 p.m. CDT, and he remained out for two hours, 14 minutes.

His first words standing on the Moon were, "That's one small step for man, a giant leap for mankind."

TWENTY MINUTES AFTER he stepped down, Aldrin followed. "Beautiful, beautiful, beautiful," he said. "A magnificent desolation."

He remained out for one hour, 44 minutes.

Their spacecraft, Eagle, landed on the moon at 3:18 p.m. CDT, and they were out of it and on the surface some six hours later.

At the end, mission control granted them extra time on the lunar surface. Armstrong was given 15 extra minutes, Aldrin 12.

EVEN WHILE THEY WERE on the lunar surface, Lick Observatory in Southern California sent a laser light beam to the Moon, aiming at the small mirror the astronauts had installed on the surface. They got a reflection back on Earth.

There were humorous moments in the awkward climbing out and in of the spacecraft. When Aldrin backed out of the hatch, he said he was "making sure not to lock it on the way out."

Armstrong, on the surface, laughed. "A pretty good thought," he said.

Once back in the spaceship, they immediately began to repressurize the cabin with oxygen. They stowed the samples of rocks and soil.

"WE'VE GOT ABOUT 20 pounds of carefully selected, if not documented, samples," Armstrong said, referring to the contents of one of two boxes filled with lunar material.

The minutes behind were unforgettable for them and for the world.

The moments ahead were still full of hazard. At 12:55 p.m. today, they are scheduled to blast off from the moon to catch up with their orbiting mothership above for the trip home.

PRESIDENT NIXON'S VOICE came to the ears of the astronauts on the Moon from the Oval Room at the White House.

"This has to be the most historic telephone call ever made," he said. "I just can't tell you how proud I am. Because of what you have done, the heavens have became part of man's world. As you talk to us from the Sea of Tranquillity, it inspires us to redouble our efforts to bring peace and tranquillity to man.

"All the people on Earth are surely one in their pride of what you have done, and one in their prayers that you will return safely."

Aldrin replied, "Thank you, Mr. President. It is a privilege to represent the people of all peaceable na-

Turn to Page 2, Col. 1

'Houston ... Tranquillity Base Here'

By SAUL PETT
(Associated Press Writer)

SPACE CENTER, Houston — Why, oh why, did we tire and age them before their appointed time?

Why did we waste them on elections and no-hitters, on bull markets and murders, on TV shows and circuses?

WHY DIDN'T WE pull out of the language long ago and save for this special moment in the story of man such words as historic and momentous, dramatic and breathtaking, fantastic and incredible?

What are we left with now except to feel a silent feeling, a wordless awe, a still reverence, perhaps for the fact that mortal men from Earth, our part of Earth, at that, have landed on the Moon?

ALL ALONG, it turns out, the astronauts had the words, the simple right words, the nouns without adjectives, the verbs without adverbs, the strong workmanlike words that would stand as tall trees in the upward path of man from the mud to the Moon.

They indulged themselves in only one metaphor. It couldn't have come at a better moment.

"The Eagle has wings," they said, and didn't it and didn't we? The lunar lander was separating from the mother ship and taking life of its own.

"SEE YOU LATER," chirpy Columbia says to departing Eagle. Later would be 30 long hours later in history after they had landed and walked on the Moon, photographed and sampled its soil, and scurried up toward home.

"Eagle, you are go for powered descent." Go, Eagle, go. Go true, go safe.

"OUR POSITION indicator shows us to be a little long," says Eagle, 40,000 feet over the Moon. Steady, Eagle.. Slow, Eagle.

"Fourteen thousand feet and coming down beautifully."

"Two thousand feet..."

"FOURTEEN hundred feet ..."

"Five hundred and forty feet." Gently, Eagle, oh, gently.

"Four hundred feet ... Face forward and hatch down ..."

"Two hundred and fifty feet .. . Two hundred and twenty feet .. . Coming down nicely ..." Lovely, Eagle. Lovely.

"One hundred feet ..."

"SEVENTY-FIVE feet ..." Oh, Eagle!

"Lights on ... Forward. Forward. Good. Forty feet ... picking up some dust ... Faint shadow ... Drifting to the right a little." Careful, Eagle, careful.

"Contact light. Okay engine stop ... Engine arm off."

HOUSTON: "We copy you down, Eagle."

"Houston ... Tranquillity Base Here. The Eagle has landed." Eagle tells Houston and the world and eternity.

Columbia: "Fantastic."

Fantastic, Eagle, fantastic. The word was made for you.

Meanwhile, Back on Earth, It's Nice

Although attention is turned on the Moon, weather continues on the Earth, and for the Madison area it is generally pleasant.

Sunday was fair and sunny with a high of 84 at 5 p.m. and a low of 65 at 5:30 a.m.

Today should continue pleasant with a forecast of sunny weather. There is zero per cent chance of rain. The high should be above 80.

More on Apollo ...

apollo 11 SOUVENIR EDITION

Wisconsin State Journal

Aldrin Asks World to Give Thanks

SPACE CENTER, Houston (UPI) — Edwin E. Aldrin Jr. Sunday asked everyone in the world to pause and give thanks for the lunar landing.

The astronaut, speaking in a calm voice from the lunar module (LM) Eagle said:

"This is the LM pilot. I'd like to take this opportunity to ask every person listening in, whoever and wherever they may be, to pause for a moment and contemplate the events of the past few hours and to give thanks in his or her own way."

Immediately afterwards, Aldrin resumed his discussion of technical matters with the ground control station.

... and the World Watches and Marvels

(Compiled From Wire Services)

America and the world held its breath Sunday and then let out a sigh of pride and relief.

Crowds screamed joyously in London's Trafalgar Square, people danced in Chile, and a Russian shouted "Hooray." Almost everyone on Earth was touched somehow by man's arrival on the Moon.

PRESIDENT Nixon and a half billion other people watched the Moon show on television, experts estimated.

Another billion couldn't see it because it was not shown in the Soviet Union or Red China. The remaining 2 billion earthlings had no sets.

There were prayers for the astronauts in churches throughout the United States and elsewhere.

IN THE U.S., a network official estimated the TV audience for the Moon walk might be 150 million, 95 per cent of total saturation.

Americans watched in homes, bars, night clubs, prisons, and on special sets or screens at race tracks, parks, plazas, and airports.

The day man came to the Moon was a warm, lazy day in much of the U.S. — a typical Sunday in July with one tremendous difference, the exhilration of knowing that two Americans had gone where no man had ever set foot before.

There was a holiday air in the nation. President Nixon's call for a national day of participation meant millions of Americans wouldn't have to show up for work today. Even if they came in late, red-eyed and yawning from a night of staring at the television set, they could be pretty sure the boss would be understanding.

AS THE long, historic afternoon wore on, Americans went about their usual Sunday ways with the world of space always within ear shot, sometimes before their eyes — the calm, staccato voices of Astronauts Neil Armstrong and Edwin Aldrin Jr. and their ground controllers. The fliers maneuvered their way to the floor of the Moon.

The voices from space and their televised images followed American to the beaches, the golf courses, the ball parks, the camping sites, all the places where they would normally spend a summer afternoon away from work.

Sunday night, there were Moon watch parties. Many vowed they would stay in front of their sets for the duration of the great adventure.

PRESIDENT Nixon sat rapt before his television set during the epochal Apollo 11 Moon landing and called it "the greatest moment of our time."

The President sat alone in his hideaway office in the Executive Office Building adjacent to the White House to view the landing on a portable color television set.

He told his press secretary, Ronald Ziegler, the last 22 seconds of the descent "were the longest I have ever lived through."

"WE'VE PROVED that we're No. 1," said Leo Vigil, 51, of Albuquerque, N.M. And, Vigil's words were echoed by most Americans.

"The Moon landing is the most fantastic thing that has ever happened," said Cecil T. Morris of Leawood, Kan. "The landing means to me just what it means to any American — pride in accomplishment."

There were dissenters. "It doesn't do any good," Mrs. Rose Rosen, 76, of New York City, said about the landing. "On this Earth there are so many people who are unhappy, forsaken and poor."

PERCY SIMPSON, 11, of Chicago, said, "I don't think they should be fooling around up there ... If God intended us to see the Moon, he'd send it down here."

Kings and presidents, prime ministers and prelates sent congratulatory cables to the Apollo 11 astronauts, in care of the Space Center at Houston, and to President Nixon.

"It is an achievement of such

Turn to Page 2, Col. 3

Wisconsin State Journal

WEATHER: Fair and Pleasant Through Wednesday. High Today Near 85. Low in 50s.

GOOD MORNING! 42 Pages, Four Sections Vol. 214, No. 295 130th Year MADISON, TUESDAY MORNING, AUGUST 25, 1970 ★ ★ ★ MORNING FINAL 10¢

VAN'S BLAST AT UW CENTER KILLS ONE AND HURTS FOUR

Sealed Off Site of Main Blast Area, Marked With X, Where Explosion Was Set

—State Journal Photo by Edwin Stein

Federal Men Head Probe; Classes Set

By CLIFFORD C. BEHNKE
Of The State Journal Staff

A powerful, pre-dawn explosion ripped through the Army Mathematics Research Center at the University of Wisconsin Monday, killing a 33-year-old researcher and injuring four other persons.

Police believe the blast originated in a small van truck parked at a loading ramp adjoining the center's south wall. The truck disintegrated into small pieces.

MILITARY intelligence officers and the FBI took charge of the intensive investigation. A spokesman for Gov. Warren P. Knowles said the two agencies would coordinate the probe because of the center's use of federal funds.

No arrests had been made Monday night.

The research center has been hit by vandals and anti-war protesters several times within the last year because of its connection with the military.

KILLED WAS Robert E. Fassnacht, 1237 E. Mifflin St. Fassnacht, the father of three children, was working on a physics project only a few feet from the blast.

Injured were:

- David Schuster, 28, of 641½ E. Dayton St., a student, who received a broken left shoulder;
- Norbert Sutter; 56, of Rt. 3, Madison, a University security guard, cuts and bruises.
- Paul Quin, 29, of 3362 Ridgeway Ave., a physics researcher, minor cuts.

An unidentified patient at University Hospitals who received a minor cut..

IN A JOINT statement, UW Pres. Fred Harvey Harrington and Madison Chancellor Edwin Young said that despite the blast the University will continue preparations for fall semester classes which begin Sept. 21.

Harrington said that the University was fortunate that the blast did not destroy a classroom building.

THE BLAST occurred at 3:42 a.m. Monday, two minutes after an anonymous caller told the Madison Police dispatcher: "Hey pig. There's a bomb in the Math Research Building on the University campus. Clear the building."

University police were on the way to the scene when the explosion ripped the building.

The explosion destroyed the interior of most of the six-story brick and re-enforced concrete structure. It also ripped through the rear portion of the old Chemistry Building located about 30 feet across Lathrop Dr. from the research center.

THE CONCUSSION broke hundreds of windows in the immediate area, dozens more as far as eight blocks away, and was heard several miles from the city.

A University engineer said after inspecting the scene that structural damage alone would probably run to between $3 and $5 million.

Damage to equipment has not yet been determined, but it will probably reach well over the $2 million mark.

THE RESEARCH center is located in a six-story addition to Sterling Hall with Van Vleck Hall to the north, Birge Hall to the east, the old Chemistry Building to the south, and University Hospitals to the west. Sterling Hall is located at the

Turn to Page 2, Col. 3

More on UW Blast, P. 4; Sec. 4, P. 1

Fund to Help Victim's Family

A memorial fund has been established for the widow and three children of Robert E. Fassnacht, the 33-year-old graduate student who was killed Monday in the explosion at the Army Mathematics Research Center.

Checks should be made out to the Robert Fassnacht Memorial Fund, 6328 Piedmont Rd., Madison, Wis., 53711.

More information is available from E.H. Behr, 271-2710 or from George E. Ott, 271-6678 at night and 262-2338 during the day.

Behr said the fund was established by members of the University of Wisconsin Physics Department.

Full Page of Explosion Photographs on Page 5

'Conspiracy of a Small Minority'

It's Part of Plot, Knowles Says

By JAMES D. SELK
Of The State Journal Staff

Gov. Warren P. Knowles Monday said he is convinced the bombing of the Army Mathematics Research Center on the University of Wisconsin campus is part of a nation-wide conspiracy of radicals bent on destroying American society.

"This I believe is a conspiracy of a very small minority who do not believe in our system of government and who are set to destroy our present way of life," the governor said.

HE MADE the statements at a hastily called news conference after a closed door meeting in his office with Mayor William Dyke, Police Chief Wilbur Emery, University Chancellor Edwin Young and other state and local officials.

The governor called on law abiding students to come forward and assist police in the investigation of the bombing which demolished the Sterling Hall center, shattered windows for blocks around, killed a young physicist, and injured four others.

"I THINK it is high time that the majority of students become aroused and that they become alerted to the fact that there is a very small minority of radicals who are the revolutionaries and the anarchists and are causing these incidents throughout the nation," Knowles said.

"I would hope that these students themselves would come forward with the information that is necessary for the enforcement officers to deal with this very difficult and complicated problem," he said.

THE GOVERNOR said he thinks members of the Weatherman faction of the now defunct Students for a Democratic Society (SDS). the Black Panthers, and other radical groups are behind much of the violence which has rocked the nation in the past several months.

But he did not single out either of the groups as being responsible for the explosion here.

Knowles repeated a pledge by University President Fred Harvey Harrington and Young that the school will begin its fall semester on schedule Sept. 21.

"WE ARE without question well organized," Knowles said of state and local forces which could be called up in an emergency to keep the campus open.

He indicated, however, that he did not plan to place the campus under martial law.

"You have to recognize there is a limitation," he said. "You can't make every campus an armed camp. People don't like that kind of surveillance."

When asked if his plans included a possible callup of National Guard troops, Knowles replied:

"WE'LL DO anything we can, within the law, to protect the lives and property of the citizens of Wisconsin."

Knowles has activated National Guard troops several times in the past several years to control demonstrators on and around the campus and the State Capitol.

Knowles visited the devastated area early Monday morning before returning to the Executive Office for a cabinet meeting and the meeting with officials concerning the bombing.

AFTER TOURING the area,

Turn to Page 2. Col. 5

No Sightseers

Mayor William D. Dyke has requested citizens to stay away from the area in the immediate vicinity of Sterling Hall.

The mayor said large crowds of onlookers could impede the investigation being conducted by authorities.

Public, Parochial School Bus Schedules, Page 12

Truck Thief Sought in Campus Explosion

By JUNE DIECKMANN
Of The State Journal Staff

Police and federal agents sought a truck thief here Monday night as a main lead to solving the pre-dawn explosion at the Army Mathematics Research Center that killed one man and injured four other persons.

Detective Capt. Stanley Davenport said the load of explosives — still unidentified — was believed to have been carried and detonated inside a truck stolen last Thursday night from the University of Wisconsin Lot 53, 1300 W. Dayton St.

MINUTE pieces of the truck, "but identifiable," were found after Monday morning's blast to identify the vehicle as one which was owned by Larry Travis, 117 Alden Dr., and stolen from the campus area lot Aug. 20 while he was vacationing in California, Davenport said.

Davenport asked anyone to call police headquarters if they saw the truck — a white 1967 Ford Falcon, small van-type Econoline with blue interior — between last Thursday and the 3:40 a.m. Monday bombing at Sterling Hall.

THE STOLEN truck apparently was driven into a service driveway, alongside Sterling Hall, and the explosives detonated while it was parked there out of street view, Davenport said evidence indicated.

About 15 FBI and Army in-

Turn to Page 2, Col. 8

First Meetings Scheduled Today in UN's Middle East Peace Bid

(c) N.Y. Times News Service

UNITED NATIONS, N.Y. — Gunnar V. Jarring announced Monday that he would open Middle East peace talks here today with the UN representatives of Israel, Jordan, and Egypt.

SECRETARY General U Thant's special representative to the Middle East said he would begin by meeting each of the three ambassadors separately in his 38th floor office here. He would not say whether there might be later joint meetings.

HE SAID he hoped that as progress was made the talks might progress to the level of foreign ministers but that he had no fixed ideas on procedure and "there are no textbooks."

Making a rare public statement after more than 2½ years of preliminary maneuvering and diplomatic pressures, Jarring refused repeatedly to an-

GUNNAR V. JARRING

Turn to Page 2. Col. 3

On the Inside . . .

. . . And Now It's Murder

See Page of Opinion

With Non-Violent Political Philosophy

Friends Recall a Dedicated Physicist

By ROGER A. GRIBBLE
Of The State Journal Staff

"He was a most unassuming appearing person — tall and lanky and soft-spoken, with a fine sense of humor. A most congenial sort of a guy.

"His political philosophy was not one of violence. Although he did not discuss the war, I do sincerely believe he was not in favor of our Vietnam involvement.

"He was a dedicated person. This is what killed him."

THIS IS HOW a friend described Robert E. Fassnacht, 33-year old University of Wisconsin researcher killed in the bomb blast that rocked the Army Mathematics Research Center here early Monday morning.

The friend, Erhard H. Behr, 1413 S. Whitney Way, a physics designer at the UW, has established a memorial fund to aid Fassnacht's widow and three children.

BEHR had known the post-graduate research assistant and his wife for five years. "We got to know him through his wife," he recalled.

Several years ago she took some experiments she was working on to the Brookhaven National Laboratory, Behr said, "and it was then that we got to know them.

"They were very dedicated, cultured people," Behr added. "We found later he'd built a harpsichord with his own hands. He played it most eloquently."

Mrs. Stephanie Fassnacht, mother of three, including year-old twins, said her husband wanted to get some experiments done. "That's why he was working late," she explained.

"We were planning to move on Wednesday and then take a trip to California," said Mrs. Fassnacht, a native of San Diego.

THE COUPLE both worked in Sterling Hall, which housed the Army Math Research Center, he on low temperature physics experiments, she on high energy physics. She is completing work toward a doctorate degree.

The UW said his work was not

ROBERT E. FASSNACHT

Turn to Page 2, Col. 6

Wisconsin State Journal

WEATHER: Mostly Cloudy, Warmer Today. Chance of Rain. High Near 38. Low in 20s.

58 Pages, Five Sections
Vol. 216, No. 137 132nd Year ★ ★ ★ MADISON, THURSDAY, FEBRUARY 17, 1972 ★ ★ ★ FINAL 10¢

'New Chapter' Opens

President Begins Journey Today

An Historic Meeting at the Wall: President Nixon and Chou En-lai

Arrives Sunday in China Capital

WASHINGTON (UPI) — President Nixon leaves Washington today on a 12-day journey to China to open "a new chapter" in relations with the world's most populous country.

On the eve of his departure, Democrats joined Republicans in wishing the President well on his 20,395-mile round trip to confer with Mao Tse-tung, Chou En-lai, and other Chinese leaders.

Senate Democratic Leader Mike Mansfield told newsmen that Nixon's trip

Related Stories on Pages 3 and 7; Reston, Page 13

could mark the beginning of a peaceful evolution in Sino-American relations, replacing more than 20 years of open hostility.

"The door has been opened by his initiative," Mansfield said.

LESS THAN AN hour before his scheduled departure at 9:30 a.m. CST, Nixon will meet with bipartisan leaders of the Senate and House, including the Democratic chairmen and ranking Republicans on major committees.

Nixon and his wife, Pat, will leave the White House by helicopter after a sendoff from their daughters Tricia Cox and Julie Eisenhower, members of the Cabinet, congressmen, government workers, and school children.

The Nixons will change to the blue, white, and silver presidential jet, "Spirit of '76," at Andrews Air Force Base, Md., for a 10-hour flight to Hawaii.

THE PRESIDENT plans to spend two nights in Hawaii and one in Guam to rest and overcome "jet lag" before his arrival in Peking on Monday morning (Sunday night in the United States).

"The post-war chapter (in relations between the U.S. and the People's Republic of China) comes to an end from the time I set foot on the soil of mainland China, and a new chapter begins," Nixon told a news conference last week.

The White House kept secret much of Nixon's agenda for his five-day stay in Peking and the one day each he will spend in

Turn to Page 2, Col. 3

Revised Itinerary

WASHINGTON (UPI) — The White House announced an updated itinerary Wednesday for President and Mrs. Nixon's trip to China.

Details of the trip after they arrive in China have not been announced fully.

9:30 a.m. (CST) Today — President and Mrs. Nixon and party depart Andrews Air Force Base en route to Kaneohe Marine Corps Air Station, Oahu, Hawaii.

3:30 p.m. HST (7:30 p.m. CST) —Presidential party arrives at Kaneohe, motors to the residence of Brig Gen. Victor Armstrong, commander of the First Marine Brigade.

Friday —President and Mrs. Nixon remain in Hawaii. No public events scheduled.

Saturday, 1:30 p.m. HST (5:30 p.m. CST)—President and Mrs. Nixon depart Kaneohe for Guam; cross International Date Line en route.

Sunday, 5:15 p.m. Guam time (1:15 a.m. CST Sunday) —Presidential party arrives at Guam International Airport; Nixons motor to the residence of Rear Adm. Paul E. Pugh, commander of naval forces in the Marianas.

Monday, 7 a.m. Guam time (3 p.m. CST Sunday) —Presidential party departs Guam en route to Shanghai.

Monday, 9 a.m. China time (7 p.m. CST Sunday) —Presidential party arrives at Hungchiao Airport, Shanghai.

Monday, 9:50 a.m. China time (7:50 p.m. CST Sunday) —Presidential party departs Shanghai Airport en route to Capitol Airport, Peking.

Monday, 11:40 a.m. China time (9:40 p.m. CST Sunday)—Presidential party arrives in Peking for formal greeting, first meeting with Chinese leaders, and banquet at Great Hall of People.

Feb. 22-25—In Peking. Schedule will include meetings; trips to Great Wall, Ming tombs, and Forbidden City; and a return banquet.

Feb. 26 — Depart Peking aboard Chinese aircraft for Hangchow. Boat ride on West Lake and banquet hosted by provincial revolutionary committee of Chekiang province. Overnight in Hangchow.

Feb. 27 —Depart Hangchow for Shanghai. Attend cultural show and Shanghai Industrial Exposition. Overnight in Shanghai.

Feb. 28 —Depart Shanghai for Washington on a direct polar flight, with refueling stop at Anchorage, Alaska.

Red Troop Buildup Growing

U.S. Warplanes Attack Artillery Guns in North

SAIGON, Thursday (AP) — American fighter-bombers launched scores of strikes Wednesday against powerful Soviet-made artillery guns inside North Vietnam and resumed pounding the targets today.

The United States Command said one Air Force F-4 jet was shot down Wednesday inside North Vietnam just north of the demilitarized zone and the two crewmen are listed as missing. Radio Hanoi claimed two planes were shot down and a number of airmen killed or captured.

THE COMMUNISTS, meanwhile, continued a massive troop buildup in South Vietnam in apparent preparation for a new offensive.

First reports said American planes destroyed at least five of the long-range 130-millimeter guns—most powerful in the enemy arsenal with a range of more than 16 miles.

A command spokesman said the guns had been installed inside North Vietnam's half of the buffer zone and just to the north of it for the first time in the Indochina war.

The raids were the heaviest inside North Vietnam since the intensive five-day bombing of last December.

THE COMMAND said the new attacks were "limited duration protective reaction air strikes against an enemy buildup of long-range artillery in and just north of the demilitarized zone."

It said the strikes "were necessary to counter a threat to the

Turn to Page 2, Col. 6

Russians Fined on Fishing Charges

ANCHORAGE, Alaska (AP) — Three Soviet officers were fined a total of $80,000 Wednesday on charges of conducting illegal fisheries support activities in United States waters.

Another $170,000 more will be paid to satisfy a civil complaint against their two ships.

The three Russians had asked that their pleas be changed from innocent to no contest.

G. Kent Edwards, U.S. attorney in Alaska, announced a $170,000 out-of-court settlement in the civil complaint against the two ships, the 362-foot processing vessel Lamut and the trawler Kolyvan. The vessels, seized by the Coast Guard last month near St. Matthew Island in the Bering Sea, are being held on Adak Island.

The fines are to be paid by the Soviet Embassy today to the Justice Dept. in Washington.

Vladimir Artemov, Igor Bovtun, and Nikolai Pavluk were charged Jan. 24. Artemov is master of an 80-vessel herring fleet operating in the Bering Sea. Bovtun and Pavluk are skippers of the two vessels seized.

Board at Mt. Horeb Can't Help Gonstead

By FRANKLIN W. IOSSI
Of The State Journal Staff

MT. HOREB — The Village Board concluded Wednesday night it legally couldn't change the property assessment of its internationally known chiropractor, C.S. Gonstead.

The board met to consider a reduction after Gonstead gave the village 30 days to reduce his nearly $67,000 in taxes by half.

HE HAD SAID if the village didn't meet his request he would give his 50-year-old business, clinic, and 78-unit Karakahl Inn motel to the Palmer College of Chiropractic, Davenport, Ia., and start anew in Florida. That would take all off the tax rolls.

The board decided it couldn't change the assessment because the taxes had been paid and budgeted for the year. Instead, it unanimously voted to write a letter to Gonstead asking that his and the village's appraisers sit down and reach an equitable agreement this spring when the village is reassessed.

"MUCH AS we'd like to help the man, our hands are tied," said Trustee Alton Lust. Most of the 40 persons in attendance disagreed with the suggestion of help.

The meeting was noteworthy for Gonstead's absence and the

Turn to Page 2, Col. 4

Warmth May Turn New Snow Into Rain

Snow returned to the area Wednesday night, but it will have to fight it out with the thermometer today to see whether it will be allowed to stay.

The temperature was around 30 when the snow began to fall and it is expected to be in the mid or upper 30s today, so the snow could easily turn to rain.

The low tonight should be in the 20s, a marked difference from the Wednesday low of 1 below zero at 5:30 a.m., and temperatures probably will drop on Friday. The high Wednesday was 31 at 8:30 p.m.

Today's Chuckle

You're getting old if you once won a prize in a dance marathon or were proposed to in a rumble seat.

Nixon Trip Might End War, Democrats' Newsletter Says

WASHINGTON (UPI) — The Democratic National Committee — basing its comment on speculation and rumor — said Wednesday it thought President Nixon might arrange a settlement of the entire Indochina war during his Peking meetings.

The Democrats, in their national newsletter Fact, said that despite Nixon's disclaimers, it was "clearly within the realm of the possible" that the President might take part in a secret summit meeting of Asian Communist leaders in Peking that would produce a comprehensive settlement.

The settlement, suggested Fact, might include an immediate ceasefire; the prompt resignation of South Vietnamese President Nguyen Van Thieu; a total United States withdrawal and return of all American prisoners by Aug. 15; national elections in the South by early December; and suspension of all U.S. military aid.

"Democrats would be found in the front ranks of those

Turn to Page 2, Col. 5

Mrs. Irving Arrested, Released Pending Hearing on Extradition

(c) N.Y. Times News Service

NEW YORK — Edith Irving was arrested by a federal marshal Wednesday in a United States District Court in New York and then released under a $250,000 personal recognizance bond pending a hearing Mar. 8 on a request by the Swiss government for her extradition.

Before leaving the courthouse, Mrs. Irving, the wife of author Clifford Irving, was fingerprinted at the direction of U.S. Magistrate Martin D. Jacobs despite a request for waiver of the procedure by Mrs. Irving's counsel, Maurice N. Nessen.

EDITH IRVING

The German-born, naturalized-Swiss wife of the controversial author was ordered to surrender her passport and was restricted by the court to the states of New York and Connecticut, where Nessen said he has a home which the Irving family plans to visit.

The Swiss government has charged her with forgery, counterfeiting, using counterfeit or forged instruments, and embezzlement and theft in the form of larceny in connection with the handling of monies intended by the McGraw-Hill Book Co. for industrialist Howard R. Hughes.

Irving said he had compiled an autobiography of Hughes and the payments were intended for Hughes in return for the material, which the company intended to publish. Spokesmen

Turn to Page 2, Col. 7

On the Inside . . .

Patterson Quits Milwaukee Bucks

See Sports Peach

Albany Recipient Can't Collect $100

Award Scholarship Cupboard Proves Bare

By ROGER A. GRIBBLE
Of The State Journal Staff

Alvin F. Kranig of Albany thinks the state of Wisconsin gave his daughter a bum check for $100.

And Kranig is trying to do something about making it good.

IT ALL started last spring when his daughter, Vikki, was given a Wisconsin Honor Scholarship upon her graduation from Albany High School. The awards are given to top graduates in all Wisconsin high schools.

Ever since 1966 those scholarships have been worth $100 when their recipients enrolled in college. Not so last fall.

WHEN VIKKI enrolled at the UW-LaCrosse she was told that the scholarship could not

JAMES JUNG

be redeemed because no state budget had yet been passed. She tried again this semester to redeem it after a state budget was finally passed. Again, to no avail.

The problem lies in the fact that the Wisconsin Honor Scholarship program was not continued by the Legislature in the 1971-73 state budget. In short, no money was appropriated to pay the scholarships.

James Jung, executive director of the State Higher Educational Aids Board (HEAB), was asked about the scholarships.

"THE GOVERNOR took the scholarships out of the budget," he explained. State high schools were warned about this in April in letters sent to all guidance counselors."

Jung said HEAB held up paying the $100 for each scholarship because it was clear the Legislature didn't intend to continue funding for the program.

"We've gotten a lot of heat on this and so have a lot of legislators," Jung complained. Two legislators, State Sen. Gordon Roseleip (R-Darlington) and State Rep. Joseph Tregoning (R-Shullsburg) have indicated they'll be at the Feb. 25 HEAB meeting to take up the matter.

Jung said high schools should have warned recipients of the scholarships that there probably would be no money appropriated by the state to pay for them.

KRANIG SAID his daughter got no such notice, and he claims that Albany High School Principal James Anseth told him the school got no notice on the matter from HEAB, Anseth could not be reached on Wednesday.

Jung said that between 700 and 800 scholarships have been given out in state high schools. When the program was eliminated it was replaced by scholarships and grants based on need.

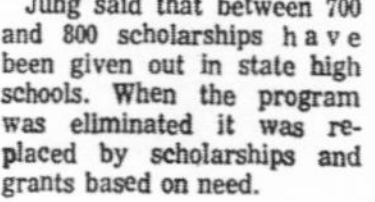

Wisconsin State Journal

WEATHER: Cloudy, Windy and Colder Today. High in Low 20s. Low Tonight Near Zero.

50 Pages, Four Sections Vol. 216, No. 138 132nd Year ★★★ MADISON, FRIDAY, FEBRUARY 18, 1972 ★★★ FINAL 10¢

KARL ARMSTRONG ARRESTED; NO CLUE TO OTHERS FOUND

Canadian police released photos of Karleton Armstrong, left and center. Photo at right is how Armstrong looked as UW student.

UW Bombing Suspect Held by Mounties

By ROBERT L. FRANZMANN
Of The State Journal Staff

TORONTO, Ont.—Karleton Lewis Armstrong's 18-month flight has ended, Royal Canadian Mounted Police (RCMP) announced here Thursday.

Accused in the United States of murder and other crimes in connection with the Aug. 24, 1970, bombing of Sterling Hall on the University of Wisconsin-Madison campus, Armstrong, 26, was arrested late Wednesday. The Sterling Hall blast killed a 33-year-old researcher, injured three others, and caused more than $1 million damage.

The RCMP said the arrest had not yet brought any leads on the location of three other Madison men also charged in the bombing.

THEY ARE Armstrong's brother, Dwight, 21, and former UW student Leo Burt, 25, and David Fine, 20. All four have been on the FBI's most wanted list since Sept. 4, 1970.

In Madison, Armstrong's father, Donald, 1721 Winchester St., was informed of the arrest by wire service newsmen shortly after noon Thursday.

The arrest in Karleton Armstrong's rooming house in Toronto's East End was quiet and inconspicuous.

"He did not resist in any way," Inspector George Potts of the RCMP headquarters in Ottawa said in a telephone interview.

So inconspicuous was the arrest that word did not leak out until the RCMP announced it Thursday afternoon.

"WE HAD reasons for not making the announcement earlier," Potts said.

Toronto authorities, however, said the arrest was not made public immediately because police hoped one or more of the other three men sought in connection with the bombing

Turn to Page 2, Col. 3

Other Stories

Sabotage Checked in Blast

LATEST

Possibility of sabotage was being checked early today after an explosion in a University of Wisconsin campus area substation critically injured a man and caused at least momentary power outage across Madison about 12:25 a.m.

The injured man was taken to University Hospital where he was listed in critical condition with extensive burns. He was tentatively identified as Pete Jabas, 20, a University of Wisconsin sophomore from Appleton.

Hospital officials said Jabas had severe third-degree burns to his "trunk and up."

POLICE LT. David Baggott said sabotage was suspected

Turn to Page 2, Col. 7

President in Hawaii En Route to Peking

KANEOHE MARINE AIR STATION, Oahu, Hawaii (UPI) — President Nixon arrived here Thursday on the way to his historic rendezvous in Peking.

The temperature was in the mid-70s as the President and Mrs. Nixon alighted from their "Spirit of '76" jetliner to the cheers and applause of an estimated 7,000 spectators.

MRS. HIRAM Fong, wife of Hawaii's Republican senator, placed a red lei, traditional Hawaiian greeting, around the President's neck.

She also draped leis around the necks of Mrs. Nixon, Secretary of State William P. Rogers, and presidential adviser Henry Kissinger.

Nixon strode to a roped-off area where the spectators stood and began mingling with them, chatting and touching the outstretched hands of children.

One group of children held up a sign which read: "Aloha President Nixon. Cub Pack 88."

BEFORE LEAVING Washington 10 hours earlier, Nixon said he hoped his unprecedented visit to the Communist Chinese mainland would help the two nations find a way to "have differences without being enemies in war."

The President was enthusiastic about a meeting with Democratic and Republican congressional leaders at the White House before his departure. He described the session as "very warm."

Nixon will spend two nights on this balmy island, plus a third on Guam, before arriving in Peking at 11:30 a.m. Monday (9:30 p.m. CST Sunday) for five days in the Chinese capital.

Flying in easy stages to keep rested and become acclimated to time changes, the Nixons scheduled no public events during their Hawaiian stay. They are quartered at the home of Brig. Gen. Victor Armstrong, commander of the First Marine Brigade.

NIXON'S ARRIVAL in Peking will be broadcast live to the U.S. by satellite, as will many of his activities in the capital and his visits to Hangchow and the great port city of Shanghai before he returns home Feb. 28.

About 1,000 Cabinet officers, diplomats, members of Congress, government employes, and school children bade the Nixons farewell on the White House south lawn Thursday morning. A nine-minute helicopter flight then took them to Andrews Air Force Base, Md., for the start of their 20,395-mile round trip.

THE NIXONS' two daughters, Mrs. Julie Eisenhower and Mrs. Tricia Cox, and men of such diverse political views as Sens. J. William Fulbright (D-Ark.) and Barry M. Goldwater (R-Ariz.) were on hand to wish the President well as he began his historic 11-day "journey for peace."

Congressional leaders whom Nixon and Kissinger briefed at the White House just before his departure reported that the President left without a formal agenda for his talks with Chinese leaders Mao Tse-tung and Chou En-lai.

IN BRIEF remarks at the departure ceremony, Nixon cautioned again against expecting any dramatic results.

Quoting from a toast Chou gave for Kissinger and his advance party in Peking last October, the President said:

"The American people are a great people. The Chinese people are a great people. The fact that they are separated by a

Turn to Page 2, Col. 6

China Trip Inside

Gusty Winds to Add Chill to New Snow

That wind is going to get colder.

The forecast calls for mostly cloudy skies with falling temperatures today. The wind was predicted to be between 15 and 25 miles per hour with gusts up to 40.

Occasional light snow may add a little to the one-tenth inch received Thursday. The skies should clear tonight with temperatures expected to be near zero.

Two Possible Methods

Officials to Seek Suspect's Return

By PATRICIA SIMMS
Of The State Journal Staff

The first steps toward returning Karleton Armstrong to Madison were taken Thursday by both federal and state authorities.

Dane County Dist. Atty. Gerald C. Nichol said that Gov. Patrick J. Lucey late Thursday officially requested the United States State Dept. to begin extradition procedures.

THERE ARE two possible methods of bringing Armstrong, wanted by the state for first-degree murder and arson and by the federal government for conspiracy and sabotage, from Toronto to Madison, Nichol said.

The first would be deportation procedures, which have already been set in motion with a hearing before an immigration officer, Nichol said.

Armstrong could be deported from the country as an undesirable, and would then be released to federal authorities in this country, U.S. Atty. John O. Olson said.

IF THE federal authorities gained custody, Armstrong probably would be tried first in Federal Court here on a seven-count indictment returned by a Federal Grand Jury here in September, 1970.

"We're hoping that Canadian officials will proceed with deportation procedures," Olson said.

On the other hand, a Canadian court last fall issued fugitive warrants for Armstrong at the request of Dane County law enforcement officers who traveled to Toronto based on the state charges of murder and arson.

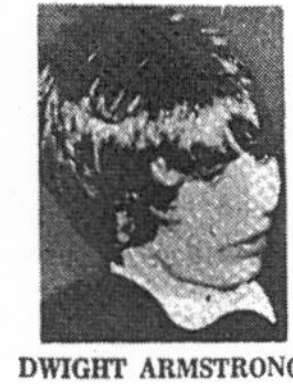

DIST. ATTY. NICHOL

"WE WANT them to act on our warrants," Nichol said.

Extradition on those warrants would mean that Armstrong would stand trial in Dane County courts first.

"Deportation could take up to three years," the district attorney said, "but extradition would probably take only four-to-six weeks."

Under extradition procedures, representatives of the district attorney's office would have to travel to Toronto and appear

Turn to Page 2, Col. 5

Glad He's Caught, Victim's Widow Says

Mrs. Robert Fassnacht, widow of a researcher killed in a 1970 University of Wisconsin bombing, said Thursday she was glad to learn of Karleton Armstrong's arrest in Canada.

"It's not a feeling of joy," Mrs. Fassnacht said, "But I'm glad he's been caught. I think people should pay for their crimes."

Mrs. Fassnacht, 34, added that she hoped the trial of Armstrong, one of four persons sought in the bombing, "doesn't turn into a big political show."

The widow said she was informed of Armstrong's arrest by her babysitter after returning from an errand.

The Fassnacht children are Christopher, 4, and twins Karen and Heidi, 2.

Mrs. Fassnacht said Christopher was aware of the circumstances of his father's death and would realize the significance of Armstrong's arrest.

3 U.S. Jets Shot Down in Strikes Against North

SAIGON, Friday (AP) — The United States Command reported today that two days of heavy air raids over North Vietnam inflicted major damage to Communist artillery and anti-aircraft defenses, but cost three American planes shot down with six crewmen missing.

THE COMMAND said in a communique that results of 125 strikes indicate that seven long-range 130-millimeter artillery guns, two surface-to-air missile sites, and five 85-millimeter anti-aircraft artillery guns were either damaged or destroyed.

In South Vietnam, the command reported, U.S. fighter-bombers uncovered a North Vietnamese staging area in the central highlands 24 miles northwest of Kontum. Bombing raids destroyed seven bunkers and a stockpile of supplies and equipment.

The command had reported earlier that one Air Force F-4 Phantom jet was downed Wednesday. It said today the two additional planes were lost Thursday.

The downing of the three planes marked the heaviest U.S. air losses over North Vietnam since last December.

All three were lost in an area less than 15 miles above the eastern portion of the demilitarized zone that separates the two Vietnams.

THE FEAR of American officials is that the big guns might be used to furnish an artillery screen for large scale North Vietnamese attacks across the border, as they were for the invasion and capture of the Plain of Jars in Laos last December.

The U. S. Command said in its weekly casualty report that two Americans were killed and

Turn to Page 2, Col. 8

area of attacks
—AP Wirephoto Map

On the Inside . . .

Hughes Moves to Nicaragua

See Story, Page 3

Today's Chuckle

Some parents have difficulty in deciding on a name for the new baby. Others have rich relatives.

Armstrong's Boss Calls Him Model Worker

TORONTO, Ont. — Karleton Lewis Armstrong, a Madison native, was a model worker, according to his employer for the last half a year in a gear factory here.

Armstrong, who was arrested by Canadian police late Wednesday in his home on Toronto's East End, "just seemed like an all-around nice guy, who never made any trouble for anybody," Ralph Reuby, owner and president of the Toronto Gear Works, Ltd., said in a telephone interview Thursday.

ARMSTRONG had been sought for 18 months by United States and Canadian authorities in connection with the fatal bombing of a University of Wisconsin-Madison building Aug. 24, 1970.

Still at large are Armstrong's younger brother, Dwight, 21, and two former UW students, David S. Fine, 20, Wilmington, Del., and Leo F. Burt, 25, Havertown, Pa.

Dwight and Karleton were last seen together in upstate New York shortly after the bombing, and police here found no evidence of the younger brother's presence in Karleton's residence.

DWIGHT ARMSTRONG

REUBY, who said Armstrong applied for a job with his small firm "five or six months ago" after reading an ad in a newspaper, said he was impressed by Armstrong's attitude at work.

"Right off the bat he seemed a cut above the guys who usually apply for a job here," Reuby said.

"Just to show you what kind of person he was, my brother, Charles, invited him to his home for Christmas dinner because he knew David (Armstrong was using the name David Weller) was alone," Reuby related.

"DAVID BROUGHT my brother's wife a book of poetry and his teenaged daughters a Beatles record when he arrived," Reuby said.

Reuby said he had not really heard much about the Madison bombing, and had never seen a picture of Armstrong.

"Oh, we have heard about the bombings at your universities, but I don't remember anything about that one in particular."

"I didn't really have anything to be suspicious about," Reuby said. "Though quite frankly, I thought he was probably one of your draft dodgers."

ARMSTRONG'S personnel file at the gear works, according to Reuby, indicates htat he had worked construction and odd jobs before applying for the machine shop job.

"He applied as a lathe operator, but I hired him as a gear machine operator, and he was a good one," Reuby said. He said Armstrong had worked both days

Turn to Page 2, Col. 3

Wisconsin State Journal

WEATHER: Fair and Warm Today. High Near 80. Low Tonight in Upper 40s.

36 Pages, Three Sections
Vol. 216, No. 225 132nd Year ★ ★ ★ MADISON, TUESDAY, MAY 16, 1972 ★ ★ ★ FINAL 10¢

MILWAUKEE MAN HELD IN SHOOTING OF WALLACE

Mrs. Cornelia Wallace kneels over wounded husband seconds after Monday's shooting at Maryland campaign rally.

—AP Wirephoto

Survival Hope Good; Doctors Fear Paralysis

LAUREL, Md. (AP) — Alabama Gov. George C. Wallace was shot and gravely wounded Monday while shaking hands with supporters after a campaign rally at a suburban shopping center.

An aide said late Monday night that doctors are optimistic he will survive the attack although there is a chance that some paralysis will remain.

A white man identified by police as Arthur Bremer, 21, Milwaukee, Wis., was arrested at the scene and quickly brought under federal and state charges.

George Magnum, a Wallace campaign aide, said Wallace, 52, struck down while making his third try for the presidency, was taken into the recovery room shortly after 9:30 p.m. CDT after about 5 hours of exploratory surgery.

A DOCTOR WHO assisted in the surgery at Holy Cross Hospital in nearby Silver Spring said Wallace was struck by five bullets, two of which caused serious

The Fourth Time in a Decade: Page 5

wounds. Magnum said one bullet was removed but another, near the spine, was left in place for the time being.

Magnum added that doctors told Wallace's wife, Cornelia, that "the governor was doing fine."

Mrs. Wallace went on television about 10:30 p.m. to read a brief statement to express her confidence that her husband will survive.

Appearing with Wallace's son and daughter beside her at the hospital, the governor's wife said: "I wanted to tell you that George is in very good condition. He has had a serious injury to his abdomen but he is out of surgery.

"THE CHILDREN AND I are going in now to speak to him. I spoke to him before the surgery. He was awake all the time. His mind was clear. He was talking to me all the way to the hospital. I feel very optimistic."

Wallace's son, George Jr., and a daughter, Peggy, flew into Washington from Alabama about 9 p.m.

Dr. James G. Galbraith, head of the University of Alabama's neurological department, said Wallace was paralyzed in the lower extremities.

The governor's wife said he had no feeling from the waist down.

In terms of total recovery from the paralysis, Dr. Galbraith said: "The outlook cannot be predicted, but it is not favorable . . . It would be unusual to get complete recovery under these circumstances."

Dr. Joseph Schanno, a vascular surgeon on the team which operated on Wallace, told a news conference a bullet lodged near the governor's spine makes it "difficult to assess the injury."

"If worse comes to worst, you could say he'd have the same disability as Franklin D. Roosesvelt."

Roosevelt suffered from paralysis of the legs caused by polio.

FEDERAL CHARGES drawn against Bremer accused him of assaulting a federal officer and violating the 1968 Civil Rights Act by assaulting a candidate for elective office. The federal officer is a Secret Service agent who was guarding Wallace and one of three other persons wounded.

The state of Maryland followed up with four charges of assault with intent to murder. He was ordered held on $200,000 bond.

Maryland State Atty. Arthur A. Marshall spoke to newsmen at Prince Georges County Hospital, where Bremer was taken for treatment of scalp lacerations and was given a medical examination.

He said Bremer has been questioned, but he would

Turn to Page 2, Col. 3

'He Never Mentioned Anything Political'

Suspect a Puzzle to His Family

By TIMOTHY L. CURRAN
Associated Press Writer

MILWAUKEE — Arthur H. Bremer, 21, a young photography student accused of shooting George C. Wallace, was described Monday as a lonely, quiet person who was something of a puzzle even to his family.

"Nobody could talk to him," Bremer's teen-age brother, Roger, said. "We never knew much about him."

BREMER LEFT the family's wood-frame South Side home last year and moved to an apartment, working as a custodian in public schools and at a private club.

Bremer's truck-driver father, William, 58, said the family "had no idea he was in Maryland. He never mentioned anything about Wallace, never mentioned anything political."

"GOD KNOWS that we hope he isn't connected with this," the father said. "If he is accused of this, he must have got really sick. We can't believe it."

"He never had a gun to my knowledge," the father said.

Another brother, Theodore, related: "He was against the radical part of the system of American life. He just stayed away from it."

STUDENTS, neighbors, and acquaintances of Bremer of-

Turn to Page 2, Col. 6

Nixon Orders Guards for Kennedy, 2 Others

From Wire Services

WASHINGTON — President Nixon offered and Sen. Edward M. Kennedy (D-Mass.) accepted temporary Secret Service protection Monday in the aftermath of the shooting of Alabama Gov. George C. Wallace.

The White House also announced that the President talked with Mrs. Wallace by phone at the hospital where her husband was undergoing surgery.

Press secretary Ronald L. Ziegler said the Alabama governor's wife reported that her husband was "conscious" at the time Nixon phoned and that she was "optimistic" about his condition.

Shortly after word of the shooting reached the White House, Ziegler said Nixon summoned Treasury Secretary John B. Connally and directed that Secret Service protection be extended to Kennedy and Reps. Shirley Chisholm (D-N.Y.) and

Turn to Page 2, Col. 8

Protesters to Hold March on Council

Anti-war protesters plan a rally on the University of Wisconsin-Madison Library Mall at 6:30 tonight to be followed by a march on the City-County Building.

The group wants to press for action on resolutions demanding withdrawal of Wisconsin resources from the Vietnam War, and an end to what it calls "police repression and brutality."

It will seek to have the City Council suspend its rules to take up the resolutions. The rally is sponsored by the United Front.

Panel Listens, Delays Action on County Executive Proposal

By RICHARD W. JAEGER
Of The State Journal Staff

Opponents of an elected county executive position Monday night pointed to results of a 1970 county-wide referendum in argument against the post, while supporters stressed the need of county leadership that answers "to all taxpayers."

Both sides of the controversial question of creating an elected executive in Dane County were hashed over before the County Judiciary Committee which conducted a public hearing on the matter.

ROBERT McDERMOTT

COMMITTEE MEMBERS indicated that they would not take action on two resolutions calling for the creation of the executive post for at least two weeks. The matter would then go to the whole County Board.

About 80 persons attended the hearing. Most of them were the same people who have appeared at other hearings on the executive issue during the past four years.

The thrust of the opposition to the executive post, which if created would replace the present appointed administrator position, was that the question was defeated in a referendum in the Nov., 1970, election.

SUPERVISORS Merton Walter, Dist. 30, Mazomanie; Robert McDermott, Dist. 26, Monona, and Edwin Hickman, Dist. 28, Middleton, charged that the move to create the executive post was an "attempt to overthrow the mandate of the people who expressed their feeling in the 1970 election."

The executive referendum lost by about 3,000 votes.

Hickman and Walter charged that the issue was up again because the news media, which had supported the executive position, "won't admit its defeat."

HICKMAN said he felt the supervisors supporting the position — 21 of them have signed the resolution — were doing so "because they fear reprisals of the newspapers who supported

Turn to Page 2, Col. 5

On the Inside . . .

Wallace Attack: An Editorial

See Page 10

Familiar, Formidable Political Figure

State Showing Gives Wallace Boost

By JAMES D. SELK
Of The State Journal Staff

Gov. George C. Wallace has been a familiar and formidable political figure in Wisconsin since he received an amazing 34 per cent of the Democratic presidential primary vote here in 1964.

GEORGE WALLACE

HE DROPPED off considerably here in the 1968 general election, in which he ran as an independent, but he popped back into the limelight last April when he ran a strong second to Sen. George S. McGovern in the Wisconsin primary, ahead of neighboring Minnesota Sen. Hubert H. Humphrey.

Wallace was clearly the most colorful figure among the large field of Democrats competing for Wisconsin's prestige and delegates Apr. 4.

He came into Wisconsin only eight days before primary day, but he came in like a gangbuster.

Wallace immediately sensed that Wisconsinites were "up to here" with high taxes, and he seized on that issue with a vengeance.

HIS ROUSING receptions at overflow auditoriums in cities throughout the state and his enthusiastic response from viewers to his 15-minute and half-hour television commercials, prompted the more conventional candidates to follow suit.

His Wisconsin appearances were well advanced, big-hall affairs, prefaced by country singers and musicians, such as folksy "Grandpa Jones" of Hee-Haw television fame.

Occasionally he had with him a Congressional Medal of Honor winner such as Gary Wetzel, Milwaukee Vietnam veteran, or an Alabama labor leader, and almost always his pretty, sharp-eyed wife, Cornelia.

He delighted his crowds with downhome rhetoric, roasting the "pointy-headed intellectuals," the "snotty newspaper editors" and the $30,000 a year "bureaucrats who walk around with their brief cases full of peanut butter sandwiches."

Although much of Wal-

Turn to Page 2, Col. 5

Wisconsin State Journal

WEATHER: Partly Sunny Today. High Near 80. Chance of Rain Tonight. Low in Mid-50s.

50 Pages, Five Sections
Vol. 217, No. 22 132nd Year ★ ★ ★ MADISON, WEDNESDAY, SEPTEMBER 6, 1972 ★ ★ ★ FINAL 10¢

ALL NINE HOSTAGES SLAIN; OLYMPIC FUTURE IN DOUBT

World Leaders Lash Attack

President, McGovern 'Outraged'

Associated Press

Expressions of horror and condemnation came Tuesday from many parts of the world after the Arab guerrilla attack on the Israeli team at the Olympic Village in Munich.

President Nixon talked by telephone from San Francisco with Israeli Premier Golda Meir, offering the "total cooperation" of the United States government.

HE LATER declared that the terrorists were "international outlaws of the worst sort who will stop at nothing to accomplish their goals."

Democratic presidential candidate George McGovern said in Portland, Ore., the act was "an outrage by any standard of humanity."

Secretary of State William P. Rogers said the U.S. had expressed its deepest condolences to the families of the victims.

Mrs. Meir in Jerusalem denounced the attack as insane terror.

UNITED NATIONS Secretary-General Kurt Waldheim called it "dastardly" and said "it was the more shocking for having taken place at the Olympic Games."

Moscow radio reported in a generally factual broadcast to the Soviet people that Soviet representatives had "expressed commiseration to the Olympic Committee . . . and expressed condolences on the deaths."

The U.S. State Dept. called the terrorists "outlaws, brigands, murderers, and an intolerable affront to society."

KING HUSSEIN of Jordan denounced the attack as "an abhorrent crime" perpetuated by "sick minds who do not belong to humanity." The king's reaction, the first by an Arab head of state, came in a telegram to West German Chancellor Willy Brandt.

In Munich, American swimmer Mark Spitz, who earlier had won a record seven gold medals, said: "As a human being and as a Jew, I am shocked and saddened by the outrageous act in the Olympic Village." He left Munich for London and will fly home today.

British Prime Minister Edward Heath, in Munich for the

Turn to Page 2, Col. 6

Hooded terrorist keeps watch on police activity from balcony of building where captives were seized.
—AP Wirephoto

Israelis Shot by Cornered Arab Captors

From Wire Services

MUNICH, Wednesday — Eleven members of Israel's Olympic team were killed Tuesday by a fanatic band of Arab terrorists.

Nine of the victims were slain in a wild gunfight at an airstrip 15 miles from Munich. The other two died 18 hours earlier when the incredible day of bloodshed began.

The murders left the future of the 20th Olympic Games, slightly more than halfway through their scheduled run, in doubt.

The guerrillas invaded the Israeli team's quarters at the Olympic Village before dawn Tuesday and shot down two Israelis. They held nine others hostage through a day of tense negotiations that ended when captors and hostages were taken by helicopter to the airport and a plane that was to fly them to Cairo.

POLICE SHARPSHOOTERS opened fire on the Arabs after the helicopters landed, but missed some because of the darkness. The guerrillas who escaped the first shots then turned their guns on the helicopters with the helpless Israelis inside, authorities reported.

There was another report that the hostages were killed by grenades when the Arabs discovered they were caught in the police trap at the airstrip.

Four of the Palestinian commandos were killed, three were captured, and one was unaccounted for, police said. One policeman was reported killed, and a helicopter pilot was seriously wounded.

Bavarian Interior Minister Bruno Merck said the Israeli hostages had agreed to go with the Arabs to Cairo. But the German authorities felt that "this would have been a certain death sentence for them . . . we had to take a chance and attempt to free the hostages."

HE SAID ONE OF THE guerrillas killed himself by exploding a hand grenade. It set fire to a helicopter with some of the hostages trapped inside — blindfolded, their hands bound, linked together with ropes. He said other guerrillas shot at fire engines to keep them from reaching the blazing helicopter.

One of the airport victims was David Berger, 28, a weightlifter who moved to Israel three years ago from Cleveland, O.

Olympic officials said a decision on whether to continue the games would be made after a memorial service this morning for the dead Israelis.

In all, the Israeli team death toll included five coaches, four weightlifters, a wrestler, and a referee.

The guerrillas were members of the militant Black September movement which has engineered a number of terrorist acts. After shooting their way into the Israeli headquarters, killing the first two Israelis, they herded the survivors together, tied their hands in front of them, and held them at gunpoint for 13

Turn to Page 2, Col. 3

More on Munich . . .

Scientist Ends 6-Month Stay in Cave

DEL RIO, Tex. (AP) — French scientist Michel Siffre emerged into daylight Tuesday after six months underground trying to see if man can break the 24-hour time cycle in which he lives.

Greeted by his wife, Nathalie, he walked to the living quarters of the above-ground crew and collapsed on a bench with his head across his arms.

"A boire, a boire (Give me a drink)," he murmured.

He later told a news conference that twice during his time under ground he achieved a 48-hour day. The average living cycle was 25 hours, he said.

The tip of his white helmet emerged from the cave at 11:49 a.m. Nathalie, dressed in a bright orange sweater and green pants, reached into the cave and helped him out.

Siffre, 33, looked around at the cloudy sky as he merged and declared: "C'est bon (It's good)."

"I am very tired," he said, "but I feel better than I did 10 years ago." The Euopean spelunker spent two months in a glacier in the French Alps in 1962.

He wore a French tricolor tucked into the open neck of his jumpsuit. He had carried the flag on all his previous underground experiments.

It was Feb. 14, St. Valentine's Day, when Siffre went down a swaying ladder to the cave that was to be his home for the next 205 days.

He aimed to prove that man, when cut off from contact with global time, can adapt his life easily from a daily cycle of 24 hours to one of 48. Throughout, his only contact with the world was by a field telephone rigged to his base camp. He had no watch, no mail, no newspapers, no radio, no means of telling time.

Siffre's experiment was backed by the French Geological Institute, the French Defense Ministry, and NASA — the U.S. National Aeronautics and Space Administration. American business firms loaned valuable computer equipment, and the Marriott Corp. of Washington provided him with frozen food identical with that used on the Apollo 16 Moon mission.

What Siffre learned during six months in the cave is expected to serve long-distance jet pilots crossing time zones, nuclear submarine crews on prolonged cruises, and astronauts.

His activities were constantly monitored by a ground crew which kept track of his health through electrodes connected to his skull.

Today's Chuckle

"A submarine," wrote the young sailor on his first test, "is a ship with water on all four sides of it."

Senate Bill Aids Lawmen's Families

WASHINGTON (AP) — The Senate approved a bill Tuesday to pay $50,000 to the dependents of policemen and firemen slain while on duty.

It would be retroactive to 1967.

The bill, passed 80-0, now goes to the House.

It also covers prison guards and National Guard troops slain while enforcing criminal laws, including highway patrol and maintenance of civil peace.

Passage of the bill was the first action of the Senate upon return from a two-week recess for the Republican National Convention.

Showers May Cool End of a Fine Day

Another fine day appeared to be in store for the Madison area today, but showers have a slight chance of moving in tonight.

The high should be about 80 in the city, following Tuesday's high of 77 at 3:30 p.m.

Night temperatures are beginning to get a bit lower. Tonight's high should be in the mid-50s.

Crowd Here Deplores Slayings, Asks Memorial at 1st UW Game

By DIANE CARMAN
Of The State Journal Staff

A rally and memorial service for the two Israelis killed by Arab terrorists at the Olympic Games in Munich was held on the University of Wisconsin Library Mall Tuesday night.

Prayers were said and comments were made by several speakers to the largely student crowd of between 400 and 500 persons.

(The service was held before the full extent of the carnage in Munich was disclosed.)

DURING THE 30-minute rally a petition was circulated requesting that a "two-minute memorial silence" be held before the Wisconsin-Northern Illinois football game on Sept. 16.

One of the rally organizers, Haim Golden, read statements from Gov. Patrick J. Lucey, State Rep. Norman Anderson, UW-Madison Chancellor H. Edwin Young, and the campaign office of Democratic presidential candidate George McGovern. State Sen. Fred Risser and State Rep. Marjorie Miller also spoke.

LUCEY EXTENDED his sympathy to the families of the slain men and condemned the incident.

The McGovern statement described the incident as one that "symbolizes the dangerous currents of violence in the world today."

The crowd was quiet, responding only once during the speeches to join in a prayer led by Rabbi Alan Lettofsky, new director of the Hillel Foundation.

TWO TORCHES were lit representing the souls of the dead Israeli and a chant for peace was sung by Cantor Leo

Turn to Page 2, Col. 5

On the Inside . . .

School Bonds' OK Faces Veto

See Sec. 4, Page 1

Police helicopter hovers over Olympic Village during tense drama.
—AP Wirephoto

Overpriced Florida Sun —The Spotlight

Problem Kids and Parents —Look Section

'Stranger in China' —People Page

Wisconsin State Journal

30¢

WEATHER: Travelers' Advisory, Cloudy, Colder, Snow Flurries Today. High 28. Low 10.

168 Pages, Sixteen Sections
Vol. 217, No. 161 133rd Year

★ ★ ★ MADISON, SUNDAY, JANUARY 28, 1973 ★ ★ ★ FINAL

Peace IN Hand; Draft Ends

Pentagon to Rely on Volunteers

WASHINGTON (UPI) — A few hours after the Vietnam ceasefire was signed in Paris, Defense Secretary Melvin R. Laird announced Saturday an immediate halt in the draft — except for doctors and dentists — and future reliance on volunteers to fill the ranks of the armed forces.

"The all-volunteer era — which our commander-in-chief, President Nixon, has promised the American people — is upon us," Laird said. "Use of the draft has ended."

Laird's order canceled his earlier plan to order draft calls for 5,000 men in the four months

History of Draft
See Story, Page 2

of March through June. There were no draft calls for January or February.

THE INDEFINITE suspension of the draft, barring a national emergency, means that the last draftees apparently will be the 2,500 who were inducted in December for two years of active duty. They were the last of 51,800 who were drafted last year.

At the height of the Vietnam war buildup in 1966, draft calls reached a peak of 364,000 men. Except for a 13-month lapse after World War II, the draft has been a continuing fact of life for millions of American young men since 1940.

The President's conscription authority under the Selective Service Act expires anyway on June 30, his target date for conversion to an all-volunteer armed force. But because the law itself is permanent, local draft boards will continue to operate, and 18-year-olds still will be required to register for the draft and to report for pre-induction physical examinations.

PENTAGON SOURCES said there was no plan to ask Congress to extend the President's draft authority past June 30, an idea that got a cool reception at the Capitol last year. The annual draft lottery to establish the order of call will continue, however, in the event there is a national emergency and Congress again authorizes a draft.

Pentagon officials said there were no plans now to draft medical personnel, but Laird retained that option because of the traditional difficulty in attracting highly paid health pro-

Turn to Page 2, Col. 6

U.S. Secretary of State William Rogers and North Vietnam's Foreign Minister Nguyen Duy Trinh sign accords.
—AP Wirephoto Via Cable From Paris

Paris Accord Halts Viet War

From Wire Services

PARIS — The United States, North and South Vietnam, and the Viet Cong signed the accord Saturday bringing an uncertain peace to Vietnam after a generation of war which killed 2.3 million persons and bitterly divided the American people.

The guns were ordered to fall silent in Vietnam at 8 a.m. today (6 p.m. CST Saturday).

While Communist demonstrators on the Avenue Kleber outside Paris' baroque International Conference Center shouted in triumph, the four signatories signed the peace settlement, toasted it in champagne, and then hurried away without public handshakes.

SECRETARY OF State William Rogers signed for the U.S. The signing was in two sessions, morning and afternoon. Half a world away the war went on the Vietnam battlefields until virtually the moment of the ceasefire hours later.

At Orly Airport after the signing and minutes before taking

27 POWs Named
SEE SEC. 4, PAGE 4

off for home, Rogers noted the ceasefire was to take place during his flight, "and very soon thereafter we have every reason to hope, and we do expect, that the ceasefire will extend to all Indochina. Then there will be no major fighting in any part of the world."

Rogers said President Nixon had set a goal of peace for a generation. "The advancement here in Paris today is a milestone in achieving this goal," he said.

THE SETTLEMENT provides a fragile peace and international control machinery intended to build a lasting one. The last 23,700 American soldiers in Vietnam will be withdrawn within 60 days and American military men held prisoner by North Vietnam — some for up to eight years — will be released during the same period.

Peace Inside

Today's Wisconsin State Journal carries extensive information on the Vietnam ceasefire which took effect at 6 p.m. CST Saturday.

PAGE 2. Last GI to die hoped for peace.

PAGE 3. Peace celebrations moderate; families of POWs, missing to learn their fate soon.

PAGE 4. Blood flows to the very end of the war; Saigon says U.S. promises to act if Reds break truce; fighting ends in war of nerves; freed POWs to get kid glove treatment.

PAGE 11. Reston comments: Truce accepted quietly.

The North Vietnamese and Viet Cong handed over a list of the POWs to the U.S., and in Washington, the Pentagon started preparations to notify their families. U.S. officials said they hoped the Communists' list might contain more than 600 names.

The accord called for internationally supervised free elections in South Vietnam. It called for no more North Vietnamese men and arms to enter South Vietnam, cutting the Ho Chi Minh Trail.

THE PREAMBLE on the four-party documents mentioned no government by name and referred only to the "parties participating in the Paris conference in Vietnam."

The agreements were built of compromises that permit the two Vietnamese sides to give them contradictory meanings

Turn to Page 2, Col. 3

Few at Peace Vigil, but Feeling Is High

By GEORGE HESSELBERG
Of The State Journal Staff

Bill Hemment paused in front of Grace Episcopal Church at 6 p.m. Saturday.

He was the only one there.

For at least two long minutes he just stared at the bell tower of the church, and when the bells started ringing to mark the end of the Vietnam war, he had to smile, perhaps to keep from crying.

HEMMENT, 27, of 323 E. Johnson St., spent a year in Vietnam, as a hospital medic in Da Nang. "I heard there were only three churches in the city that would ring their bells.

"I just had to come up here."

Across the street on the Square a car pulled up, and Dick and Lois Jellings and their two young children got out. Despite the rain, everyone in the family lit a sparkler and stood across from the church listening to the bells.

The Jellings, 4025 Steinies Dr., now were the only ones paused on the Square. The bells were chiming taps, signalling the end of 10 minutes of ringing and 12 years of war. The sparklers burned out in the rain.

"I WANTED this to be a day my children could somehow remember. Maybe their generation won't have to live through a war like this," Jellings said.

By now other people were pausing, car horns were heard around the blocks, young and old were hanging out of car windows flashing peace signs.

An elderly couple just sat quietly in their car, waiting for the ringing to stop, waiting for the war to end.

First Women MPs Since WWII Installed

FT. GORDON, Ga. (UPI) — The first women military police since World War II were graduated Friday in ceremonies at this Army base.

Brig. Gen. Mildred Bailey, commander of the Women's Army Corps, told the 21 graduates that "now the Army is permitting women to go into fields we knew all along they could do but were allowed to do only in emergencies."

Guns Roar After Truce

Fighting Dies Slowly in Land Used to War

From Wire Services

SAIGON, Sunday — The Vietnam war, which cost the United States nearly 46,000 combat deaths and $137-billion over a 12-year-period, came to an official end at 8 a.m. Saigon time today (6 p.m. Saturday CST) but at least scattered fighting continued after the deadline passed.

The ceasefire was greeted in Saigon by the sound of bells, drums, gongs, and the national anthem played by loudspeakers on street corners — and by a warning from a skeptical President Nguyen Van Thieu that "we will have to break their heads open" if the Communists violated it.

THE SOUTH Vietnamese command reported this morning that in the 24 hours ending at dawn, North Vietnamese and Viet Cong troops initiated 334 incidents throughout the country. According to government officers, that was the highest number since they began keeping a record. However, they said that during the Tet offense of 1968 a larger number of Communist troops probably was involved in the attacks.

The United States Command said two American planes were shot down Saturday afternoon while supporting government marines in northeastern Quang Tri province, and listed four airmen as missing.

Only an hour and a half before the ceasefire began, Communist gunners hit Tan Son Nhut airbase on the outskirts of Saigon with 20 122 mm. rockets, U.S. officers said. There were no report of U.S. casualties, but an oil storage area was set ablaze and one Vietnamese civilian was killed and 20 civilians wounded.

FIGHTING was also reported continuing at Tay Ninh, a provincial capital northwest of Saigon, where Communist troops Saturday infiltrated the city, apparently in an effort to seize a well-known place in which to set up a capital for their Provisional Revolutionary Government.

But reports from South Vietnamese and American officers in the field early this morning said the Communist forces had

Turn to Page 2, Col. 8

Business Profile

Today's Wisconsin State Journal contains the annual Business edition.

Called Profile, the two-section, 36-page edition features comprehensive coverage of business, industry, education, and government as well as forecasts and reviews by economic experts.

Also included in the edition are stories and photos about people, products, and places and features and reports from the State Journal's 16-county circulation area.

Today's Chuckle

These days a child who knows the value of a dollar must be mighty discouraged.

Winter Returns on Slippery Roads

The spring-like weather was just too good to last.

After declaring a truce for most of the month of January, the weatherman served notice on Madison Saturday with a chilling rain — the worst of winter is not over.

Today's forecast starts out with travelers' warnings for Madison and most of the southern part of the state. Snow flurries, freezing puddles, and colder temperatures are forecast for today.

Winds from 15 to 30 miles an hour will accompany the temperature drop which calls for a high in the upper 20s today and a low tonight near 10.

Saturday's high was 42 at noon, while the low was 31 at 12:30 a.m.

Vigilant Peace Movement Seeks New Strategies

By JOSEPH McBRIDE
Of The State Journal Staff

Reports of the death of the peace movement in Madison are greatly exaggerated.

The most prominent anti-war organization in the city, the Madison Area Peace Action Council (MAPAC), will hold a meeting this week to assess its peace-time function, and a group of concerned students will meet at 7:30 p.m. Monday in the University of Wisconsin YMCA to discuss strategy.

MRS. MARIANNE Rice, chairman of MAPAC, said that the ceasefire negotiations over the last few months did not cause a slackening of interest among the group's members.

MAPAC, a coalition of about 30 organizations, may change

MRS. RICE

its name, she said, but it will not change its purpose of keeping a vigilant eye on American military policy.

"This is not a peace with honor," she said, "because we bombed them into it."

Eddie Handell, a veteran of local anti-war protests who is now a Dane County supervisor

HANDELL

in Madison's Dist. 8, said the peace movement will continue because a war like the Vietnam War "could happen again."

"PEOPLE ARE so dedicated that they will stay together," he said. "Because there is a ceasefire doesn't mean it will keep up, and it doesn't mean there is

MRS. BOARDMAN

not going to be a war in the Philippines, Bolivia, or South Africa.

"Most people in these groups feel the war in Vietnam wasn't a mistake we just stumbled into, but rather it was planned policy, and therefore it could happen again."

Mrs. Betty Boardman, who caused a controversy in 1967 when she accompanied a Quaker shipment of medical supplies to North Vietnam, said it would be "at our peril" for the peace movement to disband now.

"NIXON AND his friends are going to get some advantage out of ending this war at this point," she said. "He's not doing it because any of us asked him to; we don't have any power right now."

Mrs. Boardman, who is active in the Wisconsin Alliance, hopes the ceasefire will cause more of a focus on local issues.

"We need practice running our affairs locally," she said. "We can't pretend to take

Turn to Page 2, Col. 4

On the Inside

● A young handicapped student learns to drive a specially equipped car in a story by Ruth Flegel on Page 5.

● Richard Jaeger reports on the State Page how nearby residents react to the prospects of a new state park in Sauk County.

● The old Queen Elizabeth, half sunk in Hong Kong Harbor, has become the world's largest marine salvage operation. See the Spotlight.

ELECTION SPECIAL

Wisconsin State Journal

WEATHER: Light Rain or Snow Ending Today. High in Low 40s. Low in Mid 20s.

56 Pages, Four Sections
Vol. 217, No. 227 133rd Year ★ ★ ★ MADISON, WEDNESDAY, APRIL 4, 1973 ★ ★ ★ FINAL 10¢

SOGLIN OUSTS DYKE IN RECORD TURNOUT

Mayor-elect Paul Soglin and wife, Diane, share victory embrace.
—State Journal Photo by J. D. Patrick

Student Vote Aids Victory Over Mayor

By MICHAEL BAUMAN
Of The State Journal Staff

Paul Soglin, carried by huge pluralities in central city districts, stopped Mayor William D. Dyke's bid for a third term by nearly 3,400 votes Tuesday.

The Eighth Dist. alderman, who will become the new mayor Apr. 17, pulled in about 52.3 per cent of the record spring election turnout to Dyke's 47.7 per

The final vote was:

Soglin	37,548
Dyke	34,179

Soglin did even better tnan had been anticipated in the student-dominated downtown districts, and secured his victory by cutting down on Dyke's expected pluralities on both the East and West Sides.

Soglin's margin in the four central city districts — the Fourth, Fifth, Eighth, and Ninth — was nearly 9,000 votes, 10,426-1,548.

In the 18 other districts of the city, Dyke outpolled Soglin, 32,631-27,122.

SOME SAMPLES of the one-sided nature of the contest in the central city were the Second

Vote by Wards: Sec. 4, Page 2

Ward of the Eighth Dist., which Soglin carried, 1,463-86; the First Ward of the Fourth Dist., which he won, 1,154-226, and the Fifth Dist.'s First Ward, where he had a 946-89 margin.

In the Ninth Dist. alone, Soglin had an edge of more than 2,400 votes — 2,845-398.

Although Dyke carried most of the outlying districts, nowhere was he able to gain the kind of overwhelming support that would have offset Soglin's edge downtown.

Soglin consistently made inroads into expected Dyke strongholds, and, when the results were in, said "We were really surprised at how well we did in the East and West Side districts."

FOR SOGLIN, Tuesday night, though, the victory could be traced to what he felt was the essential difference between his campaign and Dyke's — "a campaign on the issues against an emotional harangue."

Referring to a comment by

Turn to Page 2, Col. 3

Outcome Is All Rosy for Victor

An exultant crowd of 1500 partisans greeted Mayor-elect Paul Soglin with roses at a victory celebration in the Madison Labor Temple Tuesday night.

Across town, a sober group of 300 backers at the Sheraton Inn heard defeated Mayor William D. Dyke stoically accept his loss.

CLUTCHING A handful of roses given him as he entered the jammed Labor Temple Hall, Soglin told the crowd, "the golden coalition came together" to win the hard-fought contest.

Dyke, with his wife at his side, told his audience, "When we entered public life, we always knew there was a chance of defeat. I'm saddened at my loss, of course, but we are more sorry for people like you."

THE CONTRAST between the two gatherings was as could be expected. Each began on a somewhat tense and apprehensive note as the uncertain early returns were reported.

By 10 p.m., Soglin had firmly established the lead he was to carry through the night and the crowds at each place knew what the final results would be.

At the Sheraton, a Dyke supporter turned away from a television set and commented angrily, "You can kiss Madison goodbye."

At the Labor Temple, each new report was greeted with cheers and the crowd began growing until it jammed the hall and spilled out into the hallways.

EACH CANDIDATE appeared at his gathering shortly before 11 p.m. Each was greeted by applause. At the Labor Temple, it was exultant. At the Sheraton, it was respectful.

Dyke spoke briefly, thanking his supporters and calling the

Turn to Page 2, Col. 8

Reinke Beats Kubly in Executive's Race

By W. L. CHRISTOFFERSON
Of The State Journal Staff

County Administrator George F. Reinke handily defeated Daniel Kubly Tuesday to become Dane County's first elected executive.

The vote, with 130 of 137 wards reported, was:

Reinke	51,496
Kubly	42,160

Reinke rolled up big margins in all areas—City of Madison, suburbs and rural areas—in winning his first elective office after a career of more than 30 years as a county employe.

"I'M REALLY pleased with the voters and the way they have been consistent throughout the county," Reinke said over the noise of a victory party at his Middleton home.

"I think you'll see a real new era in county government in the next four years," Reinke said. "This new position, independent

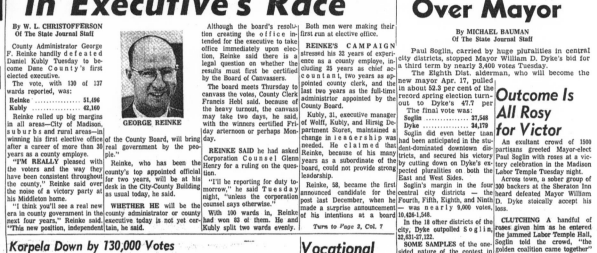

GEORGE REINKE

of the County Board, will bring real government by the people."

Reinke, who has been the county's top appointed official for two years, will be at his desk in the City-County Building as usual today, he said.

WHETHER HE will be the county administrator or county executive today is not yet certain, he said.

Although the board's resolution creating the office intended for the executive to take office immediately upon election, Reinke said there is a legal question on whether the results must first be certified by the Board of Canvassers.

The board meets Thursday to canvass the votes, County Clerk Francis Hebl said. because of the heavy turnout, the canvass may take two days, he said, with the winners certified Friday arternoon or perhaps Monday.

REINKE SAID he had asked Corporation Counsel Glenn Henry for a ruling on the question.

"I'll be reporting for duty tomorrow," he said Tuesday night, "unless the corporation counsel says otherwise."

With 100 wards in, Reinke had won 83 of them. He and Kubly split two wards evenly.

Both men were making their first run at elective office.

REINKE'S CAMPAIGN stressed his 32 years of experience as a county employe, including 25 years as chief accountant, two years as appointed county clerk, and the last two years as the full-time administrtor appointed by the County Board.

Kubly, 31, executive manager of Wolff, Kubly, and Hirsig Department Stores, maintained a change in leadership was needed. He claimed that Reinke, because of his many years as a subordinate of the board, could not provide strong leadership.

Reinke, 58, became the first announced candidate for the post last December, when he made a surprise announcement of his intentions at a board

Turn to Page 2, Col. 7

Election Bulletins

Bingo Amendment Passes

The state of Wisconsin was shouting "Bingo!" in election returns Tuesday.

On the question of whether the state should "amend or permit the Legislature to authorize bingo games" by religious, charitable, service, or fraternal groups, the yes vote led at every report.

With 3,046 of the state's 3,370 wards reporting, the vote was:

Yes	569,854
No	351,348

Equal Rights Issue Loses

Approval of the equal rights amendment to the state Constitution failed Tuesday in returns from across the state. With 3,046 of 3,370 precincts reporting, the vote was:

Yes	402,441
No	461,956

The amendment would create a section of the Constitution prohibiting "the denial or abridgement of rights and protections under the law on the basis of sex."

The first returns gave the yes a slight lead, but it then fell behind by more than 5,000 votes, cut the margin slightly, and fell back again.

3 City Aldermen Defeated

Eleven of 14 incumbents were returned to the City Council Tuesday in the Madison aldermanic elections.

Incumbents who lost were Ald. Timothy Kiefer, 16th Dist., Michael Shivers, 17th Dist., and Dale Wilson, 22nd Dist.

Since Shivers lost by only two votes, it is likely he will call for a recount.

Kiefer, Wilson, and Shivers were seeking their second terms.

All 22 seats on the council were up for grabs. The new council, including 11 new faces, will be seated Apr. 17, (Story, Sec. 4, Page 1).

2 Women Win School Posts

Mrs. Barbara Burkholder and Mrs. Nancy Harper easily won three-year terms on the Madison School Board Tuesday, far outdistancing the two male contenders.

With 69 out of 73 wards in the school district reporting the vote was: Mrs. Burkholder, 47,416 Mrs. Harper, 33,770; John Alexander, 24,312 and Charles Lem, 19,391.

The two women will replace Board President Ruth Doyle and Herbert Marcus on July 1. School Board posts are non-salaried. (Story, Sec. 4, Page 1).

Richland Drought Continues

RICHLAND CENTER — The 63-year "drought" here will continue at least another two years as 1,267 residents reaffirmed their stand against the sale of liquor in a referendum Tuesday.

The city, with a population of more than 5,000, voted 1,267 to 856 against authorizing the sale of liquor, and 1,247 to 858 against sale of beer.

Korpela Down by 130,000 Votes

Mrs. Thompson Wins Wisconsin School Post

Mrs. Barbara Thompson of Madison has won the statewide election for superintendent of public instruction, according to returns early today from most of the state wards.

Mrs. Thompson was almost 130,000 votes ahead of Ernest Korpela with 3,049 of the state's 3,370 wards counted.

THE TOTALS at midnight were:

Mrs. Thompson	515,571
Korpela	386,428

Mrs. Thompson, 36, of 6325 Landfall Dr., Madison, and Korpela, 48, of Washburn in the far northern part of Wisconsin, argued over endorsements for the new office, the politics of

MRS. THOMPSON

administering the office, and teacher strikes, while agreeing on the need for more state help for education.

This was the election for the superintendent's position which will vacated July 1 by William C. Kahl.

THE FOUR-year non-partisan position pays $25,000 a year.

Korpela's endorsement by the 45,000-member Wisconsin Education Assn. (WEA) was the major campaign issue.

Mrs. Thompson charged that the endorsement and about $25,000 in financial backing from the WEA would make Korpela indebted to the teachers organization.

Korpela said he did not fully agree with the WEA positions and had no debts to the organization.

KORPELA RECEIVED sup-

Turn to Page 2, Col. 5

Vocational Aid Veto Is Upheld

(c) N.Y. Times News Service

WASHINGTON — President Nixon won a stunning victory Tuesday as the Senate voted to uphold his veto of a politically-popular bill to supply vocational aid to the handicapped.

The vote was 60-36, four short of the two-thirds needed to override the veto. No further action is needed by the House.

THE SURPRISE Senate move would appear to indicate that Congress, despite the fact that it is numerically controlled by Democrats, is not willing to stand up to the President this year on his proposals to trim federal spending.

The vote also appeared to indicate that Democrats would be hamstrung in all efforts this year to enact bills that do not have the blessings of the President.

SHOCKED BY the vote, Mike Mansfield of Montana, the Senate Democratic leader, said glumly: "The President's in the driver's seat—at least for the time being."

The vetoed bill provided for a two-year, $2.6-billion extension of a broad program of federally matching grants to the states to aid the mentally and physically handicapped. For the first time,

Turn to Page 2, Col. 6

Severe Penalties Voted for Pushers

WASHINGTON (AP) — The Senate voted Tuesday for mandatory prison sentences for non-addicts who illegally manufacture or sell as much as one-tenth of an ounce of heroin or morphine.

For first offenders, the minimum sentence would be 10 to 30 years in addition to the penalties provided by present law. For a second offense, a life sentence would be mandatory.

In neither case would the offender be eligible for probation, suspended sentence, or parole except after serving 30 years of a life sentence.

In addition, mandatory sentences up to 30 years are provided for using or unlawfully carrying a firearm in the commission of federal crimes that threaten life or property.

Drippy Weather Supposed to Halt

Today's weather probably won't give any comfort to those awaiting real spring.

The forecast calls for occasional rain or snow ending by afternoon. The high should be in the low 40s, and the low tonight in the mid 20s. There's a 30 per cent chance of rain today.

Tuesday's high was 41 at 4 p.m., and the low was 34 at 4:20 a.m.

More Election News, Sec. 4, Pages 1, 2, 4

Justice Beilfuss Is Returned to State Supreme Court Seat

MILWAUKEE — Justice Bruce F. Beilfuss easily won a second 10-year term on the Wisconsin Supreme Court in the state's spring general elections Tuesday.

With 3,046 of the state's 3,370 wards unofficially tabulated, the vote was:

Beilfuss	570,568
Beaudry	274,284

BEAUDRY campaigned heavily, using street corners as well as normal forums to voice his message. Beilfuss traveled a more modest route, leaning more toward carefully selected campaign appointments.

An active Democrat and the father of 11 children, Beaudry, 52, a West Allis attorney, plugged away at what he called a need for the high court to permit estates to be probated in court without attorneys and to

JUSTICE BEILFUSS

end the practice of giving lawyers a percentage of the estate as a fee.

Beilfuss, 58, a former circuit judge from Neillsville, also supports probate reform but says it must come from the Legislature and not the Supreme Court.

Beilfuss said during the campaign he approved of bills now pending in the Legislature which would enable some estates to be probated administratively, without going to court and without an attorney.

HE DISAGREED, however, with Beaudry's call for the Supreme Court to reverse an earlier ruling which requires attorneys to handle all estates which go to court.

"There are legitimate interests that may be somewhat contrary to the interests of the individual seeking to probate an estate," Beilfuss said. "Things like inheritance taxes and the collection of outstanding bills owed by the deceased."

Beaudry also endorsed no-fault insurance and no-fault divorce and said the real future in the law "is going to be in the

Turn to Page 2, Col. 4

On the Inside . . .

Meat Industry Feeling Boycott

Story on Page 3

Today's Chuckle

Wife, at the airport: "Be sure to write, even if it's only a check."

Dane County Judge Races

Bruner and Torphy Are Reelected

By MAUREEN SANTINI
Of The State Journal Staff

Dane County Judges Ervin M. Bruner and Michael B. Torphy were reelected to new six-year terms Tuesday.

With 130 of 137 wards reporting, the vote for juvenile judge in County Court Branch Four was:

Bruner	62,036
Gerald C. Kops	32,213

In County Court Branch Six, the incomplete vote was:

Torphy	64,070
Stephen B. Schneider	24,720

Although both judges, who will be inaugurated Jan. 1, 1974, maintained healthy margins throughout the ballot counting, the challengers captured several wards.

JUDGE BRUNER

Kops made a good showing in several wards on Madison's East Side, particularly in the 18th Dist., which has experienced more than normal trouble with juveniles. He also won the Town of Medina and the Village of Marshall.

JUDGE TORPHY

Schneider, a Madison attorney, won 10 of the wards counted, all in Madison's central city, and particularly in heavily student-populated areas.

In both races, the challengers followed the normal campaign tactic of attacking as "ineffective" or "inactive" the records of their opponents.

The two judges appeared to rely mainly on their reputations and records, and refrained from taking defensive positions.

ALTHOUGH KOPS, 31, an assistant city attorney, was an aggressive campaigner, the race for the juvenile judge post lost much of its initial steam after Bruner received 56 per cent of the vote in the primary election.

Nevertheless, Kops continued his attacks at what he called the controversy sur-

Turn to Page 2, Col. 8

Wisconsin State Journal

WEATHER Flash Flood Watch Today. Rain Likely Through Wednesday. High mid 50s. Low 40s.

42 Pages, Five Sections
Vol. 217, No. 254 133rd Year ★ ★ ★ MADISON, TUESDAY, MAY 1, 1973 ★ ★ ★ FINAL 10¢

NIXON TAKES BLAME IN WATERGATE CASE

Atty. Gen. Richard Kleindienst resigns. —AP Wirephoto

Kleindienst, 3 Nixon Aides Go Under Pressure

WASHINGTON (UPI) — The rising tide of the Watergate scandal Monday swept from office Atty. Gen Richard G. Kleindienst and three of President Nixon's closest White House aides — H. R. Haldeman, John D. Ehrlichman, and John W. Dean III.

The President's statement announcing he had fired Dean and accepted the resignations of the other three was read at the White House while Nixon remained in seclusion at his Camp David retreat in the Maryland Mountains, where he has been since last Friday deciding how to cope with the crisis.

MONDAY NIGHT he made a nationwide radio and television address to report to the people on the ramifications of the bugging last year of Democratic National Committee headquarters—a scandal that has rocked the nation and all but paralyzed White House operations. **(See story, Cols. 7 and 8.)**

Nixon, accepting with "regret and deep appreciation" the resignation of Kleindienst, immediately named Defense Secretary Elliot L. Richardson to succeed him and take over the Watergate inquiry.

The President said Kleindienst felt he could not continue to head the Justice Dept. "now that it appears its investigation of the Watergate and related cases may implicate individuals with whom he has a close personal and professional association."

KLEINDIENST USED almost the same words in announcing last week he had removed himself from any further investigation of the Watergate affair.

Among those believed to be targets of a renewed grand jury investigation into the bizarre case are Dean, Ehrlichman, Haldeman, and Kleindienst's former boss — former Atty. Gen. John N. Mitchell, who was Nixon's campaign manager at the time of the June 17, 1972, Watergate arrests.

Haldeman and Ehrlichman remained in their White House offices Monday and there was no indication when their resignations would take effect. White House officials said they would remain for a "transition period."

A SECRETARY was also answering the phone at Dean's office, although Nixon made it clear that Dean had been fired and would be replaced by Leonard Garment.

Nixon described Ehrlichman, his chief domestic affairs adviser, and Haldeman, the powerful White House chief of staff, as "two of my closest friends and most trusted assistants."

He said his acceptance of their resignations "should not be seen by anyone as evidence of any wrong-doing by either one."

Dean reportedly has told government prosecutors that both men were involved in a concerted campaign to cover up the Watergate scandal.

PRESIDENTIAL PRESS Secretary Ronald L. Ziegler told reporters that Kleindienst, Haldeman, and Ehrlichman all decided to step down voluntarily.

But Nixon said he had "requested" the resignation of Dean, 34, the handsome White House general counsel who also has been implicated in the Wa-

Turn to Page 2, Col. 7

DEAN ERLICHMAN HALDEMAN

Elliot Richardson meets newsmen in Washington after becoming attorney general. —AP Wirephoto

Some Reservations

Nixon Stand Praised by Congress Members

WASHINGTON (UPI) — President Nixon won solid backing from Congress Monday for his housecleaning operation in the Watergate scandal, but several members said they would not be satisfied until a special prosecutor is appointed to get to the bottom of the case.

"I am very sympathetic with his position of trying to get things done with the difficulties that he has," Sen. William Saxbe (R-O.) said following Nixon's nationwide television-radio address on the scandal. "But I don't know any more about the Watergate than I did."

ASST. SENATE Democratic Leader Robert C. Byrd (D-W. Va.) urged the appointment of a special prosecutor immediately "to avoid any suspicion of a whitewash."

"The Administration must not investigate itself," he said.

Nixon said he had given Atty. Gen.-designate Elliot Richardson full authority to appoint a prosecutor to handle the case, if he chooses. But Byrd said he was "disappointed that he didn't state that this was imperative."

BEFORE THE President's speech, Sen. Barry M. Goldwater (R-Ariz.) said in North Dartmouth, Mass., that he would "expect impeachment proceedings" if it were shown that President Nixon knew or had been "dishonest" about the Watergate bugging case.

But he emphasized he did not believe Nixon "has withheld anything," and did not believe the President had prior knowledge.

Rpublican leaders weighed in with words of warm praise.

". . . Most statesmanlike and courageous appeal to principle," said Republican National Chairman George Bush.

"IT WAS fitting and proper that the President assume responsibility for the Watergate affair — and it was a most courageous act," said House GOP Leader Gerald Ford.

"The President once again has shown that in a time of crisis his stature as a man stands tall," Senate Republican Leader Hugh Scott said.

Sen. Robert Dole (R-Kan.), who has been critical of handling of the Watergate case, said Nixon "is in firm control. He is on the way to restoring confidence in the White House. I applaud his leadership."

SEN. LLOYD. Bentsen (D-Tex.) called for "an impartial and vigorous prosecutor free of

Turn to Page 2, Col. 4

Flash Flood Watch Issued for Area

The National Weather Service issued a flash flood watch today for the southern part of the state with more periods of showers and thunderstorms likely today through Wednesday.

Rains Monday dumped .83 of an inch of water on the area with little relief expected.

Cloudy skies are expected to continue with a high in the mid 50s and a low tonight near 40. Monday's high was 53 at 1 p.m. and the low 43 at 3:30 a.m.

Today's Chuckle

The happiest ending in the movies is when the guy behind you finishes his popcorn.

'Scoop' Provides Aid for College Students

EVERETT, Wash. (AP) — For the past 15 years, $31,000 has been paid out of an anonymous fund to help Washington college students.

They never knew to whom to address a letter of appreciation.

But under the new federal act requiring disclosure of congressmen's expenditures, Sen. Henry (Scoop) Jackson (D-Wash.) has been revealed as the man behind the fund. All his income from writing and speaking engagements goes into the program.

"I remember how it was," explained Jackson. "I washed dishes and waited on tables at the university. So I like to help."

Wage-Price Control Act Is Extended

WASHINGTON (UPI) — Congress passed legislation Monday extending President Nixon's wage-price control powers for one year and sent it to the White House just hours before all economic controls would have expired.

The act gives Nixon power until Apr. 30, 1974, to set and enforce guidelines for wages and prices.

Nixon is using the act now only for the relatively mild Phase III controls, which extend to health, construction, petroleum and food industries — with a rigid ceiling on meat prices. However, Administration spokesmen have indicated Nixon will place tighter controls on the economy in the face of mounting inflation.

THE SENATE passed a compromise bill by voice vote, and the House later gave it final congressional approval on a 267-115 roll call vote.

There was some fear that Republicans would try to send the bill back to the conference committee to get rid of several amendments, including one to force public disclosure of the information that big companies give the Cost of Living Council to justify major price increases.

However, the White House decided it could accept the amend-

Turn to Page 2, Col. 6

Richardson Given Probe Authority

By HARRY F. ROSENTHAL
Associated Press Writer

WASHINGTON — President Nixon told the nation Monday night he accepts final responsibility for the Watergate scandal that led him to accept the resignations of H. R. Haldeman, John D. Ehrlichman, and Atty. Gen. Richard G. Kleindienst.

In a solemn address to the nation, hours after a major shakeup in his Administration, the President said the blame belongs at the top.

PRESIDENT NIXON

"I accept it," he said in a nationally broadcast and televised address.

IN THE SHAKEUP, Nixon fired Presidential Counsel John W. Dean III and nominated Secretary of Defense Elliot L. Richardson to be attorney general.

The President gave Richardson the job of overseeing the Administration's investigation of the Watergate affair and of naming a special prosecutor to probe the bugging incident if Richardson deems one necessary.

Until late March, Nixon said he had been assured by those around him that no one in the Administration was involved in the wiretapping.

"HOWEVER, NEW information then came to me which persuaded me that there was a real possibility some of these charges were true, and suggested further that there had been an effort to conceal these facts, both from the public—from you—and from me," Nixon said.

See Editorial, Page of Opinion

Thus did Nixon disclaim any advance knowledge of the June 17 break-in at Democratic National Headquarters.

The President said he ordered an intensive new inquiry with the result to be reported "directly to me, right here in this office."

HE SAID HE was determined that the truth be brought out, no matter who was involved.

Even as he recounted the resignations of Haldeman and Ehrlichman as top White House aides, Nixon said it did not imply their guilt, and called them two of the finest public servants he had ever known.

"I wanted to be fair, but I knew that in the final analysis the integrity of this office and public faith in the integrity of this office would have to take priority over all personal considerations," Nixon said.

NIXON BEGAN by declaring that he wanted to speak "from my heart, on a subject of deep concern to every American." He concluded, 24 minutes later, asking for the nation's prayers.

"God bless America," he said. "And God bless each and every one of you."

The drama of the address recalled another moment of crisis, 21 years ago, when as vice-presidential nominee, Nixon delivered his "Checkers speech," defending the $18,235 trust fund contributed to help pay his political expenses as a United States senator from California.

NOW, IN A new time of political trauma, Nixon vowed that he would not place the blame on subordinates to whom he delegated responsibility for his 1972 campaign.

Indeed, he praised the federal

Turn to Page 2, Col. 3

'Give Me Hell,' Nixon Tells Press

WASHINGTON (AP) — After addressing the nation on Watergate, President Nixon stepped into the White House press room Monday night and told newsmen, "just continue to give me hell when you think I'm wrong."

Without advance notice, the President stepped behind a rostrum in the press briefing room and began talking into microphones that were not connected.

Looking rather grim, Nixon began by saying he and the press had had differences in the past but added: "Just continue to give me hell when you think I'm wrong. I hope I'm worthy of your trust."

With that, Nixon left the room.

Church Leader Warns Against Isolationism

U.S. Urged to Continue Generosity

The United States ought to preserve its spirit of international generosity rather than drift toward isolationism, the new general secretary of the World Council of Churches said here Monday.

"This is a better insurance of security than the kind of unhappy military alliances with rather corrupt regimes around the world," the Rev. Philip A. Potter remarked without citing specifics.

REV. PHILIP POTTER

MR. POTTER, 51, of Geneva, Switzerland, talked about America and internationalism as the council opened a three-day review of international Christianity.

Because of a decade of unhappy adventure in Southeast Asia, Americans may be tempted to abandon the "immense generosity" they demonstrated after World War II and withdraw into a militarily secure shell, he said.

BUT THEY MUST "realize they cannot go back to isolationism," he told an interviewer.

"The world has become a smaller place, and we all need each other."

"American capital is heavily invested in international firms doing business in many countries," he said. "Also, the very nature of the military balance of power shows that the United States cannot be isolationist."

The council represents more than 250 Protestant, Anglican, Eastern Orthodox, and other churches in about 90 countries, with an estimated membership of 400 million.

MR. POTTER, a black Methodist minister, said U.S. internationalism is vital to Christian missionary work as 60-70 per cent of the religion's missionary effort comes from America.

Brigalia H. Bam, a member of the council's headquarters in Geneva, described racism in South Africa as "the Nazism of our times."

Miss Bam said American racism is less serious, but cautioned: "Americans should not feel superior as long as women are denied roles in the Catholic priesthood."

AT A BANQUET Monday night in the Edgewater Hotel, Mr. Potter chided some churchmen for opposing the WCC in its fight against racism in South Africa.

He compared the fight there

Turn to Page 2, Col. 8

On the Inside . . .

Tax Reforms Are Suggested
See Page 12

Hope, Some Misgiving Expressed Here in Reaction to Nixon's Talk

President Nixon's talk to the nation Monday night brought expected mixed reaction here — with some hope and some doubt.

Gov. Patrick J. Lucey said he "so wanted to believe him (Nixon)" but that he had a "mixed" feeling over the speech.

"I find it hard to believe that he was as appalled as he claims he was when he first learned about the bugging," Lucey said. "If he was so appalled, his actions between June 17 and now didn't indicate that."

LUCEY SAID he resented the President's suggestion that scandals are "par for the course," claiming that they are not part of the normal course of politics.

GOV. LUCEY

Although the governor said he has confidence in the nomination of Elliot Richardson as attorney general, he said that Nixon would have to appoint an independent prosecutor, with full powers of investigation, subpena, and granting immunity if necessary, "If he wants to win the confidence of the American people."

DANE COUNTY Republican Party Chairman James S. Haney said:

"I think that cutting through some of the rhetorical emotion in the speech, as a Republican Party official I'm going to give the President the benefit of the doubt."

"I'm hopeful that the emotion behind Watergate will not evolve into a judicial proceeding," he said, adding that "the President can return to more important things facing him."

Haney said he felt Nixon showed "great courage" in appointing Richardson, whom he

Turn to Page 2, Col. 5

Wisconsin State Journal

MADISON, FRIDAY, JULY 12, 1974

64 Pages, 6 Sections
Vol. 218, No. 319 134th Year ★★★ WEATHER: Cloudy, Warmer, More Humid, Chance of Showers Today. High in Upper 80s. Low Near 65. ★★★ FINAL 15¢

Soglin Gets $600,000 Price

City Buys Capitol Theater

Capitol Theater, 213 State St., flanked by Singer Co. and Moon Fun Shop, involved in auditorium-plan purchase, with city-owned old Ward Co. building on right.

—State Journal Photo by L. Roger Turner

Deal Sets Stage for Auditorium

By STEVEN LOVEJOY
Of The State Journal Staff

Mayor Paul Soglin negotiated a $600,000 purchase price for the Capitol Theater with RKO-Stanley Warner on Thursday, apparently ending years of city struggling over a civic auditorium.

Soglin and Michael Duffey, director of the Central Madison Committee, returned from the negotiations with RKO head Matthew Polin in New York Thursday night and were greeted by more than 60 people at the Dane County Airport.

Soglin said the purchase price had been set at $650,000, but Polin had agreed to reduce the price by buying two tickets to the opening of the city auditorium at a price of $25,000 per ticket, leaving Madison with a total outlay of $600,000 for the theater.

THE MAYOR said he had left a check for $65,000 as earnest money for the purchase and that

Related Story: Sec. 4, Page 1

RKO Theater's attorneys will come to Madison within two weeks to finalize a contract.

"They have some very minor legal problems to work out " Soglin said, adding that the city should have title to the building in two weeks.

"The next step," Soglin said, "will be to set up an operating board and write up job descriptions. I don't know when we'll have the whole thing going."

Asked if the release of city appraisals of the building had affected the purchase, Soglin said he thought they had, and that he would have liked to have made the purchase at a price under $600,000.

CITY OFFICIALS had indicated during the day that the final contract must be approved by the City Council as a routine matter (it had approved the offer to purchase at a price up to $650,000), but Soglin said late Thursday that no further council action was necessary.

Soglin and Duffey were greeted with cheers and applause as they deplaned shortly before 9 p.m. on a flight from LaGuardia.

Duffey, whose committee is an affiliate of the Greater Madison Chamber of Commerce, had worked coordinating business support for the downtown auditorium. He said he had accompanied the mayor only as "an observer," but added that he was pleased with the purchase and the "incredible support" shown at the airport.

DUFFEY TERMED the purchase "a major step forward in the rebirth of the central city" and said it would "benefit the entire city."

"I'm happy to have had a small role in it," Duffey added,

MAYOR SOGLIN
welcomed home

"There's certainly a lot more to be done."

The Capitol Theater is expected to be used as a performing arts center-auditorium, with the adjoining former Montgomery Ward building functioning as an art center in the initial plans for the civic development.

The theater is slated to close July 25.

THE PURCHASE agreement would give the city all equipment within the theater, including fixtures, seats, and projection machinery.

According to Soglin's administrative assistant, James Rowen, the agreement also will include the purchase of the Singer Store and the Moon Fun Shop adjoining the theater.

The lease for the land under the theater lobby, not owned by RKO, will be transferred to the city, Rowen said: RKO leases the land from a local group at $15,000 per year. There are 51 years remaining on the lease, which includes an option to purchase for $275,000.

"In a couple of years, the downtown area will be really magnificent," Rowen added. "With the State St. Mall, the Capitol Concourse and the Arts Center we'll completely re-do the face of the central city."

THE MANY-YEAR controversy over city auditorium sites was still drawing fire Thursday morning as Soglin was making the purchase offer.

Ald. Eugene Parks, Dist. 5, who earlier in the week released city appraisal figures, blasted the Capitol Theater site as a "second class facility" built with "first class money."

In a morning press conference Parks contended that the building was worth only $300,000 to $400,000 and said RKO officials would be "nutty as a fruitcake and extremely arrogant to boot" if they turned down the city offer of $650,000.

Weather Taking New Sticky Turn

The heat and humidity held down by clouds and showers Thursday is expected to break through again today and Saturday.

A high in the upper 80s is expected today with a high in the low 90s on Saturday. Compared to those predictions and temperatures earlier this week, the high of 78 at 2:30 p.m. Thursday and the welcome 61 at 5:30 a.m. were chilly.

The forecast also includes increasing humidity accompanied by a chance of showers or thunderstorms today and Saturday.

The low tonight is expected to slide back to the mid 60s.

Nixon Worry Disclosed Over Watergate Impact

NIXON DEAN HALDEMAN

WASHINGTON (AP) — The House Judiciary Committee made public Thursday seven hefty volumes of Watergate evidence, including new disclosures of President Nixon's early concern about the possible impact of the break-in and coverup on the White House.

Presented to the 38-member committee in secret sessions, the thousands of pages of material represents the raw evidence on which any impeachment articles stemming from the Watergate scandal would be based.

IT WAS presented to the public in the same flat manner in which the impeachment staff laid it out for the committee — a chronological recitation of what happened on the days and weeks before and after the Watergate break-in, with no attempt to draw conclusions or point up the significance of particular events.

Nowhere in the seven volumes is there a hint of the case the staff will outline for the committee when its members begin the climactic debate the week of July 22 on whether they should recommend that the House impeach Nixon.

Nor is there any suggestion which way the committee, with its 21-17 Democratic majority, might vote.

An outline of the President's defense against Watergate allegations is suggested in an eighth volume, 242 pages long. It contained the supplementary factual information presented by Nixon's defense lawyer, James St. Clair, who sought to discredit the President's chief accuser, former White House counsel John Dean, and demonstrate that Nixon had no role in a $75,000 payment to E. Howard Hunt, the convicted Watergate conspirator.

The release of the evidence came two days after the Judiciary Committee put out its own transcripts of eight presidential conversations along with a compilation of how they differed from the White House versions, and a few days before the Senate Watergate committee is scheduled to release its final report.

Presidential press secretary Ronald Ziegler said the timing was "more than a coincidence." He said the President's foes in Congress were mounting a campaign "not to educate the public but to condition the public and manipulate it."

In the seven volumes of staff evidence, totaling more than 4,000 pages and more than 2 million words, the committee disclosed for the first time extensive excerpts from the grand jury testimony of central Watergate figures, including Nixon's former top aides.

ALSO OPENED to public view were hitherto undisclosed versions of two presidential conversations, one on June 30, 1972, less than two weeks after the break-in at Democratic national headquarters in the Watergate office building, the other a summary Nixon gave of a Mar. 17, 1973, discussion about Watergate.

The June 30 transcripts quote

Turn to Page 3

U.S. Accepts 12-Mile Limit

CARACAS, Venezuela (AP) — The United States declared Thursday its readiness to accept maritime territorial limits of 12 miles instead of the traditional 3 miles, and to recognize national "economic zones" extending up to 200 miles into the oceans.

The declaration by John R. Stevenson, U.S. chief delegate to the United Nations Conference on the Law of the Sea, was a major gesture aimed at speeding agreement on a global treaty on use of the seas.

Until Thursday, the U.S. had not stated what width it would accept for the national "economic zones" where coastal nations could claim control over fishing and minerals, but not navigation.

The "economic zone" would lie beyond the territorial limit in which a coastal nation exercises complete jurisdiction.

No Order by Nixon, Dean Says

WASHINGTON (AP) — Former White House counsel John Dean told the House impeachment inquiry Thursday that President Nixon did not direct him to arrange an alleged $75,000 hush money payment, three members of the committee said.

The three members also said, however, that Dean refused to answer the question of whether the President intended anyone to make the payment.

THEY REPORTED that Dean said that is a judgment every congressman will have to make for himself on the basis of transcripts of the Mar. 21, 1973, meeting at which Nixon discussed the payments.

Dean's testimony came in closed session under tough, hard-driving questioning from the President's lawyer, James St. Clair, and in response to some questions from members.

REP. WALTER Flowers (D-Ala.) said Dean was pressed on whether Nixon had directed the payment to Watergate conspirator E. Howard Hunt. Dean

Turn to Page 2, Col. 7

Both Sides Rest in Plumbers Case

See Page 6

today's chuckle

Said the man at the cocktail party: "That reminds me of a funny joke — I'll try to remember the ending as I go along."

top of the news

'No Knock' Repeal Voted

WASHINGTON (UPI) — The Senate voted 64-31 Thursday to repeal the controversial "no knock" provision in the federal drug laws.

An amendment to strike the provision from the law was added to an $875-million authorization measure to extend the life of the Drug Enforcement Administration for five years. The legislation must now be approved by the House.

The controversial statute, enacted in 1970, authorized federal narcotic agents and District of Columbia police to obtain court warrants to forcibly break into an individual's home or office where narcotics are suspected to exist.

Sen. Gaylord Nelson (D-Wis.) called the no-knock provisions "unnecessary, dangerous, and unconstitutional."

Princess Sued for Divorce

LONDON (UPI) — Princess Lee Radziwill, younger sister of Jaqueline Kennedy Onassis, is being sued for divorce, court sources said Thursday.

They said Prince Stanislas Radziwill's petition appeared Thursday on a list of divorce cases to be heard in the high court.

Princess Radziwill, 40, married the Polish-born prince in 1959. They have two children. Princess Radziwill now lives in New York and the prince in London.

LEE RADZIWILL
Jackie's sister

No-Tuition-Boost Backed

University of Wisconsin-Madison resident undergraduates would face no tuition increases this fall under a proposal endorsed Thursday by a Regent committee.

To be acted on by the full Regent Board today, the plan would provide for a $42 per academic year increase for freshmen and sophomores at all other campuses except Milwaukee and a $30 per year increase for juniors and seniors at those campuses. **(See Story, Sec. 4, Page 1.)**

on the inside

Land Use Plan OK Ires Towns

By W. L. CHRISTOFFERSON
Of The State Journal Staff

A land use plan was adopted by the Dane County Board Thursday night without the key provision sought by rural governments, bringing predictions of a Towns Assn. revolt.

In the end, a single word added to the bulky document near the end of three-hour debate may cause many of the county's 35 town boards to reject the plan and withdraw from the Regional Planning Commission (RPC).

SUPERVISOR Lyman Anderson, Oregon, the towns' chief spokesman on the board, predicted "trouble" when the Towns Assn. meets Wednesday, and said he expects many to carry through with their threat to pull out of the RPC.

The towns had insisted that tax relief for farmers must come before the plan could be put into effect, and asked for an amendment to the land use plan to guarantee it would not be implemented before tax reforms are enacted.

The version passed included an extra word, which Anderson said "castrated" the tax amendment.

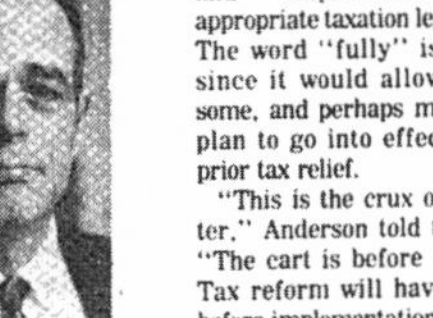

LYMAN ANDERSON
predicts trouble

THE FINAL version said that the plan "shall not be fully implemented prior to adoption and implementation of appropriate taxation legislation." The word "fully" is the key, since it would allow at least some, and perhaps most, of the plan to go into effect without prior tax relief.

"This is the crux of the matter," Anderson told the board. "The cart is before the horse. Tax reform will have to come before implementation."

Town of Middleton Clerk Ray Tanck predicted that 30 of the 35 towns would pull out of the RPC if the tax reform amendment was not passed in the form the Towns Assn. wanted.

"There's nothing unreasonable in this," Tanck said. "We'll take the land use plan if you give us the tax relief."

SOME SUPPORTERS of the plan called the Towns Assn. position blackmail, and said too many concessions had already been made to the rural interests.

Supervisor David Clarenbach, Dist. 4, Madison, said the plan was "turning into a fraud" through the adoption of amendments to pacify the rural govern-

Turn to Page 2, Col. 5

Wisconsin State Journal

MADISON, FRIDAY, AUGUST 9, 1974

48 Pages, 4 Sections
Vol. 218, No. 347 134th Year ★★★ WEATHER: Partly Cloudy With Chance of Rain Today. High in Low 80s. Low in Low 60s. ★★★ FINAL 15¢

NIXON QUITS

The end of the road — and a dream — for Richard Nixon.

Ford, wife, Betty, at home Wednesday.
— AP Wirephoto

Ford Takes Over Today

WASHINGTON (AP) — Richard Nixon resigned Thursday night, the first American President to relinquish his office, saying he did so to begin healing the wounds of the Watergate scandals.

He stepped down effective at 11 a.m. CDT today, when Vice-President Gerald Ford will become the nation's 38th President.

"The leadership of America will be in good hands," Nixon said in a nationally-televised valedictory from the Oval Office.

He said he would have preferred to fight for vindication in office, but added: "I must put the interests of America first. America needs a full time President and a full time Congress."

It could have neither, he said, with the President preoccupied by Watergate and Congress concerned with impeachment.

No Bitterness

He said he left with no bitterness toward those who had opposed him and with gratitude for those who served and supported him.

Of the Watergate role which finally forced him to surrender in the long struggle to survive in office, Nixon said:

"I would say only that if some of my judgments were wrong — and some were — they were made in what I believed at the time to be in the best interests of the nation."

Ford watched the 17-minute speech from his home in suburban Alexandria, Va. Nixon had told Ford at midday Thursday that he would be President today.

Nixon's future legal situation as a private citizen remained unclear. Watergate special prosecutor Leon Jaworski said he had no agreement or understanding with the President about the resignation.

A spokesman for Ford said Chief Justice Warren Burger was flying back from Europe to administer the presidential oath.

Leave Today

A White House spokesman said the outgoing President and his family would leave the executive mansion this morning and fly to their San Clemente, Calif., home.

The spokesman said the family would use a plane from the government's VIP fleet at Andrews Air Force Base, rather than Air Force One, the presidential jet Nixon has used for the past six years.

Ronald Ziegler, presidential adviser and press secretary, said Nixon's letter of resignation would be delivered to the office of Secretary of State Henry A. Kissinger, as required by law, before 11 a.m.

In Ford, 61, America will have for the first time a President by appointment, not election. Nixon, also 61, chose Ford to succeed Spiro Agnew, who resigned last Oct. 10 and pleaded no contest to in-

Turn to Page 2, Col. 3

Kissinger Stays as Foreign Chief

From Wire Services

WASHINGTON — Vice-President Gerald Ford announced Thursday night that Henry A. Kissinger would continue as secretary of state in the new administration.

The Kissinger appointment, the first to be made by the man who will become President at 11 a.m. CDT today, was announced by Ford as he stood in front of his home in Alexandria, Va., shortly after President Nixon's resignation speech.

FORD SAID he had asked Kissinger to stay on and that the secretary had agreed.

"Which means that he and I will be working together in the pursuit of peace as we have worked to achieve it in the past," Ford said.

Ford is expected to address the nation on television tonight.

"I think this is one of the very saddest incidents I have ever witnessed," Ford said of the President's speech.

"I THINK THE President has made one of the greatest personal sacrifices for the country, and one of the finest personal decisions on behalf of all of us as Americans, by his decision to resign as President of the United States."

Ford, 61, said he expects "a spirit of cooperation between the new President and the Congress."

"In my lifetime in public office I've had a great many adversaries in Congress," he said, "but I don't think I have any enemies in Congress."

FORD ADDED: "Let me say without any hesitation or reservation that the (Nixon foreign) policy that has achieved peace. . . will be continued as far as I'm concerned as President of the United States."

Ford, who was told by Nixon at midday of the resignation decision, met with Kissinger for an hour and 40 minutes Thursday afternoon and scheduled another session with him this morning.

After his Thursday meeting with the secretary, Ford voiced strong support for United States foreign policy and said it "is in the best interests of the country."

Ford has been receiving weekly briefings all along from either Kissinger or Maj. Gen. Brent Scowcroft, one of Kissinger's top aides at the National Security Council.

FORD WAS summoned to the White House after completing a Medal of Honor awards ceremony in nearby Blair House. Reporters swarmed around him as he left there, but he only shook his head

Turn to Page 2, Col. 6

Ford Regarded as Agent to Restore Confidence

WASHINGTON (UPI) — Official Washington reacted with more relief than sorrow Thursday at Richard Nixon's resignation and expressed hopes that Gerald Ford would restore confidence in government and get on with the fight against inflation.

"The President's resignation is clearly in the best interest of the nation," said Sen. Edward M. Kennedy (D-Mass.). "I am sure that Congress and the country will close ranks behind President Ford as America enters a period of national healing and reconciliation."

SEN. EDWARD Brooke (R-Mass.), one of the first Republicans to call for Nixon's resignation, said that if Ford "is able to curb inflation and improve the economy and if he continues the Nixon-Kissinger foreign policy, no Democrat will be able to defeat him in 1976

SEN. KENNEDY

SEN. BROOKE

'the country will be so grateful'

because the country will be so grateful."

Brooke said Ford is "able, honest, flexible, and he knows the workings of Congress. He will be able to work well with Congress. Very importantly, he listens and will take advice from sources he respects."

Ford served 25 years in the House before becoming vice-president. He was the House Republican leader a year ago at this time.

Sen. Charles Percy (R-Ill.) said the Republican Party will be helped and could have been hurt if Nixon had not resigned.

SEN. JOHN Tower (R-Tex.), one of Nixon's strongest supporters in Congress, predicted that Ford's presidential relations with Congress would be smooth.

"Ford is a creature of the Congress," Tower said. "He has no scars in his relations with us. Relations with him will be very good."

Rep. Bella Abzug (D-N.Y.), an outspoken supporter of impeachment, said constitutional government and the impeachment

Turn to Page 2, Col. 8

The Only News

An example of universal interest in President Nixon's resignation speech Thursday night:

During his talk, not one telephone call came to The Wisconsin State Journal news room, where even continually chattering teletypes' noise was almost silenced by his voice.

Two calls came to the Sports Streak — and those callers immediately said they would call back later.

House Impeach Machinery to Stop

WASHINGTON (UPI) — Speaker Carl Albert announced Thursday night after President Nixon's resignation that impeachment proceedings will "come to a halt" in the House.

Albert's statement indicated that he had rejected a proposal by Senate Democratic Leader Mike Mansfield that impeachment and a Senate trial continue regardless of whether Nixon quit.

Democratic congressional leaders also opposed a resolution introduced Thursday by Sen. Edward W. Brooke (R-Mass.) urging that Nixon be spared prosecution in the courts after his resignation.

Speech Draws Top Audience

NEW YORK (UPI) — President Nixon's resignation speech Thursday night may have had the largest television audience in American history, according to the National Broadcasting Co. (NBC).

The NBC research department estimated that 130 million Americans watched some part of the 17-minute broadcast on the three commercial networks and on public broadcasting.

The telecast of the first man setting foot on the Moon on July 20, 1969, had been the previously most watched show with an estimated 125 million persons viewing the event in the U.S.

Resignation Inside

State Leaders Express Hope

Wisconsin public figures reacted to President Nixon's resignation Thursday night with somber but optimistic statements.

Gov. Patrick J. Lucey set the tone when he called it "a sad, yet hopeful day for America."

WITH FEW exceptions, politicians of both parties put aside partisanship and expressed hope that the scars of Watergate would heal under the leadership of Gerald Ford.

Rep. Robert Kastenmeier (D-Sun Prairie), a member of the House Judiciary Committee which recommended Nixon's impeachment, called Nixon's act "a rather noble resignation" and said the country "would be better served by a healing process than the acrimony that would arise out of further impeachment process."

Joint Effort

William Christofferson of The Wisconsin State Journal staff wrote this story, based on interviews by him and Reporters Ruth Flegel, Michael Bauman, Roger Gribble, and Maureen Santini.

SEN. WILLIAM Proxmire (D-Wis.) said: "The resignation of President Nixon under these circumstances dramatizes as no other event in our history that even the President of the United States, the most powerful man in the world, must live under law."

Sen. Gaylord Nelson (D-Wis.) said that "one of the most striking ironies, I think, is that here we have a man elected as a law and order president who is losing the presidency for violations of the law."

REPUBLICANS, while expressing sadness, also saw the decision as one that would benefit their party.

President Nixon's action "will greatly improve our chances in November," said David C. Sullivan, state GOP chairman.

Sullivan said he thought the resignation would help GOP candidates at all levels. "I think the entire political picture has been helped. The cancer that people perceived to be growing in the political gut has been excised."

GOV. LUCEY
'sad, hopeful day'

WILLIAM D. Dyke, ex-Madison mayor who is the GOP candidate for governor, said: "I don't believe the events which have led to the resignation enhance the image of either one of our political parties."

Dyke took a slap at the Democratic Party, saying it was "unfortunate the Democrats did not show the same zeal 10 years ago" during the Bobby Baker scandals of President Johnson's Administration.

Rep. Vernon Thomson (R-Richland Center) said the President's involvement in the Watergate coverup "has irrevocably cost him the con-

Turn to Page 2, Col. 5

Wisconsin State Journal

MADISON, MONDAY, SEPTEMBER 9, 1974

34 Pages, Four Sections
Vol. 219, No. 11 134th Year ★★★

WEATHER: Partly Cloudy, High in Low 70s, Low Tonight in 50s. ★★★ FINAL 15¢

Shroud of Secrecy Hid Planning for Pardon

By GAYLORD SHAW

WASHINGTON (AP)—Ten days of intense secret negotiations and maneuvering preceded President Ford's granting of a full pardon Sunday to former President Richard Nixon for his role in the Watergate scandal.

Ford enlisted a criminal lawyer, described by friends as looking like "a TV sleuth . . . a very tough cop," to handle the face-to-face meetings with Nixon.

AND HE CALLED UPON another long-time lawyer friend, white haired, softspoken Philip Buchen, to coordinate preparations for his bombshell announcement.

According to reconstruction based on comments of official and unofficial sources, Ford made a tentative decision the middle of last week to grant the pardon, but did not reach a final decision until Saturday.

The reconstruction disclosed this chronology of events:

On Friday, Aug. 30, Ford called Buchen, his White House counsel, into a private meeting and told him to research historic and legal precedents for the granting of a presidential pardon to an individual before his indictment or conviction.

BUCHEN WORKED INTO the night, and then throughout the Labor Day weekend on the assignment while Ford took his family for the first time to the Camp David presidential retreat in the Maryland mountains.

After receiving Buchen's report of the legal and constitutional requirements for such an act, Ford called upon another friend, Washington lawyer, Benton Becker. He asked Becker to go to San Clemente to inform Nixon that "in all probability a pardon would be granted in the near future," according to Buchen.

Becker also was asked to complete negotiations for an agreement insuring access to Nixon's White House files during the next three years for possible use in Watergate prosecution.

Becker left Washington late Thursday for Los Angeles. He met in San Clemente with Nixon's lawyer, Herbert Miller, and the former President's closest personal aide, Ronald Ziegler. He also met, at least briefly, with Nixon.

THE AGREEMENT ON the White House papers was signed by Nixon late Friday, and Becker returned to Washington while Nixon prepared a 250-word statement to be issued after Ford signed the pardon.

White House officials insisted Ford's action was not conditioned on Nixon signing the agreement concerning his White House files or issuing a statement of contrition. But one official conceded that Ford knew "in a general way" what Nixon would say after the pardon was signed.

Strictest secrecy was applied to preparations for announcement of Ford's decision. The President led an outwardly normal schedule in the hours leading up to the disclosure.

On Saturday, for example, he spent the morning slogging across the rain-soaked fairways of Burning Tree Country Club in a golf tournament.

THEN, SATURDAY afternoon, he took visiting Soviet cosmonauts to a policeman's picnic in the Virginia countryside, introducing them to such American delicacies as hot dogs and beer.

Saturday night, however, in the privacy of the First Family's White House living quarters, Ford put the final touches on the statement disclosing his decision.

He was up early Sunday morning. Shortly before 8 a.m. he went across Lafayette Park to St. John's Episcopal church where he joined 50 other worshippers in kneeling to pray and receive communion.

Outside the church, newsmen noticed that the usually smiling Ford seemed preoccupied and somber. A reporter asked if he would play golf again Sunday, or if he had other plans.

"YOU'LL FIND OUT shortly," the President responded before stepping into his limousine for the quick ride back to the White House.

It was just moments later that reporters were told Ford would make "a major annoncement" in his Oval Office at 10:30 a.m. (9:30 a.m. CDT). But White House officials refused to disclose the nature of the announcement.

A single television film camera was set in place before Ford's Oval Office desk, which was covered with a brown felt cloth.

The small group of reporters was ushered into the office at about 11 o'clock. There they found several of Ford's closest aides, including Buchen and press secretary Jerry terHorst.

At 11:04 a.m., Ford walked into the office through a side door. He went immediately to the desk, sat down, opened a manila folder, looked toward the television crew and asked, "Are you all set?"

WHEN THEY NODDED yes, he began to read slowly the statement disclosing the action he was about to take.

For 10 minutes he talked, looking into the camera with unsmiling eyes.

Then, he paused, picked up a blue and silver felt-tip pen, and quickly signed his name to the pardon proclamation.

His statement had one more paragraph, and Ford's voice seemed to thicken with emotion as he read it: "In witness whereof, I have hereunto set my hand this eighth day of September in the year of our Lord 1974, and of the independence of the United States of America the 199th."

Still unsmiling, he rose from the desk and walked from the office.

FORD GIVES NIXON COMPLETE PARDON

Robert P. Caspersen raised his protest over President Ford's pardon of Richard Nixon Sunday by displaying an upside-down flag at half staff in his yard at 3418 Home Ave.

—State Journal Photo by Mark Perlstein

Knievel Succeeds With Rich Failure

TWIN FALLS, Ida. (UPI) — Space-age stuntman Evel Knievel parachuted in his mini-rocket into the Snake River Canyon without serious injury Sunday in a futile — but lucrative — attempt to soar across the quarter-mile gorge.

Knievel, at least $6-million richer for his seconds-long flight, explained later that he himself triggered the chutes which lowered the rocket safely to the bottom of the 600-foot-deep canyon because the rocket had begun rolling over.

BUT THE PRODUCER of the closed-circuit TV of the super-ballyhooed event said the chutes had been activated accidentally when Knievel's hand was jolted loose from the parachute trigger.

Whichever way it happened, Knievel emerged from the dented "Skycycle X-2" waving to the throngs that lined the rims of the treacherous, lava-walled canyon. He then was whisked by helicopter back to the launch site.

The blastoff came at 4:35 p.m. CDT. The red, white, and blue rocket rose from the launch pad for 8.7 seconds. Then the drag parachute popped from the tail, pulling out the main chute. The rocket floated 600 feet to the rugged canyon floor alongside the swirling waters of the river.

"The shot almost knocked me out," Knievel said afterwards.

The cyclist, whose flight made him the highest priced daredevil in history, had trouble getting off his seat belt. "Thank God I didn't go into the river or I never would have made it," he said.

AS THE "SKYCYCLE" BOUNCED to a stop Knievel's head was straight up.

Harold Conrad, chief publicist for the promoter, Top Rank, Inc., said the daredevil "suffered slight cuts."

The chutes were controlled by a "deadman stick" which was capable of triggering the chute with the release of pressure. Knievel said he activated the chutes.

He said the designer "told me many times that, if I could ever see any opposite wall of the canyon instead of sky that would mean it was rolling and I should pull the chute and, thank God he taught me that. He saved my life."

BUT JOHN BRANKER, executive producer of the closed-circuit television operation, said, "the strain of the G's (force of gravity) under direct acceleration loosed his grip on the bar."

Knievel's rocket landed just as it was supposed to — with its nose down. A pogo stick shock absorber made the craft bounce a couple of times on a rocky outcropping, then settled down on its side with Knievel's head up.

Some 30,00 spectators were massed on the south side of the 4,000-foot wide gorge in the desolate area, having paid $25 a ticket to watch the flight.

SEVERAL HOLLYWOOD STARS — including John Wayne, Steve McQueen, Elvis Presley and Dustin Hoffman — were on hand as were President Ford's sons, John, 22, and Steve, 19. And there was Bobby Riggs, tennis hustler, who beat Knievel out of a $25,000 bet by riding a motorcycle here from Las Vegas in less than 72 hours.

Knievel, 34, who assumed the first name "Evel" because it rhymed with his last name, began his career in stunt jumping at the age of nine when he rode a bicycle over an obstacle.

Now — 25 years later — he claims some 300 motorcycle jumps and only 11 crashes. His defiance of nature earned him 50 bone fractures over the years.

The rocket was the creation of Robert C. Truax, a former president of the American Rocket Society and an engineer who worked on the Polaris missile.

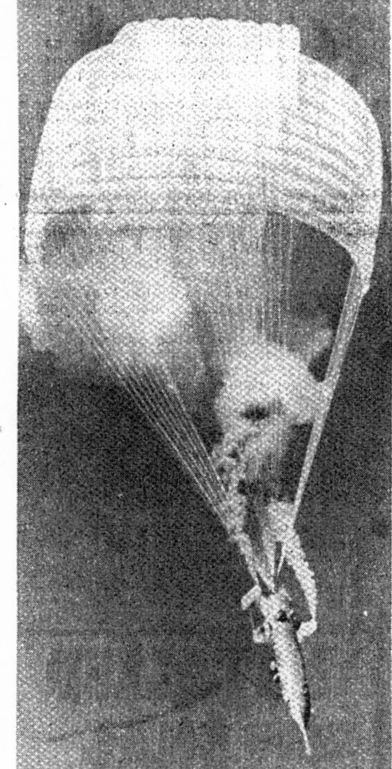

Knievel's Skycycle after midcourse correction.

—AP Wirephoto

Ford on Knievel

TWIN FALLS, Ida. (UPI) — President Ford's son John, 22, said Sunday that he would have tried the Evel Knievel jump over the Snake River Canyon for the $6-million reward.

"A man has to do his thing," John Ford said following the jump. "I'd do it for $6-million — anybody would."

The President's son, a summer ranger at Yellowstone National Park, watched the jump from the home of a friend, E. C. Connell, on the south side of the canyon. Ford said he was "turned off" by the way the event was "manufactured" through extensive publicity.

Nixon Admits Some Errors

From Wire Services

WASHINGTON — President Ford granted former President Richard Nixon an unconditional pardon Sunday for any crimes he may have committed during his term of office, an act, Ford said, that was intended to spare both Nixon and the nation further punishment in the Watergate scandals.

Nixon, in San Clemente, Calif., accepted the pardon that exempts him from indictment and trial for his role in the coverup of the Watergate burglary, and he issued a statement saying he can now see he was "wrong in not acting more decisively and more forthrightly in dealing with Watergate."

PHILIP BUCHEN, the White House counsel who advised Ford on the legal aspects of the pardon, said the "act of mercy" on the President's part was done without making any demands on Nixon and without asking the advice of the Watergate special prosecutor, Leon Jaworski, who had the legal responsibility to prosecute the case.

Buchen said he had, at the President's request, asked Jaworski that, in the event Nixon was indicted, how it long it would be before he could be brought to trial. He said Jaworski replied it would be at least nine months or more, due to the enormous amount of publicity the charges against Nixon received when the House Judiciary Committee recommended impeachment.

This was one of the reasons Ford cited for granting the pardon, saying he had concluded that "many months and perhaps more years will have to pass before Richard Nixon could hope to obtain a fair trial by jury in any jurisdiction of the United States under governing decisions of the Supreme Court."

"During this long period of delay and potential litigation, ugly passions would again be aroused, our people would again be polarized in their opinions, and the credibility of our free institutions of government would again be challenged at home and abroad," Ford said in a 10-minute statement that he read Sunday morning in the Oval Office upon signing the pardon.

A SPOKESMAN FOR Jaworski said the special prosecutor's office played no direct role in the decision to pardon Nixon but said, "obviously we accept it."

Ford's decision was not unexpected, in light of his previous statements that he thought the former President had suffered enough by being forced from office. Yet the unconditional nature of the pardon was more generous to Nixon than many had expected.

Buchen said no effort had been made to obtain acknowledgment of wrongdoing.

When Vice-President Spiro Agnew resigned last October he pleaded no contest to a charge of tax evasion and agreed to a bill of

Turn to Page 2, Col. 3

Pardon on the Inside. . .

Area People Split on Nixon Pardon

By STEVEN T. LOVEJOY
Of The State Journal Staff

Bitterness and satisfaction, combined with a large chunk of apprehension, greeted President Ford's pardon of former President Richard Nixon Sunday.

Across southern Wisconsin, the morning announcement caught most people by surprise, but not without strong opinions.

MANY GOVERNMENT officials and party leaders were unavailable for comment Sunday — off on holidays or stumping the state in last-minute campaigns for Tuesday's primary.

In Washington, Rep. Robert Kastenmeier (D-Wis.), a member of the House Judiciary Committee, termed the pardon "inappropriate" and "premature."

"I think it raises more questions than it answers," Kastenmeier said. "Former President Nixon has not been formally charged with anything, much less convicted. At the very least, Ford's action was premature."

From other points, the reaction was harsher.

IN RICHLAND CENTER, Allen Schaefer, a high school history teacher and city alderman, said, "It makes me mad. I don't like it at all, from the standpoint of history alone. We teach kids in class that a person is innocent until proven guilty in court. No there will be no court. I think Ford's action is unfair and a cop-out . . . it was done before the system had been allowed to work."

In Madison, a new city resident, Allen Bates, 14 S. Midvale

Turn to Page 2, Col. 6

today's chuckle

There is one way to protect yourself against crime. Go to a karate school and stay there.

Sure, He Makes House Calls

By WILLIAM R. WINEKE
Of The State Journal Staff

A few days after Richard M. Nixon resigned the presidency, a physician paid him a house call, apparently to check on the general state of his health.

That's the kind of service VIPs get and ordinary people don't get, right?

After all, "house calls" went out with the Model A Ford, and no doctor will make them anymore, right?

WELL, YOU MAY THINK that's right but Madison physicians insist they do make house calls.

"I don't know of a physician in this city who would categorically refuse to make a house call, asserted Dr. Blake E. Waterhouse, president of the Dane County Medical Society.

"I'll make house calls under certain conditions, like if the mother doesn't have a car and the illness isn't too severe, but I'd never make a house call for a really serious illness," added Dr. Conrad Andringa, a pediatrician at the Dean Clinic (we'll explain that philosophy later).

"Sure I make house calls if I'm asked, but don't ask me how long it's been since I was asked," said Dr. Curtis Weatherhogg, a pediatrician at the Madison Medical Center.

"I FRANKLY DON'T know a physician who would refuse to make a house call."

But, if the physicians are all that friendly, how come everyone thinks they won't leave their offices for anything more important than a martini?

It turns out that, while the physicians will make house calls, they aren't very enthusiastic about it.

"It's just not a very good way to practice medicine," Dr. Waterhouse said.

"If I'm called to someone's home, I can't perform any lab

Turn to Page 2, Col. 1

On the Inside . .

88 Are Lost in Jet Crash

See Story, Page 10

Ford Adviser terHorst Quits in Pardon Protest

(c) N. Y. Times News Service

WASHINGTON — Jerry terHorst, the White House press secretary, resigned Sunday in protest against President Ford's granting of a pardon to former President Richard Nixon.

TerHorst, a White House spokesman said Sunday night, submitted his resignation to the President earlier in the day, saying that, as a matter of conscience, he no longer could serve the Ford Administration.

"It definitely was because of the Nixon pardon," the spokesman said.

"It was a matter of conscience and Jerry's concept of equal justice."

JERRY terHORST
'matter of conscience'

It was announced that Jack Hushen, who was terHorst's deputy, would serve as acting press secretary pending a decision on a permanent appointment.

TerHorst's resignation came as a surprise. Late Sunday afternoon, he had answered reporters' questions about the pardon, giving no hint that he was displeased or that he planned to resign.

Further, he was a close friend of Ford's. The President's first act on taking office on Aug. 9 was to name terHorst as his press secretary, replacing Ronald Ziegler, who had served the Nixon Administration.

During his brief term as press secretary, terHorst had impressed reporters with his efforts to make the Ford Administration open to public exposure.

Wisconsin State Journal

MADISON, FRIDAY, AUGUST 1, 1975

44 Pages, 4 Sections
Vol. 218, No. 325 135th Year

★★★ WEATHER: Mostly Sunny and Hot Today. Chance of Thunderstorms. High ...s. ★★★ FINAL 15¢

Ex-Union Chief Hoffa Missing, Feared Slain

DETROIT (UPI) — James R (Jimmy) Hoffa, whose stormy career in union politics took him to the presidency of Teamsters International and then to prison, was reported missing—and feared dead—by his family and associates Thursday.

"I know the police suspect foul play," said L. Brooks Patterson, prosecutor for Oakland County, where Hoffa lives and where he was reported missing after he failed to return home from an appointment.

"Jimmy never has stayed out this long before without reporting in," Patterson said.

Hoffa's lawyer son, James Jr., said his family is extremely concerned.

"We just don't have anything to say, we're just waiting, hoping," James Jr. said outside the Hoffa compound at nearby Lake Orion, about 30 miles north of Detroit.

Police officially refused to comment on reports sweeping the faction-ridden union that Hoffa was kidnaped — or murdered — but a formal missing persons report was filed.

The disappearance came three weeks after the latest in a series of incidents reportedly involving rival factions in the 1.7-million-member union. A bombing destroyed a car owned by the son of the incumbent Teamsters president, Frank Fitzsimmons.

JIMMY HOFFA

The huge union is divided between Hoffa loyalists and backers of Fitzsimmons, who became president after Hoffa quit in 1971 while serving a federal prison term.

There was no indication that the incidents were linked to their rivalry, although Hoffa wants to unseat Fitzsimmons and regain the presidency himself.

Police said Hoffa, 62, was reported missing about 24 hours after he told his family that he was meeting "someone."

Robert Holmes, a teamsters vice-president, said Hoffa later telephoned home to say he was returning because the person he was to meet failed to show up.

Michigan Gov. William Milliken told newsmen in Grand Rapids late Thursday night that he understood Hoffa disappeared after planning a Wednesday night meeting with Anthony (Tony Jack) Giacalone, named in a 1963 Senate investigation of organized crime as one of the kingpins of the Detroit Mafia. Milliken did not elaborate.

Police said Hoffa's disappearance became known after authorities in Pontiac, about 25 miles north of Detroit, received an anonymous telephone call telling them where they could find his car.

Police in Bloomfield Township, another Detroit suburb, went to the location—a shopping center parking lot near a fashionable restaurant where Hoffa often ate—and found the car.

There was no sign of a struggle at the car, police said, and nothing was in the trunk. Police said they found some dirt on the front seat and a pair of white gloves on the floor in the rear.

The North American Newspaper Alliance (NANA) said Hoffa's family fears he has been murdered.

"If Jimmy hasn't turned up by now, he's dead," the report quoted a spokesman for the family as saying. "We're praying for a ransom note, but we have to face facts.

"We've had no indication he's been kidnaped," NANA said the spokesman said. "No one has called us or anything, so we have to think the worst."

Nixon Decree

State police are helping in the investigation, but the FBI is not because it apparently has no jurisdiction in the case at the moment.

Hoffa was released from prison in 1971 after then-President Richard Nixon commuted his sentence for jury tampering and mail fraud. The clemency decree barred Hoffa from union activity until 1980, which Hoffa claims was a political deal with Fitzsimmons.

Hoffa has been involved in a court battle to regain the right to participate in union politics.

Hoffa was 17 when he organized fellow warehouse workers in Detroit and obtained a Teamsters charter in 1930. Two years later, he parlayed a shipment of fresh strawberries into his first contract—by threatening to let the strawberries rot. It took him 24 hours to win a contract.

He ran for the presidency of the Detroit Joint Teamsters Council later that same year and won easily. At that time, Hoffa later said, there were no more than 100 teamsters in all of Detroit.

Two-Fisted Brawler

The years that followed were filled with arrests, bitter picket line strife and a growing reputation as a two-fisted brawler who worked 12 to 14 hours a day.

He was arrested many times, but until his first federal convictions in 1964 he had been found guilty and fined only three times.

When the stormy Dave Beck became Teamsters International president in 1952, he divided the union's jurisdiction into four regions. Hoffa became boss of the key Midwest region.

In 1957, when Beck went to prison, Hoffa became international president and inherited not only power but some of Beck's troubles with Robert F. Kennedy.

Kennedy, attorney general under his brother's presidency in the early 1960s, spearheaded the investigation and prosecution that resulted in Hoffa's conviction in 1964.

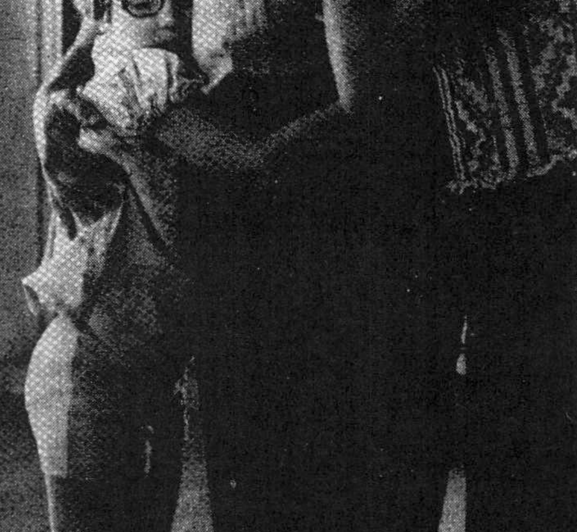

Marion Brown is welcomed home by daughters Katherine, 7, and Laura, 10.

—State Journal Photo by A. Craig Benson

Turkey Rejects Ford Offer of $50-Million Arms Gift

HELSINKI, Finland (AP) — President Ford offered Thursday to give Turkey $50-million in military aid in exchange for the reopening of 24 American bases but was turned down, according to Secretary of State Henry Kissinger.

The offer came during a breakfast meeting between the President and Turkish Prime Minister Suleyman Demirel. Kissinger said the President made the offer under provisions of United States law that allows him to waive a ban on arms aid to Turkey if it is in the American national interest.

Demirel rejected the offer as contradictory, Kissinger explained.

"Turkey takes the position that it is contradictory to give $50-million as a gift when it can't buy arms or take delivery on arms already purchased," the secretary told a news conference.

Nevertheless, the secretary said, "it is our impression that the situation is recoverable. That is, the bases can be substantially restored if the House reverses itself."

Kissinger was referring to action by the U.S. House of Representatives last week to continue the embargo against arms aid to Turkey because of Turkey's use of American military equipment to invade Cyprus a year ago.

Kissinger was asked what he understood Demirel to mean by saying that the shutdown of the bases — including some that did ultrasensitive spying on the Soviet Union — was ordered "for the time being," indicating the closings may only be temporary.

"I don't believe there was a significant change in the situation," Kissinger responded.

In Washington, the Senate voted, 47-46, late Thursday night in favor of a conditional lifting of the embargo, but the House delayed action on the measure until September.

The Soviet news agency Tass reported, meanwhile, that Demirel had met with Soviet Communist Party chief Leonid Brezhnev and Foreign Minister Andrei Gromyko and discussed Soviet-Turkish relations, the security conference here and other international issues. Tass said the meeting was held in an atmosphere of "mutual understanding."

This came amid reports from Washington that the Russians are offering helicopters to Turkey in what could be the first step in a Soviet effort to replace the U.S. as Turkey's source of military supplies.

Kissinger, asked about this, said it was "extremely unlikely" that Turkey would enter into a military relationship with Russia, its traditional enemy.

Turkish Aid Renewal Fails

WASHINGTON (AP) — A new effort to renew United States arms sales to Turkey was narrowly approved by the Senate late Thursday night but was blocked from being considered by the House until September.

Chairman Ray Madden (D-Ind.) of the House Rules Committee said he would not clear the bill for House action until Sept. 9, when Congress returns from its August vacation.

Shortly before midnight, House Minority Leader John Rhodes said he was abandoning his effort to win approval of the measure before Congress departs today for its month-long recess.

The Senate approved a conditional lifting of the 6-month-old ban on arms aid to Turkey by only one vote, 47-46. Supporters of the bill in the House forced six roll call votes against House adjournment so the bill could be considered late Thursday, but Madden steadfastly refused to clear the measure for consideration.

The vote in the Senate represented something of a victory for the Ford Administration, which wanted to have one house of Congress on record in favor of resuming aid in hopes this would bolster U.S. diplomatic efforts to restore good relations with Turkey.

Wisconsin Democrats Gaylord Nelson and William Proxmire both voted against lifting the ban.

Wilson St. Fire Damages Apartments

Fire heavily damaged the upper floor of a two-story flat at 120 W. Wilson St. early today.

The fire, which was reported by a neighbor shortly after midnight, started in the back bedroom of a second floor apartment, possibly from an electric short circuit, according to Acting District Chief Stanley Hermanson.

The fire engulfed the bedroom and moved to the attic and roof of the building. The woman occupant of the apartment was not at home at the time of the fire.

Another apartment on the second floor received extensive smoke damage. At least $5,000 in damage was reported.

The fire was under control by 1 a.m.

House Makes Final Bid to Extend Control on Oil

WASHINGTON (AP) — Congress took one final stab at keeping the lid on domestic oil prices Thursday, but the Ford Administration said it would allow full decontrol in a month rather than sit still for more delays.

Throughout an energy debate that began in January, Congress and Ford have continually rejected each others' compromise offers.

In an apparently doomed move, the House, by a 303-117 vote, passed and sent to the White House a bill to extend domestic oil price controls another six months. Federal Energy Administrator Frank Zarb said "there is no doubt" Ford will veto the measure.

Congress is packing its bags for a month-long summer vacation, beginning tonight, and cannot try for a veto override until it returns Sept. 3. Price ceilings are scheduled to expire Aug. 31 if Ford refuses to sign the extension.

That could mean a boost of up to 7 cents a gallon in the cost of gasoline at the pump.

Zarb said he does not think Congress can override a veto and restore price controls when it returns. He said the top legislative priority now should be to enact a tax on oil companies to prevent them from reaping excessive profits once controls are removed.

Ford wants to decontrol prices to encourage the development of new domestic oil supplies and lessen growing American dependence on foreign sources. He proposed doing it gradually over a 39-month period to soften the impact on consumers.

Congress rejected his plan and insists on extending controls.

Crash Kills 26

TAIPEI, Taiwan (AP) — A Taiwan domestic jetliner, trying to pull up from a second landing attempt in a driving rainstorm Thursday, skidded its wing on the runway, turned over and split into three sections, killing 26 of the 75 persons aboard.

Shark Devours Abalone Diver

HOBART, Australia (AP)—A large shark attacked an American immigrant to Australia with such violence Wednesday that he was yanked out of his abalone diving harness and completely devoured, the divers's assistant said Thursday.

The only trace of Bobby Ray Slack, 37, was one green glove and a hand net, officials said. Slack moved here from California about 10 years ago.

Tony Hitchens, 22, the mate on Slack's abalone boat, said the attack was "all over in five seconds." He said at first, when he saw the fin and tail, he thought it was a seal. Then he spotted blood and the glove and pulled up the empty diving harness with a broken air line.

Future Sound, Rocky Insists

WASHINGTON (AP) — Vice-President Nelson Rockefeller said Thursday the controversy over his political future is "a tempest in a teapot."

He told a group of reporters he has good relations with President Ford and with Howard H. (Bo) Callaway, Ford's campaign manager.

Rockefeller said he wasn't angered by statements last week by Callaway that he is Ford's "No. 1 problem" in the effort to round up backing from Southern GOP conservatives.

He said he phoned Ronald Reagan, who may challenge Ford for the 1976 Republican nomination, to thank him for defending him against criticism by Callaway.

Reagan said after Callaway's comments that the vice-president was being subjected to "shoddy treatment" by the President's associates.

UW's Brown Home, a Free, Reborn Man

By PATRICIA SIMMS
Of The State Journal Staff

In an emotional home coming at the Dane County Regional Airport, University of Wisconsin-Madison Prof. Marion Brown came home Thursday a free man.

Brown, 36, acquitted Wednesday of federal narcotics charges in Brooklyn after a four-day trial, was greeted by sudden and prolonged applause from family and friends as he and Defense Atty. Donald Eisenberg got off the plane.

There wasn't a dry eye in the house.

"We don't have to fight any longer," Brown's wife, Diane, said.

Eisenberg credited the defense victory at least partially to the Watergate mentality, where citizens are increasingly suspicious of government.

"A couple of years ago, it would have been different," Eisenberg, said. "The jury would have believed that the government was lily-white.

"Richard Nixon had a lot to do with Marion Brown's acquittal," the attorney said.

Brown seemed flushed and happy with the outcome. "It has been very unpleasant — I feel like I have been reborn," he said.

"Living with this kind of threat for a year makes it hard to get through one day at a time," Brown said, "with your family wondering every day whether you're going to be with them."

Brown, 5517 Terre Haute Ave., who spent several years in Chile as director of a Ford Foundation land development program, was charged with conspiring to smuggle 2.5 kilograms of Chilean cocaine into the United States and possessing it with intent to sell.

Eisenberg had argued that Brown was being prosecuted for his political beliefs, but Federal Judge Jacob Mishler had refused to allow Eisenberg to call government witnesses from the CIA.

Brown said the jury was waiting for him and Eisenberg at the elevator after the verdict was announced. "They told us they considered it to be a frame," the sandy-haired professor said.

"The jury knew it was political," Eisenberg said.

The defense attorney said the jury was "offended" by alleged tape recordings of telephone conversations between Brown and a government informant.

"We could tell from the outset that the tapes were fabricated," Brown said.

Brown's five daughters, ranging in age from 7 to 15, threw their arms around his neck, crying and smiling.

The small daughter of an associate who had testified on his behalf at the trial presented Brown with a single rose.

Brown, who was first indicted with 21 other persons last July, said the people of Madison had been "very decent" during the ups and downs of his case.

"There has never been any kind of pressure or social rejection," he said.

Members of his family, he said, "have been very brave and self-reliant."

"They were ready to live with it," he said, hugging his smallest daughter, who, in the happy melee, had dissolved into sobs.

"It's been a nightmare," Diane Brown said. "I'm going to forget about it."

Then it was over, the crowd cleared and Brown headed for the family station wagon and drove off, a free citizen.

"Thank you all for coming," Brown said to the 30 or so individuals who had gathered for the welcome.

Virtually unnoticed when the plane landed was former U.S. Sen. Eugene McCarthy, now an independent candidate for the presidency, who debarked steps behind Brown and Eisenberg for a campaign stop in Madison.

New Format Is Designed for You

The Wisconsin State Journal will turn fully to a 6-column format Sunday.

The reason? To make the newspaper easier to read.

The changeover from the traditional eight columns on each page is no sudden thing. In the past six months, The State Journal has used the 6-column format increasingly on Page 1, its cover pages and some inside pages.

Starting Sunday, the 6-column format will apply to all news pages and to the advertising layout.

The change was made to better serve readers, primarily through use of wider columns.

Prof. Edmund C. Arnold, chairman of the Graphic Arts and Publishing Depts. of Syracuse University and an authority on newspaper typography and design, acted as consultant to The State Journal in the changeover.

Arnold said this about the 6-column format:

"Here is a format designed for the reader. Wider columns are read more easily, more quickly, with less fatigue and with greater comprehension.

"The page arrangement presents news and advertising in a manner affording maximum comfort, convenience and pleasure to the reader."

The columns were 1⅝ inches wide under the 8-column layout; they will be 2⅛ inches wide under the 6-column layout.

Readers will find the new page slightly narrower and slightly shorter. It will be easier to handle without sacrificing space for news and advertising. One of the advantages of the 6-column design is that there are two fewer "gutters" separating columns than with eight columns on a page, thus gaining space.

"The Wisconsin State Journal has taken many steps through the years to prepare a strong, lively and consistent news report and then package it in a readable format," said Robert H. Spiegel, editor.

"Many steps have been taken through the years toward this objective . . . larger body type and cleaner headline type, an uncluttered layout, judicious use of white space for added appeal.

"Now comes the 6-column page, prompted solely to make our newspaper easier for you to read. We hope you like it."

Inside

UW Faculty Gets Pay Raise Today . . . . . Sec. 3, P. 1

Today's Chuckle

Most children hate to begin a meal on an empty stomach.

Wisconsin State Journal

MADISON, FRIDAY, SEPTEMBER 19, 1975

Vol. 282, No. 6 · 48 Pages, 4 Sections · 135th Year

★★ WEATHER: **Cloudy, windy, cooler. Chance of showers tonight, Saturday. Highs in 60s.** ★★ FINAL 15¢

PATTY HEARST CAUGHT WITH THREE COHORTS

Patty in April, 1974, holding weapon in front of SLA insignia.
—*AP Wirephoto*

Capture in Frisco ends nationwide hunt

SAN FRANCISCO (AP) — Fugitive newspaper heiress Patricia Hearst and three radical comrades were arrested Thursday, ending one of the longest and most bizarre manhunts in American history.

Miss Hearst, first the captive and then the zealous comrade-in-arms of the Symbionese Liberation Army (SAL), was arrested without resistance in a house in the city's Bernal Heights district along with fugitive Berkeley artist Wendy Yoshimura, 32.

About an hour earlier, police and federal agents working on the case arrested SLA members William and Emily Harris when they spotted them jogging on a street a few miles away.

"Thank God she's all right," Miss Hearst's mother, Catherine, said in a barely audible voice when informed of her daughter's arrest.

SLA wiped out

FBI special agent-in-charge Charles Bates said the arrests "effectively put an end to everyone we know who was in the SLA."

The arrest of Miss Hearst came less than 10 miles from the Berkeley apartment where she was kidnaped by SLA members Feb. 4, 1974.

Miss Hearst and the Harrises were arraigned before U.S. Magistrate Owen Woodruff on a variety of state and federal charges and held on $500,000 bail each pending further hearings today.

Miss Yoshimura was released to the custody of the Alameda County sheriff's office, where she is charged with possessing explosives.

Miss Hearst, 21, her auburn hair in a shag cut and dressed in a striped mauve shirt, brown jeans, sandals and tinted glasses, appeared pale as she was arraigned in a crowded courtroom on federal charges of bank robbery and firearms violations.

Standing before the magistrate with her arms folded across her chest, she answered softly "yes," when asked if her name was Patricia Campbell Hearst. It was barely a year and a half ago when she proclaimed herself "Tania," the name she had adopted as a sign of her revolutionary ardor.

Appearing pale but calm, she conferred in whispers with her attorney, Terrence Hallinan.

Defense co-counsel Ted Kleiness said Miss Hearst asked to see her parents. "She was very, very interested," Kleiness said, "she was very friendly toward us."

Father 'pleased'

Miss Hearst's father, San Francisco Examiner President Randolph Hearst, was in New York on business and said as he boarded a plane for San Francisco: "I am very pleased that things turned out the way they did."

Hearst said of the bank robbery charge against his daughter: "I don't

CHARLES BATES

think anything will happen on that score; after all she was a kidnap victim, you must remember."

The Harrises still wore the jogging outfits in which they were captured when they were arraigned on charges of federal firearms violations.

As the bearded Harris, 30, turned to leave the courtroom in a green T-shirt with lavendar shorts, he shouted: "This ain't no big deal, comrades. Long live the guerrilla!"

When he and his wife, Emily, 28, entered, both exchanged clenched fist salutes with two women and a man in the back of the room.

Bates said no single tip or informant led authorities to Miss Hearst and her comrades. He declined to give details of what finally broke the case except to say "it involved interviews with a lot of people, a lot of investigative techniques."

An FBI spokesman said the capture was the result of checking another lead in the case. He said it was "just another one of many, many, many hundreds of thousands of leads we've developed."

The FBI had been watching the house for two days.

Bates, who has handled the Hearst case since the beginning, said the four fugitives might have been living in San Francisco for as long as three weeks before the arrests.

The house where Miss Hearst was found is on the fringe of the Mission district, one of the older sections of the city. It is a working class residential section in a hilly area in the southern part of the city.

Acting Los Angeles County Dist. Atty. John Howard said Los Angeles authorities have 19 state charges pending against Miss Hearst and 18 against the Harrises, ranging from robbery to kidnaping. He said all three would be brought to Los Angeles next week for arraignment on those charges.

Miss Hearst was abducted by gun-carrying members of the SLA, described by authorities as a tiny band of white ex-college students led by black prison escapee Donald DeFreeze.

She was dragged kicking and screaming from the apartment she shared with her fiance, Steven Weed, in

Turn to Page 2, Col. 4

More on Patty . . .

Vow to fight fades

LOS ANGELES (UPI) — After six Symbionese Liberation Army (SLA) comrades were slaim by the FBI and police in a flaming house in Los Angeles on May 17, 1974, Patty Hearst swore that she, too, would fight to the end.

As it turned out, she gave up without a struggle.

Miss Hearst and William and Emily Harris escaped the encirclement of the tiny wooden home in the city's black district where SLA Field Marshal Cinque, Willie Wolfe and four white girls died.

The heiress was not heard from for more than three weeks, but on June 7, 1974, she and the Harrises sent a tape recording to a radio station.

"No matter how many they kill, the pigs can't win," Patty said. "I learned a lot from the comrades who died in the fire and I'm still learning from them. . .

"I died in that fire, but out of the ashes I was born. Our comrades didn't die in vain. The pigs only made me more determined. I renounced my class privilege when I got my name, Tania. I've never been afraid of death."

She said that since she was abducted by the SLA she had fallen in love with Wolfe.

"Neither Kujo (Wolfe's SLA nickname) or I had ever loved an individual the way we had loved each other," she said. "It's because of this I still feel determined to fight."

After a tipoff that Cinque, whose actual name was Donald DeFreeze, and other SLA members were in the south central Los Angeles area, the home was surrounded bv more than 500 FBI agents and police. More than 1,000 bullets were fired in the ensuing gun battle before the house caught fire and burned to the ground.

Killed besides DeFreeze and Wolfe were Nancy Ling Perry, Patricia Soltyzsik, Camilla Hall and Angela Atwood.

Six bodies were found in the ashes and, for a time, there was a question whether the sixth girl might be Patricia. Two days later, through dental charts, the body was identified as Miss Hall.

State Journal adds Patty Hearst news

The normal front page of the Look section has been converted to a full page of stories and pictures on the long-delayed capture of Patty Hearst. There will be an expanded Look section as part of Saturday's Wisconsin State Journal.

Inside

Football strikers back on job . Sports

Hurricane weakens but may build again

MIAMI (AP) — Eloise, the killer hurricane which charged through the Caribbean leaving thousands homeless and at least 28 persons dead, was downgraded to a tropical storm Thursday as its winds and torrential rains pelted eastern Cuba.

But the National Hurricane Center here said the storm may regain hurricane strength and possibly turn its menacing force toward the United States mainland.

More than 55,000 persons were evacuated from their homes in low-lying areas of Cuba's Oriente Province Wednesday night and Thursday as a "preventive measure," Radio Havana reported.

Packing winds of 50 miles an hour, Eloise passed over Guantanamo Thursday morning but skirted around Santiago, Cuba's second largest city, and the U.S. naval base at Guantanamo Bay where 3,000 military personnel and their dependents are based.

In Miami, hurricane center director Neil Frank said, "Weather stations in Cuba have reported no serious damage but heavy rains and the threat of flooding remain.

"If it (Eloise) continues on its predominantly western course before heading northwestward as we expect it to do tonight or tomorrow, then it probably will hit open water and gain strength," he said.

"You have to say it remains a threat to the southeastern United States but we really can't specify at this time how serious a threat," Frank said.

At 5 p.m. CDT, Eloise's disorganized center was moving west parallel to the southern coast of Cuba.

"We still expect it to head to the northwest," Frank said.

While a hurricane, Eloise hit Puerto Rico Tuesday; then moved on to the Dominican Republic and Haiti on Wednesday.

Officials said 22 persons were killed and 275 injured in Puerto Rico, and at least six more drowned in the Dominican Republic.

Power plant, line limits go to Lucey

By REID BEVERIDGE
Of The State Journal Staff

A bill regulating the locations of utility power plants and transmission lines was approved by the state Senate 30-0 Thursday and sent to the governor.

A key amendment to give farmers better access to the courts to challenge offers by utility firms when obtaining routes for transmission lines was defeated 16-15. Had the amendment prevailed, it might have delayed final enactment of the bill past next week's legislative adjournament.

Also rejected by the Senate, as it was in the Assembly, was an amendment to give local governments a veto over sites. The vote on that amendment was 19-9.

State Sen. Dale McKenna (D-Jefferson) pleaded for the amendments, accusing Gov. Patrick Lucey and the utility lobbyists of writing the bill to suit themselves.

"All others must obey local laws," McKenna said of his amendment to give local governments more control of sites.

"But it is all but the utilities under the bill. They can violate any ordinance they want."

Also rejected was an amendment to give farmers a choice between a lump sum payment for utility line easements and an annual payment.

McKenna charged some utility firms are offering $10 for a utility tower location of 90 square feet.

He charged the alternative is for the farmer to hire a lawyer, appraiser and engineer to prove the property is worth more.

STATE SEN. McKENNA

Lucey, who strongly supported the bill, praised the Legislature for enacting the bill after five years of debate.

"This is a red letter day for Wisconsin's environment, consumers and economic future," Lucey said.

"It is also testimony to the ability of our democratic process to address the problems of our day and anticipate the needs of tomorrow," Lucey said.

Under the bill, all utility companies must submit 10-year plans outlining where they want to build new electric generating plants during the decade, what kind of fuel will be used and the general size of the plants.

The PSC must hold a hearing on the plans in the general location of the proposed plant.

The comprehensive plans must be updated every two years.

Eighteen months before beginning construction, the utility firm must obtain the certificate of construction from the PSC.

No land can be bought by condemnation before the certificate is issued.

The bill does not apply to plants where the utility has already applied for the certificate, such as for Columbia II near Portage.

The utilities must include in their plans any alternate locations they might utilize if the PSC turns down their first choice.

The bill also includes a "bill of rights" for farmers whose land is crossed with a transmission line.

This bill of rights includes a requirement that the utility company must do any work with heavy equipment in the winter, when practical.

The bill of rights also requires that the farmers' land must be returned to its original condition as nearly as possible.

Today's chuckle

Every road to success provides many tempting parking places.

Wisconsin State Journal

MADISON, FRIDAY, OCTOBER 17, 1975

Vol. 282, No. 35 · 60 Pages, 6 Sections · 135th Year ★★★ WEATHER: **Mostly cloudy, cool today. High in mid 50s, low in mid 30s.** ★★★ FINAL 15¢

Nobel Prize winner Howard Temin at his laboratory work.

—State Journal photo by A. Craig Benson

County plans lower tax rate

By ANITA CLARK
Of The State Journal Staff

The Dane County tax rate for 1976 will go down if the County Board adopts the budget presented to it Thursday night.

County Executive George Reinke proposed a tax rate of $3.34 per $1,000 of equalized property value. The 1975 rate was $3.82.

The budget, described by Reinke as a stringent one, is proposed at $59.7-million, up by $1.4-million from last year.

But the amount to be raised by taxes on property owners in the county would be $14.09-million, nearly $400,000 less than in 1975.

The budget was referred to the board Finance and Personnel Committees for review before it is adopted, probably in about a month and almost certainly with changes.

The county tax levy is one of three major taxes imposed on property owners. The others are tax levies for local government and for schools.

19 new employes

Reinke's budget of $59,699,257 proposes adding 36 new positions and deleting 17 existing ones, for a net increase of 19 new employes. This is substantially less than the 44 persons hired last year or the 59 hired the year before, he said. The county has 1,462 employes authorized for 1975.

Reinke recommended $31.58-million for Health and Social Services, the county's largest division. That amount is about $3-million less than the division requested, but is $3-million more than it spent in 1975.

Recommended new positions include an airport property manager, a legislative analyst, 10 employes for the Department of Social Services, two deputies for boat and snowmobile patrol, and staff for the landfill program if the county continues to operate it.

'Wait and see'

Reinke proposed a "wait and see attitude" about retaining 39 employes now paid by federal funding which is to expire June 30, 1976. Funding could be extended, he said.

Divisions requested 167.5 new positions.

More than three hours was spent in budget hearings on the need for the two additional sheriff's deputies, Reinke said.

"At no time in the future will I approve the use of deputies on an overtime basis for boat patrol or snowmobile patrol unless there is an emergency that fully warrants charges to the overtime account," he said, after announcing that two additional deputies would be hired.

Reinke recommended $6.1-million for the Highway Dept., and said he anticipated that $300,000, in surplus funds would be available from 1975.

A separate account for sheltered workshop programs, to be allocated $300,000, was proposed by Reinke, who said the money is to be used only if the Community Mental Health Board "totally ignores the demand for a continuation of the current sheltered workshop program." Those funds are not to be available to the board, he said.

Other recommendations included

Turn to Page 2, Col. 3

GEORGE REINKE

A tentative look at your taxes

With the presentation of the Dane County budget Thursday night, all the proposed major spending components of the tax bills for Madison residents are in.

Here is what the primary taxing bodies are asking for, and the amount of change in their tax rates compared to 1975. The figures are in dollars per $1,000 of assessed valuation.

	1975	1976	Change
City of Madison	$14.70	$17.40	plus $2.70
Madison Schools	$29.17	$31.17 (maximum)	plus $2
		$29.17 (minimum)	no increase
Dane County	$3.80	$3.34	minus 46 cents
MATC	99 cents	$1.17	plus 18 cents

It is impossible to calculate exactly what the net tax rate will be for local taxpayers until the amount of state tax credits is known and until each of the taxing bodies sets a final rate, which in turn will be compiled into a total net rate for before the City Council.

However, if all the proposals were to remain intact, and stae tax credits were to remain near last year's level, the owner of a $30,000 home in Madison would expect a tax increase of about $160.

That figure includes not only the taxes themselves but an 8 percent average increase in assessments throughout the city.

Shell cuts gasoline price cent a gallon

CHICAGO (UPI) — Shell Oil Co. cut the price of gasoline nationwide by one cent a gallon Thursday, following an industry trend that is likely to end Nov. 1, an oil source said.

Shell, second behind Texaco in United States gasoline sales, became the third major oil firm to pare a penny off the price of a gallon of gas since Oct. 6 when Sun Oil Co. made the cutback. Tuesday, Exxon, the nation's third largest marketer, announced a similar reduction.

Herb Hugo, senior editor of Platts Oilgram, published in Chicago, said the trend toward lower prices began one month ago "when the effects of a decrease in demand began to be felt."

UW cancer researcher takes Nobel in stride

By ROGER A. GRIBBLE
Of The State Journal Staff

It isn't every day that a scientist wins the Nobel Prize for medicine and physiology.

Yet, University of Wisconsin-Madison Prof. Howard Temin seemed to be taking it all in stride Thursday.

Temin, 40, even rode his bike to work as usual after learning of the award through a phone call from a co-winner at 6:50 a.m.

Later, he conceded to a reporter, "No, I guess I was not completely surprised." He was nominated for the same award in 1971 for the same research.

Honored for his work with a virus which can cause cancer in chickens, he seemed determined not to let the notoriety he has achieved stop him from his work. While photographers photographed him at a microscope, he used the occasion to look at several slides rather than just posing with one slide.

His lab in the McArdle Laboratory for Cancer Research was a hectic place Thursday as Temin, a very private man, fought to find a moment to himself. "I need a minute to rest," he told a reporter before excusing himself during a hurried interview. Nobel prizes, considered among the most prestigious awards in the world, are awarded each

See other stories, photo on Page 4

year in five different fields to persons who have made valuable contributions to "the good of humanity."

The prizes consist of equal shares from the income of the estate of Swedish inventor Alfred Nobel, who died in 1896. The first Nobel prizes were awarded in 1901.

The awards are given in physics, chemistry, physiology or medicine, literature and peace.

Temin will share $143,000 with two other Nobel Prize recipients for their work on "the interactions between tumor viruses and the genetic material of the cell."

"I don't know what I'll do with the money," he said. "The most important reward a scientist can receive isn't an external award but the internal satisfaction with discovering something new and peer acceptance of your ideas. I've had peer acceptance of my work before."

A look at the record bears him out. Last year he was the recipient of an $843,000 award from the American Cancer Society which will pay two-thirds of his salary until his retirement, which could be the year 2004. The award put him in an elite group of only about 20 such scientists in the nation.

Temin said his day usually begins about 8:45 a.m. when he arrives at his office by bicycle. "I look at cell cultures and count viruses and design experiments in the morning.

"I have a luncheon seminar or meeting every day and teach a course on general virology three days a week. Then I read, write and prepare papers before going home about 5 or 5:30."

He admitted that he received many offers for other jobs. Asked whether any of them ever sound appealing, he replied, "I'm still here. That's the important thing."

Later, when asked if he planned to leave the UW like its two other Nobel Prize winners did (see page 4), he replied, "I'm not, this week, at least, going to transfer to another university."

He noted that none of his salary is paid by the state of Wisconsin and observed, "This is an indication of how

Turn to Page 2, Col. 5

Production rises sharply

Related story on Page 2

WASHINGTON (AP) — The output of the nation's mines, factories and utilities scored its largest monthly advance in nearly 11 years during September, the Federal Reserve Board reported Thursday.

The federal bank said industrial production rose 1.9 percent in September—the fifth consecutive monthly advance since the recovery from recession began in April.

The Fed said the latest advance, unlike the earlier increases, extended virtually across the economy, including raw materials and business equipment as well as the consumer goods which had initiated the advance.

The index has now climbed 5.7 percent since April.

New pill warnings drafted

WASHINGTON (UPI)—Sex hormones used in birth control pills and other drugs can result in birth defects ranging from stunted limbs to malformed hearts, the Food and Drug Administration (FDA) said Thursday.

It disclosed the findings in releasing the draft of proposed new warning labels for birth control pills which also would tell women who take them they run an increased risk of suffering fatal and non-fatal heart attacks.

The new warnings would tell the nation's 10 million women who use the pills not to take them at all if they are over 40 years of age and warned again that their use increases chances of blood clots and related problems such as strokes.

An FDA spokesman emphasized, however, that "serious adverse effects associated with the pill are relatively uncommon and birth control pills remain a safe and effective method of contraception. When taken properly, the pill is the most effective method of birth control other than sterilization."

The new labeling would advise women who wish to stop taking the pill and become pregnant to wait at least three months because "studies show there is a possible increased risk of spontaneous abortion in women who become pregnant shortly after discontinuing the pill."

The label also would advise any woman who misses one period while on the pill to have an immediate test for pregnancy to minimize the risk of damage to the developing child should she continue on the pill.

Such damage can occur, the agency said, because sex hormones such as estrogen and progestin present in the pills have resulted in some extremely rare "birth defects in children, such as heart malformations and stunted limb development" when women who become pregnant despite the pill continue taking it unaware of their condition.

At the same time, the new language would state that the FDA is certain there is at least one complication that will not result—cancer. The new labels will reaffirm there is no evidence of any link between the pill and that disease.

An FDA spokeswoman said the timing of the proposed new regulations has still not been set, but they might be put forth in a matter of weeks.

Oral contraceptives have carried warning statements, both on the package the doctor receives and on a brochure available to the patient, since 1969. The planned revision is being made, the FDA said, to take into account new research made over the past few years.

One such study, reported to the nation's doctors in an FDA "drug bulletin" in August, said women aged 30 to 39 run 2.8 times the chance of suffering a fatal heart attack if they are on the pill compared to women not using it. The risk for women aged 40 to 44 is 4.7 times higher.

The risk of suffering a non-fatal heart attack is 5.7 times greater in the 40 to 44 age group and 2.7 times greater in the 30 to 39 bracket, the same study suggested.

"FDA's obstetrics and gynecology advisory committee has recommended that patients over 40 be made thoroughly aware of the increased risk and be urged to utilize other forms of contraception," the agency said in its earlier warning.

Women with additional problems, such as diabetes, obesity and high blood pressure—or those who smoke cigarets—run an even higher risk of suffering a heart attack if they are on the pill, the studies added.

Mailman's fans protest switch

By ROBERT PFEFFERKORN
Of The State Journal Staff

Pity the poor mailmen who are replacing Lucky Jordan on Madison's West Side Hoyt Park area.

The dogs — traditional enemies of postmen everywhere — are upset and angry. So are the people.

Lucky Jordan, 1718 Winchester St., has been transferred after 10 years in the area, 24 total with the postal service, in an efficiency move.

Pity, too, James McKee and Virgil Noltner, who faced about 30 men, women and children from the neighborhood Thursday afternoon.

With Postmaster John Whitmore out of town, they faced the task of explaining to Lucky's friends — he wasn't present — that the U.S. Postal Service is not a faceless, heartless bureaucracy.

A widow, Mrs. Margaret Faber, 2530 Van Hise Ave., presented a letter at the meeting in Whitmore's office that contained upwards of 200 signatures pleading that their friend be permitted to stay.

According to the testimonials, Jordan went beyond the call of duty. He delivered mail to neighbors routinely when a family went on vacation. He pulled a child, possibly more than one, from certain tragedy in the streets.

What's more, he managed to deliver mail on time and to the right address. And then, too, one woman said, "The children love him dearly."

"We're pleased you appreciate one of our employes" said acting postmaster McKee. But only Whitmore has the power to order a new plan to keep Jor-

Turn to Page 2, Col. 1

Today's chuckle

Public relations is performing the right act at the right time — and getting credit for it.

Inside

Reds win, take Series lead — Sports

Wisconsin State Journal

Wednesday
August 17, 1977
Madison, Wisconsin
48 pages ★★★ 20 cents

Elvis Presley dead at 42

Heart attack kills king of rock 'n roll

1960: Elvis promoted to sergeant while with Army.

The late, great Elvis Presley

—AP Wirephotos

MEMPHIS, Tenn. (AP) — Elvis Presley, 42, the Mississippi boy whose rock 'n' roll guitar and gyrating hips changed American music styles, died Tuesday afternoon of heart failure.

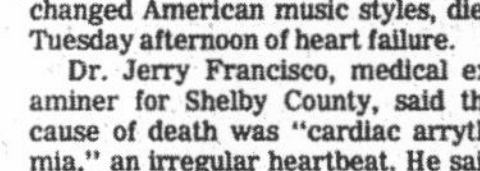

Dr. Jerry Francisco, medical examiner for Shelby County, said the cause of death was "cardiac arrythmia," an irregular heartbeat. He said "that's just another name for a form of heart attack."

Francisco said the three-hour autopsy uncovered no sign of any other diseases, and there was no sign of any drug abuse.

Presley was declared dead at 3:30 p.m CDT at Baptist Hospital, where he had been taken by a fire department ambulance after being found unconscious at his Graceland mansion.

Dr. George Nichopolous, Presley's personal physician, said Presley was last seen alive shortly after 9 a.m. Nichopoulos said Presley had been taking a number of appetite depressants, but he said they did not contribute to his death.

Elvis: A rebel who didn't need a cause

— See Look Section

Francisco said there was no sign of any drug abuse.

Gossip reporter Rona Barrett had discussed on ABC Television Tuesday morning a book in which former bodyguards alleged that Presley had been using drugs.

Presley's unconcious form was discovered at his white-columned mansion by Joe Esposito, his road manager. A girl friend, Ginger Alden, 20, was at the mansion, Nichopoulos said.

A Baptist Hospital spokesman said Esposito began resuscitation efforts and called for Nichopoulos and an ambulance.

News spread that Presley was seriously ill, and radio and television stations were inundated by telephone calls. Hundreds of people gathered at the hospital and at Presley's home. Scores of police were sent to both sites.

Presley, who had rarely emerged from his mansion grounds in recent years except for performances, had been hospitalized at Baptist in April when he cut short a tour in Louisana and returned to Memphis.

At that time, he was said to be suffering from exhaustion and intestinal flu.

In the past two years, he had also been hospitalized for eye problems and for what doctors described as a twisted colon.

He had rarely been seen in public recently, and his weight was said to have ballooned from the 175 he weighed as a young man.

However, Nichopoulos's wife said Presley was due to leave Tuesday night on an 11-day tour to begin today in Portland, Me. The Cumberland County Civic Center in Portland announced it would refund the 17,000

Turn to Page 2, Col. 1

Judge named FBI director

Judge Johnson

WASHINGTON (AP) — President Carter has chosen Federal Judge Frank Johnson, whose decisions have boosted civil rights in his native Alabama, to become FBI director, knowledgeable Administration sources said Tuesday night.

The White House planned to announce today that Carter will nominate Johnson, 58, a Republican, to succeed Clarence M. Kelley as chief of the beleaguered investigative agency. Kelley has announced plans to retire at the end of this year.

Johnson, a lifelong Alabaman, has been a federal judge for the Middle District of Alabama in Montgomery since his appointment to the bench in 1955 by President Dwight Eisenhower. Before that, he was a United States attorney.

The nomination will be subject to Senate confirmation.

The choice of Johnson ends Carter's search of more than six months for a new director to take charge of the FBI at a time when it still is suffering from disclosures of allegedly illegal intelligence-gathering tactics in the past.

The sources said Carter and Atty. Gen. Griffin Bell settled on Johnson as their choice and rejected the four candidates suggested by a citizens' committee the President assigned to screen some 200 applicants. A fifth person recommended by the committee later withdrew. None of the five suggested by the committee had a national reputation, and no strong public or congressional support developed for any of them.

In turning to Johnson, Carter and Bell went back to a man they have long sought to lure into the Administration.

Bell twice offered Johnson the job of deputy attorney general last winter but was unable to convince him to leave Alabama and his judgeship.

Johnson's best-known decisions are in the civil rights field, and he has won a towering reputation among civil rights advocates and the enmity of Alabama Gov. George Wallace.

After reviewing a suit alleging widespread violations of inmates' rights in Alabama prisons, Johnson threatened to shut down the prison system until the legislature came up with more money for improvements.

Johnson also was a pioneer in extending constitutional protection for the rights of patients in state institutions.

Today's chuckle

In the past 200 years, America has manufactured close to 100 billion pencils — and we still can't keep one by the phone.

Council bans beer, brat sales on city lands at UW games

By William R. Wineke
Of The State Journal

The City Council Tuesday night voted to ban concessions, including beer and bratwurst stands, from city property around Camp Randall stadium before University of Wisconsin football games.

The unanimous vote came after aldermen voted 15-4 to defeat a milder proposal, which would have allowed most concessions to continue but would have prohibited beer sales.

The resolution does not affect the right of the university or of private property owners to give permission for concessions.

However, in previous years, most of the concessions have been located either on city sidewalks or in the vacant city-owned areas at the intersections of Monroe St., Regent St. and Breese Terrace.

The resolution was introduced by aldermen of districts surrounding the stadium, who said community organizations in the area disagreed about the extent of the ban but did agree that beer sales should be prohibited.

Ald. Sheila Chaffee, Dist. 10, was the main proponent of a complete ban.

She referred to "85,000 fulsome folks who maraud through our neighborhoods, using them as parking lots and scattering their litter as they go."

Ald. Richard Disch, Dist. 22, who is an usher at Wisconsin football games, supported the beer ban.

"These people come to the game loaded and at half time they want to get out," he said. "We're not supposed to let them out except in emergency cases, but nine times out of 10 the emergency is that they want a brat and a beer."

But Ald. Jay Wexler, Dist. 7, termed the whole idea ridiculous and said the ban won't cut litter.

"My experience with these organizations is that the people who use them buy brats and soft drinks on their way into the stadium," he said. "My God, we've got 85,000 people coming into that area on a football day and they bring their own litter; we're not going to stop it by stopping some non-profit organizations from trying to make some money to help charity."

Wexler also said the council was being hypocritical in stopping non-profit organizations from using the property.

"For heaven's sake, this council is so used to giving money to any damn thing that comes along that it can't tell these organizations they can't make a few dollars," he said.

Demonstrators hit governor with pie

COLUMBUS, O. (UPI) — Ohio Gov. James Rhodes was struck in the face Tuesday with a pie hurled by a demonstrator protesting construction of a gym on the Kent State University campus at the opening ceremony of the 124th annual Ohio State Fair.

"Remember Kent State — move the gym," chanted the dozen demonstrators before Rhodes officially opened the fair at 6 a.m. Tuesday. Then, one of seven persons later arrested, tossed a cream pie at Rhodes, hitting him near his right eye.

The demonstrators, all claiming to be members of the Youth International Party (Yippies), said they were protesting the planned construction of a gymnasium complex at Kent State near the site where four students were shot to death by National Guardsmen during a 1970 anti-war demonstration.

Beetle fading from U.S. scene

DETROIT (AP) — The Volkswagen Beetle, that funny-looking German car which captivated a generation of youthful Americans, is sputtering to the end of its road in the United States.

Shipment to this country of the Beetle sedan, the most successful import in U.S. history, ended as the current model year expired last month. About 2,000 cars are in inventory.

VW spokesman Baron Bates said Tuesday the decision was made because sales declined while prices rose over the past decade.

"We're discontinuing the model because it is not worth it to keep up with the (federal) emissions and safety standards on so low a volume," said Bates.

He said 1977 Beetle sales through July were less than 15,000.

However, VW will continue to offer a higher-priced Beetle convertible here. Bates said projected sales are about 9,000 a year at $5,000 each, about $1,300 more than the sedan.

The VW Beetle: A still-common sight here.

—AP Wirephoto

The rear-engined, air-cooled Beetle first arrived on American shores in 1949. Just two were sold that year. But it began the import invasion of the U.S. car market and helped create demand for the small, economy car.

Since then, Americans have bought an estimated five million Beetles — more than one-quarter of the 19 million Beetles sold around the world since the car was introduced in 1945.

It is the best-selling model of all time, and it will continue to be available in Germany and other countries outside the U.S.

In 1968, VW's best year, 423,000 Beetles were sold in the U.S., starting at $1,699 apiece. "Ah, those were the days," recalled Bates. "We ruled the roost."

But the henhouse was being torn apart by the rise of the West German mark against the dollar, which forced up the U.S. price of the car and triggered a massive sales slide. Today, the car sells for $3,700.

"Devaluation (of the dollar) killed us," said Bates.

Beetle sales plummeted even more in 1975, after VW brought out the Rabbit and cut back Beetle production to step up output of the new car. VW will begin building the Rabbit in this country next year.

The Beetle's basic appeal was a reputation for dependability and, especially, a price lower than anything Detroit offered.

The basic design, by auto pioneer Ferdinand Porsche in the 1930s, changed little over the years.

Although the Beetle sedan will no longer be offered here, it has a healthy market elsewhere. VW is still producing about 1,000 Beetles a day in Germany and a dozen other countries.

Inside

Today's weather: Partly sunny

Slight chance of rain. High around 73 today. For more weather information, turn to Page 14.

Monday

June 19, 1978
Madison, Wisconsin
40 pages ★★★ 20 cents

Andy North wins U.S. Open

North blasts out of trap to Open victory on No. 18.

—AP Wirephoto

DENVER (UPI) — Andy North of Madison, Wis., struggled back from a heart-pumping string of three bogeys and a double bogey Sunday and went on to win a U.S. Open championship that no one else seemed to want.

North won by sinking a 5-foot putt on the final hole to edge Dave Stockton and J.C. Snead by one stroke.

"I'd like to be here every Sunday," North said after winning Sunday. "I feel I'm pretty much in control, that I'm in control of my destiny. It doesn't matter what any of the other guys shoot. I'm the one who can control what happens."

North, whose only previous tour victory came in the Westchester Classic last year, earned $45,000.

North, the leader after the second and third rounds, appeared in control when he took a five-shot lead with a 12-foot birdie putt on the 13th hole. But it was a struggle the rest of the way, and he needed that life-saving putt on the final hole to salvage a bogey and prevent a three-way 18-hole playoff with Snead and Stockton today.

More stories, photos in today's Sports

North stepped away from the ball twice and scratched his head on the 18th green before touching off a tumultuous ovation with his critical putt. That gave him a final round score of 74 and left him at 285, one over par for the tournament.

It was the 20th time since 1941 that the Open was won with an above-par score.

Stockton and Snead, both starting the round three strokes behind North, each closed with a 72 to share second place at 286. Two strokes farther back were Tom Weiskopf, who equalled the best round of the championship with a 68, and Hale Irwin, the first-round leader, who had a 70.

North, who had said before the round that his destiny was in his own hands, in the end staved off a field of illustrious challengers simply because no one else was up to the challenge.

After getting birdies on the fourth and fifth holes, North left the Open championship up for grabs by struggling along with five bogeys and his only double bogey in four days. But Stockton, a cool veteran with two PGA championships, was unable to take advantage as he managed only two birdies for the round. Snead had but one birdie, a 35-foot putt on No. 6.

When it was obvious that North was starting to come apart, Snead could do nothing more than par the final nine holes.

Gary Player, a winner of 114 worldwide tournaments and only one shot behind at the start of the round, was paired with North but was unable to apply the pressure. Player blew up with a 77 to finish well back at 289, tied with Jack Nicklaus (73), Tom Watson (70), Andy Bean (74), Johnny Miller (74) and Billy Kratzert (73).

Imports stir beef with farmers

N.Y. Times News Service

CHICAGO — The political waves from President Carter's decision to grant a slight increase in beef imports are washing across the Farm Belt faster than the economic ripple the administration expected from its rather modest move to slow inflation.

Earlier this month, when the White House announced its decision to raise beef imports by about 200 million pounds, or roughly 16 percent above the 1.29 billion pounds planned for this year, Secretary of Agriculture Robert Bergland described the amount as "a little dinky dab that will have no profound effect on the Consumer Price Index."

No reassurance

If that was meant to give reassurance to farmers at the same time other Carter spokesmen were telling consumers the action could save them a nickel a pound on hamburger, it did not work.

Nor did it ease the misgivings of Democratic politicians who must run for election this year in farm states, where the president's popularity in the polls had already been sagging faster than in most other parts of the country.

Farmers may make up only a tiny fraction of the electorate nationally, but they are an extremely vocal and effective minority in this part of the country, one that can easily tip the balance in a close Senate, congressional or gubernatorial race.

Sounding a wounded note that was echoed by Democratic incumbents across the Farm Belt, Sen. Dick Clark of Iowa, who is in the midst of a reelection campaign that is now viewed as more difficult than he had expected, declared:

"It is a senseless, purely political act. The president's advisers see it as a kind of agricultural Mayaguez that's supposed to demonstrate the president's firmness and decisiveness in dealing with the problem of inflation."

'Opportunistic'

He was referring to the 1975 incident in which President Ford sent Marines to rescue the American crew of the merchant ship Mayaguez from their Cambodian captors. And he was not convinced Carter's action on beef imports would have the desired results.

"I think about all it accomplishes is to make him look opportunistic and ill-informed and unwilling to listen," Clark said. "And in my judgment, that's a pretty accurate picture of it."

Reached by telephone during the recent state Democratic convention in Des Moines, the senator said he did

Turn to Page 2, Col. 1

State bands in there

Steve Sveum of Sun Prairie High School's "Cardinal Guard" played a saxaphone solo Saturday night as 29 high school marching bands from 10 states competed for $1,000 and an invitation to the Orange Bowl Parade on New Year's Eve in Miami, Fla. Live Oak High School of Morgan Hill, Calif., took top honors in the third annual national championship. Oregon High School, directed by Steve Spiwak, finished sixth in the small schools division. Other Wisconsin competitors included Wauwatosa East, Wisconsin Lutheran (Milwaukee), Verona and Hamilton (Sussex).

—State Journal photo by Joseph W. Jackson III

'Vegas East' players lose $18 an hour

ATLANTIC CITY, N.J. (AP) — Gamblers at the East's first legal casino are losing their money at an average rate of $18 an hour, according to an Associated Press review of figures released by Resorts International Hotel Casino.

Slot machine players are losing an average $18.64 per hour and table players an average $17.73 per hour, according to the AP review.

The figures are based on the casino's "win" average of $438,504 a day for its first six days of operation as reported to the New Jersey Casino Control Commission recently. The casino opened May 26.

A casino's "win" figure — actually the amount lost by gamblers — is much like the gross revenue figure of other businesses.

Taxes, labor, capital investment and other costs must be taken out before it is considered profit.

Resorts International said 55.3 percent, an average of $242,493 a day, came from its slot machines and 44.7 percent, an average of $196,011 a day, came from its gaming tables.

Charles Anderson, financial analyst for the Nevada Gaming Control Board, said it was impossible to compare the Resorts International figures with those in Nevada because of differences in reporting requirements and the large number of casinos in Nevada.

Resorts International reported about 723 of its 893 slot machines, or 81 percent, were operating for an average of slightly more than 18 hours a day during the period. The casino is open 18 hours a day on weekdays and 20 hours a day on weekends.

It also reported that about about 71 of its 84 tables, or 85 percent, were open during the period. The AP has calculated — looking at available seating — that an average of more than 600 people were playing the tables at any given time or more than 11,000 people played the tables during a casino day.

Raymond Gore, Resorts International vice president for finance, said company officials did not break down their figures to the number of gamblers or wins per hour. He said the firm believed gamblers and spectators spent about two hours each in the gaming area, or about 75,000 people a day passed through the casino.

Gambling experts said the return and win-per-hour figures are true for a large number of plays over a long period of time. They emphasized that one or a few big wins, winning streaks or a gambler's luck cannot be considered in the figures.

The casino commission said last week that bettors have the best chance to win on craps tables, where Resorts International returns 90 percent of the amount bet. Other return figures are 87 percent at baccarat, 77 percent at blackjack and roulette, and 58 percent at the wheels of fortune, according to the commission.

Resorts International officials say their nickel slot machines return 85 percent and dollar slots return 90 percent of the bet. Under New Jersey law, slot machines must return at least 83 percent.

By comparision, the New Jersey Racing Commission said the state's tracks return 83 percent of the amount bet and the New Jersey Lottery Commission says its various games return 47 percent.

Showboat upset kills UW's Fuller

Emeritus Professor Muriel L. Fuller, 65, of 1347 N. Wingra Drive, a pioneer in library science education and legislation, drowned Saturday when a tornado overturned a dinner theater-showboat on Lake Pomona in Osage County, Kan.

Professor Fuller

Miss Fuller was the retired chairman of the University of Wisconsin Extension Communication Arts Department and professor of library science at the UW-Madison.

She retired in 1977 and had continued part-time work at the UW-Extension. She was to teach a summer school course in library science at Emporia (Kan.) State University.

Her legacy in Wisconsin is evident in the improved state library systems and through her constant contact with the state system through her work with the University Extension.

Miss Fuller was instrumental in developing the Library Systems and State Aid Bill, which was made law in 1971. The legislation encouraged counties to combine their library services, making their expanded resources available to all within the counties' communities.

Miss Fuller grew up in West Salem, a small community east of La Crosse. She was graduated from La Crosse State Teachers College in 1935 and became a high school teacher before coming to Madison for library school at the UW in 1942.

After graduation, she spent 10 years in the La Crosse Public Library, first as assistant librarian, then as head librarian.

It was while in La Crosse that she began to realize the need for state legislation to improve Wisconsin libraries.

She served as consultant to the

Showboat stories and photos on Page 4

Michigan State Univesity Library after leaving La Crosse in 1953 and returned to the UW in Madison in 1962 as a library lecturer.

In 1972, she was awarded the Wisconsin Library Association's Citation of Merit for her leadership and her professional contributions to the profession on the state and national levels. Her specialty was public library administration.

She enjoyed travel and was active in the American Association of University Women, the American Civil Liberties Union and wildlife groups.

Funeral arrangements are pending.

Today's chuckle

An executive knows something about everything. A technician knows everything about something. A switchboard operator knows everything.

Inside

Today's weather: Partly cloudy, warm

Partly cloudy today, fair tonight. Highs in the low 80s. For more weather information, turn to Page 8.

Wisconsin State Journal

Saturday
February 23, 1980
Madison, Wisconsin
34 pages ★★★ 25 cents

U.S. defeats Soviets in Olympic hockey

U.S. Olympic hockey team celebrates 4-3 victory over Soviets.
—AP Laserphoto

By Don Lindstrom
State Journal Sports Writer

LAKE PLACID — Americans went beserk in Lake Placid on Friday. Their beloved Cinderella hockey team did it.

They beat the Soviets.

The hustling Americans pulled off the upset of the Games by defeating the Soviet Union 4-3 before more than 8,500 screaming fans at the Olympic Fieldhouse.

Victory came on Mike Eruzione's goal midway in the third period.

Coach Herb Brooks said — even in the light of the U.S. gold-medal achievement in 1960 — that this was the "greatest."

First loss in 12 years

The Soviets suffered their first Olympic defeat in 12 years and saw their chances of their fifth straight gold medal, and sixth in seven Olympiads, placed in jeopardy.

They will not have a chance if the U.S. beats Finland on Sunday. If, however, the Finns beat the Americans, the Soviets still have a chance. The reason? They went into the final round with two points on their 5-0 record. The U.S. went in with one point, because of its tie with Sweden in the Games' opener.

Madison's Mark Johnson, the all-American from the University of Wisconsin, scored two goals, including the third-period equalizer. Then Eruzione, a former all-American from Boston College, slammed in the winning shot.

Eruzione's 25-foot blast on Soviet goalie Vladamir Myshkin came with exactly 10 minutes remaining. Then the Americans held on — minute after minute — Brooks pleaded with them to "play your game."

U.S. in control

As the seconds wound down, the Americans controlled the puck and the flow of the game so completely Soviet Coach Vladimir Jurzinov wasn't even able to pull his goalie.

The delirious American skaters then poured onto the ice to mob goalie Jim Craig and celebrate. At the other end, the Soviets stood quietly, thoroughly dejected, waiting for the usual congratulatory line of handshakes.

It was wonderful to see; something to tuck away in the annals of your sports memory for all time.

The Americans are now in the scramble for their first gold medal since 1960. All the U.S. has to do is beat Finland. And, although Brooks regards that a monumental task, it can be done.

Brooks had prepared his team well.

They played the Soviets even through the opening minutes and got a chance on a penalty. But Johnson's tip on starting goalie Vladislav Tretjak just missed.

Then, 9 minutes, 12 seconds into the game, the Soviets scored on a slap shot by 19-year-old Vladimir Krutov on

Turn to Page 2, Col. 3

Eric Heiden will try for fifth gold today

The Wisconsin State Journal's full daily coverage of the XIII Winter Olympics continues today with sports reporter Don Lindstrom's stories, illustrated by pictures from chief photographer L. Roger Turner.

The Sports Section offers a full schedule of today's events, including Madison speed skater Eric Heiden's try for a fifth gold medal in the 10,000-meter event at 8:30 a.m. A full television schedule is in the Look Section.

Inflation explosion feared

WASHINGTON (AP) — Consumer prices surged upward 1.4 percent in January, the worst rate in 6½ years, leading a top administration official to warn Friday that "inflation is starting to explode."

The jump prompted one congressional leader to call for a fresh look at wage and price controls. But despite Friday's bleak report, the White House stood firm against mandatory controls.

The January price increase, an annual rate of more than 18 percent, compared to 13.3 percent for all of 1979, was partly due to another steep jump in fuel and housing costs. The price of gasoline rose 7.4 percent, the most ever, to an average of $1.11 per gallon for all types.

"It is beginning to appear that the underlying rate of inflation is starting to explode," said Robert Russell, director of the administration's anti-inflation agency. He said "an explosion of wage increases" also is probably inevitable.

Meanwhile, reacting to worsening inflation and the tighter money policies of the Federal Reserve Board, several major banks hiked their prime lending rates to 16½ percent, a record. Morgan Guaranty Trust Co., the nation's fifth largest, went first and was quickly followed by Bankers Trust Co. and Crocker National Bank.

The increase in prices, the worst for any month since August 1973, came despite a 0.2 percent decline in grocery store prices, and showed how bad inflation has become in the rest of the economy. Prices in January were 13.9 percent higher than a year earlier, and the annual rate of increase for the last three months was 15.6 percent.

Rep. Henry Reuss, D-Wis., chairman of the House Banking Committee, said the Carter administration "had abdicated its responsibilities" by letting inflation get out of hand.

"I think Congress would respond very fast indeed" to a comprehensive attack on inflation that included a balanced budget and mandatory wage and price controls, Reuss said. But he added that controls by themselves would be "a disaster."

White House press secretary Jody Powell told reporters Friday that anti-inflation policies "are under review as they are constantly," but he added flatly that, "mandatory wage and price controls are not under consideration."

The White House spokesman did say the administration is considering how to counter an inflationary psychology that leads to greater inflation.

A number of private economists have said in recent weeks that mandatory controls may now be needed as part of a broader anti-inflation strategy. Sen. Edward Kennedy, D-Mass., who is a presidential contender, also has called for wage and price controls.

Associated Press-NBC News polls repeatedly have shown that most Americans favor mandatory controls even though a majority doesn't think they would work.

However, the administration voiced strong new opposition to controls, despite January's price report. Charles Schultze, the president's chief economic adviser, said controls can't be maintained long enough to be effective and they are likely to harm the economy.

"In my judgment, mandatory wage and price controls are neither a quick

Turn to Page 2, Col. 4

Civic Center comes alive

By Paul Fanlund
Of The State Journal

After decades of controversy and years of planning, Madison's cavernous, modernistic Civic Center came alive in two waves Friday.

First was the formal dedication, featuring Joan Mondale, the vice president's wife, headlining a celebration of Madison's movers and shakers — the politicians, business people and art aficionados.

The dressy, hour-long affair — a review of Civic Center chronology and tribute to individual contributions — climaxed to the strains of "America the Beautiful" in the ornate Oscar Mayer Theater.

As that gathering began to disperse, a second wave started. Casually dressed passersby wandered into the $10-million center, the first unrestricted public glimpse of a project that has been the topic of a century of Madison debate.

That throng soon crowded the building in numbers equal to or larger than the dedication audience. They wandered through the Crossroads lobby area, many — engrossed in surveying the modern designs and colors — bumping into one another.

Friday marked the start of a five-week Civic Center Opening Festival, an intensive, much-publicized launching designed to acquaint residents with the center in the renovated Capitol Theater on State Street. Professional performances are being supplemented by free lunchtime concerts

(Another Civic Center story is on Page 1 of Section 4.)

and other events during the festival.

Mrs. Mondale, who toured the Civic Center before the dedication, lavishly praised Madison's citizenry and the new center. "It (the Civic Center) says the people of Madison care about the quality of their city," she said.

Mrs. Mondale, noted for her support for the arts, recently was named honorary chairperson of the Federal Council on the Arts and the Humanities by President Carter. "What Lady Bird Johnson did for flowers and trees, Joan Mondale may do for art," a recent Time magazine article said.

She said Madison's center will be "every bit as cost-effective as it is art-effective," a recurring theme among the center's boosters.

When Mrs. Mondale's appearance was announced earlier this winter, one of the center's architects pointed out the value Madison is receiving compared to inflation-plagued projects elsewhere.

During the arduous planning and construction process that lead to Friday's opening, the center suffered budget overruns, and its supporters were stung by cost criticism.

Mrs. Mondale said the Civic Center "will be active all day long with busy offices, restaurants, gallery exhibi-

Turn to Page 2, Col. 1

Chicago fire pact reached

CHICAGO (AP) — City, firefighter and labor leaders reached agreement late Friday night to end a nine-day-old strike by firemen after an earlier pact fell apart.

Details of the agreement were not announced, but Fire Commissioner Richard Albrecht said firemen could be back on the job by late today.

After more than seven hours of talks in her office, Mayor Jane Byrne and Vice President William Reddy of the Chicago Fire Union announced a written memorandum of agreement.

Reddy said the pact would be taken before the union's executive board and then before the general membership for ratification. He said a membership meeting could come this morning.

Mayor Joel Skornicka shows Joan Mondale Madison's Civic Center on Friday as Director Edgar Neiss looks on.
—State Journal photo by Edwin Stein

Inside

Today's weather: Flurries possible

Cloudy with a few flurries possible. High in the low 30s. For more weather information, turn to Page 10.

Wisconsin State Journal

Sunday

February 24, 1980
Madison, Wisconsin
174 pages ★★★ 75 cents

He's Eric the Great

By Don Lindstrom
State Journal Sports Writer

LAKE PLACID, N.Y. — Forget Jack Armstrong, and maybe Superman, too.

Now it's Eric Heiden, all-American golden miracleman.

Five individual gold medals. A feat no one in the history of the Olympic Games ever attained.

It took 56 years for the United States to win nine gold medals in speed skating. Heiden needed only 10 days to win five.

On Saturday the Madison native smashed world and Olympic records as he churned to victory in a stunning 14 minutes, 28.13 seconds in the 10,000-meter event.

It was the speed skating finale of the XIII Winter Games — 25 grueling laps — and when it was over Heiden had smashed the world record by 6.2 seconds.

The record Heiden broke was set in the ideal high altitude rink of Medeo, the Soviet Union, by Russian Viktor Leskin in 1975 — the man with whom Heiden was paired and whom he demoralized here Saturday.

And, the Olympic record? Heiden was 22.46 seconds better than the 1976 mark by Holland's Piet Kleine at Innsbruck, Austria.

"I didn't expect the times to be that fast today," said Heiden. "As I watched (Tom Erik) Oxholm and Mike Woods skate, I was scared.

"My coach (Dianne Holum) talked with me after that first pair finished, and she put me on a schedule for 14:30. During the last couple of laps she signaled that I was 2 seconds under that schedule."

Heiden finished the race and the record flashed on the scoreboard. He went around another lap, still crouched over, obviously in pain. "I kept thinking how nice it was going to be to stand up again," he said.

Heiden's five golds included five Olympic records of 38.03 seconds in the 500 meters, 1:15.18 in the 1,000, 1:55.44 in the 1,500, 7:02.29 in the 5,000, and now 14:28.13 in the 10,000.

His margins of victory ranged from 34 hundredths of a second in the 500 to 8.47 seconds in the six-mile-plus finale.

He defeated five former world record holders. He now has world records pending in three events, and still holds the total points record in World Championships.

If that isn't enough, he claims four World Sprint Championships, three men's world titles, and will try for another next weekend in Heerenveen, the Netherlands.

He has surpassed the individual performances of all-time Summer Games champion, swimmer Mark Spitz, who earned four individual golds in 1972. Spitz, however, added three golds in team events.

Now, between Heiden and 1976 Olympic swimmer Jim Montgomery, Madison can be proud of eight gold medal performances.

On this day of misty snow and before about 7,000 screaming spectators, he was like a well-oiled machine, clicking off laps in the 34-second range. He was once 2 seconds behind Leskin, who had an explosive start, but Heiden then slowly closed the gap and pulled away.

He wound up a surprising 23 seconds ahead of the former world record holder.

Woods of Milwaukee just missed the bronze medal in his skating farewell, when he placed fourth at 14: 39.53.

Woods was paired with Norway's Oxholm in the opening heat. Oxholm, one of the world's strongest distance skaters, set a tremendous pace, and wound up with the bronze medal at 14: 36.60.

Mid-race collapse

Former Olympic record holder, Piet Kleine of the Netherlands, came on strong in the sixth pair to grab silver medal honors at 14:36.03.

Leskin was seventh in 14:51.72. He can blame Heiden for his mid-race collapse. Leskin was demoralized while listening to Heiden's stunning lap times, and his medal hopes faded away amid fatigue.

The third U.S. skater, Craig Kressler of Midland, Mich., found the race too demanding, and dropped out after 7,000 meters.

Heiden's gold boosted the U.S. speed skating total to eight — two more than its 1976 total.

Heiden was especially pleased with his second pairs draw and that he was racing behind Oxholm.

'Skate my own race'

"It was a lucky draw, that's for sure. I knew then what to shoot for. When Leskin went out fast I was concerned about him and was wondering if I should attack. But Dianne told me to skate my own race.

"Leskin is the world record holder. I don't think he went out there to burn me out. If you're a smart skater, you skate your own race.

"During the race I thought about getting into the rhythm, and in the middle of the race I tried to turn off my mind. Then I started to think about how tired I was and how good it would be to have it over. It hurt."

Heiden was pleased for his distance colleague, Woods, who almost had the bronze.

"I was happy for him, until Kleine came along. Mike broke his personal record by some 20 seconds. He deserves all the recognition."

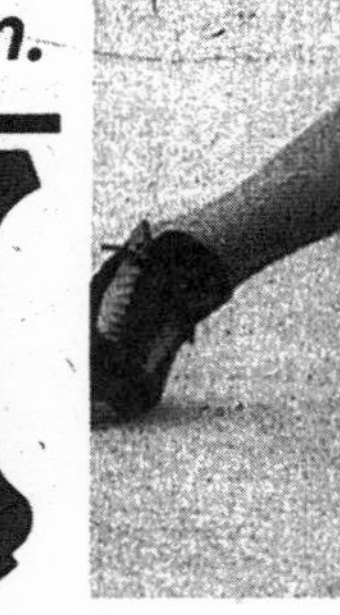

Madison's Eric Heiden: A new chapter in Olympic history.
—State Journal photo by L. Roger Turner

Khomeini raises hostage doubts

By Associated Press

A five-man, UN-sponsored commission arrived in Tehran on Saturday to begin its investigation of the deposed shah, but Ayatollah Ruhollah Khomeini said decisions about freeing the American hostages will not be made before Iranian parliamentary elections in April.

The all-powerful Iranian leader's comments, reported by Tehran Radio and monitored by BBC in London, cast the most serious doubt yet that the commission's work would lead to the quick release of the hostages. The members of the commission arrived from Geneva, Switzerland, hours after Khomeini spoke, and were met at the airport by Iran's chief of protocol, Foreign Ministry officials and ambassadors from their own countries.

Militants occupying the U.S. Embassy issued a statement late Saturday endorsing Khomeini's "decision to let the future Iranian Parliament decide (the fate of the hostages). We will obey the nation's will."

Previously, the militants had resisted efforts by President Abolhassan Bani-Sadr to negotiate an end to the crisis or take custody of the hostages, who spent their 112th day in captivity Saturday.

The militants, who have said consistently they would free the hostages only on Khomeini's orders, were sticking by their demand for the extradition of ousted Shah Mohammad Reza Pahlavi and the return of his wealth in exchange for release of some 50 Americans held captive inside the U.S. Embassy since Nov. 4.

"Today's statement has proved that Ayatollah Khomeini is a leader who is not ready for bargaining or abandoning any of the rights of the people," the militants said in their statement.

Tehran Radio quoted one member of the UN panel as telling reporters upon arrival in Iran: "The commission will try to investigate all grievances put forward by Iran against the former regime, and will try to find a speedy solution to end the crisis between Iran and America."

In Washington, State Department spokesman Hodding Carter said the commission was obligated to seek an

Turn to Page 2, Col. 1

Golden game at 10 a.m.

The U.S. Olympic hockey team's final game in its quest for a gold medal will be televised live at 10 a.m. today on Channel 27. The team, including Madisonians Mark Johnson and Bobby Suter, will face Finland.

The Wisconsin State Journal's daily coverage of the Games features a Sports interview with Johnson, the scoring star in the Friday night victory over the Soviets.

More on Eric Heiden's historic capture of five Olympic gold medals also appears in Sports.

A full television schedule of Olympic events is listed on Page 1 of Sports and in today's TV Week.

Today's weather: Mostly cloudy

Becoming mostly cloudy today, with chance of light snow this morning. Highs in the mid-20s. For more weather information, turn to Page 22.

Civic Center premiere is a dream fulfilled

By Sunny Schubert
Of The State Journal

Review on Page 4

They came, they saw and they raved. Madison society turned out en masse for the premiere performance at the new Civic Center on Saturday night — and they liked what they saw even before they heard what they'd come to hear.

The doors to the $10 million arts center were open all day, and as patrons arrived for the opening performance, they merged with strollers off the street who'd just dropped in to take a look at the renovated Capitol Theater.

Minks mingled with blue jeans, tuxedoes flanked ski jackets, and gilt pumps strode side-by-side with hiking boots down the gray carpeted pathways of the Crossroads.

But as showtime approached, as ticket holders flooded the lobby, waiting to hear opera diva Martina Arroya and the Madison Symphony Orchestra, the number of casual visitors diminished. For the rest of the evening, the Civic Center belonged to 2,200 symphony fans — many of whom had worked for years to bring the arts center to reality.

For Sid Knope, the Civic Center opening was more than realization of a long-time dream: it was a homecoming. When the Capitol Theater, which now forms the nucleus for the Civic Center, first opened almost 50 years ago, Knope was there — selling popcorn and showing people to their seats.

"I was in school at the time, at the University of Wisconsin," Knope remembered as he gazed around and up at the expanse of space surrounding the Art Center.

"I just can't believe what they've done here — what a transformation! The only disappointment is that the organ is backstage," he said as he turned to Betty and Mildred Morgan. "Remember what a thrill it used to be when that organ came up out of the floor?"

The Morgan sisters remembered, but it didn't dim their appreciation of the Civic Center. "It's like a New York opening," said Betty, glancing around at the formally clad audience crowding the lobby. "It's beautiful, and I think it's great that Madison has it."

"And the Madison Symphony Orchestra is excellent," added Mildred. "Now they have an excellent place to perform."

Joseph and Lorraine Capossela were equally happy. "I'm very impressed with the structure," said Capossela, retired news editor of The Wisconsin State Journal.

"After all these years of struggle, the people of the city of Madison have

Turn to Page 4

Madisonians and area residents alike celebrated opening night at Madison's Civic Center Saturday by attending a sold-out performance by Metropolitan Opera soprano Martina Arroyo, the Madison Symphony Orchestra, Madison Civic Chorus and several local soloists. Toasting the newly dedicated center in its "Garden Room" are Jeanne and Roth Schleck, left, and Mary and P. Goff Beach, right. Schleck is chairman of the board of First Wisconsin National Bank of Madison, and Beach is chairman of the board and chief executive office of Oscar Mayer & Co. Both couples were active promoters of the new Civic Center.

— *State Journal photo*

Wisconsin State Journal

Monday

May 19, 1980
Madison, Wisconsin
40 pages ★★★ 25 cents

Volcano blows; death toll at 8

VANCOUVER, Wash. (AP) — Mount St. Helens blew its top Sunday with a blast felt 200 miles away, belching ash and hot gas which blotted out the sun for more than 450 miles and killing at least eight people.

Mudflows and floods destroyed bridges and forced evacuation of about 2,000 people.

At least three people were missing and scenic Spirit Lake at the base of the mountain disappeared under mud and rock flows.

Late Sunday, a mile-wide wall of mud was seen oozing down the north fork of the Toutle River, snapping concrete and steel bridges like toothpicks and sweeping cars and houses in its wake.

The eruption at 6:39 a.m. CDT shot smoke and ash 9 miles into the sky and a spectacular lightning storm in the rising plume started numerous forest fires. By evening the fires covered 3,000 acres on the mountain. There were no immediate reports of lava.

In Walla Walla, 160 miles to the east, drifting ash made the sky so dark that automatic street lights went on and by evening more than a foot of ash had accumulated at Camp Baker, 15 miles west of the volcano. Ash was also reported falling in western Montana and police there said roads were closed due to near-zero visibility west and south of Missoula, about 500 miles downwind from the volcano, and ash there was a half-inch deep on the ground.

The eruption was visible in Vancouver, Wash., more than 50 miles to the southwest, and the explosion was felt in Vancouver, B.C., more than 200 miles to the north.

By Sunday evening, the once snow-covered 9,677-foot peak was reduced to about 9,100 feet, said U.S. Geological Survey spokesman Worner Gerhard. Its crater was one-half mile across.

A helicopter pilot on a rescue mission watched three persons in a pickup truck perish in flooding near the town of Toutle, said Phil Cogan, a spokesman for the state Department of Emergency Services. State officials had said earlier that five deaths were known, although details were available only on four.

The bodies of two people found at a Weyerhaeuser logging camp near the mountain were flown to Kelso, Wash., by an Air Force Reserve helicopter, said Air Force Lt. D. E. Schroeder. They were killed by heat, Schroeder said, but no more details were immediately available.

In addition to the eight deaths, two loggers were seriously burned by hot gas and cinders, said officials of the Emanuel Hpspital Burn Center in Portland.

The bodies of two of the victims were spotted in a car about 1.5 miles east of Camp Baker, which is about 15 miles west of the volcano, said Air Force Reserve Capt. Robert Wead.

"These people were fried with the heat," Wead said. "Trees and all the vegetation was laid out flat — singed, burned, steaming, sizzling — a terrible looking thing."

"The devastation on the mountainside is incredible," said Schroeder. "Trees are knocked down, animals are standing around in shock, covered with ash."

Mudflows entered both forks of the Toutle River on the north flank of the mountain in Washington's southwestern corner, swelling the river to three times its normal width, aerial observers said.

A brown wall of water reported as

Turn to Page 2, Col. 1

Mount St. Helens sends a plume of ash, smoke and debris skyward Sunday morning.

—AP Laserphoto

Sent out to die, refugees charge

KEY WEST, Fla. (AP) — Cuban authorities smiled, reported calm seas and then sent refugee-packed boats into a tempest that claimed 14 lives when an overloaded ship capsized, tearful survivors charged Sunday.

"They said the weather was good. They just stood there smiling. It was all a lie," said Eduardo Francisco Ponce, a Cuban who escaped injury in the accident Saturday.

"I don't know what happened. I lost everybody. I don't know what happened," said Ivis Guerrero, 14, who lost her father, mother, two sisters and a grandmother when the boat capsized Saturday while carrying refugees from Cuba to the United States.

Adm. John Hayes, commander of the U.S. Coast Guard, fired off a message to Cuba criticizing Cuban authorities for "the continued lack of regard for human life." He said Cuba has signed several marine safety treaties, but seems to be disregarding them.

"Thousands of refugees are encouraged to leave that country in overcrowded, unsafe vessels. This is totally inconsistent with Cuba's treaty obligations to safety of life at sea," Hayes' message said.

The Coast Guard said there was no immediate response from Cuban authorities.

At dusk Sunday, six shrimp boats loaded with more than 1,000 refugees arrived at the head of a new wave of boats. The Coast Guard reported sighting 50 to 60 boats on their way to Key West with refugees aboard.

The Coast Guard said the Florida Straits still had seas of 4 to 7 feet that were whipped up when a front blew in Saturday.

The 14 deaths, including four persons whose bodies were not recovered, raised the number of fatalities in the "Freedom Flotilla" to 25. Dozens were injured in the accident, many badly burned. The 36-foot ship, the Olo Yumi, had carried 50 passengers and a crew of two. After the ship capsized and sank, the survivors clung to debris for about 90 minutes before Coast Guard rescuers arrived.

More than 56,000 refugees have arrived at Key West since the Cuban

Turn to Page 2, Col. 1

Irate blacks prepare to overturn Dade County car in Saturday night riot in Miami.

—AP Laserphoto

14 killed in Miami riots

MIAMI (AP) — Fires, looting and sporadic shooting rocked Miami Sunday night in continued violence sparked by the acquittal of four white ex-policemen in the death of a black man.

At least 14 people were killed, 200 injured and 300 arrested on riot-related charges since violence began Saturday night, authorities said. At least three people died of gunshot wounds Sunday night.

As National Guardsmen patrolled Miami's streets, black smoke curled up from more than three dozen buildings, and the casualty toll was mounting despite a curfew. Dade County Sheriff Bobby Jones imposed the 8 p.m.-6 a.m. curfew in the most troubled area of Miami, and limited sales of firearms, explosives, gasoline and alcohol.

Schools were ordered closed today. Public bus runs were canceled.

Shouting a one-word battle cry — "McDuffie" — crowds of enraged blacks surged into Miami streets Saturday night and early Sunday after an all-white jury in Tampa found the former Dade County policemen innocent in the death of black businessman Arthur McDuffie.

Police said one man was shot, his ear cut off and tongue severed. A red rose was stuffed into his throat.

The death toll of 14 was reported by the county medical examiner, Dr. Joseph Davis. He said eight of the victims were black and six were white. Some were the victims of racial violence; others were shot by police as alleged looters.

Late Sunday, Miami Police Chief Kenneth Harms reported, "Personal violence is down. The looting and fires are up."

Gov. Bob Graham, in a broacast appeal from Tallahassee, asked residents to stay at home.

"Do your part to stop the violence and hatred," he said. "Black Americans as well as white Americans have worked long and hard since the days of the civil rights marches to secure a fair portion of the American dream for all our citizens.

"We have come too far and worked too hard to see that everything is lost

Turn to Page 2, Col. 1

Nunnery explains ideas on energy, politics, press

'My feelings on the Senate confirmation hearings are basically this: I will serve here (at the Public Service Commission) in the interim and do the best possible job I can. I will register my views as clearly and as articulately as possible before the Senate Committee on Insurance and Utilities.'

— Willie Nunnery

By Steven T. Lovejoy
Of The State Journal

When Gov. Lee Dreyfus nominated Willie Nunnery to serve on the Wisconsin Public Service Commission last month, he characterized the former director of the Division of State Energy as forceful, independent and pro-energy.

He said Nunnery was not afraid of taking unpopular stands and had demonstrated a talent for being "accurate, clear, concise and direct."

Less than a week later, the head of the Senate Insurance and Utilities Committee said an informal poll showed the committee was "not favorable" to Nunnery's appointment.

In an interview following his nomination, Nunnery created a stir when he said he had confidence in the abilities of technical engineers to make decisions on safety questions relating to nuclear power.

Shortly before his appointment, he was criticized by two legislators for an assessment that solar power and other alternate energy sources would not be a "significant impact" on Wisconsin's energy profile through the end of the decade. He responded to the criticism by saying it was an accurate assessment based on current state and federal policies — not a policy statement on the role of alternate energy sources.

Despite being "leery" of granting interviews to the press until after his Senate confirmation hearings, Nunnery talked with reporters again last week — and immediately stepped into a controversy when he suggested liberal opposition to his appointment may have been an example of a racist education theory.

Clearly, Nunnery is a man of controversy.

In an interview with The Wisconsin State Journal, Nunnery explained his ideas on energy, his entry into politics, his background and his difficulties dealing with the press.

Nunnery says his "pro-energy" philosophy is based largely in his belief that economic growth is necessary for blacks and minorities; suggests his involvement with the Republican Party

Turn to Page 4, Col. 1

Today's chuckle

Early risers are conceited in the morning and tired in the afternoon.

Rafferty is here!

Written by Gerald Dumas with drawings by Mel Crawford, Rafferty is a daily feature story for children and adults.

Rafferty and his friends — including Fieldmouse Feeney, Owl O' Grady, Mayor Foxy MacFarland and Otter O'Toole — start today on The Wisconsin State Journal Comics Page, Sec. 3, Page 2.

Inside

Today's weather: Sunny, warmer

Becoming mostly sunny by this afternoon with highs in the upper 60s. For more weather information, turn to Page 10.

New state laws

Chapters 323 tp 328, new state laws, texts, Section 4, Pages 4-8.

Iran noisily notes hostages' year: Page 6

Wisconsin State Journal

Election Extra

Wednesday

November 5, 1980
Madison, Wisconsin
64 pages ★★★★ 25 cents

Reagan landslide

President-elect Ronald Reagan

—State Journal color photo by Joseph W. Jackson III

WASHINGTON (AP) — Ronald Reagan won the White House from President Carter Tuesday night in a startling landslide that changed the face of American government.

Carter promised Reagan his "fullest support and cooperation" in the transition to Republican rule.

Reagan was gaining 51 percent of the vote, Carter 42 percent. In electoral votes, it was overwhelming: Reagan 466, Carter 68, with almost 75 percent of the precincts counted.

"I am not frightened by what lies ahead," the president-elect said, "and I don't believe the American people are frightened by what lies ahead.

"Together, we're going to do what has to be done," Reagan told a victory rally in Los Angeles. "We're going to put America back to work again."

(Reagan cemented Wisconsin's 11 electoral votes to his presidential election victory Tuesday, having made a special campaign effort to erode Carter's support in the traditionally Democratic Milwaukee area. With more than 75 percent percent of the state's wards tabulated, Reagan led 858,797 to Carter's 808,749. Reagan appeared to have held Carter's share of the Milwaukee County vote to 52 percent, too little to overcome a strong out-state showing for Reagan. With Reagan leading 47 percent to 45 percent, independent John Anderson had 132,896 votes, or 7 percent, Libertarian Ed Clark 22,538 and the Citizens Party's Barry Commoner 7,128.)

The polls were still open in the West when Carter acknowledged that his presidency was finished — an hour after telephoning Reagan to congratulate him on victory.

"He graciously offered his cooperation on the transition and I accepted it," said Reagan, who went from Hollywood to two terms as governor of Cali- presidency twice before.

Four Democratic senators fell with Carter as Republicans mounted an unexpectly strong push to take control of the Senate.

"If the trend continues, we may very well control one house of the Congress for the first time in a quarter of a century," Reagan told his cheering supporters at the Century Plaza Hotel.

Democrats limped toward renewed control of the House, but Republicans stood to gain more than 20 seats there.

As his electoral vote total soared, Reagan said he certainly hadn't looked for such a landslide. "Listen, I was happy to get 270," he said. That's what it took to win.

Then, in the hotel ballroom, before his partisans and the television cameras, Reagan said:

"There has never been a more humbling moment in my life. Even if it had been the cliffhanger we were all expecting, it would have been the same. I consider the trust you have placed in me sacred, and I will do my utmost to justify your faith."

A cliffhanger it was not. Reagan's margin rivaled history's great landslides, those of Richard Nixon in 1972, Lyndon Johnson in 1964 and Franklin Roosevelt in 1936.

Reagan had won 35 of the 50 states and led in six more. Indeed, it was so one-sided, and over so fast, that some West Coast voters were angry to hear Carter conceding before they had even cast their ballots.

So ended the longest campaign, in an electoral vote runaway that belied the forecasts of the pollsters that it would be close. It never was, from the moment the first polls closed.

With 70 percent of the nation's precincts counted, Reagan had 30.2 million votes, or 50 percent, for 462 elec-

Turn to Page 2, Col. 3

Kasten heads toward upset

By Patricia Simms
Of The State Journal

With incumbent liberal Democrats falling rapidly across the country, Republican challenger Robert Kasten Jr. headed toward an apparent upset victory over liberal U.S. Sen. Gaylord Nelson, D-Wis., in Wednesday's early morning hours.

Nelson, 64, first elected to the Senate in 1962, had acknowledged this challenge was probably his most serious contest since he defeated an incumbent Republican to win his first Senate term. With 3,184 of 3,412 wards counted, the vote was:

Robert Kasten 1,018,147
Gaylord Nelson 999,917
Bervin J. Larson 9,153

Kasten, 38, a former state legislator who ran unsuccessfully for governor in 1978, had charged that Nelson's philosophy and ideas were out of touch with the state's voters.

But Nelson, campaigning with uncharacteristic vigor, aggressively cited his own voting history on environmental issues and small business concerns.

At 1 a.m. today, Nelson told reporters in Milwaukee he was going to stay up another hour, then go to bed at 2 a.m. "And I'll wake up and see how it comes out," he said.

Nelson recollected 1948 when Democrat Harry Truman went to bed a loser and woke up a winner over GOP candidate Thomas Dewey.

Nelson aides acknowledged that the race, then stalled at a 50-50 percent split between Nelson and Kasten, was "too close to call" in the early morning hours. "I've said for months that this was going to be a close race," Nelson said, "although I must admit I didn't anticipate such a close race."

At 2:30 a.m., Nelson aides had a terse "no comment."

Nelson, who has a Senate committee chairmanship at stake in the nationwide accumulation of GOP Senate victories, may not have been able to avoid the national Republican landslide that devastated several other Democrat incumbents, including Indiana's Birch Bayh and President Carter.

The race was a squeaker, and a far cry from the comfortable 63 percent of the vote Nelson received six years ago. Aides said his vote totals coming out of Milwaukee were lower than usual, but his strength in the rural areas had increased.

As returns dribbled in, Nelson held onto a 51-48 percent edge over Kasten, then it slipped to 50-50. National televi-

Turn to Page 2, Col. 3

Robert Kasten

Today's weather: Mostly sunny

Mostly sunny today. High around 50. For more weather information, turn to Page 14.

Kastenmeier earns 12th straight term

U.S. Rep. Robert Kastenmeier, D-Wis., Tuesday bucked the conservative trend by beating Baraboo Republican James Wright in his race for a 12th consecutive term in the 2nd District.

Kastenmeier, 56, a Sun Prairie liberal, had been attacked by Wright, 37, as a congressional big spender.

But Kastenmeier charged that Wright had misrepresented his voting record. He argued that Wright's plan for a 30 percent tax cut increased defense spending and a balanced federal budget was unworkable.

Rep. Kastenmeier

As expected, Kastenmeier polled heavily in Dane County, and ended up with about 56 percent of the vote to Wright's 43 percent.

Wright's leads in some of the rural counties did not seem to be able to counter the Democrat's urban strength. With 318 of 396 wards reporting, the vote was:

Robert Kastenmeier 129,961
James Wright 99,140
Leslie G. Key 1,605

Ferris re-elected Dane sheriff

By George Hesselberg
Of The State Journal

Four-term Democrat incumbent William Ferris Jr. easily outdistanced Republican challenger Vernon Leslie in the race for Dane County sheriff Tuesday.

The race was a rematch of the 1972 sheriff's race, when Ferris upset then-incumbent Leslie.

With 120 of 140 wards reporting, the vote was:

William H. Ferris 79,440
Vernon Leslie 44,498

Sheriff Ferris

Compared with their bitter 1972 competition, the 1980 race was all feathers and yawns, with lots of yard signs and billboards but few publicized appearances by either candidate.

Ferris, 40, who rolled over two opponents in the primary, wants to continue his "administrator-first" policies that have seen him through eight relatively controversy-free years as the county's top law enforcement official.

Contacted at home late Tuesday, Ferris welcomed "this endorsement of my management style."

"I'm looking forward to these next years. For me the central issue in the county is going to be the jail. I intend to take the gloves off and go to court if necessary to do what has to be done to get that jail in order," he said.

The outspoken Leslie, 60, who returned to private business as a North Side liquor store owner after his 1972 defeat, was seeking a resurrection of his 21-year law enforcement career. He also beat two challengers for the Republican nomination.

The two candidates are as different as night and day. It was the administrator-policy-maker against the top-cop.

Ferris, fighting rumors about his health, said his re-election was vital to the survival of a number of his policies and plans, including jail expansion, cooperative enforcement efforts, recruiting and contract policing in smaller municipalities. His experience has given him "clout through knowledge," he said, stressing that "experience and knowledge are the things I can contribute."

He agreed that the sheriff's budget has grown, but said the department has assumed or been forced to take over several county operations, including lakes patrol and the airport.

Ferris, of 5733 Forsythia Place, was hospitalized for tests for four days last week, but pronounced himself in "excellent health" and recovering well from throat cancer and cancer treatments that have softened his voice and left him thin and scarred.

The two-year term job will pay a 1981 salary of $28,827, which will increase to $30,556 in 1982.

Birch Bayh

George McGovern

Election highlights

Culver, Bayh, McGovern, Magnuson lose Senate seats

WASHINGTON (AP) — Incumbent Democrats in Washington, South Dakota, Iowa and Indiana fell before Republican challengers Tuesday as the GOP bid strongly to turn Ronald Reagan's conservative landslide into control of the Senate for the first time in a quarter-century.

Veterans John Culver in Iowa, George McGovern in South Dakota, Warren Magnuson in Washington and Birch Bayh in Indiana all fell as victims to the Republican tide.

In all, GOP candidates Republicans were victorious or leading for 10 seats held by Democrats, including eight where incumbents were seeking new terms.

The only Republican incumbent in trouble was Sen. Barry Goldwater, a pre-election favorite locked in a close race with Democrat Bill Schulz. **(Details on Page 3.)**

Incumbent assemblymen leading

Many incumbent state representatives appeared to be heading for re-election Tuesday night, including several from southern Wisconsin.

Among those who appeared to be winning re-election bids were: Democrats David Travis, 37th District; Harlan Everson, 38th District; Gary Johnson, 45th District; Tom Loftus, 46th District; Jonathon Barry, 47th District; Joanne Duren, 50th District; Mary Lou Munts, 76th District, and David Clarenbach, 78th District.

Incumbent Republicans with apparently successful bids included: Joseph Tregoning, 51st District; Tommy Thompson, 79th District; James Laatsch, 80th District; Randall Radtke, 81st District, and Robert Quackenbush, 92nd District. **(Details on Sec. 2, Page 2.)**

Redford wins in 13th Senate

Back for a second try, Janice Redford of rural Cambridge trounced three challengers Tuesday in a special Democratic primary for the 13th Senate District.

Gov. Lee Dreyfus set the election after former Sen. Peter Bear, D-Madison, resigned earlier this fall. Bear defeated Mrs. Redford and a third candidate in 1978.

Mrs. Redford faces Republican Barbara Lorman of Fort Atkinson in a Dec. 2 general election. **(Details on Sec. 2, Page 2.)**

Gunderson holding slim lead

Republican Steve Gunderson, Osseo, maintained a slim lead early today over U.S. Rep. Alvin Baldus, D-Wis., in a fight for election in the Third Congressional District.

With 518 of 604 wards reporting, Gunderson led Baldus 109,156 votes to 106,645 votes. **(Earlier story, Sec. 2, Page 1.)**

Seven congressmen re-elected

Seven Wisconsin congressmen won comfortable re-elections Tuesday.

Returned to the U.S. House of Representatives were: Democrats Les Aspin, 1st District; Clement Zablocki, 4th District; Henry Reuss, 5th District; and David Obey, 7th District.

Republicans returned were: Thomas Petri, 6th District; Toby Roth, 8th District; and James Sensenbrenner, 9th District.

Wisconsin State Journal

Wednesday
January 21, 1981
Madison, Wisconsin
52 pages ★★★ 25 cents

A day to remember

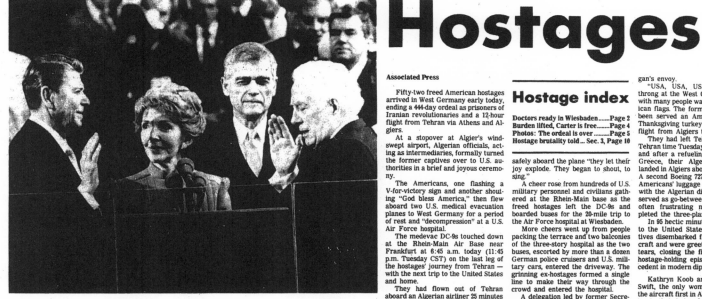

Reagan, left, takes oath from Chief Justice Warren Burger as Mrs. Reagan holds Bible. —*AP Laserphoto*

Hostages

Associated Press

Fifty-two freed American hostages arrived in West Germany early today, ending a 444-day ordeal as prisoners of Iranian revolutionaries and a 12-hour flight from Tehran via Athens and Algiers.

At a stopover at Algier's windswept airport, Algerian officials, acting as intermediaries, formally turned the former captives over to U.S. authorities in a brief and joyous ceremony.

The Americans, one flashing a V-for-victory sign and another shouting "God bless America," then flew aboard two U.S. medical evacuation planes to West Germany for a period of rest and "decompression" at a U.S. Air Force hospital.

The medevac DC-9s touched down at the Rhein-Main Air Base near Frankfurt at 6:45 a.m. today (11:45 p.m. Tuesday CST) on the last leg of the hostages' journey from Tehran — with the next trip to the United States and home.

They had flown out of Tehran aboard an Algerian airliner 25 minutes after Ronald Reagan succeeded Jimmy Carter as president at noon Tuesday in inauguration ceremonies in Washington. And as they were led to the plane, one at a time, a group of Iran's revolutionary guards crowded around, waving their fists and chanting, "Death to America!" and "God is great!"

Ali Abdelaziz, an Algerian protocol officer who was on the flight from Tehran, said when the hostages were safely aboard the plane "they let their joy explode. They began to shout, to sing."

Hostage index

A cheer rose from hundreds of U.S. military personnel and civilians gathered at the Rhein-Main base as the freed hostages left the DC-9s and boarded buses for the 20-mile trip to the Air Force hospital at Wiesbaden.

More cheers went up from people packing the terrace and two balconies of the three-story hospital as the two buses, escorted by more than a dozen German police cruisers and U.S. military cars, entered the driveway. The grinning ex-hostages formed a single line to make their way through the crowd and entered the hospital.

A delegation led by former Secretary of State Cyrus Vance, who headed the State Department when the U.S. Embassy and hostages were seized on Feb. 4, 1979, and Ambassador Walter Sotessel had formed a receiving line to greet the 52 when they disembarked at the airfield.

Carter, unable to win the hostage's freedom in the closing hours of "his watch" because of last-minute delays, was scheduled to leave for Wiesbaden about 5 a.m. CST as President Reagan's envoy.

"USA, USA, USA" cheered the throng at the West German air base, with many people waving small American flags. The former prisoners had been served an American dinner of Thanksgiving turkey on the 1,250-mile flight from Algiers to Frankfurt.

They had left Tehran at 8:55 p.m. Tehran time Tuesday (11:25 p.m. CST) and after a refueling stop in Athens, Greece, their Algerian Boeing 727 landed in Algiers about 7½ hours later. A second Boeing 727 that carried the Americans' luggage and a smaller jet with the Algerian diplomats who had served as go-betweens in the long and often frustrating negotiations completed the three-plane mission.

In 95 hectic minutes televised back to the United States, the freed captives disembarked from the Algerian craft and were greeted with hugs and tears, closing the final chapter in a hostage-holding episode withous precedent in modern diplomatic history.

Kathryn Koob and Elizabeth Ann Swift, the only women hostages, left the aircraft first in Algiers, each wearing in their hair a yellow ribbon — a gesture taken from the song, "Tie a Yellow Ribbon 'Round the Old Oak Tree," that came to symbolize America's wait for the captives.

Next came Bruce Laingen, the charge d'affaires who had been the top diplomat at the U.S. Embassy in Tehran when it was seized Nov. 4, 1979. The other hostages followed in quick

Turn to Page 2, Col. 4

Reagan

WASHINGTON (AP) — Ronald Reagan became President of the United States Tuesday, promising "an era of national renewal" at home and restraint but never surrender abroad, his inauguration blending the passage of power with a passage to freedom for 52 American hostages.

"They are now free of Iran," Reagan said, a little more than two hours after his inauguration.

Later, at his desk in the Oval Office, the president said release of the hostages "just makes the whole day perfect.

"They're on the way home."

As Jimmy Carter yielded the presidency, Iran yielded at last the captives it had held for 444 days. And so the celebration for Reagan, the parade, pageantry, music, cannon salutes, became a celebration of their freedom, too.

At the noon of inauguration, the promise of freedom had not become the fact of freedom, and Reagan did not mention the hostages in the 20-minute address he directed to "this breed called Americans," countrymen he described as the heroes of the land.

But the liberation of the captive Americans was the focus of his last briefings by Carter, and his first hours as 40th president.

And so the announcement the nation awaited came in his toast to congressional leaders at a traditional Capitol luncheon.

"And now to conclude the toast, with thanks to almighty God, I have been given a tag line, the get-off line that everyone wants for the end of a toast or a speech or anything else.

The inaugural

"Some 30 minutes ago, the planes bearing our prisoners left Iranian airspace and they are now free of Iran. So we can all drink to this one — to all of us together, doing what we all know we can do, to make this country what it should be, what it can be, what it always has been."

It was the announcement Carter had waited so long to make, but it came too late for him. So President Reagan made it, while citizen Carter flew home to Georgia.

In Plains, Carter made his own announcement to townspeople turned out to welcome him home: "Just a few moments ago on Air Force One . . . I received word officially for the first time that the aircraft carrying the 52 American hostages had cleared Iranian airspace on the first leg of the journey home and that every one of the 52 hostages was alive and well and free."

At the stroke of noon, presidential power passed from James Earl Carter Jr. of Georgia to Ronald Wilson Reagan of California, 69, oldest man ever to take office, former movie actor, former governor of California, conservative Republican.

"With all the creative energy at our command, let us begin an era of national renewal," Reagan said in his inaugural address. "Let us renew our determination, our courage and our strength. Let us renew our faith and our hope. We have every right to dream heroic dreams."

In his first act as president, Reagan signed the executive order he promised would clamp a freeze on federal hiring. "It will be my intention to curb the size and influence of the federal establishment . . ." he said in the inaugural address. He said he did not mean to do away with government but, rather, "to make it work."

A crowd estimated at 70,000 people watched the rite at the West Front of the Capitol, the monuments of American government, of Washington and Jefferson and Lincoln, shining in the sunlight of a mild January day. Reagan called those men "the giants on whose shoulders we stand."

Police estimated that 400,000 people lined the 16-block route of the inaugural parade. There were clusters of demonstrators among them, against draft registration, against the Ku Klux Klan, for the Equal Rights Amendment.

Reagan and his wife rode the ceremonial route of presidents, down Pennsylvania Avenue at the head of their own parade, standing to wave from the open roof of a black limousine.

At dusk, as the inaugural parade

Turn to Page 2, Col. 1

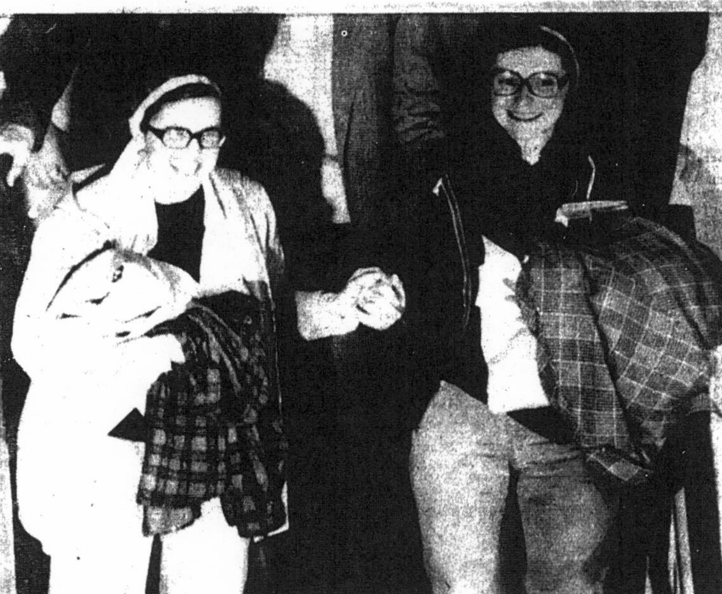

Kathryn Koob, right, and Elizabeth Ann Swift hold hands as they leave aircraft. —*AP Laserphotos*

Soldier cited by Reagan was native of Wisconsin

By Thomas W. Still
Of The State Journal

The patriotic words of a Wisconsin soldier killed in France during World War I were immortalized Tuesday in President Reagan's inaugural address.

Martin A. Treptow, an obscure Army private who died 62 years ago in a hail of enemy fire, is buried in his native Bloomer, where an American Legion post is named in his honor.

"We still have his burial flag hanging in our clubhouse," said Walden Lankey, past commander of American Legion Post 295 in Bloomer, a small city about 200 miles northwest of Madison.

"Hearing his name (in Reagan's speech) may not have meant much to the rest of the country, but it did to us," Lankey said.

Reagan recited a passage from a diary left behind by Treptow, a 24-year-old volunteer who was killed while carrying a message between entrenched battalions.

He died instantly when an artillery shell exploded at his feet.

Reagan, who mistakenly thought Treptow was buried under "a simple white marker" in Arlington National Cemetery, said in his speech:

"Under one such marker lies a young man — Martin Treptow — who left his job in a small-town barber shop in 1917 to go to France with the famed Rainbow Division. There, on the Western Front, he was killed trying to carry a message between battalions under heavy artillery fire.

"We are told that on his body was found a diary. On the flyleaf under the heading, 'My Pledge,' he had written these words: 'America must win this war. Therefore I will work, I will save, I will sacrifice, I will endure, I will fight cheerfully and do my utmost, as

Turn to Page 2, Col. 1

Today's weather: Sunny, pleasant

Becoming mostly sunny today. High around 40. For more weather information, turn to Page 16.

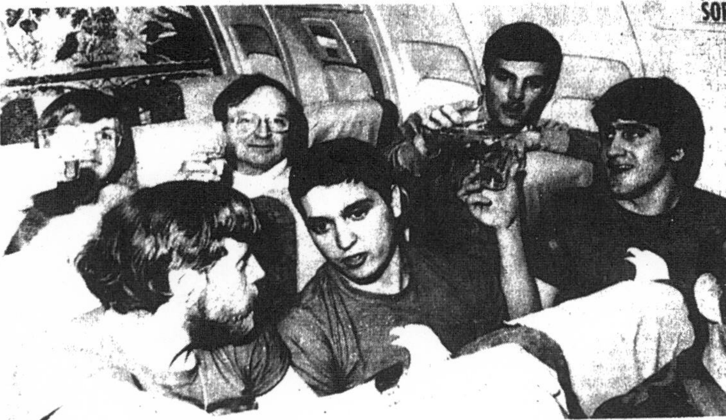

Six American hostages celebrate aboard flight out of Iran Tuesday. Back row, from left, Duane Gillette, Columbia, Pa., Leland Holland, Fairfax, Va., and Kevin Hermening, Cudahy, Wis. Front row, from left, Michael Moeller, Loup City, Neb., William Gallegos, Pueblo, Colo., and Rodney Sickman, Krakow, Mo.

Wisconsin State Journal

Tuesday
March 31, 1981
Madison, Wisconsin
48 pages ★★★ 25 cents

Reagan shot

Outlook good after chest surgery

Two Secret Service agents push the already-wounded President Reagan into his limousine outside a Washington hotel Monday.

—*AP Laserphotos*

Officers with guns drawn subdue suspect, upper left, as victims, from front to rear, Timothy McCarthy, Thomas Delahanty and James Brady lie wounded on sidewalk.

Press aide is critical; two others wounded

WASHINGTON (AP) — President Reagan was wounded in the chest Monday by a gunman who tried to assassinate him with a burst of .22-caliber bullets that critically injured his press secretary, James Brady.

Reagan "sailed through surgery" according to doctors who said he'd be ready to make White House decisions by today.

Aide fights for life

But Brady was said to be fighting for his life, a bullet through his brain.

A sandy-haired man from suburban Denver was wrestled into handcuffs moments after the assailant leveled his pistol and fired six times at Reagan from near point-blank range. The Secret Service identified him as John Warnock Hinckley Jr., 25, of Evergreen, Colo.

Near midnight, Hinckley was led into a federal courtroom and formally charged with attempting to assassinate the president, and with assaulting a Secret Service officer. He also faces a charge of assault with intent to kill a policeman.

U.S. Magistrate Arthur Burnett set a preliminary hearing for Thursday at 9 a.m. CST.

Bullet removed

Dr. Dennis O'Leary said "a really mangled bullet" was removed from Reagan's left lung. He said the president's condition was stable, the prognosis excellent, and that the president probably would be hospitalized for about two weeks.

"Honey, I forgot to duck," Reagan told his wife as he was wheeled into surgery. Then he told the surgeons he hoped they were Republicans.

A Secret Service agent and a policeman also were wounded in the mid-afternoon blaze of gunfire outside a Washington hotel where Reagan had just addressed a union convention. They were reported in serious condition but apparently not in danger.

There was no known motive, no explanation for the savage burst of gunfire that exploded as the president stood beside his limousine, ready to step inside for the one-mile ride back to the White House.

Roger Young of the FBI described the weapon as a "Saturday night special" and said it was purchased at a Dallas gun shop.

James Brady

Hinckley was booked on charges of attempted assassination of a president, and of assault with intent to kill a police officer. He was in FBI custody Monday night, awaiting arraignment.

Young, the FBI spokesman, said there had been "no problem" with Hinckley's coherence when questioned by authorities.

Monday's shooting began suddenly on an overcast Washington afternoon.

At 1:25 p.m., CST, six shots rang out, one hitting Reagan in the left chest, others felling Brady, a Secret Service agent and a policeman. Secret Service agents and police seized Hinckley.

He was wrestled to the ground outside the Washington Hilton, pinned against a wall, taken away in handcuffs.

One of Monday's eyewitnesses said the assailant, standing 10 feet from the president, "just opened up and continued squeezing the trigger."

Anxious hours later, Reagan was pronounced in good and stable condition.

Two and a half hours after emerging from surgery, Reagan joked with doctors in the recovery room, according to a White House statement.

"Despite the tubes in his mouth, he (Reagan) gave them a note that said, 'All in all, I'd rather be in Philadelphia.'"

At the White House, Vice President George Bush said, "I can reassure this nation and a watching world that the American government is functioning fully and effectively. We've had full and complete communication throughout the day."

Incision in chest

O'Leary served as spokesman for two surgeons who operated on Reagan at George Washington University Hospital. They made a 6-inch incision to remove the bullet that had penetrated about three inches into his left lung, missing his heart by several inches.

Reagan's lung collapsed, and the surgeons inserted two chest tubes to restore it.

They gave him blood transfusions, about 2½ quarts in all, to replace the blood he lost.

The wounded president walked into the hospital, "alert and awake" if a bit lightheaded, O'Leary said. At 70, the doctor said, Reagan "is physiologically very young.

"We do not believe there is any permanent injury," he added.

"He was never in any serious dan-

Turn to Page 2, Col. 1

Reagan inside

Mostly sunny; high around 66.

Wisconsin State Journal

Thursday

May 14, 1981
Madison, Wisconsin
56 pages ★★★ 30 cents

Pope survives bullets; surgery called success

From wire services

VATICAN CITY, Thursday — Pope John Paul II, shot down by a gunman as he greeted 15,000 tourists and faithful at his weekly audience in St. Peter's Square, came through 5½ hours of surgery for six wounds in "good and stable" condition, his doctors said early today.

Police quickly arrested a man identified as a right-wing Turkish terrorist who had vowed to kill the pope. He told them after the shooting Wednesday that he "couldn't care less about life."

Doctors said the prognosis remained "guarded" largely because of the risk of infection, but added that the pontiff was conscious and breathing on his own.

The attack occurred as the pope, 60, dressed in white, was shaking hands and lifting small children in his arms while being driven around the square. Suddenly, as he reached a point just outside the Vatican's bronze gate, there was a burst of gunfire.

One hand rising to his face and blood staining his garments, the pope faltered and fell into the arms of his Polish secretary, the Rev. Stanislaw Dziwisz, and his personal servant, Angelo Gugel, who were in the car with him.

The pope, the spiritual leader of nearly 600 million Roman Catholics around the world, was rushed by ambulance to Gemelli Policlinico hospital, 2 miles north of the Vatican, for surgery.

The gunman's bullets also wounded two women in the crowd, one of them American.

A press release issued early today by the Vatican and signed by the attending physicians said, "At the end of the operation, the pope recovered consciousness, breathing spontaneously, and was in good and stable cardiocirculatory condition.

"The patient came through the operation in a satisfying manner. The prognosis remains strictly guarded in part because of risks deriving from post-operative infection," the Vatican press release said.

Earlier, the director of the surgery unit at the hospital, Professor Giancarlo Castiglioni, had termed the operation "successful" and told reporters, "The pope was very lucky."

After the 5½-hour operation and blood transfusions, the pope was moved to the hospital's emergency care unit where he was expected to remain for 48 hours. The operation began at 11:00 a.m. CDT and ended at 4:25 p.m.

Castiglioni said the pope was shot twice in the lower intestine. He said one bullet passed through the body, causing another wound when it left, and another stayed in the body and was extracted by surgeons. The pope also had two slight wounds on his right arm and one on his left hand.

Castiglioni did not say how many shots were fired at the pope or how many bullets hit him.

"We have sound hopes that the pope will remain with us, that he will continue to live. He wasn't hit in vital parts but they were not light injuries. Important blood vessels were just barely missed and the pope was very lucky," Castiglioni said.

Attilio Silverstrini, Vatican secretary for public affairs, said the pope "was serene and prayed" while being taken to the hospital on the Via della Pineta Sacchetti about three-quarters of a mile from the Vatican. "He was always conscious, until when he was given anaesthesia," Silvestrini said.

A police officer who jumped onto the white jeep as soon as the pope was wounded said, "He suffered a lot, he prayed."

Shock was registered worldwide. Millions lit candles in their churches and joined the prayers of the witnesses to the shooting who immediately knelt in St. Peter's Square to pray for the pope's recovery.

The most traveled spiritual leader of the Roman Catholic church in history, John Paul's simple manner and familiar smile made him known the world over. He loved to mingle with crowds and to personally greet wellwishers.

In Washington, President Reagan — himself a victim of an assassination attempt on March 30 — said, "I'll pray for him."

"They've shot the pope! They've shot the pope!" shouted several young monks in the crowd in the southwest corner of the vast square near the Bernini colonnade. Just before he was shot, John Paul stood in his parked white jeep, beaming and waving to a crowd of 15,000 tourists and faithful.

Witnesses said the shots were fired from a distance of about 25 feet.

Two women, including Ann Odre, 58, a widow from Buffalo, N.Y., also were wounded by the bullets fired from what police described as a 9mm pistol.

Mrs. Odre was listed in "serious" condition after surgery for a wound in the chest but her

Turn to Page 2, Col. 1

Pope John Paul II

Inside

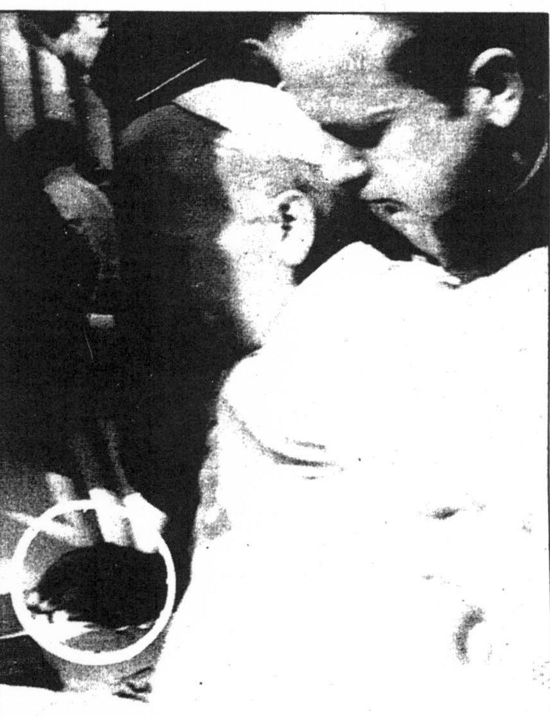

Blood can be seen on Pope John Paul's hand, circled, as he is helped by aides after being shot Wednesday in St. Peter's Square in Vatican City.
—*AP Laserphoto*

Belleville visitor was 20 feet away when shots were fired

By Thomas W. Still
Of The State Journal
©The Wisconsin State Journal

Like most of the 15,000 faithful who packed St. Peter's Square on Wednesday, Mary Gehin, 21, of Belleville, Wis., hoped for just a glimpse of Pope John Paul II.

Instead, she found herself within 20 feet of the white-clad pontiff and was clicking away on her camera when two gunshots rang out.

"A lot of people, when they heard the shots and saw the pigeons take off, thought it was firecrackers," said Miss Gehin in a telephone interview from Rome. "But I could see what was happening through my camera. I knew right away the pope had been shot."

Miss Gehin, a radiology student at Madison General Hospital, and her mother, Mrs. James (Charlotte) Gehin Jr., of rural Belleville, are touring Europe with 31 other Americans. Belleville is about 15 miles south of Madison.

Their group was merged with 110 other pilgrims, also mostly Americans, for the pope's weekly audience in the sun-drenched piazza. The Gehins were waiting between St. Peter's Basilica and the famous Bernini colonnade when the pope — standing and waving from a jeep — rolled past.

"I couldn't believe what happened; it was something I'll never forget," said Miss Gehin, who telephoned The Wisconsin State Journal from her hotel near Vatican City.

"I was about 20 feet away from where the pope was shot. He either fell or was pushed down in his jeep, and they (papal aides) just took off like a bullet," she said. "The pope was out of the area within seconds."

Miss Gehin said she took two or three pictures of the fateful moments with her 35mm camera.

"I don't know what my film shows, but I had it (the camera) focused on him," she said.

Also wounded in the assassination attempt was an American woman, Ann Odre, of Buffalo, N.Y., and Rose Hall, a Jamaican woman. Both were members of tours that had melded with Miss Gehin's group for the bus ride to Vatican City.

"I guess we were lucky not to be hit, too," Miss Gehin said. "I was just in the right place at the right time."

The Gehins apparently were the only Wisconsin residents in the tour, although the group included a number

Turn to Page 2, Col. 2

Mary Gehin

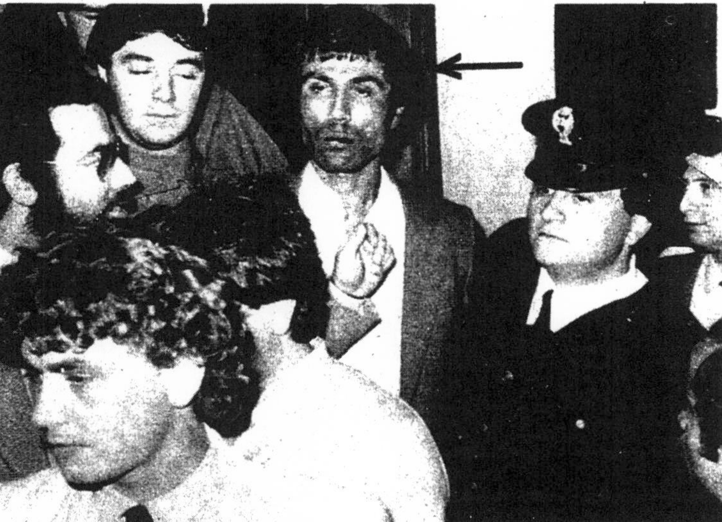

Suspect, arrow, in Italian police custody in Rome after Wednesday's shooting of pope.
—*AP Laserphoto*

Inside

Weather

Page 16

Mostly cloudy today with slight chance of showers early in the day and a high around 64. Clearing tonight, low around 40. Friday will be mostly sunny and mild, high in the low 70s. Winds will be out of the northeast at 10 to 15 miles per hour today.

Suspect tagged as Turkish terrorist

©N.Y. Times News Service

ROME — The first reports said only that he spoke no Italian, that he was young and that he had dark hair.

But within a matter of minutes, a picture of the man accused of shooting Pope John Paul II in St. Peter's Square Wednesday afternoon began to emerge — a picture of a militant Turkish terrorist, already convicted of one murder, who escaped from a maximum security prison in 1979 and then threatened in a letter to assassinate the pope.

The Turkish ambassador in Washington, Sukru Elekdag, said after the news of the shooting had flashed around the world, "The Turkish police have been under instruction to shoot him on sight."

Shortly after he was wrestled to the ground by pilgrims who had been standing near him, the alleged assailant was identified by Italian police as Mehmet Ali Agca. He gave his age as 23 and said he was Turkish. He said also that he was a student at the University for Foreigners in Perugia in central Italy, but the records of the university showed no such registration.

According to sources in Rome, Washington, New York and Ankara, Agca was convicted in February 1979 of having murdered Abdi Ipekci, the editor of the independent Turkish daily newspaper Milliyet. He was jailed. But in late November, he escaped from the military prison where he was being held, and he apparently had been in hiding since.

When he fled from the prison, he left behind a letter, addressed to Milliyet, threatening the life of the pope. If the pontiff did not cancel his visit to Turkey, which was then imminent, Agca is said to have written, he would shoot him in revenge for the attack by Moslem extremists on the Grand Mosque in Mecca earlier that year.

The attack was considered a desecration of the Islamic holy place by Moslems, and Agca charged that the incident was of American or Israeli origin. His letter denounced the pontiff as "the masked leader of the Crusades."

A partial text of the letter, made available by the Turkish police, reads as follows:

"Western imperialists who are afraid of Turkey's unity of political, military and economic power with the brotherly Islamic countries are sending Crusader Commander John Paul under the mask of a religious leader. If this ill-timed and meaningless visit is not called off, I will definitely shoot the pope. This is the only reason I escaped from prison."

His threats were taken seriously enough to warrant a tightening of the security net that surrounded the pope during his Turkish visit. There was no assassination attempt.

Although Agca gave a somewhat confusing account of his political and religious beliefs to the Italian authorities, the Turkish police labeled him a Moslem extremist, which appeared to fit in with his use of the phrase "brotherly Islamic countries" in the letter.

Agca also said at one point, however, that while he was a Turkish citi-

Turn to Page 2, Col. 1

Wisconsin State Journal

Saturday

September 26, 1981
Madison, Wisconsin
32 pages ★★★ 30 cents

Budget plan filtered out

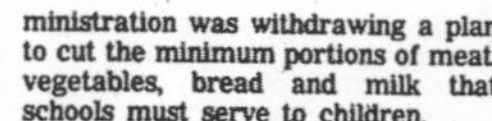

WASHINGTON (AP) — While President Reagan declared "I'm sure not going to take the blame" for a plunge in the financial markets, chief aides said Friday the quest for a balanced budget by 1984 will require further cuts in Medicaid, Medicare, federal retirement and other benefit programs.

But the administration backed off plans to cut minimum portions in the millions of school lunches served across the country. Budget Director David Stockman said that proposal was "a bureaucratic goof that we're going to change."

Stock and bond prices plunged and interest rates rose on the markets Friday, an apparent indication that Wall Street wasn't much encouraged by Reagan's economic address to the nation Thursday night. The Dow industrials closed 11.13 points lower, a 16-month low.

Asked if he took the market's performance as a vote of no confidence, Reagan snapped "That keeps us even.

"I'm going to go by the phone calls and telegrams that have been coming in since last night's speech, and they are running three or four to one and better in our favor," he said.

Stockman confirmed that the administration was withdrawing a plan to cut the minimum portions of meat, vegetables, bread and milk that schools must serve to children.

Meanwhile, Republican leaders said Congress likely will cut the defense budget next year by more than the $2 billion recommended by the president.

Senate Majority Leader Howard Baker, R-Tenn., said his colleagues "almost certainly" will go deeper. House Republican Leader Robert Michael of Illinois agreed, though he said a proposal from liberal GOP members to slash $9 billion from defense goes too far.

Treasury Secretary Donald Regan, Stockman and Murray Weidenbaum, chairman of the president's Council of Economic Advisers, met with reporters to amplify the president's pitch Thursday night for additional spending reductions.

The president recommended across-the-board reductions of 12 percent in non-defense and non-benefit programs, slashing the federal work force by 75,000 jobs, cutting back on federal-loan guarantees and abolishing the departments of Education and Energy to achieve $13 billion in savings for the fiscal year that begins next Thursday.

Also included was a call for $3 billion in additional tax revenues through the elimination of "abuses and obsolete incentives in the tax code."

"When we first announced our economic recovery effort last February our national illness was clearly inflation. . . . This new round of reductions is simply one more initiative in that effort" to fight inflation, the Treasury secretary said.

Included in the president's proposals is a plan to reduce the government's mandated-benefit payments to individuals — "entitlements" — by $27.6 billion over the next three years.

Regan denied that the further entitlement cuts represent a retreat from the president's pledge to keep intact the "social safety net" of welfare and

Turn to Page 2, Col. 1

President Reagan and Chief Justice Warren Burger pose for pictures with new Justice Sandra Day O'Connor.
—AP color Laserphoto

Court's 'brethren' get a sister

©Knight-Ridder News Service

WASHINGTON — After 101 men, there is a woman on the Supreme Court.

Sandra Day O'Connor, wearing a simple belted pink dress, arose Friday afternoon from the chair used by the first chief justice, John Marshall, walked up to the high-court bench, swore to defend the Constitution against all enemies, donned a black robe and made history.

She took the seat reserved for newcomers, next to her friend and fellow Arizonan, Justice William Rehnquist.

From the vantage of President and Mrs. Reagan and more than 300 invited guests and reporters, O'Connor and Rehnquist sat on the far right of the justices' mahogany bench in the somber marble-columned courtroom. The general public was excluded.

Chief Justice Warren Burger welcomed her and wished her "a long life and a long, happy career."

He then assigned her to supervise the federal courts in the Sixth Circuit, which covers the states of Kentucky, Michigan, Ohio and Tennessee.

To some onlookers, the scene was life imitating art, a scene out of "First Monday In October," a current comic film about the first woman justice.

O'Connor, at 51, also is the youngest justice on a court dominated by men well past normal retirement age.

Five of the nine justices, appointed by Presidents Eisenhower, Johnson and Nixon, are over 70.

O'Connor, having won the confirmation plaudits of the Senate Judiciary Committee and the full Senate by votes of 17-0 and 99-0, will find little unanimity among her new male colleagues on the most controversial issues of the day.

For years, the justices have been split, often with a single vote separating them, on cases involving school desegregation, affirmative action, abortion, state aid to religion, obscenity, government regulation and the death penalty.

A conservative on many issues, O'Connor is expected to make little difference in the court's fragile balance because she replaces the retired Potter Stewart, who voted conservatively on school busing, affirmative action, school prayer, health and safety regulations and other bitterly debated subjects.

O'Connor joins a court with several vexing and far-reaching legal questions on its calendar.

Among the problems already accepted for court review are these:

Sex — Can the federal government cut off funds to schools guilty of sex discrimination against teachers and professors in hiring and promotions? The court will consider conflicting lower court verdicts in cases from New Haven, Conn., and Seattle University.

Mental — Do mental patients committed to institutions have a constitutional right to refuse anti-psychotic medicines?

Aliens — Must states provide free public education to the children of illegal aliens? This is an important case in Texas, California, New York, Illinois, Florida and other areas with large Hispanic populations. A lower court ruled Texas may not charge tuition because it would unconstitutionally keep hundreds of thousands of children in the lowest level of society.

Charity — Minnesota exempts from charity reporting requirements any religious organization that receives more than half its contributions from members, rather than the general public. Does such a law unconstitutionally favor establishment religions while discriminating against unpopular sects?

Free speech — Can a private college bar an uninvited person from expressing political views on its campus? The dispute arose at Princeton University, where Chris Schmid was arrested in 1978 for distributing U.S. Labor Party leaflets. Princeton says academic freedom is at stake.

College — Should a state-owned university be allowed to bar students from using its buildings for religious worship or teaching?

Court OKs death arrest

By Mary Frances Schjonberg
Of The State Journal

Madison police acted legally when they arrested Wayne Drogsvold without a warrant as a suspect in the killing of a man in May 1979, the state Court of Appeals, 4th District, ruled Friday.

Dane County District Attorney James Doyle said the ruling, which overturned a decision by Dane County Judge Michael Torphy, was important to the Drogsvold case and to the question of police behavior.

James Fortney, 30, of Chicago, was killed May 21, 1979, at the Sportsman's Bar, 205 S. Baldwin St., when a shot was fired from outside through the window of the bar.

After about two hours of investigation, six Madison police officers surrounded Drogsvold's Femrite Drive home, knocked on the door and arrested him about 1 a.m. May 22.

During their investigation, officers learned Drogsvold had been in a nearby tavern before the shooting, carrying a loaded rifle and making derogatory remarks about black people. Drogsvold is white and Fortney was black.

Drogsvold was charged with first-degree murder but the complaint was dismissed in June 1979 and immediately filed again. Drogsvold's attorney asked the court late that summer to suppress statements Drogsvold made to the police after his arrest and to suppress other evidence.

In June 1980, Torphy agreed with the defense and said the statements and evidence could not be used against Drogsvold. Doyle argued against that ruling in the Court of Appeals in May.

Drogsvold has been free on bail since a few days after his arrest.

The Court of Appeals ruling, written by Judge Paul Gartzke, said Madison police were justified in not waiting

Turn to Page 2, Col. 1

Weather Page 8

Rain ending early today, becoming partly sunny with a chance for afternoon showers and thunderstorms; high in upper-70s. Tonight and Sunday partly cloudy, breezy and cooler. Tonight's low in upper-40s. High Sunday in mid-60s. Probability of measurable rain 40 percent today.

Tau Kappa Epsilon's Bucky Badger was well dressed for a rainy-day Homecoming Friday at 216 Langdon St.
—State Journal color photo by Edwin Stein

Jury verdict mixed on coach nickname

By George Hesselberg
Of The State Journal

The future looks "Rosy" for "Plunkie" McClain. Or was that "Caboose" McClain?

From "Caboose" to "Plunkie," "Digger" to "Sparky," Badger sports fans have united to solve a problem that threatens the future of UW football.

The object was to find a nickname for Dave McClain, coach of the University of Wisconsin-Madison football team, which plays the 1981 Homecoming game today against Western Michigan.

The logic for this search was the following:

Since the Badgers have a chance at a successful season, the coach, for tradition's sake, needs a nickname. Taking up The State Journal's invitation to send in nickname nominations, readers sent in more than 50 ideas following last week's article.

Most writers signed their letters as "avid" fans. Here are some of the nominations received in the mail this week:

For originality, "Milkdud" McClain was a good choice. "He turned a dud of a Badger team into a great team and the "milk" represents the Dairy state," said Chip Kuchenan, of Madison.

Another thoughtful suggestion came from Steve Ellsworth, of Belleville, who nominated "DEWEY" McClain, as in "Defensive Excellence Wins Every Year."

"Skeets" McClain would fit, said John T. Maclean, Middleton, or how about "Cruiser" short for "Crusade" McClain, from Irene Johns, of Dodgeville?

"Rosy" McClain, from John Damon, of Madison, because "he has a rosy complexion." Thelma Hill of Madison thought of "Big Red" McClain.

"Plunkie" McClain, because "I feel he really gave us a plunker when his team beat Michigan," wrote Mrs. F. Halsey Kraege.

"Win" McClain. "If Wisconsin goes back to the old ways, forget about "Win" and call him "Loser" McClain," said Pat Malone, Portage.

"Boom-Boom" McClain. "It's got a nice ring to it," thought Amy Jewell, Plain.

There were several nominations for "Big Mac" McClain, and five persons thought "Digger" would be nice. There were also several anonymous letters suggesting that McClain already had a nickname, "Scooter," used when he was a coach at Ohio State.

Thinking ahead, Ed Hickman wrote, "By the time you get this, Wisconsin will have been beaten by UCLA 28-7 so I would suggest "One Shot" McClain." Sterling Johnson, of Madison, took an entomological view, suggesting "Sting" McClain or "Bee" McClain.

Kathryn E. Hampel, of Madison, mixed her sports and came up with "Brew" McClain, and Earl Seifert of Jefferson thought up "Buck" McClain.

Thinking offensively, Bill Noltner of Monona suggested "Trix" McClain.

"Now that the offense appears to be alive and well," said Carl Campbell, of Middleton, "we should call him "Gunner" McClain."

He deserves to be called "Dapper Dave" McClain, said Mrs. Anne Mueller, Monroe. The 2:30 p.m. class at St. Coletta's school in Jefferson thought "Scruffy" McClain was a fitting nickname.

There were even a few pro-wrestler types suggested by B. Colden, of Waterloo, who mentioned "Masher or Crunch" McClain. Don Huebner, Jr., of Edgerton, picked a combination that

Turn to Page 2, Col. 1

Car-train crash kills five

Associated Press

Five persons were killed in a car-train accident in Jefferson County Friday night, authorities said.

A Sheriff's Department spokesman said the crash occurred about 9 p.m. at a rail crossing along Switzke Road, just north of Highway 18.

Details were not available.

The deaths raised the 1981 Wisconsin traffic fatality toll to 708 Friday, compared with 727 on the same date last year.

Wisconsin State Journal

Monday

October 11, 1982
Madison, Wisconsin
40 pages * 30 cents**

Brewers St. Louis bound

Ecstatic chaos erupted on the field at Milwaukee County Stadium Sunday as Brewers players and fans joined in celebrating victory.

—State Journal color photo by Joseph W. Jackson III

By Bill Brophy
State Journal sports reporter

MILWAUKEE — For the second consecutive week they had been marked off by some as a team that didn't deserve to win a championship. They blew a four-game lead in the last five days of the regular season and had to beat Baltimore on the last day of the season to win the American League East Division title.

Emotionally drained, the Milwaukee Brewers then lost the first two games of the American League Championship Series to California. They came back, however, to set baseball history on a magical Sunday afternoon at a theater called County Stadium with a 4-3 victory over the Angels.

Cecil Cooper's bases-loaded single with two outs in the seventh inning and Pete Ladd's dramatic relief job in the ninth inning put a Milwaukee team into the World Series for the first time since the Braves lost the world title 24 years ago. The Brewers became the first team in the 13-year history of the playoffs to lose the first two games of a league championship series and come back to win the pennant.

"It took me away from being a goat," said Cooper, who had only two hits in his previous 19 at-bats in the playoff series before poking his game-winner. "And I would have been the goat. When I looked at my wife while I was in the on-deck circle, I knew this was going to my at-bat."

You can win 2 Series tickets

The Milwaukee Brewers are in the World Series, and if you turn to Section 2, Page 4, you can find out how you can win two tickets to the fourth game, which will be played in Milwaukee next Saturday.

You'll have to answer a few baseball trivia questions to win. You should start work on that right away, because the deadline for entries is noon Thursday.

See the two-column "World Series" ad on Page 4 of Sports.

The Brewers will open the World Series Tuesday night in St. Louis, which defeated the Atlanta Braves in three consecutive games to win the National League Championship Series. Game Two of the best-of-seven series will be in St. Louis Wednesday night. Games Three and Four of the Series will be in Milwaukee Friday night and Saturday afternoon. Game Five, if necessary, will be in Milwaukee next Sunday afternoon and Games Six and Seven, if necessary, will be in St. Louis Oct. 19 and 20.

The Brewers relished their first pennant in the 13-year history of the franchise. It may not have been the wild celebration of Baltimore, but it was emotional. Team President Bud Selig hugged each of his players and Manager Harvey Kuenn in the crowded clubhouse. He huddled with Cooper in the corner of the locker room for several minutes before being swooped up by his team and thrown in the shower.

"When I came here," said Cooper, who was acquired by the Brewers in 1975 from Boston, "things were bad and Mr. Selig came to me and promised that he would put a team together. I'm just so glad to be a part of it."

"This club can not be intimidated," said Pete Vuckovich, who pitched out of trouble for most of the first six innings and left the game in the seventh with the Brewers trailing, 3-2. "They just keep coming at you. If you're a pitcher on this team, you have to try your damndest because these guys won't let you give anything else."

The heroes in the biggest victory of the Brewer franchise once again kept with the oft-repeated theme of Kuenn, who said often in the champagne soaked clubhouse, "this is a group of 25 guys who are molded into one."

Bob McClure relieved Vuckovich in the seventh inning and threw a double play ball to "Mr. October," Reggie

Turn to Page 2, Col. 5

Polish union calls for strike

WARSAW, Poland (AP) — Solidarity's fugitive leaders Sunday called for a four-hour, nationwide strike on Nov. 10, responding swiftly to the outlawing of their independent union.

"At every enterprise, and at every department a clandestine committee preparing the protest of Nov. 10 should be organized," said the statement dated Oct. 9 and signed by four of the underground union's leaders.

"The course of the protest will decide the further strategy of the unions."

The statement called for the strike on the second anniversary of Solidarity's registration by a Warsaw court.

Noting that Poland's parliament, the Sejm, Friday banned Polish unions and imposed severe limits on any new unions, it said: "Solidarity exists and will exist, no matter if someone likes it or not."

Archbishop Glemp

That phrase was taken from a speech by Solidarity's founder-leader Lech Walesa, who along with more than 600 other union leaders has been interned since martial law was imposed Dec. 13 and the independent union was suspended. The statement was signed by the three Solidarity leaders still at large: Bogdan Lis of Gdansk, Zbigniew Bujak of Warsaw and Wladyslaw Hardek of Krakow. Piotr Bednorz signed in place of Wladyslaw Frasyniuk, who was captured last Tuesday.

Earlier Sunday, Roman Catholic Primate Jozef Glemp accused martial law authorities of "embittering the nation" and several Warsaw priests urged calm as other signs of protest emerged against the outlawing of Solidarity.

Nine senior Solidarity leaders interned in Warsaw's Bialoleka prison sent a letter condemning the ban and

Turn to Page 2, Col. 5

Israel sets conditions for Lebanon pullout

©N.Y. Times News Service

JERUSALEM — Israel announced Sunday its troops would not withdraw from Lebanon until the Beirut government signed a security agreement with Israel and all Israeli prisoners in Syrian and Palestinian hands were returned.

The decision came in a Cabinet meeting designed to set forth Israel's bargaining position in the upcoming negotiations for a mutual Syrian and Israeli departure from Lebanon. The talks with Syria are being held through American mediation.

The Cabinet repeated its earlier demand that the Palestine Liberation Organization leave the country first, before the mutual withdrawal begins.

However, some Israeli officials indicated this was merely an opening argument, leaving open the possibility that should Syria agree to take PLO units along on any pullout, Israel would accept such an arrangement.

"If the Syrians tell us tomorrow that they want to leave, together with

Turn to Page 2, Col. 1

Brewer fans go wild

MILWAUKEE (AP) — Milwaukee's main downtown thoroughfares became scenes of near bedlam Sunday night as thousands of revelers celebrated the city's first major league baseball pennant in a quarter century.

Police stood by helplessly as young people jumped atop cars of passers-by or rocked them back and forth after the throng, in effect, forced the closing of Wisconsin Avenue, the main street.

Other cars with occupants leaning out of windows careened through side streets with horns blowing.

It was reminiscent of the street celebrations that occurred when the Braves, then of Milwaukee, won the National League pennant in 1957 and 1958.

"We're No. 1," was the repeated cheer Sunday night.

It all started early Sunday night at County Stadium when the Milwaukee Brewers won the American League pennant with a 4-3 victory over the California Angels.

When Rod Carew grounded out in the ninth, sealing the Angels' fate, hundreds of fans, led mainly by bleacherites, jumped over the barriers and rushed to the infield. The scene was total confusion.

The fans ripped up the bases while the public address announcer begged them to leave the field.

The billboard flashed a sign: "Please leave the field. Due to the recent rain, the playing field can be easily damaged. It is important that the field be ready for next weekend's World Series."

The fans paid no heed. For almost an hour they milled about on the infield and outfield. They were told that the players would come out to make a bow, but not until the field was cleared.

"It's pandemonium," one fan who

Turn to Page 6, Col. 1

Today's chuckle

The best thing to save for your old age is yourself.

Inside

Weather

Page 10

Today cloudy, windy and cool with a 20-percent chance for showers; high in the mid-50s. Southwest to west winds 15 to 25 mph. Tonight and Tuesday continued mostly cloudy and cool with a chance for showers; low in the low 40s; high Tuesday in the low 50s.

Wisconsin State Journal

Sunday
June 19, 1983
Madison, Wisconsin
●●● $1

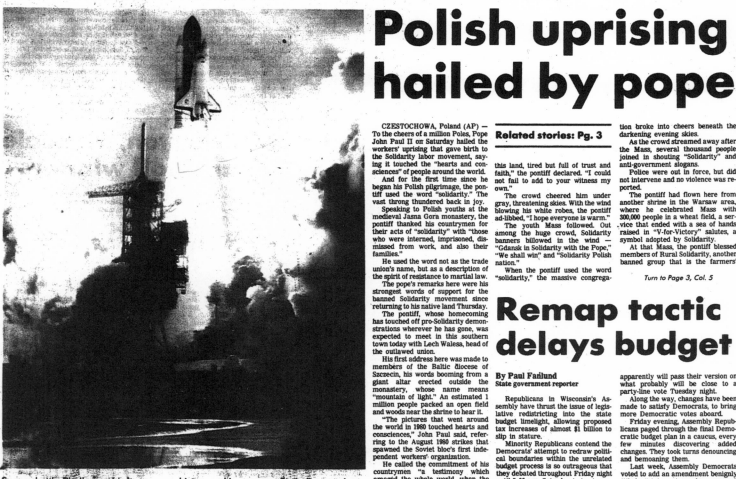

Space shuttle Challenger blasts away on history-making voyage Saturday morning.
—*AP Laserphoto*

Space is no longer men-only for U.S.

CAPE CANAVERAL, Fla. (AP) — After 22 years and 57 men, the United States put a woman in space Saturday. Sally Ride, a 32-year-old astrophysicist, went right to work, sending a Canadian satellite spinning out of space shuttle Challenger's cargo bay.

"It sure is fun," she told Mission Control during her first hour in space.

And, by the end of the day, she had not changed her mind. As Mission Control bid the astronauts a good night and thanked them for a great day, Ms. Ride exclaimed: "If you think it was a great day for you, you should have been up here."

Neither Ms. Ride nor her four male crewmates aboard Challenger made note of the breakup of a men-only group. But as fire belched from the tail of the shuttle at the beginning of Flight Seven, the voice of launch control exulted: "Liftoff, liftoff of STS-7 and America's first woman astronaut!"

On the shuttle's seventh turn around Earth, she conducted critical checkout procedures and then pushed the button that ejected the $24-million Anik-C communications satellite at a precise point over the Pacific Ocean, southwest of Hawaii.

"This makes the orbiter three for three on PAM deploy," said Ms. Ride after the successful release. She referred to the "Payload Assist Module," the small system that had ejected two satellites on a previous flight.

Her fellow mission specialist, John Fabian, said, "As previously advertised, we deliver."

Forty-five minutes later, the satellite's own rocket motor fired, the first of two "burns" that will place Anik-C in a parking orbit over the Pacific.

The Anik-C will bring satellite pay-TV to receiving dishes in millions of American homes.

Ms. Ride's husband, Steve Hawley, — an astronaut who is to fly in space for the first time next year — bade her farewell from launch control.

"Sally, have a ball," he said. A crowd estimated at half-a-million urged her upward. Many donned T-shirts with the slogan: "Ride, Sally Ride."

The trip has other significant "firsts." If all goes well, Challenger will make the shuttle program's first round trip, Florida-to-Florida, landing at a concrete Kennedy Space Center strip next Friday at 7:53 a.m. And never before have five people gone into orbit on one ship, prompting this boast from NASA: "Space shuttle Challenger has delivered to space the largest human payload of all time — four men, one woman."

In his weekly radio address, President Reagan called Ms. Ride an example of the great strides women have made. He wished the crew well and added, "Nancy and I look forward to being on hand to greet them when they land next Friday."

Ms. Ride acted as commander Robert Crippen's flight engineer on the spectacular climb from launch pad 39A over the Atlantic.

The flight was 2½ hours old when Crippen — the only crew member who has flown a shuttle before — reported the crew was making use of slack time by straightening

Turn to Page 2, Col. 5

Joyce, Dale Ride moments after liftoff.
—*AP Laserphoto*

Daughter in orbit, mom, dad confident

CAPE CANAVERAL, Fla. (AP) — The impact of her daughter's historic flight didn't hit Joyce Ride until several minutes after Sally Ride had disappeared off the face of the Earth.

"It really got to me when they said they're downrange and if there's any problem they'll land in Dakar (Senegal)," Mrs. Ride said after her daughter and four male astronauts soared into orbit aboard the space shuttle Challenger.

Other than that, there were no worries. Asked if he was anxious during the countdown and thundering liftoff, Dale Ride, the astronaut's father, confidently answered, "No, not at all. It's a great program."

Relatives of the 32-year-old spacewoman chatted briefly with reporters after the 6:33 a.m. launch.

Mrs. Ride greeted reporters with a wide grin and a cocked arm, issuing a mocking demand that no one pose the ultimate dumb question.

"The first one who asks how I feel gets it," she said, wielding a cup of water as her weapon.

Following the launch, the Rides chatted with feminist leader Gloria Steinem, who watched the launch at the VIP site with Jane Fonda and hundreds of other space agency guests.

Polish uprising hailed by pope

CZESTOCHOWA, Poland (AP) — To the cheers of a million Poles, Pope John Paul II on Saturday hailed the workers' uprising that gave birth to the Solidarity labor movement, saying it touched the "hearts and consciences" of people around the world.

And for the first time since he began his Polish pilgrimage, the pontiff used the word "solidarity." The vast throng thundered back in joy.

Speaking to Polish youths at the medieval Jasna Gora monastery, the pontiff thanked his countrymen for their acts of "solidarity" with "those who were interned, imprisoned, dismissed from work, and also their families."

He used the word not as the trade union's name, but as a description of the spirit of resistance to martial law.

The pope's remarks here were his strongest words of support for the banned Solidarity movement since returning to his native land Thursday.

The pontiff, whose homecoming has touched off pro-Solidarity demonstrations wherever he has gone, was expected to meet in this southern town today with Lech Walesa, head of the outlawed union.

His first address here was made to members of the Baltic diocese of Szczecin, his words booming from a giant altar erected outside the monastery, whose name means "mountain of light." An estimated 1 million people packed an open field and woods near the shrine to hear it.

"The pictures that went around the world in 1980 touched hearts and consciences," John Paul said, referring to the August 1980 strikes that spawned the Soviet bloc's first independent workers' organization.

He called the commitment of his countrymen "a testimony which amazed the whole world, when the Polish worker stood up for himself with the gospel in his hand and a prayer on his lips."

The pope also spoke emotionally about the monastery's Black Madonna, a symbol of independence throughout Poland. He said the holy icon's eyes were "tear-filled and sad."

"I could not fail to speak at least briefly about these great problems, which are situated mainly in the consciousness and hearts of the people of

Related stories: Pg. 3

this land, tired but full of trust and faith," the pontiff declared. "I could not fail to add to your witness my own."

The crowd cheered him under gray, threatening skies. With the wind blowing his white robes, the pontiff ad-libbed, "I hope everyone is warm."

The youth Mass followed. Out among the huge crowd, Solidarity banners billowed in the wind — "Gdansk in Solidarity with the Pope," "We shall win" and "Solidarity Polish nation."

When the pontiff used the word "solidarity," the massive congregation broke into cheers beneath the darkening evening skies.

As the crowd streamed away after the Mass, several thousand people joined in shouting "Solidarity" and anti-government slogans.

Police were out in force, but did not intervene and no violence was reported.

The pontiff had flown here from another shrine in the Warsaw area, where he celebrated Mass with 300,000 people in a wheat field, a service that ended with a sea of hands raised in "V-for-Victory" salutes, a symbol adopted by Solidarity.

At that Mass, the pontiff blessed members of Rural Solidarity, another banned group that is the farmers'

Turn to Page 3, Col. 5

Today's chuckle

Growing up: When you start beating your dad on the golf course. Maturity: When you let him win.

Remap tactic delays budget

By Paul Fanlund
State government reporter

Republicans in Wisconsin's Assembly have thrust the issue of legislative redistricting into the state budget limelight, allowing proposed tax increases of almost $1 billion to slip in stature.

Minority Republicans contend the Democrats' attempt to redraw political boundaries within the unrelated budget process is so outrageous that they debated throughout Friday night until 5:30 a.m. Saturday to try to amplify their position.

GOP lawmakers portray the reapportionment issue as sort of a budgetary last straw.

Democratic Gov. Anthony Earl proposed his 1983-85 state budget last February. Democrats who control the Legislature's Joint Finance Committee (12-2) amended it. Democrats who control the Senate (19-14), and a majority of Assembly Democrats who control the lower house (57-40) have agreed to their own package of amendments.

In accordance with an agreement reached early Saturday morning, Republicans will have six more hours to denounce the Democratic budget Tuesday afternoon, then Democrats apparently will pass their version on what probably will be close to a party-line vote Tuesday night.

Along the way, changes have been made to satisfy Democrats, to bring more Democratic votes aboard.

Friday evening, Assembly Republicans paged through the final Democratic budget plan in a caucus, every few minutes discovering added changes. They took turns denouncing and bemoaning them.

Last week, Assembly Democrats voted to add an amendment benignly titled a "state cartography program." Sponsor David Travis, D-Madison, said his plan makes technical adjustments to a remapping ordered by a panel of federal judges last year.

Republicans reacted with fury, saying the Travis amendment cunningly makes strong GOP districts even more Republican and leaves alone heavily Democratic Milwaukee, then makes contested districts more Democratic. The bottom line, they say, is an arrogant attempt by Democrats to indefinitely consolidate their majorities.

Republicans have virtually no leverage. If Assembly Speaker Thomas Loftus, D-Sun Prairie, and

Turn to Page 2, Col. 1

Volcker retained as Fed chief

©N.Y. Times News Service

WASHINGTON — Ending months of speculation that has roiled the financial markets, President Reagan announced Saturday he would reappoint Paul Volcker to another four-year term as chairman of the Federal Reserve Board.

Taking time from his regular Saturday radio address for what he said was "a news flash," Reagan told listeners he telephoned Volcker Saturday morning and asked him to accept the reappointment.

"He's agreed to do so," the president said. "And I couldn't be more pleased. He is as dedicated as I am to continuing the fight against inflation. And with him as chairman of the Fed, I know we'll win that fight."

Volcker's tight-money policies in 1981 and 1982 were credited by most economists with helping to bring down the nation's inflation rate, and by critics with causing the recession.

"As I have said on a number of occasions, I do believe we now have a rare opportunity to achieve sustained growth on a firm foundation of stability," Volcker said. "I am sure I can speak for the entire Federal Reserve System as to our commitment to work toward that objective."

Volcker was appointed chairman by President Carter in 1979. His appointment to a new term, beginning Aug. 6, is subject to approval by the Senate, but he was not expected to have much difficulty winning confirmation.

In the regular Democratic response to Reagan's address, Sen. Thomas Eagleton of Missouri, said, "I vigorously support President Reagan's reappointment of Paul Volcker."

Another Democratic senator, Gary Hart of Colorado, who is seeking his party's presidential nomination, issued a statement saying "to the

Paul Volcker

degree this represents a continuation of the policies of the past two years," the selection "could be a disaster for our economy and for the unemployed."

Arthur Levitt Jr., president of the American Stock Exchange, said he applauded the president's decision, adding Volcker "has done an outstanding job."

The Federal Reserve System is the central banking authority of the United States and primary regulator of the nation's commercial banks. The board also controls the growth or contraction of the nation's money supply, thereby affecting interest rates.

The other candidates Reagan had been considering were believed to be Alan Greenspan, former chairman of the Council of Economic Advisers; Preston Martin, vice chairman of the Federal Reserve Board, and Paul McCracken, former chairman of the Council of Economic Advisers.

Inside

Weather

Page 16

Twenty-percent chance of lingering showers during the morning hours today, then becoming partly cloudy. High today in the high 70s to low 80s. East to southeast winds at 5-10 mph. Partly cloudy tonight, low in the low 60s. Monday, chance of showers, high in the low 80s.

Wisconsin State Journal

Saturday
June 9, 1984
Madison, Wisconsin
★★★ 30 cents

Path of destruction

Barneveld tornado toll: 9 dead, scores injured

By Chuck Martin
and other staff members
Of The State Journal

The death toll reached nine by early today in the aftermath of a south-central Wisconsin tornado that the meteorologist in charge of the National Weather Service in Madison called "the worst one I've ever seen."

All of the dead were in Barneveld, an Iowa County community about 25 miles west of Madison that officials said was 90-percent destroyed.

About 500 of Barneveld's 607 people were homeless Friday night, and 25 remained in hospitals in Dodgeville and Madison.

Officials estimated that 50 more people were homeless along the unusually wide 13-mile path of destruction the tornado wrought through eastern Iowa County and western Dane County. In Black Earth in western Dane County, at least 24 homes were damaged, at least eight destroyed.

Parts of farmsteads in the storm's way were reduced to pieces of wood and metal scattered over fields.

State officials Friday night said they will ask for $18 million to $20 million in federal aid to help rebuild.

Gov. Anthony Earl, who toured the area Friday, called the destruction "as extensive as anything I've ever seen."

For those who saw the destruction, the tornado inspired awe and horror. For those involved, it tested body and mind. For all, it produced stories that lay bare the human condition — stories of death, kindness, spirit and poignancy.

● At Memorial Hospital of Iowa County in Dodgeville, Mary Ann Myers was being treated for injuries. A blanket was draped over her nightgown — once pink, now a dirty rose.

"Oh yes," she said, "I can tell you what happened. . . . By the way, I am a village trustee (in Barneveld) — not that it matters at this point because the village isn't there anymore."

● Dave Olson of Black Earth received bruises when the tornado lifted him from his bedroom and deposited him 40 feet outside his house.

● James Slewitzke came to Barneveld from his Mosinee home earlier in the week to help his sister, Elaine Slewitzke, with painting chores. Both died in the tornado.

● On a farmstead about two miles north of Blue Mounds State Park, two barns were piles of rubble. Fields were littered with debris. Thirty feet from one of the barns, the farmhouse stood undamaged.

● Sightseers hindered Friday's cleanup and prompted law enforcement officers to warn people to stay away from Barneveld today. The Madison Police Department sent at least five officers to Barneveld Friday night to protect property against looters.

● A 5-year-old child was the first storm victim to be brought to Memorial Hospital in Dodgeville. The child was not seriously injured and told nurses to "help the older people first."

● Less than an hour after the storm struck Barneveld, residents of nearby Dodgeville organized a shelter for the homeless at a school.

The tornado that devastated Barneveld was part of a storm system that produced 49 reported tornadoes throughout the Midwest. Killer tornadoes struck Missouri and Iowa as well as Wisconsin.

The Barneveld tornado was the deadliest of Friday's storms and the

Turn to Page 2, Col. 1

The dead

Nine people were identified Friday by the Iowa County Sheriff's Department as having been killed in the tornado that struck Barneveld early Friday.

Three members of the Bruce Simon family — Bruce and Jill and their daughter, Cassandra, 8, were killed. An infant son, Trevor James Simon, was injured and hospitalized in serious condition at University Hospital in Madison.

The other six were Ralph Hammerly, an adult; Kirk Holland, an adult; Matthew Aschliman, an infant; Bob Arneson, an adult; Elaine Slewitzke and her brother, James Slewitzke, of Mosinee, who had come to Barneveld to help his sister paint her house.

Ages were not available, said Iowa County Coroner Dr. Timothy Correll. The dead were taken to the Iowa County Memorial Hospital.

The devastation in downtown Barneveld is starkly illustrated. The view looks northeast along the tornado's path.

—State Journal photo by Joseph W. Jackson III

The end of a devastating day

BARNEVELD — The sunset Friday was one of the most beautiful of the year.

As the sun dropped behind the Iowa County hills overlooking Barneveld, the optical illusion it presented made it seem as large as a barn.

It was quiet in Barneveld Friday night; all the people were gone.

The tornado that destroyed the village early Friday left Barneveld a virtual ghost town. Its only inhabitants were police officers and National Guardsmen.

The trees were silhouetted against the peach sky, leaves gone, branches snapped.

But those birds that remained in Barneveld sang their evening songs, just as they had the night before.

There were no lights and virtually no traffic. The residents had come earlier to view their demolished homes; now, the only vehicles were squad cars and jeeps.

Those homes left standing were stripped naked to public view.

The businesses were gone. The churches were gone. The school was damaged.

One house was lifted from its foundation and tipped on its side. Someone tacked a new "For Sale" sign to one wall.

— By William R. Wineke

Tornado special

Pull out this special 8-page tornado section for easy reading and saving. The regular front-page news begins on Page 5.

Some were lucky to recall nightmare

By Ron Seely
Regional reporter

BARNEVELD — At 12:50 a.m. Friday, this was like any other sleeping village in the Wisconsin countryside — at 1 a.m., it was gone, literally blown from the Earth and there was nothing but rubble, the sickening smell of plaster and gas, the dazed survivors, the wounded, the dead.

It happened, some said, in 20 seconds, preceded only by an ominous silence, a tremendous bolt of lightning that many will remember forever as a warning that something terrible was about to happen and then the eerie, high-pitched whistle of the tornado itself as it did its work.

Ruth Ann Koebke, 33, had been uneasy earlier in the evening when, during the Tonight Show, a tornado watch flashed across the television screen. But the family — Ruth and her husband, Dale, their daughter, Carren, 7, and Lauren, 11 — went to bed after the show and slept. Until that bolt of lightning. She'll never forget the lightning.

"It was like," she recalled, "someone was saying 'This is your last chance,' "

The family plucked the pet guinea pig from its cage and went to the basement as the tornado destroyed the village around them. When it seemed that the storm had passed, Koebke ventured up the dark stairs and outside.

"He came back in tears," Mrs. Koebke said. "A grown man and he was weeping."

Just two blocks north, Bobby Schaller, his wife, Cindy and Mark and Melanie, their son and daughter, were in their second-floor bedrooms when they saw the lightning. Even before they could rise from their beds, the wooden-frame house began shaking. They knew from the strange whistle outside what was happening and they headed for the stairs. But before they reached the stairs, the house disintegrated beneath them. Schaller, still in the bedroom, felt the floor drop from beneath him and watched as the wall in front of him fell away.

"I dove into the bathroom and rode the floor down," he said. "The whole house shook. It only took 10 seconds, if that long, and it was done. I didn't even open my eyes. I didn't want to look. I thought my life was over."

Seconds later, Schaller opened his eyes. He was on the ground with the bathroom in shambles around him but he was unhurt. He heard screams, saw his son pinned under a door frame, alive but apparently not badly hurt. He heard his wife and moments later found her beneath the roof of the house just a few feet away, a gash in her back two inches deep. She was hospitalized later and treated.

At about 12:45 a.m. Dick Ehlert, an off-duty dispatcher with the Iowa County Sheriff's Department, ran with his family down the basement stairs of his Barneveld home. As he ran he yelled into a walkie-talkie, alerting the Iowa County Sheriff's Department that Barneveld was getting hit. His was the first word the county received that anything was amiss. Later, after the storm passed, Ehlert called in again and said "the whole town was blown away." The dispatcher on duty refused to believe him at first.

All of these things happened on the village's West Side, soon after the tornado touched down and began following its course to the northeast. It pounded its way through the small downtown, reduced it to piles of bricks and wood, and terrified

Turn to Page 2, Col. 1

Wisconsin State Journal

Saturday

September 7, 1985
Madison, Wisconsin
★★★ **35 cents**

Worst Wisconsin air crash kills 31 at Milwaukee field

Searchers check debris but find no survivors after Friday afternoon's Midwest Express Airlines crash at Milwaukee's Gen. Billy Mitchell Field.

—State Journal photos by Carolyn Pflasterer.

Flight originated in Madison

By George Hesselberg
Of The State Journal

More on Pages 2,3

A Midwest Express Airlines jet went into a roll, crashed and burned moments after takeoff from Milwaukee's Mitchell Field Friday afternoon, killing all 31 passengers and crew members on board.

It is the worst crash in Wisconsin aviation history.

More than 1,500 persons have died in air disasters worldwide this year, a record.

Three passengers, including one Madison resident, boarded the Midwest plane in Madison, the flight's origination point, an airline spokesman said.

The lone Madison victim was identified by Midwest as Paulette Chandler, of 702 Oneida Place. She was the former wife of Madison businessman Leonard Mattioli. She was on her way to Atlanta to visit a sister, a family friend said.

All of the victims, including nine from Wisconsin, had been identified by early today. The two others who boarded in Madison were identified by Midwest as William Epsilantis, of Georgia, and Nancy Mani, of Savannah, Ga.

Robert Goudreau, a spokesman for the Kimberly-Clark Corp., which owns Midwest Express, said it was very likely Kimberly-Clark employees were aboard the flight. Company workers often drive to Madison to catch flights for the weekend, he said.

Midwest Express transported relatives and friends from Atlanta, the flight's destination, to Milwaukee to aid in identifying the bodies.

Federal transportation investigators were at the crash scene, but the cause of the accident was not immediately determined.

The DC-9 jetliner Flight Number 105 took off from Madison for Milwaukee at 2:20 p.m. Thursday. The continuing flight from Milwaukee headed for Atlanta at 3:17 p.m., two minutes behind schedule.

Moments after a takeoff into

Turn to Page 2, Col. 3

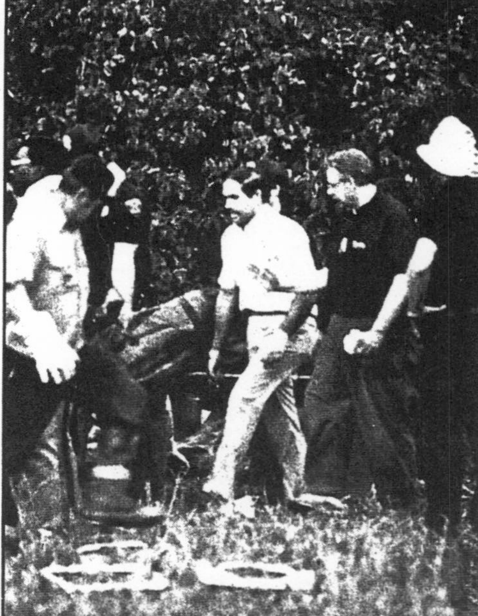

Clergyman, second from right, offers prayer for victim.

Former Mrs. Mattioli among victims

Paulette Chandler, 40, of 702 Oneida Place, former wife of Leonard Mattioli, chairman of American TV and Applicance, was the only Madison resident killed in Friday's Milwaukee plane crash.

Weather

Partly sunny, warm and humid, with a 30-percent chance for thunderstorms; high in the upper 80s and south winds at 5-15 mph. Tonight, a 40-percent chance for thunderstorms, continued humidity; low in the upper 60s. Sunday, continued 30-percent chance for showers. **More on Page 12.**

Ms. Chandler was on her way to visit her sister, Barbara de Felice of Atlanta.

Originally from Chicago, Ms. Chandler met Mattioli in high school. They were married and moved to Rochester, N.Y., where their two sons, Joe, 17, and Tom, 19, were born. The family moved to Madison in 1970, when Mattioli took over American TV, which was founded by his brother.

Ms. Chandler had diverse interests, including calligraphy, portraits, photo realism and public speaking. For a short time she was interested in sky diving. She also recorded radio commercials for her husband's business.

She started her own calligraphy business in 1979, and her skill at artistic lettering was praised by local artists. She sold artistically lettered mottos and sayings in the Dane County area. Although she no longer operated the calligraphy business, a friend said she still was interested in the art.

She was active in several Madison organizations, especially the Art League. She was taking courses at Madison Area Technical College.

A friend described her as an "outgoing, happy-type person."

Mattioli and Ms. Chandler were divorced in 1982.

The other victims were:

Crew:
Dan Martin, Appleton.
Bill Weiss, Appleton.
Amy Bain, Milwaukee.
Sharon Herb, Milwaukee.

Passengers:
Baranello, Thomas; Georgia.
Christopher, Nick; Grafton.
Connelly, John; Appleton, Wis.
Danhope, Mike; Alpharetta, Ga.
Davis, Calvern; Georgia.
Decandia, Nick; Appleton.
Dupuis, Michael; Georgia.
Epsilantis, William; Georgia.
Hargrove, Charles; N.C.
Medley, Darla; Norcross, Ga.
Helms, Donald; Decatur, Ga.
Holt, Kurt; Atlanta.
Hynson, Steve; Georgia.
Jenkins, Donald F.; Appleton.
Lunsford, Celeste; Georgia.
Mani, Nancy; Savannah, Ga.
McGibboney, Frank; Stone Mountain, Ga.
Pope, Richard; Douglasville, Ga.
Schmuhl, Ray; Ga.
Simmons, J. Scott; Savannah, Ga.
Simpson, Elkin; LaGrange, Ga.
Skagen, John; Georgia.
Sooy, Don;, Milburne, Ga.
Sweet, Earl; Georgia.
Tuck, John L.; Georgia.
Waters, Ricky; Mapleton, Ga.

Wisconsin State Journal

Wednesday

January 29, 1986
Madison, Wisconsin
★★★ 35 cents

Shuttle's tragic flight

Nation mourns as NASA seeks clues

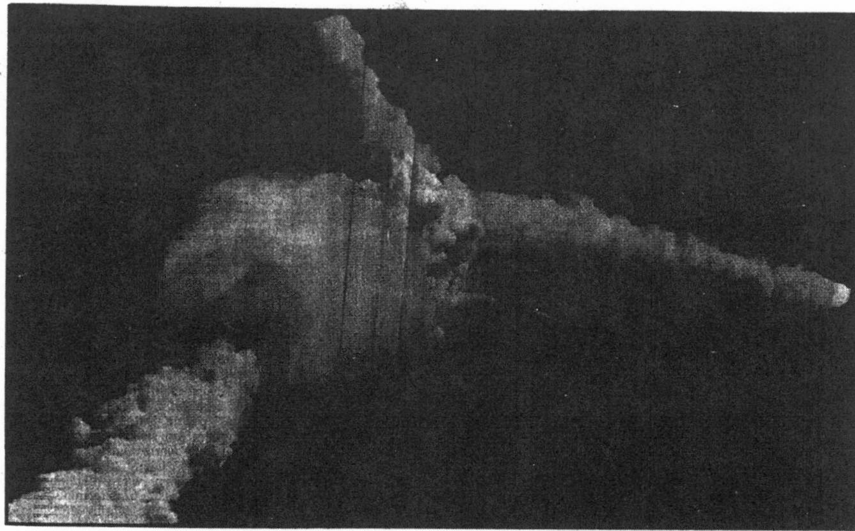

Space shuttle Mission 51-L disintegrates 74 seconds after liftoff at Kennedy Space Center Tuesday.

—AP Laserphoto

By Howard Benedict

CAPE CANAVERAL, Fla. (AP) — A catastrophic explosion blew apart the space shuttle Challenger 74 seconds after liftoff Tuesday, sending schoolteacher Christa McAuliffe and six NASA astronauts to a fiery death in the sky eight miles out from Kennedy Space Center.

"We mourn seven heroes," said President Reagan.

The accident defied quick explanation, though a slow-motion replay seemed to show a flame or other abnormality on one of two peel-away rocket boosters followed by the detonation of the shuttle's huge external fuel tank. The tank-turned-fireball destroyed Challenger high above the Atlantic while crew families and NASA officials watched in despair from the Cape.

Other observers noted the boosters continued to fly crazily through the sky after the explosion, indicating the problem might have originated in the giant tank itself.

"We will not speculate as to the specific cause of the explosion based on that footage," said Jesse Moore, NASA's top shuttle administrator. National Aeronautics and Space Administration officials are organizing an investigating board and Moore said it will take a "careful review" of all data "before we can reach any conclusions."

The explosion followed an apparently flawless launch, delayed two hours as officials analyzed the danger from icicles that formed in the frosty Florida morning along the shuttle's new launch pad.

"There were no signs of abnormalities on the screens" as flight controllers monitored Challenger's liftoff and ascent, a source said. The source, at the Johnson Space Center in Houston, said the blast occurred "unexpectedly and with absolutely no warning."

Mission Control reported there had been no indication of any problem with the three shuttle engines, its twin solid boosters or any other system and that the shuttle just suddenly blew apart 10 miles high and eight miles downrange of Cape Canaveral.

Reagan, in an Oval Office address after he postponed his State of the Union message because of the tragedy, reaffirmed his commitment to the shuttle program and said, "The future doesn't belong to the fainthearted, it belongs to the brave."

"We will continue our quest in space," he said. "There will be more shuttle flights and more shuttle crews and, yes, more volunteers, more civilians, more teachers in space."

He added: "Nothing stops here."

NASA announced it had suspended its ambitious 1986 shuttle schedule, however.

"We're obviously not going to pick up any flight activity until we fully understand what the circumstances were relative to launch," Moore said.

He declined to speculate about how long an investigation might take, saying only that flight safety was the agency's first priority.

NASA delayed its announcement that there appeared to be no survivors until it had conducted search-and-rescue efforts. Even before Moore's statement, it seemed impossible anyone could survive such a cataclysmic explosion.

The crew included Mrs. McAuliffe and six NASA astronauts: commander Francis R. Scobee, 46, pilot Michael J. Smith, 40; Judith Resnik, 36; Ronald E. McNair, 35; Ellison S. Onizuka, 39; and Gregory B. Jarvis, 41.

Col. John Shults, director of Defense Department contingency operations here, said a search armada of helicopters, ships and planes had spotted several pieces of debris floating in the Atlantic.

"We have seen several pieces, what looked to be about five or 10 feet long and a couple feet wide," he said. The debris will be recovered and brought to a hangar at nearby Patrick Air Force Base.

NASA said most of the debris being found consisted of the thermal tiles that coat the outside of the orbiter to protect it from the heat of re-entering the atmosphere.

Shults said debris from the shattered shuttle fell into the ocean in an area between 50 and 130 miles southeast of the launch site. He said the water there was 70 to 200 feet deep.

"It's a terrible thing," Reagan told reporters. "I just can't get out of my mind her (Mrs. McAuliffe's) husband, her children, as well as the families of the others on board."

"Oh, my God, no!" exclaimed first lady Nancy Reagan, who was watching the launch in the White House family quarters.

New Hampshire schoolchildren were drawn to this launch, the shuttle program's 25th, because of the presence of Mrs. McAuliffe, the first "common citizen" chosen to make a space flight. They screamed and fought back tears. Americans everywhere watched in disbelief as television networks replayed the shuttle explosion.

Lost along with the $1.2-billion spacecraft were a $100-million satellite that was to have become an important part of NASA's space-based shuttle communications network and a smaller $10-million payload that was to have studied Halley's comet.

It was the second disaster to strike NASA's pioneering space program. On Jan. 27, 1967, astronauts Virgil "Gus" Grissom, Edward White and Roger Chaffee burned to death while preparing for an Apollo flight when a fire destroyed their capsule during a training drill.

As Challenger fell in pieces, debris was so heavy that for several minutes NASA di-

Turn to Page 3, Col. 1

Inside

- **President Reagan, in an address to the nation on the shuttle tragedy Tuesday, said, "There will be more shuttle flights and more shuttle crews and, yes, more volunteers, more civilians, more teachers in space." More on Page 3.**
- A blast of party horns and cheers turned quickly to silence and stunned disbelief as 1,200 Concord (N.H.) High School pupils watched the space shuttle Challenger rise into the sky and explode into pieces. "It's awful. Just too awful even to contemplate," Concord High Principal Charles Foley said as he fought back tears. **More on Page 3.**
- For brief profiles of each of the seven crew members aboard the space shuttle Challenger when it exploded in a fireball shortly after liftoff from Cape Canaveral on Tuesday **see Page 4.**
- Several Wisconsin residents have flown space shuttle missions and at least two men are now in Houston training for 1986 shuttle flights. **More on Page 4.**
- "Oh dear God in heaven," sobbed Mary Weullenwebber of Concord, N.H., as the Kennedy Space Center loudspeaker announced, "The vehicle has exploded." Ms. Weullenwebber was one of a dozen parents in Florida as chaperones for a class of 19 third-graders. **More on the eyewitnesses on Page 5.**
- Foreign leaders reacted quickly Tuesday to the explosion of Challenger sending messages of condolence and support to Washington. From personal messages from world leaders to moments of silence in legislative bodies, the world expressed its grief. **More on Page 5.**

The family of teacher-astronaut Christa McAuliffe realizes the horror after Challenger blew apart shortly after liftoff. Mrs. McAuliffe's sister, Betsy, left, and parents, Grace and Ed Corrigan, console each other after the explosion.

—AP Laserphoto

Challenger's final words

SPACE CENTER, Houston (AP) — Words from space shuttle Challenger were all routine through the 74 seconds of flight. There was silence after the spacecraft erupted into a fireball.

Here is a transcript of those seconds as recorded by NASA and released to the Associated Press. NASA officials did not immediately have a written transcript of the conversations and the times they occurred.

Launch control public information commentator Hugh Harris: 10-9-8-7-6, we have main engine start, 4-3-2-1, and liftoff. Liftoff of the 25th space shuttle mission. And it has cleared the tower.

Pilot Mike Smith: Roll program.

Mission Control spacecraft communicator: Roger, roll, Challenger.

Mission Control public information Commentator Steve Nesbitt: Roll program confirmed. Challenger now heading down range. The engines are throttling down now at 94 percent. Normal throttle for most of the flight is 104 percent. We'll throttle down to 65 percent shortly. Engines at 65 percent. Three engines running normally. Three good fuel cells. Three good APUs (auxiliary power units). Velocity 2,257 feet per second (1,400 miles per hour), altitude 4.3 nautical miles (4.9 statute miles), downrange distance 3 nautical miles (3.4 statute miles). Engines throttling up, three engines now 104 percent.

Mission Control spacecraft communicator: Challenger, go at throttle up.

Smith: Roger, go at throttle up.

(Fireball occurs)

Nesbitt: We're at a minute 15 seconds, velocity 2,900 feet per second (1,977 mph) altitude 9 nautical miles (10.35 statute miles), range distance 7 nautical miles (8.05 statute miles)

Long silence.

Nesbitt: Flight controllers are looking very carefully at the situation. Obviously a major malfunction. We have no downlink (communications).

Francis R. Scobee, 46
Spacecraft commander
Cle Elum, Wash.

Michael J. Smith, 40,
Mission's pilot
Beaufort, N.C.

Christa McAuliffe, 37
High school teacher
Concord, N.H.

Judith A. Resnik, 36
Mission specialist
Akron, Ohio

Ronald E. McNair, 35
Mission specialist
Lake City, S.C.

Ellison S. Onizuka, 39
Mission specialist
Kealakekua, Hawaii

Gregory B. Jarvis, 41
Payload specialist
Detroit

Wisconsin State Journal

Wednesday
April 30, 1986
Madison, Wisconsin
★★★ **35 cents**

Soviet meltdown feared

©N.Y. Times, AP

Swedish scientists said Tuesday they were convinced that the radioactive core of a Soviet power-generating reactor melted after an accident last weekend, making it the worst nuclear power plant disaster in history.

They said their conclusion was based partly on discussions with Soviet experts, who sought advice Tuesday from the Swedes on handling the accident.

In Washington, senators were briefed on the disaster and Sen. Patrick Leahy, D-Vt., told reporters he had seen nothing to substatiate reports that 2,000 people were killed in the accident.

Swedish scientists also said their own analysis of atmospheric samples from Sweden's east coast, more than 700 miles from the Chernobyl station in the Ukraine, supported the view that a meltdown had occurred at the plant.

"It is clear what happened," said Frigyes Reich, a chief engineer at Sweden's Nuclear Inspection Board, a Government agency. "The nuclear plant's reactor core has melted, in part or even completely."

On Page 2:
- **U.S. watches for cloud**
- **5 reactors lack shells**
- **Futures prices up**

One technical fact that points to a meltdown, one nuclear expert said, is that measurable amounts of cesium are contained in the radioactivity coming from the Soviet Union. In accident planning for reactors, operators typically assume that at worst, about 10 percent of the radioactive core will be vaporized and that the releases from any small accident will therefore be volatile elements, such as iodine and rare gases. The presence of the less-volatile cesium, the scientist said, suggests a more serious incident.

U.S. intelligence sources also reported a meltdown.

Arms control administrator Kenneth Adelman told Congress that Soviet claims of only two deaths were "frankly preposterous" and called the incident "the most catastrophic nuclear disaster in history."

He said temperatures reached as high as 4,000 degrees (Centigrade, or 7,232 Fahrenheit) at the graphite-cooled reactor and added, "The graphite is burning and will continue to burn for a good number of days."

In Bali, White House spokesman Larry Speakes, traveling with the president, called on the Soviet Union to minimize the danger to other countries by providing full information about the incident, and repeated a U.S. offer of technical help in containing fire and radiation from the accident. There has been no response from the Soviet Union.

The White House has established a special interagency task force to coordinate the government's response to the accident, Speakes said.

Leahy, D-Vt., vice chairman of the Senate Intelligence Committee, said after a CIA briefing Tuesday, "I've seen nothing that indicates that huge numbers of people are dead. It could be two, 12 or two dozen. Certainly the blast itself would have killed anyone in the immediate area."

But Leahy said he had seen nothing to confirm a report that 2,000 people had been killed.

Emerging from the CIA briefing, Sen. Malcolm Wallop, R-Wyo., told reporters, "As we understand it, the building itself was essentially destroyed . . . One would have to assume there is contamination flowing everywhere within that 30-kilometer radius. You've got a hot radioactive core and it's still burning."

The estimates are that the radiation levels are "100,000 to 200,000 to perhaps a million times greater than anything that was contemplated at the worst point in the appraisal of Three Mile Island," Wallop said, attributing that assertion to information he received at the briefing.

"There are extensive levels of radiation, some of which are high enough to cause instantaneous death, some of which will cause death in days or weeks," Wallop said. "There is a hot fire burning and no ready way of putting it out."

It was understood that much of the U.S. intelligence information was gathered by a KH-11 spy satellite, but

Turn to Page 2, Col. 5

February edition of Soviet Life magazine published this photo of Chernobyl.
—AP Laserphoto

Accident's agony likely to linger

©Knight-Ridder News Service

The death toll from the Soviet Union's nuclear reactor accident may rise for weeks as more people succumb to the painful effects of radiation poisoning, experts said Tuesday.

"At first they would have a lot of vomiting, diarrhea, cramps," said Dr. Robert Hattner, chief of nuclear medicine at the University of California at San Francisco.

"Then as they became more and more infected and dehydrated, their minds would become affected. They would become sleepy. You would see bleeding under the skin, bleeding with the slightest trauma, bleeding in the gastrointestinal tract, high fevers."

Although Soviet officials announced two people died in the accident at the Chernobyl power plant in the Ukraine, there were unconfirmed reports of up to 2,000 dead.

If those reports are true, Hattner said, 10 times that number could die within a few weeks from exposure to high levels of radiation.

And both the wounded and the dying would find themselves in a medical system that, like our own, is ill-equipped to handle a radioactive disaster of this magnitude, he said.

"It would be impossible," he said. "There wouldn't be enough physicians. There wouldn't be enough medicine. There wouldn't be enough beds or nurses to observe them. You'd get into this crunch where you have to select the healthiest patients, the ones who seem most likely to survive.

"The others you would just ignore."

American experts are hampered in their assessment of the accident by a lack of information.

But they do know a great deal about what radiation does to the human body.

At very high levels of radiation exposure, death comes almost immediately from damage to the central nervous system, said Roland Finston, director of health physics at Stanford University Medical Center. It is unlikely that levels got this high in the Soviet accident.

At slightly lower levels, radiation kills cells in the lining of the small intestine that normally absorb nutrients. Without this cell barrier, plasma and blood leak out of the blood vessels and intestinal bacteria are free to enter. Victims die of dehydration, shock and infection within two weeks.

Next, radiation damages bone marrow, where white blood cells are produced. The body loses its ability to fight infection and to clot blood. Although this stage of poisoning can be treated with transfusions, antibiotics and intravenous fluids, patients are at great risk of dying for 10 to 12 weeks.

Meanwhile, radioactive gases can damage the lungs, leaving behind the scar tissue called fibrosis.

"If you get through the first 60 days," Finston said, "you're not likely to die of any systemic damage. You then have the delayed effects of cancer to contend with."

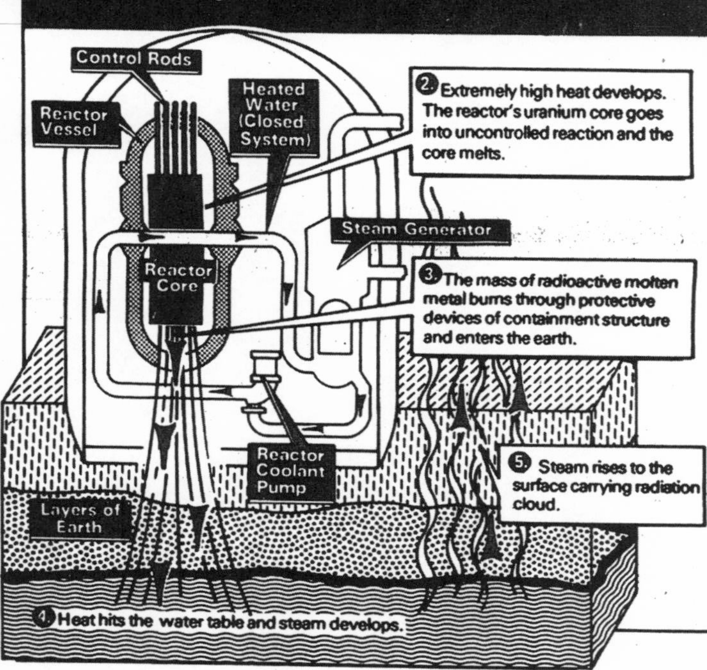
HOW A MELTDOWN OCCURS
1. Meltdown begins when fuel rods overheat
Control Rods
Reactor Vessel
Heated Water (Closed System)
2. Extremely high heat develops. The reactor's uranium core goes into uncontrolled reaction and the core melts.
Steam Generator
Reactor Core
3. The mass of radioactive molten metal burns through protective devices of containment structure and enters the earth.
Reactor Coolant Pump
Layers of Earth
5. Steam rises to the surface carrying radiation cloud.
4. Heat hits the water table and steam develops.

Soviet secrecy, pride to blame

By Lars-Erik Nelson
©N.Y. Daily News

News analysis

WASHINGTON — The world's worst nuclear accident was spawned by Soviet pride and made worse by Soviet secrecy, U.S. experts said Tuesday.

They predicted the radioactive leak at Chernobyl will prove to be a diplomatic and economic disaster for the Kremlin — and maybe for the U.S.

By cloaking an accident involving nuclear power, a frightening and little understood technology, in needless but traditional mystery, the Soviets left even their closest allies to guess whether their lives were at risk and allowed the fears of the world to run free.

Even the Soviets were frightened enough by the Chernobyl disaster to request foreign help — from West Germany and Sweden — in coping with it. "That's unique in our history," said George Vest, director general of the U.S. Foreign Service and a former nuclear-technology negotiator with the Soviets.

"They did two really extraordinary things — they admitted that an accident occurred, and they asked for foreign help," Vest said.

Ironically, although the Soviets are clearly at fault for the mishap, the United States is likely to suffer as well from the inevitable secondary reaction.

"I think you'll see a new wave of protests by both Europeans and Americans against everything nuclear — whether reactors or missiles, Soviet or American," said William Hyland, editor of Foreign Affairs quarterly and a leading Soviet affairs expert.

Joseph Yager of the Brookings Institution said the Soviets have most likely created new problems for themselves with West European environmental groups that have campaigned against both nuclear power and nuclear weapons.

In the past, groups like West Germany's Green Party have focused their protests on U.S. nuclear weapons or their own countries' nuclear-power programs. "This accident will remind them that the Soviet program looks dangerous, too," Yager said.

The Soviet Union let itself in for the Chernobyl accident by placing too much confidence in its engineering skills, said Professor Joseph Nye of the John F. Kennedy School of Government in Cambridge, Mass. Nye also was a State Department nuclear negotiator.

"We used to argue with them about the risks of running a nuclear plant without a containment structure to hold in a possible radiation leak," Nye said. "They assured us their engineering was so precise that a containment shield was just a needless barrier. They had a technological optimism that just made us marvel."

The Soviet Union may have taken shortcuts on radiation shielding to save money, Nye and others said. "They were taking chances, and now they're paying the price," another expert said. "We couldn't build reactors like that in this country."

A CIA study of Soviet energy sources noted, with unconscious envy, that Soviet nuclear engineers never had to contend with the public protests and congressional scrutiny that have forced U.S. nuclear-power companies to be supercareful about radia-

Turn to Page 2, Col. 5

Shuttle seal failure inevitable

© N.Y. Times News Service

WASHINGTON — New and unpublished test results show that a failure of a safety seal on the space-shuttle Challenger virtually was inevitable because of a combination of cold temperatures on the morning of the launching and design flaws.

The test results, conducted for the presidential panel studying the accident and summarized for the New York Times, determined that the joint sometimes would begin to fail at temperatures as high as 50 degrees. National Aeronautics and Space Administration officials testified that they felt confident the shuttle could be launched at lower temperatures without any undue risk to the crew.

The Challenger was launched in 36-degree weather, but investigators estimate that the temperature of the joint that contained the failed seal was about 28 degrees, a temperature at which failure is more likely than not, the tests show.

The analysis is expected to serve as the centerpiece of the presidential commission's report, due in early June. On Monday, panel members received a summary of the results.

The findings, when taken with testimony before the commission, suggest that the middle-level NASA officials from the Marshall Space Flight Center who decided to go ahead with the launching, despite warnings about the low temperature from engineers working for the manufacturer of the booster rocket, acted with virtually no knowledge of the performance limitations of the joints and the synthetic rubber rings that were relied on to seal them.

The report also concludes:

✔ Seconds after Challenger broke apart, a second joint on the right-hand solid-fuel booster rocket, which was veering out of control, also ruptured and a "plume" of flame appeared. While the second failure did not contribute to the accident and probably was caused by aerodynamic stress, it appears to buttress fears that the joint was unduly fragile.

✔ On each flight, the re-usable booster rocket segments "ballooned" about 0.02 inch and never recovered their original shape. NASA officials were not aware of this phenomenon until after the shuttle accident.

✔ Investigators no longer believe that the final breakup of the Challenger was caused when the nose cone of the booster crashed into the area that separated liquid hydrogen and liquid oxygen in the external fuel tank. Instead, evidence indicates that a breach of the bottom of the external tank 64.66 seconds into flight led to a structural failure, and the tank collapsed from the bottom up.

✔ Contrary to earlier belief, the shuttle never exploded. Instead, the mass of flame and smoke seen in the film of the last seconds of the Challenger came from a flash fire as liquid hydrogen and oxygen burned off in the atmosphere. The shuttle, one investigator said, "just fell apart."

Weather

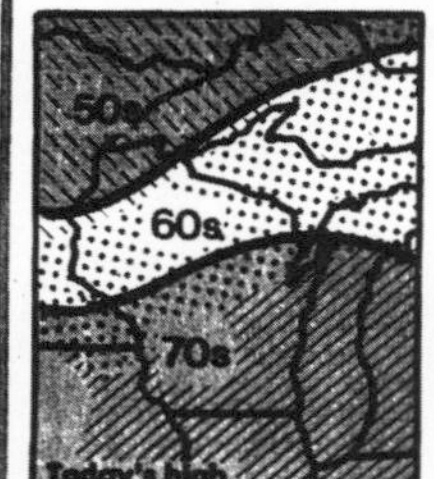
50s
60s
70s
Today's high
Showers
Storms
Snow
Rain

Source: Weather Central

Today: Scattered showers and thunderstorms ending, becoming partly cloudy and windy. **Tonight:** Partly cloudy, windy and cooler. Low near 40. **More on Page 9.**

B. La Follette dropping of lawsuit is questioned

By George Hesselberg
Of The State Journal

A Justice Department investigation and subsequent informal resolution of a deceptive-sales-practices complaint in 1983 was cited Tuesday as an example of a lobbyist's influence over Attorney General Bronson La Follette.

Steven Nicks, an assistant attorney general who once headed La Follette's Office of Consumer Protection, questioned whether a lunch meeting La Follette had with lobbyist James Boullion convinced La Follette to drop an already-approved lawsuit.

La Follette said Tuesday night the lawsuit was not an appropriate remedy to the complaints, that he does not recall having lunch with Boullion the day of the meetings, and that it wouldn't have mattered anyway.

The lawsuit, aimed at deceptive practices of a cemetery-vault sales operation in Madison represented by Boullion, had won La Follette's support for filing at a morning briefing, said Nicks.

La Follette then went to lunch with Boullion, Nicks said. Later that afternoon, at a meeting that included Boullion, La Follette ordered that the lawsuit not be filed.

Instead of the lawsuit, La Follette asked the Justice Department to accept a "voluntary assurance" from the cemetery firm. A voluntary assurance is a signed promise that the company will not engage in any further illegal practices.

The morning and afternoon meetings were in La Follette's office in "late April or early May" of 1983,

Turn to Page 2, Col. 1

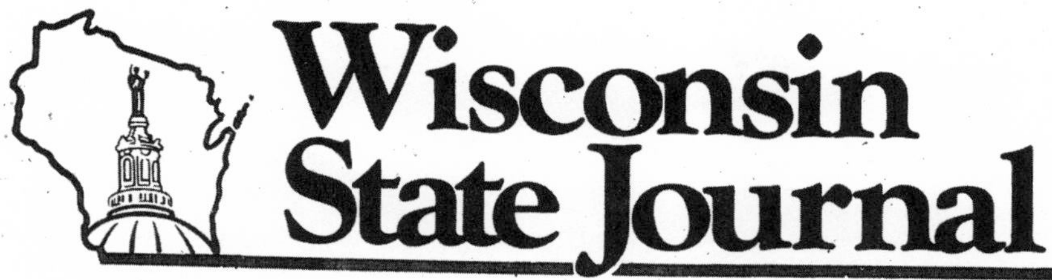

Wisconsin State Journal

Wednesday
November 5, 1986
Madison, Wisconsin
★★★ 35 cents

It'll be Gov. Thompson

Sen. Kasten is re-elected

By Paul A. Rix
Of The State Journal

Republican Robert Kasten, who spent $3 million defending his conservative record, overcame an early deficit to defeat Democrat Edward Garvey in Tuesday's nip-and-tuck U.S. Senate contest.

With returns pouring in from rural areas, Kasten staged an early morning rally to overtake Garvey, who refused to concede defeat at 1:15 a.m. Kasten won with 52 percent of the vote to 48 percent for Garvey. With 3,332 of 3,449 wards reporting, the vote was:

Robert Kasten	**727,322**
Edward Garvey	**680,574**

Both CBS and ABC television projected Kasten the winner before midnight.

"We have re-elected a Republican senator in Wisconsin for the first time since 1956," Kasten said in a 1:30 a.m. victory speech at the Orchard Inn in Menomonee Falls.

Pre-election polls showed Kasten running ahead of Garvey.

It was believed the candidates waged the most negative statewide campaign ever. Instead of explaining their differences on issues, they unleashed televised personal attacks, part of a national trend toward negative campaigning.

Kasten, 44, a conservative and a backer of President Reagan, narrowly defeated former Democratic Sen. Gaylord Nelson in 1980. He is considered close to the banking, insurance and business communities that contributed thousands of dollars to his campaign.

Dems king of the Hill
—Details, Pages 15-16

Kasten, a member of the Senate Appropriations Committee, voted for aid to the Nicaraguan Contras, chemical weapons and the Strategic Defense Initiative.

Kasten attended private school in Milwaukee, then Choate, the University of Arizona and Columbia University. He was elected to the state Senate in 1972 and the U.S. House in 1974 and again in 1976. Kasten is married.

Born and raised in Wisconsin, Garvey, 46, was graduated from the University of Wisconsin and its Law School. He practiced law in Minnesota, then was executive director of the National Football League Players Association in 1971-83. He was state deputy attorney general for two years.

Garvey, married and father of three daughters, had backing from organized labor, consumer groups and environmental activists.

Smear tactics and money dominated the campaign. Garvey accused Kasten of skirting debates and distorting his record as executive director of the players union.

In a state where the other U.S. senator, Democrat William Proxmire, spent almost nothing in his 1982 campaign, Kasten and Garvey will set spending records. The Federal Election Commission reported Kasten spent $3 million and Garvey $1 million by mid-October.

Senate

Robert Kasten

Governor

Tommy Thompson

Attorney general

Donald Hanaway

Congress

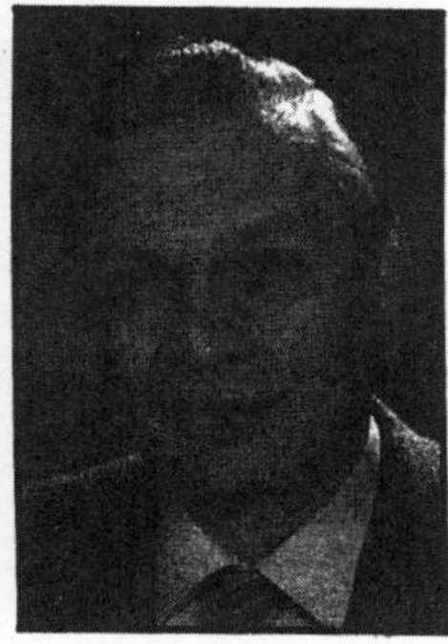

Robert Kastenmeier

By Doug Mell
State government reporter

Rep. Tommy Thompson will end his 20-year legislative career in early January by taking the oath of office for governor.

Thompson, the Assembly Republican minority leader from Elroy, beat Gov. Anthony Earl in Tuesday's election by a margin of 53 percent to 47 percent. With 3,332 of 3,449 wards reporting, the vote was:

Tommy Thompson	**773,458**
Anthony Earl	**683,172**

Thompson appeared before jubilant supporters at 1:05 a.m. today at the Concourse Hotel in downtown Madison to claim victory.

He gave a "thumbs up" signal to the crowd and held high the hands of the state's new lieutenant governor, state Sen. Scott McCallum, R-Fond du Lac.

"We have been very humbled and very gratified by the tremendous amount of support shown here tonight," Thompson said.

"We are looking for a better Wisconsin," Thompson said, "a Wisconsin that is going to be productive, going to be pro-jobs, pro-growth and pro-family."

He said he will work to get Wisconsin's spending under control.

He called Earl "a very fine individual" and said he still considers Earl a friend, despite the criticisms Thompson leveled at the Earl administration during the campaign.

Earl appeared 20 minutes later at Madison's Inn on the Park to congratulate Thompson.

"It's awfully important that we feel we left the state in better condition than we inherited it four years ago," Earl said, and urged supporters to continue fighting for progressive ideals.

Thompson will have to work with a state Senate and Assembly that have Democratic majorities. Thompson said he hoped leaders of both houses would unify with his administration to do what is best for Wisconsin.

Earl took an early lead but there were immediate indications he did not fare as hoped in places like Milwaukee County. Earl supporters wanted 60 percent of the vote out of the populous Milwaukee County but it appeared he wouldn't do that well.

Earl, 50, promoted his record in erasing the budget deficit and improving the economic conditions he inherited from Republican Gov. Lee Dreyfus.

Thompson, 44, based his campaign on criticism of what he called the overspending and excessive taxation policies of the Earl administration. Other criticisms focused on too-high welfare benefits and Earl's support of a 450-inmate prison in the Milwaukee area.

Thompson claimed that Earl made Wisconsin a "social laboratory" for trendy liberal programs like marital property reform pay-equity initiatives for female state employees.

Earl suffered from poor popularity among state residents for much of his term, a situation that baffled political observers.

There were indications as the race progressed, however, that Earl had lost some of his support from groups like organized labor and environmentalists because of the measures he took to improve opportunities for business people.

Earl was elected four years ago with 57 percent of the vote over Republican Terry Kohler.

Thompson, an attorney, has served in the Legislature for 20 years. His wife, Sue Ann, is a teacher in Elroy. They have three children.

Earl, an attorney, is a former Assembly majority leader, secretary of the Department of Administration and head of the Department of Natural Resources.

Also on the ballot were Kathryn Christensen, of the Labor-Farm Party, and two independents.

Hanaway boots La Follette out

By Susan Lampert Smith
Of The State Journal

State Sen. Donald Hanaway defeated the magic La Follette name in Tuesday's election, handing Attorney General Bronson La Follette his first defeat in six runs for that office.

With 2,715 of 3,449 wards (79 percent) reporting, the vote was:

Donald Hanaway	**610,728**
Bronson La Follette	**546,875**
Dennis Boyer	**24,781**

In traditionally Democratic Dane County, with 149 of 158 wards in, Republican Hanaway beat Democrat La Follette 56,210 votes to 48,796. Farm Labor candidate Boyer, 37, picked up 8,391 Dane County votes.

Speaking from his Green Bay campaign headquarters this morning, Hanaway, 52, said the campaign's "basic issue was clean government, integrity in government and public trust."

"There is a great amount of work that needs to be done in the attorney general's office and in the Department of Justice," Hanaway told his supporters. "I'm anxious to get to that work."

La Follette, 50, could not be reached for comment.

La Follette has been attorney general for 15 years. In previous elections he stomped opponents; this year he was hobbled by ethics questions.

Last month, the State Ethics Board fined La Follette $500 for having a Justice Department attorney do work for Superlog Ventures, Inc. a firm in which La Follette held stock. La Follette's ties to lobbyist James Boullion, another Superlog investor, were also questioned.

But La Follette is the grandson of Progressive pioneer Sen. "Fighting Bob" La Follette, and some observers predicted name recognition would help him overcome the bad publicity.

La Follette said he did nothing wrong and called the ethics board decision a vindication.

La Follette first won election as attorney general in 1964. He won four attorney general elections, but lost when he ran for governor against Warren Knowles in 1968.

Kastenmeier a winner

U.S. Rep. Robert Kastenmeier, a liberal Democrat whose House career has spanned parts of four decades, was re-elected with room to spare in southern Wisconsin's 2nd Congressional District.

Kastenmeier, a long-time member of the House Judiciary Committee and one of the most unreconstructed liberals in Congress, overcame Republican Ann Haney's edge in 10 outlying counties with a solid victory in populous Dane County. With 342 of 413 wards reporting, the vote was:

Robert Kastenmeier	**93,539**
Ann Haney	**71,926**

Haney, who served as state insurance commissioner and Regulation and Licensing Department secretary under former Gov. Lee Dreyfus, was a novice campaigner but was expected to give Kastenmeier a stiff test. Haney said Tuesday night she plans to run again in 1988.

"We thought this would be a reasonably close election," said Kastenmeier, who said his victory was a referendum on President Reagan's policies. ". . . This is part of a national trend."

Kastenmeier, 62, campaigned largely on his record, citing his accomplishments in areas of civil rights, court administration and privacy rights. Haney, 37, stressed her background in state government, business and farming, telling voters that she would put more emphasis on economic development.

Election digest

D. La Follette, Charles Smith win

Two Democratic incumbents were handily winning re-election to two constitutional offices in returns Tuesday.

Secretary of State Douglas La Follette was beating an old La Follette Progressive, former state Sen. Clifford "Tiny" Krueger, while State Treasurer Charles Smith was well ahead of his two opponents. **Details on Page 4.**

Battle set: Dems control Legislature

While Republicans were winning the major statewide offices, Democrats made slight gains on their majorities in the state Assembly and Senate.

No local legislators were defeated. Assembly Democrats knocked off at least two incumbents and will have as many as 54 of the 99 seats. In the Senate, Democrats apparently will have 20 of the 33 seats. **Details on Page 5.**

Some courthouse incumbents out

Several incumbent courthouse officeholders in area counties were swept out of office in Tuesday's general election. Changes came in Crawford, Richland, Rock, Jefferson, Dodge, and Vernon counties. **Details on Section 3, Page 13.**

New Dane Co. voter turnout record

Tuesday's general election proved an upset, too, for dour predictions of light voter turnout. Dane County Clerk Carol Little said it appeared Tuesday's countywide turnout would set a new record, topping the 51 percent figure set in 1982. In the city of Madison, an estimated 59 percent of eligible voters went to the polls. Statewide figures were not available.

Dems build edge in House of Representatives

— Details on Page 16

More governor's mansions turning to GOP

— Details on Page 17

State anti-abortion referendums failing

— Details on Page 17

McFarland wins Madison Council seat

— Details on Page 5

Weather/inside

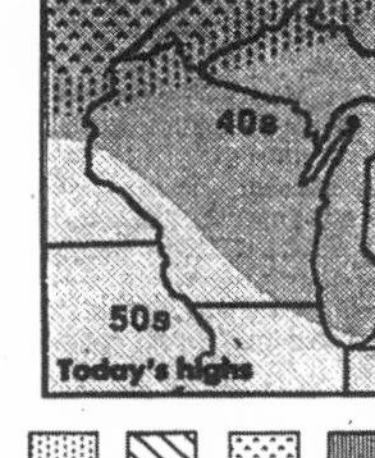

Rain Thunderstorms Snow Ice

Source: Weather Central

Today: Partly to mostly cloudy and a little warmer. High of 48 with east winds becoming south 7 to 15 mph. **Tonight:** Partly cloudy. Low near 33 with south winds turning to the west at 5 to 12 mph. **Details on Page 20.**

Freedom near?

Terry Waite, the Anglican go-between in the Lebanon hostage affair, said Tuesday there were "reasonably strong" expectations that the release of two more Americans might be imminent. **Details on Page 2.**

Hasenfus plea

Captured American mercenary Eugene Hasenfus said Tuesday he would ask the Nicaraguan government to show compassion if he is found guilty of terrorism and other crimes. **Details on Page 2.**

Football playoffs

Cambridge, Monroe, Milton and Wisconsin Dells were winners in the first round of the WIAA football playoffs. **Details in Sports.**

Iran reports expulsion of former Reagan aide

NICOSIA, Cyprus (AP) — The speaker of Iran's Majlis (Parliament) said Tuesday President Reagan sent an envoy to Tehran to try to improve U.S.-Iranian relations but he was arrested, confined for five days and expelled.

The official Islamic Republic News Agency quoted speaker Hashemi Rafsanjani as saying Robert McFarlane, former national security adviser, and four other Americans arrived aboard a plane carrying military equipment for Iran.

Rafsanjani's statement, in a speech marking the seventh anniversary of the takeover of the U.S. Embassy in Tehran, followed published reports in the Middle East that American hostage David Jacobsen was freed Sunday as a result of negotiations between Iran and the United States.

Rafsanjani did not mention any negotiations and the news agency did not say when the McFarlane visit occurred. But the Beirut magazine Al-Shiraa reported McFarlane went to Tehran in September.

Reagan, McFarlane and U.S. government officials had no comment.

Asked about the report that military equipment was involved, White House spokesman Larry Speakes reaffirmed a U.S. ban on weapons sales to that nation.

"As long as Iran advocates the use of terrorism, the U.S. embargo will continue," Speakes told reporters.

According to the IRNA report, Rafsanjani described the American mission to Tehran as a futile attempt by Washington to mend relations with the Islamic government of the Ayatollah Ruhollah Khomeini.

The United States broke diplomatic relations with Iran in 1979 when the U.S. Embassy was seized and Americans taken hostage.

Rafsanjani said McFarlane brought a Bible signed by Reagan and a cake that he described as "a key to open Iran-U.S. relations."

THE TRAGEDY AT CITY-COUNTY

Saturday, January 16, 1988, Madison, Wis., *** 35 cents, 50¢ outside Dane County

'I'm going to kill everybody'

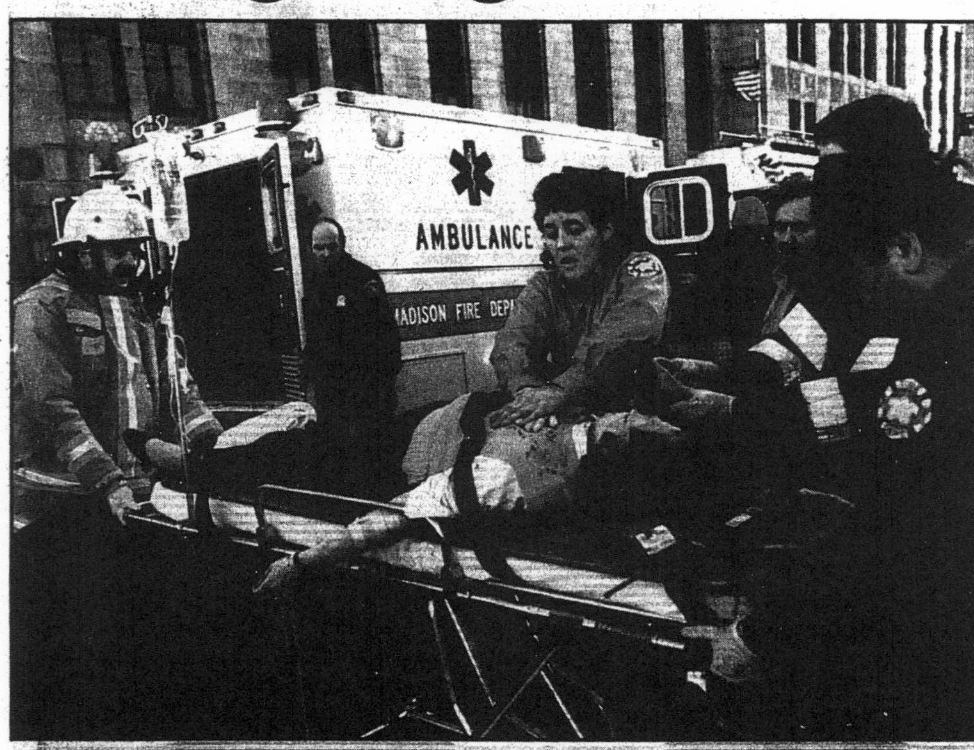

Paramedics fight to save the life of Eleanor Townsend, one of three victims of a gunman in the City-County Building.

—*State Journal photo by L. Roger Turner*

A troubled man, a gun, and 2 die

By Monte Hanson
Police reporter

Authorities and survivors today are trying to make sense of a murderous rampage that terrorized the City-County Building Friday, killing the Dane County coroner and a part-time secretary.

Answers, police hope, will come from Aaron J. Lindh, a 19-year-old Madison man who was shot down by a sheriff's deputy to end the midday violence that stunned Downtown Madison.

The gunman lurched through ground-floor offices and corridors about 12:45 p.m., shooting apparently at random, killing the two, wounding another man and scattering office workers and visitors.

Finally, Deputy Louis Molnar confronted Lindh in a hallway.

Molnar said he futilely tried to convince Lindh to surrender his weapon while the suspect yelled, "I'm going to kill you. I'm going to kill everybody, and I don't care if you kill me."

Molnar, who said he could not bring himself to kill the man, shot Lindh in the chest and stomach. Lindh was in stable condition in Meriter-Methodist Hospital Friday night following two hours of surgery for gunshot wounds.

Dead are Clyde "Bud" Chamberlain Jr., Dane County coroner and father of three, and Eleanor Townsend, a part-time secretary in the county corporation office and mother of two.

Another victim, Erik H. Erickson, 45, of McFarland, was in serious condition Friday night at Meriter-Madison General Hospital.

Erickson, personnel director for the state Department of Justice, was shot behind the left ear. A hospital spokesman said Erickson's prognosis was good and that there was no apparent brain damage.

"We don't think there was motive in this — that it was a random situation," said Madison Police Chief David Couper. "People do strange things sometimes."

Lindh was scheduled to stand trial Feb. 1 in Dane County Circuit Court on a charge of reckless use of a weapon. Police said they did not know whether Friday's shootings were related to the charge.

Authorities said they did not believe Lindh was stalking the three people who were shot. In all likelihood, police said, they happened to be in the line of fire when he began shooting.

Police said Lindh acted alone. There were erroneous early reports that a second suspect was being sought.

The suspect apparently walked into the building carrying a .22-caliber semi-automatic Ruger rifle concealed under his coat. The gun, which

Clyde Chamberlain

was sawed off on both ends, was about 2 feet long, police said. There were an estimated 40 rounds remaining in the gun when police recovered the weapon.

One witness reported seeing a nervous Lindh in the ground-floor coffee shop near the coroner's office shortly before the shootings.

He also was in the Madison Police Department detective bureau to ask about a burglary in which he was the victim.

From the detective bureau, Lindh walked up a hallway to the southeast corner of the building to the Dane County Sheriff's Department reception area. He allegedly entered the room and fired the gun an undetermined number of times.

Townsend, 40, of 4610 Judy Lane, was delivering paperwork from her office to the sheriff's department when she was shot twice in the back of the head. She died on the way to the hospital. Erickson was in the reception area to pay a parking ticket.

From there, the suspect headed northeast along a hallway in the direction of the Coroner's Office. Sheriff's Deputy John Cavanaugh, hearing the shooting and yells for help, peeked through a doorway along the corridor and saw Lindh half-running from one side of the hall to the other. Cavanaugh shot once at the suspect and missed.

Then the suspect ran into the coroner's office, where police said he made threats before shooting and killing Chamberlain. Police said Chamberlain, 62, of 2213 Lakeland Ave., was hit at least once at the front base of the neck.

When Lindh left the office, he was confronted by Molnar and Lt. John Van Dinter, also of the sheriff's department. Molnar, seeking cover in the nearby coffee shop doorway, tried to convince Lindh to put down his weapon. Van Dinter stood around the corner just north of the coffee shop. When Lindh refused to relinquish his gun and walked toward the officer, Molnar shot him twice.

Shooting suspect known as chronic troublemaker

By Joe Beck
Of The State Journal

Before Friday, Aaron Lindh, 19, seemed to be just one of countless troubled youths marked as chronic troublemakers — but hardly capable of murder.

Few people expect someone they know to be accused of a crime like the one in which Lindh is now a suspect. People who have known Lindh from childhood or more recently were stunned to learn of the bloody shootout in the City-County Building.

But there was one recent brush with the law in which Lindh was accused of showing a bad temper with a gun.

He is scheduled to be tried in Circuit Court Feb. 1 on a charge of reckless use of a weapon at his apartment at 113 E. Gorham St.

The criminal complaint says Lindh asked two guests to leave during a party Nov. 1.

One of the witnesses asked Lindh, "Can I at least finish my glass of water?" Lindh went to another room and emerged with a .22 cal. handgun that he pointed at the complainant's midsection, according to the criminal complaint.

Police officers responding to the call say they found a spent .22 caliber shell on a dresser in Lindh's bedroom and at least 15 more cartridges on the floor.

Lindh is the adopted child of John and Mary Lindh, 1209 Juniper St., on the East Side near East Washington Avenue and Highway 51.

He was the only black child in an all-white neighborhood of ranch-style homes. All members of his adoptive family, which includes four sisters and two brothers are white.

Former neighbors remember him as being much like other boys, playing baseball, basketball and football after school.

But one neighborhood woman recalled some troubling characteristics.

"He had quite a temper," she said. "He had to have things his way."

The obvious turmoil in his life began several years ago when, neighbors said, he broke into a neighbor's home to watch television, and later broke into the same home to steal money. Then he started a fire in his basement and was referred to a program for juvenile arsonists. The

Turn to Page 2, Col. 1

Aaron Lindh

'He had quite a temper. . . . He had to have things his way.'
Neighbor of Lindh

Deputy agonized before he fired

By George Hesselberg
Of The State Journal

"What the hell was that? Sounds like firecrackers," thought Lou Molnar as he poked his head out of a corner cubicle on the ground floor of the City-County Building.

It was about 12:45 p.m., Friday.

In the next three minutes, Molnar, a short, chunky, happy-go-lucky sheriff's deputy who "never had any trouble shooting at paper targets," would face a kill-or-be-killed decision.

And neither would happen.

In an interview at a Madison apartment Friday night with The Wisconsin State Journal, Molnar said he shot armed murder suspect Aaron J. Lindh only after numerous warnings to the suspect to "put the gun down."

The suspect begged the uniformed deputy Molnar to kill him.

Molnar said he was ready to shoot the suspect in the chest from 15 feet away, but "I thought, I can't kill this guy, so I lowered the aim to the stomach."

That decision probably saved the suspect's life.

Molnar said he was "busy shuffling papers and reading reports" Friday afternoon. His office is right across from the coroner's office.

"I heard what sounded like four firecrackers going off down the hall and I thought, what the hell was that," said Molnar.

"I took two steps into the hall and saw (deputy) John Cavanaugh. He said there was a guy with a gun who just shot somebody and he told me to watch out.

"I looked the other way down the hall and saw this big bullet hole in the wall, so I draw my gun and step out of the office and ease against the wall," he said.

As Molnar reached the intersection with the wide hallway that passes in front of the coroner's office, he saw Dr. Billy Bauman "come running out of the office."

"And I was looking down the barrel of a rifle," he said.

The rifle-holder, a black man wearing black-rimmed glasses and a three-quarter length tweed-type coat, was standing in the coroner's office when Molnar heard him say:

"I'm going to kill you. I'm going to kill everybody and I don't care if you kill me."

Molnar said he did not know that Coroner Bud Chamberlain lay dying on the floor.

Molnar kept his own gun aimed at the suspect and "then I realized I got no cover."

Molnar crept up to the wall adjacent to the coroner's office and, in sight of the suspect, told him, "Drop the gun, stay where you are. I am a police officer."

The suspect kept walking toward Molnar and responded, again, with: "I'm going to kill everybody, I'm going to kill you."

At this point, Dane County Sher-

Turn to Page 12, Col. 5

Tragedy at the City-County Building
A gunman's rampage leaves a deadly trail

Floor plan of the area of the City-County Building where the shootings took place
3. County Coroner Clyde 'Bud' Chamberlain slain
4. Deputy Molnar shoots gunman
Coroner's office
WILSON STREET ENTRANCE
Molnars' position
Coffee shop
2. Deputy Cavanaugh fires at gunman as he runs down the corridor. The shot misses
1. The gunman shoots and wounds Erickson, shoots and kills Townsend
The gunman was reportedly seen in the coffee shop and the police department area prior to the shootings
Police Department area
Sheriff's office
CARROLL STREET ENTRANCE

'It happened so fast, it was the longest three minutes of my life.'
Deputy Lou Molnar

Shots, screams; witnesses flee

By Marv Balousek and Joe Beck
Of The State Journal

Mail carrier Robert Haakenstad was eating lunch Friday afternoon at the ground-floor coffee shop in the City-County Building when a man came up to him and asked for a light.

"I reached for the lighter in my pocket, and he said, 'no, no, no,'" Haakenstad said. "He took my cigarette instead of the lighter."

Haakenstad said the man, about 5 feet 8 inches tall, slim and wearing an overcoat, seemed nervous as he paced up and down the hallway, then disappeared.

The man apparently went to a Sheriff's Department office and began a shooting spree that left two dead and one injured. The shootings terrorized county employees who work on the ground floor and routinely walk the hallway.

Donald Garczynski and Brent Markart, printing operators in the county Division of Printing and Services, were seated on red stools along the hallway counter, eating lunch.

"I heard three gunshots coming from up the hall," Markart said. "Then I heard a woman moaning and screaming. I saw this guy running fast into the coroner's office. Then I heard four more shots."

Garczynski also saw a man run into the coroner's office. "He was just like a blur, just scooting into the coroner's office," he said.

Jerry Olsen, an accountant in the county controller's office, was drinking a can of pop at the counter. The first shot did not startle him. "We didn't know if it was a door that slammed shut or something," he said. He said he heard a woman scream and shout, "Don't." He heard six shots in all.

Anthony Diederich, another controller's-office accountant, was sitting next to Olsen when the shooting began. "It sounded muffled," he said. "It didn't sound like what I thought a gun would sound like."

The shots sent people at the coffee-shop counter scrambling for cover. Markart hid behind a door leading to the garage. Garczynski ran to the printing office and locked the door. Haakenstad ducked into the mailroom. Olsen and several others ran to the emergency government office down the hall.

"We let everyone in, and then we

Turn to Page 12, Col. 1

TRAVEL
JAMAICA
For the beach bum, the choices are many
See 14E

SHOWCASE
A silver symphony
Orchestra turns 25
See 1H

LOOK
Turtle trouble
Zoologist strives to save state's turtles
See 1D

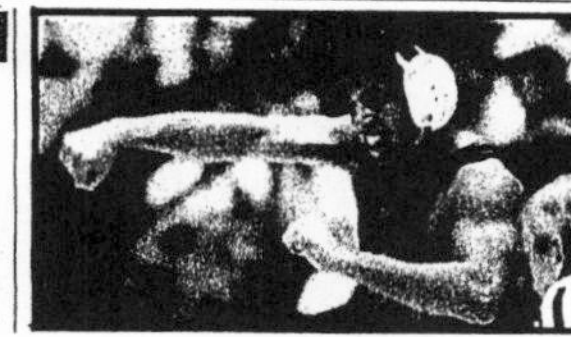

SPORTS
Mat mania
State coverage
See 1E, 10E

UW loses in overtime at hockey
See 1E

WISCONSIN

STATE JOURNAL

SUNDAY/FEBRUARY 24, 1991 MADISON, WISCONSIN *** $1.50

Allied firestorm begins

Bush: 'A final phase'

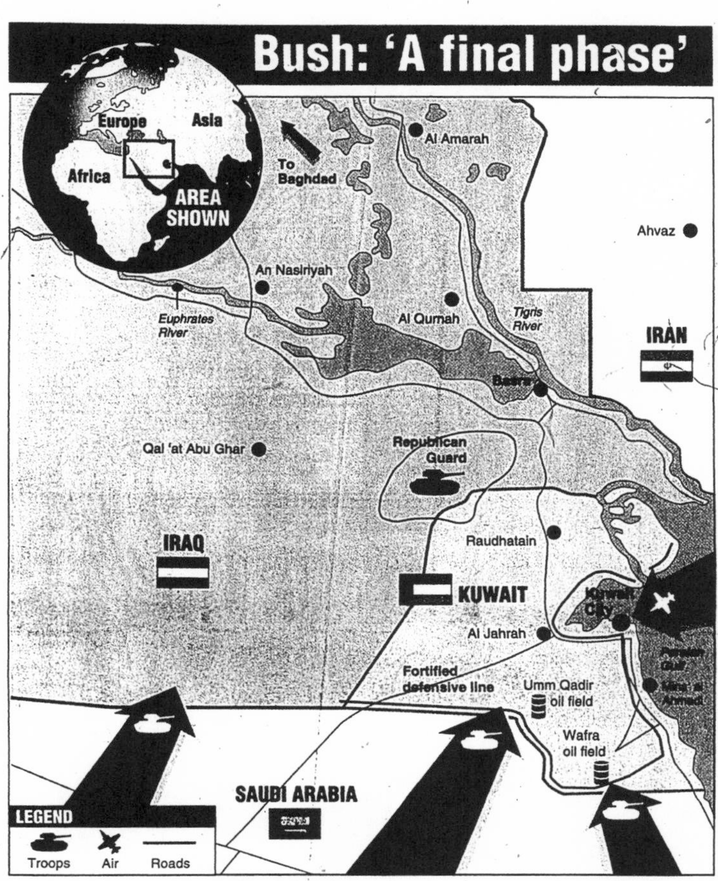

SOURCES: The Times Atlas of the World, The National Geographic Society,1991 World Almanac, Knight-Ridder Graphics Network, The Associated Press.

WSJ graphic/**KENNETH A. MILLER**

Troops march on Iraq, Kuwait

State Journal wire services

DHAHRAN, Saudi Arabia — A vast, multi-pronged land attack against Iraqi forces began two hours before dawn today after President Bush's deadline for the start of an Iraqi withdrawal from Kuwait slipped by with no sign in word or deed that President Saddam Hussein would comply.

Hundreds of tanks and tens of thousands of allied troops began racing into Iraq and Kuwait behind a deafening artillery and naval gunfire barrage shortly after 4 o'clock this morning, which was 7 p.m. Saturday, CST.

Field reports said that American columns, kicking up enormous clouds of dust as they dashed across the desert, quickly penetrated about six miles into enemy territory, with large numbers of Iraqi troops surrendering.

U.S. soldiers punched through two stretches of the border between Saudi Arabia and Kuwait, with one northward thrust near the town of Wafra and another eastward into the Umm Qadir oil field, a Kuwaiti government source said.

The troops had driven more than nine miles into Kuwait toward the oil field and eight miles toward Wafra shortly before 8 p.m. CST, he said. A Saudi military source confirmed the penetrations.

The Kuwaiti official also reported heavy helicopter activity over Kuwait City, which he thought was a landing by U.S. Marines from ships in the Persian Gulf, aimed at seizing and securing the national airport. Marine units controlled Faylakah Island, 20 miles offshore

Please turn to Troops, Page 2

Somber Bush tells nation his goal is 'right and just'

Knight-Ridder Newspapers

After 38 days of relentless air assaults against Iraq and two days of ill-fated diplomatic negotiations, President Bush Saturday ordered what is expected to be the largest ground attack since World War II.

"The liberation of Kuwait has now entered a final phase," Bush said in a brief televised address to the nation at 9 p.m. Saturday CST. The invasion "seeks to do that which is right and just."

Bush said he was confident that coalition forces would "swiftly and decisively accomplish their mission" despite an estimated half-million Iraqi troops dug into defensive positions and the potential of heavy American casualties.

White House spokesman Marlin Fitzwater said the president's "mood is somber, very serious. He understands the magnitude of this operation and the risks involved . . . He knows this is a very dangerous mission."

Fitzwater said the allies "have no way of knowing how long it will take or how much resistance we'll run into."

The land war started at 7 p.m. CST under the cover of darkness, eight hours after Iraqi President Saddam Hussein failed to meet a deadline to withdraw his occupying army.

In Iraq's first response to the ground war, that country's UN ambassador, Abdul-Amir al-Anbari, told reporters in New York: "Iraq will never surrender. A lot of Americans will die also."

Please turn to Bush, Page 2

Incinerator flap burns 3 counties

By Susan Lampert Smith
Regional reporter

MUSCODA — This week, the taxpayers of Iowa, Grant and Richland counties begin the task of paying back $17.25 million for a dream that went up in toxic smoke.

But the principal and interest costs of the failed Muscoda Waste to Energy incinerator project will be felt well beyond the borders of those counties. Because the counties haven't budgeted or haven't released the $517,000 that must be deposited by Thursday to make a payment on the bonds, money that was supposed to have come from incinerator profits, they automatically will trigger a loan from the State Trust Fund, tying up money that could be lent for other public works projects.

"I feel bad about it," said Steve Gauger, secretary to the state Board of Commissioners of Public Lands, which voted in 1987 to support the counties by guaranteeing the $8.3 million in bonds. "I'd

Please turn to Page 6A, Col. 1

INSIDE

TODAY'S FORECAST
Variable cloudiness. High 27. Continued mostly cloudy tonight. Low 10. Details/Back page.

State Journal photo/L. ROGER TURNER

J.W. Jung president John C. Jung scoops seeds from old storage drawers.

Springtime comes early to Randolph

Mail-order seed company prepares for the new season

By Steve Hopkins
Wisconsin State Journal

For a long time, beginning in the last century and extending to the middle of this century, there were more mail-order seed companies scattered about the country than you could poke a garden hoe at.

Business was good. Gardening for most Americans then was a nutritional and an economic necessity. There were no handy neighborhood garden centers. The seed catalog and the U.S. mail were vital links in the nation's food chain.

"Thirty years ago," the late E.B. White observed from his farm in Maine in 1960, "almost every house along this road was hooked up to a family cow . . . Most homeowners planted a garden, raised fruits and vegetables and berries, and put their harvest in jars against a long winter."

It was like that. We were a rural people, and that did not change much until after World War II. There were no chain supermarkets in the early part of the century, with long rows of canned foods and with well-stocked freezer aisles and fresh produce departments.

The seed catalog was a necessity, and its arrival was an eagerly anticipated event. With it would come the promise of good things to grow, and, perhaps more than that, an affirmation that there would be yet another spring.

With the arrival of the catalogs, the lamps in small town and farm parlors throughout the country would burn brightly far into the night. There were flower and vegetable varieties to choose from — marigolds and astors and zinnias and impatiens, sweet peppers and onions and snow peas and parsnips.

The order blanks would slowly and painstakingly be filled and put out for the mail carrier to pick up. There would be the long, agonizing wait for the packages to arrive.

Super highways, easy travel, the growth of shopping malls and urban garden centers and better economic times all signaled an end to reliance on the mails. But ordering by catalog was a tradition that, once established, did not easily fade.

There are fewer mail-order seed companies now than there were at mid-century. Increasing operational costs, the growth of urban garden centers and, in some cases, lack of heirs to carry on the family businesses all have taken their toll.

But the names of those that are left roll as easily from the tongue as the sweet spring sap from a Vermont sugar maple — George W.

Please turn to Page 11A, Col. 1

WISCONSIN  STATE JOURNAL

JULY 25, 1991 | MADISON, WISCONSIN | 50 CENTS

THURSDAY

State Journal photo/MEG THENO

Wild thing

Maybe it's the glossy finish or rich coat of color, but something about a shiny mustang can sure turn heads — not a Ford mustang but a Nevada mustang, wild and desert-dusted. Above, Jeff Morris of Springfield, Tenn., tries to halter one before it's loaded for travel from the Waukesha Expo Center. **Details in Look/1C.**

NATION

Hostage probe moves

House Democratic leaders are going ahead with an inquiry into whether the 1980 Reagan-Bush campaign conspired with Iran to delay release of American hostages, sources say. **Details/3A.**

WORLD

Croatia's killing fields

Nature has blessed the golden wheat land of eastern Croatia with a bumper crop this year. But in Yugoslavia's political crisis, men with guns roam the fields and the harvest is often death. **Details/7A.**

METRO

Blacks' rights violated

A federal office has found the civil rights of black UW-Madison students were violated by a visiting professor who gave the students poor grades in a foreign language class. **Details/1D.**

SPORTS

A linebacker's roots

What was boyhood in Fort Atkinson like for John Offerdahl, a Pro Bowl linebacker for the National Football League's Miami Dolphins? You might be surprised. **Details/1B.**

MONEY

Sauk gamble pays

A few years ago, Sauk City took a gamble and invested in an industrial park. Now it is paying off in hometown jobs and a larger tax base. **Details/8B.**

■ **Fair time:** The Rock County 4-H Fair, long one of the more popular fairs in the area, keeps growing. **Details/8B.**

QUOTE/UNQUOTE

'I think hunting is more important to Mr. Baker this weekend than talks about our economic situation.'

Davadorjin Ganbold

a key figure in Mongolia's attempted transition from socialism to democracy on Secretary of State James Baker's stop en route to the Moscow summit. **Details/10A**

INSIDE

TODAY'S FORECAST

Partly cloudy and comfortable. High 76. Mostly clear and cool tonight. Low 54. **Details/Back page.**

New planet? Or false alarm?

Boston Globe

British astronomers have discovered what they believe to be the first planet outside the solar system, an object with 10 times Earth's mass that is orbiting the burned-out remnant of an exploded star.

If confirmed, the discovery would be a milestone in astronomy — the long-sought proof that planets exist elsewhere — capping a flurry of similar reports in recent years that have either been disproved or remain unconfirmed. But some astronomers doubt the validity of this latest claim.

The planet the astronomers say they discovered is orbiting around the rapidly spinning collapsed core of a massive star about 30,000 light-years — nearly 200 billion billion miles — from Earth that exploded long ago in a cataclysm called a supernova.

The astronomers, Andrew Lyne, Matthew Bailes and Setnam Shemar of Nuffield Radio Astronomy Laboratories at England's University of Manchester, base their conclusions on variations in the pulses of radio waves from a pulsar, a collapsed star that emits regular bursts of energy.

The pulses of energy are normally more regular than the ticking of a clock, but the astronomers found that those from a pulsar called PSR1829-10 varied in length in a regular way, increasing gradually for six months, then decreasing for the next six. They concluded that the pulsar was being tugged back and forth by a planet orbiting it once every six months.

"We believe that this is the first detection of a planetary-sized body outside the solar system," the astronomers wrote in a paper published today in the journal Nature.

For years, the discovery of a planet around another star has been a kind of holy grail for astronomers, because finding even one such planet would dramatically increase the odds that planets are common in the universe and thus increase the odds that life exists elsewhere.

The discovery of a planet orbiting a pulsar would be unexpected and difficult to explain, because standard theories hold that pulsars form in colossal explosions and any planets that had orbited the original star would not have survived.

New world

British astronomers claim to have discovered the first known planet outside our solar system. The planet orbits a very dense, compact star called a neutron star.

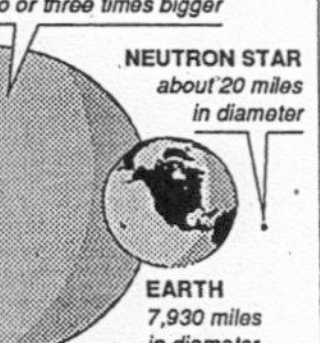

The neutron star and its planet are about 20,000-30,000 light years from Earth, in the direction of the center of our galaxy.

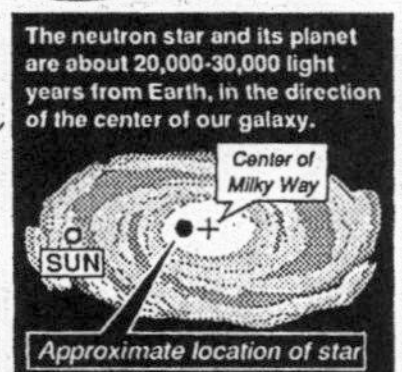

The planet orbits its star at about the distance that Venus is from our sun. Its orbit takes six months. The discovery was made by analyzing pulses of radio waves from the star. The pulses varied in speed as the orbiting planet pulled the star back and forth.

Neutron stars spin and emit pulses of electromagnetic energy.

Source: Nature, Discovering the Universe

AP/Karl Tate

Busy accident scene

State Journal photos/L. ROGER TURNER

Rescue workers from several communities scramble to treat five people injured in a two-car accident at Highway 12-18 and Highway AB at noon Wednesday. Melody L. Bryant, 16, of 1302 Droster Road, went through a stop sign on AB, and hit a car driven by Jeff Thomas, 31, of Cottage Grove, state police said. Thomas' 1989 Chevrolet rolled several times and landed upright in the ditch. Josh Barns, 13, riding in Bryant's car, was in fair condition at University Hospital Wednesday night.

Befriended, then killed

Victims were drugged, strangled, dismembered

By Lisa Holewa
Associated Press

MILWAUKEE — A man in whose apartment parts of 11 bodies were found told police he drugged and strangled the victims then dismembered them and boiled some of their skulls for keeping, authorities said Wednesday.

One victim was identified as a Chicago man, who family said disappeared this month after going to a downtown Milwaukee mall after leaving his job as an office cleaner.

In an affidavit submitted in Milwaukee County Circuit Court, Police Lt. David Kane wrote that Jeffrey L. Dahmer, 31, told police he met his victims at taverns or shopping malls and lured them to his apartment for photographs.

"Dahmer further stated that he would drug these individuals and usually strangle them and then he would dismember the bodies, often boiling the heads to remove flesh so he could retain the skulls," the affidavit said.

"Mr. Dahmer further stated that he took Polaroid photographs of a number of these persons while they were still alive, after he had killed them, and of their heads and body parts after he had dismembered them," it said.

Circuit Judge Frank Crivello accepted

Please turn to Page 2A, Col. 1

More on murders

Probation visits waived

By Kim Schneider
Wisconsin State Journal

Jeffrey Dahmer was just one of 121 convicted criminals on the caseload of Milwaukee probation agent Donna Chester.

Because the convicted sex offender had a steady job and apartment, Chester's supervisors allowed her to skip the monthly visits she was supposed to make to his home.

It wasn't until a handcuffed man flagged down police while fleeing a man who tried to kill him that officers learned what was inside Dahmer's apartment: the bodies of at least 11 people, chopped up into parts.

Milwaukee Police Chief Philip Arreola said the fact that a probation officer had never visited the home was a "damning indictment" of the judicial system.

Gov. Tommy Thompson also has asked corrections chief Patrick Fiedler to look into why Dahmer, 31, was free despite a 1989 conviction for molesting a 13-year-old Milwaukee boy, said Scott Jensen, Thompson's chief of staff.

While the Department of Corrections is reviewing the case, a spokesman said he isn't sure either the system or the probation officer are to blame.

"There was a lot of evidence he was doing all right," spokesman Joe Scislowicz said. "Most people who have a residence and a steady, good-paying job tend to stay out of trouble. This is such an exception."

Dahmer served 10 months in jail before he was released in March 1990 on five years probation. After his release, he returned to his job at the Ambrosia Chocolate Co., one he held for eight years. He has remained in the same apartment since his release. And he has been given a "considerable amount" of attention in the form of other conditions of his probation, which Scislowicz said were confidential.

Scislowicz said there is no way of knowing if home visits would have made a difference. "If he hadn't done it at home, would he have done it someplace else in some other way?" he asked.

Scislowicz said the Department of Corrections is not likely to point a finger at the agent, who was allowed by a supervisor to waive the home visits. Under regular policy, the agent would have visited Dahmer, considered to be on "maximum supervision," at least once a month. A waiver can be made for several reasons, including a heavy workload and the dangerousness of a neighborhood, something Scislowicz said could have been a factor.

Chester's caseload was 121 people, compared to the state average of 70, he said.

"It's difficult to be 100 percent with every client," he said. "You hit one of these every once in a while. The agents are always destroyed by it. These people are put out there and they're asked to make judgments. They do it day in, day out, week in, week out. By luck of the draw, if you want to call it luck, someone gets a case like this."

Shamir counters hard-liners' threats

JERUSALEM (AP) — Prime Minister Yitzhak Shamir, facing threats by right-wing allies Wednesday to quit his Cabinet, restated his refusal to negotiate with Palestinians from Jerusalem and his opposition to yielding territory to the Arabs.

But he insisted it was time to start negotiations and hinted government policy could change during talks. "Sometimes you arrive at something you did not intend," he said on Israel television.

Shamir said Israel should accept Syrian President Hafez Assad's offer to negotiate directly as a "challenge."

Yitzhak Shamir

His interview seemed intended to counter hard-liners' threats to quit his Cabinet if he accepts a U.S. plan for a one-time peace conference leading to direct negotiations with the Palestinians and Arab states.

PLO chief Yasser Arafat complained in a broadcast interview Wednesday that the U.S.-proposed talks ignored Palestinian rights: He said Washington had violated a promise to push for participation by Palestinians from Jerusalem.

"We are watching the American-Israeli designs which completely conceal the subject of Jerusalem and which abort completely the Palestinian people's national and political rights," Arafat said on Radio Monte Carlo, monitored in Cyprus.

Shamir took a hard line on what is sure to be the central issue of any future talks: land.

"You know my position. I don't believe in territorial compromise," he said.

"Our land is very small. ... Where in the world would you find people who are ready to give up the territory of ... their homeland? And I believe with all my heart and soul that we are connected forever with our homeland."

Right-wingers fear Secretary of State James Baker's efforts to start talks will lead Israel to cede the Golan Heights, West Bank and Gaza Strip, captured in the 1967 Middle East war.

An interviewer asked if Shamir believed the Golan Heights were an inseparable part of Israel. "You put it very well," he replied.

However, he seemed to indicate that things might change as negotiations progressed.

Shamir was jovial and expansive, claiming a triumph for Israeli diplomacy in finally getting the Arabs to accept direct negotiations, which the Jewish state has demanded for 43 years.

He said disagreement continued over Palestinian representation.

Israel expected the Palestinians to attend as part of a Jordanian delegation, he said, but sought assurances that no PLO members would attend. Israel views the Palestine Liberation Organization as a terrorist group.

Asked if he would accept Palestinians from Arab east Jerusalem, also captured in 1967 and annexed, Shamir replied: "Under no circumstances."

Palestinians demand a negotiator from east Jerusalem because they want east Jerusalem to be their capital.

He laughed off hard-liners' threats to topple his government, expressing confidence he could dissuade them from quiting.

Politicians and newspapers judged Shamir popular enough to override the opposition and skirt other issues menacing the talks.

WISCONSIN  STATE JOURNAL

★★★★

NOVEMBER 4, 1992 MADISON, WISCONSIN 50 CENTS

'Together we can do it'

Convention center building, borrowing OK'd

By Marv Balousek and Joel Broadway
Wisconsin State Journal

Voters in Madison early today appeared to have approved a referendum on construction of the Monona Terrace convention center.

The decision came only after a long evening of nail-biting for center supporters as results trickled into the city clerk's office.

Madison voters cast their ballots on a two-part referendum question. The first part asked whether the city should build the center at a cost not to exceed $63.5 million in 1992 dollars. The second part asked whether the city should borrow $12 million to help finance the cost.

More voters supported building the center than borrowing the money. With 68 of 70 wards reporting, the vote on building the center was:

Yes	49,807
No	43,825

On the borrowing question, the vote was:

Yes	45,677
No	43,192

Supporters who gathered to celebrate at the Concourse Hotel remained cautious about the outcome until well past midnight.

"I think everybody's feeling very optimistic right now," said Ken Opin, co-chairman of the It's Wright for Wisconsin Committee. "I'd really like to let loose and start celebrating."

Earlier, a glum Mayor Paul Soglin predicted the referendum could lose based on analysis of his own polling data. Later, he was pleased that he had been wrong.

" The people are willing to make sacrifices at a very difficult time ," he said, adding that the center will expand the city's economy and help develop resources to deal with problems like poverty and lack of child care.

A small group of center opponents kept up a vigil in the city clerk's office, poring over results as they trickled in.

The vote reversed a recent trend of losing referendums in the city. Last spring, voters approved a referendum on shoreline development that prevented Madison from building a swimming pool at Olin Park.

In 1989, 60 percent of Madison voters turned down a similar referendum to build a $46 million convention center at the same Law Park location.

That referendum was on the same ballot in which Mayor Paul Soglin won election over incumbent Joseph Sensenbrenner. At that time, Gov. Tommy Thompson endorse the proposed center but it was opposed by State Street merchants and others.

Unlike that convention center plan, the current proposal is based on a design by prairie-style architect Frank Lloyd Wright first conceived in the late 1930s. The design was revamped by Taliesin Associates, Wright's architectural firm. Wright died in 1959.

Because of the Wright design, proponents said the center could become a tourist attraction.

Opponents said the city should spend its money instead to prevent library branch closings and possible cuts in police services.

Associated Press

President-elect Gov. Bill Clinton gives final thumbs up after voting in Little Rock, Ark., Tuesday.

Clinton wins in all regions

By Art Dalglish
Cox News Service

Bill Clinton was elected the 42nd president of the United States on Tuesday, riding a wave of economic pain and anti-incumbent feeling that sent a legion of fresh faces to Washington.

Clinton told a euphoric throng in Little Rock, Ark., that his goal as president was to create "a new spirit of community" in which Americans would "be interested not just in getting, but in giving."

"Together we can do it," the president-elect said, repeating one of his favorite campaign phrases.

With some Western polls still open at 9:48 p.m. CST, all four television networks declared the Democratic ticket of Clinton and Sen. Al Gore of Tennessee the winners. Clinton was projected the winner in 31 states with 362 electoral votes, far more than the 270 needed for victory.

President Bush, the Republican

Please turn to Page 2A, Col. 1

State voters pick Clinton

State Journal staff

In a victory that the state's Democrats called "historic," Wisconsin voters approved a change of residence for Bill Clinton — from the Arkansas statehouse to the nation's White House.

Jon Sender, executive director of the state Democratic Party, said Clinton's campaign and resulting victory was like none he has seen.

"Bill Clinton connects with the voters," Sender said. "I've seen him dog-tired and he gets off a plane and he hits the ground and wades into a crowd and he's energized."

That special quality — a quality that Democrats who worked in the state compared to the campaigning skills of John F. Kennedy — won Clinton Wisconsin and the nation, Sender said. **See story/2A.**

WEDNESDAY

Our NBA preview

Larry Bird and Magic Johnson are retired, but Michael Jordan is still around and he has a chance to make history. He will be trying to lead the Chicago Bulls to a third straight National Basketball Association title. For our team-by-team preview of the season that begins Friday, see **Sports/1B, 3B.**

MONEY

Low income, high taxes

Net incomes declined for Wisconsin's farmers last year but their property taxes soared, two studies show. **Details/8B.**

■ **No boost:** The government's leading indicators show a pretty flat economy for the next year. **Details/8B.**

QUOTE/UNQUOTE

'Nobody would argue with his horsepower, but you could also bottle his ego and sell it to the insecure.'

Anonymous assistant U.S. attorney about federal prosecutor Thomas Scorza, who fights gangs in Chicago. **Details/14A.**

TODAY'S FORECAST

Cloudy, breezy and cold with a chance for flurries. High 34. Tonight: Continued cloudy and cold. Low 27. **Details/Back page.**

Feingold positively overwhelms Kasten

By Jeff Mayers
State government reporter

Riding a mood of change and a reserve of good will, Russ Feingold beat two-term Republican incumbent Bob Kasten in a landslide to cap an improbable five-year campaign that will give Wisconsin two Democratic U.S. senators for the first time since 1980.

Feingold, a progressive Middleton state senator who had little statewide identity six months ago, won a longshot primary and general election campaign to take back the Senate seat the conservative Kasten nabbed from Gaylord Nelson and Democrats in 1980.

And Feingold — who celebrated election night with wife Mary, their four children and hundreds of supporters at the Holiday Inn West in Middleton — did it with a positive grass roots campaign that recalled themes used so successfully by former Wisconsin Sen. William Proxmire.

"We have shown money is not the only thing in politics," said Feingold, outspent nearly 3-to-1 by Kasten — $3.75 million to $1.5 million, according to campaign estimates. "We have served notice on all politicians — it's time to clean up."

"Next stop, Washington," added Feingold, mimicking his "back of the hand" television ad campaign. "After we take a little time off."

Feingold also did it with Senate election margins not seen in Wisconsin since Proxmire — 70 percent of the vote in the Sept. 8 Democratic primary and possibly more than 55 percent of the vote in the general election. Herb Kohl, whom Feingold will join in the U.S. Senate, was elected with about 52 percent of the vote in 1988 after Proxmire retired.

With 3,219 of 3,589 wards reporting, the vote was:

Russ Feingold	1,153,032
Bob Kasten	991,456

Feingold apparently was swept to victory by a huge turnout that included many independent, young and minority voters who also went big for Democratic presidential nominee Bill Clinton but were undercounted in tighter pre-election polls, analysts said.

"I think everything broke well for both Clinton and Feingold in the final days," said Larry Longley, a Democratic activist and political science professor at Appleton's Lawrence University.

Ross Perot voters also likely

Please turn to Page 3A, Col. 1

State Journal photo/MEG THENO

Russ Feingold raises his hands in victory.

ELECTION '92

Klug easily re-elected to House

By Phil McDade
Wisconsin State Journal

U.S. Rep. Scott Klug achieved something that was rare Tuesday night — an easy Republican victory.

In an election when Republicans throughout Wisconsin lost or struggled, Klug won a convincing victory Tuesday over Democrat Ada Deer in the 2nd Congressional District race.

"Two years ago, a lot of people took a leap of faith with us," Klug said of his upset win in 1990 over longtime Democrat Rep. Robert Kastenmeier. "I think we've done a good job of spending time in the district and we have a moderate voting record."

Deer conceded the race at 10:30 p.m. after returns showed Klug running well in Madison and beating her badly in the rest of the district.

Klug credited his supporters for his victory.

"We had a number of people willing to work very hard for us throughout the district," he said. "It's really their triumph as much as mine."

With 337 of 384 wards reporting, the vote was:

Klug	163,699
Deer	96,881

"I am proud of the way I ran in this election," Deer said in her concession speech. "Our campaign was remarkable in many respects."

Klug had racked up some big margins in Madison suburbs, winning Waunakee by a 3-to-1 margin and Sun Prairie with 70 percent of the vote.

With his victory, the first-term incumbent solidified his hold on a seat long considered safely in the Democratic corner.

Klug ran well in the Democratic stronghold of Madison. He won several West Side wards and lost by only a few hundred votes in strong Democratic wards on the Isthmus.

Klug's win came despite a poor showing statewide by other Republicans. President Bush lost Wisconsin to Democrat Bill Clinton, and U.S. Sen. Robert Kasten lost by a wide margin to Democrat Russ Feingold, of Middleton.

But Klug said his victory was proof of his ability to attract voters willing to split their ballots between Democrats and Republicans.

"I think this area has changed in that it's much more moderate than people think it is," he said.

Deer came into the general election with momentum following an upset win over state Rep. David Clarenbach in the Democratic primary.

But Deer never capitalized on that victory, and ran an uneven campaign that featured mixed messages on why she should be elected to Congress.

WISCONSIN  STATE JOURNAL

FEBRUARY 27, 1993 MADISON, WISCONSIN ★★★ 50 CENTS

SATURDAY

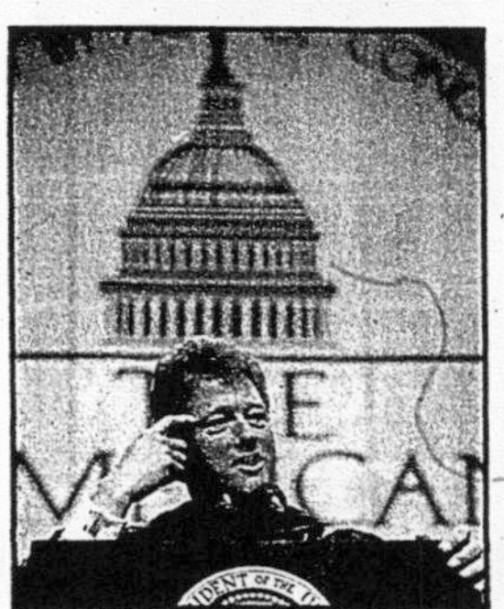

Associated Press

'And so I say to you in the face of all the pressures to do the reverse, we must compete, not retreat.'

President Clinton

telling U.S. allies in speech at American University in Washington, D.C., Friday the United States is getting its economic house in order and they should respond by opening markets. **Details/3A.**

SPORTS

UW, Gophers tie

Wisconsin lost a two-goal lead to post a 4-4 tie with Minnesota in the WCHA Friday night. Details/1D.

LOOK

Ellerbee's advice

Former newswoman Linda Ellerbee offered teachers her "personal, flexible rules for dealing with change" during her talk Friday in Madison. Rule No. 1: "If you believe with all your heart you are right, do it your way." Details/1C.

■ **Religious advice:** When Hollywood gets holy, the Rev. Gregory Coiro steps in. The Catholic friar has helped TV and movie producers get their facts straight on such projects as "Sister Act." Details/1C.

COMING SUNDAY

■ Don't miss the Wisconsin State Journal's Book of Business, the second part of this year's economic report, in Sunday's State Journal. This handy, 40-page section is full of vital information for your business or consumer decisions.

MONEY

Home sales stay hot

Sales of existing homes continue their torrid pace into 1993 in Wisconsin, even though sales slacked off a bit in Dane County. Details/8B.

■ **Boost:** Consumer spending helped push economic growth to the highest level in five years. Details/8B.

INDEX

TODAY'S FORECAST

Partly cloudy. High 28. Tonight: Becoming mostly clear. Low 6. **Details/Back page.**

Bigger the Powerball, harder the haul

By Mike Dorsher
Higher education reporter

Even though the estimated jackpot for tonight's Powerball lottery drawing is a record $42 million, bettors as a whole will get no more than a 64-cent return on their dollar, according to a UW-Madison math professor.

In fact, there's less than a 31 percent chance anyone will win the jackpot tonight, Professor David Griffeath said, even though more than 20 million tickets are expected to be sold. That's based on the theory of "binomial distributions," said Griffeath, who teaches statistics courses and specializes in probabilities.

The expected return on each bet is restrained by the possibility the jackpot will be split by two or more people with the winning number — and that becomes a significant possibility with 20 million tickets sold.

Normally, however, the Powerball jackpot hovers closer to $10 million and there are only a few million tickets sold for each drawing. Then the expected return on each $1 bet is less than 38 cents.

At that rate, it would be smarter for lottery players to bet on Supercash, Griffeath agreed. Even though Supercash's jackpot is set at $250,000 everyday, the chances of winning it are much better than the odds of winning the Powerball or Megabucks jackpots.

Supercash always has an expected return of 51.6 cents on a $1 bet. The expected return on Powerball isn't that high until the jackpot reaches about $20 million, and it isn't that high on Megabucks until its jackpot reaches $2.6 million.

When neither jackpot is that large, the scratch card games offer the best expected return, at 60 cents on the dollar. But most scratch games offer a top prize of $1,000 or less, so don't count on retiring with your winnings.

The only thing you can count on by playing the lottery, Griffeath said, is steadily reducing your wealth. He called it a "diabolical drain" that makes Las Vegas slot machines look like founts of philanthropy.

Having said that, Griffeath acknowledged the field of probability owes a debt to gambling, because it arose out of the elaborate games of chance engaged in by 17th century aristocrats. Even today, he uses gambling situations as examples and exercises in many classes he teaches.

So although Griffeath never plays the lottery — even when the jackpot reaches $42 million — "our field is tainted by its roots in this area," he said.

Profs stay put

By Mike Dorsher
Higher education reporter

Interim Chancellor David Ward declared victory Friday in the faculty retention war, saying UW-Madison has been able to keep 76 percent of the professors wooed by other universities.

UW-Madison suffered in the mid-1980s as star faculty left for higher-paying jobs, but "in the last three years the story is good," Ward told the Wisconsin State Journal editorial board.

Ward

Two things turned the tide, Ward said: UW-Madison's ability to match offers by reallocating funds within its budget and the bicoastal recession, which forced many other top universities to rein in their recruiting budgets.

Frankly, some of the faculty who left recently will not be missed, Ward said, while others had to leave due to personal circumstances. Less than 10 percent left because UW-Madison couldn't match their new salary, Ward said.

Moreover, Ward and former Chancellor Donna Shalala have had enough money to recruit some faculty stars of their own. Among them, Ward mentioned professors William Cronon in history, David Sorkin in Jewish studies, Morton Gernsbacher in psychology, Kerry VanDell in business and Deborah VanDell in education psychology.

As a result, UW-Madison's faculty remains among the top 10 in the nation among public universities and among the top 15 overall, Ward asserted, citing national surveys of administrators.

The reason UW-Madison isn't ranked that high by U.S. News & World Report or other popular surveys, Ward said, is that its students are not quite of the same caliber as its faculty. He said that's mostly because UW-Madison accepts a larger percentage of its home-state students than do top universities in more populous states, such as Michigan and Illinois.

Although UW-Madison turns aways students every year, it could still improve its student body by more aggressive recruiting of Wisconsin's top high school graduates, Ward acknowledged. It probably would behoove the university to attract more National Merit scholars and produce a Rhodes scholar or two, he said.

"Maybe we need the same attitude toward getting the best students that we have in getting the best faculty."

As for his own future, Ward said he will carry on with Shalala's energy and initiatives if he is selected to succeed her as UW-Madison chancellor. But Ward said he would be more detail-oriented and listen more if he beats out the crowd expected to apply for one of the nation's top jobs in higher education.

If Ward is not selected as the new chancellor this summer, he probably will move on within a year rather than revert to being provost, he said. Meanwhile, he has rejected applying to become chancellor of the Illinois-Urbana campus and his wife, Judith Ward, has withdrawn her application to become UW System vice president for university relations.

Judith Ward will remain a UW System associate vice president and even that will be reviewed, David Ward said, if he is selected to head the Madison campus.

Trade center bombed

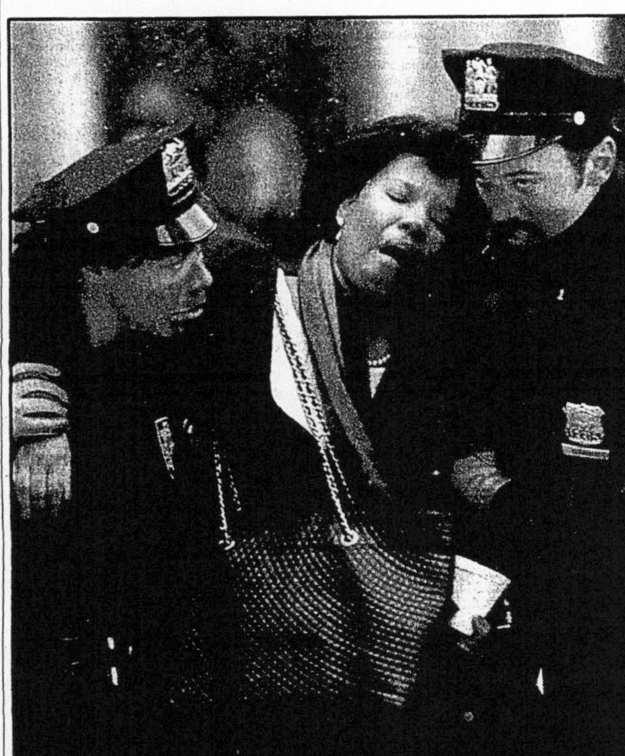

Two New York City police officers help an injured woman away from the scene near the World Trade Center in New York Friday after an underground explosion rocked the twin 110-story buildings.

At least five dead, 600 hurt in New York

By Tom Hays
Associated Press

NEW YORK — An explosion apparently caused by a car bomb in an underground garage rocked the 110-story World Trade Center on Friday, killing at least five people, injuring 600 and forcing thousands to flee down dark, smoke-filled stairs.

A pregnant woman was plucked off the roof of one of the two towers by a helicopter. About 200 kindergartners and elementary school children were stranded for hours on the observation deck. Other people were trapped in elevators, or in rubble in the garage and a train station beneath it.

SPECIAL REPORT

Hundreds poured out of the towers into the streets of lower Manhattan, gasping, their faces black with soot, after groping their way from as high as the 105th floor. Others on upper floors stayed put to await help, and broke windows as the smoke reached them.

Eight disabled people were trapped for nine hours on the 94th floor before they were taken to the roof and removed by helicopter, the last people out of the building, the Port Authority said. In all, 23 people were rescued from the towers by helicopter.

The towers, the world's second-largest buildings, shuddered with the noontime explosion. Thick black smoke billowed in minutes to the top of both buildings, where some 130,000 people work or visit each day.

The blast created a 200-foot-by-100-foot crater six stories deep in the parking garage, witnesses said.

A terrorist task force of federal and city investigators believed that a car bomb caused the blast, James Fox, an assistant director of the FBI who heads its New York office, told The New York Times. He said no bomb fragments had been found.

After the blast, authorities received at least nine telephone calls claiming responsibility, said Jack Killorin, spokesman for the Bureau of Alcohol, Tobacco and Firearms in Washington.

Asked whether a bomb was used, he said, "There was nothing that we saw

Please turn to Page 2A, Col. 3

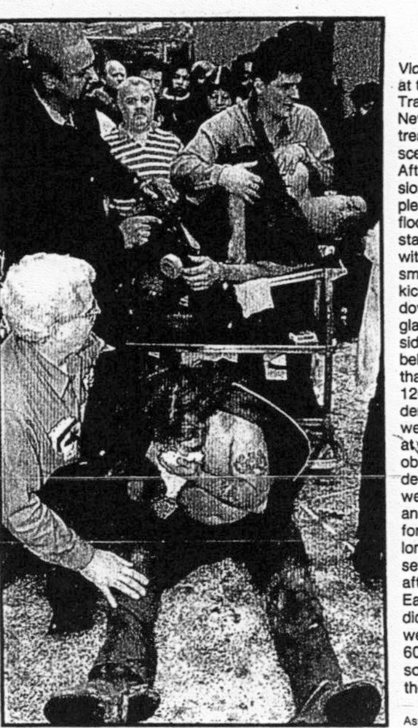

Victims of a fire at the World Trade Center in New York are treated at the scene Friday. After the explosion, many people on upper floors fled down stairwells filled with thick, black smoke. Others kicked out windows, sending glass to the sidewalks below. More than 200 pupils, 120 of them kindergartners, were stranded at the center's observation deck. They were given milk and snacks before making the long walk down several hours after the blast. Early reports indicated there were at least 600 injuries associated with the blast.

Associated Press photos

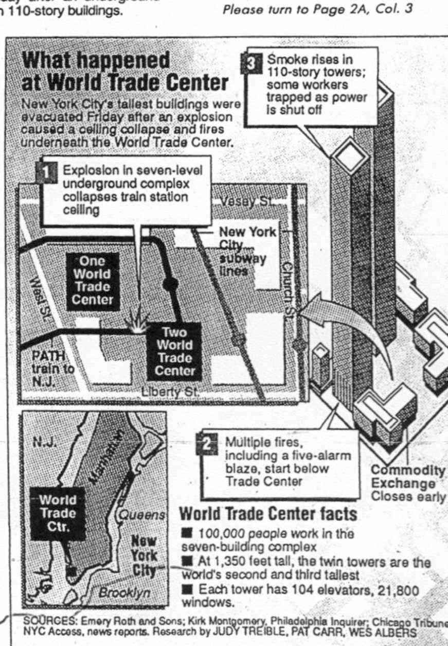

Knight-Ridder Tribune / JEFF DIONISE, RON CODDINGTON

WISCONSIN  STATE JOURNAL

APRIL 20, 1993 MADISON, WISCONSIN 50 CENTS

'It was his final lie'

Koresh had vowed children would be safe

By Rachel Boehm and Lee Hancock
Dallas Morning News

WACO, Texas — Moments before David Koresh gave orders to set fire to the Branch Davidian compound, he told his followers that the children would be safe, the FBI said Monday.

Koresh said the children were tucked away in a buried bus that served as the group's bunker. The FBI said authorities spotted the bodies of some of the children inside that bunker late in the day.

But after the blaze devastated the wooden compound, authorities discovered that Koresh once again had lied: The children, authorities believe, died inside the living quarters on the second floor of the compound.

"It was his final lie," FBI Special Agent Bob Ricks said in an afternoon briefing that detailed the fiery devastation that Koresh ordered. He was believed to have died, along with 85 members of his cult, including 24 children.

Throughout the 51-day standoff, Koresh went back on his word more than once. He repeatedly had promised authorities and even his attorneys that suicide wasn't "in the cards." At one point early in the standoff, he promised to surrender if his taped sermon was aired.

But beneath the broken promises, there always was the prophecy of violence.

"From the very beginning, he said that the people in there were going to be killed, and they were going to do it with an armed conflict with law enforcement," Ricks said Monday. "It was to our benefit that we were able to prevent the second part of his prophecy from being realized, and that's to take as many law enforcement people as possible."

No law enforcement officials suffered serious injuries in Monday's confrontation and, despite early sporadic fire from within the compound, federal agents didn't return fire, according to Ricks.

"We had concerns early on with regard to possible suicide," he said.

He said FBI negotiators asked the cult leader on at least four separate instances to promise that he would not lead a mass suicide, and he gave his word.

When his attorneys also pressed the issue, Ricks said, "He promised them that suicide was never in the cards."

That's what authorities believe he did Monday. Federal officials said two cult members set fire to the compound. The orders came shortly after tear gas began to enter the cinder-block bunker where Koresh was holed up with his "leadership."

Koresh's assurances Monday that the children were safe and his promises that he wouldn't lead a mass suicide were not the only times the self-professed prophet broke his word.

Last Wednesday, Koresh sent out word that he would surrender after he finished a manuscript in which he would reveal the contents of the seven seals in the Book of Revelation in the Bible. His attorney, Dick DeGuerin of Houston, said that when it came time to surrender, Koresh, in fact, would be the first to walk out.

Flames engulf the Branch Davidian compound Monday. The tower in the center of the photo appears to be the observation deck shown in the graphic below.

Associated Press

Events leading up to cult compound fire

Federal officials said cult members set fire to their compound at Waco, Texas, Monday, after FBI agents rammed buildings with armored vehicles and spread tear gas within them in an effort to end the 51-day standoff.

Cultists' fate uncertain
Cult leader David Koresh and 95 followers, reportedly including 24 children, were in the building; some cultists may have escaped

Underground bunker
Observation deck
David Koresh's living quarters
Gymnasium
M728 Combat Engineer Vehicle (modified M60 tank)
Main entrance
Bradley Fighting Vehicles

Within two hours: Compound destroyed

How tear gas was injected
Tip of battering ram released tear gas after breaking through structure
M728

How events unfolded

1. **Shortly before 5 a.m.:** Federal agents warn cultists to surrender or be gassed
2. **Shortly after 5 a.m.:** Agents tear holes in building, using a combat engineering vehicle equipped with a battering ram; the vehicle disperses tear gas through holes
3. **Throughout morning:** Incursions continue around all the buildings
4. **Shortly after noon:** Cult members reportedly set fire to compound in two places; wind spreads flames quickly

SOURCE: News reports, research by PAT CARR

Knight-Ridder Tribune/RON CODDINGTON and JEFF DIONISE

TUESDAY FOCUS: SIEGE ENDS IN INFERNO

24 children believed to be among dead

By Deborah Tedford and Kathy Fair
Houston Chronicle

WACO, Texas — The children of David Koresh's doomsday cult were so prepared for the final battle between good and evil that when bullets rained down on their commune seven weeks ago they believed it was a prophecy fulfilled.

But that was only the beginning. The end came Monday in fire.

It is estimated that twenty-four children died in the blaze. Where they were in the compound and whether they died of smoke inhalation, burns or other causes remain unanswered questions. One 16-year-old girl is known to have survived, and was taken to a Dallas hospital. (See story, 3A.)

Authorities speculated that some members and children might have taken poison, but that could not be confirmed.

For weeks, Koresh had maintained that 17 children lived in the compound. But authorities said the actual count was 24 because cult leader David Koresh considered those over age 10 to be adults. The youngest child presumed dead was believed to be a 1-year-old girl.

Early in the 51-day siege, 21 children were released from the compound, and Monday they were being shielded from news reports of the tragedy, according to an official with the state's Child Protective Services office.

Joyce Sparks, who heads the Child Protective Services abuse investigations unit, said the agency believes that the children were put in danger by their parents during the gun battle with federal agents Feb. 28.

"It doesn't appear that the parents made any particular effort to protect," Sparks said. "They weren't taken to one place to keep them out of the line of fire. They were all over.

"Basically, the children reported seeing bullets come through. They talked about seeing the bullet holes and seeing people who were hit."

Recent interviews with state caseworkers revealed that the cult children viewed the war atmosphere of that raid as almost normal.

"Some (of the children) said, 'Well, that's what we

Please turn to Page 2A, Col. 1

TUESDAY

Dinomania

Dinosaurs are showcased on the cover of the latest Time magazine, moviemakers are rushing to finish their dinosaur flicks and there's a glut of dinosaur food, books, toys and fashions on the market.

And dinomaniacs want more.

Here it is today: News about a new dinosaur coming soon to the UW-Madison Geology Museum, on 1D; a dinosaur quiz, jokes, food, software, quilt and more on 1C and 3C; and a letter to the editor, column and David Letterman Top 10 list all about preschoolers' favorite dinosaur, Barney, all on 7A.

MONEY

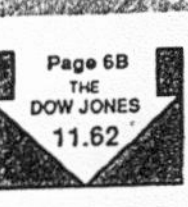

Beer's back: Huber has begun bottling and canning beer, but the returnable bottle line is still closed. **Details/8B.**

INDEX

40s
Superior
30s
La Crosse
Green Bay
MADISON
Milwaukee
40s

TODAY'S FORECAST
Occasional rain, possibly mixed with snow. High 41. Tonight: Rain ending. Low 29. **Details/Back page.**

S.D. governor dies in crash

8 die in air tragedy in Iowa

DUBUQUE, Iowa (AP) — A plane carrying South Dakota Gov. George Mickelson and seven other people crashed in eastern Iowa after reporting engine failure Monday. There were no survivors.

Jackson County Sheriff Bob Lyons said "everyone on board is dead."

Mickelson's body wasn't immediately identified. However, Dick Vohs, an aide to Iowa Gov. Terry Branstad, said the airplane's passenger list included Mickelson. Janelle Toman, press secretary for Mickelson, confirmed Mickelson was on the plane.

Rose Marie Ambrosy, who owns the farm where the plane crashed, said no bystanders on the ground were hurt.

Mickelson, 52, a Republican, was serving his second term. He was elected governor in 1986 and won another four-year term in 1990. He also served six years in the South Dakota House, where he was speaker in 1979-80.

The plane was returning to South Dakota from Cincinnati when it crashed after reporting engine trouble.

The twin-engine turboprop had been headed for an emergency landing at the Dubuque airport when it struck a barn and silo about 15 miles southwest of Dubuque at about 4 p.m., said Sandra Campbell, a spokeswoman at the Federal Aviation Administration regional office at Kansas City, Mo.

The Mitsubishi turboprop plane is registered to the Department of Transportation of the state of South Dakota.

"The pilot reported a lost engine and lost pressurization. The aircraft then was handed off to the Dubuque tower for clearance to land. It was the nearest location," Campbell said.

Heavy rain was reported in the area at the time, but the FAA said it had not determined if it was a factor in the crash.

Investigators from the National Transportation Safety Board were en route to the crash site.

Mickelson's death means Lt. Gov. Walter Dale Miller takes over the governor's office.

"What a tragedy. We lost the heart out of South Dakota," said the Democratic leader of the South Dakota Senate, Roger McKellips.

The other victims were Roger Hainje, director of the Sioux Falls Development Foundation; state Economic Development Commissioner Roland Dolly; state Energy Policy Commissioner Ron Reed; Sioux Falls banker Dave Birkeland; Angus Anson of Northern States Power Co. in Sioux Falls; and two pilots from Pierre, S.D., Ron Becker and Dave Hansen.

Former South Dakota Gov. Bill Janklow said he knew all those aboard the plane.

George Mickelson

"Angus Anson worked for me. Dave Hansen was my security chief, and Ron Becker was my pilot. He taught me how to fly," Janklow said. "Everyone of these people was a leader."

Gov. Tommy Thompson, who was a friend of Mickelson's, was saddened by the news.

"We're really going to miss him," Thompson said. "He was such a great guy and such a good governor." Thompson praised Mickelson for being a national leader on health care and rural issues.

Mickelson, the son of former Gov. George T. Mickelson, followed his father's political footsteps and was elected South Dakota's governor in 1986. His father was governor from 1947 to 1951.

Mickelson is survived by his wife, Linda, and three children.

State Journal reporter Joel Broadway contributed to this report.

Chicago parents get probation

2 girls left alone could return home in 'couple of months'

By Jim Paul
Associated Press

GENEVA, Ill. — The couple accused of leaving their two young children alone at home while they went on a vacation to Mexico agreed to plead guilty Monday to contributing to the neglect of a child.

David and Sharon Schoo's daughters, now in state-supervised foster care, could be back in their parents' custody within "a couple of months," defense attorney Gerard Kepple said after a hearing in Kane County Circuit Court.

Nicole, 10, and Diana, 4, will visit their parents within a week and make overnight and weekend visits before being permanently returned home, he said.

Under the plea agreement, the Schoos will each be sentenced to two years of probation and will perform 200 hours of community service, Assistant State's Attorney John Barsanti said.

The couple thus avoided being tried on 64 counts, including neglect of children, endangering the life of a child, aggravated battery, abandonment, cruelty to children and unlawful possession of marijuana.

Barsanti said the Schoos' activities will be limited and they will be monitored electronically at home. They will be free to go to work, counseling or their community service work.

Authorities said the couple left their daughters alone while they spent nine days on vacation. The parents were arrested Dec. 29 at O'Hare International Airport as they returned from Acapulco.

Prosecutors said the Schoos also left the girls home alone during a previous four-day trip.

In announcing the indictments in February, Kane County State's Attorney David Akemann said the mistreatment of the children went beyond being left in the house alone without an adult.

He said one girl had been locked repeatedly in a room and another in a crawl space for seven hours, and that the Schoos beat both children with a belt and pulled their hair. One girl was scratched on the chest and abdomen, and kicked in the ribs, he said.

Authorities learned the children were alone after they ran to a neighbor's house for help when a smoke alarm was accidentally triggered in their split-level home in St. Charles, a western suburb of Chicago.

The children have been in foster care and their parents have not been allowed to see them.

David Schoo, 45, was an engineer with a smoke-alarm manufacturing company, which will not confirm whether he still works there. Sharon Schoo, 35, is a homemaker.

MONEY

at HOME *in* MILTON BURDICK CO.

1E

TRAVEL

ALOHA HAWAII

Kauai is island's essence

1H

DAYBREAK

The MEADOW

A HALLOWEEN STORY

1G

SPORTS

BADGERS 13-10!

Ohio State next See 1D

WISCONSIN  STATE JOURNAL

SUNDAY/OCTOBER 31, 1993 MADISON, WISCONSIN ★★★ $1.50

'You couldn't breathe'

Crowd surge injures scores at stadium

By Nathan Seppa
Wisconsin State Journal

At least 68 people were injured at Camp Randall Stadium on Saturday, eight seriously, when fans rushed the field at the end of a University of Wisconsin football game — pinning dozens against an iron railing at the base of the stands and trampling others.

A total of 16 people, including two in critical condition and four others also in intensive care, remained in hospitals late Saturday night with various neurological and orthopedic injuries, according to hospital reports.

All 11 of those admitted to University Hospital were women. St. Mary's Hospital and Meriter-Park Hospital refused to identify patients who were admitted.

One injured student was Sari Weinstein, a UW-Madison psychology senior from Minnetonka, Minn., who had been pulseless and not breathing but was alert when she was admitted to Meriter-Park Hospital. She was listed in serious condition Saturday night.

Five of the patients in intensive care were at University Hospital, and one at Meriter-Park.

The last seconds of Wisconsin's 13-10 win over Michigan had just ticked away when an estimated 12,000 elated fans in the student section rose up and swooped down the stands, seemingly in unison.

But the cascade stopped abruptly at the three-foot-high railing, crushing people in the front row. Uniformed security police tried to hold the crowd back.

They failed, and backed off. The force of the crowd broke the railing from its concrete moorings along a 40-yard stretch around the corner of the north end zone, sending people sprawling onto the frigid asphalt track.

Those who couldn't scramble free were either pressed against parts of the railing that was still standing, got trampled or were pinned against another

Please turn to Page 2A, Col. 1

■ Police reaction/2A
■ Joe Panos saves lives/3A
■ 20 years of unruly behavior/4A
■ Editorial/11A

State Journal photos/MEG THENO

Fans in front of the student section pile up in the aftermath of UW's victory over Michigan. At one point people, according to one eyewitness, were "piled 10 feet high."

'I was watching my friends being crushed'

State Journal staff

With two minutes left in the game, Scott Noland and three of his friends were preparing to storm the field to celebrate the Badger victory.

But as the game ended, the crowd in sections O and P started pushing harder and harder. When the fence gave way, Noland, 24, jumped over the twisted metal, turned around and started picking a fence post off the buried crowd.

Noland said he passed over the less seriously injured — those with bruises or broken bones — and kept digging to see if the people underneath were all right.

That's when he found Sari Weinstein, lying on the cement steps. She wasn't breathing.

"She had turned completely blue and lifeless," Noland said from Meriter Hospital-Park, where Weinstein was in serious condition Saturday night.

Noland said he and an unidentified UW-Madison football player immobilized Weinstein as best they could and lifted her onto a bleacher. They started giving her mouth-to-mouth resuscitation (not CPR) and Weinstein responded with short, irregular breaths, Noland said.

Noland's story is one of many to come out of the

Please turn to Page 3A, Col. 1

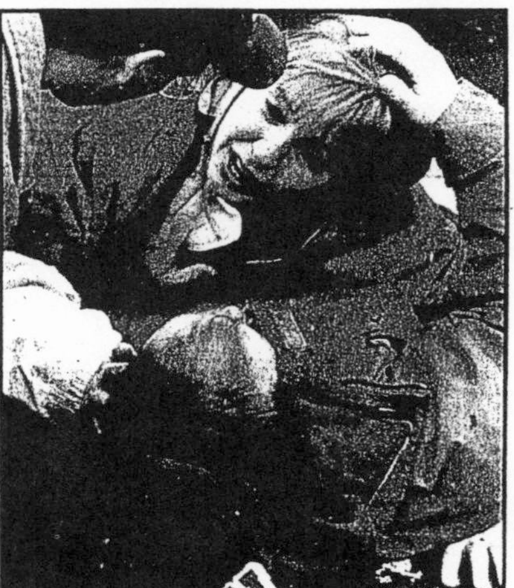

A crush of fans following Saturday's Badger football game sent more than 60 people to area hospitals. Here, the field becomes a makeshift medical center as a woman tries to comfort one of the victims.

UW-Madison officials search for answers

By Mike Dorsher
Higher education reporter

UW-Madison Chancellor David Ward hopes students will be so horrified by the injuries and pandemonium at Saturday's football game that they will never again try to surge onto the field.

Ward hopes that because there were no immediate answers to what could have been done to prevent the dozens of inadvertent injuries — or how to avert a repeat tragedy this Saturday when the Badgers host Ohio State in an even bigger game.

"Any event like this is so unprecedented that it almost provides protection for the next game," Ward said after a news conference at the University Police station.

He rejected any notion that the surge meant UW-Madison students cannot control themselves. "Events of that nature don't seem to have any reflection on the character of an institution," the chancellor said.

Ward began the news conference by saying the university will launch a two-phase investigation into the post-game eruption. The first phase will be a short-term review and plan for handling the crowd at this week's Ohio State game. The second phase will be a long-term "thorough investigation" of what went wrong, he said.

Much of what officials do next will be determined by their review of TV and videotapes that captured the crowd surge and security reaction, said University Police Chief Susan Riseling.

"I'm not sure there's a plan for the surge we saw today, but that's what we have to try to figure out," she said.

Asked if there was a chance the Ohio State game would be canceled, Ward said, "I think that's unlikely." The only reason the game might be canceled is out of "respect for the casualties," he said. "That would be the variable rather than whether we could provide safety."

But safety is the utmost consideration, he added. "The game is not the most important thing."

Athletic Director Pat Richter said he was confident that some "reasonable solutions" could be found in time for this Saturday's game. Meanwhile, he said university counselors will meet with the football team to talk about the terrible epilogue to their wonderful performance.

About a dozen Badger players were still on the field when the students surged into the north end zone. Some of them pulled fans from the crush and helped care for the injured.

Richter, who has seen dozens of games at Camp Randall Stadium since leading the Badgers to the

Please turn to Page 4A, Col. 5

Superior 35/22
Wausau 35/21
Eau Claire 36/22
Green Bay 37/25
La Crosse 37/22
Madison 38/23
Milwaukee 38/27

Madison Forecast:
Today: Partly cloudy and cold. High 38.
Tonight: Partly cloudy and continued cold. Low 23.
Details/back page

Knight-Ridder Tribune/ANITA JONES

Clinton trying to clear lanes of 'information superhighway'

By Carol Jouzaitis
Chicago Tribune

WASHINGTON — Inside the White House, presidential image-makers and spin doctors are busily preparing for the coming revolution in information technology.

No longer content with handing out paper copies of news releases and speeches to reporters, President Clinton's media team distributes thousands of White House materials electronically to the public through computer networks.

Want to know how Clinton intends to reform the health care system? Call up a copy of his proposals on your home computer. Interested in Vice President Al Gore's ideas for reinventing the federal government? Find them listed on a computerized bulletin board. Looking for a complete, unedited version of what Press Secretary Dee Dee Myers said about Haiti today? Get it on your personal computer.

"Information is power," Jonathon Gill, who runs the electronic distribution project in the Clinton media affairs office, said. "We want this information readily available to all."

It isn't surprising that the Clinton White House is the first to go

Please turn to Page 8A, Col. 1

ROSE BOWL SPECIAL section inside!

TRAVEL — QUEBEC BY RAIL 6B

OUTLOOK

Comparing health care proposals 1B

DAYBREAK

WHO MADE A DIFFERENCE 1F

HOME — NEW BUNGALOWS

1I

SPORTS — BOWL WRAP-UP
Florida, 41-7
Florida St., 18-16
1D

WISCONSIN STATE JOURNAL

SUNDAY/JANUARY 2, 1994 MADISON, WISCONSIN ★★★ $1.50

BUCKY ROLLS IN ROSES!

Bruins see red as Badgers win, 21-16

By Vic Feuerherd
Assistant sports editor

PASADENA, Calif. — The Rose Bowl may never be the same again. It's certain that University of Wisconsin football will never be the same again.

The Badgers won their first Rose Bowl Saturday, holding on to defeat UCLA, 21-16. It was only the fourth time the Badgers had made the trip to Pasadena.

UW fans overwhelmed this game, so affectionately known as the "Granddaddy of Them All," with Badger red and white consuming some 60,000 to 70,000 of the seats filled by the crowd of 101,237.

"I told them this was like a home field advantage with the crowd," UW coach Barry Alvarez said afterward. "This win also was for the great fans of Wisconsin."

"It was almost like playing in Camp Randall, except the ground was a little softer," senior offensive tackle and co-captain Joe Panos said following the victory. "They really helped us."

The Badgers helped themselves, as well, forcing six turnovers, an interception and a Rose Bowl record five fumble recoveries, that contributed to two of their three touchdowns against the Bruins.

Tailback Brent Moss was named the game's most valuable player after scoring twice on runs of three yards and one yard and gaining 158 yards on 36 carries. Moss, who led the Big Ten Conference in rushing this season, went over the 100-yard mark for the 12th straight time.

UW quarterback Darrell Bevell scored the final touchdown on a 21-yard run with 10 minutes, 52 seconds remaining.

It proved to be the decisive score because UCLA would score once more to bring it to 21-16, and then march 47 yards in the final 1:43 without any timeouts before Badgers defensive tackle Mike Thompson's game-ending tackle at the UW 15-yard line.

"This gives our program a lot of credibility," Alvarez said.

State Journal photo/SCOTT SEID

Badgers Tarek Saleh (42), Kenny Gales (3) Chad Cascadden, with helmet raised, and Jason Levine (53) celebrate the Rose Bowl victory.

Fans do celebration right

By Susan Lampert Smith
Wisconsin State Journal

PASADENA, Calif. — A new kind of smog licked at those mansions atop the San Gabriel mountains Saturday. It was a little spicy, a little greasy and carried with it the smell of a thousand brats grilling.

Maniac Badgers fans turned Arroyo Boulevard into Breese Terrace Saturday. They tailgated, they drank beer, they painted big Ws on their naked chests.

And inside, the Rose Bowl looked

Please turn to Page 8A, Col. 1

Winnebagos divvy up casino profits

Gaming cited for reducing welfare cases

By Ron Seely
Wisconsin State Journal

For Wisconsin's Winnebago tribe, the jingling bells of the slot machines at the tribe's Ho-Chunk Casino near Wisconsin Dells heralded a bountiful Christmas this year.

Checks of $1,200 were mailed to each of the tribe's 4,700 members in the last couple of weeks. The money came from $5.6 million in gambling profits the tribe's business council voted to set aside for payments to each enrolled tribal member.

The checks could not have come at a better time, said tribal member Lance Talmadge.

"It was a welcome surprise," said Talmadge. "It made for a little more of a joyous season. Our kids are no different than any other kids. They look forward to Christmas. Many parents were able to better provide for their families."

With the payments, the Winnebagos become one of the first of Wisconsin's tribes to distribute profits from gambling directly to tribal members. Other tribes, such as the Oneidas, have voted against the per capita payments, choosing instead to use all of the gambling income to improve social programs and other tribal services on the reservations.

The Winnebagos are doing this, too, according to Tribal Chairwoman JoAnn Jones. But the tribe's business council voted this fall to share some of the bounty directly. According to a plan filed with the federal Bureau of Indian Affairs, the Winnebagos have allocated 46 percent of their gambling profits to the promotion of tribal economic development, 22 percent to the operation of tribal programs, and 30.5 percent to general tribal welfare. The rest goes to charitable donations and to pay for local government services.

Jones said direct payments come from the money set aside for general tribal welfare; money from the same pot goes toward scholarships and tribal education programs including Head Start. Direct payments to tribal members can be made up to four times a year, Jones said.

In a survey by the Wisconsin State Journal last year, the Winnebagos reported gambling profits of $18 million in 1992. The tribe's gaming operations were the second most profitable among Wisconsin's tribes; the Oneidas reported profits of $37 million in 1992.

But the Winnebago gambling profits are expected to increase dramatically this year with the opening of the tribe's expanded casino just south of Wisconsin Dells. The tribe spent $20 million on an expansion of its existing casino; the operation now boasts 86,000 square feet, 1,200 slot machines, 48 blackjack tables, and 925 employees. Tribal officials estimate the casino will bring in $150 million in revenue and $30 million in profits during its first year of operation.

The casino's parking lot has been jammed since its opening in October. The success of the casino this fall and during the early weeks of winter have made for a far different season from recent years when the old casino was the site of vio-

Please turn to Page 2A, Col. 1

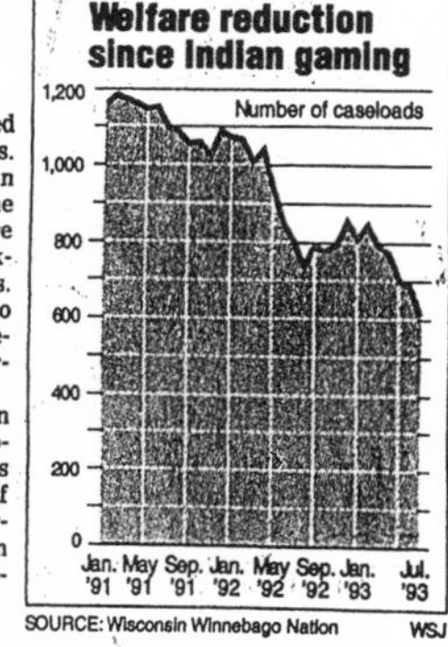

SOURCE: Wisconsin Winnebago Nation WSJ

INSIDE

Superior 5/-9
Wausau 12/3
Eau Claire 18/4
Green Bay 15/9
La Crosse 19/10
Madison 19/11
Milwaukee 24/17
Chicago 26/17

Madison Forecast:
Today: Cloudy with a chance of snow. High 19. **Tonight:** Cloudy with snow continuing. Low 11.
Details/back page

Fixing a broken welfare system

Clinton team seeks answers

By Anthony Flint
Boston Globe

WASHINGTON — It is perhaps the ultimate domestic policy puzzle, an emotionally charged quagmire that has defied a half-dozen presidents: the task of fixing the flawed U.S. welfare system without abandoning the vulnerable and poor.

Mary Jo Bane and David Ellwood, two former Harvard professors recruited by President Clinton to be the chief architects of his attempt at reform, are finding out just how precarious a balancing act it really is.

Charged with fulfilling Clinton's campaign promise to "end welfare as we know it," Bane and Ellwood must confront liberals opposed to tough measures such as limiting benefits to two years.

But they also face conservatives and moderate Democrats who worry they won't be tough enough — that in the process of tearing down one safety net, they may build a new one: costly new entitlement programs such as day care so single mothers can work; child support guarantees and other incentives to keep families together; education and job training programs; subsidies for private employers who hire welfare recipients; and new public-sector jobs.

So it is that Ellwood, 39, and Bane, 51, former collaborators at Harvard's Kennedy School of Government, have had to look beyond their own liberal instincts, developed over years in academia as two of the nation's top poverty experts. There will be radical change, they vow.

"Work, family, responsibility," Ellwood said in an interview with Bane, repeating the moderate mantra for changing the underlying attitude about welfare. Transform that, he said, and the sprawling bureaucracy will be brought to heel.

"We're trying to change fundamentally the culture of what goes on here," said Ellwood, a labor economist whose 1988 book "Poor Support: Poverty in the American Family" inspired Clinton on the campaign trail. "From the day you walk into that welfare office, we should be focusing on what it is going to take to focus on getting a job so you can support your family.

"Right now, it's geared toward paperwork and writing checks," he said. "We should be in the business of helping people help themselves, not in the welfare business."

Bane, a former Brookline, Mass.,

Please turn to Page 6A, Col. 1

- Key issue ignored/1B

WISCONSIN  STATE JOURNAL

THURSDAY/APRIL 20, 1995 MADISON, WISCONSIN *** 50 CENTS

Terror in the heartland

Blast shakes America to its roots; search seeks 'evil cowards'

By Judy Gibbs
Associated Press

OKLAHOMA CITY — A car bomb ripped deep into America's heartland Wednesday, killing at least 31 people and leaving 200 missing in a blast that gouged a nine-story hole in a federal office building.

The dead included at least 12 youngsters, some of whom had just been dropped off by their parents at a day-care center.

There was no immediate claim of responsibility for the attack, the deadliest U.S. bombing in 75 years.

At least 200 people were injured — 58 critically, according to Fire Chief Gary Marrs — and scores were feared trapped in the rubble of the Alfred Murrah Federal Building more than nine hours after the bombing.

Two people were pulled from the rubble Wednesday night but died a short time later, said Assistant Fire Chief Jon Hansen.

Hansen said a woman who was trapped in the basement said there were two others down there. She didn't know if they were dead or alive.

The death toll was certain to rise.

"Our firefighters are having to crawl over corpses in areas to get to people that are still alive," Hansen said.

Attorney General Janet Reno refused to comment on who might have been behind the attack. President Clinton called the bombers "evil cowards," and Reno said the government would seek the death penalty against them.

The bomb was believed to be in a mini-van with Texas plates, owned by National Rental Car, said Oklahoma City Police Sgt. Kim Hughes. An axle of the vehicle was found about two blocks from the scene, said a police source who requested anonymity.

Their clothes torn off, victims covered in glass and plaster emerged bloodied and crying from the building, which looked as if a giant bite had been taken out of it.

Cables and other debris dangled from the floors like tangled streamers in a scene that brought to mind the car bombings at the U.S. Embassy and Marine barracks in Beirut in 1983.

"I dove under that table," said Brian Espe, a state veterinarian who was giving a slide presentation on the fifth floor. "When I came out, I could see daylight if I looked north and daylight if I looked west."

Mayor Ron Norick said the blast, which left a crater 30 feet long and 8 feet deep, was caused by a car bomb. He said the car had been outside.

"Obviously, no amateur did this," Gov. Frank Keating said. "Whoever did this was an animal."

Police Sgt. Bill Martin said at least 26 people were killed, 12 of them children.

Earlier in the day, paramedic Heather Taylor said 17 children were dead at the scene, a figure later disputed by police. Dr. Carl Spengler, one of the first doctors at the scene, said the children, all at the day-care center, ranged in age from 1 to 7, and some were burned beyond recognition.

The search continued after nightfall, with about 100 Oklahoma Army National Guard soldiers activated to help with rescue and security operations in the downtown area.

The explosion, similar to the terrorist car bombing that killed six people and injured 1,000 at New York's World Trade Center in 1993, occurred just after 9 a.m., when most of the more than 500 federal employees were in their offices.

The blast could be felt 30 miles away. Black smoke streamed across the skyline, and glass, bricks and other debris

Please see EXPLOSION, Page 2A

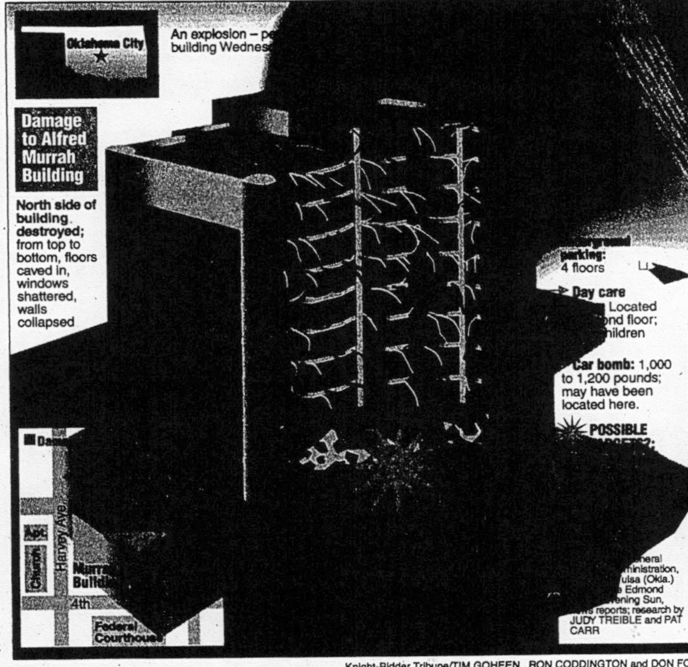

Knight-Ridder Tribune/TIM GOHEEN, RON CODDINGTON and DON FOLEY

Associated Press photos

An Oklahoma City firefighter carries a child injured in an explosion Wednesday at the Alfred Murrah Federal Building in Oklahoma City.

SPECIAL REPORT

'I couldn't go back in the nursery; there were no children alive'

By Max Baker and Roland Martin
Fort Worth Star-Telegram

OKLAHOMA CITY — Billy Baay's white sweatshirt and white pants were splattered with dried blood as he choked back tears and talked haltingly of his day of horror.

A former construction worker, now employed at a pizza parlor, Baay rushed to the Alfred Murrah Federal Building Wednesday morning to help search the crumbling debris for survivors and victims of a terrorist bomb.

What he found was that children, some of them babies, had borne the brunt of the explosion.

"We pulled six babies out and took them to a makeshift morgue at the Methodist church," Baay said. "I couldn't go back in the nursery; there were no children alive."

The blast occurred at the start of the work day as parents were dropping off their youngsters at the day-care center on the second floor of the building, just above the spot where a car bomb exploded.

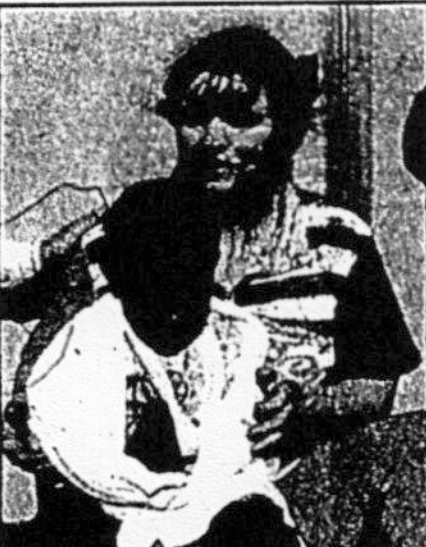

An unidentified injured woman holds an injured child following the explosion.

Toys and games were scattered amid broken glass and other debris on the street.

Frantic parents searched for their missing children.

One woman who survived the blast stood outside the building and screamed for her child. Rescuers ushered her away just before they brought out a victim they believed to be her dead son.

"At the time it blew up, the place should have been full," said Dr. Carl Spengler, one of the first doctors at the scene.

Ken McAffrey, 43, a paramedic in Vietnam, said he had never seen such destruction.

"There was nothing you could do for any of them when they came out," said McAffrey, describing several children and a woman pulled from the building.

In the chaos, no one was certain the exact number of children in the center, but of up to 40 estimated to be there, only two were known to be alive late Wednesday — one in surgery and one in intensive care. The dead ranged in age from 1 to 7, and some were

Please see CHILDREN, Page 2A

INSIDE

Magician won't be bound by Madison

Story in Daybreak/1C

Bucks playoff hopes alive

Story in Sports/1E

State residents support death penalty

Story in Local/1B

INDEX

Madison Forecast: **Today:** Cloudy, a chance of showers High 54. **Tonight:** Showers continuing Low 39.
Details/back page

Menards eyes East Side site

Eau Claire-based Menards is negotiating the purchase of an 11-acre site north of East Towne and east of Kohl's Department Store on which to build a home repair and furnishings store.

The new Madison store would be one of the larger ones in the Menards chain, a company spokesman said, and would provide 150 to 200 full- and part-time jobs.

Ray Zeier of 2211 N. Stoughton Road, who owns the land, said, "We haven't closed yet (on the purchase) but we're well beyond an option to purchase."

Marv Prochaska, vice president for real estate in Menards' general office, said, "We haven't bought the land yet, but we have a purchase contract."

The new store would offer basically the same products as the other stores here but would total about 150,000 square feet.

The far West Side store is 53,000 square feet and the one in Monona is 100,000 square feet, Prochaska said.

Prochaska said Menards hopes to start construction in Madison this fall and have the store ready to open next summer.

He declined to estimate the cost of the store.

Menards has 105 stores in nine Midwestern states.

The company has stores at 8115 Mineral Point Road and 6401 Copps Ave. in Monona. It also has stores in Janesville, Milwaukee, Oshkosh, Appleton and Green Bay.

A second Appleton store and ones in Fond du Lac and Plover are under construction.

— Roger Gribble

How much kick in your beer?

Court rules breweries may list alcohol content

By Richard Carelli
Associated Press

WASHINGTON — How much alcohol is in that bottle of beer? Breweries won the right to put alcohol content on their beer labels Wednesday when the Supreme Court said it was a matter of free speech — and none of the government's business.

The ruling was a sobering blow to longstanding government efforts to keep beer-makers from bragging about the strength of their brews.

The unanimous decision was a victory for the Coors Brewing Co., which challenged the law in 1987. Coors said there was no evidence to support the government's fears that the disclosure of alcohol content would set off beer strength wars.

The court rejected a Clinton administration attempt to reinstate a 1935 law that banned alcohol-content labels except where state law required such a listing.

Justice Clarence Thomas, writing for the court, said the government's interest in "combatting strength wars" is valid. But he called the post-Prohibition law an irrational effort to thwart such wars and promote sobriety among beer drinkers.

> 'If a consumer wants to know how much (alcohol) he's getting he can call me up I'll give him the exact number.'
>
> **Hans Kestler**
> **brew master,**
> **Joseph Huber Brewing Co.**

The unanimous ruling means brewers now are free to put such information on labels in the 40 states where there has been no requirement to do so.

The 10 states that require alcohol-content labels are Arkansas, California, Colorado, Kansas, Massachusetts, Minnesota, Missouri, Montana, Oklahoma and Oregon.

Hans Kestler, vice president of brewing and brew master of the Joseph Huber Brewing Co. in Monroe, Wis., whose beers include Huber and Berghoff, said he thinks beer makers should have the right to decide if they want to disclose their alcohol content. "If you want to put it on, you put it on. If you don't, you don't," said Kestler.

He said companies have different reasons for wanting to disclose alcohol content.

"The trend is to put it on Coors because they are low in content and others want to put it on because they are higher," he said.

He said that although Huber executives have not decided if they will begin labeling, alcohol content is public information.

"We have beers as low as 2.8 and above 5 (percent alcohol). If a consumer wants to know how much he's getting, he can call me up I'll give him the exact number," Kestler said. "We don't hide anything."

Coors succeeded in its challenge of the federal law that banned the alcohol-content information from labels but not from advertisements.

In a concurring opinion, Justice John Paul Stevens criticized the law as "nothing more than an attempt to blindfold the public."

State Journal reporter Lee Hawkins contributed to this story.

■ Other Supreme Court decisions/7A

© 1995 Wisconsin State Journal

WISCONSIN  STATE JOURNAL

WEDNESDAY/OCTOBER 4, 1995 MADISON, WISCONSIN 50 CENTS

Beyond the verdict

Blacks, whites understood the trial in different ways

By Donna St. George and Vanessa Gallman
Knight-Ridder Newspapers

WASHINGTON — If O.J. Simpson's acquittal by a mostly black jury delivered one message loud and clear, it may have been that blacks and whites in America inhabit different worlds.

That much was evident in St. Louis, where law professor Leland Ware, who is black, watched the dramatic finale to the Simpson trial Tuesday in a faculty office filled with white colleagues. "They were expressionless, they were numb," Ware said. "But black people I know were smiling."

At historically black Howard University, in Washington, black students erupted with cheers when the verdict — acquitting Simpson of the murders of ex-wife Nicole Brown Simpson and her friend Ronald Goldman — was announced. They hugged each other, jumped up and down and punched their fists into the air.

Many whites and blacks clearly understood the Simpson trial in different ways.

"The blacks brought to the case a set of experiences that made them very skeptical of the police to begin with," said Ware, who studies race relations. "Once that Fuhrman thing came up, I think that was the end of it, quite frankly."

But from the white point of view, says Frederick Lynch, a professor at Claremont McKenna College, in Claremont, Calif., the

Please see **VERDICT,** Page 4A

Associated Press

O.J. Simpson, center, walks into his Brentwood, Calif., estate with his friend Al Cowlings, left, and an unidentified man after he was acquitted of the double-murder of his ex-wife Nicole Brown and Ronald Goldman in Los Angeles Tuesday.

INSIDE

World Dairy Expo starts today

Story in Money/8B

American League, National League divisional playoffs under way

Story in Sports/1B

Assembly relaxes restrictive gun laws

Madison's handgun ban would be thrown out

By Mike Flaherty
Legislative reporter

The Wisconsin Assembly Tuesday voted to end Madison's 25-year-old ban on handguns — and every ban like it around the state.

Over angry objections from urban lawmakers, state representatives overwhelmingly passed a bill that would replace all the state's local gun ordinances with a statewide gun law that is relatively relaxed.

Under state law, felons and the mentally ill are forbidden from owning guns, but there are few other restrictions.

By contrast, it has been illegal in Madison for the last quarter century to buy a gun. As of this year, it is also illegal to own an assault rifle, a handgun with a barrel shorter than 4 inches and several types of exploding ammunition.

The reason the bill (AB69) is needed, explained Rep. Steve Freese, R-Dodgeville, is that there are 1,920 communities in Wisconsin and each one has a different gun law.

For hunters or target shooters who travel around the state to pursue their sport, the community ordinances are a nightmare of complexity, he said.

Some community laws, such as Madison's, are extraordinarily strict, too, added Rep. Sheryl Albers, R-Loganville.

"Madison can fine you $1,500 for a gun with a magazine that can hold more than 15 rounds — including a bolt-action .22 (caliber rifle)," she said. "If the ordinances hadn't been so strict in the first place, this bill wouldn't have been needed."

But urban legislators were outraged.

"This bill has nothing to do with the right to bear arms or the winning of the Revolutionary War," said Rep. Antonio Riley, D-Milwaukee, a member whose father was shot to death in Chicago when Riley was a boy. Local governments face different problems with guns and have to be free to respond, he said.

"This bill is a disgrace," said Jim O'Keefe, a lobbyist and spokesman for the city of Madison. "This bill imposes the same gun standards in Madison and Milwaukee as it does on Eastman," he said, noting that Eastman in southwestern Wisconsin is the small, rural community from which the bill's Republican author, Rep. DuWayne Johnsrud, hails.

O'Keefe added that Madison has a record of being one of the safest cities of its size in the nation, and the gun law is one of the reasons. "This makes it easier to own a handgun, and easier to use a handgun in Madison,"

What makes the bill particularly galling, he added, is that Republicans won control of the Legislature arguing that local communities are best able to govern, not state government.

The bill passed 69-29 early Tuesday and was sent to the Senate.

Madison residents absorb the outcome

The innocent verdicts in O.J. Simpson's double-murder trial have changed the way many Madison-area residents think about race, the justice system and spouse abuse.

Wherever a TV flickered at noon Tuesday, the normal flow of events halted as area residents watched the verdict announcement from a Los Angeles courtroom.

Wisconsin State Journal reporters filed the following reports from around Madison.

Vera Court: cheers, devastation

It was absolutely silent in the Vera Court Neighborhood Center on Madison's North Side when the verdicts were read.

Seven people — four African-American women who work at the center, two white Madison police officers and one white man who said he works in the Vera Court area — stared at the blaring TV set in the large tiled recreation room.

Darlene Horner, president of the Vera Court Neighborhood Association, was so tense that she climbed up onto the ping-pong table and buried her head in the net as the "not guilty" pronouncements came down.

Cheers of "Not guilty!" rose up from Horner and Brenda Bankston, a receptionist at the neighborhood center.

Associated Press photos

Left: Fred Goldman, father of murder victim Ronald Goldman, rubs his eyes as he holds a news conference after O.J. Simpson was acquitted Tuesday morning. At center is Ronald Goldman's stepmother, Patti, and back right is prosecutor Hank Goldberg. At far right is an unidentified family member. **Right:** Robert Graham stands outside the Criminal Courts Building in Los Angeles Tuesday holding the latest edition of the Pasadena, Calif., Star-News announcing that O.J. Simpson has been found not guilty.

Bankston said she believes Simpson was "framed" by police. But if he weren't so rich, Bankston said, Simpson probably would've been convicted.

"Without money, what would you have? That jail door clanking in your face."

Sharron Hubbard-Mayer, an outreach worker at the neighborhood center, disagreed.

"If you have money ... you can play with the system longer, appealing and appealing," she said. "But I don't think it means you win."

But Dane County social worker Joan Bethel was crestfallen, saying as she stared at the screen, "I can't believe it. I can't."

Bethel said she was "devastated" by the verdict because she believes Simpson is guilty. But she blamed sloppy police work and a jury swept up in emotions for the acquittal.

"Somehow, I had to believe the jurors must have had a sense of the racial overtones — what it would've done to the city," Bethel said. "I really felt the jury felt he was guilty ... but not beyond a reasonable doubt. Given the evidence they were given, they were forced to come back with a verdict of not guilty."

The two police officers declined to comment on the case.

While Horner and Bankston favored the "not guilty" verdicts, their reasons were complex. Bankston believes Simpson is innocent. Horner, on the other hand, believes jury members acquitted Simpson because they — like she — don't trust the police.

Horner said when her brother was murdered 10 years ago in Chicago, the police reaction was, "They don't know who did it. They weren't looking for anyone. They told me if I found out who did it, let them know."

Horner said it's common knowledge in her old neighborhood that three young men undergoing gang initiation killed her 54-year-old brother. Their skin, Horner said, was found under his fingernails. No one was ever arrested in the case, she said.

She complained that in Madison, when police "stop Afro-Americans, they come out with their gun drawn."

Pointing directly at the chest of a white reporter, Horner said, "They don't do that to you."

— Dee J. Hall

Park Street bar: anger, cynicism

Minutes before the verdicts were announced, the lone black customer at Bennett's On The

Please see **REACTION,** Page 2A

Complete coverage inside

UW surgeon denies overbilling allegations

Ward recommends doctor's dismissal

By Richard W. Jaeger
Wisconsin State Journal

Dr. Allan Levin, a nationally known neurosurgeon at University Hospital, denied Tuesday that he overbilled patients as charged in a dismissal recommendation made by UW-Madison Chancellor David Ward.

Levin's attorney, John Markson of Madison, said the longtime UW surgeon will appeal Ward's recommendation that Levin be fired from the UW faculty and the hospital staff. Markson said he will meet with university officials next week to set a hearing date.

UW officials confirmed that Ward has sent a letter to Levin recommending his dismissal based on the findings of an internal investigation that alleges he overbilled patients at the Spinal Cord Injury Clinic by more than $100,000 since 1989.

Ward was not available for comment Tuesday. He was attending a conference out of town.

Levin, who has been on the Medical School faculty since 1973, would not comment on the allegations. Markson denied they have merit.

The allegations, according to university officials, stem from an audit conducted by the Clinical Practice Plan, which governs the money earned by Medical School faculty members who provide patient care.

Dr. Venkat Rao, president of the CPP and a member of the hospital staff, verified that an audit had been conducted and found that "one physician seemed to have billed patients for services while he was out of town." Rao, however, would not verify that Levin was that physician.

Rao said that after the discovery of the alleged billing practices, an independent survey was done that found there were "no similar patterns by other physicians."

Markson said the audit findings showed errors in billings made under Levin's name for physicians who were filling in for him during his absence.

Markson said the fees were divided among Levin and his associates at the hospital. "There was no double-billing and Dr. Levin did not benefit from the error."

Markson said that according to Levin's preliminary accounting, the billing errors over the past seven years amount to less than half of the $100,000 alleged in Ward's complaint and are less than 1 percent of Levin's total billings during that period.

According to hospital officials, Levin is among the highest paid physicians at University Hospital. He is a tenured member of the faculty and his earnings, including faculty salary, have been estimated at more than $500,000.

Hospital and clinic officials said that when the final accounting of Levin's billings is completed, the university will have to refund money to patients and their insurance companies.

INDEX

Madison Forecast:
Today: Partly sunny early; mostly cloudy late. High 68.
Tonight: A chance for showers. Low 50.
Details/back page

© 1996 Wisconsin State Journal

WISCONSIN STATE JOURNAL

50 CENTS ★★★

FRIDAY/APRIL 5, 1996 MADISON, WISCONSIN

INSIDE

Easter is hopping on the e-trail

The celebration of Easter has its place on the World Wide Web

Story in Daybreak/1C

Clinton signs farm bill ending traditional subsidies

Story in Money/8B

Platteville's Ryan candidate at Drake

Story in Sports/1B

City is losing money on Monona Shores

By Jonnel LiCari
Wisconsin State Journal

During the first six months the city owned the Monona Shores apartments on the South Side it has lost $22,500.

And since the city has delayed finding a developer to rehabilitate the apartments, it likely will have to renovate some apartments itself and start renting them out, according to memos written this week by George Austin, the city's planning director.

As part of a plan to revitalize the Broadway-Simpson neighborhood — an area beset by crime and poverty — Madison's Community Development Authority bought the apartments off West Broadway for $1.95 million last August.

No new apartments were being rented and several buildings were being mothballed, so that many tenants in the 295-unit development could move into empty apartments and not be evicted when the rehabilitation started. Four buildings were mothballed to reduce operating costs and only 94 of the units are occupied. That resulted in a shortfall between revenue from rent and operating expenditures.

Last month the CDA rejected proposals for the area from two developers, Gorman and Co. and the Paszko Group, and it's now back where it started. The CDA has not yet requested new proposals for developing the area.

Faced with many more months of ownership, the city wants to find a way to make the a profit or at least stem the financial loss.

"Now that the CDA will be owning Monona Shores longer than we anticipated, some decisions need to be made on the property's interim operations," Austin said in a April 2 memo to CDA members.

"I'm recommending that 14 units be rehabed for occupancy ...," Austin wrote. "In addition, rents, which have not been raised in three years at the complex, should be increased by 5 (percent)."

The CDA will discuss the future of the project Tuesday.

According to documents included in the CDA's agenda for the meeting, the 14 units could be fixed up for rental at a cost of $49,610. The city could recoup the cost in several months through the rent. In a year, the city would collect about $104,220 in rent if all 14 units were rented, the documents said.

It was not in the city's plans to operate the apartments. It originally wanted to find a developer for the Monona Shores buildings before implementing a broad revitalization plan for the neighborhood. But Austin is suggesting that the entire redevelopment plan and a tax incremental financing district be created before the CDA seeks another developer.

One criticism of the CDA during the first process was that it didn't know what it wanted when it asked for development proposals.

This new approach, Austin wrote in another memo to the CDA, would allow it to hold public hearings on what people want to see happen in the neighborhood before a plan in undertaken.

Ald. Tim Bruer, 14th District, who represents the area, said it is in the city's interest to move quickly with the project.

The city is losing money in lost taxes on the property, he said. "Although it is a much better place to live than it was even a year ago we're continuing to support and underwrite a poverty pocket."

"They (CDA members) recognized when they came in here they would lose money but that they would be losing money for a short period of time," he added.

Bruer also said the city has to show its lender, Bank One, that it is moving forward.

"What does the CDA do in terms of their obligation to Bank One?" he asked. "By yearend they should have their ducks in a row."

FOCUS: AUTHORITIES CHARGE UNABOMBER SUSPECT

Adding up the evidence

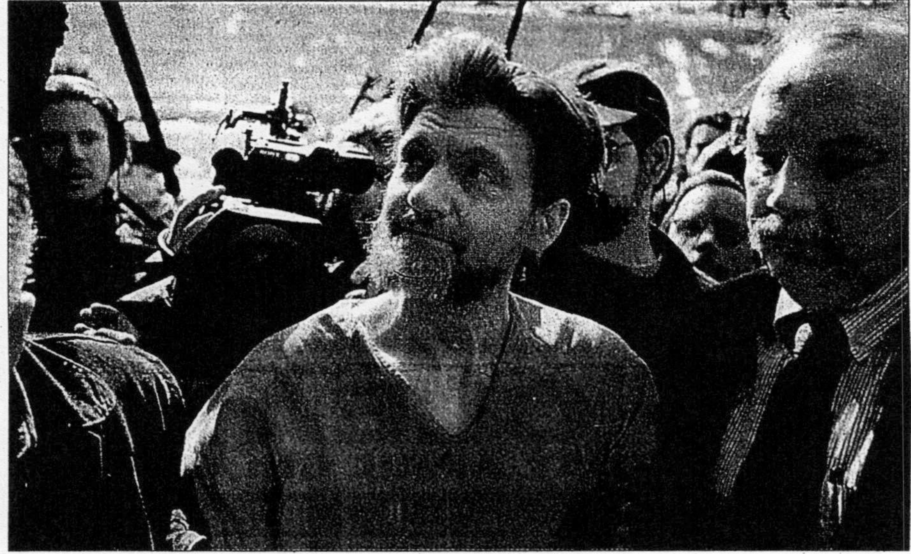

Associated Press

Theodore John Kaczynski, the suspected Unabomber, is escorted by U.S. marshals Thursday into the federal courthouse in Helena, Mont.

Former math professor had partially assembled bomb

By Nicholas K. Geranios
Associated Press

HELENA, Mont. — Investigators found a partially assembled pipe bomb, chemicals and meticulous notes on making explosives in the mountain cabin of the former Berkeley math professor suspected of being the Unabomber, federal officials said Thursday.

Theodore John Kaczynski, 53, was charged Thursday with possessing the bomb components and was held without bail. Appearing before a judge, Kaczynski, bearded and thin, said he was mentally competent and couldn't afford his own lawyer.

The charge made no mention of the Unabomber's string of bombing attacks, which killed three people and injured 23 in 18 years. Federal officials said the charge was designed to hold Kaczynski while agents build a case.

The FBI again searched Kaczynski's hand-built, 16-by-20-foot cabin Thursday. Federal officials said the search could last several days.

"It's going very slowly because we're not sure if it's booby-trapped," said a federal agent speaking on condition of anonymity. "We have an explosives ordnance team X-raying everything before we touch it."

> 'It's going very slowly because we're not sure if it's booby-trapped. We have an explosives ordnance team X-raying everything before we touch it.'
>
> **Federal agent**

The cabin has no electricity and no running water, which would appear to match the Unabomber's aversion to modern society and technology.

FBI agents had been staking out Kaczynski's cabin near the Continental Divide for several weeks, ever since his mother and brother in the Chicago area notified authorities that they had stumbled across some of his old writings while cleaning out the house they were putting up sale and found them similar to the Unabomber's anarchist manifestos.

Kaczynski was taken into custody by federal agents Wednesday so they could search his cabin in the wilderness 50 miles northwest of Helena.

A key question went unanswered: How could Kaczynski, described by neighbors as going everywhere on foot or on an old bicycle, have mailed bombs from locations including San Francisco, Oakland, Calif., Sacramento, Calif., and Chicago? Other bombs were left in cities around the country.

Dick Lundberg, a neighbor, said he sometimes gave Kaczynski rides into Helena. Plane connections were available there.

Asked about the possibility of accomplices, one federal agent said: "This guy is a loner. He wouldn't work with someone else."

FBI and Bureau of Alcohol, Tobacco and Firearms agents found a partially completed

Please see **UNABOMBER,** Page 2A

■ **Neighbors describe** Kaczynski/**2A**

Rayovac verdict rejected

Judge throws out harassment award

By Cary Segall
Wisconsin State Journal

A federal judge Thursday threw out a jury verdict that said the work environment at Rayovac was sexually hostile to women.

U.S. District Judge Barbara Crabb also said the jury wrongly decided last November that the Madison company forced Kristie Alvey to quit after she complained to a state agency about sexually suggestive conduct at company parties and meetings.

Rayovac had agreed to pay Alvey $300,000 for her emotional damage, the maximum allowed under federal law, if the verdict was upheld. Alvey also was awarded $39,387 in back pay.

But Crabb said the numerous sexual jokes and comments at company functions were merely boorish and vulgar, not sexual harassment under federal law.

"The laws are not designed to purge the workplace of vulgarity, bad manners or boorishness not intended to demean or intimidate female employees," Crabb wrote.

But Crabb upheld a jury ruling that said Rayovac retaliated against Alvey by cutting her job responsibilities after she complained to the state Equal Rights Division in 1993 about being sexually harassed at the company.

Rayovac spokesman John Daggett said the company "is pleased that this court removes a cloud from Rayovac's hard-working employees that was created by the original verdict and the press stories.

"We have always maintained that Ms. Alvey was not a victim of illegal sexual harassment at Rayovac," Daggett added in a press release. "Rayovac has not and would not condone or permit a sexually hostile work environment."

Alvey had worked at the company since 1989 and was a business analyst supervising three people when she quit in 1994.

She filed the state complaint after a business meeting in Palm Springs, Calif. She claimed Ken Biller, Rayovac's vice president of manufacturing, walked her to her hotel room after a company party and wouldn't leave. She claimed Biller forcibly kissed her twice and said he wanted to make love to

Please see **AWARD,** Page 2A

Surf's up

Some UW Internet users stray to Penthouse Web site

Associated Press

UW-Madison computer users were second among academic visitors to Penthouse Magazine's World Wide Web page between December and January, but officials say the visits were only a tiny fraction of campus Internet traffic.

The magazine said that, from Dec. 21 to Jan. 20, UW computer users made 7,337 visits to its Web site, second to the University of Minnesota, with 8,751 visits.

"I guess it was a rough winter," said Keith Ferrell, Penthouse's director of Internet and online services.

With 80 to 90 percent of the Madison campus' 39,000 students signed up for the Internet and 20,000 faculty and staff members with access, too, the number of visits to Penthouse wasn't very high, UW officials said.

It was not immediately apparent if both students and UW-Madison staff had visited the Penthouse site.

"We hope they're using it for their studies, but it sounds like some of them are using it for other things as well," said Brian Rust, marketing director for the UW Division of Information Technology.

Students who stray from strictly academic use of the university's Internet resources could do worse than Penthouse, Rust added.

"I'm sure there are things out there that are more distasteful," he said.

Associate Dean of Students Roger Howard said the UW is only beginning to tackle the issue of appropriate use of the Internet.

Associated Press

President Clinton hugs Melissa Moss outside St. John's Episcopal Church Thursday after Commerce Secretary Ron Brown's memorial service. Moss is a former Democratic National Committee and Commerce Department employee.

Brown's plane lacked flight data gear

Pentagon claims it couldn't afford a 'black box'

State Journal news services

WASHINGTON — The plane that crashed Wednesday in Croatia, killing Commerce Secretary Ronald Brown and all others aboard, was not equipped with gear that records pilots' voices or flight data because the Air Force couldn't afford it, the Pentagon said Thursday.

Such equipment, required for military aircraft built after 1974 and for all commercial airliners, provides flight and crew information that is often essential in piecing together the cause of accidents.

"Having that information today is essential in determining what happened to that airplane," said Roger Rozelle, director of publications for the Flight Safety Foundation, an Arlington, Va., group supported by airline companies and aircraft manufacturers.

Brown was among 35 people killed Wednesday when their military plane crashed into a hillside near Dubrovnik, a Croatian port on the Adriatic Sea. The victims included members of Brown's staff and a dozen top U.S. business executives interested in rebuilding Bosnia's economy.

The 23-year-old airplane Brown and his delegation were killed in had neither a flight-data recorder — which automatically records such data as flight speed, heading, altitude and positions of key controls — nor a cockpit voice recorder, which tapes conversations among pilots and crew members in the cockpit.

The reason, said a senior Air Force official, is that installing the gear would have cost some $7 million.

The plane was fitted, however, with a ground proximity warning system, which sounds an alarm if the airplane is flying too low for safety. But it is not built to warn of an imminent collision with a vertical structure such as a mountainside.

Army Gen. John Shalikashvili, chairman of the Joint Chiefs of Staff, told reporters in Boston that the recording devices, often called "black boxes," are not considered essential safety gear by the military because they can't prevent a plane from crashing.

"Black boxes have nothing to do with the safety of an airplane, because they simply allow you to reconstruct later on what happened," Shalikashvili said.

Meanwhile, U.S. investigators were arriving at the site Thursday to try to determine what caused the T-43, the U.S. military version of a Boeing 737, to crash into the hill, known locally as Sveti Ivan, or Saint John.

The bodies began arriving Thursday at a makeshift morgue set up at the airport. The White House said Army Brig. Gen. Michael Canavan identified Brown's body.

■ **Brown's death just part** of difficult week for African Americans/**3A**

■ **World leaders** fondly recall commerce secretary/**7A**

■ **Business community** feels void/**8B**

INDEX

Madison Forecast:
Today: Partly cloudy with continued cold conditions. High 40.
Tonight: Continued partly cloudy and cold. Low 19.

Details/back page

Brett Favre poster

BACK OF LOCAL, 14C

PACKERS BEGIN TITLE DEFENSE

Full preview of tonight's game vs. Chicago Bears

8 p.m. on Ch. 27

SPORTS, 1B

Packing a school lunch? Keep it simple

DAYBREAK, 1D

WISCONSIN  STATE JOURNAL

★★★

MONDAY/SEPTEMBER 1, 1997 MADISON, WISCONSIN 50 CENTS

1961-1997

Princess Diana

Charles escorts his 'English rose' back to London

By Maureen Johnson
Associated Press

LONDON — Prince Charles brought Princess Diana home for the last time Sunday, escorting the body of his "English rose" back to the land where their storybook romance ended in sorrow and scandal, a nation now plunged into grief and outrage over a stunning final tragedy.

A jet carrying the somber prince and the coffin bearing his ex-wife's remains landed outside London 16 hours after Diana died from injuries suffered when her automobile, chased by paparazzi, crashed in a Paris traffic tunnel.

Outside her London palace home, mourners heaped flowers in tribute to the much-admired Diana. But the sadness mixed with anger — outrage at a press that pursued the princess relentlessly in life, and may have contributed to her death.

French police were investigating the role seven pursuing paparazzi may have played in the early Sunday morning tragedy, which also took the lives of the 36-year-old Diana's new beau, the millionaire Dodi Fayed, and their chauffeur.

The red-tailed jet from Paris landed at the Northholt air base, where a grim array of dignitaries, led by Prime Minister Tony Blair, had gathered under leaden skies. A Royal Air Force honor guard solemnly bore the coffin, draped in a flag signifying the presence of the monarch, from the aircraft to a waiting hearse.

"How difficult things were for her from time to time, I am sure we can only guess at," Blair said earlier in the day. "But people everywhere … they liked her, they loved her, they regarded her as one of the people."

After the brief airport ceremony, Charles flew back to Scotland to be with the couple's two sons, Princes William, 15, and Harry, 12.

Diana's body was moved from a private mortuary to the Chapel Royal at St. James's Palace just after midnight, Buckingham Palace said today. Charles

Please see DIANA, Page 6A

Associated Press

The Rev. Martin Draper leads pallbearers carrying the Royal Standard-draped coffin holding the remains of Diana, Princess of Wales, from the Salpetriere Hospital in Paris Sunday to a waiting hearse.

Paris prosecutor focuses on paparazzi, seized film

By Elaine Ganley
Associated Press

PARIS — Police seized about 20 rolls of film from the paparazzi who pursued Princess Diana and were developing it for clues to the crash that killed her and her companion, sources close to the investigation said Sunday.

Police sources, speaking on condition of anonymity, said the film was confiscated from seven free-lance photographers working mainly for the Stills, Gamma and Sipa agencies.

The photographers — six Frenchmen and a Macedonian — were placed in formal custody Sunday as authorities tried to determine whether they were in any way responsible for the tunnel crash that killed the Princess of Wales; her millionaire companion, Dodi Fayed; and their driver.

Police detained the seven at the crash scene early Sunday morning and questioned them throughout the day. Prosecutors can hold them for up to 48 hours without charges, and the police sources said they would spend Sunday night in custody. Police did not release their names.

Witnesses said the photographers, riding motorcycles, had swarmed the Mercedes sedan before it entered the tunnel along the Seine River just north of the Eiffel Tower. Within seconds, the car slammed into a concrete piling, spun and hit a tunnel wall, crumpling in a mass of twisted steel. Fayed and the chauffeur were killed instantly; Diana died at a hospital a few hours later.

"We want the entire truth," Fayed's family lawyer, Bernard Darteville, told French television Sunday evening, while calling for a separate judicial inquiry.

"It seems to me to be a case of involuntary homicide," he said.

France Info radio said at least some of the photographers took pictures before help arrived — and one of the photographers was beaten at the scene by horrified witnesses. Police impounded two motorcycles and a scooter.

"This investigation will determine more particularly the role that these people may have played in the genesis of the accident," the Paris prosecutor's office said in a brief statement issued Sunday.

The Italian photographer who snapped a photo of Diana embracing Fayed that started a bidding war among tabloids around the world last month said he was told photographers were no longer

Please see PAPARAZZI, Page 6A

Princess Diana's final hours

Events leading to deaths of Princess Diana and Dodi Fayed:

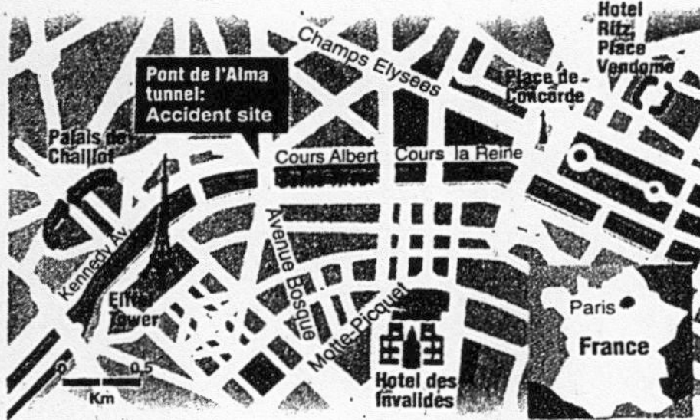

Saturday afternoon:
► Princess Diana, Dodi Al Fayed arrive in Paris

Saturday 11:30 p.m.
► Diana and Dodi leave the Hotel Ritz after dinner

Sunday 12:35 a.m.
► Commercial photographers on motorcycles pursue Diana and Dodi's Mercedes

► Mercedes heads into tunnel at Pont de l'Alma, speeding to elude paparazzi

► Driver loses control of car; it slams into concrete post, bounces into the wall

► Dodi and driver killed instantly, Dodi's bodyguard severly injured

Sunday 4 a.m.
► Diana dies from cardiac arrest at the Salpetriere Hospital

SOURCE: News reports

Knight-Ridder Tribune/TIM BARKER

Unions have reason to celebrate holiday

Success in UPS strike indicates comeback

By Phil McDade
Wisconsin State Journal

Dave Poklinkoski will find himself celebrating Labor Day this year with, well, something to celebrate.

It didn't used to be that way.

Labor unions, beaten up for the better part of the past two decades, now find themselves on the rebound. The recent battle between the Teamsters and United Parcel Service has been widely viewed as a victory for organized labor, and the latest example of renewed vigor in the labor movement.

"It's about time we won a battle," said Poklinkoski, a storeroom worker at Madison Gas and Electric Co. and president of the International Brotherhood of Electrical Workers Local 2304.

"You have to get your members involved in fighting for your future," he said. "That's what the Teamsters did and that's we've done in our local, and that's made a big difference."

Area labor leaders say they've turned a corner in their battle for

Please see LABOR DAY, Page 3A

Today: Warm, humid. High 86. Winds: SSW 5-10 mph.
Tonight: T-storm possible. Low 62.
Details/back page

The good and bad of gaming

Local officials in Sauk County have seen both sides firsthand

FOCUS

Recent comments by Madison Mayor Sue Bauman that seemed to soften the city's long-standing opposition to a casino have spurred a debate about what it would mean to the city. In a two-part series, the State Journal examines the renewed controversy over a Madison casino.

SUNDAY: Madison casino prospects cause stir.

TODAY: Lake Delton's casino: A mixed blessing.

By Ron Seely
Wisconsin State Journal

LAKE DELTON — Madison officials curious about what it's like to have a casino in town might want to have a chat with the Steinhorsts.

That would be Butch and Dean. They're cousins.

Butch is the sheriff of Sauk County, home to the Ho-Chunk Casino in the town of Lake Delton. Dean is the mayor of Baraboo, a city of about 9,000 just down the road from the casino.

Both are in positions that require them to deal with the neighboring casino in some fashion every day or so. Both say the casino has been a mixed blessing, bringing dollars and tourists to the area but also creating new and sometimes difficult demands on police and fire departments, as well as rescue squads.

"It's definitely had an impact," Dean Steinhorst said. "There are more people in the area because of it."

He said the casino runs shuttle buses to city motels, which are busier since the arrival of gambling.

But Dean said he's seen the dark side of gambling, too. "I've seen a lot of families torn apart," he said. "I've seen homes lost and farms lost."

Butch Steinhorst, as sheriff, deals even more frequently with the problems a casino can bring. Although the casino has its own security force, Steinhorst's officers still have to drive there frequently to as-

Please see GAMING, Page 3A

For home opener, it's Boise State; your guide/1D

•158th Year — No. 249 © 1997 Wisconsin State Journal

WISCONSIN

STATE JOURNAL

★★★ 50 CENTS

SATURDAY/SEPTEMBER 6, 1997 MADISON, WISCONSIN

Mother Teresa, friend to the poor

Mother Teresa, 1910-1997

Beloved nun with endless compassion dies at 87 of heart attack in Calcutta

By Bikas Das
Associated Press

CALCUTTA, India — Mother Teresa, the Roman Catholic nun revered for her tireless dedication to the world's most wretched, died Friday surrounded by grieving sisters of her order. She was 87.

Crowds of weeping people stood in the rain before dawn outside her Missionaries of Charity home in central Calcutta. Pope John Paul II, President Clinton and other world leaders praised Mother Teresa and her commitment to the poor.

With Mother Teresa gone, "there is less love in the world, less compassion, less light," said President Jacques Chirac of France. "She leaves us a strong message which has no borders and which goes beyond faith: helping, listening, solidarity. The world is in mourning."

The frail, 4-foot-11-inch nun, who was born in Europe but became an Indian citizen during her six decades on the subcontinent, had suffered heart problems and other ailments for years and gave up leadership of her order in March because she was too ill to do the job.

Her successor, Sister Nirmala, told reporters that Mother Teresa died of a heart attack.

Mother Teresa's last words were, "I cannot breathe," said a close friend, Sunita Kumar. She said Mother Teresa then slumped down in her bed.

Nuns of the Missionaries of Charity indicated the funeral is tentatively planned for Wednesday, the 51st anniversary of the day Mother Teresa received what she said was a calling from Jesus "to serve him among the poorest of the poor."

A spokeswoman reached at the Missionaries of Charity office said no definite funeral arrangements had been made.

Mother Teresa's body was taken to a chapel at the convent and laid, with hands clasped, in the simple habit worn by members of her order — a blue-trimmed white sari and a long-sleeved blouse

The Vatican said Pope John Paul II would celebrate Mass for her today at Castel Gandolfo, his summer residence outside Rome.

Working in the slums of Calcutta 50 years ago, Mother Teresa started taking in the destitute dying in gutters, sheltering infants abandoned in trash heaps, soothing lepers' wounds and helping the insane.

A British TV documentary about her in 1969 brought "the saint of the gutters" international attention, and volunteers and donations poured in to the religious order she founded.

That allowed her to spread her work around the globe, with more than 500 missions in 100 countries by mid-1990, from the hovels of Third World nations to the ghettos of New York. She received the Nobel Peace Prize in 1979.

Although India is predominantly Hindu, Mother Teresa was widely regarded as a national treasure who transcended religious divisions.

"The world, and especially India, is poorer by her passing away," said India's prime minister, Inder Kumar Gujral. "Hers was a life devoted to bring love, peace and joy to people, whom the world generally shuns."

■ **Mother Teresa's** mission, miracles/1C

Walkout ends, for now

State Journal photo/CRAIG SCHREINER

By 9 a.m. Friday morning, students had been dismissed at La Follette High School. Only about 100 of the school's nearly 1,500 students showed up for classes. Junior Adam Milkowski waits for a ride home in the school's empty commons area.

District, teachers ordered to 'cool off,' resume talks

By Phil Brinkman
Education reporter

At the urging of a Dane County judge, the Madison School District and its teachers union agreed Friday to a three-week "cooling off" period, ending a walkout by teachers and sending the two sides back to the bargaining table.

The agreement, approved by Circuit Judge Richard Callaway in a court order, set aside for the moment the volatile question of sanctions against the union for Friday's illegal strike, or "sick-in."

That gave both sides the chance to claim they won after the hastily arranged court hearing. The hearing was originally called to take up a district request filed earlier in the day for a court order to force the teachers to return to the job.

"This is a major victory for MTI," said John Matthews, executive director of Madison Teachers Inc., the teachers union.

For weeks, the union has accused the district of dragging out teacher contract negotiations by not giving its lead negotiator, Jon Anderson, authority to approve proposals on his own. The contract expired June 30.

Callaway's ruling requires that both sides have people at the bargaining table who can make such decisions.

Please see **TEACHER,** Page 3A

State Journal photo/L. ROGER TURNER

A sign for Madison Teachers Inc., the teachers union, hangs on a door leading to an empty classroom Friday.

INSIDE

Other strike coverage

On Page 3A:

■ Students talk about the strike

■ Scenes from around the district

On Page 1B:

■ An hour at Glendale Elementary

■ Teachers: Pain, frustration, resolve

On Page 3B:

■ Other Dane County districts

■ Parents react to Friday's news

Breaking tradition, Queen Elizabeth II addresses mourners

By Fawn Vrazo
and Jeffrey Fleishman
Knight-Ridder Newspapers

LONDON — Queen Elizabeth II heaped praise upon her late former daughter-in-law Princess Diana Friday night in a virtually unprecedented address that palace officials said was the monarch's first live broadcast in nearly 40 years.

"What I say to you now, as your queen and a grandmother, I say from my heart," said the queen, hatless and wearing simple street clothes as she stood against a backdrop of mourners milling outside Buckingham Palace.

Friday's four-minute address by the queen was the royal family's pointed response to heavy criticism leveled at it by Britons for the family's seeming coldness and indifference toward the death of Diana, who was killed in a Paris car crash Sunday along with her millionaire boyfriend, Dodi Fayed, and his driver, Henri Paul. It was also a rare public discussion by the queen of personal matters.

"First, I want to pay tribute to Diana myself," the queen said. "She was an exceptional and gifted human being. In good times and bad she never lost her capacity to smile and laugh, nor to inspire others with her warmth and kindness. I admired and respected her for her energy and her commitment to others, and especially for her devotion to her two boys. . . . I hope that (today) we can all, wherever we are, join in expressing our grief at Diana's loss and gratitude for her all-too-short life."

The 36-year-old Diana, Princess of Wales, was to be eulogized and buried today in what is being called the largest public event in Britain's history. A crowd estimated at up to 6 million was expected to stand in somber attendance as her coffin was carried on a horse-drawn carriage in a silent procession through London's central streets.

In a sudden change late Friday, Diana's family, the Spencers, decided she will not be buried as planned in the small rural church of St. Mary of the Virgin in Great Brington, where 20 generations of her family are interred. Instead, her burial will be on the private grounds of her family's estate in nearby Althorp — a move that apparently was taken because local residents feared the small church would be overwhelmed by visitors who would turn it into a public shrine.

In London, the queen, her husband Philip, Diana's former husband Prince Charles and their two sons, Princes William, 15, and Harry, 12, appeared in public to personally greet mourners standing outside Buckingham Palace and St. James's Palace, where Diana's body lay until Friday night. In what was viewed as another attempt to repair their tattered image, members of the royal family had returned to the capital a day early from Balmoral Castle in Scotland, where they had been secluded since Diana's death.

There were moving scenes in central London Friday afternoon as the two young princes, with faint smiles on their faces, were hugged and patted by crying mourners who reached out to them across the barricades.

Earlier Friday, the family of Fayed, the millionaire boyfriend who died with Diana, said that the two of them had been in a relationship "that was a sincere one on both sides" and confirmed that Fayed had given Diana a $215,000 diamond ring just hours before they died.

At some point, Fayed had written a poem to Diana that was in-

Please see **DIANA,** Page 4A

■ Text of queen's address/6A

COMING SUNDAY

Special report

The State Journal will provide expanded coverage Sunday of Princess Diana's funeral, including a full-color picture page.

Thompson picks Hamblin for county sheriff

By Ed Treleven
Wisconsin State Journal

Gary Hamblin, a state Justice Department agent since 1968, will take over Monday as Dane County sheriff.

Hamblin, 51, joined by his wife, Madison Ald. Susan Hamblin, 9th District, was introduced Friday as Gov. Tommy Thompson's pick to succeed Sheriff Rick Raemisch.

Hamblin became the third consecutive gubernatorial pick for the post, after the appointment of Jerome Lacke in 1981 and Thompson's selection of Raemisch in 1990.

Raemisch has resigned to take a job with Martin Security Corp. His last day as sheriff will be Sunday.

Hamblin

Hamblin is leaving a job as director of the state Gaming Enforcement Bureau. He will probably be sworn in Monday, but details were being worked out. He said he plans to run for re-election in November 1998.

"I say that not having set foot in the office," he joked. "Come Monday, that may be different."

Hamblin, a 1968 graduate of UW-Eau Claire and a 1991 FBI Academy graduate, was also director of the Division of Narcotics Enforcement Bureau from 1990 to 1992 and director of the Narcotics and Dangerous Drugs Bureau from 1988 to 1990.

Hamblin said he has no specific plans for changes in the sheriff's office but said staffing, the source of budget wrangling between former County Executive Rick Phelps and Raemisch, is one area that needs immediate attention.

"It's been difficult to maintain full staffing levels," Hamblin said. "Deputies have been required to work overtime, and that needs to be addressed."

Hamblin also said he plans to take advantage of the sheriff's job to finally get involved in the community as a law enforcement officer, something he's had little chance to do during his years with the Justice Department.

Raemisch, who was listed as a reference on Hamblin's resume, said he was at first troubled by the thought that someone might take his post who wouldn't care as much about the job as he did.

"My fears are gone now with the appointment of Gary Hamblin as sheriff," he said.

The salary for the position is $77,000 per year.

INDEX

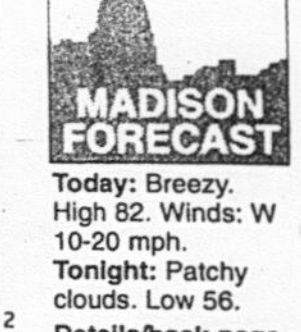

Today: Breezy. High 82. Winds: W 10-20 mph.
Tonight: Patchy clouds. Low 56.
Details/back page

150th Year — No. 22 © 1998 Wisconsin State Journal

WISCONSIN  STATE JOURNAL

★★★ 50 CENTS

THURSDAY JANUARY 22, 1998 MADISON, WISCONSIN

INSIDE

Badgers lose to Illinois, 62-48

See Page 3C

Two Packers posters for the price of one!

See pages 8C and 8F

Mining bill locked up for the night

Politicking to resume today; fate of the Crandon mine is at stake

By Andrew Blasko
Associated Press

State Assembly work stalled late Wednesday night on a bill that would require companies seeking to open mines to first show that similar mines operated without environmental damage elsewhere.

Republicans and Democrats came out of closed-door caucuses accusing each other of trying to delay the bill because they couldn't agree on key details — such as defining the meaning of pollution.

Finally, just before midnight, lawmakers agreed, 51-46, to make the bill and any amendments a special order of business today, with action to resume at noon and to continue until completed.

The Assembly, with foes and backers of a proposed mine near Crandon looking on from the gallery, took up the bill and other mining-related measures at 4 p.m. Wednesday.

Lawmakers passed amendments making minor changes in the Senate-passed moratorium bill on votes of 52-46 and 55-43 before recessing to party caucuses that continued for hours.

The bill's backers had wanted it passed without changes so that it could go to the governor for signing. Any amendments must go back to the Senate for consideration before the Legislature ends its current session in March.

About 55 of the bill's supporters and opponents were in attendance as the debate began, many wearing T-shirts expressing their views because signs are banned in the gallery.

Supporters wore orange shirts with blue letters saying "No Amendments," calling on lawmakers to make no changes and pass the bill. Opponents wore green T-shirts with white lettering, reading "Mining Matters."

Vonna Brooks, a marketing planner with Harnischfeger Corp. of Milwaukee, which makes above-ground mining equipment, said the company opposes the bill because

Please see **MINING,** Page 3A

Student eyes spot on School Board

West junior wants to 'reconnect teens with politics again'

By Phil Brinkman
Education reporter

Hoping to rally his slumbering generation, Ben Wikler has picked an unlikely place to start the revolution: the Madison School Board.

Wikler, an earnest and soft-spoken junior at West High School, is leading a campaign to return a non-voting student member to the board.

"I'm trying to reconnect teens with politics again," said Wikler, a self-described progressive.

The proposal would revive the practice, abandoned in the late 1970s, of having a student representative attend all board meetings and join in discussions. The board's ad hoc policy committee could act on the request as early as today, when it meets at the district headquarters, 545 W. Dayton St., at noon.

Wikler and three colleagues at West and Shabazz City High School — Jessica Murname, Jim Ploeser and Stephanie Yau — say they want to give students a voice on the board, which they say has been unresponsive to their concerns.

They've put together an elaborate plan for electing the representative and appointing a student advisory council to make sure schools' concerns are passed along to that person.

B. Wikler

The student would not vote and could not attend closed-door meetings where such sensitive topics as expulsions and contract negotiations are discussed. Similar representatives already serve on 136 of the state's 426 school boards.

"Students will no longer have the feeling that decisions affecting their lives are being made by people with no accountability to them," Wikler said.

Equally important is the potential for student representatives to develop leadership skills, said Wikler, who has worked on several political campaigns and hopes to run for office one day.

Wikler, 16, is used to making his voice heard. As a seventh-grader at Hamilton Middle School, he started the alternative Hamilton Free Press, which once referred to a former assistant principal known to be a strict disciplinarian as a "dictator."

Currently, he edits the Yellow Press, a satirical student paper.

Board members and administrators say they like the proposal but have raised a number of concerns, chief among them whether any student would find the minutiae of budgets and policy-making interesting.

The last time this was tried, "I think we wore them down and bored them to death and they just dropped out," Memorial High School Principal Carolyn Taylor said.

But Wikler said the type of students apt to run for the office "do have a taste for that kind of thing."

"People don't reach out to the students much right now," Wikler said. "If they did, I think they'd be pleasantly surprised."

Pope's message: Bring Cuba back into the world

Associated Press

Top: Members of the Jesus Mary and Joseph Church in Havana, Cuba, pray at the Plaza of the Revolution Wednesday waiting for the motorcade of Pope John Paul II to pass. **Above:** Cuban President Fidel Castro, right, greets the pope at Jose Marti Airport Wednesday.

Castro (dressed in suit, not fatigues) greets pontiff

By Victor L. Simpson
Associated Press

HAVANA — Pope John Paul II, a "messenger of truth and hope," began a historic pilgrimage Wednesday to Cuba, land of hardship, embattled faith and an aging, struggling revolution.

President Fidel Castro, dressed in a double-breasted blue suit instead of his usual fatigues, was among those waiting to greet John Paul.

Four children, dressed in white, held up a box of Cuban soil so the pontiff could continue his tradition of kissing the ground as he arrived.

"John Paul the Second! The whole world loves you!" the crowd chanted.

For more than an hour, at the center of world attention in the televised airport ceremony, the 77-year-old white-clad pope and the gray-bearded 71-year-old revolutionary moved easily together. The Cuban leader aided the bent and ailing pontiff, offering his hand at the pope's elbow.

Things may not be so solicitous when the two hold their substantive session today.

Castro hopes the visit will gain stature for his revolution and support for an end to the more than three-decade-old U.S. economic embargo. The Cuban church hopes the visit will help it expand its influence.

In his airport remarks, John Paul said he was praying that Cuba "may offer to everyone a climate of freedom, mutual trust, social justice and lasting peace." Castro said if there have been difficulties between the church and his revolutionary government, "the revolution is not to blame."

Standing at an airport lectern under a blazing sun, the pope celebrated this "happy and long-awaited day" and spoke out on the U.S.-Cuban standoff that has long isolated this communist nation.

"May Cuba, with all its magnificent potential, open itself up to the world, and may the world open itself up to Cuba," he declared.

And he firmly endorsed what he called the "legitimate desires" of the Roman Catholic Church in Cuba — its quest for more privileges under Castro's government.

"I wish to say with the same force as at the beginning of my pontificate: 'Do not be afraid to open your hearts to Christ.' Allow him to come into your lives, into your families, into society," he said.

Castro, in his address, denounced the U.S. embargo as "genocide" and sought to identify his revolution's ideals with those of the church.

■ **Cuban socialism hurting** families/3A

FOCUS: PRESIDENT ACCUSED

Clinton denies having affair with intern, covering it up

■ **Kenneth Starr is investigating whether the president and a friend asked the woman to lie about the alleged dalliance.**

By Jodi Enda and Angie Cannon
Knight Ridder Newspapers

WASHINGTON — Facing down the most grave accusations ever launched against his presidency, President Clinton Wednesday firmly denied allegations that he had an affair with a 21-year-old White House intern and then engaged in illegal efforts to cover it up.

"That is not true. That is not true," Clinton said in an interview with PBS. "I did not ask anyone to tell anything other than the truth.

"There is no improper relationship," he added.

Lewinsky

The president's denial followed news reports that independent prosecutor Kenneth Starr is investigating whether Clinton and a close friend, Vernon Jordan, advised the young woman to lie about a sexual relationship that allegedly spanned 1½ years during Clinton's presidency. It echoed a denial made last week by the former intern, Monica Lewinsky, who is now 24.

Despite the denials, Starr's office is exploring whether Clinton broke the law by encouraging Lewinsky to lie under oath to lawyers for Paula Jones, who has filed a sexual-harassment lawsuit against the president. In fact, Starr sent a subpoena to the White House Wednesday afternoon seeking documents concerning the Lewinsky allegations.

White House spokeswoman Nanda Chitre said the administration will cooperate.

Lewinsky, who began working as a volunteer

Please see **CLINTON,** Page 4A

INDEX

Today: Flurries. High 28. Winds: NE 8-16 mph.
Tonight: Snow develops again. Low 20.
Details/back page

Big East Side housing plan passes

Council approves a development with more than 3,000 units

By Dean Mosiman
City government reporter

The stage is set for the biggest master-planned development in Madison history.

The City Council this week approved the Sprecher Neighborhood Development Plan, a blueprint for 1,425 acres of rolling countryside on the far East Side.

It means developer Donald Hovde of Madison can start the formal approval process for a residential and commercial project in the area, which is bounded by Interstate 90, Door Creek Valley, Interstate 94 and Cottage Grove Road.

Hovde unveiled a development proposal in March 1996 and has since worked with the city and others to create the neighborhood plan. He said the project would be built over 15 years and would ultimately increase the city's tax base by $500 million.

The developer could not be reached for comment, and it's unclear whether he intends to modify his earlier proposal, which called for 3,500 housing units on 765 acres.

He or any other developer must still get required subdivision, site plan and zoning approvals.

"This is just the first step," city planning unit director Brad Murphy said.

But the process will be easier with a 34-page neighborhood plan that considers everything from open space to streets.

About 1,051 acres, or 74 percent of the 1,425-acre planning area, is in the city, and the rest is in the town of Blooming Grove. The city anticipates annexing it all.

The neighborhood plan envisions a town center that could host anything from a branch public library to a pizza parlor near the intersection of I-90 and Cottage Grove Road.

The plan calls for a smaller business area on Milwaukee Street west of Sprecher Road, and a 74-acre commercial district northeast of Milwaukee and Sprecher.

It sets aside 331 acres of open space, including fields, picnic shelters and other facilities in the Door Creek corridor.

And it includes a 22-acre public school and park site between I-90 and Sprecher Road, and a 32-acre church site just east of Sprecher.

Low- and medium-density housing would hug commercial centers or major parks, although a variety of housing types and densities can be built in all areas.

The plan allows for a maximum 3,785 dwelling units.

The city ironed out most wrinkles by the time the plan reached the Plan Commission and City Council, city planner Dave Larson said.

Concerns about density, traffic, drainage and location of a water tower have largely been resolved, agreed town of Blooming Grove Chairman Tom Anderson.

Any lingering problems can be addressed when specific development proposals are reviewed, Anderson said.

Sprecher neighborhood plan

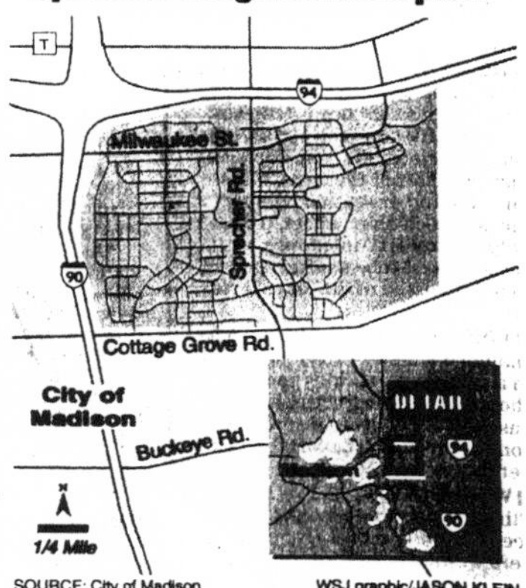

SOURCE: City of Madison
WSJ graphic/JASON KLEIN

DAYBREAK/1C
Life a page-turner for Madison author Jacquelyn Mitchard

SPORTS/1D
Madison Mad Dogs win playoff over Green Bay Bombers

SPORTS/1D
Craig Newsome making his return tonight for Packers

NATION/2A
Kenneth Starr may be in trouble for leaks in Lewinsky case

WISCONSIN STATE JOURNAL

★★★ 50 CENTS

SATURDAY/AUGUST 8, 1998 MADISON, WISCONSIN

SPECIAL REPORT: U.S. EMBASSIES BOMBED

Motive unknown in deadly attacks

U.S. Ambassador Prudence Bushnell, right, is helped from the area of the U.S. Embassy on Friday in Nairobi, Kenya.

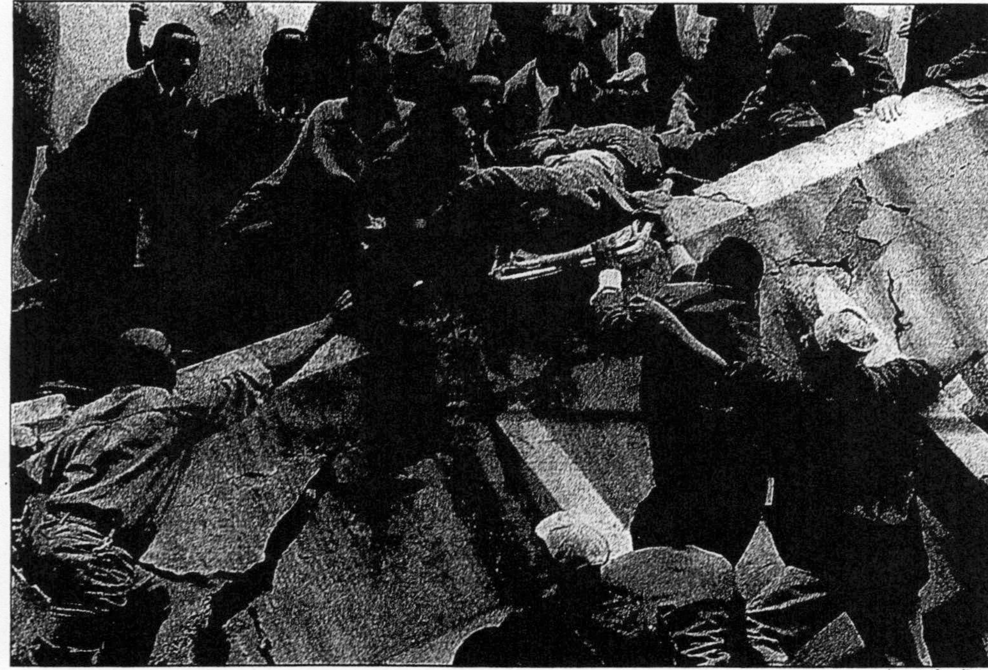

Associated Press Photos

Rescue workers carry an injured woman over the rubble of a collapsed building next to the U.S. Embassy on Friday in Nairobi, Kenya.

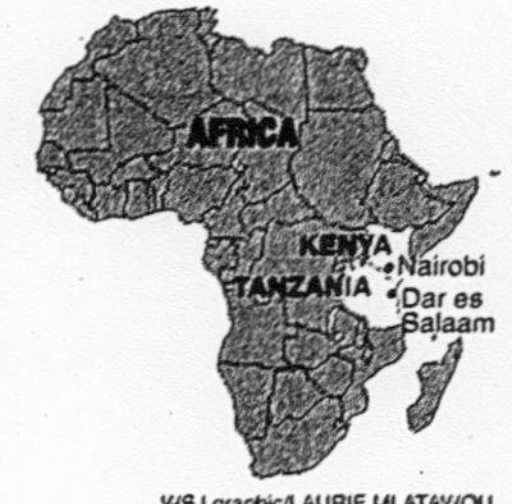

AFRICA
KENYA
Nairobi
TANZANIA
Dar es Salaam

WSJ graphic/LAURIE MLATAWOU

Dozens missing in embassy rubble

By James C. McKinley Jr.
New York Times

NAIROBI, Kenya — In what U.S. officials described as coordinated terrorist attacks, two massive bombs exploded minutes apart outside the U.S. Embassies in Kenya and Tanzania late Friday morning, killing at least 80 people, including eight Americans.

President Clinton condemned the attacks as abhorrent and inhuman acts of cowardice. He vowed to bring those responsible to justice "no matter what or how long it takes."

■ U.S. embassies present big target/**3A**
■ Teams sent to aid victims, find clues/**3A**

In Nairobi, an enormous explosion ripped through downtown around 10:35 a.m., turning the busy Haile Selassie Avenue into a scene of carnage and destruction that left more than 1,600 people injured and dozens still missing long after night fell.

The blast, which leveled a three-story building containing a secretarial school and destroyed the rear half of the U.S. Embassy next door, dismembered more than a dozen people passing on foot and incinerated dozens of others in their seats in three nearby buses.

Just minutes before, a bomb re-

Please see **ATTACKS**, Page 3A

No motive in fatal shooting; man in jail

Man, 18, killed outside suspect's apartment building

By Brenda Ingersoll
Police reporter

Police don't know why a 30-year-old divorced father and Oscar Mayer worker allegedly pumped several bullets into a man outside his apartment building.

"We know *what* happened," town of Madison Detective Mike J. Gehn said, "but we really don't know *why*."

Renaldo E. Gettridge of the town of Madison is jailed on suspicion of first-degree intentional homicide. An employee of Oscar Mayer Foods Corp., he apparently has no criminal record.

Police said he shot Mack C. Dixon, 18, a La Follette High School dropout, at 11:48 p.m. Thursday in a parking lot behind 2717 Granada Way, where Gettridge has lived since February.

"There's no indication they knew each other before," town officer David M. Dresser said, "but we don't know for sure. They got into some kind of argument."

Alive when he reached University Hospital, Dixon was pronounced dead of multiple wounds at 1:14 a.m. Friday. An autopsy was to be held today.

Dixon had two adult convictions and was released last summer from the Ethan Allen boys' reformatory.

Please see **SHOOTING**, Page 5A

The victim

Dixon

Mack Dixon, 18, died early Friday after being shot in a parking lot at 2717 Granada Way. Police arrested Renaldo Gettridge, 30, on tentative charges of first-degree intentional homicide.

The suspect

Gettridge

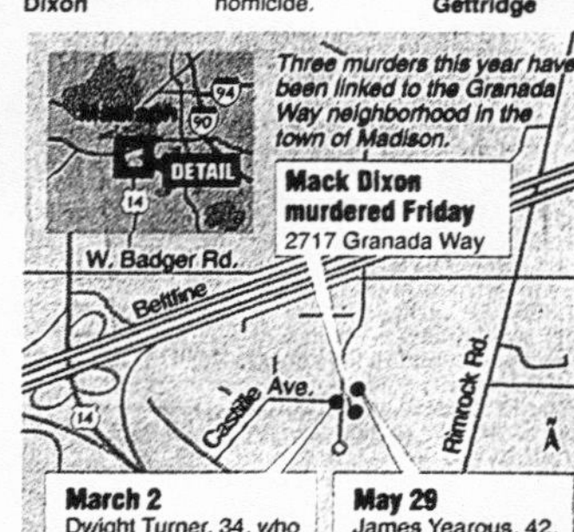

Three murders this year have been linked to the Granada Way neighborhood in the town of Madison.
94
90
DETAIL
14
Mack Dixon murdered Friday
2717 Granada Way
W. Badger Rd.
Beltline
Castille Ave.
Rimrock Rd.
March 2
Dwight Turner, 34, who police believe may have been killed near Granada Way and Castille Avenue before his body was dumped in the town of Cottage Grove. No arrests have been made.
May 29
James Yearous, 42, who was stabbed repeatedly in his apartment at 2613 Granada Way. Ervin Schad, 18, is jailed on charges of first-degree intentional homicide.

WSJ graphic

FDA panel backs drug for rheumatoid arthritis

Associated Press

BETHESDA, Md. — The first new drug in over a decade for rheumatoid arthritis won the backing of government advisers Friday — with a warning that it must be taken very carefully by women who have not yet gone through menopause.

Arava, made by Hoechst Marion Roussel, does not cure crippling rheumatoid arthritis. But it appears to work as well as the gold-standard treatment, a cancer drug, at treating swollen, painful joints. And it appears to slow the progression of the debilitating disease.

"This drug does good things in joints," said Dr. Kenneth Brandt of Indiana University, before fellow advisers to the Food and Drug Administration recommended unanimously that Arava be approved for sale.

The FDA is not bound by its advisers' recommendations, but typically follows them.

Rheumatoid arthritis affects about 2 million Americans, the vast majority of them women.

It is not the kind of arthritis that plagues the elderly as their joints essentially wear out. Instead, rheumatoid arthritis is an autoimmune disease — the immune system goes awry and attacks patients' own cartilage. It typically strikes between ages 25 and 50.

The best treatment today is methotrexate, a cancer drug. But it causes side effects, and its effectiveness wanes over time, leaving patients with few options.

INDEX

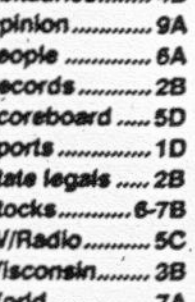

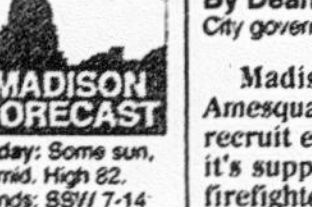

MADISON FORECAST

Today: Some sun, humid. High 82. Winds: SSW 7-14 mph.
Tonight: Patchy clouds, fog. Low 66.
Details/back page

Amesqua wants to dump recruiting list

By Dean Mosiman
City government reporter

Madison Fire Chief Debra Amesqua wants to stop using a fire recruit eligibility list a year before it's supposed to expire — and the firefighters' union is miffed.

The move could be costly and could undermine efforts to boost staffing, union president Joe Conway Jr. said Friday.

It further strains relations between Amesqua and Fire Fighters Local 311, which recently voted no-confidence in Amesqua.

The city's Police and Fire Commission, with assistance from an $80,000 consultant, produced an eligibility list of 135 candidates in late 1997 that is supposed to last through December 1999.

Amesqua used the list for the most recent class, in which five of 17 recruits failed to graduate. She will use it for 10-person classes starting Monday and in November.

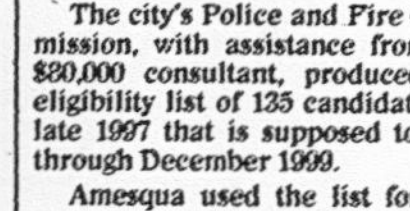

Mayor Sue Bauman has tentatively agreed to boost staffing from 58 to 62 firefighters daily, starting Sept. 1. To do so, the union is using "creative staffing" measures such as sending extra personnel home when beyond full strength, and using floating shifts. The city is supposed to start recruit classes Monday, in November and in April to make sure the department has enough firefighters.

Amesqua said she wants to abandon the list after November because she is concerned about the quality of candidates and because it may not have enough diversity.

She said she wants to improve the process that produces the list, and that those on it now can reapply. She is confident that a new list can be ready for an April class.

Conway disagreed. Amesqua began the last two classes two months late with a list in hand, and it will be very difficult to move through the process of checks, interviews and tests needed to produce a new eligibility list and start a class by April, he said.

Conway said he is unsure if the union will continue to provide creative staffing measures if a recruit class doesn't start around April. That may mean more overtime costs or reduced staffing, he said.

Bauman, who has voiced increasing frustration with Amesqua, said she knew the chief wants to abandon the list but is unsure why or when.

"The question for me is, if we don't have people on the list to hire, why is that?" she said.

City Council president Tim Bruer, 14th District, said he is concerned about people on the current list filing lawsuits and the erosion of staffing levels.

150th Year — No. 354 © 1998 Wisconsin State Journal

WISCONSIN  STATE JOURNAL

★★★

SUNDAY/DECEMBER 20, 1998 MADISON, WISCONSIN $1.75

IMPEACHED

Two counts against Clinton go to Senate

President refuses Republican calls for him to resign

By Steven Thomma, Raja Mishra and David Hess
Knight Ridder Newspapers

WASHINGTON — Casting a permanent stain on a man who once dreamed of a gloried place in American history, the House of Representatives on Saturday impeached President William Jefferson Clinton and, for only the second time in the nation's two centuries, urged the Senate to remove a president from office.

Carried almost entirely by Republican votes, the House charged Clinton with committing "high crimes and misdemeanors," the grave offenses envisioned by the framers of the Constitution as grounds to step in between elections and impeach a sitting president.

If convicted in the Senate, Clinton would automatically be removed from office and Vice President Al Gore would immediately become the nation's 43rd president. There is no appeal.

The House approved two articles of impeachment accusing Clinton of lying under oath and obstructing justice to conceal an extramarital affair with former aide Monica Lewinsky. Two other articles were defeated.

If convicted in the Senate, Clinton would automatically be removed from office and Vice President Al Gore would immediately become the nation's 43rd president. There is no appeal.

Republicans who pushed the impeachment of the Democratic president called on him to resign and spare the nation from what could be a long and disruptive trial.

In a stunning effort to lend weight to that argument, the House speaker-designate, Rep. Bob Livingston, R-La., said he would set an example for Clinton and resign from Congress because of reve-

Please see **PRESIDENT,** Page 3A

Associated Press

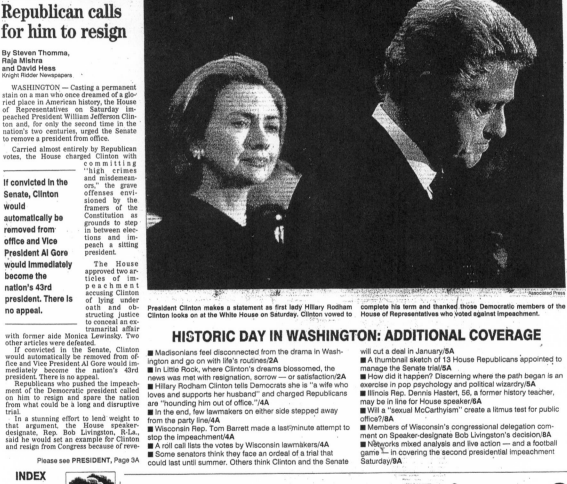

President Clinton makes a statement as first lady Hillary Rodham Clinton looks on at the White House on Saturday. Clinton vowed to complete his term and thanked those Democratic members of the House of Representatives who voted against impeachment.

Livingston's move to quit shocks colleagues

By Frank Greve and David Hess
Knight Ridder Newspapers

WASHINGTON — House Speaker-designate Bob Livingston dumbfounded Congress Saturday by announcing his intention to resign from the House after his admissions of past sexual indiscretions. He challenged President Clinton to follow his example.

Livingston's decision, overshadowed only by the impeachment of the president that ensued, threw House Republicans, who have lost two speakers in six weeks, into temporary chaos.

A low-key former wrestling coach, Rep. Dennis Hastert, R-Ill., is seen as a moderate who could be effective in unifying party factions.

But within a few hours Rep. Dennis Hastert, R-Ill., a 12-year veteran of Congress, emerged as a leading contender for the speaker's job. A low-key former wrestling coach, Hastert is seen as a moderate who could be effective in unifying party factions.

Hastert is a favorite of Republican Whip Tom DeLay, R-Texas, the influential third-ranking Republican leader, and also won the endorsement of outgoing Speaker Newt Gingrich, R-Ga.

Rep. Tom Davis, R-Va., said a grass-roots group of 40 members met minutes after Livingston's resignation and decided to nominate Hastert before "Denny had even decided to run."

Davis said Gingrich told Republican caucus members that Hastert was the only person with the qualities to hold the party together in the House.

DeLay, a controversial figure who has avidly pursued President Clinton's impeachment, said he thought about pursuing the leadership post himself but decided against making the move because

Please see **QUIT,** Page 3A

HISTORIC DAY IN WASHINGTON: ADDITIONAL COVERAGE

INDEX

MADISON FORECAST

Today: Light snow and cold. High 24. Winds: NNE 8-16 mph.
Tonight: Colder. Low 16.
Details/back page

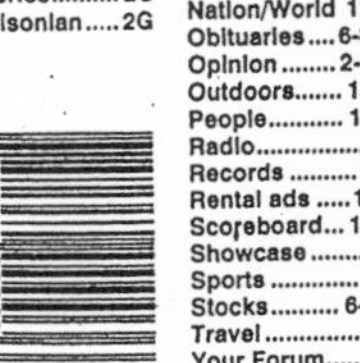

U.S. halts bombing of Iraq

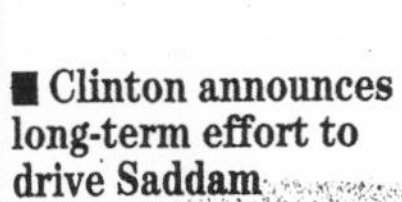

■ Clinton announces long-term effort to drive Saddam from power.

By Scott Shepard and Larry Kaplow
Cox News Service

WASHINGTON — After four days of massive airstrikes against the soldiers and facilities Saddam Hussein relies upon to retain power in Iraq, President Clinton ordered an end to the bombing Saturday and announced a long-term strategy to work with anti-Saddam forces to topple the dictator.

Declaring that the objectives of Operation Desert Fox have been achieved, Clinton said the United States and its allies would now "intensify our engagement with the Iraqi opposition groups, prudently and effectively" to end Saddam's regime. He said the United States would help any "new leadership" that emerges in Iraq.

Saddam

"Over the long term, the best way to end the threat that Saddam poses to his own people and the region is for Iraq to have a different government," Clinton said in a brief announcement at the White House. "We hope that we will return Iraq to its rightful place in the community of nations."

In London, British Prime Minister Tony Blair, backing the president's long-term strategy, addressed himself to the Iraqi people, saying, "We have a common enemy in Saddam."

Clinton said the United States and its allies will retain a significant military force in the region that will be used again in the event that there is evidence of Saddam threatening his neighbors or resuming efforts to build weapons of mass destruction. He also said economic sanctions against Iraq would continue.

Although Iraqi officials indicated earlier in the day that they would no longer allow United Nations weapons inspectors in the country, Clinton expressed hope that the inspection process could resume.

Iraq remained defiant, however, as protests and tensions spread throughout the Arab world, which began observing Ramadan, a holy Muslim month. Rioters in Damascus, Syria, attacked the U.S. and British embassies and broke into the U.S. ambassador's residence. And officials in the United Arab Emirates, Iran and Egypt called on Clinton to halt the bombings.

"I tell you that Iraq will continue to defend its land, policy and dignity. . . . We will fight until the last citizen," Iraqi Vice President Taha Yassin Ramadan told a news conference in Baghdad. He also vowed that the mission of the U.N. Special Commission, known as UNSCOM, is over.

The commission was created at the end of the 1991 Persian Gulf War to oversee the destruction of banned Iraqi weapons and the means to produce them.

"Everything related to inspections and the Special Commission is now behind us," Ramadan said.

After the president's announcement, Cohen said the four-day, 70-hour operation had successfully hit 100 targets, with a minimum number of civilian casualties. He said U.S. and British forces in the conflict had not suffered any casualties.

Before Saturday's attacks, the

Please see **BOMBING,** Page 13A

A vote for kindness

Story by Hesselberg

DAYBREAK, 1G

Should cranberry law change?

LOCAL, 1C

Struggles of Brent Moss

Interview with '94 Rose Bowl MVP

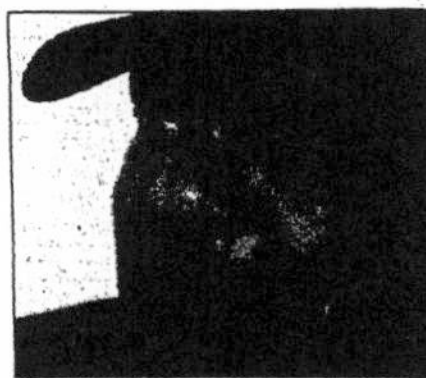

SPORTS, 1D

Your regular Saturday State Journal begins on Page 3A

160th Year — No. 2 © 1999 Wisconsin State Journal

WISCONSIN STATE JOURNAL

SATURDAY / JANUARY 2, 1999 MADISON, WISCONSIN 50 CENTS

RETURN TO THE ROSES

BADGERS 38 BRUINS 31

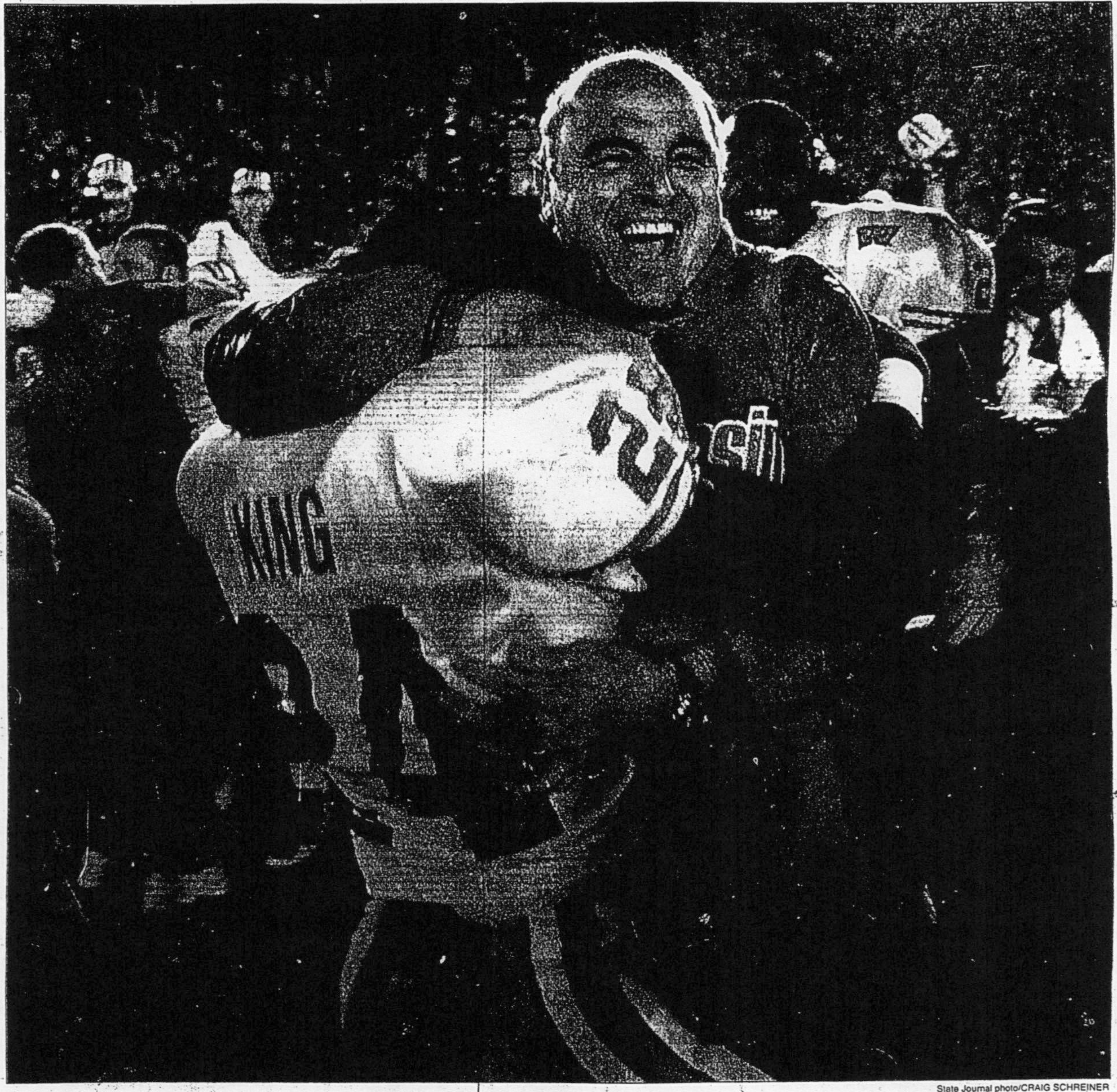

State Journal photo/CRAIG SCHREINER

Wisconsin coach Barry Alvarez and Badgers sophomore Donte King find plenty to celebrate Friday in Pasadena, Calif. The Badgers, who were nine-point underdogs, beat UCLA in the Rose Bowl, 38-31.

Badgers silence doubters

Thrilling Rose Bowl victory over UCLA makes UW 11-1

By Andy Baggot
Sports reporter

PASADENA, Calif. — For months, they have been in quiet, desperate pursuit of national respect.

The chase ended here Friday on a pristine southern California afternoon. Members of the University of Wisconsin football team cradled their redemption along with the Rose Bowl trophy, both of which came by virtue of a dramatic 38-31 victory over UCLA before 93,872 onlookers.

The triumph came five years to the day after UW claimed a 21-16 victory over UCLA to win its first Rose Bowl.

The second conquest came with an estimated 50,000 UW fans on hand to cheer every move the Badgers (11-1) made during this riveting shootout.

In the process of setting a school record for victories in a season, UW muzzled a slew of critics who insisted this team did not belong here because of a soft non-conference schedule and because of the perception it was inferior to fellow Big Ten Conference co-champion Ohio State.

One CBS analyst went so far as to opine the Badgers, who were listed as nine-point underdogs, were the worst team ever to play in the Rose Bowl. But with a host of national media on hand, UW coach Barry Alvarez declined an opportunity to gloat.

"I'm not trying to stick this game down anybody's throat," he said. "There's no reason to do that."

Because his team already had.

"I talk to our kids all the time about making a statement on the field," Alvarez said.

Junior tailback Ron Dayne tied a Rose Bowl record with four touchdowns and finished just short of another standard with 246 rushing yards on 27 carries. The Rose Bowl record for rushing yards in a game is 247, set by Charles White of USC in 1980.

"Take away Ron Dayne and we win the game," UCLA all-America offensive tackle Kris Farris said. "He's the best in the nation."

Dayne did his work despite feeling the effects of a torn right pectoral muscle sustained in the regular-season finale Nov. 21 against Penn State.

"It's a great feeling," Dayne said.

SPECIAL ROSE BOWL SECTION INSIDE

Roaring sea of Red

UW fans' impact is deafening, definite

By Susan Lampert Smith
Wisconsin State Journal

PASADENA, Calif. — Things were loud, loud, loud down here in the throat of Wisconsin's most-voluble player.

This beast, the student section in the north end of the Rose Bowl, produced a roar that knocked the ball out of UCLA's hands, caused a game-winning interception and forced UCLA to waste two timeouts the Bruins could have used as it saw its season melt away into a 38-31 Wisconsin win.

"Our 12th man helped us," coach Barry Alvarez said on national television, seconds after the 12th man had screamed its way to a second Rose Bowl championship in five years. The beast paid homage by bowing to game MVP Ron Dayne, who appeared on the big screen above the section to be weeping as openly as some of his fellow students in section 10.

These are the fans who kept a steady chant of "O-VER RA-TED" directed at the UCLA Bruins, who were once-national title contenders.

The 50,000 Wisconsin fans may have been a smaller group than the 70,000 who saw the game in 1994, but they were just as loud, again turning the Rose Bowl into

Please see FANS, Page 2A

100th Year — No. 44 © 1999 Wisconsin State Journal

WISCONSIN  STATE JOURNAL

★★★ 50 CENTS
SATURDAY/FEBRUARY 13, 1999 MADISON, WISCONSIN

ACQUITTED

Clinton sets out to rebuild his presidency

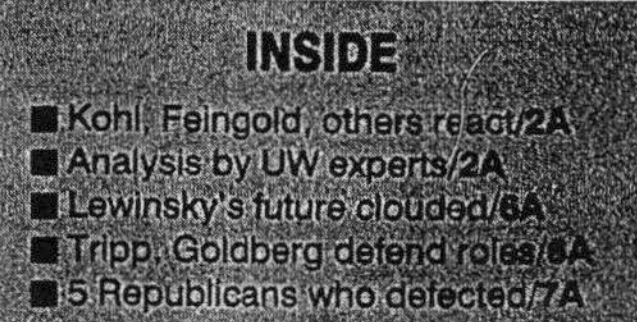

Tangled web of legal issues is still pending

By David Jackson
The Dallas Morning News

WASHINGTON — The impeachment battle is over, but it's only a cease-fire in the scandal wars.

Independent counsel Kenneth Starr is still investigating President Clinton and his associates on a variety of fronts, some of which could rekindle the firefight that sparked impeachment.

Starr himself is also under investigation, including a Justice Department review that some Republicans suggest is payback for the Monica Lewinsky investigation.

Above all looms the big question: Will Starr try to obtain a criminal indictment of President Clinton before his term expires in 2001? He has retained consultants who argue that the Constitution permits indictments of sitting presidents.

Charles Bakaly, the independent counsel's spokesman, declined to comment on Starr's plans.

In coming months, Starr will also be called on to defend his investigation of Clinton's actions during the Paula Jones sexual-misconduct lawsuit, including the president's relationship with Lewinsky.

Some Senate Democrats cited what they called Starr's overaggressive tactics as a reason to support acquittal of the president on two impeachment articles.

"Did Mr. Starr respect the rule of law?" asked Sen. Richard Durbin, D-Ill.

On the other hand, Sen. Slade Gorton, R-Wash., who favored an article charging obstruction of justice, condemned "the president's attempt to derail the independent counsel's inquiry."

Starr's overall inquiry still includes pending trials against two Clinton associates, former Justice Department official Webster Hubbell and former business partner Susan McDougal. Both cases stem from Starr's initial assignment, the Whitewater land deal.

Prosecutors also are preparing to try an ex-friend of Kathleen Willey, the former White House volunteer who accused Clinton of an improper sexual advance.

All three defendants have accused Starr of improper tactics designed to get at the president and first lady Hillary Rodham Clinton.

After his tax indictment last year, Hubbell said, "The office of independent counsel can indict my

Please see **PENDING,** Page 3A

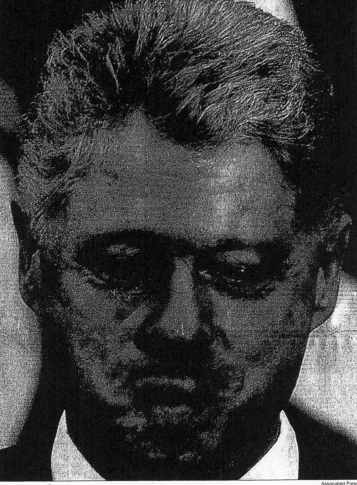

Associated Press

"I want to say again to the American people how profoundly sorry I am for what I said and did to trigger these events and the great burden they have imposed on the Congress and on the American people," President Clinton said outside the White House on Friday after his acquittal by the Senate. He added: "This can be and this must be a time of reconciliation and renewal for America."

New York Times

WASHINGTON — The Senate on Friday acquitted President William Jefferson Clinton on two articles of impeachment, falling short of even a majority vote on either of the charges against him, perjury and obstruction of justice.

Bill Clinton has survived, again.

And he issued another apology.

"I want to say again to the American people how profoundly sorry I am for what I said and did to trigger these events and the great burden they have imposed on the Congress and on the American people," Clinton said in a statement in the Rose Garden.

But, he said, the outcome of his trial presented an opportunity: "This can be and this must be a time of reconciliation and renewal for America."

After leaving the Rose Garden. Clinton telephoned several Democratic senators to thank them. Then, in a display of the business-as-usual briskness that carried him through his yearlong crisis, he met with his foreign policy team to begin preparing for an overnight trip to Mexico on Sunday.

Hoping to mold history's judgment, Clinton is bent on remaking his protean presidency once again, his friends and advisers say.

After a harrowing year of scandal and investigation, the five-week Senate trial of the president — only the second in the nation's 210-year history — came to a climax with the roll calls to determine Clinton's fate.

The vote

By all 100 Senators on charges against President Clinton:

1 PERJURY

"Willfully provided perjurious, false and misleading testimony" to special prosecutor Kenneth Starr's grand jury

Yes: 45	Dem. 0	Rep. 45	**No: 55**	Dem. 45	Rep. 10

2 OBSTRUCTION OF JUSTICE

Encouraged Monica Lewinsky to submit a false affidavit, hide gifts

Yes: 50	Dem. 0	Rep. 50	**No: 50**	Dem. 45	Rep. 5

SOURCE: AP KRT

"Is respondent William Jefferson Clinton guilty or not guilty?" asked Chief Justice William Rehnquist. In a hushed chamber, with senators standing one by one to pronounce Clinton guilty or not guilty, the Senate rejected the charge of perjury 55-45, with 10 Republicans voting against conviction.

They are Sens. John Chafee, R-R.I.; Susan Collins, R-Maine; Slade Gorton, R-Wash.; James Jeffords, R-Vt.; Richard Shelby, R-Ala.; Olympia Snowe, R-Maine; Alen Specter, R-Pa.; Ted Stevens, R-Alaska; Fred Thompson, Tenn.; and John Warner, R-Va.

It then split 50-50 on a second article accusing Clinton of obstruction of justice in concealing his affair with Monica Lewinsky. Five Republicans — Chaffee, Collins, Jeffords, Snowe and Specter — broke ranks on the obstruction of justice charge.

No Democrats voted to convict on either charge, and it would have taken a dozen of them, and all 55 Republicans, to reach the two-thirds majority of 67 senators required for conviction.

"It is, therefore, ordered and adjudged that the

Please see **ACQUIT,** Page 3A

INDEX

Today: Sunny, cold. High 32. Winds: NW 12-25 mph.
Tonight: Mostly clear, cold. Low 16.
Details/back page

Four tried to reduce powers of chief justice

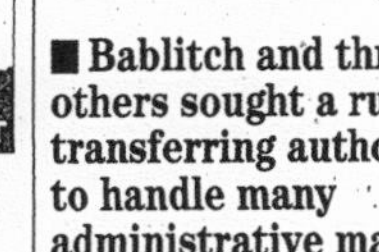

■ **Bablitch and three others sought a rule transferring authority to handle many administrative matters.**

By Cary Segall
Wisconsin State Journal

Four Wisconsin Supreme Court justices tried last October to strip Chief Justice Shirley Abrahamson of some of her constitutional power to run the court system.

Justices Bill Bablitch, Pat Crooks, Don Steinmetz and Jon Wilcox proposed a lengthy rule that would have given much of the court's administrative power to four justices chosen by a majority of the seven-member court.

They backed off when Justice Ann Walsh Bradley, upset about a provision that would have limited the ability of justices to get help from court employees, threatened to sue.

"I wouldn't let them make me a potted plant," Bradley said Friday. "I threatened to sue when they were going to try and limit my ability to do my job."

The initial proposal and its evolution into a watered-down rule adopted unanimously in January is detailed in a series of drafts released by the court Friday.

The court made the records public after they were requested

Abrahamson Bablitch

under the state Open Records Law by the Wisconsin State Journal and other newspapers.

The first rule would have required that a long list of administrative matters be handled by the group of four before they could be considered by the full court.

In addition to personnel access, areas included were: grants, publications, conferences, projects, awards, furnishings, decorations, hiring, scheduling, equipment, appointments, use of facilities and spending.

Bablitch said Friday the proposal was an effort by the four to have some say in programs Abrahamson has started since becoming chief in 1996.

"The ultimate objective through all of this was to give the entire court, not just the chief justice, knowledge and approval of all administrative matters," Bablitch said.

He said Abrahamson, who has started numerous public outreach projects, hasn't let her colleagues know what she's doing. He said the four would release a statement today detailing their concerns.

Bablitch, Crooks and Wilcox have called lawyers across the state on behalf of Sharren Rose, a Green Bay lawyer running against Abrahamson for the court in an election April 6, according to seven lawyers who have been called by the three or know lawyers who have been called.

Most of the lawyers didn't want to be named because they may appear before the court. But Stevens Point lawyer Jerry O'Brien, who has endorsed Rose, said last week the three told him there are seri-

Please see **COURT,** Page 3A

Spelling Bee today

LOCAL, 4B

UW women beat Ohio State in OT

SPORTS, 1D

Bus fire survivor speaks out

Guest column

OPINION, 9A

Fancy fliers

City kicks off first kite festival

LOCAL, 1,3B

BREAKAWAY/1D

Wood you build a canoe?

LOCAL/1C

Ka-boom!

Advice for attending Rhythm & Booms fireworks display

MONEY/8B

Green power

Three wind projects begin this month in Wisconsin

SPORTS/1B

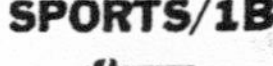

Who's No. 1?

Tom Oates' predictions

160th Year — No. 181 © 1999 Wisconsin State Journal

WISCONSIN STATE JOURNAL

★★★ 50 CENTS

WEDNESDAY, JUNE 30, 1999 MADISON, WISCONSIN

ANOTHER $50 MILLION!

Frautschi doubles his gift for arts district

State Journal photo/CRAIG SCHREINER

The announcement of Jerry Frautschi's gift of an additional $50 million to build a Downtown Madison arts district brought surprise, applause and tears Tuesday at Monona Terrace. Here, Frautschi is hugged after the news conference by Lisa Thurrell, artistic director of Kanopy Dance.

By Dean Mosiman
City government reporter

Jerry Frautschi inspired cheers and tears of joy Tuesday by doubling his gift to $100 million for a Downtown Madison arts district block.

The gift, thought to be the largest single donation ever for an arts project in the United States, was announced as Frautschi's private Overture Foundation unveiled conceptual design plans for the most expensive building project in city history.

The plans, unveiled before a crowd of more than 200 city officials, arts supporters and others gathered at the Monona Terrace Convention Center, would dramatically transform the entire Madison Civic Center block bounded by State, North Fairchild, North Henry and West Mifflin streets.

Overture would build a new 2,200- to 2,400-seat multi-purpose theater, renovate the Oscar Mayer Theater into new space for the Madison Children's Museum, expand the Madison Art Center, and create three small- to mid-size performance spaces.

The venues would have separate entrances to enliven the streets they face, but be connected inside.

The project would preserve some of the Oscar Mayer Theatre's interior and the facade of the landmark Yost building on the corner of State and North Fairchild streets. It would significantly alter or perhaps remove the Bank One building on the corner of North Fairchild and West Mifflin streets. All other buildings would be demolished for new construction.

No city funds beyond the current $1.2 million operating subsidy for the Civic Center will be sought, Overture President George Austin said.

If management issues are resolved and necessary permits secured, phased construction could start by late 2000 and be completed by 2004, Austin said.

The proposal and gift were met by awe and praise, questions on management, maintenance, traffic and parking, and concerns about historic preservation.

The ambitious conceptual design is far more expensive than Frautschi's initial $50 million gift announced last July, Austin said.

When Austin announced Frautschi's intent to double his gift to $100 million, the auditorium erupted in cheers, whoops and hollers, and a sustained standing ovation for a beaming Frautschi, who was seated in the audience.

"I knew I had to fund whatever was

Please see **ARTS**, Page 2A

■ Arts groups react/**2A**
■ Hesselberg on Frautschi/**2A**
■ Quotes of the day/**2A**
■ Arts scene timeline/**3A**
■ Area businesses face decisions/**3A**

An artist's rendering of what the proposed Downtown arts district might look like, looking down Fairchild Street from State Street. As pictured, the proposed theater is far left, the proposed mid-sized theater is in the middle, and at far right is the proposed entrance to the renovated Isthmus Playhouse.

ANALYSIS

Don't mourn loss of theater

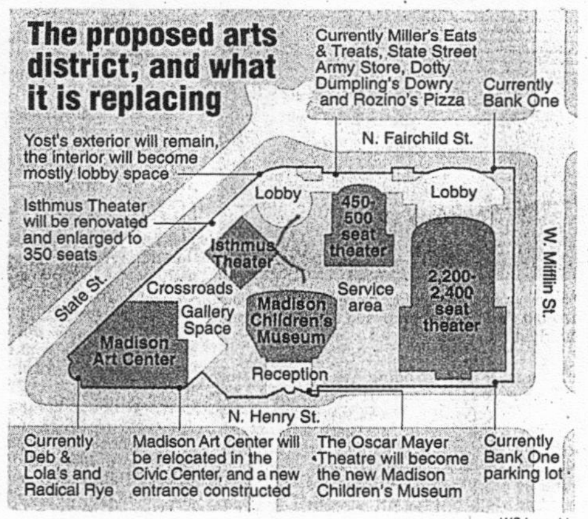

WSJ graphic

Oscar Mayer served purpose and will continue to do so

By Tom Alesia
Wisconsin State Journal

The Oscar Mayer Theatre became a punching bag Tuesday.

Take your pick from the criticism fired at the 2,200-seat facility from various arts leaders:

Awful sound. Awful seats. Awful ventilation. Awful backstage. Awful sightlines. Awful restrooms. Awful stage space. Awful exterior.

"It is not a good facility," Madison Civic Center Director Bob D'Angelo said flatly after the press conference. (Bet Bob doesn't plan to use that line as the theater's slogan to promote next fall's season.)

After all, he's booked a stellar season, featuring Kiri Te Kanawa, Emanuel Ax, Itzhak Perlman, Martha Graham Dance Company, "Show Boat," Ladysmith Black Mambazo and dozens of other world-renowned acts.

In other words, we've got it good now.

So don't expect the new theater — likely to open in late 2002 — to increase the caliber of

Please see **ANALYSIS**, Page 3A

Medicare drug plan unveiled

Price of prescription subsidy: $24 a month

By Larry Lipman
Cox News Service

WASHINGTON — President Clinton offered a plan Tuesday to modernize the 1960s-era Medicare program by including a prescription drug benefit and increased competition among managed care plans.

Republicans in Congress immediately criticized the plan for not providing enough protection against catastrophic medical expenses and offering lavish coverage for the wealthy.

"In a nation bursting with prosperity, no senior should have to choose between buying food and buying medicine," Clinton said, unveiling his plan in the White House East Room.

Clinton's plan would offer the 38 million elderly and disabled Medicare beneficiaries the option of having the government subsidize half of their drug costs up to $1,000 beginning in 2002 and $5,000 when fully implemented by 2008.

Plan participants would pay $24 a month for the voluntary Medicare Part D drug program. The premium would rise to $44 by 2008. The drug benefit would cost the federal government $118 billion over 10 years, much of which the administration expects would be offset by reduced spending on hospitals and other treatment because seniors were receiving proper medication.

■ Preventive care emphasized/4A

Elderly with incomes below 135 percent of the poverty line — currently $11,000 for individuals, $17,000 for couples — would not have to pay drug premiums.

"This is a drug benefit our seniors can afford at a price America can afford," Clinton said.

Other facets of the plan include increased competition among managed care plans to cover a core set of benefits and elimination of deductibles and copayments for Medicare-approved preventive care services such as cancer screenings.

"The plan is credible, sensible and fiscally responsible. It will secure the health of Medicare while improving the health of our seniors," Clinton said.

Tuesday's announcement fulfilled Clinton's promise last March to offer his own reform plan after the Bipartisan Medicare Reform Commission failed to issue a recommendation to Congress.

The commission's leaders, Sen. John Breaux, D-La., and Rep. Bill Thomas, R-Calif., said they saw Clinton's plan as a positive development — although both were critical of numerous provisions.

Clinton's proposal does little to change Medicare's basic structure, but with an infusion of the projected federal surplus, it gives the program a sound fiscal future well into the next century.

Without changes, Medicare Part A, which pays for hospital charges out of the payroll tax, is expected to be depleted by 2015. Clinton's plan would shift 15 percent of the budget surplus, nearly $800 billion over the next 15 years, into the Part A trust fund, extending its life until 2027.

After years of failing to provide a drug benefit because it was considered too expensive, the fight now is likely to be over how rather than whether to provide a prescription drug benefit.

Madison boy to inherit writer Shel Silverstein's fortune

Children's author, songwriter leaves at least $20 million

By Dee J. Hall
Wisconsin State Journal

A 15-year-old Madison boy will inherit at least $20 million from his late father, Shel Silverstein, the well-known cartoonist, songwriter, poet and children's author who died in May.

An attorney for the estate of Silverstein confirmed that the teen-ager is the sole heir to the fortune of the reclusive author, who sold 14 million books and wrote dozens of popular songs. The boy's family asked that his name not be revealed to protect his privacy.

Silverstein, whose main residence was in Key West, Fla., was found dead of a heart attack May 10 at his home. Although media reports put his age at 66, court documents filed in Monroe County, Fla., say he was 68.

"He (the teen-ager) was the only heir. There was no will, and it all goes to him," said Robert Gunn, a West Palm Beach, Fla., attorney who is helping handle the estate.

Under Florida law, the boy stands to inherit Silverstein's entire fortune when he turns 18.

According to attorneys for the estate, Silverstein and the boy's mother never married. When contacted at her home, the mother declined comment, saying "I am a mother trying to protect my child — that's my viewpoint."

Silverstein

Michael McCloud, a close friend of Silverstein's from Key West, said Silverstein had a good relationship with his son and the boy's mother. The two often visited Silverstein at his tiny Key West home, a 700-square-foot place considered big by local standards, McCloud said.

"He had a front yard big enough to park a bicycle in and a backyard big enough for a party of four," said McCloud, a singer and songwriter.

McCloud said Silverstein, who was known for his quirky, subversive and sometimes raunchy humor, was extremely private. Even though they knew each other for more than 15 years, McCloud says he doesn't know whether Silverstein ever married. Biographies of Silverstein

Please see **INHERIT**, Page 7A

INDEX

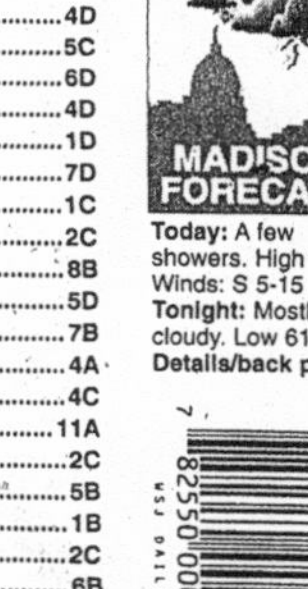

Today: A few showers. High 74. Winds: S 5-15 mph. **Tonight:** Mostly cloudy. Low 61. **Details/back page**

7 82550 00001 2 WSJ DAILY

160th Year — No. 196 © 1999 Wisconsin State Journal

WISCONSIN  STATE JOURNAL

★★★

THURSDAY/JULY 15, 1999 MADISON, WISCONSIN 50 CENTS

MILLER PARK TRAGEDY

Crane falls on unfinished stadium; 3 die

By Scott Milfred and Susan Lampert Smith
Wisconsin State Journal

MILWAUKEE — A giant crane used for building Miller Park collapsed Wednesday onto the unfinished stadium, crumpling over the structure, killing three workers and injuring five others, authorities said.

"It looks like a bomb went off," Milwaukee County Sheriff Lev Baldwin said of the collapse, which was reported at 5:14 p.m. "It's treacherous and unbelievable."

Firefighters had made three passes through the rubble late Wednesday to look for other victims but had not found any. Body-sniffing dogs were brought in to search through the night.

The injured crane operator and other workers were taken to Froedtert Memorial Lutheran Hospital. The crane operator, 64, whose name was not released, was in satisfactory condition with a broken hip, said hospital spokesman Mark McLaughlin.

The injured man has 47 years of experience as a crane operator, including 15 years on the crane that collapsed, McLaughlin said.

The crane, nicknamed "Big Blue," collapsed while trying to lift a section of the retractable roof. Strong winds in the area were gusting to about 30 mph at the time, although authorities would not say whether wind may have caused the accident.

There was no word on how Wednesday's accident would affect the timetable for the stadium, scheduled to open next season.

The Brewers' scheduled home game was postponed for tonight against the Kansas City Royals in the existing Milwaukee County Stadium, which is adjacent to the site of the new one.

The ballpark was born in controversy in the Legislature in 1995, and financial wrangling continued, delaying the construction start until November 1996 and costing Milwaukee the 1999 All-Star Game, which was played Tuesday in Boston.

A state audit released in June found the project will cost $399.4 million, an increase of $77 million over the original budget.

Construction has resulted in a few accidents.

Last month, several workers were injured when a steel girder being lowered into position collided with an aerial basket.

A worker fell 60 feet on May 10 and was hospitalized about a week with multiple injuries. The federal Occupational Safety and Health administration fined the construction firms $4,500 for safety violations in that accident.

John Anderson, chief steward of the state building inspectors Local 333, raised concerns about state oversight of the massive project, saying, "our union has had a concern that there should be more state inspectors on that project."

But Thompson's chief of staff Robert Woods said the state did add an employee to oversee construction, although he said the person may not be a union member.

"We do have an inspector on site, but they're not there for

Please see CRANE, Page 2A

Associated Press

The remains of the 567-foot-tall construction crane known as "Big Blue" drape across the unfinished Milwaukee Brewers' Miller Park, where three workers were killed and at least five injured Wednesday afternoon. The crane was lifting 400-ton roof sections when it collapsed.

■ Chronology/2A
■ Miller Park at a glance/3A
■ Officials, fans shocked/3A
■ 'Big Blue' facts, figures/3A

WSJ graphic

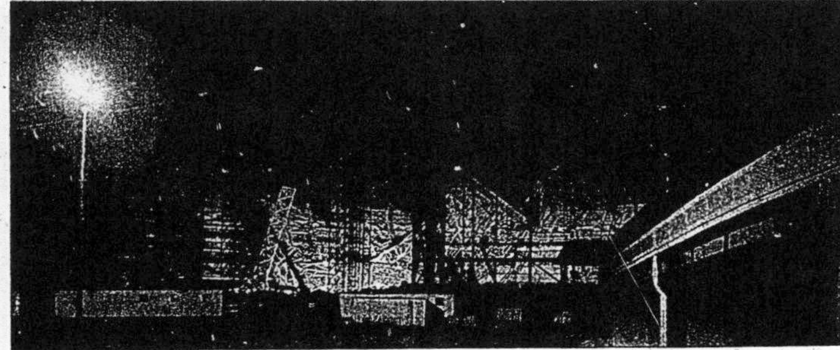

SARAH B. TEWS/WSJ photo

Floodlights illuminate the wreckage in Miller Park on Wednesday night as rescue workers searched for more victims after the collapse of a construction crane lifting a roof section.

DANE COUNTY FAIR

SARAH B. TEWS/WSJ photo

Who is Joe Sarbacker pulling into the Dane County Fair? Find out on 3B.

Affordable AIDS drug could save babies

■ At $4 dollars a treatment, developing countries could get a powerful new weapon.

By Lauran Neergaard
AP medical writer

WASHINGTON — Scientists working in Uganda have discovered a dramatically more effective way to prevent pregnant women from spreading the AIDS virus to their babies: a drug treatment that costs just $4 per mother and could save up to 1,000 newborns a day.

The drug nevirapine already is widely sold around the world to treat AIDS. But the new study found it is 47 percent more effective than the therapy now recommended in developing countries for preventing mother-to-baby transmission of the AIDS virus.

The discovery, announced Wednesday by U.S. scientists, could finally boost AIDS prevention among the world's poorest countries because for the first time the nations most afflicted by the AIDS epidemic could afford to buy babies some protection.

"You're talking about the possibility of preventing infection in up to 1,000 babies per day for a cost that is really very minor," said Dr. Anthony Fauci of the U.S. National Institutes of Health, which funded the research. "Now all of a sudden it falls, at least in some countries, within the realm of affordability."

"This research provides real hope that we may be able to protect many of Africa's next generation from the ravages of AIDS," said Uganda's health minister, Crispus Kiyonga, in a statement.

One of the greatest successes in the fight against AIDS is using the drug AZT to lower pregnant women's chances of spreading the deadly virus to their newborns. In the United States and other wealthy countries, infected mothers typically receive five months of AZT, a therapy that cuts in half their babies' risk of infection.

But that treatment can cost more than $1,000, far beyond what developing countries can afford.

Last year, scientists discovered that giving far fewer AZT doses, starting during labor, could protect newborns, although not as effectively as the treatment Americans get. But even that "short-course AZT therapy" was too expensive for many countries.

Nevirapine is a cheaper AIDS drug. Although it works against the same viral target as AZT, it stays in the body for a longer time, crosses the placenta and even gets into breast milk.

Widespread use of nevirapine could prevent between 300,000 and 400,000 babies a year from contracting HIV at birth, the NIH said.

The new study has implications for American women, too: If a woman goes into labor without having had prenatal AZT treatment, doctors could consider giving her nevirapine, Fauci said.

INDEX

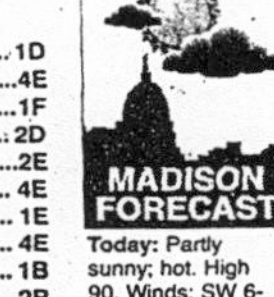

MADISON FORECAST

Today: Partly sunny; hot. High 90. Winds: SW 6-12 mph.
Tonight: Partly cloudy. Low 68.
Details/back page

RHYTHM

Psychosexual journey

'Eyes Wide Shut' hits screen on Friday

NATION/4A

Radio uproar

Radical public station KPFA fights changes

SPORTS/1C

Trash talking's rich history

Packers' Brett Favre among best of 'em

MONEY/1F

Vegging out?

State may lose canning ranking

DAYBREAK/1E

Sarong way to dress?

Pondering a new style for men

RHYTHM

Intro to Introversion

Meet the teens who survived the Battle of the Bands

SPORTS/1C

On the rise

Madison's Steinhauer finds success on LPGA Tour

WISCONSIN STATE JOURNAL

★★★ CENTS

150th Year — No. 203 © 1999 Wisconsin State Journal

THURSDAY, JULY 22, 1999 MADISON, WISCONSIN

Bodies recovered from JFK Jr. plane

Burial at sea planned this morning for Kennedy

By Erica Noonan
Associated Press

AQUINNAH, Mass. — Navy divers found the bodies of John F. Kennedy Jr., his wife and sister-in-law in the wreckage of Kennedy's plane Wednesday, ending the painful, five-day vigil their families endured during the search of the waters off Martha's Vineyard.

The bodies were brought to shore Wednesday night and taken to the medical examiner's office for autopsies.

A Navy destroyer, the USS Briscoe, was headed to Cape Cod for Kennedy's burial at sea at 9 a.m. today, sources said, speaking on condition of anonymity. The sources did not know whether all three victims would be involved.

Bruce Fisher, the head of a business that leases out guides to help vessels navigate through unfamiliar waters, said his office was called by Navy officials Wednesday night and told there would likely be cremations and a burial of the ashes at sea.

The bodies were found 116 feet below the surface after ships from the Navy, Coast Guard and National Oceanic and Atmospheric Administration spent the night scouring a site 7½ miles southwest of Martha's Vineyard.

After a search that had the nation transfixed since Saturday, the plane's body, or fuselage, was spotted by underwater cameras at 11:30 p.m. Tuesday. The bodies o[illegible] three victims were found in the fuselage, Coast Guard Rear Adm. Richard

Please see **KENNEDY,** Page 3A

Associated Press photos

ABOVE: Sen. Edward Kennedy, D-Mass., center with sunglasses, is flanked by Douglas Kennedy at left and Edward Kennedy Jr., as well as Rep. Patrick Kennedy, D-R.I., left front, and Maxwell Kennedy, far right, as the casket bearing the remains of one of the victims is placed into a van in Woods Hole, Mass. TOP: Edward Kennedy, front, stands with his son Patrick as they motor out Wednesday on a Coast Guard patrol boat to the site where John F. Kennedy Jr.'s plane crashed off Martha's Vineyard, Mass.

Searchers have recovered the bodies of John F. Kennedy Jr., Carolyn Bessette Kennedy and Lauren Bessette from the submerged fuselage.

Mass.
Martha's Vineyard
Gay Head
Airport
DETAIL

Graphic/LEE HULTENG/KRT

Clinton authorized extending search

Knight Ridder Newspapers

■ The science of the search/3A

WASHINGTON — On the day divers located the bodies of John F. Kennedy Jr., his wife and sister-in-law, President Clinton said he personally authorized extending the search effort beyond what would be done for other Americans because the Kennedy family played a special role in American life and deserved special attention.

Long close to the Kennedy family, Clinton said Wednesday he agreed to extend the search effort Sunday when told the Coast Guard was confident it could recover Kennedy's plane and body if given more time.

"Because of the role of the Kennedy family in our national lives and because of the enormous losses that they have sustained in our lifetimes, I thought it was appropriate to give them a few more days," Clinton said in response to a question about the search at a White House news conference.

"If anyone believes that was wrong, the Coast Guard is not at fault, I am," Clinton added.

Clinton's decision came when it was clear that Kennedy, his wife and her sister were dead and the massive search and rescue effort became a search and recovery operation.

"The rescue and recovery efforts that were undertaken were consistent with what would have been done in any other case," Clinton said of the first two days.

Clinton said he spoke Monday with Coast Guard Rear Adm. Richard Larrabee, "at a time when the operation might normally have ceased." Clinton said it was Larrabee who suggested spending more time on the search, "because of the circumstances here and because of who's involved."

Though Clinton did not mention it, there also was concern in the government that if it did not recover Kennedy's body and the airplane wreckage, scavengers or souvenir hunters would. The same improvements in technology used by the Coast Guard and Navy also are available to private concerns like the one that discovered the Titanic.

Given the obsession and conspiracy theories that still surround the assassination of Kennedy's father, a missing plane and missing body might have fueled rampant speculation and theories.

Madison College troubled

■ The financial situation forces a re-examination of strategy and makes school this fall unlikely.

By Phil Brinkman
Wisconsin State Journal

Nearly a year after it was forced to close because of financial difficulties, Madison College still has not dug out from under a pile of debt.

The money problems and uncertainties about the future direction of the school all but guarantee it won't reopen this fall, school officials say.

"The reality is, there has to be money, and if it opens it won't be run the way it was before," said the Rev. Stephen Stauffacher, pastor of Capitoland Christian Center and a member of the college's board of trustees.

Stauffacher, who took over the ailing school from its last president, Charles Wilkerson, in October, originally hoped to reopen the facility at 760 E. Verona Road in the town of Verona last January.

Stauffacher said he was moved to intervene to save the attached Birchwood Court senior housing center, where his church had offered services for seven years.

At the time, Stauffacher said, he knew the school had $2 million in debts, acquired when the college purchased the retirement facility in the hopes of setting up a new campus and dormitory.

But the actual debt turned out to be several hundred thousand dollars more, after students were given their tuition money back and contractors demanded to be paid.

"Who knows? It could be bigger," Stauffacher said this week of the college's debt.

Officials were also taken aback by a consultant's report that said the school needed to offer more advanced instruction to compete with other colleges.

In the last decade, Stauffacher said, six in 10 two-year business colleges have folded. If it is to succeed, the school, which started before the Civil War as Madison Business College, has to offer more than basic skills, Stauffacher said.

"So we decided to get this in perspective," Stauffacher said of eventually reopening the school. "We said, 'If it takes us two years to do it, let's take two years.' "

Stauffacher said his first concern was saving the nursing home, and he said he'd sell the school property and go back to renting if that's what it took.

Meanwhile, the state Department of Justice is continuing its investigation into whether Wilkerson lured members of the college's failed football team from out of state with false promises of financial help.

"It's likely to be a while yet" before the investigation is complete, said Jim Haney, spokesman for Attorney General James Doyle.

Wilkerson, who sunk much of his own money in the college, moved to Texas late last year, where he said he and his wife were so broke they had to move in with one of their children.

INDEX

MADISON FORECAST

Today: Hazy, hot and humid. High 92. Winds: W 6-12 mph.
Tonight: Warm and muggy. Low 68.
Details/back page

State technical colleges attract more minority students

By Dee J. Hall
Wisconsin State Journal

Aggressive efforts boosted the number of minority students attending Wisconsin technical colleges by 39 percent during the 1990s, a report issued Wednesday says.

At Madison Area Technical College, the numbers are even brighter, said Calvin Williams, affirmative action officer for the college.

The Wisconsin Technical College System Board said the number of minorities participating in programs and classes at the technical colleges was 43,012 in 1998, up from 30,860 in 1990.

In 1998, roughly 10.1 percent of the student population was racial and ethnic minority members — equal to the state's minority population. That compares with a 7.3 percent minority population in 1990. The percentages are estimates since a certain number of students each year don't report their racial or ethnic makeup.

"On the one hand, we're pleased that there is an increase and it's a pretty significant increase — but that's because we've been working at it," said Deborah Mahaffey, director of student and support services for the system.

But Mahaffey said the report did highlight some areas for improvement. For one thing, the technical colleges could do more to recruit minority students right out of high school, Mahaffey said.

Technical college minority attendance

Minority student population, Wisconsin Technical College System, 1990 and 1998:

YEAR	WHITE	MINORITY	N/A	% MINORITY*
1998	367,794	43,012	29,896	10.1%
1990	389,672	30,860	27,187	7.3%

*The percent minority is calculated using only students reporting membership in an ethnic/racial group.

SOURCE: Wisconsin Technical College System Board WSJ graphic

And, she said, the system will examine whether minority students who enroll in the technical colleges fulfill their goals — be they two-year associate degrees, extra job training, one-year certificates or preparation for college. Minority graduation figures for the system don't accurately reflect the success rate for minorities since many students are attending for reasons other than obtaining a degree, she said.

The technical college system, which includes 16 colleges with multiple campuses, has been striving to increase minority participation since a governor's task force in 1990 concluded minorities were under-represented in the system.

LaVerne Dixon, who heads the effort to recruit and retain minority students, said the state has been funding aggressive efforts for the past several years. The system spent $464,000 last year on programs across the state to draw minority students in, she said,

Please see **MINORITIES,** Page 3A

ENVELOPES INSIDE

DAYBREAK/1G

She'll forgive, but never forget

Attempted murder a tie that binds for Jackie Millar

SPORTS/1F

Local star at Lambeau

Madison's Donald Hayes returns with Panthers

150th Year — No. 346 © 1999 Wisconsin State Journal

WISCONSIN STATE JOURNAL

★★★ SUNDAY, DECEMBER 12, 1999 MADISON, WISCONSIN $1.75

JOHN MANIACI/WSJ photo

Check 'n Go on East Washington Avenue is part of a payday lending industry that's growing at an explosive rate in Wisconsin.

Critics say payday lenders prey on people in financial binds, and proposed legislation seeks to provide remedies.

Interest of 500%

■ Short-term lenders say they fill a void.

By Rick Barrett
Business reporter

Dramatic growth of payday lenders that often charge 500 percent interest is driving a push in the Legislature for a law to protect consumers.

At the root of the problem: Although this has been one of the most prosperous decades of the century, easy credit and an endless array of tempting goods has encouraged people to live beyond their means. This new comfort with debt, combined with a lack of regulation, has opened the door for explosive growth in the short-term loan industry.

Yet critics of payday lenders say they prey on stressed consumers and those just trying to make ends meet, encouraging them to borrow more — at exorbitant rates.

"The short-term fix for small amounts of money, to tide people over from payday to payday, has produced a financial tidal wave of problems," said state Sen. Judy Robson, D-Beloit, sponsor of legislation to cap payday loans at a 36 percent annual interest rate.

Payday loan companies profiting

The number of payday loan companies in Wisconsin is up, and so is business. From 1996 through 1998 loan amounts were up 1,213 percent. Loans in millions of dollars:

1996 (17 companies; 80,000 loans) $11.2

1997 (64 companies; 350,618 loans) $73.9

1998 (162 companies; 630,300 loans) $147.1

NOTE: In 1999 there are about 194 companies

SOURCE: WSJ research WSJ graphic

Bearing names like Check 'n Go, Check Into Cash, and Check Mart, the number of payday lending outlets in the state has mushroomed from 17 in 1996 to nearly 200, according to Wisconsin Department of Financial Institutions records.

And payday lenders have increased their Wisconsin business from 80,000 loans totaling $11.2 million in 1996 to 630,300 loans totaling $147.1 million in 1998, state records show.

Mostly, the companies write two-week loans to workers against their paychecks in a process that

Please see **LOANS,** Page 4A

Heisman is his!

UW's Ron Dayne is crowned college football's best player

SOUVENIR SECTION

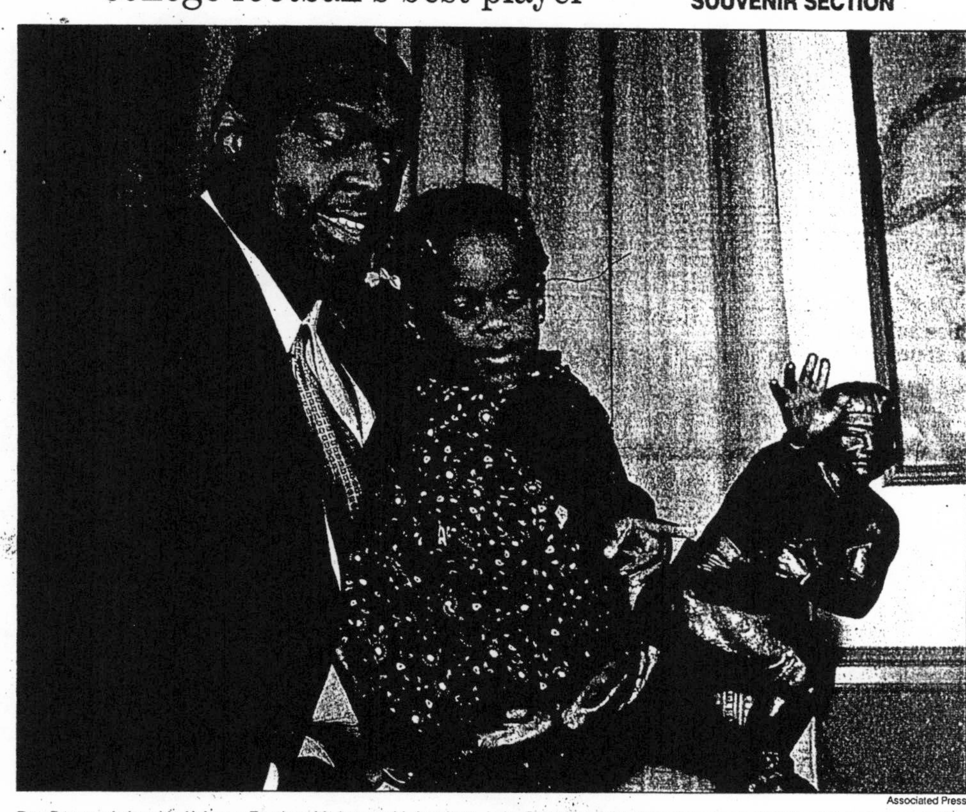

Associated Press

Ron Dayne admires his Heisman Trophy with 2-year-old daughter, Jada, Saturday night at the Downtown Athletic Club in New York City. The UW tailback rushed into college football history by winning the Heisman, college football's ultimate individual honor.

Y's fight highlights tax-exemption issue

■ When institutions don't have to pay property taxes, others have to pay more.

By Jeff Mayers
Capitol bureau chief

A nasty debate over the tax-exempt status of YMCA fitness facilities is casting attention onto an often overlooked reason for the constant pressure on property taxes.

Many personal and real-estate property tax exemptions — 20 pages of them are laid out in a state guidebook for assessors — eat away at the property tax base. The more exemptions there are, the more non-exempt property taxpayers — homeowners and businesses — pay for school costs, police and fire protection, garbage pickup and other municipal services.

There is little dispute that government property should be tax exempt, but there also are many privately owned parcels that are tax exempt. There are property tax exemptions for land occupied by archaeological sites, nonprofit hospitals, labor temples, veterans' memorial halls, benevolent nursing and retirement homes, and religious properties. There's even one for nonprofit youth hockey

Please see **TAX,** Page 3A

Tax-exempt private property

State and local privately owned property that was tax exempt in 1998.

State

38% Churches ($5.33 billion)
20.3% Housing ($2.85 billion)
16.8% Medical ($2.35 billion)
12.1% Education ($1.69 billion)
7.9% Public benefit* ($1.1 billion)
4.9% Other ($0.69 billion)

Madison

47.2% Churches ($249.1 million)
18.4% Housing ($97.1 million)
13.8% Medical ($72.7 million)
13.3% Public benefit* ($70.3 million)
6.2% Education ($32.5 million)
1.2% Other ($6.1 million)

* Includes YMCAs

SOURCE: Dept. of Revenue, City of Madison Assessor's Office WSJ graphic

Panama Canal ready to bid U.S. goodbye

■ Noon on Dec. 31 marks the end of U.S. control. Will Panama try to squeeze the region dry, and what about China?

By Thomas Ginsberg
Knight Ridder Newspapers

BALBOA, Panama — Down the road from the Panama Canal, next to a vacant American high school, a giant digital clock rises in the tropical sky, displaying rapidly dwindling hours and seconds.

The clock, unlike many worldwide, is counting down not to the end of the year but to noon on Dec. 31. That's when the old order here is to give way to the new. It's the moment when, finally, the Yankees will go home.

The United States will at that instant formally hand over the waterway. The Panama Canal — conceived by Spain, started by France, and completed by the United States — will become Panama's canal.

A ceremony Tuesday will mark the final withdrawal of all U.S. armed forces from Panama. On Dec. 31, a moment of symbolism, apprehension and high hope, the formal handover will take place.

"The face of colonialism ... is

Please see **PANAMA,** Page 8A

WEATHER

Today Partly sunny. High 38. Winds: SW 6-12 mph.

Tonight Partly cloudy. Low 28. **Details/ back page**

TOMORROW

Legislators take advantage of technology to do their jobs more effectively.

INDEX

ROSE BOWL GAME DAY: 1D

WISCONSIN STATE JOURNAL

50 CENTS

161st Year — No. 1 © 2000 Wisconsin State Journal

SATURDAY, JANUARY 1, 2000 MADISON, WISCONSIN

A new age!

■ Millennium rides in on hope and joy
■ Y2K threat passes with few glitches

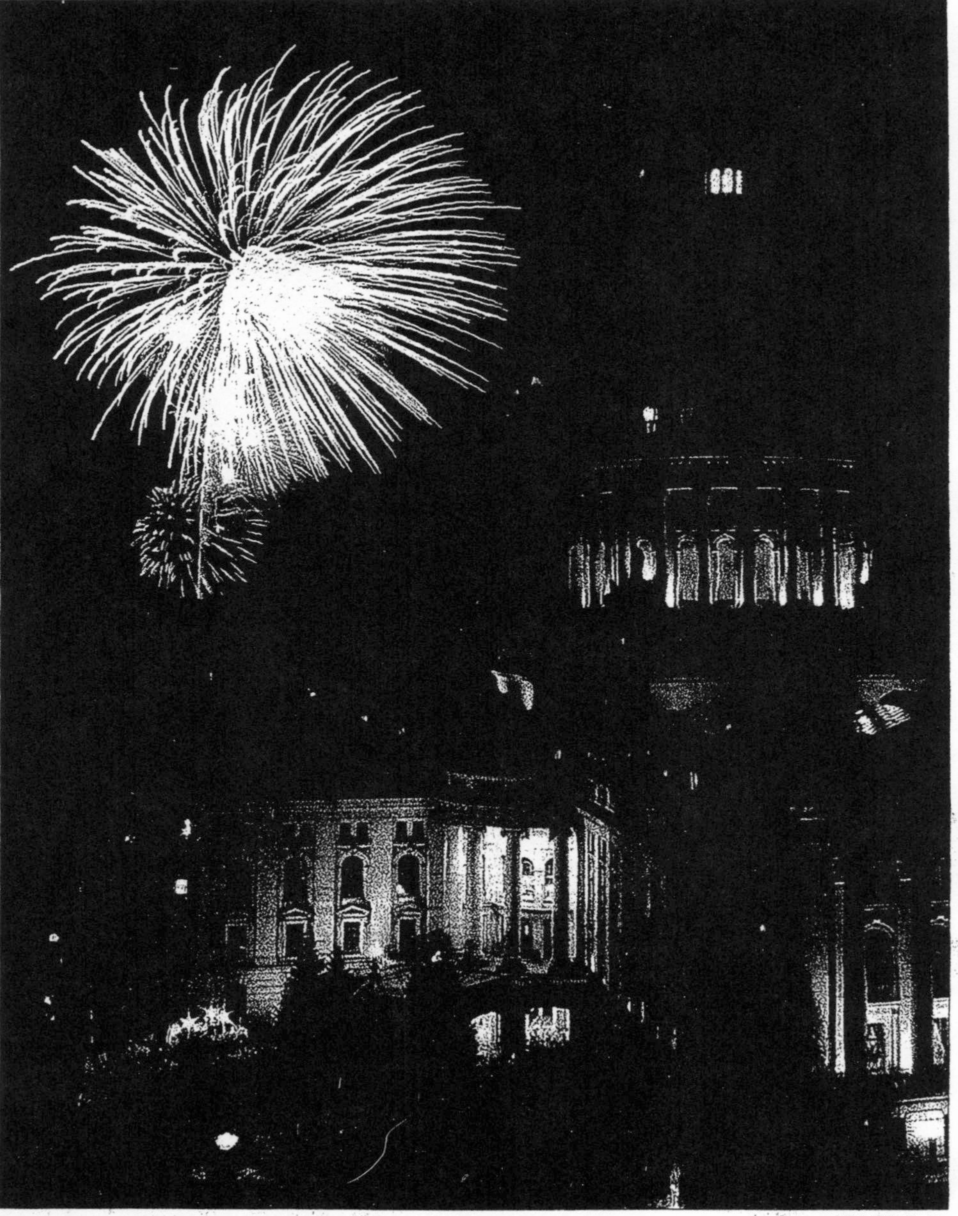

STEVE APPS/WSJ photo

Millennium Booms fireworks explode over the Madison Capitol Friday night to celebrate the new year.

By Patricia Hoftiezer Simms
Wisconsin State Journal

Despite worldwide expectations of millennial misconduct, humans and their machines behaved better than expected as the year jubilantly rolled over to 2000.

In Tonga and Kiribati, in London, Paris, Beijing and Wisconsin, people reveled.

Linked by satellite TV, the world's nearly 200 countries, in their 24 time zones, celebrated. South Sea islanders sang Handel's "Hallelujah Chorus." Buddhist monks prayed for peace in Japan and a German choir sang in a church in Nazareth, Israel.

In Russia, the bombshell was political, not technological, as longtime president Boris Yeltsin resigned.

Seattle was subdued, but New York's Times Square was the scene of a wild street party for an estimated 1 million people. From the harbor in Sydney, Australia, to the Eiffel Tower in Paris, fireworks exploded across the world.

Fireworks also flooded the Madison skies, and good hearts rose to the occasion.

A couple in country-western getup were set to marry at 11:59 p.m. Friday at Club Tavern and Grille in Middleton.

A 5-pound 8-ounce boy, son of Karen and Andy Derrick of Beaver Dam, was born at 48 minutes past midnight by Caesarean section at Meriter Hospital — the first baby born at a Madison hospital in the year 2000.

State and county Y2K preparedness teams were all smiles, and on State Street, David Haltom, a kazoo-carrying student from Springfield, Mo., was craving a brat. "Brats and a kazoo. That's New Year's Eve in Wisconsin."

Shortly after midnight, a swelling crowd smashed bottles and glasses, threw bottles and rocks at cars and tore down street signs at the three-way intersection of North Broom, West Gilman and State streets. Madison police shut down State Street from Lake Street to Gilman Street.

New Year's Eve joy was also marred locally by the death of a man in a traffic crash north of the Dane County Regional Airport.

As for technology, the world's computers appear to have survived the Year 2000 rollover.

As midnight passed in the first industrialized nations of New Zealand, Australia and Japan, there were no reports of major disruptions in gas, water and electricity distribution systems.

Nor were there reports of major infrastructure problems in the less-developed nations, from China, through India, and across the vast African continent.

In Wisconsin, a malfunctioning clock was the biggest problem utilities experienced. That was blamed on faulty reception of a satellite signal, Wisconsin Electric spokesman Mike John said.

In Washington, there was so little news coming from the Y2K Information Coordination Center Friday that some television technicians popped in a video — "Apocalypse Now."

State Journal staff and wire services contributed to this report.

YELTSIN QUITS

MOSCOW — Pleading for forgiveness, Boris Yeltsin resigned Friday as Russia's president, clearing the way for his handpicked successor to lead the world's largest nation into a new age and fix the mistakes he admitted having made through eight chaotic years.

Putin

Prime Minister Vladimir Putin, who will be acting president until elections are held in March, signed a document granting Yeltsin broad immunity from prosecution, inviting speculation that a deal had been made to entice Yeltsin into early retirement. Details/9A

NEW ZEALAND

Sam Lanauze stands with his horse, Dribbles, as they watch the first sunrise of the new millennium on Mt. Hakepa on Pitt Island, New Zealand, early today. Pitt Island is one of the first inhabited land masses in the world to see 2000.

INDONESIA

A young couple kiss to celebrate 2000 as others dance in a pool of bubbles at a disco on Kuta Beach, Bali, shortly after midnight today.

FRANCE

In Paris, the Eiffel Tower dances in a dazzling ballet of fiery colors before popping its cork to spew symbolic bubbles. Crowds of Parisians and tourists then descended on the Champs-Elysees to keep going until dawn.

CHINA

Chinese and foreigners walk along the Great Wall of China at Badaling, north of Beijing, early today. Hundreds gathered to tour the Great Wall, which was lit up for the occasion.

WASHINGTON, D.C.

With an extravagant fireworks display dancing up the sides of the Washington Monument as the 21st century arrived in America, President Clinton called on the nation to fear not the future but to "welcome it, embrace it and create it."

ENGLAND

As Big Ben hit midnight and world air traffic control computers rolled into 2000 Greenwich Mean Time, Queen Elizabeth II lights a beacon as she travels to the Millennium Dome.

SOUTH AFRICA

South African President Thabo Mbeki, right, and former president Nelson Mandela toast in the new millennium on Robben Island in Cape Town, South Africa, early today.

INSIDE

Y2K: Were we fooled?/3A

★★★ WISCONSIN  STATE JOURNAL

MORE COVERAGE OF BADGERS' WIN IN SPORTS

SUNDAY, JANUARY 2, 2000 MADISON, WISCONSIN $1.75

17 BADGERS  CARDINAL 9

Sweet repeat!

Badgers achieve a Big Ten first by posting back-to-back Rose Bowl wins

JOHN MANIACI/WSJ photo

Badgers linebacker Donnel Thompson, left, a former Madison West athlete, and tackle Chris McIntosh are all smiles as they talk with UW Coach Barry Alvarez following the University of Wisconsin's 17-9 victory over Stanford in the Rose Bowl game on Saturday.

Dayne named MVP in milestone victory

By Andy Baggot
Sports reporter

PASADENA, Calif. — When you are first to reach the mountain top you do not quibble about the aesthetics.

The University of Wisconsin football team became the first in Big Ten Conference history to win consecutive Rose Bowls Saturday when it outlasted Stanford, 17-9.

Looking very much like a team that had not played in 49 days, the fourth-ranked Badgers (10-2) never established an offensive rhythm and struggled in the face of penalties and tactical breakdowns.

But thanks to some stellar defense and a highly memorable curtain-closing performance by Heisman Trophy-winning tailback Ron Dayne, UW followed up its 38-31 win over UCLA last New Year's Day with a milestone triumph before an announced crowd of 93,731 at the Rose Bowl.

"It's a great feeling," said Dayne, who capped his brilliant Badgers career with a 34-carry, 200-yard effort that earned him Most Valuable Player honors for the second straight year. "We were able to accomplish our goals from the beginning. After we lost two games (to Cincinnati and Michigan in September), I guess this is our reward. I'm

Please see **BADGERS**, Page 2A

CRAIG SCHREINER/WSJ photo

Ron Dayne hoists his Rose Bowl MVP trophy Saturday.

When game was ugly, Badger fans were snarly

By Elizabeth Brixey
Wisconsin State Journal

PASADENA, Calif. — Wisconsin fans didn't lose faith Saturday. But at the half, when Stanford was leading 9-3 in the Rose Bowl, they wavered. They groused and muttered. They jeered at Stanford's fans and marching band in unprintable language.

"Barry's going to have to kick some booty in the locker room," said UW-Madison alum Hilde Surbaugh, the rhinestones in her Badger-red sunglasses twinkling in the hide-and-go-seek sun.

"They didn't play well offensively. No consistency," said Clarence Stensby, who played right guard for the Badgers in the 1953 Rose Bowl game, which they lost to Southern California. "But we have the whole next half. It's a 60-minute game."

Sure enough, a couple of minutes into the second half, Heisman Trophy winner Ron Dayne scored a touchdown and Wisconsin took the lead. Later, quarterback Brooks Bollinger got a touchdown on a 1-yard plunge, and the Badgers hung on for a 17-9 victory.

Team loyalty and colorful, sometimes naughty school spirit was abundant at Wisconsin's third trip to the Rose Bowl under Coach Barry Alvarez. In a damp chill that felt like an October day in Madison, Badger fans went nuts not only for the players but for Bucky Badger in his red cape, the UW Marching Band and the cheerleaders.

The stadium drew 93,731 people — and it looked like a tight squeeze in plenty of places — but the fans leaped to their feet over and over, ringing cowbells when they were happy and making

Please see **FANS**, Page 2A

Inside

Inside your *SUNDAY* State Journal . . .

SHOWCASE/1F

Movie mania

Previews of the Oscars, Wisconsin Film Festival

SPORTS/1D

B.C. upsets UW

Season ends suddenly as top-ranked Badgers lose 4-1

On to the finals

UW wins 78-60 to reach WNIT title game

DAYBREAK/1G

Robin's world

Some concerned about status of state bird

CLASSIFIED/1I

Employment Opportunities

	New Jobs	Total Jobs
General	132	190
Office/clerical	130	148
Health care	106	118
Total jobs in today's paper		1,096

161st Year — No. 85 © 2000 Wisconsin State Journal

★★★ WISCONSIN STATE JOURNAL

SUNDAY, MARCH 26, 2000 MADISON, WISCONSIN $1.75

Four sure!

Indianapolis, here come the Badgers

The Final Four

In Indianapolis Semifinals, April 1

■ Wisconsin (22-13) vs. Michigan State (30-7), approximately 7 p.m.

■ Florida-Oklahoma State winner vs. North Carolina-Tulsa winner, 4:42 p.m.

Championship

■ April 3, 8:18 p.m.

Inside

■ Final Four ticket info/3A

■ Complete coverage of Saturday's game in Sports/1D

By Tom Mulhern
Sports reporter

ALBUQUERQUE, N.M. — They grew up watching Final Four celebrations on television, so they knew what to do. They just never imagined it could really happen to them.

When the clock hit zeros Saturday and the unfathomable had become reality — the University of Wisconsin men's basketball team had won the NCAA tournament West regional with a 64-60 victory over Purdue — the UW players embraced on the court, quickly donned their Final Four T-shirts and hats and headed straight for the biggest section of Badgers fans.

Several players jumped on media tables, waved to the crowd and chanted "Final Four." The hardest thing was believing all this was actually taking place.

"I never would have imagined in my wildest dreams doing that, a Final Four celebration," junior forward Andy Kowske said. "There's no words that can describe it."

The celebration, including the ritual of cutting down the nets, was among the most emotional and euphoric following a UW sporting event in recent memory.

"It's unbelievable," junior forward Maurice Linton said. "You saw a couple guys

Please see BADGERS, Page 3A

Associated Press

The Badgers, with Mike Kelley in the center, leap for joy after completing their stunning run through the West region with Saturday's victory over Purdue.

ANDY MANIS/photo

Senior basketball player Jon Bryant, the West regional most valuable player, body surfs through the crowd at Camp Randall Stadium early today.

Badgers bask in some good Camp Randall karma

By Beth Williams and Brenda Ingersoll
Wisconsin State Journal

About 30,000 fans — from screaming students and gray-haired graduates to future Badger fans in strollers — turned out early today to bask in the fact that the University of Wisconsin will make its first Final Four appearance since 1941.

"What is there in life after this?" UW-Madison senior Ed Murray, co-chairman of the Badger Student Fan Club, asked shortly before the triumphant men's basketball team arrived at Camp Randall Stadium for a welcome-home celebration around 12:30 a.m.

He wasn't the only one think-

Please see KARMA, Page 3A

Russia soaks up U.S. aid; no end in sight

By Julia Malone
Cox News Service

WASHINGTON -- In the years after the Soviet Union's disintegration, the United States has sent Russia more than $7 billion to safeguard its nuclear arsenal, feed its people, prop up its space program and nourish the seedlings of a private enterprise economy.

The results have been, by almost all accounts, less than stellar.

Russia's economy has taken a nose-dive. Its space program fell behind in building its components for the International Space Station, creating delays for the project and cost overruns for U.S. taxpayers.

And despite a six-year effort and a half-billion dollars in U.S. assistance, only a small amount of Russia's nuclear materials are now stored in secure buildings.

Even so, there are few signs that America is about to cut off the aid spigot, now that acting President Vladimir Putin, the former KGB officer, moves toward becoming Russia's second democratically

Please see RUSSIA, Page 4A

Inside

■ Excerpts from an interview with UW-Madison Chancellor David Ward/6A

Ward sees creative UW future

By Elizabeth Brixey
Higher education reporter

In the 21st century, UW-Madison will see new subjects, new ways of teaching and new ways to pay for everything, says outgoing Chancellor David Ward.

"The campus is beginning to accept that . . . there are going to be new subjects, recombinations of subjects," he said. "I see us moving way ahead of a lot of other institutions on that."

Chancellor since 1993, the 61-year-old geography professor announced recently that he will step down at the end of the year, first to take a sabbatical and then to return to teaching and research.

Last week, Ward sat down for an hour in his Bascom Hall office to talk about the future at UW-Madison and public universities generally.

"Historically, the public university has been a place that has been

Please see WARD, Page 7A

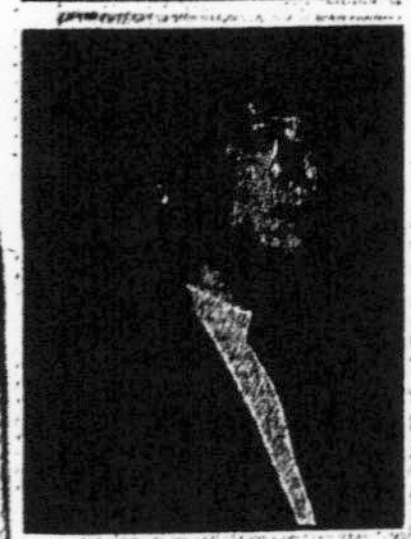

Diane Sykes

Age: 42
Hometown: Bayside
Education: Bachelor's degree from Northwestern University, 1980; law degree from Marquette University, 1984
Judicial career: Milwaukee County Circuit Court, 1992-99; Wisconsin Supreme Court, 1999-2000

Tipping the court's scales

■ Election will play a key role in determining the political slant of the state Supreme Court.

By Cary Segall
Wisconsin State Journal

People who know Wisconsin Supreme Court candidates Diane Sykes and Louis Butler say they have starkly different legal views, but each would be a fine high court justice.

"One good thing about this election is you have two candidates who are intellectually up to the task and I would rank Louie and Diane very close," says Howard Eisenberg, dean of Marquette University Law School.

But Eisenberg, who knows both candidates well and is backing neither, says they are worlds apart politically.

He says Sykes, 42, who was appointed to the court in September by Gov. Tommy Thompson to serve the last year of the

Please see COURT, Page 10A

Louis Butler

Age: 48
Hometown: Milwaukee
Education: Bachelor's degree from Lawrence University, 1973; law degree from UW-Madison, 1977
Judicial career: Milwaukee Municipal Court, 1992-present

■ A closer look at the two candidates and their decisions./10A

WEATHER

Today Mostly sunny. High 63. Winds: SW 12-25 mph.

Tonight Rain showers. Low 42. **Details/ back of Local**

TOMORROW

Who will join the Badgers and Michigan State in the NCAA tournament Final Four? Today's regional title games match Florida vs. Oklahoma State in the East and North Carolina vs. Tulsa in the South.

INDEX

Inside your *SUNDAY* State Journal . . .

YOUR FORUM/1B
How our privacy is threatened

INSIDE

SPORTS/1D
Badgers top gun

UW quarterback Brooks Bollinger is ready for a bigger role

DAYBREAK/1G

Will the TIE DIE?

CLASSIFIED/1I
Employment Opportunities

	New jobs	Total jobs
General	117	193
Office/clerical	113	129
Health care	86	100
Total jobs in today's paper		1,035

WISCONSIN STATE JOURNAL
SUNDAY, APRIL 23, 2000 MADISON, WISCONSIN $1.75

Elian is back in father's arms

EASTER SUNDAY

SARAH B. TEWS/WSJ photo

The Easter resurrection is portrayed in stained glass at St. James Catholic Church in Madison.

Reflecting on the meaning of Easter

■ It's about more than colored eggs and candy — a lot more.

By William R. Wineke
Wisconsin State Journal

The Rev. Kenneth Gast, pastor of Eastside Evangelical Lutheran Church, recalls meeting with a century-old parishioner in a nursing home.

"She said, 'I'm 100 years old; I don't have much to look forward to, anymore.' I told her, 'You've got the best thing to look forward to, resurrection and being with Jesus Christ forever,'" Gast reported.

The elderly parishioner quickly agreed.

To Gast, the story is a reminder that Easter Sunday is about more than colored eggs, candy and fragrant lilies.

This is a day that Christians throughout the Western world celebrate as confirmation that Jesus was raised from the dead after being crucified by Roman soldiers.

Eastern Orthodox churches, which follow a slightly different church year, will celebrate the resurrection on April 30.

Whatever the date, the idea that

Please see EASTER, Page 3A

In local
■ Christian Scientists observe Easter in their usual understated methods/1E

Inside

Use of force controversy
■ RIGHT: Elian Gonzalez is held by fisherman Donato Dalrymple inside Lazaro Gonzalez's bedroom early Saturday as Border Patrol agents storm the Miami home. The Clinton administration defended its use of force, but the chaotic scene also drew harsh criticism. Story/5A

The scene
■ Map details Saturday morning's frantic few minutes/5A

In Miami
■ Cuban-Americans express outrage at Elian's removal/5A

In Cuba
■ Elian's grandparents grateful for father-son reunion/5A

In Madison
■ Local Cuban-Americans fault Miami relatives/5A

What's ahead
■ Legal battle still could be long one/12A

Opinion
■ State Journal editorial/3B

Media
■ Dramatic photo sparks public relations war/3B

RIGHT: Elian Gonzalez arrived at Andrews Air Force Base, Md., at 9:42 a.m. Saturday and was immediately reunited with his father, Juan Miguel Gonzalez.

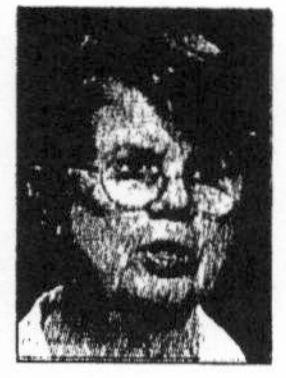

"That is what this case is still all about — the bond between a father and a son."
Attorney General Janet Reno

Associated Press photos

Federal agents carry Elian Gonzalez out of his Miami relatives' home shortly after 5:15 a.m. Saturday.

Standoff ends as boy is seized in pre-dawn raid

By Rick Bragg
New York Times

MIAMI — Armed U.S. immigration agents smashed their way into the Little Havana home of Elian Gonzalez's Miami relatives before dawn on Saturday, took the sobbing 6-year-old boy from a bedroom closet and flew him to a reunion with his father outside Washington.

As demonstrators wept in rage and coughed from pepper spray and tear gas, the agents wrapped the child in a blanket and carried him to an airport to fly him to Washington. The action touched off a fury in the streets outside the home where Cuban exiles have kept a vigil.

"What's happening? What's happening?" Elian said in Spanish as he was taken away. "Help me. Help me."

The agents, wearing shirts with the words "INS FEDERAL OFFICER" in bold yellow letters, ended a bitter standoff between Miami's exile community and a federal government that stopped fruitless negotiations with the child's defiant great-uncle and a community that saw Elian as a symbol of freedom and a precious victory, now perhaps lost, over President Fidel Castro of Cuba.

"God, how could you have performed only half a miracle?" asked a frantic, weeping Marisleysis Gonzalez, a 21-year-old cousin who had been the boy's closest

Please see ELIAN, Page 4A

Researchers are probing the potential, not just the problems, of aging

Maintaining that zest for life

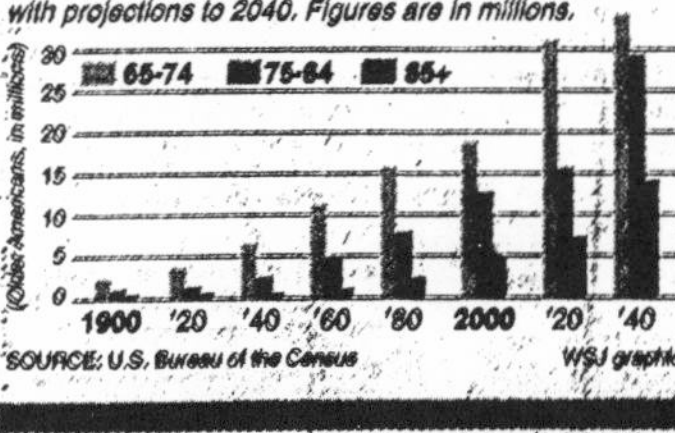

By Patricia Hoftiezer Simms
Health reporter

Americans are paying attention to the elderly as never before.

For one thing, demographers are predicting the U.S. population over 65 will swell in the next few decades: some call it the "longevity revolution."

People like Janet Misch, 92, represent the fastest-growing segment of America's older population: the "oldest old," those at least 85 years of age.

Two years ago, Misch moved from New York City to the Meriter Retirement Center on South Henry Street.

She has close family here, a daughter and son-in-law. With hearing becoming more difficult, she navigates more slowly.

"It's very difficult to get older," she said. "But I love my life. I do. I don't feel 92 a bit. I feel much younger."

Absorbed in a flurry of exploration, scientists are now beginning to believe that positive mental health among the elderly affects their

Please see LIFE, Page 2A

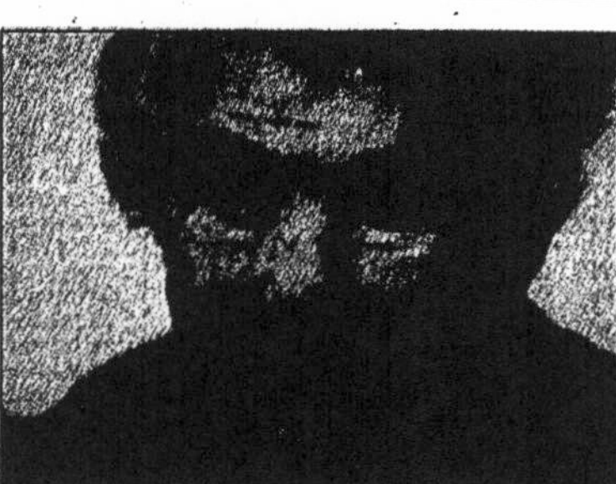

CRAIG SCHREINER/WSJ photo

"I'm not down in the dumps about anything," says Gene McFadden, 87.

The Later Years

First in a series.
Today: Good mental health can affect the way the body ages.
April 23: Many older Americans are struggling to be able to live independently.
May 7: Nursing homes provide a last resort for the growing elderly population.

■ Research, helpful tips, how to get involved/2A

WEATHER

Today Sunshine. High 66. Winds: SE 8-16 mph.

Tonight Cloudy. Low 38. Details/back of Local

TOMORROW
It's National TV-Turnoff Week and we'll tell you how you can spend the week with your kids without the tube.

LOCAL: New sewage rules go into effect/**1C** **SPORTS:** Venus Williams wins at Wimbledon/**1D**

WISCONSIN  **STATE JOURNAL**

★★★ SUNDAY, JULY 9, 2000 MADISON, WISCONSIN $1.75

Badgers' shoe discounts may violate NCAA rules

After being told by State Journal, university launches its own investigation

By Andy Hall and Tom Mulhern
Wisconsin State Journal

At least eight members of last season's University of Wisconsin NCAA Final Four men's basketball team and 14 members of the Rose Bowl champion football team accepted unadvertised discounts at a shoe store, in possible violation of NCAA rules.

Badger players also may have violated National Collegiate Athletic Association rules by accepting special credit arrangements and exchanging university-issued Reebok shoes for merchandise at The Shoe Box in Black Earth, 25 miles northwest of Madison, store documents and interviews with store owner Steve Schmitt and nine current or former employees show.

Members of the men's basketball and football teams accepted discounts more than twice as generous as those generally available to other UW students at the store. Some players brought along friends and relatives who also received the discounts.

Those findings from a two-month Wisconsin State Journal investigation prompted UW officials on Friday to launch their own investigation and notify the NCAA and Big Ten Conference of possible rules violations.

UW's top NCAA compliance official sought to address rumors of improper Shoe Box discounts eight months ago but said he found no evidence of wrongdoing.

"It would appear there is information there that ought to be of concern to the university," NCAA spokesman Wally Renfro said when informed of the newspaper's findings. He declined further comment.

NCAA rules bar university athletes from receiving discounts and credit arrangements unless the same benefits are "generally available to the institution's students." Athletes are forbidden to exchange university-issued supplies, such as shoes, for other items.

"We're always concerned when any possible violation of rules occurs," UW Athletic Director Pat Richter said. "It appears that may have been the case here."

Asked by the State Journal whether he has ever worried that players may be violating NCAA standards, Schmitt replied, "Not really, no. Like I say, everybody gets, as far as I'm concerned, the same treatment here."

Schmitt said he prides himself on the way he provides discounts to many types of customers, including UW students who

Please see UW, Page 8A

One football player's bill

This is one of five UW football players' bills that Steve Schmitt, owner of The Shoe Box, provided. On such bills, which are mailed to players, Schmitt commonly includes a greeting to the player. Jamar Fletcher, a star UW cornerback, is from St. Louis and apparently shares Schmitt's passion for that city's teams. Schmitt discounted Fletcher's bill in the sample below.

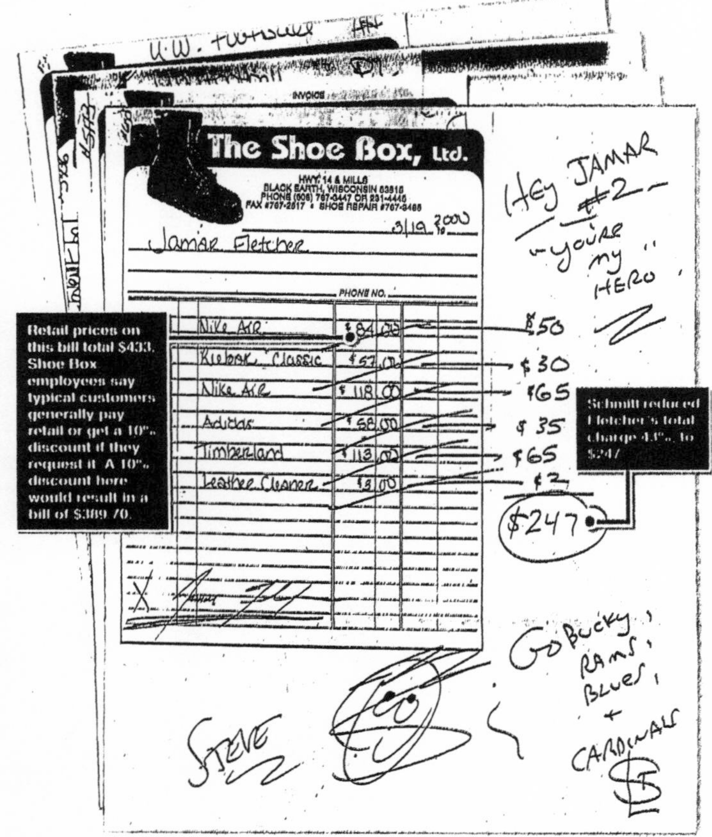

WSJ graphic

Inside

- Excerpts of NCAA bylaws/8A
- University of Wisconsin officials will try to persuade the NCAA that any violations are minor/9A
- A profile of Shoe Box owner Steve Schmitt and how he operates his business/9A
- Ron Dayne was a frequent shopper at The Shoe Box/9A

STEVE APPS/WSJ photo

Steve Schmitt, owner of The Shoe Box

What's at stake

Allegations:

Based on Shoe Box documents and interviews with owner Steve Schmitt and nine current or former store employees:

- At least 22 members of last season's University of Wisconsin men's basketball and football teams accepted unadvertised discounts from Schmitt.
- Players received lenient treatment when tardy in repaying debts on interest-free Shoe Box credit accounts.
- Players exchanged university-issued Reebok shoes for The Shoe Box merchandise.

NCAA violations:

UW athletes may have violated NCAA requirement that they receive discounts and credit arrangements only if they're widely available to other students. NCAA rules also prohibit athletes from exchanging university-issued supplies, such as shoes, for other merchandise.

Penalties:

Athletes violating NCAA rules may be forced to sit out games and pay the value of special benefits they've received. Teams and the university may face a range of penalties, depending on the seriousness of the offense, including reprimand, loss of NCAA tournament accomplishments, cancellation of TV appearances or ban on postseason play.

Sources: Wisconsin State Journal research, NCAA rules

In the eyes of the beholder

SARAH B. TEWS/WSJ photo

Ron Reth of Racine looks at glass items while shopping at the Art Fair on the Square in Madison on Saturday. Reth was shopping at Virginia artist Phillip Nolley's Quintessence Glass booth. See story/1C.

Coke's deal in schools may end

■ Madison would be the first large district in the nation not to renew the exclusive vending contract.

By Doug Erickson
Education reporter

The Madison School District appears poised to dump its exclusive vending contract with Coke, apparently becoming the first large school district in the nation to do an about-face on the issue.

School Board members are scheduled to begin discussing Monday whether to approve a two-year extension of the original three-year contract, which expires next month.

But five of seven board members already say they oppose renewal, citing concerns about corporate influence in public education and the dubious nutritional value of soft drinks.

Their decision is expected to reverberate nationally.

"Madison is going to be the first major district to enter into a contract, experience that contract for a few years, and then back out of it," said Andrew Hagelshaw of the Center for Commercial-Free Public Education in Oakland, Calif. "We hope other school districts will look at what happened in Madison and think twice before signing a contract."

Hagelshaw estimates that about 175 large school districts now have exclusive beverage contracts.

For many residents, Madison's contract has always been about as popular as New Coke. The School Board narrowly approved the original contract in 1997 amid considerable public opposition,

Please see COKE, Page 10A

Missile defense system sent back to drawing board

■ After latest failure, Clinton may have to assess the viability of the project.

By John Aloysius Farrell
The Boston Globe

WASHINGTON — The Pentagon's failure to intercept a target warhead in Saturday's predawn test of its experimental missile defense system intensifies doubts about plans to begin deployment of the multibillion-dollar high-tech weapon.

It was the second failure in three tests of the antimissile system, which the Defense Department hopes to build and deploy within the next five years to guard the United States against long-range missiles fired by North Korea, Iran or other potential antagonists.

Undersecretary of Defense Jack Gansler acknowledged Saturday that the missile defense system was "a high-risk program" and that "you wouldn't like, if you had the time, . . . to make a go-ahead decision of any sort on the basis of what we've seen so far."

President Clinton and Secretary of Defense William S. Cohen will "have to make an assessment of whether or not it is still critical to try to make the 2005 date," Gansler said.

But because of the rapid spread of ballistic missile technology and the abbreviated building season in northern climes, the United States might decide to proceed with initial construction of the necessary radar installation on Shemya Island,

Please see MISSILES, Page 14A

Judge battles government over gunboat graveyard's treasures

■ Man claims he owns the Civil War ships because they were left on his property. The government disagrees.

By Helen O'Neill
AP national writer

MONTGOMERY, La. — The judge's town car tears along the dirt road, bumping to a halt in the middle of a muddy field. Pine trees rustle in the bluffs. A snowy egret glides along a pond.

But the judge's mind is racing back 136 years, to a time when the crackle of musket-fire flew across the meadow and the smell of gunpowder filled the air. A time when the ponderous Red River meandered through this spot, and gunboats struggled to navigate its shallow waters.

Two of the ships are still here — buried 40 feet beneath Mike Wahlder's boots.

"I just want the whiskey and the guns," booms Wahlder, a blustery 65-year-old Social Security judge who lives on a plantation, owns thousands of acres in the area and calls the Civil War wrecks the pride of his "backyard".

The truth is, no one knows if any whiskey or guns exist, and if they do, it's not clear who would get them: Wahlder, who owns the land, or the U.S. government, which claims the ships.

Over the years, the river changed course around the wrecks and it now flows 150 feet to the west. The boats were covered by sediment, and eventually, by woodland.

The judge would like to dig them up.

Wahlder has no personal ties to these ships. He jokes that his family's only connection to the Civil War is the fact that some of his ancestors were Confederate deserters.

But he loves the smell of history as much as the smell of a challenge.

This is a man who, at age 21, spotted a beautiful woman in a travel brochure, tracked her to Israel and married her.

A man who challenged David Duke for the U.S. Senate in 1990,

Please see BOATS, Page 3A

7 82550 00003 6
WSJ SUNDAY

WEATHER

Today Hot, humid. High 90. Winds: SW 10-18 mph.

Tonight Warm. Low 68. **Details/ back of Local**

TOMORROW

Work at the UW Arboretum signals the beginning of what is a new emphasis on preserving and understanding the effigy mounds built in such profusion in this area some 1,000 years ago by Late Woodland Indians. In Focus.

INDEX

GORE PAYS VISIT
Candidate fires up supporters at rally in Milwaukee
◆ LOCAL/B1

CHANGES AT WEAC
Union reduces job security for its top managers
◆ LOCAL/B1

METS BEAT CARDS
6-5 victory puts New York ahead in series, 2-0
◆ SPORTS/C1

★★★ 50 CENTS

F R I D A Y

Wisconsin State Journal

FRIDAY, OCTOBER 13, 2000 MADISON, WISCONSIN

'A SENSELESS ACT OF TERRORISM'

Blast rips U.S. ship; at least 6 are killed

Associated Press

The U.S. Navy released this view of damage to the port side of the Arleigh Burke class guided missile destroyer USS Cole after a suspected terrorist bomb exploded during a refueling operation in the port of Aden, Yemen, on Thursday.

Warship was refueling at Yemen port when bomb exploded

By Robert Burns
AP military writer

WASHINGTON — In a sinister slip through Navy security, suicide bombers in a small boat tore a huge hole in a U.S. warship Thursday at a refueling stop in a Yemeni harbor on the Arabián Peninsula, U.S. officials say. The blast killed at least six members of the crew, injured 35 and left 11 missing.

The crippled ship was tilting slightly in the harbor at Aden, Yemen, but the Navy said it was not in danger of sinking.

No one has claimed responsibility, Defense Secretary William Cohen told a Pentagon news conference.

President Clinton said the attack on the USS Cole, one of the world's most advanced warships, appeared to be an act of terrorism, the worst against the U.S. military since the bombing of an Air Force barracks in Saudi Arabia in 1996 that killed 19 troops.

"We will find out who was responsible and hold them accountable," Clinton pledged.

He dispatched to Yemen investigative teams from the FBI, the State Department and the Pentagon. Clinton also ordered a heightened state of alert for all U.S. military installations around the world.

After the attack, ambulances rushed to the port, and Americans working with Yemeni authorities cordoned off the area. Yemeni police sources said without elaboration that a number of people had been detained for questioning; it was not clear whether any were suspects.

The State Department issued a worldwide alert, saying it was extremely concerned about the possibility of violence against U.S. citizens and interests. Americans were urged to maintain "a high level of vigilance."

In a parallel travel warning, Americans were advised to defer all travel to Israel, the West Bank and Gaza, and those already there were told to stay at home or get to a safe location. Americans were warned not to go to Yemen.

Yemeni President Ali Abdullah Saleh talked with Secretary of State Madeleine Albright, pledged his cooperation in the investigation and

Please see **SHIP**, Page A15

◆ Families await news at home port/**A7**

Flags lowered

WASHINGTON — U.S. flags will be lowered to half-staff at public buildings and military installations in respect for the sailors killed Thursday in a terrorist attack on the U.S. Navy destroyer Cole on the Arabian Peninsula.

President Clinton ordered the action in a proclamation. The president directed that flags remain lowered until sunset Monday.

— Associated Press

The explosion, according to witnesses

A small boat exploded alongside the destroyer USS Cole Thursday morning in Aden, killing at least six U.S. sailors and injuring dozens more; 11 crew members are missing.

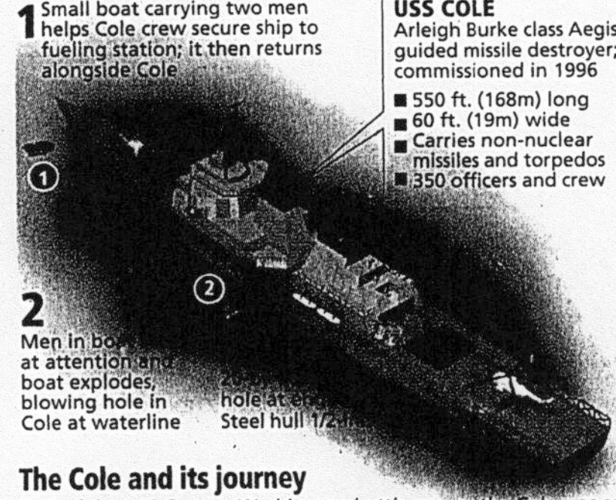

The Cole and its journey

Part of the USS George Washington battle group, the Cole was en route to the Persian Gulf with a crew of about 350. The explosion occurred at Aden, where the Cole was in port for refueling:

1. June 21: Left Norfolk, Va.; scheduled to return Dec. 21

2. Monday: Sailed through Suez Canal into Red Sea

3. Thursday: Stopped at Aden, Yemen, for a 4-hour refueling stop

4. Destination: Bahrain

SOURCES: U.S. Navy, AP, Reuters, KRT News in Motion

KRT, AP graphic

Peace fades as rockets fly

Both sides in Mideast unleash pent-up rage.

By Ibrahim Hazboun
Associated Press

Associated Press

Palestinian leader Yasser Arafat kisses 20-year-old Raid Mady wounded by Israeli forces during the recent clashes in the Gaza Strip, during Arafat's visit to the Gaza hospital on Thursday.

GAZA CITY, Gaza Strip — In a day of incendiary violence that left Mideast peacemaking in ashes, Israeli helicopters rocketed Palestinian leader Yasser Arafat's compound Thursday in retaliation for the mutilation of three Israeli soldiers by a mob of enraged Palestinians.

Late Thursday, the possibility of a four-way summit was revived during a conference call among President Clinton, Egyptian President Hosni Mubarak and Palestinian leader Yasser Arafat, according to U.S. officials who spoke on condition of anonymity. British sources went a step further, saying Mubarak had issued invitations to the Israeli and Palestinian leaders to attend a summit meeting in the coming days.

Please see **PEACE**, Page A15

Inside

◆ Arab-Americans protest/A7
◆ Experts assess situation/A7
◆ A tragic day in Ramallah/A13

Bad day in Mideast brings a bad day on Wall Street

AP, State Journal staff

The Dow Jones industrial average plunged 379 points Thursday, nearly dropping below 10,000, as new Mideast violence and soaring oil prices compounded worries about weak company profits.

The NASDAQ composite index fell to its lowest close this year.

Events in the Middle East spark fears that oil prices will soar, said Dan Julie, portfolio manager for Members Capital Advisers, CUNA Mutual Group's investment affiliate, in Madison.

"Inflation concerns start growing rampant when oil prices rise," Julie said.

Home Depot led the Dow's decline after the retailer became the latest blue chip company to warn it would not meet third-quarter expectations.

Home Depot handles finances well, Julie said, so the news jarred investors. "If one of the 'stars' misses, everybody's going to have some trouble."

The Dow closed down 379.21 at 10,034.58, the lowest it's been since March. It was its fifth-largest point drop ever.

Broader markets also fell. The NASDAQ composite closed down 93.81 to 3,074.68 — its lowest close of 2000. The Standard & Poor's 500 index tumbled 34.81 to 1,329.78.

◆ Optimism turns to caution/**C12**

Lawyer ordered to pay ex-client $2.6 million

Wrongly convicted man had sued, claiming attorney didn't seek DNA tests that would have cleared him of rape.

By Ed Treleven
Courts reporter

Nunnery

Hicks

A Dane County jury Thursday ordered the attorney of a man wrongly convicted of rape to pay him more than $2.6 million, ruling the lawyer didn't seek crucial DNA tests that might have exonerated his client.

In time, one UW-Madison expert said, the man's lawyer may not be the only one to be challenged by an ex-client for not making use of DNA evidence.

Anthony Hicks, who spent 4½ years in prison, sued his trial attorney, Willie Nunnery, in 1997. Hicks claimed Nunnery neglected during his 1991 trial to seek DNA tests on hair root tissue samples that might have proven he did not commit the rape. Nunnery should have known those tests were available, Hicks said.

The lawsuit, heard before Dane County Circuit Judge Steven Ebert, also alleged that Nunnery failed to pursue a witness before the trial who would have bolstered Hicks' alibi.

After deliberations that lasted about an hour, the jury of three men and three women decided Nunnery was negligent on both counts and that Hicks might have been found innocent at trial had Nunnery taken those steps. They awarded Hicks $2,606,950.

Hicks' attorney, Jeff Scott Olson, had asked the jury for $2.5 million for lost wages and the pain and humiliation Hicks suffered from the rape conviction.

"It's closure for myself and my family," Hicks said moments after the verdict. "It's now time to move forward."

Hicks will head home to Houston, where he moved with

Please see **HICKS**, Page A12

WEATHER

Today Partly sunny. High 70. Winds: SW 8-16 mph.

Tonight Mostly cloudy. Low 50. **Details/back of Local**

TOMORROW

Complete coverage of Dick Cheney's visit to Dane County.

INSIDE

161st Year — No. 287 © 2000 Wisconsin State Journal

NADER'S DAY
Candidate dismisses claims he's sabotaging Gore's hopes
◆ LOCAL/B1

STATE TOURNAMENTS
Girls volleyball, boys soccer tournaments begin today
◆ SPORTS/C1

RECALL ON BLINDS
Cords from window blinds have caused child strangulation
◆ BUSINESS/F1

★★★ THURSDAY 50 CENTS

Wisconsin State Journal

THURSDAY, NOVEMBER 2, 2000 MADISON, WISCONSIN

BUILDING AN ARTS DISTRICT

Dazzling and historic

◆ Glass and light are stars of the design for the exterior, and traditional elements are preserved.

◆ At night, glass features will glow like beacons.

An overhead look at a model for the Overture Center.

RENDERING COURTESY CESAR PELLI & ASSOCIATES
A look at the proposed Overture Center, from the North Fairchild Street perspective.

By Dean Mosiman
Wisconsin State Journal

It blends a glassy cutting edge with history.

And architect Cesar Pelli got mostly praise Wednesday for his design of the Overture Foundation's $100 million Downtown arts block, the most expensive building project in city history.

The design has no single character or style, but instead combines striking new icons and historic elements.

"The new parts are definitely very contemporary," Pelli said. "They are crisp, simple, friendly and designed with a northern climate and a northern light in mind."

Overture, using a $100 million gift from businessman Jerry Frautschi, intends to redevelop the entire 200 block of State Street, which includes the Madison Civic Center and Madison Art Center.

The arts block will be called Overture Center.

"I think we're giving the community what it wanted — to keep historic elements yet incorporating contemporary, modern parts to it," Frautschi said.

The historic Yost-Kessenich building facade will be capped with a prominent, crystalline dome and will serve as the

Please see **ARTS DISTRICT**, Page A4

CRAIG SCHREINER/WSJ
This is how North Fairchild Street looked on Wednesday afternoon, a stark contrast to how it will appear when the Overture Center is completed.

What's next

◆ 4-8 p.m., Nov. 8. Overture Foundation will host an open house to view Cesar Pelli's design and meet with the design team at the Madison Civic Center.
◆ Early 2001. Overture submits final design and land use plans for city review and approvals.
◆ June 2001. First phase of construction begins, including the new 2,250-seat performance hall.
◆ Late 2003-2004. Performances begin in the new hall. Second phase of construction starts, including remodeling of Oscar Mayer Theatre, Isthmus Playhouse and Madison Art Center.
◆ End of 2005. Construction complete.

Inside

ANALYSIS

Everyone wins, and some are big winners

By Tom Alesia
Wisconsin State Journal

There was another big Overture Foundation press conference Wednesday with Madison arts angel Jerry Frautschi looking mortified (yet again) as lengthy, heartfelt applause greeted recognition of his $100 million donation.

He tightened his face and folded his arms in the audience, like someone who hates being the center of attention on his birthday.

Get on with it, he seemed to wish.

Enter international heavyweight architect Cesar Pelli who unveiled drawings and neat mini-models of what Madison's arts-and-entertainment Ground Zero will resemble — and this was Wednesday's purpose — from the exterior.

It's easy to get lost in Overture hoopla. There are more layers to this project's formation than the biggest, juiciest hamburger at Dotty Dumpling's Dowry.

To understand what's up after Wednesday's announcement, here are two essentials:

1. The buildings, all connected, will feature

Please see **ANALYSIS**, Page A5

Boyfriend sought in slaying

Mother of 2-year-old shot in duplex on Pflaum Road.

By Brenda Ingersoll and Ed Treleven
Wisconsin State Journal

An arrest warrant was issued Wednesday for Christopher Nelson, 29, in the fatal shooting of Kari Jo Hodges, the mother of his 2-year-old son, police said.

Nelson left the couple's rented duplex at 709 Pflaum Road after the Tuesday night shooting, leaving behind both their Jeep Cherokee and Oldsmobile.

Nelson, a Chicago native, is wanted for first-degree intentional homicide.

Hodges

The shooting happened "within the context of ongoing, troubled domestic relations," Madison police spokesman Dave Gouran said. "The child is the truest victim, because he's lost his mother and for all intents and purposes, his father. What a way to start out life."

The toddler has been placed with his maternal grandmother. There was no reason to think drugs were involved in the death, Gouran said.

Nelson, a car washer at an East Side auto body and paint shop, has a Dane County criminal history dating to 1992, including a charge of possession with intent to sell marijuana. He pleaded no contest

Please see **SLAYING**, Page A13

CHANCELLOR FINALIST PROFILE

Her current campus is like a twin

By Dee J. Hall
Wisconsin State Journal

Nancy Cantor is a well-known social psychologist who studies how people set goals, how they reach those goals and how they react if they don't succeed.

This week, Cantor herself could become a case study as the 48-year-old provost of the University of Michigan-Ann Arbor vies for the job of UW-Madison chancellor.

Cantor

Cantor, whom acquaintances say packs a high amount of energy into her diminutive frame, is one of three finalists for the job. She was on campus Wednesday to meet UW-Madison faculty, staff and students and to answer questions from the press.

In three separate settings, Cantor was relaxed, friendly and self-assured. And she emphasized her main themes: creating a diverse campus; building a "civic university" with strong ties to

Please see **CANTOR**, Page A13

Our profiles of the finalists for the UW-Madison chancellor's job begin today with Nancy Cantor, who was at UW-Madison Wednesday. John Wiley and Susan Westerberg Prager will be on campus today. Look for profiles on them Friday.

7 82550 00001 2

WEATHER

Today Spotty showers. High 64. Winds: SE 12-22 mph.

Tonight Partly cloudy. Low 39. **Details/back of Local**

SUNDAY

Our voter guide will look at the top races, both national and local, to be decided in Tuesday's election.

INSIDE

ELECTION SPECIAL

★★★☆

W E D N E S D A Y

50 CENTS

Wisconsin State Journal

WEDNESDAY, NOVEMBER 8, 2000 MADISON, WISCONSIN WWW.MADISON.COM

It's Bush, maybe

He's ready to claim victory, but Florida still too close to call

HOW WE VOTED

U.S. SENATE

1,419,394 Herb Kohl, Democrat (I)

861,379 John Gillespie, Republican

3,259 of 3,572 wards reporting

Third term for Kohl

U.S. Sen. Herb Kohl, a two-term Democratic incumbent, easily defeated Republican John Gillespie. **Page A2**

Clinton victorious

First lady **Hillary Rodham Clinton**, left, swept to a history-making victory Tuesday and captured a Senate seat in New York but Democrats struggled to end the Republicans' six-year reign in the Senate. **Page A10**

U.S. HOUSE

Wisconsin races

Republican Paul Ryan won a second term in Wisconsin's 1st Congressional District. **Page A3**

House up for grabs

Before the election, the Republicans held a 222-209 majority in the House. Whichever party prevails, the majority is expected to be even smaller than it is currently. **Page A10**

STATE LEGISLATURE

Senate, Assembly appear to be split

Wisconsin Democrats turned back Republican efforts to wrest control of the state Senate. The GOP kept control of the Assembly. **Page A5**

ALSO INSIDE

Yes on Lambeau

The sale of Lambeau Field naming rights to ease taxpayer costs for stadium renovation won approval of Brown County residents. **Page A4**

Beloit supports casino, La Crosse County doesn't

Voters in Beloit supported a proposed Indian casino, while La Crosse County voters rejected a similar proposal there. **Page A4**

Blanchard wins

Brian Blanchard rode a wave of local Democratic support to become Dane County's next district attorney. **Page A8**

Associated Press

George W. Bush appeared to go over the top of the 270 Electoral College votes needed to win, but a late rush of votes for Gore in Florida may change the outcome.

By Ron Fournier
Associated Press

Texas Gov. George W. Bush fought Al Gore in an agonizingly close presidential election Tuesday that gave voters a choice of four more years of Democratic rule or a Republican "fresh start." Television networks projected Bush the winner, igniting GOP celebrations in Austin.

The vice president called Bush to congratulate him on his victory, according to Republican aides.

Republicans were clinging to precarious control of Congress as the GOP bid to hold the House, Senate and presidency since after the 1952 election.

In the most dramatic election in decades, it all came down to Florida. AP's analysis showed the narrowest of margins with final votes still being tallied in several Democratic counties. The networks projected a Bush victory that would put him over the top and that sparked gloom in the Gore camp in Nashville and triumphant cheers in Texas.

A Bush victory would give America its second father-son presidents after John Adams (1797-01) and John Quincy Adams (1825-29).

Bush was said to be poised to claim his prize.

Florida would give Bush 271 votes in the Electoral College, one over the majority needed to claim the presidency. Just thousands of votes separated the two candidates in Florida out of almost 6 million cast, and the margin was sure to require a recount.

Presidential results

Here is a state-by-state breakdown of the vote for president. Electoral votes are noted on the map.

Electoral College vote

To win the presidency, 270 electoral votes are needed. The number won as of 1:30 a.m. Wed.:

Bush 271 Gore 249

Popular vote

The percentage of votes won as of 12:45 a.m. Wed.:
83% of precincts reporting

Bush.. **49%** Nader........ **2%**
Gore.. **48%** Buchanan.. **Less than 1%**

Note: Percentages don't add up to 100% due to rounding.
SOURCE: Compiled from AP wire reports

AP

Several states were still to close to call.

With Florida officials continuing their tally, the New York Times said Bush had won and congratulated him on "the amazing political feat of laping to the White House after only six years in public office."

With the election so tight, Democrats were sure to second-guess Gore's refusal to involve President Clinton in his campaign. They also were sure to rue the day that Green Party candidate Ralph Nader entered the race and siphoned off Gore votes in several key states.

Florida had been the epicenter of the campaign and Tuesday night was chaotic. At one point news organizations said Gore was the winner, but they backtracked as more votes were counted and Bush eased ahead.

Republicans retained control of the Senate — if narrowly — and looked likely to keep a small majority in the House as well. Bush or Gore,

Please see **RACE**, Page A11

RACE IN WISCONSIN

Bush, Gore dead heat in state

By Doug Erickson
Wisconsin State Journal

Republican George W. Bush and Democrat Al Gore remained in a dead heat for Wisconsin's 11 electoral votes early today, even though Florida appeared to be the pivotal state in electing the next president.

As of 2:30 a.m., only Florida, Oregon and Wisconsin were still up for grabs.

With 90 percent of Wisconsin wards reporting, Bush had 1,137,680 votes, or 48 percent, compared with 1,122,808, or 47 percent, for Gore, unofficial results showed. Green Party candidate Ralph Nader was a distant third with 84,135 or 4 percent.

At 1:18 a.m., television stations reported that Florida went to Bush and handed him the election. Republicans at the Concourse Hotel in Madison erupted in wild yelps and dancing that lasted five minutes. Then they started yelling "Tommy, Tommy, Tommy," trying to lure Gov. Tommy Thompson from interviews with national news media to address the home crowd.

Please see **STATE**, Page A11

U.S. HOUSE OF REPRESENTATIVES

2nd Congressional District

155,825 Tammy Baldwin, Democrat (I)

146,711 John Sharpless, Republican

399 of 405 wards reporting

Baldwin narrowly defeats Sharpless

She pledges to continue her fight for universal health care.

By Scott Milfred
Wisconsin State Journal

Wisconsin's first and only woman in Congress narrowly claimed victory early today in her hard-fought and expensive re-election campaign against Republican challenger John Sharpless.

"We did it!" Tammy Baldwin declared to a jubilant crowd of supporters at the Monona Terrace Convention Center about 12:30 a.m.

"Our victory tonight was more than a victory of one candidate over another," she said. "It is a rare victory of personal activism."

Sharpless hadn't conceded the race yet. But with most wards reporting, Baldwin was almost sure to hold her narrow lead.

Baldwin pledged to continue her fight for universal health care, recalling stories of local people having trouble affording or finding medical care and insurance.

"This is why we do all the work we do" to get re-elected, she said.

Baldwin also pledged to strengthen schools, protect the environment, keep Social Security and Medicare solvent and protect minorities from discrimination.

Sharpless was hoping that a strong showing by Republican Texas Gov. George W. Bush in Wisconsin would help his chances.

The presidential race in the Badger State was too close to call early today. Democratic presidential candidates have carried the state in the last three elections.

Please see **BALDWIN**, Page A8

161st Year — No. 313 © 2000 Wisconsin State Journal

WEATHER

Today
Cloudy; shower.
High 45.
Winds: NW
10-20 mph.

Tonight
Mostly cloudy.
Low 29.
Details/back of Local

INSIDE

Camp Randall to be renovated

$99.7 million plan clears first hurdle. **Page C1**

ENDOSTATIN TESTS
Researchers say new cancer treatment is safe and promising
◆ NATION/A6

APPRAISING ANTIQUES
Leigh and Leslie Keno of 'Antiques Roadshow' have built national reputation
◆ CLICK/D1

MR. OFFENSE
Badgers brace for Hoosiers quarterback Antwaan Randle El
◆ SPORTS/C1

★★★ F R I D A Y 50 CENTS

Wisconsin State Journal

FRIDAY, NOVEMBER 10, 2000 MADISON, WISCONSIN

Wiley set to get top job at UW

Chancellor decision expected today from Regents

By Elizabeth Brixey
Higher education reporter

John Wiley will be recommended today to the UW Board of Regents for appointment as chancellor of UW-Madison, the Wisconsin State Journal has learned.

Wiley, who has been provost of UW-Madison for five years, was one of three finalists to oversee the campus of more than 41,000 students.

The closely guarded announcement is expected to follow a late-morning closed session of the board, during which it will consider the recommendation of a special Regents' committee and University of Wisconsin System President Katharine Lyall.

Wiley wouldn't comment Thursday evening on the decision. Lyall, who would be Wiley's boss, couldn't be reached.

As chancellor, Wiley would be the chief executive officer of UW-Madison and responsible for all of its programs. He would replace Chancellor David Ward, who announced in March that he will step down at the end of the year to teach and conduct higher education policy research.

The other finalists were Nancy Cantor, provost at the University of Michigan-Ann Arbor, and Susan

Please see WILEY, Page A17

Wiley

ELECTION 2000

GEORGE W. BUSH

FLORIDA RECOUNT

AL GORE

Gore hints at fight to finish

As George W. Bush's lead over the vice president in Florida slips, Democrats look to the courts for help.

By Jodi Enda
Knight Ridder Newspapers

WASHINGTON — Two days after the presidential election produced no official winner, Vice President Al Gore's campaign said Thursday that it would aggressively pursue victory in Florida, even if it meant going to court and delaying the election's outcome.

A two-day Florida recount, triggered by Texas Gov. George W. Bush's razor-thin victory in the state, remained unfinished Thursday but appeared to narrow the gap to an even smaller margin.

The difference was so slim that no result can be conclusive without absentee ballots still arriving from Americans overseas. According to an unofficial Associated Press tally of the recount in 66 of the state's 67 counties by Thursday night, Bush led by only 229 votes out of nearly 6 million cast.

The original count showed Bush leading by 1,784 votes.

Secretary of State Katherine Harris released a new total from a recount of 53 of Florida's 67 counties Thursday that she said showed Bush ahead by exactly the same margin of 1,784. A top aide to Harris, a Republican and Bush supporter, said it was "completely coincidental."

Among the 14 counties not included in Harris' count were three where the AP's tally showed Gore gaining more than 1,350 votes and Bush gaining only 63 votes.

Harris said the state would not certify the recount until Tuesday and would not tally the incoming absentee ballots until Nov. 17.

The narrow count, the threat of legal challenges and the outstanding absentee ballots provoked a suspenseful and tense day in which officials from both camps sniped at each other on national television while their candidates remained in seclusion.

Besides monitoring the recount and exploring legal action, Democrats waged a political offensive with the help of such luminaries as former

Please see ELECTION, Page A17

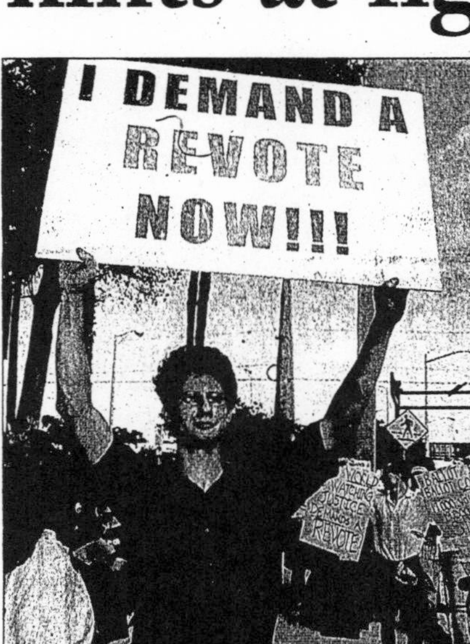

An unidentified person holds a sign outside of the Palm Beach Government building Thursday, in West Palm Beach, Fla., where the Palm Beach Board of Elections is based.

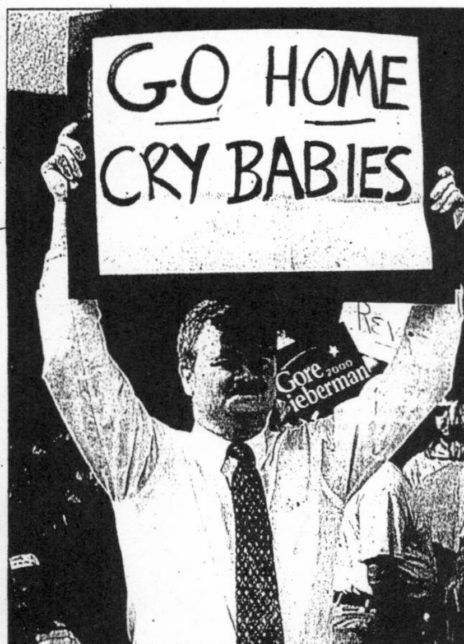

Associated Press photos

Chris Hammon of Palm Beach, Fla., demonstrates at a rally in front of the Palm Beach County elections office, on Thursday in West Palm Beach, Fla. About 300 demonstrators attended the rally.

Inside

Gore camp's road to reversing election fraught with obstacles

Following long legal and political traditions, judges usually have been extremely reluctant to overturn results.

By Chris Mondics and Lenny Savino
Knight Ridder Newspapers

WASHINGTON — Al Gore's campaign faces high legal hurdles if it goes to court to try to overturn election results in Florida, as it hinted Thursday it might.

Judges at both the state and federal levels, following long legal and political traditions, usually have been extremely reluctant to reverse elections and have done so only in instances of fraud or extreme irregularities.

To intervene would open a Pandora's box of time-consuming legal assaults and multiple challenges and possibly would undermine the election process itself, legal experts said Thursday.

While a handful of Florida elections have been reversed based on evidence of fraud, legal experts said they knew of no elections overturned because ballots had been confusingly designed. That's the allegation in the principal pending case, in Palm Beach County, Fla.

"One reason courts don't step in and shouldn't step in is because it would be easy to say 'My guy didn't win and I'm going to come up with a reason' for challenging the election," said Susan Low Bloch, a professor of constitutional law at Georgetown University Law Center in Washington. "You don't want that kind of hindsight and second guessing."

Yet so much about this election is unprecedented that legal experts were reluctant

Please see LAW, Page A18

Judge proceeds after man collapses

By Cary Segall
Wisconsin State Journal

U.S. District Judge John Shabaz plowed ahead with a hearing Wednesday while the defendant was sprawled partially conscious on the floor after suffering a mini-stroke.

Shabaz, who is known for abhorring delay, had stepped into his courtroom just after defendant Craig Gorsuch, who has a history of strokes, had collapsed and struck his head on a chair while falling.

The judge acknowledged that Gorsuch was unavailable and then continued the scheduling conference while rescue workers rushed to the scene.

Shabaz said Thursday that he proceeded because he expected the conference to last only 60 to 90 seconds and he didn't want to "inconvenience the parties."

Gorsuch's lawyer, Mark Brown, said his client had complained to marshals about numbness in his right arm but said he could proceed. Then, Brown said, Gorsuch stated that he had to leave, stood up and collapsed.

Brown said the marshals called 911 and Shabaz then entered the courtroom and saw Gorsuch on the floor.

An audio tape of the conference indicates Shabaz started dictating the new schedule, then paused briefly about 40 seconds into the hearing when a radio in the courtroom relayed news of the paramedics' arrival at the courthouse.

He then continued for about 40 seconds more before paramedics entered the courtroom and carted Gorsuch away.

Shabaz delayed the hearing for about 15 minutes to hear another case and then continued for about seven minutes without the defendant.

The judge told Brown and Assistant U.S. Attorney Rita Rumbelow that he was rescheduling a trial that had been moved by Magistrate Judge Steve Crocker from Dec. 4 to Jan. 8 because Brown recently took the case after Gorsuch fired his first lawyer.

Shabaz moved the trial back to Dec. 4.

Gorsuch, 42, of Portage, was treated at University Hospital and then returned to the Dane County Jail, where he is being held on a charge of possessing guns after being convicted of slapping his wife.

161st Year — No. 315 © 2000 Wisconsin State Journal

7 82550 00001 2
WSJ DAILY

WEATHER

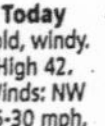

Today Cold, windy. High 42. Winds: NW 15-30 mph.

Tonight Mainly clear. Low 28. **Details/back of Local**

SUNDAY

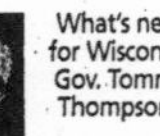

What's next for Wisconsin Gov. Tommy Thompson?

INSIDE

ANTI-SMOKING
Lung cancer decreases 14 percent in California
NATION/A12

MARKETS TUMBLE
PC Gateway warning prompts tech selloff, stock downturn
BUSINESS/C10

HAPPY ANNIVERSARY
Community radio station WORT celebrates 25 years at 8 p.m. today
CLICK/D1

★★★ 50 CENTS

FRIDAY

Wisconsin State Journal

FRIDAY, DECEMBER 1, 2000 MADISON, WISCONSIN

Associated Press

A motorcade containing a rental truck carrying some 460,000 ballots from Palm Beach County arrives in Tallahassee, Fla., on Thursday.

Florida's legislators will name electors

Bush and Gore continue to slug it out in the courts.

By David Barstow
New York Times

TALLAHASSEE, Fla. — Taking its first formal step to intervene in the outcome of the presidential election, a select committee of Florida's Republican-dominated Legislature recommended on Thursday that a special session be held "as soon as practicable" to name Florida's 25 electors.

Inside
- Following that yellow truck/A7
- Bush looks ahead, meets with Powell/A9
- U.S. Supreme Court case might not settle it/A9

Based on the recommendation, the speaker of the Florida House of Representatives and the president of the Florida Senate were expected to summon lawmakers to the state Capitol next week, possibly as early as Tuesday.

It was unclear how long the special session would last, but Republican legislators said on Thursday that they were determined to ratify George W. Bush's slate of electors before Dec. 12, the deadline for naming electors to the Electoral College.

"He who hesitates is lost," Rep. Johnnie Byrd, co-chairman of the select committee, said shortly before

Please see **ELECTORS,** Page A15

Thursday's developments
- A committee of the Florida Legislature recommended a special session as early as next week to name the state's presidential electors. Republicans control both houses and would likely make George W. Bush president-elect.
- In the U.S. Supreme Court, lawyers for Bush argued that the Florida Legislature has the power to name the state's presidential electors. Lawyers for Vice President Al Gore said the Legislature had no such authority.

What's next
- The U.S. Supreme Court will hear oral arguments today on Bush's request to overturn a Florida Supreme Court ruling that allowed for an extended recount.

DICK BENNETT RETIRES

'I am at peace'

CRAIG SCHREINER/WSJ photos

Dick Bennett, who brought the Badgers into the national spotlight with last season's Final Four appearance, said he is retiring because he no longer has the energy to coach.

He took UW basketball to glory of Final Four

By Vic Feuerherd
Wisconsin State Journal

When Dick Bennett arrived at UW-Madison in the spring of 1995, he said it would take five years to bring the men's basketball program to a level of national respectability. Two weeks into his sixth season, he decided his original timetable was correct.

Dick Bennett coverage on A10, A11 and in Sports. Editorial/ A14

Just eight months after leading the Badgers to the Promised Land of college basketball, the NCAA Final Four, Bennett called it quits, formally announcing Thursday afternoon that he was retiring as UW's coach effective immediately. Friends and associates said Bennett simply "ran out of gas."

It brought to an end a 36-year era synonymous with Wisconsin basketball, where Bennett was a high school coach in Mineral Point, West Bend and Eau Claire, and a college coach at UW-Stevens Point and UW-Green Bay before joining the Badgers.

"Those who know me well enough know that any job worth doing is worth doing well," said Bennett, who in the days leading up to the announcement had publicly questioned his ability to motivate his team. "If I'm slipping, it's not fair to you."

Bennett, 57, shared with a packed audience at the Kohl

Please see **BENNETT,** Page A15

Bennett did it his way — and that wore him out

Brad Soderberg, the person who stood to gain the most by Dick Bennett's unexpected departure, summed it up best.

TOM OATES

"I really think it's a sad day for Wisconsin basketball," said Soderberg, named the acting men's basketball coach for the University of Wisconsin following Bennett's abrupt retirement Thursday.

Indeed, we will all miss the homespun, homegrown coach who did his prep work in the high schools and colleges of

Please see **OATES,** Page A10

Brad Soderberg, center, takes over as acting head coach after serving as an assistant under Bennett since 1995.

Wisconsin's educational system makes the grade

The Badger state is in good standing when measured against other states in the nation.

By Anita Clark
Wisconsin State Journal

Wisconsin received good grades on a national report card Thursday ranking states on higher education.

The state's best grade, an A-minus, came on preparing high school students for college.

In Wisconsin, 55 percent of high school students take upper-level math, compared to 59 percent in top states like Massachusetts.

State-by-state differences illustrate the way college opportunities depend on where you live, as well as on family resources and ethnicity, according to the report card.

Called "Measuring Up 2000," the 188-page report comes from the National Center for Public Policy and Higher Education, a 2-year-old nonpartisan organization with offices in San Jose, Calif., and Washington, D.C.

"Despite the accomplishments of American higher education, its benefits are unevenly and often unfairly distributed and do not reflect the distribution of talent in America," said James Hunt Jr., governor of North Carolina and chairman of the center's board.

No state received straight As. Some states showed a huge gap between scores. New York, for example, won As and Bs in four categories but received a D-minus on affordability.

The report card defines higher education as all education and training beyond high school, including public and private institutions.

It used 30 statistical measures in five categories: preparation of students, participation in higher education, affordability, completion rates and benefits to society of having well-educated citizens.

On that benefits category, Wisconsin received its lowest grade, a B-minus. Twenty-five percent of the adult population has at least a bachelor's degree, compared to 34 percent in top states.

The Badger state also trailed slightly on measures of skill levels and economic and civic benefits, like voting and philanthropy, tied to education.

The national report was released as Gov. Tommy Thompson and more than 800 educational, civic and business leaders gathered in Milwaukee to map strategies for economic success.

"This report confirms many of the positive perceptions about Wisconsin's educational system that were discussed" at the meeting, University of Wisconsin System President Katharine Lyall said Thursday.

The national report card will be updated in 2002 and 2004.

◆ **On the Internet:** *www.highereducation.org*

How Wisconsin scores for higher education

	WISCONSIN	Illinois	Iowa	Michigan	Minnesota
Preparation	A-	A	B	B	C+
Participation	B	A	B	B+	B-
Affordability	B+	A	B	C	A
Completion	B	C+	A-	C+	B+
Benefits	B-	B-	C+	B	A

Wisconsin preparation: A-

K-12 student achievement
Eighth-graders scoring at or above "proficient" on the national assessment exam:

	Wis.	Top states
Math	32%	33%
Reading	33%	38%
Writing	28%	31%

Wisconsin affordability: B+

Family ability to pay
Percent of income needed to pay for college expenses, minus financial aid:

	Wis.	Top states
Community college	23%	17%
Public 4-year	18%	19%
Private 4-year	50%	30%

SOURCE: The National Center for Public Policy and Higher Education WSJ

161st Year — No. 336 © 2000 Wisconsin State Journal
7 82550 00001 2
WSJ DAILY

WEATHER

Today Light snow. High 32. Winds: NW 6-12 mph.

Tonight A few flurries. Low 18. **Details/back of Local**

COMING SUNDAY

A tribute to the USS Wisconsin, the largest and last of U.S. battleships.

INSIDE

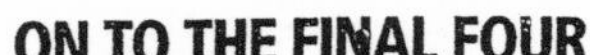

ON TO THE FINAL FOUR

UW women play Southern California in a national semifinal tonight

SPORTS/B1

PLAZA TAVERN PENALTY

Popular campus-area bar and grill may be fined and briefly closed

LOCAL/D1

CELEBRATING BACH

Madison Symphony Orchestra to pay tribute to composer

DAYBREAK/G1

★★★

THURSDAY

50 CENTS

Wisconsin State Journal

THURSDAY, DECEMBER 14, 2000 MADISON, WISCONSIN

"This is America and we put country before party. We will stand together behind our new president."
AL GORE

ELECTION 2000

"I was not elected to serve one party, but to serve one nation."
GEORGE W. BUSH

A winner — at last

GORE'S CONCESSION

Associated Press

In a brief address tinged with patriotism and light humor, Vice President Al Gore concedes the presidential election Wednesday night to George W. Bush.

With race lost, Gore urges unity

By G. Robert Hillman
The Dallas Morning News

WASHINGTON — For Al Gore, the long, exhausting struggle for the presidency ended Wednesday night next door to the White House.

Addressing the nation from his office at the Old Executive Office Building, Gore bowed out 36 days after Election Day.

"For the sake of our unity as a people and the strength of our democracy, I offer my concession," he said.

At the end of the tightest presidential race in more than a century, Gore pledged his support to Republican George W. Bush, who will be moving into the Oval Office.

"What remains of partisan rancor must now be put aside, and may God bless his stewardship of this country" Gore said during his televised address, which lasted less than 10 minutes.

It was a gracious, personal statement that his aides said not only bore his mark but his desire to help heal

Please see **GORE**, Page A5

President-elect George W. Bush begins a new campaign as he moves quickly to unify nation

Associated Press

President-elect George W. Bush stands with his wife, Laura, Texas House Speaker Pete Laney and Texas Lt. Gov. Rick Perry, top, after addressing the nation from the chambers of the Texas House of Representatives in Austin.

By Tom Raum
Associated Press

AUSTIN, Texas — President-elect George W. Bush, preparing to enter the White House without a voting majority, called upon the nation Wednesday night to "put politics behind us and work together" on education, Social Security, Medicare and tax relief after a wrenching election.

"Our nation must rise above a house divided," Texas' Republican governor asserted in reaching out to try to heal deep partisan wounds. In a special appeal to supporters of Democratic rival Al Gore, Bush pledged: "Whether you voted for me or not, I will do my best to serve your interests, and I will work to earn your respect."

"I will give it my all," he declared in a nationally televised address from the spacious chamber of the Texas House of Representatives an hour after Gore delivered a graceful, generous concession speech that also called for national reconciliation and unity.

"I hope the long wait of the last five weeks will heighten a desire to move beyond the bitterness and partisanship of the recent past," Bush said.

The president-elect received what he said was "a gracious call" from Gore shortly before the vice president delivered his own speech, a call that "I know was difficult for him to make."

Please see **BUSH**, Page A5

Presidential election returns

A summary of the vote and what's next:

Popular vote

Al Gore	**50,158,094**
George W. Bush	**49,820,518**

Electoral vote

George W. Bush	**271**
Al Gore	**267**

What's next?

Dec. 18	Electoral College members meet in each state, cast votes
Jan. 5* 2001	Congress conducts official tally of electoral votes, declares winner
Jan. 20	Inauguration Day; president sworn into office

*Date Senate will meet; House yet to decide

SOURCE: News reports

Inside

TOMMY THOMPSON'S FUTURE

Time for a Cabinet job?

Many expect the Wisconsin governor's name will be included in the Bush administration.

By Phil Brinkman
State government reporter

Now that the country's chief political question has been settled, another is coming into sharper focus in Wisconsin: What's next for Gov. Tommy Thompson?

Wednesday's concession by Vice President Al Gore clears the way for president-elect George W. Bush to begin naming a Cabinet. Many expect Thompson's name will be included in that list.

Thompson, who initially fed the speculation with breezy but vague answers to reporters' questions, has clamped his mouth shut on the matter in recent weeks.

Thompson's brother, Tomah Mayor Ed Thompson, said vice president-elect Dick Cheney, who's heading up Bush's transition team, told the governor to be in Washington on Wednesday, The Associated Press has reported.

Tommy Thompson did travel to Washington on Wednesday and planned to stay through today, but aides insist his only business there is to attend a meeting of the Amtrak board of directors, which he chairs. He has no plans, they say, to meet with the Bush transition team.

But friends and associates say the governor would be very interested in a White

Please see **THOMPSON**, Page A5

SARAH B. TEWS/WSJ photo

Much of Gov. Tommy Thompson's days recently have been filled with budget briefings. Some speculate that the new year and new administration in the White House may mean a new job for Thompson.

ANALYSIS

Bush presidency will be tested early and often

By Ken Moritsugu and Jonathan S. Landay
Knight Ridder Newspapers

WASHINGTON — Now it's time to run the country. As an untested George W. Bush takes the helm of the world's sole superpower, the challenges could come hard and fast.

The outlook for America and the world is far cloudier than it was on that sunny Saturday afternoon in Iowa just 18 months ago, when Bush entered a campaign that boiled down to a common theme: who could best ensure continued peace and prosperity.

Now, the economy is slowing, the stock market is tumbling and winter heating bills are soaring. Overseas, Israeli-Palestinian violence is raising fears of a wider Middle East conflict, and Saddam Hussein is undercutting U.S. efforts to isolate Iraq.

While Bush is surrounding himself with veteran advisers, many of them from the administration of his father, former

Please see **ANALYSIS**, Page A5

161st Year — No. 349 © 2000 Wisconsin State Journal

WEATHER

Today Some sun. High 24. Winds: WNW 10-20 mph.

Tonight Mostly cloudy. Low 14. **Details/back of Local**

TOMORROW

The Dane County Board takes up a resolution for support for "quiet zones" along rail corridors.

INSIDE

A CONFESSION
Rev. Jesse Jackson reveals affair, child out of wedlock
NATION/A3

ANNEX FIRE
Another popular music club damaged
LOCAL/B1

MORE SEATS
Camp Randall renovation to put capacity over 86,000
SPORTS/C1

WOMEN'S
Badgers 90
Minnesota 67

RAYOVAC CUTS
Company to close Wonewoc plant, eliminate 240 jobs
BUSINESS/C10

★★★

FRIDAY

50 CENTS

Wisconsin State Journal

FRIDAY, JANUARY 19, 2001 MADISON, WISCONSIN

Shoe Box reports released by UW

Records indicate recruits — already signed and on campus — got unadvertised discounts, too.

By Andy Hall
Wisconsin State Journal

Current UW-Madison athletes accepted more than $23,000 in unadvertised discounts at a local shoe store, in violation of NCAA rules, public records released Thursday reveal.

Reports compiled by university investigators say that in addition several unidentified recruits, who had signed to play for the Badgers and already were on campus, received shoe discounts last summer, in possible violation of a National Collegiate Athletic Association rule barring teams' prospects from obtaining special benefits.

The rule is intended to prevent a team from gaining an advantage over competitors, and violations could lead to harsh punishment of the university.

The 160 pages of university investigators' reports, released in response to a Wisconsin State Journal public-records lawsuit, indicate that 121 current athletes improperly accepted discounts totaling more than $23,000 at The Shoe Box, 25 miles northwest of Madison in Black Earth.

NCAA rules forbid athletes from receiving better deals than those generally offered to other students.

Punishments for the 121 athletes were announced last year, but the extent of the discounts and the possible involvement of recruits wasn't disclosed until Thursday.

Athletes committing violations were required to pay a charity the amount of benefits received and, depending on the size of their violations, faced a mix of suspensions from games and community service.

Citing a federal privacy law, the

Please see UW, Page A7

"Wisconsin has sought more waivers from federal programs than any other state. Now, it's time for me to put up."
GOV. TOMMY THOMPSON

Thompson sailing smoothly

Associated Press

Tommy Thompson, left, nominated for secretary of health and human services, is accompanied by the current secretary, Donna Shalala, and former senator Bob Dole at Thursday's Senate Finance Committee hearing on Thompson's confirmation.

Overwhelming bipartisan support for confirmation

State Journal wire services, staff

WASHINGTON — Gov. Tommy Thompson sailed through his first Senate confirmation hearing Thursday, already opening the door to a political compromise that could scuttle one of his new boss' controversial campaign proposals.

Wisconsin's 14-year Republican governor received overwhelming bipartisan support from the Senate Finance Committee, which is considering his nomination to head the Department of Health and Human Services.

Thompson, 59, said during the hearing that the incoming Bush administration will push for quick bipartisan agreement on a federal prescription drug benefit under Medicare — even if that means abandoning President-elect George W. Bush's plan to give grants to the states to provide drug coverage for poor seniors.

"While comprehensive reform may take some time to achieve, the American people are demanding a prescription drug benefit today," Thompson said. "We must move immediately to help millions of low-income senior citizens who cannot afford the life-preserving prescription drugs they so desperately need."

Thompson said the administration would be willing to set aside Bush's proposal if Republicans and Democrats can agree on a program under Medicare, the federal health insurance program for the

Please see THOMPSON, Page A9

Today

◆ Tommy Thompson testifies before the Senate Committee on Health, Education, Labor and Pensions, 9 a.m.

◆ TV: C-SPAN2, which is Ch. 17 for cable television subscribers in Madison, wasn't scheduled to broadcast the hearing live, although it might be aired later in the day. An updated schedule for CSPAN and CSPAN2 may be viewed on the World Wide Web at *www.c-span.org*.

Ashcroft

Inside

◆ Thompson must be careful not to give too much away during confirmation hearings/A9

◆ Missouri Supreme Court Judge Ronnie White testified that attorney general nominee John Ashcroft misrepresented White's record in maneuvering to have the Senate turn down the judge's nomination to the federal bench/A3

◆ Other confirmation hearings/A4

CRAIG SCHREINER/WSJ

Linda Chappetto, left, and Jamie Kuhn listen to the confirmation hearing via an Internet broadcast while working at the state Capitol.

Clinton rides off, but not into sunset

His parting advice to Bush: Don't choke off prosperity or withdraw U.S. from world.

By Marc Lacey
New York Times

Associated Press

President Clinton sits in the Oval Office after bidding farewell to the nation in his final address as president.

WASHINGTON — President Clinton said goodbye to the nation Thursday night, using his final televised address to look back at his administration's accomplishments and warn the incoming president against retrenching from the world or squandering the country's economic prosperity.

Clinton wished President-elect George W. Bush well. But he also bluntly repeated the policy differences he has with his successor, the ones that he hammered away at during the hard-fought presidential campaign.

Clinton spoke of the economic good times that have marked his years in office and urged Bush not to veer away from fiscal responsibility. He never mentioned Bush's tax cut plan directly, but he was clearly trying to nudge the new administration to scale it back in favor of continuing to pay down the debt.

"Staying on that course will bring lower interest rates, greater prosperity, and the opportunity to meet our big challenges," Clinton said. "If we choose wisely, we can pay down the debt, deal with the retirement of the baby boomers, invest

Please see CLINTON, Page A7

"America cannot and must not disentangle itself from the world. If we want the world to embody our shared values, then we must assume a shared responsibility."
PRESIDENT CLINTON
In his farewell address

BadgerCare gets waiver from federal government

By Patricia Simms
Health reporter

The federal government Thursday gave a long-awaited final blessing to Wisconsin's popular BadgerCare program, which provides health insurance to the working poor and their children.

A waiver from the U.S. Department of Health and Human Services means that BadgerCare can use federal Children's Health Insurance Program (CHIP) dollars to cover parents and children equally.

The decision gives Wisconsin an additional $2 million in federal money for the fiscal year that ends June 30, as well as an average $6 million a year in the next two-year budget cycle, said state Health and Family Services Secretary Joe Leean.

"It's not just the additional $2 million this year," Leean said. "This waiver not only means more federal dollars, but I think it's a stamp of approval that this was the right approach from day one."

BadgerCare, a creation of Republican Gov. Tommy Thompson, is the nation's first program to target adults as a means of providing health insurance to entire families. It has exceeded initial enrollment projections by more than 10,000 people, Leean said.

When BadgerCare started in 1999, Wisconsin got permission to include parents as well as children but had to use scarcer Medicaid dollars to pay for the more costly adult services.

Wisconsin then asked for federal permission to use between $3 million and $4 million of unused children's insurance dollars for adults this biennium.

The waiver, which will permit use of the children's insurance money for adults in subsequent years, is expected to relieve some of the financial pressure on BadgerCare.

Instead of seeking $13.5 million to plug the financial hole in this year's BadgerCare budget, Leean said only $11.5 million will be needed.

U.S. Rep. Tom Barrett, D-Milwaukee, who has championed the waiver in Washington, said the move should encourage state legislators.

"It shows the Legislature that the federal government is receptive to the changes it has made," Barrett said, "and it vastly improves the chances that the state Legislature will put more money in as well."

Barrett said the waiver announcement was a milestone for Wisconsin health care. "This is the next step toward universal health care," he said.

The CHIP program was created in 1997 to insure poor children.

162nd Year — No. 19 © 2001 Wisconsin State Journal

WEATHER

Today Brisk and cold. High 18. Winds: N 10-20 mph.

Tonight Very cold. Low 0. Details/back of Local

TOMORROW

Washington awaits a new president and a weekend of celebration as George W. Bush takes the oath of office on Saturday.

INSIDE

BENNETT AFTER BASKETBALL

Former coach talks about retirement, his old team and maybe getting back into the game

SPORTS/D1

Minnesota 8
Badgers 2

BABY BOOM

A big year for births in Madison

LOCAL/C1

CLIMB HIGH

Women age 40 and up hit the rock wall

DAYBREAK/G1

★★★ $1.75

THE SUNDAY

Wisconsin State Journal

SUNDAY, JANUARY 21, 2001 MADISON, WISCONSIN

THE BUSH INAUGURATION

'A nation of character'

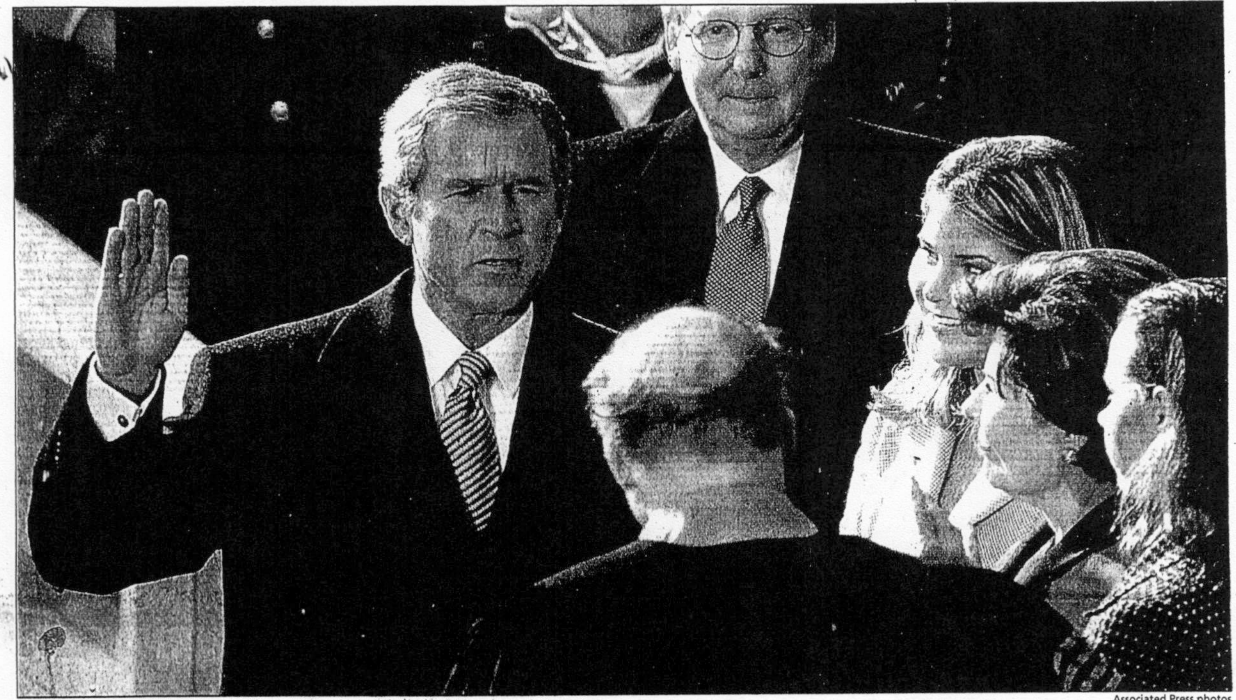

Associated Press photos

George W. Bush takes the oath of office from Chief Justice William Rehnquist, becoming the 43rd President of the United States.

CLINTON'S PARDONS

McDougal, Patty Hearst make the list

By Marc Lacey
New York Times

WASHINGTON — With just hours to go in his presidency, Bill Clinton on Saturday issued pardons to more than 100 people, including former CIA Director John Deutch, former Housing Secretary Henry Cisneros and Susan McDougal, a former Clinton business partner who was jailed in the Whitewater scandal.

Others issued presidential pardons in one of Clinton's last official acts were his half-brother, Roger, who pleaded guilty to distributing cocaine in Arkansas, and Patricia Hearst Shaw, the heiress who robbed a San Francisco bank in 1974 after being kidnapped by the Symbionese Liberation Army.

Please see CLINTON, Page A12

Inside

President Bush embraces his father, former President Bush, while former President Clinton looks on.

THE AGENDA

Bush's to-do list includes reacting

By Richard W. Stevenson
New York Times

WASHINGTON — When George W. Bush walked into the White House Saturday, his desk was clean, but his to-do list was long and getting longer.

Power shortages in California are threatening to set off an economic and political crisis. Peace negotiations in the Middle East are again approaching a critical stage. Bush's choice for attorney general is under attack from Democrats on Capitol Hill.

The economic outlook is murky, and the stock market is edgy. Bush must make a critical choice within weeks about whether to proceed with a version of a national missile defense system. He has a stack of initiatives he wants to send to Congress, but he has not yet formulated a budget to show how he will pay for them.

Bush and his aides have

Please see REACTING, Page A7

THE NEW PRESIDENT

He tells Americans: Give until it hurts

By Ken Herman
Cox News Service

WASHINGTON — George Walker Bush, born into politics but late to come to the game, took the oath of office Saturday as the nation's 43rd president and his family's second.

In a 15-minute inaugural address to a damp, chilly crowd that stretched far beyond the Capitol grounds, Bush promised action on education, military improvements, Social Security and other topics, but spent more time talking about how Congress works rather than what it works on.

Bottom line: Bush wants better behavior in a capital known for cut-throat partisanship. He called on the nation's leaders and lawmakers to "live up to the calling we share."

"Today we affirm a new commitment to live out our nation's promise through civility, courage, compassion and character," said Bush. "America at its best matched a commitment to principle with a concern for civility. A civil society demands from each of us good will and respect, fair dealing and forgiveness."

"Civility is not a tactic or a sentiment. It is the determined choice of trust over cynicism, of community over chaos," he said. "And this commitment, if we keep it, is the way to shared accomplishment."

In his characteristic unflowery way, Bush re-urged the ideal embodied 40 years ago

Please see BUSH, Page A6

Decision time Monday over school boundary struggle

By Doug Erickson
Education reporter

Four months of sometimes bruising work by a Madison School District committee will face a final test Monday, when the School Board is expected to decide how to resolve elementary school crowding.

Together with smaller changes already approved by the board, 690 children would shift to different schools next year, or about 6 percent of the district's 11,278 elementary students.

Although the number of students affected is relatively small, the proposed boundary changes and program adjustments touched off heated discourse among hundreds of parents in pockets across the city.

The level of emotion was anticipated and, in some ways, was a positive sign, said School Board member Carol Carstensen, chairwoman of the three-member Long Range Planning Committee. The committee held about a dozen meetings on the issue.

"It's a reflection of the quality of our schools that people say, 'We like where we are, our kids are doing well, and we don't want to change,' " she said.

While specific boundary change proposals were hotly

Please see BOUNDARIES, Page A5

If you go

◆ What: Madison School Board meeting.
◆ Where: Doyle Administration Building, 545 W. Dayton St.
◆ When: 6 p.m. Monday. The boundary-change issue is the third item on the agenda.

Inside

◆ A look at the recommendations, by school/A5

162nd year — No. 21 © 2001 Wisconsin State Journal

7 82550 00003 6
WSJ SUNDAY

WEATHER

Today
Partly sunny.
High 23.
Winds: WNW 10-20 mph.

Tonight
More clouds.
Low 14.
Details/ back of Local

TOMORROW

Many Native American tribal leaders are wondering where they will fit in to President Bush's plans.

INSIDE

EMPLOYMENT LISTINGS

	New	Total
General	97	148
Office/clerical	114	141
Health care	79	107

Total jobs in today's paper: 1,078

SPECIAL SEDER
UW student organizes event for women on campus
LOCAL/B1

THE PERFECT GIG
Anna Purnell is teacher by day, jazz musician by night
DAYBREAK/C1

DiMASTER
Masters rookie Chris DiMarco leads Woods
SPORTS/F1

★★★ 50 CENTS

SATURDAY

Wisconsin State Journal

SATURDAY, APRIL 7, 2001 MADISON, WISCONSIN

Parents ask court to clear their name

Their suit asks that therapists be held responsible for what they say were false claims of abuse.

By Cary Segall
Wisconsin State Journal

Charles and Karen Johnson were torn up when one of their adult daughters accused them of abusing her as a child, and they believe her therapists should be held responsible.

But two lower courts threw out their lawsuit, so they watched with trepidation Friday as their last hope — the Wisconsin Supreme Court — heard arguments in their case.

"There is no truth to the accusations we have been hit with, and it has totally devastated our family," said Charles Johnson, a retired plastic surgeon, after the arguments.

"We're doing it for other families and our daughter, too, to know the truth," added Karen Johnson, a retired nurse.

The Johnsons, of St. Louis, Mo., said their daughter claimed her father had sexually abused her and her mother physically abused her when she was 3 and living in Madison about 30 years ago.

The Johnsons' lawyer, Bill Smoler, told the court that Dane County Circuit Judge Dan Moeser and the 4th District Court of Appeals wrongly concluded the Johnsons' lawsuit couldn't proceed because their estranged daughter hasn't waived her right to keep her treatment records confidential.

The appeals court decided, 2-1, last July that the lawsuit couldn't be fairly resolved without the records and that it was more important to protect the confidentiality of the therapist-patient relationship.

But Smoler told the justices it was more important to hold therapists Kay Phillips, Jeff Hollowell and Tim Reisenauer responsible for implanting false memories of sexual abuse.

He said the therapists had used "recovered memory therapy" in treating the Johnsons' daughter in Madison and Oconomowoc and that the method had been totally discredited in the scientific community.

"Society has a reason to try and stop this kind of therapy," Smoler said.

He also said he might be able to prove his case without the records or convince the daughter to release them.

But the therapists' lawyers, David McFarlane and Mario Mendoza, said their clients couldn't defend themselves without the records and the privilege was important to assure patients they speak in confidence.

"Peope are going in and sharing their deepest feelings and traumas and concerns," McFarlane said.

The justices' comments indicated they're likely to give the Johnsons a chance to proceed, but a decision isn't expected until the end of June.

BALL ONE!

Associated Press

President Bush throws out the first ceremonial pitch to open Miller Park, the Milwaukee Brewers' new stadium, during opening day ceremonies Friday in Milwaukee. The Brewers beat the Cincinnati Reds in the home opener.

Miller Park opens in style

Bush tosses the first pitch . . . in the dirt.

By Susan Lampert Smith
Wisconsin State Journal

MILWAUKEE — Miller Park began making memories Friday night.

If you were one of the 42,024 people who fought their way through traffic and security blockades to attend opening night of the snazzy new ballpark, you have a kaleidoscope of memories to press in your scrapbook.

You saw the president of the United States take the mound for the ceremonial pitch, wind up and shank it right into the red dirt in front of a scrambling Brewers' manager Davey Lopes.

You smelled the smell of a new ball park: equal parts new carpet, old beer and that secret stadium sauce.

You roared for Robin Yount, the former Brewer announcer Bob Uecker still introduces as "the keeyid," and flashed one of thousands of cameras when baseball commissioner Bud Selig took the mound (and delivered the other honorary pitch right to Lopes.)

You saw a bald eagle soar down from Bernie Brewer's chalet to the pitcher's mound while kids from every Wisconsin county waved a huge flag.

And, oh yes, you saw a little baseball, watching the Brewers beat the Cincinnati Reds 5-4.

If you weren't at Miller Park, clip this out anyway, since someday you'll swear you were here. How else to explain a million people who claim they were at County Stadium when the Milwaukee Braves played in the World Series or the 2 million who swear they

Please see **BREWERS,** Page A5

CRAIG SCHREINER/WSJ

A Robin Yount look-alike enjoys the tailgating outside Miller Park Friday.

Inside

Senate passes reduced tax cut

President fails to get all the package he wanted

By James Kuhnhenn
Knight Ridder Newspapers

WASHINGTON — The Senate approved a federal budget outline Friday that trims President Bush's tax cut to $1.2 trillion over 10 years, denying him outright victory on the top legislative goal of his young presidency.

Senators approved the $1.2 trillion cut 65-35, despite weeks of tough lobbying for a bigger tax cut by Bush and Vice President Dick Cheney. Bush had been pushing his $1.6 trillion, 10-year tax cut for more than a year and made it one of the defining issues of his presidential campaign.

Fifteen Democrats — including Sen. Herb Kohl of Wisconsin — voted for the smaller $1.2 trillion measure. That was a significant level of Democratic support for a tax cut much higher than the $750 billion tax cut preferred by their party's leaders. (Sen. Russ Feingold, D-Wis., voted against it.)

The Senate did not vote on Bush's $1.6 trillion proposal because GOP leaders recognized they did not have the votes to pass it.

Though this budget plan is not binding on Congress, the vote illustrated the difficulties of maneuvering Bush's agenda through a Senate that is split evenly between Democrats and Republicans. But White House aides and Republi-

Please see **BUDGET,** Page A5

Madison property values at record level; construction soars in city

The value of the average home leaped from $149,831 to $161,500.

By Brenda Ingersoll
Wisconsin State Journal

A strong local economy pushed property values in Madison to a record high this year, which portends higher assessments for most taxpayers.

Construction and new assessments increased the city's overall property value by 9.3 percent to a record $12.5 billion, the assessor's office reported Friday. New construction accounted for 42 percent of the real estate valuation, said Ray Fisher, city revenue director.

"One of the things probably fueling the increase in valuation is interest rates being changed (reduced) this year," Fisher said. "When people buy houses, they don't have to pay as much on their monthly installments. We have a very healthy economy. You read the national newspapers and they say everything's going to hell in a hand basket, but you can't say that about Madison."

The impact on taxes won't be determined until later this year after local taxing entities — the city, Dane County and schools — arrive at their budgets for tax bills that go out in early December. They set their spending, factor in revenues and then rely on property taxes to balance their budgets.

The new values are "a pretty impressive increase," Mayor Sue Bauman said. "It shows that

Please see **VALUES,** Page A9

◆ Assessment changes by neighborhood/A9

162nd Year — No. 97 © 2001 Wisconsin State Journal

WEATHER

Today Warm and windy. High 70. Winds: SW 15-30 mph.

Tonight Partly cloudy. Low 46. **Details/ back of Local**

COMING SUNDAY

A willow furniture maker.

INSIDE

DO OR DIE FOR BUCKS
What: Charlotte at Milwaukee
When: 2 p.m. TV: WMTV
SPORTS/D1

Sam Cassell

FUNERAL FINANCES
Baby boomers are shopping around and saving money
BUSINESS/E1

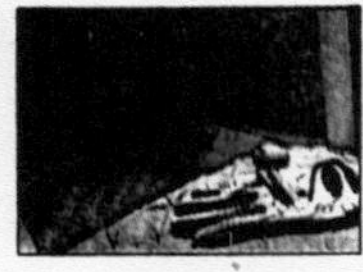

DREAM DEALS
Hunted down some second-hand steals
DAYBREAK/G1

★★★ $1.75

SUNDAY
Wisconsin State Journal
SUNDAY, MAY 20, 2001 MADISON, WISCONSIN WWW.MADISON.COM

A Wisconsin State Journal investigation finds legislative caucus employees use state work time, supplies and offices for campaign purposes, in possible violation of state law.

State employees secretly campaign

By Dee J. Hall
Wisconsin State Journal

Employees at four state agencies secretly campaign for legislative candidates on state time and from their state offices in apparent violation of the law, a Wisconsin State Journal investigation revealed.

The employees work for four partisan legislative caucuses that cost taxpayers an estimated $3.9 million a year.

The caucuses, one each for Assembly Democrats and Republicans and one for each party in the Senate, are officially charged with helping lawmakers with legislative tasks such as researching bills, drafting news releases and printing newsletters.

The state Ethics Board has advised legislators and their employees that it is illegal to campaign on state time or with state resources. But a State Journal investigation involving hundreds of records and interviews with more than 70 people found that the caucuses operate as secret campaign machines, especially during the election season.

"It's not confined to either the Democrats or Republicans, but I would say it happens on a wholesale basis and it's barely disguised anymore," said Greg DiMiceli, who was ousted last year from the Senate Republican Caucus (SRC) along with three others when state Sen. Mary Panzer took over GOP leadership in the Senate.

"It (campaigning) is almost the reason now for the existence of the caucuses," he said.

Among the State Journal's findings:

◆ The state caucus offices serve as campaign central for many legislative races, performing a variety of campaign functions in their government offices including coordinating advertising, providing lists of registered voters, designing brochures and giving out advice.

◆ Most candidates interviewed by the State Journal said they were unaware that caucus workers were prohibited

Please see **SECRET CAMPAIGNS**, Page A6

STEVE APPS/WSJ photos

When visitors arrive at two Assembly legislative caucuses, there is no government insignia that alerts them to the fact that they are entering a state office, where campaign activity is forbidden. The Assembly caucuses are at 17 S. Fairchild St. Similar offices for the Democratic and Republican Senate caucuses are at 1 S. Pinckney St.

Tracking campaign activity at the caucuses

Former staffers, legislators and candidates say campaign activity is widespread inside the state's four legislative caucuses. Documents obtained by the State Journal support those claims.

This catering bill for a Democratic campaign event was sent to Matthew Pagel at the taxpayer-funded funded Assembly Democratic Caucus office at 17 S. Fairchild St. Pagel said he was sent the bill by mistake after the organizer of the event failed to show up.

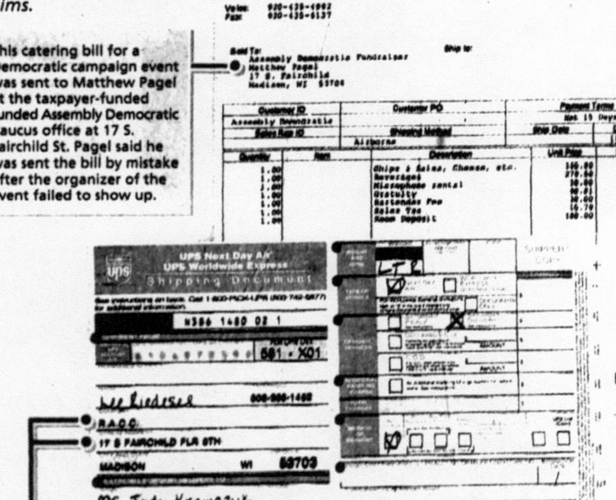
Ms. Judy Krawczyk
Krawczyk for Assembly
2294 Manitowoc Rd
Green Bay, WI 54311

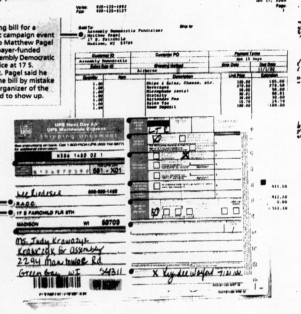

Mailing labels, such as this one addressed to then-candidate Judy Krawczyk before her election to the state Assembly, list the shipper as the privately-funded Republican Assembly Campaign Committee (RACC) — but show a return address for the taxpayer-funded Assembly Republican Caucus, 17 S. Fairchild St.

SOURCE: State Journal research

LAURA SPARKS/WSJ graphic

ABOUT THE SERIES

Caucuses: Secret campaign machines

A Wisconsin State Journal investigation involving more than 70 interviews and hundreds of documents scrutinized the work of the Legislature's four taxpayer-funded caucuses.

What are the caucuses?

They are teams of partisan employees who help legislators research issues, develop policy, design newsletters and communicate with constituents and the media. There are two caucuses in the Senate — one for each party — and two in the Assembly.

What the State Journal found

Caucus employees also routinely do political campaign work on state time or at their state offices. Regulators say state law prohibits both.

Coming Monday

Almost since their inception in 1967, state legislators have questioned the need for — and the activities of — the caucuses.

Coming Tuesday

Members of one caucus may have violated state campaign laws by working with an independent campaign group in the 2000 election.

INSIDE: ◆ State Journal finds questionable caucus phone calls/**A6** ◆ Ethics and campaign laws explained/**A6** ◆ How caucuses, legislative campaign committees, work together/**A6** ◆ Caucus staff told to keep campaigning secret/**A7**

Graduation day

SARAH B TEWS/WSJ

UW-Madison graduate Bridgette Leonard helps classmate Katee Anderson fix her cap in preparation for pre-commencement photographs outside the Kohl Center on Saturday. Leonard is from Osceola, and Anderson is from Red Wing, Minn. Story/C1

Unsolicited e-mail can be x-rated

And the governor and legislators want to curtail the messages known as 'spam.'

By Brenda Ingersoll
Wisconsin State Journal

If you've got e-mail, you've got spam.

With apologies to Hormel, spam is a derogatory term for unsolicited commercial e-mail. Just about everyone seems to get it. A sample: an ad promising to enlarge a part of the male anatomy blares, "Women get this for your boyfriend/husband. It really works! Click Here Now To Be Amazed, 18 And Over Only Please!!"

Gov. Scott McCallum and some legislators don't like this sort of solicitation. A provision that would make sending X-rated spam a Class A misdemeanor, unless it includes the words "Adult Advertisement" in the subject line, is part of McCallum's budget bill. Sen. Joanne Huelsman, R-Waukesha, says she's gotten pornographic e-mail at her Senate office. "Why is someone dumb enough to send this to a legislative office?" she

Please see **X-RATED**, Page A9

State in line for prescription drug money

Representatives think a federal drug-assistance program could be in place as soon as next year.

By Scott Milfred
State government reporter

Wisconsin is in line to get tens of millions of federal dollars to help people 65 and older pay for prescription drugs, members of the state's congressional delegation agree.

But big questions remain: When is the money coming? How much will it be? What strings are attached?

Even more important to people like Bob Silvers, 80, of Madison, is whether the federal prescription drug program called "Immediate Helping Hand" will help him.

Silvers, a retired printer, spends $6,745 of his annual $21,000 income on 10 drugs to treat prostate and skin cancer, glaucoma, shingles and Crohn's disease.

Please see **PRESCRIPTION**, Page A14

WEATHER

Today Partly sunny. High 74. Winds: ESE 7-14 mph.

Tonight Showers, storms. Low 52. **Details/ back of Local**

TOMORROW

Brooklyn Elementary School will lose 120 years of teaching experience when Betty Manson, Chris Johnson, Mary Weigand and Tom Sinks retire at the end of the school year.

INSIDE

PICTORIAL TRIBUTE INSIDE

SOUVENIR SECTION

Wisconsin State Journal

TUESDAY, SEPTEMBER 11, 2001 MADISON, WISCONSIN WWW.MADISON.COM

Capitol shines again

Joseph W. Jackson III/WSJ

In the dome's oculus, or eye, rings of gold-painted flourishes and daylight from 20 windows surround the mural "Resources of Wisconsin" by Edwin Blashfield. The tile mosaics were created by Kenyon Cox and depict Justice, top, and Government, bottom. During its cleaning and restoration, scaffolding filled the rotunda so workers could reach the dome.

ATOP the Isthmus' highest point, the state Capitol constantly beckons to those viewing it in Madison and from surrounding hilltops.

It is ubiquitous with Madison, and a view of its noble dome will often boost a property's value.

This month, with the completion of its $141 million, 11-year restoration, the Capitol's interior is restored to its original grandeur and its Bethel granite exterior is as white as it was the day it was finished.

Those walking through its doors will appreciate architect George B. Post's historic designs that make it worthy of its new place as a National Historic Landmark.

What will be less apparent is that it is as technologically advanced as the brand new State Justice Center a block away.

— Lisa Schuetz

★★★ 50 CENTS

SPECIAL REPORT

Wisconsin State Journal

WEDNESDAY, SEPTEMBER 12, 2001 MADISON, WISCONSIN WWW.MADISON.COM

'ACT OF WAR'

◆ Bush vows justice after worst terrorist attack stuns nation
◆ Thousands feared dead; rescuers dig for survivors
◆ Hijacked jets destroy World Trade Center, damage Pentagon

By Scott Shepard and Shelley Emling
Cox News Service

WASHINGTON — Unknown enemies waged war against America Tuesday with horrendous attacks on the chief symbols of U.S. military and financial power, causing untold deaths and sparking unprecedented fear and thirst for revenge.

The day of horror and sorrow began when two of four commercial jetliners hijacked nearly simultaneously crashed into the giant towers of the World Trade Center in New York. Soon afterward, another plowed into the Pentagon just outside the nation's capital. The fourth crashed 80 miles southeast of Pittsburgh, possibly bound for the presidential retreat at Camp David, Md.

"The search is under way for those who are behind these evil acts," President Bush said in an evening address intended to calm the nation's fears but also to focus the "quiet, unyielding anger" of his countrymen.

"I have directed the full resources of our intelligence and law enforcement communities to find those responsible and bring them to justice," the president added. "We will make no distinction between the terrorists who committed these acts and those who harbor them."

The government assumed a war footing after the most deadly attack ever on American civilians. Hundreds are known dead, and it is almost certain to eclipse the 1,178 Americans killed in the surprise Japanese attack that led to the United States' entry into World War II 60 years ago.

Please see **ATTACK**, Page A16

INSIDE

Associated Press

A shell of the facade of one of the twin towers of New York's World Trade Center rises above the rubble after both towers were destroyed when two hijacked planes flew into the building 18 minutes apart Tuesday morning. It was the most devastating terrorist attack ever waged against the United States.

162nd Year — No. 255 © 2001 Wisconsin State Journal

WEATHER

Today Partly sunny. High 74. Winds: SW 8-16 mph.

Tonight A stray shower. Low 52. **Details/ back of Local**

TOMORROW

The aftermath: U.S. hunts for terrorists while the search for bodies continues.

INSIDE

★★★

SPECIAL REPORT

50 CENTS

Wisconsin State Journal

THURSDAY, SEPTEMBER 13, 2001 MADISON, WISCONSIN WWW.MADISON.COM

Out of darkness: clues

Associated Press photos

Firefighters and rescue workers pulled out at least five survivors from the wreckage of the World Trade Center in New York City by Wednesday evening. They had recovered 82 bodies. Thousands of people died in the terrorist attack that destroyed the twin towers Tuesday.

Officials begin unraveling complex plot

By Warren P. Strobel and Daniel de Vise
Knight Ridder Newspapers

WASHINGTON — Launching perhaps the largest criminal investigation in U.S. history, federal and state authorities raided hotel rooms and searched for vehicles from Maine to Florida on Wednesday as they began uncovering the complex plot that led to the deadly terrorist attacks on the World Trade Center and the Pentagon.

Investigators in the FBI-led probe tracked down hundreds of potential leads on their first full day, scouring clues left behind by the suicide terrorists, from rental cars and hotel rooms to Arabic-language piloting manuals.

The early evidence indicated that 20 or more hijackers commandeered the four jetliners and steered them into the seats of U.S. economic and military power. The terrorists may have been divided into separate, self-contained groups, some crossing into the United States from Canada recently. Others may have been here for some time, law enforcement authorities said.

Among them was a 33-year-old man who was on the passenger list of one of the hijacked planes. He had also been taking flying lessons in South Florida.

"A number of the suspected hijackers were trained as pilots in the United States," Attorney General John Ashcroft told a news conference.

"The four planes were hijacked by between three and six individuals per plane, using knives and box-cutters, and in some cases making bomb threats," Ashcroft said. "Our government has credible evidence that the White House and Air Force One were targets."

FBI Director Robert Mueller said law enforcement authorities have identified many of the hijackers by name, and efforts are now under way to find their associates.

Mueller said the investigation involves 4,000 of the bureau's agents, 3,000 support staff and 400 lab technicians. Some

Please see CLUES, Page A14

"The four planes were hijacked by between three and six individuals per plane, using knives and box-cutters, and in some cases making bomb threats. Our government has credible evidence that the White House and Air Force One were targets."

JOHN ASHCROFT
U.S. Attorney General

SEARCH FOR SURVIVORS

'Thousands and thousands and thousands of dead'

Amid overpowering rubble, rescue workers dig for survivors and bodies.

By Ken Moritsugu and Mark Fazlollah
Knight Ridder Newspapers

NEW YORK — With fires still smoldering and other buildings in danger of collapsing more than 24 hours after the terrorist attack, rescue workers at the World Trade Center began the enormous task Wednesday of removing tons of ash-strewn debris, trying to find survivors and digging out the bodies.

"There are thousands and thousands and thousands of dead," said Dr. Ira Warheit, a volunteer medical worker on the scene.

By that night, only 82 bodies had been recovered and at least five people had been pulled out alive, New York Mayor Rudolph Giuliani said. About 20,000 people worked in the two towers and tens of thousands more in other buildings at the World Trade Center, though many escaped before the buildings collapsed. About 300 firefighters and 70 police officers were also missing.

"I really think this is a situation we're going to be living with for a while, which is we'll only know whether we've saved someone or recovered someone's body when that actually happens," Giuliani said at a news conference. He apologized that he could not offer anything more concrete to relatives desperate for information.

As a funnel of brownish smoke continued to rise from the site, people throughout the city took to the streets to search for their loved ones. Some wore sandwich boards with photographs of the missing. Others passed out fliers.

The scene at the World Trade Center site looked like the aftermath of war. One tower looked

Please see SEARCH, Page A14

INSIDE

President Bush, accompanied by Secretary of Defense Donald Rumsfeld, left, examines the devastation at the Pentagon Wednesday. Bush thanked weary rescuers at the Pentagon and the destroyed World Trade Center in New York.

CLOSER TO HOME

We share our sorrow

From chapels to college campuses, we found places to share our grief and shock. Many of us gathered around the modern communal hearth of flickering television screens to watch burning buildings and piles of rubble in New York City and Washington, D.C.

In Stoughton, students circled an American flag flying at half-staff to pray for our nation. "Give our country the strength and wisdom to do what is right," said Christina Stanek, the student organizer.

At Edgewood College in Madison, students met on the lawn in a vigil for peace. While on local talk radio, some of us cried for vengeance.

◆ Susan Lampert Smith's report/**A3**

162nd Year — No. 256 © 2001 Wisconsin State Journal

WEATHER

Today Much cooler. High 62. Winds: NNE 8-16 mph.

Tonight Mostly clear. Low 42. **Details/ back of Local**

TOMORROW

War on America: The United States hunts for terrorists while the search for bodies continues.

INSIDE

BADGERS, NFL CALL OFF GAMES/B1 **FULL-PAGE COLOR FLAG INSIDE TODAY**

★★★ 50 CENTS

FRIDAY

Wisconsin State Journal

FRIDAY, SEPTEMBER 14, 2001 MADISON, WISCONSIN WWW.MADISON.COM

WAR ON AMERICA

Bush: We'll win this war

Congress prepares to send the president $40 billion for the task

By Scott Shepard
Cox News Service

WASHINGTON — President Bush stepped forward Thursday to lead America into what he called the "first war of the 21st century" as his administration fingered Saudi exile Osama bin Laden as a key suspect in the suicidal terrorist attacks in New York and Washington.

"The nation must understand, this is now the focus of my administration," Bush told reporters in the Oval Office after an emotional and nationally televised telephone call to New York Mayor Rudolph Giuliani and the state's governor, George Pataki.

"I weep and mourn with America. ... I wish I could comfort every single family whose lives have been affected," the president said, blinking back tears. "My resolve is steady and strong about winning this war that has been declared on America ... the first war of the 21st century," he added.

But the targets and scope of such a war were far from clear.

ABC News reported late Thursday that authorities has taken 10 people into custody at two of New York's major airports after they attempted to board commercial flights with knives and fake identification. ABC said four had open tickets to various U.S. cities dated Sept. 11, the date of Tuesday's attacks.

"This is a new kind of war, and this government will adjust," Bush said earlier in the day in his first meeting with reporters since the attacks.

At the State Department, Secretary of State Colin Powell, who was the nation's top military official in the 1991 war

Please see **WAR,** Page A15

Associated Press

President Bush declares today a national day of prayer and remembrance

Meeting with reporters for the first time since Tuesday's attacks, President Bush vowed to win at any cost what he called the "first war of the 21st century."

Today, he will lead the nation in a day of prayer at the Washington National Cathedral and fly to New York to inspect the devastation and recovery efforts there.

◆ Bush's proclamation/A2

Associated Press

John Potts waves a U.S. flag as a Delta plane loaded with passengers takes off from Dallas-Fort Worth International airport in Grapevine, Texas, on Thursday. Air traffic had been grounded since Tuesday.

Flag buying and flying increases

The biggest patriotic buying spree in recent memory is taking place across the nation and at home.

By Susan Lampert Smith
and Richard A. Jaeger
Wisconsin State Journal

Today's the day to fly your American flag — if you can find one.

Monroe is among a number of Wisconsin communities and schools that have declared today Red, White & Blue Day.

"Here in Monroe, we're asking everyone to fly their flags and to wear red, white and blue," Mayor Bill Ross said. "We want to show that everyone here in Monroe is behind our country and whatever it needs to do to correct this situation."

Patriotic colors are also going to be the norm today in the Black Hawk School District, along the Wisconsin and Illinois border.

"We're having Red, White and Blue Day for our whole district," High School Principal Jerry Mortimer said. He said the students at the district's schools in South Wayne and Gratiot are planning to gather around the flag pole to recite the Pledge of Allegiance as a group this morning.

Tonight's football game will also be a chance for the community to express its patriotism.

"Before the band plays the national anthem, we're going to have a minute of silence, and then the mixed chorus is going to sing a beautiful song called 'Wings,'" he said. "We'll have a thousand people here."

At the new Rome Corners Intermediate School in Oregon, students are also being encouraged to wear the colors of the flag today.

Please see **FLAG,** Page A6

◆ Tips on flying the flag properly/A2

Excruciating search continues

Associated Press

Rachel Uchitel makes an emotional plea as she searches for her fiance James Andrew O'Grady outside Bellevue Hospital in Manhattan on Thursday. O'Grady was working on the 104th floor of Tower 2 of New York's World Trade Center that was destroyed in the terrorist attack on Tuesday. Thousands of anguished people, many holding photographs of their missing loved ones, waited for some word about their fate. Mayor Rudolph Giuliani said 4,763 people are known to be missing, although authorities expect that number to go much higher. Story/A3

THE INVESTIGATION

More terrorists may be on loose

Several people trying to board planes are detained by authorities.

By John Solomon
Associated Press

WASHINGTON — U.S. investigators pressed Thursday to identify terrorist collaborators who may still be in a position to strike more Americans, and agents located critical "black boxes" from two of Tuesday's hijacked planes.

Four U.S. officials, speaking on condition of anonymity, told The Associated Press that authorities are investigating the possibility that some terrorists involved with Tuesday's plots are still at large.

Five men who tried to board a plane Thursday in New York were being questioned, officials said. One of the men had a false pilot's identification. The five were identified as the same men who had tried to board a plane around the time of Tuesday's hijackings, but were turned away.

The FBI sent the airline industry a list of 52 people wanted for questioning. Airlines were asked to alert agents if any of the individuals were spotted.

Please see **TERRORISTS,** Page A15

Deadly cost

Here is a tally of victims and people missing as a result of the Sept. 11 terrorist attacks.

New York
◆ **Confirmed dead:** 94
◆ **Dead which have been identified:** 46
◆ **Missing:** 4,763, including about 300 firefighters and 60 NYPD and Port Authority police officers.
◆ **Injured:** 3,800

Washington
◆ **Believed dead:** 126
◆ **Injured:** 94 treated at area hospitals, including at least 10 in critical condition.
Pennsylvania
◆ **Confirmed dead:** 45

Airline crashes
◆ **Confirmed dead:**
American Airlines Flight 11: 92
American Airlines Flight 77: 64
United Airlines Flight 175: 65
United Airlines Flight 93: 45

SOURCE: *AP wire reports* AP

INSIDE

Pentagon death toll
◆ A Pentagon official says about 190 people died in the attack there. **Page A3**

A sustained strike
◆ A Pentagon official said the United States will launch sustained military strikes against those responsible and their support systems. **Page A4**

Missing family
◆ Five Wisconsin families awaited word Thursday on the fate of missing relatives. **Page A5**

In the classroom
◆ University of Wisconsin System classes will close at noon but Madison School District will remain open today. **Page A5**

Planes in the air
◆ Jetliners returned to the nation's skies, carrying nervous passengers who faced strict new security measures. **Page B8**

Markets reopen Monday
◆ Stock market officials announced that trading will resume Monday. **Page B8**

162nd Year — No. 257 © 2001 Wisconsin State Journal
7 82550 00001 2
WSJ DAILY

WEATHER

Today Comfortable. High 60. Winds: NE 7-14 mph.

Tonight Chilly. Low 44. **Details/ back of Local**

TOMORROW

Investigators press forward and cleanup and recovery efforts continue.

INSIDE

NEW LIFE FOR AN OLD THEATER/D1 **THE MEANING OF 'I LOVE YOU'/B1**

★★★ MONDAY 50 CENTS

Wisconsin State Journal

MONDAY, SEPTEMBER 17, 2001 MADISON, WISCONSIN WWW.MADISON.COM

Beware our 'full wrath'

◆ That's message to nations hosting terrorists ◆ Bush is zeroing in on suspect bin Laden

By Tom Raum
Associated Press

WASHINGTON — President Bush, vowing not to be "cowed by evildoers," pledged a crusade against terrorists Sunday as top administration officials on Sunday zeroed in on Saudi exile Osama bin Laden and Afghanistan's Taliban militia for possible retribution for last week's terrorist attacks.

"No question, he is the prime suspect. No question about that," Bush said, brushing off a reported denial of responsibility by bin Laden.

As Bush sought to rally Americans to get on with their lives and jobs, administration officials asserted on the Sunday talk shows that nations that harbor terrorists would face the "full wrath" of the United States.

They emphasized that the battle against terrorism would

Please see **WRATH,** Page A11

Inside

STEVE APPS/WSJ photos

Madison firefighters prepare to raise a huge American flag on the King Street corner of the Capitol Square for Sunday afternoon's "Wisconsin Salute to the American Spirit." The flag was suspended between the raised ladders of two fire trucks during the ceremony.

Cheney: Economy is down, but it will bounce back

By Ken Moritsugu
Knight Ridder Newspapers

NEW YORK — U.S. stock markets prepared to reopen today amid a growing belief by economists and government officials that last week's terrorist attacks may have plunged the wounded American economy into a recession.

Vice President Dick Cheney, speaking Sunday on NBC's "Meet the Press," acknowledged the economy may be in recession but expressed confidence that it will bounce back later this year.

"I would hope the American people would, in effect, stick their thumb in the eye of the terrorists and say that they've got great confidence in the country, great confidence in our economy, and not let what's happened here in any way throw off their normal level of economic activity," he said.

What economists are struggling to judge, more so than whether the country is technically in a recession, is how much the attack will delay an economic recovery.

Please see **ECONOMY,** Page A11

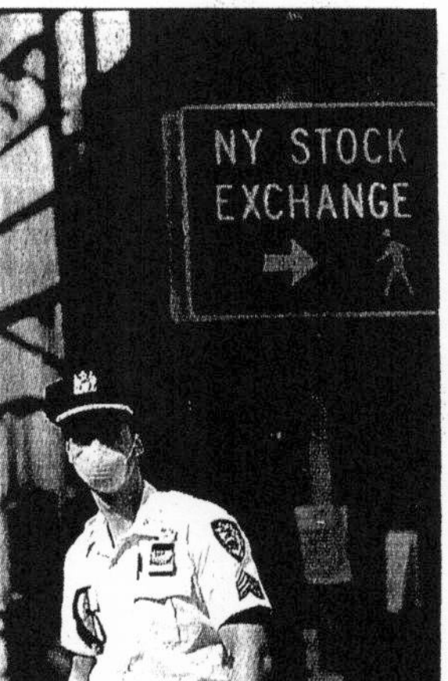

Associated Press

A police officer patrols near the New York Stock Exchange on Sunday as preparations continued for reopening the stock markets this morning. They have been closed since Tuesday.

At Capitol, a strong showing of support

By Deborah Kades
Wisconsin State Journal

As the mournful tones of taps sounded across the state Capitol grounds Sunday, a tribute to the lives lost in last week's terrorism attacks, Minako Voeltz, 13, gave in to tears.

The Madison teen worries that her father, Chan, a Navy reservist, could find himself in a dangerous situation as America gears up to fight terrorism.

"I know he'd want to help, but I can't imagine losing my dad," she said, dabbing the corners of her eyes with her sweat shirt sleeves.

Minako isn't the only person to take the attacks to heart. As people filled churches to overflowing across the county, as many as 5,000 Wisconsin residents came together at the Capitol to mourn the lives lost, and those irrevocably changed, when hijacked jets crashed into the World Trade Center, the Pentagon and a field in Pennsylvania.

Under a picture-perfect blue sky, the 132nd Army Band of the Wisconsin National Guard played the national anthem and "God Bless America" in between speeches from politicians, clergymen, and spokesmen for police officers and firefighters.

Brig. Gen. Al Wilkening of the Wisconsin National Guard assured state residents that the 10,000 men and women in the state Guard are ready to answer the nation's call to action.

Everyone from toddlers on parents' shoulders to teens and seniors listened reverently.

Much of the crowd was a sea of blue and green, with uniformed police officers and firefighters from across the state standing somberly, shoulder to shoulder.

"We're here to show our support for our lost brothers and sisters in New York and Washington," said Rob Indrebo, a firefighter from Eau Claire. "You feel so helpless in Wisconsin, because you want to go out there and help. It's important for us to show our support in any way we can."

And although a sense of loss pervaded the event, each speaker urged the country to move forward.

"Today, more than ever, let us all recognize that we are in this together, and let us say to the world that this tragedy has made us stronger, not weaker," said Gov. Scott McCallum.

Hoping to make schools gay-harassment-free

The new liaison specialist for Madison schools is listening and learning the newly created job.

By Doug Erickson
Education reporter

Hours before Bonnie Augusta was to give a speech Wednesday, she discarded the one she'd written and started over.

The day before, terrorists had killed what appears to be thousands in New York, Washington, D.C., and Pennsylvania. As she stood before a group made up mostly of gay and lesbian educators in Madison, Augusta spoke of intolerance and the fear of perceived differences.

"Airplane crashes did not kill anyone yesterday," she said. "Neither did fire nor falling buildings. It was hate. Hate killed people yesterday."

She urged the 40 people at the annual meeting of the local chapter of the Gay Lesbian and Straight Education Network to fight the ignorance that leads to misperceptions and to battle intolerance in all its forms.

It was a well-received speech, moving some to tears. It also was a speech close to Augusta's heart. In her new job with the Madison School District, she is trying to do exactly what her speech urged, she said.

Augusta is the district's first resource teacher for those who are gay, lesbian, bisexual or transgender. The School Board created the position in February amid controversy, and the district now is thought to be among only a handful in the country with a full-time employee to address harassment of gay students and staffers.

Augusta, a 25-year district veteran, began the new position July 1 and is paid $54,023 annually.

The mood at Wednesday's meeting was celebratory, with many people hugging and encouraging Augusta. A Room of One's Own, a local feminist bookstore, gave her $1,000 credit to buy resource books.

"I'm just glad we're not waiting for the rest of the country to do this," said Rachel Potter,

Please see **AUGUSTA,** Page A7

STEVE APPS/WSJ

Sherman Middle School Principal Ann Yehle, left, talks with Bonnie Augusta during a meeting of the school's climate action team. Yehle had asked Augusta to contribute her expertise on gay and lesbian issues to the team, which is working to reduce harassment at the school.

162nd Year — No. 260 © 2001 Wisconsin State Journal

WEATHER

Today: Spotty showers. High 66; Winds: SW 7-14 mph.

Tonight: Mostly cloudy. Low 52. Details/ back of Local

TOMORROW

Play for Peace movement comes to Madison. In Daybreak

INSIDE

BADGERS KEEP BOWL HOPES ALIVE
Bollinger, UW beat Iowa 34-28
SPORTS/D1

D'BACKS FORCE GAME 7 TONIGHT
Arizona routs Yankees 15-2

2001 WOLMAN AWARD WINNER
Joseph McClain
LOCAL/C1

★★★ $1.75

SUNDAY

Wisconsin State Journal

SUNDAY, NOVEMBER 4, 2001 MADISON, WISCONSIN WWW.MADISON.COM

Anthrax 'second wave' of attacks

THE SECRET FIGHT OF AFGHANISTAN'S WOMEN

Associated Press photos

All Afghan women are forced to cover themselves entirely with burqas. The Revolutionary Association of the Women of Afghanistan, or RAWA, uses the covering to its advantage, hiding banned schoolbooks and other illegal literature.

They wage war with books

A women's group called RAWA conducts illegal classes for girls and breaks other rules of the Taliban.

By Liz Sly
Chicago Tribune

JALOZAI REFUGEE CAMP, Pakistan — The head-to-toe robe that women in Afghanistan are compelled to wear by the Taliban regime represents to many the most overtly sinister symbol of the absolute subjugation of that country's women. It restricts air supply, shuts out the light, inhibits movement and snuffs out individuality, turning women into indistinguishable blobs.

But from within the prison of their cloth cages, Afghan women are fighting back.

Using their burqas as cloaks for covert activities, a group of dedicated Afghan women is waging a secret war against the Taliban's suppression of women's rights. The Revolutionary Association of the Women of Afghanistan, or RAWA, advocates a modest agenda of gender equality. But in the context of Taliban-ruled Afghanistan, it is a movement as radical and as revolutionary as any of the militant Islamic organizations America is battling in its war on terrorism.

Afghan women attend a school run by RAWA in Quetta, Pakistan. Inside Afghanistan, RAWA runs secret schools for girls and women, an extremely dangerous undertaking. In Pakistan, the group operates freely, but organizers keep a low profile because of death threats from Taliban loyalists and fundamentalist religious groups.

Their weapons are simple but potent in a country in which women are banned from attending school, forbidden to hold jobs, forced to hide their faces and risk a whipping if they laugh in public. They conduct illegal school classes for girls. They advocate nail polish. They secretly photograph evidence of Taliban atrocities, which they post on their Web site, *www.rawa.org*. They hold covert political awareness classes at which Afghan women are taught the basics of human rights.

"Our main motive is to make them aware that they have rights and that they can fight for them," said Weeda Mansoor, 36, one of RAWA's 11-member leadership collective, speaking at one of the group's bases at the Jalozai refugee camp in Pakistan.

Please see **RAWA,** Page A12

Administration misjudged its severity: Bush

By Michael Kranish
Boston Globe

WASHINGTON — President Bush said Saturday that anthrax cases represent a "second wave of terrorist attacks" on the country and acknowledged that his administration originally had underestimated the severity of the problem.

He also said anthrax "apparently can be passed from one letter to another," an assertion that could make Americans wary of even letters that don't look suspicious on the outside.

Bush spoke on a day of heightened tension from new alerts. Police provided extra security at the World Series in Phoenix. California authorities kept guard at major bridges. The Immigration and Naturalization Service detained three men in New Jersey as a result of the anthrax inquiry.

In Washington, Treasury Department officials isolated a suspicious letter and sent it for testing. The letter bore the same Trenton, N.J., postmark as anthrax-laced mail sent to New York and Washington.

Bush, delivering the Saturday

Please see **BUSH,** Page A5

WAR ON TERROR

Inside

- Tom Ridge, above, faces unique 'Homeland Security' challenge/A3
- Tajikistan agrees to consider further helping U.S.-led campaign/A9
- In videotaped statement, Osama bin Laden denounces United Nations/A9
- Marines using Harrier jump jets launch strikes on Taliban/A9

In Your Forum

- The propaganda war/B1
- The media's job: Neutrality vs. objectivity/B1

Madison's anthrax 'history'

- Columnist George Hesselberg explains /G1

ANALYSIS

Attacks put an end to 'me-first' lifestyle

Although President Bush hasn't asked them for much, Americans seem ready to sacrifice.

By Dick Polman
Knight Ridder Newspapers

Forget war and sacrifice for a moment. Let us revisit the America that existed one year ago, on the eve of a tight presidential election, and ponder the blase pursuits of a society that belongs in a time capsule.

Half of all voting-age Americans were planning to boycott the Bush-Gore contest, an apparently low-stakes affair that at times seemed to hinge on whether the Democrat's pompous behavior was worse than the Republican's propensity for mangling syntax.

Downloaders of Internet music were alarmed at the prospect of paying a fee for Napster. Film-goers were weighing the new "Charlie's Angels" film against the old TV show. Consumers were buying more cigars,

Please see **LIFESTYLE,** Page A7

Papers sue state boards on caucus-deal records

The Ethics and Elections boards refused to turn over documents.

By Phil Brinkman
State government reporter

The Wisconsin State Journal and the Milwaukee Journal Sentinel plan to go to court to try to force two state agencies to turn over records of their review of alleged illegal campaign activity by the legislative caucuses.

In a complaint to be filed in Dane County Circuit Court on Monday, the newspapers allege the state Ethics and Elections boards failed to comply with the state's open records law when they refused requests for the documents last month.

The two boards secretly negotiated a pact to eliminate the staffs of the legislative caucuses, impose fines and reform legislative work rules, in exchange for agreeing not to pursue any penalties against legislators or caucus staffers.

"We are never especially comfortable suing our own state government, but the behavior of these public bodies in secret, and apparently in collusion, is outrageous," said Frank Denton, editor of the State Journal. "This back-room deal is totally alien to the Wisconsin tradition of clean and open government. We need to get to the bottom of it."

Please see **CAUCUS,** Page A6

Taxi accident injures 11 near Camp Randall Stadium

STEVE APPS/WSJ

Madison Fire Department paramedics treat a pedestrian who was among 11 people injured Saturday when a taxi jumped a curb on University Avenue near Camp Randall Stadium before the UW-Madison football game against Iowa. The cab driver and 10 pedestrians were taken to local hospitals. Police reported no serious injuries. Story/C1

THE GOVERNOR'S RACE

Anything goes in unpredictable contest

Four Democrats are in the field, with Gov. McCallum the only Republican so far.

By Scott Milfred
State government reporter

Crowded, unpredictable and incredibly expensive, the race for governor in Wisconsin culminates one year from Tuesday.

At least one Republican, four Democrats and a third-party candidate with a famous last name hope to win the state's top job on Nov. 5, 2002.

"It's a wide-open race," said U.S. Rep. Tom Barrett, a Democratic candidate for governor from Milwaukee. "I don't think anybody should be measuring for new drapes in that office yet."

Republican strategists agree that 2002 will be the most competitive gubernatorial race in more than a decade. Yet they insist incumbent Gov. Scott McCallum, who inherited the job Feb. 1, is still the guy to beat.

"He's the governor, and there are a lot of advantages that come with that," said Republican strategist Brandon Scholz. "If he can make the case he's been able to manage the state

Please see **GOVERNOR,** Page A6

WEATHER

Today: Sunshine; nice. High 54. Winds: NW 5-10 mph.

Tonight: Clear and cool. Low 30. Details/ back of Local

INSIDE

TOMORROW

Bacterial detectives are still chasing the E. coli infection that sickened at least 35 people last month at UW-Madison Stock Pavilion.

INSIDE: WIAA FOOTBALL PLAYOFFS

Div. 1: Janesville Parker 34, Middleton 13
Div. 2: Milton 34, Verona 12
Div. 3: Waunakee 21, Monona Grove 20
WIAA playoff coverage/D1, D4.-5

Bush speaks to U.N., calls for world unity
WORLD/A9

BEARS VS. PACKERS
NOON, AT CHICAGO,
WMSN (CH. 47)

SPORTS/D1

A Harry Potter primer on books, films, the legend
SHOWCASE/F1

Help fill Empty Stockings
ENVELOPE INSIDE, STORY/C1

★★★

V E T E R A N S   D A Y

$1.75

Wisconsin State Journal

SUNDAY, NOVEMBER 11, 2001 MADISON, WISCONSIN WWW.MADISON.COM

JOHN MANIACI/WSJ

A deer clears Highway 78 near Prairie du Sac earlier this fall, although many others aren't so lucky. State wildlife officials say they're struggling to convince people of the need to control the growing deer herd.

Hunters don't accept DNR's deer herd data

Agency struggles to convince them that there are too many deer in Wisconsin.

By Ron Seely
Environment reporter

In the 1940s, Wisconsin conservationist Aldo Leopold was practically tarred and feathered for suggesting there were too many deer in the state.

Leopold, who established one of the nation's first wildlife ecology programs at the UW-Madison, even proposed killing more deer, especially does. This, in those days, was blasphemy among hunters. Good sportsmanship meant shooting only bucks, leaving the females to reproduce and sustain the herd size.

Leopold's fight is still being fought by today's wildlife managers, even as the first statewide gun deer hunt of the new millennium approaches. The season begins Saturday. The Department of Natural Resources estimates the size of the deer herd at about 1.8 million animals.

Please see **DEER**, Page A5

◆ Deer season overview/**D12**

Taliban took power during civil war

The illiterate farmers and students were initially supported by Pakistan and ordinary Afghans.

By Earleen Fisher
Associated Press

The last battle of the Cold War was fought in the harsh beauty of Afghanistan by the proxy warriors of the United States and the Soviet Union and by the Red Army itself.

Now the first battle of America's declared war on terrorism has been launched in the same nation of graveyards — where crude cemeteries hold not only the million or more people killed since the Soviet invasion but also the dead ideologies and ambitions of those who sought to reshape Afghanistan to their own will.

How did it come to this? The last two decades hold a key.

The Soviet Union invaded its southern neighbor in 1979 to prop up a Kremlin-clone government that had seized power the previous year. Nearly 10 years later its army withdrew, defeated by a fractious array of U.S.-supported mujahedeen, or Islamic holy warriors.

But the mujahedeen, who received arms and money from Pakistan and Arab nations as well as from America, couldn't stop battling each

Please see **TALIBAN**, Page A11

Campaign accusations spread in Statehouse

Memos reveal campaign activity at legislative offices

These documents show that electioneering occurs in the Capitol even though it is prohibited by law.

Campaign thank-you invitation
Assembly Republican staffers were told in this invitation to reply to the office of Rep. Bonnie Ladwig, R-Racine, if they wanted to attend a post-election party at a Downtown bar after work.

Ladwig

TO: All members of the Assembly, and Members- Elect

FROM: Speaker Scott Jensen
Majority Leader Mickey Foti
Assistant Majority Leader Bonnie Ladwig
Speaker Pro Temp Steve Freese
Caucus Chair Mark Green
Vice Caucus Chair Dan Vrakas
Caucus Secretary Carol Owens
Sgt. At Arms Dean Kaufert
Jt. Finance Chair John Gard

RE: Leadership Elections

DATE: November 5, 1998

Congratulations to all of you on your re-election to the State Assembly!!! Some of us had races that we barely pulled off, others of us had an easy cruise to victory, and were able to help out our colleagues. Either way we all worked together, and came out the victors.

I think we all realize that this was one of the hardest fought battles in a long time. Members and their staff have given so much time and effort to the cause, and I think it is obvious that we could not have done this without the help of our loyal staff. Without them, hundreds of thousands of records would never have been entered, over twenty thousand envelopes would never have been hand addressed, literature would never have been personally delivered to thousand of houses throughout the state, and that last push of annoying phone calls would have never been made.

As a thank you to all of our members and to all of our staff, our Assembly leadership [illegible] thank you [illegible] elections.
Please reserve this time on your calendars, and we will be letting staff know shortly.

If you defiantly do not plan on attending, please call Judi Rhodes in Rep. Ladwig's office (266-9171) so we can get a general head count for food.

A staffer's final letter
Dan Kroll left this letter for Doug Burnett, chief of staff for Senate Majority Leader Chuck Chvala, D-Madison, on Kroll's last day as Chvala's press secretary.

Chvala

Wednesday, February 12, 1997

Doug:

Chuck took care of his interests, and now I am going to take care of mine. I won't be in anymore. Chuck can [illegible] the rest of the month severance pay, family leave [illegible] anything.

The file that you no doubt are most interested in – the campaign file – is in the lower right drawer of my desk. At the front of that file is the disk that contains most or all of my campaign writing. You might want to check the C drive for anything else.

Thanks [illegible]

Aides asked to campaign
Assembly Republican staffers were told to contact the offices of Reps. Eugene Hahn, R-Cambria, and Rick Skindrud, R-Mount Horeb, to work on their campaigns.

Skindrud

SWARM

To: Republican Colleagues

From: Rob Richard, SWARM Coordinator

Date: July 28, 1998

Re: Local state races and misc. items

For those of you willing to help out with elections in the Madison area, Rep. Skindrud and Rep. Hahn will be needing your assistance throughout this campaign season with lit drops, parades, mailings and phones. I know that many of you will be unable to travel outside of the Dane County area, so any effort you can give to the local races will be most appreciated.

If you want to volunteer in these races, please call the office of Rep. Skindrud or Rep. Hahn. Their staff will set everything up as far as departing times and/or rides. The Democrats always target these seats, so it is important that we work harder than they do to keep these seats in GOP hands.

SOURCE: State Journal research by Dee J. Hall
LAURA SPARKS/WSJ graphic

Activity in Capitol is routine among some legislators and aides

By Dee J. Hall
Wisconsin State Journal

Campaigning has been common in the offices of some state lawmakers and not confined to the soon-to-be-defunct legislative caucuses, according to Capitol sources and documents obtained by the Wisconsin State Journal.

Despite state laws prohibiting campaigning with state resources, seven staffers said campaigning directly out of the Capitol is routine among some lawmakers and reaches into the ranks of the legislative leaders. Campaign-related documents stretching from 1994 to 2001 also show that such activity takes place in some legislative offices.

On Nov. 1, work rules aimed at eliminating illegal campaigning took effect for lawmakers and their employees as a result of a State Journal investigation that revealed widespread campaign activity at the four partisan legislative caucuses.

Late last month, a former aide to Senate Majority Leader Chuck Chvala, one of the two most powerful lawmakers in Wisconsin, came forward to say he often witnessed and participated in campaign activity on state time during his year in Chvala's office. Former press secretary Dan Kroll said he believes he was fired in

Please see **ACTIVITY**, Page A7

Inside

Coming Monday

A Democratic legislative aide ran his own campaign for the Edgerton City Council and the campaigns of three other council candidates directly out of his Capitol office during 2001, also possibly violating state law.

Local arts community deals with the aftermath of terrorist attacks

Nonprofit groups must carefully try to assess the public's reaction.

By Amanda Henry and Natasha Kassulke
Wisconsin State Journal

How did you feel in the weeks after Sept. 11? Be precise: What were your exact needs and desires, your sense of right and wrong? Now, how will you feel in six months? What about next year?

Take that uncertainty and try to turn it into a business plan, and you'll have some sense of the plight of Madison's arts community in the wake of the terrorist attacks. The old adage has it that the show must go on, but the "biz" has never seen anything like this. The national news has been full of stories of Broadway shows folding, high-profile events canceled, movies and TV shows postponed.

While losses in the millions may not hobble Hollywood, with its vast margin for error, the position of local nonprofits is more precarious. What, if any, has been the impact of the terrorist attacks on the cultural life of our community?

Two months later, the answers are ambiguous, and far from uniform.

Live theater saw a dramatic drop for one to two weeks, then a return to normal. A few pop and rock shows were canceled or postponed, but there have been just as many sellouts. Fine art outlets with an out-of-town customer base have suffered, but ticket sales for classical concerts are setting records.

As with all of the repercussions of terrorism, what we are seeing in the arts community is a preliminary reaction. Poised between their belief in the country's need for creative release and an ailing economy, local arts groups are treading carefully. It doesn't take much to plunge a nonprofit into the red. Where there are problems on the art or business end, this fall and winter may push some organizations over the edge. Elsewhere, we may see arts groups putting on fewer shows, with smaller budgets and a reduced staff.

On the other hand, as we struggle to describe our reactions to Sept. 11, news anchors and politicians won't have all the answers, and the desire for national unity will need

Please see **ARTS**, Page A10

162nd year — No. 314 © 2001 Wisconsin State Journal

7 82550 00003 6
WSJ SUNDAY

WEATHER

Today
Sunny, brisk.
High 50.
Winds: SW
10-20 mph.

Tonight
Mainly clear.
Low 32.
Details/ back of Local

INSIDE

INSIDE

Madison's Holiday Parade on the Capitol Square pleases young and old alike.
In Local/C1

WILD ABOUT HARRY

RHYTHM: Review of 'Sorcerer's Stone'
DAYBREAK: Meet our contest winner
INSIDE TODAY

STATE FOOTBALL

Waunakee, Lancaster play for championships today
SPORTS/C1

★★★

THURSDAY

50 CENTS

Wisconsin State Journal

NOVEMBER 15, 2001 | MADISON, WISCONSIN | WWW.MADISON.COM

Taliban tries to flee from U.S. airstrikes

Islamic militia losing control of strongholds

By Kathy Gannon
Associated Press

KABUL, Afghanistan — The rout of the Taliban accelerated Wednesday with the Islamic militia losing control of Jalalabad in the east, once-loyal Pashtun tribesmen joining in the revolt in the south and many of their fighters fleeing into the mountains to evade U.S. airstrikes.

The Taliban is "in retreat virtually all over the country," Vice President Dick Cheney said in Washington.

A day after seizing the capital, Kabul, elements of the Northern Alliance consolidated their power by taking over the defense and interior ministries — temporary measures, the alliance insisted, until a U.N.-supervised political settlement representing all ethnic groups.

In the south, there were reports — although impossible to confirm — of fighting in the streets of Kandahar, the Taliban's birthplace.

Many of Afghanistan's 23 or more Pashtun groups appeared to have risen up against the Taliban, Pentagon spokesman Rear Adm. John Stufflebeem said. "Whether or not they're working in concert, we don't know," he told reporters in Washington.

Please see **TALIBAN,** Page A9

Associated Press

Keith Helton, left, Lexia Campbell, center, and Anne Marie Lake celebrate Wednesday the freedom of Heather Mercer and Dayna Curry. The three are at Antioch Community Church in Waco, Texas. Mercer, Curry and six other foreign aid workers had been held captive by the Taliban in Afghanistan on charges of preaching Christianity.

Inside

Aid workers airlifted from Afghanistan

Eight are safe in Pakistan.

By Dan Chapman and Bob Deans
Cox News Service

ISLAMABAD, Pakistan — Eight foreign aid workers, including two Americans, who had been jailed by the Taliban militia were free and in good health in Pakistan early today after being airlifted from Afghanistan by U.S. special forces helicopters.

The aid workers had been held for three months and placed on trial for preaching Christianity, outlawed under the harsh Islamic regime now on the run in Afghanistan.

"I'm thankful they're safe, and I'm pleased with our military for conducting this operation," said President Bush at his ranch in Crawford, Texas, where he is hosting Russian President Vladimir Putin as part of a three-day summit. "I'm also thankful for the folks in Afghanistan

Please see **WORKERS,** Page A9

Arts endowment gift thrills city, resident groups

Pleasant T. Rowland Foundation announces challenge grant for Overture performers.

By Dean Mosiman
Wisconsin State Journal

Less than 2½ years before the first show at Overture Center, a familiar philanthropist delivered a financial blockbuster.

The Pleasant T. Rowland Foundation on Wednesday announced a $23 million endowment challenge grant for nine resident groups of the new arts facility.

The foundation will match, dollar for dollar, endowment money raised by the organizations through 2006, Rowland said.

Although thrilled about Overture Center, resident groups have been concerned about the higher costs of playing there and reworking financial plans. Rowland's husband, W. Jerome Frautschi, donated $100 million to redevelop the 200 block of State Street into a world-class performing and visual arts center.

"This gift will ensure that for generations to come Madisonians will be able to enjoy truly great performances in a truly great facility," said Rowland, founder of the successful American Girl doll business.

The CTM Madison Family Theater Co. will now be able to offer more guest artists, choreographers and orchestras, said artistic director Nancy Thurow.

The gift appears to be the largest arts endowment gift in the city's history.

"It's phenomenal," Mayor Sue Bauman said. "Between Jerry and Pleasant, we have a couple that there's no comparison with anywhere in the country."

George Tzougros, executive director of the

Please see **ARTS,** Page A13

Matching grants

Amount of endowment money Pleasant T. Rowland Foundation will match through 2006

Wisconsin Symphony Orchestra
$5 million

Wisconsin Chamber Orchestra
$5 million

Madison Art Center
$2.5 million

Madison Children's Museum
$2 million

CTM
Madison Family Theatre Company
$2 million

Madison Opera
$2 million

Madison Repertory Theatre
$2 million

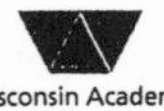

Wisconsin Academy of Sciences, Arts, Letters
$1.5 million

madisonballet
Madison Ballet
$1 million

WSJ graphic

Putins get firsthand look at Bushes' ranch

Associated Press

President Bush and first lady Laura Bush greet Russian President Vladimir Putin and his wife, Lyudmila Putin, seen holding a rose that she gave to Laura Bush, at the Bush ranch in Crawford, Texas, Wednesday. The two presidents are in the midst of a three-day summit, which ends today and included the Putins' visit to the Bush ranch. See story/A3

Elections Board drops investigation of GOP caucus aiding private group

Board says the evidence is too inconclusive for trial.

By Phil Brinkman
State government reporter

The state Elections Board voted Wednesday to drop its investigation into whether state workers illegally helped a private group coordinate attack ads against Assembly Democratic candidates last fall, saying the evidence it had gathered so far was too inconclusive to take before a judge.

"It's not worth our resources to go further," Elections Board executive director Kevin Kennedy conceded after the board's 7-1 vote. Chairwoman Jeralyn Wendelberger, the Democratic Party's designee on the board, was the only one to vote to continue the probe.

Although the board could revive the investigation if new evidence of wrongdoing surfaces, it chose to leave any further questioning to Dane County District Attorney Brian Blanchard, who is conducting his own probe of possible illegal campaign activity by legislators and staff.

The board's investigation was in response to a complaint filed after a Wisconsin State Journal story last May.

That story detailed claims by Lyndee Wall, former executive assistant to the Assembly Republican Caucus, headed by Assembly Speaker Scott Jensen, R-Waukesha.

Wall said she and two other caucus staffers helped independent political consultant Todd Rongstad produce, address and mail controversial campaign radio ads before the Nov. 7, 2000, election.

Some of the work took place in the caucus' state office on South Fairchild Street, Wall said.

Rongstad, who worked for the caucus from 1994 to 1997, left state service to form a number of private political groups known for their stridently negative campaign ads.

In October 2000, Wall said,

Please see **CAUCUS,** Page A13

Rongstad

Wall

Red Cross money to aid terror victims

All donations for disaster relief will go to people affected.

By Patricia Simms
Health reporter

A dramatic announcement by the American Red Cross in Washington on Wednesday means all $7.6 million raised by the Red Cross in Wisconsin for disaster relief since Sept. 11 will go directly to people affected by the terrorist attacks.

So will the entire $543 million raised nationally by the Red Cross' Liberty Fund.

Under fire for holding back more than $200 million of the donations for future terrorist attacks, Red Cross leaders reversed that plan.

Officials said programs that had been part of the Liberty Fund — such as the Strategic Blood Reserve, community outreach and Armed Forces services — will continue but be funded from other sources.

Among those eligible for money will be survivors of the attacks and their families, those with homes damaged in the attacks and those unemployed because their workplaces are in lower Manhattan, officials said.

For the Red Cross' Badger Chapter, the decision means about 90 percent of the $650,000 collected in its five-county region since Sept. 11 will go for direct relief, said Executive Director Phillip Hansen. Donors earmarked 10 percent for general operations.

"It's what the American people want," he said.

In Washington, new Red Cross chief executive officer Harold Decker acknowledged the agency's misstep. "We deeply regret that our activities over the past eight weeks have not been as sharply focused as America wants, nor as focused as the victims of this tragedy deserve," Decker said.

Hansen said all gifts to the Badger chapter with names and addresses are acknowledged with a letter that says where the money was directed.

The Red Cross also said direct support costs would be covered by the interest earned on the Liberty Fund, if possible, and the Red Cross Family Gift Program was extended from three months to a year.

162nd Year — No. 319 © 2001 Wisconsin State Journal

WEATHER

Today Clouds and sun. High 68. Winds: SW 10-20 mph.

Tonight Partly cloudy. Low 46. **Details/ back of Local**

TOMORROW

The dish on "Don Giovanni." In DayBreak

INSIDE

Badgers 97
Cleveland St. 55

MSO, TAYLOR PLAN BUSY HOLIDAY SEASON

DAYBREAK/D1

No health benefits from 'light' cigarettes
NATION/A3

Warm weather blamed for low deer kill
LOCAL/B1

★★★ 50 CENTS

W E D N E S D A Y

Wisconsin State Journal

NOVEMBER 28, 2001 MADISON, WISCONSIN WWW.MADISON.COM

5 charged in Internet fraud case

Four of the Madison residents are teens.

By Ed Treleven
Courts reporter

Five Madison residents — four of them teen-agers — were charged Tuesday with wide-ranging Internet fraud that involved stolen credit card numbers, hacked e-mail accounts and solicitations for pornographic Web sites.

A 62-page criminal complaint charges Heath S. Beecher, Alex J. Meunier and Nathan Peterson, all 18, and Meghan N. Peterson, 22, with felonies that include conspiracy to commit theft through false representation, unauthorized access to computer files to obtain property, identity theft to obtain items of value, credit card fraud and forgery.

A 16-year-old juvenile was also charged in the scheme, which allegedly netted $42,805 in credit card purchases.

"I think it's safe to say this is one of the more extensive jobs of investigation that the district attorney's office has handled," Dane County District Attorney Brian Blanchard said. "It involved at least three search warrants and a lot of work by computer specialists in the Madison Police Department."

The complaint alleges the five used credit card numbers stolen from customers at a restaurant and ordered goods from retail Web sites. Items were delivered to empty houses near the homes of the five, mostly on the Northeast Side, and picked up there, the complaint states.

Meunier and Nathan Peterson told police that they also harvested credit card numbers by sending official-looking messages to customers nationwide of Internet service providers, asking them to re-send credit card and social security numbers, the complaint states.

Beecher, Meunier, Nathan Peterson and the juvenile also allegedly made money by "spamming," sending mass e-mail messages advertising pornographic Web sites. Porn sites paid them based on how many customers signed up. They allegedly used hacked e-mail accounts to send out the porn ads.

MORE MOLD AT CHAVEZ

School district cancels classes after findings

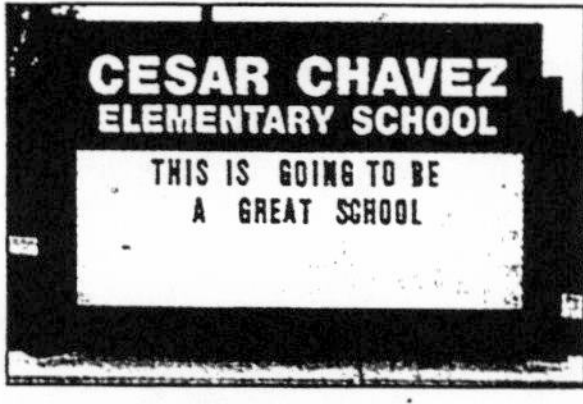

CESAR CHAVEZ
ELEMENTARY SCHOOL
THIS IS GOING TO BE
A GREAT SCHOOL

The sign at Chavez Elementary speaks to the staff's high hopes when the new school opened in August.

JOSEPH W. JACKSON III/WSJ photos

Kindergarten teacher Linda Mattson-Childs removes items from her Chavez Elementary School classroom Tuesday as workers from Onyx Environmental, Milwaukee, seal windows. Mold found in 14 rooms at the school could explain flu-like symptoms among staff and students.

14 rooms are now known to be contaminated with mold at the recently opened Chavez Elementary School.

By Doug Erickson
and Patricia Simms
Wisconsin State Journal

The Madison School District canceled classes for today at Chavez Elementary School after mold was found in two more classrooms and an office.

Fourteen rooms — 11 of them classrooms — are now known to be contaminated. District officials thought they'd found all of the mold Monday after inspecting vinyl baseboards in all rooms. Tuesday, mold was found on drywall above ceiling tiles in the additional rooms.

The district will complete inspections above ceilings today, said district spokesman Ken Syke.

"Because we're going to be in all of the rooms, it would be extremely difficult to do the inspections with students and teachers there," he said.

The district plans to update parents at a meeting tonight.

Mold found in the new Chavez Elementary may have been caused by the presence of leaking water during the building's construction.

If you go

◆ What: Community meeting to discuss mold problems at Madison's Chavez Elementary School.

◆ Where: Chavez Elementary, 3502 Maple Grove Drive.

◆ When: 7 tonight.

Tuesday, classes were held as scheduled, with displaced classrooms moved to other parts of the school.

As workers sealed windows and wiped down furniture around them, kindergarten teachers took a last-chance sweep through their classrooms. The kindergarten wing is among areas that will

Please see MOLD, Page A7

◆ Facts about indoor mold/A7

Suspected terror nest is bombed

Key figures said to be there

By Robert Burns
AP military writer

WASHINGTON — The Pentagon ordered airstrikes Tuesday on an Afghan compound southeast of Kandahar after receiving information it was being used by senior leaders of the Taliban and of al-Qaida and another alleged terrorist group, Defense Secretary Donald Rumsfeld said.

The information about the target came into U.S. Central Command in Tampa, Fla., while Rumsfeld was visiting.

U.S. F-16 jets and B-1B bombers attacked two targets, military officials said.

Rumsfeld said the compound was thought to hold leaders of the ruling Taliban militia; Osama bin Laden's al-Qaida organization; and Wafa, a Saudi humanitarian aid organization that was among several groups named by the United States as alleged money conduits for bin Laden.

At Central Command, Gen. Tommy Franks, the commander running the war, said U.S. forces in Afghanistan are searching more than 40 laboratories and other facilities suspected of conducting secret work on chemical, biological or nuclear weapons. So far, none has yielded clear evidence of such work, he said, adding that if any such weapons material were found, its removal would be "non-negotiable."

Franks said there are now two main areas of focus for finding bin Laden, the chief suspect in the Sept. 11 terrorist attacks. One is Kandahar, southern stronghold of the Taliban government, and the other is an area between Kabul, the capital, and Khyber Pass to the east, including the key city of Jalalabad and the Tora Bora mountain base, Franks said.

But Rumsfeld interjected, "They are not the only places we are paying attention to." He did not elaborate.

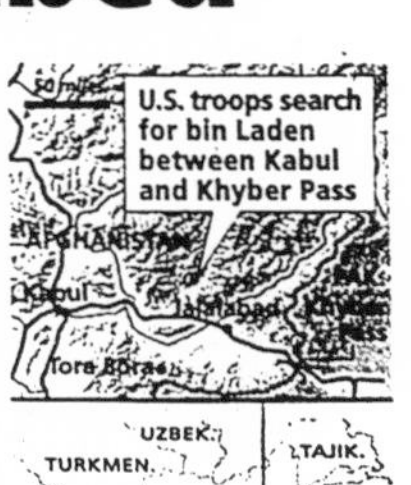

KRT, AP graphic

WAR ON TERROR

603 people held in terrorism probe

◆ Attorney General John Ashcroft said Tuesday that 104 people have been charged with federal crimes in the terrorism probe, and 603 people remain in custody, including some alleged members of Osama bin Laden's terrorist network. Page A3

Former king gains support among factions

◆ The former king of Afghanistan has emerged as the first choice among the Afghan factions meeting in Germany to lead an interim government, officials said on the opening day of talks. Page A5

Also inside

◆ Americans didn't panic after Sept. 11, pollsters say, and they firmly support the war/A3

◆ Northern Alliance says it has put down uprising by Taliban prisoners/A5

Boarded-up building causes South Side stir

JOHN MANIACI/WSJ

Madison neighborhood officer Tom Grosse, right, with town of Madison neighborhood officer Jeff Garton on Tuesday check a board that had been partly pried from the front door of an apartment building at 2414 Cypress Way on the city's South Side.

Police found crack pipes and other drug paraphernalia there.

By Dean Mosiman
City government reporter

It might not turn a head in Milwaukee or Chicago.

But residents, police and city officials are concerned about a boarded-up apartment building near the heart of a drug and prostitution trade on the South Side.

The beat-up, four-unit brick building with plywood in the windows and a broken-down chain-link fence at 2414 Cypress Way is a blight and subject to break-ins, they said.

The building, vacant for months, is a visual scar for children at nearby Lincoln Elementary School or the Early Childhood Learning Center, they said.

Before the owner boarded it up a few weeks ago, police found discarded crack pipes and other drug paraphernalia and used condoms in the building, neighborhood officer Tom Grosse said. Since then, people have made repeated attempts to get inside, others said.

"You look at this and say, 'Is this really Madison?' " said neighborhood leader and landlord John Lucille, who owns four apartment buildings on nearby Badger Road.

In fact, Lucille on Monday used his own tools to secure plywood that had been busted from a back window and side door.

Lucille said he has lost potential tenants because of the situation.

"I'm trying to bring quality tenants to this area," he said. "They see the boarded-up building and you lose them."

Please see BUILDING, Page A4

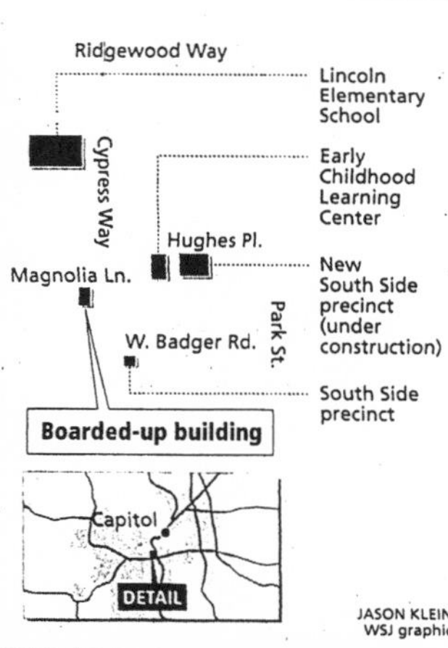

JASON KLEIN
WSJ graphic

162nd Year — No. 332 © 2001 Wisconsin State Journal

WEATHER

Today
Rain/snow mix.
High 38.
Winds: NE
6-12 mph.

Tonight
Cloudy; flurry.
Low 33.
Details/
back of Local

TOMORROW

A look behind the scenes of the Rep's "Guys on Ice." In Daybreak

INSIDE

Notre Dame coach Davie gets the boot
SPORTS/C1

AREA NONPROFITS BIG ON COOKBOOKS
DAYBREAK/D1

Students get a virtual tour of France
LOCAL/B1

★★★ MONDA[Y] 50 CENTS

Wisconsin State Journal

DECEMBER 3, 2001 MADISON, WISCONSIN WWW.MADISON.COM

TERROR IN THE MIDDLE EAST

Bombings called bloodiest in the history of Israel

Latest blast on bus kills 15 in Haifa

By Michael Matza
Knight Ridder Newspapers

HAIFA, Israel — Twelve hours after timed terrorist attacks killed 10 Israelis in the heart of Jerusalem, another suicide bomber attacked this northern port city Sunday, killing 15 people in a massive explosion aboard a crosstown bus carrying students, soldiers and retirees.

The front of the red-and-white bus was grotesquely twisted and burned. Its roof was buckled, its seats were mangled, its sides were blown out. Witnesses said the bus traveled downhill, out of control, for 100 yards after the explosion, crushing two pedestrians to death before slamming to rest against a utility pole.

At least one body hung from the waist out of the bus, arms extended over the sill of a window. Ambulance driver Shimon Suissa, 30, and senior medic Avi Amar, 38, said they had brought out four bodies, all apparently students.

The attack capped what Israeli television called the bloodiest 24 hours of terrorism in the country's history. In other violence Sunday, several Israelis and Palestinians were killed or wounded, prompting renewed calls for the government to get tough with Palestinian leader Yasser Arafat's Palestinian Authority.

U.S. special envoy Anthony Zinni condemned the attack on the bus as "evil," and Israeli Prime Minister Ariel Sharon cut short a visit to Washington to meet with President Bush. Bush denounced the bombings as "horrific acts of murder" and pressed Arafat to immediately crack down on militants.

The Palestinian militant group Hamas, which had vowed to avenge Israel's killing of one of its leaders last month, claimed responsibility for the attack.

Zinni, who came to the Middle East last week on an open-ended mission to broker a Palestinian-

Please see **ISRAEL**, Page A8

Associated Press

Mourners cry at the funeral of Nir Haftsadi at Mt. Herzl military cemetery in Jerusalem Sunday. Haftsadi, 19, was an Israeli soldier killed Saturday night when two Palestinian suicide bombers blew themselves up at a crowded downtown Jerusalem pedestrian mall, killing ten and wounding more than 150.

Associated Press

Mordechai Haftsadi waves goodbye to his son Nir, after his casket is lowered into the ground during his funeral at Mt. Herzl military cemetery in Jerusalem on Sunday. Haftsadi, 19, an Israeli soldier, was killed Saturday night in the suicide attack.

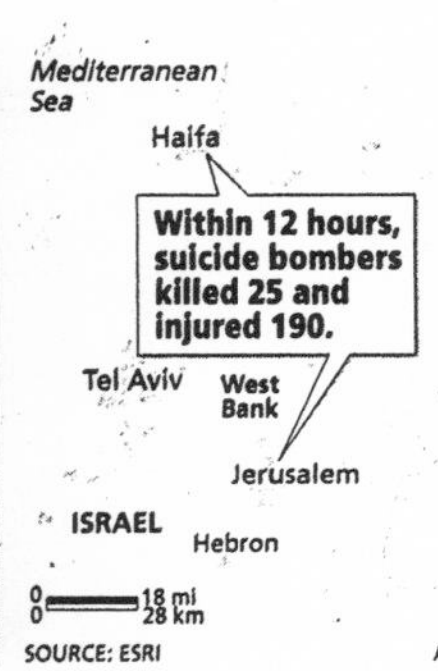

Inside

◆ Palestinian militants vow massive escalation of violence/A5

AMA mulls paying donors for organs

The notion of financial incentives for donations has been considered taboo.

By Paul Elias
AP biotechnology writer

SAN FRANCISCO — As the nation's need for organ transplants continues to outstrip supply, the American Medical Association on Sunday grappled with a possible solution once thought taboo: paying dying would-be donors and their families for vital organs.

Such financial incentives are illegal, banned by Congress in 1984, and as a result people needing organ transplants must rely strictly on volunteers, a system that is failing, said many doctors attending the AMA's 2001 Interim Meeting of the House of Delegates, the association's 549-member policy-setting body.

An AMA committee, the Council on Ethical and Judicial Affairs, is recommending that the association support studies to determine if financial incentives will motivate more organ donations.

Some 15,000 people die each year awaiting organ transplants, as only one-third of potentially valuable organs are donated, according to the United Network for Organ Sharing, a nonprofit agency.

"We have a nationwide crisis and altruism doesn't seem to be hacking it right now."

FRANK RIDDICK JR.
AMA Council on Ethical and Judicial Affairs

Most donation decisions must be made by families of people who die suddenly and unexpectedly, and most families in those situations decline to offer up their dead relatives for donations.

"We have a nationwide crisis and altruism doesn't seem to be hacking it right now," said Dr. Frank Riddick Jr., chairman of the Council on Ethical and Judicial Affairs.

Riddick's council was to make its recommendation to the full AMA today. The AMA will decide, perhaps as early as Tuesday, if it will adopt the council's recommendation.

The proposal has drawn passionate opposition from many AMA attendees, who view financial incentives as unethical.

If the AMA does agree to test financial incentives, Congress would have to change current law to permit a study.

A congressional bill introduced in May would allow a donor family a $10,000 tax credit in exchange for donated organs.

Ringing doorbells to collect Keys recall signatures

Some residents praise the volunteer, a UW Medical School faculty member, others bawl him out.

By Doug Erickson
Education reporter

Steve Clark approached the first home with some trepidation. He had never done this before — go door to door for a cause.

Nobody answered at the first two homes. At the third door, Mickey Rath's face lit up when Clark told her he was circulating a petition to force a recall election of Madison School Board member Bill Keys.

"I was wondering when someone was going to come by," said Rath, in her mid-60s, who signed the petition with her husband.

"I'm just so against (Keys) for being so arrogant that he wouldn't stand up for the pledge at that School Board meeting."

But at the next home, Clark got a quick rebuke.

"Not a chance," said Sandy DeBeers, who declined to sign the petition. "I believe in Bill Keys and so does my wife. It's absurd that we're wasting money on this."

And so it went for more than an hour Saturday as Clark, 47, an associate professor at UW Medical School, walked the streets of the Tamarack Trails neighborhood on Madison's far West Side.

Organizers of the recall say hundreds of volunteers such as Clark have picked up petitions and are circulating them around town. The group began the effort Nov. 12 and

Please see **RECALL**, Page A7

ANDY MANIS/photo

Steve Clark finds an eager petition signer in Kathleen Gragg, who said she was "totally outraged" by Madison School Board member Bill Keys' position on the Pledge of Allegiance. Clark is a volunteer with a group hoping to force a recall election of Keys. He spent Saturday morning collecting signatures against Keys in Gragg's neighborhood on the city's far West Side.

Parents looking for ways to block porn on the Web

Some have given up on government regulation and are monitoring more.

By Anick Jesdanun
AP Internet writer

NEW YORK — With 7-year-old Adam at her side, Sherra Schwartau typed "Boston Terriers" into an online search engine. Instead of information Adam could use for a school report on dogs, they got a porn site.

"As Mom is scrambling trying to close the screen, he goes, 'What was that?' " Schwartau said.

Score another for the pornographers, who, since Schwartau's incident three years ago, have gotten even smarter about tricking Internet users into visiting their sites.

Rather than looking to

Please see **PORN**, Page A4

"One company, one group, one nonprofit can't do it all."

DONNA RICE HUGHES
commission member

162nd Year — No. xx © 2001 Wisconsin State Journal

WEATHER

Today
Sun and clouds.
High 52.
Winds: SW
10-20 mph.

Tonight
Partly cloudy.
Low 47.
Details/ back of Local

TOMORROW

The Lussier Teen Center and Loft has a bold look thanks to a group of young artists.
In Daybreak

INSIDE

AMERICA LOSING OBESITY BATTLE
NATION/A5

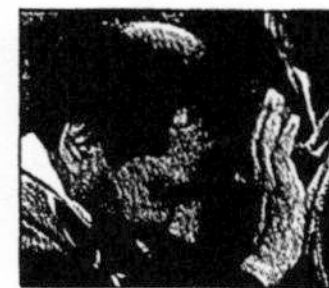

SUICIDE ATTACKERS STORM INDIA PARLIAMENT
WORLD/A11

BADGERS	74
DRAKE	61

★★★ 50 CENTS

F R I D A Y

Wisconsin State Journal

DECEMBER 14, 2001 MADISON, WISCONSIN WWW.MADISON.COM

THE TRANSCRIPT OF BIN LADEN TAPE/A6

'They were overjoyed when the first plane hit the building, so I said to them: Be patient.'

"I suppose everyone will be able to draw your own conclusion about it. For myself, I never had any doubt as to who was responsible for the September 11th attacks."

DONALD RUMSFELD
Defense secretary

"This totally vindicates the action that we, the U.S. and the international coalition have taken in Afghanistan."

JACK STRAW
British foreign secretary

"Until and unless he's brought to justice or eliminated, he's probably going to kill a lot more innocent human beings."

RUDOLPH GIULIANI
New York mayor

"This is totally out of context and does not represent at all the understanding of Islam and the teachings of the Koran."

SAYYID M. SYEED
secretary general of Islamic Society of North America

KEY EXCERPTS FROM OSAMA BIN LADEN . . .

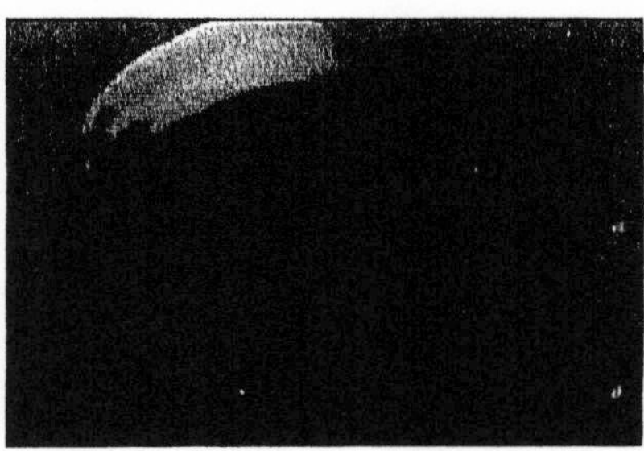

"We calculated in advance the number of casualties from the enemy, who would be killed based on the position of the tower. We calculated that the floors that would be hit would be three or four floors. I was the most optimistic of them all. (. . . Inaudible) Due to my experience in this field, I was thinking that the fire from the gas in the plane would melt the iron structure of the building and collapse the area where the plane hit and all the floors above it only. This is all that we had hoped for."

◆

"We were at (. . . inaudible) when the event took place. We had notification since the previous Thursday that the event would take place that day. We had finished our work that day and had the radio on. It was 5:30 p.m. our time. I was sitting with Dr. Ahmad Abu-al-(Khair). Immediately, we heard the news that a plane had hit the World Trade Center. We turned the radio station to the news from Washington. The news continued and (there was) no mention of the attack until the end. At the end of the newscast, they reported that a plane just hit the World Trade Center. . . . After a little while, they announced that another plane had hit the World Trade Center. The brothers who heard the news were overjoyed by it."

◆

"The brothers, who conducted the operation, all they knew was that they have a martyrdom operation and we asked each of them to go to America, but they didn't know anything about the operation, not even one letter. But they were trained and we did not reveal the operation to them until they are there and just before they boarded the planes."

Computer experts: Bin Laden tape authentic/A6

Smiling bin Laden revels in attacks

He tells how surprised he was by the total collapse of the towers.

By Richard Whittle
The Dallas Morning News

WASHINGTON — Smiling serenely, Osama bin Laden gloats and boasts about the Sept. 11 destruction of the World Trade Center in a videotape released by the Bush administration Thursday to show that the Saudi fugitive masterminded the atrocity.

The leader of the al-Qaida terrorist network, speaking in Arabic to an admirer described as an "unidentified sheik," says that he knew the date of the attacks on New York and Washington five days before they occurred.

"We calculated in advance the number of casualties from the enemy who would be killed based on the position of the tower," bin Laden cheerfully recalls at dinner with the sheik and two al-Qaida leaders.

As segments of the tape were replayed on television

Please see **BIN LADEN,** Page A6

WAR ON TERROR

◆ As U.S. planes strafed and bombed al-Qaida positions, Afghan tribesmen and U.S. special forces may have cornered Osama bin Laden and his fighters Thursday in a snowy mountain canyon near the Pakistan border. A11

◆ In the Mideast, many Arabs said the scratchy video released Thursday doesn't provide evidence of bin Laden's guilt and may even have been fabricated. A11

Appearance of town of Pleasant Springs as a tax haven can be deceiving

The average home assessment in the town has soared.

By Marv Balousek
and Lesley Rogers Barrett
Wisconsin State Journal

Inside

◆ Dane County property taxes by community/A15
◆ Calculate your tax/A15

As property tax bills hit the mail this month, the town of Pleasant Springs appears at first glance to be Dane County's tax haven.

The town, which hugs the shoreline of Lake Kegonsa, had a tax rate of $13.27 per $1,000 assessed property value for all taxing bodies, the lowest among the county's 61 municipalities.

The estimated tax bill on a county-average $146,106 home also was the lowest at $2,054.

But those figures don't reflect the town's property reevaluation this year that boosted assessments by 47 percent.

The average home assessment in the town rose from $122,511 last year to $179,717 this year, according to figures from the county treasurer.

"We've had a fair amount of new construction," said town chairman Ken Schuck.

Higher assessments mean taxing bodies can set lower tax rates and collect more money.

A tax bill includes levies for public schools, municipal and county government, vocational schools and state forestry.

Other communities with rapidly rising average assessments this year are the town of Dane, $89,464 last year to $114,616 this year, Shorewood Hills, $292,860 to $365,736 and the town of Mazomanie, $101,571 to $127,094.

County Treasurer Dave Gawenda said 55 municipalities have picked up their printed tax bills from his office.

To compare tax bills in Dane County communities, the State Journal calculated tax bills in each community for a $146,106 home, the countywide average value.

162nd Year — No. 348 © 2001 Wisconsin State Journal

WEATHER

Today
Cloudy.
High 36.
Winds: ENE 6-12 mph.

Tonight
Mostly cloudy.
Low 26.
Details/ back of Local

TOMORROW

Dave Barry's gift guide. In Daybreak.

INSIDE

Experts track chronic wasting disease
LOCAL/B1

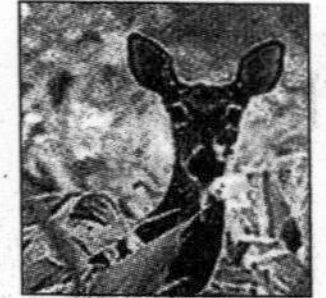

PORTRAITS GO BACK IN TIME
DAYBREAK/D1

Big storm losses at American Family
BUSINESS/C10

★★★ 50 CENTS

WEDNESDAY

Wisconsin State Journal

MARCH 6, 2002 MADISON, WISCONSIN WWW.MADISON.COM

Governor firm on aid cuts

He continues to push for eliminating shared revenue

McCallum highlights

Highlights of Gov. Scott McCallum's State of the State address:

◆ Says "our will is strong," despite "a faltering national economy" and "evil" from terrorism.

◆ Sticks with plan to cut by $700 million and then eliminate shared revenue, the state's main form of aid to local governments.

◆ Urges local governments to "put our differences behind" us and "work together" to consolidate and shrink the size of government in Wisconsin.

◆ Pledges to speed up the formation of a task force to look for ways to eliminate state mandates on local governments.

◆ Repeats pledge to "oppose any budget solution that includes higher taxes."

◆ Acknowledges his plan to fix a $1.1 billion budget deficit has been controversial but also has changed the debate "from how we spend money to how we can save money."

◆ Says he'll unveil a statewide business plan this spring.

◆ Says a goal is to raise Wisconsin's per capita income above the national average by the end of 2005.

By Scott Milfred
State government reporter

Gov. Scott McCallum softened his tone but continued to fight for deep cuts in aid to local governments Tuesday during an annual State of the State address.

McCallum, who six weeks ago called local leaders "big spenders," changed his tack in front of a joint session of the Legislature and a statewide public television audience.

McCallum urged local government officials to "embrace a new spirit of partnership" with the state. The governor complimented Madison Mayor Sue Bauman and others for pushing to consolidate local services.

"Their efforts to save money . . . are gaining new momentum," McCallum said. "In town halls and city councils across the state, and right here in the Capitol, already the debate has changed from how we spend money to how we can save money."

Yet the Republican governor made it clear he's sticking with his plan to cut by $700 million and eliminate in 2004 shared revenue, the state's main form of aid to cities, counties, villages and towns.

"Those who argue that the shared revenue

Please see **SPEECH,** Page A8

SPEECH REACTION

Governor credited with gentler delivery

But Democrats say he offers no new solutions to fix the state's deficit.

By Phil Brinkman
State government reporter

Republicans and Democrats alike credited Gov. Scott McCallum with toning down his budget rhetoric in his first State of the State speech Tuesday.

But while Republicans praised the governor for reiterating his core themes of no new taxes and protecting programs serving children and the needy, Democrats expressed disappointment that the speech offered no new solutions for solving the state's $1.1 billion budget deficit.

Instead, the governor stuck to his plan to balance the budget by cutting shared revenue, the state's main aid program to local government.

"The more conciliatory tone was welcome," Assembly Minority Leader Spencer Black, D-Madison, said, noting the contrast

Please see **REACTION,** Page A8

ABOVE: Gov. Scott McCallum gives his State of the State address to the Legislature and Wisconsin residents on Tuesday in the state Capitol. Behind him are Assembly Speaker Scott Jensen, R-Waukesha, left, and Senate President Fred Risser, D-Madison.

LEFT: Assembly Minority Leader Spencer Black, D-Madison, left, and Rep. Michael Lehman, R-Hartford, listen as the governor outlines his and the state's successes during the past year and his plans for the future.

CRAIG SCHREINER/WSJ photos

Ryan Penney

Ryan is coach of year; Penney's on first team

University of Wisconsin men's basketball coach Bo Ryan, who in his first season led the Badgers to their first regular-season Big Ten title since 1947, was named conference Coach of the Year Tuesday.

The vote of the media covering the conference makes Ryan the first UW-Madison coach to receive the award.

In addition, UW-Madison junior Kirk Penney was made a member of the all-Big Ten first team by the coaches and the media. Senior Charlie Wills received honorable mention on the coaches' team.

Story in Sports/C1

Emotions run high over loitering law

Council's override of mayor's veto very unlikely.

By Dean Mosiman
City government reporter

After hearing stories of drug dealers terrorizing neighborhoods and police discriminating against minorities, the Madison City Council early today was still contentiously debating the fate of the city's controversial loitering law.

The law, passed in 1997 but with time limits, makes it illegal to loiter for the purpose of selling drugs.

The council two weeks ago voted 11-7 to make the law permanent. But Mayor Sue Bauman vetoed the law over concern the law isn't working and discriminates against blacks. She wants the council to extend the law a year or two while police develop other strategies.

Unless the council musters 14 votes to override the mayor's veto, considered very unlikely, the law expires today.

Last year, most citations issued were to blacks. Most who were ticketed lived outside the neighborhood and had a history of drugs, violence or both.

The four-plus hour debate was passionate and emotional.

At one point, landlord John Lucille said Bauman "doesn't have a clue what's going on." The mayor bristled and tried to berate Lucille before council members said she was out of order. Bauman then turned control of the meeting to council president Gary Poulson so she could speak later.

Supporters called the law an important tool to fight open-air drug dealing.

"It's about drug dealers taking over our neighborhood and having us live in fear," resident Cindy Donais said.

Among supporters were residents from the Burr Oaks neighborhood, where the law was most used last year, the police and the Apartment Association of South Central Wisconsin.

Opponents — including the Equal Opportunities Commission, the NAACP and the American Civil Liberties Union — said the law is a "sugar pill" and has a disparate impact on blacks.

Study: Big-city air pollution raises lung cancer death risk

By Lindsey Tanner
AP medical writer

CHICAGO — Long-term exposure to the air pollution in some of America's biggest metropolitan areas significantly raises the risk of dying from lung cancer and is about as dangerous as living with a smoker, a study of a half-million people found.

The study echoes previous research and provides the strongest evidence yet of the health dangers of the pollution levels found in many big cities and even some smaller ones, according to the researchers from Brigham Young University and New York University.

The risk is from what scientists call combustion-related fine particulate matter — soot emitted by cars and trucks, coal-fired power plants and factories.

The study appears in today's Journal of the American Medical Association.

It involved 500,000 adults who enrolled in 1982 in an American Cancer Society survey on cancer prevention. The researchers examined participants' health records through 1998 and analyzed data on annual air pollution averages in the cities where participants lived.

◆ **On the Internet:**

JAMA: *jama.ama-assn.org*

EPA: *www.epa.gov*

Deadly air pollution

A study found that fine-particulate air pollution — soot emitted from cars and trucks and coal-fired power plants and factories — was linked to an increased risk of lung cancer death.

Increase in deaths for every 10 micrograms of air pollution

Lung cancer	+8%
Heart and lung-related causes	+6%

Annual fine-particulate pollutant averages for some cities, in micrograms

Los Angeles	23.9
Chicago	20.2
Washington	18.9
New York	18.4

SOURCE: Journal of the American Medical Association; Environmental Protection Agency AP

U.S.-led coalition forces close in on al-Qaida

An American commander says they're inching up snow-covered mountains, trying to reach hideouts.

By Kathy Gannon
Associated Press

GARDEZ, Afghanistan — Hundreds of Taliban and al-Qaida fighters were killed in fierce fighting Tuesday as U.S.-led coalition forces pressed their offensive in the rugged mountains of eastern Afghanistan, the American commander of the operation said.

U.S. forces in the region said as many as 800 opposition fighters had been seen moving toward the battle since the American-led offensive, dubbed Operation Anaconda, was launched on Saturday.

"We caught several hundred of them with RPGs (rocket-propelled grenades) and mortars heading toward the fight. We body slammed them today and killed hundreds of those guys," said Maj. Gen. Frank L. Hagenbeck, the commander of the operation near Gardez, 75 miles south of Kabul, the

Please see **FORCES,** Page A7

◆ Troops deal with stiff resistance, harsh conditions/A5

162nd Year — No. 65 © 2002 Wisconsin State Journal

WEATHER

Today
Milder.
High 38.
Winds: SW
8-16 mph.

Tonight
Mostly cloudy.
Low 26.
Details/ back of Local

INSIDE

TOMORROW

Rosie O'Donnell's big news causes nary a ripple.
In Daybreak

Soderberg the coach at St. Louis ▸
SPORTS/C1

Singh leads rain-delayed Masters
SPORTS/C1

A NEW LEADER IN VENEZUELA
Chavez out; interim president named
WORLD/A5

UW honors grad wounded as Mideast reporter
LOCAL/B1

Anthony Shadid

★★★

SATURDAY

50 CENTS

Wisconsin State Journal

APRIL 13, 2002 MADISON, WISCONSIN WWW.MADISON.COM

Powell nixes meeting with Arafat after suicide bomb

Associated Press photos

Israeli police and paramedics work at the scene of a suicide bombing that killed six people in Jerusalem on Friday.

Secretary of State Colin Powell, left, failed to secure a timetable for Israeli troop withdrawal from Prime Minister Ariel Sharon during their meeting Friday in Jerusalem.

MIDEAST AT A GLANCE

◆ **Bombing delays Powell visit:** A suicide bombing in the heart of Jerusalem killed six people Friday, compelling Secretary of State Colin Powell to postpone today's meeting with Yasser Arafat.

◆ **Little progress in talks:** Powell met with Israeli Prime Minister Ariel Sharon but failed to persuade Sharon to agree on a timetable for withdrawing Israeli troops.

◆ **A look ahead:** Powell's spokesman, Richard A. Boucher, said that a meeting on Sunday with Arafat had not been ruled out, but demanded that Arafat condemn the bombing.

◆ **Quote:** Jerusalem Mayor Ehud Olmert: "I never thought there was any hope (for Powell to succeed)."

Inside

◆ Standoff at the Church of the Nativity continues/**A5**

◆ Palestinian refugees forced to flee Jenin/**A7**

Palestinian leader ignores U.S. demands

By Charles A. Radin
The Boston Globe

JERUSALEM — U.S. Secretary of State Colin Powell Friday night called off his meeting today with Palestinian Authority President Yasser Arafat after a suicide bomber struck in central Jerusalem and Arafat ignored American demands that he condemn the attack.

President Bush joined Powell in asking Arafat to speak out against the latest terror attack, as he has in the past. But Arafat did not condemn Friday's attack, which killed six people. The Al Aqsa Martyrs' Brigade, which is aligned with Arafat, claimed responsibility.

A helicopter carrying Powell to inspect Israel's northern border, the scene of dozens of recent rocket attacks by the Iranian-backed Islamic extremist group Hezbollah, hovered for a time over the devastation,

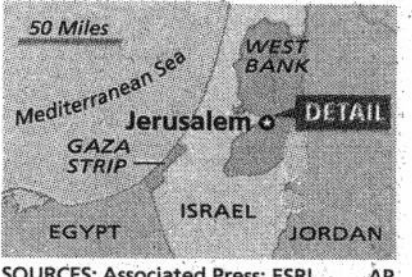

SOURCES: Associated Press; ESRI AP

and late Friday night State Department officials said the meeting with Arafat was off, at least for now.

Powell was expected to meet today with religious leaders and relief agency officials at the U.S. Consulate.

Even before the bombing, Powell backed away from the

Please see **MIDEAST**, Page A9

UW to hike fees to park on campus

By Dean Mosiman
City government reporter

To ease demand on precious parking spots, UW-Madison is raising parking permit rates, offering commuter alternatives and making other changes for fall.

"It's going to reach quite a few people," Transportation Services Director Lance Lunsway said.

The university has 11,000 stalls, fewest per capita in the Big 10, officials said. About 250 employees still need parking assignments.

The crunch will worsen as stalls are lost for construction projects, officials said.

"There is little we can do to create more parking on this campus," Chancellor John Wiley said. "But we can provide incentives for commuters to try other forms of transportation."

To help pay for alternatives and new parking garages, the university is raising the cost of permits closer to what city and state employees pay.

University permits, which now cost between $200 and $980 a year, will jump to $400, $650 and $990, depending on location. It costs $1,128 a year to park in the city's State Street-Capitol garage.

The university intends to make cheaper spaces available to those making less money, and to base fees on salary in the fall of 2003.

To free space, those with emeritus status must pay for annual permits, and after-hours permits will be eliminated.

And to get people out of cars, the university will offer free city bus passes to faculty and staff. Students already pay $1.38 million a year in fees for passes.

UW-Madison parking changes

◆ Annual permits will cost $400, $650 or $990, depending on location.

◆ University faculty and staff will be offered free Madison Metro bus passes useable anytime.

◆ Another lot will be added to the Park and Rides program, in which drivers can park and catch a shuttle to various locations for $162 a year.

◆ Capacity on the free campus bus service will be increased.

◆ Those with emeritus status must apply and pay for the same pool of permits available to other faculty and staff, but free daily permits will be available.

◆ Those with permits have a primary lot and one, rather than four, alternate lots.

◆ After-hour permits will be eliminated to increase evening access to general lots.

◆ Application forms will be handled online.

Vogt quits as Historical Society head

He cites stress of budget problems as he takes job in Delaware.

By George Hesselberg
Wisconsin State Journal

The state's budget turmoil Friday claimed one more victim at the Wisconsin Historical Society. The director since 1996, George Vogt, quit to take a job at a private institution in Delaware. He cited the stress of recent budget problems as the reason for leaving.

Vogt

"The legislative process and the budget process here have taken a physical toll, and it is just really, really hard to operate when your stomach is in orbit non-stop," said Vogt.

He had ominous words for his successor: "I don't see an end to this for another biennium or maybe two. I think the

Please see **VOGT**, Page A7

LEAVING DOWNTOWN

Alliant moves to new headquarters

The energy company will operate in the American Center business park.

By Judy Newman
Business reporter

Workers still have stair rails to finish and reception desks to install, but Alliant Energy Corp.'s move to its new $47 million headquarters on the far Northeast Side is in full swing.

Four semitrailers full of company records and office supplies will be unloaded today at the sprawling building at 4902 N. Biltmore Lane in the fast-growing American Center business park.

The four-story building, with a façade of brick and concrete panels, features a circular driveway leading up to a round hub — Alliant officials call it the rotunda — and a wing of offices sprouting from two sides. The design bears some resemblance to the state Capitol and it's no accident.

Architect Rob Eszerins of Opus North Corp., Milwaukee, based the project on a classic Greek design.

"And then he came to

Please see **ALLIANT**, Page A9

CRAIG SCHREINER/WSJ

Mayflower Moving employee Charles Timmons and a co-worker roll a plastic-wrapped cart of office materials to a truck. Alliant Energy Corp. workers will be moved out of the company's long-time Downtown offices at 222 W. Washington Ave.

Skunk Hill given new designation

Skunk Hill, a bluff in the center of Wisconsin, was once a sacred site for American Indians who journeyed there to practice traditional religions that had been repressed on their reservations.

On Friday, dozens of Americans Indians, many of them tribal elders, journeyed to Madison to watch a state board name the hill as a state historic site and nominate the Wood County site to the National Register of Historic Places.

◆ Story/B1

163rd Year — No. 103 © 2002 Wisconsin State Journal

WEATHER

Today Clouds, sun. High 62°. Winds: N 5-10 mph.

Tonight Partly cloudy. Low 44°. **Details/ back of Local**

INSIDE

INSIDE

West leaves Harvard for Princeton
Cornel West, the prominent professor of Afro-American studies at Harvard, is leaving for Princeton, nearly four months after publicly sparring with Harvard's new president. **PAGE A3**

NBA DRAFT
YAO IS TOP PICK
◆ BUCKS SELECT TENNESSEE FORWARD MARCUS HAISLIP: IN SPORTS

Study says pill does not raise risk of breast cancer

NATION/A10

Rhythm & Booms: A musical blast

RHYTHM

GET IN THE MONEY

MILLIONAIRE MONEY INSIDE

★★★ 50 CENTS

THURSDAY

Wisconsin State Journal

JUNE 27, 2002 MADISON, WISCONSIN WWW.MADISON.COM

File photo

State Sen. Brian Burke, D-Milwaukee, withdrew from the state attorney general's race May 10 after his legal bills became public.

Burke charged with 18 felonies

Senator accused of using state resources for campaign, shaking down lobbyists and destroying evidence

SARAH B. TEWS/WSJ

Dane County District Attorney Brian Blanchard, right, announces criminal charges Wednesday against state Sen. Brian Burke, D-Milwaukee. Burke is accused of misconduct in office, lying about expenses, altering public records and withholding subpoenaed documents. With Blanchard in the City-County Building in Madison was David Collins, director of the white collar crimes bureau of the state Department of Justice.

By Phil Brinkman and Dee J. Hall
Wisconsin State Journal

State Sen. Brian Burke, once considered the leading candidate for attorney general, was charged Wednesday with 18 felonies, including using state resources to run his campaign, trading votes for cash and destroying evidence.

The criminal complaint, filed in Dane County Circuit Court, accuses Burke, co-chairman of the Legislature's powerful budget committee, of "systematically and repeatedly breaking the law" in his quest to become the state's top law enforcement officer, said Dane County District Attorney Brian Blanchard.

Over the last year, Burke, D-Milwaukee, transformed his Capitol office into a virtual campaign bazaar, Blanchard said, shaking down lobbyists for campaign donations and using staffers to call contributors. Lobbyists who didn't give were called "deadbeats."

When some staffers took partial leaves to work on his campaign, Burke arranged substantial raises for them at taxpayer expense rather than have the campaign make up their salaries, according to the complaint.

As investigators began closing in on his office, Burke ordered

Please see **BURKE,** Page A15

Inside

◆ Any legislators convicted of a felony would be removed from office/**A14**

◆ Charges against Burke may be only the beginning/**A14**

◆ Criminal complaint says Burke manipulated his payroll to hide his staff's campaign activity/**A15**

The charges

Brian Burke

◆ Misconduct in public office (14 counts) including hiring staffers to work on Burke's campaign for attorney general on state time, asking lobbyists for donations in exchange for support on bills and falsifying expense vouchers.

◆ Fraudulently concealing public records (two counts) by altering calendar entries in his state computer.

◆ Withholding and altering subpoenaed documents (one count each).

Each is a felony carrying a possible penalty of five years in prison, except for fraudulently concealing public records, which carries a possible penalty of 10 years.

Others

Tanya Bjork (aide to Burke)

◆ Soliciting campaign contributions on state property and fraudulently manipulating data. Both are misdemeanors punishable by up to, respectively, six months and nine months in jail.

Raghu Devaguptapu (aide to Burke)

◆ Soliciting campaign contributions on state property (five counts), punishable by fines of up to $500 for each offense.

Brian Burke

File photo

File photo

Students in Madison, including those shown here from Black Hawk Middle School, recite the Pledge of Allegiance in the classroom. Wednesday's appeals court ruling declaring pledge recitations unconstitutional does not immediately affect Wisconsin.

'Under God' in pledge ruled unconstitutional

The 9th U.S. Circuit Court of Appeals says "under God" phrase endorses religion.

By Doug Erickson
Education reporter

In a ruling reminiscent of a wrenching debate in Madison last fall, a federal appeals court declared that the Pledge of Allegiance is unconstitutional because the phrase "one nation under God" violates the separation of church and state.

Wednesday's ruling, if allowed to stand, means schoolchildren can no longer be led in group recitations of the pledge, at least not in the nine Western states covered by the court.

Wisconsin is not one of those nine states and is not directly affected by the decision. But the issues it raises have been fiercely argued since last fall, when the state Legislature began requiring schools to offer either the pledge or the national anthem daily in grades one through 12.

Pledge of Allegiance

I pledge allegiance to the flag of the United States of America, and to the Republic, for which it stands, one nation **under God,** indivisible, with liberty and justice for all.

Please see **PLEDGE,** Page A12

◆ Senate condemns ruling/**A3**

Broken neck killed child left in closed car

Police say the parents were distracted and left the boy, 1, in the car in 90-degree weather.

By Kathleen Ostrander
Rock County correspondent

BELOIT — A 1-year-old boy died of a broken neck after his parents left him in a closed car and became distracted while fixing a gate that had allowed the family dog to get loose, police said Wednesday.

Daytona Brewster, who had his first birthday a week ago, died Tuesday afternoon in front of his family's Shore Drive home.

Investigators aren't sure if heat in the closed-up car caused the child to have a seizure that led to the fatal injury or if his neck became tangled in a strap while he tried to escape his carrier seat.

"Given the situation, the

Please see **CHILD,** Page A17

Professor says he's found a safe, natural mosquito repellent

A North Carolina bug expert claims to have discovered a natural compound that's more safe and effective than DEET in repelling mosquitoes. In tests, people stuck their arms into boxes full of human-biting mosquitoes. No mosquitoes bit — 12 hours after the compound was applied.

◆ **Story/A5**

Bush denounces WorldCom for inflating profits

Wall Street is shaken by the news of $3 billion in fraud committed by the telecommunications giant.

By Tom Raum
Associated Press

WASHINGTON — President Bush called WorldCom's revelation of billions in disguised expenses "outrageous," announced a government investigation and said he could understand why jittery investors have come to doubt "the balance sheet of corporate America."

Meanwhile, the chairman of the Securities and Exchange Commission said Wednesday his agency filed fraud charges against WorldCom. Harvey Pitt said the action in federal court in New York was partly aimed at preventing the destruction of documents by WorldCom and payouts to executives while the SEC investigates.

WorldCom, which owns the carrier MCI and is second only to AT&T in the long-distance market, disclosed that more than $3 billion of expenses in 2001 and $797 million in the first quarter of 2002 were wrongly listed on company books as capital expenses, thus artificially raising profits.

Bush on Wednesday called for more corporate accountability and said the recent string of accounting scandals has contributed to declines in stock prices.

"We will fully investigate and hold people accountable for misleading not only shareholders but employees as well," Bush said on the opening day of an eight-nation economic summit in the Canadian Rockies.

Senate Majority Leader Tom Daschle, D-S.D., said there must be "aggressive enforcement of the law. And if laws were broken, somebody needs to go to jail."

Also Wednesday, the House voted overwhelmingly to authorize a 77 percent boost in the SEC's budget, raising it to $776 million for the fiscal year beginning Oct. 1. "It is absolutely vital for the SEC to have the necessary resources to protect investors," said Rep. Michael Oxley, R-Ohio, chairman of the House Financial Services Committee.

Bush's comments underscored the administration's concerns over a growing crisis of confidence in corporate America's behavior that has taken a toll on the stock investments of millions of people and could threaten a fragile economic recovery.

◆ More on the scandal/**E1**
◆ G-8 summit begins/**A13**

163rd Year — No. 178 © 2002 Wisconsin State Journal

7 82550 00001 2
WSJ DAILY

WEATHER

Today
Less humid.
High 82.
Winds: NW
6-12 mph.

Tonight
Comfortable.
Low 62.
Details/back of Local

INSIDE

LOCAL/B1

Concerts on the Square

The summer's first Concert on the Square began at 7 p.m. Wednesday, but the rush for good patches of lawn began hours earlier.